DOING
ETHICS

Moral Reasoning and Contemporary Issues

FIFTH EDITION

Lewis Vaughn

W. W. NORTON & COMPANY, INC.

NEW YORK • LONDON

W. W. Norton & Company has been independent since its founding in 1923, when William Warder Norton and Mary D. Herter Norton first published lectures delivered at the People's Institute, the adult education division of New York City's Cooper Union. The firm soon expanded its program beyond the Institute, publishing books by celebrated academics from America and abroad. By midcentury, the two major pillars of Norton's publishing program—trade books and college texts—were firmly established. In the 1950s, the Norton family transferred control of the company to its employees, and today—with a staff of four hundred and a comparable number of trade, college, and professional titles published each year—W. W. Norton & Company stands as the largest and oldest publishing house owned wholly by its employees.

Editor: Ken Barton
Project Editors: Taylere Peterson, Katie Callahan, and Sujin Hong
Editorial Assistant: Katie Pak
Manuscript Editor: Norma Sims Roche
Managing Editor, College: Marian Johnson
Managing Editor, College Digital Media: Kim Yi
Production Manager: Benjamin Reynolds
Media Editor: Samantha Held
Media Assistant: Ava Bramson
Marketing Manager, Philosophy: Michael Moss
Design Director: Rubina Yeh
Permissions Manager: Megan Schindel
Permissions Associate: Elizabeth Trammell
Composition: SixRedMarbles—Brattleboro, VT
Manufacturing: LSC Communications—Crawfordsville, IN

Permission to use copyrighted material is included as a footnote on the first page of each reading.

ISBN: 978-0-393-64026-7

W. W. Norton & Company, Inc., 500 Fifth Avenue, New York, NY 10110-0017

wwnorton.com

W. W. Norton & Company Ltd., 15 Carlisle Street, London W1D 3BS

1 2 3 4 5 6 7 8 9 0

CONTENTS

PART 3: THEORIES OF MORALITY

CHAPTER 6   **Nonconsequentialist Theories: Do Your Duty**   132

PART 4: ETHICAL ISSUES

PREFACE

This fifth edition of *Doing Ethics* contains the most extensive additions, updates, and improvements of any previous version. The aims that have shaped this text from the beginning have not changed: to help students (1) see why ethics matters to society and to themselves; (2) understand core concepts (theories, principles, values, virtues, and the like); (3) become familiar with the background (scientific, legal, and otherwise) of contemporary moral problems; and (4) know how to apply critical reasoning to those problems—to assess moral judgments and principles, construct and evaluate moral arguments, and apply and critique moral theories. This book, then, tries hard to provide the strongest possible support to teachers of applied ethics who want students, above all, to think for themselves and competently do what is often required of morally mature persons—that is, to *do ethics*.

These goals are reflected in the book's extensive introductions to concepts, cases, and issues; its large collection of readings and exercises; and its chapter-by-chapter coverage of moral reasoning—perhaps the most thorough introduction to these skills available in an applied ethics text. This latter theme gets systematic treatment in five chapters, threads prominently throughout all the others, and is reinforced everywhere by "Critical Thought" text boxes prompting students to apply critical thinking to real debates and cases. The point of all this is to help students not just study ethics but to become fully involved in the ethical enterprise and the moral life.

NEW FEATURES

- A new chapter on campus free speech, hate speech, speech codes, speech and violence, and news-making conflicts: Chapter 16—Free Speech on Campus. It includes five readings by notable free speech theorists and commentators.

- A new stand-alone chapter on an increasingly influential approach to ethics: Chapter 8—Feminist Ethics and the Ethics of Care. It includes two new readings by important theorists in the field.

- A new chapter on the justice of health care—who should get it, who should supply it, and who should pay for it: Chapter 11—Delivering Health Care.

- A new chapter on immigration, immigration policy, and contemporary conflicts over the treatment of immigrants: Chapter 20—The Ethics of Immigration. It includes recent research on some widely believed but erroneous ideas about U.S. immigration, as well as five readings that represent contrasting perspectives on the subject.

- A substantially revised chapter on social equality, now covering race, racism, racial prejudice, discrimination, white privilege, and affirmative action: Chapter 14—Racism, Equality, and Discrimination. It includes four new readings on racism and inequality by prominent participants in the ongoing debates.

- A revised chapter on sexuality, now including examinations not only of sexual behavior but also of campus sexual assault, rape, harassment, and hookup culture: Chapter 15—Sexual Morality.

- A greatly expanded chapter on personal liberty, now including discussions and readings on using drugs and owning guns: Chapter 17—Drugs, Guns, and Personal Liberty.

- New sections in Chapter 4—The Power of Moral Theories, on social contract theory and one called "Devising a Coherent Moral Theory" that shows by example how one might develop a plausible theory of morality.

- A new focus on climate change in the environmental ethics chapter and more emphasis on torture and drone warfare in the political violence chapter.

- Eleven new readings by women writers.

- Thirty-seven new readings in all to supplement the already extensive collection of essays.

- New pedagogical elements: the inclusion of key terms at the end of each chapter; the addition of end-of-chapter review and discussion questions; and several new "Cases for Analysis"—now called "Ethical Dilemmas."

ORGANIZATION

Part 1 (Fundamentals) prepares students for the tasks enumerated above. Chapter 1 explains why ethics is important and why thinking critically about ethical issues is essential to the examined life. It introduces the field of moral philosophy, defines and illustrates basic terminology, clarifies the connection between religion and morality, and explains why moral reasoning is crucial to moral maturity and personal freedom. Chapter 2 investigates a favorite doctrine of undergraduates—ethical relativism—and examines its distant cousin, emotivism.

Part 2 (Moral Reasoning) consists of Chapters 3 and 4. Chapter 3 starts by reassuring students that moral reasoning is neither alien nor difficult but is simply ordinary critical reasoning applied to ethics. They've seen this kind of reasoning before and done it before. Thus, the chapter focuses on identifying, devising, diagramming, and evaluating moral arguments and encourages practice and competence in finding implied premises, testing moral premises, assessing nonmoral premises, and dealing with common argument fallacies.

Chapter 4 explains how moral theories work and how they relate to other important elements in moral experience: considered judgments, moral arguments, moral principles and rules, and cases and issues. It reviews major theories and shows how students can evaluate them using plausible criteria.

Part 3 (Theories of Morality, Chapters 5–8) covers key theories in depth—utilitarianism, ethical egoism, social contract theory, Kant's theory, natural law theory, virtue ethics, feminist ethics, and the ethics of care. Students see how each theory is applied to moral issues and how their strengths and weaknesses are revealed by applying the criteria of evaluation.

In Part 4 (Ethical Issues), each of thirteen chapters explores a timely moral issue through discussion and relevant readings: abortion, euthanasia and physician-assisted suicide, health care, animal welfare, environmental ethics, racism and equality, sexual morality, free speech on campus, drug use, gun ownership, capital punishment, political violence, terrorism, torture, immigration, and global economic justice. Every chapter supplies legal, scientific, and other background information on the issue; discusses how major theories have been applied to the problem; examines arguments that have been used in the debate; and includes additional cases for analysis with questions. The readings are a mix of well-known essays and surprising new voices, both classic and contemporary.

PEDAGOGICAL FEATURES

In addition to "Critical Thought" boxes and "Ethical Dilemmas," the end-of-chapter questions, and the key terms, there are other pedagogical devices:

- "Quick Review" boxes that reiterate key points or terms mentioned in previous pages
- Text boxes that discuss additional topics or issues related to main chapter material
- Chapter summaries
- Suggestions for further reading for each issues chapter
- Glossary

RESOURCES

This Fifth Edition is accompanied by InQuizitive, Norton's award-winning formative, adaptive online quizzing program. InQuizitive activities, written by Dan Lowe of University of Colorado Boulder, motivate students to learn the core concepts and theories of moral reasoning so that they're prepared to think critically about ethical issues. The text is also supported by a full test bank, lecture slides, and a coursepack of assignable quizzes and discussion prompts that loads into most learning management systems. Access these resources at **digital.wwnorton.com/doingethics5**.

EBOOK

Norton Ebooks give students and instructors an enhanced reading experience at a fraction of the cost of a print textbook. Students are able to have an active reading experience and can take notes, bookmark, search, highlight, and even read offline. As an instructor, you can even add your own notes for students to see as they read the text. Norton Ebooks can be viewed on—and synced among—all computers and mobile devices. Access the ebook for *Doing Ethics* at **digital.wwnorton.com/doingethics5**.

ACKNOWLEDGMENTS

The silent partners in this venture are the many reviewers who helped in countless ways to make the book better. They include Marshall Abrams (University of Alabama at Birmingham), Harry Adams (Prairie View A&M University), Alex Aguado (University of North Alabama), Edwin Aiman (University of Houston), Daniel Alvarez (Colorado State University), Peter Amato (Drexel University), Robert Bass (Coastal Carolina University), Ken Beals (Mary Baldwin College), Helen Becker (Shepherd University), Paul Bloomfield (University of Connecticut), Robyn Bluhm (Old Dominion University), Vanda Bozicevic (Bergen Community College), Brent Braga (Northland Community and Technical College), Joy Branch (Southern Union State Community College), Barbara A. Brown (Community College of Allegheny County), Mark Raymond Brown (University of Ottawa), David C. Burris (Arizona Western College), Matthew Burstein (Washington and Lee University), Gabriel R. Camacho (El Paso Community College), Jay Campbell (St. Louis Community College at Meramec), Kenneth Carlson (Northwest Iowa Community College), Jeffrey Carr (Illinois State University), Alan Clark (Del Mar College), Andrew J. Cohen (Georgia State University), Elliot D. Cohen (Indian River State College), Robert Colter (Centre College), Timothy Conn (Sierra College), Guy Crain (University of Oklahoma), Sharon Crasnow (Norco College), Kelso Cratsley (University of Massachusetts, Boston), George Cronk (Bergen Community College), Kevin DeCoux (Minnesota West Community and Technical College), Lara Denis (Agnes Scott College), Steve Dickerson (South Puget Sound Community College), Nicholas Diehl (Sacramento City College), Robin S. Dillon (Lehigh University), Peter Dlugos (Bergen Community College), Matt Drabek (University of Iowa), David Drebushenko (University of Southern Indiana), Clint Dunagan (Northwest Vista College), Paul Eckstein (Bergen Community College), Andrew Fiala (California

State University, Fresno), Stephen Finlay (University of Southern California), Matthew Fitzsimmons (University of North Alabama), Tammie Foltz (Des Moines Area Community College), Tim Fout (University of Louisville), Dimitria Gatzia (University of Akron), Candace Gauthier (University of North Carolina, Wilmington), Mark Greene (University of Delaware), Kevin Guilfoy (Carroll University), Katherine Guin (The College at Brockport: SUNY), Meredith Gunning (University of Massachusetts, Boston), Don Habibi (University of North Carolina, Wilmington), Barbara M. Hands (University of North Carolina, Greensboro), Craig Hanks (Texas State University), Jane Haproff (Sierra College), Ed Harris (Texas A&M University), Carol Hay (University of Massachusetts Lowell), Blake Heffner (Raritan Valley Community College), Marko Hilgersom (Lethbridge Community College), Andrew J. Hill (St. Philip's College), John Holder III (Pensacola Junior College), Mark Hollifield (Clayton College and State University), Margaret Houck (University of South Carolina), Michael Howard (University of Maine, Orono), Frances Howard-Snyder (Western Washington University), Kenneth Howarth (Mercer County Community College), Louis F. Howe, Jr. (Naugatuck Valley Community College), Kyle Hubbard (Saint Anselm College), Robert Hull (Western Virginia Wesleyan College), Amy Jeffers (Owens Community College), Vicki Jenkins (Ivy Tech Community College, Timothy Jessen (Ivy Tech Community College, Bloomington), John Johnston (College of the Redwoods), Marc Jolley (Mercer University), Frederik Kaufman (Ithaca College), Thomas D. Kennedy (Berry College), W. Glenn Kirkconnell (Santa Fe College), Donald Knudsen (Montgomery County Community College), Gilbert Kohler (Shawnee Community College), Thomas Larson (Saint Anselm College), Matt Lawrence (Long Beach City College), Clayton Littlejohn (Southern Methodist University), Jessica Logue (University of Portland), Ian D. MacKinnon (The University of Akron), Tim Madigan (St. John Fisher College), Ernâni Magalhães (West Virginia University), Daniel Malotky (Greensboro College), Luke Manning (Auburn University), Ron Martin (Lynchburg College), Michael McKeon (Barry University), Katherine Mendis (Hunter College, CUNY), Joshua Mills-Knutsen (Indiana University Southeast), Michael Monge (Long Beach City College), Louisa Lee Moon (Mira Costa College), Eric Moore (Longwood University), Jon S. Moran (Southwest Missouri State University), Dale Murray (Virginia Commonwealth University), Elizabeth Murray (Loyola Marymount University), Richard Musselwhite (North Carolina Central University), Thomas Nadelhoffer (Dickinson College), Jay Newhard (East Carolina University), Marcella Norling (Orange Coast College), Charles L. North (Southern New Hampshire University), Robert F. O'Connor (Texas State University), Jeffrey P. Ogle (Metropolitan State University of Denver), Don Olive (Roane State Community College), Leonard Olson (California State University, Fresno), Jessica Payson (Bryn Mawr College), Gregory E. Pence (University of Alabama), Donald Petkus (Indiana University School of Public and Environmental Affairs), Trisha Philips (Mississippi State University), Thomas M. Powers (University of Delaware), Marjorie Price (University of Alabama), Netty Provost (Indiana University, Kokomo), Elisa Rapaport (Molloy College), Michael Redmond (Bergen Community College), Daniel Regan (Villanova University), Joseph J. Rogers (University of Texas, San Antonio), John Returra (Lackawanna College), Robert M. Seltzer (Western Illinois University), Edward Sherline (University of Wyoming), Aeon J. Skoble (Bridgewater Community College), Eric Snider (Lansing Community College), Eric Sotnak (University of Akron), Susanne Sreedhar (Boston University), Piers H.G. Stephens (University of Georgia), Grant Sterling (Eastern Illinois University), John Stilwell (University of Texas at Dallas), Tyler Suggs (Virginia Tech), Michele Svatos (Eastfield College), David Svolba (Fitchburg State University), Allen Thompson (Virginia Commonwealth University), Peter B. Trumbull (Madison College),

Donald Turner (Nashville State Community College), Julie C. Van Camp (California State University, Long Beach), Michelle Rehwinkel Vasilinda (Tallahassee Community College), Kris Vigneron (Columbus State Community College), Christine Vitrano (Brooklyn College, CUNY), Mark Vopat (Youngstown State University), Matt Waldschlagel (University of North Carolina, Wilmington), Steve Wall (Hillsborough Community College), Bill Warnken (Granite State College), Jamie Carlin Watson (Young Harris College), Rivka Weinberg (Scripps College), Cheryl Wertheimer (Butler Community College), Monique Whitaker (Hunter College, CUNY), Phillip Wiebe (Trinity Western University), Jonathan Wight (University of Richmond), John Yanovitch (Molloy College), Steven Zusman (Waubonsee Community College), and Matt Zwolinski (University of San Diego). Thank you all.

PART

1

Fundamentals

CHAPTER 1

Ethics and the Examined Life

Ethics, or **moral philosophy**, is the philosophical study of morality. **Morality** refers to beliefs concerning right and wrong, good and bad—beliefs that can include judgments, values, rules, principles, and theories. These beliefs help guide our actions, define our values, and give us reasons for being the persons we are. (*Ethical* and *moral*, the adjective forms, are often used to mean simply "having to do with morality," and *ethics* and *morality* are sometimes used to refer to the moral norms of a specific group or individual, as in "Greek ethics" or "Russell's morality.") Ethics, then, addresses the powerful question that Socrates formulated twenty-four hundred years ago: how ought we to live?

The scope and continued relevance of this query suggest something compelling about ethics: you cannot escape it. You cannot run away from all the choices, feelings, and actions that accompany ideas about right and wrong, good and bad—ideas that persist in your culture and in your mind. After all, for much of your life, you have been assimilating, modifying, or rejecting the ethical norms you inherited from your family, community, and society. Unless you are very unusual, from time to time you deliberate about the rightness or wrongness of actions, embrace or reject particular moral principles or codes, judge the goodness of your character or intentions (or someone else's), perhaps even question (and agonize over) the soundness of your own moral outlook when it conflicts with that of others. In other words, you are involved in ethics—you *do ethics*. Even if you try to remove yourself from the ethical realm by insisting that all ethical concepts are irrelevant or empty, you assume a particular view—a theory, in the broadest sense—about morality and its place in your life. If at some point you are intellectually brave enough to wonder whether your moral beliefs rest on some coherent supporting considerations, you will see that you cannot even begin to sort out such considerations without—again—doing ethics. In any case, in your life you must deal with the rest of the world, which turns on moral conflict and resolution, moral decision and debate.

What is at stake when we do ethics? In an important sense, the answer is *everything we hold dear*. Ethics is concerned with values—specifically, *moral values*. Through the sifting and weighing of moral values we determine what the most important things are in our lives, what is worth living for, and what is worth dying for. We decide what is the greatest good, what goals we should pursue in life, what virtues we should cultivate, what duties we should or should not fulfill, what value we should put on human life, and what pain and perils we should be willing to endure for notions such as the common good, justice, and rights.

Does it matter whether the state executes a criminal who has the mental capacity of a ten-year-old? Does it matter who actually writes the term paper you turn in and represent as your own? Does it matter whether we can easily save a drowning child but casually decide not to? Does it matter whether young girls in Africa undergo painful genital mutilation for reasons of custom or religion? Do these actions and a million others just as controversial matter at all? Most of us—regardless of our opinion on these issues—would say that they matter a great deal. If they matter, then ethics matters, because these are ethical concerns requiring careful reflection using concepts and reasoning peculiar to ethics.

But even though ethics is inescapable and important, you are still free to take the easy way out, and many people do. You are free *not* to think too deeply or too systematically about ethical concerns. You can simply embrace the moral beliefs and norms given to you by your family and your society. You can accept them without question or serious examination. In other words, you can try *not* to do ethics. This approach can be simple and painless—at least for a while—but it has some drawbacks.

First, it undermines your personal freedom. If you accept and never question the moral beliefs handed to you by your culture, then those beliefs are not really yours—and they, not you, control the path you take in life. Only if you critically examine these beliefs *yourself* and decide for *yourself* whether they have merit will they be truly yours. Only then will you be in charge of your own choices and actions.

Second, the no-questions-asked approach increases the chances that your responses to moral dilemmas or contradictions will be incomplete, confused, or mistaken. Sometimes in real life moral codes or rules do not fit the situations at hand, or moral principles conflict with one another, or entirely new circumstances are not covered by any moral policy at all. Solving these problems requires something that a hand-me-down morality does not include: the intellectual tools to critically evaluate (and reevaluate) existing moral beliefs.

Third, if there is such a thing as intellectual moral growth, you are unlikely to find it on the safe route. To not do ethics is to stay locked in a kind of intellectual limbo, where exploration in ethics and personal moral progress are barely possible.

The philosopher Paul Taylor suggests that there is yet another risk in taking the easy road. If someone blindly embraces the morality bequeathed to him by his society, he may very well be a fine embodiment of the rules of his culture and accept them with certainty. But he will lack the ability to defend his beliefs by rational argument against criticism. What happens when he encounters others who also have very strong beliefs that contradict his? "He will feel lost and bewildered," Taylor says, and his confusion might leave him disillusioned about morality. "Unable to give an objective, reasoned justification for his own convictions, he may turn from dogmatic certainty to total skepticism. And from total skepticism it is but a short step to an 'amoral' life. . . . Thus the person who begins by accepting moral beliefs blindly can end up denying all morality."[1]

There are other easy roads—roads that also bypass critical and thoughtful scrutiny of morality. We can describe most of them as various forms of subjectivism, a topic that we examine closely in the next chapter. You may decide, for example, that you can establish all your moral beliefs by simply consulting your feelings. In situations calling for moral judgments, you let your emotions be your guide. If it feels right, it *is* right. Alternatively, you may come to believe that moral realities are relative to each person, a view known as *subjective relativism* (also covered in the next chapter). That is, you think that what a person believes or approves of determines the rightness or wrongness of actions. If you believe that abortion is wrong, then it *is* wrong. If you believe it is right, then it *is* right.

But these facile roads through ethical terrain are no better than blindly accepting existing norms. Even if you want to take the subjectivist route, you still need to examine it critically to see if there are good reasons for choosing it—otherwise your choice is arbitrary and therefore not really yours. And unless you thoughtfully consider the merits of moral beliefs (including subjectivist beliefs), your chances of being wrong about them are substantial.

Ethics does not give us a royal road to moral truth. Instead, it shows us how to ask critical questions about morality and systematically seek answers supported by good reasons. This is a tall order because, as we have seen, many of the questions in ethics are among the toughest we can ever ask—and among the most important in life.

THE ETHICAL LANDSCAPE

The domain of ethics is large, divided into several areas of investigation and cordoned off from related subjects. So let us map the territory carefully. As the term *moral philosophy* suggests, ethics is a branch of philosophy. A very rough characterization of *philosophy* is the systematic use of critical reasoning to answer the most fundamental questions in life. Moral philosophy, obviously, tries to answer the fundamental questions of morality. The other major branches of philosophy address other basic questions; these branches are *logic* (the study of correct reasoning), *metaphysics* (the study of the fundamental nature of reality), and *epistemology* (the study of knowledge). As a division of philosophy, ethics does its work primarily through critical reasoning: the careful, systematic evaluation of statements, or claims. Critical reasoning is a process used in all fields of study, not just in ethics. The main components of this process are the evaluation of logical arguments and the careful analysis of concepts.

Science also studies morality, but not in the way that moral philosophy does. Its approach is known as **descriptive ethics**—the *scientific* study of moral beliefs and practices. Its aim is to describe and explain how people actually behave and think when dealing with moral issues and concepts. This kind of empirical research is usually conducted by sociologists, anthropologists, and psychologists. In contrast, the focus of moral philosophy is not what people actually believe and do, but what they *should* believe and do. The point of moral philosophy is to determine what actions are right (or wrong) and what things are good (or bad).

Philosophers distinguish three major divisions in ethics, each one representing a different way

to approach the subject. The first division is **normative ethics**—the study of the principles, rules, or theories that guide our actions and judgments. (The word *normative* refers to norms, or standards, of judgment—in this case, norms for judging rightness and goodness.) The ultimate purpose of doing normative ethics is to try to establish the soundness of moral norms, especially the norms embodied in a comprehensive moral system, or moral theory. We do normative ethics when we use critical reasoning to demonstrate that a moral principle is justified, or that a professional code of conduct is contradictory, or that one proposed moral theory is better than another, or that a person's motive is good. Should the rightness of actions be judged by their consequences? Is happiness the greatest good in life? Is utilitarianism a good moral theory? Such questions are the preoccupation of normative ethics.

Another major division of ethics is **metaethics**—the study of the meaning and logical structure of moral beliefs. It asks not whether an action is right or whether a person's character is good. It takes a step back from these concerns and asks more fundamental questions about them: What does it mean for an action to be *right*? Is *good* the same thing as *desirable*? How can a moral principle be justified? Is there such a thing as moral truth? To do normative ethics, we must assume certain things about the meaning of moral terms and the logical relationships among them. But the job of metaethics is to question all these assumptions, to see if they really make sense.

Finally, there is **applied ethics**—the application of moral norms to specific moral issues or cases, particularly those in a profession such as medicine or law. Applied ethics in these fields goes under names such as medical ethics, journalistic ethics, and business ethics. In applied ethics we study the results derived from applying a moral principle or theory to specific circumstances. The purpose of the exercise is to learn something important about either the moral characteristics of the situation or the adequacy of the moral norms. Did the doctor do right in performing that abortion? Is it morally permissible for scientists to perform experiments on people without their consent? Was it right for the journalist to distort her reporting to aid a particular side in the war? Questions like these drive the search for answers in applied ethics.

In every division of ethics, we must be careful to distinguish between *values* and *obligations*. Sometimes we may be interested in concepts or judgments of *value*—that is, about what is morally *good*, *bad*, *blameworthy*, or *praiseworthy*. We properly use these kinds of terms to refer mostly to persons, character traits, motives, and intentions. We may say "She is a good person" or "He is to blame for that tragedy." At other times, we may be interested in concepts or judgments of *obligation*—that is, about what is obligatory, or a duty, or what we should or ought to do. We use these terms to refer to *actions*. We may say "She has a duty to tell the truth" or "What he did was wrong."

When we talk about value in the sense just described, we mean *moral* value. If she is a good person, she is good in the moral sense. But we can also talk about *nonmoral* value. We can say that things such as televisions, rockets, experiences, and works of art (things other than persons, intentions, and so forth) are good, but we mean "good" only in a nonmoral way. It makes no sense to assert that televisions or rockets in themselves are morally good or bad. Perhaps a rocket could be used to perform an action that is morally wrong. In that case, the action would be immoral, while the rocket itself would still have only nonmoral value.

Many things in life have value for us, but they are not necessarily valuable in the same way. Some things are valuable because they are a means to something else. We might say that gasoline is good because it is a means to make a gas-powered vehicle work, or that a pen is good because it can be used to write a letter. Such things are said to be **instrumentally**, or **extrinsically**, **valuable**—they are valuable as a means to something else.

Some things, however, are valuable for their own sakes. They are valuable simply because they are what they are, without being a means to something else. Things that have been regarded as valuable in themselves include happiness, pleasure, virtue, and beauty. These things are said to be **intrinsically valuable**—they are valuable in themselves.

THE ELEMENTS OF ETHICS

We all do ethics, and we all have a general sense of what is involved. But we can still ask, What are the elements of ethics that make it the peculiar enterprise that it is? We can include at least the following factors:

The Preeminence of Reason

Doing ethics typically involves grappling with our feelings, taking into account the facts of the situation (including our own observations and relevant knowledge), and trying to understand the ideas that bear on the case. But above all, it involves, even requires, critical reasoning—the consideration of reasons for whatever statements (moral or otherwise) are in question. Whatever our view on moral issues and whatever moral outlook we subscribe to, our commonsense moral experience suggests that if a moral judgment is to be worthy of acceptance, it must be supported by good reasons, and our deliberations on the issue must include a consideration of those reasons.

The backbone of critical reasoning generally, and moral reasoning in particular, is logical argument. This kind of argument—not the angry-exchange type—consists of a statement to be supported (the assertion to be proved, the conclusion) and the statements that do the supporting (the reasons for believing the statement, the premises). With such arguments, we try to show that a moral judgment is or is not justified, that a moral principle is or is not sound, that an action is or is not morally permissible, or that a moral theory is or is not plausible.

> ## QUICK REVIEW
>
> **ethics** (or **moral philosophy**)—The philosophical study of morality.
>
> **morality**—Beliefs concerning right and wrong, good and bad; they can include judgments, values, rules, principles, and theories.
>
> **descriptive ethics**—The scientific study of moral beliefs and practices.
>
> **normative ethics**—The study of the principles, rules, or theories that guide our actions and judgments.
>
> **metaethics**—The study of the meaning and logical structure of moral beliefs.
>
> **applied ethics**—The application of moral norms to specific moral issues or cases, particularly those in a profession such as medicine or law.
>
> **instrumentally** (or **extrinsically**) **valuable**—Valuable as a means to something else.
>
> **intrinsically valuable**—Valuable in itself, for its own sake.

Our use of critical reasoning and argument helps us keep our feelings about moral issues in perspective. Feelings are an important part of our moral experience. They make empathy possible, which gives us a deeper understanding of the human impact of moral norms. They can also serve as internal alarm bells, warning us of the possibility of injustice, suffering, and wrongdoing. But they are unreliable guides to moral truth. They may simply reflect our own emotional needs, prejudices, upbringing, culture, and self-interests. Careful reasoning, however, can inform our feelings and help us decide moral questions on their merits.

The Universal Perspective

Logic requires that moral norms and judgments follow the *principle of universalizability*—the idea that a moral statement (a principle, rule, or judgment) that applies in one situation must apply in all other situations that are relevantly similar. If you say, for example, that lying is wrong in a particular situation, then you implicitly agree that lying is wrong for anyone in relevantly similar situations. If you say that killing in self-defense is morally permissible, then you say in effect that killing in self-defense is permissible for everyone in relevantly similar situations. It cannot be the case that an action performed by A is *wrong* while the same action performed by B in relevantly similar circumstances is *right*. It cannot be the case that the moral judgments formed in these two situations must differ just because two different people are involved.

This point about universalizability also applies to reasons used to support moral judgments. If reasons apply in a specific case, then those reasons also apply in all relevantly similar cases. It cannot be true that reasons that apply in a specific case do not apply to other cases that are similar in all relevant respects.

The Principle of Impartiality

From the moral point of view, all persons are considered equal and should be treated accordingly. This sense of impartiality is implied in all moral statements. It means that the welfare and interests of each individual should be given the same weight as the welfare and interests of all others. Unless there is a morally relevant difference between people, we should treat them the same: we must treat equals equally. We would think it outrageous for a moral rule to say something like "Everyone must refrain from stealing food in grocery stores—except for Mr. X, who may steal all he wants." Imagine that there is no morally relevant reason for making this exception for stealing food; Mr. X is exempted merely because, say, he is a celebrity known for outrageous behavior. We not only would object to this rule but might even begin to wonder if it was a genuine moral rule at all, because it lacks impartiality. Similarly, we would reject a moral rule that says something like "Everyone is entitled to basic human rights—except Native Americans." Such a rule would be a prime example of discrimination based on race. We can see this blatant partiality best if we ask what morally relevant difference there is between Native Americans and everyone else. Differences in income, social status, skin color, ancestry, and the like are not morally relevant. Apparently there are no morally relevant differences. Because there are none, we must conclude that the rule sanctions unfair discrimination.

We must keep in mind, however, that sometimes there are good reasons for treating someone differently. Imagine a hospital that generally gives equal care to patients, treating equals equally. But suppose a patient comes to the hospital in an ambulance because she has had a heart attack and will die without immediate care. The hospital staff responds quickly, giving her faster and more sophisticated care than other patients receive. The situation is a matter of life and death—a good reason for *not* treating everyone the same and for providing the heart attack patient with special consideration. This instance of discrimination is justified.

The Dominance of Moral Norms

Not all norms are moral norms. There are legal norms (laws, statutes), aesthetic norms (for judging artistic creations), prudential norms (practical considerations of self-interest), and others. Moral norms seem to stand out from all these in an interesting way: they dominate. Whenever moral principles or values conflict in some way with nonmoral principles or values, the moral considerations usually override the others. Moral considerations seem more important, more critical, or more weighty. A principle of prudence such as "Never help a stranger" may be well justified, but it must yield to any moral principle that contradicts it, such as "Help a stranger in an emergency if you can do so without endangering yourself." An aesthetic norm that somehow involved violating a moral principle would have to take a backseat to the moral considerations. A law

that conflicted with a moral principle would be suspect, and the latter would have to prevail over the former. Ultimately the justification for civil disobedience is that specific laws conflict with moral norms and are therefore invalid. If we judge a law to be bad, we usually do so on moral grounds.

RELIGION AND MORALITY

Many people believe that morality and religion are inseparable—that religion is the source or basis of morality and that moral precepts are simply what God says should be done. This view is not at all surprising, because all religions imply or assert a perspective on morality. The three great religions in the Western tradition—Christianity, Judaism, and Islam—provide their believers with commandments or principles of conduct that are thought to constitute the moral law, the essence of morality. For their millions of adherents, the moral law is the will of God, and the will of God is the moral law. In the West, at least, the powerful imprint of religion is evident in secular laws and in the private morality of believers and unbelievers alike. Secular systems of morality—for example, those of the ancient Greek philosophers, Immanuel Kant, the utilitarians, and others—have of course left their mark on Western ethics. But they have not moved the millions who think that morality is a product exclusively of religion.

So what is the relationship between religion and morality? For our purposes, we should break this question into two parts: (1) What is the relationship between religion and *ethics* (the philosophical study of morality)? and (2) What is the relationship between religion and *morality* (beliefs about right and wrong)? The first question asks about how religion relates to the kind of investigation we conduct in this book—the use of experience and critical reasoning to study morality. The key point about the relationship is that whatever your views on religion and morality, an open-minded expedition into ethics is more useful and empowering than you may realize, especially now, at the beginning of your journey into moral philosophy. You may believe, for example, that God determines what is right and wrong, so there is no need to apply critical reasoning to morality—you just need to know what God says. But this judgment—and similar dismissals of ethics—would be premature, as we will see.

Believers Need Moral Reasoning

It is difficult—perhaps impossible—for most people to avoid using moral reasoning. Religious people are no exception. One reason is that religious moral codes (such as the Ten Commandments) and other major religious rules of conduct are usually vague, laying out general principles that may be difficult to apply to specific cases. (Secular moral codes have the same disadvantage.) For example, we may be commanded to love our neighbor, but what neighbors are included—people of a different religion? people who denounce our religion? the gay or lesbian couple? those who steal from us? the convicted child molester next door? the drug dealers on the corner? the woman who got an abortion? Also, what does loving our neighbor demand of us? How does love require us to behave toward the drug dealers, the gay couple, or the person who denounces our religion? If our terminally ill neighbor asks us in the name of love to help him kill himself, what should we do? Does love require us to kill him—or to refrain from killing him? And, of course, commandments can conflict—as when, for example, the only way to avoid killing an innocent person is to tell a lie, or the only way to save the life of one person is to kill another. All these situations force the believer to interpret religious directives, to try to apply general rules to specific cases, to draw out the implications of particular views—in other words, to do ethics.

When Conflicts Arise, Ethics Steps In

Very often moral contradictions or inconsistencies confront the religious believer, and only moral reasoning can help resolve them. Believers sometimes disagree with their religious leaders on moral issues.

Adherents of one religious tradition may disagree with those from another tradition on whether an act is right or wrong. Sincere devotees in a religious tradition may wonder if its moral teachings make sense. In all such cases, intelligent resolution of the conflict of moral claims can be achieved only by applying a neutral standard that helps sort out the competing viewpoints. Moral philosophy supplies the neutral standard in the form of critical thinking, well-made arguments, and careful analysis. No wonder then that many great religious minds—Aquinas, Leibniz, Descartes, Kant, Maimonides, Averroës, and others—have relied on reason to examine the nature of morality. In fact, countless theists have regarded reason as a gift from God that enables human beings to grasp the truths of science, life, and morality.

Moral Philosophy Enables Productive Discourse

Any fruitful discussions about morality undertaken between people from different religious traditions or between believers and nonbelievers will require a common set of ethical concepts and a shared procedure for deciding issues and making judgments. Ethics provides these tools. Without them, conversations will resolve nothing, and participants will learn little. Without them, people will talk past each other, appealing only to their own religious views. Furthermore, in a pluralistic society, most of the public discussions about important moral issues take place in a context of shared values such as justice, fairness, equality, and tolerance. Just as important, they also occur according to an unwritten understanding that (1) moral positions should be explained, (2) claims should be supported by reasons, and (3) reasoning should be judged by common rational standards. These skills, of course, are at the heart of ethics.

Now consider the second question introduced above: What is the relationship between religion and morality? For many people, the most interesting query about the relationship between religion

CRITICAL THOUGHT: Ethics, Religion, and Tough Moral Issues

How can we hope to grapple with complex moral issues that have emerged only in recent years? Can religion alone handle the job? Consider the following case:

> According to a report by CNN, Jack and Lisa Nash made history when they used genetic testing to save the life of their six-year-old daughter, Molly, by having another child. Molly had a rare genetic disorder known as Fanconi anemia, which prevents the generation of bone marrow and produces a fatal leukemia. Molly's best chance to live was to get a transplant of stem cells from the umbilical cord of a sibling, and Molly's parents were determined to give her that sibling, brother Adam. Through genetic testing (and in vitro fertilization), Jack and Lisa were able to select a child who would not be born with a particular disease (Fanconi anemia, in this case) but also would help a sibling combat the disease by being the optimal tissue

match for a transplant—a historic combination. As Lisa Nash said, "I was going to save Molly no matter what, and I wanted Molly to have siblings."*

Is it right to produce a child to save the life or health of someone else? More to the point, do the scriptures of the three major Western religions provide any guidance on this question? Do any of these traditions offer useful methods for productively discussing or debating such issues with people of different faiths? How might ethics help with these challenges? Is it possible to formulate a reasonable opinion on this case *without doing ethics?* Why or why not?

*"Genetic Selection Gives Girl a Brother and a Second Chance," CNN.com, October 3, 2000, http://archives.cnn.com/2000/HEALTH/10/03/testube.brother/index.html (December 8, 2005).

and morality is this: Is God the maker of morality? That is, is God the author of the moral law? Those who answer yes are endorsing a theory of morality known as the *divine command theory*. It says that right actions are those that are willed by God, that God literally defines right and wrong. Something is right or good only because God makes it so. In the simplest version of the theory, God can determine right and wrong because he is omnipotent. He is all-powerful—powerful enough even to create moral norms. In this view, God is a divine lawgiver, and his laws constitute morality.

In general, believers are divided on whether the divine command theory gives an accurate account of the source of morality. Notable among the theory's detractors are the great theistic philosophers Gottfried Leibniz (1646–1716) and Thomas Aquinas (1225–1274). And conversely, as odd as it may sound, some nonbelievers have subscribed to it. In

The Brothers Karamazov (1879–1880), the character Ivan Karamazov declares, "If God doesn't exist, everything is permissible." This very sentiment was espoused by, among others, the famous atheist philosopher Jean-Paul Sartre.

Both religious and secular critics of the divine command theory believe that it poses a serious dilemma, one first articulated by Socrates two and a half millennia ago. In the dialogue *Euthyphro*, Socrates asks, Is an action morally right because God wills it to be so, or does God will it to be so because it is morally right? Critics say that if an action is right only because God wills it (that is, if right and wrong are dependent on God), then many heinous crimes and evil actions would be right if God willed them. If God willed murder, theft, or torture, these deeds would be morally right. If God has unlimited power, he could easily will such actions. If the rightness of an action depended on God's will alone, he could not have reasons for willing what he wills. No reasons would be available or required. Therefore, if God commanded an action, the command would be without reason, completely arbitrary. Neither the believer nor the nonbeliever would think this state of affairs plausible. On the other hand, if God wills an action because it is morally right (if moral norms are independent of God), then the divine command theory must be false. God does not create rightness; he simply knows what is right and wrong and is subject to the moral law just as humans are.

For some theists, this charge of arbitrariness is especially worrisome. Leibniz, for example, rejects the divine command theory, declaring that it implies that God is unworthy of worship:

> In saying, therefore, that things are not good according to any standard of goodness, but simply by the will of God, it seems to me that one destroys, without realizing it, all the love of God and all his glory; for why praise him for what he has done, if he would be equally praiseworthy in doing the contrary? Where will be his justice and his wisdom if he has only a certain despotic power, if arbitrary will takes the place of reasonableness, and if in accord with the definition of tyrants, justice consists in that which is pleasing to the most powerful?[2]

Defenders of the divine command theory may reply to the arbitrariness argument by contending that God would never command us to commit heinous acts, because God is all-good. Because of his supreme goodness, he would will only what is good. Some thinkers, however, believe that such reasoning renders the very idea of God's goodness meaningless. As one philosopher says,

> [O]n this view, the doctrine of the goodness of God is reduced to nonsense. It is important to religious believers that God is not only all-powerful and all-knowing, but that he is also good; yet if we accept the idea that good and bad are defined by reference to God's will, this notion is deprived of any meaning. What could it mean to say that God's commands are good? If "X is good" means "X is commanded by God," then "God's commands are good" would mean only "God's commands are commanded by God," an empty truism.[3]

In any case, it seems that through critical reasoning we can indeed learn much about morality and the moral life. After all, there are complete moral systems (some of which are examined in this book) that are not based on religion, that contain genuine moral norms indistinguishable from those embraced by religion, and that are justified not by reference to religious precepts but by careful thinking and moral arguments. As the philosopher Jonathan Berg says, "Those who would refuse to recognize as adequately justified any moral beliefs not derived from knowledge of or about God, would have to refute the whole vast range of arguments put by Kant and all others who ever proposed a rational basis for ethics!"[4] Moreover, if we can do ethics—if we can use critical reasoning to discern moral norms certified by the best reasons and evidence—then critical reasoning is sufficient to guide us to moral standards and values. We obviously can do ethics (as the following chapters demonstrate), so morality is both accessible and meaningful to us whether we are religious or not.

CHAPTER REVIEW

SUMMARY

Ethics is the philosophical study of morality, and morality consists of beliefs concerning right and wrong, good and bad. These beliefs can include judgments, principles, and theories. Participating in the exploration of morality—that is, doing ethics—is inescapable. We all must make moral judgments, assess moral norms, judge people's character, and question the soundness of our moral outlooks. A great deal is at stake when we do ethics, including countless decisions that determine the quality of our lives.

You can decide to forgo any ethical deliberations and simply embrace the moral beliefs and norms you inherited from your family and culture.

But this approach undermines your freedom, for if you accept without question whatever moral beliefs come your way, they are not really yours. Only if you critically examine them for yourself are they truly yours.

The three main divisions of ethics proper are normative ethics (the study of the moral norms that guide our actions and judgments), metaethics (the study of the meaning and logical structure of moral beliefs), and applied ethics (the application of moral norms to specific moral issues or cases).

Ethics involves a distinctive set of elements. These include the preeminence of reason, the universal perspective, the principle of impartiality, and the dominance of moral norms.

Some people claim that morality depends on God, a view known as the divine command theory. Both theists and nontheists have raised doubts about this doctrine. The larger point is that doing ethics—using critical reasoning to examine the moral life—can be a useful and productive enterprise for believer and nonbeliever alike.

KEY TERMS

ethics or **moral philosophy** (p. 3)
morality (p. 3)
descriptive ethics (p. 5)
normative ethics (p. 5)
metaethics (p. 5)
applied ethics (p. 5)
instrumentally or **extrinsically valuable** (p. 6)
intrinsically valuable (p. 6)

EXERCISES

Review Questions

1. When can it be said that your moral beliefs are not really yours? (p. 3)
2. In what ways are we forced to do ethics? What is at stake in these deliberations? (pp. 3–4)
3. What is the unfortunate result of accepting moral beliefs without questioning them? (pp. 4–5)
4. Can our feelings be our sole guide to morality? Why or why not? (pp. 4–5)

5. What are some questions asked in normative ethics? (p. 5)
6. What is the difference between normative ethics and metaethics? (p. 5)
7. What is the dilemma about God and morality that Socrates posed in *Euthyphro*? (pp. 10–11)
8. What kinds of moral contradictions or inconsistencies confront religious believers? (pp. 8–9)
9. What are the premises in the arbitrariness argument against the divine command theory? (p. 10)
10. Does the principle of impartiality imply that we must always treat equals equally? Why or why not? (pp. 7–8)

Discussion Questions

1. Do you think that morality ultimately depends on God (that God is the author of the moral law)? Why or why not?
2. Do you believe that you have absorbed or adopted without question most of your moral beliefs? Why or why not?
3. Formulate an argument against the divine command theory, then formulate one for it.
4. Give an example of how you or someone you know has used reasons to support a moral judgment.
5. Identify at least two normative ethical questions that you have wondered about in the past year.
6. Name two things (such as persons, objects, experiences) in your life that you consider intrinsically valuable. Name three that are instrumentally valuable.
7. How do your feelings affect the moral judgments you make? Do they *determine* your judgments? Do they inform them? If so, how?
8. What is the logic behind the principle of universalizability? Cite an example of how the principle has entered into your moral deliberations.
9. How does racial discrimination violate the principle of impartiality?

10. What is the "dominance of moral norms"? Does it strike you as reasonable? Or do you believe that sometimes nonmoral norms can outweigh moral ones? If the latter, provide an example.

ETHICAL DILEMMAS

1. You are the mayor of a major city, and you want to keep the streets as clean as possible. You send the city's street sweepers to the more affluent neighborhoods, but you ignore the poorer neighborhoods because the poor residents pay less in taxes than the rich people do. Is this practice a violation of the impartiality principle? Why or why not?

2. You try to live strictly by the moral rules contained in your religion's moral code. The two most important rules are "Be merciful" (don't give people what they deserve) and "Be just" (give people exactly what they deserve). Now suppose a man is arrested for stealing food from your house, and the police leave it up to you whether he should be prosecuted for his crime or set free. Should you be merciful and set him free, or be just and make sure he is appropriately punished? How do you resolve this conflict of rules? Can your moral code resolve it? To what moral principles or theories do you appeal?

3. Suppose you are an engineer building a road across a mountain. From a prudential point of view, it would be easier and cheaper to build it through a family's farm. This option would require compelling the family to move, which would be an extreme hardship for them. From a moral point of view, the family should be allowed to stay on their farm. Which view should take precedence?

FURTHER READING

Anita L. Allen, *New Ethics: A Guided Tour of the Twenty-First-Century Moral Landscape* (New York: Miramax, 2004).

Aristotle, *Nicomachean Ethics,* book 2, parts 1 and 4.

Simon Blackburn, *Being Good: A Short Introduction to Ethics* (Oxford: Oxford University Press, 2002).

Donald M. Borchert and David Stewart, *Exploring Ethics* (New York: Macmillan, 1986).

Steven M. Cahn and Joram G. Haber, eds., *Twentieth Century Ethical Theory* (Englewood Cliffs, NJ: Prentice Hall, 1995).

William K. Frankena, *Ethics,* 2nd ed. (Englewood Cliffs, NJ: Prentice Hall, 1973).

Bernard Gert, *Morality: Its Nature and Justification* (New York: Oxford University Press, 1998).

Brooke Noel Moore and Robert Michael Stewart, *Moral Philosophy: A Comprehensive Introduction* (Belmont, CA: Mayfield, 1994).

Dave Robinson and Chris Garrett, *Introducing Ethics,* ed. Richard Appignanesi (New York: Totem Books, 2005).

Peter Singer, ed., *A Companion to Ethics,* corr. ed. (Oxford: Blackwell, 1993).

Paul Taylor, *Principles of Ethics: An Introduction* (Encino, CA: Dickenson, 1975).

Jacques P. Thiroux, *Ethics: Theory and Practice,* 3rd ed. (New York: Macmillan, 1986).

Thomas F. Wall, *Thinking Critically about Moral Problems* (Belmont, CA: Wadsworth, 2003).

G. J. Warnock, *The Object of Morality* (London: Methuen, 1971).

READINGS

From *What Is the Socratic Method?*

CHRISTOPHER PHILLIPS

The Socratic method is a way to seek truths by your own lights.

It is a system, a spirit, a method, a type of philosophical inquiry, an intellectual technique, all rolled into one.

Socrates himself never spelled out a "method." However, the Socratic method is named after him because Socrates, more than any other before or since, models for us *philosophy practiced*—philosophy as deed, as way of living, as something that any of us can do. It is an *open system* of philosophical inquiry that allows one to interrogate from many vantage points.

Gregory Vlastos, a Socrates scholar and professor of philosophy at Princeton, described Socrates' method of inquiry as "among the greatest achievements of humanity." Why? Because, he says, it makes philosophical inquiry "a common human enterprise, open to every man." Instead of requiring allegiance to a specific philosophical viewpoint or analytic technique or specialized vocabulary, the Socratic method "calls for common sense and common speech." And this, he says, "is as it should be, for how many should live is every man's business."

I think, however, that the Socratic method goes beyond Vlastos' description. It does not merely call for common sense but examines what common sense *is*. The Socratic method asks: Does the common sense of our day offer us the greatest potential for self-understanding and human excellence? Or is the prevailing common sense in fact a roadblock to realizing this potential?

Vlastos goes on to say that Socratic inquiry is by no means simple, and "calls not only for the highest degree of mental alertness of which anyone is capable" but also for "moral qualities of a high order: sincerity,

humility, courage." Such qualities "protect against the possibility" that Socratic dialogue, no matter how rigorous, "would merely grind out . . . wild conclusions with irresponsible premises." I agree, though I would replace the quality of sincerity with honesty, since one can hold a conviction sincerely without examining it, while honesty would require that one subject one's convictions to frequent scrutiny.

A Socratic dialogue reveals how different our outlooks can be on concepts we use every day. It reveals how different our philosophies are, and often how tenable—or untenable, as the case may be—a range of philosophies can be. Moreover, even the most universally recognized and used concept, when subjected to Socratic scrutiny, might reveal not only that there is *not* universal agreement, after all, on the meaning of any given concept, but that every single person has a somewhat different take on each and every concept under the sun.

What's more, there seems to be no such thing as a concept so abstract, or question so off base, that it can't be fruitfully explored [using the Socratic method]. In the course of Socratizing, it often turns out to be the case that some of the most so-called abstract concepts are intimately related to the most profoundly relevant human experiences. In fact, it's been my experience that virtually any question can be plumbed Socratically. Sometimes you don't know what question will have the most lasting and significant impact until you take a risk and delve into it for a while.

What distinguishes the Socratic method from mere nonsystematic inquiry is the sustained attempt to explore the ramifications of certain opinions and then offer compelling objections and alternatives. This scrupulous and exhaustive form of inquiry in many ways

"Socratic method" to think through difficult philosophical issues. To see the Socratic method applied to ethics, read the excerpt from Plato's *Euthyphro* that follows on p. 16.

resembles the scientific method. But unlike Socratic inquiry, scientific inquiry would often lead us to believe that whatever is not measurable cannot be investigated. This "belief" fails to address such paramount human concerns as sorrow and joy and suffering and love.

Instead of focusing on the outer cosmos, Socrates focused primarily on human beings and their cosmos within, utilizing his method to open up new realms of self-knowledge while at the same time exposing a great deal of error, superstition, and dogmatic nonsense. The Spanish-born American philosopher and poet George Santayana said that Socrates knew that "the foreground of human life is necessarily moral and practical" and that "it is so even so for artists"—and even for scientists, try as some might to divorce their work from these dimensions of human existence.

Scholars call Socrates' method the *elenchus,* which is Hellenistic Greek for *inquiry* or *cross-examination.* But it is not just any type of inquiry or examination. It is a type that reveals people to themselves, that makes them see what their opinions really amount to. C. D. C. Reeve, professor of philosophy at Reed College, gives the standard explanation of an elenchus in saying that its aim "is not simply to reach adequate definitions" of such things as virtues; rather, it also has a "moral reformatory purpose, for Socrates believes that regular elenctic philosophizing makes people happier and more virtuous than anything else. . . . Indeed philosophizing is so important for human welfare, on his view, that he is willing to accept execution rather than give it up."

Socrates' method of examination can indeed be a vital part of existence, but I would not go so far as to say that it *should* be. And I do not think that Socrates felt that habitual use of this method "makes people happier." The fulfillment that comes from Socratizing comes only at a price—it could well make us *unhappier,* more uncertain, more troubled, as well as more fulfilled. It can leave us with a sense that we *don't* know the answers after all, that we are much further from knowing the answers than we'd ever realized before engaging in Socratic discourse. And this is fulfilling—and exhilarating and humbling and perplexing.

* * *

There is no neat divide between one's views of philosophy and of life. They are overlapping and kindred views. It is virtually impossible in many instances to *know* what we believe in daily life until we engage others in dialogue. Likewise, to discover our philosophical views, we must engage with ourselves, with the lives we already lead. Our views form, change, evolve, as we participate in this dialogue. It is the only way truly to discover what philosophical colors we sail under. Everyone at some point preaches to himself and others what he does not yet practice; everyone acts in or on the world in ways that are in some way contradictory or inconsistent with the views he or she confesses or professes to hold. For instance, the Danish philosopher Søren Kierkegaard, the influential founder of existentialism, put Socratic principles to use in writing his dissertation on the concept of irony in Socrates, often using pseudonyms so he could argue his own positions with himself. In addition, the sixteenth-century essayist Michel de Montaigne, who was called "the French Socrates" and was known as the father of skepticism in modern Europe, would write and add conflicting and even contradictory passages in the same work. And like Socrates, he believed the search for truth was worth dying for.

The Socratic method forces people "to confront their own dogmatism," according to Leonard Nelson, a German philosopher who wrote on such subjects as ethics and theory of knowledge until he was forced by the rise of Nazism to quit. By doing so, participants in Socratic dialogue are, in effect, "*forcing* themselves to be free," Nelson maintains. But they're not just confronted with their own dogmatism. In the course of a [Socratic dialogue], they may be confronted with an array of hypotheses, convictions, conjectures and theories offered by the other participants, and themselves—all of which subscribe to some sort of dogma. The Socratic method requires that—honestly and openly, rationally and imaginatively—they confront the dogma by asking such questions as: What does this mean? What speaks for and against it? Are there alternative ways of considering it that are even more plausible and tenable?

At certain junctures of a Socratic dialogue, the "forcing" that this confrontation entails—the insistence that each participant carefully articulate her singular philosophical perspective—can be upsetting. But that is all to the good. If it never touches any nerves, if it doesn't upset, if it doesn't mentally and spiritually challenge and perplex, in a wonderful and exhilarating way, it is not Socratic dialogue. This "forcing" opens us up to the varieties of experiences of others—whether through direct dialogue, or through other means, like drama or books, or through a work of art or a dance. It compels us to explore alternative perspectives, asking what might be said for or against each.

* * *

From *The Euthyphro*
Plato

* * *

Euthyphro. Piety . . . is that which is dear to the gods, and impiety is that which is not dear to them.

Socrates. Very good, Euthyphro; you have now given me the sort of answer which I wanted. But whether what you say is true or not I cannot as yet tell, although I make no doubt that you will prove the truth of your words.

Euthyphro. Of course.

Socrates. Come, then, and let us examine what we are saying. That thing or person which is dear to the gods is pious, and that thing or person which is hateful to the gods is impious, these two being the extreme opposites of one another. Was not that said?

Euthyphro. It was.

Socrates. And well said?

Euthyphro. Yes, Socrates, I thought so; it was certainly said.

Socrates. And further, Euthyphro, the gods were admitted to have enmities and hatreds and differences?

Euthyphro. Yes, that was also said.

Socrates. And what sort of difference creates enmity and anger? Suppose for example that you and I, my good friend, differ about a number; do differences of this sort make us enemies and set us at variance with one another? Do we not go at once to arithmetic, and put an end to them by a sum?

Plato, *The Euthyphro*, translated by Benjamin Jowett.

Euthyphro. True.

Socrates. Or suppose that we differ about magnitudes, do we not quickly end the differences by measuring?

Euthyphro. Very true.

Socrates. And we end a controversy about heavy and light by resorting to a weighing machine?

Euthyphro. To be sure.

Socrates. But what differences are there which cannot be thus decided, and which therefore make us angry and set us at enmity with one another? I dare say the answer does not occur to you at the moment, and therefore I will suggest that these enmities arise when the matters of difference are the just and unjust, good and evil, honourable and dishonourable. Are not these the points about which men differ, and about which when we are unable satisfactorily to decide our differences, you and I and all of us quarrel, when we do quarrel?

Euthyphro. Yes, Socrates, the nature of the differences about which we quarrel is such as you describe.

Socrates. And the quarrels of the gods, noble Euthyphro, when they occur, are of a like nature?

Euthyphro. Certainly they are.

Socrates. They have differences of opinion, as you say, about good and evil, just and unjust, honourable and dishonourable: there would have been no quarrels among them, if there had been no such differences—would there now?

Euthyphro. You are quite right.

Socrates. Does not every man love that which he deems noble and good, and hate the opposite of them?

Euthyphro. Very true.

Socrates. But, as you say, people regard the same things, some as just and others as unjust,—about these they dispute; and so there arise wars and fightings among them.

Euthyphro. Very true.

Socrates. Then the same things are hated by the gods and loved by the gods, and are both hateful and dear to them?

Euthyphro. True.

Socrates. And upon this view the same things, Euthyphro, will be pious and also impious?

Euthyphro. So I should suppose.

Socrates. Then, my friend, I remark with surprise that you have not answered the question which I asked. For I certainly did not ask you to tell me what action is both pious and impious: but now it would seem that what is loved by the gods is also hated by them. And therefore, Euthyphro, in thus chastising your father you may very likely be doing what is agreeable to Zeus but disagreeable to Cronos or Uranus, and what is acceptable to Hephaestus but unacceptable to Hera, and there may be other gods who have similar differences of opinion.

Euthyphro. But I believe, Socrates, that all the gods would be agreed as to the propriety of punishing a murderer: there would be no difference of opinion about that.

Socrates. Well, but speaking of men, Euthyphro, did you ever hear any one arguing that a murderer or any sort of evil-doer ought to be let off?

Euthyphro. I should rather say that these are the questions which they are always arguing, especially in courts of law: they commit all sorts of crimes, and there is nothing which they will not do or say in their own defence.

Socrates. But do they admit their guilt, Euthyphro, and yet say that they ought not to be punished?

Euthyphro. No; they do not.

Socrates. Then there are some things which they do not venture to say and do: for they do not venture to argue that the guilty are to be unpunished, but they deny their guilt, do they not?

Euthyphro. Yes.

Socrates. Then they do not argue that the evil-doer should not be punished, but they argue about the fact of who the evil-doer is, and what he did and when?

Euthyphro. True.

Socrates. And the gods are in the same case, if as you assert they quarrel about just and unjust, and some of them say while others deny that injustice is done among them. For surely neither God nor man will ever venture to say that the doer of injustice is not to be punished?

Euthyphro. That is true, Socrates, in the main.

Socrates. But they join issue about the particulars—gods and men alike; and, if they dispute at all, they dispute about some act which is called in question, and which by some is affirmed to be just, by others to be unjust. Is not that true?

Euthyphro. Quite true.

Socrates. Well then, my dear friend Euthyphro, do tell me, for my better instruction and information, what proof have you that in the opinion of all the gods a servant who is guilty of murder, and is put in chains by the master of the dead man, and dies because he is put in chains before he who bound him can learn from the interpreters of the gods what he ought to do with him, dies unjustly; and that on behalf of such an one a son ought to proceed against his father and accuse him of murder. How would you show that all the gods absolutely agree in approving of his act? Prove to me that they do, and I will applaud your wisdom as long as I live.

Euthyphro. It will be a difficult task; but I could make the matter very clear indeed to you.

Socrates. I understand; you mean to say that I am not so quick of apprehension as the judges: for to them you will be sure to prove that the act is unjust, and hateful to the gods.

Euthyphro. Yes indeed, Socrates; at least if they will listen to me.

Socrates. But they will be sure to listen if they find that you are a good speaker. There was a notion that came into my mind while you were speaking; I said to myself: "Well, and what if Euthyphro does prove to me that all the gods regarded the death of the serf as unjust, how do I know anything more of the nature of piety and impiety? for granting that this action may be hateful to the gods, still piety and impiety are not adequately defined by these distinctions, for that which is hateful to the gods has been shown to be also pleasing and dear to them." And therefore, Euthyphro, I do not ask you to prove this; I will suppose, if you like, that all the gods condemn and abominate such an action. But I will amend the definition so far as to say that what all the gods hate is impious, and what they love pious or holy; and what some of them love and others hate is both or neither. Shall this be our definition of piety and impiety?

Euthyphro. Why not, Socrates?

Socrates. Why not! Certainly, as far as I am concerned, Euthyphro, there is no reason why not. But whether this admission will greatly assist you in the task of instructing me as you promised, is a matter for you to consider.

Euthyphro. Yes, I should say that what all the gods love is pious and holy, and the opposite which they all hate, impious.

Socrates. Ought we to enquire into the truth of this, Euthyphro, or simply to accept the mere statement on our own authority and that of others? What do you say?

Euthyphro. We should enquire; and I believe that the statement will stand the test of enquiry.

Socrates. We shall know better, my good friend, in a little while. The point which I should first wish to understand is whether the pious or holy is beloved by the gods because it is holy, or holy because it is beloved of the gods.

Euthyphro. I do not understand your meaning, Socrates.

Socrates. I will endeavour to explain: we speak of carrying and we speak of being carried, of leading and being led, seeing and being seen. You know that in all such cases there is a difference, and you know also in what the difference lies?

Euthyphro. I think that I understand.

Socrates. And is not that which is beloved distinct from that which loves?

Euthyphro. Certainly.

Socrates. Well; and now tell me, is that which is carried in this state of carrying because it is carried, or for some other reason?

Euthyphro. No; that is the reason.

Socrates. And the same is true of what is led and of what is seen?

Euthyphro. True.

Socrates. And a thing is not seen because it is visible, but conversely, visible because it is seen; nor is a thing led because it is in the state of being led, or carried because it is in the state of being carried, but the converse of this. And now I think, Euthyphro, that my meaning will be intelligible; and my meaning is, that any state of action or passion implies previous action or passion. It does not become because it is becoming, but it is in a state of becoming because it becomes; neither does it suffer because it is in a state of suffering, but it is in a state of suffering because it suffers. Do you not agree?

Euthyphro. Yes.

Socrates. Is not that which is loved in some state either of becoming or suffering?

Euthyphro. Yes.

Socrates. And the same holds as in the previous instances; the state of being loved follows the act of being loved, and not the act the state.

Euthyphro. Certainly.

Socrates. And what do you say of piety, Euthyphro; is not piety, according to your definition, loved by all the gods?

Euthyphro. Yes.

Socrates. Because it is pious or holy, or for some other reason?

Euthyphro. No, that is the reason.

Socrates. It is loved because it is holy, not holy because it is loved?

Euthyphro. Yes.

Socrates. And that which is dear to the gods is loved by them, and is in a state to be loved of them because it is loved of them?

Euthyphro. Certainly.

Socrates. Then that which is dear to the gods, Euthyphro, is not holy, nor is that which is holy loved of God, as you affirm; but they are two different things.

Euthyphro. How do you mean, Socrates?

Socrates. I mean to say that the holy has been acknowledged by us to be loved of God because it is holy, not to be holy because it is loved.

Euthyphro. Yes.

Socrates. But that which is dear to the gods is dear to them because it is loved by them, not loved by them because it is dear to them.

Euthyphro. True.

Socrates. But, friend Euthyphro, if that which is holy is the same with that which is dear to God, and is loved because it is holy, then that which is dear to God would have been loved as being dear to God; but if that which dear to God is dear to him because loved by him, then that which is holy would have been holy because loved by him. But now you see that the reverse is the case, and that they are quite different from one another. For one (Θεοφιλὲς) is of a kind to be loved because it is loved, and the other (ο'σιον) is loved because it is of a kind to be loved. Thus you appear to me, Euthyphro, when I ask you what is the essence of holiness, to offer an attribute only, and not the essence—the attribute of being loved by all the gods. But you still refuse to explain to me the nature of holiness. And therefore, if you please, I will ask you not to hide your treasure, but to tell me once more what holiness or piety really is, whether dear to the gods or not (for that is a matter about which we will not quarrel) and what is impiety?

Euthyphro. I really do not know, Socrates, how to express what I mean. For somehow or other our arguments, on whatever ground we rest them, seem to turn around and walk away from us.

* * *

CHAPTER 2

Subjectivism, Relativism, and Emotivism

Consider the following: Abdulla Yones killed his sixteen-year-old daughter Heshu in their apartment in west London. The murder was an example of an "honor killing," an ancient tradition still practiced in many parts of the world. Using a kitchen knife, Yones stabbed Heshu eleven times and slit her throat. He later declared that he *had* to kill her to expunge a stain from his family, a stain that Heshu had caused by her outrageous behavior. What was outrageous behavior to Yones, however, would seem to many Westerners to be typical teenage antics, annoying but benign. Heshu's precise offense against her family's honor is unclear, but the possibilities include wearing makeup, having a boyfriend, and showing an independent streak that would be thought perfectly normal throughout the West. In some countries, honor killings are sometimes endorsed by the local community or even given the tacit blessing of the state.

What do you think of this time-honored way of dealing with family conflicts? Specifically, what is your opinion regarding the *morality* of honor killing? Your response to this question is likely to reveal not only your view of honor killing but your overall approach to morality as well. Suppose your response is something like this: "Honor killing is morally *wrong*—wrong no matter where it's done or who does it." With this statement, you implicitly embrace moral **objectivism**—the theory that moral truths exist and that they do so independently of what individuals or societies think of them. In other words, there are moral facts, and they are not human inventions, fictions, or preferences. However, you need not hold that objective

principles are rigid rules that have no exceptions (a view known as *absolutism*) or that they must be applied in exactly the same way in every situation and culture.

On the other hand, let us say that you assess the case like this: "In societies that approve of honor killing, the practice is morally right; in those that do not approve, it is morally wrong. My society approves of honor killing, so it is morally right." If you believe what you say, then you are a cultural relativist. **Cultural relativism** is the view that an action is morally right if one's culture approves of it. Moral rightness and wrongness are therefore relative to cultures. So in one culture, an action may be morally right; in another culture, it may be morally wrong.

Perhaps you prefer an even narrower view of morality, and so you say, "Honor killing may be right for you, but it is most certainly not right for me." If you mean this literally, then you are committed to another kind of relativism called **subjective relativism**—the view that an action is morally right if one approves of it. Moral rightness and wrongness are relative not to cultures but to individuals. An action, then, can be right for you but wrong for someone else. Your approving of an action makes it right. There is therefore no objective morality, and cultural norms do not make right or wrong—individuals make right or wrong.

Finally, imagine that you wish to take a different tack regarding the subject of honor killing. You say, "I abhor the practice of honor killing"—but you believe that in uttering these words you are saying nothing that is true or false. You believe that despite what your statement seems to mean, you are simply expressing your emotions. You therefore hold to **emotivism**—the view that moral utterances are neither true nor false but are instead expressions of emotions or attitudes. So in your sentence about honor killing, you are not stating a fact—you are merely emoting and possibly trying to influence someone's behavior. Even when emotivists express a more specific preference regarding other people's behavior—by saying, for instance, "No one should commit an honor killing"—they are still not making a factual claim. They are simply expressing a preference, and perhaps hoping to persuade other people to see things their way.

These four replies represent four distinct perspectives (though certainly not the *only* perspectives) on the meaning and import of moral judgments. Moreover, they are not purely theoretical, but real and relevant. People actually live their lives (or try to) as moral objectivists, or relativists, or emotivists, or some strange and inconsistent mixture of these. (There is an excellent chance, for example, that you were raised as an objectivist but now accept some form of relativism—or even try to hold to objectivism in some instances and relativism in others.)

In any case, the question that you should ask (and that ethics can help you answer) is not whether you in fact accept any of these views, but whether you are justified in doing so. Let us see, then, where an examination of reasons for and against them will lead.

SUBJECTIVE RELATIVISM

What view of morality could be more tempting (and convenient) than the notion that an action is right if someone approves of it? Subjective relativism says that action X is right for Ann if she approves of it yet wrong for Greg if he disapproves of it. Thus action X can be both right and wrong—right for Ann but wrong for Greg. A person's approval of an action *makes it right* for that person. Action X is not

> ### QUICK REVIEW
>
> **objectivism**—The theory that moral truths exist and that they do so independently of what individuals or societies think of them.
>
> **cultural relativism**—The view that an action is morally right if one's culture approves of it. *Implications*: that cultures are morally infallible, that social reformers can never be morally right, that moral disagreements between individuals in the same culture amount to arguments over whether someone disagrees with her culture, that other cultures cannot be legitimately criticized, and that moral progress is impossible.
>
> **subjective relativism**—The view that an action is morally right if one approves of it. *Implications*: that individuals are morally infallible and that genuine moral disagreement between individuals is nearly impossible.
>
> **emotivism**—The view that moral utterances are neither true nor false but are expressions of emotions or attitudes. *Implications*: that people cannot disagree over the moral facts because there are no moral facts, that presenting reasons in support of a moral utterance is a matter of offering nonmoral facts that can influence someone's attitude, and that nothing is actually good or bad.

objectively right (or wrong). It is right (or wrong) relative to individuals. In this way, moral rightness becomes a matter of personal taste. If to Ann strawberry ice cream tastes good, then it is good (for her). If to Greg strawberry ice cream tastes bad, then it is bad (for him). There is no such thing as strawberry ice cream tasting good objectively or generally. Likewise, the morality of an action depends on Ann's and Greg's moral tastes.

Many people claim they are subjective relativists—until they realize the implications of the doctrine

Judge Not?

Jesus said "Judge not that ye be not judged." Some have taken this to mean that we should not make moral judgments about others, and many who have never heard those words are convinced that to judge others is to be insensitive, intolerant, or absolutist. Professor Jean Bethke Elshtain examines this attitude and finds it both mistaken and harmful.

> I have also found helpful the discussion of the lively British philosopher, Mary Midgley. In her book *Can't We Make Moral Judgments?* Midgley notes our contemporary search for a nonjudgmental politics and quotes all those people who cry, in effect, "But surely it's always wrong to make moral judgments." We are not permitted to make anyone uncomfortable, to be "insensitive." Yet moral judgment of "some kind," says Midgley, "is a necessary element to our thinking." Judging involves our whole nature—it isn't just icing on the cake of self-identity. Judging makes it possible for us to "find our way through a whole forest of possibilities."

Midgley argues that Jesus was taking aim at sweeping condemnations and vindictiveness: he was not trashing the "whole faculty of judgment." Indeed, Jesus is making the "subtle point that while we cannot possibly avoid judging, we can see to it that we judge fairly, as we would expect others to do to us." This is part and parcel, then, of justice as fairness, as a discernment about a particular case and person and deed. Subjectivism in such matters—of the "I'm okay, you're okay," variety—is a cop-out, a way to stop forming and expressing moral judgments altogether. This strange suspension of specific moments of judgment goes hand-in-glove, of course, with an often violent rhetoric of condemnation of whole categories of persons, past and present—that all-purpose villain, the Dead White European Male, comes to mind.*

*Jean Bethke Elshtain, "Judge Not?" *First Things*, no. 46, pp. 36–40, October 1994. Reprinted by permission of the publisher.

that are at odds with our commonsense moral experience. First, subjective relativism implies that in the rendering of any moral opinion, each person is incapable of being in error. Each of us is *morally infallible*. If we approve of an action—and we are sincere in our approval—then that action is morally right. We literally cannot be mistaken about this, because our approval makes the action right. If we say that inflicting pain on an innocent child for no reason is right (that is, we approve of such an action), then the action is right. Our moral judgment is correct, and it cannot be otherwise. Yet if anything is obvious about our moral experience, it is that we are *not* infallible. We sometimes *are* mistaken in our moral judgments. We are, after all, not gods.

By all accounts, Adolf Hitler approved of (and ordered) the extermination of vast numbers of

innocent people, including six million Jews. If so, by the lights of subjective relativism, his facilitating those deaths was morally right. It seems that the totalitarian leader Pol Pot approved of his murdering more than a million innocent people in Cambodia. If so, it was right for him to murder those people. But it seems obvious that what these men did was wrong and that their approving of their actions did not make the actions right. Because subjective relativism suggests otherwise, it is a dubious doctrine.

Another obvious feature of our commonsense moral experience is that from time to time we have moral disagreements. Maria says that capital punishment is right, but Carlos says that it is wrong. This seems like a perfectly clear case of two people disagreeing about the morality of capital punishment.

Subjective relativism, however, implies that such disagreements cannot happen. Subjective relativism says that when Maria states that capital punishment is right, she is just saying that she approves of it. And when Carlos states that capital punishment is wrong, he is just saying that he disapproves of it. But they are not really disagreeing, because they are merely describing their attitudes toward capital punishment. In effect, Maria is saying "This is my attitude on the subject," and Carlos is saying "Here is my attitude on the subject." But these two claims are not opposed to each other. They are about different subjects, so both statements could be true. Maria and Carlos might as well be discussing how strawberry ice cream tastes to each of them, for nothing that Maria says could contradict what Carlos says. Because genuine disagreement is a fact of our moral life, and subjective relativism is inconsistent with this fact, the doctrine is implausible.

In practice, subjective relativism is a difficult view to hold consistently. At times, of course, you can insist that an action is right for you but wrong for someone else. But you may also find yourself saying something like "Pol Pot committed absolutely heinous acts; he was evil," or "What Hitler did was wrong"—and what you mean is that what Pol Pot and Hitler did was objectively wrong, not just wrong relative to you. Such slides from subjective relativism to objectivism suggest a conflict between these two perspectives and the need to resolve it through critical reasoning.

CULTURAL RELATIVISM

To many people, the idea that morality is relative to culture is obvious. It seems obvious primarily because modern sociology has left no doubt that people's moral judgments differ from culture to culture. The moral judgments of people in other cultures are often shockingly different from our own. In some societies, it is morally permissible to kill infants at birth, burn widows alive with the bodies of their husbands, steal and commit acts of treachery, surgically remove the clitorises of young girls for no medical reason, kill one's elderly parents, have multiple husbands or wives, and make up for someone's death by murdering others. Among some people, it has been considered morally acceptable to kill those of a different sexual orientation, lynch persons with a different skin color, and allow children to die by refusing to give them available medical treatment. (These latter acts have all been practiced in subcultures within the United States, so not all such cultural differences happen far from home.) It is only a small step from acknowledging this moral diversity among cultures to the conclusion that cultures determine moral rightness and that objective morality is a myth.

The philosopher Walter T. Stace (1886–1967) illustrates how easily this conclusion has come to many in Western societies:

> It was easy enough to believe in a single absolute morality in older times when there was no anthropology, when all humanity was divided clearly into two groups, Christian peoples and the "heathen." Christian peoples knew and possessed the one true morality. The rest were savages whose moral ideas could be ignored. But all this changed. Greater knowledge has brought greater tolerance. We can no longer exalt our own moralities as alone true, while dismissing all other moralities as false or inferior. The investigations of anthropologists have shown that there exist side by side in the world a bewildering variety of moral codes. On this topic endless volumes have been written, masses of evidence piled up. Anthropologists have ransacked the Melanesian Islands, the jungles of New Guinea, the steppes of Siberia, the deserts of Australia, the forests of central Africa, and have brought back with them countless examples of weird, extravagant, and fantastic "moral" customs with which to confound us. We learn that all kinds of horrible practices are, in this, that, or the other place, regarded as essential to virtue. We find that there is nothing, or next to nothing, which has always and everywhere been regarded as morally good by all men. Where then is our universal morality? Can we, in face of all this evidence, deny that it is nothing but an empty dream?[1]

Here, Stace spells out in rough form the most common argument for cultural relativism, an inference from differences in the moral beliefs of cultures to the conclusion that cultures make morality. Before we conclude that objectivism is in fact an empty dream, we should state the argument more precisely and examine it closely. We can lay out the argument like this:

1. People's judgments about right and wrong differ from culture to culture.

2. If people's judgments about right and wrong differ from culture to culture, then right and wrong are relative to culture, and there are no objective moral principles.

3. Therefore, right and wrong are relative to culture, and there are no objective moral principles.

A good argument gives us good reason to accept its conclusion, and an argument is good if its logic is solid (the conclusion follows logically from the premises) *and* the premises are true. So is the foregoing argument a good one? We can see right away that the logic is in fact solid. That is, the argument is valid: the conclusion does indeed follow from the premises. The question then becomes whether the premises are true. As we have seen, Premise 1 is most certainly true. People's judgments about right and wrong do vary from culture to culture. But what of Premise 2? Does the diversity of views about right and wrong among cultures show that right and wrong are determined by culture, that there are no universal moral truths? There are good reasons to think this premise false.

CRITICAL THOUGHT: "Female Circumcision" and Cultural Relativism

In recent years many conflicts have flared between those who espouse universal human rights and those who embrace cultural relativism. One issue that has been a flash point in these contentious debates is a practice called *female genital cutting* (FGC). Other names include *female circumcision* and *female genital mutilation*.

In FGC, all or part of the female genitals are removed. The procedure, used mostly in Africa and the Middle East, is usually performed on girls between the ages of four and eight, but sometimes on young women. A report in the *Yale Journal of Public Health* states that in Sudan, 89 percent of girls receive FGC and that the cutting tools used "include knives, scissors, razors, and broken glass. The operation is typically performed by elderly women or traditional birth attendants, though increasing numbers of doctors are taking over these roles."* The practice occurs for various reasons, including religious and sociological ones, and is defended by some who say that it prepares girls for their role in society and marriage and discourages illicit sex.

Public health officials regard FGC as a serious health problem. It can cause reproductive tract infections, pain during intercourse, painful menstruation, complications during childbirth, greater risk of HIV infection, bleeding, and even death. International health agencies denounce FGC, but many say that no one outside a culture using FGC has a right to criticize the practice.

Do you think that FGC is morally permissible? If you judge the practice wrong, are you appealing to some notion of objective morality? If you judge it permissible, are you doing so because you are a cultural relativist? In either case, explain your reasoning.

*Sarah Cannon and Daniel Berman, "Cut Off: The Female Genital-Cutting Controversy," *Yale Journal of Public Health* 1, no. 2 (2004).

Premise 2 says that because there are disagreements among cultures about right and wrong, there must not be any universal standards of right and wrong. But even if the moral judgments of people in various cultures do differ, such differences in themselves do not show that morality is relative to culture. Just because people in different cultures have different views about morality, their disagreement does not prove that no view can be objectively correct—no more than people's disagreements about the size of a house show that no one's opinion about it can be objectively true. Suppose Culture 1 endorses infanticide, but Culture 2 does not. Such a disagreement does not demonstrate that both cultures are equally correct or that there is no objectively correct answer. After all, it is possible that infanticide is objectively right (or wrong) and that the relevant moral beliefs of either Culture 1 or Culture 2 are false.

Another reason to doubt the truth of Premise 2 comes from questioning how deep the disagreements among cultures really are. Judgments about the rightness of actions obviously do vary across cultures. But people can differ in their moral judgments not just because they accept different moral principles, but also because they have divergent *nonmoral* beliefs. They may actually embrace the *same* moral principles, but their moral judgments conflict because their nonmoral beliefs lead them to apply those principles in very different ways. If so, the diversity of moral judgments across cultures does not necessarily indicate deep disagreements over fundamental moral principles or standards. Here is a classic example:

> [T]he story is told of a culture in which a son is regarded as obligated to kill his father when the latter reaches age sixty. Given just this much information about the culture and the practice in question it is tempting to conclude that the members of that culture differ radically from members of our culture in their moral beliefs and attitudes. We, after all, believe it is immoral to take a human life, and regard patricide as especially wrong. But suppose

that in the culture we are considering, those who belong to it believe (a) that at the moment of death one enters heaven; (b) one's physical and mental condition in the afterlife is exactly what it is at the moment of death; and (c) men are at the peak of their physical and mental powers when they are sixty. Then what appeared at first to be peculiarities in moral outlook on the part of the cultural group in question regarding the sanctity of life and respect for parents, turn out to be located rather in a nonmoral outlook of the group. A man in that culture who kills his father is doing so out of concern for the latter's well-being—to prevent him, for example, from spending eternity blind or senile. It is not at all clear that, if we shared the relevant nonmoral beliefs of this other culture, we would not believe with them that sons should kill their fathers at the appropriate time.[2]

To find similar examples, we need not search for the exotic. In Western cultures we have the familiar case of abortion, an issue hotly debated among those who at first glance appear to be disagreeing about moral principles. But in fact the disputants agree about the moral principle involved: that murder (unjustly killing a person) is morally wrong. What they do disagree about is a nonmoral factual matter—whether the fetus is an entity that can be murdered (that is, whether it is a person). Disagreement over the nonmoral facts masks substantial agreement on fundamental moral standards.

The work of several anthropologists provides some evidence for these kinds of disagreements as well as for the existence of cross-cultural moral agreement in general. The social psychologist Solomon Asch, for instance, maintains that differing moral judgments among societies often arise when the same moral principles are operating but the particulars of cultural situations vary.[3] Other observers claim that across numerous diverse cultures we can find many common moral elements such as prohibitions against murder, lying, incest, and adultery and obligations of fairness, reciprocity, and consideration toward parents and children.[4] Some philosophers argue that a core set of moral values—including, for example, truth telling and prohibitions against murder—*must* be universal, otherwise cultures would not survive.

These points demonstrate that Premise 2 of the argument for cultural relativism is false. The argument therefore gives us no good reasons to believe that an action is right simply because one's culture approves of it.

For many people, however, the failure of the argument for cultural relativism may be beside the point. They find the doctrine appealing mainly because it seems to promote the humane and enlightened attitude of tolerance toward other cultures. Broad expanses of history are drenched with blood and marked by cruelty because of the evil of intolerance—religious, racial, political, and social. Tolerance therefore seems a supreme virtue, and cultural relativism appears to provide a justification and vehicle for it. After all, if all cultures are morally equal, does not cultural relativism both entail and promote tolerance?

We should hope that tolerance does reign in a pluralistic world, but there is no necessary connection between tolerance and cultural relativism. For one thing, cultural relativists cannot consistently advocate tolerance. To advocate tolerance is to advocate an objective moral value. But if tolerance is an objective moral value, then cultural relativism must be false, because it says that there are no objective moral values. So instead of justifying tolerance toward all, cultural relativism actually undercuts universal tolerance. Moreover, according to cultural relativism, intolerance can be justified just as easily as tolerance can. If a culture approves of intolerance, then intolerance is right for that culture. If a culture approves of tolerance, then tolerance is right for that culture. Cultural relativists are thus committed to the view that intolerance can in fact be justified, and they cannot consistently claim that tolerance is morally right everywhere.

At this point we are left with no good reasons to believe that cultural relativism is true. But the problems for the doctrine are deeper than that. Like subjective relativism, it has several implications that render it highly implausible.

First, like subjective relativism, cultural relativism implies moral infallibility—that a culture simply cannot be mistaken about a moral issue. If it approves of an action, then that action is morally right, and there is no possibility of error as long as the culture's approval is genuine. But, of course, cultural infallibility in moral matters is flagrantly implausible, just as individual infallibility is. At one time or another, cultures have sanctioned witch burning, slavery, genocide, racism, rape, human sacrifice, and religious persecution. Does it make any sense to say that they could not have been mistaken about the morality of these actions?

Cultural relativism also has the peculiar consequence that social reformers of every sort would *always be wrong*. Their culture would be the ultimate authority on moral matters, so if they disagreed with their culture, they could not possibly be right. If their culture approved of genocide, genocide would be right, and antigenocide reformers would be wrong to oppose the practice. In this upside-down world, the antigenocide reformers would be immoral, and the genocidal culture would be the real paragon of righteousness. Reformers such as Martin Luther King Jr., Mahatma Gandhi, Mary Wollstonecraft (champion of women's rights), and Frederick Douglass (American abolitionist) would be great crusaders—for immorality. Our moral experience, however, suggests that cultural relativism has matters exactly backward. Social reformers have often been right when they claimed their cultures were wrong, and this fact suggests that cultural relativism is wrong about morality.

Where cultural relativism holds, if you have a disagreement with your culture about the rightness of an action, you automatically lose. You are in error by definition. But what about a disagreement among members of the same society? What does such a disagreement amount to? It amounts to something very strange, according to cultural relativism. When two people in the same culture disagree on a moral issue, what they are really disagreeing about—the only thing they can rationally disagree about—is whether their society endorses a particular view. After all, society makes actions right by approving or disapproving of them. According to cultural relativism, if René and Michel (both members of society X) are disagreeing about capital punishment, their disagreement must actually be about whether society X approves of capital punishment. Because right and wrong are determined by one's culture, René and Michel are disagreeing about what society X says. But this view of moral disagreement is dubious, to say the least. When we have a moral disagreement, we do not think that the crux of it is whether our society approves of an action. We do not think that deciding a moral issue is simply a matter of polling the public to see which way opinion leans. We do not think that René and Michel will ever find out whether capital punishment is morally permissible by consulting public opinion. Determining whether an action is right is a very different thing from determining what most people think. This odd consequence of cultural relativism suggests that the doctrine is flawed.

One of the more disturbing implications of cultural relativism is that cultures cannot be legitimately criticized from the outside. If a culture approves of the actions that it performs, then those actions are morally right, regardless of what other cultures have to say about the matter. One society's practices are as morally justified as any other's, as long as the practices are socially sanctioned. This consequence of cultural relativism may not seem too worrisome when the societies in question are long dead. But it takes on a different tone when the societies are closer to us in time. Consider the 1994 genocide committed in Rwanda in which a million people died. Suppose the killers' society (their tribe) approved of the murders. Then the genocide was morally justified. And what of Hitler's "final solution"—the murder of millions of Jews in World War II? Say that German society approved of Hitler's actions (and those of the men who

carried out his orders). Then Hitler's final solution was morally right; engineering the Holocaust was morally permissible. If you are a cultural relativist, you cannot legitimately condemn these monstrous deeds. Because they were approved by their respective societies, they were morally justified. They were just as morally justified as the socially sanctioned activities of Albert Schweitzer, Jonas Salk, or Florence Nightingale. But all this seems implausible. We do in fact sometimes criticize other cultures and believe that it is legitimate to do so.

Contrary to the popular view, rejecting cultural relativism (embracing moral objectivism) does not entail intolerance. In fact, it provides a plausible starting point for tolerance. A moral objectivist realizes that she can legitimately criticize other cultures—and that people of other cultures can legitimately criticize her culture. A recognition of this fact together with an objectivist's sense of fallibility can lead her to an openness to criticism of her own culture and to acceptance of everyone's right to disagree.

We not only criticize other cultures but also compare the past with the present. We compare the actions of the past with those of the present and judge whether moral progress has been made. We see that slavery has been abolished, that we no longer burn witches, that we recognize racism as evil—then we judge that these changes represent moral progress. For moral relativists, however, there is no objective standard by which to compare the ways of the past with the ways of the present. Societies of the past approved or disapproved of certain practices, and contemporary societies approve or disapprove of them, and no transcultural moral assessments can be made. But if there is such a thing as moral progress, then there must be some cross-cultural moral yardstick by which we can evaluate actions. There must be objective standards by which we can judge that actions of the present are better than those of the past. If there are no objective moral standards, our judging that we are in fact making moral progress is hard to explain.

Finally, there is a fundamental difficulty concerning the application of cultural relativism to moral questions: the doctrine is nearly impossible to use. The problem is that cultural relativism applies to societies (or social groups), but we all belong to several societies, and there is no way to choose which one is the proper one. What society do you belong to if you are an Italian American Buddhist living in Atlanta, Georgia, who is a member of the National Organization for Women and a breast cancer support group? The hope of cultural relativists is that they can use the doctrine to make better, more enlightened moral decisions. But this society-identification problem seems to preclude any moral decisions, let alone enlightened ones.

What, then, can we conclude from our examination of cultural relativism? We have found that the basic argument for the view fails; we therefore have no good reasons to believe that the doctrine is true. Beyond that, we have good grounds for thinking the doctrine false. Its surprising implications regarding moral infallibility, moral reformers, moral progress, the nature of moral disagreements within societies, and the possibility of cross-cultural criticism show it to be highly implausible. The crux of the matter is that cultural relativism does a poor job of explaining some important features of our moral experience. A far better explanation of these features is that some form of moral objectivism is true.

EMOTIVISM

The commonsense view of moral judgments is that they ascribe moral properties to such things as actions and people and that they are therefore statements that can be true or false. This view of moral judgments is known as *cognitivism.* The opposing view, called *noncognitivism,* denies that moral judgments are statements that can be true or false; it holds that they do not ascribe properties to anything. Probably the most famous

noncognitivist view is emotivism, which says that moral judgments cannot be true or false because they do not make any claims—they merely express emotions or attitudes. For the emotivist, moral utterances are something akin to exclamations that simply express approving or disapproving feelings: "Violence against women—disgusting!" or "Shoplifting—love it!"

The English philosopher A. J. Ayer (1910–1989), an early champion of emotivism, is clear and blunt about what a moral utterance such as "Stealing money is wrong" signifies. This sentence, he says,

> expresses no proposition which can be either true or false. It is as if I had written "Stealing money!!"—where the shape and thickness of the exclamation marks show, by a suitable convention, that a special sort of moral disapproval is the feeling which is being expressed. It is clear that there is nothing said here which can be true or false. . . . For in saying that a certain type of action is right or wrong, I am not making any factual statement, not even a statement about my own state of mind.[5]

If moral judgments are about feelings and not the truth or falsity of moral assertions, then ethics is a very different sort of inquiry than most people imagine. As Ayer says,

> [A]s ethical judgements are mere expressions of feeling, there can be no way of determining the validity of any ethical system, and, indeed, no sense in asking whether any such system is true. All that one may legitimately enquire in this connection is, What are the moral habits of a given person or group of people, and what causes them to have precisely those habits and feelings? And this enquiry falls wholly within the scope of the existing social sciences.[6]

The emotivist points out that in addition to expressing feelings and attitudes, moral utterances also function to influence people's attitudes and behavior. So the sentence "Stealing money is wrong" not only expresses feelings of disapproval but can also influence others to have similar feelings and act accordingly.

Emotivists also take an unusual position on moral disagreements. They maintain that moral disagreements are not conflicts of beliefs, as is the case when one person asserts that something is true and another person asserts that it is not true. Instead, moral disagreements are *disagreements in attitude.* Jane has positive feelings or a favorable attitude toward abortion, but Ellen has negative feelings or an unfavorable attitude toward abortion. The disagreement is emotive, not cognitive. Jane may say "Abortion is right," and Ellen may say "Abortion is wrong," but they are not really disagreeing over the facts. They are expressing conflicting attitudes and trying to influence each other's attitude and behavior.

Philosophers have criticized emotivism on several grounds, and this emotivist analysis of disagreement has been a prime target. As you might suspect, their concern is that this notion of disagreement is radically different from our ordinary view. Like subjective relativism, emotivism implies that disagreements in the usual sense are impossible. People cannot disagree over the moral facts, because there are no moral facts. But we tend to think that when we disagree with someone on a moral issue, there really is a conflict of statements about what is the case. Of course, when we are involved in a conflict of beliefs, we may also experience conflicting attitudes. But we do not think that we are *only* experiencing a disagreement in attitudes.

Emotivism also provides a curious account of how reasons function in moral discourse. Our commonsense view is that a moral judgment is the kind of thing that makes a claim about moral properties and that such a claim can be supported by reasons. If someone asserts "Euthanasia is wrong," we may sensibly ask her what reasons she has for believing that claim. If she replies that there are no reasons to back up her claim or that moral utterances are not the kinds of things that can be supported by reasons, we would probably think that she misunderstood the question or the nature of morality. For the emotivist, "moral" reasons have a very

different function. Here reasons are intended not to support statements (because there are no moral statements) but to influence the emotions or attitudes of others. Because moral utterances express emotions or attitudes, "presenting reasons" is a matter of offering nonmoral facts that can influence those emotions and attitudes. Suppose A has a favorable attitude toward abortion, and B has an unfavorable one (that is, A and B are having a disagreement in attitude). For A, to present reasons is to provide information that might cause B to have a more favorable attitude toward abortion.

This conception of the function of reasons, however, implies that good reasons encompass *any* nonmoral facts that can alter someone's attitude. On this view, the relevance of these facts to the judgment at hand is beside the point. The essential criterion is whether the adduced facts are sufficiently influential. They need not have any logical or cognitive connection to the moral judgment to be changed. They may, for example, appeal to someone's ignorance, arrogance, racism, or fear. But we ordinarily suppose that reasons *should* be relevant to the cognitive content of moral judgments. Moreover, we normally make a clear distinction between influencing someone's attitudes and showing (by providing reasons) that a claim is true—a distinction that emotivism cannot make.

The final implication of emotivism is also problematic: there is no such thing as goodness or badness. We cannot legitimately claim that anything is good or bad, because these properties do not exist. To declare that something is good is simply to express positive emotions or a favorable attitude toward it. We may say that pain is bad, but badness (or goodness) is not a feature of pain. Our saying that pain is bad is just an expression of our unfavorable attitude toward pain.

Suppose a six-year-old girl is living in a small village in Syria during the civil war between President Bashar al-Assad's Baathist government and rebel forces. Assad's henchmen firebomb the village, destroying it and incinerating everyone except the girl, who is burned from head to toe and endures excruciating pain for three days before she dies. Suppose that we are deeply moved by this tragedy as we consider her unimaginable suffering and we remark, "How horrible. The little girl's suffering was a very bad thing."[7] When we say something like this, we ordinarily mean that the girl's suffering had a certain moral property: that the suffering was bad. But according to emotivism, her suffering had no moral properties at all. When we comment on the girl's suffering, we are simply expressing our feelings; the suffering itself was neither good nor bad. But this view of things seems implausible. Our moral experience suggests that some things in fact are bad and some are good.

The philosopher Brand Blanshard (1892–1987) makes the point in the following way:

> [T]he emotivist is cut off by his theory from admitting that there has been anything good or evil in the past, either animal or human. There have been Black Deaths, to be sure, and wars and rumours of war; there have been the burning of countless women as witches, and the massacre in the Katyn forest, and Oswiecim, and Dachau, and an unbearable procession of horrors; but one cannot meaningfully say that anything evil has ever happened. The people who suffered from these things did indeed take up attitudes of revulsion toward them; we can now judge that they took them; but in such judgments we are not saying that anything evil occurred. . . . [Emotivism], when first presented, has some plausibility. But when this is balanced against the implied unplausibility of setting down as meaningless every suggestion that good or evil events have ever occurred, it is outweighed enormously.[8]

Obviously, emotivism does not fare well when examined in light of our commonsense moral experience. We must keep in mind, though, that common sense is fallible. On the other hand, we should not jettison common sense in favor of another view unless we have good reasons to do so. In the case of emotivism, we have no good reasons to prefer it over common sense—and we have good grounds for rejecting it.

CHAPTER REVIEW

SUMMARY

Subjective relativism is the view that an action is morally right if one approves of it. A person's approval makes the action right. This doctrine (as well as cultural relativism) is in stark contrast to *moral objectivism,* the view that moral truths exist and that they do so independently of what individuals or societies think of them. Subjective relativism, though, has some troubling implications. It implies that each person is morally infallible and that individuals can never have a genuine moral disagreement.

Cultural relativism is the view that an action is morally right if one's culture approves of it. The argument for this doctrine is based on the diversity of moral judgments among cultures: because people's judgments about right and wrong differ from culture to culture, right and wrong must be relative to culture, and there are no objective moral principles. This argument is defective, however, because the diversity of moral views does not imply that morality is relative to cultures. In addition, the alleged diversity of basic moral standards among cultures may be only apparent, not real. Societies whose moral judgments conflict may be differing not over moral principles but over nonmoral facts.

Some think that tolerance is entailed by cultural relativism. But there is no necessary connection between tolerance and the doctrine. Indeed, the cultural relativist cannot consistently advocate tolerance while maintaining his relativist standpoint. To advocate tolerance is to advocate an objective moral value. But if tolerance is an objective moral value, then cultural relativism must be false, because it says that there are no objective moral values.

Like subjective relativism, cultural relativism has some disturbing consequences. It implies that cultures are morally infallible, that social reformers can never be morally right, that moral disagreements between individuals in the same culture amount to arguments over whether they disagree with their culture, that other cultures cannot be legitimately criticized, and that moral progress is impossible.

Emotivism is the view that moral utterances are neither true nor false but are expressions of emotions or attitudes. It leads to the conclusion that people can disagree only in attitude, not in beliefs. People cannot disagree over the moral facts, because there are no moral facts. Emotivism also implies that presenting reasons in support of a moral utterance is a matter of offering nonmoral facts that can influence someone's attitude. It seems that any nonmoral facts will do, as long as they affect attitudes. Perhaps the most far-reaching implication of emotivism is that nothing is actually good or bad. There simply are no properties of goodness and badness. There is only the expression of favorable or unfavorable emotions or attitudes toward something.

KEY TERMS
objectivism (p. 20)
cultural relativism (p. 20)
subjective relativism (p. 20)
emotivism (p. 21)

EXERCISES

Review Questions

1. Does objectivism entail intolerance? Why or why not? (p. 20)
2. Does objectivism require absolutism? Why or why not? (p. 20)
3. How does subjective relativism differ from cultural relativism? (p. 20)
4. What is emotivism? How does emotivism differ from objectivism? (p. 21)
5. How does subjective relativism imply moral infallibility? (p. 22)
6. According to moral subjectivism, are moral disagreements possible? Why or why not? (pp. 22–23)
7. What is the argument for cultural relativism? Is the argument sound? Why or why not? (pp. 23–26)
8. Does the diversity of moral outlooks in cultures show that right and wrong are determined by culture? Why or why not? (pp. 24–26)

9. According to the text, how is it possible for people in different cultures to disagree about moral judgments and still embrace the same fundamental moral principles? (pp. 25–26)
10. Is there a necessary connection between cultural relativism and tolerance? Why or why not? (p. 26)
11. What does cultural relativism imply about the moral status of social reformers? (p. 26)
12. What is the emotivist view of moral disagreements? (p. 29)
13. According to emotivism, how do reasons function in moral discourse? (p. 29)

Discussion Questions

1. Are you a subjective relativist? If so, how did you come to adopt this view? If not, what is your explanation for not accepting it?
2. Suppose a serial killer approves of his murderous actions. According to subjective relativism, are the killer's actions therefore justified? Do you believe a serial killer's murders are justified? If not, is your judgment based on a subjective relativist's perspective or an objectivist perspective?
3. Are you a cultural relativist? Why or why not?
4. Suppose a majority of the German people approved of Hitler's murdering six million Jews in World War II. Would this approval make Hitler's actions morally justified? If so, why? If not, why not—and what moral outlook are you using to make such a determination?
5. When cultural relativists say that every culture should embrace a policy of tolerance, are they contradicting themselves? If so, how? If cultural relativism were true, would this fact make wars between societies less or more likely? Explain your answer.
6. If you traveled the world and saw that cultures differ dramatically in their moral judgments, would you conclude from this evidence that cultural relativism was true? Why or why not?
7. According to a cultural relativist, would the civil rights reforms that Martin Luther King Jr. sought be morally right or wrong? Do *you* think

that his efforts at reform were morally wrong? What are your reasons for your decision?

8. Do you believe that there has been moral progress in the past thousand years of human history? Why or why not?

9. Suppose a deer that had been shot by a hunter writhed in agony for days before dying. You exclaim, "How she must have suffered! Her horrendous pain was a bad thing." In this situation, does the word *bad* refer to any moral properties? Is there really something *bad* about the deer's suffering—or is your use of the word just a way to express your horror without making any moral statement at all? Explain your answers.

ETHICAL DILEMMAS

1. In Western societies, some cultural subgroups believe it is morally permissible to kill anyone who criticizes their religion. Do you agree or disagree with this view? On what grounds? Is your position relativist or objectivist?

2. Suppose you are a social reformer campaigning against your culture's practice of systematically discriminating against the poorest people in your society. Do you think your stance is morally right—or is your culture right while you are wrong? Why?

3. Suppose you accept (approve of) premarital sex. Is it possible for you to be mistaken about this issue? Why or why not? Does your answer suggest that you are a subjective relativist?

FURTHER READING

A. J. Ayer, *Language, Truth and Logic* (1936; reprint, New York: Dover, 1952).

Brand Blanshard, "Emotivism," in *Reason and Goodness* (1961; reprint, New York: G. Allen and Unwin, 1978).

Donald M. Borchert and David Stewart, "Ethical Emotivism," in *Exploring Ethics* (New York: Macmillan, 1986).

Richard B. Brandt, chapter 11 in *Ethical Theory: The Problems of Normative and Critical Ethics* (Englewood Cliffs, NJ: Prentice Hall, 1959).

Jean Bethke Elshtain, "Judge Not?" *First Things,* no. 46 (October 1994): 36–40.

Fred Feldman, chapter 11 in *Introductory Ethics* (Englewood Cliffs, NJ: Prentice Hall, 1978).

Chris Gowans, "Moral Relativism," in *Stanford Encyclopedia of Philosophy*, Spring 2004 ed., ed. Edward N. Zalta, http://plato.stanford.edu/archives/spr2004/entries/moral-relativism (March 1, 2015).

Melville Herskovits, *Cultural Relativism: Perspectives in Cultural Pluralism,* ed. Frances Herskovits (New York: Random House, 1972).

J. L. Mackie, *Ethics: Inventing Right and Wrong* (Harmondsworth: Penguin, 1977).

James Rachels, "Subjectivism," in *A Companion to Ethics*, ed. Peter Singer, corr. ed. (Oxford: Blackwell, 1993), 432–41.

Theodore Schick Jr. and Lewis Vaughn, chapter 5 in *Doing Philosophy: An Introduction through Thought Experiments,* 2nd ed. (Boston: McGraw-Hill, 2003).

Walter T. Stace, "Ethical Relativism," in *The Concept of Morals* (1937; reprint, New York: Macmillan, 1965).

Paul Taylor, chapter 2 in *Principles of Ethics: An Introduction* (Encino, CA: Dickenson, 1975).

David Wong, "Relativism," in *A Companion to Ethics*, ed. Peter Singer, corr. ed. (Oxford: Blackwell, 1993), 442–50.

READINGS

From *Anthropology and the Abnormal*
Ruth Benedict

Modern social anthropology has become more and more a study of the varieties and common elements of cultural environment and the consequences of these in human behavior. For such a study of diverse social orders primitive peoples fortunately provide a laboratory not yet entirely vitiated by the spread of a standardized worldwide civilization. Dyaks and Hopis, Fijians and Yakuts are significant for psychological and sociological study because only among these simpler peoples has there been sufficient isolation to give opportunity for the development of localized social forms. In the higher cultures the standardization of custom and belief over a couple of continents has given a false sense of the inevitability of the particular forms that have gained currency, and we need to turn to a wider survey in order to check the conclusions we hastily base upon this near-universality of familiar customs. Most of the simpler cultures did not gain the wide currency of the one which, out of our experience, we identify with human nature, but this was for various historical reasons, and certainly not for any that gives us as its carriers a monopoly of social good or of social sanity. Modern civilization, from this point of view, becomes not a necessary pinnacle of human achievement but one entry in a long series of possible adjustments.

These adjustments, whether they are in mannerisms like the ways of showing anger, or joy, or grief in any society, or in major human drives like those of sex, prove to be far more variable than experience in any one culture would suggest. In certain fields, such as that of religion or of formal marriage arrangements, these wide limits of variability are well known and can be fairly described. In others it is not yet possible to give a generalized account, but that does not absolve us of the task of indicating the significance of the work that has been done and of the problems that have arisen.

One of these problems relates to the customary modern normal-abnormal categories and our conclusions regarding them. In how far are such categories culturally determined, or in how far can we with assurance regard them as absolute? In how far can we regard inability to function socially as diagnostic of abnormality, or in how far is it necessary to regard this as a function of the culture?

As a matter of fact, one of the most striking facts that emerge from a study of widely varying cultures is the ease with which our abnormals function in other cultures. It does not matter what kind of "abnormality" we choose for illustration, those which indicate extreme instability, or those which are more in the nature of character traits like sadism or delusions of grandeur or of persecution, there are well-described cultures in which these abnormals function at ease and with honor, and apparently without danger or difficulty to the society.

The most notorious of these is trance and catalepsy. Even a very mild mystic is aberrant in our culture. But most peoples have regarded even extreme psychic manifestations not only as normal and desirable, but even as characteristic of highly valued and gifted individuals. This was true even in our own cultural background in that period when Catholicism made the ecstatic experience the mark of sainthood. It is hard for us, born and brought up in a culture that makes no use of the experience, to realize how important a role it may play and how many individuals are capable of it, once it has been given an honorable place in any society.

* * *

Cataleptic and trance phenomena are, of course, only one illustration of the fact that those whom we regard as abnormals may function adequately in other cultures. Many of our culturally discarded traits are selected for elaboration in different societies. Homosexuality is an excellent example, for in this case our attention is not constantly diverted, as in the consideration of trance, to the interruption of routine activity which it implies. Homosexuality poses the problem very simply. A tendency toward this trait in our culture exposes an individual to all the conflicts to which all aberrants are always exposed, and we tend to identify the consequences of this conflict with homosexuality. But these consequences are obviously local and cultural. Homosexuals in many societies are not incompetent, but they may be such if the culture asks adjustments of them that would strain any man's vitality. Wherever homosexuality has been given an honorable place in any society, those to whom it is congenial have filled adequately the honorable roles society assigns to them. Plato's *Republic* is, of course, the most convincing statement of such a reading of homosexuality. It is presented as one of the major means to the good life, and it was generally so regarded in Greece at that time.

The cultural attitude toward homosexuals has not always been on such a high ethical plane, but it has been varied. Among many American Indian tribes there exists the institution of the berdache, as the French called them. These men-women were men who at puberty or thereafter took the dress and the occupations of women. Sometimes they married other men and lived with them. Sometimes they were men with no inversion, persons of weak sexual endowment who chose this role to avoid the jeers of the women. The berdaches were never regarded as of first-rate supernatural power, as similar men-women were in Siberia, but rather as leaders in women's occupations, good healers in certain diseases, or, among certain tribes, as the genial organizers of social affairs. In any case, they were socially placed. They were not left exposed to the conflicts that visit the deviant who is excluded from participation in the recognized patterns of his society.

* * *

No one civilization can possibly utilize in its mores the whole potential range of human behavior. Just as there are great numbers of possible phonetic articulations, and the possibility of language depends on a selection and standardization of a few of these in order that speech communication may be possible at all, so the possibility of organized behavior of every sort, from the fashions of local dress and houses to the dicta of a people's ethics and religion, depends upon a similar selection among the possible behavior traits. In the field of recognized economic obligations or sex tabus this selection is as nonrational and subconscious a process as it is in the field of phonetics. It is a process which goes on in the group for long periods of time and is historically conditioned by innumerable accidents of isolation or of contact of peoples. In any comprehensive study of psychology, the selection that different cultures have made in the course of history within the great circumference of potential behavior is of great significance.

Every society, beginning with some slight inclination in one direction or another, carries its preference farther and farther, integrating itself more and more completely upon its chosen basis, and discarding those types of behavior that are uncongenial. Most of these organizations of personality that seem to us most incontrovertibly abnormal have been used by different civilizations in the very foundations of their institutional life. Conversely the most valued traits of our normal individuals have been looked on in differently organized cultures as aberrant. Normality, in short, within a very wide range, is culturally defined. It is primarily a term for the socially elaborated segment of human behavior in any culture; and abnormality, a term for the segment that that particular civilization does not use. The very eyes with which we see the problem are conditioned by the long traditional habits of our own society.

It is a point that has been made more often in relation to ethics than in relation to psychiatry. We do not any longer make the mistake of deriving the morality of our own locality and decade directly from the inevitable constitution of human nature. We do not elevate it to the dignity of a first principle. We recognize that morality differs in every society, and is a convenient term for socially approved habits. Mankind has always preferred to say, "It is a morally good," rather than "It is habitual," and the fact of this preference is matter enough for a critical science of ethics. But historically the two phrases are synonymous.

The concept of the normal is properly a variant of the concept of the good. It is that which society has approved. A normal action is one which falls well within the limits of expected behavior for a particular society. Its variability among different peoples is essentially a function of the variability of the behavior patterns that different societies have created for themselves, and can never be wholly divorced from a consideration of culturally institutionalized types of behavior.

Each culture is a more or less elaborate working-out of the potentialities of the segment it has chosen. In so far as a civilization is well integrated and consistent within itself, it will tend to carry farther and farther, according to its nature, its initial impulse toward a particular type of action, and from the point of view of any other culture those elaborations will include more and more extreme and aberrant traits.

Each of these traits, in proportion as it reinforces the chosen behavior patterns of that culture, is for that culture normal. Those individuals to whom it is congenial either congenitally, or as the result of childhood sets, are accorded to prestige in that culture, and are not visited with the social contempt or disapproval which their traits would call down upon them in a society that was differently organized. On the other hand, those individuals whose characteristics are not congenial to the selected type of human behavior in that community are the deviants, no matter how valued their personality traits may be in a contrasted civilization.

* * *

I have spoken of individuals as having sets toward certain types of behavior, and of these sets as running sometimes counter to the types of behavior which are institutionalized in the culture to which they belong. From all that we know of contrasting cultures it seems clear that differences of temperament occur in every society. The matter has never been made the subject of investigation, but from the available material it would appear that these temperament types are very likely of universal recurrence. That is, there is an ascertainable range of human behavior that is found wherever a sufficiently large series of individuals is observed. But the proportion in which behavior types stand to one another in different societies is not universal. The vast majority of the individuals in any group are shaped to the fashion of that culture. In other words, most individuals are plastic to the moulding force of the society into which they are born. In a society that values trance, as in India, they will have supernormal experience. In a society that institutionalizes homosexuality, they will be homosexual. In a society that sets the gathering of possessions as the chief human objective, they will amass property. The deviants, whatever the type of behavior the culture has institutionalized, will remain few in number, and there seems no more difficulty in moulding the vast malleable majority to the "normality" of what we consider an aberrant trait, such as delusions of reference, than to the normality of such accepted behavior patterns as acquisitiveness. The small proportion of the number of the deviants in any culture is not a function of the sure instinct with which that society has built itself upon the fundamental sanities, but of the universal fact that, happily, the majority of mankind quite readily take any shape that is presented to them.

* * *

Trying Out One's New Sword
MARY MIDGLEY

All of us are, more or less, in trouble today about trying to understand cultures strange to us. We hear constantly of alien customs. We see changes in our

Mary Midgley, "Trying Out One's New Sword," in *Heart and Mind: The Varieties of Moral Experience* (Brighton, Sussex: Harvester Press, 1981), pp. 69–75. Reprinted by permission of David Higham Associates.

lifetime which would have astonished our parents. I want to discuss here one very short way of dealing with this difficulty, a drastic way which many people now theoretically favour. It consists in simply denying that we can ever understand any culture except our own well enough to make judgements about it. Those who recommend this hold that the world is sharply divided into separate societies, sealed units, each with its own system of thought. They feel that the respect and tolerance due from one system to another forbids us ever to take up a critical position to any other culture. Moral judgment, they suggest, is a kind of coinage valid only in its country of origin.

I shall call this position 'moral isolationism'. I shall suggest that it is certainly not forced upon us, and indeed that it makes no sense at all. People usually take it up because they think it is a respectful attitude to other cultures. In fact, however, it is not respectful. Nobody can respect what is entirely unintelligible to them. To respect someone, we have to know enough about him to make a *favourable* judgement, however general and tentative. And we do understand people in other cultures to this extent. Otherwise a great mass of our most valuable thinking would be paralysed.

To show this, I shall take a remote example, because we shall probably find it easier to think calmly about it than we should with a contemporary one, such as female circumcision in Africa or the Chinese Cultural Revolution. The principles involved will still be the same. My example is this. There is, it seems, a verb in classical Japanese which means 'to try out one's new sword on a chance wayfarer'. (The word is *tsujigiri,* literally 'crossroads-cut'.) A samurai sword had to be tried out because, if it was to work properly, it had to slice through someone at a single blow, from the shoulder to the opposite flank. Otherwise, the warrior bungled his stroke. This could injure his honour, offend his ancestors, and even let down his emperor. So tests were needed, and wayfarers had to be expended. Any wayfarer would do—provided, of course, that he was not another Samurai. Scientists will recognize a familiar problem about the rights of experimental subjects.

Now when we hear of a custom like this, we may well reflect that we simply do not understand it; and therefore are not qualified to criticize it at all, because we are not members of that culture. But we are not members of any other culture either, except our own. So we extend the principle to cover all extraneous cultures, and we seem therefore to be moral isolationists. But this is, as we shall see, an impossible position. Let us ask what it would involve.

We must ask first: Does the isolating barrier work both ways? Are people in other cultures equally unable to criticize *us*? This question struck me sharply when I read a remark in *The Guardian* by an anthropologist about a South American Indian who had been taken into a Brazilian town for an operation, which saved his life. When he came back to his village, he made several highly critical remarks about the white Brazilians' way of life. They may very well have been justified. But the interesting point was that the anthropologist called these remarks 'a damning indictment of Western civilization'. Now the Indian had been in that town about two weeks. Was he in a position to deliver a damning indictment? Would we ourselves be qualified to deliver such an indictment on the Samurai, provided we could spend two weeks in ancient Japan? What do we really think about this?

My own impression is that we believe that outsiders can, in principle, deliver perfectly good indictments—only, it usually takes more than two weeks to make them damning. Understanding has degrees. It is not a slapdash yes-or-no matter. Intelligent outsiders can progress in it, and in some ways will be at an advantage over the locals. But if this is so, it must clearly apply to ourselves as much as anybody else.

Our next question is this: Does the isolating barrier between cultures block praise as well as blame? If I want to say that the Samurai culture has many virtues, or to praise the South American Indians, am I prevented from doing *that* by my outside status? Now, we certainly do need to praise other societies in this way. But it is hardly possible that we could praise them effectively if we could not, in principle, criticize them. Our praise would be worthless if it rested on no definite grounds, if it did not flow from some understanding. Certainly we may need to praise things which we do not *fully* understand. We say 'there's something very good here, but I can't quite make out what it is yet'. This happens when we want to learn from strangers. And we can learn from strangers. But to do this we have to distinguish between those strangers who are worth learning from and those who are not. Can we then judge which is which?

This brings us to our third question: What is involved in judging? Now plainly there is no question here of sitting on a bench in a red robe and sentencing people. Judging simply means forming an opinion, and expressing it if it is called for. Is there anything wrong about this? Naturally, we ought to avoid forming—and expressing—*crude* opinions, like that of a simple-minded missionary, who might dismiss the whole Samurai culture as entirely bad, because non-Christian. But this is a different objection. The trouble with crude opinions is that they are crude, whoever forms them, not that they are formed by the wrong people. Anthropologists, after all, are outsiders quite as much as missionaries. Moral isolationism forbids us to form *any* opinions on these matters. Its ground for doing so is that we don't understand them. But there is much that we don't understand in our own culture too. This brings us to our last question: If we can't judge other cultures, can we really judge our own? Our efforts to do so will be much damaged if we are really deprived of our opinions about other societies, because these provide the range of comparison, the spectrum of alternatives against which we set what we want to understand. We would have to stop using the mirror which anthropology so helpfully holds up to us.

In short, moral isolationism would lay down a general ban on moral reasoning. Essentially, this is the programme of immoralism, and it carries a distressing logical difficulty. Immoralists like Nietzsche are actually just a rather specialized sect of moralists. They can no more afford to put moralizing out of business than smugglers can afford to abolish customs regulations. The power of moral judgement is, in fact, not a luxury, not a perverse indulgence of the self-righteous. It is a necessity. When we judge something to be bad or good, better or worse than something else, we are taking it as an example to aim at or avoid. Without opinions of this sort, we would have no framework of comparison for our own policy, no chance of profiting by other people's insights or mistakes. In this vacuum, we could form no judgements on our own actions.

Now it would be odd if Homo sapiens had really got himself into a position as bad as this—a position where his main evolutionary asset, his brain, was so little use to him. None of us is going to accept this sceptical diagnosis. We cannot do so, because our

involvement in moral isolationism does not flow from apathy, but from a rather acute concern about human hypocrisy and other forms of wickedness. But we polarize that concern around a few selected moral truths. We are rightly angry with those who despise, oppress or steamroll other cultures. We think that doing these things is actually *wrong*. But this is itself a moral judgement. We could not condemn oppression and insolence if we thought that all our condemnations were just a trivial local quirk of our own culture. We could still less do it if we tried to stop judging altogether.

Real moral scepticism, in fact, could lead only to inaction, to our losing all interest in moral questions, most of all in those which concern other societies. When we discuss these things, it becomes instantly clear how far we are from doing this. Suppose, for instance, that I criticize the bisecting Samurai, that I say his behaviour is brutal. What will usually happen next is that someone will protest, will say that I have no right to make criticisms like that of another culture. But it is most unlikely that he will use this move to end the discussion of the subject. Instead, he will justify the Samurai. He will try to fill in the background, to make me understand the custom, by explaining the exalted ideals of discipline and devotion which produced it. He will probably talk of the lower value which the ancient Japanese placed on individual life generally. He may well suggest that this is a healthier attitude than our own obsession with security. He may add, too, that the wayfarers did not seriously mind being bisected, that in principle they accepted the whole arrangement.

Now an objector who talks like this is implying that it *is* possible to understand alien customs. That is just what he is trying to make me do. And he implies, too, that if I do succeed in understanding them, I shall do something better than giving up judging them. He expects me to change my present judgement to a truer one—namely, one that is favourable. And the standards I must use to do this cannot just be Samurai standards. They have to be ones current in my own culture. Ideals like discipline and devotion will not move anybody unless he himself accepts them. As it happens, neither discipline nor devotion is very popular in the West at present. Anyone who appeals to them may well have to do some more arguing to make *them* acceptable, before he can use them to explain the Samurai. But if he does succeed here, he will have persuaded us, not just that there was something to be said for them in ancient Japan, but that there would be here as well.

Isolating barriers simply cannot arise here. If we accept something as a serious moral truth about one culture, we can't refuse to apply it—in however different an outward form—to other cultures as well, wherever circumstance admit it. If we refuse to do this, we just are not taking the other culture seriously. This becomes clear if we look at the last argument used by my objector—that of justification by consent of the victim. It is suggested that sudden bisection is quite in order, *provided* that it takes place between consenting adults. I cannot now discuss how conclusive this justification is. What I am pointing out is simply that it can only work if we believe that *consent* can make such a transaction respectable—and this is a thoroughly modern and Western idea. It would probably never occur to a Samurai; if it did, it would surprise him very much. It is *our* standard. In applying it, too, we are likely to make another typically Western demand. We shall ask for good factual evidence that the wayfarers actually do have this rather surprising taste—that they are really willing to be bisected. In applying Western standards in this way, we are not being confused or irrelevant. We are asking the questions which arise *from where we stand,* questions which we can see the sense of. We do this because asking questions which you can't see the sense of is humbug. Certainly we can extend our questioning by imaginative effort. We can come to understand other societies better. By doing so, we may make their questions our own, or we may see that they are really forms of the questions which we are asking already. This is not impossible. It is just very hard work. The obstacles which often prevent it are simply those of ordinary ignorance, laziness and prejudice.

If there were really an isolating barrier, of course, our own culture could never have been formed. It is no scaled box, but a fertile jungle of different influences—Greek, Jewish, Roman, Norse, Celtic and so forth, into which further influences are still pouring—American, Indian, Japanese, Jamaican, you name it. The moral isolationist's picture of separate, unmixable cultures is quite unreal. People who talk about British history usually stress the value of this fertilizing mix, no doubt rightly. But this is not just an odd fact about Britain. Except for the very smallest and most remote, all cultures are formed out of many streams. All have the problem of digesting and assimilating things which, at the start, they do not understand. All have the choice of learning something from this challenge, or, alternatively, of refusing to learn, and fighting it mindlessly instead.

This universal predicament has been obscured by the fact that anthropologists used to concentrate largely on very small and remote cultures, which did not seem to have this problem. These tiny societies, which had often forgotten their own history, made neat, self-contained subjects for study. No doubt it was valuable to emphasize their remoteness, their extreme strangeness, their independence of our cultural tradition. This emphasis was, I think, the root of moral isolationism. But, as the tribal studies themselves showed, even there the anthropologists were able to interpret what they saw and make judgements—often favourable—about the tribesmen. And the tribesmen, too, were quite equal to making judgements about the anthropologists—and about the tourists and Coca-Cola salesmen who followed them. Both sets of judgements, no doubt, were somewhat hasty, both have been refined in the light of further experience. A similar transaction between us and the Samurai might take even longer. But that is no reason at all for deeming it impossible. Morally as well as physically, there is only one world, and we all have to live in it.

PART
2

Moral Reasoning

CHAPTER 3

Evaluating Moral Arguments

This much is clear: we cannot escape the ethical facts of life. We often must make moral judgments, assess moral principles or rules, contend with moral theories, and argue the pros and cons of moral issues. Typically we do all of these things believing that in one way or another they *really matter*.

Because we think that ethics (that is, moral *philosophy*) matters, it follows that moral *reasoning* matters, for we could make little headway in these difficult waters without the use of reasons and arguments. Along the way we may take into account our feelings, desires, beliefs, and other factors, but getting to our destination depends mostly on the quality of our moral reasoning. Through moral reasoning we assess what is right and wrong, good and bad, virtuous and vicious. We make and dismantle arguments for this view and for that. In our finest moments, we follow the lead of reason in the search for answers, trying to rise above subjectivism, prejudice, and confusion.

In this chapter you will discover (if you haven't already) that you are no stranger to moral reasoning. Moral reasoning is ordinary critical reasoning applied to ethics. Critical reasoning (or critical thinking) is the careful, systematic evaluation of statements or claims. We use critical reasoning every day to determine whether a statement is worthy of acceptance—that is, whether it is true. We harness critical reasoning to assess the truth of all sorts of claims in all kinds of contexts—personal, professional, academic, philosophical, scientific, political, and ethical. Moral reasoning, then, is not a type of reasoning that you have never seen before.

We therefore begin this chapter with the basics of critical reasoning. The focus is on the skills that are at the heart of this kind of thinking—the formulation and evaluation of logical arguments. The rest of the chapter is about applying critical reasoning to the claims and arguments of ethics.

CLAIMS AND ARGUMENTS

When you use critical reasoning, your ultimate aim is usually to figure out whether to accept, or believe, a statement—either someone else's statement or one of your own. A **statement**, or claim, is an assertion that something is or is not the case; it is either true or false. These are statements:

- The ship sailed on the wind-tossed sea.

- I feel tired and listless.

- Murder is wrong.

- 5 + 5 = 10.

- A circle is not a square.

These statements assert that something is or is not the case. Whether you accept them, reject them, or neither, they are still statements because they are assertions that can be either true or false.

The following, however, are not statements; they do not assert that something is or is not the case:

- Why is Anna laughing?

- Is abortion immoral?

- Hand me the screwdriver.

- Don't speak to me.

- Hello, Webster.

- For heaven's sake!

A fundamental principle of critical reasoning is that we should not accept a statement as true without good reasons. If a statement is supported by good reasons, we are entitled to believe it. The better the reasons supporting a statement, the more likely it is to be true. Our acceptance of a statement, then, can vary in strength. If a statement is supported by strong reasons, we are entitled to believe it strongly. If it is supported by weaker reasons, our belief should likewise be weaker. If the reasons are equivocal—if they do not help us decide one way or another—we should suspend judgment until the evidence is more definitive.

Reasons supporting a statement are themselves statements. To lend credence to another claim, these supporting statements may assert something about scientific evidence, expert opinion, relevant examples, or other considerations. In this way they provide reasons for believing that a statement is true, that what is asserted is actual. When this state of affairs exists—when at least one statement attempts to provide reasons for believing another statement—we have an **argument**. An argument is a group of statements, one of which is supposed to be supported by the rest. An argument in this sense, of course, has nothing to do with the common notion of arguments as shouting matches or vehement quarrels.

In an argument, the supporting statements are known as **premises**; the statement being supported is known as a **conclusion**. Consider these arguments:

Argument 1. Capital punishment is morally permissible because it helps to deter crime.
Argument 2. If John killed Bill in self-defense, he did not commit murder. He did act in self-defense. Therefore, he did not commit murder.

Argument 3. Telling a white lie is morally permissible. We should judge the rightness of an act by its impact on human well-being. If an act increases human well-being, then it is right. Without question, telling a white lie increases human well-being, because it spares people's feelings; that's what white lies are for.

These arguments are fairly simple. In Argument 1, a single premise ("because it helps to deter crime") supports a straightforward conclusion—"Capital punishment is morally permissible." Argument 2 has two premises: "If John killed Bill in self-defense, he did not commit murder" and "He did act in self-defense." And the conclusion is "Therefore, he did not commit murder." Argument 3 has three premises: "We should judge the rightness of an act by its impact on human well-being," "If an act increases human well-being, then it is right," and "Without question, telling a white lie increases human well-being, because it spares people's feelings." Its conclusion is "Telling a white lie is morally permissible."

As you can see, these three arguments have different structures. Argument 1, for example, has just one premise, but Arguments 2 and 3 have two and three premises. In Arguments 1 and 3, the conclusion is stated first; in Argument 2, last. Obviously, arguments can vary dramatically in their number of premises, in the placement of premises and conclusion, and in the wording of each of these parts. But all arguments share a common pattern: at least one premise is intended to support a conclusion. This pattern is what makes an argument an argument.

Despite the simplicity of this premise-conclusion arrangement, though, arguments are not always easy to identify. They can be embedded in long passages of nonargumentative prose, and nonargumentative prose can often look like arguments. Consider:

The number of abortions performed in this state is increasing. More and more women say that they favor greater access to abortion. This is an outrage.

Do you see an argument in this passage? You shouldn't, because there is none. The first two sentences are meant to be assertions of fact, and the last one is an expression of indignation. There is no premise providing reasons to accept a conclusion. But what if we altered the passage to make it an argument? Look:

> The number of abortions performed in this state is increasing, and more and more women say that they favor greater access to abortion. Therefore, in this state the trend among women is toward greater acceptance of abortion.

This is now an argument. There is a conclusion ("Therefore, in this state the trend among women is toward greater acceptance of abortion") supported by two premises ("The number of abortions performed in this state is increasing, and more and more women say that they favor greater access to abortion"). We are given reasons for accepting a claim.

Notice how easy it would be to elaborate on the nonargumentative version, adding other unsupported claims and more expressions of the writer's attitude toward the subject matter. We would end up with a much longer passage piled high with more assertions—but with no argument in sight. Often those who write such passages believe that because they have stated their opinion, they have presented an argument. But a bundle of unsupported claims—however clearly stated—does not an argument make. Only when reasons are given for believing one of these claims is an argument made.

Learning to distinguish arguments from nonargumentative material takes practice. The job gets easier, however, if you pay attention to **indicator words**. Indicator words are terms that often appear in arguments and signal that a premise or conclusion may be nearby. Notice that in the argument about abortion, the word *therefore* indicates that the conclusion follows, and in Argument 1 the word *because* signals the beginning of a premise. In addition to *therefore,* common conclusion indicators

include *consequently, hence, it follows that, thus, so, it must be that,* and *as a result.* Besides *because,* some common premise indicators are *since, for, given that, due to the fact that, for the reason that, the reason being, assuming that,* and *as indicated by.*

Understand that indicator words are not foolproof evidence that a premise or conclusion is near. Sometimes words that often function as indicators appear when no argument at all is present. Indicator words are simply hints that an argument may be close by.

Probably the most reliable way to identify arguments is to *look for the conclusion first.* When you know what claim is being supported, you can more easily see what statements are doing the supporting. A true argument always has something to prove. If there is no statement that the writer is trying to convince you to accept, no argument is present.

Finally, understand that *argumentation* (the presentation of an argument) is not the same thing as *persuasion.* To offer a good argument is to present reasons why a particular assertion is true. To persuade someone of something is to influence her opinion by any number of means, including emotional appeals, linguistic or rhetorical tricks, deception, threats, propaganda, and more. Reasoned argument does not necessarily play any part at all. You may be able to use some of these ploys to persuade people to believe a claim. But if you do, you will not have established that the claim is worth believing. On the other hand, if you articulate a good argument, then you prove something—and others just might be persuaded by your reasoning.

ARGUMENTS GOOD AND BAD

A good argument shows that its conclusion is worthy of belief or acceptance; a bad argument fails to show this. A good argument gives you good reasons to accept a claim; a bad argument proves nothing. So the crucial question is, How can you tell which is which? To start, you can learn more about different

CRITICAL THOUGHT: The Morality of Critical Thinking

You might be surprised to learn that some philosophers consider reasoning itself a moral issue. That is, they think that believing a claim without good reasons (an unsupported statement) is immoral. Probably the most famous exposition of this point comes from the philosopher and mathematician W. K. Clifford (1845–79). He has this to say on the subject:

> It is wrong always, everywhere, and for anyone, to believe anything upon insufficient evidence. If a man, holding a belief which he was taught in childhood or persuaded of afterwards, keeps down and pushes away any doubts which arise about it in his mind . . . and regards as impious those questions which cannot easily be asked without disturbing it—the life of that man is one long sin against mankind.*

Do you agree with Clifford? Can you think of a counterexample to his argument—that is, instances in which believing without evidence would be morally permissible? Suppose the power of reason is a gift from God to be used to help you live a good life. If so, would believing without evidence (failing to use critical thinking) be immoral?

*W. K. Clifford, "The Ethics of Belief," in *The Rationality of Belief in God*, ed. George I. Mavrodes (Englewood Cliffs, NJ: Prentice Hall, 1970), 159–60.

kinds of arguments and what makes them good or bad.

There are two basic types of arguments: deductive and inductive. **Deductive arguments** are supposed to give logically conclusive support to their conclusions. **Inductive arguments**, on the other hand, are supposed to offer only probable support for their conclusions.

Consider this classic deductive argument:

All men are mortal.

Socrates is a man.

Therefore, Socrates is mortal.

It is deductive because the support offered for the conclusion is meant to be absolutely unshakable. When a deductive argument actually achieves this kind of conclusive support, it is said to be **valid**. In a valid argument, if the premises are true, then the conclusion absolutely has to be true. In the Socrates argument, if the premises are true, the conclusion *must be true*. The conclusion follows inexorably from the premises. The argument is therefore valid. When a deductive argument does not offer conclusive support for the conclusion, it is said to be **invalid**. In an invalid argument, it is not the case that if the premises are true, the conclusion must be true. Suppose the first premise of the Socrates argument was changed to "All ducks are mortal." Then the argument would be invalid because even if the premises were true, the conclusion would not necessarily be true. The conclusion would not follow inexorably from the premises.

Notice that the validity or invalidity of an argument is a matter of its *form,* not its content. The structure of a deductive argument renders it either valid or invalid, and validity is a separate matter from the truth of the argument's statements. Its statements (premises and conclusion) may be either true or false, but that has nothing to do with validity. Saying that an argument is valid means that it has a particular form that ensures that if the premises are true, the conclusion can be nothing but true. There is no way that the premises can be true and the conclusion false.

Recall that there are indicator words that point to the presence of premises and conclusions. There are also indicator words that suggest (but do not prove) that an argument is deductive. Some of the more common are *it necessarily follows that, it must be the case that, it logically follows that, conclusively,* and *necessarily.*

Now let us turn to inductive arguments. Examine this one:

Almost all the men at this college have high SAT scores.

Therefore, Julio (a male student at the college) probably has high SAT scores.

This argument is inductive because it is intended to provide probable, not decisive, support to the conclusion. That is, the argument is intended to show only that, at best, the conclusion is probably true. With any inductive argument, it is possible for the premises to be true and the conclusion false. An inductive argument that manages to actually give probable support to the conclusion is said to be **strong**. In a strong argument, if the premises are true, the conclusion is probably true (more likely to be true than not). The SAT argument is strong. An inductive argument that does not give probable support to the conclusion is said to be **weak**. In a weak argument, if the premises are true, the conclusion is not probable (not more likely to be true than not true). If we change the first premise in the SAT argument to "Twenty percent of the men at this college have high SAT scores," the argument would be weak.

Like deductive arguments, inductive ones are often accompanied by indicator words. These terms include *probably, likely, in all probability, it is reasonable to suppose that, odds are,* and *chances are.*

Good arguments provide you with good reasons for believing their conclusions. You now know that good arguments must be valid or strong. But they must also have true premises. Good arguments must both have the right form (be valid or strong) and have reliable content (have true premises). Any argument that fails in either of these respects is a bad argument. A valid argument with true premises is said to be **sound**; a strong argument with true premises is said to be **cogent**.

To evaluate an argument is to determine whether it is good or not, and establishing that requires you to check the argument's form and the truth of its premises. You can check the truth of premises in many different ways. Sometimes you can see immediately that a premise is true (or false). At other times you may need to examine a premise more closely or even do some research. Assessing an argument's form is also usually a straightforward process. With inductive arguments, common sense may be all that's required to see whether they are strong or weak (whether the conclusions follow from the premises). With deductive arguments, just thinking about how the premises are related to the conclusion is often sufficient. In all cases, the key to correctly and efficiently determining the validity or strength of arguments is practice.

Fortunately, there are some techniques that can improve your ability to check the validity of deductive arguments. Some deductive forms are so common that just being familiar with them can give you a big advantage. Let's look at some of them.

To begin, understand that you can easily indicate an argument's form by using a kind of standard shorthand, with letters standing for statements. Consider, for example, this argument:

If Maria walks to work, then she will be late.

She is walking to work.

Therefore, she will be late.

Here's how we symbolize this argument's form:

If p, then q.

p.

Therefore, q.

We represent each statement with a letter, thereby laying bare the argument's skeletal form. The first premise is a compound statement, consisting of two constituent statements, p and q. This particular argument form is known as a *conditional*. A conditional argument has at least one conditional premise—a premise in an if-then pattern

(If *p*, then *q*). The two parts of a conditional premise are known as the *antecedent* (which begins with *if*) and the *consequent* (which follows *then*).

This argument form happens to be very common—so common that it has a name, *modus ponens,* or affirming the antecedent. The first premise is conditional ("If Maria walks to work, then she will be late"), and the second premise affirms the antecedent of that conditional ("She is walking to work"). This form is *always valid:* if the premises are true, the conclusion *has to be true.* Any argument that has this form will be valid regardless of the subject matter.

Another frequently occurring form is known as *modus tollens,* or denying the consequent:

If Maria walks to work, then she will be late.

She will not be late.

Therefore, she will not walk to work.

Symbolized, *modus tollens* looks like this:

If *p,* then *q.*

Not *q.*

Therefore, not *p.*

Modus tollens is always valid, no matter what statements you plug into the formula.

Here are two more common argument forms. These, however, are *always invalid.*

Denying the antecedent:

If Maria walks to work, then she will be late.

She will not walk to work.

Therefore, she will not be late.

If *p,* then *q.*

Not *p.*

Therefore, not *q.*

Affirming the consequent:

If Maria walks to work, then she will be late.

She will be late.

Therefore, she will walk to work.

If *p,* then *q.*

q.

Therefore, *p.*

Do you see the problem with these two? In the first one (denying the antecedent), even a false antecedent (if Maria will not walk to work) doesn't mean that she will not be late. Maybe she will sit at home and be late, or be late for some other reason. When the antecedent is denied, the premises can be true and the conclusion false—clearly an invalid argument. In the second argument (affirming the consequent), even a true consequent (if Maria will be late) doesn't mean that she will walk to work. Some other factor besides her walking could cause Maria to be late. Again, the premises can be true while the conclusion is false—definitely invalid.

Consider one last form, the hypothetical syllogism (*hypothetical* means *conditional;* a *syllogism* is a three-statement deductive argument):

If Maria walks to work, then she will be late.

If she is late, she will be fired.

Therefore, if Maria walks to work, she will be fired.

If *p,* then *q.*

If *q,* then *r.*

Therefore, if *p,* then *r.*

The hypothetical syllogism is a valid argument form. If the premises are true, the conclusion must be true.

Obviously, if *modus ponens, modus tollens*, and the hypothetical syllogism are always valid, then any arguments you encounter that have the same form will also be valid. And if denying the antecedent and affirming the consequent are always invalid, any arguments you come across that have the same form will also be invalid. The best way to make use of these facts is to memorize each argument form so you can tell right away when an argument matches one of them—and thereby see immediately that it is valid (or invalid).

But what if you bump into a deductive argument that does not match one of these common forms? You can try the *counterexample method*. This approach is based on a fundamental fact that you already know: *it is impossible for a valid argument to have true premises and a false conclusion.* So to test the validity of an argument, you first invent a twin argument that has exactly the same form as the argument you are examining—but you try to give this new argument true premises and a false conclusion. If you can construct such an argument, you have proven that your original argument is invalid.

Suppose you want to test this argument for validity:

If capital punishment deters crime, then the number of death row inmates will decrease over time.

But capital punishment does not deter crime.

Therefore, the number of death row inmates will not decrease over time.

You can probably see right away that this argument is an example of denying the antecedent, an invalid form. But for the sake of example, let's use the counterexample method in this case. Suppose we come up with this twin argument:

If lizards are mammals, then they have legs.

But they are not mammals.

Therefore, they do not have legs.

We have invented a twin argument that has true premises and a false conclusion, so we know that the original argument is invalid.

IMPLIED PREMISES

Most of the arguments that we encounter in everyday life are embedded in larger tracts of nonargumentative prose—in essays, reports, letters to the editor, editorials, and the like. The challenge is to pick out the premises and conclusions and evaluate the assembled arguments. In many cases, though, there is an additional obstacle: some premises may

---

QUICK REVIEW

statement—An assertion that something is or is not the case.

argument—A group of statements, one of which is supposed to be supported by the rest.

premise—A supporting statement in an argument.

conclusion—The statement supported in an argument.

indicator words—Terms that often appear in arguments to signal the presence of a premise or conclusion, or to indicate that an argument is deductive or inductive.

deductive argument—An argument that is supposed to give logically conclusive support to its conclusion.

inductive argument—An argument that is supposed to offer probable support to its conclusion.

valid argument—A deductive argument that does in fact provide logically conclusive support for its conclusion.

invalid argument—A deductive argument that does not offer logically conclusive support for the conclusion.

strong argument—An inductive argument that does in fact provide probable support for its conclusion.

weak argument—An inductive argument that does not give probable support to the conclusion.

sound argument—A valid argument with true premises.

cogent argument—A strong argument with true premises.

---

be implied instead of stated. Sometimes the premises are implicit because they are too obvious to mention; readers mentally fill in the blanks. But in most cases, implicit premises should not be left unstated. It is often unclear what premises have been assumed, and unless these are spelled out, argument evaluation becomes difficult or impossible. More to the point, unstated premises are often the most dubious parts of an argument. This problem is especially common in moral arguments, in which the implicit premises are frequently the most controversial and the most in need of close scrutiny.

Here is a typical argument with an unstated premise:

> The use of condoms is completely unnatural. They have been manufactured for the explicit purpose of interfering with the natural process of procreation. Therefore, the use of condoms should be banned.

In this argument, the first two sentences constitute a single premise, the gist of which is that using condoms is unnatural. The conclusion is that the use of condoms should be banned. This conclusion, however, does not follow from the stated premise. There is a logical gap between premise and conclusion. The argument will work only if the missing premise is supplied. Here's a good possibility: "Anything that interferes with a natural process should not be allowed." The argument then becomes:

> The use of condoms is completely unnatural. They have been manufactured for the explicit purpose of interfering with the natural process of procreation. Anything that interferes with a natural process should not be allowed. Therefore, the use of condoms should be banned.

By adding the implicit premise, we have filled out the argument, making it valid and a little less mysterious. But now that the missing premise has been brought out into the open, we can see that it is dubious or, at least, controversial. Should everything that interferes with a natural process be banned? If so, we would have to ban antibiotics, anticancer drugs, deodorants, and automobiles. (Later in this chapter, ways to judge the truth of moral premises are discussed.)

When you evaluate an argument, you should try to explicitly state any implied premise (or premises) when (1) there seems to be a logical gap between premises or between premises and the conclusion and (2) the missing material is not a commonsense assumption. In general, the supplied premise should make the argument valid (when the argument is supposed to be deductive) or strong (when the argument is supposed to be inductive). It should also be *plausible* (as close to the truth as possible) and *fitting* (coinciding with what you think is the author's intent). The point of these stipulations is that when you supply a missing premise, you should be fair and honest, expressing it in such a way that the argument is as solid as possible and in keeping with the author's purpose. Adding a premise that renders an argument ridiculous is easy, and so is distorting the author's intent—and with neither tack are you likely to learn anything or uncover the truth.

Be aware, though, that some arguments are irredeemably bad, and no supplied premise that is properly made can save them. They cannot be turned into good arguments without altering them beyond recognition or original intent. You need not take these arguments seriously, and the responsibility of recasting them lies with those who offer them.

DECONSTRUCTING ARGUMENTS

In the real world, arguments do not come neatly labeled, their parts identified and their relationships laid bare. So you have to do the labeling and connecting yourself, and that can be hard work. Where are the premises and the conclusion? Are there implied premises? What statements are irrelevant to the argument, just background or window dressing? How are all these pieces related? Fortunately there is a tool that can help you penetrate all the verbiage to uncover the essential argument (or arguments) within: *argument diagramming*.

So let's try to diagram the argument in this passage:

In 2003 the United States attacked Iraq and thereby started a war. President Bush justified his decision to go to war by saying that the action was necessary to preempt Iraq from launching a military strike against the United States. But the obvious question about the war has hardly been addressed and rarely answered: Was the United States morally justified in going to war against Iraq? I think just war theory gives us an answer. The theory says a preemptive attack against a state is justified only if that state presents a substantial danger that is "immediate and imminent." That is, to meet this criterion, an attack by an aggressor nation must be in the final planning stages—an attack must not be merely feared, but about to happen. If invading Iraq were justified, there would have been clear indications of Iraq's final preparations to attack the United States. But there were no such indications. There was only a fantasy about Iraq's having weapons of mass destruction, and in the Bush administration, there was only the fear that the Iraqis were up to no good. In addition, because there was no serious attempt by the United States to try to find a peaceful solution, the war was premature and therefore unjust. Most news accounts at the time reveal that steps by the United States to head off war were halfhearted at best. Finally, the war was unjustified because it violated the moral standard that must be met by any war: the cause of the war must be just. Consequently we are forced to conclude that the war in Iraq was not morally justified.

The first step is to number all the statements for identification and underline any premise or conclusion indicator words. (Note: We count an if-then, or conditional, statement as one statement, and we count multiple statements in a compound sentence separately.) Next we search for the conclusion and draw a <u>double line</u> under it. Locating the conclusion can then help us find the premises, which we tag by <u>underlining</u> them. The marked-up passage should then look like this:

(1) In 2003 the United States attacked Iraq and thereby started a war. (2) President Bush justified his decision

to go to war by saying that the action was necessary to preempt Iraq from launching a military strike against the United States. (3) But the obvious question about the war has hardly been addressed and rarely answered: Was the United States morally justified in going to war against Iraq? (4) I think just war theory gives us an answer. (5) The theory says a preemptive attack against a state is justified only if that state presents a substantial danger that is "immediate and imminent." (6) That is, to meet this criterion, an attack by an aggressor nation must be in the final planning stages—an attack must not be merely feared, but about to happen. (7) <u>If invading Iraq were justified, there would have been clear indications of Iraq's final preparations to attack the United States.</u> (8) <u>But there were no such indications.</u> (9) There was only a fantasy about Iraq's having weapons of mass destruction, (10) and in the Bush administration, there was only the fear that the Iraqis were up to no good. (11) <u>In addition, because there was no serious attempt by the United States to try to find a peaceful solution, the war was premature and therefore unjust.</u> (12) <u>Most news accounts at the time reveal that steps by the United States to head off war were halfhearted at best.</u> (13) <u>Finally, the war was unjustified because it violated the moral standard that must be met by any war: the cause of the war must be just.</u> (14) <u>Consequently we are forced to conclude that the war in Iraq was not morally justified.</u>

A key reason for diagramming is to distinguish the premises and conclusions from everything else: background information, redundancies, asides, clarifications, illustrations, and any other material that is logically irrelevant to the argument (or arguments). So the next step is to cross out these irrelevancies, like this:

(1) ~~In 2003 the United States attacked Iraq and thereby started a war that continues to this day.~~ (2) ~~President Bush justified his decision to go to war by saying that the action was necessary to preempt Iraq from launching a military strike against the United States.~~ (3) ~~But the obvious question about the war has hardly been addressed and rarely answered: Was the United States morally justified in going to war against Iraq?~~ (4) ~~I think just war theory gives us an answer.~~ (5) ~~The theory says a preemptive attack against a state is justified only if that state presents a substantial danger that is "immediate and~~

imminent." (6) ~~That is, to meet this criterion, an attack by an aggressor nation must be in the final planning stages—an attack must not be merely feared, but about to happen.~~ (7) <u>If invading Iraq were justified, there would have been clear indications of Iraq's final preparations to attack the United States.</u> (8) <u>But there were no such indications.</u> (9) ~~There was only a fantasy about Iraq's having weapons of mass destruction,~~ (10) ~~and in the Bush administration, there was only the fear that the Iraqis were up to no good.~~ (11) <u>In addition, because there was no serious attempt by the United States to try to find a peaceful solution, the war was premature and therefore unjust.</u> (12) <u>Most news accounts at the time reveal that steps by the United States to head off war were halfhearted at best.</u> (13) <u>Finally, the war was unjustified because it violated the moral standard that must be met by any war: the cause of the war must be just.</u> (14) <u>Consequently we are forced to conclude that the war in Iraq was not morally justified.</u>

We now can see that most of this passage is logically extraneous material. Statements 1 through 6 are background information and introductory remarks. Statement 3, for example, is an assertion of the issue to be addressed in the passage. Statements 9 and 10 are embellishments of Statement 8.

The premises and conclusion are asserted in Statements 7, 8, 11, 12, 13, and 14:

> (7) If invading Iraq were justified, there would have been clear indications of Iraq's final preparations to attack the United States.
> (8) But there were no such indications.
> (11) In addition, because there was no serious attempt by the United States to try to find a peaceful solution, the war was premature and therefore unjust.
> (12) Most news accounts at the time reveal that steps by the United States to head off war were halfhearted at best.
> (13) Finally, the war was unjustified because it violated the moral standard that must be met by any war: the cause of the war must be just.
> (14) Consequently we are forced to conclude that the war in Iraq was not morally justified.

But how are these statements related? To find out, we draw a diagram. Using the numbers to represent the premises and conclusion, we write down the number for the conclusion and place the numbers for the premises above it. Then, to show how the premises support the conclusion, we draw arrows from the premises to the conclusion. Each arrow indicates the logical connection between premise and conclusion, representing such expressions as "Premise 11 supports the Conclusion (14)" or "the Conclusion (14) is supported by Premise 11." Here's the completed diagram:

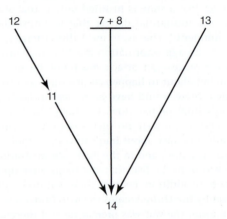

In the simplest relationship depicted here, Premise 13 provides direct support to the conclusion (14). Premise 11 also supplies direct support to the conclusion, and this premise in turn is backed up by Premise 12. (See how an arrow goes from 11 to 14, and then from 12 to 11.) Premises 7 and 8 are linked to the conclusion in a different way, reflecting the fact that some premises are *dependent* and some are *independent*. An independent premise (such as Premise 13) supports a conclusion without relying on any other premises; a dependent premise gives little or no support on its own and requires the assistance of at least one other premise. Premises 7 and 8 are dependent premises and are joined by a plus sign to represent this fact. Together, Premises 7 and 8 provide support to the conclusion; they give a reason for accepting it. But if either premise is deleted, the remaining premise can provide no substantial support.

As you work through the diagramming exercises at the end of this chapter, you will come to understand why diagramming arguments can be so useful. You will learn a great deal about the structure of arguments—which is a prerequisite for being able to devise, deconstruct, and evaluate them.

MORAL STATEMENTS AND ARGUMENTS

When we deliberate about the rightness of our actions, make careful moral judgments about the character or behavior of others, or strive to resolve complex ethical issues, we are usually making or critiquing moral arguments—or trying to. And rightly so. To a remarkable degree, moral arguments are the vehicles that move ethical thinking and discourse along. The rest of this chapter should give you a demonstration of how far skill in devising and evaluating moral arguments can take you.

Arguments, as you will recall, are made up of statements (premises and conclusions), and thus moral arguments are too. What makes an argument a moral argument is that its conclusion is always a moral statement. A **moral statement** is a statement affirming that an action is right or wrong or that a person (or one's motive or character) is good or bad. These are moral statements:

- Capital punishment is wrong.
- Jena should not have lied.
- You ought to treat him as he treated you.
- Tania is a good person.
- Cruelty to animals is immoral.

Notice the use of the terms *wrong, should, ought, good,* and *immoral.* Such words are the mainstays of moral discourse, though some of them (for example, *good* and *wrong*) are also used in nonmoral senses.

Nonmoral statements are very different. They do not affirm that an action is right or wrong or that a person is good or bad. They assert that a

state of affairs is actual (true or false) but do not assign a moral value to it. Most of the statements that we encounter every day are nonmoral. Of course, nonmoral statements may assert nonmoral normative judgments, such as "This is a good library" or "Jack ought to invest in stocks," but they are clearly not moral statements. They may also describe a state of affairs that touches on moral concerns—without *being* moral statements. For example:

- Many people think that capital punishment is wrong.
- Jena did not lie.
- You treated him as he treated you.
- Tania tries to be a good person.
- Animals are treated cruelly.

Now we can be more specific about the structure of moral arguments. A typical moral argument consists of premises and a conclusion, just as any other kind of argument does, with the conclusion being a moral statement, or judgment. The premises, however, are a combination of the moral and nonmoral. At least one premise must be a moral statement affirming a moral principle or rule (a general moral standard), and at least one premise must be a nonmoral statement about a state of affairs, usually a specific type of action. Beyond these simple requirements, the structure of moral arguments can vary in standard ways: there may be many premises or few; premises may be implicit or overt; and extraneous material may be present or absent. Take a look at this moral argument:

1. Committing a violent act to defend yourself against physical attack is morally permissible.

2. Assaulting someone who is attacking you is a violent act of self-defense.

3. Therefore, assaulting someone who is attacking you is morally permissible.

Premise 1 is a moral statement asserting a general moral principle about the rightness of a category of actions (violent acts in self-defense). Premise 2 is a nonmoral statement about the characteristics of a specific kind of action (violent acts against someone who is attacking you). It asserts that a specific kind of action falls under the general moral principle expressed in Premise 1. Premise 3, the conclusion, is a moral judgment about the rightness of the specific kind of action in light of the general moral principle.

Why must we have at least one premise that is a moral statement? Without a moral premise, the argument would not get off the ground. We cannot infer a moral statement (conclusion) from a nonmoral statement (premise). That is, we cannot reason that a moral statement must be true because a nonmoral state of affairs is actual. Or as philosophers say, we cannot establish what *ought to be* or *should be* solely on the basis of on what *is*. What if our self-defense argument contained no moral premise? Look:

2. Assaulting a person who is attacking you is a violent act of self-defense.
3. Therefore, assaulting a person who is attacking you is morally permissible.

The conclusion no longer follows. It says something about the rightness of an action, but the premise asserts nothing about rightness—it just characterizes the nonmoral aspects of an action. Perhaps the action described is morally permissible, or perhaps it is not—Premise 2 does not say.

Another example:

1. Not using every medical means available to keep a seriously ill newborn infant alive is allowing the infant to die.
3. Therefore, not using every medical means available to keep a seriously ill newborn infant alive is wrong.

As it stands, this argument is flawed. The conclusion (a moral statement) does not follow from the nonmoral premise. Even if we know that "not using every medical means" is equivalent to allowing a seriously ill newborn to die, we cannot then conclude that the action is wrong. We need a premise making that assertion:

2. Allowing seriously ill newborn infants to die is wrong.

Here's the complete argument:

1. Not using every medical means available to keep a seriously ill newborn infant alive is allowing the infant to die.
2. Allowing seriously ill newborn infants to die is wrong.
3. Therefore, not using every medical means available to keep a seriously ill newborn infant alive is wrong.

A nonmoral premise is also necessary in a moral argument. Why exactly? Recall that the conclusion of a typical moral argument is a moral judgment, or claim, about a particular kind of action. The moral premise is a general moral principle, or standard, concerning a wider category of actions. But we cannot infer a statement (conclusion) about a *particular kind of action* from a moral statement (premise) about a *broad category of actions*—unless we have a nonmoral premise to link the two. We saw, for example, that we cannot infer from the general principle that "committing a violent act to defend yourself . . . is morally permissible" the conclusion that "assaulting a person who is attacking you is morally permissible" unless a nonmoral premise tells us that assaulting a person who is attacking you is an instance of self-defense. (The nonmoral premise may seem obvious here, but not everyone would agree that violence against a person who is attacking you is an example of self-defense. Some might claim that such violence is an unnecessary act of retaliation or revenge.) The role of the nonmoral premise, then, is to affirm that the general moral principle does indeed apply to the particular case.

Unfortunately, both moral and nonmoral premises are often left unstated in moral arguments. As we noted earlier, making implicit premises explicit is always a good idea, but in moral arguments it is critical. The unseen premises (of which an argument may have several) are the ones most likely to be dubious or unfounded, a problem that can arise whether an argument is yours or someone else's. Too many times, unstated premises are assumptions that you may be barely aware of; they might be the true, unacknowledged source of disagreement between you and others. No premise should be left unexamined. (We'll learn more about assessing the truth of premises in the next section.)

The general guidelines for uncovering unstated premises discussed earlier apply to moral arguments—but we need to add a proviso. Remember, in a moral argument, as in any other kind of argument, you have good reason to look for implicit premises if there is a logical gap between premises and the missing premise is not simply common sense. And any premise you supply should be both plausible and fitting. But note: The easiest way to identify implied premises in a moral argument is to treat it as *deductive*. Approaching moral arguments this way helps you not only to find implied premises but also to assess the worth of *all* the premises. Consider this example:

1. The use of capital punishment does not deter crime.

2. Therefore, the use of capital punishment is immoral.

This is an invalid argument. Even if the premise is true, the conclusion does not follow from it. The argument needs a premise that can bridge the gap between the current premise and the conclusion. So we should ask, "What premise can we add that will be plausible and fitting *and* make the argument valid?" This premise will do: "Administering a punishment to criminals that does not deter crime is immoral." The argument then becomes:

1. Administering a punishment to criminals that does not deter crime is immoral.

2. The use of capital punishment does not deter crime.

3. Therefore, the use of capital punishment is immoral.

Now the argument is valid, and trying to make it valid has helped us find at least one premise that might work. Moreover, if we know that the argument is valid, we can focus our inquiry on the truth of the premises. After all, if there is something wrong with a valid argument (that is, if the argument is not sound), we know that the trouble is in the premises—specifically, that at least one premise must be false. To put it another way, whether or not such an argument is a good argument depends entirely on the truth of the premises.

As it turns out, our added premise is a general moral principle. And like many implied premises, it is questionable. Deterrence is not necessarily the only reason for administering punishment. Some would say that justice is a better reason; others, that rehabilitation is. (The second premise is also dubious, but we won't worry about that now.)

In any case, if the supplied premise renders the argument valid, and the premise is plausible and fitting, we can then conclude that we have filled out the argument properly. We can then examine the resulting argument and either accept or reject it. And if we wish to explore the issue at greater depth, we can overhaul the argument altogether to see what we can learn. We can radically change or add premises until we have a sound argument or at least a valid one with plausible premises.

TESTING MORAL PREMISES

But how can we evaluate moral premises? After all, we cannot check them by consulting a scientific study or opinion poll as we might when examining nonmoral premises. Usually the best approach is to use counterexamples.

If we want to test a universal generalization such as "All dogs have tails," we can look for counterexamples—instances that prove the generalization false. All we have to do to show that the statement "All dogs have tails" is false is to find one tailless dog. And a thorough search for tailless dogs is a way to check the generalization. Likewise, if we want to test a moral premise (a variety of universal generalization), we can look for counterexamples.

Examine this valid moral argument:

1. Causing a person's death is wrong.
2. Individuals in a deep, irreversible coma are incapacitated persons.
3. "Pulling the plug" on someone in a deep, irreversible coma is causing a person to die.
4. Therefore, "pulling the plug" on someone in a deep, irreversible coma is wrong.

Premise 1 is the moral premise, a general moral principle about killing. Premises 2 and 3 are nonmoral premises. (Premise 2 is entailed by Premise 3, but we separate the two to emphasize the importance to this argument of the concept of personhood.) Statement 4, of course, is the conclusion, the verdict that causing someone in a deep coma to die is immoral.

Is Premise 1 true? It is at least dubious, because counterexamples abound in which the principle seems false. Is it wrong to kill one person to save a hundred? Is it wrong to kill a person in self-defense? Is it wrong to kill a person in wartime? As it stands, Premise 1 seems implausible.

To salvage the argument, we can revise Premise 1 (as well as Premise 3) to try to make it impervious to counterexamples. We can change it like this:

1. Causing the death of a person who is incapacitated is wrong.
2. Individuals in a deep, irreversible coma are incapacitated persons.
3. "Pulling the plug" on someone in a deep, irreversible coma is causing an incapacitated person to die.
4. Therefore, "pulling the plug" on someone in a deep, irreversible coma is wrong.

Premise 1 now seems a bit more reasonable. In its current form, it rules out the counterexamples involving self-defense and war. But it does not escape the killing-to-save-lives counterexample. In some circumstances it may be morally permissible to kill someone to save many others, even if the person is incapacitated. To get around this problem, we can amend Premise 1 so the counterexample is no longer a threat (and make a corresponding change in the conclusion). For example:

1. Causing the death of a person who is incapacitated is wrong, except to save lives.
2. Individuals in a deep, irreversible coma are incapacitated persons.
3. "Pulling the plug" on someone in a deep, irreversible coma is causing an incapacitated person to die.
4. Therefore, "pulling the plug" on someone in a deep, irreversible coma is wrong, except to save lives.

Premise 1 now seems much closer to being correct than before. It may not be flawless, but it is much improved. By considering counterexamples, we have made the whole argument better.

Checking a moral premise against possible counterexamples is a way to consult our considered moral judgments, a topic we broached in Chapter 1 and take up again in Part 3 (Theories of Morality). If our considered moral judgments are at odds with a moral premise that is based on a cherished moral principle or moral theory, we may have a prima facie (at first sight) reason to doubt not only the premise but also the principle or theory from which it is derived. We may then need to reexamine the claims involved and how they are related. If we do, we may find that our judgments are on solid ground and the premise, principle, or theory needs to be adjusted—or vice versa. If our purpose is solely to evaluate a moral premise in an argument, we need not carry our investigation this far. But we should understand that widening our investigation may sometimes be appropriate and that our moral beliefs are often more interconnected than we might realize. Our ultimate goal should be to ensure that all our moral beliefs are as logically consistent as we can make them.

ASSESSING NONMORAL PREMISES

Sometimes the sticking point in a moral argument is not a moral premise but a nonmoral one—a claim about a nonmoral state of affairs. Often people on both sides of a dispute may agree on a moral principle but differ dramatically on the nonmoral facts. Usually these facts concern the consequences of an action or the characteristics of the parties involved. Does pornography cause people to commit sex crimes? Does capital punishment deter crime? Is a depressed person competent to decide whether to commit suicide? When does a fetus become viable? Are African Americans underrepresented among executives in corporate America? Does gay marriage undermine the institution of heterosexual marriage? These and countless other questions arise—and must be answered—as we try to develop and analyze moral arguments.

The most important principle to remember is that nonmoral premises, like all premises, *must be supported by good reasons.* As we have already seen, simply believing or asserting a claim does not make it so. We should insist that our own nonmoral premises and those of others be backed by reliable

> **QUICK REVIEW**
>
> - Look for an implicit premise when (1) there seems to be a logical gap between premises or between premises and the conclusion and (2) the missing material is not a commonsense assumption.
> - Any supplied unstated premise should be valid or strong, plausible, and fitting.
> - A typical moral argument has at least one moral premise and at least one nonmoral premise.
> - The easiest way to identify implied premises in a moral argument is to treat it as deductive.
> - Test moral premises with counterexamples.
>
> **moral statement**—A statement affirming that an action is right or wrong or that a person (or one's motive or character) is good or bad.
>
> **nonmoral statement**—A statement that does not affirm that an action is right or wrong or that a person (or one's motive or character) is good or bad.

scientific research, the opinions of trustworthy experts, pertinent examples and analogies, historical records, or our own background knowledge (claims that we have excellent reasons to believe).

Ensuring that nonmoral premises are supported by good reasons is sometimes difficult but always worth the effort. The process begins by simply asking, "Is this statement true?" and "What reasons do I have for believing this?"

In your search for answers, keep the following in mind:

1. *Use reliable sources.* If you have reason to doubt the accuracy of a source, do not use it. Doubt it if it produces statements you know to be false, ignores reliable data (such as the latest scientific research), or has a track record of presenting inaccurate information or dubious arguments. Make sure that any

experts you rely on are in fact experts in their chosen field. In general, true experts have the requisite education and training, the relevant experience in making reliable judgments, and a good reputation among peers.

Probably every major moral issue discussed in this book is associated with numerous advocacy groups, each one devoted to promoting its particular view of things. Too often the information coming from many of these groups is unreliable. Do not automatically assume otherwise. Double-check any information you get from them with sources you know are reliable and see if it is supported by scientific studies, expert opinion, or other evidence.

2. *Beware when evidence conflicts.* You have good reason to doubt a statement if it conflicts with other statements you think are well supported. If your nonmoral premise is inconsistent with another claim you believe is true, you cannot simply choose the one you like best. To resolve the conflict, you must evaluate them both by weighing the evidence for each one.

3. *Let reason rule.* Deliberating on moral issues is serious business, often involving the questioning of cherished views and the stirring of strong feelings. Many times the temptation to dispense with reason and blindly embrace a favorite outlook is enormous. This common—and very human—predicament can lead us to veer far from the relevant evidence and true nonmoral premises. Specifically, we may reject or disregard evidence that conflicts with what we most want to believe. We may even try to pretend that the conflicting evidence actually supports our preconceptions. Yet resisting the relevant evidence is just one side of the coin. We may also look for and find only evidence that supports what we want to believe, going around the world to confirm our prejudices.

Our best chance to avert these tendencies is to try hard to be both critical and fair—to make a deliberate effort to examine *all* the relevant evidence, both for and against our preferred beliefs.

After all, the point of assessing a moral argument is to discover the truth. We must be brave enough to let the evidence point where it will.

AVOIDING BAD ARGUMENTS

Recall that a good argument has true premises plus a conclusion that follows from those premises. A bad argument fails at least one of these conditions—it has a false premise or a conclusion that does not follow. This failure, however, can appear in many different argument forms, some of which are extremely common. These common bad arguments are known as *fallacies*. They are so distinctive and are used so often that they have been given names and are usually covered in courses on critical reasoning. Though flawed, fallacies are often persuasive and are frequently employed to mislead the unwary—even in (or *especially* in) moral reasoning. The best way to avoid using fallacies—or being taken in by them—is to study them so you know how they work and can easily identify them. The following is a brief review of the fallacies that are most prevalent in moral argumentation.

Begging the Question

Begging the question is the fallacy of arguing in a circle—that is, trying to use a statement as both a premise in an argument and the conclusion of that argument. Such an argument says, in effect, *p* is true because *p* is true. That kind of reasoning, of course, proves nothing.

For example:

1. Women in Muslim countries, regardless of their social status and economic limitations, are entitled to certain rights, including but not necessarily limited to suffrage.

2. Therefore, all women in Muslim countries have the right to vote in political elections.

This argument is equivalent to saying "Women in Muslim countries have a right to vote because women in Muslim countries have a right to vote." The conclusion merely repeats the premise but in different words. The best protection against circular reasoning is a close reading of the argument.

Equivocation

The fallacy of **equivocation** assigns two different meanings to the same term in an argument. Here's an example that, in one form or another, is commonplace in the abortion debate:

1. A fetus is an individual that is indisputably human.
2. A human is endowed with rights that cannot be invalidated, including a right to life.
3. Therefore, a fetus has a right to life.

This argument equivocates on the word *human*. In Premise 1, the term means physiologically human, as in having human DNA. This claim, of course, is indeed indisputable. But in Premise 2, *human* is used in the sense of *person*—that is, an individual having full moral rights. Since the premises refer to two different things, the conclusion does not follow. If you are not paying close attention, though, you might not detect the equivocation and accept the argument as it is.

Appeal to Authority

This fallacy consists of relying on the opinion of someone thought to be an expert who is not. An expert, of course, can be a source of reliable information—but only if he really is an authority in the designated subject area. A true expert is someone who is both knowledgeable about the facts and able to make reliable judgments about them. Ultimately, experts are experts because they carefully base their opinions on the available evidence.

We make a fallacious **appeal to authority** when we (1) cite experts who are not experts in the field under discussion (though they may be experts in some other field) or (2) cite nonexperts as experts. Expertise in one field does not automatically carry over to another, and even nonexperts who are prestigious and famous are still nonexperts. In general, on subjects outside an expert's area of expertise, her opinions are no more reliable than those of nonexperts.

Two rules of thumb should guide your use of expert opinion. First, if a claim conflicts with the consensus of opinion among experts, you have good reason to doubt the claim. Second, if experts disagree about a claim, you again have good reason to doubt it.

Appeal to Emotion

Emotions have a role to play in the moral life. In moral arguments, however, the use of emotions alone as substitutes for premises is a fallacy. We commit this fallacy when we try to convince someone to accept a conclusion not by providing them with relevant reasons but by appealing only to fear, guilt, anger, hate, compassion, and the like. For example:

> The defendant is obviously guilty of murder in this case. Look at him in the courtroom—he's terrifying and menacing. And no one can ignore the way he stabbed that girl and mutilated her body. And her poor parents. . . .

The question here is whether the defendant committed the crime, and the feelings of fear and pity that he evokes are not relevant to it. But if the question were about the anguish or torment inflicted on the victim or her parents, then our feelings of empathy would indeed be relevant—and so would any pertinent moral principles or theories.

Slippery Slope

The **slippery slope** fallacy is the use of dubious premises to argue that doing a particular action will inevitably lead to other actions that will result in disaster, so that first action should not be done. This way of arguing is perfectly legitimate if the premises are solid—that is, if there are good reasons to believe that the first step really will lead to ruin. Consider:

1. Rampant proliferation of pornography on the Internet leads to obsession with pornographic materials.
2. Obsession with pornographic materials disrupts relationships, and that disruption leads to divorce.
3. Therefore, we should ban pornography on the Internet.

Perhaps the chain of events laid out here could actually occur, but we have been given no reason to believe that it would. (You can see that this argument is also missing a moral premise.) Scientific evidence showing that this sequence of cause and effect does occur as described would constitute good reason to accept Premises 1 and 2.

Faulty Analogy

The use of an analogy to argue for a conclusion is known, not surprisingly, as argument by analogy. It is a type of inductive argument that says because two things are alike in some ways, they must be alike in some additional way. For example:

1. Humans feel pain, care for their young, live in social groups, and understand nuclear physics.
2. Apes also feel pain, care for their young, and live in social groups.
3. Therefore, apes can understand nuclear physics.

In argument by analogy, the probability that the conclusion is true depends on the relevant similarities between the two things being compared. The greater the relevant similarities, the more likely it is that the conclusion is true. Humans and apes are relevantly similar in several ways, but the question is, Are they relevantly similar enough to render the conclusion probable? In this case, though humans and apes are similar in some ways, they are not relevantly similar enough to adequately support the conclusion. Humans and apes have many differences—the most relevant of which for this argument is probably in the physiology of their brains and in their capacity for advanced learning.

Arguments by analogy are common in moral reasoning. For example:

1. When a neighbor needs your help (as when he needs to borrow your garden hose to put out a fire in his house), it is morally permissible to lend the neighbor what he needs.
2. Britain is a neighbor of the United States, and it is in dire need of help to win the war against Germany.
3. Therefore, it is morally permissible for the United States to lend Britain the material and equipment it needs to defeat Germany.

This is roughly the moral argument that President Franklin Roosevelt made during World War II to convince Americans to aid Britain in its struggle. The strength of the argument depends on the degree of similarity between the two situations described. At the time, many Americans thought the argument strong.

The fallacy of **faulty analogy** is argument by an analogy that is weak. In strong arguments by analogy, not only must the degree of similarity be great, but the similarities must also be relevant. This means that the similarities must relate specifically to the conclusion. Irrelevant similarities cannot strengthen an argument.

Appeal to Ignorance

This fallacy consists of arguing that the *absence of evidence* entitles us to believe a claim. Consider these two arguments:

- No one has proven that the fetus is not a person, so it is in fact a person.

- It is obviously false that a fetus is a person, because science has not proven that it is a person.

Both of these arguments are **appeals to ignorance**. The first one says that because a statement has not been proven false, it must be true. The second one has things the other way around: because a statement has not been proven true, it must be false. The problem in both of these cases is that a *lack* of evidence cannot be evidence for anything. A dearth of evidence simply indicates that we are ignorant of the facts. If having no evidence could prove something, we could prove all sorts of outrageous claims. We could argue that because no one has proven that there are no space aliens controlling all our moral decisions, there are in fact space aliens controlling all our moral decisions.

Straw Man

Unfortunately, the **straw man** fallacy is rampant in debates about moral issues. It amounts to misrepresenting someone's claim or argument so it can be more easily refuted. For example, suppose you are trying to argue that a code of ethics for your professional group should be secular so that it can be appreciated and used by as many people as possible, regardless of their religious views. Suppose further that your opponent argues against your claim in this fashion:

> X obviously wants to strip religious faith away from every member of our profession and to banish religion from the realm of ethics. We should not let this happen. We should not let X have his way. Vote against the secular code of ethics.

This argument misrepresents your view, distorting it so that it seems outrageous and unacceptable. Your opponent argues against the distorted version and then concludes that your (original) position should be rejected.

The straw man fallacy is not just a bad argument— it flies in the face of the spirit of moral reasoning, which is about seeking understanding through critical thinking and honest and fair exploration of issues. If you agree with this approach, then you should not use the straw man fallacy— and you should beware of its use by others.

Appeal to the Person

Appeal to the person (also known as *ad hominem*) is the fallacy of arguing that a claim should be rejected solely because of the characteristics of the person who makes it. Look at these:

- We should reject Alice's assertion that cheating on your taxes is wrong. She's a political libertarian.

- Jerome argues that we should all give a portion of our income to feed the hungry people of the world. But that's just what you'd expect a rich guy like him to say. Ignore him.

- Maria says that animals have rights and that we shouldn't use animal products on moral grounds. Don't believe a word of it. She owns a fur coat—she's a big hypocrite.

In each of these arguments, a claim is rejected on the grounds that the person making it has a particular character, political affiliation, or motive. Such personal characteristics, however, are irrelevant to the truth of a claim. A claim must stand or fall on its own merits. Whether a statement is true or false, it must be judged according to the quality of the reasoning and evidence behind it. Bad people can construct good arguments; good people can construct bad arguments.

Hasty Generalization

Hasty generalization is a fallacy of inductive reasoning. It is the mistake of drawing a conclusion about an entire group of people or things based on an undersized sample of the group.

- In this town three pro-life demonstrators have been arrested for trespassing or assault. I'm telling you, pro-lifers are lawbreakers.

• In the past thirty years, at least two people on death row in this state have been executed and later found to be innocent by DNA evidence. Why is the state constantly executing innocent people?

QUICK REVIEW

begging the question—The fallacy of arguing in a circle—that is, trying to use a statement as both a premise in an argument and the conclusion of that argument. Such an argument says, in effect, *p* is true because *p* is true.

equivocation—The fallacy of assigning two different meanings to the same term in an argument.

appeal to authority—The fallacy of relying on the opinion of someone thought to be an expert who is not.

slippery slope—The fallacy of using dubious premises to argue that doing a particular action will inevitably lead to other actions that will result in disaster, so that first action should not be done.

faulty analogy—The use of a flawed analogy to argue for a conclusion.

appeal to ignorance—The fallacy of arguing that the absence of evidence entitles us to believe a claim.

straw man—The fallacy of misrepresenting someone's claim or argument so it can be more easily refuted.

appeal to the person—The fallacy (also known as *ad hominem*) of arguing that a claim should be rejected solely because of the characteristics of the person who makes it.

hasty generalization—The fallacy of drawing a conclusion about an entire group of people or things based on an undersized sample of the group.

In the first argument, a conclusion is drawn about all people with pro-life views from a sample of just three people. When it is spelled out plainly, the leap in logic is clearly preposterous. Yet such preposterous leaps are extremely common. In the second argument, the conclusion is that wrongful executions in the state happen frequently. This conclusion, though, is not justified by the tiny sample of cases.

WRITING AND SPEAKING ABOUT MORAL ISSUES

A common view about ethics is that arguing about morality is unproductive, unenlightening, frustrating, unsatisfying—and therefore pointless. A typical moral disagreement can go like this:

"The university should ban alcohol everywhere on campus," says X. "Drinking is immoral, whether on campus or off."

"You sound like the administration hacks. They're all idiots!" says Y.

X: "They're not *all* idiots. Some are nice."

Y: "Wrong. They're idiots, and they drink plenty of alcohol every day. Alcohol helps them forget they're idiots."

X: "What about Professor Jones? She doesn't drink."

Y: "Yeah, but she's boring. And for a college professor, being boring is the worst moral failing imaginable."

This exchange really *is* pointless; it's going nowhere. It's the kind of conversation that gives moral discourse a bad name. As we've seen, proper discussions about moral issues—whether in written or oral form—are not at all pointless. They are often productive, thought-provoking, even enlightening. You may not always like where the conversation ends up (what conclusions are arrived at), but you will probably think the trip is worthwhile.

Good moral essays or conversations have several essential elements, without which no progress could be made in resolving the issue at hand.

1. *A claim to be proved.* Almost always, the point of writing or speaking about a moral issue is to resolve it—that is, to determine whether the central moral claim or statement (a judgment, principle, or theory) is true. Is it the case that same-sex marriage is wrong (or right)? Is it true that Maria's action is morally permissible (or impermissible)? Should actions always be judged right or wrong according to the consequences they produce? To answer such questions is to resolve the issue at hand, and resolving the issue at hand is the point of the written or spoken discourse. Without a clear idea of the claim in question, the essay or conversation will meander, as it does in the previous example.

In an essay, the claim should be spelled out (or sometimes implied) in the first one or two paragraphs. In a conversation, it is most often mentioned (or understood) at the beginning. In either case, it is by grasping the claim that we come to understand the point of it all and to follow the thread of the discussion.

In the most productive moral essays or conversations, something else is made apparent early on: the reason the claim is worth discussing in the first place. This means making sure that the meaning of the claim is clear and that its implications are apparent. Sometimes this step requires only a sentence or two, but usually much more explaining is necessary. Just as essential is ensuring that readers or listeners understand why anyone would *want* to address the issue—why the issue is deemed important enough to warrant an essay or serious conversation. Often all that's required is a brief explanation of how the issue directly affects people's lives. How, for example, might attitudes and lives change if everyone agreed that same-sex marriage was morally permissible? Or how differently might we view the world if all moral judgments were based on the consequences of actions?

Many times, the best reason for dealing with a particular moral issue is that others have addressed it and we want to disagree or agree with their response. So we might say, "Juan argues that using illicit drugs is morally right, but I think he's wrong on several counts." Or, "In the debates over abortion, many commentators have asserted that a human fetus is a person with moral standing. But there are at least three reasons for rejecting this view." Or, "Does science prove that persons do not have free will? Some philosophers think so. But I, along with many astute commentators, beg to differ."

2. *An argument for or against the claim.* By now, you know that the essence of moral reasoning, the means for resolving (or trying to resolve) a moral issue, and the overall shape of an essay or conversation about a moral claim is the moral argument. The common pattern in an essay is to follow the introduction (where the moral claim is stated) with a moral argument. Likewise, in a truly rewarding conversation on a moral issue, the main event is the presentation of a moral argument and the ensuing discussion about the quality of that argument (whether the premises are true and whether the conclusion logically follows from them).

Setting forth the argument involves explaining and amplifying each premise and supporting it with evidence (expert opinion, studies, statistics), examples, or analogies. The aim is to demonstrate clearly and carefully that the conclusion follows from the premises and that the premises are true.

In a worthwhile oral debate, the elements are much the same. Enough time and attention must be allowed for giving and explaining an argument and for thoughtful responses to that argument.

3. *Consideration of alternative views.* In any good essay or conversation about moral issues, presenting an argument is not enough. There must be space or time to consider alternative views on the subject. Specifically, there should be an honest and thorough assessment of objections to your argument and its conclusion. Students are often reluctant to take this step because they think it will weaken their

case. But the opposite is true. When you carefully consider contrary opinions, you gain credibility, because you show that you are fair-minded and careful. You demonstrate to readers or listeners that you are aware of possible objections and that you have good replies to them. Would you trust the assertions of someone who dogmatically pushes his own view and ignores or dismisses out of hand anyone who disagrees? Remember that a logical argument is not a quarrel or spat and that a truly productive debate is not a competition or shouting match. In ethics, written and oral approaches to moral issues are honest searches for truth and sincere exchanges of ideas.

In an essay, an assessment of objections can come early or late but usually appears after the presentation of the argument. In conversation, objections may be taken up throughout and be addressed as interlocutors raise them. Mutual respect and fairness is a necessity in oral debate. Speakers must be given a chance to have their say—to present arguments, raise objections, or respond to objections.

Handling objections properly involves both summarizing and examining them. We should always avoid the fallacies mentioned earlier, of course, but in considering alternative views, we need to be especially alert to the *straw man*. Because the essence of the straw man fallacy is the misrepresenting of someone's claim or argument so it can be more easily refuted, inserting the fallacy into discussions is both dishonest and counterproductive. And by using it, you miss an opportunity to spot weaknesses in your case, which means you also miss a chance to strengthen it.

CHAPTER REVIEW

SUMMARY

An argument is a group of statements, one of which is supposed to be supported by the rest. To be more precise, an argument consists of one or more premises

and a conclusion. In a good argument, the conclusion must follow from the premises, and the premises must be true.

Arguments come in two basic types: deductive and inductive. Deductive arguments are meant to give logically conclusive support for their conclusions. A deductive argument that actually provides this kind of support is said to be valid. If it also has true premises, it is said to be sound. An inductive argument is meant to provide probable support for its conclusion. An inductive argument that actually provides this kind of support is said to be strong. If it also has true premises, it is said to be cogent.

Deductive arguments come in different forms. Some of these forms are known to be valid; some, invalid. Knowing these patterns helps you determine the validity of deductive arguments. Using the counterexample method can also aid your analysis.

The typical moral argument consists of at least one moral premise and at least one nonmoral premise. The best approach to evaluating moral arguments is to treat them as deductive. This tack enables you to uncover implicit premises. Implicit premises are often moral premises, which may be controversial or dubious. They can be tested through the use of counterexamples.

In moral reasoning, you frequently encounter fallacies—forms of bad arguments that arise repeatedly. Some of those you are most likely to come across are begging the question, equivocation, appeal to authority, slippery slope, faulty analogy, appeal to ignorance, straw man, appeal to the person, and hasty generalization.

KEY TERMS
statement (p. 41)
argument (p. 42)
premise (p. 42)
conclusion (p. 42)
indicator words (p. 43)
deductive argument (p. 44)
inductive argument (p. 44)
valid argument (p. 44)
invalid argument (p. 44)
strong argument (p. 45)

weak argument (p. 45)
sound argument (p. 45)
cogent argument (p. 45)
moral statement (p. 51)
nonmoral statement (p. 51)
begging the question (p. 56)
equivocation (p. 57)
appeal to authority (p. 57)
slippery slope (p. 58)
faulty analogy (p. 58)
appeal to ignorance (p. 59)
straw man (p. 59)
appeal to the person (p. 59)
hasty generalization (p. 59)

EXERCISES

Review Questions

1. Are all persuasive arguments valid? Recount a situation in which you tried to persuade someone of a view by using an argument. (p. 44)
2. Can a valid deductive argument ever have false premises? Why or why not? (p. 44)
3. Are the premises of a cogent argument always true? Is the conclusion always true? Explain. (p. 45)
4. What is the term designating a valid argument with true premises? a strong argument with true premises? (p. 45)
5. Is the following argument form valid or invalid? Why or why not? (p. 45)

   If p, then q.

   p.

   Therefore, q.
6. Is the following argument form valid or invalid? Why or why not? (p. 46)

   If p, then q.

   If q, then r.

   Therefore, if p, then r.
7. What is the counterexample method? (p. 47)
8. What kinds of premises must a moral argument have? (p. 57)
9. What is the best method for evaluating moral premises? (pp. 54–55)

10. Explain the method for locating implied premises. (pp. 47–48)

Discussion Questions

1. Is it immoral to believe a claim without evidence? Why or why not?
2. If moral reasoning is largely about providing good reasons for moral claims, where do feelings enter the picture? Is it possible to present a good argument that you feel strongly about? If so, provide an example of such an argument.
3. Which of the following passages are arguments (in the sense of displaying critical reasoning)? Explain your answers.
   - If you harm someone, they will harm you.
   - Racial profiling is wrong. It discriminates against racial groups, and discrimination is wrong.
   - If you say something that offends me, I have the right to prevent you from saying it again. After all, words are weapons, and I have a right to prevent the use of weapons against me.
4. What is the difference between persuading someone to believe a claim and giving them reasons to accept it? Can a good argument be persuasive? Why or why not?
5. Why do you think people are tempted to use the straw man fallacy in disagreements on moral issues? How do you feel when someone uses this fallacy against you?

Argument Exercises

Diagram the following arguments. Exercises marked with an asterisk (*) have answers in Answers to Argument Exercises at the end of the text.

*1. If John works out at the gym daily, he will be healthier. He is working out at the gym daily. So he will be healthier.
2. If when you are in a coma you are no longer a person, then giving you a drug to kill you would not be murder. In a coma, you are in fact not a person. Therefore, giving you the drug is not murder.

*3. Ghosts do not exist. There is no reliable evidence showing that any disembodied persons exist anywhere.

4. If you smoke, your heart will be damaged. If your heart is damaged, your risk of dying due to heart problems will increase. Therefore, smoking can increase your risk of dying due to heart problems.

*5. The mayor is soft on crime. He cut back on misdemeanor enforcement and told the police department to be more lenient with traffic violators.

6. Grow accustomed to the belief that death is nothing to us, since every good and evil lie in sensation. However, death is the deprivation of sensation. Therefore, death is nothing to us.

*7. The president is either dishonest or incompetent. He's not incompetent, though, because he's an expert at getting self-serving legislation through Congress. I guess he's just dishonest.

8. Most Republicans are conservatives, and Kurt is a Republican. Therefore, Kurt is probably a conservative. Therefore Kurt is probably opposed to increases in welfare benefits, because most conservatives are opposed to increased welfare benefits.

*9. Can people without strong religious beliefs be moral? Countless people have been nonbelievers or nontheists and still behaved according to lofty moral principles; for example, the Buddhists of Asia and the Confucianists of China. Consider also the great secular philosophers, from the ancient Greeks to the likes of David Hume and Bertrand Russell. So it's not true that those without strong religious beliefs cannot be moral.

10. Jan is a student at Harvard. No student at Harvard has won a Pulitzer prize. Therefore, Jan has not won a Pulitzer.

*11. We shouldn't pay the lawnmower guy so much money because he never completes the work, and he will probably just gamble the money away because he has no self-control.

12. Either Manny, Mo, or Jack crashed the car. Manny couldn't have done it, because he was sleeping in his room and was observed the whole time. Mo couldn't have done it, because he was out of town at the time and has witnesses to prove it. So the guy who crashed the car had to be Jack.

FURTHER READING

Richard Feldman, *Reason and Argument,* 2nd ed. (Upper Saddle River, NJ: Prentice Hall, 1999).

Richard M. Fox and Joseph P. DeMarco, *Moral Reasoning: A Philosophic Approach to Applied Ethics,* 2nd ed. (Fort Worth, TX: Harcourt College Publishers, 2001).

Brooke Noel Moore and Richard Parker, *Critical Thinking,* 7th ed. (Boston: McGraw-Hill, 2004).

Lewis Vaughn, *The Power of Critical Thinking: Effective Reasoning about Ordinary and Extraordinary Claims*, 5th ed. (New York: Oxford University Press, 2016).

CHAPTER 4

The Power of Moral Theories

Recall that Part 1 (Fundamentals) gave you a broad view of our subject, outlining the major concerns of moral philosophy, the function of moral judgments and principles, the nature of moral problems, the elements of our common moral experience, and the challenges of moral relativism and emotivism. Part 2 (Moral Reasoning) covered ethics at the ground level—the fundamentals of critical reasoning as applied to everyday moral claims, arguments, and conflicts. Here in Part 3 (Chapters 4–7) we touch again on a great deal of this previous material as we explore a central concern of contemporary ethics: moral theory.

THEORIES OF RIGHT AND WRONG

Whatever else the moral life entails, it surely has moral reasoning at its core. We act, we feel, we choose, and in our best moments, we are guided by the sifting of reasons and the weighing of arguments. Much of the time, we expect—and want—this process to yield plausible moral judgments. We confront the cases that unsettle us and hope to respond to them with credible assessments of the right and the good. In making these judgments, we may appeal to moral standards—principles or rules that help us sort out right and wrong, good and bad. Our deliberations may even work the other way around: moral judgments may help us mold moral principles. If we think carefully about our own deliberations, however, we will probably come to understand that this interplay between moral judgments and principles cannot be the whole story of moral reasoning. From time to time we step back from

such considerations and ask ourselves if a trusted moral principle is truly sound, whether a conflict of principles can be resolved, or if a new principle can handle cases that we have never had to address before. When we puzzle over such things, we enter the realm of moral theory. We theorize—trying to use, make, or revise a moral theory or a piece of one.

A **moral theory** is an explanation of what makes an action right or what makes a person or thing good. Its focus is not the rightness or goodness of specific actions or persons but the very nature of rightness or goodness itself. Moral theories concerned with the goodness of persons or things are known as *theories of value*. Moral theories concerned with the rightness or wrongness of actions are called *theories of obligation*. In this text, we focus mostly on theories of obligation and, unless otherwise indicated, will use the more general term *moral theories* to refer to them. A moral theory in this sense, then, is an explanation of what makes an action right or wrong. It says, in effect, that a particular action is right (or wrong) because it has *this* property or characteristic.

Moral theories and theorizing are hard to avoid. To wonder what makes an action right is to theorize. To try *not* to think much about morality but to rely on your default moral theory—the one you inherited from your family or culture—is of course to live by the lights of a moral theory. To reject all moral theories, to deny the possibility of objective morality, or to embrace a subjectivist view of right and wrong is to have a particular overarching view of morality, a view that in the broadest sense constitutes a moral theory or part of one.

Moral Theories versus Moral Codes

A moral theory explains what makes an action right; a moral code is simply a set of rules. We value a moral theory because it identifies for us the essence of rightness and thereby helps us make moral judgments, derive moral principles, and resolve conflicts between moral statements. A moral code is much less useful than a moral theory. The rules in a moral code inevitably conflict but provide no means for resolving their inconsistencies. Rules saying "Do not kill" and "Protect human life," for example, will clash when the only way to protect human life is to kill. Also, rules are always general—usually too general to cover many specific situations that call for a moral decision—yet not general enough (in the way that theories are) to help us deal with such an array of specifics. How does a rule insisting "Children must obey their parents" apply when the parents are criminally insane or under the influence of drugs, or when there are no parents, just legal guardians? To make the rule apply, we would have to interpret it—and that gets us back into the realm of moral theory.

The point is that moral codes may have their place in the moral life, but they are no substitute for a plausible moral theory. Rules are rules, but a moral theory can help us see beyond the rules.

A moral theory provides us with very general norms, or standards, that can help us make sense of our moral experiences, judgments, and principles. (Some moral theories feature only *one* overarching standard.) The standards are meant to be general enough and substantial enough to inform our moral reasoning—to help us assess the worth of less general principles, to shed light on our moral judgments, to corroborate or challenge aspects of our moral experience, and even to generate new lower-level principles if need be.

Moral theories and moral arguments often work together. A statement expressing a moral theory may itself act as the moral premise in an argument. More often, an argument's moral premise is ultimately backed by a moral theory from which the moral premise (principle or rule) is derived. Testing the premise may require examining one or more supporting principles or perhaps the most general norm (the theory) itself.

Classic utilitarianism (covered in the next chapter) is an example of a simple moral theory, one based on a single, all-encompassing standard: right actions are those that directly produce the greatest overall happiness, everyone considered. What matters most are the consequences of actions. Thus, in a particular situation, if there are only two possible actions, and action X produces, say, 100 units of overall happiness for everyone involved (early utilitarians were the first to use this strange-sounding notion of *units* of happiness), while action Y produces only 50 units, action X is the morally right action to perform. The theory therefore identifies what is thought to be the most important factor in the moral life (happiness) and provides a procedure for making judgments about right and wrong actions.

Should we therefore conclude that a moral theory is the final authority in moral reasoning? Not at all. A moral theory is not like a mathematical axiom. From a moral theory we cannot derive in strict logical fashion principles or judgments that will solve all the problems of our real-world cases. Because moral theories are by definition general and theoretical, they cannot by themselves give us precisely tailored right answers. But neither can we dispense with moral theories and rely solely on judgments about particular cases and issues. In the field of ethics, most philosophers agree that carefully made moral judgments about cases and issues are generally reliable data that we should take very seriously. Such opinions are called **considered moral judgments**, because they are formed after careful deliberation that is as free of bias as possible.

Our considered moral judgments (including the principles or rules sanctioned by those judgments) by themselves, however, are sometimes of limited use. They may conflict. They may lack sufficient justification. A moral theory provides standards that can help overcome these limitations.

So where does theory fit in our moral deliberations? Theory plays a role along with judgments and principles or rules. In trying to determine the morally right thing to do in a specific case, we may find ourselves reflecting on just one of these elements or on all of them at once. We may, for example, begin by considering the insights embodied in our moral theory, which give some justification to several relevant principles. In light of these principles, we may decide to perform a particular action. But we may also discover that our considered moral judgment in the case conflicts with the deliverances of the relevant principles or even with the overarching theory. Depending on the weight we give to the particular judgment, we may decide to adjust the principles or the theory so that it is compatible with the judgment. A moral theory can crystallize important insights in morality and thereby give us general guidance as we make judgments about cases and issues. But the judgments—if they are indeed trustworthy—can compel us to reconsider the theory.

The ultimate goal in this give-and-take of theory and judgment (or principle) is a kind of close coherence between the two—what has come to be known as *reflective equilibrium.*[1] They should fit together as closely as possible, with maximum agreement between them. This process is similar to the one used in science to reconcile theory and experimental data, a topic we address in more detail later in this chapter.

MAJOR THEORIES

Moral philosophers have traditionally grouped theories of morality into two major categories: consequentialist (or teleological) and nonconsequentialist (or deontological). In general, **consequentialist theories** say that what makes an action right is its *consequences.* Specifically, the rightness of an action depends on the amount of good it produces. A consequentialist theory may define the good in different ways—as, for example, pleasure, happiness, well-being, flourishing, or knowledge. But however *good* is defined, the morally right action is the one that results in the most favorable balance of good over bad.

Nonconsequentialist theories say that the rightness of an action does *not* depend entirely on its consequences. It depends primarily, or completely, on the nature of the action itself. To a nonconsequentialist, the balance of good over bad that results from an action may matter little or not at all. What is of primary concern is the *kind* of action in question. To a consequentialist, telling a lie may be considered wrong because it leads to more unhappiness than other actions do. To a nonconsequentialist, telling a lie may be considered wrong simply because it violates an exceptionless rule. Thus, by nonconsequentialist lights, an action could be morally right even though it produces less good than any alternative action.

Consequentialist Theories

There are several consequentialist theories, each differing from the others on who is to benefit from goods or what kinds of goods are to be pursued. But two theories have received the most attention from moral philosophers: utilitarianism and ethical egoism.

Utilitarianism says that the morally right action is the one that produces the most favorable balance of good over evil, everyone considered. That is, the right action maximizes the good (however *good* is defined) better than any alternative action, everyone considered. Utilitarianism insists that *everyone* affected by an action must be included in any proper calculation of overall consequences. The crucial factor is how much net good is produced when everyone involved is counted.

Moral philosophers distinguish two major types of utilitarianism according to whether judgments of rightness focus on individual acts (without reference to rules) or on rules that cover various categories of acts. **Act-utilitarianism** says that right actions are those that *directly* produce the greatest overall good, everyone considered. The consequences that flow directly from a particular act are all that matter; rules are irrelevant to this calculation. In act-utilitarianism, each situation calling for a moral judgment is unique and demands a new calculation of the balance of good over evil. Thus, breaking a promise may be right in one situation and wrong in another, depending on the consequences. **Rule-utilitarianism**, on the other hand, says that the morally right action is the one *covered by a rule* that if generally followed would produce the most favorable balance of good over evil, everyone considered. The consequences of generally following a rule are of supreme importance—not the direct consequences of performing a particular action. Specific rules are justified because if people follow them all the time (or most of the time), the result will be a general maximization of good over evil. We are to follow such rules consistently, even if doing so in a particular circumstance results in bad consequences.

Ethical egoism says that the morally right action is the one that produces the most favorable balance of good over evil *for oneself.* That is, in every situation the right action is the one that advances one's own best interests. In each circumstance, the ethical egoist must ask, "Which action, among all possible actions, will result in the most good *for me?*" Ironically, it may be possible for an ethical egoist to consistently practice this creed without appearing to be selfish or committing many selfishly unkind acts. The egoist may think that *completely* disregarding the welfare of others is not in his or her best interests. After all, people tend to resent such behavior and may respond accordingly. Nevertheless, the bottom line in all moral deliberations is whether an action maximizes the good for

the egoist. This approach to morality seems to radically conflict with commonsense moral experience as well as with the basic principles of most other moral theories.

Nonconsequentialist Theories

Nonconsequentialist (deontological) theories also take various forms. They differ on, among other things, the number of foundational principles or basic rules used and the ultimate basis of those principles.

By far the most influential nonconsequentialist theory is that of Immanuel Kant (1724–1804). Kant wants to establish as the foundation of his theory a single principle from which all additional maxims can be derived, a principle he calls the **categorical imperative**. One way that he states his principle is "Act only on that maxim through which you can at the same time will that it should become a universal law."[2] (Kant insists that he formulates just one principle but expresses it in several different forms; the forms, however, seem to be separate principles.) The categorical imperative, Kant says, is self-evident—and therefore founded on reason. The principle and the maxims derived from it are also universal (applying to all persons) and absolutist, meaning that they are moral laws that have no exceptions. **Kant's theory**, then, is the view that the morally right action is the one done in accordance with the categorical imperative.

For Kant, every action implies a rule or maxim that says, in effect, always do this in these circumstances. An action is right, he says, if and only if you could rationally will the rule to be universal—to have everyone in a similar situation always act according to the same rule. Breaking promises is wrong because if the implied rule (something like "Break promises whenever you want") were universalized (if everyone followed the rule), then no promise anywhere could be trusted, and the whole convention of promise making would be obliterated—and no one would be willing to live in such a world. In other words, universalizing the breaking of promises would result in a logically contradictory state of affairs, a situation that makes no moral sense.

Notice again the stark contrast between utilitarianism and Kant's theory. For the former, the rightness of an action depends solely on its consequences, on what results the action produces for everyone involved. For the latter, the consequences of actions for particular individuals never enter into the equation. An action is right if and only if it possesses a particular property—the property of according with the categorical imperative, of not involving a logical contradiction.

Another notable nonconsequentialist view is the theory of natural law. **Natural law theory** says that the morally right action is the one that follows the dictates of nature. What does nature have to do with ethics? According to the most influential form of this theory (traditional natural law theory), the natural world, including humankind, exhibits a rational order in which everything has its proper place and purpose, with each thing given a specific role to play by God. In this grand order, natural laws reflect how the world is as well as how it should be. People are supposed to live according to natural law—that is, they are to fulfill their rightful, *natural* purpose. To act morally, they must act naturally; they must do what they were designed to do by God. They must obey the absolutist moral rules that anyone can read in the natural order.

A natural law theorist might reason like this: Lying is immoral because it goes against human nature. Truth telling is natural for humans because they are social creatures with an inborn tendency to care about the welfare of others. Truth telling helps humans get along, maintain viable societies, and show respect for others. Lying is therefore unnatural and wrong. Another example: Some natural law theorists claim that "unnatural" sexual activity is immoral. They argue that because the natural purpose of sex is procreation, and such practices as homosexual sex or anal sex have nothing to do with procreation, these practices are immoral.

QUICK REVIEW

moral theory—An explanation of what makes an action right or what makes a person or thing good.

considered moral judgment—A moral assessment that is as free from bias and distorting passions as possible. We generally trust such a judgment unless there is a reason to doubt it.

consequentialist theory—A theory asserting that what makes an action right is its consequences.

nonconsequentialist theory—A theory asserting that the rightness of an action does not depend on its consequences.

utilitarianism—A theory asserting that the morally right action is the one that produces the most favorable balance of good over evil, everyone considered.

act-utilitarianism—A utilitarian theory asserting that the morally right action is the one that directly produces the most favorable balance of good over evil, everyone considered.

rule-utilitarianism—A utilitarian theory asserting that the morally right action is the one covered by a rule that, if generally followed, would produce the most favorable balance of good over evil, everyone considered.

ethical egoism—A theory asserting that the morally right action is the one that produces the most favorable balance of good over evil for oneself.

categorical imperative—An imperative that we should follow regardless of our particular wants and needs; also, the principle that defines Kant's theory.

Kant's theory—A theory asserting that the morally right action is the one done in accordance with the categorical imperative.

(continued)

natural law theory—A theory asserting that the morally right action is the one that follows the dictates of nature.

divine command theory—A theory asserting that the morally right action is the one that God commands.

prima facie principle—A principle that applies in a situation unless exceptions are justified.

negative right—A person's right that obligates others not to interfere with that person's obtaining something.

positive right—A person's right that obligates others to help that person obtain something.

retributive justice—The fair use of punishment for wrongdoing.

distributive justice—The fair distribution of society's benefits and costs (such as income, taxes, jobs, and public service).

self-evident statement—An assertion that a person is justified in believing merely by understanding it, such as "No bachelors are married."

Another critical aspect of the traditional theory is that it insists that humans can discover what is natural, and thus moral, through reason. God has created a natural order and given humans the gift of rationality to correctly apprehend this order. This means that any rational person—whether religious or not—can discern the moral rules and live a moral life.

One of the simplest nonconsequentialist theories is the **divine command theory**, a view discussed in Chapter 1. It says that the morally right action is the one that God commands. An action is right if and only if God says it is. The rightness of an action does not depend in any way on its consequences. According to the divine command theory, an action may be deemed right even though it does *not* maximize the good, or deemed wrong even if it does maximize the good. It may

incorporate one principle only (the core principle that God makes rightness) or the core principle plus several subordinate rules, as is the case with divine command views that designate the Ten Commandments as a God-made moral code.

EVALUATING THEORIES

We come now to the question that moral philosophers have been asking in one way or another for centuries: Is this moral theory a *good* theory? That is, is it true? Does it reliably explain what makes an action right? As we have seen, not all moral theories are created equal. Some are better than others; some are seriously flawed; and some, though imperfect, have taught the world important lessons about the moral life.

The next question, of course, is, How do we go about answering the first question? At first glance, it seems that impartially judging the worth of a moral theory is impossible, because we all look at the world through our own tainted lens, our own moral theory or theory fragments. However, our review of subjectivism and relativism (see Chapter 2) suggests that this worry is overblown. More to the point, there are plausible criteria that we can use to evaluate the adequacy of moral theories (our own and those of others), standards that moral philosophers and others have used to appraise even the most complex theories of morality. These are what we may call the *moral criteria of adequacy*.

The first step in assessing any theory (before using these criteria) is to ensure that the theory meets the minimum requirement of *coherence*. A moral theory that is coherent is *eligible* to be evaluated using the criteria of adequacy. A coherent theory is internally consistent, which means that its central claims are consistent with one another—they are not contradictory. An internally consistent theory would not assert, for example, both that (1) actions are right if and only if they are natural and that (2) it is morally right to use unnatural means to save a life. Contradictory claims assert both that something *is* and *is not* the case; one statement says X and another says not-X. When claims conflict in this way, we know that at least one of them is false. So if two substantial claims in a theory are contradictory, one of the claims must be false—and the theory is refuted. This kind of inconsistency is such a serious shortcoming in a moral theory that further evaluation of it would be unnecessary. It is, in fact, not eligible for evaluation. Ineligible theories would get low marks on each criterion of adequacy.

Eligible moral theories are a different matter. Unlike ineligible theories, they are not guaranteed to fare poorly when evaluated, and testing their mettle with the moral criteria of adequacy is almost always revealing. But how do we use these criteria? The answer is that we apply them in much the same way and for a few of the same reasons that scientists apply their criteria to scientific theories.

Scientific theories are introduced to explain data concerning the causes of events—why something happens as it does or why it is the way it is. Usually scientists devise several theories (explanations) of a phenomenon, ensuring that each one is minimally adequate for evaluation. Then they try to determine which of these is best, which offers the best explanation for the data in question, for they know that the best theory is the one most likely to be true. To discover which is the best, they must judge each theory according to some generally accepted standards—the scientific criteria of adequacy. One criterion, for example, is *conservatism:* how well a theory fits with what scientists already know. A scientific theory that conflicts with existing knowledge (well-established facts, scientific laws, or extensively confirmed theories) is not likely to be true. On the other hand, the more conservative a theory is (that is, the less it conflicts with existing knowledge), the more likely it is to be true. All things being equal, a conservative theory is better than one that is not conservative. Another criterion is *fruitfulness:* how many successful novel predictions the theory makes. The more such predictions, the more plausible the theory is.

Now consider the following criteria of adequacy for moral theories:

Criterion 1: Consistency with Considered Moral Judgments

To be worth evaluating, a plausible scientific theory must be consistent with the data it was introduced to explain. A theory meant to explain an epidemic, for example, must account for the nature of the disease and the method of transmission. Otherwise it is a very poor theory. A moral theory must also be consistent with the data it was introduced to explain. A moral theory is supposed to explain what makes an action right, and the data relevant to that issue are our considered moral judgments.

Recall that considered moral judgments are views that we form after careful deliberation under conditions that minimize bias and error. They are therefore thought to have considerable weight as reasons or evidence in moral matters, even though they can be mistaken and other considerations (such as an established moral principle or a well-supported theory) can sometimes overrule them.

A moral theory that is inconsistent with trustworthy judgments is at least dubious and likely to be false and in need of drastic overhaul or rejection. There is something seriously wrong, for example, with a theory that approves of the murder of innocent people, the wanton torture of children, or the enslavement of millions of men and women. As we will see in the next chapter, inconsistency with considered moral judgments can be the undoing of even the most influential and attractive moral theories.

Consider Theory 1. It says that right actions are those that enhance the harmonious functioning of a community. On the face of it, this theory appears to be a wise policy. But it seems to imply that certain heinous acts are right. It suggests, for example, that if killing an innocent person would enhance a community's harmonious functioning, killing that person would be right. This view conflicts

Considered Moral Judgments

The philosopher John Rawls devised the notion of reflective equilibrium and put heavy emphasis on the quality of moral judgments in his own moral theory. This is what he has to say about the nature of considered moral judgments:

> Now, as already suggested, [considered judgments] enter as those judgments in which our moral capacities are most likely to be displayed without distortion. Thus in deciding which of our judgments to take into account we may reasonably select some and exclude others. For example, we may discard those judgments made with hesitation, or in which we have little confidence. Similarly, those given when we are upset or frightened, or when we stand to gain one way or the other can be left aside. All these judgments are likely to be erroneous or to be influenced by an excessive attention to our own interests. Considered judgments are simply those rendered under conditions favorable to the exercise of the sense of justice, and therefore in circumstances where the more common excuses and explanations for making a mistake do not obtain. The person making the judgment is presumed, then, to have the ability, the opportunity, and the desire to reach a correct decision (or at least, not the desire not to). Moreover, the criteria that identify these judgments are not arbitrary. They are, in fact, similar to those that single out considered judgments of any kind.*

*John Rawls, *A Theory of Justice,* rev. ed. (Cambridge, MA: Harvard University Press, Belknap Press, 1999), 42.

dramatically with our considered moral judgment that murdering an innocent person just to make a community happy is wrong. Theory 1 should be rejected.

Criterion 2: Consistency with Our Moral Experiences

As we saw earlier, a good scientific theory should be conservative. It should, in other words, be consistent with scientific background knowledge—with the many beliefs that science has already firmly established. Likewise, a plausible moral theory should be consistent with moral background knowledge—with what we take to be the fundamental facts of our moral experience. Whatever our views on morality, few of us would deny that we do in fact have these experiences:

- We sometimes make moral judgments.

- We often give reasons for particular moral beliefs.

- We are sometimes mistaken in our moral beliefs.

- We occasionally have moral disagreements.

- We occasionally commit wrongful acts.

As is the case with theories that conflict with considered moral judgments, a theory in conflict with these experiences is at least dubious and probably false. A moral theory is inconsistent with the moral life if it implies that we do not have one or more of these basic moral experiences.

Suppose Theory 2 says that our feelings alone determine whether actions are right—that if our feelings lead us to believe that an action is right, then it is right. But this theory suggests that we are *never* mistaken in our moral beliefs, for if our feelings determine what is right, we cannot be wrong. Whatever we happen to feel tells us what actions are right. Our moral experience, however, is good evidence that we are *not* morally infallible. Theory 2 therefore is problematic, to say the least.

Could we possibly be mistaken about our moral experience? Yes. It is possible that our experience of the moral life is illusory. Perhaps we are morally infallible after all, or maybe we do not actually

CRITICAL THOUGHT: A 100 Percent All-Natural Theory

Imagine that you come across a theory based on this moral standard: Only actions that are "natural" are morally right; "unnatural" actions are wrong. We can call it the *all-natural theory*. It defines natural actions as (1) those done in accordance with the normal biological urges and needs of human beings, (2) those that reflect typical human psychological tendencies and patterns, and (3) those that help ensure the survival of the human species. (This approach should not be confused with the more sophisticated and historically important natural law theory.) An all-natural theorist might view these actions as morally permissible: walking, talking, eating, having sex, cooperating with others, caring for loved ones, teaching children, creating art, growing food, building shelters, going to war, solving problems, and protecting the environ-

ment. Impermissible actions might include building spaceships, using birth control, using performance-enhancing drugs, being a loner or a hermit, and intervening in reproductive processes (as in cloning, abortion, fertility treatments, in vitro fertilization, and stem cell research).

Is this a good theory? Is it internally inconsistent? (For example, do the three definitions of natural actions conflict? Would applying Definition 3 contradict the results of applying Definitions 1 and 2?) Is the all-natural theory consistent with our considered moral judgments? (Hint: Would it condone murder? Would it conflict with our usual concepts of justice?) If it is not consistent, supply an example (a counterexample). Is the theory consistent with our moral experience? Give reasons for your answer. Is the theory useful? If not, why not?

make moral judgments. But like our considered moral judgments, our commonsense moral experiences carry weight as evidence—good evidence that the moral life is, for the most part, as we think it is. We are therefore entitled to accept this evidence as trustworthy unless we have good reason to think otherwise.

Criterion 3: Usefulness in Moral Problem Solving

Good scientific theories increase our understanding of the world, and greater understanding leads to greater usefulness—the capacity to solve problems and answer questions. The more useful a scientific theory is, the more credibility it acquires. A good moral theory is also useful—it helps us solve moral problems in real-life situations. It helps us make reliable judgments about moral principles and actions and resolve conflicts among conflicting judgments and principles and within the theory

itself. A major reason for devising a moral theory is to obtain this kind of practical guidance.

Usefulness is a necessary, though not sufficient, characteristic of a good moral theory. This means that all good theories are useful, but usefulness alone does not make a moral theory good. It is possible for a bad theory to be useful as well (to be useful but fail some other criterion of adequacy). But any moral theory that lacks usefulness is a dubious theory.

Now we can be more specific about the similarities between science and ethics in handling theory and data. In science, the interaction between a theory and the relevant data is dynamic. The theory is designed to explain the data, so the data help shape the theory. But a plausible theory can give scientists good reasons to accept or reject specific data or to reinterpret them. Both the theory and the data contribute to the process of searching for the truth. Scientists work to get the balance between these two just right. They try to ensure a very close fit between them—so close that there is no need for major alterations in either the theory or the data. In ethics, the link between theory and data (considered moral judgments) is similar. Considered moral judgments help shape theory (and its principles or rules), and a good theory sheds light on judgments and helps adjudicate conflicts between judgments and other moral statements. As in science, we should strive for a strong logical harmony between theory, data, and subordinate principles.

Remember, though, that theory evaluation is not a mechanical process, and neither is the application of theories to moral problems. There is no formula or set of instructions for applying our three criteria to a theory. Neither is there a calculating machine for determining how much weight to give each criterion in particular situations. We must make an informed judgment about the importance of particular criteria in each new instance. Nevertheless, applying the criteria is not a subjective, arbitrary affair. It is rational and objective—like, for example, the diagnosis of an illness, which is based on the educated judgment of a physician using appropriate guidelines.

Now suppose you apply the moral criteria of adequacy and reach a verdict on the worth of a theory: you reject it. Should this verdict be the end of your inquiry? In general, no. There is often much to be learned from even seriously defective theories. Many philosophers who reject utilitarianism,

for example, also believe that it makes a valuable point that any theory should take into account: the consequences of actions do matter. Judiciously applying the criteria of adequacy to a theory can help us see a theory's strengths as well as its weaknesses. Such insights can inspire us to improve any moral theory—or perhaps create a new one.

You will get a chance to see firsthand how theory evaluation is done. In Chapters 5 and 6, we will apply the moral criteria of adequacy to several major moral theories.

DEVISING A COHERENT MORAL THEORY

By now you know that we are all chronic moral theorizers. We can't help ourselves. We usually operate on the ground level of ethics, making judgments about the rightness or wrongness of particular actions or the moral worth of particular people or motives, trying to align our lives with moral norms that we think rest on a solid footing. But sometimes we must take a bird's-eye view of morality to see how these particulars are related, whether they reveal a pattern that informs the moral life, and whether the moral principles we embrace are really worth embracing. In other words, we *theorize*.

In the next few pages, I show you how I do some of this big-picture theorizing. I try to work out a plausible moral theory of obligation—an explanation of what makes an action right or wrong. I base this theory on what I consider the best aspects of the moral theories discussed earlier and on the elements of the moral life in which we have the greatest confidence.

Moral Common Sense

As we have seen, some of the more influential theories of the past—utilitarianism, Kant's theory, and natural law theory—offer invaluable moral insights. But each one overlooks at least one feature that seems vital to morality and to any adequate moral theory. Some leave out the consequences of

---

QUICK REVIEW

The Moral Criteria of Adequacy

Criterion 1: Consistency with considered judgments.
Criterion 2: Consistency with our moral experiences.
Criterion 3: Usefulness in moral problem solving.

actions, some the claims of autonomy and rights, and some the demands of justice. I think the absence of these elements constitutes a disabling flaw for these theories. But if this assessment is correct—if our best theories to date are not entirely adequate to the task of providing moral guidance and ethical understanding—how can we expect to devise something better? What are our prospects for improving on what we have?

I think our prospects are good. Recall that we are all capable of forming considered moral judgments, the assessments we make about cases and principles after careful reflection that is as clear and unbiased as possible. These judgments—what some call our moral common sense—are fallible and revisable, but they can constitute credible evidence in favor of particular judgments or principles. They are used regularly by philosophers not only to formulate principles and theories but also to test them for soundness. When a judgment or principle or theory or value seems questionable, we usually fall back on our most trusted data: our considered moral judgments.

Our considered moral judgments tell us that wantonly killing people is wrong, that slavery is a moral abomination, that equals must be treated equally, that respecting the rights of innocent people is morally required, and that inflicting undeserved and unnecessary suffering on others is evil. We are rightly suspicious of any theory that says otherwise. We should have more confidence in our considered moral judgment that abusing babies is wrong than in any theory that condones it. Of course, our moral common sense can be in error; we can be wrong about what at first seems obvious; and a good moral theory can show us that a considered moral judgment should be revised. But we are entitled to trust the urgings of common sense unless we have good reasons to doubt them. Utilitarianism, Kant's theory, and natural law theory have all been found wanting, in large part because they conflict in some way with our considered moral judgments. Our moral common sense, then,

is the starting point of our theorizing as well as the corroboration of what we learn.

Building a Moral Theory

Here is one way a moral theory is built: Suppose we begin with our data—our considered moral judgments rendered about specific cases. We judge that the actions in these cases are morally wrong, and then we look for what these wrong actions have in common. Suppose we notice that all of them share the property of being instances in which people are prevented from exercising their autonomy (their capacity for self-governance). Perhaps a doctor operates on them without their consent, or they are denied their right to live and work where they choose, or they are forced to practice a religion they despise. After much reflection, we think we see a moral principle threading through these cases: people have a right of self-determination. But to avoid jumping to conclusions, we examine many similar cases, and this forces us to modify our principle, perhaps a little bit or perhaps a lot. And our modified principle sheds new light on our cases, perhaps revealing that some of them are not really instances of wrongdoing after all. We gather more considered moral judgments, and we think they suggest other principles. Ultimately we may conclude that all our principles can be summed up in one dominant principle (as is the case with utilitarianism). Or perhaps we are left with an apparently irreducible set of principles that seem to cover all our moral duties (as in natural law theory). In either situation, we continually test the principles to determine if they lead to reasonable judgments, and we check the plausibility of the judgments by comparing them with the principles. The idea is to eliminate conflicts between the two and to achieve the closest possible agreement between them. Thus, common sense shapes theory, and theory informs common sense.

So in developing a moral theory, we begin with what we know or think we know. And through much critical reflection on our data and the generalizations arising from them, we can formulate a theory—a work in progress—and a more or less useful guide to the moral life.

Prima Facie Principles

But what shape would an adequate moral theory take? The overall structure of a moral theory of obligation depends largely on the number of fundamental principles it has and whether those principles are absolute—that is, whether they are rigid rules that allow no exceptions. Utilitarianism has a single ultimate rule (the principle of utility), and so does Kant's theory (the categorical imperative). For these theories, no principles are more basic. Each basic principle is also absolute; the rule must always be followed in every circumstance. There is no clause that says the rule must be strictly adhered to except in circumstance X or Y. Other theories, however, feature not one but several fundamental principles, which may or may not be absolute. Natural law theory, for example, is based on a handful of absolute rules. But some theories that also contain more than one basic rule reject absolutism.

Of these possible theory configurations, I think only the latter type is plausible. Deep down, we may all want moral principles to be reassuringly sturdy and absolute, but I think this is a false hope. It seems that for any absolute moral principle, we can always find counter-examples in which adhering strictly to the rule can lead to immoral actions and unpalatable results. Kant offers the example of the poor unfortunate who runs from an insane murderer and hides in a friend's house. When the friend is asked for the whereabouts of the murderer's prey, he has a choice: he can lie and save his friend's life, or he can tell the truth and doom her. Kant thinks he must tell the truth, even if the result is a tragic loss of life. According to Kant, we must do right though the heavens fall. His absolutism compels him to obey the letter of the law. But our considered moral judgments seem to suggest that in situations like this, saving a life is far more important than telling the truth. If the stakes are high enough—if obeying an absolute rule would cause, say, death and destruction—violating the rule would appear to be the right thing to do.

Our moral common sense also tells us, I think, that there must be more than one basic moral rule that defines our duties. More than one primary rule must be necessary, because we obviously have many basic duties, and we cannot derive them all from one another or from one overarching principle. Our duty to benefit others is distinct from our duty to respect their rights; if anything, these are *competing* duties. Utilitarianism and Kant's theory, which boast just one ultimate rule, have trouble accounting for these disparate obligations.

Any theory that consists of two or more fundamental rules must explain how those rules relate to one another. For the absolutist, multiple rules lead to a serious problem: they will inevitably produce irresolvable contradictions. Honoring one rule may force the violation of another. Suppose an absolutist theory consists of just two rules: "Care for loved ones in dire need" and "Keep your promises." Suppose you promise to take your mother to see a Broadway show, something she has looked forward to for years, but on that same night your son becomes seriously ill and will suffer horribly if you do not tend to him. If you keep your promise and take your mother to the show, your son will suffer; if you take care of your son, you will break your promise to your mother. You cannot obey one rule without violating the other. In absolutist theories consisting of two or more basic rules, such contradictions are common, and they render the theories implausible. Various attempts have been made by absolutists to answer this kind of criticism, but in my opinion none of these efforts has succeeded or ever will succeed.

I think nonabsolutist, multiple-rule theories have a much better way of dealing with conflicting rules. Their approach hinges on the concept of **prima facie principles**—principles that apply in a situation unless exceptions are justified. Exceptions are justified when two rules conflict (when both rules apply, but it is not possible to obey both) and one is considered weightier than the other. Viewing the duties in the mother-son case as prima facie would require us to decide which duty was more important and therefore which should be performed. The two rules represent *apparent* duties, but after weighting the duties appropriately, only one constitutes our *actual* duty. This approach to conflicting rules aligns better with our moral common sense: we know that our duties sometimes collide, that a duty can be overridden by a weightier one, and that occasionally we must break the rules in order to do the right thing. We also seem to have a sense that prima facie duties remain fundamentally important even when they are overridden.

So I think that an adequate moral theory, however it is fleshed out, must be based on more than one principle, and the principles should be prima facie (nonabsolute) and irreducible (they cannot be derived from one another).

Three Rules

The next issue to consider is what these principles are and how they function in the theory. On this point, theories of prima facie principles can differ substantially in both the content of the principles and their number. W.D. Ross (1877–1967), the first philosopher to devise a theory of prima facie duties, thought there were at least seven prima facie duties: duties of *fidelity* (keeping promises, telling the truth); *reparation* (making amends for a wrongful act); *gratitude* (acknowledging services done for us by others); *justice* (distributing benefits and burdens fairly); *beneficence* (benefiting others); *self-improvement* (enhancing our own virtue or intelligence); and *non-maleficence* (not injuring others).[3] More recently, philosophers have tended to argue for a smaller set of prima facie principles—for example, four (autonomy, justice, beneficence, and non-maleficence), or two (justice and beneficence).

These variations may seem to make the task of developing an acceptable theory fairly complex,

but the job is actually simpler than it might initially appear. First, principles that may seem fundamental can often be subsumed under fewer, more basic principles, with the highest-level principles supporting subordinate ones. Second, the flawed theories of the past have helped us see that the moral life is defined by a relatively small number of general norms or core values. We have learned from utilitarianism and other consequentialist theories that any plausible moral theory must take into account the effects of actions and the demands of beneficence and non-maleficence, and we have seen in Kant's theory and other nonconsequentialist views the supreme importance of autonomy, rights, and justice. For most theorists, these concerns define the full spectrum of moral norms that inform the moral life. Although philosophers have parsed these general norms in different ways, there is plenty of agreement about what they are.

If all of these assumptions are correct, then a satisfactory moral theory that reflects the facts of the moral life should comprise a small number of prima facie principles covering all the duties endorsed by our considered moral judgments. Absolute rules and a structure dominated by a single sovereign principle cannot be features of this theory.

With these requirements in mind, I want to argue for a theory that rests on three prima facie principles: respect, justice, and beneficence. These three, I think, can cover all our basic moral duties while simplifying the process of identifying and weighing obligations. For particular cases, we would have to specify how, and to what, the principles should be applied, but this process is a necessity for any theory of general norms. As is the case with all theories consisting of more than one moral norm, the principles will often conflict. As suggested earlier, the tension is resolved by weighing and balancing the prima facie principles to ascertain actual duties—our "all things considered" obligations.

Respect refers to respect for persons, the guiding value of Kant's theory and other nonconsequentialist theories. Respect is owed all persons equally, because they have intrinsic worth and dignity due to their autonomy—that is, to their capacity for rational decisions, autonomous action, and moral choices. Kant made this point by insisting that we must always treat persons as ends in themselves, never merely as a means to an end (a tool to be used for someone else's purposes). Another way to express this is to say that, as persons, we have *rights*—specifically, **negative rights**, which obligate others not to interfere with our obtaining something. (In my theoretical scheme, **positive rights**—the rights that obligate others to help us obtain something—fall under the principle of beneficence.) Persons have the right not to be treated in certain ways: not to be used or regarded as if they were mere instruments, and not to have their autonomous actions and free choices thwarted or constrained. The principle of respect therefore would prohibit, among other things, lying to persons, cheating them, coercing them, falsely imprisoning them, and manipulating them.

This principle of respect can accommodate most of Ross's prima facie duties. It supports what he calls duties of fidelity, reparation, gratitude, and self-improvement. We can view this latter duty as an obligation to respect ourselves, to more fully develop those capacities that make us persons.

Duties of respect can override the moral weight of an action's consequences. In general, we may not violate the rights of persons, even if the violation would benefit them or others. We would probably condemn a policy that mandated discrimination against a minority just so the majority could be happy. We would not countenance medical experiments on people without their knowledge and consent—even if the experiments were needed to search for a cancer cure.

Respect, however, does not always trump utility. It is, after all, a *prima facie* duty. In some cases we might be justified in flouting the principle of respect, but we would need very strong reasons to do so. For example, if by jailing an innocent person we could thwart a terrorist attack that would kill a thousand people, we would most likely favor jailing the person. From a moral standpoint, the loss of so many lives seems far more important than the injustice of false imprisonment.

The principle of *justice* requires that persons be treated fairly and that they get what is due them. **Retributive justice** concerns the fair use of punishment for wrongdoing. **Distributive justice** (what I will focus on here) is about the fair distribution of society's benefits and costs (such as income, privileges, taxes, health care, jobs, and public service). The essence of this principle is that equals must be treated equally. A rule that applies to someone in a particular situation must apply to anyone else in a relevantly similar situation. Justice, then, reflects a central fact about the moral life: morality requires impartiality. Racial discrimination is contrary to justice because it treats one group differently than it does another, even though no morally relevant differences exist between them.

Like the principle of respect, the justice principle generally overrides concerns about consequences. In fact, one of the strongest criticisms of utilitarianism is that its emphasis on maximizing happiness or welfare is often at odds with our considered moral judgments about justice. Justice demands equal treatment of persons, but utilitarianism seeks to produce the best balance of good over evil, which may or may not amount to the equal treatment of equals.

I think the proper way to take consequences into account is through the prima facie principle of *beneficence*. This principle is about the good and bad effects of actions, the nonmoral consequences of what we do or don't do. It says we have a qualified duty to benefit others and to avoid causing them harm. This obligation has three different dimensions: (1) we should not deliberately harm others (should not kill, hurt, disable, rob, or terrorize them, for example); (2) we should act to benefit others (to prevent harm or evil, remove harm or evil, and promote good); and (3) we should strive to produce the most favorable balance of good over evil effects, everyone considered (the utilitarian standard). It is possible to view these three options as separate principles in their own right, but I think that approach would muddle the essential difference between our first two principles (respect and justice) and beneficence, because the former are not primarily concerned with the consequences of actions, but the latter is.

In some cases we may see that only one element of beneficence is relevant—either Option 1 or Option 2. But often *both* of these options apply, and when considering whether to benefit or not to harm persons, we must decide which duty is weightier. Either consideration may override any obligation to maximize utility. Suppose a physician wants to try an experimental treatment that might cure a patient's disease but will also cause permanent damage to her lungs. The overriding principle would be not to cause such harm, even if the benefit to be gained is substantial. A third possibility is that both principles apply and that each duty comes with costs and benefits. We then must make a utilitarian calculation (Option 3) to determine the best solution.

The prohibition against deliberately harming others is a common feature in moral theories: intentionally harming people is always deemed prima facie wrong. Our duty calls not for some action but for *not* performing an action. In most interactions with others, we have an implicit duty not to harm them, but not necessarily a duty to benefit them or to maximize their welfare. If we are driving a heavy truck on a busy highway, for example, our strongest duty is likely to be to refrain from intentionally or carelessly harming other drivers and pedestrains, but we may not have an obligation to benefit them (by, say, continually yielding the right of way to them). And we would not ordinarily have a duty to maximize their good.

It seems that our duty to benefit others (prevent harm, remove harm, and promote good) does not demand that we help *all* persons. Our considered moral judgments tell us that we may have an obligation to promote the welfare of our family, friends, and others we are close to, but we do not have an equally strong duty to help the rest of the world. Treating everyone with such beneficence would not be the fulfillment of a duty but the performance of a supererogatory act (above the call of duty). We might have a duty to help those in the rest of the world, but that duty cannot be as weighty as the one we have to our loved ones.

We are also not obliged to make *extreme* sacrifices to help those with whom we have no relationship. The principle of beneficence, for example, does not insist that we risk our lives and our health to aid a stranger. Nevertheless I think we may have at least a limited obligation to help those with whom we have no connection. We surely must sometimes have a "duty of rescue"—an obligation to try to save a stranger in serious peril when we have the wherewithal to do so without extreme risk or cost to ourselves. If we can easily save a drowning man without too much risk or trouble to ourselves, we may be obligated to do so. And if we have such a duty of rescue, we may have other duties of beneficence in morally equivalent circumstances.

Because my proposed theory consists of principles that are prima facie, conflicts between them are less of a problem than they are in absolutist views. Much of the time, weighing and balancing principles to determine our actual duties is straightforward, though sometimes difficult. In each situation that calls for a moral judgment, the basic pattern of our deliberations is something like this: (1) we discern which principles (respect, justice, and beneficence) apply; (2) we weigh them according to their importance in the case; (3) we determine which principle dominates; and (4) we decide what action best fits with this analysis.

The most challenging part of this process is determining the weight of the basic principles. Even if we know what those principles are, we still have to figure out their relative importance in context. But there is no formula or algorithm to help us with this. Even a rough but firm ranking of principles—in which, say, respect would always outweigh justice, and justice would always outweigh beneficence—would be a tremendous help. But there is no such formula or ranking, and there cannot be one, because the relative importance of the principles fluctuates depending on the details of the case. Sometimes justice may carry the most moral weight, sometimes respect or beneficence.

Our only option is to rely on our reason and experience—that is, our considered moral judgments and the theory that provides the perspective and insight to these judgments. We must work without a net while trying to grasp at answers, and we will occasionally fail. But this difficulty of assigning weight to principles without detailed instructions is also a feature of other moral theories. And as discussed earlier, in their search for the best theory to explain a set of data, scientists must also decide the importance of divergent criteria—and do it without a precise decision-making formula. These judgments are like the ones that a physician makes when diagnosing a disease in a particular patient. There are usually rules of thumb to follow, but in the end, the physician must use her best judgment to arrive at an answer. Such judgments are not formulaic, but they are rational and far from arbitrary.

Self-Evidence

As you can see, my proposed theory appeals at every turn to our moral common sense. But some people might ask, "Who says our considered judgments are reliable guides to moral truth? Why should we trust common sense to identify the true moral principles, especially given that we know it to be fallible and sometimes unreliable?" For example, in response to the claim that utilitarianism conflicts with our moral common sense, some utilitarians have said, in effect, "That's too bad for common sense."

One facile response to this disparagement of common sense is to ask, "Doesn't every theory ultimately rely on common sense? Isn't the utilitarian's

principle of utility itself founded on common sense, because the principle is not supported by a more basic principle?"

But I think a more serious defense of moral common sense and our fundamental moral principles is possible. I want to argue, as several contemporary moral theorists do, that many of our basic moral principles are self-evident.[4] I don't have the space here to fully defend this claim, but I can point out a few considerations that support it.

A **self-evident statement** is one that you are justified in believing merely by understanding it. Here are some self-evident assertions: "Whatever has a shape has a size"; "No bachelors are married"; and "If A is larger than B, and B is larger than C, then A is larger than C." If you understand what these statements mean, then you are justified in believing them, and you need no special faculty to discern their truth. You don't need to gather evidence or conduct experiments to know them; you know them as soon as you grasp their meaning, whether you understand them immediately or after long reflection. If someone insists that the statement "No bachelors are married" is not true, it is up to him to provide a counterexample—to cite a circumstance in which the statement would not be true. If he cannot, then he has no reasons supporting his assertion that the statement is false; his assertion is groundless. This is the only kind of response we can make to those who reject beliefs that we consider to be self-evidently true.

I take it that the following are self-evident moral beliefs (which are also prima facie moral principles):

- Equals should be treated equally.

- It is wrong to punish the innocent.

- It is wrong to inflict unnecessary and undeserved suffering.

- It is wrong to torture people for fun.

I have come to know these statements in the same way that I come to know nonmoral truths—

through reason and reflection, not by any extraordinary faculties or irrational process.

As in the case of nonmoral statements, if someone thinks that "It is wrong to inflict unnecessary and undeserved suffering" is not true, it is up to her to cite circumstances in which the statement would be false. If she cannot, then her rejection of the principle is unwarranted.

If there are self-evident moral truths, it is reasonable to expect that some of our prima facie principles arising from our considered moral judgments are in fact self-evident. Their self-evidence would explain why we have such confidence in some moral principles—so much confidence that we would sooner give up a theory that denied those principles than the principles themselves. If at least some of my proposed theory's prima facie principles are self-evident, then the theory (and theories like it) is on firmer ground than some might think.

The hard truth about moral theorizing is that it never seems to result in a widely accepted, complete, or unblemished theory. My proposal is no exception to the rule. But it does have the advantage of incorporating what I regard as the most manifest and least questionable elements of the moral life.

CHAPTER REVIEW

SUMMARY

A moral theory is an explanation of what makes an action right or what makes a person or thing good. Theories concerned with the rightness or wrongness of actions are known as *theories of obligation* (or, in this text, simply *moral theories*). A moral theory is interconnected with considered moral judgments and principles. Considered moral judgments can shape a theory, and a theory can shed light on judgments and principles.

The two major types of moral theories are consequentialist and nonconsequentialist. Consequentialist

theories say that what makes an action right is its consequences. Nonconsequentialist theories say that the rightness of an action does not depend entirely on its consequences. Consequentialist theories include utilitarianism (both act- and rule-utilitarianism) and ethical egoism; nonconsequentialist theories include Kant's theory, natural law theory, and divine command theory.

Because not all theories are of equal worth, we must try to discover which one is best—a task that we can perform by applying the moral criteria of adequacy to theories. The three criteria are (1) consistency with considered moral judgments, (2) consistency with our moral experiences, and (3) usefulness in moral problem solving.

KEY TERMS
moral theory (p. 65)
considered moral judgment (p. 66)
consequentialist theory (p. 67)
nonconsequentialist theory (p. 67)
utilitarianism (p. 67)
act-utilitarianism (p. 68)
rule-utilitarianism (p. 68)
ethical egoism (p. 68)
categorical imperative (p. 68)
Kant's theory (p. 68)
natural law theory (p. 69)
divine command theory (p. 70)
prima facie principle (p. 76)
negative right (p. 78)
positive right (p. 78)
retributive justice (p. 78)
distributive justice (p. 78)
self-evident statement (p. 80)

EXERCISES

Review Questions

1. Is a moral theory the final authority in moral reasoning? Why or why not? (p. 66)
2. What is the difference between a moral theory and a moral code? (p. 66)
3. How can a moral theory be used in a moral argument? (p. 66)

4. What is a considered moral judgment? (p. 66)
5. What are the two main categories of moral theories? (p. 67)
6. What is utilitarianism? ethical egoism? (pp. 67–68)
7. According to Kant's moral theory, what makes an action right? (pp. 68–69)
8. What are the three moral criteria of adequacy? (pp. 71–74)

Discussion Questions

1. Do you try to guide your moral choices with a moral code or a moral theory, or both? If so, how?
2. Suppose you try to use the Ten Commandments as a moral code to help you make moral decisions. How would you resolve conflicts between commandments? Does your approach to resolving the conflicts imply a moral theory? If so, can you explain the main idea behind the theory?
3. What considered moral judgments have you made or appealed to in the past month? Do you think that these judgments reflect a moral principle or moral theory you implicitly appeal to? If so, what is it?
4. Would you describe your approach to morality as consequentialist, nonconsequentialist, or some combination of both? What reasons do you have for adopting this particular approach?
5. Give an example of a possible conflict between a consequentialist theory and a considered moral judgment. (Show how these two may be inconsistent.)
6. Provide an example of a conflict between a nonconsequentialist theory and a moral judgment based on the consequences of an action.
7. Using the moral criteria of adequacy, evaluate act-utilitarianism.
8. Using the moral criteria of adequacy, evaluate natural law theory.

ETHICAL DILEMMAS

1. Suppose your friend puts forth several arguments in an effort to convince you that all abortions are morally wrong. You already have strong views to the contrary, and you know she is a member of an anti-abortion group that advocates violence. In light of these facts, should you dismiss her arguments out of hand? Why or why not? What would constitute a good reason for rejecting her arguments?
2. You believe that all illegal immigrants should be deported. You have no reasons for believing this; you were simply taught to believe it by your parents. Is it morally right for you to adhere to such a view without good reasons? Do you have a moral duty to apply critical reasoning to your belief? Why or why not?
3. Your grandmother is near death in the hospital, barely conscious but in great pain. She has terminal cancer, and her medical team assures you that she may linger in this state for a week at most but will never recover. A year ago she made you promise that no matter how much she suffers, you are not to allow anyone to shorten her life by removing her ventilator or by letting her doctors administer "terminal sedation"—medication that relieves pain while slowly ending life (a legal form of euthanasia). You can hardly bear to see her in such agony. Should you keep your promise to her and ensure that she lingers in horrible suffering, or should you break your promise and request terminal sedation or removal of all life support?

FURTHER READING

John D. Arras and Nancy K. Rhoden, "The Need for Ethical Theory," in *Ethical Issues in Modern Medicine*, 3rd ed. (Mountain View, CA: Mayfield, 1989).

Richard B. Brandt, *Ethical Theory: The Problems of Normative and Critical Ethics* (Englewood Cliffs, NJ: Prentice Hall, 1959).

C. D. Broad, *Five Types of Ethical Theory* (1930; reprint, London: Routledge & Kegan Paul, 1956).

John Hospers, *Human Conduct: Problems of Ethics,* shorter ed. (New York: Harcourt Brace Jovanovich, 1972).

John Rawls, "Some Remarks about Moral Theory," in *A Theory of Justice,* rev. ed. (Cambridge, MA: Harvard University Press, Belknap Press, 1999).

PART
3

Theories of Morality

CHAPTER 5

Consequentialist Theories: Maximize the Good

There is something in consequentialist moral theories that we find appealing, something simple and commonsensical that jibes with everyday moral experience. This attractive core is the notion that right actions must produce the best balance of good over evil. Never mind (for now) how *good* and *evil* are defined. The essential concern is how much good can result from actions performed. In this chapter, we examine the plausibility of this consequentialist maxim and explore how it is worked out in its two most influential theories: ethical egoism and utilitarianism.

ETHICAL EGOISM

Ethical egoism is the theory that the right action is the one that advances one's own best interests. It is a provocative doctrine, in part because it forces us to consider two opposing attitudes in ourselves. On the one hand, we tend to view selfish or flagrantly self-interested behavior as wicked, or at least troubling. Self-love is bad love. We frown on people who trample others in life to get to the head of the line. On the other hand, sometimes we want to look out for number one, to give priority to our own needs and desires. We think, If we do not help ourselves, who will? Self-love is good love.

Ethical egoism says that one's only moral duty is to promote the most favorable balance of good over evil for oneself. Each person must put his or her own welfare first. Advancing the interests of others is part of this moral equation only if it helps promote one's own good. Yet this extreme self-interest is not necessarily selfishness. Selfish acts

advance one's own interests regardless of how others are affected. Self-interested acts promote one's own interests but not necessarily to the detriment of others. To further your own interests you may actually find yourself helping others. To gain some advantage, you may perform actions that are decidedly unselfish.

Just as we cannot equate ethical egoism with selfishness, neither can we assume it is synonymous with self-indulgence or recklessness. An ethical egoist does not necessarily do whatever she desires to do or whatever gives her the most immediate pleasure. She does what is in her best interests, and instant gratification may not be in her best interests. She may want to spend all her money at the casino or work eighteen hours a day, but over the long haul doing so may be disastrous for her. Even ethical egoists have to consider the long-term effects of their actions. They also have to take into account their interactions with others. At least most of the time, egoists are probably better off if they cooperate with others, develop reciprocal relationships, and avoid actions that antagonize people in their community or society.

Ethical egoism comes in two forms—one applying the doctrine to individual *acts* and one to relevant *rules*. **Act-egoism** says that to determine right action, you must apply the egoistic principle to individual acts. Act A is preferable to act B because it promotes your self-interest better. **Rule-egoism** says that to determine right action, you must see if an act falls under a rule that if consistently followed would maximize your self-interest. Act A is preferable to act B because it falls under a rule that maximizes your self-interest better than any other relevant rule applying to act B. An ethical egoist can define self-interest in various ways. The Greek philosopher Epicurus (341–270 B.C.E.), a famous ethical egoist from whose name we derive the words *epicure* and *epicurean,* gave a hedonist answer: The greatest good is pleasure, and the greatest evil, pain. The duty of a good ethical egoist is to maximize pleasure for oneself. (Contrary to legend, Epicurus thought that wanton overindulgence in the delights of the senses was not in one's best interests. He insisted that the best pleasures were those of the contemplative life and that extravagant pleasures such as drunkenness and gluttony eventually lead to misery.) Other egoistic notions of the greatest good include self-actualization (fulfilling one's potential), security and material success, satisfaction of desires, acquisition of power, and the experience of happiness.

To many people, ethical egoism may sound alien, especially if they have heard all their lives about the noble virtue of altruism and the evils of self-centeredness. But consider that self-interest is a pillar on which the economic system of capitalism is built. In a capitalist system, self-interest is supposed to drive people to seek advantages for themselves in the marketplace, compelling them to compete against one another to build a better mousetrap at a lower price. Economists argue that the result of this clash of self-interests is a better, more prosperous society.

Applying the Theory

Suppose Rosa is a successful executive at a large media corporation, and she has her eye on a vice president's position, which has just become vacant. Vincent, another successful executive in the company, also wants the VP job. Management wants to fill the vacancy as soon as possible, and they are trying to decide between the two most qualified candidates—Rosa and Vincent. One day Rosa discovers some documents left near a photocopier and quickly realizes that they belong to Vincent. One of

them is an old memo from the president of a company where Vincent used to work. In it, the president lambastes Vincent for botching an important company project. Rosa knows that despite what she reads in the memo, Vincent has had an exemplary professional career in which he has managed most of his projects extremely well. In fact, she believes that the two of them are about equal in professional skills and accomplishments. She also knows that if management sees the memo, they will almost certainly choose her over Vincent for the VP position. She figures that Vincent has probably left the documents there by mistake and will soon return to retrieve them. Impulsively, she makes a copy of the memo for herself.

Now she is confronted with a moral choice. Let us suppose that she has only three options. First, she can destroy her copy of the memo and forget about the whole incident. Second, she can discredit Vincent by showing it to management, thereby securing the VP slot for herself. Third, she can achieve the same result by discrediting Vincent surreptitiously: she can simply leave a copy where management is sure to discover it. Let us also assume that she is an act-egoist who defines her self-interest as self-actualization. Self-actualization for her means developing into the most powerful, most highly respected executive in her profession while maximizing the virtues of loyalty and honesty.

So, by the lights of her act-egoism, what should Rosa do? Which choice is in her best interests? Option 1 is neutral regarding her self-interest. If she destroys her copy of the memo, she will neither gain nor lose an advantage for herself. Option 2 is more complicated. If she overtly discredits Vincent, she will probably land the VP spot—a feat that fits nicely with her desire to become a powerful executive. But such a barefaced sabotaging of someone else's career will probably trouble management, and their loss of some respect for Rosa will impede future advancement in her career. They may also come to distrust her. Rosa's backstabbing will also probably erode the trust and respect of her subordinates (those who report to her). If so, their performance may suffer, and any deficiencies in Rosa's subordinates will reflect on her leadership skills. Over time, she may be able to regain the respect of management through dazzling successes in her field, but the respect and trust of others may be much harder to regain. Option 2 involves the unauthorized, deceitful use of personal information against another person—not an action that encourages the virtue of honesty in Rosa. In fact, her dishonesty may weaken her moral resolve and make similar acts of deceit more probable. Like Option 2, Option 3 will probably secure the VP job for Rosa. But because the deed is surreptitious, it will probably not diminish the respect and trust of others. There is a low probability, however, that Rosa's secret will eventually be uncovered—especially if Vincent suspects Rosa, which is likely. If she is found out, the damage done to her reputation (and possibly her career) may be greater than that caused by the more up-front tactic of Option 2. Also like Option 2, Option 3 may weaken the virtue of honesty in Rosa's character.

Given this situation and Rosa's brand of act-egoism, she should probably go with Option 3—but only if the risk of being found out is extremely low. Option 3 promotes her self-interest dramatically by securing the coveted job at a relatively low cost (a possible erosion of virtue). Option 2 also lands the job but at a very high cost—a loss of other people's trust and respect, a possible decrease in her chances for career advancement, damage to her professional reputation, and a likely lessening of a virtue critical to Rosa's self-actualization (honesty).

If Rosa believes that the risks to her career and character involved in Options 2 and 3 are too high, she should probably choose Option 1. This choice will not promote her best interests, but it will not diminish them either.

Would Rosa's action be any different if judged from the perspective of rule-egoism? Suppose Rosa, like many other ethical egoists, thinks that her actions should be guided by this rule (or something like it): People should be honest in their dealings with others—that is, except in insignificant matters (white lies), they should not lie to others or mislead them. She believes that adhering to this prohibition against dishonesty is in her best interests. The rule, however, disallows Options 2 and 3, for they involve significant deception. Only Option 1 is left. But if obeying the rule will lead to a major setback for her interests, Rosa may decide to ignore it in this case (or reject it altogether as contrary to the spirit of ethical egoism). If so, she may have to fall back to act-egoism and decide in favor of Option 3.

Evaluating the Theory

Is ethical egoism a plausible moral theory? Let us find out by examining arguments in its favor and applying the moral criteria of adequacy.

The primary argument for ethical egoism depends heavily on a scientific theory known as **psychological egoism**, the view that the motive for all our actions is self-interest. Whatever we do, we do because we want to promote our own welfare. Psychological egoism, we are told, is simply a description of the true nature of our motivations. We are, in short, born to look out for number one.

Putting psychological egoism to good use, the ethical egoist reasons as follows: We can never be morally obligated to perform an action that we cannot possibly do. This is just an obvious fact about morality. Because we are *not able* to prevent a hurricane from blasting across a coastal city, we are *not morally obligated* to prevent it. Likewise, because we are not able to perform an action except out of self-interest (the claim of psychological egoism), we are not morally obligated to perform an action unless motivated by self-interest. That is, we are morally obligated to do only what our self-interest motivates us to do. Here is the argument stated more formally:

1. We are not able to perform an action except out of self-interest (psychological egoism).

2. We are not morally obligated to perform an action unless motivated by self-interest.

3. Therefore, we are morally obligated to do only what our self-interest motivates us to do.

Notice that even if psychological egoism is true, this argument does not establish that an action is right if and only if it promotes one's self-interest (the claim of ethical egoism). But it does demonstrate that an action cannot be right unless it at least promotes one's self-interest. To put it another way, an action that does not advance one's own welfare cannot be right.

Is psychological egoism true? Many people think it is, and they offer several arguments in its favor. One line of reasoning is that psychological egoism is true because experience shows that all our actions are in fact motivated by self-interest. In other words, all our actions—including seemingly altruistic ones—are performed to gain some benefit for ourselves. This argument, however, is far from conclusive. Sometimes people do perform altruistic acts because doing so is in their best interests. Smith may contribute to charity because such generosity furthers his political ambitions. Jones may do volunteer work for the Red Cross because it looks good on her résumé. But people also seem to do things that are *not* motivated by self-interest. They sometimes risk their lives by rushing into a burning building to rescue a complete stranger. They may impair their health by donating a kidney to prevent one of their children from dying. Explanations that appeal to self-interest in such cases seem implausible. Moreover, people often have self-destructive habits (for example, drinking excessively and driving recklessly)—habits that are unlikely to be in anyone's best interests.

Some ethical egoists may argue in a slightly different vein: People get satisfaction (or happiness or pleasure) from what they do, including their so-called unselfish or altruistic acts. Therefore, they perform unselfish or altruistic actions because doing so gives them satisfaction. A man saves a child from a burning building because he wants the emotional satisfaction that comes from saving a life. Our actions, no matter how we characterize them, are all about self-interest.

This argument is based on a conceptual confusion. It says that we perform selfless acts to achieve satisfaction. Satisfaction is the object of the whole exercise. But if we experience satisfaction in performing an action, that does not show that our goal in performing the action is satisfaction. A much more plausible account is that we desire something other than satisfaction and then experience satisfaction as a result of getting what we desired. Consider, for example, our man who saves the child from a fire. He rescues the child and feels satisfaction—but he could not have experienced that satisfaction unless he already had a desire to save the child or cared what happened to her. If he did not have such a desire or care about her, how could he have derived any satisfaction from his actions? To experience satisfaction he had to have a desire for something other than his own satisfaction. The moral of the story is that satisfaction is the result of getting what we want—not the object of our desires.

This view fits well with our own experience. Most often when we act according to some purpose, we are not focused on, or aware of, our satisfaction. We concentrate on obtaining the real object of our efforts, and when we succeed, we then feel satisfaction.

The philosopher Joel Feinberg makes a similar point about the pursuit of happiness. He asks us to imagine a person, Jones, who has no desire for much of anything—except happiness. Jones has no interest in knowledge for its own sake, the beauty of nature, art and literature, sports, crafts, or business. But Jones does have "an overwhelming passion for, a complete preoccupation with, his own happiness. The one desire of his life is to be happy."[1] The irony is that using this approach, Jones will *not* find happiness. He cannot pursue happiness directly and expect to find it. To achieve happiness, he must pursue other aims whose pursuit yields happiness as a by-product. We must conclude that it is not the

---

Can Ethical Egoism Be Advocated?

Some critics of ethical egoism say that it is a very strange theory because its adherents cannot urge others to become ethical egoists! The philosopher Theodore Schick Jr. makes the point:

> Even if ethical egoism did provide necessary and sufficient conditions for an action's being right, it would be a peculiar sort of ethical theory, for its adherents couldn't consistently advocate it. Suppose that someone came to an ethical egoist for moral advice. If the ethical egoist wanted to do what is in his best interest, he would not tell his client to do what is in her best interest because her interests might conflict with his. Rather, he would tell her to do what is in his best interest.

Such advice has been satirized on national TV. Al Franken, a former writer for *Saturday Night Live* and author of *Rush Limbaugh Is a Big Fat Idiot and Other Observations,* proclaimed on a number of *Saturday Night Live* shows in the early 1980s that whereas the 1970s were known as the "me" decade, the 1980s were going to be known as the "Al Franken" decade. So whenever anyone was faced with a difficult decision, the individual should ask herself, "How can I most benefit Al Franken?"*

*Theodore Schick Jr., in *Doing Philosophy: An Introduction through Thought Experiments*, by Theodore Schick Jr. and Lewis Vaughn, 2nd ed. (Boston: McGraw-Hill, 2003), 327.

---

case that our only motivation for our actions is the desire for happiness (or satisfaction or pleasure).

These reflections show that psychological egoism is a dubious theory, and if we construe self-interest as satisfaction, pleasure, or happiness, the theory seems false. Still, some may not give up the argument from experience (mentioned earlier), insisting that when properly interpreted, all our actions (including those that seem purely altruistic or unselfish) can be shown to be motivated by self-interest. All the counterexamples that seem to suggest that psychological egoism is false actually are evidence that it is true. Smith's contributing to charity may look altruistic, but he is really trying to impress a woman he would like to date. Jones's volunteer work at the Red Cross may seem unselfish, but she is just trying to cultivate some business contacts. Every counterexample can be reinterpreted to support the theory.

Critics have been quick to charge that this way of defending psychological egoism is a mistake. It renders the theory untestable and useless. It ensures that no evidence could possibly count against it, and therefore it does not tell us anything about self-interested actions. Anything we say about such actions would be consistent with the theory. Any theory that is so uninformative could not be used to support another theory—including ethical egoism.

So far we have found the arguments for ethical egoism ineffective. Now we can ask another question: Are there any good arguments *against* ethical egoism? This is where the moral criteria of adequacy come in.

Recall that an important first step in evaluating a moral theory (or any other kind of theory) is to determine if it meets the minimum requirement of coherence, or internal consistency. As it turns out, some critics of ethical egoism have brought the charge of logical or practical inconsistency against the theory. But in general these criticisms seem to fall short of a knockout blow to ethical egoism. Devising counterarguments that can undercut the criticisms seems to be a straightforward business. Let us assume, then, that ethical egoism is in fact eligible for evaluation using the moral criteria of adequacy.

We begin with Criterion 1, consistency with considered moral judgments. A major criticism of ethical egoism is that it is *not* consistent with many of our considered moral judgments—judgments that seem highly plausible and commonsensical. Specifically, ethical egoism seems to sanction actions that we would surely regard as abominable. Suppose a young man visits his elderly, bedridden father. When he sees that no one else is around, he uses a pillow to smother the old man in order to collect on his life insurance. Suppose, too, that the action is in the son's best interests; it will not cause the least bit of unpleasant feeling in him, and the crime will remain his own terrible secret. According to ethical egoism, this heinous act is morally right. The son has done his duty.

An ethical egoist might object to this line by saying that *refraining* from committing evil acts is actually endorsed by ethical egoism—one's best interests are served by refraining. You should not murder or steal, for example, because it might encourage others to do the same to you, or it might undermine trust, security, or cooperation in society, which would not be in your best interests. For these reasons, you should obey the law or the rules of conventional morality (as the rule-egoist might do).

But following the rules is clearly not always in one's best interests. Sometimes committing a wicked act really does promote one's own welfare. In the case of the murdering son, no one will seek revenge for the secret murder, cooperation and trust in society will not be affected, and the murderer will suffer no psychological torments. There seems to be no downside here—but the son's rewards for committing the deed will be great. Consistently looking out for one's own welfare sometimes requires rule violations and exceptions. In fact, some argue that the interests of ethical egoists may be best served when they urge everyone else to obey the rules while they themselves secretly break them.

If ethical egoism does conflict with our considered moral judgments, it is questionable at best.

But it has been accused of another defect as well: it fails Criterion 2, consistency with our moral experiences.

One aspect of morality is so fundamental that we may plausibly view it as a basic fact of the moral life: moral impartiality, or treating equals equally. We know that in our dealings with the world, we are supposed to take into account the treatment of others as well as that of ourselves. The moral life is lived with the wider world in mind. We must give all persons their due and treat all equals equally, for in the moral sense we are all equals. Each person is presumed to have the same rights as—and to have interests that are just as important as those of—everyone else, unless we have good reason for thinking otherwise. If one person is qualified for a job, and another person is equally qualified, we would be guilty of discrimination if we hired one and not the other based solely on race, sex, skin color, or ancestry. These factors are not morally relevant. People who do treat equals unequally in such ways are known as racists, sexists, bigots, and the like. Probably the most serious charge against ethical egoism is that it discriminates against people in the same fashion. It arbitrarily treats the interests of some people (oneself) as more important than the interests of all others (the rest of the world)—even though there is no morally relevant difference between the two.

The failure of ethical egoism to treat equals equally seems a serious defect in the theory. It conflicts with a major component of our moral existence. For many critics, this single defect is enough reason to reject the theory.

Recall that Criterion 3 is usefulness in moral problem solving. Some philosophers argue that ethical egoism fails this standard because the theory seems to lead to contradictory advice or conflicting actions. If real, this problem constitutes a significant failing of the theory. But this criticism depends on controversial assumptions about ethical egoism or morality in general, so we will not dwell on it here. Our analysis of ethical egoism's

---

QUICK REVIEW

act-egoism—The theory that to determine right action, you must apply the egoistic principle to individual acts.

rule-egoism—The theory that to determine right action, you must see if an act falls under a rule that, if consistently followed, would maximize your self-interest.

psychological egoism—The view that the motive for all our actions is self-interest.

---

problems using the first two criteria should be sufficient to raise serious doubts about the theory.

UTILITARIANISM

Are you a utilitarian? To find out, consider the following scenario: After years of research, a medical scientist—Dr. X—realizes that she is just one step away from developing a cure for all known forms of heart disease. Such a breakthrough would save hundreds of thousands of lives—perhaps millions. The world could finally be rid of heart attacks, strokes, heart failure, and the like, a feat as monumental as the eradication of deadly smallpox. That one last step in her research, however, is technologically feasible but morally problematic. It involves the killing of a single healthy human being to examine the person's heart tissue under a microscope just seconds after the heart stops beating. The crucial piece of information needed to perfect the cure can be acquired only as just described; it cannot be extracted from the heart of a cadaver, an accident victim, someone suffering from a disease, or a person who has been dead for more than sixty seconds. Dr. X decides that the benefits to humanity from the cure are just too great to ignore. She locates a suitable candidate for the operation: a homeless man with no living relatives and no friends—someone who would not be missed. Through some elaborate subterfuge she manages to secretly do what needs to be done, killing the man and successfully performing the operation. She formulates the cure and saves countless lives. No one ever discovers how she obtained the last bit of information she needed to devise the cure, and she feels not the slightest guilt for her actions.

Did Dr. X do right? If you think so, then you may be a utilitarian. A utilitarian is more likely to believe that Dr. X's action was right because of its consequences: it brought about consequences that were more good than bad. One man died, but countless others were saved. If you think that Dr. X did wrong, you may be a nonconsequentialist. A nonconsequentialist is likely to believe that Dr. X did wrong because of the nature of her action: it was murder. The consequences are beside the point.

In this example, we get a hint of some of the elements that have made utilitarianism so attractive (and often controversial) to so many. First, whether or not we agree with the utilitarian view in this case, we can see that it has some plausibility. We tend to think it entirely natural to judge the morality of an action by the effects that it has on the people involved. To decide if we do right or wrong, we want to know whether the consequences of our actions are good or bad, whether they bring pleasure or pain, whether they enhance or diminish the welfare of ourselves and others. Second, the utilitarian formula for distinguishing right and wrong actions seems exceptionally straightforward. We simply calculate which action among several possible actions has the best balance of good over evil, everyone considered—and act accordingly. Moral choice is apparently reduced to a single moral principle and simple math. Third, at least sometimes, we all seem to be utilitarians. We may tell a white lie because the truth would hurt someone's feelings. We may break a promise because keeping it causes more harm than good. We may want a criminal punished not because he broke the law but because the punishment may deter him from future crimes. We justify such departures from conventional morality on the grounds that they produce better consequences.

Utilitarianism is one of the most influential moral theories in history. The English philosopher Jeremy Bentham (1748–1832) was the first to fill out the theory in detail, and the English philosopher and economist John Stuart Mill (1806–1873) developed it further. In their hands utilitarianism became a powerful instrument of social reform. It provided a rationale for promoting women's rights, improving the treatment of prisoners, advocating animal rights, and aiding the poor—all radical ideas in Bentham's and Mill's day. In the twenty-first century, the theory still has a strong effect on moral and policy decision making in many areas, including health care, criminal justice, and government.

Classic utilitarianism—the kind of act-utilitarianism formulated by Bentham—is the simplest form of the theory. It affirms the principle that the right action is the one that directly produces the best balance of happiness over unhappiness for all concerned. Happiness is an intrinsic good—the *only* intrinsic good. What matters most is how much net happiness comes directly from performing an action (as opposed to following a rule that applies to such actions). To determine the right action, we need only compute the amount of happiness that each possible action generates and choose the one that generates the most. There are no rules to take into account—just the single, simple utilitarian principle. Each set of circumstances calling for a moral choice is unique, requiring a new calculation of the varying consequences of possible actions.

Bentham called the utilitarian principle the **principle of utility** and asserted that all our actions can be judged by it. (Mill called it the **greatest happiness principle**.) As Bentham says,

> By the principle of utility is meant that principle which approves or disapproves of every action whatsoever, according to the tendency which it appears to have to augment or diminish the happiness of the party whose interest is in question: or, what is the same thing in other words, to promote or to oppose that happiness. . . .
>
> By utility is meant that property in any object, whereby it tends to produce benefit, advantage, pleasure, good, or happiness, (all this in the present case comes to the same thing) or (what comes again to the same thing) to prevent the happening of mischief, pain, evil, or unhappiness to the party whose interest is considered[.][2]

The principle of utility, of course, makes the theory consequentialist. The emphasis on happiness or pleasure makes it hedonistic, for happiness is the only intrinsic good.

As you can see, there is a world of difference between the moral focus of utilitarianism (in all its forms) and that of ethical egoism. The point of ethical egoism is to promote one's own good. An underlying tenet of utilitarianism is that you should promote the good of *everyone concerned* and that everyone *counts equally*. When deliberating about which action to perform, you must take into account the happiness of everyone who will be affected by your decision as well as your own—and no one is to be given privileged status. Such evenhandedness requires a large measure of impartiality, a quality that plays a role in every plausible moral theory. Mill says it best:

> [T]he happiness which forms the utilitarian standard of what is right in conduct, is not the agent's own happiness, but that of all concerned. As between his own happiness and that of others, utilitarianism requires him to be as strictly impartial as a disinterested and benevolent spectator.[3]

In classic act-utilitarianism, knowing how to total the amount of utility, or happiness, generated by various actions is essential. Bentham's answer to this requirement is the *hedonic calculus,* which quantifies happiness and handles the necessary calculations. His approach is straightforward in conception but complicated in the details: For each possible action in a particular situation, determine the total amount of happiness or unhappiness produced by it for one individual (that is, the *net* happiness—happiness minus unhappiness). Gauge the level of happiness with seven basic characteristics such as intensity, duration, and fecundity (how likely the pleasure or pain is to be followed by more pleasure or pain). Repeat this process for all individuals involved and sum their happiness or unhappiness to arrive at an overall net happiness for that particular action. Repeat for each possible action. The action with the best score (the most happiness or least unhappiness) is the morally right one.

Notice that in this arrangement, only the *total amount* of net happiness for each action matters. How the happiness is distributed among the persons involved does not figure into the calculations. This means that an action that affects ten people and produces 100 units of happiness is to be preferred over an action that affects those same ten people but generates only 50 units of happiness—even if most of the 100 units go to just one individual, and the 50 units divide equally among the ten. The aggregate of happiness is decisive; its distribution is not. Classic utilitarianism, though, does ask that any given amount of happiness be spread among as many people as possible—thus the utilitarian slogan "The greatest happiness for the greatest number."

Both Bentham and Mill define happiness as pleasure. In Mill's words,

> The creed which accepts as the foundation of morals *utility,* or the *greatest happiness principle,* holds that actions are right in proportion as they tend to promote happiness, wrong as they tend to produce the reverse of happiness. By "happiness" is intended pleasure, and the absence of pain; by "unhappiness," pain, and the privation of pleasure.[4]

They differ, though, on the nature of happiness and on how it should be measured. Bentham thinks that happiness varies only in quantity—different actions produce different amounts of happiness. To judge the intensity, duration, or fecundity of happiness is to calculate its quantity. Mill contends

that happiness can vary in quantity *and* quality. There are lower pleasures, such as eating, drinking, and having sex, and there are higher pleasures, such as pursuing knowledge, appreciating beauty, and creating art. The higher pleasures are superior to the lower ones. The lower ones can be intense and enjoyable, but the higher ones are qualitatively better and more fulfilling. In this scheme, a person enjoying a mere taste of a higher pleasure may be closer to the moral ideal than a hedonistic glutton who gorges on lower pleasures. Thus Mill declared, "It is better to be a human being dissatisfied than a pig satisfied; better to be Socrates dissatisfied than a fool satisfied."[5] In Bentham's view, the glutton—who acquires a larger quantity of pleasure—would be closer to the ideal.

The problem for Mill is to justify his hierarchical ranking of the various pleasures. He tries to do so by appealing to what the majority prefers—that is, the majority of people who have experienced both the lower and higher pleasures. But this approach probably will not help, because people can differ drastically in how they rank pleasures. It is possible, for example, that a majority of people who have experienced a range of pleasures would actually disagree with Mill's rankings. In fact, any effort to devise such rankings using the principle of utility seems unlikely to succeed.

Many critics have argued that the idea of defining right action in terms of some intrinsic nonmoral good (whether pleasure, happiness, or anything else) is seriously problematic. Attempts to devise such a definition have been fraught with complications—a major one being that people have different ideas about what things are intrinsically valuable. Some utilitarians have tried to sidestep these difficulties by insisting that maximizing utility means maximizing people's *preferences,* whatever they are. This formulation seems to avoid some of the difficulties just mentioned but falls prey to another: some people's preferences may be clearly objectionable when judged by almost any moral standard, whether utilitarian or nonconsequentialist. Some people, after all, have ghastly preferences—preferences, say, for torturing children or killing innocent people for fun. Some critics say that repairing this preference utilitarianism to avoid sanctioning objectionable actions seems unlikely without introducing some nonutilitarian moral principles such as justice, rights, and obligations.

Like act-utilitarianism, rule-utilitarianism aims at the greatest good for all affected individuals, but it maintains that we travel an indirect route to that goal. In rule-utilitarianism, the morally right action is not the one that directly brings about the greatest good, but the one covered by a rule that, if followed consistently, produces the greatest good for all. In act-utilitarianism, we must examine each action to see how much good (or evil) it generates. Rule-utilitarianism would have us first determine what rule an action falls under, then see if that rule would be likely to maximize utility if everyone followed it. In effect, the rule-utilitarian asks, "What if everyone followed this rule?"

An act-utilitarian tries to judge the rightness of actions by the consequences they produce, occasionally relying on "rules of thumb" (such as "Usually we should not harm innocents") merely to save time. A rule-utilitarian, however, tries to follow every valid rule—even if doing so may not maximize utility in a specific situation.

In our example featuring Dr. X and the cure for heart disease, an act-utilitarian might compare the net happiness produced by performing the lethal operation and by not performing it, opting finally for the former because it maximizes happiness. A rule-utilitarian, on the other hand, would consider what moral rules seem to apply to the situation. One rule might be "It is permissible to conduct medical procedures or experiments on people without their full knowledge and consent in order to substantially advance medical science." Another one might say "Do not conduct medical procedures or experiments on people without their full knowledge and consent." If the first rule is generally followed, happiness is not likely to be maximized in the long run. Widespread adherence to this rule would encourage medical scientists and physicians to murder patients for the good of science. Such practices would outrage people and cause them to fear and distrust science and the medical profession, leading to the breakdown of the entire health care system and most medical research. But if the second rule is consistently adhered to, happiness is likely to be maximized over the long haul. Trust in physicians and medical scientists would be maintained, and promising research could continue as long as it was conducted with the patient's consent. The right action, then, is for Dr. X *not* to perform the gruesome operation.

Applying the Theory

Let us apply utilitarianism to another type of case. Imagine that for more than a year a terrorist has been carrying out devastating attacks in a developing country, killing hundreds of innocent men, women, and children. He seems unstoppable. He always manages to elude capture. In fact, because of his stealth, the expert assistance of a few accomplices, and his support among the general population, he will most likely never be captured or killed. The authorities have no idea where he hides or where he will strike next. But they are sure that he will go on killing indefinitely. They have tried every tactic they know to put an end to the slaughter, but it goes on and on. Finally, as a last resort, the chief of the nation's antiterrorist police orders the arrest of the terrorist's family—a wife and seven children. The chief intends to kill the wife and three of the children right away (to show that he is serious), then threaten to kill the remaining four unless the terrorist turns himself in. There is no doubt that the chief will make good on his intentions, and there is excellent reason to believe that the terrorist will indeed turn himself in rather than allow his remaining children to be executed.

Suppose that the chief has only two options: (1) refrain from murdering the terrorist's family

Peter Singer, Utilitarian

The distinguished philosopher Peter Singer is arguably the most famous (and controversial) utilitarian of recent years. Many newspaper and magazine articles have been written about him, and many people have declared their agreement with, or vociferous opposition to, his views. This is how one magazine characterizes Singer and his ideas:

> *The New Yorker* calls him "the most influential living philosopher." His critics call him "the most dangerous man in the world." Peter Singer, the De Camp Professor of Bioethics at Princeton University's Center for Human Values, is most widely and controversially known for his view that animals have the same moral status as humans. . . .
>
> Singer is perhaps the most thoroughgoing philosophical utilitarian since Jeremy Bentham. As such, he believes animals have rights because the relevant moral consideration is not whether a being can reason or talk but whether it can suffer. Jettisoning the traditional distinction between humans and nonhumans, Singer distinguishes instead between persons and non-persons. Persons are beings that feel, reason, have self-awareness, and look forward to a future. Thus, fetuses and some very impaired human beings are not persons in his view and have a lesser moral status than, say, adult gorillas and chimpanzees.
>
> Given such views, it was no surprise that anti-abortion activists and disability rights advocates loudly decried the Australian-born Singer's appointment at Princeton last year. Indeed, his language regarding the treatment of disabled human beings is at times appallingly similar to the eugenic arguments used by Nazi theorists concerning "life unworthy of life." Singer, however, believes that only parents, not the state, should have the power to make decisions about the fates of disabled infants.*

*Peter Singer, "The Pursuit of Happiness: Peter Singer Interviewed by Ronald Bailey," *Reason Magazine*, December 2000. Reprinted with permission from Reason Magazine and Reason.com.

and continue with the usual antiterrorist tactics (which have only a tiny chance of being successful); or (2) kill the wife and three of the children and threaten to kill the rest (a strategy with a very high chance of success). According to utilitarianism, which action is right?

As an act-utilitarian, the chief might reason like this: Action 2 would probably result in a net gain of happiness, everyone considered. Forcing the terrorist to turn himself in would save hundreds of lives. His killing spree would be over. The general level of fear and apprehension in the country might subside, and even the economy—which has slowed because of terrorism—might improve. The prestige of the antiterrorism chief and his agents might increase. On the downside, performing Action 2 would guarantee that four innocent people (and perhaps eight) would lose their lives, and the terrorist (whose welfare must also be included in the calculations) would be imprisoned for life or executed. In addition, many citizens would be disturbed by the killing of innocent people and the flouting of the law by the police, believing that these actions are wrong and likely to set a dangerous precedent. Over time, though, these misgivings might diminish. All things considered, then, Action 2 would probably produce more happiness than unhappiness. Action 1, on the other hand, maintains the status quo. It would allow the terrorist to continue murdering innocent people and spreading fear throughout the land—a decidedly unhappy result. It clearly would produce more unhappiness than happiness. Action 2, therefore, would produce the most happiness and would therefore be the morally right option.

As a rule-utilitarian, the chief might make a different choice. He would have to decide what rules would apply to the situation, then determine which one, if consistently followed, would yield the most utility. Suppose he must decide between Rule 1 and Rule 2. Rule 1 says, "Do not kill innocent people in order to prevent terrorists from killing other innocent people." Rule 2 says, "Killing innocent people is permissible if it helps to stop terrorist attacks." The chief might deliberate as follows: We can be confident that consistently following Rule 2 would have some dire consequences for society. Innocent people would be subject to arbitrary execution, civil rights would be regularly violated, the rule of law would be severely compromised, and trust in government would be degraded. In fact, adhering to Rule 2 might make people more fearful and less secure than terrorist attacks would; it would undermine the very foundations of a free society. In a particular case, killing innocent people to fight terror could possibly have more utility than not killing them. But whether such a strategy would be advantageous to society over the long haul is not at all certain. Consistently following Rule 1 would have none of these unfortunate consequences. If so, a society living according to Rule 1 would be better off than one adhering to Rule 2, and therefore the innocent should not be killed to stop the terrorist.

Evaluating the Theory

Bentham and Mill do not offer ironclad arguments demonstrating that utilitarianism is the best moral theory. Mill, however, does try to show that the principle of utility is at least a plausible basis for the theory. After all, he says, humans by nature desire happiness and nothing but happiness. If so, then happiness is the standard by which we should judge human conduct, and therefore the principle of utility is the heart of morality. But this kind of moral argument is controversial because it reasons from what *is* to what *should be*. In addition, as pointed out in the discussion of psychological egoism, the notion that happiness is our sole motivation is dubious.

What can we learn about utilitarianism by applying the moral criteria of adequacy? Let us begin with classic act-utilitarianism and deal with rule-utilitarianism later. We can also postpone discussion of the minimum requirement of coherence, because critics have been more inclined to charge rule-utilitarianism than act-utilitarianism with having significant internal inconsistencies.

If we begin with Criterion 1 (consistency with considered moral judgments), we run into what some have called act-utilitarianism's most serious problem: it conflicts with commonsense views about justice. Justice requires equal treatment of persons. It demands, for example, that goods such as happiness be distributed fairly—that we not harm one person to make several other persons

---

QUICK REVIEW

principle of utility—Bentham's "principle which approves or disapproves of every action whatsoever, according to the tendency which it appears to have to augment or diminish the happiness of the party whose interest is in question."

greatest happiness principle—Mill's principle that "holds that actions are right in proportion as they tend to promote happiness, wrong as they tend to produce the reverse of happiness."

social contract theory—The doctrine that morality arises from a social contract that self-interested and rational people would abide by in order to secure a degree of peace, prosperity, and safety.

happy. Utilitarianism says that everyone should be included in utility calculations, but it does not require that everyone get an equal share. Consider this famous scenario from the philosopher H. J. McCloskey:

> While a utilitarian is visiting an area plagued by racial tension, a black man rapes a white woman. Race riots ensue, and white mobs roam the streets, beating and lynching black people as the police secretly condone the violence and do nothing to stop it. The utilitarian realizes that by giving false testimony, he could bring about the quick arrest and conviction of a black man whom he picks at random. As a result of this lie, the riots and the lynchings would stop, and innocent lives would be spared. As a utilitarian, he believes he has a duty to bear false witness to punish an innocent person.

If right actions are those that maximize happiness, then it seems that the utilitarian would be doing right by framing the innocent person. The innocent person, of course, would experience unhappiness (he might be sent to prison or even executed), but framing him would halt the riots and prevent many other innocent people from being killed, resulting in a net gain in overall happiness. Framing the innocent is unjust, though, and our considered moral judgments would be at odds with such an action. Here the commonsense idea of justice and the principle of utility collide. The conflict raises doubts about act-utilitarianism as a moral theory.

Here is another famous example:

> This time you are to imagine yourself to be a surgeon, a truly great surgeon. Among other things you do, you transplant organs, and you are such a great surgeon that the organs you transplant always take. At the moment you have five patients who need organs. Two need one lung each, two need a kidney each, and the fifth needs a heart. If they do not get those organs today, they will all die; if you find organs for them today, you can transplant the organs and they will all live. But where to find the lungs, the kidneys, and the heart? The time is almost up when a report is brought to you that a young man who has just come into your clinic for his yearly check-up has exactly the right blood type and is in excellent health. Lo, you have a possible donor. All you need do is cut him up and distribute his parts among the five who need them. You ask, but he says, "Sorry. I deeply sympathize, but no." Would it be morally permissible for you to operate anyway?[6]

This scenario involves the possible killing of an innocent person for the good of others. There seems little doubt that carrying out the murder and transplanting the victim's organs into five other people (and thus saving their lives) would maximize utility (assuming, of course, that the surgeon's deed would not become public and he would suffer no untoward psychological effects). Compared with the happiness produced by doing the transplants, the unhappiness of the one unlucky donor seems minor. Therefore, according to act-utilitarianism, you (the surgeon) should commit the murder and do the transplants. But this choice appears to conflict with our considered moral judgments. Killing the healthy young man to benefit the five unhealthy patients seems unjust.

Look at one final case. Suppose a tsunami devastates a coastal area of Singapore. Relief agencies arrive on the scene to distribute food, shelter, and medical care to 100 tsunami victims—disaster aid that amounts to, say, 1,000 units of happiness. There are only two options for the distribution of the 1,000 units. Option 1 is to divide the 1,000 units equally among all 100 victims, supplying 10 units to each person. Option 2 is to give 901 units to one victim (who happens to be the richest man in the area) and 99 units to the remaining victims, providing 1 unit per person. Both options distribute the same amount of happiness to the victims—1,000 units. Following the dictates of act-utilitarianism, we would have to say that the two actions (options) have equal utility and so are equally right. But this conclusion seems wrong. It seems unjust to distribute the units of happiness so unevenly when all recipients are equals in all morally relevant respects. Like the other examples, this one suggests that act-utilitarianism may be an inadequate theory.

Detractors make parallel arguments against the theory in many cases besides those involving injustice. A familiar charge is that act-utilitarianism conflicts with our commonsense judgments both about people's rights and about their obligations to one another. Consider first this scenario about rights: Mr. Y is a nurse in a care facility for the elderly. He tends to many bedridden patients who are in pain most of the time, are financial and emotional burdens to their families, and are not expected to live more than a few weeks. Despite their misery, they do not wish for death; they want only to be free of pain. Mr. Y, an act-utilitarian, sees that there would be a lot more happiness in the world and less pain if these patients died sooner rather than later. He decides to take matters into his own hands, so he secretly gives them a drug that kills them quietly and painlessly. Their families and the facility staff feel enormous relief. No one will ever know what Mr. Y has done, and no one suspects foul play. He feels no guilt—only immense satisfaction knowing that he has helped make the world a better place.

If Mr. Y does indeed maximize happiness in this situation, then his action is right, according to act-utilitarianism. Yet most people would probably say that he violated the rights of his patients. The commonsense view is that people have certain rights that should not be violated merely to create a better balance of happiness over unhappiness.

Another typical criticism of act-utilitarianism is that it appears to fly in the face of our considered moral judgments about our obligations to other people. Suppose Ms. Z must decide between two actions: Action 1 will produce 1,001 units of happiness; Action 2, 1,000 units. The only other significant difference between them is that Action 1 entails the breaking of a promise. By act-utilitarian lights, Ms. Z should choose Action 1 because it yields more happiness than Action 2 does. But we tend to think that keeping a promise is more important than a tiny gain in happiness. We often try to keep our promises even when we know that doing so will result in a decrease in utility. Some say that if our obligations to others sometimes outweigh considerations of overall happiness, then act-utilitarianism must be problematic.[7]

What can an act-utilitarian say to rebut these charges? One frequent response goes like this: The scenarios put forth by critics (such as the cases just cited) are misleading and implausible. They are always set up so that actions regarded as immoral produce the greatest happiness, leading us to conclude that utilitarianism conflicts with commonsense morality and therefore cannot be an adequate moral theory. But in real life these kinds of actions almost never maximize happiness. In the case of Dr. X, her crime would almost certainly be discovered by physicians or other scientists, and she would be exposed as a murderer. This revelation would surely destroy her career, undermine patient-physician trust, tarnish the reputation of the scientific community, dry up funding for legitimate research, and prompt countless lawsuits. Scientists might even refuse to use the data from Dr. X's research because she obtained them through a heinous act. As one philosopher put it, "Given a clearheaded view of the world as it is and a realistic understanding of man's nature, it becomes more and more evident that injustice will never have, in the long run, greater utility than justice.... Thus injustice becomes, in actual practice, a source of great social disutility."[8]

The usual response to this defense is that the act-utilitarian is probably correct that most violations of commonsense morality do not maximize happiness—but at least some violations do. At least sometimes, actions that have the best consequences do conflict with our credible moral principles or considered moral judgments. The charge is that the act-utilitarian cannot plausibly dismiss all counterexamples, and only one counterexample is required to show that maximizing utility is not a necessary and sufficient condition for right action.[9]

Unlike ethical egoism, act-utilitarianism (as well as rule-utilitarianism) does not fail Criterion

2 (consistency with our moral experiences), so we can move on to Criterion 3 (usefulness in moral problem solving). On this score, some scholars argue that act-utilitarianism deserves bad marks. Probably their most common complaint is what has been called the *no-rest problem*. Utilitarianism (in all its forms) requires that in our actions we *always* try to maximize utility, everyone considered. Say you are watching television. Utilitarianism would have you ask yourself, "Is this the best way to maximize happiness for everyone?" Probably not. You could be giving to charity or working as a volunteer for the local hospital or giving your coat to a homeless person or selling everything you own to buy food for hungry children. Whatever you are doing, there is usually something else you could do that would better maximize net happiness for everyone.

If act-utilitarianism does demand too much of us, then its usefulness as a guide to the moral life is suspect. One possible reply to this criticism is that the utilitarian burden can be lightened by devising rules that place limits on supererogatory actions. Another reply is that our moral common sense is simply wrong on this issue—we *should* be willing to perform, as our duty, many actions that are usually considered supererogatory. If necessary, we should be willing to give up our personal ambitions for the good of everyone. We should be willing, for example, to sacrifice a very large portion of our resources to help the poor.

To some, this reply seems questionable precisely because it challenges our commonsense moral intuitions—the very intuitions that we use to measure the plausibility of our moral judgments and principles. Moral common sense, they say, can be mistaken, and our intuitions can be tenuous or distorted—but we should cast them aside only for good reasons.

But a few utilitarians directly reject this appeal to common sense, declaring that relying so heavily on such intuitions is a mistake:

> Admittedly utilitarianism does have consequences which are incompatible with the common moral

consciousness, but I tended to take the view "so much the worse for the common moral consciousness." That is, I was inclined to reject the common methodology of testing general ethical principles by seeing how they square with our feelings in particular instances.[10]

These utilitarians would ask, Isn't it possible that in dire circumstances, saving a hundred innocent lives by allowing one to die would be the best thing to do even though allowing that one death would be a tragedy? Aren't there times when the norms of justice and duty *should* be ignored for the greater good of society?

To avoid the problems that act-utilitarianism is alleged to have, some utilitarians have turned to rule-utilitarianism. By positing rules that should be consistently followed, rule-utilitarianism seems to align its moral judgments closer to those of common sense. And the theory itself is based on ideas about morality that seem perfectly sensible:

> In general, rule utilitarianism seems to involve two rather plausible intuitions. In the first place, rule utilitarians want to emphasize that moral rules are important. Individual acts are justified by being shown to be in accordance with correct moral rules. In the second place, utility is important. Moral rules are shown to be correct by being shown to lead, somehow, to the maximization of utility. . . . Rule utilitarianism, in its various forms, tries to combine these intuitions into a single, coherent criterion of morality.[11]

But some philosophers have accused the theory of being internally inconsistent. They say, in other words, that it fails the minimum requirement of coherence. (If so, we can forgo discussion of our three moral criteria of adequacy.) They argue as follows: Rule-utilitarianism says that actions are right if they conform to rules devised to maximize utility. Rules with exceptions or qualifications, however, maximize utility better than rules without them. For example, a rule like "Do not steal except in these circumstances" maximizes utility better than the rule "Do not steal." It seems, then, that the best rules are those with amendments that make them as specific as possible to particular cases. But if the rules were changed in this way to maximize utility, they would end up mandating the same actions that act-utilitarianism does. They all would say, in effect, "Do not do this except to maximize utility." Rule-utilitarianism would lapse into act-utilitarianism.

Some rule-utilitarians respond to this criticism by denying that rules with a lot of exceptions would maximize utility. They say that people might fear for their own well-being when others make multiple exceptions to rules. You might be reassured by a rule such as "Do not harm others," but feel uneasy about the rule "Do not harm others except in this situation." What if you end up in that particular situation?

Those who criticize the theory admit that it is indeed possible for an exception-laden rule to produce more unhappiness than happiness because of the anxiety it causes. But, they say, it is also possible for such a rule to generate a very large measure of happiness—large enough to more than offset any ill effects spawned by rule exceptions. If so, then rule-utilitarianism could easily slip into act-utilitarianism, thus exhibiting all the conflicts with commonsense morality that act-utilitarianism is supposed to have.

LEARNING FROM UTILITARIANISM

Regardless of how much credence we give to the arguments for and against utilitarianism, we must admit that the theory seems to embody a large part of the truth about morality. First, utilitarianism begs us to consider that the consequences of our actions do indeed make a difference in our moral deliberations. Whatever factors work to make an action right (or wrong), surely the consequences of what we do must somehow be among them. Even if lying is morally wrong primarily because of the kind of act it is, we cannot plausibly think that a lie that saves a thousand lives is morally equivalent to one that changes nothing. Sometimes our considered moral judgments may tell us that an action is right regardless of the good (or evil) it does. And sometimes they may say that the good it does matters a great deal.

Second, utilitarianism—perhaps more than any other moral theory—incorporates the principle of impartiality, a fundamental pillar of morality itself. Everyone concerned counts equally in every moral decision. As Mill says, when we judge the rightness of our actions, utilitarianism requires us to be "as strictly impartial as a disinterested and benevolent spectator." Discrimination is forbidden, and equality reigns. We would expect no less from a plausible moral theory.

Third, utilitarianism is through and through a moral theory for promoting human welfare. At its core is the moral principle of beneficence—the obligation to act for the well-being of others. Beneficence is not the whole of morality, but to most people it is at least close to its heart.

SOCIAL CONTRACT THEORY

So far we have examined several moral theories and observed that each is based on, and justified by, some distinctive fundamental feature. For utilitarianism, that feature is utility; for the divine command theory, God's will; for Kant's theory, the categorical imperative. But suppose you don't believe in any of these justifying principles. You think the universe is entirely physical—just atoms in motion, devoid of divinity and purpose. You believe reason can never yield an authoritative rational principle like the categorical imperative, and you are sure that utilitarianism is hopelessly unrealistic because people can never be trusted to promote the common good. At their core, people are egoistic and self-interested. And in service to their own needs and desires, they will, given the chance, commit all manner of horrific cruelties and vile wrongs. In such a world, on what foundation can morality rest? In such a perilous and corrosive environment, how can morality ever find a foothold?

CRITICAL THOUGHT: Cross-Species Transplants: What Would a Utilitarian Do?

Like any adequate moral theory, utilitarianism should be able to help us resolve moral problems, including new moral issues arising from advances in science and medicine. A striking example of one such issue is cross-species transplantation, the transplanting of organs from one species to another, usually from nonhuman animals to humans. Scientists are already bioengineering pigs so that their organs will not provoke tissue rejection in human recipients. Pigs are thought to be promising organ donors because of the similarities between pig and human organs. Many people are in favor of such research because it could open up new sources of transplantable organs, which are now in short supply and desperately needed by thousands of people whose organs are failing.

Would an act-utilitarian be likely to condone cross-species transplants of organs? If so, on what grounds? Would the unprecedented, "unnatural" character of these operations bother a utilitarian? Why or why not? Would you expect an act-utilitarian to approve of cross-species organ transplants if they involved the killing of one hundred pigs for every successful transplant? If only a very limited number of transplants could be done successfully each year, how do you think an act-utilitarian would decide who gets the operations? Would she choose randomly? Would she ever be justified (by utilitarian considerations) in, say, deciding to save a rich philanthropist while letting a poor person die for lack of a transplant?

For some, the answer is **social contract theory** (or *contractarianism*). This doctrine says that morality arises from a social contract that self-interested and rational people abide by in order to secure a degree of peace, prosperity, and safety. Without such an agreement, life would be nearly unlivable, with each person competing with everyone else to promote his or her own interests, to grab as much wealth and power as possible, and to defend his or her person and property against all comers. Humanity, as the saying goes, would be red in tooth and claw. But such a dog-eat-dog world is in no one's interests. Only in a world where people restrain their greed and try to cooperate with one another can they achieve a modestly satisfying and secure life. And this kind of restraint and cooperation, says the social contract theorist, is possible only through a social contract in which people agree to obey practical, beneficial rules as long as everyone else does the same. Obedience means relinquishing some personal freedom and giving up the option to kill, wound, and cheat our neighbors at will, but it also ensures a better life and a measure of protection from the ravages of continual conflict and fear. From this social contract comes morality, for the rules *constitute* morality. Morality comprises the social rules that are in everyone's best interests to heed. In a well-ordered society, the rules are embodied in laws and policies, enforced by the state and recognized by most citizens as necessary and legitimate. They are deemed legitimate because they are the result of an agreement among rational equals who understand that the contract, however restrictive, is for the best.

Hobbes's Theory

The first well-developed social contract theory in modern times was devised by the British philosopher and linguist Thomas Hobbes (1588–1679). He argues for the necessity of a social contract by first giving us a glimpse of a world without one.

In his masterpiece *Leviathan*, he presents a pessimistic picture of human beings in their natural, unfettered, lawless state. They are, he says, greedy, selfish, violent, self-destructive, and desperate. Their cutthroat struggle for advantage and survival rages on and on because they are roughly equal in strength and ability, ensuring that no one can win. So conflict, chaos, death, and loss reign—and humankind is reduced to living in a horrifying and gruesome "state of nature." This state is not merely a Hobbesian construct: it arises in the real world when there is a breakdown in the forces that preserve law and order—in times of revolution, war, natural disaster, famine, and civil unrest. According to Hobbes,

> Hereby it is manifest, that during the time men live without a common power to keep them all in awe, they are in that condition which is called war; and such a war, as is of every man, against every man. . . .
>
> Whatsoever therefore is consequent to a time of war, where every man is enemy to every man; the same is consequent to the time; wherein men live without other security, than what their own strength, and their own invention shall furnish them withal. In such condition, there is no place for industry; because the fruit thereof is uncertain: and consequently no culture of the earth; no navigation, nor use of the commodities that may be imported by sea; no commodious building; no instruments of moving, and removing such things as require much force; no knowledge of the face of the earth; no account of time; no arts; no letters; no society; and which is worst of all, continual fear, and danger of violent death; and the life of man, solitary, poor, nasty, brutish, and short.[12]

As long as people continue to trample others on the way to steal the biggest piece of pie, life will remain a "war of every man against every man." The only rational alternative, says Hobbes, is to accept a social contract that mandates cooperation and restraint. By following the rules, everyone wins. The agreement prohibits contract breaking as well as harming, threatening, and defrauding others, because such behavior threatens the peace and prosperity that the social contract makes possible.

But people are people, and they will renege on the deal if given half a chance. So what's needed is a fearsome, powerful person or persons to enforce the rules, to threaten punishment, and to deliver it swiftly to rule breakers. Specifically, what's required is an absolute sovereign, what Hobbes refers to as the Leviathan (the name of a terrifying monster mentioned in the Bible). The Leviathan's job is to ensure that the social contract is honored and that agreements are kept. His subjects agree to cede to him much of their freedom and right of self-determination in exchange for an orderly and secure society.

Before the Leviathan rules society, Hobbes says, there is no right and wrong:

> [In the state of nature] nothing can be unjust. The notions of right and wrong, justice and injustice have there no place. . . . It is consequent also to the same condition, that there be no propriety, no dominion, no mine and thine distinct; but only that to be every man's, that he can get; and for so long, as he can keep it.[13]

Morality comes into existence only when the Leviathan takes control and guarantees the strength and stability of the social contract.

Evaluating the Theory

Many thinkers have tried to improve on Hobbes's theory or offer alternatives, and as a result, several types of social contract theory have been put forth. But let's limit our discussion to Hobbes's theory (and those like it). Like every major moral theory, Hobbesian social contract theory has both appealing and questionable features, so let's examine both.

On the positive side, the theory provides an answer to skeptics and relativists who question whether morality is objective or consists of a set of beliefs we merely happen to accept. It says that morality is objective because it consists of the rules—the standards of right and wrong—that rational members of society have determined to be most beneficial for all. The source of morality is therefore apparent. We need not ask—as we would with many other theories—whether it is based on God's will, nature, or pure reason. Its rules make peaceful coexistence and productive cooperation possible, and they are the very rules that would be enacted by rational people of equal status whose goal is to see that the rules benefit everyone.

These attributes ensure that, at least in one respect, Hobbes's theory scores high on the moral criterion of usefulness: there is no mystery about how to find out if an action is morally right or wrong. The social rules are those that promote social harmony. It is clear that theft, murder, fraud, promise breaking, exploitation, intolerance, and other malicious acts are contrary to social order, so they are immoral.

But why should we be moral in the first place? Or to put it another way, What is the purpose of morality? This is a difficult question for any moral theory. The social contract answer is straightforward: We should be moral in a society where the rules are generally followed because we are better off doing so. In addition, breaking the rules would bring punishment from the Leviathan, and trying to avoid the pain of such punishment is rational.

Philosophers have faulted Hobbes's theory on several counts. Among the most important of these is the charge that few people have ever actually *consented* to the terms of a social contract. (Critics make this point against other forms of the theory, not just Hobbes's.) The essence of a contract is that people freely agree to abide by its terms. Presumably, if they don't give their consent, they are not obliged to obey the contract's rules. But who has explicitly agreed to be bound by a social contract? Who has raised their right hand and sworn

allegiance or signed on the dotted line? Most people have not.

Some defenders of social contract theory reply that people may not have given their explicit consent, but they surely have given their *implicit* consent. By enjoying the social and material advantages that the social contract makes possible, these advocates say, people implicitly agree to abide by its rules. If they accept the benefits, they tacitly agree to shoulder the obligations.

But this notion of implicit consent will not do. There are many who benefit from living in a well-ordered society, but we cannot plausibly say they consented to be bound by any social contract. People are born into a particular society without their consent; they have no choice in the matter. They do not agree to be part of the social order. And as adults, many may hate the society they find themselves in but cannot leave it because the political, financial, and social costs of trying to emigrate may be prohibitive. In any case, it is hard to see how such citizens could be said to implicitly accept a social contract.

At this point the contractarian might say that we can be duty-bound to obey the moral tenets of a social contract even if we *don't* consent to it, either explicitly or implicitly. Our moral duties are established not because we accept the social contract from which they come, but because the contract is one that we *would* embrace if we were rational individuals searching for rules that would best serve everyone's interests. The social contract, in other words, is hypothetical but nevertheless binding. This is how most contemporary contractarians view social contracts: they see them as fictions—but very useful fictions. For example, today's most influential social contract theory comes from the philosopher John Rawls (1921–2002). He attempted to determine what moral principles a society would accept if they were arrived at through a hypothetical give-and-take that was as fair and impartial as possible. According to Rawls, such principles are what "free and rational persons concerned to further their own interests would accept in an initial position of equality as defining the fundamental terms of their association."[14]

There is a stronger objection that has been made against Hobbes's theory and contractarian theories generally: the category of individuals that we normally think should have moral status is restricted. Living beings have moral status if they are suitable candidates for moral concern or respect. This means we cannot treat them just any way we want; we have direct moral duties to them. We know that normal, rational, adult human beings have full moral status—they deserve our highest level of respect and consideration no matter their social situation. And we typically think that vulnerable individuals—for example, the severely disabled, the very poor, nonhuman animals, children, and infants—also have moral status: they also deserve a measure of our respect and consideration. But critics charge that social contract theories conflict with these intuitions. The theories generally hold that the only ones who have moral status are those who can legitimately be party to a social contract (the contractors), and that the only ones who can participate in a social contract are those for whom participation would be mutually beneficial. The vulnerable individuals who cannot take part in this give-and-take for mutual benefit may have no moral status and no rights.

Modern contractarians have responded to these complaints in several ways. Their general contention is that although vulnerable individuals may not be contractors, it does not follow that they can be mistreated or left unprotected. They point out, for example, that it may be mutually advantageous for society to care for disabled children because some contractors (namely, parents) care about such children, and this concern makes the benevolent treatment of disabled children a matter of the parents' self-interest. Also, it may be in everyone's interests for society to care for the elderly, the chronically ill, and victims of accidents, because in the future we all may find ourselves in one of these situations. Or benefiting the vulnerable could be viewed as a psychological need of contractors, so fulfilling this need by helping the vulnerable may be in every contractor's best interests.

CHAPTER REVIEW

SUMMARY

Ethical egoism is the theory that the right action is the one that advances one's own best interests. It promotes self-interested behavior but not necessarily selfish acts. The ethical egoist may define his self-interest in various ways—as pleasure, self-actualization, power, happiness, or other goods. The most important argument for ethical egoism relies on the theory known as psychological egoism, the view that the motive for all our actions is self-interest. Psychological egoism, however, seems to ignore the fact that people sometimes do things that are not in their best interests. It also seems to misconstrue the relationship between our actions and the satisfaction that often follows from them. We seem to desire something other than satisfaction and then experience satisfaction as a result of getting what we desire.

Utilitarianism is the view that the morally right action is the one that produces the most favorable balance of good over evil, everyone considered. Act-utilitarianism says that right actions are those that directly produce the greatest overall happiness, everyone considered. Rule-utilitarianism says that the morally right action is the one covered by a rule that if generally followed would produce the most favorable balance of good over evil, everyone considered.

Critics argue that act-utilitarianism is not consistent with our considered moral judgments about justice. In many possible scenarios, the action that maximizes utility in a situation also seems blatantly unjust. Likewise, the theory seems to collide with our notions of rights and obligations. Again, it seems relatively easy to imagine scenarios in which utility is maximized while rights or obligations are short-changed. An act-utilitarian might respond to these points by saying that such examples are unrealistic—that in real life, actions thought to be immoral almost never maximize happiness.

Rule-utilitarianism has been accused of being internally inconsistent—of easily collapsing into act-utilitarianism. The charge is that the rules that maximize happiness best are specific to particular cases, but such rules would sanction the same actions that act-utilitarianism does.

Regardless of criticisms lodged against it, utilitarianism offers important insights into the nature of morality: The consequences of our actions surely do matter in our moral deliberations and in our lives. The principle of impartiality is an essential part of moral decision making. And any plausible moral theory must somehow take into account the principle of beneficence.

Social contract theory is the view that morality arises from a social contract that self-interested and rational people would abide by to secure a degree of security and prosperity. Restraint and cooperation are possible only through a social contract in which people agree to obey practical, beneficial rules as long as everyone else does the same.

KEY TERMS

act-egoism (p. 85)
rule-egoism (p. 85)
psychological egoism (p. 87)
principle of utility (p. 92)
greatest happiness principle (p. 92)
social contract theory (p. 101)

EXERCISES

Review Questions

1. What is ethical egoism? What is the difference between act- and rule-egoism? (p. 85)
2. What is psychological egoism? (p. 87)

3. What is the psychological egoist argument for ethical egoism? (pp. 87–88)
4. Is psychological egoism true? Why or why not? (pp. 88–89)
5. In what way is ethical egoism not consistent with our considered moral judgments? (p. 90)
6. What is the principle of utility? (p. 92)
7. According to Hobbes, where does morality come from? (p. 102)
8. What is the difference between act- and rule-utilitarianism? (p. 94)
9. How do act- and rule-utilitarians differ in their views on rules? (p. 94)
10. Is act-utilitarianism consistent with our considered moral judgments regarding justice? Why or why not? (pp. 96–98)

Discussion Questions

1. Is psychological egoism based on a conceptual confusion? Why or why not?
2. Why do critics regard ethical egoism as an inadequate moral theory? Are the critics right? Why or why not?
3. How would your life change if you became a consistent act-utilitarian?
4. How would your life change if you became a consistent rule-utilitarian?
5. To what was Mill referring when he said, "It is better to be a human being dissatisfied than a pig satisfied"? Do you agree with this statement? Why or why not?
6. If you were on trial for your life (because of an alleged murder), would you want the judge to be an act-utilitarian, a rule-utilitarian, or neither? Why?
7. Do you agree with Hobbes's view of human nature? Why or why not?
8. Does act-utilitarianism conflict with commonsense judgments about rights? Why or why not?
9. Is there such a thing as a supererogatory act—or are all right actions simply our duty? What would an act-utilitarian say about supererogatory acts?

10. Suppose you had to decide which one of a dozen dying patients should receive a lifesaving drug, knowing that there was only enough of the medicine for one person. Would you feel comfortable making the decision as an act-utilitarian would? Why or why not?

ETHICAL DILEMMAS

1. Suppose you are an act-utilitarian, and you must choose between two courses of action. In the first action, you could make a stranger very happy by giving her $100. In the second action, you could make another stranger even happier by giving him the same amount of money—but this action would involve breaking a promise to a friend. According to act-utilitarianism, which action is the morally right one? Do you agree with this choice? Why or why not?

2. Imagine that your preferred moral theory implies that racial discrimination is morally permissible—an implication that is in direct conflict with your considered moral judgments. Would such a conflict suggest to you that the theory must be defective? Why or why not?

3. Suppose your preferred moral theory is based entirely on love—that is, you believe that right actions are those that issue from a feeling of empathy, compassion, or mercy. Now imagine that a homeless man assaults you and steals your wallet, and then you see him do the same thing to two other people. How would your love theory apply to this case? Would there be a conflict between love and the principle of justice or the community's moral standards? Would your theory lead you to go against your considered moral judgments? Assess the worth of the love theory.

FURTHER READING

Jeremy Bentham, "Of the Principle of Utility," in *An Introduction to the Principles of Morals and Legislation* (1789; reprint, Oxford: Clarendon Press, 1879).

C. D. Broad, "Egoism as a Theory of Human Motives," in *Twentieth Century Ethical Theory,* ed. Steven M. Cahn and Joram G. Haber (Englewood Cliffs, NJ: Prentice Hall, 1995).

Steven M. Cahn and Joram G. Haber, eds., *Twentieth Century Ethical Theory* (Englewood Cliffs, NJ: Prentice Hall, 1995).

Fred Feldman, "Act Utilitarianism: Pro and Con," in *Introductory Ethics* (Englewood Cliffs, NJ: Prentice Hall, 1978).

William Frankena, "Utilitarianism, Justice, and Love," in *Ethics,* 2nd ed. (Englewood Cliffs, NJ: Prentice Hall, 1973).

C. E. Harris, "The Ethics of Utilitarianism," in *Applying Moral Theories,* 3rd ed. (Belmont, CA: Wadsworth, 1997).

Kai Nielsen, "A Defense of Utilitarianism," *Ethics* 82 (1972): 113–24.

Robert Nozick, "The Experience Machine," in *Anarchy, State and Utopia* (New York: Basic Books, 1974).

Louis P. Pojman, ed., *The Moral Life: An Introductory Reader in Ethics and Literature,* 2nd ed. (New York: Oxford University Press, 2004).

John Rawls, *A Theory of Justice* (Cambridge, MA: Harvard University Press, 1999).

John Simmons, *Political Philosophy* (New York: Oxford University Press, 2008).

J. J. C. Smart, "Extreme and Restricted Utilitarianism," in *Essays Metaphysical and Moral: Selected Philosophical Papers* (Oxford: Blackwell, 1987).

Paul W. Taylor, "Ethical Egoism," in *Principles of Ethics: An Introduction* (Encino, CA: Dickenson, 1975).

Bernard Williams, "A Critique of Utilitarianism," in *Utilitarianism: For and Against,* ed. J. J. C. Smart and Bernard Williams (Cambridge: Cambridge University Press, 1973).

Jonathan Wolff, *An Introduction to Political Philosophy* (Oxford: Oxford University Press, 2006).

READINGS

Egoism and Altruism

LOUIS P. POJMAN

Universal ethical egoism is the theory that everyone ought always to serve his or her own self-interest. That is, everyone ought to do what will maximize one's own expected utility or bring about one's own greatest happiness, even if it requires harming others. Ethical egoism is utilitarianism reduced to the pinpoint of the single individual ego. Instead of advocating the greatest happiness for the greatest number, as utilitarianism does, it advocates the greatest happiness for myself, whoever I may be. It is a self-preoccupied prudence, urging one to postpone enjoyment today for long-term benefits. In its more sophisticated form, it compares life to a competitive game, perhaps a war-game, and urges each person to *try* to win in the game of life.

In her books *The Virtue of Selfishness* and *Atlas Shrugged,* Ayn Rand argues that selfishness is a virtue and altruism a vice, a totally destructive idea that leads to the undermining of individual worth. She defines *altruism* as the view that

> any action taken for the benefit of others is good, and any action taken for one's own benefit is evil. Thus, the beneficiary of an action is the only criterion of moral value—and so long as the beneficiary is anybody other than oneself, anything goes.[1]

As such, altruism is suicidal:

> If a man accepts the ethics of altruism, his first concern is not how to live his life, but how to sacrifice it. . . . Altruism erodes men's capacity to grasp the value of an individual life; it reveals a mind from which the reality of a human being has been wiped out.

Since finding happiness is the highest goal and good in life, altruism, which calls on us to sacrifice our happiness for the good of others, is contrary to our highest good.

From Louis P. Pojman, "Egoism and Altruism: A Critique of Ayn Rand," *Philosophy: The Quest for Truth,* 10th ed., 461–65. © 2016 by Oxford University Press, Inc. By permission of Oxford University Press, USA.

Her argument seems to go like this:

1. The perfection of one's abilities in a state of happiness is the highest goal for humans. We have a moral duty to attempt to reach this goal.
2. The ethics of altruism prescribes that we sacrifice our interests and lives for the good of others.
3. Therefore, the ethics of altruism is incompatible with the goal of happiness.
4. Ethical egoism prescribes that we seek our own happiness exclusively, and as such it is consistent with the happiness goal.
5. Therefore ethical egoism is the correct moral theory.

Ayn Rand's argument for the virtue of selfishness is flawed by the fallacy of a false dilemma. It simplistically assumes that absolute altruism and absolute egoism are the only alternatives. But this is an extreme view of the matter. There are plenty of options between these two positions. Even a predominant egoist would admit that (analogous to the paradox of hedonism) sometimes the best way to reach self-fulfillment is for us to forget about ourselves and strive to live for goals, causes, or other persons. Even if altruism is not required (as a duty), it may be permissible in many cases. Furthermore, self-interest may not be incompatible with other-regarding motivation. Even the Second Great Commandment set forth by Moses and Jesus states not that you must always sacrifice yourself for the other person, but that you ought to love your neighbor *as* yourself (Lev. 19:19; Matt. 23). Self-interest and self-love are morally good things, but not at the expense of other people's legitimate interests. When there is moral conflict of interests, a fair process of adjudication needs to take place.

But Rand's version of egoism is only one of many. We need to go to the heart of ethical egoism: the thesis that our highest moral duty is always to promote our individual interests. Let us focus on the alleged problems of this thesis.

FOUR CRITICISMS OF ETHICAL EGOISM

The Inconsistent Outcomes Argument

Brian Medlin argues that ethical egoism cannot be true because it fails to meet a necessary condition of morality, that of being a guide to action. He claims that it will be like advising people to do inconsistent things based on incompatible desires.[2] His argument goes like this:

1. Moral principles must be universal and categorical.
2. I must universalize my egoist desire to come out on top over Tom, Dick, and Harry.
3. But I must also prescribe Tom's egoist desire to come out on top over Dick, Harry, and me (and so on).
4. Therefore I have prescribed incompatible outcomes and have not provided a way of adjudicating conflicts of desire. In effect, I have said nothing.

The proper response to this is that of Jesse Kalin, who argues that we can separate our beliefs about ethical situations from our desires.[3] He likens the situation to a competitive sports event, in which you believe that your opponent has a right to try to win as much as you, but you desire that you, not he, will in fact win. An even better example is that of the chess game in which you recognize that your opponent ought to move her bishop to prepare for checkmate, but you hope she won't see the move. Belief that A ought to do Y does not commit you to wanting A to do Y.

The Publicity Argument

On the one hand, in order for something to be a moral theory it seems necessary that its moral principles be publicized. Unless principles are put forth as universal prescriptions that are accessible to the public, they cannot serve as guides to action or as aids in resolving conflicts of interest. But on the other hand, it is not in the egoist's self-interest to publicize them. Egoists would rather that the rest of us be altruists. (Why did Nietzsche and Rand write books announcing their positions? Were the royalties taken in by announcing ethical egoism worth the price of letting the cat out of the bag?)

Thus it would be self-defeating for the egoist to argue for her position, and even worse that she should convince others of it. But it is perfectly possible to have a private morality that does not resolve conflicts of interest. So the egoist should publicly advocate standard principles of traditional morality—so that society doesn't break down—while adhering to a private, nonstandard, solely self-regarding morality. So, if you're willing to pay the price, you can accept the solipsistic-directed norms of egoism.

If the egoist is prepared to pay the price, egoism could be a consistent system that has some limitations. Although the egoist can cooperate with others in limited ways and perhaps even have friends—so long as their interests don't conflict with his—he has to be very careful about preserving his isolation. The egoist can't give advice or argue about his position—not sincerely at least. He must act alone, atomistically or solipsistically in moral isolation, for to announce his adherence to the principle of egoism would be dangerous to his project. He can't teach his children the true morality or justify himself to others or forgive others.

The Paradox of Egoism

The situation may be even worse than the sophisticated, self-conscious egoist supposes. Could the egoist have friends? And if limited friendship is possible, could he or she ever be in love or experience deep friendship? Suppose the egoist discovers that in the pursuit of the happiness goal, deep friendship is in his best interest. Can he become a friend? What is necessary to deep friendship? A true friend is one who is not always preoccupied about his own interest in the relationship but who forgets about himself altogether, at least sometimes, in order to serve or enhance the other person's interest. "Love seeketh not its own." It is an altruistic disposition, the very opposite of egoism. So the *paradox of egoism* is that in order to reach the goal of egoism one must give up egoism and become (to some extent) an altruist, the very antithesis of egoism.

The Argument from Counterintuitive Consequences

The final argument against ethical egoism is that it is an absolute ethics that not only permits egoistic behavior but demands it. Helping others at one's own expense is not only not required, it is morally wrong. Whenever I do not have good evidence that my helping you will end up to my advantage, I must refrain from helping you. If I can save the whole of Europe and Africa from destruction by pressing a button, then so long as there is nothing for me to gain by it, it is wrong for me to press that button. The Good Samaritan was, by this logic, morally wrong in helping the injured victim and not collecting payment for his troubles. It is certainly hard to see why the egoist should be concerned about environmental matters if he or she is profiting from polluting the environment. (For example, if the egoist gains 40 hedons in producing P, which produces pollution that in turn causes others 1,000 dolors—units of suffering—but suffers only 10 of those dolors himself, then by an agent-maximizing calculus he is morally obligated to produce P.) There is certainly no obligation to preserve scarce natural resources for future generations. "Why should I do anything for posterity?" the egoist asks "What has posterity ever done for me?"

In conclusion, we see that ethical egoism has a number of serious problems. It cannot consistently publicize itself, nor often argue its case. It tends towards solipsism and the exclusion of many of the deepest human values, such as love and deep friendship. It violates the principle of fairness, and, most of all, it entails an absolute prohibition on altruistic behavior, which we intuitively sense as morally required (or, at least, permissible).

EVOLUTION AND ALTRUISM

If sheer unadulterated egoism is an inadequate moral theory, does that mean we ought to aim at complete altruism, total self-effacement for the sake of others? What is the role of self-love in morality? An interesting place to start answering these queries is with the new field of sociobiology, which theorizes that social structures and behavioral patterns, including morality, have a biological base, explained by evolutionary theory.

In the past, linking ethics to evolution meant justifying exploitation. Social Darwinism justified imperialism and the principle that "Might makes right" by saying that survival of the fittest is a law of nature. This philosophy lent itself to a promotion of ruthless egoism. This is nature's law, "nature red in tooth and claw." Against this view ethologists such as Robert Ardrcy and Konrad Lorenz argued for a more benign view of the animal kingdom—one reminiscent of Rudyard Kipling's, in which the animal kingdom survives by cooperation, which is at least as important as competition. On Ardrey's and Lorenz's view it is the group or the species, not the individual, that is of primary importance.

With the development of sociobiology—in the work of E. O. Wilson but particularly the work of Robert Trivers, J. Maynard Smith, and Richard Dawkins—a theory has come to the fore that combines radical individualism with limited altruism. It is not the group or the species that is of evolutionary importance but the gene, or, more precisely, the gene type. Genes—the parts of the chromosomes that carry the blueprints for all our natural traits (e.g., height, hair color, skin color, intelligence)—copy themselves as they divide and multiply. At conception they combine with the genes of a member of the opposite sex to form a new individual.

In his fascinating sociobiological study, Richard Dawkins describes human behavior as determined evolutionarily by stable strategies set to replicate the gene.[4] This is not done consciously, of course, but by the invisible hand that drives consciousness. We are essentially gene machines.

Morality—that is, successful morality—can be seen as an evolutionary strategy for gene replication. Here's an example: Birds are afflicted with life-endangering parasites. Because they lack limbs to enable them to pick the parasites off their heads, they—like much of the animal kingdom—depend on the ritual of mutual grooming. It turns out that nature has evolved two basic types of birds in this regard: those who are disposed to groom anyone (the non-prejudiced type?), and those who refuse to groom anyone but who present themselves for grooming. The former type of bird Dawkins calls "Suckers" and the latter "Cheaters."

In a geographical area containing harmful parasites and where there are only Suckers or Cheaters, Suckers will do fairly well, but Cheaters will not survive, for want of cooperation. However, in a Sucker population in which a mutant Cheater arises, the Cheater will prosper, and the Cheater gene-type will multiply. As the Suckers are exploited, they will gradually die out. But if and when they become too few to groom the Cheaters, the Cheaters will start to die off too and eventually become extinct.

Why don't birds all die off, then? Well, somehow nature has come up with a third type, call them "Grudgers." Grudgers groom all and only those who reciprocate in grooming them. They groom each other and Suckers, but not Cheaters. In fact, once caught, a Cheater is marked forever. There is no forgiveness. It turns out then that unless there are a lot of Suckers around, Cheaters have a hard time of it—harder even than Suckers. However, it is the Grudgers that prosper. Unlike Suckers, they don't waste time messing with unappreciative Cheaters, so they are not exploited and have ample energy to gather food and build better nests for their loved ones.

J. L. Mackie argues that the real name for Suckers is "Christian," one who believes in complete altruism, even turning the other cheek to one's assailant and loving one's enemy. Cheaters are ruthless egoists who can survive only if there are enough naive altruists around. Whereas Grudgers are *reciprocal* altruists who have a rational morality based on cooperative self-interest, Suckers, such as Socrates and Jesus, advocate "turning the other cheek and repaying evil with good."[5] Instead of a Rule of Reciprocity, "I'll scratch your back if you'll scratch mine," the extreme altruist substitutes the Golden Rule, "If you want the other fellow to scratch your back, you scratch his—even if he won't reciprocate."

The moral of the story is this: Altruist morality (so interpreted) is only rational given the payoff of eternal life (with a scorekeeper as Woody Allen says). Take that away, and it looks like a Sucker system. What replaces the "Christian" vision of submission and saintliness is the reciprocal altruist with a tit-for-tat morality,

someone who is willing to share with those willing to cooperate.

Mackie may caricature the position of the religious altruist, but he misses the subtleties of wisdom involved (Jesus said, "Be as wise as serpents but as harmless as doves"). Nevertheless, he does remind us that there is a difference between core morality and complete altruism. We have duties to cooperate and reciprocate, but no duty to serve those who manipulate us nor an obvious duty to sacrifice ourselves for people outside our domain of special responsibility. We have a special duty of high altruism toward those in the close circle of our concern, namely, our family and friends.

CONCLUSION

Martin Luther once said that humanity is like a man who, when mounting a horse, always falls off on the opposite side, especially when he tries to overcompensate for his previous exaggerations. So it is with ethical egoism. Trying to compensate for an irrational, guilt-ridden, Sucker altruism of the morality of self-effacement, it falls off the horse on the other side, embracing a Cheater's preoccupation with self-exaltation that robs the self of the deepest joys in life. Only the person who mounts properly, avoiding both extremes, is likely to ride the horse of happiness to its goal.

NOTES

1. Ayn Rand, *The Virtue of Selfishness* (New American Library, 1964), pp. vii and 27–32; 80ff.

2. Brian Medlin, "Ultimate Principles and Ethical Egoism," *Australasian Journal of Philosophy* (1957), pp. 111–118; reprinted in Louis Pojman, *Ethical Theory*, pp. 91–95.

3. See Jesse Kalin, "In Defense of Egoism," in *Ethical Theory*, 4th ed., ed. Louis Pojman (Wadsworth, 2002), p. 95f.

4. Richard Dawkins, *The Selfish Gene* (Oxford University Press, 1976), Ch. 10.

5. J. L. Mackie, "The Law of the Jungle: Moral Alternatives and Principles of Evolution," *Philosophy* 53 (1978).

From *Utilitarianism*

John Stuart Mill

CHAPTER II.
WHAT UTILITARIANISM IS

* * *

The creed which accepts, as the foundation of morals, Utility, or the Greatest Happiness Principle, holds that actions are right in proportion as they tend to promote happiness, wrong as they tend to produce the reverse of happiness. By happiness is intended pleasure, and the absence of pain; by unhappiness, pain, and the privation of pleasure. To give a clear view of the moral standard set up by the theory, much more requires to be said; in particular, what things it includes in the ideas of pain and pleasure; and to what extent this is left an open question. But these supplementary explanations do not affect the theory of life on which this theory of morality is grounded—namely, that pleasure, and freedom from pain, are the only things desirable as ends; and that all desirable things (which are as numerous in the utilitarian as in any other scheme) are desirable either for the pleasure inherent in themselves, or as means to the promotion of pleasure and the prevention of pain.

Now, such a theory of life excites in many minds, and among them in some of the most estimable in feeling and purpose, inveterate dislike. To suppose that life has (as they express it) no higher end than pleasure—no better and nobler object of desire and pursuit—they designate as utterly mean and grovelling; as a doctrine worthy only of swine, to whom the followers of Epicurus were, at a very early period, contemptuously likened; and modern holders of the doctrine are occasionally made the subject of equally polite comparisons by its German, French, and English assailants.

When thus attacked, the Epicureans have always answered, that it is not they, but their accusers, who represent human nature in a degrading light; since the accusation supposes human beings to be capable of no pleasures except those of which swine are capable.

John Stuart Mill, *Utilitarianism*, Chapter 2 (edited).

If this supposition were true, the charge could not be gainsaid, but would then be no longer an imputation; for if the sources of pleasure were precisely the same to human beings and to swine, the rule of life which is good enough for the one would be good enough for the other. The comparison of the Epicurean life to that of beasts is felt as degrading, precisely because a beast's pleasures do not satisfy a human being's conceptions of happiness. Human beings have faculties more elevated than the animal appetites, and when once made conscious of them, do not regard anything as happiness which does not include their gratification. I do not, indeed, consider the Epicureans to have been by any means faultless in drawing out their scheme of consequences from the utilitarian principle. To do this in any sufficient manner, many Stoic, as well as Christian elements require to be included. But there is no known Epicurean theory of life which does not assign to the pleasures of the intellect, of the feelings and imagination, and of the moral sentiments, a much higher value as pleasures than to those of mere sensation. It must be admitted, however, that utilitarian writers in general have placed the superiority of mental over bodily pleasures chiefly in the greater permanency, safety, uncostliness, &c., of the former—that is, in their circumstantial advantages rather than in their intrinsic nature. And on all these points utilitarians have fully proved their case; but they might have taken the other, and, as it may be called, higher ground, with entire consistency. It is quite compatible with the principle of utility to recognise the fact, that some *kinds* of pleasure are more desirable and more valuable than others. It would be absurd that while, in estimating all other things, quality is considered as well as quantity, the estimation of pleasures should be supposed to depend on quantity alone.

If I am asked, what I mean by difference of quality in pleasures, or what makes one pleasure more valuable than another, merely as a pleasure, except its being greater in amount, there is but one possible answer. Of two pleasures, if there be one to which all or almost all who have experience of both give a decided preference, irrespective of any feeling of moral obligation to prefer it, that is the more desirable pleasure. If one of the two is, by those who are competently acquainted with both, placed so far above the other that they prefer it, even though knowing it to be attended with a greater amount of discontent, and would not resign it for any quantity of the other pleasure which their nature is capable of, we are justified in ascribing to the preferred enjoyment a superiority in quality, so far outweighing quantity as to render it, in comparison, of small account.

Now it is an unquestionable fact that those who are equally acquainted with, and equally capable of appreciating and enjoying, both, do give a most marked preference to the manner of existence which employs their higher faculties. Few human creatures would consent to be changed into any of the lower animals, for a promise of the fullest allowance of a beast's pleasures; no intelligent human being would consent to be a fool, no instructed person would be an ignoramus, no person of feeling and conscience would be selfish and base, even though they should be persuaded that the fool, the dunce, or the rascal is better satisfied with his lot than they are with theirs. They would not resign what they possess more than he, for the most complete satisfaction of all the desires which they have in common with him. If they ever fancy they would, it is only in cases of unhappiness so extreme, that to escape from it they would exchange their lot for almost any other, however, undesirable in their own eyes. A being of higher faculties requires more to make him happy, is capable probably of more acute suffering, and is certainly accessible to it at more points, than one of an inferior type; but in spite of these liabilities, he can never really wish to sink into what he feels to be a lower grade of existence. We may give what explanation we please of this unwillingness; we may attribute it to pride, a name which is given indiscriminately to some of the most and to some of the least estimable feelings of which mankind are capable; we may refer it to the love of liberty and personal independence, an appeal to which was with the Stoics one of the most effective means for the inculcation of it; to the love of power, or the love of excitement, both of which do really enter into and

contribute to it: but its most appropriate appellation is a sense of dignity, which all human beings possess in one form or other, and in some, though by no means in exact, proportion to their higher faculties, and which is so essential a part of the happiness of those in whom it is strong, that nothing which conflicts with it could be, otherwise than momentarily, an object of desire to them. Whoever supposes that this preference takes place at a sacrifice of happiness—that the superior being, in anything like equal circumstances, is not happier than the inferior—confounds the two very different ideas, of happiness, and content. It is indisputable that the being whose capacities of enjoyment are low, has the greatest chance of having them fully satisfied; and a highly-endowed being will always feel that any happiness which he can look for, as the world is constitute, is imperfect. But he can learn to bear its imperfections, if they are at all bearable; and they will not make him envy the being who is indeed unconscious of the imperfections, but only because he feels not at all the good which those imperfections qualify. It is better to be a human being dissatisfied than a pig satisfied; better to be Socrates dissatisfied than a fool satisfied. And if the fool, or the pig, is of a different opinion, it is because they only know their own side of the question. The other party to the comparison knows both sides.

It may be objected, that many who are capable of the higher pleasures, occasionally, under the influence of temptation, postpone them to the lower. But this is quite compatible with a full appreciation of the intrinsic superiority of the higher. Men often, from infirmity of character, make their election for the nearer good, though they know it to be the less valuable; and this no less when the choice is between two bodily pleasures, than when it is between bodily and mental. They pursue sensual indulgences to the injury of health, though perfectly aware that health is the greater good. It may be further objected, that many who begin with youthful enthusiasm for everything noble, as they advance in years sink into indolence and selfishness. But I do not believe that those who undergo this very common change, voluntarily choose the lower description of pleasures in preference to the higher. I believe that before they devote themselves exclusively to the one, they have already become incapable of the other. Capacity for the nobler feelings is in most natures a very tender plant, easily killed, not only by hostile influences, but by mere want of sustenance; and in the majority of young persons it speedily dies away if the occupations to which their position in life has devoted them, and the society into which it has thrown them, are not favourable to keeping that higher capacity in exercise. Men lose their high aspirations as they lose their intellectual tastes, because they have not time or opportunity for indulging them; and they addict themselves to inferior pleasures, not because they deliberately prefer them, but because they are either the only ones to which they have access, or the only ones which they are any longer capable of enjoying. It may be questioned whether any one who has remained equally susceptible to both classes of pleasures, ever knowingly and calmly preferred the lower; though many, in all ages, have broken down in an ineffectual attempt to combine both.

From this verdict of the only competent judges, I apprehend there can be no appeal. On a question which is the best worth having of two pleasures, or which of two modes of existence is the most grateful to the feelings, apart from its moral attributes and from its consequences, the judgment of those who are qualified by knowledge of both, or, if they differ, that of the majority among them, must be admitted as final. And there needs be the less hesitation to accept this judgment respecting the quality of pleasures, since there is no other tribunal to be referred to even on the question of quantity. What means are there of determining which is the acutest of two pairs, or the intensest of two pleasurable sensations, except the general suffrage of those who are familiar with both? Neither pains nor pleasures are homogeneous, and pain is always heterogeneous with pleasure. What is there to decide whether a particular pleasure is worth purchasing at the cost of a particular pain, except the feelings and judgment of the experienced? When, therefore, those feelings and judgment declare the pleasures derived from the higher faculties to be preferable *in kind,* apart from the question of intensity, to those of which the animal nature, disjoined from the higher faculties, is susceptible, they are entitled on this subject to the same regard.

I have dwelt on this point, as being a necessary part of a perfectly just conception of Utility or Happiness, considered as the directive rule of human conduct. But it is by no means an indispensable condition to the acceptance of the utilitarian standard; for that standard is not the agent's own greatest happiness, but the greatest amount of happiness altogether; and if it may possibly be doubted whether a noble character is always the happier for its nobleness, there can be no doubt that it makes other people happier, and that the world in general is immensely a gainer by it. Utilitarianism, therefore, could only attain its end by the general cultivation of nobleness of character, even if each individual were only benefited by the nobleness of others, and his own, so far as happiness is concerned, were a sheer deduction from the benefit. But the bare enunciation of such an absurdity as this last, renders refutation superfluous.

According to the Greatest Happiness Principle, as above explained, the ultimate end, with reference to and for the sake of which all other things are desirable (whether we are considering our own good or that of other people), is an existence exempt as far as possible from pain, and as rich as possible in enjoyments, both in point of quantity and quality; the test of quality, and the rule for measuring it against quantity, being the preference felt by those who, in their opportunities of experience, to which must be added their habits of self-consciousness and self-observation, are best furnished with the means of comparison. This being, according to the utilitarian opinion, the end of human action, is necessarily also the standard of morality; which may accordingly be defined, the rules and precepts for human conduct, by the observance of which an existence such as has been described might be, to the greatest extent possible, secured to all mankind; and not to them only, but, so far as the nature of things admits, to the whole sentient creation.

* * *

I must again repeat, what the assailants of utilitarianism seldom have the justice to acknowledge, that the happiness which forms the utilitarian standard of what is right in conduct, is not the agent's own happiness, but that of all concerned. As between his own happiness and that of others, utilitarianism requires him to be as strictly impartial as a disinterested and benevolent spectator. In the golden rule of Jesus of Nazareth, we read the complete spirit of the ethics of utility. To do as one would be done by, and to love one's neighbour as oneself, constitute the ideal perfection of utilitarian morality. As the means of making the nearest approach to this ideal, utility would enjoin, first, that laws and social arrangements should place the happiness, or (as speaking practically it may be called) the interest, of every individual, as nearly as possible in harmony with the interest of the whole; and secondly, that education and opinion, which have so vast a power over human character, should so use that power as to establish in the mind of every individual an indissoluble association between his own happiness and the good of the whole; especially between his own happiness and the practice of such modes of conduct, negative and positive, as regard for the universal happiness prescribes: so that not only he may be unable to conceive the possibility of happiness to himself, consistently with conduct opposed to the general good, but also that a direct impulse to promote the general good may be in every individual one of the habitual motives of action, and the sentiments connected therewith may fill a large and prominent place in every human being's sentient existence. If the impugners of the utilitarian morality represented it to their own minds in this its true character, I know not what recommendation possessed by any other morality they could possibly affirm to be wanting to it: what more beautiful or more exalted developments of human nature any other ethical system can be supposed to foster, or what springs of action, not accessible to the utilitarian, such systems rely on for giving effect to their mandates.

* * *

It may not be superfluous to notice a few more of the common misapprehensions of utilitarian ethics, even those which are so obvious and gross that it might appear impossible for any person of candour and intelligence to fall into them: since persons, even of considerable mental endowments, often give themselves so little trouble to understand the bearings of any opinion against which they entertain a prejudice, and men are in general so little conscious of this voluntary ignorance as a defect, that the vulgarest misunderstandings of ethical doctrines are continually met with in the deliberate writings of persons of the greatest pretensions both to high principle and to philosophy. We not uncommonly hear the doctrine of utility inveighed against as a *godless* doctrine. If it be necessary to say anything at all against so mere an assumption, we may say that the question depends upon what idea we have formed of the moral character of the Deity. If it be a true belief that God desires, above all things, the happiness of his creatures, and that this was his purpose in their creation, utility is not only not a godless doctrine, but more profoundly religious than any other. If it be meant that utilitarianism does not recognise the revealed will of God as the supreme law of morals, I answer, that an utilitarian who believes in the perfect goodness and wisdom of God, necessarily believes that whatever God has thought fit to reveal on the subject of morals, must fulfil the requirements of utility in a supreme degree. But others besides utilitarians have been of opinion that the Christian revelation was intended, and is fitted, to inform the hearts and minds of mankind with a spirit which should enable them to find for themselves what is right, and incline them to do it when found, rather than to tell them, except in a very general way, what it is: and that we need a doctrine of ethics, carefully followed out, to *interpret* to us the will of God. Whether this opinion is correct or not, it is superfluous here to discuss; since whatever aid religion, either natural or revealed, can afford to ethical investigation, is as open to the utilitarian moralist as to any other. He can use it as the testimony of God to the usefulness or hurtfulness of any given course of action, by as good a right as others can use it for the indication of a transcendental law, having no connexion with usefulness or with happiness.

Again, Utility is often summarily stigmatized as an immoral doctrine by giving it the name of Expediency, and taking advantage of the popular use of that term to contrast it with Principle. But the Expedient, in the sense in which it is opposed to the Right, generally means that which is expedient for the particular interest of the agent himself: as when a minister sacrifices the interest of his country to keep himself in place. When it means anything better than this, it means that which is expedient for some immediate object, some temporary purpose, but which violates a rule whose observance is expedient in a much higher degree. The Expedient, in this sense, instead of being the same thing with the useful, is a branch of the hurtful. Thus, it would often be expedient, for the purpose of getting over some momentary embarrassment, or attaining some object immediately useful to ourselves or others, to tell a lie. But inasmuch as the cultivation in ourselves of a sensitive feeling on the subject of veracity, is one of the most useful, and the enfeeblement of that feeling one of the most hurtful, things to which our conduct can be instrumental; and inasmuch as any, even unintentional, deviation from truth, does that much towards weakening the trustworthiness of human assertion, which is not only the principal support of all present social well-being, but the insufficiency of which does more than any one thing that can be named to keep back civilisation, virtue, everything on which human happiness on the largest scale depends; we feel that the violation, for a present advantage, of a rule of such transcendent expediency, is not expedient, and that he who, for the sake of a convenience to himself or to some other individual, does what depends on him to deprive mankind of the good, and inflict upon them the evil, involved in the greater or less reliance which they can place in each other's word, acts the part of one of their worst enemies. Yet that even this rule, sacred as it is, admits of possible exceptions, is acknowledged by all moralists; the chief of which is when the withholding of some fact (as of information from a malefactor, or of bad news from a person dangerously ill) would preserve some one (especially a person other than oneself) from great and unmerited evil, and when the withholding can only be effected by denial. But in order that the exception may not extend itself beyond the need, and may have the least possible effect in weakening reliance on veracity, it ought to be recognized, and, if possible, its limits defined; and if the principle of utility is good for anything, it must be good for weighing these conflicting utilities against one another, and marking out the region within which one or the other preponderates.

* * *

From *A Theory of Justice*

JOHN RAWLS

THE ROLE OF JUSTICE

Justice is the first virtue of social institutions, as truth is of systems of thought. A theory however elegant and economical must be rejected or revised if it is untrue; likewise laws and institutions no matter how efficient and well-arranged must be reformed or abolished if they are unjust. Each person possesses an inviolability founded on justice that even the welfare of society as a whole cannot override. For this reason justice denies

From John Rawls, *A Theory of Justice*, rev. ed. (Cambridge: Harvard University Press, 1999) 3–6, 10–15, 52–54. Copyright © 1971, 1999 by the President and Fellows of Harvard College. Reprinted by permission of the publisher.

that the loss of freedom for some is made right by a greater good shared by others. It does not allow that the sacrifices imposed on a few are outweighed by the larger sum of advantages enjoyed by many. Therefore in a just society the liberties of equal citizenship are taken as settled, the rights secured by justice are not subject to political bargaining or to the calculus of social interests. The only thing that permits us to acquiesce in an erroneous theory is the lack of a better one; analogously, an injustice is tolerable only when it is necessary to avoid an even greater injustice. Being first virtues of human activities, truth and justice are uncompromising.

These propositions seem to express our intuitive conviction of the primacy of justice. No doubt they are expressed too strongly. In any event I wish to inquire whether these contentions or others similar to them are sound, and if so how they can be accounted for. To this end it is necessary to work out a theory of justice in the light of which these assertions can be interpreted and assessed. I shall begin by considering the role of the principles of justice. Let us assume, to fix ideas, that a society is a more or less self-sufficient association of persons who in their relations to one another recognize certain rules of conduct as binding and who for the most part act in accordance with them. Suppose further that these rules specify a system of cooperation designed to advance the good of those taking part in it. Then, although a society is a cooperative venture for mutual advantage, it is typically marked by a conflict as well as by an identity of interests. There is an identity of interests since social cooperation makes possible a better life for all than any would have if each were to live solely by his own efforts. There is a conflict of interests since persons are not indifferent as to how the greater benefits produced by their collaboration are distributed, for in order to pursue their ends they each prefer a larger to a lesser share. A set of principles is required for choosing among the various social arrangements which determine this division of advantages and for underwriting an agreement on the proper distributive shares. These principles are the principles of social justice: they provide a way of assigning rights and duties in the basic institutions of society and they define the appropriate distribution of the benefits and burdens of social cooperation.

Now let us say that a society is well-ordered when it is not only designed to advance the good of its members but when it is also effectively regulated by a public conception of justice. That is, it is a society in which (1) everyone accepts and knows that the others accept the same principles of justice, and (2) the basic social institutions generally satisfy and are generally known to satisfy these principles. In this case while men may put forth excessive demands on one another, they nevertheless acknowledge a common point of view from which their claims may be adjudicated. If men's inclination to self-interest makes their vigilance against one another necessary, their public sense of justice makes their secure association together

possible. Among individuals with disparate aims and purposes a shared conception of justice establishes the bonds of civic friendship; the general desire for justice limits the pursuit of other ends. One may think of a public conception of justice as constituting the fundamental charter of a well-ordered human association.

Existing societies are of course seldom well-ordered in this sense, for what is just and unjust is usually in dispute. Men disagree about which principles should define the basic terms of their association. Yet we may still say, despite this disagreement, that they each have a conception of justice. That is, they understand the need for, and they are prepared to affirm, a characteristic set of principles for assigning basic rights and duties and for determining what they take to be the proper distribution of the benefits and burdens of social cooperation. Thus it seems natural to think of the concept of justice as distinct from the various conceptions of justice and as being specified by the role which these different sets of principles, these different conceptions, have in common.[1] Those who hold different conceptions of justice can, then, still agree that institutions are just when no arbitrary distinctions are made between persons in the assigning of basic rights and duties and when the rules determine a proper balance between competing claims to the advantages of social life. Men can agree to this description of just institutions since the notions of an arbitrary distinction and of a proper balance, which are included in the concept of justice, are left open for each to interpret according to the principles of justice that he accepts. These principles single out which similarities and differences among persons are relevant in determining rights and duties and they specify which division of advantages is appropriate. Clearly this distinction between the concept and the various conceptions of justice settles no important questions. It simply helps to identify the role of the principles of social justice.

Some measure of agreement in conceptions of justice is, however, not the only prerequisite for a viable human community. There are other fundamental social problems, in particular those of coordination, efficiency, and stability. Thus the plans of individuals need to be fitted together so that their activities are compatible with one another and they can all be carried through without anyone's legitimate expectations being severely disappointed. Moreover, the execution of these plans should lead to the achievement of social ends in ways that are efficient and consistent with justice. And finally, the scheme of social cooperation must be stable: it must be more or less regularly complied with and its basic rules willingly acted upon; and when infractions occur, stabilizing forces should exist that prevent further violations and tend to restore the arrangement. Now it is evident that these three problems are connected with that of justice. In the absence of a certain measure of agreement on what is just and unjust, it is clearly more difficult for individuals to coordinate their plans efficiently in order to insure that mutually beneficial arrangements are maintained. Distrust and resentment corrode the ties of civility, and suspicion and hostility tempt men to act in ways they would otherwise avoid. So while the distinctive role of conceptions of justice is to specify basic rights and duties and to determine the appropriate distributive shares, the way in which a conception does this is bound to affect the problems of efficiency, coordination, and stability. We cannot, in general, assess a conception of justice by its distributive role alone, however useful this role may be in identifying the concept of justice. We must take into account its wider connections; for even though justice has a certain priority, being the most important virtue of institutions, it is still true that, other things equal, one conception of justice is preferable to another when its broader consequences are more desirable.

* * *

THE MAIN IDEA OF THE THEORY OF JUSTICE

My aim is to present a conception of justice which generalizes and carries to a higher level of abstraction the familiar theory of the social contract as found, say, in Locke. Rousseau, and Kant.[2] In order to do this we are not to think of the original contract as one to enter a particular society or to set up a particular form of government. Rather, the guiding idea is that the principles of justice for the basic structure of society are the object of the original agreement. They are the

principles that free and rational persons concerned to further their own interests would accept in an initial position of equality as defining the fundamental terms of their association. These principles are to regulate all further agreements; they specify the kinds of social cooperation that can be entered into and the forms of government that can be established. This way of regarding the principles of justice I shall call justice as fairness.

Thus we are to imagine that those who engage in social cooperation choose together, in one joint act, the principles which are to assign basic rights and duties and to determine the division of social benefits. Men are to decide in advance how they are to regulate their claims against one another and what is to be the foundation charter of their society. Just as each person must decide by rational reflection what constitutes his good, that is, the system of ends which it is rational for him to pursue, so a group of persons must decide once and for all what is to count among them as just and unjust. The choice which rational men would make in this hypothetical situation of equal liberty assuming for the present that this choice problem has a solution, determines the principles of justice.

In justice as fairness the original position of equality corresponds to the state of nature in the traditional theory of the social contract. This original position is not, of course, thought of as an actual historical state of affairs, much less as a primitive condition of culture. It is understood as a purely hypothetical situation characterized so as to lead to a certain conception of justice.[3] Among the essential features of this situation is that no one knows his place in society, his class position or social status, nor does any one know his fortune in the distribution of natural assets and abilities, his intelligence, strength, and the like. I shall even assume that the parties do not know their conceptions of the good or their special psychological propensities. The principles of justice are chosen behind a veil of ignorance. This ensures that no one is advantaged or disadvantaged in the choice of principles by the outcome of natural chance or the contingency of social circumstances. Since all are similarly situated and no one is able to design principles to favor his particular condition, the principles of justice are the result of a fair agreement or bargain. For given the circumstances of the original position, the symmetry of everyone's relations to each other, this initial situation is fair between individuals as moral persons, that is, as rational beings with their own ends and capable, I shall assume, of a sense of justice. The original position is, one might say, the appropriate initial status quo, and thus the fundamental agreements reached in it are fair. This explains the propriety of the name "justice as fairness": it conveys the idea that the principles of justice are agreed to in an initial situation that is fair. The name does not mean that the concepts of justice and fairness are the same, any more than the phrase "poetry as metaphor" means that the concepts of poetry and metaphor are the same.

Justice as fairness begins, as I have said, with one of the most general of all choices which persons might make together, namely, with the choice of the first principles of a conception of justice which is to regulate all subsequent criticism and reform of institutions. Then, having chosen a conception of justice, we can suppose that they are to choose a constitution and a legislature to enact laws, and so on, all in accordance with the principles of justice initially agreed upon. Our social situation is just if it is such that by this sequence of hypothetical agreements we would have contracted into the general system of rules which defines it. Moreover, assuming that the original position does determine a set of principles (that is, that a particular conception of justice would be chosen), it will then be true that whenever social institutions satisfy these principles those engaged in them can say to one another that they are cooperating on terms to which they would agree if they were free and equal persons whose relations with respect to one another were fair. They could all view their arrangements as meeting the stipulations which they would acknowledge in an initial situation that embodies widely accepted and reasonable constraints on the choice of principles. The general recognition of this fact would provide the basis for a public acceptance of the corresponding principles of justice. No society can, of course, be a scheme of cooperation which men enter voluntarily in a literal sense; each person finds himself placed at birth in some particular position in some particular society, and the nature of this position materially affects his life prospects. Yet a society satisfying the principles of justice as fairness comes as close as a society can to being a voluntary scheme, for it meets the principles which free and equal persons would assent to under circumstances that are fair. In this sense its members are autonomous and the obligations they recognize self-imposed.

One feature of justice as fairness is to think of the parties in the initial situation as rational and mutually disinterested. This does not mean that the parties are egoists, that is, individuals with only certain kinds of interests, say in wealth, prestige, and domination. But they are conceived as not taking an interest in one another's interests. They are to presume that even their spiritual aims may be opposed, in the way that the aims of those of different religions may be opposed. Moreover, the concept of rationality must be interpreted as far as possible in the narrow sense, standard in economic theory, of taking the most effective means to given ends. I shall modify this concept to some extent, as explained later, but one must try to avoid introducing into it any controversial ethical elements. The initial situation must be characterized by stipulations that are widely accepted.

In working out the conception of justice as fairness one main task clearly is to determine which principles of justice would be chosen in the original position. To do this we must describe this situation in some detail and formulate with care the problem of choice which it presents. These matters I shall take up in the immediately succeeding chapters. It may be observed, however, that once the principles of justice are thought of as arising from an original agreement in a situation of equality, it is an open question whether the principle of utility would be acknowledged. Offhand it hardly seems likely that persons who view themselves as equals, entitled to press their claims upon one another, would agree to a principle which may require lesser life prospects for some simply for the sake of a greater sum of advantages enjoyed by others. Since each desires to protect his interests, his capacity to advance his conception of the good, no one has a reason to acquiesce in an enduring loss for himself in order to bring about a greater net balance of satisfaction. In the absence of strong and lasting benevolent impulses, a rational man would not accept a basic structure merely because it maximized the algebraic sum of advantages irrespective of its permanent effects on his own basic rights and interests. Thus it seems that the principle of utility is incompatible with the conception of social cooperation among equals for mutual advantage. It appears to be inconsistent with the idea of reciprocity implicit in the notion of a well-ordered society. Or, at any rate, so I shall argue.

I shall maintain instead that the persons in the initial situation would choose two rather different principles: the first requires equality in the assignment of basic rights and duties, while the second holds that social and economic inequalities, for example inequalities of wealth and authority are just only if they result in compensating benefits for everyone, and in particular for the least advantaged members of society. These principles rule out justifying institutions on the grounds mat the hardships of some are offset by a greater good in the aggregate. It may be expedient but it is not just that some should have less in order that others may prosper. But there is no injustice in the greater benefits earned by a few provided that the situation of persons not so fortunate is thereby improved. The intuitive idea is that since everyone's well-being depends upon a scheme of cooperation without which no one could have a satisfactory life, the division of advantages should be such as to draw forth the willing cooperation of everyone taking part in it, including those less well situated. The two principles mentioned seem to be a fair basis on which those better endowed, or more fortunate in their social position, neither of which we can be said to deserve, could expect the willing cooperation of others when some workable scheme is a necessary condition of the welfare of all.[4] Once we decide to look for a conception of justice that prevents the use of the accidents of natural endowment and the contingencies of social circumstance as counters in a quest for political and economic advantage, we are led to these principles. They express the result of leaving aside those aspects of the social world that seem arbitrary from a moral point of view.

The problem of the choice of principles, however, is extremely difficult. I do not expect the answer I shall

suggest to be convincing to everyone. It is, therefore, worth noting from the outset that justice as fairness, like other contract views, consists of two parts: (1) an interpretation of the initial situation and of the problem of choice posed there, and (2) a set of principles which, it is argued, would be agreed to. One may accept the first part of the theory (or some variant thereof), but not the other, and conversely. The concept of the initial contractual situation may seem reasonable although the particular principles proposed are rejected. To be sure, I want to maintain that the most appropriate conception of this situation does lead to principles of justice contrary to utilitarianism and perfectionism, and therefore that the contract doctrine provides an alternative to these views. Still, one may dispute this contention even though one grants that the contractarian method is a useful way of studying ethical theories and of setting forth their underlying assumptions.

Justice as fairness is an example of what I have called a contract theory. Now there may be an objection to the term "contract" and related expressions, but I think it will serve reasonably well. Many words have misleading connotations which at first are likely to confuse. The terms "utility" and "utilitarianism" are surely no exception. They too have unfortunate suggestions which hostile critics have been willing to exploit; yet they are clear enough for those prepared to study utilitarian doctrine. The same should be true of the term "contract" applied to moral theories. As I have mentioned, to understand it one has to keep in mind that it implies a certain level of abstraction. In particular, the content of the relevant agreement is not to enter a given society or to adopt a given form of government, but to accept certain moral principles. Moreover, the undertakings referred to are purely hypothetical: a contract view holds that certain principles would be accepted in a well-defined initial situation.

The merit of the contract terminology is that it conveys the idea that principles of justice may be conceived as principles that would be chosen by rational persons, and that in this way conceptions of justice may be explained and justified. The theory of justice is a part, perhaps the most significant part, of the theory of rational choice. Furthermore, principles of justice deal with conflicting claims upon the advantages won by social cooperation; they apply to the relations among several persons or groups. The word "contract" suggests this plurality as well as the condition that the appropriate division of advantages must be in accordance with principles acceptable to all parties. The condition of publicity for principles of justice is also connoted by the contract phraseology. Thus, if these principles are the outcome of an agreement, citizens have a knowledge of the principles that others follow. It is characteristic of contract theories to stress the public nature of political principles. Finally there is the long tradition of the contract doctrine. Expressing the tie with this line of thought helps to define ideas and accords with natural piety. There are then several advantages in the use of the term "contract." With due precautions taken, it should not be misleading.

A final remark. Justice as fairness is not a complete contract theory. For it is clear that the contractarian idea can be extended to the choice of more or less an entire ethical system, that is, to a system including principles for all the virtues and not only for justice. Now for the most part I shall consider only principles of justice and others closely related to them; I make no attempt to discuss the virtues in a systematic way. Obviously if justice as fairness succeeds reasonably well, a next step would be to study the more general view suggested by the name "rightness as fairness." But even this wider theory fails to embrace all moral relationships, since it would seem to include only our relations with other persons and to leave out of account how we are to conduct ourselves toward animals and the rest of nature. I do not contend that the contract notion offers a way to approach these questions which are certainly of the first importance; and I shall have to put them aside. We must recognize the limited scope of justice as fairness and of the general type of view that it exemplifies. How far its conclusions must be revised once these other matters are understood cannot be decided in advance.

* * *

TWO PRINCIPLES OF JUSTICE

I shall now state in a provisional form the two principles of justice that I believe would be agreed to in the original position The first formulation of these principles is tentative. As we go on I shall consider several formulations and approximate step by step the final statement to be given much later. I believe that doing this allows the exposition to proceed in a natural way.

The first statement of the two principles reads as follows.

First: each person is to have an equal right to the most extensive scheme of equal basic liberties compatible with a similar scheme of liberties for others.

Second: social and economic inequalities are to be arranged so that they are both (a) reasonably expected to be to everyone's advantage, and (b) attached to positions and offices open to all.

* * *

These principles primarily apply, as I have said, to the basic structure of society and govern the assignment of rights and duties and regulate the distribution of social and economic advantages. Their formulation presupposes that, for the purposes of a theory of justice, the social structure may be viewed as having two more or less distinct parts, the first principle applying to the one, the second principle to the other. Thus we distinguish between the aspects of the social system that define and secure the equal basic liberties and the aspects that specify and establish social and economic inequalities. Now it is essential to observe that the basic liberties are given by a list of such liberties. Important among these are political liberty (the right to vote and to hold public office) and freedom of speech and assembly: liberty of conscience and freedom of thought: freedom of the person, which includes freedom from psychological oppression and physical assault and dismemberment (integrity of the person); the right to hold personal property and freedom from arbitrary arrest and seizure as defined by the concept of the rule of law. These liberties are to be equal by the first principle.

The second principle applies, in the first approximation, to the distribution of income and wealth and to the design of organizations that make use of differences in authority and responsibility. While the distribution of wealth and income need not be equal, it must be to everyone's advantage and at the same time, positions of authority and responsibility must be accessible to all. One applies the second principle by holding positions open, and then, subject to this constraint, arranges social and economic inequalities so that everyone benefits.

These principles are to be arranged in a serial order with the first principle prior to the second. This ordering means that infringements of the basic equal liberties protected by the first principle cannot be justified, or compensated for, by greater social and economic advantages. These liberties have a central range of application within which they can be limited and compromised only when they conflict with other basic liberties. Since they may be limited when they clash with one another, none of these liberties is absolute; but however they are adjusted to form one system, this system is to be the same for all. It is difficult, and perhaps impossible, to give a complete specification of these liberties independently from the particular circumstances—social, economic, and technological—of a given society. The hypothesis is that the general form of such a list could be devised with sufficient exactness to sustain this conception of justice. Of course, liberties not on the list, for example, the right to own certain kinds of property (e.g., means of production) and freedom of contract as understood by the doctrine of laissez-faire are not basic; and so they are not protected by the priority of the first principle. Finally, in regard to the second principle, the distribution of wealth and income, and positions of authority and responsibility, are to be consistent with both the basic liberties and equality of opportunity.

The two principles are rather specific in their content, and their acceptance rests on certain assumptions that I must eventually try to explain and justify. For the present, it should be observed that these principle are a special case of a more general conception of justice that can be expressed as follows.

> All social values—liberty and opportunity, income and wealth, and the social bases of self-respect—are to be distributed equally unless an unequal distribution of any, or all, of these values is to everyone's advantage.

Injustice, then, is simply inequalities that are not to the benefit of all. Of course, this conception is extremely vague and requires interpretation.

NOTES

1. Here I follow H. L. A. Hart, *The Concept of Law* (Oxford, The Clarendon Press, 1961), pp. 155–159.

2. As the text suggests, I shall regard Locke's *Second Treatise of Government,* Rousseau's *The Social Contract,* and Kant's ethical works beginning with *The Foundations of the Metaphysics of Morals* as definitive of the contract tradition. For all of its greatness, Hobbes's *Leviathan* raises special problems. A general historical survey is provided by J. W. Gough, *The Social Contract,* 2nd ed. (Oxford, The Clarendon Press, 1957), and Otto Gierke, *Natural Law and the Theory of Society.* trans. with an introduction by Ernest Barker (Cambridge, The University Press, 1934). A presentation of the contract view as primarily an ethical theory is to be found in G. R. Grice, *The Grounds of Moral Judgment* (Cambridge, The University Press, 1967). See also §19, note 30.

3. Kant is clear that the original agreement is hypothetical. See *The Metaphysics of Morals,* pt. I *(Rechtslehre),* especially §§47, 52; and pt. II of the essay "Concerning the Common Saying: This May Be True in Theory but It Does Not Apply in Practice," in *Kant's Political Writings,* ed. Hans Reiss and trans. by H. B. Nisbet (Cambridge, The University Press, 1970), pp. 73–87. See Georges Vlachos, *La Pensée politique de Kant* (Paris, Presses Universitaires de France, 1962), pp. 326–335; and J. G. Murphy, *Kant: The Philosophy of Right* (London, Macmillan, 1970), pp. 109–112, 133–136, for a further discussion.

4. For the formulation of this intuitive idea I am indebted to Allan Gibbard.

The Entitlement Theory of Justice

ROBERT NOZICK

The term "distributive justice" is not a neutral one. Hearing the term "distribution," most people presume that some thing or mechanism uses some principle or criterion to give out a supply of things. Into this process of distributing shares some error may have crept. So it is an open question, at least, whether *re*distribution should take place; whether we should do again what has already been done once, though poorly. However, we are not in the position of children who have been given portions of pie by someone who now makes last minute adjustments to rectify careless cutting. There is no *central* distribution, no person or group entitled to control all the resources, jointly deciding how they are to be doled out. What each person gets, he gets from others who give to him in exchange for something, or as a gift. In a free society, diverse persons control different resources, and new holdings arise out of the voluntary exchanges and actions of persons. There is no more a distributing or distribution of shares than there is a distributing of mates in a society in which persons choose whom they shall marry. The total result is the product of many individual decisions which the different individuals involved are entitled to make. Some uses of the term "distribution," it is true, do not imply a previous distributing appropriately judged by some criterion (for example, "probability distribution"); nevertheless, . . . it would be best to use a terminology that clearly is neutral. We shall speak of people's holdings; a principle of justice in holdings describes (part of) what justice tells us (requires) about holdings. I shall state first what I take to be the correct view about justice in holdings, and then turn to the discussion of alternate views.

THE ENTITLEMENT THEORY

The subject of justice in holdings consists of three major topics. The first is the *original acquisition of*

holdings, the appropriation of unheld things. This includes the issues of how unheld things may come to be held, the process, or processes, by which unheld things may come to be held, the things that may come to be held by these processes, the extent of what comes to be held by a particular process, and so on. We shall refer to the complicated truth about this topic, which we shall not formulate here, as the principle of justice in acquisition. The second topic concerns the *transfer of holdings* from one person to another. By what processes may a person transfer holdings to another? How may a person acquire a holding from another who holds it? Under this topic come general descriptions of voluntary exchange, and gift and (on the other hand) fraud, as well as reference to particular conventional details fixed upon in a given society. The complicated truth about this subject (with placeholders for conventional details) we shall call the principle of justice in transfer. (And we shall suppose it also includes principles governing how a person may divest himself of a holding, passing it into an unheld state.)

If the world were wholly just, the following inductive definition would exhaustively cover the subject of justice in holdings.

1. A person who acquires a holding in accordance with the principle of justice in acquisition is entitled to that holding.
2. A person who acquires a holding in accordance with the principle of justice in transfer, from someone else entitled to the holding, is entitled to the holding.
3. No one is entitled to a holding except by (repeated) applications of 1 and 2.

The complete principle of distributive justice would say simply that a distribution is just if everyone is entitled to the holdings they possess under the distribution.

A distribution is just if it arises from another just distribution by legitimate means. The legitimate means of moving from one distribution to another are specified by the principle of justice in transfer. The legitimate first "moves" are specified by the principle of justice in acquisition.[1] Whatever arises from a just situation by just steps is itself just. The means of change specified by the principle of justice in transfer preserve justice.

* * *

Not all actual situations are generated in accordance with the two principles of justice in holdings: the principle of justice in acquisition and the principle of justice in transfer. Some people steal from others, or defraud them, or enslave them, seizing their product and preventing them from living as they choose, or forcibly exclude others from competing in exchanges. None of these are permissible modes of transition from one situation to another. And some persons acquire holdings by means not sanctioned by the principle of justice in acquisition. The existence of past injustice (previous violations of the first two principles of justice in holdings) raises the third major topic under justice in holdings: the rectification of injustice in holdings. If past injustice has shaped present holdings in various ways, some identifiable and some not, what now, if anything, ought to be done to rectify these injustices? What obligations do the performers of injustice have toward those whose position is worse than it would have been had the injustice not been done? Or, than it would have been had compensation been paid promptly? How, if at all, do things change if the beneficiaries and those made worse off are not the direct parties in the act of injustice, but, for example, their descendants? Is an injustice done to someone whose holding was itself based upon an unrectified injustice? How far back must one go in wiping clean the historical slate of injustices? What may victims of injustice permissibly do in order to rectify the injustices being done to them, including the many injustices done by persons acting through their government? I do not know of a thorough or theoretically sophisticated treatment of such issues. Idealizing greatly, let us suppose theoretical investigation will produce a principle of rectification. This principle uses historical information about previous situations and injustices done in them (as defined by the first two

principles of justice and rights against interference), and information about the actual course of events that flowed from these injustices, until the present, and it yields a description (or descriptions) of holdings in the society. The principle of rectification presumably will make use of its best estimate of subjunctive information about what would have occurred (or a probability distribution over what might have occurred, using the expected value) if the injustice had not taken place. If the actual description of holdings turns out not to be one of the descriptions yielded by the principle, then one of the descriptions yielded must be realized.[2]

The general outlines of the theory of justice in holdings are that the holdings of a person are just if he is entitled to them by the principles of justice in acquisition and transfer, or by the principle of rectification of injustice (as specified by the first two principles). If each person's holdings are just, then the total set (distribution) of holdings is just.

* * *

HISTORICAL PRINCIPLES AND END-RESULT PRINCIPLES

The general outlines of the entitlement theory illuminate the nature and defects of other conceptions of distributive justice. The entitlement theory of justice in distribution is *historical;* whether a distribution is just depends upon how it came about. In contrast, *current time-slice principles* of justice hold that the justice of a distribution is determined by how things are distributed (who has what) as judged by some *structural* principle(s) of just distribution. A utilitarian who judges between any two distributions by seeing which has the greater sum of utility and, if the sums tie, applies some fixed equality criterion to choose the more equal distribution, would hold a current time-slice principle of justice. As would someone who had a fixed schedule of trade-offs between the sum of happiness and equality. According to a current time-slice principle, all that needs to be looked at, in judging the justice of a distribution, is who ends up with what; in comparing any two distributions one need look only at the matrix presenting the distributions. No further information need be fed into a principle of justice. It is a consequence of such principles of justice that any two structurally identical distributions are equally just. (Two distributions are structurally identical if they present the same profile, but perhaps have different persons occupying the particular slots. My having ten and your having five, and my having five and your having ten are structurally identical distributions.) Welfare economics is the theory of current time-slice principles of justice. The subject is conceived as operating on matrices representing only current information about distribution. This, as well as some of the usual conditions (for example, the choice of distribution is invariant under relabeling of columns), guarantees that welfare economics will be a current time-slice theory, with all of its inadequacies.

Most persons do not accept current time-slice principles as constituting the whole story about distributive shares. They think it relevant in assessing the justice of a situation to consider not only the distribution it embodies, but also how that distribution came about. If some persons are in prison for murder or war crimes, we do not say that to assess the justice of the distribution in the society we must look only at what this person has, and that person has, and that person has, . . . at the current time. We think it relevant to ask whether someone did something so that he *deserved* to be punished, deserved to have a lower share. Most will agree to the relevance of further information with regard to punishments and penalties. Consider also desired things. One traditional socialist view is that workers are entitled to the product and full fruits of their labor; they have earned it; a distribution is unjust if it does not give the workers what they are entitled to. Such entitlements are based upon some past history. No socialist holding this view would find it comforting to be told that because the actual distribution *A* happens to coincide structurally with the one he desires *D, A* therefore is no less just than *D;* it differs only in that the "parasitic" owners of capital receive under *A* what the workers are entitled to under *D,* and the workers receive under *A* what the owners are

entitled to under *D,* namely very little. This socialist rightly, in my view, holds onto the notions of earning, producing, entitlement, desert, and so forth, and he rejects current time-slice principles that look only to the structure of the resulting set of holdings. (The set of holdings resulting from what? Isn't it implausible that how holdings are produced and come to exist has no effect at all on who should hold what?) His mistake lies in his view of what entitlements arise out of what sorts of productive processes.

We construe the position we discuss too narrowly by speaking of *current* time-slice principles. Nothing is changed if structural principles operate upon a time sequence of current time-slice profiles and, for example, give someone more now to counterbalance the less he has had earlier. A utilitarian or an egalitarian or any mixture of the two over time will inherit the difficulties of his more myopic comrades. He is not helped by the fact that *some* of the information others consider relevant in assessing a distribution is reflected, unrecoverably, in past matrices. Henceforth, we shall refer to such unhistorical principles of distributive justice, including the current time-slice principles, as *end-result principles* or *end-state principles.*

In contrast to end-result principles of justice, *historical principles* of justice hold that past circumstances or actions of people can create differential entitlements or differential deserts to things. An injustice can be worked by moving from one distribution to another structurally identical one, for the second, in profile the same, may violate people's entitlements or deserts; it may not fit the actual history.

PATTERNING

The entitlement principles of justice in holdings that we have sketched are historical principles of justice. To better understand their precise character, we shall distinguish them from another subclass of the historical principles. Consider, as an example, the principle of distribution according to moral merit. This principle requires that total distributive shares vary directly with moral merit; no person should have a greater share than anyone whose moral merit is greater. (If moral merit could be not merely ordered but measured on an interval or ratio scale, stronger principles could be formulated.) Or consider the principle that results by substituting "usefulness to society" for "moral merit" in the previous principle. Or instead of "distribute according to moral merit," or "distribute according to usefulness to society," we might consider "distribute according to the weighted sum of moral merit, usefulness to society, and need," with the weights of the different dimensions equal. Let us call a principle of distribution *patterned* if it specifies that a distribution is to vary along with some natural dimension, weighted sum of natural dimensions, or lexicographic ordering of natural dimensions. And let us say a distribution is patterned if it accords with some patterned principle. (I speak of natural dimensions, admittedly without a general criterion for them, because for any set of holdings some artificial dimensions can be gimmicked up to vary along with the distribution of the set.) The principle of distribution in accordance with moral merit is a patterned historical principle, which specifies a patterned distribution. "Distribute according to I.Q." is a patterned principle that looks to information not contained in distributional matrices. It is not historical, however, in that it does not look to any past actions creating differential entitlements to evaluate a distribution; it requires only distributional matrices whose columns are labeled by I.Q. scores. The distribution in a society, however, may be composed of such simple patterned distributions, without itself being simply patterned. Different sectors may operate different patterns, or some combination of patterns may operate in different proportions across a society. A distribution composed in this manner, from a small number of patterned distributions, we also shall term "patterned." And we extend the use of "pattern" to include the overall designs put forth by combinations of end-state principles.

Almost every suggested principle of distributive justice is patterned: to each according to his moral merit, or needs, or marginal product, or how hard he tries, or the weighted sum of the foregoing, and so on. The principle of entitlement we have sketched is *not* patterned.[3] There is no one natural dimension or weighted sum or combination of a small number of

natural dimensions that yields the distributions generated in accordance with the principle of entitlement. The set of holdings that results when some persons receive their marginal products, others win at gambling, others receive a share of their mate's income, others receive gifts from foundations, others receive interest on loans, others receive gifts from admirers, others receive returns on investment, others make for themselves much of what they have, others find things, and so on, will not be patterned.

* * *

HOW LIBERTY UPSETS PATTERNS

It is not clear how those holding alternative conceptions of distributive justice can reject the entitlement conception of justice in holdings. For suppose a distribution favored by one of these non-entitlement conceptions is realized. Let us suppose it is your favorite one and let us call this distribution D_1; perhaps everyone has an equal share, perhaps shares vary in accordance with some dimension you treasure. Now suppose that Wilt Chamberlain is greatly in demand by basketball teams, being a great gate attraction. (Also suppose contracts run only for a year, with players being free agents.) He signs the following sort of contract with a team: In each home game, twenty-five cents from the price of each ticket of admission goes to him. (We ignore the question of whether he is "gouging" the owners, letting them look out for themselves.) The season starts, and people cheerfully attend his team's games; they buy their tickets, each time dropping a separate twenty-five cents of their admission price into a special box with Chamberlain's name on it. They are excited about seeing him play; it is worth the total admission price to them. Let us suppose that in one season one million persons attend his home games, and Wilt Chamberlain winds up with $250,000, a much larger sum than the average income and larger even than anyone else has. Is he entitled to this income? Is this new distribution D_2, unjust? If so, why? There is *no* question about whether each of the people was entitled to the control over the resources they held in D_1; because that was the distribution (your favorite) that (for the purposes of argument) we assumed was acceptable. Each of these persons *chose* to give twenty-five cents of their money to Chamberlain. They could have spent it on going to the movies, or on candy bars, or on copies of *Dissent* magazine, or of *Monthly Review*. But they all, at least one million of them, converged on giving it to Wilt Chamberlain in exchange for watching him play basketball. If D_1 was a just distribution, and people voluntarily moved from it to D_2, transferring parts of their shares they were given under D_1 (what was it for if not to do something with?), isn't D_2 also just? If the people were entitled to dispose of the resources to which they were entitled (under D_1), didn't this include their being entitled to give it to, or exchange it with, Wilt Chamberlain? Can anyone else complain on grounds of justice? Each other person already has his legitimate share under D_1. Under D_1, there is nothing that anyone has that anyone else has a claim of justice against. After someone transfers something to Wilt Chamberlain, third parties *still* have their legitimate shares; *their* shares are not changed. By what process could such a transfer among two persons give rise to a legitimate claim of distributive justice on a portion of what was transferred, by a third party who had no claim of justice on any holding of the others *before* the transfer?[4] To cut off objections irrelevant here, we might imagine the exchanges occurring in a socialist society, after hours. After playing whatever basketball he does in his daily work, or doing whatever other daily work he does, Wilt Chamberlain decides to put in *overtime* to earn additional money. (First his work quota is set; he works time over that.) Or imagine it is a skilled juggler people like to see, who puts on shows after hours.

Why might someone work overtime in a society in which it is assumed their needs are satisfied? Perhaps because they care about things other than needs. I like to write in books that I read, and to have easy access to books for browsing at odd hours. It would be very pleasant and convenient to have the resources of Widener Library in my back yard. No society, I assume, will provide such resources close to each person who would like them as part of his regular allotment (under

D_1). Thus, persons either must do without some extra things that they want, or be allowed to do something extra to get some of these things. On what basis could the inequalities that would eventuate be forbidden? Notice also that small factories would spring up in a socialist society, unless forbidden. I melt down some of my personal possessions (under D_1) and build a machine out of the material. I offer you, and others, a philosophy lecture once a week in exchange for your cranking the handle on my machine, whose products I exchange for yet other things, and so on. (The raw materials used by the machine are given to me by others who possess them under D_1, in exchange for hearing lectures.) Each person might participate to gain things over and above their allotment under D_1. Some persons even might want to leave their job in socialist industry and work full time in this private sector. I shall say something more about these issues in the next chapter. Here I wish merely to note how private property even in means of production would occur in a socialist society that did not forbid people to use as they wished some of the resources they are given under the socialist distribution D_1. The socialist society would have to forbid capitalist acts between consenting adults.

The general point illustrated by the Wilt Chamberlain example and the example of the entrepreneur in a socialist society is that no end-state principle or distributional patterned principle of justice can be continuously realized without continuous interference with people's lives. Any favored pattern would be transformed into one unfavored by the principle, by people choosing to act in various ways; for example, by people exchanging goods and services with other people, or giving things to other people, things the transferrers are entitled to under the favored distributional pattern. To maintain a pattern one must either continually interfere to stop people from transferring resources as they wish to, or continually (or periodically) interfere to take from some persons resources that others for some reason chose to transfer to them.

* * *

REDISTRIBUTION AND PROPERTY RIGHTS

Apparently, patterned principles allow people to choose to expend upon themselves, but not upon others, those resources they are entitled to (or rather, receive) under some favored distributional pattern D_1. For if each of several persons chooses to expend some of his D_1 resources upon one other person, then that other person will receive more than his D_1 share, disturbing the favored distributional pattern. Maintaining a distributional pattern is individualism with a vengeance! Patterned distributional principles do not give people what entitlement principles do, only better distributed. For they do not give the right to choose what to do with what one has; they do not give the right to choose to pursue an end involving (intrinsically, or as a means) the enhancement of another's position. To such views, families are disturbing; for within a family occur transfers that upset the favored distributional pattern. Either families themselves become units to which distribution takes place, the column occupiers (on what rationale?), or loving behavior is forbidden. We should note in passing the ambivalent position of radicals toward the family. Its loving relationships are seen as a model to be emulated and extended across the whole society, at the same time that it is denounced as a suffocating institution to be broken and condemned as a focus of parochial concerns that interfere with achieving radical goals. Need we say that it is not appropriate to enforce across the wider society the relationships of love and care appropriate within a family, relationships which are voluntarily undertaken?[5] Incidentally, love is an interesting instance of another relationship that is historical, in that (like justice) it depends upon what actually occurred. An adult may come to love another because of the other's characteristics; but it is the other person, and not the characteristics, that is loved. The love is not transferrable to someone else with the same characteristics, even to one who "scores" higher for these characteristics. And the love endures through changes of the characteristics that gave rise to it. One loves the particular person one actually encountered. Why love is historical, attaching to persons in this way and not to characteristics, is an interesting and puzzling question.

Proponents of patterned principles of distributive justice focus upon criteria for determining who is to receive holdings; they consider the reasons for which someone should have something, and also the total picture of holdings. Whether or not it is better to give than to receive, proponents of patterned principles ignore giving altogether. In considering the distribution of goods, income, and so forth, their theories are theories of recipient justice; they completely ignore any right a person might have to give something to someone. Even in exchanges where each party is simultaneously giver and recipient, patterned principles of justice focus only upon the recipient role and its supposed rights. Thus discussions tend to focus on whether people (should) have a right to inherit, rather than on whether people (should) have a right to bequeath or on whether persons who have a right to hold also have a right to choose that others hold in their place. I lack a good explanation of why the usual theories of distributive justice are so recipient oriented; ignoring givers and transferrers and their rights is of a piece with ignoring producers and their entitlements. But why is it *all* ignored?

Patterned principles of distributive justice necessitate *re*distributive activities. The likelihood is small that any actual freely-arrived-at set of holdings fits a given pattern; and the likelihood is nil that it will continue to fit the pattern as people exchange and give. From the point of view of an entitlement theory, redistribution is a serious matter indeed, involving, as it does, the violation of people's rights. (An exception is those takings that fall under the principle of the rectification of injustices.) From other points of view, also, it is serious.

Taxation of earnings from labor is on a par with forced labor.[6] Some persons find this claim obviously true: taking the earnings of n hours labor is like taking n hours from the person; it is like forcing the person to work n hours for another's purpose. Others find the claim absurd. But even these, *if* they object to forced labor, would oppose forcing unemployed hippies to work for the benefit of the needy.[7] And they would also object to forcing each person to work five extra hours each week for the benefit of the needy. But a system that takes five hours' wages in taxes does not seem to them like one that forces someone to work five hours, since it offers the person forced a wider range of choice in activities than does taxation in kind with the particular labor specified. (But we can imagine a gradation of systems of forced labor, from one that specifies a particular activity, to one that gives a choice among two activities, to . . . ; and so on up.) Furthermore, people envisage a system with something like a proportional tax on everything above the amount necessary for basic needs. Some think this does not force someone to work extra hours, since there is no fixed number of extra hours he is forced to work, and since he can avoid the tax entirely by earning only enough to cover his basic needs. This is a very uncharacteristic view of forcing for those who *also* think people are forced to do something *whenever* the alternatives they face are considerably worse. However, *neither* view is correct. The fact that others intentionally intervene, in violation of a side constraint against aggression, to threaten force to limit the alternatives, in this case to paying taxes or (presumably the worse alternative) bare subsistence, makes the taxation system one of forced labor and distinguishes it from other cases of limited choices which are not forcings.

The man who chooses to work longer to gain an income more than sufficient for his basic needs prefers some extra goods or services to the leisure and activities he could perform during the possible nonworking hours; whereas the man who chooses not to work the extra time prefers the leisure activities to the extra goods or services he could acquire by working more. Given this, if it would be illegitimate for a tax system to seize some of a man's leisure (forced labor) for the purpose of serving the needy, how can it be legitimate for a tax system to seize some of a man's goods for that purpose? Why should we treat the man whose happiness requires certain material

goods or services differently from the man whose preferences and desires make such goods unnecessary for his happiness? Why should the man who prefers seeing a movie (and who has to earn money for a ticket) be open to the required call to aid the needy, while the person who prefers looking at a sunset (and hence need earn no extra money) is not? Indeed, isn't it surprising that redistributionists choose to ignore the man whose pleasures are so easily attainable without extra labor, while adding yet another burden to the poor unfortunate who must work for his pleasures? If anything, one would have expected the reverse. Why is the person with the nonmaterial or nonconsumption desire allowed to proceed unimpeded to his most favored feasible alternative, whereas the man whose pleasures or desires involve material things and who must work for extra money (thereby serving whomever considers his activities valuable enough to pay him) is constrained in what he can realize? Perhaps there is no difference in principle. And perhaps some think the answer concerns merely administrative convenience. (These questions and issues will not disturb those who think that forced labor to serve the needy or to realize some favored end-state pattern is acceptable.) In a fuller discussion we would have (and want) to extend our argument to include interest, entrepreneurial profits, and so on. Those who doubt that this extension can be carried through, and who draw the line here at taxation of income from labor, will have to state rather complicated patterned *historical* principles of distributive justice, since end-state principles would not distinguish *sources* of income in any way. It is enough for now to get away from end-state principles and to make clear how various patterned principles are dependent upon particular views about the sources or the illegitimacy or the lesser legitimacy of profits, interest, and so on; which particular views may well be mistaken.

What sort of right over others does a legally institutionalized end-state pattern give one? The central core of the notion of a property right in *X*, relative to which other parts of the notion are to be explained, is the right to determine what shall be done with X; the right to choose which of the constrained set of options concerning X shall be realized or attempted. The constraints are set by other principles or laws operating in the society; in our theory, by the Lockean rights people possess (under the minimal state). My property rights in my knife allow me to leave it where I will, but not in your chest. I may choose which of the acceptable options involving the knife is to be realized. This notion of property helps us to understand why earlier theorists spoke of people as having property in themselves and their labor. They viewed each person as having a right to decide what would become of himself and what he would do, and as having a right to reap the benefits of what he did.

* * *

When end-result principles of distributive justice are built into the legal structure of a society, they (as do most patterned principles) give each citizen an enforceable claim to some portion of the total social product; that is, to some portion of the sum total of the individually and jointly made products. This total product is produced by individuals laboring, using means of production others have saved to bring into existence, by people organizing production or creating means to produce new things or things in a new way. It is on this batch of individual activities that patterned distributional principles give each individual an enforceable claim. Each person has a claim to the activities and the products of other persons, independently of whether the other persons enter into particular relationships that give rise to these claims, and independently of whether they voluntarily take these claims upon themselves, in charity or in exchange for something.

Whether it is done through taxation on wages or on wages over a certain amount, or through seizure of profits, or through there being a big *social pot* so that it's not clear what's coming from where

and what's going where, patterned principles of distributive justice involve appropriating the actions of other persons. Seizing the results of someone's labor is equivalent to seizing hours from him and directing him to carry on various activities. If people force you to do certain work, or unrewarded work, for a certain period of time, they decide what you are to do and what purposes your work is to serve apart from your decisions. This process whereby they take this decision from you makes them a *part-owner* of you; it gives them a property right in you. Just as having such partial control and power of decision, by right, over an animal or inanimate object would be to have a property right in it.

End-state and most patterned principles of distributive justice institute (partial) ownership by others of people and their actions and labor. These principles involve a shift from the classical liberals' notion of self-ownership to a notion of (partial) property rights in *other* people.

* * *

May a person emigrate from a nation that has institutionalized some end-state or patterned distributional principle? For some principles (for example, Hayek's) emigration presents no theoretical problem. But for others it is a tricky matter. Consider a nation having a compulsory scheme of minimal social provision to aid the neediest (or one organized so as to maximize the position of the worst-off group); no one may opt out of participating in it. (None may say, "Don't compel me to contribute to others and don't provide for me via this compulsory mechanism if I am in need.") Everyone above a certain level is forced to contribute to aid the needy. But if emigration from the country were allowed, anyone could choose to move to another country that did not have compulsory social provision but otherwise was (as much as possible) identical. In such a case, the person's *only* motive for leaving would be to avoid participating in the compulsory scheme of social provision. And if he does leave, the needy in his initial country will receive no (compelled) help from him. What rationale yields the result that the person be permitted to emigrate, yet forbidden to stay and opt out of the compulsory scheme of social provision? If providing for the needy is of overriding importance, this does militate against allowing internal opting out; but it also speaks against allowing external emigration. (Would it also support, to some extent, the kidnapping of persons living in a place without compulsory social provision, who could be forced to make a contribution to the needy in your community?) Perhaps the crucial component of the position that allows emigration solely to avoid certain arrangements, while not allowing anyone internally to opt out of them, is a concern for fraternal feelings within the country. "We don't want anyone here who doesn't contribute, who doesn't care enough about the others to contribute." That concern, in this case, would have to be tied to the view that forced aiding tends to produce fraternal feelings between the aided and the aider (or perhaps merely to the view that the knowledge that someone or other voluntarily is not aiding produces unfraternal feelings).

NOTES

1. Applications of the principle of justice in acquisition may also occur as part of the move from one distribution to another. You may find an unheld thing now and appropriate it. Acquisitions also are to be understood as included when, to simplify, I speak only of transitions by transfers.

2. If the principle of rectification of violations of the first two principles yields more than one description of holdings, then some choice must be made as to which of these is to be realized. Perhaps the sort of considerations about distributive justice and equality that I argue against play a legitimate role in *this* subsidiary choice. Similarly, there may be room for such considerations in deciding which otherwise arbitrary features a statute will embody, when such features are unavoidable because other considerations do not specify a precise line; yet a line must be drawn.

3. One might try to squeeze a patterned conception of distributive justice into the framework of the entitlement conception, by formulating a gimmicky obligatory "principle of transfer" that would lead to the pattern. For example, the principle that if one has more than the mean income one must transfer everything one holds above the mean to persons below the mean so as to bring them up to (but not over) the mean. We can formulate a criterion for a "principle of transfer" to rule out such obligatory transfers, or we can say that no correct principle of transfer, no principle of transfer in a free society will be like this. The former is probably the better course, though the latter also is true.

Alternatively, one might think to make the entitlement conception instantiate a pattern, by using matrix entries that express the relative strength of a person's entitlements as measured by some real-valued function. But even if the limitation to natural dimensions failed to exclude this function, the resulting edifice would *not* capture our system of entitlements to *particular* things.

4. Might not a transfer have instrumental effects on a third party, changing his feasible options? (But what if the two parties to the transfer independently had used their holdings in this fashion?) I discuss this question below, but note here that this question concedes the point for distributions of ultimate intrinsic non instrumental goods (pure utility experiences, so to speak) that are transferable. It also might be objected that the transfer might make a third party more envious because it worsens his position relative to someone else. I find it incomprehensible how this can be thought to involve a claim of justice. . . .

Here and elsewhere in this chapter, a theory which incorporates elements of pure procedural justice might find what I say acceptable, *if* kept in its proper place; that is, if background institutions exist to ensure the satisfaction of certain conditions on distributive shares. But if these institutions are not themselves the sum or invisible-hand result of people's voluntary (nonaggressive) actions, the constraints they impose require justification. At no point does *our* argument assume any background institutions more extensive than those of the minimal night-watchman state, a state limited to protecting persons against murder, assault, theft, fraud, and so forth.

5. One indication of the stringency of Rawls' difference principle, which we attend to in the second part of this chapter, is its inappropriateness as a governing principle even within a family of individuals who love one another. Should a family devote its resources to maximizing the position of its least well off and least talented child, holding back the other children or using resources for their education and

development only if they will follow a policy through their lifetimes of maximizing the position of their least fortunate sibling? Surely not. How then can this even be considered as the appropriate policy for enforcement in the wider society? (I discuss below what I think would be Rawls' reply: that some principles apply at the macro level which do not apply to micro-situations.)

6. I am unsure as to whether the arguments I present below show that such taxation merely *is* forced labor; so that "is on a par with" means "is one kind of." Or alternatively, whether the arguments emphasize the great similarities between such taxation and forced labor, to show it is plausible and illuminating to view such taxation in the light of forced labor. This latter approach would remind one of how John Wisdom conceives of the claims of metaphysicians.

7. Nothing hangs on the fact that here and elsewhere I speak loosely of *needs,* since I go on, each time, to reject the criterion of justice which includes it. If, however, something did depend upon the notion, one would want to examine it more carefully. For a skeptical view, see Kenneth Minogue, *The Liberal Mind,* (New York: Random House, 1963), pp. 103–112.

CHAPTER 6

Nonconsequentialist Theories: Do Your Duty

For the consequentialist, the rightness of an action depends entirely on the effects of that action (or of following the rule that governs it). Good effects make the deed right; bad effects make the deed wrong. But for the nonconsequentialist (otherwise known as a *deontologist*), the rightness of an action can never be measured by such a variable, contingent standard as the quantity of goodness brought into the world. Rightness derives not from the consequences of an action but from its nature, its right-making characteristics. An action is right (or wrong) not because of what it produces but because of what it *is*. Yet for all their differences, both consequentialist and deontological theories contain elements that seem to go to the heart of morality and our moral experience. So in this chapter, we look at ethics through a deontological lens and explore the two deontological theories that historically have offered the strongest challenges to consequentialist views: Kant's moral theory and natural law theory.

KANT'S ETHICS

The German philosopher Immanuel Kant (1724–1804) is considered one of the greatest moral philosophers of the modern era. Many scholars would go further and say that he is *the* greatest moral philosopher of the modern era. As a distinguished thinker of the Enlightenment, he sought to make reason the foundation of morality. For him, reason alone leads us to the right and the good. Therefore, to discover the true path we need not appeal to utility, religion, tradition, authority, happiness, desires, or intuition. We need only heed the dictates

of reason, for reason informs us of the moral law just as surely as it reveals the truths of mathematics. Because of each person's capacity for reason, he or she is a sovereign in the moral realm, a supreme judge of what morality demands. What morality demands (in other words, our duty) is enshrined in the moral law—the changeless, necessary, universal body of moral rules.

In Kant's ethics, right actions have moral value only if they are done with a "good will"—that is, a will to do your duty for duty's sake. To act with a good will is to act with a desire to do your duty *simply because it is your duty*, to act out of pure reverence for the moral law. Without a good will, your actions have no moral worth—even if they accord with the moral law, even if they are done out of sympathy or love, even if they produce good results. Only a good will is unconditionally good, and only an accompanying good will can give your talents, virtues, and actions moral worth. As Kant explains,

Nothing can possibly be conceived in the world, or even out of it, which can be called good without qualification, except a *good will.* Intelligence, wit, judgement, and the other *talents* of the mind, however they may be named, or courage, resolution, perseverance, as qualities of temperament, are undoubtedly good and desirable in many respects; but these gifts of nature may also become extremely bad and mischievous if the will which is to make use of them, and which, therefore, constitutes what is called *character,* is not good. It is the same with the *gifts of fortune.* Power, riches, honour, even health, and the general well-being and contentment with one's condition which is called *happiness,* inspire pride, and often presumption, if there is not a good will to correct the influence of these on the mind. . . . A good will is good not because of what it performs or effects, not by its aptness for the attainment of some proposed end, but simply by virtue of the volition—that is, it is good in itself, and considered by itself is to be esteemed much higher than all that can be brought about by it in favour of any inclination, nay, even of the sum-total of all inclinations.[1]

So to do right, we must do it for duty's sake, motivated solely by respect for the moral law. But how do we know what the moral law is? Kant sees the moral law as a set of principles, or rules, stated in the form of imperatives, or commands. Imperatives can be *hypothetical* or *categorical*. A **hypothetical imperative** tells us what we should do if we have certain desires: for example, "If you need money, work for it" or "If you want orange juice, ask for it." We should obey such imperatives only if we desire the outcomes specified. A **categorical imperative**, however, is not so iffy. It tells us that we should do something in all situations *regardless of our wants and needs*. A moral categorical imperative expresses a command such as "Do not steal" or "Do not commit suicide." Such imperatives are universal and unconditional, containing no stipulations contingent on human desires or preferences. Kant says that the moral law consists entirely of categorical imperatives. They are the authoritative expression of our moral duties. Because they are the products of rational insight and we are rational agents, we can straightforwardly access, understand, and know them as the great truths that they are.

Kant says that all our duties, all the moral categorical imperatives, can be logically derived from a principle that he calls *the* categorical imperative. It tells us to "act only on that maxim through which you can at the same time will that it should become a universal law."[2] (Kant actually devised three statements, or versions, of the principle, the one given here and two others; in the next few pages we will examine only the two most important ones.) Kant believes that every action implies a general rule, or

maxim. If you steal a car, then your action implies a maxim such as "In this situation, steal a car if you want one." So the first version of the categorical imperative says that an action is right if you could will the maxim of an action to become a moral law applying to all persons. That is, an action is permissible if (1) its maxim can be universalized (if everyone can consistently act on the maxim in similar situations) and (2) you would be willing to let that happen. If you can so will the maxim, then the action is right (permissible). If you cannot, the action is wrong (prohibited). Right actions pass the test of the categorical imperative; wrong actions do not.

Some of the duties derived from the categorical imperative are, in Kant's words, perfect duties and some, imperfect duties. **Perfect duties** are those that absolutely must be followed without fail; they have no exceptions. Some perfect duties cited by Kant include duties not to break a promise, not to lie, and not to commit suicide. **Imperfect duties** are not always to be followed; they do have exceptions. As examples of imperfect duties, Kant mentions duties to develop your talents and to help others in need.

Kant demonstrates how to apply the first version of the categorical imperative to several cases, the most famous of which involves a lying promise. Imagine that you want to borrow money from someone, and you know you will not be able to repay the debt. You also know that you will get the loan if you falsely promise to pay the money back. Is such deceptive borrowing morally permissible? To find out, you have to devise a maxim for the action and ask whether you could consistently will it to become a universal law. Could you consistently will everyone to act on the maxim, "If you need money, make a lying promise to borrow some"? Kant's emphatic answer is no. If all persons adopted this rule, then they would make lying promises to obtain loans. But then everyone would know that such promises are false, and the practice of giving loans based on a promise would no longer exist, because no promises could be trusted.

CRITICAL THOUGHT: Sizing Up the Golden Rule

The Golden Rule—"Do unto others as you would have them do unto you"—has some resemblance to Kant's ethics and has been, in one form or another, implicit in many religious traditions and moral systems. Moral philosophers generally think that it touches on a significant truth about morality. But some have argued that taken by itself, without the aid of any other moral principles or theory, the Golden Rule can lead to implausible conclusions and absurd results. Here is part of a famous critique by Richard Whately (1787–1863):

> Supposing any one should regard this golden rule as designed to answer the purpose of a complete system of morality, and to teach us the difference of right and wrong; then, if he had let his land to a farmer, he might consider that the farmer would be glad to be excused paying any rent for it, since he would himself, if he were the farmer, prefer having the land rent-free; and that, therefore, the rule of doing as he would be done by requires him to give up all his property. So also the shopkeeper might, on the same principle,

think that the rule required him to part with his goods under prime cost, or to give them away, and thus to ruin himself. Now such a procedure would be *absurd*. . . .

> You have seen, then, that the golden rule was far from being designed to impart to men the first notions of justice. On the contrary, it *presupposes* that knowledge; and if we had *no* such notions, we could not properly apply the rule. But the real design of it is to put us on our guard against the danger of being blinded by self-interest.*

How does the Golden Rule resemble Kant's theory? How does it differ? Do you agree with Whately's criticism? Why or why not? How could the Golden Rule be qualified or supplemented to blunt Whately's critique? John Stuart Mill said that the Golden Rule was the essence of utilitarianism. What do you think he meant by this?

*Richard Whately, quoted in Louis P. Pojman and Lewis Vaughn, *The Moral Life* (New York: Oxford University Press, 2007), 353–54.

The maxim, if acted on by everyone, would defeat itself. As Kant says, the "maxim would necessarily destroy itself as soon as it was made a universal law."[3] Therefore, you cannot consistently will the maxim to become a universal law. The action, then, is not morally permissible.

Kant believes that besides the rule forbidding the breaking of promises, the categorical imperative generates several other duties. Among these he includes prohibitions against committing suicide, lying, and killing innocent people.

Some universalized maxims may fail the test of the categorical imperative (first version) not by being self-defeating (as in the case of a lying promise) but by constituting rules that you would not want everyone else to act on. (Remember that an

action is permissible if everyone can consistently act on it in similar situations *and* you would be willing to let that happen.) Kant asks us to consider a maxim that mandates *not* contributing anything to the welfare of others or aiding them when they are in distress. If you willed this maxim to become a universal moral law (if everyone followed it), no self-defeating state of affairs would obtain. Everyone could conceivably follow this rule. But you probably would not want people to act on this maxim, because one day *you* might need *their* help and sympathy. Right now you might will the maxim to become universal law, but later, when the tables are turned, you might regret that policy. The inconsistency lies in wanting the rule to be universalized and not wanting it to be universalized. Kant says that this alternative kind of inconsistency shows that the action embodied in the maxim is not permissible.

Kant's second version of the categorical imperative is probably more famous and influential than the first. (Kant believed the two versions to be virtually synonymous, but they seem to be distinct principles.) He declares, "So act as to treat humanity, whether in thine own person or in that of any other, in every case as an end withal, never as means only."[4] This rule—the **means-ends principle**—says that we must always treat people (including ourselves) as ends in themselves, as creatures of great intrinsic worth, never merely as things of instrumental value, never merely as tools to be used for someone else's purpose.

This statement of the categorical imperative reflects Kant's view of the status of rational beings, or persons. Persons have intrinsic value and dignity because they, unlike the rest of creation, are rational agents who are free to choose their own ends, legislate their own moral laws, and assign value to things in the world. Persons are the givers of value, so they must have ultimate value. They therefore must always be treated as ultimate ends and never merely as means.

Kant's idea is that people not only have intrinsic worth—they also have *equal* intrinsic worth. Each rational being has the same inherent value as every other rational being. This equality of value cannot be altered by, and has no connection to, social and economic status, racial and ethnic considerations, or the possession of prestige or power. Any two persons are entitled to the same moral rights, even if one is rich, wise, powerful, and famous—and the other is not.

To treat people merely as a means rather than as an end is to fail to recognize the true nature and status of persons. Because people are by nature free, rational, autonomous, and equal, we treat them merely as a means if we do not respect these attributes—if we, for example, interfere with their right to make informed choices by lying to them,

inhibit their free and autonomous actions by enslaving or coercing them, or violate their equality by discriminating against them. For Kant, lying or breaking a promise is wrong because to do so is to use people merely as a means to an end rather than as an end in themselves.

Sometimes we use people to achieve some end, yet our actions are not wrong. To see why, we must understand that there is a moral difference between treating people as a means and treating them *merely*, or *only*, as a means. We may treat a mechanic as a means to repair our cars, but we do not treat him merely as a means if we also respect his status as a person. We do not treat him only as a means if we neither restrict his freedom nor ignore his rights.

As noted earlier, Kant insists that the two versions of the categorical imperative are two ways of stating the same idea. But the two principles seem to be distinct, occasionally leading to different conclusions about the rightness of an action. The maxim of an action, for example, may pass the first version (be permissible) by being universalizable but fail the second by not treating persons as ends. A more plausible approach is to view the two versions not as alternative tests but as a single two-part test that an action must pass to be judged morally permissible. So before we can declare a maxim a bona fide categorical imperative, we must be able to consistently will it to become a universal law *and* know that it would have us treat persons not only as means but as ends.

Applying the Theory

How might a Kantian decide the case of the antiterrorist chief of police, discussed in Chapter 5, who considers killing a terrorist's wife and children? Recall that the terrorist is murdering hundreds of innocent people each year and that the chief has good reasons to believe that killing the wife and children (who are also innocent) will end the terrorist's attacks. Recall also the verdicts on this case rendered from the act- and rule-utilitarian perspectives. By act-utilitarian lights, the chief should kill some of the terrorist's innocent relatives (and threaten to kill others). The rule-utilitarian view, however, is that the chief should *not* kill them.

Suppose the maxim in question is "When the usual antiterrorist tactics fail to stop terrorists from killing many innocent people, the authorities should kill (and threaten to kill) the terrorists' relatives." Can we consistently will this maxim to become a universal law? Does this maxim involve treating persons merely as a means to an end rather than as an end in themselves? To answer the first question, we should try to imagine what would happen if everyone in the position of the relevant authorities followed this maxim. Would any inconsistencies or self-defeating states of affairs arise? We can see that the consequences of universalizing the maxim would not be pleasant. The authorities would kill the innocent—actions that could be as gruesome and frightening as terrorist attacks. But our willing that everyone act on the maxim would not be self-defeating or otherwise contradictory. Would we nevertheless be willing to live in a world where the maxim was universally followed? Again, there seems to be no good reason why we could not. The maxim therefore passes the first test of the categorical imperative.

To answer the second (means-ends) question, we must inquire whether following the maxim would involve treating someone merely as a means. The obvious answer is yes. This antiterrorism policy would use the innocent relatives of terrorists as a means to stop terrorist acts. Their freedom and their rights as persons would be violated. The maxim therefore fails the second test, and the acts sanctioned by the maxim would not be permissible. From the Kantian perspective, using the innocent relatives would be wrong no matter what—regardless of how many lives the policy would save or how much safer the world would be. So in this case, the Kantian verdict would coincide with that of rule-utilitarianism but not that of act-utilitarianism.

Evaluating the Theory

Kant's moral theory meets the minimum requirement of coherence and is generally consistent with our moral experience (Criterion 2). In some troubling ways, however, it seems to conflict with our commonsense moral judgments (Criterion 1) and appears to have some flaws that restrict its usefulness in moral problem solving (Criterion 3).

As we saw earlier, some duties generated by the categorical imperative are absolute—they are, as Kant says, perfect duties, allowing no exceptions whatsoever. We have, for example, a perfect (exceptionless) duty not to lie—ever. But what should we do if lying is the only way to prevent a terrible tragedy? Suppose a friend of yours comes to your house in a panic and begs you to hide her from an insane man intent on murdering her. No sooner do you hide her in the cellar than the insane man appears at your door with a bloody knife in his hand and asks where your friend is. You have no doubt that the man is serious and that your friend will in fact be brutally murdered if the man finds her. Imagine that you have only two choices (and saying "I don't know" is not one of them): either you lie to the man and thereby save your friend's life, or you tell the man where she is hiding and guarantee her murder. Kant actually considers such a case and renders this verdict on it: you should tell the truth though the heavens fall. He says, as he must, that the consequences of your action here are irrelevant. Yet Kant's answer seems contrary to our considered moral judgments. Moral common sense seems to suggest that in a case like this, saving a life would be much more important than telling the truth.

Another classic example involves promise keeping, which is also a perfect duty. Suppose you promise to meet a friend for lunch, and on your way to the restaurant you are called on to help someone injured in a car crash. No one else can help her, and she will die unless you render aid. But if you help her, you will break your promise to meet your friend. What should you do? Kant would say that come what may, your duty is to keep your promise to meet your friend. Under these circumstances, however, keeping the promise just seems wrong.

These scenarios are significant because, contrary to Kant's view, they suggest that we have no absolute, or exceptionless, moral duties. We can easily imagine many cases like those just mentioned. Moreover, we can also envision situations in which we must choose between two allegedly perfect duties, each one prohibiting some action. We cannot fulfill both duties at once, and we must make a choice. Such conflicts provide plausible evidence against the notion that there are exceptionless moral rules.[5]

Conflicts of duties, of course, are not just deficiencies under Criterion 1. They also indicate difficulties with Criterion 3. Like many moral theories, Kant's system fails to provide an effective means of resolving major conflicts of duties.

Some additional inconsistencies with our considered moral judgments seem to arise from applications of the first version of the categorical imperative. Remember that the first version says that an action is permissible if everyone can consistently act on it and if you would be willing to have that happen. At first glance, it seems to guarantee that moral rules are universally fair. But it makes the acceptability of a moral rule depend largely on whether *you personally* are willing to live in a world that conforms to the rule. If you are not willing to live in such a world, then the rule fails the first version of the categorical imperative, and your conforming to the rule is wrong. But if you are the sort of person who would prefer such a world, then conforming to the rule would be morally permissible. This subjectivity in Kant's theory could lead to the sanctioning of heinous acts of all kinds. Suppose the rule is "Kill everyone with dark skin" or "Murder all Jews." Neither rule would be contradictory if universalized; everyone could consistently act on it. Moreover, if you were willing to have everyone act on it—even willing to be killed if *you* have dark skin or are a Jew—then acts endorsed by the rule would be permissible. Thus the first version seems to bless acts that are clearly immoral.

Critics say that another difficulty with Kant's theory concerns the phrasing of the maxims to be universalized. Oddly enough, Kant does not provide any guidance for how we should state a rule

---

Kant, Respect, and Personal Rights

Respect is the guiding value of Kantian ethics. Respect is owed all persons equally, Kant says, because they have intrinsic worth and dignity due to their autonomy—that is, their capacity for rational decisions, autonomous action, and moral choices. Kant made this point by insisting that we must always treat persons as ends in themselves, never merely as a means to an end (as tools to be used for someone else's purposes). Another way to express this is to say that, as persons, we have *rights*—specifically, *negative rights*, which obligate others not to interfere with our obtaining something. (*Positive rights* are rights that obligate others to help us obtain something.) Persons have the right not to be treated in certain ways: not to be used or regarded as if they were mere instruments, and not to have their autonomous actions and free choices thwarted or constrained. The principle of respect therefore would prohibit, among other things, lying to persons, cheating them, coercing them, falsely imprisoning them, discriminating against them, and manipulating them. Their negative rights can be violated or overridden only for very strong reasons.

describing an action, an oversight that allows us to word a rule in many different ways. Consider, for example, our duty not to lie. You might state the relevant rule like this: "Lie only to avoid injury or death to others." But you could also say "Lie only to avoid injury, death, or embarrassment to anyone who has green eyes and red hair" (a group that includes you and your relatives). Neither rule would lead to an inconsistency if everyone acted on it, so they both describe permissible actions. The second rule, though, is obviously not morally acceptable. More to the point, it shows that we can use the first version of the categorical imperative to sanction all sorts of immoral acts if we state the rule *in enough detail*. This result suggests not only a problem with Criterion 1 but also a limitation on the usefulness of the theory, a fault measured by Criterion 3. Judging the rightness of an action is close to impossible if the language of the relevant rule can change with the wind.

It may be feasible to remedy some of the shortcomings of the first version of the categorical imperative by combining it with the second. Rules such as "Kill everyone with dark skin" or "Lie only to avoid injury, death, or embarrassment to anyone who has green eyes and red hair" would be unacceptable because they would allow people to be treated merely as a means. But the means-ends principle itself appears to be in need of modification. The main difficulty is that our duties not to use people merely as a means can conflict, and Kant provides no counsel on how to resolve such dilemmas. Say, for example, that hundreds of innocent people are enslaved inside a brutal Nazi concentration camp, and the only way we can free them is to kill the Nazis guarding the camp. We must therefore choose between allowing the prisoners to be used merely as a means by the Nazis or using the Nazis merely as a means by killing them to free the prisoners.

Here is another example, a classic case from the philosopher C. D. Broad:

> Again, there seem to be cases in which you must either treat A or treat B, not as an end, but as a means. If we isolate a man who is a carrier of typhoid, we are

treating him merely as a cause of infection to others. But, if we refuse to isolate him, we are treating other people merely as means to his comfort and culture.[6]

Kant's means-ends principle captures an important truth about the intrinsic value of persons. But apparently we cannot fully implement it, because sometimes we are forced to treat people merely as a means and not as an end in themselves.

LEARNING FROM KANT'S THEORY

Despite these criticisms, Kant's theory has been influential because it embodies a large part of the whole truth about morality. At a minimum, it promotes many of the duties and rights that our considered moral judgments lead us to embrace. Furthermore, it emphasizes three of morality's most important features: (1) universality, (2) impartiality, and (3) respect for persons.

Kant's first version of the categorical imperative rests firmly on universality—the notion that the moral law applies to all persons in relevantly similar situations. Impartiality requires that the moral law apply to everyone in the same way, that no one can claim a privileged moral status. In Kantian ethics, double standards are inherently bad. Ethical egoism fails as a moral theory in large part because it lacks this kind of impartiality. The first version of the categorical imperative, in contrast, enshrines impartiality as essential to the moral life. Kant's principle of respect for persons (the means-ends imperative) entails a recognition that persons have ultimate and inherent value, that they should not be used merely as a means to utilitarian ends, that equals should be treated equally, and that there are limits to what can be done to persons for the sake of good consequences. To many scholars, the central flaw of utilitarianism is that it does not incorporate a fully developed respect for persons. But in Kant's theory, the rights and duties of persons override any consequentialist calculus.

So Kantian ethics has many of the most important qualities that we associate with adequate moral theories. And no one has explained better than Kant why persons deserve full respect and how we are to determine whether persons are getting the respect they deserve.

NATURAL LAW THEORY

The natural law theory of morality comes to us from ancient Greek and Roman philosophers (most notably, Aristotle and the Stoics) through the theologian and philosopher Thomas Aquinas (1225–1274). Aquinas molded it into its most influential form and bequeathed it to the world and the Roman Catholic Church, which embraced it as its official system of ethics. To this day, the theory is the primary basis for the church's views on abortion, homosexuality, euthanasia, and other controversial issues.

Here we focus on the traditional version of the theory derived from Aquinas. This form is theistic, assuming a divine lawgiver that has given us the gift of reason to comprehend the order of nature. But there are other natural law theories of a more recent vintage that dispense with the religious elements, basing objective moral standards on human nature and the natural needs and interests of humans.

According to Aquinas, at the heart of the traditional theory is the notion that right actions are those that accord with the natural law—the moral principles that we can "read" clearly in the very structure of nature itself, including human nature. We can look into nature and somehow uncover moral standards because nature is a certain way: it is rationally ordered and *teleological* (goal-directed), with every part having its own purpose or end at which it naturally aims. From this notion about nature, traditional natural law theorists draw the following conclusion: How nature *is* reveals how it *should be*. The goals to which nature inclines reveal the values that we should embrace and the moral purposes to which we should aspire.

In conformity with an inherent natural purpose or goal—that is, according to natural law—an acorn develops into a seedling, then into a sapling, and finally into an oak. The end toward which the acorn strives is the good (for acorns)—that is, to be a well-formed and well-functioning oak. Natural law determines how an oak functions—*and* indicates how an oak should function. If the oak does not function according to its natural purpose (if, for example, it is deformed or weak), it fails to be as it should be, deviating from its proper path laid down in natural law. Likewise, humans have a nature—a natural function and purpose unique among all living things. In human nature, in the mandates of the natural law for humanity, are the aims toward which human life strives. In these teleological strivings, in these facts about what human nature *is*, we can perceive what it *should be*.

What is it, exactly, that human nature aims at? Aquinas says that humans naturally incline toward preservation of human life, avoidance of harm, basic functions that humans and animals have in common (sexual intercourse, raising offspring, and the like), the search for truth, the nurturing of social ties, and behavior that is benign and reasonable. For humans, these inclinations constitute the good—the good of human flourishing and well-being. Our duty, then, is to achieve the good, to fully realize the goals to which our nature is already inclined. As Aquinas says,

> [T]his is the first precept of law, that *good is to be done and promoted, and evil is to be avoided*. All other precepts of the natural law are based upon this; so that all things which the practical reason naturally apprehends as man's good belong to the precepts of the natural law under the form of things to be done or avoided.
>
> Since, however, good has the nature of an end, and evil, the nature of the contrary, hence it is that all those things to which man has a natural inclination are naturally apprehended by reason as good, and consequently as objects of pursuit, and their contraries as evil, and objects of avoidance. Therefore, the order of the precepts of the natural law is according to the order of natural inclinations.[7]

In this passage, Aquinas refers to the aspect of human nature that enables us to decipher and implement the precepts of natural law: reason. Humans, unlike the rest of nature, are rational creatures, capable of understanding, deliberation, and free choice. Because all of nature is ordered and rational, only rational beings such as humans can peer into it and discern the inclinations in their nature, derive from the natural tendencies the natural laws, and apply the laws to their actions and their lives. Humans have the gift of reason (a gift from God, Aquinas says), and reason gives us access to the laws. Reason therefore is the foundation of morality. Judging the rightness of actions, then, is a matter of consulting reason, of considering rational grounds for moral beliefs.

It follows from these points that the natural (moral) laws are both objective and universal. The general principles of right and wrong do not vary from person to person or culture to culture. The dynamics of each situation may alter how a principle is applied, and not every situation has a relevant principle, but principles do not change with the tide. The natural laws are the natural laws. Further, not only are they binding on all persons, but they can be known by all persons. Aquinas insists that belief in God or inspiration from above is not a prerequisite for knowledge of morality. A person's effective use of reason is the only requirement.

Like Kant's categorical imperative, traditional natural law theory is, in the main, strongly absolutist. Natural law theorists commonly insist on several exceptionless rules. Directly killing the innocent is always wrong (which means that direct abortion is always wrong). Use of contraceptives is always wrong (on the grounds that it interferes with the natural human inclination toward procreation). Homosexuality is always wrong (again because it thwarts procreation). For Aquinas, lying, adultery, and blasphemy are always wrong.

As we have seen, moral principles—especially absolutist rules—can give rise to conflicts of duties. Kant's view on conflicting perfect duties is that such inconsistencies cannot happen. The natural law tradition gives a different answer: conflicts between duties are possible, but they can be resolved by applying the **doctrine of double effect**. This principle pertains to situations in which an action has both good and bad effects. It says that performing a good action may be permissible even if it has bad effects, but performing a bad action for the purpose of achieving good effects is never permissible. More formally, in a traditional interpretation of the doctrine, an action is permissible if four conditions are met:

1. *The action is inherently (without reference to consequences) either morally good or morally neutral.* That is, the action itself must at least be morally permissible.

2. *The bad effect is not used to produce the good effect (though the bad may be a side effect of the good).* Killing a fetus to save the mother's life is never permissible. However, using a drug to cure the mother's life-threatening disease—even though the fetus dies as a side effect of the treatment— may be permissible.

3. *The intention must always be to bring about the good effect.* For any given action, the bad effect may occur, and it may even be foreseen, but it must not be intended.

4. *The good effect must be at least as important as the bad effect.* The good of an action must be proportional to the bad. If the bad heavily outweighs the good, the action is not permissible. The good of saving your own life in an act of self-defense, for example, must be at least as great as the bad of taking the life of your attacker.

The doctrine of double effect is surprisingly versatile. Natural law theorists have used it to navigate moral dilemmas in medical ethics, reproductive health, warfare, and other life-and-death issues, as we will see in the next section.

Applying the Theory

Traditional natural law theory and its double-effect doctrine figure prominently in obstetrics cases in which a choice must be made between harming a pregnant woman or harming her fetus. A typical scenario goes something like this: A pregnant woman has cancer and will die unless she receives chemotherapy to destroy the tumors. If she does take the chemotherapy, the fetus will die. Is it morally permissible for her to do so?

In itself, the act of taking the chemotherapy is morally permissible. There is nothing inherently wrong with using a medical treatment to try to cure a life-threatening illness. So the action meets Condition 1. We can also see that the bad effect (killing the fetus) is not used to produce the good effect (saving the woman's life). Receiving

the chemotherapy is the method used to achieve the good effect. The loss of the fetus is an indirect, unintended result of the attempt to destroy the cancer. The action therefore meets Condition 2. The intention behind the action is to kill the cancer and thereby save the woman's life—not to kill the fetus. The woman and her doctors know that the unfortunate consequence of treating the cancer will be the death of the fetus. They foresee the death, but their intention is not to kill the fetus. Thus, the action meets Condition 3. Is the good effect proportional to the bad effect? In this case, a life is balanced against a life, the life of the woman and the life of the fetus. From the natural law perspective, both sides of the scale seem about equal in importance. If the good effect to be achieved for the woman was, say, a nicer appearance through cosmetic surgery, and the bad effect was the death of the fetus, the two sides would not have the same level of importance. But in this case, the action does meet Condition 4. Because the action meets all four conditions, receiving the chemotherapy is morally permissible for the woman.

Now let us examine a different kind of scenario. Remember that earlier in this chapter, we applied both utilitarianism and Kant's theory to the antiterrorism tactic of killing a terrorist's relatives. To stop the murder of many innocent people by a relentless terrorist, the authorities consider killing his wife and three of his children and threatening to kill the remaining four children. What verdict would the doctrine of double effect yield in this case?

The good effect of this action is preventing the deaths of innocent citizens; the bad effect is the killing of other innocents. Right away we can see that the action, in itself, is not morally good. Directly killing the innocent is never permissible, so the action does not meet Condition 1. Failing to measure up to even one condition shows the action to be prohibited, but we will continue our analysis anyway. Is the bad effect used to produce the good effect? Yes. The point of the action is to prevent

QUICK REVIEW

hypothetical imperative—An imperative that tells us what we should do if we have certain desires.

categorical imperative—An imperative that we should follow regardless of our particular wants and needs; also, the principle that defines Kant's ethical system.

perfect duty—A duty that has no exceptions.

imperfect duty—A duty that has exceptions.

means-ends principle—The rule that we must always treat people (including ourselves) as ends in themselves, never merely as a means.

doctrine of double effect—The principle that performing a good action may be permissible even if it has bad effects, but performing a bad action for the purpose of achieving good effects is never permissible; any bad effects must be unintended.

CRITICAL THOUGHT: Double Effect and the "Trolley Problem"

Consider the following thought experiment, first proposed by the philosopher Philippa Foot and set forth here by the philosopher Judith Jarvis Thomson:

> Suppose you are the driver of a trolley. The trolley rounds a bend, and there come into view ahead five track workmen, who have been repairing the track. The track goes through a bit of a valley at that point, and the sides are steep, so you must stop the trolley if you are to avoid running the five men down. You step on the brakes, but alas they don't work. Now you suddenly see a spur of track leading off to the right. You can turn the trolley onto it, and thus save the five men on the straight track ahead. Unfortunately, Mrs. Foot has arranged that there is one track workman on that spur of track. He can no more get off the track in

time than the five can, so you will kill him if you turn the trolley onto him. Is it morally permissible for you to turn the trolley?*

If you were the driver of the trolley, which option would you choose? Would you consider it morally permissible to turn the trolley onto the one workman to save the other five? Why or why not? What would the doctrine of double effect have you do in this case? Does your moral intuition seem to conflict with what the doctrine would have you do? What reasons can you give for the choice you make?

*Judith Jarvis Thomson, "Critical Thought: Double Effect and the 'Trolley Problem,'" *Yale Law Journal*, vol. 94, no. 6, May 1985. Reprinted with permission from the Yale Law Journal.

further terrorist killings, and the means to that end is killing the terrorist's wife and children. The bad is used to achieve the good. So the action does not meet Condition 2, either. It does, however, meet Condition 3 because the intention behind the action is to bring about the good effect, preventing further terrorist killings. Finally, if we view the good effect (preventing the deaths of citizens) as comparable to the bad effect (the killing of the terrorist's wife and children), we should infer that the action meets Condition 4. In any case, because the action fails Conditions 1 and 2, we have to say that killing members of the terrorist's family is not permissible.

As suggested earlier, a Kantian theorist would be likely to agree with this decision, and a rule-utilitarian would probably concur. However, judging that the good consequences outweigh the bad, an act-utilitarian might very well say that killing the wife and children to prevent many other deaths would be not only permissible, but obligatory.

Evaluating the Theory

Traditional natural law theory appears to contain no crippling internal inconsistencies, so we will regard it as an eligible theory for evaluation. But it does encounter difficulties with Criteria 1 and 3.

The theory seems to fall short of Criterion 1 (it conflicts with commonsense moral judgments) in part because of its absolutism, a feature that also encumbers Kant's theory. As we have seen, natural law theorists maintain that some actions are *always* wrong: for example, intentionally killing the innocent, impeding procreation (through contraception, sterilization, or sexual preferences), or lying. Such absolutes, though, can lead to moral judgments that seem to diverge from common sense. The absolute prohibition against directly killing the innocent, for example, could actually result in great loss of life in certain extreme circumstances. Imagine that a thousand innocent people are taken hostage by a homicidal madman, and the only way to save the lives of nine hundred and ninety-nine is to intentionally kill one of them. If the one is not killed, all one thousand will die. Most of us would probably regard the killing of the one hostage as a tragic but necessary measure to prevent a massive loss of life. The alternative—letting them all die—would seem a much greater tragedy. But many natural law theorists would condemn the killing of the one innocent person even if it would save the lives of hundreds.

Similarly, suppose a pregnant woman will die unless her fetus is aborted. Would it be morally permissible for her to have the abortion? Given the natural law prohibition against killing the innocent, many natural law theorists would say no. Aborting the fetus would be wrong, even to save the mother's life. But most people would probably say that this view contradicts our considered moral judgments.

The absolutism of natural law theory arises from the notion that nature is authoritatively teleological. Nature aims toward particular ends that are ordained by the divine, and the values inherent in this arrangement cannot and must not be ignored or altered. How nature *is* reveals how it *should be*. Period. But the teleological character of nature has never been established by logical argument or empirical science—at least not to the satisfaction of most philosophers and scientists. In fact, science (including evolutionary theory) suggests that nature is not teleological at all, but instead random and purposeless, changing and adapting according to scientific laws, blind cause and effect, chance mutation, and competition among species. Moreover, the idea that values can somehow be extracted from the facts of nature is as problematic for natural law theory as it is for ethical egoism and utilitarianism. From the fact that humans have a natural inclination toward procreation it does not follow that discouraging procreation through contraception is morally wrong.

Natural law theory seems to falter on Criterion 3 (usefulness) because, as just mentioned, discovering what values are inscribed in nature is

problematic. The kinds of moral principles that we might extract from nature depend on our conception of nature, and such conceptions can vary. Taking their cue from Aquinas, many natural law theorists see the inclinations of human nature as benign; others, as fundamentally depraved. Historically, humans have shown a capacity for both great good and monstrous evil. Which inclination is the true one? And even if we could accurately identify human inclinations, there seems to be no reliable procedure for uncovering the corresponding moral values or telling whether moral principles should be absolutist.

LEARNING FROM NATURAL LAW

Like Kantian ethics, natural law theory is universalist, objective, and rational, applying to all persons and requiring that moral choices be backed by good reasons. The emphasis on reason makes morality independent of religion and belief in God, a distinction also found in Kant's ethics. At the heart of natural law theory is a strong respect for human life, an attitude that is close to, but not quite the same thing as, Kant's means-ends principle. Respect for life or persons is, of course, a primary concern of our moral experience and seems to preclude the kind of wholesale end-justifies-the-means calculations that are a defining characteristic of many forms of utilitarianism.

Natural law theory emphasizes a significant element in moral deliberation that some other theories play down: intention. In general, intention plays a larger role in natural law theory than it does in Kant's categorical imperative. To many natural law theorists, the rightness of an action often depends on the intentions of the moral agent performing it. In our previous example of the pregnant woman with cancer, the intention behind the act of taking the chemotherapy is to kill the cancer, not the fetus, though the fetus dies because of the treatment. So the action is thought to be morally permissible. If the intention had been to kill the fetus directly, the action would have been deemed wrong. In our everyday moral experience, we frequently take intentions into account in evaluating an action. We usually would think that there must be some morally relevant difference between a terrorist's intentionally killing ten people and a police officer's accidentally killing those same ten people while chasing the terrorist, though both scenarios result in the same tragic loss of life.

CHAPTER REVIEW

SUMMARY

Kant's moral theory is perhaps the most influential of all nonconsequentialist approaches. In his view, right actions have moral value only if they are done with a "good will"—for duty's sake alone. The meat of Kant's theory is the categorical imperative, a principle that he formulates in three versions. The first of the two versions we discuss says that an action is right if you could will the maxim of that action to become a moral law applying to all persons. An action is permissible if (1) its maxim can be universalized (if everyone can consistently act on it) and (2) you would be willing to have that happen. The second version of the categorical imperative says that we must always treat people as ends in themselves and never merely as means to an end.

Kant's theory seems to conflict with our common-sense moral judgments (Criterion 1) and has flaws that limit its usefulness in moral problem solving (Criterion 3). The theory falters under Criterion 1 mainly because some duties generated by the categorical imperative are absolute. Absolute duties can conflict, and Kant provides no way to resolve these inconsistencies, a failure under Criterion 3. Furthermore, counterexamples suggest that we have no genuine absolute duties.

Natural law theory is based on the notion that right actions are those that accord with natural law—the moral principles embedded in nature itself. How nature *is* reveals how it *should be*. The inclinations of human nature reveal the values that humans should live by. Aquinas, who gave us the most influential form of natural law theory, says that humans naturally incline toward preservation of human life, procreation, the search for truth, community, and benign and reasonable behavior. Like Kant's theory, traditional natural law theory is absolutist, maintaining that some actions are always wrong. These immoral actions include directly killing the innocent, interfering with procreation, and lying. The theory's absolutist rules do occasionally conflict, and the proposed remedy for any such inconsistencies is the doctrine of double effect. That principle applies to situations in which an action produces both good and bad effects. It says that performing a good action may be permissible even if it has bad effects, but performing a bad action for the purpose of achieving good effects is never permissible. Despite the double-effect doctrine, the theory's biggest weakness is still its absolutism, which seems to mandate actions that conflict with our considered moral judgments. In some cases, for example, the theory might require someone to allow hundreds of innocent people to die just to avoid the direct killing of a single person.

KEY TERMS
hypothetical imperative (p. 133)
categorical imperative (p. 133)
perfect duty (p. 133)
imperfect duty (p. 133)
means-ends principle (p. 135)
doctrine of double effect (p. 140)

EXERCISES
Review Questions
1. What is the significance of a "good will" in Kant's ethics? (pp. 132–133)
2. What is the difference between a hypothetical and a categorical imperative? (p. 133)
3. What is the moral principle laid out in the first version of Kant's categorical imperative? (p. 133)

4. What is the difference between perfect and imperfect duties? (p. 133)
5. How does Kant distinguish between treating someone as a means and treating someone *merely* as a means? (p. 135)
6. How can the absolutism of Kant's theory lead to judgments that conflict with moral common sense? (pp. 136–137)
7. How might the subjectivity of Kant's theory lead to the sanctioning of heinous acts? (p. 137)
8. What is natural law theory? (pp. 139–140)
9. According to natural law theorists, how can nature reveal anything about morality? (pp. 139–140)
10. According to Aquinas, what is the good that human nature aims at? (p. 139)
11. According to natural law theory, how are moral principles objective? How are they universal? (p. 140)
12. What is the doctrine of double effect? (p. 140)
13. How can the absolutism of natural law theory lead to moral judgments that conflict with moral common sense? (p. 143)

Discussion Questions

1. Which moral theory—Kant's or natural law—seems more plausible to you? Why?
2. What elements of Kant's theory do you think could or should be part of any viable moral theory?
3. In what way is Kant's ethics independent of (not based on) religious belief? Is natural law theory independent of religious belief? Why or why not?
4. According to Kant, why is breaking a promise or lying immoral? Do you agree with Kant's reasoning? Why or why not?
5. How might your life change if you completely embraced Kant's theory of morality?
6. How might your life change if you adopted the natural law theory of morality?
7. Would a Kantian and a natural law theorist agree on whether having an abortion is moral? Why or why not?

8. Do you believe, as Kant does, that there are perfect (absolute) duties? Why or why not?
9. According to the textbook, natural law theory generates judgments that conflict with commonsense morality. Do you agree with this assessment? Why or why not?
10. Is natural law theory more plausible than utilitarianism? Why or why not?

ETHICAL DILEMMAS

Explain how Kant's theory could be applied in the following scenarios to determine the proper course of action.

1. Julie and Chan have been dating for three months, and their relationship has slowly blossomed into one of sincere affection and trust. At the time they began dating, Chan had a sexually transmitted disease, but he never disclosed this information to Julie. Without Julie's knowledge, Chan sought treatment and was eventually cured of the infection. Chan has kept his secret from the beginning and has no intention of ever revealing it to anyone. How would Kant evaluate this situation? Would he approve or disapprove of Chan's actions?
2. Imagine a World War II scenario in which German soldiers strap innocent people to the front of their tanks to dissuade Allied troops from firing on the vehicles. If the Allies hold their fire, their positions will be overrun, and hundreds of their troops will be killed. The Allied commander gives the order for his troops to shoot at the tanks, knowing that the civilians will perish. Should the Allies have killed these innocents?

Explain how natural law theory could be applied in the following scenario to determine the proper course of action.

3. A scientist is conducting an experiment using one hundred adult subjects, hoping to finally discover a cure for liver cancer. Conducting this one last study is the only way to identify the substance that can cure the disease and save the

lives of countless people. But the experiment causes long-lasting, horrible pain in the subjects, and they will not be able to benefit in any way from the study's success. The researcher would ordinarily never be able to enlist any subjects for the study because of these two facts, so to ensure the cooperation of the subjects, he lies to them: he says that being a part of the study will be painless and that it will increase their life span. The study is completed, the cure is found, and the subjects spend the next year in agony. What would natural law theory say about the scientist's actions?

FURTHER READING

Stephen Buckle, "Natural Law," in *A Companion to Ethics,* ed. Peter Singer, corr. ed. (Oxford: Blackwell, 1993).

John Finnis, *Natural Law and Natural Rights* (Oxford: Clarendon Press; New York: Oxford University Press, 1980).

C. E. Harris, chapters 6 and 8 in *Applying Moral Theories,* 3rd ed. (Belmont, CA: Wadsworth, 1997).

Mark Murphy, "The Natural Law Tradition in Ethics," in *Stanford Encyclopedia of Philosophy*, Winter 2002 ed., ed. Edward N. Zalta, http://plato.stanford.edu/archives/win2002/entries/natural-law-ethics (1 March 2015).

Kai Nielsen, *Ethics without God* (London: Pemberton; Buffalo, NY: Prometheus, 1973).

Robert Nozick, *Anarchy, State and Utopia* (New York: Basic Books, 1974).

Onora O'Neill, "Kantian Ethics," in *A Companion to Ethics,* ed. Peter Singer, corr. ed. (Oxford: Blackwell, 1993).

Louis P. Pojman, "Natural Law," in *Ethics: Discovering Right and Wrong,* 4th ed. (Belmont, CA: Wadsworth, 2002).

James Rachels, chapter 9 in *The Elements of Moral Philosophy,* 4th ed. (Boston: McGraw-Hill, 2003).

Paul Taylor, chapter 5 in *Principles of Ethics: An Introduction* (Encino, CA: Dickenson, 1975).

Thomas Aquinas, *Summa Theologica,* in *Basic Writings of Saint Thomas Aquinas,* ed. and annotated by Anton C. Pegis (New York: Random House, 1945).

Robert N. Van Wyk, chapters 4 and 6 in *Introduction to Ethics* (New York: St. Martin's, 1990).

READINGS

From *Fundamental Principles of the Metaphysic of Morals*
IMMANUEL KANT

* * *

Nothing can possibly be conceived in the world, or even out of it, which can be called good, without qualification, except a *good will*. Intelligence, wit, judgement, and the other talents of the mind, however, they may be named, or courage, resolution, perseverance, as qualities of temperament, are undoubtedly good and desirable in many respects; but these gifts of nature may also become extremely bad and mischievous if the will which is to make use of them, and which, there-

Immanuel Kant, *Fundamental Principles of the Metaphysic of Morals,* trans. Thomas K. Abbott (edited).

fore, constitutes what is called *character,* is not good. It is the same with the *gifts of fortune*. Power, riches, honour, even health, and the general well-being and contentment with one's condition which is called *happiness,* inspire pride, and often presumption, if there is not a good will to correct the influence of these on the mind, and with this also to rectify the whole principle of acting and adapt it to its end. The sight of a being who is not adorned with a single feature of a pure and good will, enjoying unbroken prosperity, can never give pleasure to an impartial rational spectator. Thus a good will appears to constitute the indispensable condition even of being worthy of happiness.

There are even some qualities which are of service to this good will itself and may facilitate its action, yet which have no intrinsic unconditional value, but always presuppose a good will, and this qualifies the esteem that we justly have for them and does not permit us to regard them as absolutely good. Moderation in the affections and passions, self-control, and calm deliberation are not only good in many respects, but even seem to constitute part of the intrinsic worth of the person; but they are far from deserving to be called good without qualification, although they have been so unconditionally praised by the ancients. For without the principles of a good will, they may become extremely bad, and the coolness of a villain not only makes him far more dangerous, but also directly makes him more abominable in our eyes than he would have been without it.

A good will is good not because of what it performs or effects, not by its aptness for the attainment of some proposed end, but simply by virtue of the volition— that is, it is good in itself, and considered by itself is to be esteemed much higher than all that can be brought about by it in favour of any inclination, nay, even of the sum-total of all inclinations. Even if it should happen that, owing to special disfavour of fortune, or the niggardly provision of a step-motherly nature, this will should wholly lack power to accomplish its purpose, if with its greatest efforts it should yet achieve nothing, and there should remain only the good will (not, to be sure, a mere wish, but the summoning of all means in our power), then, like a jewel, it would still shine by its own light, as a thing which has its whole value in itself. Its usefulness or fruitfulness can neither add nor take away anything from this value. It would be, as it were, only the setting to enable us to handle it the more conveniently in common commerce, or to attract to it the attention of those who are not yet connoisseurs, but not to recommend it to true connoisseurs, or to determine its value.

There is, however, something so strange in this idea of the absolute value of the mere will, in which no account is taken of its utility, that notwithstanding the thorough assent of even common reason to the idea, yet a suspicion must arise that it may perhaps really be the product of mere high-flown fancy, and that we may have misunderstood the purpose of nature in assigning reason as the governor of our will. Therefore we will examine this idea from this point of view.

* * *

To be beneficent when we can is a duty; and besides this, there are many minds so sympathetically constituted that, without any other motive of vanity or self-interest, they find a pleasure in spreading joy around them and can take delight in the satisfaction of others so far as it is their own work. But I maintain that in such a case an action of this kind, however proper, however amiable it may be, has nevertheless no true moral worth, but is on a level with other inclinations, e.g., the inclination to honour, which, if it is happily directed to that which is in fact of public utility and accordant with duty and consequently honourable, deserves praise and encouragement, but not esteem. For the maxim lacks the moral import, namely, that such actions be done from duty, not from inclination. Put the case that the mind of that philanthropist were clouded by sorrow of his own, extinguishing all sympathy with the lot of others, and that, while he still has the power to benefit others in distress, he is not touched by their trouble because he is absorbed with his own; and now suppose that he tears himself out of this dead insensibility, and performs the action without any inclination to it, but simply from duty, then first has his action its genuine moral worth. Further still, if nature has put little sympathy in the heart of this or that man; if he, supposed to be an upright man, is by temperament cold and indifferent to the sufferings of others, perhaps because in respect of his own he is provided with the special gift of patience and fortitude and supposes, or even requires, that others should have the same—and such a man would certainly not be the meanest product of nature— but if nature had not specially framed him for a philanthropist, would he not still find in himself a source from whence to give himself a far higher worth than that of a good-natured temperament could be? Unquestionably. It is just in this that the moral worth of the character is brought out which is incomparably the highest of all, namely, that he is beneficent, not from inclination, but from duty.

* * *

Thus the moral worth of an action does not lie in the effect expected from it, nor in any principle of action which requires to borrow its motive from this expected effect. For all these effects—agreeableness of one's condition and even the promotion of the happiness of others—could have been also brought about by other causes, so that for this there would have been no need of the will of a rational being; whereas it is in this alone that the supreme and unconditional good can be found. The pre-eminent good which we call moral can therefore consist in nothing else than the conception of law in itself, which certainly is only possible in a rational being, in so far as this conception, and not the expected effect, determines the will. This is a good which is already present in the person who acts accordingly, and we have not to wait for it to appear first in the result.

* * *

But what sort of law can that be, the conception of which must determine the will, even without paying any regard to the effect expected from it, in order that this will may be called good absolutely and without qualification? As I have deprived the will of every impulse which could arise to it from obedience to any law, there remains nothing but the universal conformity of its actions to law in general, which alone is to serve the will as a principle, i.e., I am never to act otherwise than so that I could also will that my maxim should become a universal law. Here, now, it is the simple conformity to law in general, without assuming any particular law applicable to certain actions, that serves the will as its principle and must so serve it, if duty is not to be a vain delusion and a chimerical notion. The common reason of men in its practical judgements perfectly coincides with this and always has in view the principle here suggested. Let the question be, for example: May I when in distress make a promise with the intention not to keep it? I readily distinguish here between the two significations which the question may have: Whether it is prudent, or whether it is right, to make a false promise? The former may undoubtedly often be the case. I see clearly indeed that it is not enough to extricate myself from a present difficulty by means of this subterfuge, but it must be well considered whether there may not hereafter spring from this lie much greater inconvenience than that from which I now free myself, and as, with all my supposed cunning, the consequences cannot be so easily foreseen but that credit once lost may be much more injurious to me than any mischief which I seek to avoid at present, it should be considered whether it would not be more prudent to act herein according to a universal maxim and to make it a habit to promise nothing except with the intention of keeping it. But it is soon clear to me that such a maxim will still only be based on the fear of consequences. Now it is a wholly different thing to be truthful from duty, and to be so from apprehension of injurious consequences. In the first case, the very notion of the action already implies a law for me; in the second case, I must first look about elsewhere to see what results may be combined with it which would affect myself. For to deviate from the principle of duty is beyond all doubt wicked; but to be unfaithful to my maxim of prudence may often be very advantageous to me, although to abide by it is certainly safer. The shortest way, however, and an unerring one, to discover the answer to this question whether a lying promise is consistent with duty, is to ask myself, "Should I be content that my maxim (to extricate myself from difficulty by a false promise) should hold good as a universal law, for myself as well as for others?" and should I be able to say to myself, "Every one may make a deceitful promise when he finds himself in a difficulty from which he cannot otherwise extricate himself?" Then I presently become aware that while I can will the lie, I can by no means will that lying should be a universal law. For with such a law there would be no promises at all, since it would be in vain to allege my intention in regard to my future actions to those who would not believe this allegation, or if they over hastily did so would pay me back in my own coin. Hence my maxim, as soon as it should be made a universal law, would necessarily destroy itself.

I do not, therefore, need any far-reaching penetration to discern what I have to do in order that my will may be morally good. Inexperienced in the course of the world, incapable of being prepared for all its contingencies, I only ask myself: Canst thou also will that thy maxim should be a universal law? If not, then it must be rejected, and that not because of a disadvantage accruing from it to myself or even to others, but because it cannot enter as a principle into a possible universal legislation, and reason extorts from me immediate respect for such legislation. I do not indeed as yet discern on what this respect is based (this the philosopher may inquire), but at least I understand this, that it is an estimation of the worth which far outweighs all worth of what is recommended by inclination, and that the necessity of acting from pure respect for the practical law is what constitutes duty, to which every other motive must give place, because it is the condition of a will being good in itself, and the worth of such a will is above everything.

* * *

Nor could anything be more fatal to morality than that we should wish to derive it from examples. For every example of it that is set before me must be first itself tested by principles of morality, whether it is worthy to serve as an original example, i.e., as a pattern; but by no means can it authoritatively furnish the conception of morality. Even the Holy One of the Gospels must first be compared with our ideal of moral perfection before we can recognise Him as such; and so He says of Himself, "Why call ye Me (whom you see) good; none is good (the model of good) but God only (whom ye do not see)?" But whence have we the conception of God as the supreme good? Simply from the idea of moral perfection, which reason frames a priori and connects inseparably with the notion of a free will. Imitation finds no place at all in morality, and examples serve only for encouragement, i.e., they put beyond doubt the feasibility of what the law commands, they make visible that which the practical rule expresses more generally, but they can never authorize us to set aside the true original which lies in reason and to guide ourselves by examples.

* * *

From what has been said, it is clear that all moral conceptions have their seat and origin completely a priori in the reason, and that, moreover, in the commonest reason just as truly as in that which is in the highest degree speculative; that they cannot

be obtained by abstraction from any empirical, and therefore merely contingent, knowledge; that it is just this purity of their origin that makes them worthy to serve as our supreme practical principle, and that just in proportion as we add anything empirical, we detract from their genuine influence and from the absolute value of actions; that it is not only of the greatest necessity, in a purely speculative point of view, but is also of the greatest practical importance, to derive these notions and laws from pure reason, to present them pure and unmixed, and even to determine the compass of this practical or pure rational knowledge, i.e., to determine the whole faculty of pure practical reason; and, in doing so, we must not make its principles dependent on the particular nature of human reason, though in speculative philosophy this may be permitted, or may even at times be necessary; but since moral laws ought to hold good for every rational creature, we must derive them from the general concept of a rational being. In this way, although for its application to man morality has need of anthropology, yet, in the first instance, we must treat it independently as pure philosophy, i.e., as metaphysic, complete in itself (a thing which in such distinct branches of science is easily done); knowing well that unless we are in possession of this, it would not only be vain to determine the moral element of duty in right actions for purposes of speculative criticism, but it would be impossible to base morals on their genuine principles, even for common practical purposes, especially of moral instruction, so as to produce pure moral dispositions, and to engraft them on men's minds to the promotion of the greatest possible good in the world.

But in order that in this study we may not merely advance by the natural steps from the common moral judgement (in this case very worthy of respect) to the philosophical, as has been already done, but also from a popular philosophy, which goes no further than it can reach by groping with the help of examples, to metaphysic (which does not allow itself to be checked by anything empirical and, as it must measure the whole extent of this kind of rational knowledge, goes as far as ideal conceptions, where even examples fail us), we must follow and clearly describe the practical faculty of reason, from the general rules of its determination to the point where the notion of duty springs from it.

Everything in nature works according to laws. Rational beings alone have the faculty of acting according to the conception of laws—that is, according to principles, that is, have a will. Since the deduction of actions from principles requires reason, the will is nothing but practical reason. If reason infallibly determines the will, then the actions of such a being which are recognised as objectively necessary are subjectively necessary also, that is, the will is a faculty to choose that only which reason independent of inclination recognises as practically necessary, that is, as good. But if reason of itself does not sufficiently determine the will, if the latter is subject also to subjective conditions (particular impulses) which do not always coincide with the objective conditions; in a word, if the will does not in itself completely accord with reason (which is actually the case with men), then the actions which objectively are recognised as necessary are subjectively contingent, and the determination of such a will according to objective laws is obligation, that is to say, the relation of the objective laws to a will that is not thoroughly good is conceived as the determination of the will of a rational being by principles of reason, but which the will from its nature does not of necessity follow.

The conception of an objective principle, in so far as it is obligatory for a will, is called a command (of reason), and the formula of the command is called an imperative.

All imperatives are expressed by the word ought [or shall], and thereby indicate the relation of an objective law of reason to a will, which from its subjective constitution is not necessarily determined by it (an obligation). They say that something would be good to do or to forbear, but they say it to a will which does not always do a thing because it is conceived to be good to do it. That is practically good, however, which determines the will by means of the conceptions of reason, and consequently not from subjective causes, but objectively, that is, on principles which are valid for every rational being as such. It is distinguished from the pleasant, as that which influences the will only by means of sensation from merely subjective causes, valid only for the sense

of this or that one, and not as a principle of reason, which holds for every one.

* * *

Now all imperatives command either hypothetically or categorically. The former represent the practical necessity of a possible action as means to something else that is willed (or at least which one might possibly will). The categorical imperative would be that which represented an action as necessary of itself without reference to another end, that is, as objectively necessary.

Since every practical law represents a possible action as good and, on this account, for a subject who is practically determinable by reason, necessary, all imperatives are formulae determining an action which is necessary according to the principle of a will good in some respects. If now the action is good only as a means to something else, then the imperative is hypothetical; if it is conceived as good in itself and consequently as being necessarily the principle of a will which of itself conforms to reason, then it is categorical.

Thus the imperative declares what action possible by me would be good and presents the practical rule in relation to a will which does not forthwith perform an action simply because it is good, whether because the subject does not always know that it is good, or because, even if it know this, yet its maxims might be opposed to the objective principles of practical reason.

Accordingly the hypothetical imperative only says that the action is good for some purpose, possible or actual. In the first case it is a problematical, in the second an assertorial practical principle. The categorical imperative which declares an action to be objectively necessary in itself without reference to any purpose, i.e., without any other end, is valid as an apodeictic (practical) principle.

* * *

Finally, there is an imperative which commands a certain conduct immediately, without having as its condition any other purpose to be attained by it. This imperative is categorical. It concerns not the matter of the action, or its intended result, but its form and the principle of which it is itself a result; and what is essentially good in it consists in the mental disposition, let the consequence be what it may. This imperative may be called that of morality.

* * *

[The] question how the imperative of morality is possible, is undoubtedly one, the only one, demanding a solution, as this is not at all hypothetical, and the objective necessity which it presents cannot rest on any hypothesis, as is the case with the hypothetical imperatives. Only here we must never leave out of consideration that we cannot make out by any example, in other words empirically, whether there is such an imperative at all, but it is rather to be feared that all those which seem to be categorical may yet be at bottom hypothetical. For instance, when the precept is: "Thou shalt not promise deceitfully"; and it is assumed that the necessity of this is not a mere counsel to avoid some other evil, so that it should mean: "Thou shalt not make a lying promise, lest if it become known thou shouldst destroy thy credit," but that an action of this kind must be regarded as evil in itself, so that the imperative of the prohibition is categorical; then we cannot show with certainty in any example that the will was determined merely by the law, without any other spring of action, although it may appear to be so. For it is always possible that fear of disgrace, perhaps also obscure dread of other dangers, may have a secret influence on the will. Who can prove by experience the non-existence of a cause when all that experience tells us is that we do not perceive it? But in such a case the so-called moral imperative, which as such appears to be categorical and unconditional, would in reality be only a pragmatic precept, drawing our attention to our own interests and merely teaching us to take these into consideration.

We shall therefore have to investigate a priori the possibility of a categorical imperative, as we have not in this case the advantage of its reality being given in experience, so that [the elucidation of] its possibility should be requisite only for its explanation, not for its establishment. In the meantime it may be discerned beforehand that the categorical imperative alone has the purport of a practical law; all the rest may indeed be called principles of the will but not laws, since whatever is only necessary for the attainment of some

arbitrary purpose may be considered as in itself contingent, and we can at any time be free from the precept if we give up the purpose; on the contrary, the unconditional command leaves the will no liberty to choose the opposite; consequently it alone carries with it that necessity which we require in a law.

Secondly, in the case of this categorical imperative or law of morality, the difficulty (of discerning its possibility) is a very profound one. It is an a priori synthetical practical proposition; and as there is so much difficulty in discerning the possibility of speculative propositions of this kind, it may readily be supposed that the difficulty will be no less with the practical.

* * *

In this problem we will first inquire whether the mere conception of a categorical imperative may not perhaps supply us also with the formula of it, containing the proposition which alone can be a categorical imperative; for even if we know the tenor of such an absolute command, yet how it is possible will require further special and laborious study, which we postpone to the last section.

When I conceive a hypothetical imperative, in general I do not know beforehand what it will contain until I am given the condition. But when I conceive a categorical imperative, I know at once what it contains. For as the imperative contains besides the law only the necessity that the maxims shall conform to this law, while the law contains no conditions restricting it, there remains nothing but the general statement that the maxim of the action should conform to a universal law, and it is this conformity alone that the imperative properly represents as necessary.

* * *

There is therefore but one categorical imperative, namely, this: Act only on that maxim whereby thou canst at the same time will that it should become a universal law.

Now if all imperatives of duty can be deduced from this one imperative as from their principle, then, although it should remain undecided what is called duty is not merely a vain notion, yet at least we shall be able to show what we understand by it and what this notion means.

Since the universality of the law according to which effects are produced constitutes what is properly called nature in the most general sense (as to form), that is the existence of things so far as it is determined by general laws, the imperative of duty may be expressed thus: Act as if the maxim of thy action were to become by thy will a universal law of nature.

We will now enumerate a few duties, adopting the usual division of them into duties to ourselves and to others, and into perfect and imperfect duties.

* * *

1. A man reduced to despair by a series of misfortunes feels wearied of life, but is still so far in possession of his reason that he can ask himself whether it would not be contrary to his duty to himself to take his own life. Now he inquires whether the maxim of his action could become a universal law of nature. His maxim is: "From self-love I adopt it as a principle to shorten my life when its longer duration is likely to bring more evil than satisfaction." It is asked then simply whether this principle founded on self-love can become a universal law of nature. Now we see at once that a system of nature of which it should be a law to destroy life by means of the very feeling whose special nature it is to impel to the improvement of life would contradict itself and, therefore, could not exist as a system of nature; hence that maxim cannot possibly exist as a universal law of nature and, consequently, would be wholly inconsistent with the supreme principle of all duty.

2. Another finds himself forced by necessity to borrow money. He knows that he will not be able to repay it, but sees also that nothing will be lent to him unless he promises stoutly to repay it in a definite time. He desires to make this promise, but he has still so much conscience as to ask himself: "Is it not unlawful and inconsistent with duty to get out of a difficulty in this way?" Suppose however that he resolves to do so: then the maxim of his action would be expressed thus: "When I think myself in want of money, I will borrow money and promise to repay it, although I know that I never can do so." Now this principle of self-love or

of one's own advantage may perhaps be consistent with my whole future welfare; but the question now is, "Is it right?" I change then the suggestion of self-love into a universal law, and state the question thus: "How would it be if my maxim were a universal law?" Then I see at once that it could never hold as a universal law of nature, but would necessarily contradict itself. For supposing it to be a universal law that everyone when he thinks himself in a difficulty should be able to promise whatever he pleases, with the purpose of not keeping his promise, the promise itself would become impossible, as well as the end that one might have in view in it, since no one would consider that anything was promised to him, but would ridicule all such statements as vain pretences.

3. A third finds in himself a talent which with the help of some culture might make him a useful man in many respects. But he finds himself in comfortable circumstances and prefers to indulge in pleasure rather than to take pains in enlarging and improving his happy natural capacities. He asks, however, whether his maxim of neglect of his natural gifts, besides agreeing with his inclination to indulgence, agrees also with what is called duty. He sees then that a system of nature could indeed subsist with such a universal law although men (like the South Sea islanders) should let their talents rest and resolve to devote their lives merely to idleness, amusement, and propagation of their species—in a word, to enjoyment; but he cannot possibly will that this should be a universal law of nature, or be implanted in us as such by a natural instinct. For, as a rational being, he necessarily wills that his faculties be developed, since they serve him and have been given him, for all sorts of possible purposes.

4. A fourth, who is in prosperity, while he sees that others have to contend with great wretchedness and that he could help them, thinks: "What concern is it of mine? Let everyone be as happy as Heaven pleases, or as he can make himself; I will take nothing from him nor even envy him, only I do not wish to contribute anything to his welfare or to his assistance in distress!" Now no doubt if such a mode of thinking were a universal law, the human race might very well subsist and doubtless even better than in a state

in which everyone talks of sympathy and goodwill, or even takes care occasionally to put it into practice, but, on the other side, also cheats when he can, betrays the rights of men, or otherwise violates them. But although it is possible that a universal law of nature might exist in accordance with that maxim, it is impossible to will that such a principle should have the universal validity of a law of nature. For a will which resolved this would contradict itself, inasmuch as many cases might occur in which one would have need of the love and sympathy of others, and in which, by such a law of nature, sprung from his own will, he would deprive himself of all hope of the aid he desires.

These are a few of the many actual duties, or at least what we regard as such, which obviously fall into two classes on the one principle that we have laid down. We must be able to will that a maxim of our action should be a universal law. This is the canon of the moral appreciation of the action generally. Some actions are of such a character that their maxim cannot without contradiction be even conceived as a universal law of nature, far from it being possible that we should will that it should be so. In others this intrinsic impossibility is not found, but still it is impossible to will that their maxim should be raised to the universality of a law of nature, since such a will would contradict itself. It is easily seen that the former violate strict or rigorous (inflexible) duty; the latter only laxer (meritorious) duty. Thus it has been completely shown how all duties depend as regards the nature of the obligation (not the object of the action) on the same principle.

* * *

Now I say: man and generally any rational being exists as an end in himself, not merely as a means to be arbitrarily used by this or that will, but in all his actions, whether they concern himself or other rational beings, must be always regarded at the same time as an end. All objects of the inclinations have only a conditional worth, for if the inclinations and the wants founded on them did not exist, then their object would be without value. But the inclinations, themselves being sources of want, are so far from having an absolute worth for which they should be desired that on the contrary it must be the universal wish

of every rational being to be wholly free from them. Thus the worth of any object which is to be acquired by our action is always conditional. Beings whose existence depends not on our will but on nature's, have nevertheless, if they are irrational beings, only a relative value as means, and are therefore called things; rational beings, on the contrary, are called persons, because their very nature points them out as ends in themselves, that is as something which must not be used merely as means, and so far therefore restricts freedom of actions (and is an object of respect). These, therefore, are not merely subjective ends whose existence has a worth for us as an effect of our action, but objective ends, that is, things whose existence is an end in itself; an end moreover for which no other can be substituted, which they should subserve merely as means, for otherwise nothing whatever would possess absolute worth; but if all worth were conditioned and therefore contingent, then there would be no supreme practical principle of reason whatever.

If then there is a supreme practical principle or, in respect of the human will, a categorical imperative, it must be one which, being drawn from the conception of that which is necessarily an end for everyone because it is an end in itself, constitutes an objective principle of will, and can therefore serve as a universal practical law. The foundation of this principle is: rational nature exists as an end in itself. Man necessarily conceives his own existence as being so; so far then this is a subjective principle of human actions. But every other rational being regards its existence similarly, just on the same rational principle that holds for me: so that it is at the same time an objective principle, from which as a supreme practical law all laws of the will must be capable of being deduced. Accordingly the practical imperative will be as follows: So act as to treat humanity, whether in thine own person or in that of any other, in every case as an end withal, never as means only. We will now inquire whether this can be practically carried out.

* * *

To abide by the previous examples:

Firstly, under the head of necessary duty to oneself: He who contemplates suicide should ask himself whether his action can be consistent with the idea of humanity as an end in itself. If he destroys himself in order to escape from painful circumstances, he uses a person merely as a mean to maintain a tolerable condition up to the end of life. But a man is not a thing, that is to say, something which can be used merely as means, but must in all his actions be always considered as an end in himself. I cannot, therefore, dispose in any way of a man in my own person so as to mutilate him, to damage or kill him. (It belongs to ethics proper to define this principle more precisely, so as to avoid all misunderstanding, for example, as to the amputation of the limbs in order to preserve myself as to exposing my life to danger with a view to preserve it, etc. This question is therefore omitted here.)

Secondly, as regards necessary duties, or those of strict obligation, towards others: He who is thinking of making a lying promise to others will see at once that he would be using another man merely as a mean, without the latter containing at the same time the end in himself. For he whom I propose by such a promise to use for my own purposes cannot possibly assent to my mode of acting towards him and, therefore, cannot himself contain the end of this action. This violation of the principle of humanity in other men is more obvious if we take in examples of attacks on the freedom and property of others. For then it is clear that he who transgresses the rights of men intends to use the person of others merely as a means, without considering that as rational beings they ought always to be esteemed also as ends, that is, as beings who must be capable of containing in themselves the end of the very same action.

* * *

Thirdly, as regards contingent (meritorious) duties to oneself: It is not enough that the action does not violate humanity in our own person as an end in itself, it must also harmonize with it. Now there are in humanity capacities of greater perfection, which belong to the end that nature has in view in regard to humanity in ourselves as the subject: to neglect these might perhaps be consistent with the maintenance of humanity as an end in itself, but not with the advancement of this end.

* * *

Looking back now on all previous attempts to discover the principle of morality, we need not wonder why they all failed. It was seen that man was bound to laws by duty, but it was not observed that the laws to which he is subject are only those of his own giving, though at the same time they are universal, and that he is only bound to act in conformity with his own will; a will, however, which is designed by nature to give universal laws. For when one has conceived man only as subject to a law (no matter what), then this law required some interest, either by way of attraction or constraint, since it did not originate as a law from his own will, but this will was according to a law obliged by something else to act in a certain manner. Now by this necessary consequence all the labour spent in finding a supreme principle of duty was irrevocably lost. For men never elicited duty, but only a necessity of acting from a certain interest. Whether this interest was private or otherwise, in any case the imperative must be conditional and could not by any means be capable of being a moral command. I will therefore call this the principle of autonomy of the will, in contrast with every other which I accordingly reckon as heteronomy.

The conception of the will of every rational being as one which must consider itself as giving in all the maxims of its will universal laws, so as to judge itself and its actions from this point of view—this conception leads to another which depends on it and is very fruitful, namely that of a kingdom of ends.

By a kingdom I understand the union of different rational beings in a system by common laws. Now since it is by laws that ends are determined as regards their universal validity, hence, if we abstract from the personal differences of rational beings and likewise from all the content of their private ends, we shall be able to conceive all ends combined in a systematic whole (including both rational beings as ends in themselves, and also the special ends which each may propose to himself), that is to say, we can conceive a kingdom of ends, which on the preceding principles is possible.

For all rational beings come under the law that each of them must treat itself and all others never merely as means, but in every case at the same time as ends in themselves. Hence results a systematic union of rational being by common objective laws, that is, a kingdom which may be called a kingdom of ends, since what these laws have in view is just the relation of these beings to one another as ends and means. It is certainly only an ideal.

A rational being belongs as a member to the kingdom of ends when, although giving universal laws in it, he is also himself subject to these laws. He belongs to it as sovereign when, while giving laws, he is not subject to the will of any other.

A rational being must always regard himself as giving laws either as member or as sovereign in a kingdom of ends which is rendered possible by the freedom of will. He cannot, however, maintain the latter position merely by the maxims of his will, but only in case he is a completely independent being without wants and with unrestricted power adequate to his will.

Morality consists then in the reference of all action to the legislation which alone can render a kingdom of ends possible. This legislation must be capable of existing in every rational being and of emanating from his will, so that the principle of this will is never to act on any maxim which could not without contradiction be also a universal law and, accordingly, always so to act that the will could at the same time regard itself as giving in its maxims universal laws. If now the maxims of rational beings are not by their own nature coincident with this objective principle, then the necessity of acting on it is called practical necessitation, that is, duty. Duty does not apply to the sovereign in the kingdom of ends, but it does to every member of it and to all in the same degree.

* * *

From *Summa Theologica*, First Part of the Second Part

St. Thomas Aquinas

QUESTION 91.
OF THE VARIOUS KINDS OF LAW.

* * *

First Article.
Whether There Is an Eternal Law?

Objection 1. It would seem that there is no eternal law. Because every law is imposed on someone. But there was not someone from eternity on whom a law could be imposed: since God alone was from eternity. Therefore no law is eternal.

Obj. 2. Further, promulgation is essential to law. But promulgation could not be from eternity: because there was no one to whom it could be promulgated from eternity. Therefore no law can be eternal.

Thomas Aquinas, *Summa Theologica*, First Part of the Second Part, Questions 91 and 94 (edited). Translated by Fathers of the English Dominican Province, 1911.

Obj. 3. Further, a law implies order to an end. But nothing ordained to an end is eternal: for the last end alone is eternal. Therefore no law is eternal.

On the contrary, Augustine says: *That Law which is the Supreme Reason cannot be understood to be otherwise than unchangeable and eternal.*

I answer that . . . a law is nothing else but a dictate of practical reason emanating from the ruler who governs a perfect community. Now it is evident, granted that the world is ruled by Divine Providence . . . that the whole community of the universe is governed by Divine Reason. Wherefore the very Idea of the government of things in God the Ruler of the universe, has the nature of a law. And since the Divine Reason's conception of things is not subject to time but is eternal, according to Proverbs 8:23, therefore it is that this kind of law must be called eternal.

Reply Obj. 1. Those things that are not in themselves, exist with God, inasmuch as they are foreknown and preordained by Him, according to Romans

4:17: *Who calls those things that are not, as those that are.* Accordingly the eternal concept of the Divine law bears the character of an eternal law, in so far as it is ordained by God to the government of things foreknown by Him.

Reply Obj. 2. Promulgation is made by word of mouth or in writing; and in both ways the eternal law is promulgated: because both the Divine Word and the writing of the Book of Life are eternal. But the promulgation cannot be from eternity on the part of the creature that hears or reads.

Reply Obj. 3. The law implies order to the end actively, in so far as it directs certain things to the end; but not passively—that is to say, the law itself is not ordained to the end—except accidentally, in a governor whose end is extrinsic to him, and to which end his law must needs be ordained. But the end of the Divine government is God Himself, and His law is not distinct from Himself. Wherefore the eternal law is not ordained to another end.

Second Article.
Whether There Is in Us a Natural Law?

Objection 1. It would seem that there is no natural law in us. Because man is governed sufficiently by the eternal law: for Augustine says that *the eternal law is that by which it is right that all things should be most orderly.* But nature does not abound in superfluities as neither does she fail in necessaries. Therefore no law is natural to man.

Obj. 2. Further, by the law man is directed, in his acts, to the end . . . But the directing of human acts to their end is not a function of nature, as is the case in irrational creatures, which act for an end solely by their natural appetite; whereas man acts for an end by his reason and will. Therefore no law is natural to man.

Obj. 3. Further, the more a man is free, the less is he under the law. But man is freer than all the animals, on account of his free-will, with which he is endowed above all other animals. Since therefore other animals are not subject to a natural law, neither is man subject to a natural law.

On the contrary, A gloss on Romans 2:14: *When the Gentiles, who have not the law, do by nature those things that are of the law,* comments as follows: *Although they have no written law, yet they have the natural law, whereby each one knows, and is conscious of, what is good and what is evil.*

I answer that . . . law, being a rule and measure, can be in a person in two ways: in one way, as in him that rules and measures; in another way, as in that which is ruled and measured, since a thing is ruled and measured, in so far as it partakes of the rule or measure. Wherefore, since all things subject to Divine providence are ruled and measured by the eternal law . . . ; it is evident that all things partake somewhat of the eternal law, in so far as, namely, from its being imprinted on them, they derive their respective inclinations to their proper acts and ends. Now among all others, the rational creature is subject to Divine providence in the most excellent way, in so far as it partakes of a share of providence, by being provident both for itself and for others. Wherefore it has a share of the Eternal Reason, whereby it has a natural inclination to its proper act and end: and this participation of the eternal law in the rational creature is called the natural law. Hence the Psalmist after saying (Psalms 4:6): *Offer up the sacrifice of justice,* as though someone asked what the works of justice are, adds: *Many say, Who showeth us good things?* in answer to which question he says: *The light of Thy countenance, O Lord, is signed upon us:* thus implying that the light of natural reason, whereby we discern what is good and what is evil, which is the function of the natural law, is nothing else than an imprint on us of the Divine light. It is therefore evident that the natural law is nothing else than the rational creature's participation of the eternal law.

Reply Obj. 1. This argument would hold, if the natural law were something different from the eternal law: whereas it is nothing but a participation thereof, as stated above.

Reply Obj. 2. Every act of reason and will in us is based on that which is according to nature . . . : for every act of reasoning is based on principles that are known naturally, and every act of appetite in respect of the means is derived from the natural appetite in respect of the last end. Accordingly the first direction of our acts to their end must needs be in virtue of the natural law.

Reply Obj. 3. Even irrational animals partake in their own way of the Eternal Reason, just as the rational creature does. But because the rational creature partakes thereof in an intellectual and rational manner, therefore the participation of the eternal law in the rational creature is properly called a law, since a law is something pertaining to reason . . . Irrational creatures, however, do not partake thereof in a rational manner, wherefore there is no participation of the eternal law in them, except by way of similitude.

Third Article.
Whether There Is a Human Law?

Objection 1. It would seem that there is not a human law. For the natural law is a participation of the eternal law . . . Now through the eternal law *all things are most orderly,* as Augustine states. Therefore the natural law suffices for the ordering of all human affairs. Consequently there is no need for a human law.

Obj. 2. Further, a law bears the character of a measure. . . . But human reason is not a measure of things, but vice versa. . . . Therefore no law can emanate from human reason.

Obj. 3. Further, a measure should be most certain. . . . But the dictates of human reason in matters of conduct are uncertain, according to Book of Wisdom 9:14: *The thoughts of mortal men are fearful, and our counsels uncertain.* Therefore no law can emanate from human reason.

On the contrary, Augustine distinguishes two kinds of law, the one eternal, the other temporal, which he calls human.

I answer that . . . a law is a dictate of the practical reason. Now it is to be observed that the same procedure takes place in the practical and in the speculative reason: for each proceeds from principles to conclusions . . . Accordingly we conclude that just as, in the speculative reason, from naturally known indemonstrable principles, we draw the conclusions of the various sciences, the knowledge of which is not imparted to us by nature, but acquired by the efforts of reason, so too it is from the precepts of the natural law, as from general and indemonstrable principles, that the human reason needs to proceed to the more particular determination of certain matters. These particular determinations, devised by human reason,

are called human laws, provided the other essential conditions of law be observed . . . Wherefore Tully [Cicero] says in his *Rhetoric* that *justice has its source in nature; thence certain things came into custom by reason of their utility; afterwards these things which emanated from nature and were approved by custom, were sanctioned by fear and reverence for the law.*

Reply Obj. 1. The human reason cannot have a full participation of the dictate of the Divine Reason, but according to its own mode, and imperfectly. Consequently, as on the part of the speculative reason, by a natural participation of Divine Wisdom, there is in us the knowledge of certain general principles, but not proper knowledge of each single truth, such as that contained in the Divine Wisdom; so too, on the part of the practical reason, man has a natural participation of the eternal law, according to certain general principles, but not as regards the particular determinations of individual cases, which are, however, contained in the eternal law. Hence the need for human reason to proceed further to sanction them by law.

Reply Obj. 2. Human reason is not, of itself, the rule of things: but the principles impressed on it by nature, are general rules and measures of all things relating to human conduct, whereof the natural reason is the rule and measure, although it is not the measure of things that are from nature.

Reply Obj. 3. The practical reason is concerned with practical matters, which are singular and contingent: but not with necessary things, with which the speculative reason is concerned. Wherefore human laws cannot have that inerrancy that belongs to the demonstrated conclusions of sciences. Nor is it necessary for every measure to be altogether unerring and certain, but according as it is possible in its own particular genus.

Fourth Article.
Whether There Was Any Need for a Divine Law?

Objection 1. It would seem that there was no need for a Divine law. Because . . . the natural law is a participation in us of the eternal law. But the eternal law is a Divine law . . . Therefore there was no need for a Divine law in addition to the natural law, and human laws derived therefrom.

Obj. 2. Further, it is written (Ecclesiastes 15:14) that *God left man in the hand of his own counsel.* Now counsel is an act of reason . . . Therefore man was left to the direction of his reason. But a dictate of human reason is a human law . . . Therefore there is no need for man to be governed also by a Divine law.

Obj. 3. Further, human nature is more self-sufficing than irrational creatures. But irrational creatures have no Divine law besides the natural inclination impressed on them. Much less, therefore, should the rational creature have a Divine law in addition to the natural law.

On the contrary, David prayed God to set His law before him, saying (Psalms 118:33): *Set before me for a law the way of Thy justifications, O Lord.*

I answer that, Besides the natural and the human law it was necessary for the directing of human conduct to have a Divine law. And this for four reasons. First, because it is by law that man is directed how to perform his proper acts in view of his last end. And indeed if man were ordained to no other end than that which is proportionate to his natural faculty, there would be no need for man to have any further direction of the part of his reason, besides the natural law and human law which is derived from it. But since man is ordained to an end of eternal happiness which is inproportionate to man's natural faculty . . . therefore it was necessary that, besides the natural and the human law, man should be directed to his end by a law given by God.

Secondly, because, on account of the uncertainty of human judgment, especially on contingent and particular matters, different people form different judgments on human acts; whence also different and contrary laws result. In order, therefore, that man may know without any doubt what he ought to do and what he ought to avoid, it was necessary for man to be directed in his proper acts by a law given by God, for it is certain that such a law cannot err.

Thirdly, because man can make laws in those matters of which he is competent to judge. But man is not competent to judge of interior movements, that are hidden, but only of exterior acts which appear: and yet for the perfection of virtue it is necessary for man to conduct himself aright in both kinds of acts.

Consequently human law could not sufficiently curb and direct interior acts; and it was necessary for this purpose that a Divine law should supervene.

Fourthly, because, as Augustine says, human law cannot punish or forbid all evil deeds: since while aiming at doing away with all evils, it would do away with many good things, and would hinder the advance of the common good, which is necessary for human intercourse. In order, therefore, that no evil might remain unforbidden and unpunished, it was necessary for the Divine law to supervene, whereby all sins are forbidden.

And these four causes are touched upon in Psalms 118:8, where it is said: *The law of the Lord is unspotted,* i.e. allowing no foulness of sin; *converting souls,* because it directs not only exterior, but also interior acts; *the testimony of the Lord is faithful,* because of the certainty of what is true and right; *giving wisdom to little ones,* by directing man to an end supernatural and Divine.

Reply Obj. 1. By the natural law the eternal law is participated proportionately to the capacity of human nature. But to his supernatural end man needs to be directed in a yet higher way. Hence the additional law given by God, whereby man shares more perfectly in the eternal law.

Reply Obj. 2. Counsel is a kind of inquiry: hence it must proceed from some principles. Nor is it enough for it to proceed from principles imparted by nature, which are the precepts of the natural law, for the reasons given above: but there is need for certain additional principles, namely, the precepts of the Divine law.

Reply Obj. 3. Irrational creatures are not ordained to an end higher than that which is proportionate to their natural powers: consequently the comparison fails.

Fifth Article.
Whether There Is But One Divine Law?

Objection 1. It would seem that there is but one Divine law. Because, where there is one king in one kingdom there is but one law. Now the whole of mankind is compared to God as to one king, according to Psalms 46:8: *God is the King of all the earth.* Therefore there is but one Divine law.

Obj. 2. Further, every law is directed to the end which the lawgiver intends for those for whom he makes the law. But God intends one and the same thing for all men; since according to 1 Timothy 2:4: *He will have all men to be saved, and to come to the knowledge of the truth.* Therefore there is but one Divine law.

Obj. 3. Further, the Divine law seems to be more akin to the eternal law, which is one, than the natural law, according as the revelation of grace is of a higher order than natural knowledge. Therefore much more is the Divine law but one.

On the contrary, The Apostle says (Hebrews 7:12): *The priesthood being translated, it is necessary that a translation also be made of the law.* But the priesthood is twofold, as stated in the same passage, viz. the levitical priesthood, and the priesthood of Christ. Therefore the Divine law is twofold, namely the Old Law and the New Law.

I answer that . . . distinction is the cause of number. Now things may be distinguished in two ways. First, as those things that are altogether specifically different, e.g., a horse and an ox. Secondly, as perfect and imperfect in the same species, e.g., a boy and a man: and in this way the Divine law is divided into Old and New. Hence the Apostle (Galatians 3:24, 25) compares the state of man under the Old Law to that of a child *under a pedagogue*; but the state under the New Law, to that of a full grown man, who is *no longer under a pedagogue*.

Now the perfection and imperfection of these two laws is to be taken in connection with the three conditions pertaining to law, as stated above. For, in the first place, it belongs to law to be directed to the common good as to its end . . . This good may be twofold. It may be a sensible and earthly good; and to this, man was directly ordained by the Old Law: wherefore, at the very outset of the law, the people were invited to the earthly kingdom of the Chananaeans (Exodus 3:8, 17). Again it may be an intelligible and heavenly good: and to this, man is ordained by the New Law. Wherefore, at the very beginning of His preaching, Christ invited men to the kingdom of heaven, saying (Matthew 4:17): *Do penance, for the kingdom of heaven is at hand.* Hence Augustine says that *promises of temporal goods are contained in the Old Testament, for which reason it is called old; but the promise of eternal life belongs to the New Testament.*

Secondly, it belongs to the law to direct human acts according to the order of righteousness: wherein also the New Law surpasses the Old Law, since it directs our internal acts, according to Matthew 5:20: *Unless your justice abound more than that of the Scribes and Pharisees, you shall not enter into the kingdom of heaven.* Hence the saying that *the Old Law restrains the hand, but the New Law controls the mind.*

Thirdly, it belongs to the law to induce men to observe its commandments. This the Old Law did by the fear of punishment: but the New Law, by love, which is poured into our hearts by the grace of Christ, bestowed in the New Law, but foreshadowed in the Old. Hence Augustine says that *there is little difference between the Law and the Gospel—fear and love.*

Reply Obj. 1. As the father of a family issues different commands to the children and to the adults, so also the one King, God, in His one kingdom, gave one law to men, while they were yet imperfect, and another more perfect law, when, by the preceding law, they had been led to a greater capacity for Divine things.

Reply Obj. 2. The salvation of man could not be achieved otherwise than through Christ, according to Acts 4:12: *There is no other name . . . given to men, whereby we must be saved.* Consequently the law that brings all to salvation could not be given until after the coming of Christ. But before His coming it was necessary to give to the people, of whom Christ was to be born, a law containing certain rudiments of righteousness unto salvation, in order to prepare them to receive Him.

Reply Obj. 3. The natural law directs man by way of certain general precepts, common to both the perfect and the imperfect: wherefore it is one and the same for all. But the Divine law directs man also in certain particular matters, to which the perfect and imperfect do not stand in the same relation. Hence the necessity for the Divine law to be twofold, as already explained.

* * *

QUESTION 94.
OF THE NATURAL LAW.

First Article.
Whether the Natural Law Is a Habit?

Objection 1. It would seem that the natural law is a habit. Because, as the Philosopher [Aristotle] says, *there are three things in the soul: power, habit, and passion.* But the natural law is not one of the soul's powers: nor is it one of the passions; as we may see by going through them one by one. Therefore the natural law is a habit.

Obj. 2. Further, Basil says that the conscience or *synderesis is the law of our mind*; which can only apply to the natural law. But the *synderesis* is a habit. . . . Therefore the natural law is a habit.

Obj. 3. Further, the natural law abides in man always . . . But man's reason, which the law regards, does not always think about the natural law. Therefore the natural law is not an act, but a habit.

On the contrary, Augustine says that *a habit is that whereby something is done when necessary.* But such is not the natural law: since it is in infants and in the damned who cannot act by it. Therefore the natural law is not a habit.

I answer that, A thing may be called a habit in two ways. First, properly and essentially: and thus the natural law is not a habit. For . . . the natural law is something appointed by reason, just as a proposition is a work of reason. Now that which a man does is not the same as that whereby he does it: for he makes a becoming speech by the habit of grammar. Since then a habit is that by which we act, a law cannot be a habit properly and essentially.

Secondly, the term habit may be applied to that which we hold by a habit: thus faith may mean that which we hold by faith. And accordingly, since the precepts of the natural law are sometimes considered by reason actually, while sometimes they are in the reason only habitually, in this way the natural law may be called a habit. Thus, in speculative matters, the indemonstrable principles are not the habit itself whereby we hold those principles, but are the principles the habit of which we possess.

Reply Obj. 1. The Philosopher [Aristotle] proposes to discover the genus of virtue; and since it is evident that virtue is a principle of action, he mentions only those things which are principles of human acts, viz. powers, habits and passions. But there are other things in the soul besides these three: there are acts; thus *to will* is in the one that wills; again, things known are in the knower; moreover its own natural properties are in the soul, such as immortality and the like.

Reply Obj. 2. *Synderesis* is said to be the law of our mind, because it is a habit containing the precepts of the natural law, which are the first principles of human actions.

Reply Obj. 3. This argument proves that the natural law is held habitually; and this is granted.

To the argument advanced in the contrary sense we reply that sometimes a man is unable to make use of that which is in him habitually, on account of some impediment: thus, on account of sleep, a man is unable to use the habit of science. In like manner, through the deficiency of his age, a child cannot use the habit of understanding of principles, or the natural law, which is in him habitually.

Second Article.
Whether the Natural Law Contains Several Precepts, or Only One?

Objection 1. It would seem that the natural law contains, not several precepts, but one only. For law is a kind of precept. . . . If therefore there were many precepts of the natural law, it would follow that there are also many natural laws.

Obj. 2. Further, the natural law is consequent to human nature. But human nature, as a whole, is one; though, as to its parts, it is manifold. Therefore, either there is but one precept of the law of nature, on account of the unity of nature as a whole; or there are many, by reason of the number of parts of human nature. The result would be that even things relating to the inclination of the concupiscible faculty belong to the natural law.

Obj. 3. Further, law is something pertaining to reason . . . Now reason is but one in man. Therefore there is only one precept of the natural law.

On the contrary, The precepts of the natural law in man stand in relation to practical matters, as the first principles to matters of demonstration. But there are several first indemonstrable principles. Therefore there are also several precepts of the natural law.

I answer that . . . the precepts of the natural law are to the practical reason, what the first principles of demonstrations are to the speculative reason; because both are self-evident principles. Now a thing is said to be self-evident in two ways: first, in itself; secondly, in relation to us. Any proposition is said to be self-evident in itself, if its predicate is contained in the notion of the subject: although, to one who knows not the definition of the subject, it happens that such a proposition is not self-evident. For instance, this proposition, *Man is a rational being,* is, in its very nature, self-evident, since who says *man,* says *a rational being*: and yet to one who knows not what a man is, this proposition is not self-evident. Hence it is that, as Boethius says, certain axioms or propositions are universally self-evident to all; and such are those propositions whose terms are known to all, as, *Every whole is greater than its part,* and, *Things equal to one and the same are equal to one another.* But some propositions are self-evident only to the wise, who understand the meaning of the terms of such propositions: thus to one who understands that an angel is not a body, it is self-evident that an angel is not circumscriptively in a place: but this is not evident to the unlearned, for they cannot grasp it.

Now a certain order is to be found in those things that are apprehended universally. For that which, before aught else, falls under apprehension, is *being,* the notion of which is included in all things whatsoever a man apprehends. Wherefore the first indemonstrable principle is that *the same thing cannot be affirmed and denied at the same time,* which is based on the notion of *being* and *not-being*: and on this principle all others are based . . . Now as *being* is the first thing that falls under the apprehension simply, so *good* is the first thing that falls under the apprehension of the practical reason, which is directed to action: since every agent acts for an end under the aspect of good. Consequently the first principle of practical reason is one founded on the notion of good, viz. that *good is that which all things seek after.* Hence this is the first precept of law, that *good is to be done and pursued, and evil is to be avoided.* All other precepts of the natural law are based upon this: so that

whatever the practical reason naturally apprehends as man's good (or evil) belongs to the precepts of the natural law as something to be done or avoided.

Since, however, good has the nature of an end, and evil, the nature of a contrary, hence it is that all those things to which man has a natural inclination, are naturally apprehended by reason as being good, and consequently as objects of pursuit, and their contraries as evil, and objects of avoidance. Wherefore according to the order of natural inclinations, is the order of the precepts of the natural law. Because in man there is first of all an inclination to good in accordance with the nature which he has in common with all substances: inasmuch as every substance seeks the preservation of its own being, according to its nature: and by reason of this inclination, whatever is a means of preserving human life, and of warding off its obstacles, belongs to the natural law. Secondly, there is in man an inclination to things that pertain to him more specially, according to that nature which he has in common with other animals: and in virtue of this inclination, those things are said to belong to the natural law, *which nature has taught to all animals,* such as sexual intercourse, education of offspring and so forth. Thirdly, there is in man an inclination to good, according to the nature of his reason, which nature is proper to him: thus man has a natural inclination to know the truth about God, and to live in society: and in this respect, whatever pertains to this inclination belongs to the natural law; for instance, to shun ignorance, to avoid offending those among whom one has to live, and other such things regarding the above inclination.

Reply Obj. 1. All these precepts of the law of nature have the character of one natural law, inasmuch as they flow from one first precept.

Reply Obj. 2. All the inclinations of any parts whatsoever of human nature, e.g. of the concupiscible and irascible parts, in so far as they are ruled by reason, belong to the natural law, and are reduced to one first precept, as stated above: so that the precepts of the natural law are many in themselves, but are based on one common foundation.

Reply Obj. 3. Although reason is one in itself, yet it directs all things regarding man; so that whatever can be ruled by reason, is contained under the law of reason.

Third Article.
Whether All Acts of Virtue Are Prescribed by the Natural Law?

Objection 1. It would seem that not all acts of virtue are prescribed by the natural law. Because . . . it is essential to a law that it be ordained to the common good. But some acts of virtue are ordained to the private good of the individual, as is evident especially in regards to acts of temperance. Therefore not all acts of virtue are the subject of natural law.

Obj. 2. Further, every sin is opposed to some virtuous act. If therefore all acts of virtue are prescribed by the natural law, it seems to follow that all sins are against nature: whereas this applies to certain special sins.

Obj. 3. Further, those things which are according to nature are common to all. But acts of virtue are not common to all: since a thing is virtuous in one, and vicious in another. Therefore not all acts of virtue are prescribed by the natural law.

On the contrary, Damascene says that *virtues are natural.* Therefore virtuous acts also are a subject of the natural law.

I answer that, We may speak of virtuous acts in two ways: first, under the aspect of virtuous; secondly, as such and such acts considered in their proper species. If then we speak of acts of virtue, considered as virtuous, thus all virtuous acts belong to the natural law. For it has been stated that to the natural law belongs everything to which a man is inclined according to his nature. Now each thing is inclined naturally to an operation that is suitable to it according to its form: thus fire is inclined to give heat. Wherefore, since the rational soul is the proper form of man, there is in every man a natural inclination to act according to reason: and this is to act according to virtue. Consequently, considered thus, all acts of virtue are prescribed by the natural law: since each one's reason naturally dictates to him to act virtuously. But if we speak of virtuous acts, considered in themselves, i.e. in their proper species, thus not all virtuous acts are prescribed by the natural law: for many things are done virtuously, to which nature does not incline at first; but which, through the inquiry of reason, have been found by men to be conducive to well-living.

Reply Obj. 1. Temperance is about the natural concupiscences of food, drink and sexual matters, which are indeed ordained to the natural common good, just as other matters of law are ordained to the moral common good.

Reply Obj. 2. By human nature we may mean either that which is proper to man—and in this sense all sins, as being against reason, are also against nature, as Damascene states: or we may mean that nature which is common to man and other animals; and in this sense, certain special sins are said to be against nature; thus contrary to sexual intercourse, which is natural to all animals, is unisexual lust, which has received the special name of the unnatural crime.

Reply Obj. 3. This argument considers acts in themselves. For it is owing to the various conditions of men, that certain acts are virtuous for some, as being proportionate and becoming to them, while they are vicious for others, as being out of proportion to them.

Fourth Article.
Whether the Natural Law Is the Same in All Men?

Objection 1. It would seem that the natural law is not the same in all. For it is stated in the Decretals that *the natural law is that which is contained in the Law and the Gospel.* But this is not common to all men; because, as it is written (Romans 10:16), *all do not obey the gospel.* Therefore the natural law is not the same in all men.

Obj. 2. Further, *Things which are according to the law are said to be just.* . . . But . . . nothing is so universally just as not to be subject to change in regard to some men. Therefore even the natural law is not the same in all men.

Obj. 3. Further . . . to the natural law belongs everything to which a man is inclined according to his nature. Now different men are naturally inclined to different things; some to the desire of pleasures, others to the desire of honors, and other men to other things. Therefore there is not one natural law for all.

On the contrary, Isidore says: *The natural law is common to all nations.*

I answer that . . . to the natural law belongs those things to which a man is inclined naturally: and among these it is proper to man to be inclined to act according to reason. Now the process of reason is from the common to the proper . . . The speculative reason, however, is differently situated in this matter, from the practical reason. For, since the speculative reason is busied chiefly with the necessary things, which cannot be otherwise than they are, its proper conclusions, like the universal principles, contain the truth without fail. The practical reason, on the other hand, is busied with contingent matters, about which human actions are concerned: and consequently, although there is necessity in the general principles, the more we descend to matters of detail, the more frequently we encounter defects. Accordingly then in speculative matters truth is the same in all men, both as to principles and as to conclusions: although the truth is not known to all as regards the conclusions, but only as regards the principles which are called common notions. But in matters of action, truth or practical rectitude is not the same for all, as to matters of detail, but only as to the general principles: and where there is the same rectitude in matters of detail, it is not equally known to all.

It is therefore evident that, as regards the general principles whether of speculative or of practical reason, truth or rectitude is the same for all, and is equally known by all. As to the proper conclusions of the speculative reason, the truth is the same for all, but is not equally known to all: thus it is true for all that the three angles of a triangle are together equal to two right angles, although it is not known to all. But as to the proper conclusions of the practical reason, neither is the truth or rectitude the same for all, nor, where it is the same, is it equally known by all. Thus it is right and true for all to act according to reason: and from this principle it follows as a proper conclusion, that goods entrusted to another should be restored to their owner. Now this is true for the majority of cases: but it may happen in a particular case that it would be injurious, and therefore unreasonable, to restore goods held in trust; for instance, if they are claimed for the purpose of fighting against one's country. And this principle will be found to fail the more, according as we descend further into detail, e.g. if one were to say that goods held in trust should be restored with such and such a guarantee, or in such and such a way; because the greater the

number of conditions added, the greater the number of ways in which the principle may fail, so that it be not right to restore or not to restore.

Consequently we must say that the natural law, as to general principles, is the same for all, both as to rectitude and as to knowledge. But as to certain matters of detail, which are conclusions, as it were, of those general principles, it is the same for all in the majority of cases, both as to rectitude and as to knowledge; and yet in some few cases it may fail, both as to rectitude, by reason of certain obstacles (just as natures subject to generation and corruption fail in some few cases on account of some obstacle), and as to knowledge, since in some the reason is perverted by passion, or evil habit, or an evil disposition of nature; thus formerly, theft, although it is expressly contrary to the natural law, was not considered wrong among the Germans, as Julius Caesar relates.

Reply Obj. 1. The meaning of the sentence quoted is not that whatever is contained in the Law and the Gospel belongs to the natural law, since they contain many things that are above nature; but that whatever belongs to the natural law is fully contained in them. Wherefore Gratian, after saying that *the natural law is what is contained in the Law and the Gospel,* adds at once, by way of example, *by which everyone is commanded to do to others as he would be done by.*

Reply Obj. 2. The saying of the Philosopher is to be understood of things that are naturally just, not as general principles, but as conclusions drawn from them, having rectitude in the majority of cases, but failing in a few.

Reply Obj. 3. As, in man, reason rules and commands the other powers, so all the natural inclinations belonging to the other powers must needs be directed according to reason. Wherefore it is universally right for all men, that all their inclinations should be directed according to reason.

Fifth Article.
Whether the Natural Law Can Be Changed?

Objection 1. It would seem that the natural law can be changed. Because on Ecclesiastes 17:9, *He gave them instructions, and the law of life,* the gloss says: *He wished the law of the letter to be written, in order to correct the law of nature.* But that which is corrected is changed. Therefore the natural law can be changed.

Obj. 2. Further, the slaying of the innocent, adultery, and theft are against the natural law. But we find these things changed by God: as when God commanded Abraham to slay his innocent son (Genesis 22:2); and when he ordered the Jews to borrow and purloin the vessels of the Egyptians (Exodus 12:35); and when He commanded Osee to take to himself *a wife of fornications* (Hosea 1:2). Therefore the natural law can be changed.

Obj. 3. Further, Isidore says that *the possession of all things in common, and universal freedom, are matters of natural law.* But these things are seen to be changed by human laws. Therefore it seems that the natural law is subject to change.

On the contrary, It is said in the Decretals: *The natural law dates from the creation of the rational creature. It does not vary according to time, but remains unchangeable.*

I answer that, A change in the natural law may be understood in two ways. First, by way of addition. In this sense nothing hinders the natural law from being changed: since many things for the benefit of human life have been added over and above the natural law, both by the Divine law and by human laws.

Secondly, a change in the natural law may be understood by way of subtraction, so that what previously was according to the natural law, ceases to be so. In this sense, the natural law is altogether unchangeable in its first principles: but in its secondary principles, which, as we have said, are certain detailed proximate conclusions drawn from the first principles, the natural law is not changed so that what it prescribes be not right in most cases. But it may be changed in some particular cases of rare occurrence, through some special causes hindering the observance of such precepts.

Reply Obj. 1. The written law is said to be given for the correction of the natural law, either because it supplies what was wanting to the natural law; or because the natural law was perverted in the hearts of some men, as to certain matters, so that they esteemed those things good which are naturally evil; which perversion stood in need of correction.

Reply Obj. 2. All men alike, both guilty and innocent, die the death of nature: which death of nature is inflicted by the power of God on account of original sin, according to 1 Kings 2:6: *The Lord killeth and maketh alive.* Consequently, by the command of God, death can be inflicted on any man, guilty or innocent, without any injustice whatever. In like manner adultery is intercourse with another's wife; who is allotted to him by the law emanating from God. Consequently intercourse with any woman, by the command of God, is neither adultery nor fornication. The same applies to theft, which is the taking of another's property. For whatever is taken by the command of God, to Whom all things belong, is not taken against the will of its owner, whereas it is in this that theft consists. Nor is it only in human things, that whatever is commanded by God is right; but also in natural things, whatever is done by God, is, in some way, natural . . .

Reply Obj. 3. A thing is said to belong to the natural law in two ways. First, because nature inclines thereto: e.g. that one should not do harm to another. Secondly, because nature did not bring in the contrary: thus we might say that for man to be naked is of the natural law, because nature did not give him clothes, but art invented them. In this sense, *the possession of all things in common and universal freedom* are said to be of the natural law, because, to wit, the distinction of possessions and slavery were not brought in by nature, but devised by human reason for the benefit of human life. Accordingly the law of nature was not changed in this respect, except by addition.

Sixth Article.
Whether the Law of Nature Can Be Abolished from the Heart of Man?

Objection 1. It would seem that the natural law can be abolished from the heart of man. Because on Romans 2:14, *When the Gentiles who have not the law,* etc. a gloss says that *the law of righteousness, which sin had blotted out, is graven on the heart of man when he is restored by grace.* But the law of righteousness is the law of nature. Therefore the law of nature can be blotted out.

Obj. 2. Further, the law of grace is more efficacious than the law of nature. But the law of grace is blotted out by sin. Much more therefore can the law of nature be blotted out.

Obj. 3. Further, that which is established by law is made just. But many things are enacted by men, which are contrary to the law of nature. Therefore the law of nature can be abolished from the heart of man.

On the contrary, Augustine says: *Thy law is written in the hearts of men, which iniquity itself effaces not.* But the law which is written in men's hearts is the natural law. Therefore the natural law cannot be blotted out.

I answer that . . . there belong to the natural law, first, certain most general precepts, that are known to all; and secondly, certain secondary and more detailed precepts, which are, as it were, conclusions following closely from first principles. As to those general principles, the natural law, in the abstract, can nowise be blotted out from men's hearts. But it is blotted out in the case of a particular action, in so far as reason is hindered from applying the general principle to a particular point of practice, on account of concupiscence

or some other passion . . . But as to the other, i.e. the secondary precepts, the natural law can be blotted out from the human heart, either by evil persuasions, just as in speculative matters errors occur in respect of necessary conclusions; or by vicious customs and corrupt habits, as among some men, theft, and even unnatural vices, as the Apostle states, were not esteemed sinful.

Reply Obj. 1. Sin blots out the law of nature in particular cases, not universally, except perchance in regard to the secondary precepts of the natural law, in the way stated above.

Reply Obj. 2. Although grace is more efficacious than nature, yet nature is more essential to man, and therefore more enduring.

Reply Obj. 3. This argument is true of the secondary precepts of the natural law, against which some legislators have framed certain enactments which are unjust.

Morality as a System of Hypothetical Imperatives

PHILIPPA FOOT

There are many difficulties and obscurities in Kant's moral philosophy, and few contemporary moralists will try to defend it all; many, for instance, agree in rejecting Kant's derivation of duties from the mere form of law expressed in terms of a universally legislative will. Nevertheless, it is generally supposed, even by those who would not dream of calling themselves his followers, that Kant established one thing beyond doubt—namely, the necessity of distinguishing moral judgments from hypothetical imperatives. That moral judgments cannot be hypothetical imperatives has come to seem an unquestionable truth. It will be argued here that it is not.

Philippa Foot, "Morality as a System of Hypothetical Imperatives," *Philosophical Review*, vol. 81, no. 3 (July 1972): 305–16.

In discussing so thoroughly Kantian a notion as that of the hypothetical imperative, one naturally begins by asking what Kant himself meant by a hypothetical imperative, and it may be useful to say a little about the idea of an imperative as this appears in Kant's works. In writing about imperatives Kant seems to be thinking at least as much of statements about what ought to be or should be done, as of injunctions expressed in the imperative mood. He even describes as an imperative the assertion that it would be "good to do or refrain from doing something"[1] and explains that for a will that "does not always do something simply because it is presented to it as a good thing to do" this has the force of a command of reason. We may therefore think of Kant's imperatives as statements to the effect that something ought to be done or that it would be good to do it.

The distinction between hypothetical imperatives and categorical imperatives, which plays so important a part in Kant's ethics, appears in characteristic form in the following passages from the *Foundations of the Metaphysics of Morals:*

> All imperatives command either hypothetically or categorically. The former present the practical necessity of a possible action as a means to achieving something else which one desires (or which one may possibly desire). The categorical imperative would be one which presented an action as of itself objectively necessary, without regard to any other end.[2]
>
> If the action is good only as a means to something else, the imperative is hypothetical; but if it is thought of as good in itself, and hence as necessary in a will which of itself conforms to reason as the principle of this will, the imperative is categorical.[3]

The hypothetical imperative, as Kant defines it, "says only that the action is good to some purpose" and the purpose, he explains, may be possible or actual. Among imperatives related to actual purposes Kant mentions rules of prudence, since he believes that all men necessarily desire their own happiness. Without committing ourselves to this view it will be useful to follow Kant in classing together as "hypothetical imperatives" those telling a man what he ought to do because (or if) he wants something and those telling him what he ought to do on grounds of self-interest. Common opinion agrees with Kant in insisting that a moral man must accept a rule of duty whatever his interests or desires.[4]

Having given a rough description of the class of Kantian hypothetical imperatives it may be useful to point to the heterogeneity within it. Sometimes what a man should do depends on his passing inclination, as when he wants his coffee hot and should warm the jug. Sometimes it depends on some long-term project, when the feelings and inclinations of the moment are irrelevant. If one wants to be a respectable philosopher one should get up in the mornings and do some work, though just at that moment when one should do it the thought of being a respectable philosopher leaves one cold. It is true nevertheless to say of one, at that moment, that one wants to be a respectable philosopher,[5] and this can be the foundation of a desire-dependent hypothetical imperative. The term "desire" as used in the original account of the hypothetical imperative was meant as a grammatically convenient substitute for "want," and was not meant to carry any implication of inclination rather than long-term aim or project. Even the word "project," taken strictly, introduces undesirable restrictions. If someone is devoted to his family or his country or to any cause, there are certain things he wants, which may then be the basis of hypothetical imperatives, without either inclinations or projects being quite what is in question. Hypothetical imperatives should already be appearing as extremely diverse; a further important distinction is between those that concern an individual and those that concern a group. The desires on which a hypothetical imperative is dependent may be those of one man, or may be taken for granted as belonging to a number of people, engaged in some common project or sharing common aims.

Is Kant right to say that moral judgments are categorical, not hypothetical, imperatives? It may seem that he is, for we find in our language two different uses of words such as "should" and "ought," apparently corresponding to Kant's hypothetical and categorical imperatives, and we find moral judgments on the "categorical" side. Suppose, for instance, we have advised a traveler that he should take a certain train, believing him to be journeying to his home. If we find that he has decided to go elsewhere, we will most likely have to take back what we said: the "should" will now be unsupported and in need of support. Similarly, we must be prepared to withdraw our statement about what he should do if we find that the right relation does not hold between the action and the end—that it is either no way of getting what he wants (or doing what he wants to do) or not the most eligible among possible means. The use of "should" and "ought" in moral contexts is, however, quite different. When we say that a man should do something and intend a moral judgment we do not have to back up what we say by considerations about his interests or his desires; if no such connection can be found the "should" need not be withdrawn. It follows that the agent cannot rebut an assertion about what, morally speaking, he should do by showing that the action is not ancillary to his interests or desires. Without such a connection the "should" does not stand unsupported and in need of support; the support that *it* requires is of another kind.[6]

There is, then, one clear difference between moral judgments and the class of "hypothetical imperatives" so far discussed. In the latter "should" is used "hypothetically," in the sense defined, and if Kant were merely drawing attention to this piece of linguistic usage his point would be easily proved. But obviously Kant meant more than this; in describing moral judgments as non-hypothetical—that is, categorical imperatives—he is ascribing to them a special dignity and necessity which this usage cannot give. Modern philosophers follow Kant in talking, for example, about the "unconditional requirement" expressed in moral judgments. These tell us what we have to do whatever our interests or desires, and by their inescapability they are distinguished from hypothetical imperatives.

The problem is to find proof for this further feature of moral judgments. If anyone fails to see the gap that has to be filled it will be useful to point out to him that we find "should" used non-hypothetically in some non-moral statements to which no one attributes the special dignity and necessity conveyed by the description "categorical imperative." For instance, we find this non-hypothetical use of "should" in sentences enunciating rules of etiquette, as, for example, that an invitation in the third person should be answered in the third person, where the rule does not *fail to apply* to someone who has his own good reasons for ignoring this piece of nonsense, or who simply does not care about what, from the point of view of etiquette, he should do. Similarly, there is a non-hypothetical use of "should" in contexts where something like a club rule is in question. The club secretary who has told a member that he should not bring ladies into the smoking room does not say, "Sorry, I was mistaken" when informed that this member is resigning tomorrow and cares nothing about his reputation in the club. Lacking a connection with the agent's desires or interests, this "should" does not stand "unsupported and in need of support"; it requires only the backing of the rule. The use of "should" is therefore "non-hypothetical" in the sense defined.

It follows that if a hypothetical use of "should" gives a hypothetical imperative, and a non-hypothetical use of "should" a categorical imperative, then "should" statements based on rules of etiquette, or rules of a club, are categorical imperatives. Since this would not be accepted by defenders of the categorical imperative in ethics, who would insist that these other "should" statements give hypothetical imperatives, they must be using this expression in some other sense. We must therefore ask what they mean when they say that "You should answer . . . in the third person" is a hypothetical imperative. Very roughly the idea seems to be that one may reasonably ask why anyone should bother about what should$_e$ (should from the point of view of etiquette) be done, and that such considerations deserve no notice unless reason is shown. So although people give as their reason for doing something the fact that it is required by etiquette, we do not take this consideration as *in itself giving us reason to act*. Considerations of etiquette do not have any automatic reason-giving force, and a man might be right if he denied that he had reason to do "what's done."

This seems to take us to the heart of the matter, for, by contrast, it is supposed that moral considerations necessarily give reasons for acting to any man. The difficulty is, of course, to defend this proposition which is more often repeated than explained. Unless it is said, implausibly, that all "should" or "ought" statements give reasons for acting, which leaves the old problem of assigning a special categorical status to moral judgment, we must be told what it is that makes the moral "should" relevantly different from the "shoulds" appearing in normative statements of other kinds.[7] Attempts have sometimes been made to show that some kind of irrationality is involved in ignoring the "should" of morality: in saying "Immoral—so what?" as one says "Not *comme il faut*—so what?" But as far as I can see these have all rested on some illegitimate assumption, as, for instance, of thinking that the amoral man, who agrees that some piece of conduct is immoral but takes no notice of that, is inconsistently disregarding a rule of conduct that he has accepted; or again of thinking it inconsistent to desire that others will not do to one what one proposes to do to them. The fact is that the man who rejects morality because he sees no reason to obey its rules can be convicted of villainy but not of inconsistency. Nor will his action necessarily be irrational. Irrational actions are those in which a man in some way defeats his own purposes, doing what is calculated to be disadvantageous or to frustrate his ends. Immorality does not *necessarily* involve any such thing.

It is obvious that the normative character of moral judgment does not guarantee its reason-giving force. Moral judgments are normative, but so are judgments of manners, statements of club rules, and many others. Why should the first provide reasons for acting as the others do not? In every case it is because there is a background of teaching that the non-hypothetical "should" can be used. The behavior is required, not simply recommended, but the question remains as to why we should do what we are required to do. It is true that moral rules are often enforced much more strictly than the rules of etiquette, and our reluctance to press the non-hypothetical "should" of etiquette may be one reason why we think of the rules of etiquette as hypothetical imperatives. But are we then to say that there is nothing behind the idea that moral judgments are categorical imperatives but the relative stringency of our moral teaching? I believe that this may have more to do with the matter than the defenders of the categorical imperative would like to admit. For if we look at the kind of thing that is said in its defense we may find ourselves puzzled about what the words can even mean unless we connect them with the feelings that this stringent teaching implants. People talk, for instance, about the "binding force" of morality, but it is not clear what this means if not that we *feel* ourselves unable to escape. Indeed the "inescapability" of moral requirements is often cited when they are being contrasted with hypothetical imperatives. No one, it is said, escapes the requirements of ethics by having or not having particular interests or desires. Taken in one way this only reiterates the contrast between the "should" of morality and the hypothetical "should," and once more places morality alongside of etiquette. Both are inescapable in that behavior does not cease to offend against either morality or etiquette because the agent is indifferent to their purposes and to the disapproval he will incur by flouting them. But morality is

supposed to be inescapable in some special way and this may turn out to be merely the reflection of the way morality is taught. Of course, we must try other ways of expressing the fugitive thought. It may be said, for instance, that moral judgments have a kind of necessity since they tell us what we "must do" or "have to do" whatever our interests and desires. The sense of this is, again, obscure. Sometimes when we use such expressions we are referring to physical or mental compulsion. (A man has to go along if he is pulled by strong men, and he has to give in if tortured beyond endurance.) But it is only in the absence of such conditions that moral judgments apply. Another and more common sense of the words is found in sentences such as "I caught a bad cold and had to stay in bed" where a penalty for acting otherwise is in the offing. The necessity of acting morally is not, however, supposed to depend on such penalties. Another range of examples, not necessarily having to do with penalties, is found where there is an unquestioned acceptance of some project or role, as when a nurse tells us that she has to make her rounds at a certain time, or we say that we have to run for a certain train.[8] But these too are irrelevant in the present context, since the acceptance condition can always be revoked.

No doubt it will be suggested that it is in some other sense of the words "have to" or "must" that one has to or must do what morality demands. But why should one insist that there must be such a sense when it proves so difficult to say what it is? Suppose that what we take for a puzzling thought were really no thought at all but only the reflection of our *feelings* about morality? Perhaps it makes no sense to say that we "have to" submit to the moral law, or that morality is "inescapable" in some special way. For just as one may feel as if one is falling without believing that one is moving downward, so one may feel as if one has to do what is morally required without believing oneself to be under physical or psychological compulsion, or about to incur a penalty if one does not comply. No one thinks that if the word "falling" is used in a statement reporting one's sensations it must be used in a special sense. But this kind of mistake may be involved in looking for the special sense in which one "has to" do what morality demands. There is no difficulty about the idea that we feel we *have to* behave morally, and given the psychological conditions of the learning of moral behavior it is natural that we should have such feelings. What we cannot do is quote them in support of the doctrine of the categorical imperative. It seems, then, that in so far as it is backed up by statements to the effect that the moral *is* inescapable, or that we *do* have to do what is morally required of us, it is uncertain whether the doctrine of the categorical imperative even makes sense.

The conclusion we should draw is that moral judgments have no better claim to be categorical imperatives than do statements about matters of etiquette. People may indeed follow either morality or etiquette without asking why they should do so, but equally well they may not. They may ask for reasons and may reasonably refuse to follow either if reasons are not to be found.

It will be said that this way of viewing moral considerations must be totally destructive of morality, because no one could ever act morally unless he accepted such considerations as in themselves sufficient reason for action. Actions that are truly moral must be done "for their own sake," "because they are right," and not for some ulterior purpose. This argument we must examine with care, for the doctrine of the categorical imperative has owed much to its persuasion.

Is there anything to be said for the thesis that a truly moral man acts "out of respect for the moral law" or that he does what is morally right because it is morally right? That such propositions are not prima facie absurd depends on the fact that moral judgment concerns itself with a man's reasons for acting as well as with what he does. Law and etiquette require only that certain things are done or left undone, but no one is counted as charitable if he gives alms "for the praise of men," and one who is honest only because it pays him to be honest does not have the virtue of honesty. This kind of consideration was crucial in shaping Kant's moral philosophy. He many times contrasts acting out of respect for the moral law with acting from an ulterior motive, and what is more from one that is self-interested. In the early *Lectures on Ethics* he gave the principle of truth-telling under a system of

hypothetical imperatives as that of not lying *if it harms one* to lie. In the *Metaphysics of Morals* he says that ethics cannot start from the ends which a man may propose to himself, since these are all "selfish."[9] In the *Critique of Practical Reason* he argues explicitly that when acting not out of respect for the moral law but "on a material maxim" men do what they do for the sake of pleasure or happiness.

> All material practical principles are, as such, of one and the same kind and belong under the general principle of self love or one's own happiness.[10]

Kant, in fact, was a psychological hedonist in respect of all actions except those done for the sake of the moral law, and this faulty theory of human nature was one of the things preventing him from seeing that moral virtue might be compatible with the rejection of the categorical imperative.

If we put this theory of human action aside, and allow as ends the things that seem to be ends, the picture changes. It will surely be allowed that quite apart from thoughts of duty a man may care about the suffering of others, having a sense of identification with them, and wanting to help if he can. Of course he must want not the reputation of charity, nor even a gratifying role helping others, but, quite simply, their good. If this is what he does care about, then he will be attached to the end proper to the virtue of charity and a comparison with someone acting from an ulterior motive (even a respectable ulterior motive) is out of place. Nor will the conformity of his action to the rule of charity be merely contingent. Honest action may happen to further a man's career; charitable actions do not *happen* to further the good of others.

Can a man accepting only hypothetical imperatives possess other virtues besides that of charity? Could he be just or honest? This problem is more complex because there is no one end related to such virtues as the good of others is related to charity. But what reason could there be for refusing to call a man a just man if he acted justly because he loved truth and liberty, and wanted every man to be treated with a certain minimum respect? And why should the truly honest man not follow honesty for the sake of the good that honest dealing brings to men? Of course, the usual difficulties can be raised about the rare case in which no good is foreseen from an individual act of honesty. But it is not evident that a man's desires could not give him reason to act honestly even here. He wants to live openly and in good faith with his neighbors; it is not all the same to him to lie and conceal.

If one wants to know whether there could be a truly moral man who accepted moral principles as hypothetical rules of conduct, as many people accept rules of etiquette as hypothetical rules of conduct, one must consider the right kind of example. A man who demanded that morality should be brought under the heading of self-interest would not be a good candidate, nor would anyone who was ready to be charitable or honest only so long as he felt inclined. A cause such as justice makes strenuous demands, but this is not peculiar to morality, and men are prepared to toil to achieve many ends not endorsed by morality. That they are prepared to fight so hard for moral ends—for example, for liberty and justice—depends on the fact that these are the kinds of ends that arouse devotion. To sacrifice a great deal for the sake of etiquette one would need to be under the spell of the emphatic "$ought_e$." One could hardly be devoted to behaving *comme il faut*.

In spite of all that has been urged in favor of the hypothetical imperative in ethics, I am sure that many people will be unconvinced and will argue that one element essential to moral virtue is still missing. This missing feature is the recognition of a *duty* to adopt those ends which we have attributed to the moral man. We have said that he *does* care about others, and about causes such as liberty and justice; that it is on this account that he will accept a system of morality. But what if he never cared about such things, or what if he ceased to care? Is it not the case that he *ought* to care? This is exactly what Kant would say, for though at times he sounds as if he thought that morality is not concerned with ends, at others he insists that the adoption of ends such as the happiness of others is itself dictated by morality.[11] How is this proposition to be regarded by one who rejects all talk about the binding force of the moral law? He will agree that a moral man has moral ends and cannot be indifferent to matters such as suffering and injustice. Further, he

will recognize in the statement that one *ought* to care about these things a correct application of the non-hypothetical moral "ought" by which society is apt to voice its demands. He will not, however, take the fact that he $ought_m$ to have certain ends as in itself reason to adopt them. If he himself is a moral man then he cares about such things, but not "because he ought." If he is an amoral man he may deny that he has any reason to trouble his head over this or any other moral demand. Of course he may be mistaken, and his life as well as others' lives may be most sadly spoiled by his selfishness. But this is not what is urged by those who think they can close the matter by an emphatic use of "ought." My argument is that they are relying on an illusion, as if trying to give the moral "ought" a magic force.[12]

This conclusion may, as I said, appear dangerous and subversive of morality. We are apt to panic at the thought that we ourselves, or other people, might stop caring about the things we do care about, and we feel that the categorical imperative gives us some control over the situation. But it is interesting that the people of Leningrad were not similarly struck by the thought that only the *contingent* fact that other citizens shared their loyalty and devotion to the city stood between them and the Germans during the terrible years of the siege. Perhaps we should be less troubled than we are by fear of defection from the moral cause; perhaps we should even have less reason to fear it if people thought of themselves as volunteers banded together to fight for liberty and justice and against inhumanity and oppression. It is often felt, even if obscurely, that there is an element of deception in the official line about morality. And while some have been persuaded by talk about the authority of the moral law, others have turned away with a sense of distrust.

NOTES

1. *Foundations of the Metaphysics of Morals*, Sec. II, trans. by L. W. Beck.

2. *Ibid.*

3. *Ibid.*

4. According to the position sketched here we have three forms of the hypothetical imperative: "If you want *x* you

should do *y*," "Because you want *x* you should do *y*," and "Because *x* is in your interest you should do *y*." For Kant the third would automatically be covered by the second.

5. To say that at that moment one wants to be a respectable philosopher would be another matter. Such a statement requires a special connection between the desire and the moment.

6. I am here going back on something I said in an earlier article ("Moral Beliefs," *Proceedings of the Aristotelian Society, 1958–1959*) where I thought it necessary to show that virtue must benefit the agent. I believe the rest of the article can stand.

7. To say that moral considerations are *called* reasons is blatantly to ignore the problem.

8. I am grateful to Rogers Albritton for drawing my attention to this interesting use of expressions such as "have to" or "must."

9. Pt. II, Introduction, sec. II.

10. Immanuel Kant, *Critique of Practical Reason*, trans. by L. W. Beck, p. 133.

11. See, e.g., *The Metaphysics of Morals*, pt. II, sec. 30.

12. See G. E. M. Anscombe, "Modern Moral Philosophy," *Philosophy* (1958). My view is different from Miss Anscombe's, but I have learned from her.

CHAPTER 7

Virtue Ethics: Be a Good Person

Consequentialist moral theories are concerned with the consequences of actions, for the consequences determine the moral rightness of conduct. The production of good over evil is the essence of morality. Nonconsequentialist moral theories are concerned with the moral nature of actions, for the right-making characteristics of actions determine the rightness of conduct. Virtue ethics, however, takes a different turn. **Virtue ethics** is a theory of morality that makes virtue the central concern. When confronted with a moral problem, a utilitarian or a Kantian theorist asks, "What should I *do*?" But a virtue ethicist asks, in effect, "What should I *be*?" For the former, moral conduct is primarily a matter of following or applying a moral principle or rule to a particular situation, and morality is mainly duty-based. For the latter, moral conduct is something that emanates from a person's moral virtues, from his or her moral character, not from obedience to moral laws. In this chapter we try to understand both the main attractions and the major criticisms of this virtue-centered approach to ethics and the moral life.

THE ETHICS OF VIRTUE

Most modern virtue ethicists trace their theoretical roots back to the ancients, most notably to Aristotle (384–322 B.C.E.). His ethics is a coherent, virtue-based view that interlocks with his broader philosophical concerns—his theories about causation, society, self, education, mind, and metaphysics. He says the moral life consists not in following moral rules that stipulate right actions

but in striving to be a particular kind of person—a virtuous person whose actions stem naturally from virtuous character.

For Aristotle, every living being has an end toward which it naturally aims. Life is teleological; it is meant not just to *be* something but to *aspire toward* something, to fulfill its proper function. What is the proper aim of human beings? Aristotle argues that the true goal of humans—their greatest good—is ***eudaimonia***, which means "happiness" or "flourishing" and refers to the full realization of the good life. To achieve *eudaimonia*, human beings must fulfill the function that is natural and distinctive to them: living fully in accordance with reason. The life of reason entails a life of virtue because the virtues themselves are rational modes of behaving. Thus Aristotle says, "Happiness is an activity of the soul in accordance with complete or perfect virtue." The virtuous life both helps human beings *achieve* true happiness and *is the realization of* true happiness. Virtues make you good, *and* they help you have a good life.

A **virtue** is a stable disposition to act and feel according to some ideal or model of excellence. It is a deeply embedded character trait that can affect actions in countless situations. Aristotle distinguishes between intellectual and moral virtues. Intellectual virtues include wisdom, prudence, rationality, and the like. Moral virtues include fairness, benevolence, honesty, loyalty, conscientiousness, and courage. He believes that intellectual virtues can be taught, just as logic and mathematics can be taught. But moral virtues can be learned only through practice:

CRITICAL THOUGHT: Learning Virtues in the Classroom

Years ago the *New York Times* reported that the teaching of traditional virtues such as honesty and civility was becoming more common in public schools. The article highlighted Paul Meck, an elementary school guidance counselor who spent much of his time teaching students about virtues and values. Meck's approach was to visit classrooms and lead discussions on such topics as honesty, friendship, and shoplifting. When he talked to younger students, he played his guitar and sang lyrics that underscored his points. "Whether through song, discussion or simply a straightforward lecture," the reporter noted, "there is an effort afoot to awaken the interest of youngsters in these subjects."*

Would Aristotle approve of the methods cited here (song, discussion, lecture)? Why or why not? What type of virtue education would he approve of? Which approach—Aristotle's or the one mentioned in this news article—do you think would be most effective? Give reasons for your answer.

*Gene I. Maeroff, "About Education; Values Regain Their Popularity," *New York Times*, Science Desk, April 10, 1984.

[M]oral virtue comes about as a result of habit. . . . From this it is also plain that none of the moral virtues arises in us by nature. . . . [B]ut the virtues we get by first exercising them, as also happens in the case of the arts as well. For the things we have to learn before we can do them, we learn by doing them, e.g. men become builders by building and lyreplayers by playing the lyre; so too we become just by doing just acts, temperate by doing temperate acts, brave by doing brave acts.[1]

Aristotle's notion of a moral virtue is what he calls the "**Golden Mean**," a balance between two behavioral extremes. A moral virtue (courage, for example) is the midpoint between excess (an excess of courage, or foolhardiness) and deficit (a deficit of courage, or cowardice). For Aristotle, then, the virtuous—and happy—life is a life of moderation in all things.

Modern virtue ethicists follow Aristotle's lead in many respects. Some thinkers take issue with his teleological theory of human nature and his concept of a virtue as a mean between opposing tendencies. And some have offered interesting alternatives to his virtue ethics. But almost all virtue theories owe a debt to Aristotle in one way or another.

Like Aristotle, contemporary virtue ethicists put the emphasis on quality of character and virtues (character traits), rather than on adherence to particular principles or rules of right action. They are of course concerned with doing the right thing, but moral obligations, in their view, are derived from virtues. These thinkers are, for example, less likely to ask whether lying is wrong in a particular situation than whether the action or person is honest or dishonest, or whether honesty precludes lying in this case, or whether an exemplar of honesty (say, Gandhi or Jesus) would lie in these circumstances.

Contemporary virtue ethicists are also Aristotelian in believing that a pure duty-based morality of rule adherence represents a barren, one-dimensional conception of the moral life. First, they agree with Aristotle that the cultivation of virtues is not merely a moral requirement—it is a way (some would say the *only* way) to ensure human flourishing and the good life. Second, they maintain that a full-blown ethics must take into account motives, feelings, intentions, and moral wisdom—factors that they think duty-based morality neglects. This view contrasts dramatically with Kant's duty-based ethics. He argues that to act morally is simply to act out of duty—that is, to do our duty *because* it is our duty. We need not act out of friendship, loyalty, kindness, love, or sympathy. But in virtue ethics, acting from such motivations is a crucial part of acting from a virtuous character, for virtues are stable dispositions that naturally include motivations and feelings. Contrast the action of someone who methodically aids his sick mother solely out of a sense of duty with the person who tends to her mother out of sympathy, love, and loyalty (perhaps in addition to a sense of duty). Most people would probably think that the latter is a better model of the moral life, while the former seems incomplete.

VIRTUE IN ACTION

If moral rules are secondary in virtue ethics, how does a virtue ethicist make moral decisions or guide his or her conduct or judge the behavior of others? Suppose Helen, a conscientious practitioner of Aristotelian virtue ethics, hears William lie to a friend to avoid paying a debt. She does not have to appeal to a moral rule such as "Do not lie" to know that William's action is an instance of dishonesty (or untruthfulness) and that William himself is dishonest. She can see by his actions that he lacks the virtue of honesty.

But to Helen, honesty is more than just a character trait: it is also an essential part of human happiness and flourishing. In her case, honesty is a virtue that she has cultivated for years by behaving honestly and truthfully in a variety of situations (not just in cases of lying). She has taken such trouble in part because cultivating this virtue has helped her become the kind of person she wants to be. She has developed the disposition to act honestly; acting honestly is part of who she is. She sometimes relies on moral rules (or moral rules of thumb) to make moral decisions, but she usually does not need them, because her actions naturally reflect her virtuous character.

In addition, Helen's trained virtues not only guide her actions but also inspire the motivations and feelings appropriate to the actions. Helen avoids dishonest dealings, and she does so because that is what a virtuous person would do, because she has compassion and sympathy for innocent people who are cheated, and because dishonesty is not conducive to human happiness and flourishing.

What guidance can Helen obtain in her strivings toward a moral ideal? Like most virtue ethicists, she looks to moral exemplars—people who embody the virtues and inspire others to follow in their steps. (For exemplars of honesty, Helen has several moral heroes to choose from—Socrates, Gandhi, Jesus, the Buddha, Thomas Aquinas, and many others.) As the philosopher Louis Pojman says of virtue systems,

> The primary focus is not on abstract reason but on ideal types of persons or on actual ideal persons. Discovering the proper moral example and imitating that person or ideal type thus replace casuistic reason as the most significant aspects of the moral life. Eventually, the apprentice-like training in virtue gained by imitating the ideal model results in a virtuous person who spontaneously does what is good.[2]

EVALUATING VIRTUE ETHICS

A case can be made for virtue ethics based on how well it seems to explain important aspects of the moral life. Some philosophers, for example, claim that the virtue approach offers a more plausible explanation of the role of motivation in moral actions than duty-based moral systems do. By Kantian lights your conduct may be morally acceptable even if you, say, save a friend's life out of a sense of duty alone (that is, without any sincere regard for your friend). But this motivation—your calculating sense of duty—seems a very cold and anemic motivation indeed. Virtue theorists would say that a more natural and morally appropriate response would be to save your friend primarily out of compassion, love, loyalty, or something similar—and these motives are just what we would expect from a virtuous person acting from fully developed virtues.

Some philosophers also remind us that virtue ethics puts primary emphasis on being a good person and living a good life, a life of happiness and flourishing. They say that these aims are obviously central to the moral life and should be part of any adequate theory of morality. Duty-based moral systems, however, pay much less attention to these essential elements.

Many duty-based theorists are willing to concede that there is some truth in both these claims. They believe that motivation for moral action cannot be derived entirely from considerations of duty, just as appropriate motivation cannot be based solely on virtuous character. And they recognize that the moral life involves more than merely honoring rules and principles. As Aristotle insists, there should be room for moral achievement in morality, for striving toward moral ideals. But even if these claims of the virtue ethicist are true, it does not follow that traditional virtue ethics is the best moral theory or that an ethics without duties or principles is plausible.

Virtue-based ethics seems to meet the minimum requirement of coherence, and it appears to be generally consistent with our commonsense moral judgments and moral experience. Nevertheless critics have taken it to task, with most of the strongest criticisms centering on alleged problems with applying the theory—in other words, with usefulness (Criterion 3).

The critics' main contention is that appeals to virtues or virtuous character without reference to principles of duty cannot give us any useful guidance in deciding what to do. Suppose we are trying to decide what to do when a desperately poor stranger steals money from us. Should we have him arrested? Give him even more money? Ignore the whole affair? According to virtue ethics, we should do what a virtuous person would do, or do what moral exemplars such as Jesus or Buddha would do, or do what is benevolent or conscientious. But what exactly *would* a virtuous person do? Or what precisely *is* the benevolent or conscientious action? As many philosophers see it, the problem is that virtue ethics says that the right action is the one performed by the virtuous person and that the

virtuous person is the one who performs the right action. But this is to argue in a circle and to give us no help in figuring out what to do. To avoid this circularity, they say, we must appeal to some kind of moral standard or principle to evaluate the action itself. Before we can decide if a person is virtuous, we need to judge if her actions are right or wrong—and such judgments take us beyond virtue ethics.

Some argue in a similar vein by pointing out that a person may possess all the proper virtues and still be unable to tell right from wrong actions. Dr. Green may be benevolent and just and still not know if stem cell research should be continued or stopped, or if he should help a terminal patient commit suicide, or if he should perform a late-term abortion. Likewise, we know that it is possible for a virtuous person to act entirely from virtue—and still commit an immoral act. This shows, critics say, that the rightness of actions does not necessarily (or invariably) depend on the content of one's character. We seem to have independent moral standards—independent of character considerations—by which we judge the moral permissibility of actions.

The virtue theorist can respond to these criticisms by asserting that there is actually plenty of moral guidance to be had in statements about virtues and vices. According to the virtue ethicist Rosalind Hursthouse,

[A] great deal of specific action guidance could be found in rules employing the virtue and vice terms ("v-rules") such as "Do what is honest/charitable; do not do what is dishonest/uncharitable." (It is a noteworthy feature of our virtue and vice vocabulary that, although our list of generally recognised virtue terms is comparatively short, our list of vice terms is remarkably, and usefully, long, far exceeding anything that anyone who thinks in terms of standard deontological rules has ever come up with. Much invaluable action guidance comes from avoiding courses of action that would be irresponsible, feckless, lazy, inconsiderate, uncooperative, harsh, intolerant, selfish, mercenary, indiscreet, tactless, arrogant . . . and on and on.)[3]

CRITICAL THOUGHT: Warrior Virtues and Moral Disagreements

A 2005 report from *Voice of America* told of a dispute over the war in Iraq among highly regarded war veterans. Democratic Representative John Murtha, a decorated Marine Corps veteran who fought in Vietnam, was a strong supporter of the military—but thought the war in Iraq was a disaster and demanded that U.S. forces be withdrawn from Iraq within six months. Democratic Senator John Kerry, also a decorated veteran of the Vietnam War, disagreed with Murtha's timetable for troop withdrawal. He proposed that troops start to leave Iraq later, in early 2007. Republican Senator John McCain, a former Navy fighter pilot and POW in the Vietnam conflict, supported the president's view that the troops should stay in Iraq until the job was done.*

Assume that all these men were honorable and had all the appropriate warrior virtues such as courage and loyalty. If they were then comparably virtuous in the ways indicated, how could they have disagreed about the conduct of the war? Suppose they all possessed exactly the same virtues to exactly the same degree and had access to the same set of facts about the war. Would it still have been possible for them to disagree? Why or why not? Do you think that any of these considerations suggest that virtue ethics may be a flawed moral theory? Why or why not?

*Jim Malone, "Waning US Iraq War Support Stirs New Comparisons to Vietnam Conflict," *VOANews.com* (November 22, 2005), http://www.51voa.com/VOA_Standard _English/VOA_Standard_3636.html (January 9, 2015).

Hursthouse believes we can discover our moral duties by examining terms that refer to virtues and vices because moral guidance is implicit in these terms.

Another usefulness criticism crops up because of apparent conflicts between virtues. What should you do if you have to choose between performing or not performing a particular action, and each option involves the same two virtues but in contradictory ways? Suppose your best friend is on trial for murder, and under oath you must testify about what you know of the case—and what you know will incriminate her. The question is, Should you lie? If you lie to save your friend, you will be loyal but dishonest. If you tell the truth, you will be honest but disloyal. The virtues of loyalty and honesty conflict; you simply cannot be both loyal and honest. Virtue ethics says you should act as a virtuous person would. But such advice gives you no guidance on how to

do that in this particular case. You need to know which virtue is more important in this situation, but virtue ethics does not seem to provide a useful answer.

The proponent of virtue ethics has a ready reply to this criticism: some duty-based moral theories, such as Kantian ethics, are also troubled by conflicts (conflicts of rules or principles, for example). Obviously the existence of such conflicts is not a fatal flaw in duty-based ethics, and so it must not be in virtue approaches either. When principles seem to conflict, the duty-based theorist must determine if the conflict is real and, if so, if it can be resolved (by, say, weighting one principle more than another). Virtue ethics, the argument goes, can exercise the same kinds of options. Some might observe, however, that incorporating a weighting rule or similar standard into virtue ethics seems to make the theory a blend of duty-based and virtue-based features.

LEARNING FROM VIRTUE ETHICS

Why does the ancient moral tradition of virtue ethics persist—and not just persist, but thrive, even enjoying a revival in modern times? Many thinkers would say that virtue ethics is alive and well because it is sustained by an important ethical truth: virtue and character are large, unavoidable constituents of our moral experience. As moral creatures, we regularly judge the moral permissibility of actions—*and* assess the goodness of character. If someone commits an immoral act (kills an innocent human being, for example), it matters to us whether the act was committed out of compassion (as in euthanasia), benevolence, loyalty, revenge, rage, or ignorance. The undeniable significance of virtue in morality has obliged many philosophers to consider how best to accommodate virtues into their principle-based theories of morality or to recast those theories entirely to give virtues a larger role.

The rise of virtue ethics has also forced many thinkers to reexamine the place of principles in morality. If we have virtues, do we need principles? Most philosophers would probably say yes and agree with the philosopher William Frankena that "principles without traits [virtues] are impotent and traits without principles are blind":

> To be or to do, that is the question. Should we construe morality as primarily a following of certain principles or as primarily a cultivation of certain dispositions and traits? Must we choose? It is hard to see how a morality of principles can get off the ground except through the development of dispositions to act in accordance with its principles, else all motivation to act on them must be of an *ad hoc* kind, either prudential or impulsively altruistic. Moreover, morality can hardly be content with a mere conformity to rules, however willing and self-conscious it may be, unless it has no interest in the spirit of its law but only in the letter. On the other hand, one cannot conceive of traits of character except as including dispositions and tendencies to act in certain ways in certain circumstances. Hating involves being disposed to kill or harm, being just involves tending to do just acts (acts that conform to the principle of justice) when the occasion calls. Again, it is hard to see how we could know what traits to encourage or inculcate if we did not subscribe to principles, for example, to the principle of utility, or to those of benevolence and justice.[4]

Kant would have us act out of duty alone, granting no bonus points for acting from virtue. Utilitarianism doesn't require, but also doesn't reject, virtuous motives. Yet virtue seems to be as much a part of our moral experience as moral disagreements, moral errors, and moral reasoning. The question is not whether we should care about virtues but how much we should care and how we can incorporate them into our lives.

CHAPTER REVIEW

SUMMARY

Virtue ethics is a moral theory that makes virtue the central concern. In virtue ethics, moral conduct is supposed to radiate naturally from moral virtues. That is, moral actions are derived from virtues. A virtue is a stable disposition to act and feel according to an ideal or model of excellence.

Most modern virtue ethicists take their inspiration from Aristotle. He argues that humankind's greatest good is happiness, or *eudaimonia*. To achieve happiness, human beings must fulfill their natural function—to live fully in accordance with reason. To live this way is to cultivate the virtues, for they are rational ways of being and flourishing. Aristotle suggests that a moral virtue is a Golden Mean, a midpoint between two extreme ways of behaving. So he says that the good life is a life in the middle, a life of moderation.

Virtue theorists think that acting out of duty alone is a distortion of true morality. A full-blown morality, they insist, must include motives, emotions, intentions, and moral wisdom. Acting morally means acting from virtue—from the appropriate motives and feelings, taking all the factors of the situation into account.

Virtue-based ethics seems to meet the minimum requirement of coherence, and it fits with our commonsense moral judgments and experience. But it has been accused of not being useful. The main criticism is that appeals to virtue alone (sans principles) give us little or no guidance about how to act. Critics argue that virtue ethics defines virtue in terms of right actions and defines right actions in terms of virtue. But this is circular reasoning and provides no help for making moral decisions. Virtue theorists, however, can reply that guidance in moral decision making is in fact available—it is inherent in statements about virtues and vices.

KEY TERMS

virtue ethics (p. 172)
eudaimonia (p. 172)
virtue (p. 172)
Golden Mean (p. 173)

EXERCISES

Review Questions

1. What are the strengths and weaknesses of Aristotle's virtue ethics theory? (pp. 174–176)
2. What does Aristotle mean when he says that the virtuous life helps us *achieve* happiness and *is* happiness? (p. 172)
3. How does virtue ethics differ from duty-based ethics? (p. 172)
4. In what way is Aristotle's virtue ethics considered teleological? (p. 172)

5. What, according to Aristotle, must humans do to achieve *eudaimonia?* (p. 172)
6. What is a virtue? Give three examples of moral virtues. Give two examples of intellectual virtues. (p. 172)
7. What important elements do virtue ethicists think are missing from traditional duty-based ethics? (p. 174)
8. How do virtue ethicists use moral exemplars? (p. 175)
9. Does virtue ethics seem to offer a more plausible explanation of the role of motivation in moral actions than does Kantian ethics? If so, how? (p. 175)
10. What is the chief argument against virtue ethics? How can the virtue ethicist respond? (p. 175)

Discussion Questions

1. For Aristotle, what is the central task in morality and how does it differ from the central task in utilitarianism?
2. How does Aristotle's conception of the virtuous life differ from Kant's?
3. Is Aristotle's notion of the Golden Mean helpful in identifying the virtues in any situation? Why or why not?
4. Kant says that to act morally is to act out of duty. How does this differ from the virtue ethics approach? Are you likely to admire someone who always acts out of duty alone? Why or why not?
5. Compare the advantages and disadvantages of act-utilitarianism and virtue ethics. Which do you think is the better theory? How would you combine the two approaches to fashion a better theory?
6. William Frankena says that morality requires both principles and virtues. Do you agree? Why or why not?

ETHICAL DILEMMAS

Explain how virtue ethics could be applied in the following scenarios to determine the proper course of action.

1. You are walking across town, and a homeless person bumps into you, takes your wallet, and runs away. What would a virtuous person do in this instance? Should the guiding virtue be compassion? fairness? honesty?

2. You are a physician treating a terminally ill woman who is in a great deal of pain that no drug can relieve. She says she has lived a full life and now wants you to end her anguish by helping her die quickly and quietly. She has no known relatives. The American Medical Association's code of ethics absolutely forbids physician-assisted suicide, and the hospital where she is a patient has a similar policy. But you want to alleviate her agony and give her a chance to die with dignity. What would a virtuous person do?

3. Your father has stolen $30,000 from his employer to pay for surgery that his sister desperately needs. Without the surgery, she will be dead within six months. Only you know about his crime. You also know that no one will ever know who stole the money unless you report the theft to the authorities. Should you turn your father in to the police? Should you keep quiet about the matter? What would a virtuous person do?

FURTHER READING

G. E. M. Anscombe, "Modern Moral Philosophy," *Philosophy* 33, no. 124 (January 1958): 1–19.

Philippa Foot, "Virtues and Vices," in *Virtues and Vices and Other Essays in Moral Philosophy* (Berkeley: University of California Press, 1978).

William K. Frankena, "Ethics of Virtue," in *Ethics,* 2nd ed. (Englewood Cliffs, NJ: Prentice Hall, 1973).

Rosalind Hursthouse, "Virtue Ethics," in *Stanford Encyclopedia of Philosophy*, Fall 2003 ed., ed. Edward N. Zalta, http://plato.stanford/archives/fall2003/entries/ethics-virtue/ (March 1, 2015).

Alasdair MacIntyre, "The Nature of the Virtues," in *After Virtue: A Study in Moral Theory* (Notre Dame, IN: University of Notre Dame Press, 1984).

Greg Pence, "Virtue Theory," in *A Companion to Ethics,* ed. Peter Singer, corr. ed. (Oxford: Blackwell, 1993).

READINGS

From *Nicomachean Ethics*

ARISTOTLE

BOOK I

1

Every art and every inquiry, and similarly every action and pursuit, is thought to aim at some good; and for this reason the good has rightly been declared to be that at which all things aim. But a certain difference is found among ends; some are activities, others are products apart from the activities that produce them. Where there are ends apart from the actions, it is the nature of the products to be better than the activities.

Aristotle, *Nichomachean Ethics,* trans. W. D. Ross, books I and II, (edited) (eBooks@Adelaide, 2004).

Now, as there are many actions, arts, and sciences, their ends also are many; the end of the medical art is health, that of shipbuilding a vessel, that of strategy victory, that of economics wealth. But where such arts fall under a single capacity—as bridle-making and the other arts concerned with the equipment of horses fall under the art of riding, and this and every military action under strategy, in the same way other arts fall under yet others—in all of these the ends of the master arts are to be preferred to all the subordinate ends; for it is for the sake of the former that the latter are pursued. It makes no difference whether the activities themselves are the ends of the actions, or something else apart from the activities, as in the case of the sciences just mentioned.

2

If, then, there is some end of the things we do, which we desire for its own sake (everything else being desired for the sake of this), and if we do not choose everything for the sake of something else (for at that rate the process would go on to infinity, so that our desire would be empty and vain), clearly this must be the good and the chief good. Will not the knowledge of it, then, have a great influence on life? Shall we not, like archers who have a mark to aim at, be more likely to hit upon what is right? If so, we must try, in outline at least, to determine what it is, and of which of the sciences or capacities it is the object. It would seem to belong to the most authoritative art and that which is most truly the master art. And politics appears to be of this nature; for it is this that ordains which of the sciences should be studied in a state, and which each class of citizens should learn and up to what point they should learn them; and we see even the most highly esteemed of capacities to fall under this, e.g. strategy, economics, rhetoric; now, since politics uses the rest of the sciences, and since, again, it legislates as to what we are to do and what we are to abstain from, the end of this science must include those of the others, so that this end must be the good for man. For even if the end is the same for a single man and for a state, that of the state seems at all events something greater and more complete whether to attain or to preserve; though it is worth while to attain the end merely for one man, it is finer and more godlike to attain it for a nation or for city-states. These, then, are the ends at which our inquiry aims, since it is political science, in one sense of that term.

* * *

3

Now each man judges well the things he knows, and of these he is a good judge. And so the man who has been educated in a subject is a good judge of that subject, and the man who has received an all-round education is a good judge in general. Hence a young man is not a proper hearer of lectures on political science; for he is inexperienced in the actions that occur in life, but its discussions start from these and are about these; and, further, since he tends to follow his passions, his study

will be vain and unprofitable, because the end aimed at is not knowledge but action. And it makes no difference whether he is young in years or youthful in character; the defect does not depend on time, but on his living, and pursuing each successive object, as passion directs. For to such persons, as to the incontinent, knowledge brings no profit; but to those who desire and act in accordance with a rational principle knowledge about such matters will be of great benefit. These remarks about the student, the sort of treatment to be expected, and the purpose of the inquiry, may be taken as our preface.

4

Let us resume our inquiry and state, in view of the fact that all knowledge and every pursuit aims at some good, what it is that we say political science aims at and what is the highest of all goods achievable by action. Verbally there is very general agreement; for both the general run of men and people of superior refinement say that it is happiness, and identify living well and doing well with being happy; but with regard to what happiness is they differ, and the many do not give the same account as the wise. For the former think it is some plain and obvious thing, like pleasure, wealth, or honour; they differ, however, from one another—and often even the same man identifies it with different things, with health when he is ill, with wealth when he is poor; but, conscious of their ignorance, they admire those who proclaim some great ideal that is above their comprehension. Now some thought that apart from these many goods there is another which is self-subsistent and causes the goodness of all these as well. To examine all the opinions that have been held were perhaps somewhat fruitless; enough to examine those that are most prevalent or that seem to be arguable.

* * *

5

Let us, however, resume our discussion from the point at which we digressed. To judge from the lives that men lead, most men, and men of the most vulgar type, seem (not without some ground) to identify the good, or happiness, with pleasure; which is the reason why they love the life of enjoyment. For there are, we may say, three prominent types of life—that just mentioned, the political, and thirdly the contemplative life. Now the mass of mankind are evidently quite slavish in their tastes, preferring a life suitable to beasts, but they get some ground for their view from the fact that many of those in high places share the tastes of Sardanapallus. A consideration of the prominent types of life shows that people of superior refinement and of active disposition identify happiness with honour, for this is, roughly speaking, the end of the political life. But it seems too superficial to be what we are looking for, since it is thought to depend on those who bestow honour rather than on him who receives it, but the good we divine to be something proper to a man and not easily taken from him. Further, men seem to pursue honour in order that they may be assured of their goodness; at least it is by men of practical wisdom that they seek to be honoured, and among those who know them, and on the ground of their virtue; clearly, then, according to them, at any rate, virtue is better. And perhaps one might even suppose this to be, rather than honour, the end of the political life. But even this appears somewhat incomplete; for possession of virtue seems actually compatible with being asleep, or with lifelong inactivity, and, further, with the greatest sufferings and misfortunes; but a man who was living so no one would call happy, unless he were maintaining a thesis at all costs. But enough of this; for the subject has been sufficiently treated even in the current discussions. Third comes the contemplative life, which we shall consider later.

The life of money-making is one undertaken under compulsion, and wealth is evidently not the good we are seeking; for it is merely useful and for the sake of something else. And so one might rather take the aforenamed objects to be ends; for they are loved for themselves. But it is evident that not even these are ends; yet many arguments have been thrown away in support of them. Let us leave this subject, then.

* * *

7

Let us again return to the good we are seeking, and ask what it can be. It seems different in different actions and arts; it is different in medicine, in strategy, and

in the other arts likewise. What then is the good of each? Surely that for whose sake everything else is done. In medicine this is health, in strategy victory, in architecture a house, in any other sphere something else, and in every action and pursuit the end; for it is for the sake of this that all men do whatever else they do. Therefore, if there is an end for all that we do, this will be the good achievable by action, and if there are more than one, these will be the goods achievable by action.

So the argument has by a different course reached the same point; but we must try to state this even more clearly. Since there are evidently more than one end, and we choose some of these (e.g. wealth, flutes, and in general instruments) for the sake of something else, clearly not all ends are final ends; but the chief good is evidently something final. Therefore, if there is only one final end, this will be what we are seeking, and if there are more than one, the most final of these will be what we are seeking. Now we call that which is in itself worthy of pursuit more final than that which is worthy of pursuit for the sake of something else, and that which is never desirable for the sake of something else more final than the things that are desirable both in themselves and for the sake of that other thing, and therefore we call final without qualification that which is always desirable in itself and never for the sake of something else.

Now such a thing happiness, above all else, is held to be; for this we choose always for self and never for the sake of something else, but honour, pleasure, reason, and every virtue we choose indeed for themselves (for if nothing resulted from them we should still choose each of them), but we choose them also for the sake of happiness, judging that by means of them we shall be happy. Happiness, on the other hand, no one chooses for the sake of these, nor, in general, for anything other than itself.

From the point of view of self-sufficiency the same result seems to follow; for the final good is thought to be self-sufficient. Now by self-sufficient we do not mean that which is sufficient for a man by himself, for one who lives a solitary life, but also for parents, children, wife, and in general for his friends and fellow citizens, since man is born for citizenship. But some limit must be set to this; for if we extend our requirement to ancestors and descendants and friends' friends we are in for an infinite series. Let us examine this question, however, on another occasion; the self-sufficient we now define as that which when isolated makes life desirable and lacking in nothing; and such we think happiness to be; and further we think it most desirable of all things, without being counted as one good thing among others—if it were so counted it would clearly be made more desirable by the addition of even the least of goods; for that which is added becomes an excess of goods, and of goods the greater is always more desirable. Happiness, then, is something final and self-sufficient, and is the end of action.

Presumably, however, to say that happiness is the chief good seems a platitude, and a clearer account of what it is still desired. This might perhaps be given, if we could first ascertain the function of man. For just as for a flute-player, a sculptor, or an artist, and, in general, for all things that have a function or activity, the good and the 'well' is thought to reside in the function, so would it seem to be for man, if he has a function. Have the carpenter, then, and the tanner certain functions or activities, and has man none? Is he born without a function? Or as eye, hand, foot, and in general each of the parts evidently has a function, may one lay it down that man similarly has a function apart from all these? What then can this be? Life seems to be common even to plants, but we are seeking what is peculiar to man. Let us exclude, therefore, the life of nutrition and growth. Next there would be a life of perception, but it also seems to be common even to the horse, the ox, and every animal. There remains, then, an active life of the element that has a rational principle; of this, one part has such a principle in the sense of being obedient to one, the other in the sense of possessing one and exercising thought. And, as 'life of the rational element' also has two meanings, we must state that life in the sense of activity is what we mean; for this seems to be the more proper sense of the term. Now if the function of man is an activity of soul which follows or implies a rational principle, and if we say 'a so-and-so' and 'a good so-and-so' have a function which is the same in kind, e.g. a lyre, and a good lyre-player, and so without qualification in all

cases, eminence in respect of goodness being added to the name of the function (for the function of a lyre-player is to play the lyre, and that of a good lyre-player is to do so well): if this is the case, and we state the function of man to be a certain kind of life, and this to be an activity or actions of the soul implying a rational principle, and the function of a good man to be the good and noble performance of these, and if any action is well performed when it is performed in accordance with the appropriate excellence: if this is the case, human good turns out to be activity of soul in accordance with virtue, and if there are more than one virtue, in accordance with the best and most complete.

But we must add 'in a complete life.' For one swallow does not make a summer, nor does one day; and so too one day, or a short time, does not make a man blessed and happy.

* * *

BOOK II

1

Virtue, then, being of two kinds, intellectual and moral, intellectual virtue in the main owes both its birth and its growth to teaching (for which reason it requires experience and time), while moral virtue comes about as a result of habit, whence also its name (*ēthikē*) is one that is formed by a slight variation from the word *ethos* (habit). From this it is also plain that none of the moral virtues arises in us by nature; for nothing that exists by nature can form a habit contrary to its nature. For instance the stone which by nature moves downwards cannot be habituated to move upwards, not even if one tries to train it by throwing it up ten thousand times; nor can fire be habituated to move downwards, nor can anything else that by nature behaves in one way be trained to behave in another. Neither by nature, then, nor contrary to nature do the virtues arise in us; rather we are adapted by nature to receive them, and are made perfect by habit.

Again, of all the things that come to us by nature we first acquire the potentiality and later exhibit the activity (this is plain in the case of the senses; for it was not by often seeing or often hearing that we got these senses, but on the contrary we had them before we used them, and did not come to have them by using them); but the virtues we get by first exercising them, as also happens in the case of the arts as well. For the things we have to learn before we can do them, we learn by doing them, e.g. men become builders by building and lyre-players by playing the lyre; so too we become just by doing just acts, temperate by doing temperate acts, brave by doing brave acts.

This is confirmed by what happens in states; for legislators make the citizens good by forming habits in them, and this is the wish of every legislator, and those who do not effect it miss their mark, and it is in this that a good constitution differs from a bad one.

Again, it is from the same causes and by the same means that every virtue is both produced and destroyed, and similarly every art; for it is from playing the lyre that both good and bad lyre-players are produced. And the corresponding statement is true of builders and of all the rest; men will be good or bad builders as a result of building well or badly. For if this were not so, there would have been no need of a teacher, but all men would have been born good or bad at their craft. This, then, is the case with the virtues also; by doing the acts that we do in our transactions with other men we become just or unjust, and by doing the acts that we do in the presence of danger, and being habituated to feel fear or confidence, we become brave or cowardly. The same is true of appetites and feelings of anger; some men become temperate and good-tempered, others self-indulgent and irascible, by behaving in one way or the other in the appropriate circumstances. Thus, in one word, states of character arise out of like activities. This is why the activities we exhibit must be of a certain kind; it is because the states of character correspond to the differences between these. It makes no small difference, then, whether we form habits of one kind or of another from our very youth; it makes a very great difference, or rather all the difference.

2

Since, then, the present inquiry does not aim at theoretical knowledge like the others (for we are inquiring not in order to know what virtue is, but in order

to become good, since otherwise our inquiry would have been of no use), we must examine the nature of actions, namely how we ought to do them; for these determine also the nature of the states of character that are produced, as we have said. Now, that we must act according to the right rule is a common principle and must be assumed—it will be discussed later, i.e. both what the right rule is, and how it is related to the other virtues. But this must be agreed upon beforehand, that the whole account of matters of conduct must be given in outline and not precisely, as we said at the very beginning that the accounts we demand must be in accordance with the subject-matter; matters concerned with conduct and questions of what is good for us have no fixity, any more than matters of health. The general account being of this nature, the account of particular cases is yet more lacking in exactness; for they do not fall under any art or precept but the agents themselves must in each case consider what is appropriate to the occasion, as happens also in the art of medicine or of navigation.

But though our present account is of this nature we must give what help we can. First, then, let us consider this, that it is the nature of such things to be destroyed by defect and excess, as we see in the case of strength and of health (for to gain light on things imperceptible we must use the evidence of sensible things); both excessive and defective exercise destroys the strength, and similarly drink or food which is above or below a certain amount destroys the health, while that which is proportionate both produces and increases and preserves it. So too is it, then, in the case of temperance and courage and the other virtues. For the man who flies from and fears everything and does not stand his ground against anything becomes a coward, and the man who fears nothing at all but goes to meet every danger becomes rash; and similarly the man who indulges in every pleasure and abstains from none becomes self-indulgent, while the man who shuns every pleasure, as boors do, becomes in a way insensible; temperance and courage, then, are destroyed by excess and defect, and preserved by the mean.

But not only are the sources and causes of their origination and growth the same as those of their destruction, but also the sphere of their actualization will be the same; for this is also true of the things which are more evident to sense, e.g. of strength; it is produced by taking much food and undergoing much exertion, and it is the strong man that will be most able to do these things. So too is it with the virtues; by abstaining from pleasures we become temperate, and it is when we have become so that we are most able to abstain from them; and similarly too in the case of courage; for by being habituated to despise things that are terrible and to stand our ground against them we become brave, and it is when we have become so that we shall be most able to stand our ground against them.

* * *

4

The question might be asked, what we mean by saying that we must become just by doing just acts, and temperate by doing temperate acts; for if men do just and temperate acts, they are already just and temperate, exactly as, if they do what is in accordance with the laws of grammar and of music, they are grammarians and musicians.

Or is this not true even of the arts? It is possible to do something that is in accordance with the laws of grammar, either by chance or at the suggestion of another. A man will be a grammarian, then, only when he has both done something grammatical and done it grammatically; and this means doing it in accordance with the grammatical knowledge in himself.

Again, the case of the arts and that of the virtues are not similar; for the products of the arts have their goodness in themselves, so that it is enough that they should have a certain character, but if the acts that are in accordance with the virtues have themselves a certain character it does not follow that they are done justly or temperately. The agent also must be in a certain condition when he does them; in the first place he must have knowledge, secondly he must choose the acts, and choose them for their own sakes, and thirdly his action must proceed from a firm and unchangeable character. These are not reckoned in as conditions of the possession of the arts, except the bare knowledge; but as a condition of the possession of the virtues knowledge has little or no weight, while the other conditions count not for a little but for everything, i.e. the very conditions which result from often doing just and temperate acts.

Actions, then, are called just and temperate when they are such as the just or the temperate man would do; but it is not the man who does these that is just and temperate, but the man who also does them as just and temperate men do them. It is well said, then, that it is by doing just acts that the just man is produced, and by doing temperate acts the temperate man; without doing these no one would have even a prospect of becoming good.

But most people do not do these, but take refuge in theory and think they are being philosophers and will become good in this way, behaving somewhat like patients who listen attentively to their doctors, but do none of the things they are ordered to do. As the latter will not be made well in body by such a course of treatment, the former will not be made well in soul by such a course of philosophy.

5

Next we must consider what virtue is. Since things that are found in the soul are of three kinds—passions, faculties, states of character, virtue must be one of these. By passions I mean appetite, anger, fear, confidence, envy, joy, friendly feeling, hatred, longing, emulation, pity, and in general the feelings that are accompanied by pleasure or pain; by faculties the things in virtue of which we are said to be capable of feeling these, e.g. of becoming angry or being pained or feeling pity; by states of character the things in virtue of which we stand well or badly with reference to the passions, e.g. with reference to anger we stand badly if we feel it violently or too weakly, and well if we feel it moderately; and similarly with reference to the other passions.

Now neither the virtues nor the vices are passions, because we are not called good or bad on the ground of our passions, but are so called on the ground of our virtues and our vices, and because we are neither praised nor blamed for our passions (for the man who feels fear or anger is not praised, nor is the man who simply feels anger blamed, but the man who feels it in a certain way), but for our virtues and our vices we are praised or blamed.

Again, we feel anger and fear without choice, but the virtues are modes of choice or involve choice. Further, in respect of the passions we are said to be moved, but in respect of the virtues and the vices we are said not to be moved but to be disposed in a particular way.

For these reasons also they are not faculties; for we are neither called good nor bad, nor praised nor blamed, for the simple capacity of feeling the passions; again, we have the faculties by nature, but we are not made good or bad by nature; we have spoken of this before. If, then, the virtues are neither passions nor faculties, all that remains is that they should be states of character.

Thus we have stated what virtue is in respect of its genus.

6

We must, however, not only describe virtue as a state of character, but also say what sort of state it is. We may remark, then, that every virtue or excellence both brings into good condition the thing of which it is the excellence and makes the work of that thing be done well; e.g. the excellence of the eye makes both the eye and its work good; for it is by the excellence of the eye that we see well. Similarly the excellence of the horse makes a horse both good in itself and good at running and at carrying its rider and at awaiting the attack of the enemy. Therefore, if this is true in every case, the virtue of man also will be the state of character which makes a man good and which makes him do his own work well.

How this is to happen we have stated already, but it will be made plain also by the following consideration of the specific nature of virtue. In everything that is continuous and divisible it is possible to take more, less, or an equal amount, and that either in terms of the thing itself or relatively to us; and the equal is an intermediate between excess and defect. By the intermediate in the object I mean that which is equidistant from each of the extremes, which is one and the same for all men; by the intermediate relatively to us that which is neither too much nor too little—and this is not one, nor the same for all. For instance, if ten is many and two is few, six is the intermediate, taken in terms of the object;

for it exceeds and is exceeded by an equal amount; this is intermediate according to arithmetical proportion. But the intermediate relatively to us is not to be taken so; if ten pounds are too much for a particular person to eat and two too little, it does not follow that the trainer will order six pounds; for this also is perhaps too much for the person who is to take it, or too little—too little for Milo, too much for the beginner in athletic exercises. The same is true of running and wrestling. Thus a master of any art avoids excess and defect, but seeks the intermediate and chooses this—the intermediate not in the object but relatively to us.

If it is thus, then, that every art does its work well—by looking to the intermediate and judging its works by this standard (so that we often say of good works of art that it is not possible either to take away or to add anything, implying that excess and defect destroy the goodness of works of art, while the mean preserves it; and good artists, as we say, look to this in their work), and if, further, virtue is more exact and better than any art, as nature also is, then virtue must have the quality of aiming at the intermediate. I mean moral virtue; for it is this that is concerned with passions and actions, and in these there is excess, defect, and the intermediate. For instance, both fear and confidence and appetite and anger and pity and in general pleasure and pain may be felt both too much and too little, and in both cases not well; but to feel them at the right times, with reference to the right objects, towards the right people, with the right motive, and in the right way, is what is both intermediate and best, and this is characteristic of virtue. Similarly with regard to actions also there is excess, defect, and the intermediate. Now virtue is concerned with passions and actions, in which excess is a form of failure, and so is defect, while the intermediate is praised and is a form of success; and being praised and being successful are both characteristics of virtue. Therefore virtue is a kind of mean, since, as we have seen, it aims at what is intermediate.

Again, it is possible to fail in many ways (for evil belongs to the class of the unlimited, as the Pythagoreans conjectured, and good to that of the limited), while to succeed is possible only in one way (for which reason also one is easy and the other difficult—to miss the mark easy, to hit it difficult); for these reasons also, then, excess and defect are characteristic of vice, and the mean of virtue;

> For men are good in but one way, but bad in many.

Virtue, then, is a state of character concerned with choice, lying in a mean, i.e. the mean relative to us, this being determined by a rational principle, and by that principle by which the man of practical wisdom would determine it. Now it is a mean between two vices, that which depends on excess and that which depends on defect; and again it is a mean because the vices respectively fall short of or exceed what is right in both passions and actions, while virtue both finds and chooses that which is intermediate. Hence in respect of its substance and the definition which states its essence virtue is a mean, with regard to what is best and right an extreme.

But not every action nor every passion admits of a mean; for some have names that already imply badness, e.g. spite, shamelessness, envy, and in the case of actions adultery, theft, murder; for all of these and suchlike things imply by their names that they are themselves bad, and not the excesses or deficiencies of them. It is not possible, then, ever to be right with regard to them; one must always be wrong. Nor does goodness or badness with regard to such things depend on committing adultery with the right women, at the right time, and in the right way, but simply to do any of them is to go wrong. It would be equally absurd, then, to expect that in unjust, cowardly, and voluptuous action there should be a mean, an excess, and a deficiency; for at that rate there would be a mean of excess and of deficiency, an excess of excess, and a deficiency of deficiency. But as there is no excess and deficiency of temperance and courage because what is intermediate is in a sense an extreme, so too of the actions we have mentioned there is no mean nor any excess and deficiency, but however they are done they are wrong; for in general there is neither a mean of excess and deficiency, nor excess and deficiency of a mean.

7

We must, however, not only make this general statement, but also apply it to the individual facts. For among statements about conduct those which are general apply more widely, but those which are particular are more genuine, since conduct has to do with individual cases, and our statements must harmonize with the facts in these cases. We may take these cases from our table. With regard to feelings of fear and confidence courage is the mean; of the people who exceed, he who exceeds in fearlessness has no name (many of the states have no name), while the man who exceeds in confidence is rash, and he who exceeds in fear and falls short in confidence is a coward. With regard to pleasures and pains—not all of them, and not so much with regard to the pains—the mean is temperance, the excess self-indulgence. Persons deficient with regard to the pleasures are not often found; hence such persons also have received no name. But let us call them 'insensible'.

With regard to giving and taking of money the mean is liberality, the excess and the defect prodigality and meanness. In these actions people exceed and fall short in contrary ways; the prodigal exceeds in spending and falls short in taking, while the mean man exceeds in taking and falls short in spending. (At present we are giving a mere outline or summary, and are satisfied with this; later these states will be more exactly determined.) With regard to money there are also other dispositions—a mean, magnificence (for the magnificent man differs from the liberal man; the former deals with large sums, the latter with small ones), an excess, tastelessness and vulgarity, and a deficiency, niggardliness; these differ from the states opposed to liberality, and the mode of their difference will be stated later. With regard to honour and dishonour the mean is proper pride, the excess is known as a sort of 'empty vanity', and the deficiency is undue humility; and as we said liberality was related to magnificence, differing from it by dealing with small sums, so there is a state similarly related to proper pride, being concerned with small honours while that is concerned with great. For it is possible to desire honour as one ought, and more than one ought, and less, and the man who exceeds in his desires is called ambitious, the man who falls short unambitious, while the intermediate person has no name. The dispositions also are nameless, except that that of the ambitious man is called ambition. Hence the people who are at the extremes lay claim to the middle place;

and we ourselves sometimes call the intermediate person ambitious and sometimes unambitious, and sometimes praise the ambitious man and sometimes the unambitious. The reason of our doing this will be stated in what follows; but now let us speak of the remaining states according to the method which has been indicated.

With regard to anger also there is an excess, a deficiency, and a mean. Although they can scarcely be said to have names, yet since we call the intermediate person good-tempered let us call the mean good temper; of the persons at the extremes let the one who exceeds be called irascible, and his vice irascibility, and the man who falls short an inirascible sort of person, and the deficiency inirascibility.

There are also three other means, which have a certain likeness to one another, but differ from one another: for they are all concerned with intercourse in words and actions, but differ in that one is concerned with truth in this sphere, the other two with pleasantness; and of this one kind is exhibited in giving amusement, the other in all the circumstances of life. We must therefore speak of these two, that we may the better see that in all things the mean is praiseworthy, and the extremes neither praiseworthy nor right, but worthy of blame. Now most of these states also have no names, but we must try, as in the other cases, to invent names ourselves so that we may be clear and easy to follow. With regard to truth, then, the intermediate is a truthful sort of person and the mean may be called truthfulness, while the pretence which exaggerates is boastfulness and the person characterized by it a boaster, and that which understates is mock modesty and the person characterized

by it mock-modest. With regard to pleasantness in the giving of amusement the intermediate person is ready-witted and the disposition ready wit, the excess is buffoonery and the person characterized by it a buffoon, while the man who falls short is a sort of boor and his state is boorishness. With regard to the remaining kind of pleasantness, that which is exhibited in life in general, the man who is pleasant in the right way is friendly and the mean is friendliness, while the man who exceeds is an obsequious person if he has no end in view, a flatterer if he is aiming at his own advantage, and the man who falls short and is unpleasant in all circumstances is a quarrelsome and surly sort of person.

* * *

9

That moral virtue is a mean, then, and in what sense it is so, and that it is a mean between two vices, the one involving excess, the other deficiency, and that it is such because its character is to aim at what is intermediate in passions and in actions, has been sufficiently stated. Hence also it is no easy task to be good. For in everything it is no easy task to find the middle, e.g. to find the middle of a circle is not for every one but for him who knows; so, too, any one can get angry—that is easy—or give or spend money; but to do this to the right person, to the right extent, at the right time, with the right motive, and in the right way, that is not for every one, nor is it easy; wherefore goodness is both rare and laudable and noble.

* * *

The Need for More Than Justice
ANNETTE C. BAIER

In recent decades in North American social and moral philosophy, alongside the development and discussion of widely influential theories of justice, taken as Rawls takes it as the 'first virtue of social institutions,'[1] there has been a counter-movement gathering strength, one coming from some interesting sources. For some of the most outspoken of the diverse group who have in a variety of ways been challenging the assumed supremacy of justice among the moral and social virtues are members of those sections of society whom one might have expected to be especially aware of the supreme importance of justice, namely blacks and women. Those who have only recently seen the correction or partial correction of long-standing racist and sexist injustices to their race and sex, are among the philosophers now suggesting that justice is only one virtue among many, and one that may need the presence of the others in order to deliver its own undenied value. Among these philosophers of the philosophical counterculture, as it were—but an increasingly large counterculture—I include Alasdair MacIntyre, Michael Stocker, Lawrence Blum, Michael Slote, Laurence Thomas, Claudia Card, Alison Jaggar, Susan Wolf and a whole group of men and women, myself included, who have been influenced by the writings of Harvard educational psychologist Carol Gilligan, whose book *In a Different Voice* (Harvard 1982; hereafter D.V.) caused a considerable stir both in the popular press and, more slowly, in the philosophical journals.

Let me say quite clearly at this early point that there is little disagreement that justice is *a* social value of very great importance, and injustice an evil. Nor would those who have worked on theories of justice want to deny that other things matter besides justice. Rawls, for example, incorporates the value of freedom into his account of justice, so that denial of basic

freedoms counts as injustice. Rawls also leaves room for a wider theory of the right, of which the theory of justice is just a part. Still, he does claim that justice is the 'first' virtue of social institutions, and it is only that claim about priority that I think has been challenged. It is easy to exaggerate the differences of view that exist, and I want to avoid that. The differences are as much in emphasis as in substance, or we can say that they are differences in tone of voice. But these differences do tend to make a difference in approaches to a wide range of topics not just in moral theory but in areas like medical ethics, where the discussion used to be conducted in terms of patients' rights, of informed consent, and so on, but now tends to get conducted in an enlarged moral vocabulary, which draws on what Gilligan calls the ethics of *care* as well as that of *justice*.

For 'care' is the new buzz-word. It is not, as Shakespeare's Portia demanded, mercy that is to season justice, but a less authoritarian humanitarian supplement, a felt concern for the good of others and for community with them. The 'cold jealous virtue of justice' (Hume) is found to be too cold, and it is 'warmer' more communitarian virtues and social ideals that are being called in to supplement it. One might say that liberty and equality are being found inadequate without fraternity, except that 'fraternity' will be quite the wrong word, if as Gilligan initially suggested, it is *women* who perceive this value most easily. ('Sorority' will do no better, since it is too exclusive, and English has no gender-neuter word for the mutual concern of siblings.) She has since modified this claim, allowing that there are two perspectives on moral and social issues that we all tend to alternate between, and which are not always easy to combine, one of them what she called the justice perspective, the other the care perspective. It is increasingly obvious that there are many male philosophical spokespersons for the care perspective (Laurence Thomas, Lawrence Blum, Michael Stocker) so that it cannot be the prerogative of women. Nevertheless Gilligan still wants to claim that women are most unlikely to take *only* the justice perspective, as some men are claimed to, at least

Annette C. Baier, "The Need for More Than Justice," *Canadian Journal of Philosophy,* supplementary vol. 13 (1988): 41–56. Published by University of Calgary Press. Reprinted with permission of University of Calgary Press.

until some mid-life crisis jolts them into 'bifocal' moral vision (see D.V., ch. 6).

Gilligan in her book did not offer any explanatory theory of why there should be any difference between female and male moral outlook, but she did tend to link the naturalness to women of the care perspective with their role as primary care-takers of young children, that is with their parental and specifically maternal role. She avoided the question of whether it is their biological or their social parental role that is relevant, and some of those who dislike her book are worried precisely by this uncertainty. Some find it retrograde to hail as a special sort of moral wisdom an outlook that may be the product of the socially enforced restriction of women to domestic roles (and the reservation of such roles for them alone). For that might seem to play into the hands of those who still favor such restriction. (Marxists, presumably, will not find it so surprising that moral truths might depend for their initial clear voicing on the social oppression, and memory of it, of those who voice the truths.) Gilligan did in the first chapter of D.V. cite the theory of Nancy Chodorow (as presented in *The Reproduction of Mothering* [Berkeley 1978]) which traces what appears as gender differences in personality to early social development, in particular to the effects of the child's primary care-taker being or not being of the same gender as the child. Later, both in 'The Conquistador and the Dark Continent: Reflections on the Nature of Love' (*Daedalus* [Summer 1984]), and 'The Origins of Morality in Early Childhood' (in press), she develops this explanation. She postulates two evils that any infant may become aware of, the evil of detachment or isolation from others whose love one needs, and the evil of relative powerlessness and weakness. Two dimensions of moral development are thereby set—one aimed at achieving satisfying community with others, the other aiming at autonomy or equality of power. The relative predominance of one over the other development will depend both upon the relative salience of the two evils in early childhood, and on early and later reinforcement or discouragement in attempts made to guard against these two evils. This provides the germs of a theory about *why,* given current customs of childrearing, it should be mainly women who are not content with only the moral outlook that

she calls the justice perspective, necessary though that was and is seen by them to have been to their hard won liberation from sexist oppression. They, like the blacks, used the language of rights and justice to change their own social position, but nevertheless see limitations in that language, according to Gilligan's findings as a moral psychologist. She reports their discontent with the individualist more or less Kantian moral framework that dominates Western moral theory and which influenced moral psychologists such as Lawrence Kohlberg, to whose conception of moral maturity she seeks an alternative. Since the target of Gilligan's criticism is the dominant Kantian tradition, and since that has been the target also of moral philosophers as diverse in their own views as Bernard Williams, Alasdair MacIntyre, Philippa Foot, Susan Wolf, Claudia Card, her book is of interest as much for its attempt to articulate an alternative to the Kantian justice perspective as for its implicit raising of the question of male bias in Western moral theory, especially liberal-democratic theory. For whether the supposed blind spots of that outlook are due to male bias, or to nonparental bias, or to early traumas of powerlessness or to early resignation to 'detachment' from others, we need first to be persuaded that they *are* blind spots before we will have any interest in their cause and cure. Is justice blind to important social values, or at least only one-eyed? What is it that comes into view from the 'care perspective' that is not seen from the 'justice perspective'?

Gilligan's position here is mostly easily described by contrasting it with that of Kohlberg, against which she developed it. Kohlberg, influenced by Piaget and the Kantian philosophical tradition as developed by John Rawls, developed a theory about typical moral development which saw it to progress from a pre-conventional level, where what is seen to matter is pleasing or not offending parental authority-figures, through a conventional level in which the child tries to fit in with a group, such as a school community, and conform to its standards and rules, to a post-conventional critical level, in which such conventional rules are subjected to tests, and where those tests are of a Utilitarian, or, eventually, a Kantian sort—namely ones that require respect for each person's individual rational will, or autonomy, and conformity to any implicit social contract such wills are deemed to have made, or to any hypothetical ones they would make if thinking clearly. What was found when Kohlberg's questionnaires (mostly by verbal response to verbally sketched moral dilemmas) were applied to female as well as male subjects, Gilligan reports, is that the girls and women not only scored generally lower than the boys and men, but tended to *revert* to the lower stage of the conventional level even after briefly (usually in adolescence) attaining the post-conventional level. Piaget's finding that girls were deficient in 'the legal sense' was confirmed.

These results led Gilligan to wonder if there might not be a quite different pattern of development to be discerned, at least in female subjects. She therefore conducted interviews designed to elicit not just how far advanced the subjects were towards an appreciation of the nature and importance of Kantian autonomy, but also to find out what the subjects themselves saw as progress or lack of it, what conceptions of moral maturity they came to possess by the time they were adults. She found that although the Kohlberg version of moral maturity as respect for fellow persons, and for their rights as equals (rights including that of free association), did seem shared by many young men, the women tended to speak in a different voice about morality itself and about moral maturity. To quote Gilligan, 'Since the reality of interconnexion is experienced by women as given rather than freely contracted, they arrive at an understanding of life that reflects the limits of autonomy and control. As a result, women's development delineates the path not only to a less violent life but also to a maturity realized by interdependence and taking care' (D.V., 172). She writes that there is evidence that 'women perceive and construe social reality differently from men, and that these differences center around experiences of attachment and separation . . . because women's sense of integrity appears to be intertwined with an ethics of care, so that to see themselves as women is to see themselves in a relationship of connexion, the major changes in women's lives would seem to involve changes in the understanding and activities of care' (D.V., 171). She contrasts this progressive understanding of care, from merely pleasing others to helping and nurturing, with the sort of progression that is involved

in Kohlberg's stages, a progression in the understanding, not of mutual care, but of mutual *respect,* where this has its Kantian overtones of distance, even of some fear for the respected, and where personal autonomy and *in*dependence, rather than more satisfactory interdependence, are the paramount values.

This contrast, one cannot but feel, is one which Gilligan might have used the Marxist language of alienation to make. For the main complaint about the Kantian version of a society with its first virtue justice, constructed as respect for equal rights to formal goods such as having contracts kept, due process, equal opportunity including opportunity to participate in political activities leading to policy and law-making, to basic liberties of speech, free association and assembly, religious worship, is that none of these goods do much to ensure that the people who have and mutually respect such rights will have any other relationships to one another than the minimal relationship needed to keep such a 'civil society' going. They may well be lonely, driven to suicide, apathetic about their work and about participation in political processes, find their lives meaningless and have no wish to leave offspring to face the same meaningless existence. Their rights, and respect for rights, are quite compatible with very great misery, and misery whose causes are not just individual misfortunes and psychic sickness, but social and moral impoverishment.

What Gilligan's older male subjects complain of is precisely this sort of alienation from some dimly glimpsed better possibility for human beings, some richer sort of network of relationships. As one of Gilligan's male subjects put it, 'People have real emotional needs to be attached to something, and equality does not give you attachment. Equality fractures society and places on every person the burden of standing on his own two feet' (D.V., 167). It is not just the difficulty of self-reliance which is complained of, but its socially 'fracturing' effect. Whereas the younger men, in their college years, had seen morality as a matter of reciprocal non-interference, this old man begins to see it as reciprocal attachment. 'Morality is . . . essential . . . for creating the kind of environment, interaction between people, that is a prerequisite to the fulfillment of individual goals. If you want other people not to interfere with your pursuit of whatever you are into, you have to play the game,' says the spokesman for traditional liberalism (D.V., 98). But if what one is 'into' is interconnexion, interdependence rather than an individual autonomy that may involve 'detachment,' such a version of morality will come to seem inadequate. And Gilligan stresses that the interconnexion that her mature women subjects, and some men, wanted to sustain was not merely freely chosen interconnexion, nor interconnexion between equals, but also the sort of interconnexion that can obtain between a child and her unchosen mother and father, or between a child and her unchosen older and younger siblings, or indeed between most workers and their unchosen fellow workers, or most citizens and their unchosen fellow citizens.

A model of a decent community different from the liberal one is involved in the version of moral maturity that Gilligan voices. It has in many ways more in common with the older religion-linked versions of morality and a good society than with the modern Western liberal idea. That perhaps is why some find it so dangerous and retrograde. Yet it seems clear that it also has much in common with what we call Hegelian versions of moral maturity and of social health and malaise, both with Marxist versions and with so-called right-Hegelian views.

Let me try to summarize the main differences, as I see them, between on the one hand Gilligan's version of moral maturity and the sort of social structures that would encourage, express and protect it, and on the other the orthodoxy she sees herself to be challenging. I shall from now on be giving my own interpretation of the significance of her challenges, not merely reporting them. The most obvious point is the challenge to the individualism of the Western tradition, to the fairly entrenched belief in the possibility and desirability of each person pursuing his own good in his own way, constrained only by a minimal formal common good, namely a working legal apparatus that enforces contracts and protects individuals from undue interference by others. Gilligan reminds us that noninterference can, especially for the relatively powerless, such as the very young, amount to neglect, and even between equals can be isolating and alienating. On her less individualist version of individuality, it

becomes defined by responses to dependence and to patterns of interconnexion, both chosen and unchosen. It is not something a person *has,* and which she then chooses relationships to suit, but something that develops out of a series of dependencies and interdependencies, and responses to them. This conception of individuality is not flatly at odds with, say, Rawls' Kantian one, but there is at least a difference of tone of voice between speaking as Rawls does of each of us having our own rational life plan, which a just society's moral traffic rules will allow us to follow, and which may or may not include close association with other persons, and speaking as Gilligan does of a satisfactory life as involving 'progress of affiliative relationship' (D.V., 170) where 'the concept of identity expands to include the experience of interconnexion' (D.V., 173). Rawls can allow that progress to Gilligan-style moral maturity may be *a* rational life plan, but not a moral constraint on every life-pattern. The trouble is that it will not do just to say 'let this version of morality be an optional extra. Let us agree on the essential minimum, that is on justice and rights, and let whoever wants to go further and cultivate this more demanding ideal of responsibility and care.' For, first, it cannot be satisfactorily cultivated without closer cooperation from others than respect for rights and justice will ensure, and second, the encouragement of some to cultivate it while others do not could easily lead to exploitation of those who do. It obviously *has* suited some in most societies well enough that others take on the responsibilities of care (for the sick, the helpless, the young) leaving them free to pursue their own less altruistic goods. Volunteer forces of those who accept an ethic of care, operating within a society where the power is exercised and the institutions designed, redesigned, or maintained by those who accept a less communal ethic of minimally constrained self-advancement, will not be the solution. The liberal individualists may be able to 'tolerate' the more communally minded, if they keep the liberals' rules, but it is not so clear that the more communally minded can be content with just those rules, nor be content to be tolerated and possibly exploited.

For the moral tradition which developed the concept of rights, autonomy and justice is the same tradition that provided 'justifications' of the oppression of those whom the primary right-holders depended on to do the sort of work they themselves preferred not to do. The domestic work was left to women and slaves, and the liberal morality for right-holders was surreptitiously supplemented by a different set of demands made on domestic workers. As long as women could be got to assume responsibility for the care of home and children, and to train their children to continue the sexist system, the liberal morality could continue to be the official morality, by turning its eyes away from the contribution made by those it excluded. The long unnoticed moral proletariat were the domestic workers, mostly female. Rights have usually been for the privileged. Talking about laws, and the rights those laws recognize and protect, does not in itself ensure that the group of legislators and rights-holders will not be restricted to some elite. Bills of rights have usually been proclamations of the rights of some in-group, barons, landowners, males, whites, non-foreigners. The 'justice perspective,' and the legal sense that goes with it, are shadowed by their patriarchal past. What did Kant, the great prophet of autonomy, say in his moral theory about women? He said they were incapable of legislation, not fit to vote, that they needed the guidance of more 'rational' males.[2] Autonomy was not for them, only for first-class, really rational persons. It is ironic that Gilligan's original findings in a way confirm Kant's views—it seems that autonomy really may not be for women. Many of them reject that ideal (D.V., 48), and have been found not as good at making rules as are men. But where Kant concludes—'so much the worse for women,' we can conclude—'so much the worse for the male fixation on the special skill of drafting legislation, for the bureaucratic mentality of rule worship, and for the male exaggeration of the importance of independence over mutual interdependence.'

It is however also true that the moral theories that made the concept of a person's rights central were not just the instruments for excluding some persons, but also the instruments used by those who demanded that more and more persons be included in the favored group. Abolitionists, reformers, women, used the language of rights to assert their claims to inclusion in the group of full members of a community. The tradition of liberal moral theory has in fact developed so as to include the women it had for so long excluded, to include the poor as well as rich, blacks and whites, and so on. Women like Mary Wollstonecraft used the male moral theories to good purpose. So we should not be wholly ungrateful for those male moral theories, for all their objectionable earlier content. They were undoubtedly patriarchal, but they also contained the seeds of the challenge, or antidote, to this patriarchal poison.

But when we transcend the values of the Kantians, we should not forget the facts of history—that those values were the values of the oppressors of women. The Christian church, whose version of the moral law Aquinas codified, in his very legalistic moral theory, still insists on the maleness of the God it worships, and jealously reserves for males all the most powerful positions in its hierarchy. Its patriarchical prejudice is open and avowed. In the secular moral theories of men, the sexist patriarchal prejudice is today often less open, not as blatant as it is in Aquinas, in the later natural law tradition, and in Kant and Hegel, but is often still there. No moral theorist today would say that women are unfit to vote, to make laws, or to rule a nation without powerful male advisors (as most queens had), but the old doctrines die hard. In one of the best male theories we have, John Rawls's theory, a key role is played by the idea of the 'head of a household.' It is heads of households who are to deliberate behind a 'veil of ignorance' of historical details, and of details of their own special situation, to arrive at the 'just' constitution for a society. Now of course Rawls does not think or say that these 'heads' are fathers rather than mothers. But if we have really given up the age-old myth of women needing, as Grotius put it, to be under the 'eye' of a more 'rational' male protector and master, then how do families come to have any one 'head,' except by the death or desertion of one parent? They will either be two-headed, or headless. Traces of the old patriarchal poison still remain in even the best contemporary moral theorizing. Few may actually say that women's place is in the home, but there is much muttering, when unemployment figures rise, about how the relatively recent flood of women into the work force complicates the problem, as if it would be a good thing if women just went back home whenever unemployment rises, to leave the available jobs for the men. We still do not really have a wide acceptance of the equal rights of women to employment outside the home. Nor do we have wide acceptance of the equal duty of men to perform those domestic tasks which in no way depend on special female anatomy, namely cooking, cleaning, and the care of weaned children. All sorts of stories (maybe true stories), about children's need for one 'primary' parent, who must be the mother if the mother breast-feeds the child, shore up the unequal division of domestic responsibility between mothers and fathers, wives and husbands. If we are really to transvalue the values of our patriarchal past, we need to rethink all of those assumptions, really test those psychological theories. And how will men ever develop an understanding of the 'ethics of care' if they continue to be shielded or kept from that experience of caring for a dependent child, which complements the experience we all have had of being cared for as dependent children? These experiences form the natural background for the development of moral maturity as Gilligan's women saw it.

Exploitation aside, why would women, once liberated, not be content to have their version of morality merely tolerated? Why should they not see themselves as voluntarily, for their own reasons, taking on *more* than the liberal rules demand, while having no quarrel with the content of those rules themselves, nor with their remaining the only ones that are expected to be generally obeyed? To see why, we need to move on to three more differences between the Kantian liberals (usually contractarians) and their critics. These concern the relative weight put on relationships between equals, and the relative weight put on freedom of choice, and on the authority of intellect over emotions. It is a typical feature of the dominant moral theories and traditions, since Kant, or perhaps since Hobbes, that relationships between equals or those who are deemed equal in some important sense, have been the relations that morality is concerned primarily to regulate. Relationships between those who are clearly unequal in power, such as parents and children, earlier and later generations in relation to one

another, states and citizens, doctors and patients, the well and the ill, large states and small states, have had to be shunted to the bottom of the agenda, and then dealt with by some sort of 'promotion' of the weaker so that an appearance of virtual equality is achieved. Citizens collectively become equal to states, children are treated as adults-to-be, the ill and dying are treated as continuers of their earlier more potent selves, so that their 'rights' could be seen as the rights of equals. This pretence of an equality that is in fact absent may often lead to desirable protection of the weaker, or more dependent. But it somewhat masks the question of what our moral relationships *are* to those who are our superiors or our inferiors in power. A more realistic acceptance of the fact that we begin as helpless children, that at almost every point of our lives we deal with both the more and the less helpless, that equality of power and interdependency, between two persons or groups, is rare and hard to recognize when it does occur, might lead us to a more direct approach to questions concerning the design of institutions structuring these relationships between unequals (families, schools, hospitals, armies) and of the morality of our dealings with the more and the less powerful. One reason why those who agree with the Gilligan version of what morality is about will not want to agree that the liberals' rules are a good minimal set, the only ones we need pressure *everyone* to obey, is that these rules do little to protect the young or the dying or the starving or any of the relatively powerless against neglect, or to ensure an education that will form persons to be *capable* of conforming to an ethics of care and responsibility. Put baldly, and in a way Gilligan certainly has not put it, the liberal morality, if unsupplemented, may *unfit* people to be anything other than what its justifying theories suppose them to be, ones who have no interest in each others' interests. Yet some must take an interest in the next generation's interests. Women's traditional work, of caring for the less powerful, especially for the young, is obviously socially vital. One cannot regard any version of morality that does not ensure that it gets well done as an adequate 'minimal morality,' any more than we could so regard one that left any concern for more distant future generations an optional extra. A moral theory, it can plausibly be claimed, cannot regard concern for new and future persons as an optional charity left for those with a taste for it. If the morality the theory endorses is to sustain itself, it must provide for its own continuers, not just take out a loan on a carefully encouraged maternal instinct or on the enthusiasm of a self-selected group of environmentalists, who make it their business or hobby to be concerned with what we are doing to mother earth.

The recognition of the importance for all parties of relations between those who are and cannot but be unequal, both of these relations in themselves and for their effect on personality formation and so on other relationships, goes along with a recognition of the plain fact that not all morally important relationships can or should be freely chosen. So far I have discussed three reasons women have not to be content to pursue their own values within the framework of the liberal morality. The first was its dubious record. The second was its inattention to relations of inequality or its pretence of equality. The third reason is its exaggeration of the scope of choice, or its inattention to unchosen relations. Showing up the partial myth of equality among actual members of a community, and of the undesirability of trying to pretend that we are treating all of them as equals, tends to go along with an exposure of the companion myth that moral obligations arise from freely *chosen* associations between such equals. Vulnerable future generations do not choose their dependence on earlier generations. The unequal infant does not choose its place in a family or nation, nor is it treated as free to do as it likes until some association is freely entered into. Nor do its parents always choose their parental role, or freely assume their parental responsibilities any more than we choose our power to affect the conditions in which later generations will live. Gilligan's attention to the version of morality and moral maturity found in women, many of whom had faced a choice of whether or not to have an abortion, and who had at some point become mothers, is attention to the perceived inadequacy of the language of rights to help in such choices or to guide them in their parental role. It would not be much of an exaggeration to call the Gilligan 'different voice' the voice of the potential parents. The emphasis

on care goes with a recognition of the often unchosen nature of the responsibilities of those who give care, both of children who care for their aged or infirm parents, and of parents who care for the children they in fact have. Contract soon ceases to seem the paradigm source of moral obligation once we attend to parental responsibility, and justice as a virtue of social institutions will come to seem at best only first equal with the virtue, whatever its name, that ensures that each new generation is made appropriately welcome and prepared for their adult lives.

This all constitutes a belated reminder to Western moral theorists of a fact they have always known, that as Adam Ferguson, and David Hume before him emphasized, we are born into families, and the first society we belong to, one that fits or misfits us for later ones, is the small society of parents (or some sort of child-attendants) and children, exhibiting as it may both relationships of near equality and of inequality in power. This simple reminder, with the fairly considerable implications it can have for the plausibility of contractarian moral theory, is at the same time a reminder of the role of human emotions as much as human reason and will in moral development as it actually comes about. The fourth feature of the Gilligan challenge to liberal orthodoxy is a challenge to its typical *rationalism,* or intellectualism, to its assumption that we need not worry what passions persons have, as long as their rational wills can control them. This Kantian picture of a controlling reason dictating to possibly unruly passions also tends to seem less useful when we are led to consider what sort of person we need to fill the role of parent, or indeed want in any close relationship. It might be important for father figures to have rational control over their violent urges to beat to death the children whose screams enrage them, but more than control of such nasty passions seems needed in the mother or primary parent, or parent-substitute, by most psychological theories. They need to love their children, not just to control their irritation. So the emphasis in Kantian theories on rational control of emotions, rather than on cultivating desirable forms of emotion, is challenged by Gilligan, along with the challenge to the assumption of the centrality of autonomy, or relations between equals, and of freely chosen relations.

The same set of challenges to 'orthodox' liberal oral theory has come not just from Gilligan and other women, who are reminding other moral theorists of the role of the family as a social institution and as an influence on the other relationships people want to or are capable of sustaining, but also, as I noted at the start, from an otherwise fairly diverse group of men, ranging from those influenced by both Hegelian and Christian traditions (MacIntyre) to all varieties of other backgrounds. From this group I want to draw attention to the work of one philosopher in particular, namely Laurence Thomas, the author of a fairly remarkable article[3] in which he finds sexism to be a more intractable social evil than racism. . . . Thomas makes a strong case for the importance of supplementing a concern for justice and respect for rights with an emphasis on equally needed virtues, and on virtues seen as appropriate *emotional* as well as rational capacities. Like Gilligan (and unlike MacIntyre) Thomas gives a lot of attention to the childhood beginnings of moral and social capacities, to the role of parental love in making that possible, and to the emotional as well as the cognitive development we have reason to think both possible and desirable in human persons.

It is clear, I think, that the best moral theory has to be a cooperative product of women and men, has to harmonize justice and care. The morality it theorizes about is after all for all persons, for men and for women, and will need their combined insights. As Gilligan said (D.V., 174), what we need now is a 'marriage' of the old male and the newly articulated female insights. If she is right about the special moral aptitudes of women, it will most likely be the women who propose the marriage, since they are the ones with moral natural empathy, with the better diplomatic skills, the ones more likely to shoulder responsibility and take moral initiative, and the ones who find it easiest to empathize and care about how the other party feels. Then, once there is this union of male and female moral wisdom, we maybe can teach each other the moral skills each gender currently lacks, so that the gender difference in moral outlook that Gilligan found will slowly become less marked.

NOTES

1. John Rawls, *A Theory of Justice* (Harvard University Press).

2. Immanuel Kant, *Metaphysics of Morals*, sec. 46.

3. Laurence Thomas, 'Sexism and Racism: Some Conceptual Differences,' *Ethics* 90 (1980), 239–50; republished in *Philosophy, Sex and Language*, Vetterling-Braggin, ed. (Totowa, NJ: Littlefield Adams 1980).

CHAPTER 8

Feminist Ethics and the Ethics of Care

Beyond the moral theorizing of Aquinas, Kant, Hobbes, and Mill, there is a different approach to moral thinking and feeling that constitutes a serious challenge to them: **feminist ethics**. Feminist ethics is not a moral theory so much as an alternative way of looking at the concepts and concerns of the moral life. It is an approach focused on women's interests and experiences and devoted to supporting the moral equality of women and men.

Those who see ethics from this perspective are reacting to some hard facts. One is that most of the great ethical theorists (and many of their followers, past and present) have assumed that women are somehow morally inferior to men—less rational, less important, less mature, or less moral. Coupled with this bias is a trend that is even more alarming: most women throughout the world are in a thousand ways second-class citizens (or worse). By law, by religion, or by custom, they are the victims of violence, stereotype, bigotry, coercion, forced dependence, and social, political, and professional inequality. Modern Western societies are as guilty of some of these evils as many countries in the developing world.

In the West, some ways of thinking and feeling have been regarded as characteristic of women, and these ways, whether distinctive of women or not, have been largely neglected by moral philosophers (who have traditionally been men). According to the feminist philosopher Alison M. Jaggar,

> Western moral theory is said to embody values that are "masculine," insofar as they are associated, empirically, normatively, or symbolically with

men. For instance, western ethics is alleged to prefer the supposedly masculine or male-associated values of independence, autonomy, intellect, will, wariness, hierarchy, domination, culture, transcendence, product, asceticism, war and death over the supposedly feminine or female-associated values of interdependence, community, connection, sharing, emotion, body, trust, absence of hierarchy, nature, immanence, process, joy, peace and life.[1]

Some moral issues are more likely to arise from women's experiences than men's, and these, too, have been overlooked:

> Issues of special concern to women are said to have been ignored by modern moral philosophers, who have tended to portray the domestic realm as an arena outside the economy and beyond justice, private in the sense of being beyond the scope of legitimate political regulation. Even philosophers like Aristotle or Hegel (1770–1831), who give some ethical importance to the domestic realm, have tended to portray the home as an arena in which the most fully human excellences are incapable of being realized. . . . [Feminist philosophers] argued that the philosophical devaluation of the domestic realm made it impossible to raise questions about the justice of the domestic division of labor, because it obscured the far-reaching social significance and creativity of women's work in the home, and concealed, even legitimated, the domestic abuse of women and girls.[2]

In the past few decades, feminist philosophers and other thinkers (mostly women but some men) have tried to shed light on all of these dark corners. The result—still an ongoing project—is feminist ethics and its grandchild, the ethics of care.

FEMINIST ETHICS

Feminists are a diverse group with contrasting viewpoints, so it should not be a surprise that they approach feminist ethics in different ways and arrive at different conclusions. Still, some generalizations are possible.

An emphasis on personal relationships. For the most part, traditional moral theories have been concerned with what we could call "public life"—the realm in which unrelated individuals try to figure out how to behave toward one another and how to ensure that, among strangers, justice is done, rights are respected, and utility is maximized. The focus has been mostly on moral judgments and theories pertaining to people as separate members of the community, the polity, and the culture. But feminist ethics narrows down the area of moral concern to the interconnected and familiar small group—to the people with whom we have close personal relationships. The relationships of interest are the ties of kinship, the bonds of friendship, or the connections between caregivers and the cared-for—the sphere of the domestic and the private. This is the realm of intimate relationships, sexual behavior, child rearing, and family struggles—the place we all come from and perhaps never leave, and where we live a large part of our moral lives.

Differing views on moral principles. Some feminist philosophers resist the temptation to map out moral actions according to moral principles. Whereas Kant wants to reduce all moral deliberation to adherence to a single rule (the categorical imperative), some feminists demur. They argue that principles such as autonomy, justice, and utility are too general and too unwieldy to be of much use in the complicated, multifaceted arena of the domestic, social, and personal. Many feminist philosophers, however, are comfortable with moral principles and see them as essential to moral reasoning. Some of these thinkers are working within the context of traditional moral theories and see these frameworks as compatible with feminist ethics.

CRITICAL THOUGHT: Feminist Ethics in History

The increased contemporary focus on feminist ethics is new, but important work in the area is not. Rosemarie Tong and Nancy Williams explain:

> Feminist approaches to ethics, as well as debates about the gendered nature of morality, are not recent developments. During the eighteenth and nineteenth centuries, a wide variety of thinkers including Mary Wollstonecraft, John Stuart Mill, Catherine Beecher, Charlotte Perkins Gilman, and Elizabeth Cady Stanton addressed topics related to "women's morality." Each of these thinkers raised questions such as: Are women's "feminine" traits the product of nature/biology or are they instead the outcome of social conditioning? Are moral virtues as well as gender traits connected with one's affective as well as cognitive capacities,

> indeed with one's physiology and psychology? If so, should we simply accept the fact that men and women have different moral virtues as well as different gender traits and proceed accordingly? If not, should we strive to get men and women to adhere to the same morality: a one-size-fits-all human morality?*

What would be the social implications of scientific proof that alleged feminine traits are entirely the result of either biology or social conditioning?

*Rosemarie Tong and Nancy Williams, "Feminist Ethics," in *Stanford Encyclopedia of Philosophy*, Winter 2016 ed. Edward N. Zalta, https://plato.stanford.edu/archives/win2016/entries/feminism-ethics/.

Contrasting attitudes toward impartiality. Recall that the principle of impartiality is regarded as a defining characteristic of morality itself. Impartiality says that from the moral point of view, all persons are considered equal and should be treated accordingly. But in the domestic sphere we are anything but impartial. We are naturally partial to the people we care about—our family and friends. Typically we would not think of treating our spouse the same way we treat a store clerk or the bus driver. We have moral duties to the former that we do not have to the latter. Some feminists (most notably care ethicists) make these duties central to their moral outlook instead of ignoring them as Kant and Mill would have us do.

A higher regard for emotions. As we've seen, Kant has no place for emotions in his theory. Reading our moral duties off the categorical imperative is all that is required. But feminist philosophers have greater respect for the emotional side of our lives than many non-feminist ethicists do. Moral philosophers of all stripes recognize the importance of emotions. They understand that emotions can alert us to moral evil, provide the motivation to pursue the good, and enable us to empathize with the suffering of others. (Moral philosophers also caution that feelings without thinking are blind, and thinking without feelings makes for a sterile morality.)

An emphasis on the nonideal. Feminist thinkers take issue with the tendency of traditional moral theories to assume an idealized view of human beings, their capacities, and their social interactions. These philosophers charge that to the traditional theorist, the world consists of atomistic individuals with perfect rationality living in an idealized society without oppression, where moral agents are unaffected by poor living conditions and unjust institutions. As feminist philosopher Sarah Clark Miller says,

> Ideal theories commence and operate from the best of what humans can be, conveniently overlooking the ways in which we break down, fail, and fall apart . . . But real life is much messier and involves humans who are often irrational, who have histories of oppression, who only sometimes follow rules, and who have a variety of complex needs. . . . Many feminist ethicists appreciate the value of the nonideal and make it a cornerstone of feminist ethics.[3]

THE ETHICS OF CARE

The **ethics of care** is a good example of feminist ethics. It is a perspective on moral issues that emphasizes close personal relationships and moral virtues such as compassion, faithfulness, kindness, love, and sympathy. It contrasts dramatically with traditional moral theories preoccupied with principles and legalistic moral reasoning.

Much of the interest in the ethics of care was sparked by research done by the psychologist Carol Gilligan on how men and women think about moral problems.[4] She maintained that men and women think in radically different ways when making moral decisions. In moral decision making, she said, men deliberate about rights, justice, and rules; women, on the other hand, focus on personal relationships, caring for others, and being aware of people's feelings, needs, and viewpoints. She dubbed these two approaches the *ethic of justice* and the *ethic of care.* Later she rejected the notion that women and men have distinct traits or essences that lead them to different styles of moral reasoning. She now denies that these two styles are inherently linked to being male or female.

More recent research has raised doubts about whether there really is a gap between the moral thinking styles of men and women. But these findings do not dilute the relevance of caring to ethics. The ethics of care, regardless of any empirical underpinnings, is a reminder that caring is a vital and inescapable part of the moral life—a conclusion that few philosophers would deny. If virtues are a part of the moral life (as they surely are), and if caring (or compassion, sympathy, or love) is a virtue, then there must be a place for caring alongside principles of moral conduct and moral reasoning. The philosopher Annette C. Baier, an early proponent of the ethics of care, makes a case for both care and justice: "It is clear, I think, that the best moral theory has to be a cooperative product of women and men, has to harmonize justice and care. The morality it theorizes about is after all for all persons, for men and women, and will need their combined insights."[5]

Here is the feminist philosopher Virginia Held explaining the need for care in the moral life:

> [T]he central focus of the ethics of care is on the compelling moral salience of attending to and meeting the needs of the particular others for whom we take responsibility. Caring for one's child, for instance, may well and defensibly be at the forefront of a person's moral concerns. The ethics of care recognizes that human beings are dependent for many years of their lives, that the moral claim of those dependent on us for the care they need is pressing, and that there are highly important moral aspects in developing the relations of caring that enable human beings to live and progress. All persons need care for at least their early years. Prospects for human progress and flourishing hinge fundamentally on the care that those needing it receive, and the ethics of care stresses the moral force of the responsibility to respond to the needs of the dependent. Many persons will become ill and dependent for some periods of their later lives, including in frail old age, and some who

are permanently disabled will need care the whole of their lives. Moralities built on the image of the independent, autonomous, rational individual largely overlook the reality of human dependence and the morality for which it calls. The ethics of care attends to this central concern of human life and delineates the moral values involved. It refuses to relegate care to a realm "outside morality."[6]

CHAPTER REVIEW

SUMMARY

Feminist ethics is an alternative way of looking at the concepts and concerns of the moral life. It is an approach focused on women's interests and experiences and devoted to supporting the moral equality of women and men. The main elements of this approach are an emphasis on personal relationships, a suspicion of moral principles, the rejection of impartiality, and a greater respect for emotions.

The ethics of care is a perspective on moral issues that emphasizes personal relationships and the virtues of compassion, love, sympathy, and the like. It can be thought of as an essential element in virtue ethics. The ethics of care is a reminder that caring is a crucial part of the moral life. Many philosophers have acknowledged this fact by trying to incorporate care into moral theories containing principles.

KEY TERMS
feminist ethics (p. 196)
ethics of care (p. 198)

EXERCISES

Review Questions

1. How does feminist ethics differ from Kantian ethics? (pp. 197–198)
2. What attitudes did many of the great ethical theorists have toward women? (p. 196)

3. What ways of feeling and thinking have been regarded in the West as characteristic of women? (p. 196)
4. What kinds of moral issues are more likely to arise from women's experiences than men's? (p. 196)
5. What elements of the moral life does feminist ethics emphasize? What elements does it deemphasize? (pp. 197–198)
6. Why do feminist philosophers think an ethics of care is needed? (p. 198)
7. What are the hard facts that have helped to propel the rise of feminist ethics? (p. 196)
8. What are some of the fundamental elements of the ethics of care? (p. 198)
9. What is Annette Baier's claim about care and justice? (p. 199)
10. What is Carol Gilligan's thesis about moral thinking? (p. 198)

Discussion Questions

1. What features of feminist ethics do you find most plausible? Why?
2. Do you think moral principles such as justice and rights have a place in any good moral theory? Why or why not?
3. What part do you think emotions should play in morality?
4. Do you believe there are innate differences in the ways men and women deliberate about moral issues? Or do you think any differences are the result of cultural influences? Explain.
5. Do you believe there are situations in which impartiality is important in moral reasoning? If not, why not? If so, give an example.
6. Suppose you have an opportunity to either (1) send $800 to Africa to save a dozen people from starvation or (2) give the money to your little sister to buy books for college. Which would you do? Why?
7. What is the attitude of feminist ethics toward moral principles? Compare it with Kant's view.
8. Are there instances of moral decision making in which moral impartiality is not appropriate? Explain.

ETHICAL DILEMMAS

Explain how feminist ethics or the ethics of care could be applied in the following scenarios to determine the proper course of action.

1. Suppose your best friend is in the hospital battling a serious illness and would deeply appreciate a visit from you. But you are also on spring break and, after a very stressful semester, need to forget about all your commitments and just relax. What might the ethics of care have you do? What is a utilitarian likely to do?
2. You want to help your brother overcome a serious addiction to drugs. You know that because he is a member of your family, you have a duty to help him. But your main reason for trying to help is that you love him and care what happens to him. Which of these two motivating factors (duty and love) would Kant approve of, and which would he reject? How might the attitude of someone who embraces feminist ethics differ from Kant's response?
3. Imagine that your town has been hit by a tornado, and you are in a position to rescue only one of a dozen people who are nearby and trapped in demolished houses. The victim who happens to be farthest from you, but still reachable, is your mother. Which of these twelve people should you rescue? Who would you rescue if feminist ethics was your preferred moral outlook? Who would you rescue if you were a strict act-utilitarian?

FURTHER READING

Carol Gilligan, *In a Different Voice: Psychological Theory and Women's Development* (Cambridge, MA: Harvard University Press, 1982).

Carol Hay, *Kantianism, Liberalism, and Feminism: Resisting Oppression* (New York: Palgrave Macmillan, 2013).

Virginia Held, *Feminist Morality: Transforming Culture, Society, and Politics* (Chicago: University of Chicago Press, 1993).

Virginia Held, *The Ethics of Care* (Oxford: Oxford University Press, 2006).

Alison M. Jaggar, *Feminist Politics and Human Nature* (Totowa, NJ: Allenheld, 1983).

Alison M. Jaggar, "Feminist Ethics," in *Encyclopedia of Ethics*, ed. Lawrence C. Becker and Charlotte B. Becker (New York: Garland, 1992), 361–70.

Martha Nussbaum, "The Feminist Critique of Liberalism," in *Women's Voices, Women's Rights*, ed. A. Jeffries (Boulder, CO: Westview Press, 1999).

Susan Moller Okin, *Justice, Gender, and the Family* (New York: Basic Books, 1989).

Rosemarie Tong and Nancy Williams, "Feminist Ethics," in *Stanford Encyclopedia of Philosophy*, Winter 2016 ed., ed. Edward N. Zalta, https://plato.stanford.edu /archives/win2016/entries/feminism-ethics/.

Mary Wollstonecraft, *A Vindication of the Rights of Woman*, ed. M. Brody (London: Penguin, 1988).

READINGS

Feminist Ethics

ALISON M. JAGGAR

Feminist approaches to ethics, often known collectively as feminist ethics, are distinguished by an explicit commitment to correcting male biases they perceive in traditional ethics, biases that may be manifest in rationalizations of women's subordination, or in disregard for, or disparagement of, women's moral experience. Feminist ethics, by contrast, begins from the convictions that the subordination of women is morally wrong and that the moral experience of women is as worthy of respect as that of men. The practical goals of feminist ethics, then, are the following: first, to articulate moral critiques of actions and practices that perpetuate women's subordination; second, to prescribe morally justifiable ways of resisting such actions and practices; and, third, to envision morally desirable alternatives that will promote women's emancipation. The meta-ethical goal of feminist ethics is to develop theoretical understandings of the nature of morality that treat women's moral experience respectfully, though never uncritically.

Just as feminist ethics may be identified by its explicit commitment to challenging perceived male bias in ethics, so approaches that do not express such a commitment may be characterized as nonfeminist.

Alison M. Jaggar, "Feminist Ethics," in *Encyclopedia of Ethics*, ed. Lawrence C. Becker and Charlotte B. Becker (New York: Garland Publishing, 1992). Reproduced by permission of Taylor and Francis Group, LLC, a division of Informa plc.

Nonfeminist approaches to ethics are not necessarily anti-feminist or male-biased; they may or may not be so.

THE DEVELOPMENT OF CONTEMPORARY FEMINIST ETHICS

The history of western philosophy includes a number of isolated but indisputable instances of moral opposition to women's subordination. Noteworthy examples are Mary Wollstonecraft's (1759–1797) *A Vindication of the Rights of Woman* (1792), John Stuart Mill's (1806–1873) *The Subjection of Women* (1869), Frederick Engels' (1820–1895) *The Origin of the Family, Private Property and the State* (1884), and Simone de Beauvoir's (1908–1986) *The Second Sex* (1949).

In the late 1960s, however, as part of a general resurgence of feminist activism, an unprecedented explosion of feminist ethical debate occurred, first among the general public, soon in academic discourse. Actions and practices whose gendered dimensions hitherto either had been unnoticed or unchallenged now became foci of public and philosophical attention, as feminists subjected them to outspoken moral critique, developed sometimes dramatic strategies for opposing them, and proposed alternatives that nonfeminists often perceived as dangerously radical. First grassroots and soon academic feminist perspectives were articulated on topics such as abortion, equality of opportunity, domestic labor, portrayals of women in the media, and a variety of issues concerning sexuality, such as rape and compulsory heterosexuality. A little later, feminists displayed increasing ethical concern about pornography, reproductive technology, so-called surrogate motherhood, militarism, the environment and the situation of women in developing nations.

Despite the long history of feminist ethical debate, the term "feminist ethics" itself did not come into general use until the late 1970s or early 1980s. At this time, a number of feminists began expressing doubts about the possibility of fruitfully addressing so-called women's issues in terms of the conceptual apparatus supplied by traditional ethical theory. For instance, a rights framework was alleged by some to distort discussions of abortion insofar as it constructed pregnancy and motherhood as adversarial situations. Other feminists charged that certain assumptions widely accepted by traditional ethical theory were incompatible with what was now beginning to be claimed as a distinctively feminine moral experience or sensibility. Contract theory, for instance, was criticized for postulating a conception of human individuals as free, equal, independent and mutually disinterested, a conception claimed by some to be contrary to the moral experience of most women. Even the requirement of impartiality, usually taken as a defining feature of morality, became the object of feminist criticism insofar as it was alleged to generate prescriptions counter to many women's moral intuitions. Some feminists began to speculate that traditional ethics was more deeply male-biased and needed more fundamental rethinking than they had realized hitherto.

Such speculations were fuelled by the much-publicized work of developmental psychologist Carol Gilligan, whose 1982 book, *In a Different Voice: Psychological Theory and Women's Development*, seemed to demonstrate empirically that the moral development of women was significantly different from that of men. Claiming that females tend to fear separation or abandonment while males, by contrast, tend to perceive closeness as dangerous, Gilligan reported that girls and women often construe moral dilemmas as conflicts of responsibilities rather than of rights and seek to resolve those dilemmas in ways that will repair and strengthen webs of relationship. Furthermore, Gilligan described females as supposedly less likely than males to make or justify moral decisions by the application of abstract moral rules; instead, she claimed girls and women were more likely to act on their feelings of love and compassion for particular individuals. Gilligan concluded that whereas men typically adhere to a morality of justice, whose primary values are fairness and equality, women often adhere to a morality of care, whose primary values are inclusion and protection from harm. For this reason, studies of moral development based exclusively on a morality of justice do not provide an appropriate standard for measuring female moral development and may be said to be male-biased.

Many feminists seized on Gilligan's work as offering evidence for the existence of a characteristically feminine approach to morality, an approach assumed to provide the basis for a distinctively feminist ethics. For some, indeed, feminist ethics became and remains synonymous with an ethics of care. Just how an ethics of care should be delineated, however, was far from evident; nor was it clear whether it should supplement or supplant an ethics of justice. Many feminists today are exploring such questions, even though the connection between women and care is challenged by some psychologists who allege Gilligan's samples to be nonrepresentative, her methods of interpreting her data suspect, and her claims impossible to substantiate, especially when the studies are controlled for occupation and class.

Regardless of empirical findings in moral psychology, debate continues over whether the fundamental tenets of western ethics are male biased in some sense: if not in the sense that they express a moral sensibility characteristic of men rather than women, then perhaps in that they promote a culturally masculine image of moral psychology, discourage preoccupation with issues defined culturally as feminine, or in other ways covertly advance men's interests over women's. Since feminism is essentially a normative stance, and since its meaning is continually contested by feminists themselves, all feminists are constantly engaged in ethical reflection. In this sense, feminist ethics is practiced both inside and outside the academy. Within the academy, its main practitioners are scholars in philosophy, religion and jurisprudence. These scholars represent a variety of philosophical traditions, secular and religious, Anglo-American and continental European; in challenging perceived male bias in those traditions, they draw extensively on feminist scholarship in other disciplines, such as literature, history and psychology.

Scholarly work in feminist ethics often is also responsive to the ethical reflections of nonacademic feminists as these occur, for instance, in much feminist fiction and poetry. In addition, a considerable body of nonfiction, written by nonacademics and directed towards a nonacademic audience, presents itself as feminist ethics. Popular feminist books and journals frequently engage in ethical consideration of moral or public policy issues and sometimes also offer more general discussions of supposedly "masculine" and "feminine" value systems. There are even grassroots journals of feminist ethics, such as *Lesbian Ethics,* published in the United States, and *Gossip: A Journal of Lesbian Feminist Ethics,* published in the United Kingdom. *Feminist Ethics,* published in Canada, seeks to combine academic scholarship with accessibility to a general audience. One may note striking parallels between many of the claims made by feminists inside the academy and those on the outside.

Those who currently claim the field of feminist ethics are mainly, though not exclusively, white western women. Nevertheless, a few male philosophers are doing significant work in feminist ethics, and people of color have produced a considerable amount of writing, both fiction and nonfiction, that seems compatible with the moral and theoretical inspiration of feminist ethics. It is predictable that women would be more likely than men to identify themselves as feminists, and both nonwesterners and western people of color are less likely than western whites either to be philosophers or, because of feminism's racist history, to be feminists. "Womanist" is a term that many African American authors currently prefer to "feminist" but they might not object to the description of their work as feminist ethics if feminism could be cleansed of racism and ethnocentrism.

FEMINIST CRITICISMS OF WESTERN ETHICS

Since most feminist ethics is done in a western context, it is western ethics, particularly (though not exclusively) the European Enlightenment tradition, that is the most frequent target of feminist critique. The feminist challenges to this tradition may be grouped conveniently under five main headings.

Lack of concern for women's interests. Many of the major theorists, such as Aristotle (384–322 B.C.) and Rousseau (1712–1778), are accused of having given insufficient consideration to women's interests, a lack of concern expressed theoretically by their prescribing for women allegedly feminine virtues such as obedience, silence, and faithfulness. Some feminists charge that many contemporary ethical discussions continue the tendency to regard women as instrumental to male-dominated institutions, such as the family or the state; in debates on abortion, for instance, the pregnant woman may be portrayed as little more than a container or environment for the fetus, while debates on reproductive technology are alleged to assume frequently that infertility is a problem only for heterosexual married women, i.e., women defined in relationship to men.

Neglect of "women's issues." Issues of special concern to women are said to have been ignored by modern moral philosophers, who have tended to portray the domestic realm as an arena outside the economy and beyond justice, private in the sense of being beyond the scope of legitimate political regulation. Even philosophers like Aristotle or Hegel (1770–1831), who give some ethical importance to the domestic realm, have tended to portray the home as an arena in which the most fully human excellences are incapable of being realized. Feminist philosophers began early to criticized this conceptual bifurcation of social life. They pointed out that the home was precisely that realm to which women historically had been confined, and that it had become symbolically associated with the feminine, despite the fact that heads of households were paradigmatically male. They argued that the philosophical devaluation of the domestic realm made it impossible to raise questions about the justice of the domestic division of labor, because it obscured the far-reaching social significance and creativity of women's work in the home, and concealed, even legitimated, the domestic abuse of women and girls.

Denial of women's moral agency. Women's moral agency is said to have often been denied, not simply by excluding women from moral debate or ignoring their contributions, but through philosophical claims to the effect that women lack moral reason. Such claims were made originally by Aristotle, but they have been elaborated and refined by modern theorists such as Rousseau, Kant (1724–1804), Hegel, and Freud (1856–1939).

Depreciation of "feminine" values. Western moral theory is said to embody values that are "masculine," insofar as they are associated, empirically, normatively, or symbolically, with men. For instance, western ethics is alleged to prefer the supposedly masculine or male-associated values of independence, autonomy, intellect, will, wariness, hierarchy, domination, culture, transcendence, product, asceticism, war and death over the supposedly feminine or female-associated values of interdependence, community, connection, sharing, emotion, body, trust, absence of hierarchy, nature, immanence, process, joy, peace and life. Claims like this are common in both popular and academic feminist writings on ethics.

Devaluation of women's moral experience. Finally, prevailing western conceptualizations of the nature of morality, moral problems, and moral reasoning are also charged with being masculine insofar as they too are associated with men, an association that again may be empirical, symbolic or normative. For instance, feminists have accused modern moral theory of being excessively preoccupied with rules, obsessed with impartiality and exclusively focussed on discrete deeds. In addition, feminists have charged modern moral theory with taking the contract as the paradigmatic moral relation and construing moral rationality so narrowly as to exclude emotions of assessment, sometimes called moral emotions. All these characteristics have been asserted to be masculine in some sense. A feminine approach to ethics, by contrast, has been supposed to avoid assuming that individuals ordinarily are free, equal and independent; to take more account of the specificities of particular contexts; and to be more likely to resolve moral dilemmas by relying on empathic feeling rather than by appealing to rules.

Not all feminists endorse all of the above clusters of criticisms—and even where they agree with the general statement, they may well disagree over its applicability in the case of specific philosophers or debates. Despite such differences of relative detail, feminists tend generally to agree on the first three clusters of criticisms, whose correction seems not only attainable in principle within the framework of Enlightenment moral theory but even to be required by that framework. However, there is sharp feminist disagreement on the last two clusters of criticisms, especially the fifth, which obviously contains clear parallels with a number of nonfeminist criticisms of Enlightenment ethics made by proponents of, for example, situation ethics, virtue ethics, communitarianism and postmodernism.

COMMON MISCONSTRUALS OF FEMINIST ETHICS

Feminist ethics has sometimes been construed, both by some of its proponents and some of its critics, as a simple inversion of the criticisms listed above. In other words, it has sometimes been identified with one or more of the following: putting women's interests first; focusing exclusively on so-called women's issues; accepting women (or feminists) as moral experts or authorities; substituting "female" (or feminine) for "male" (or masculine) values; or extrapolating directly from women's moral experience. These characterizations of feminist ethics are sufficiently pervasive that it is worth noting just why they cannot be correct.

1. Putting women's interests first occasionally has been recommended as a way of achieving a "woman-centered" ethics that transcends the covert bias of a supposed humanism grounded in fact on male norms. Whatever might be said for or against this recommendation, however, it cannot be definitive of feminist ethics. This is because the formula, as it stands, raises more questions than it answers insofar as it fails to specify not only which women's interests should be preferred over which men's (or children's) and in what circumstances, but also what should be done

about conflicts of interest between women and even how interests should be identified at all. Most obviously, feminist ethics cannot be identified with "putting women's interests first" simply because many feminists would refuse to accept and, indeed, be morally outraged by what they would perceive as blatant partiality and immorality.

2. Feminist ethics certainly is concerned to address issues of special concern to women, issues that have been neglected by modern moral theory, but it cannot be identified with an exclusive focus on such issues. This is partly because nonfeminists as well as feminists have addressed these issues—and, indeed, are doing so increasingly as feminism grows stronger and more articulate. It is also because feminism rejects the notion that moral issues can be divided cleanly into those that are and those that are not of special concern to women. On the one hand, since men's and women's lives are inextricably intertwined, there are no "women's issues" that are not also men's issues; the availability or otherwise of child care and abortion, for instance, has significant consequences for the lives of men as well as women. On the other hand, since men and women typically are not what lawyers call "similarly situated" relative to each other, it is difficult to think of any moral or public policy ("human") issue in which women do not have a special interest. For instance, such "human" issues as war, peace and world starvation have special significance for women because the world's hungry are disproportionately women (and children), because women are primarily those in need of the social services neglected to fund military spending, and because women benefit relatively little from militarism and the weapons industries. For these reasons, it would be a mistake to identify feminist ethics with attention to some explicitly gendered subset of ethical issues. On the contrary, rather than being limited to a restricted ethical domain, feminist ethics has *enlarged* the traditional concerns of ethics, both through identifying previously unrecognized ethical issues and by introducing fresh perspectives on issues already acknowledged as having an ethical dimension.

3. Feminist ethics certainly is being developed by feminists, most of whom are women, but this does not imply, of course, that any women, or even feminists, therefore should be regarded as moral experts whose moral authority is beyond question. Not only are there deep disagreements among women and even among feminists such that it would be difficult to know whom to select as an expert, but many painful examples of the failure of insight or principle on the part of feminist leaders also demonstrate only too clearly that no women, even feminists, are morally infallible.

4. There are also serious difficulties with thinking of feminist ethics as the substitution of female or feminine for male or masculine values. These difficulties include problems with establishing that *any* values are male or female in the sense of being generally held by men or women, when both women's and men's values vary so much, both within cultures as well as across them. Similar problems confront attempts to establish that certain values are masculine or feminine in the sense of being considered socially appropriate for individuals of one gender or the other. Again, norms of masculinity and femininity vary not only between societies but even within the same society along such axes as class and ethnicity: some social groups, for instance, value physical health, strength or athletic prowess in women; others value physical fragility, weakness or incompetence. But even if certain values could be identified in some sense as male or female, masculine or feminine, the conclusive objection to identifying feminist ethics with the elaboration of female or feminine values is that the femin*ine* is not necessarily the femin*ist*. Indeed, since the feminine typically has been constructed in circumstances of male domination, it is likely to be quite opposed to the feminist. Personal charm, for example, may be valued not only *in* women but also *by* them; even if charm were, in these senses, a feminine value, however, it would seem at least as likely to undermine feminist goals as to promote them.

5. Similar problems apply to defining feminist ethics as the systematic extrapolation of women's moral experience, exclusive of men's. While no approach to morality can be adequate if it ignores the moral experience of women, it seems most unlikely that women generally are similar enough to each other and

different enough from men that a single distinctively female or feminine approach to ethics can be identified. Attempts to establish such an identification frequently commit the fallacy of generalizing about the experience of *all* or *most* women from the moral experience of *some* women; this seems to have been one flaw at least in Gilligan's earlier work. Again, even if a distinctively femin*ine* approach to morality could be identified, perhaps in terms of symbolic or normative connections with women rather than empirical ones, there is no reason to suppose that such an approach would be femin*ist*. Indeed, given the feminist commitment to a critical rethinking of cultural constructions of both masculinity and femininity, there is good *prima facie* reason to suppose that it would not.

MINIMUM CONDITIONS OF ADEQUACY FOR FEMINIST ETHICS

Even though feminist ethics is far broader and more open than it appears in the foregoing misconstruals, its goals are sufficiently specific, especially when taken in conjunction with its criticisms of traditional ethics, as to generate certain minimum conditions of adequacy for any approach to ethics that purports to be feminist.

1. First of all, feminist ethics can never begin by assuming that women and men are similarly situated—although it may discover that this is the case in certain respects in specific contexts. In addition, not only does feminist ethics need constant vigilance to detect subtle as well as blatant manifestations of gender privilege, it must also be sensitive to the ways in which gendered norms are different for different groups of women—or in which the same norms, such as a cultural preference for slimness or blondness, affect different groups of women differently. Ultimately feminism's concern for *all* women means that feminist ethics must address not only "domestic" issues of racism or homophobia or class privilege but also such international issues as environmental destruction, war, and access to world resources.

2. In order to offer guides to action that will tend to subvert rather than reinforce the present systematic subordination of women, feminist approaches to ethics must understand individual actions in the context of broader social practices, evaluating the symbolic and cumulative implications of action as well as its immediately observable consequences. They must be equipped to recognize covert as well as overt manifestations of domination, subtle as well as blatant forms of control, and they must develop sophisticated accounts of coercion and consent. Similarly, they must provide the conceptual resources for identifying and evaluating the varieties of resistance and struggle in which women, particularly, have engaged. They must recognize the often unnoticed ways in which women and other members of the underclass have refused cooperation and opposed domination, while acknowledging the inevitability of collusion and the impossibility of totally clean hands. In short, feminist approaches to ethics must be transitional and nonutopian, often extensions of, rather than alternatives to, feminist political theory, exercises in non-ideal rather than ideal theory.

3. Since most of most women's lives have been excluded from that domain conceptualized as public, a third requirement for feminist approaches to ethics is that they should be able to provide guidance on issues of so-called private life: intimate relations, sexuality and childrearing. Thus, they must articulate the moral dimensions of issues that may not hitherto have been recognized as moral. In addition, we have seen that feminist approaches to ethics must provide appropriate guidance for dealing with national and international issues, strangers and foreigners. In developing the conceptual tools for undertaking these tasks, feminist ethics cannot assume that moral concepts developed originally for application to the so-called public realm, concepts such as impartiality or exploitation, are appropriate for use in the so-called private; neither can it assume that concepts such as care, developed in intimate relationships, will necessarily be helpful in the larger world. Indeed, the whole distinction between public and private life must be examined critically by feminist ethics, with no prior assumptions as to whether the distinction should be retained, redrawn or rejected.

4. Finally, feminist ethics must take the moral experience of all women seriously, though not, of course,

uncritically. Though what is *feminist* often will turn out to be very different from what is *feminine,* a basic respect for women's moral experience is necessary to acknowledging women's capacities as moralists and to countering traditional stereotypes of women as less than full moral agents, as childlike or close to nature. Furthermore, empirical claims about differences in the moral sensibility of women and men make it impossible to assume that any approach to ethics will be unanimously accepted if it fails to consult the moral experience of women. Additionally, it seems plausible to suppose that women's distinctive social experience may make them especially perceptive regarding the implications of domination, especially gender domination, and especially well equipped to detect the male bias that feminists believe has pervaded so much of male-authored western moral theory.

Most feminist, and perhaps even many non feminist, philosophers might well find the general statement of these conditions quite uncontroversial, but they will inevitably disagree sharply over when the conditions have been met. Not only may feminists disagree with nonfeminists, but they are likely even to differ with each other over, for instance, what are women's interests, what are manifestations of domination and coercion, how resistance should be expressed, and which aspects of women's moral experience are worth developing and in which directions.

Those who practice feminist ethics thus may be seen both as united by a shared project and as diverging widely in their views as to how this project may be accomplished. Their divergences result from a variety of philosophical differences, including differing conceptions of feminism itself, which, as we have seen, is [a] constantly contested concept. The inevitability of such divergence means that feminist ethics can never be identified in terms of a specific range of topics, methods or orthodoxies. While feminist ethics is distinguished by its explicit commitment to developing approaches to ethics that will respect women's moral experience and avoid rationalizing women's subordination, attempts to define it more precisely or substantively than this are likely to disregard the richness and variety of feminist moral thinking and prematurely foreclose the feminist moral debate.

CURRENT CONCERNS IN FEMINIST ETHICS

Despite the scope and diversity of feminist ethics, certain current preoccupations may be identified. These preoccupations are not definitive of feminist ethics, but they are characteristic of its present stage of development. (They are also, sometimes in different ways, preoccupations of much contemporary nonfeminist ethics.) They include concern with issues of universality and particularity, sociality and individuality, moral emotion and moral rationality. These concerns are not independent of each other and they may be discerned underlying many contemporary feminist approaches to practical issues, such as equality, health care, or the environment, as well as being foci of feminist reflection on such traditional philosophical issues as moral subjectivity and moral epistemology.

Feminist challenges to traditional views of moral subjectivity are not limited to assertions (*contra* Aristotle, Rousseau, Kant and Hegel) that women are as capable as men of moral virtue or rationality. Instead, many feminists have drawn on and extended nonfeminist criticisms of the basic model of the moral self most characteristic of Enlightenment moral theory, a model derived from Descartes (1596–1650) and portraying the self as disembodied, asocial, autonomous, unified, rational and essentially similar to all other selves. This model, of course, has been under attack for over a century from, among others, Marxists, Freudians, contemporary communitarians, and postmodernists. Feminists often share many conclusions with such nonfeminist critics of Enlightenment theory, but they arrive at those conclusions by different routes, and often they add to them the claim that the Cartesian model is male-biased (as well as class- and possibly race-biased), in that it reflects the interests and values of European bourgeois men and either ignores divergent interests and values or portrays them as less than fully human.

One source of feminist challenge to the Cartesian self is a growing philosophical interest in embodiment. This itself springs partly from feminist outrage over the male control and exploitation of women's bodies, partly from the feminist recognition that much of the responsibility for physical reproduction and bodily maintenance traditionally has been assigned to women—both of which reinforce symbolic western associations between women and the body. Philosophical reflection that begins from the body tends to highlight features of human nature very different from those emphasized by Cartesianism: temporality rather than timelessness, growth and decay rather than changelessness, particularity rather than universality, sociality rather than isolation. These features, in turn, tend to generate concerns for ethics different from those that dominated much Enlightenment theory: inequality, dependence and interdependence, specificity, social embeddedness and historical community now must all be recognized as permanent circumstances of moral life, never to be avoided or transcended by focusing on equality, independence, autonomy, generality, isolated individuals, ideal communities or the universal human condition. It does not escape feminist authors that concern with precisely the former circumstances has been claimed by many to be distinctively feminine—preoccupying women in virtue of their social situation, associated symbolically with women or defined culturally as appropriate to women.

Conceiving moral subjects as embodied also has psychological implications: insofar as their identity is significantly constituted by their specific social relationships (relationships determined at least in part by the social meaning attributed to bodily characteristics such as parentage, age or sex), moral subjects conceived in this way are revealed as likely to be moved by considerations of particular attachment as much as abstract concern for duty, care as much as respect, solidarity as much as dignity, responsibility as much as right. Many feminists currently argue that much Enlightenment moral psychology is inadequate insofar as it fails to take adequate account of these propensities, conceiving them at best as morally irrelevant, at worst as morally subversive. In addition, noting the ways in which the psyche is shaped by social practices, especially childrearing and other gendered practices, many feminists criticize the common Enlightenment assumption that people are essentially alike, rational and autarchic. Noting the significance of fantasy in our lives, they deny that consciousness is transparent and unified and that individuals always know their own interests best. In general, they challenge much

Enlightenment moral psychology for its failure to recognize that, if autonomy exists at all, it is an achievement with complex material and social preconditions.

That people in fact have certain psychological propensities of course does not entail that those propensities are morally relevant, let alone morally desirable; on the other hand, an adequate moral theory cannot be grounded in a psychology that is descriptively inadequate. Many feminists claim that much Enlightenment moral psychology is so alien to the ways in which people in fact do act and think morally that it cannot serve even as an acceptable reconstruction of moral reasoning. For instance, by failing to appreciate the moral significance of the psychological characteristics noted above, it offers a model of moral rationality that is unduly narrow in disregarding emotion, and likely to generate morally repugnant conclusions that ignore our responsibility for the welfare of others, neglect the claims of conventional morality, and undervalue the moral weight of particular relationships. Some feminists go on to argue that most Enlightenment models of moral rationality are not only empirically and morally inadequate but also serve, insofar as they are culturally accepted, as oppressive norms for those social groups, including perhaps some groups of women, whose moral thinking is stigmatized as amoral or immoral for failing to conform to these models.

Morality on most Enlightenment views is a system of rationally justified rules or principles that guide action in specific cases. Many contemporary feminists, by contrast, deny that morality is reducible to rules and assert the impossibility of justifying the claims of ethics by appeal to a universal, impartial reason. They charge that undue emphasis on the epistemological importance of moral rules obscures the crucial role of moral insight, virtue and character in determining the right course of action. Some give a feminist twist to this essentially Aristotelian criticism by claiming that excessive reliance on rules reflects a juridical-administrative interest that is characteristic of modem masculinity—contemporary women, by contrast, are claimed to be more likely to disregard conventionally accepted moral rules because such rules are insensitive to the specificities of particular situations. Some feminists assert, therefore, that a morality of rule devalues the moral wisdom of women and gives insufficient weight to such supposedly feminine virtues as kindness, generosity, helpfulness and sympathy.

Though many feminists continue to defend various versions of Enlightenment moral theory, many others are concerned not merely to criticize them but also to develop alternatives to them—alternatives that will avoid their perceived shortcomings while meeting the conditions of adequacy identified earlier. Thus, contemporary feminists are exploring ways of thinking about moral subjects that are sensitive

both to their concrete particularity and their intrinsic shared value—the ideal expressed in Enlightenment claims about common humanity, equality and impartiality; developing "particularist" epistemologies that recognize the moral validity of immediate, emotion-laden responses to particular others while avoiding subjective relativism; and finding ways of simultaneously acknowledging and criticizing the claims of conventional morality—known colloquially as living with contradictions. They are exploring these approaches in the context of developing feminist perspectives on many of the most pressing moral issues of our time.

The Ethics of Care as Moral Theory

Virginia Held

The ethics of care is only a few decades old. Some theorists do not like the term 'care' to designate this approach to moral issues and have tried substituting 'the ethic of love,' or 'relational ethics,' but the discourse keeps returning to 'care' as the so far more satisfactory of the terms considered, though dissatisfactions with it remain. The concept of care has the advantage of not losing sight of the work involved in caring for people and of not lending itself to the interpretation of morality as ideal but impractical to which advocates of the ethics of care often object. Care is both value and practice.

By now, the ethics of care has moved far beyond its original formulations, and any attempt to evaluate it should consider much more than the one or two early works so frequently cited. It has been developed as a moral theory relevant not only to the so-called private realms of family and friendship but to medical practice, law, political life, the organization of society, war, and international relations.

Virginia Held, "The Ethics of Care as Moral Theory," in *The Ethics of Care* (Oxford: Oxford University Press, 2006), 9–20. © 2006 by Oxford University Press, Inc. By permission of Oxford University Press, USA.

The ethics of care is sometimes seen as a potential moral theory to be substituted for such dominant moral theories as Kantian ethics, utilitarianism, or Aristotelian virtue ethics. It is sometimes seen as a form of virtue ethics. It is almost always developed as emphasizing neglected moral considerations of at least as much importance as the considerations central to moralities of justice and rights or of utility and preference satisfaction. And many who contribute to the understanding of the ethics of care seek to integrate the moral considerations, such as justice, which other moral theories have clarified, satisfactorily with those of care, though they often see the need to reconceptualize these considerations.

FEATURES OF THE ETHICS OF CARE

Some advocates of the ethics of care resist generalizing this approach into something that can be fitted into the form of a moral theory. They see it as a mosaic of insights and value the way it is sensitive to contextual nuance and particular narratives rather than making the abstract and universal claims of more familiar moral theories. Still, I think one can discern among various versions of the ethics of care a number of major features.

First, the central focus of the ethics of care is on the compelling moral salience of attending to and meeting the needs of the particular others for whom we take responsibility. Caring for one's child, for instance, may well and defensibly be at the forefront of a person's moral concerns. The ethics of care recognizes that human beings are dependent for many years of their lives, that the moral claim of those dependent on us for the care they need is pressing, and that there are highly important moral aspects in developing the relations of caring that enable human beings to live and progress. All persons need care for at least their early years. Prospects for human progress and flourishing hinge fundamentally on the care that those needing it receive, and the ethics of care stresses the moral force of the responsibility to respond to the needs of the dependent. Many persons will become ill and dependent for some periods of their later lives, including in frail old age, and some who are permanently disabled will need care the whole of their lives. Moralities built on the image of the independent, autonomous, rational individual largely overlook the reality of human dependence and the morality for which it calls. The ethics of care attends to this central concern of human life and delineates the moral values involved. It refuses to relegate care to a realm "outside morality." How caring for particular others should be reconciled with the claims of, for instance, universal justice is an issue that needs to be addressed. But the ethics of care starts with the moral claims of particular others, for instance, of one's child, whose claims can be compelling regardless of universal principles.

Second, in the epistemological process of trying to understand what morality would recommend and what it would be morally best for us to do and to be, the ethics of care values emotion rather than rejects it. Not all emotion is valued, of course, but in contrast with the dominant rationalist approaches, such emotions as sympathy, empathy, sensitivity, and responsiveness are seen as the kind of moral emotions that need to be cultivated not only to help in the implementation of the dictates of reason but to

better ascertain what morality recommends. Even anger may be a component of the moral indignation that should be felt when people are treated unjustly or inhumanely, and it may contribute to (rather than interfere with) an appropriate interpretation of the moral wrong. This is not to say that raw emotion can be a guide to morality; feelings need to be reflected on and educated. But from the care perspective, moral inquiries that rely entirely on reason and rationalistic deductions or calculations are seen as deficient.

The emotions that are typically considered and rejected in rationalistic moral theories are the egoistic feelings that undermine universal moral norms, the favoritism that interferes with impartiality, and the aggressive and vengeful impulses for which morality is to provide restraints. The ethics of care, in contrast, typically appreciates the emotions and relational capabilities that enable morally concerned persons in actual interpersonal contexts to understand what would be best. Since even the helpful emotions can often become misguided or worse—as when excessive empathy with others leads to a wrongful degree of self-denial or when benevolent concern crosses over into controlling domination—we need an *ethics* of care, not just care itself. The various aspects and expressions of care and caring relations need to be subjected to moral scrutiny and *evaluated*, not just observed and described.

Third, the ethics of care rejects the view of the dominant moral theories that the more abstract the reasoning about a moral problem the better because the more likely to avoid bias and arbitrariness, the more nearly to achieve impartiality. The ethics of care respects rather than removes itself from the claims of particular others with whom we share actual relationships. It calls into question the universalistic and abstract rules of the dominant theories. When the latter consider such actual relations as between a parent and child, if they say anything about them at all, they may see them as permitted and [indicative of] a preference that a person may have. Or they may recognize a universal obligation for all parents to care for their children. But they do not permit actual relations ever to take priority over the requirements of impartiality. As Brian Barry expresses this view, there can be universal rules permitting people to favor their friends in certain contexts, such as deciding to whom to give holiday gifts, but the latter partiality is morally acceptable only because universal rules have already so judged it. The ethics of care, in contrast, is skeptical of such abstraction and reliance on universal rules and questions the priority given to them. To most advocates of the ethics of care, the compelling moral claim of the particular other may be valid even when it conflicts with the requirement usually made by moral theories that moral judgments be universalizeable, and this is of fundamental moral importance. Hence the potential conflict between care and justice, friendship and impartiality, loyalty and universality. To others, however, there need be no conflict if universal judgments come to incorporate appropriately the norms of care previously disregarded.

Annette Baier considers how a feminist approach to morality differs from a Kantian one and Kant's claim that women are incapable of being fully moral because of their reliance on emotion rather than reason. She writes, "Where Kant concludes 'so much the worse for women,' we can conclude 'so much the worse for the male fixation on the special skill of drafting legislation, for the bureaucratic mentality of rule worship, and for the male exaggeration of the importance of independence over mutual interdependence.'"

Margaret Walker contrasts what she sees as feminist "moral understanding" with what has traditionally been thought of as moral "knowledge." She sees the moral understanding she advocates as involving "attention, contextual and narrative appreciation, and communication in the event of moral deliberation." This alternative moral epistemology holds that "the adequacy of moral understanding decreases as its form approaches generality through abstraction."

The ethics of care may seek to limit the applicability of universal rules to certain domains where they are more appropriate, like the domain of law, and resist their extension to other domains. Such rules may simply be inappropriate in, for instance, the contexts of family and friendship, yet relations in these domains should certainly be *evaluated,* not merely described, hence morality should not be limited to abstract rules. We should be able to give moral guidance concerning actual relations that are trusting, considerate, and caring and concerning those that are not.

Dominant moral theories tend to interpret moral problems as if they were conflicts between egoistic individual interests on the one hand, and universal moral principles on the other. The extremes of "selfish individual" and "humanity" are recognized, but what lies between these is often overlooked. The ethics of care, in contrast, focuses especially on the area between these extremes. Those who conscientiously care for others are not seeking primarily to further their own *individual* interests; their interests are intertwined with the persons they care for. Neither are they acting for the sake of *all others* or *humanity in general;* they seek instead to preserve or promote an actual human relation between themselves and *particular others.* Persons in caring relations are acting for self-and-other together. Their characteristic stance is neither egoistic nor altruistic; these are the options in a conflictual situation, but the well-being of a caring relation involves the cooperative well-being of those in the relation and the well-being of the relation itself.

In trying to overcome the attitudes and problems of tribalism and religious intolerance, dominant moralities have tended to assimilate the domains of family and friendship to the tribal, or to a source of the unfair favoring of one's own. Or they have seen the attachments people have in these areas as among the nonmoral private preferences people are permitted to pursue if restrained by impartial moral norms. The ethics of care recognizes the *moral* value and importance of relations of family and friendship and the need for *moral* guidance in these domains to understand how existing relations should often be changed and new ones developed. Having grasped the value of caring relations in such contexts as these more personal ones, the ethics of care then often examines social and political arrangements in the light of these values. In its more developed forms, the ethics of care as a feminist ethic offers suggestions for the radical transformation of society. It demands not just equality for women in existing structures of society but equal consideration for the experience that reveals the values, importance, and moral significance, of caring.

A fourth characteristic of the ethics of care is that like much feminist thought in many areas, it reconceptualizes traditional notions about the public and the private. The traditional view, built into the dominant moral theories, is that the household is a private sphere beyond politics into which government, based on consent, should not intrude. Feminists have shown how the greater social, political, economic, and cultural power of men has structured this "private" sphere to the disadvantage of women and children, rendering them vulnerable to domestic violence without outside interference, often leaving women economically dependent on men and subject to a highly inequitable division of labor in the family. The law has not hesitated to intervene into women's private decisions concerning reproduction but has been highly reluctant to intrude on men's exercise of coercive power within the "castles" of their homes.

Dominant moral theories have seen "public" life as relevant to morality while missing the moral significance of the "private" domains of family and friendship. Thus the dominant theories have assumed that morality should be sought for unrelated, independent, and mutually indifferent individuals assumed to be equal. They have posited an abstract, fully rational "agent as such" from which to construct morality, while missing the moral issues that arise between interconnected persons in the contexts of family, friendship, and social groups. In the context of the family, it is typical for relations to be between persons with highly unequal power who did not choose the ties and obligations in which they find themselves enmeshed. For instance, no child can choose her parents yet she may well have obligations to care for them. Relations of this kind are standardly noncontractual, and conceptualizing them as contractual would often undermine or at least obscure the trust on which their worth depends. The ethics of care addresses rather than neglects moral issues arising in relations among the unequal and dependent, relations that are often laden with emotion and involuntary, and then notices how often these attributes apply not only in the household but in the wider society as well. For instance, persons do not choose which gender, racial, class, ethnic, religious, national, or cultural groups to be brought up in, yet these sorts of ties may be important aspects of who they are and how their experience can contribute to moral understanding.

A fifth characteristic of the ethics of care is the conception of persons with which it begins. This will be dealt with in the next section.

THE CRITIQUE OF LIBERAL INDIVIDUALISM

The ethics of care usually works with a conception of persons as relational, rather than as the self-sufficient independent individuals of the dominant moral theories. The dominant theories can be interpreted as importing into moral theory a concept of the person developed primarily for liberal political and economic theory, seeing the person as a rational, autonomous agent, or a self-interested individual. On this view, society is made up of "independent, autonomous units who cooperate only when the terms of cooperation are such as to make it further the ends of each of the parties," in Brian Barry's words. Or, if they are Kantians, they refrain from actions that they could not will to be universal laws to which all fully rational and autonomous individual agents could agree. What such views hold, in Michael Sandel's critique of them, is that "what separates us is in some important sense prior to what connects us—epistemologically prior as well as morally prior. We are distinct individuals first and *then* we form relationships. In Martha Nussbaum's liberal feminist morality, "the flourishing of human beings taken one by one is both analytically and normatively prior to the flourishing" of any group.

The ethics of care, in contrast, characteristically sees persons as relational and interdependent, morally and epistemologically. Every person starts out as a child dependent on those providing us care, and we remain interdependent with others in thoroughly fundamental ways throughout our lives. That we can think and act as if we were independent depends on a network of social relations making it possible for us to do so. And our relations are part of what constitute our identity. This is not to say that we cannot become autonomous; feminists have done much interesting work developing an alternative conception of autonomy in place of the liberal individualist one. Feminists have much experience rejecting or reconstituting relational ties that are oppressive. But it means that from the perspective of an ethics of care, to construct morality *as if* we were Robinson Crusoes, or, to use Hobbes's image, mushrooms sprung from nowhere, is misleading. As Eva Kittay writes, this conception fosters the illusion that society is composed of free, equal, and independent individuals who can choose to associate with one another or not. It obscures the very real facts of dependency for everyone when they are young, for most people at various periods in their lives when they are ill or old and infirm, for some who are disabled, and for all those engaged in unpaid "dependency work." And it obscures the innumerable ways persons and groups are interdependent in the modern world.

Not only does the liberal individualist conception of the person foster a false picture of society and the persons in it, it is, from the perspective of the ethics of care, impoverished also as an ideal. The ethics of care values the ties we have with particular other persons and the actual relationships that partly constitute our identity. Although persons often may and should reshape their relations with others—distancing themselves from some persons and groups and developing or strengthening ties with others—the autonomy sought within the ethics of care is a capacity to reshape and cultivate new relations, not to ever more closely resemble the unencumbered abstract rational self of liberal political and moral theories. Those motivated by the ethics of care would seek to become more admirable relational persons in better caring relations.

Even if the liberal ideal is meant only to instruct us on what would be rational in the terms of its ideal model, thinking of persons as the model presents them has effects that should not be welcomed. As Annette Baier writes, "Liberal morality, if unsupplemented, may *unfit* people to be anything other than what its justifying theories suppose them to be, ones who have no interest in each others' interests." There is strong empirical evidence of how adopting a theoretical model can lead to behavior that mirrors it. Various studies show that studying economics, with its "repeated and intensive exposure to a model whose unequivocal prediction" is that people will decide what to do on the basis of self-interest, leads economics students to be less cooperative and more inclined to free ride than other students.

The conception of the person adopted by the dominant moral theories provides moralities at best suitable for legal, political, and economic interactions between relative strangers, once adequate trust exists for them to form a political entity. The ethics of care is, instead, hospitable to the relatedness of persons. It sees many of our responsibilities as not freely entered into but presented to us by the accidents of our embeddedness in familial and social and historical contexts. It often calls on us to *take* responsibility, while liberal individualist morality focuses on how we should leave each other alone. The view of persons as embedded and encumbered seems fundamental to much feminist thinking about morality and especially to the ethics of care.

JUSTICE AND CARE

Some conceptions of the ethics of care see it as contrasting with an ethic of justice in ways that suggest one must choose between them. Carol Gilligan's suggestion of alternative perspectives in interpreting and organizing the elements of a moral problem lent itself to this implication; she herself used the metaphor of the ambiguous figure of the vase and the faces, from psychological research on perception, to illustrate how one could see a problem as either a problem of justice or a problem of care, but not as both simultaneously.

An ethic of justice focuses on questions of fairness, equality, individual rights, abstract principles, and the consistent application of them. An ethic of care focuses on attentiveness, trust, responsiveness to need, narrative nuance, and cultivating caring relations. Whereas an ethic of justice seeks a fair solution between competing individual interests and rights, an ethic of care sees the interests of carers and cared-for as importantly intertwined rather than as simply competing. Whereas justice protects equality and freedom, care fosters social bonds and cooperation.

These are very different emphases in what morality should consider. Yet both deal with what seems of great moral importance. This has led many to explore how they might be combined in a satisfactory morality.

One can persuasively argue, for instance, that justice is needed in such contexts of care as the family, to protect against violence and the unfair division of labor or treatment of children. One can also persuasively argue that care is needed in such contexts of justice as the streets and the courts, where persons should be treated humanely, and in the way education and health and welfare should be dealt with as social responsibilities. The implication may be that justice and care should not be separated into different "ethics," that, in Sara Ruddick's proposed approach, "justice is always seen in tandem with care."

Few would hold that considerations of justice have no place at all in care. One would not be caring well for two children, for instance, if one showed a persistent favoritism toward one of them that could not be justified on the basis of some such factor as greater need. The issues are rather what constellation of values have priority and which predominate in the practices of the ethics of care and the ethics of justice. It is quite possible to delineate significant differences between them. In the dominant moral theories of the ethics of justice, the values of equality, impartiality, fair distribution, and noninterference have priority; in practices of justice, individual rights are protected, impartial judgments are arrived at, punishments are deserved, and equal treatment is sought. In contrast, in the ethics of care, the values of trust, solidarity, mutual concern, and empathetic responsiveness have priority; in practices of care, relationships are cultivated, needs are responded to, and sensitivity is demonstrated.

An extended effort to integrate care and justice is offered by Diemut Bubeck. She makes clear that she "endorse[s] the ethic of care as a system of concepts, values, and ideas, arising from the practice of care as an organic part of this practice and responding to its material requirements, notably the meeting of needs." Yet her primary interest is in understanding the exploitation of women, which she sees as tied to the way women do most of the unpaid work of caring. She argues that such principles as equality in care and the minimization of harm are tacitly, if not explicitly, embedded in the practice of care, as carers whose capacities and time for engaging in caring labor are limited must decide how to respond to various others in need of being cared for. She writes that "far from being extraneous impositions . . . considerations of justice arise from within the practice of care itself and therefore are an important part of the ethic of care, properly understood." The ethics of care must thus also concern itself with the justice (or lack of it) of the ways the tasks of caring are distributed in society. Traditionally, women have been expected to do most of the caring work that needs to be done; the sexual division of labor exploits women by extracting unpaid care labor from them, making women less able than men to engage in paid work. "Femininity" constructs women as carers, contributing to the constraints by which women are pressed into accepting the sexual division of labor. An ethic of care that extols caring but that fails to be concerned with how the burdens of caring are distributed contributes to the exploitation of women, and of the minority groups whose members perform much of the paid but ill-paid work of caring in affluent households, in day care centers, hospitals, nursing homes, and the like.

The question remains, however, whether justice should be thought to be incorporated into any ethic of care that will be adequate or whether we should keep the notions of justice and care and their associated ethics conceptually distinct. There is much to be said for recognizing how the ethics of care values interrelatedness and responsiveness to the needs of particular others, how the ethics of justice values fairness and rights, and how these are different emphases. Too much integration will lose sight of these valid differences. I am more inclined to say that an adequate, comprehensive moral theory will have to include the insights of both the ethics of care and the ethics of justice, among other insights, rather than that either of these can be incorporated into the other in the sense of supposing that it can provide the grounds for the judgments characteristically found in the other. Equitable caring is not necessarily better caring, it is fairer caring. And humane justice is not necessarily better justice, it is more caring justice.

Almost no advocates of the ethics of care are willing to see it as a moral outlook less valuable than the dominant ethics of justice. To imagine that the concerns of care can merely be added on to the dominant theories, as, for instance, Stephen Darwall suggests, is seen as unsatisfactory. Confining the ethics of care to the private sphere while holding it unsuitable for public life, as Nel Noddings did at first and as many accounts of it suggest, is also to be rejected. But how care and justice are to be meshed without losing sight of their differing priorities is a task still being worked on.

My own suggestions for integrating care and justice are to keep these concepts conceptually distinct and to delineate the domains in which they should have priority. In the realm of law, for instance, justice and the assurance of rights should have priority, although the humane considerations of care should not be absent. In the realm of the family and among friends, priority should be given to expansive care, though the basic requirements of justice surely should also be met. But these are the clearest cases; others will combine moral urgencies. Universal human rights (including the social and economic ones as well as the political and civil) should certainly be respected, but promoting care across continents may be a more promising way to achieve this than mere rational recognition. When needs are desperate, justice may be a lessened requirement on shared responsibility for meeting needs, although this rarely excuses violations of rights. At the level of what constitutes a society in the first place, a domain within which rights are to be assured and care provided, appeal must be made to something like the often weak but not negligible caring relations among persons that enable them to recognize each other as members of the same society. Such recognition must eventually be global; in the meantime, the civil society without which the liberal institutions of justice cannot function presume a background of some degree of caring relations rather than of merely competing individuals . . . Furthermore, considerations of care provide a more fruitful basis than considerations of justice for deciding much about how society should be structured, for instance, how extensive or how restricted markets should be . . . And in the course of protecting the rights that ought to be recognized, such as those to basic necessities, policies that express the caring of the community for all its members will be better policies than those that grudgingly, though fairly, issue an allotment to those deemed unfit.

Care is probably the most deeply fundamental value. There can be care without justice: There has historically been little justice in the family, but care and life have gone on without it. There can be no justice without care, however, for without care no child would survive and there would be no persons to respect.

Care may thus provide the wider and deeper ethics within which justice should be sought, as when persons in caring relations may sometimes compete and in doing so should treat each other fairly, or, at the level of society, within caring relations of the thinner kind we can agree to treat each other for limited purposes as if we were the abstract individuals of liberal theory. But although care may be the more fundamental value, it may well be that the ethics of care does not itself provide adequate theoretical resources for dealing with issues of justice. Within its appropriate sphere and for its relevant questions, the ethics of justice may be best for what we seek. What should be resisted is the traditional inclination to expand the reach of justice in such a way that it is mistakenly imagined to be able to give us a comprehensive morality suitable for all moral questions.

IMPLICATIONS FOR SOCIETY

Many advocates of the ethics of care argue for its relevance in social and political and economic life. Sara Ruddick shows its implications for efforts to achieve peace. I argue that as we see the deficiencies of the contractual model of human relations within the household, we can see them also in the world beyond and begin to think about how society should be reorganized to be hospitable to care, rather than continuing to marginalize it. We can see how not only does every domain of society need transformation in light of the values of care but so would the relations between such domains if we took care seriously, as care would move to the center of our attention and become a primary concern of society. Instead of a society dominated by conflict restrained by law and preoccupied with economic gain, we might have a society that saw as its most important task the flourishing of children and the development of caring relations, not only in personal contexts but among citizens and using governmental institutions. We would see that instead of abandoning culture to the dictates of the marketplace, we should make it possible for culture to develop in ways best able to enlighten and enrich human life.

Joan Tronto argues for the political implications of the ethics of care, seeing care as a political as well as moral ideal advocating the meeting of needs for care as "the highest social goal." She shows how unacceptable are current arrangements for providing care: "Caring activities are devalued, underpaid, and disproportionately occupied by the relatively powerless in society." Bubeck, Kittay, and many others argue forcefully that care must be seen as a public concern, not relegated to the private responsibility of women, the inadequacy and arbitrariness of private charities, or the vagaries and distortions of the market. In her recent book *Starting at Home*, Noddings explores what a caring society would be like.

When we concern ourselves with caring relations between more distant others, this care should not be thought to reduce to the mere "caring about" that has little to do with the face-to-face interactions of caring labor and can easily become paternalistic or patronizing. The same characteristics of attentiveness, responsiveness to needs, and understanding situations from the points of view of others should characterize caring when the participants are more distant. This also requires the work of understanding and of expending varieties of effort.

Given how care is a value with the widest possible social implications, it is unfortunate that many who look at the ethics of care continue to suppose it is a "family ethics," confined to the "private" sphere. Although some of its earliest formulations suggested this, and some of its related values are to be seen most clearly in personal contexts, an adequate understanding of the ethics of care should recognize that it elaborates values as fundamental and as relevant to political institutions and to how society is organized, as those of justice. Perhaps its values are even more fundamental and more relevant to life in society than those traditionally relied on.

Instead of seeing the corporate sector, and military strength, and government and law as the most important segments of society deserving the highest levels of wealth and power, a caring society might see the tasks of bringing up children, educating its members, meeting the needs of all, achieving peace and treasuring the environment, and doing these in the best ways possible to be that to which the greatest social efforts of all should be devoted. One can recognize that something comparable to legal constraints and police enforcement, including at a global level, may always be necessary for special cases, but also that caring societies could greatly decrease the need for them. The social changes a focus on care would require would be as profound as can be imagined.

The ethics of care as it has developed is most certainly not limited to the sphere of family and personal relations. When its social and political implications are understood, it is a radical ethic calling for a profound restructuring of society. And it has the resources for dealing with power and violence . . .

THE ETHICS OF CARE AND VIRTUE ETHICS

Insofar as the ethics of care wishes to cultivate in persons the characteristics of a caring person and the skills of activities of caring, might an ethic of care be assimilated to virtue theory?

To some philosophers, the ethics of care is a form of virtue ethics. Several of the contributors to the volume *Feminists Doing Ethics* adopt this view. Leading virtue theorist Michael Slote argues extensively for the position that caring is the primary virtue and that a morality based on the motive of caring can offer a general account of right and wrong action and political justice.

Certainly there are some similarities between the ethics of care and virtue theory. Both examine practices and the moral values they embody. Both see more hope for moral development in reforming practices than in reasoning from abstract rules. Both understand that the practices of morality must be cultivated, nurtured, shaped.

Until recently, however, virtue theory has not paid adequate attention to the practices of caring in which women have been so heavily engaged. Although this might be corrected, virtue theory has characteristically seen the virtues as incorporated in various traditions or traditional communities. In contrast, the ethics of care as a feminist ethic is wary of existing traditions and traditional communities: Virtually all are patriarchal. The ethics of care envisions caring not as practiced under male domination, but as it should be practiced in postpatriarchal society, of which we do not yet have traditions or wide experience. Individual egalitarian families are still surrounded by inegalitarian social and cultural influences.

In my view, although there are similarities between them and although to be caring is no doubt a virtue, the ethics of care is not simply a kind of virtue ethics. Virtue ethics focuses especially on the states of character of individuals, whereas the ethics of care concerns itself especially with caring *relations*. Caring relations have primary value.

If virtue ethics is interpreted, as with Slote, as primarily a matter of motives, it may neglect unduly the labor and objective results of caring, as Bubeck's emphasis on actually meeting needs highlights. Caring is not only a question of motive or attitude or virtue. On the other hand, Bubeck's account is unduly close to a utilitarian interpretation of meeting needs, neglecting that care *also* has an aspect of motive and virtue. If virtue ethics is interpreted as less restricted to motives, and if it takes adequate account of the results of the virtuous person's activities for the persons cared for, it may better include the concerns of the ethics of care. It would still, however, focus on the dispositions of individuals, whereas the ethics of care focuses on social relations and the social practices and values that sustain them. The traditional Man of Virtue may be almost as haunted by his patriarchal past as the Man of Reason. The work of care has certainly not been among the virtuous activities to which he has adequately attended.

The ethics of care, in my view, is a distinctive ethical outlook, distinct even from virtue ethics. Certainly it has precursors, and such virtue theorists as Aristotle, Hume, and the moral sentimentalists contribute importantly to it. As a feminist ethic, the ethics of care is certainly not a mere description or generalization of women's attitudes and activities as developed under patriarchal conditions. To be acceptable, it must be a *feminist* ethic, open to both women and men to adopt. But in being feminist, it is different from the ethics of its precursors and different as well from virtue ethics.

The ethics of care is sometimes thought inadequate because of its inability to provide definite answers in cases of conflicting moral demands. Virtue theory has similarly been criticized for offering no more than what detractors call a "bag of virtues," with no clear indication of how to prioritize the virtues or apply their requirements, especially when they seem to conflict. Defenders of the ethics of care respond that the adequacy of the definite answers provided by, for instance, utilitarian and Kantian moral theories is illusory. Cost-benefit analysis is a good example of a form of utilitarian calculation that purports to provide clear answers to questions about what we ought to do, but from the point of view of moral understanding, its answers are notoriously dubious. So, too, often are casuistic reasonings about deontological rules. To advocates of the ethics of care, its alternative moral epistemology seems better. It stresses sensitivity to the multiple relevant considerations in particular contexts, cultivating the traits of character and of relationship that sustain caring, and promoting the dialogue that corrects and enriches the perspective of any one individual. The ethics of care is hospitable to the methods of discourse ethics, though with an emphasis on actual dialogue that empowers its participants to express themselves rather than on discourse so ideal that actual differences of viewpoint fall away.

* * *

PART
4

Ethical Issues

CHAPTER 9

Abortion

If somehow you had unobstructed access for a single day to all the public and private dramas provoked by the issue of abortion, you might see scenes like this: a forty-year-old mother of five agonizing over whether she should terminate her pregnancy (which is both unexpected and unwanted); anti-abortion activists shouting "Thou shall not kill!" at a woman hurrying inside a clinic that performs abortions; a frightened sixteen-year-old rape victim having an abortion against her family's wishes; a Catholic bishop asserting on the eleven o'clock news that abortion in any form is murder; the head of an abortion rights organization declaring in a CNN interview that anti-abortion activists are violent and dangerous; a politician getting elected solely because he favors a constitutional amendment to ban virtually all abortions; two women who have been friends for years disagreeing bitterly about whether a fetus has a right to life; and state legislators angrily debating a bill requiring any woman seeking an abortion to watch a fifteen-minute video titled "The Tragedy of Abortion."

Such scenes are emblematic of the abortion issue in that they are intensely emotional and usually accompanied by uncritical or dogmatic thinking. Passions surge because abortion touches on some of our deepest values and most basic beliefs. When we grapple with the issue of abortion, we must consider whose rights (the mother's or the unborn's) carry the most moral weight, what the meaning of *human being* or *person* is, when—if ever—the unborn achieves personhood, how having an abortion affects the health and mind of the mother, how much importance to assign to

our most fundamental moral principles, and much more. For many women, the abortion controversy is *personal,* involving judgments about their own bodies, their own health and happiness, and their own inner turmoil provoked by life-and-death decisions. Uncritical acceptance of particular moral perspectives on abortion seems to be the norm for people on all sides of the debate. Often, discussion of the issue is reduced to shouting; informed reflection, to knee-jerk conclusions; and reasoned argument, to cases built on assumptions never questioned.

In this chapter, we try to do better, relying heavily on critical reasoning and striving for a more objective approach. We begin with a review of the (nonmoral) facts of abortion—biological, medical, psychological, semantic, and legal. Then we consider how the moral theories discussed in previous chapters can be applied to this issue. Finally, we examine a range of common arguments in the debate, from liberal to conservative as well as some intermediate positions.

ISSUE FILE: BACKGROUND

Abortion (also called *induced abortion*) is the deliberate termination of a pregnancy by surgical or medical (with drugs) means. The unintentional termination of a pregnancy (due to a medical disorder or injury) is known as a *spontaneous abortion,* or *miscarriage.* An abortion performed to protect the life or health of the mother is referred to as a **therapeutic abortion**. Therapeutic abortions are usually not thought to be morally problematic. (The Roman

Catholic stance, however, is that induced abortion is always wrong, though the unintended death of the fetus during an attempt to save the mother's life is morally permissible.) But induced abortions are intensely controversial and are the focus of the ongoing moral debate.

Throughout our discussion of abortion in this chapter, we will use the word *fetus* to refer to the unborn during its entire development from conception to birth. But technically, the term indicates a particular phase of this development. Development begins at **conception**, or fertilization, when a sperm cell enters an ovum and the two merge into a single cell called a *zygote*. The zygote contains a complete set of forty-six chromosomes, half of them from the mother, half from the father—all the genetic information needed to make a unique human individual. Over the next few days the zygote inches down the fallopian tube toward the uterus, expanding as cells divide. In three to five days it reaches the uterus, where it grows in a tiny orb of cells called a *blastocyst*. By day ten the blastocyst fully implants itself in the lining of the uterus, and from implantation until the eighth week after fertilization it is known technically as an *embryo*. In the embryonic phase, most major organs form (though the brain and spinal cord will keep developing during pregnancy), and the embryo grows to just over an inch long. At about the third week the embryo first acquires a human shape; by the eighth, doctors can detect brain activity. From the end of the eighth week until birth (approximately week forty), the embryo is known in medical terminology as a *fetus*.

In the abortion debate, certain other aspects of fetal development are thought by some to be of special significance. For example, usually at about sixteen to twenty weeks, the mother can feel the fetus moving, an event known as **quickening**. At about twenty-three or twenty-four weeks, the fetus may be able to live outside the uterus, a state referred to as **viability**.

Abortion methods vary depending largely on the stage of a woman's pregnancy. Within the first seven weeks or so, drugs can be used to induce an abortion. A combination of mifepristone (RU-486) and prostaglandins (hormonelike agents that provoke uterine contractions) can force the embryo out of the uterus and through the vagina. This approach, sometimes called a *medical* or *medication abortion*, has an extremely high success rate.

With a method known as *menstrual aspiration* (or *manual vacuum aspiration*), an abortion can be performed in the first three weeks. In this procedure, a physician expands the opening of the uterus (the cervix) and uses a syringe to draw out the embryo from the uterine wall. Up until twelve weeks of pregnancy (the period when most abortions are performed, also called the *first trimester*), a method called *suction curettage* (or *dilation and suction curettage*) is often used. A physician widens the cervix, then inserts a thin, flexible tube through it and into the uterus itself. A vacuum device attached to the other end of the tube then provides suction to empty the uterus. A method often used after twelve weeks is *dilation and evacuation*. After the cervix is opened up, forceps and suction are used to extract the fetus. A nonsurgical technique used in some late abortions involves inducing the contractions of labor so the fetus is expelled from the uterus. To force the contractions, physicians often use drugs as well as *saline injection,* the substitution of saltwater for amniotic fluid in the uterus.

Like any medical procedure, abortion poses some risk of complications. Its risks, however, are relatively low. Fewer than 0.05 percent of women who have a first-trimester abortion suffer from a major complication. The risk of death for women who have an abortion at eight weeks or earlier is 0.3 deaths per hundred thousand abortions. The risk of death for abortions performed at eighteen weeks or later is 6.7 per hundred thousand. The health risks linked to abortion are directly related to the timing of the procedure. The earlier in the pregnancy an abortion is performed, the lower the risk.

Abortion in the United States: Facts and Figures

- Nearly half (45 percent) of all pregnancies among U.S. women in 2011 were unintended, and about four in ten of these were terminated by abortion.

- Nineteen percent of pregnancies (excluding miscarriages) in 2014 ended in abortion.

- Approximately 926,200 abortions were performed in 2014, down 12 percent from 1.06 million in 2011. In 2014, some 1.5 percent of women aged fifteen to forty-four had an abortion.

- The abortion rate in 2014 was 14.6 abortions per thousand women aged fifteen to forty-four, down 14 percent from 16.9 per thousand in 2011. This is the lowest rate ever observed in the United States; in 1973, the year abortion became legal, the rate was 16.3 per thousand.

- Seventeen percent of abortion patients in 2014 identified as mainline Protestant, 13 percent as evangelical Protestant, and 24 percent as Catholic; 38 percent reported no religious affiliation, and the remaining 8 percent reported some other affiliation.

- More than half of all U.S. abortion patients in 2014 were in their twenties: patients aged twenty to twenty-four obtained 34 percent of all abortions, and patients aged twenty-five to twenty-nine obtained 27 percent.

- Twelve percent of abortion patients in 2014 were adolescents: those aged eighteen to nineteen accounted for 8 percent of all abortions, fifteen-to seventeen-year-olds for 3 percent, and those younger than fifteen for 0.2 percent.

- White patients accounted for 39 percent of abortion procedures in 2014, blacks for 28 percent, Hispanics for 25 percent, and patients of other races and ethnicities for 9 percent.

- In 2014, 59 percent of abortions were obtained by women who had had at least one birth.

- In 2014, nearly half of the women seeking an abortion were living with a male partner, and 14 percent of them were married.

- The reasons patients gave for having an abortion underscored their understanding of the responsibilities of parenthood and family life. The three most common reasons—each cited by three-fourths of patients—were concern for or responsibility to other individuals; the inability to afford raising a child; and the belief that having a baby would interfere with work, school, or the ability to care for dependents. Half said they did not want to be a single parent or were having problems with their husband or partner.

- A first-trimester abortion is one of the safest medical procedures and carries minimal risk—less than 0.05 percent—of major complications that might necessitate hospital care.

- Leading experts have concluded that among women who have an unplanned pregnancy, the risk of mental health problems is no greater if they have a single first-trimester abortion than if they carry the pregnancy to term.

- The risk of death associated with abortion increases with the length of pregnancy, from 0.3 for every hundred thousand abortions at or before eight weeks to 6.7 per hundred thousand at eighteen weeks or later.

- Medication abortions accounted for 31 percent of all nonhospital abortions in 2014 and for 45 percent of abortions before nine weeks' gestation.*

*Derived from "Fact Sheet" and "National Reproductive Health Profile," data compiled and developed by the Alan Guttmacher Institute, January 2017, January 2018, www.guttmacher.org (March 7, 2018).

When we try to evaluate arguments in the abortion debate, we must distinguish between the moral question (Is abortion right?) and the legal one (What should the law allow?). Our main concern here is the former, not the latter. But to be fully informed about the issue, we should understand, at least in general terms, what the law does allow. In 1973, in the landmark case of *Roe v. Wade*, the United States Supreme Court ruled that a woman has a constitutional, but not unlimited, right to obtain an abortion in a range of circumstances. According to the court, in the first trimester of pregnancy, the woman's right is unrestricted. The decision to have an abortion is up to the woman in consultation with her physician. After the first trimester, a state may regulate (but not ban) abortion to protect the health of the mother. After viability, however, a state may regulate and even forbid abortions in the interests of "the potentiality of human life," except when abortion is necessary to preserve the health or life of the woman.[1]

In *Roe* the court maintained that a woman's right to an abortion is based on a fundamental right of personal privacy and that this right, derived from several constitutional amendments, applies to numerous situations involving reproduction, families, and children. The court also pointed out that the word *person* as used in the Constitution "does not include the unborn" and that "the unborn have never been recognized in the law as persons in the whole sense."[2]

Over the next thirty years the Court handed down other abortion decisions that clarified or supplemented *Roe*. Among other things, the justices prohibited or constrained the use of Medicaid (a government entitlement program) to subsidize abortions; forbade the use of public employees and facilities to perform abortions (except to save the life of the mother); declared that a woman seeking an abortion does not have to notify her husband of her intent; affirmed that states may not impose restrictions that present an "undue burden," or excessive impediment, to women seeking abortions; and held that states may require a girl under eighteen to obtain either the informed consent of a parent or a court order before getting an abortion.

MORAL THEORIES

How would a utilitarian judge the moral permissibility of abortion? How would a Kantian theorist or a natural law theorist evaluate it? Let us take utilitarianism first. An act-utilitarian would say that an abortion is morally right if it results in the greatest overall happiness, everyone considered. To argue for abortion, she might point to all the unhappiness that could be caused by the mother's remaining pregnant against her wishes: the mother's impaired mental and physical health (and possible death), her loss of personal freedom and future opportunities, financial strain on the mother as well as on her family, the anguish of being pregnant as a result of rape or incest, the agony of bringing a seriously impaired baby to term only to see it die later, and the stress that all these social and financial problems would have on a child after birth. The philosopher Mary Anne Warren cites a possible consequentialist argument that says when women do not have the option of abortion, unhappiness can be created on a *global* scale:

> In the long run, access to abortion is essential for the health and survival not just of individual women and families, but also that of the larger social and biological systems on which all our lives depend. Given the inadequacy of present methods of contraception and the lack of universal access to contraception, the avoidance of rapid population growth generally requires some use of abortion. Unless population growth rates are reduced in those impoverished societies where they remain high, malnutrition and starvation will become even more widespread than at present.[3]

An act-utilitarian, of course, could also argue against abortion on exactly the same grounds— the overall happiness (or unhappiness) brought

Majority Opinion in *Roe v. Wade*

Seven justices concurred with the U.S. Supreme Court's opinion in *Roe v. Wade,* including Justice Harry Blackmun, who wrote it. Here is an excerpt:

> This right of privacy, whether it be founded in the Fourteenth Amendment's concept of personal liberty and restrictions upon state action, as we feel it is, or, as the District Court determined, in the Ninth Amendment's reservation of rights to the people, is broad enough to encompass a woman's decision whether or not to terminate her pregnancy. . . .
>
> [A]ppellant and some *amici* argue that the woman's right is absolute and that she is entitled to terminate her pregnancy at whatever time, in whatever way, and for whatever reason she alone chooses. With this we do not agree. Appellant's arguments that Texas either has no valid interest at all in regulating the abortion decision, or no interest strong enough to support any limitation upon the woman's sole determination, are unpersuasive. The Court's decisions recognizing a right of privacy also acknowledge that some state regulation in areas protected by that right is appropriate. As noted above, a State may properly assert important interests in safeguarding health, in maintaining medical standards, and in protecting potential life. At some point in pregnancy,
>
> these respective interests become sufficiently compelling to sustain regulation of the factors that govern the abortion decision. The privacy right involved, therefore, cannot be said to be absolute. . . .
>
> We, therefore, conclude that the right of personal privacy includes the abortion decision, but that this right is not unqualified and must be considered against important state interests in regulation. . . .
>
> [This] decision leaves the State free to place increasing restrictions on abortion as the period of pregnancy lengthens, so long as those restrictions are tailored to the recognized state interests. The decision vindicates the right of the physician to administer medical treatment according to his professional judgment up to the points where important state interests provide compelling justifications for intervention. Up to those points, the abortion decision in all its aspects is inherently, and primarily, a medical decision, and basic responsibility for it must rest with the physician. If an individual practitioner abuses the privilege of exercising proper medical judgment, the usual remedies, judicial and intra-professional, are available.*

*Roe v. Wade, 410 U.S. 113, 153–54, 165–66 (1973).

about by particular actions. She could contend, for example, that *not* having an abortion would produce more net happiness than having one because having one would cause the mother tremendous psychological pain, because the happiness brought into the world with the birth of the child would be considerable, and because the social stigma of having an abortion would be extremely painful for both the mother and her family.

A rule-utilitarian could also view abortion as either morally right or wrong depending on the rule being followed and how much net happiness

results from adhering to it. He could argue on various grounds that generally following a rule such as "Abortion is not morally permissible except to save the mother's life" would maximize happiness. Or he could claim that generally following this rule instead would maximize happiness: "Abortion is morally permissible for any reason during the first trimester and always in cases of rape, incest, fetal impairment, and serious threats to the mother's health or life."

A premise (often unstated) in many arguments about abortion is that the fetus is (or is not) a

person—an entity with full moral rights. In general, utilitarian arguments about abortion do not depend heavily, if at all, on whether the fetus is regarded as a person. Whether the fetus is a person is not likely to dramatically affect the hedonic calculus. The main issue is not personhood but utility. For the Kantian theorist, however, the moral status of the fetus is likely to matter much more. (Whether Kant himself thought the fetus a person is an open question.) If the Kantian maintains that the fetus is a person—that is, an end in itself, a thing of intrinsic value and dignity—then he would insist that it has all the rights and is due all the respect that any other person has. This would mean that the unborn should not be regarded as just another quantity in a utilitarian calculation of consequences. Like any adult human, the fetus has rights, and these rights cannot be overridden merely for utility's sake. Only for the most compelling moral reasons can these rights be set aside. A Kantian might say that one such reason is self-defense: killing a person in self-defense is permissible. He might therefore argue

---

ABORTION AND THE SCRIPTURES

Do the Jewish or Christian scriptures forbid abortion? Many people believe that they do, but the philosopher James Rachels argues that they do not:

> It is difficult to derive a prohibition of abortion from either the Jewish or the Christian Scriptures. The Bible does not speak plainly on the matter. There are certain passages, however, that are often quoted by conservatives because they seem to suggest that fetuses have full human status. One of the most frequently cited passages is from the first chapter of Jeremiah, in which God is quoted as saying: "Before I formed you in the womb I knew you, and before you were born I consecrated you." These words are presented as though they were God's endorsement of the conservative position: They are taken to mean that the unborn, as well as the born, are "consecrated" to God.
>
> In context, however, these words obviously mean something quite different. Suppose we read the whole passage in which they occur:
>
>> Now the word of the Lord came to me saying, "Before I formed you in the womb I knew you, and before you were born I consecrated you; I appointed you a prophet to the nations." Then I said, "Ah, Lord God! Behold, I do not know how to speak, for I am only a youth." But the Lord said to me, "Do not say, 'I am only a youth' for to all to whom I send you you shall go, and whatever I command you you shall speak. Be not afraid of them, for I am with you to deliver you," says the Lord.
>
> Neither abortion, the sanctity of fetal life, nor anything else of the kind is being discussed in this passage. Instead, Jeremiah is asserting his authority as a prophet. He is saying, in effect, "God authorized me to speak for him; even though I resisted, he commanded me to speak." But Jeremiah puts the point more poetically; he has God saying that God had intended him to be a prophet even before Jeremiah was born. . . .
>
> The scriptural passage that comes closest to making a specific judgment about the moral status of fetuses occurs in the 21st chapter of Exodus. This chapter is part of a detailed description of the law of the ancient Israelites. Here the penalty for murder is said to be death; however, it is also said that if a pregnant woman is caused to have a miscarriage, the penalty is only a fine, to be paid to her husband. Murder was not a category that included fetuses. The Law of Israel apparently regarded fetuses as something less than full human beings.*

*James Rachels, from *The Elements of Moral Philosophy*, 4th Ed. pp. 59–60. Copyright © 2003 McGraw Hill Education. Reprinted with permission.

that if the mother's life is being threatened by the fetus she carries (if being pregnant is somehow life-threatening), therapeutic abortion is permissible, just as killing someone who is trying to kill you is permissible. In this view, abortion would seem to be only rarely justified.

On the other hand, if the Kantian does not regard the fetus as a person, he may believe that abortion is often justified to protect the rights and dignity of the mother, who *is* a person. In other words, the fetus—like any other nonperson—can be used as a means to an end, whereas the mother must be treated as an end in herself.

Traditional natural law theorists would view abortion very differently, for two reasons. First, to them, there is no question about the moral status of the fetus: it is a person with full moral rights. Second, the theory is very clear about the treatment of innocent persons: it is always morally wrong to directly kill the innocent. So the direct, intentional killing of a fetus through abortion is never permissible. According to the doctrine of double effect, killing an innocent person for the purpose of achieving some greater good is immoral. But indirectly, unintentionally killing an innocent person while trying to do good may be permissible. Therefore, intentionally killing a fetus through abortion, even to save the mother's life, is wrong. But trying to, say, cure a pregnant woman's cancer by performing a hysterectomy on her or giving her chemotherapy—treatment that has the unintended side effect of aborting the fetus—may be morally acceptable. In this view, very few abortions are morally acceptable.

MORAL ARGUMENTS

Arguments for and against abortion are plentiful and diverse, their quality ranges from good to bad, and their conclusions vary from conservative ("pro-life") to liberal ("pro-choice"), with several moderate positions in between. We can sum up the central issue of the debate like this: *When, if ever,*

QUICK REVIEW

abortion—The deliberate termination of a pregnancy by surgical or medical (with drugs) means.

therapeutic abortion—An abortion performed to protect the life or health of the mother.

conception—The merging of a sperm cell and an ovum into a single cell; also called fertilization.

quickening—The point in fetal development when the mother can feel the fetus moving (at about sixteen to twenty weeks).

viability—The stage of fetal development at which the fetus is able to survive outside the uterus.

person—A being thought to have full moral rights.

is abortion morally permissible? Recall that in ethics the proper response to such a question is to provide good reasons for a particular position. The usual fireworks that accompany the abortion debate—strident denunciations of the other side, appeals to emotion and pity, extremist rhetoric, exaggerated claims, political posturing, and the like—are not appropriate, not germane, and not helpful. So here we try to cut through all that and examine a few of the main arguments offered for a range of views.

The conservative position is that abortion is never, or almost never, morally permissible. Typically the "almost never" refers to situations in which abortion may be permissible to save the life of the mother. (Generally, both the liberal and conservative positions hold that abortion may be permissible to save the mother's life, usually on the grounds that the mother has a right of self-defense. But as mentioned earlier, the Roman Catholic position is that in any case, the death of the fetus must be unintended.)

Like many arguments about abortion, the conservative case is built on a proposition about the moral status of the fetus. For most conservatives, the fetus is a person (a human being, as some would say) with full moral rights, the same rights that any adult human has, and these rights emerge at the moment of conception. Of course, the moral right at the heart of it all is the right to life. Taking the life of a fetal person is just as immoral as killing an innocent adult human.

Here is one version of the conservative argument:

1. The unborn is obviously a human life.

2. It is wrong to take a human life.

3. Abortion is the taking of a human life.

4. Therefore, abortion is wrong.

To evaluate this argument (or *any* argument), we must determine (1) whether the conclusion follows from the premises; and (2) whether the premises are true. A cursory glance at this argument might suggest that the conclusion does follow from the premises and that the premises are true. But we must be careful. This argument commits the fallacy of equivocation. The term *human life* is assigned two different meanings in the premises, rendering the argument invalid. In Premise 1, "human life" means something like "biologically human"—an entity with human DNA, an entity that is from the human species. But in Premises 2 and 3, the term means "person"—a being entitled to full moral rights. If "human life" is used in different senses in the premises, then the argument is not valid (the conclusion does not follow from the premises)— even if the premises, using their respective meanings of the term, are true. As it stands, Premise 1 is unmistakably true: a fetus born of human parents with human DNA is certainly biologically human. And in its present form, Premise 2 is also true: the killing of a person is indeed wrong (except perhaps to save a life). Still, the argument fails and does not provide us with good reasons to accept the conclusion.

Yet there are conservative arguments that do not equivocate. Consider this one:

1. The unborn is an innocent person from conception.

2. It is wrong to kill an innocent person.

3. Abortion is the killing of an innocent person.

4. Therefore, abortion is wrong.

This argument is valid. The only significant difference between it and the previous one is Premise 1, which asserts that the unborn is a being with full moral rights from the very moment of fertilization. If Premise 1 is true, then the argument is sound—the premises are true and the conclusion follows from them.

But *is* the premise true? The conservative insists that it is and can argue for it in this fashion. Birth is generally thought to be the point at which the fetus is most clearly (and legally) a person. The development of the unborn from conception to birth, however, is one continuous process, with no obvious points along the way that might signal a transition into personhood. Moreover, whatever essential properties a born human has that make it a person seem to be present at the moment of conception. Therefore, because no unambiguous point of personhood can be located in this process, the most reasonable option is to identify personhood with conception.

Opponents of this argument contend that it is fallacious. We may not be able to pinpoint a precise moment when day becomes night, they say, but that does not mean that day *is* night. Likewise, we may not be able to determine the precise point in the continuous process of human development when a zygote becomes a full-fledged person. But that does not mean that a zygote is a person.

The conservative, however, can propose a more nuanced reason for supposing that conception marks the beginning of personhood:

> One evidence of the nonarbitrary character of the line drawn [at conception] is the difference of probabilities on either side of it. If a spermatozoon is destroyed, one destroys a being which had a chance of far less

State Abortion Laws

The legal status of abortion has been shaped not only by the U.S. Supreme Court but also by many state statutes, some of which have been struck down by the court, and some that have been left standing but are still challenged by many organizations and groups. Here's a brief summary of current state requirements:

- *Physician and hospital requirements*: Thirty-eight states require an abortion to be performed by a licensed physician. Nineteen states require an abortion to be performed in a hospital after a specified point in the pregnancy, and nineteen states require the involvement of a second physician after a specified point.

- *Gestational limits*: Forty-three states prohibit abortions, generally except when necessary to protect the woman's life or health, after a specified point in pregnancy.

- *"Partial-birth" abortion*: Nineteen states have laws in effect that prohibit "partial-birth" abortion. Three of these laws apply only to postviability abortions.

- *Coverage by private insurance*: Eleven states restrict coverage of abortion in private insurance plans, most often limiting coverage to cases in which the woman's life would be endangered if the pregnancy were carried to term. Most states allow the purchase of additional abortion coverage at an additional cost.

- *Refusal*: Forty-five states allow individual health care providers to refuse to participate in an abortion. Forty-two states allow institutions to refuse to perform abortions, sixteen of which limit refusal to private or religious institutions.

- *State-mandated counseling*: Sixteen states mandate that women be given counseling before an abortion that includes information on at least one of the following: the purported link between abortion and breast cancer (five states), the ability of a fetus to feel pain (twelve states), or long-term mental health consequences for the woman (six states).

- *Waiting periods*: Twenty-seven states require a woman seeking an abortion to wait a specified period of time, usually twenty-four hours, between when she receives counseling and when the procedure is performed. Fourteen of these states have laws that effectively require the woman to make two separate trips to the clinic to obtain the procedure.

- *Parental involvement*: Thirty-seven states require some type of parental involvement in a minor's decision to have an abortion. Twenty-six states require one or both parents to consent to the procedure, while eleven require that one or both parents be notified.*

*Derived from "An Overview of Abortion Laws," data compiled by the Alan Guttmacher Institute, August 1, 2017, www.guttmacher.org (August 17, 2017).

---

than 1 in 200 million of developing into a reasoning being, possessed of the genetic code, a heart and other organs, and capable of pain. If a fetus is destroyed, one destroys a being already possessed of the genetic code, organs and sensitivity to pain, and one which had an 80 percent chance of developing further into a baby outside the womb who, in time, would reason.

The positive argument for conception as the decision moment of humanization is that at conception the new being receives the genetic code. It is this genetic information which determines his characteristics, which is the biological carrier of the possibility of human wisdom, which makes him a self-evolving being. A being with a human genetic code is man.[4]

Others who oppose abortion argue that although the fetus may not be a person, it has the *potential* to become a person and is therefore entitled to the same rights as full-fledged persons. But critics reject this view:

> This argument is implausible, since in no other case do we treat the potential to achieve some status entailing certain rights as itself entailing those same rights. For instance, every child born in the United States is a potential voter, but no-one under the age of 18 has the right to vote in that country. If a fetus is a potential person, then so is an unfertilized human ovum, together with enough viable spermatozoa to achieve fertilization; yet few would seriously suggest that *these* living human entities should have full and equal moral status.[5]

The liberal position is that abortion is always (or almost always) permissible. Like the conservative's argument, the liberal's is based on a particular view of the moral status of the fetus. But in opposition to the conservative view, the liberal asserts that the fetus is not a person, not a being with full moral rights. Abortion therefore is morally permissible because the fetus does not possess a right to life (unlike the mother, who has a full complement of rights). Generally, for the liberal, the event that makes the unborn a person is not conception but birth.

Here is a version of a common liberal argument:

1. The unborn is not a person until birth (and thus does not have a right to life).

2. It is wrong to kill an innocent person.

3. Abortion before birth would not be the killing of an innocent person.

4. If abortion before birth is not the killing of an innocent person, it is permissible.

5. Therefore, abortion before birth is permissible.

Notice that this argument and the conservative one have a common premise: it is wrong to kill an innocent person. Thus the liberal and the conservative agree on the immorality of murder. Their disagreement is not over this fundamental moral principle, but over the nature of persons and who does or does not qualify as such an entity. Premise 1, then, is the crux of the liberal's argument (just as Premise 1 is the heart of the conservative's argument). How might the liberal defend this premise?

The obvious approach is to plausibly explain what a person is and then show that the fetus does not qualify as one. The most influential argument along these lines is that of Mary Anne Warren. "What characteristics entitle an entity to be considered a person?" she asks. What criteria, for example, would we use to decide whether alien beings encountered on an unknown planet deserve to be treated morally or treated as, say, a source of food? How would we tell whether the creatures are persons? Warren says that the characteristics most important to our idea of personhood are (1) consciousness, (2) the ability to reason, (3) self-motivated activity, (4) the capacity to communicate, and (5) the presence of self-concepts and self-awareness. Any being that has all of these traits we would surely regard as a person. Even a being that has only some of these traits would probably qualify as a person. More to the point, Warren says, we must admit that any being that has none of these traits is unquestionably *not* a person. And since a fetus lacks all these, we have to conclude that it, too, is not a person.

These considerations suggest that being genetically human is not the same thing as being a person in the moral sense, the sense of having full moral rights. As Warren notes,

> Now if [these five traits] are indeed the primary criteria of personhood, then it is clear that genetic humanity is neither necessary nor sufficient for establishing that an entity is a person. Some human beings are not people [persons], and there may well be people who are not human beings. A man or woman whose consciousness has been permanently obliterated but who remains alive is a human being which is no longer a person; defective human beings, with no appreciable mental capacity, are not and presumably never

will be people; and a fetus is a human being which is not yet a person, and which therefore cannot coherently be said to have full moral rights. Citizens of the next century should be prepared to recognize highly advanced, self-aware robots or computers, should such be developed, and intelligent inhabitants of other worlds, should such be found, as people in the fullest sense, and to respect their moral rights.[6]

Against the liberal's argument, the conservative can lodge the following objections. First, he can point out that if Warren's view of personhood is

CRITICAL THOUGHT: Fact-checking Abortion Claims

Because abortion is so controversial, and because conflicts over it are so intense, abortion debates often abound in falsehoods and half-truths. Here are some recent examples, along with the verdicts of the fact-checking website PolitiFact.com:

Claim	Verdict
"Abortion providers like Planned Parenthood do little more than provide abortions."—Sean Duffy	False
"Toomey and Trump will ban abortion and punish women who have them."—NARAL Pro-Choice America	False
"Today in America, between 40 and 50 percent of all African-American babies, virtually 1-in-2, are killed before they are born."—Trent Franks	Mostly False
Ohio budget item later signed into law by Gov. John Kasich requires women seeking an abortion to undergo a "mandatory vaginal probe."—Rachel Maddow	False
Birth control pioneer Margaret Sanger "believed that people like me should be eliminated."—Ben Carson	False
Attorney general candidate Brad Schimel "is in cahoots with Wisconsin Right to Life to make abortion a crime in Wisconsin."—Chris Taylor	Mostly False
"A salesclerk at Hobby Lobby who needs contraception . . . is not going to get that service through her employer's health care plan because her employer doesn't think she should be using contraception."—Hillary Clinton	Mostly False
"Upwards of 90 percent" of women seeking an abortion decide not to have an abortion after seeing an ultrasound.—Rachel Campos-Duffy	False
Mitt Romney "backed a bill that outlaws all abortions, even in cases of rape and incest."—Barack Obama	False

Can you trust advocacy groups such as NARAL and National Right to Life to provide accurate information about abortion? Do you accept every claim they make just because you agree with their stand on the abortion issue? How would you fact-check an abortion claim that you're not sure of?

correct, then a fetus is not a person—but neither is a newborn. After all, it is doubtful that a newborn (or perhaps even an older baby) can meet Warren's criteria for personhood. If a newborn is not a person, then killing it—the crime of infanticide—would seem to be permissible. But we tend to think that infanticide is obviously wrong.

To this criticism the liberal may say that though a newborn is not a person, it still has value—either because it is a potential person or because it is valued by others. The liberal might even argue that though a baby is not a person, infanticide should never be permitted because it is a gruesome act that cheapens life or cultivates a callous attitude toward it.

The conservative can offer a related objection to the liberal's position. The liberal argument implies that the unborn is a person at birth, but not a person a day or even an hour *before* birth, and therefore that abortion is immoral after birth but permissible an hour before. But because the physiological and psychological differences between the newborn and unborn are virtually nil, the liberal's distinction seems both arbitrary and ghastly.

The moderate rejects the claim that abortions are almost never permissible (as conservatives say) as well as the notion that they almost always are (as liberals maintain). In a variety of ways, moderates take intermediate positions between these two ends of the spectrum, asserting that abortion may be justified in more cases than conservatives would allow and fewer than liberals would like.

One moderate approach is to argue that the fetus becomes a person (and acquires full rights) at some time after conception and before birth—at viability, quickening, sentience (sensory experience), or some other notable milestone. Each of these points, however, is problematic in one way or another. The viability of the fetus (the point when it can survive outside the womb) is largely a function of modern medical know-how. Physicians are getting better at sustaining fetal life outside the womb, gradually pushing viability further back toward conception. But this observation suggests, implausibly, that personhood depends on medical expertise. Quickening, the first detection of fetal movement by the mother, signifies nothing that can be plausibly linked to personhood. It does not indicate the start of fetal movement—the fetus begins moving in the very first week of life. Sentience refers to consciousness, specifically the capacity to have sense experiences. If being sentient (especially the capacity to feel pleasure and pain) is proof of personhood, then personhood must not arise in the fetus until the second trimester, when neurological pathways are developed enough to make sense experience possible. But why should we regard sentience as a marker for personhood in the first place? Kittens, birds, crabs, and spiders are sentient, but few of us would insist that they are persons with full moral rights.

Some moderate positions can be mapped out without reference to the issue of personhood. The most impressive argument for this sort of view is that of Judith Jarvis Thomson. She contends that even if we grant that the fetus is a person with full moral rights, abortion still may be permissible in certain cases—more cases than the conservative would permit and fewer than the liberal would. She argues that the fetus has a right to life, but not a right to sustain that life by using the mother's body against her will. To underscore her argument, Thomson asks us to consider this strange scenario:

> You wake up in the morning and find yourself back to back in bed with an unconscious violinist. A famous unconscious violinist. He has been found to have a fatal kidney ailment, and the Society of Music Lovers has canvassed all the available medical records and found that you alone have the right blood type to help. They have therefore kidnapped you, and last night the violinist's circulatory system was plugged into yours, so that your kidneys can be used to extract poisons from his blood as well as your own. The director of the hospital now tells you, "Look, we're sorry the Society of Music Lovers did this to you—we would never have permitted it if we had known. But still, they did it, and the violinist now is plugged into you. To unplug you would be to kill him. But never mind, it's only for nine months. By then he will

have recovered from his ailment, and can safely be unplugged from you."[7]

Would you agree to such an arrangement? Would you be morally obligated to do so? The violinist, like all persons, has a right to life. But does this right, in Thomson's phrase, "[outweigh] your right to decide what happens in and to your body"? Thomson concludes that the unborn's right to life does not entail the right to use the mother's body without her consent; the mother has a right to defend herself against unauthorized exploitation of her body. Abortion then is morally permissible when pregnancy is forced on the mother—that is, in cases of rape, incest, and defective contraception. (Like most people involved in the abortion debate, Thomson also thinks that abortion is morally acceptable to save the life of the mother.)

While laying out her argument, Thomson makes a distinction that further moderates her views. She points out that though women have a right to terminate a pregnancy in some cases, they do not have a right to "secure the death of the unborn child":

> It is easy to confuse these two things in that up to a certain point in the life of the fetus it is not able to survive outside the mother's body; hence removing it from her body guarantees its death. But they are importantly different. I have argued that you are not morally required to spend nine months in bed, sustaining the life of that violinist; but to say this is by no means to say that if, when you unplug yourself, there is a miracle and he survives, you then have a right to turn round and slit his throat. You may detach yourself even if this costs him his life; you have no right to be guaranteed his death, by some other means, if unplugging yourself does not kill him.[8]

Here is a greatly simplified version of Thomson's basic argument:

1. Whether or not the unborn has a right to life, it does not have a right to sustain its life by using the mother's body against her will.

2. The mother has a right to defend herself against the unborn's use of her body against her will (a right to have an abortion).

3. The unborn uses the mother's body against her will when the pregnancy is the result of rape, incest, or defective contraception.

4. Therefore, abortion is permissible in cases of rape, incest, or defective contraception.

Probably the most common criticism of this argument is that the mother may in fact not have the right to disconnect herself from the fetus if she bears some responsibility for being connected. In the case of Thomson's violinist, the woman was not at all responsible for being connected to him. However, if the woman's own actions somehow precipitated her being attached to the violinist, then she would be responsible for her predicament and thus would have no right to disconnect herself. Likewise, this objection goes, if a woman consents to sexual intercourse and knows that her actions can lead to pregnancy, she bears some responsibility for getting pregnant and therefore has no right to abort the fetus, even though it is using her body to survive. If this view is right, an abortion would seem to be justified only in cases of rape, when the woman is clearly not responsible for her pregnancy.

CHAPTER REVIEW

SUMMARY

Abortion is the deliberate termination of a pregnancy by surgical or medical means. Therapeutic abortions are those performed to protect the life of the mother. An abortion can be performed at any point in the development of the unborn—from conception to birth.

Abortion methods vary depending on how long the woman has been pregnant. Very early abortions can be done with drugs. Other types of abortions are performed by widening the cervix and drawing out the embryo from the uterus with a syringe (manual vacuum aspiration), by opening the cervix and using a thin suction tube to empty the uterus (suction curettage), by using forceps and suction to extract the fetus (dilation and evacuation), and by using drugs or saline solution to cause contractions to expel the fetus from the uterus.

In 1973, in the famous case *Roe v. Wade,* the United States Supreme Court ruled that a woman has a constitutional, but limited, right to obtain an abortion. According to the court, in the first trimester, the woman's right is unrestricted. The decision to have an abortion is up to the woman in consultation with her physician. After the first trimester, a state may regulate but not ban abortion to protect the health of the mother. After the fetus reaches viability, a state may regulate and even forbid abortions in the interests of the fetus, except when an abortion is necessary to preserve the health or life of the woman.

Major moral theories offer different perspectives on the issue of abortion. An act-utilitarian would argue that an abortion is morally right (or wrong) depending on its consequences. A rule-utilitarian could also judge abortion to be either morally right or wrong depending on the rule being followed and how much net happiness results from adhering to it. A Kantian theorist is likely to judge the issue according to the moral status of the fetus. If the Kantian believes that the fetus is a person, then she would say that the fetus has full moral rights and that these rights cannot be overridden on utilitarian grounds. If she does not think the fetus a person, she may believe that abortion is sometimes justified to protect the rights and dignity of the mother.

Arguments for and against abortion can be roughly grouped into three major categories—conservative, liberal, and moderate. The conservative position is that abortion is never, or almost never, morally permissible. The conservative case is built on the supposition that the fetus is a person with full moral rights. The liberal position is that abortion is always, or almost always, permissible. The liberal asserts that the fetus is not a person and therefore does not have a right to life. The moderate can take a number of intermediate positions between these two extremes, asserting on various grounds that abortion may be permissible in more situations than would be allowed by the conservative

and in fewer situations than would be accepted by the liberal. A moderate position can be formulated by arguing that the unborn is a person some time after conception and before birth—perhaps at viability, quickening, or sentience.

KEY TERMS
abortion (p. 221)
therapeutic abortion (p. 221)
conception (p. 222)
quickening (p. 222)
viability (p. 222)
person (p. 226)

EXERCISES
Review Questions

1. What is a therapeutic abortion? (p. 221)
2. At what point in a woman's pregnancy is the fetus thought to be viable? (p. 222)
3. What is a zygote? a blastocyst? (p. 222)
4. What was the U.S. Supreme Court's ruling in *Roe v. Wade*? (p. 224)
5. What is an abortion? (p. 221)
6. In *Roe v. Wade*, the court held that a woman's right to an abortion was based on what fundamental right? (p. 224)
7. In the last few years, has the abortion rate in the United States been going down or up? (p. 223)
8. In 2011, what percentage of unintended pregnancies were terminated by abortion? (p. 223)
9. In 2014, white patients accounted for what percentage of abortion procedures? What percentage of patients were black? (p. 223)
10. Do most medical experts think that abortion in the first trimester is relatively safe? (p. 223)

Discussion Questions

1. Why is personhood such an important concept in abortion debates?
2. How might an act-utilitarian judge the moral permissibility of abortion?

3. What is the conservative argument against abortion?

4. What is the liberal argument for a woman's right to an abortion?

5. What is Thomson's argument for a woman's right to an abortion? Is it sound?

6. What is Warren's abortion argument? Is it sound?

7. Why does Warren reject the argument that because a fetus has a potential to become a person, it has the same rights as a full-fledged person?

8. Is being genetically human the same thing as being a person? Why or why not?

9. What argument can the conservative lodge against Warren's view?

10. What claims about abortion does the moderate reject? Do you agree? Why or why not?

FURTHER READING

Daniel Callahan, "Abortion Decisions: Personal Morality," in *Abortion: Law, Choice and Morality* (New York: Macmillan, 1970).

Sidney Callahan, "A Case for Pro-Life Feminism," *Commonweal* 25 (April 1986): 232–38.

Jane English, "Abortion and the Concept of a Person," *Canadian Journal of Philosophy* 5, no. 2 (October 1975): 233–43.

Joel Feinberg, "Abortion," in *Matters of Life and Death,* ed. Tom Regan, 3rd ed. (New York: McGraw-Hill, 1993).

Ronald Munson, "Abortion," in *Intervention and Reflection: Basic Issues in Medical Ethics,* ed. Ronald Munson, 7th ed. (Belmont, CA: Wadsworth, 2004).

John T. Noonan Jr., "An Almost Absolute Value in History," in *The Morality of Abortion: Legal and Historical Perspectives,* ed. John T. Noonan Jr. (Cambridge, MA: Harvard University Press, 1970).

Louis P. Pojman and Francis J. Beckwith, eds., *The Abortion Controversy: 25 Years After Roe v. Wade: A Reader,* 2nd ed. (Belmont, CA: Wadsworth, 1998).

Roe v. Wade, 410 U.S. 113, 113–67 (1973). Justice Harry Blackmun, Majority Opinion of the Court.

Michael Tooley, *Abortion and Infanticide* (Oxford: Clarendon Press; New York: Oxford University Press, 1983).

ETHICAL DILEMMAS

1. Aborting Daughters

The illegal abortion of female foetuses solely to ensure that families have sons is widely practised within some ethnic communities in Britain and has resulted in significant shortfalls in the proportion of girls, according to an investigation by The Independent.

The practice of sex-selective abortion is now so commonplace that it has affected the natural 50:50 balance of boys to girls within some immigrant groups and has led to the "disappearance" of between 1,400 and 4,700 females from the national census records of England and Wales, we can reveal.

A government investigation last year found no evidence that women living in the UK, but born abroad, were preferentially aborting girls. However, our deeper statistical analysis of data from the 2011 National Census has shown widespread discrepancies in the sex ratio of children in some immigrant families, which can only be easily explained by women choosing to abort female foetuses in the hope of becoming quickly pregnant again with a boy. The findings will reignite the debate over whether pregnant women should be legally allowed to know the sex of their babies following ultrasound scans at 13 weeks.*

Do you think sex-selection abortions are morally permissible? What reasons can you provide to back up your view? Some Chinese parents could argue that such abortions are acceptable on utilitarian grounds: aborting female fetuses prevents economic harm to the family. Is this a good moral argument? Why or why not?

*Steve Connor, "The Lost Girls: Illegal Abortion Widely Used by Some UK Ethnic Groups to Avoid Daughters 'Has Reduced Female Population by Between 1,500 and 4,700,'" *The Independent*, January 15, 2014, https://www.independent.co.uk/news/science/the-lost-girls-illegal-abortion-widely-used-by-some-uk-ethnic-groups-to-avoid-daughters-has-reduced-9059790.html. Reprinted by permission of ESI Media.

2. Parental Notification

USA Today—Sabrina Holmquist trained as a physician in low-income neighborhoods in the Bronx, N.Y. She says she often saw pregnant teenagers in desperate health and family crises, including some girls who had been abused at home. That, Holmquist says, led her to believe that doctors sometimes should be able to perform abortions on minors without informing a parent.

But in Texas, Linda W. Flower, who practiced obstetrics for two decades, disagrees. She says that in the vast majority of cases in which a teenage girl seeks an abortion, a parent's guidance is helpful and needed. Flower says she knows of young women who have regretted having abortions.

The doctors' views reflect the dueling arguments in the first abortion case to come before the Supreme Court in five years: a New Hampshire dispute that tests whether a state may bar physicians from performing an abortion on a girl younger than 18 unless one of her parents has been notified at least 48 hours in advance—even in instances in which the girl faces a health emergency.

The case, to be heard by the court Wednesday, is the first abortion dispute before the justices since 2000, when they voted 5–4 to strike down Nebraska's ban on a procedure that critics call "partial birth" abortion because the ban lacked an exception for cases in which the woman's health was at risk. The new dispute tests whether such a health exception should be required in parental-involvement mandates, which have been passed in various forms by 43 states.[†]

Which doctor do you think is right about parental notification? Under what circumstances, if any, do you think it morally permissible for an under-eighteen girl to have an abortion without notifying a parent or guardian? when the girl's life is at stake? when she is a victim of sexual abuse, including incest? Would it be reasonable to require parental notification in *all* cases without exception?

†Joan Biskupic, "High Court Case May Signal Shift on Abortion" from USA Today, February 7, 2006. © 2006 Gannett-USA Today. All rights reserved. Used by permission and protected by the Copyright Laws of the United States. The printing, copying, redistribution, or retransmission of this Content without express written permission is prohibited. www.usatoday.com.

3. Abortion to Avert Health Risks

Medical News Today—The European Court of Human Rights on Tuesday began considering the appeal of a Polish woman who says that in 2000 she was denied an abortion despite warnings from physicians that she could become blind if she continued the pregnancy, the *Scotsman* reports (Neighbour, *Scotsman,* 2/8). Alicja Tysiac—who has three children—alleges that Poland's abortion law violated her rights under Article 8 and Article 14 of the European Convention for the Protection of Human Rights and Fundamental Freedoms, which guarantee "respect for privacy and family life" and "prohibition of discrimination," respectively. Polish law allows abortion only if a woman has been raped, if there is danger to the life of the woman or if the fetus will have birth defects, according to the *Jurist* (Onikepe, *Jurist,* 2/8). The European Court could rule that Tysiac's rights were violated but cannot mandate that Poland change its abortion laws (*Reuters,* 2/7).[‡]

Should Alicja Tysiac have been permitted an abortion even though her life was not at risk? Why or why not? How serious must pregnancy-related health problems be before a risk-lowering abortion is permissible (if ever)? When such health dangers are involved, why should—or should not—a woman be allowed to decide for herself about whether to have an abortion?

[‡]Kaiser Daily Health Policy Report, "European Court of Human Rights Considers Appeal of Polish Woman," published in *Medical News Today*, February 10, 2006. Copyright © 2005 The Henry J. Kaiser Family Foundation. Reprinted with permission.

READINGS

A Defense of Abortion

JUDITH JARVIS THOMSON

Most opposition to abortion relies on the premise that the fetus is a human being, a person, from the moment of conception. The premise is argued for, but, as I think, not well. Take, for example, the most common argument. We are asked to notice that the development of

Judith Jarvis Thomson, excerpts from "A Defense of Abortion." *Philosophy & Public Affairs* 1(1): 47–66. Copyright © 1971 Blackwell Publishing Ltd. Reproduced with permission of Blackwell Publishing Ltd.

a human being from conception through birth into childhood is continuous; then it is said that to draw a line, to choose a point in this development and say "before this point the thing is not a person, after this point it is a person" is to make an arbitrary choice, a choice for which in the nature of things no good reason can be given. It is concluded that the fetus is, or anyway that we had better say it is, a person from the moment of conception. But this conclusion does not follow. Similar things might be said about the development of an acorn into an oak tree, and it does not follow that acorns are oak trees, or that we had better say they are. Arguments of this form are sometimes called "slippery slope arguments"—the phrase is perhaps self-explanatory—and it is dismaying that opponents of abortion rely on them so heavily and uncritically.

I am inclined to agree, however, that the prospects for "drawing a line" in the development of the fetus look dim. I am inclined to think also that we shall probably have to agree that the fetus has already become a human person well before birth. Indeed, it comes as a surprise when one first learns how early in its life it begins to acquire human characteristics. By the tenth week, for example, it already has a face, arms and legs, fingers and toes; it has internal organs, and brain activity is detectable. On the other hand, I think that the premise is false, that the fetus is not a person from the moment of conception. A newly fertilized ovum, a newly implanted clump of cells, is no more a person than an acorn is an oak tree. But I shall not discuss any of this. For it seems to me to be of great interest to ask what happens if, for the sake of argument, we allow the premise. How, precisely, are we supposed to get from there to the conclusion that abortion is morally impermissible? Opponents of abortion commonly spend most of their time establishing that the fetus is a person, and hardly any time explaining the step from there to the impermissibility of abortion. Perhaps they think the step too simple and obvious to require much comment. Or perhaps instead they are simply being economical in argument. Many of those who defend abortion rely on the premise that the fetus is not a person, but only a bit of tissue that will become a person at birth; and why pay out more arguments than you have to? Whatever the explanation, I suggest that the step they take is neither easy nor obvious, that it calls for closer examination than it is commonly given, and that when we do give it this closer examination we shall feel inclined to reject it.

I propose, then, that we grant that the fetus is a person from the moment of conception. How does the argument go from here? Something like this, I take it. Every person has a right to life. So the fetus has a right to life. No doubt the mother has a right to decide what shall happen in and to her body; everyone would grant that. But surely a person's right to life is stronger and more stringent than the mother's right to decide what happens in and to her body, and so outweighs it. So the fetus may not be killed; an abortion may not be performed.

It sounds plausible. But now let me ask you to imagine this. You wake up in the morning and find yourself back to back in bed with an unconscious violinist. A famous unconscious violinist. He has been found to have a fatal kidney ailment, and the Society of Music Lovers has canvassed all the available medical records and found that you alone have the right blood type to help. They have therefore kidnapped you, and last night the violinist's circulatory system was plugged into yours, so that your kidneys can be used to extract poisons from his blood as well as your own. The director of the hospital now tells you, "Look, we're sorry the Society of Music Lovers did this to you—we would never have permitted it if we had known. But still, they did it, and the violinist now is plugged into you. To unplug you would be to kill him. But never mind, it's only for nine months. By then he will have recovered from his ailment, and can safely be unplugged from you." Is it morally incumbent on you to accede to this situation? No doubt it would be very nice of you if you did, a great kindness. But do you *have* to accede to it? What if it were not nine months, but nine years? Or longer still? What if the director of the hospital says, "Tough luck, I agree, but you've now got to stay in bed, with the violinist plugged into you, for the rest of your life. Because remember this. All persons have a right to life, and violinists are persons. Granted you have a right to decide what happens in and to your body, but a person's right to life outweighs your right to decide what happens in and to your body. So you cannot ever be unplugged from him." I imagine you would regard this as outrageous, which suggests that something really is wrong with that plausible-sounding argument I mentioned a moment ago.

In this case, of course, you were kidnapped; you didn't volunteer for the operation that plugged the violinist into your kidneys. Can those who oppose abortion on the ground I mentioned make an exception for a pregnancy due to rape? Certainly. They can say that persons have a right to life only if they didn't come into existence because of rape; or they can say that all persons have a right to life, but that some have less of a right to life than others, in particular, that those who came into existence because of rape have less. But these statements have a rather unpleasant sound. Surely the question of whether you have a right to life at all, or how much of it you have, shouldn't turn on the question of whether or not you are the product of a rape. And in fact the people who oppose abortion on the ground I mentioned do not make this distinction, and hence do not make an exception in case of rape.

Nor do they make an exception for a case in which the mother has to spend the nine months of her pregnancy in bed. They would agree that would be a great pity, and hard on the mother; but all the same, all persons have a right to life, the fetus is a person, and so on. I suspect, in fact, that they would not make an exception for a case in which, miraculously enough, the pregnancy went on for nine years, or even the rest of the mother's life.

Some won't even make an exception for a case in which continuation of the pregnancy is likely to shorten the mother's life; they regard abortion as impermissible even to save the mother's life. Such cases are nowadays very rare, and many opponents of abortion do not accept this extreme view. All the same, it is a good place to begin: a number of points of interest come out in respect to it.

1. Let us call the view that abortion is impermissible even to save the mother's life "the extreme view." I want to suggest first that it does not issue from the argument I mentioned earlier without the addition of some fairly powerful premises. Suppose a woman has become pregnant, and now learns that she has a cardiac condition such that she will die if she carries the baby to term. What may be done for her? The fetus, being a person, has a right to life, but as the mother is a person too, so has she a right to life. Presumably they have an equal right to life. How is it supposed to come out that an abortion may not be performed? If mother and child have an equal right to life, shouldn't we perhaps flip a coin? Or should we add to the mother's right to life her right to decide what happens in and to her body, which everybody seems to be ready to grant—the sum of her rights now outweighing the fetus' right to life?

The most familiar argument here is the following. We are told that performing the abortion would be directly killing[1] the child, whereas doing nothing would not be killing the mother, but only letting her die. Moreover, in killing the child, one would be killing an innocent person, for the child has committed no crime, and is not aiming at his mother's death. And then there are a variety of ways in which this might be continued. (1) But as directly killing an innocent person is always and absolutely impermissible, an abortion may not be performed. Or, (2) as directly killing an innocent person is murder, and murder is always and absolutely impermissible, an abortion may not be performed. Or, (3) as one's duty to refrain from directly killing an innocent person is more stringent than one's duty to keep a person from dying, an abortion may not be performed. Or, (4) if one's only options are directly killing an innocent person or letting a person die, one must prefer letting the person die, and thus an abortion may not be performed.

Some people seem to have thought that these are not further premises which must be added if the conclusion is to be reached, but that they follow from the very fact that an innocent person has a right to life. But this seems to me to be a mistake, and perhaps the simplest way to show this is to bring out that while we must certainly grant that innocent persons have a right to life, the theses in (1) through (4) are all false. Take (2), for example. If directly killing an innocent person is murder, and thus is impermissible, then the mother's directly killing the innocent person inside her is murder, and thus is impermissible. But it cannot seriously be thought to be murder if the mother performs an abortion on herself to save her life. It cannot seriously be said that she *must* refrain, that she *must* sit passively by and wait for her death. Let us look again at the case of you and the violinist. There you are, in bed with the violinist, and the director of the hospital says to you, "It's all most distressing, and I deeply sympathize, but you see this is putting an additional strain on your kidneys, and you'll be dead within the month. But you *have* to stay where you are all the same. Because unplugging you would be directly killing an innocent violinist, and that's murder, and that's impermissible." If anything in the world is true, it is that you do not commit murder, you do not do what is impermissible, if you reach around to your back and unplug yourself from that violinist to save your life.

The main focus of attention in writings on abortion has been on what a third party may or may not do in answer to a request from a woman for an abortion. This is in a way understandable. Things being as they are, there isn't much a woman can safely do to abort herself. So the question asked is what a third party may do, and what the mother may do, if it is mentioned at all, is deduced, almost as an afterthought, from what it is concluded that third parties may do. But it seems to me that to treat the matter in this way is to refuse to grant to the mother that very status of person which is so firmly insisted on for the fetus. For we cannot simply read off what a person may do from what a third party may do. Suppose you find yourself trapped in a tiny house with a growing child. I mean a very tiny house, and a rapidly growing child—you are already up against the wall of the house and in a few minutes you'll be crushed to death. The child on the other hand won't be crushed to death; if nothing is done to stop him from growing he'll be hurt, but in the end he'll simply burst open the house and walk out a free man. Now I could well understand it if a bystander were to say, "There's nothing we can do for you. We cannot choose between your life and his, we cannot be the ones to decide who is to live, we cannot intervene." But it cannot be concluded that you too can do nothing, that you cannot attack it to save your life. However innocent the child may be, you do not have to wait passively while it crushes you to death. Perhaps a pregnant woman is vaguely felt to have the status of house, to which we don't allow the right of self-defense. But if the woman houses the child, it should be remembered that she is a person who houses it.

I should perhaps stop to say explicitly that I am not claiming that people have a right to do anything whatever to save their lives. I think, rather, that there are drastic limits to the right of self-defense. If someone threatens you with death unless you torture someone else to death, I think you have not the right, even to save your life, to do so. But the case under consideration here is very different. In our case there are only two people involved, one whose life is threatened, and one who threatens it. Both are innocent: the one who is threatened is not threatened because of any fault, the one who threatens does not threaten because of any fault. For this reason we may feel that we bystanders cannot intervene. But the person threatened can.

In sum, a woman surely can defend her life against the threat to it posed by the unborn child, even if doing so involves its death. And this shows not merely that the theses in (1) through (4) are false; it shows also that the extreme view of abortion is false, and so we need not canvass any other possible ways of arriving at it from the argument I mentioned at the outset.

2. The extreme view could of course be weakened to say that while abortion is permissible to save the mother's life, it may not be performed by a third party, but only by the mother herself. But this cannot be right either. For what we have to keep in mind is that the mother and the unborn child are not like two tenants in a small house which has, by an unfortunate mistake, been rented to both: the mother *owns* the house. The fact that she does adds to the offensiveness of deducing that the mother can do nothing from the supposition that third parties can do nothing. But it does more than this: it casts a bright light on the supposition that third parties can do nothing. Certainly it lets us see that a third party who says "I cannot choose between you" is fooling himself if he thinks this is impartiality. If Jones has found and fastened on a certain coat, which he needs to keep him from freezing, but which Smith also needs to keep him from freezing, then it is not impartiality that says "I cannot choose between you" when Smith owns the coat. Women have said again and again "This body is *my* body!" and they have reason to feel angry, reason to feel that it has been like shouting into the wind. Smith, after all, is hardly likely to bless us if we say to him, "Of course it's your coat, anybody would grant that it is. But no one may choose between you and Jones who is to have it."

We should really ask what it is that says "no one may choose" in the face of the fact that the body that houses the child is the mother's body. It may be simply a failure to appreciate this fact. But it may be something more interesting, namely the sense that one has a right to refuse to lay hands on people, even where it would be just and fair to do so, even where justice seems to require that somebody do so. Thus justice might call for somebody to get Smith's coat back from Jones, and yet you have a right to refuse to be the one to lay hands on Jones, a right to refuse to do physical violence to him. This, I think, must be granted. But then what should be said is not "no one may choose," but only "*I* cannot choose," and indeed not even this, but "*I* will not *act*," leaving it open that somebody else can or should, and in particular that anyone in a position of authority, with the job of securing people's rights, both can and should. So this is no difficulty. I have not been arguing that any given third party must accede to the mother's request that he perform an abortion to save her life, but only that he may.

I suppose that in some views of human life the mother's body is only on loan to her, the loan not being one which gives her any prior claim to it. One who held this view might well think it impartiality to say "I cannot choose." But I shall simply ignore this possibility. My own view is that if a human being has any just, prior claim to anything at all, he has a just, prior claim to his own body. And perhaps this needn't be argued for here anyway, since, as I mentioned, the arguments against abortion we are looking at do grant that the woman has a right to decide what happens in and to her body.

But although they do grant it, I have tried to show that they do not take seriously what is done in granting it. I suggest the same thing will reappear even more clearly when we turn away from cases in which the mother's life is at stake, and attend, as I propose we now do, to the vastly more common cases in which a woman wants an abortion for some less weighty reason than preserving her own life.

3. Where the mother's life is not at stake, the argument I mentioned at the outset seems to have a much stronger pull. "Everyone has a right to life, so the unborn person has a right to life." And isn't the child's right to life weightier than anything other than the mother's own right to life, which she might put forward as ground for an abortion?

This argument treats the right to life as if it were unproblematic. It is not, and this seems to me to be precisely the source of the mistake.

For we should now, at long last, ask what it comes to, to have a right to life. In some views having a right to life includes having a right to be given at least the bare minimum one needs for continued life. But suppose that what in fact *is* the bare minimum a man needs for continued life is something he has no right at all to be given? If I am sick unto death, and the only thing that will save my life is the touch of Henry Fonda's cool hand on my fevered brow, then all the same, I have no right to be given the touch of Henry Fonda's cool hand on my fevered brow. It would be frightfully nice of him to fly in from the West Coast to provide it. It would be less nice, though no doubt well meant, if my friends flew out to the West Coast and carried Henry Fonda back with them. But I have no right at all against anybody that he should do this for me. Or again, to return to the story I told earlier, the fact that for continued life that violinist needs the continued use of your kidneys does not establish that he has a right to be given the continued use of your kidneys. He certainly has no right against you that *you* should give him continued use of your kidneys. For nobody has any right to use your kidneys unless you give him such a right; and nobody has the right against you that you shall give him this right—if you do allow him to go on using your kidneys, this is a kindness on your part, and not something he can claim from you as his due. Nor has he any right against anybody else that *they* should give him continued use of your kidneys. Certainly he had no right against the Society of Music Lovers that they should plug him into you in the first place. And if you now start to unplug yourself, having learned that you will otherwise have to spend nine years in bed with him, there is nobody in the world who must try to prevent you, in order to see to it that he is given something he has a right to be given.

Some people are rather stricter about the right to life. In their view, it does not include the right to be given anything, but amounts to, and only to, the right not to be killed by anybody. But here a related difficulty arises. If everybody is to refrain from killing that violinist, then everybody must refrain from doing a great many different sorts of things. Everybody must refrain from slitting his throat, everybody must refrain from shooting him—and everybody must refrain from unplugging you from him. But does he have a right against everybody that they shall refrain from unplugging you from him? To refrain from doing this is to allow him to continue to use your kidneys. It could be argued that he has a right against us that *we* should allow him to continue to use your kidneys. That is, while he had no right against us that we should give him the use of your kidneys, it might be argued that he anyway has a right against us that we shall not now intervene and deprive him of the use of your kidneys. I shall come back to third-party interventions later. But certainly the violinist has no right against you that *you* shall allow him to continue to use your kidneys. As I said, if you do allow him to use them, it is a kindness on your part, and not something you owe him.

The difficulty I point to here is not peculiar to the right to life. It reappears in connection with all the other natural rights; and it is something which an adequate account of rights must deal with. For present purposes it is enough just to draw attention to it. But I would stress that I am not arguing that people do not have a right to life—quite to the contrary, it seems to me that the primary control we must place on the acceptability of an account of rights is that it should turn out in that account to be a truth that all persons have a right to life. I am arguing only that having a right to life does not guarantee having either a right to be given the use of or a right to be allowed continued use of another person's body—even if one needs it for life itself. So the right to life will not serve the opponents of abortion in the very simple and clear way in which they seem to have thought it would.

4. There is another way to bring out the difficulty. In the most ordinary sort of case, to deprive someone of what he has a right to is to treat him unjustly. Suppose a boy and his small brother are jointly given a box of chocolates for Christmas. If the older boy takes the box and refuses to give his brother any of the chocolates, he is unjust to him, for the brother has been given a right to half of them. But suppose that, having learned that otherwise it means nine years in bed with that violinist, you unplug yourself from him. You surely are not being unjust to him, for you gave him no right to use your kidneys, and no one else can have

given him any such right. But we have to notice that in unplugging yourself, you are killing him; and violinists, like everybody else, have a right to life, and thus in the view we were considering just now, the right not to be killed. So here you do what he supposedly has a right you shall not do, but you do not act unjustly to him in doing it.

The emendation which may be made at this point is this: the right to life consists not in the right not to be killed, but rather in the right not to be killed unjustly. This runs a risk of circularity, but never mind: it would enable us to square the fact that the violinist has a right to life with the fact that you do not act unjustly toward him in unplugging yourself, thereby killing him. For if you do not kill him unjustly, you do not violate his right to life, and so it is no wonder you do him no injustice.

But if this emendation is accepted, the gap in the argument against abortion stares us plainly in the face: it is by no means enough to show that the fetus is a person, and to remind us that all persons have a right to life—we need to be shown also that killing the fetus violates its right to life, i.e., that abortion is unjust killing. And is it?

I suppose we may take it as a datum that in a case of pregnancy due to rape the mother has not given the unborn person a right to the use of her body for food and shelter. Indeed, in what pregnancy could it be supposed that the mother has given the unborn person such a right? It is not as if there were unborn persons drifting about the world, to whom a woman who wants a child says "I invite you in."

But it might be argued that there are other ways one can have acquired a right to the use of another person's body than by having been invited to use it by that person. Suppose a woman voluntarily indulges in intercourse, knowing of the chance it will issue in pregnancy, and then she does become pregnant; is she not in part responsible for the presence, in fact the very existence, of the unborn person inside her? No doubt she did not invite it in. But doesn't her partial responsibility for its being there itself give it a right to the use of her body? If so, then her aborting it would be more like the boy's taking away the chocolates, and less like your unplugging yourself from the violinist—doing so would be depriving it of what it does have a right to, and thus would be doing it an injustice.

And then, too, it might be asked whether or not she can kill it even to save her own life: If she voluntarily called it into existence, how can she now kill it, even in self-defense?

The first thing to be said about this is that it is something new. Opponents of abortion have been so concerned to make out the independence of the fetus, in order to establish that it has a right to life, just as its mother does, that they have tended to overlook the possible support they might gain from making out that the fetus is *dependent* on the mother, in order to establish that she has a special kind of responsibility for it, a responsibility that gives it rights against her which are not possessed by any independent person—such as an ailing violinist who is a stranger to her.

On the other hand, this argument would give the unborn person a right to its mother's body only if her pregnancy resulted from a voluntary act, undertaken in full knowledge of the chance a pregnancy might result from it. It would leave out entirely the unborn person whose existence is due to rape. Pending the availability of some further argument, then, we would be left with the conclusion that unborn persons whose existence is due to rape have no right to the use of their mothers' bodies, and thus that aborting them is not depriving them of anything they have a right to and hence is not unjust killing.

And we should also notice that it is not at all plain that this argument really does go even as far as it purports to. For there are cases and cases, and the details make a difference. If the room is stuffy, and I therefore open a window to air it, and a burglar climbs in, it would be absurd to say, "Ah, now he can stay, she's given him a right to the use of her house—for she is partially responsible for his presence there, having voluntarily done what enabled him to get in, in full knowledge that there are such things as burglars, and that burglars burgle." It would be still more absurd to say this if I had had bars installed outside my windows, precisely to prevent burglars from getting in, and a burglar got in only because of a defect in the bars. It remains equally absurd if we imagine it is not a burglar who climbs in, but an innocent person who blunders

or falls in. Again, suppose it were like this: people-seeds drift about in the air like pollen, and if you open your windows, one may drift in and take root in your carpets or upholstery. You don't want children, so you fix up your windows with fine mesh screens, the very best you can buy. As can happen, however, and on very, very rare occasions does happen, one of the screens is defective; and a seed drifts in and takes root. Does the person-plant who now develops have a right to the use of your house? Surely not—despite the fact that you voluntarily opened your windows, you knowingly kept carpets and upholstered furniture, and you knew that screens were sometimes defective. Someone may argue that you are responsible for its rooting, that it does have a right to your house, because after all you *could* have lived out your life with bare floors and furniture, or with sealed windows and doors. But this won't do—for by the same token anyone can avoid a pregnancy due to rape by having a hysterectomy, or anyway by never leaving home without a (reliable!) army.

It seems to me that the argument we are looking at can establish at most that there are *some* cases in which the unborn person has a right to the use of its mother's body, and therefore *some* cases in which abortion is unjust killing. There is room for much discussion and argument as to precisely which, if any. But I think we should sidestep this issue and leave it open, for at any rate the argument certainly does not establish that all abortion is unjust killing.

5. There is room for yet another argument here, however. We surely must all grant that there may be cases in which it would be morally indecent to detach a person from your body at the cost of his life. Suppose you learn that what the violinist needs is not nine years of your life, but only one hour: all you need do to save his life is to spend one hour in that bed with him. Suppose also that letting him use your kidneys for that one hour would not affect your health in the slightest. Admittedly you were kidnapped. Admittedly you did not give anyone permission to plug him into you. Nevertheless it seems to me plain you *ought* to allow him to use your kidneys for that hour—it would be indecent to refuse.

Again, suppose pregnancy lasted only an hour, and constituted no threat to life or health. And suppose that a woman becomes pregnant as a result of rape. Admittedly she did not voluntarily do anything to bring about the existence of a child. Admittedly she did nothing at all which would give the unborn person a right to the use of her body. All the same it might well be said, as in the newly emended violinist story, that she *ought* to allow it to remain for that hour—that it would be indecent in her to refuse.

Now some people are inclined to use the term "right" in such a way that it follows from the fact that you ought to allow a person to use your body for the hour he needs, that he has a right to use your body for the hour he needs, even though he has not been given that right by any person or act. They may say that it follows also that if you refuse, you act unjustly toward him. This use of the term is perhaps so common that it cannot be called wrong; nevertheless it seems to me to be an unfortunate loosening of what we would do better to keep a tight rein on. Suppose that box of chocolates I mentioned earlier had not been given to both boys jointly, but was given only to the older boy. There he sits, stolidly eating his way through the box, his small brother watching enviously. Here we are likely to say "You ought not to be so mean. You ought to give your brother some of those chocolates." My own view is that it just does not follow from the truth of this that the brother has any right to any of the chocolates. If the boy refuses to give his brother any, he is greedy, stingy, callous—but not unjust. I suppose that the people I have in mind will say it does follow that the brother has a right to some of the chocolates, and thus that the boy does act unjustly if he refuses to give his brother any. But the effect of saying this is to obscure what we should keep distinct, namely the difference between the boy's refusal in this case and the boy's refusal in the earlier case, in which the box was given to both boys jointly, and in which the small brother thus had what was from any point of view clear title to half.

A further objection to so using the term "right" that from the fact that A ought to do a thing for B, it follows that B has a right against A that A do it for him, is that it is going to make the question of whether or not a man has a right to a thing turn on how easy it is to provide him with it; and this seems not merely unfortunate, but morally unacceptable. Take the case of Henry Fonda again. I said earlier that I had no right to the touch of his cool hand on my fevered brow, even though I needed it to save my life. I said it would be frightfully nice of him to fly in from the West Coast to provide me with it, but that I had no right against him that he should do so. But suppose he isn't on the West Coast. Suppose he has only to walk across the room, place a hand briefly on my brow—and lo, my life is saved. Then surely he ought to do it, it would be indecent to refuse. Is it to be said "Ah, well, it follows that in this case she has a right to the touch of his hand on her brow, and so it would be an injustice in him to refuse"? So that I have a right to it when it is easy for him to provide it, though no right when it's hard? It's rather a shocking idea that anyone's rights should fade away and disappear as it gets harder and harder to accord them to him.

So my own view is that even though you ought to let the violinist use your kidneys for the one hour he needs, we should not conclude that he has a right to do so—we should say that if you refuse, you are, like the boy who owns all the chocolates and will give none away, self-centered and callous, indecent in fact, but not unjust. And similarly, that even supposing a case in which a woman pregnant due to rape ought to allow the unborn person to use her body for the hour he needs, we should not conclude that he has a right to do so; we should conclude that she is self-centered, callous, indecent, but not unjust, if she refuses. The complaints are no less grave; they are just different. However, there is no need to insist on this point. If anyone does wish to deduce "he has a right" from "you ought," then all the same he must surely grant that there are cases in which it is not morally required of you that you allow that violinist to use your kidneys, and in which he does not have a right to use them, and in which you do not do him an injustice if you refuse. And so also for mother and unborn child. Except in such cases as the unborn person has a right to demand it—and we were leaving open the possibility that there may be such cases—nobody is morally *required* to make large sacrifices, of health, of all other interests and concerns, of all other duties and commitments, for nine years, or even for nine months, in order to keep another person alive.

6. We have in fact to distinguish between two kinds of Samaritan: the Good Samaritan and what we might call the Minimally Decent Samaritan. The story of the Good Samaritan, you will remember, goes like this:

> A certain man went down from Jerusalem to Jericho, and fell among thieves, which stripped him of his raiment, and wounded him, and departed, leaving him half dead.
>
> And by chance there came down a certain priest that way; and when he saw him, he passed by on the other side.
>
> And likewise a Levite, when he was at the place, came and looked on him, and passed by on the other side.
>
> But a certain Samaritan, as he journeyed, came where he was; and when he saw him he had compassion on him.
>
> And went to him, and bound up his wounds, pouring in oil and wine, and set him on his own beast, and brought him to an inn, and took care of him.
>
> And on the morrow, when he departed, he took out two pence, and gave them to the host, and said unto him, "Take care of him; and whatsoever thou spendest more, when I come again, I will repay thee."
>
> (Luke 10:30–35)

The Good Samaritan went out of his way, at some cost to himself, to help one in need of it. We are not told what the options were, that is, whether or not the priest and the Levite could have helped by doing less than the Good Samaritan did, but assuming they could have, then the fact they did nothing at all shows they were not even Minimally Decent Samaritans, not because they were not Samaritans, but because they were not even minimally decent.

These things are a matter of degree, of course, but there is a difference, and it comes out perhaps most clearly in the story of Kitty Genovese, who, as you will remember, was murdered while thirty-eight people watched or listened, and did nothing at all to help her. A Good Samaritan would have rushed out to give direct assistance against the murderer. Or perhaps we had better allow that it would have been a Splendid Samaritan who did this, on the ground that it would have involved a risk of death for himself. But the thirty-eight not only did not do this, they did not

even trouble to pick up a phone to call the police. Minimally Decent Samaritanism would call for doing at least that, and their not having done it was monstrous.

After telling the story of the Good Samaritan, Jesus said "Go, and do thou likewise." Perhaps he meant that we are morally required to act as the Good Samaritan did. Perhaps he was urging people to do more than is morally required of them. At all events it seems plain that it was not morally required of any of the thirty-eight that he rush out to give direct assistance at the risk of his own life, and that it is not morally required of anyone that he give long stretches of his life—nine years or nine months—to sustaining the life of a person who has no special right (we were leaving open the possibility of this) to demand it.

Indeed, with one rather striking class of exceptions, no one in any country in the world is *legally* required to do anywhere near as much as this for anyone else. The class of exceptions is obvious. My main concern here is not the state of the law in respect to abortion, but it is worth drawing attention to the fact that in no state in this country is any man compelled by law to be even a Minimally Decent Samaritan to any person; there is no law under which charges could be brought against the thirty-eight who stood by while Kitty Genovese died. By contrast, in most states in this country women are compelled by law to be not merely Minimally Decent Samaritans, but Good Samaritans to unborn persons inside them. This doesn't by itself settle anything one way or the other, because it may well be argued that there should be laws in this country—as there are in many European countries—compelling at least Minimally Decent Samaritanism. But it does show that there is a gross injustice in the existing state of the law. And it shows also that the groups currently working against liberalization of abortion laws, in fact working toward having it declared unconstitutional for a state to permit abortion, had better start working for the adoption of Good Samaritan laws generally, or earn the charge that they are acting in bad faith.

I should think, myself, that Minimally Decent Samaritan laws would be one thing, Good Samaritan laws quite another, and in fact highly improper. But we are not here concerned with the law. What we should ask is not whether anybody should be compelled by law to be a Good Samaritan, but whether we must accede to a situation in which somebody is being compelled—by nature, perhaps—to be a Good Samaritan. We have, in other words, to look now at third-party interventions. I have been arguing that no person is morally required to make large sacrifices to sustain the life of another who has no right to demand them, and this even where the sacrifices do not include life itself; we are not morally required to be Good Samaritans or anyway Very Good Samaritans to one another. But what if a man cannot extricate himself from such a situation? What if he appeals to us to extricate him? It seems to me plain that there are cases in which we can, cases in which a Good Samaritan would extricate him. There you are, you were kidnapped, and nine years in bed with that violinist lie ahead of you. You have your own life to lead. You are sorry, but you simply cannot see giving up so much of your life to the sustaining of his. You cannot extricate yourself, and ask us to do so. I should have thought that—in light of his having no right to the use of your body—it was obvious that we do not have to accede to your being forced to give up so much. We can do what you ask. There is no injustice to the violinist in our doing so.

7. Following the lead of the opponents of abortion, I have throughout been speaking of the fetus merely as a person, and what I have been asking is whether or not the argument we began with, which proceeds only from the fetus' being a person, really does establish its conclusion. I have argued that it does not.

But of course there are arguments and arguments, and it may be said that I have simply fastened on the wrong one. It may be said that what is important is not merely the fact that the fetus is a person, but that it is a person for whom the woman has a special kind of responsibility issuing from the fact that she is its mother. And it might be argued that all my analogies are therefore irrelevant—for you do not have that special kind of responsibility for that violinist, Henry Fonda does not have that special kind of responsibility for me. And our attention might be drawn to the fact that men and women both *are* compelled by law to provide support for their children.

I have in effect dealt (briefly) with this argument in section 4 above; but a (still briefer) recapitulation now may be in order. Surely we do not have any such "special responsibility" for a person unless we have assumed it, explicitly or implicitly. If a set of parents do not try to prevent pregnancy, do not obtain an abortion, and then at the time of birth of the child do not put it out for adoption, but rather take it home with them, then they have assumed responsibility for it, they have given it rights, and they cannot *now* withdraw support from it at the cost of its life because they now find it difficult to go on providing for it. But if they have taken all reasonable precautions against having a child, they do not simply by virtue of their biological relationship to the child who comes into existence have a special responsibility for it. They may wish to assume responsibility for it, or they may not wish to. And I am suggesting that if assuming responsibility for it would require large sacrifices, then they may refuse. A Good Samaritan would not refuse—or anyway, a Splendid Samaritan, if the sacrifices that had to be made were enormous. But then so would a Good Samaritan assume responsibility for that violinist; so would Henry Fonda, if he is a Good Samaritan, fly in from the West Coast and assume responsibility for me.

8. My argument will be found unsatisfactory on two counts by many of those who want to regard abortion as morally permissible. First, while I do argue that abortion is not impermissible, I do not argue that it is always permissible. There may well be cases in which carrying the child to term requires only Minimally Decent Samaritanism of the mother, and this is a standard we must not fall below. I am inclined to think it a merit of my account precisely that it does *not* give a general yes or a general no. It allows for and supports our sense that, for example, a sick and desperately frightened fourteen-year-old schoolgirl, pregnant due to rape, may *of course* choose abortion, and that any law which rules this out is an insane law. And it also allows for and supports our sense that in other cases resort to abortion is even positively indecent. It would be indecent in the woman to request an abortion, and indecent in a doctor to perform it, if she is in her seventh month, and wants the abortion just to avoid the

nuisance of postponing a trip abroad. The very fact that the arguments I have been drawing attention to treat all cases of abortion, or even all cases of abortion in which the mother's life is not at stake, as morally on a par ought to have made them suspect at the outset.

Secondly, while I am arguing for the permissibility of abortion in some cases, I am not arguing for the right to secure the death of the unborn child. It is easy to confuse these two things in that up to a certain point in the life of the fetus it is not able to survive outside the mother's body; hence removing it from her body guarantees its death. But they are importantly different. I have argued that you are not morally required to spend nine months in bed, sustaining the life of that violinist; but to say this is by no means to say that if, when you unplug yourself, there is a miracle and he survives, you then have a right to turn round and slit his throat. You may detach yourself even if this costs him his life; you have no right to be guaranteed his death, by some other means, if unplugging yourself does not kill him. There are some people who will feel dissatisfied by this feature of my argument. A woman may be utterly devastated by the thought of a child, a bit of herself, put out for adoption and never seen or heard of again. She may therefore want not merely that the child be detached from her, but more, that it die. Some opponents of abortion are inclined to regard this as beneath contempt—thereby showing insensitivity to what is surely a powerful source of despair. All the same, I agree that the desire for the child's death is not one which anybody may gratify, should it turn out to be possible to detach the child alive.

At this place, however, it should be remembered that we have only been pretending throughout that the fetus is a human being from the moment of conception. A very early abortion is surely not the killing of a person, and so is not dealt with by anything I have said here.

NOTE

1. The term "direct" in the arguments I refer to is a technical one. Roughly, what is meant by "direct killing" is either killing as an end in itself, or killing as a means to some end, for example, the end of saving someone else's life.

On the Moral and Legal Status of Abortion

MARY ANNE WARREN

We will be concerned with both the moral status of abortion, which for our purposes we may define as the act which a woman performs in voluntarily terminating, or allowing another person to terminate, her pregnancy, and the legal status which is appropriate for this act. I will argue that, while it is not possible to produce a satisfactory defense of a woman's right to obtain an abortion without showing that a fetus is not a human being, in the morally relevant sense of that term, we ought not to conclude that the difficulties involved in determining whether or not a fetus is human make it impossible to produce any satisfactory solution to the problem of the moral status of abortion. For it is possible to show that, on the basis of intuitions which we may expect even the opponents of abortion to share, a fetus is not a person, and hence not the sort of entity to which it is proper to ascribe full moral rights.

Of course, while some philosophers would deny the possibility of any such proof, others will deny that there is any need for it, since the moral permissibility of

Mary Anne Warren, excerpts from "On the Moral and Legal Status of Abortion" in *The Monist* Volume 57, pp. 43–61. Copyright © *The Monist: An International Quarterly Journal of General Philosophical Inquiry*, The Hegeler Institute, Peru, IL. Reprinted by permission.

abortion appears to them to be too obvious to require proof. But the inadequacy of this attitude should be evident from the fact that both the friends and the foes of abortion consider their position to be morally self-evident. Because proabortionists have never adequately come to grips with the conceptual issues surrounding abortion, most if not all, of the arguments which they advance in opposition to laws restricting access to abortion fail to refute or even weaken the traditional antiabortion argument, i.e., that a fetus is a human being, and therefore abortion is murder.

These arguments are typically of one of two sorts. Either they point to the terrible side effects of the restrictive laws, e.g., the deaths due to illegal abortions, and the fact that it is poor women who suffer the most as a result of these laws, or else they state that to deny a woman access to abortion is to deprive her of her right to control her own body. Unfortunately, however, the fact that restricting access to abortion has tragic side effects does not, in itself, show that the restrictions are unjustified, since murder is wrong regardless of the consequences of prohibiting it; and the appeal to the right to control one's body, which is generally construed as a property right, is at best a rather feeble argument for the permissibility of abortion. Mere ownership does not give me the right to kill innocent people whom I find on my property, and indeed I am apt to be held responsible if such people injure themselves while on my property. It is equally unclear that I have any moral right to expel an innocent person from my property when I know that doing so will result in his death.

Furthermore, it is probably inappropriate to describe a woman's body as her property, since it seems natural to hold that a person is something distinct from her property, but not from her body. Even those who would object to the identification of a person with his body, or with the conjunction of his body and his mind, must admit that it would be very odd to describe, say, breaking a leg, as damaging one's property, and much more appropriate to describe it as injuring one*self*. Thus it is probably a mistake to argue that the right to obtain an abortion is in any way derived from the right to own and regulate property.

But however we wish to construe the right to abortion, we cannot hope to convince those who consider abortion a form of murder of the existence of any such right unless we are able to produce a clear and convincing refutation of the traditional antiabortion argument, and this has not, to my knowledge, been done. With respect to the two most vital issues which that argument involves, i.e., the humanity of the fetus and its implication for the moral status of abortion, confusion has prevailed on both sides of the dispute.

Thus, both proabortionists and antiabortionists have tended to abstract the question of whether abortion is wrong to that of whether it is wrong to destroy a fetus, just as though the rights of another person were not necessarily involved. This mistaken abstraction has led to the almost universal assumption that if a fetus is a human being, with a right to life, then it follows immediately that abortion is wrong (except perhaps when necessary to save the woman's life), and that it ought to be prohibited. It has also been generally assumed that unless the question about the status of the fetus is answered, the moral status of abortion cannot possibly be determined.

* * *

Judith Thomson is . . . the only writer I am aware of who has seriously questioned this assumption; she has argued that, even if we grant the antiabortionist his claim that a fetus is a human being, with the same right to life as any other human being, we can still demonstrate that, in at least some and perhaps most cases, a woman is under no moral obligation to complete an unwanted pregnancy.[1] Her argument is worth examining, since if it holds up it may enable us to establish the moral permissibility of abortion without becoming involved in problems about what entitles an entity to be considered human, and accorded full moral rights. To be able to do this would be a great gain in the power and simplicity of the proabortion position, since, although I will argue that these problems can be solved at least as decisively as can any other moral problem, we should certainly be pleased to be able to avoid having to solve them as part of the justification of abortion.

On the other hand, even if Thomson's argument does not hold up, her insight, i.e., that it requires *argument* to show that if fetuses are human then abortion is properly classified as murder, is an extremely valuable one. The assumption she attacks is particularly invidious, for it amounts to the decision that it is appropriate, in deciding the moral status of abortion, to leave the rights of the pregnant woman out of consideration entirely, except possibly when her life is threatened. Obviously, this will not do; determining what moral rights, if any, a fetus possesses is only the first step in determining the moral status of abortion. Step two, which is at least equally essential, is finding a just solution to the conflict between whatever rights the fetus may have, and the rights of the woman who is unwillingly pregnant. While the historical error has been to pay far too little attention to the second step, Ms. Thomson's suggestion is that if we look at the second step first we may find that a woman has a right to obtain an abortion *regardless* of what rights the fetus has.

Our own inquiry will also have two stages. In Section I, we will consider whether or not it is possible to establish that abortion is morally permissible even on the assumption that a fetus is an entity with a full-fledged right to life. I will argue that in fact this cannot be established, at least not with the conclusiveness which is essential to our hopes of convincing those who are skeptical about the morality of abortion, and that we therefore cannot avoid dealing with the question of whether or not a fetus really does have the same right to life as a (more fully developed) human being.

In Section II, I will propose an answer to this question, namely, that a fetus cannot be considered a member of the moral community, the set of beings with full and equal moral rights, for the simple reason that it is not a person, and that it is personhood, and not genetic humanity, . . . which is the basis for membership in this community. I will argue that a fetus, whatever its stage of development, satisfies none of the basic criteria of personhood, and is not even enough *like* a person to be accorded even some of the same rights on the basis of this resemblance. Nor, as we will see, is a fetus's *potential* personhood a threat to the morality of abortion, since, whatever the rights of potential people may be, they are invariably overridden in any conflict with the moral rights of actual people.

I

We turn now to Professor Thomson's case for the claim that even if a fetus has full moral rights, abortion is still morally permissible, at least sometimes, and for some reasons other than to save the woman's life. Her argument is based upon a clever, but I think faulty, analogy. She asks us to picture ourselves waking up one day, in bed with a famous violinist. Imagine that you have been kidnapped, and your bloodstream hooked up to that of the violinist, who happens to have an ailment which will certainly kill him unless he is permitted to share your kidneys for a period of nine months. No one else can save him, since you alone have the right type of blood. He will be unconscious all that time, and you will have to stay in bed with him, but after the nine months are over he may be unplugged, completely cured, that is provided that you have cooperated.

Now then, she continues, what are your obligations in this situation? The antiabortionist, if he is consistent, will have to say that you are obligated to stay in bed with the violinist: for all people have a right to life, and violinists are people, and therefore it would be murder for you to disconnect yourself from him and let him die [p. 238]. But this is outrageous, and so there must be something wrong with the same argument when it is applied to abortion. It would certainly be commendable of you to agree to save the violinist, but it is absurd to suggest that your refusal to do so would be murder. His right to life does not obligate you to do whatever is required to keep him alive; nor does it justify anyone else in forcing you to do so. A law which required you to stay in bed with the violinist would clearly be an unjust law, since it is no proper function of the law to force unwilling people to make huge sacrifices for the sake of other people toward whom they have no such prior obligation.

Thomson concludes that, if this analogy is an apt one, then we can grant the antiabortionist his claim that a fetus is a human being, and still hold that it is at least sometimes the case that a pregnant woman has the right to refuse to be a Good Samaritan towards the fetus, i.e., to obtain an abortion. For there is a great gap between the claim that *x* has a right to life, and the claim that *y* is obligated to do whatever is necessary to keep *x* alive, let alone that he ought to be forced to do so. It is *y*'s duty to keep *x* alive only if he has somehow contracted a *special* obligation to do so; and a woman who is unwillingly pregnant, e.g., who was raped, has done nothing which obligates her to make the enormous sacrifice which is necessary to preserve the conceptus.

This argument is initially quite plausible, and in the extreme case of pregnancy due to rape it is probably conclusive. Difficulties arise, however, when we try to specify more exactly the range of cases in which abortion is clearly justifiable even on the assumption that the fetus is human. Professor Thomson considers it a virtue of her argument that it does not enable us to conclude that abortion is *always* permissible. It would, she says, be "indecent" for a woman in her seventh month to obtain an abortion just to avoid having to postpone a trip to Europe. On the other hand, her argument enables us to see that "a sick and desperately frightened schoolgirl pregnant due to rape may *of course* choose abortion, and that any law which rules this out is an insane law" [p. 246]. So far, so good; but what are we to say about the woman who becomes pregnant not through rape but as a result of her own carelessness, or because of contraceptive failure, or who gets pregnant intentionally and then changes her mind about wanting a child? With respect to such cases, the violinist analogy is of much less use to the defender of the woman's right to obtain an abortion.

Indeed, the choice of a pregnancy due to rape, as an example of a case in which abortion is permissible even if a fetus is considered a human being, is extremely significant; for it is only in the case of pregnancy due to rape that the woman's situation is adequately analogous to the violinist case for our intuitions about the latter to transfer convincingly. The crucial difference between a pregnancy due to rape and the *normal* case of an unwanted pregnancy is that in the normal case, we cannot claim that the woman is in no way responsible for her predicament; she could have remained chaste, or taken her pills more faithfully, or abstained on dangerous days, and so on. If, on the other hand, you are kidnapped by strangers, and hooked up to a strange violinist, then you are free

of any shred of responsibility for the situation, on the basis of which it could be argued that you are obligated to keep the violinist alive. Only when her pregnancy is due to rape is a woman clearly just as nonresponsible.[2]

Consequently, there is room for the antiabortionist to argue that in the normal case of unwanted pregnancy a woman has, by her own actions, assumed responsibility for the fetus. For if *x* behaves in a way which he could have avoided, and which he knows involves, let us say, a 1 percent chance of bringing into existence a human being, with a right to life, and does so knowing that if this should happen then that human being will perish unless *x* does certain things to keep him alive, then it is by no means clear that when it does happen *x* is free of any obligation to what he knew in advance would be required to keep that human being alive.

The plausibility of such an argument is enough to show that the Thomson analogy can provide a clear and persuasive defense of a woman's right to obtain an abortion only with respect to those cases in which the woman is in no way responsible for her pregnancy, e.g., where it is due to rape. In all other cases, we would almost certainly conclude that it was necessary to look carefully at the particular circumstances in order to determine the extent of the woman's responsibility, and hence the extent of her obligation. This is an extremely unsatisfactory outcome, from the viewpoint of the opponents of restrictive abortion laws, most of whom are convinced that a woman has a right to obtain an abortion regardless of how and why she got pregnant.

Of course a supporter of the violinist analogy might point out that it is absurd to suggest that forgetting her pill one day might be sufficient to obligate a woman to complete an unwanted pregnancy. And indeed it *is* absurd to suggest this. As we will see, the moral right to obtain an abortion is not in the least dependent upon the extent to which the woman is responsible for her pregnancy. But unfortunately, once we allow the assumption that a fetus has full moral rights, we cannot avoid taking this absurd suggestion seriously. Perhaps we can make this point more clear by altering the violinist story just enough to make it more analogous to a normal unwanted pregnancy and less to a pregnancy due to rape, and then seeing whether it is still obvious that you are not obligated to stay in bed with the fellow.

Suppose, then, that violinists are peculiarly prone to the sort of illness the only cure for which is the use of someone else's bloodstream for nine months, and that because of this there has been formed a society of music lovers who agree that whenever a violinist is stricken they will draw lots and the loser will, by some means, be made the one and only person capable of saving him. Now then, would you be obligated to cooperate in curing the violinist if you had voluntarily joined this society, knowing the possible consequences, and then your name had been drawn and you had been kidnapped? Admittedly, you did not promise ahead of time that you would, but you did deliberately place yourself in a position in which it might happen that a human life would be lost if you did not. Surely this is at least a prima facie reason for supposing that you have an obligation to stay in bed with the violinist. Suppose that you had gotten your name drawn deliberately; surely *that* would be quite a strong reason for thinking that you had such an obligation.

It might be suggested that there is one important disanalogy between the modified violinist case and the case of an unwanted pregnancy, which makes the woman's responsibility significantly less, namely, the fact that the fetus *comes into existence* as the result of the woman's actions. This fact might give her a right to refuse to keep it alive, whereas she would not have had this right had it existed previously, independently, and then as a result of her actions become dependent upon her for its survival.

My own intuition, however, is that x has no more right to bring into existence, either deliberately or as a foreseeable result of actions he could have avoided, a being with full moral rights (y), and then refuse to do what he knew beforehand would be required to keep that being alive, then he has to enter into an agreement with an existing person, whereby he may be called upon to save that person's life, and then refuse to do so when so called upon. Thus, x's responsibility for y's existence does not seem to lessen his obligation to keep y alive, if he is also responsible for y's being in a situation in which only he can save him.

Whether or not this intuition is entirely correct, it brings us back once again to the conclusion that once we allow the assumption that a fetus has full moral rights it becomes an extremely complex and difficult question whether and when abortion is justifiable. Thus the Thomson analogy cannot help us produce a clear and persuasive proof of the moral permissibility of abortion. Nor will the opponents of the restrictive laws thank us for anything less; for their conviction (for the most part) is that abortion is obviously *not* a morally serious and extremely unfortunate, even though sometimes justified act, comparable to killing in self-defense or to letting the violinist die, but rather is closer to being a morally neutral act, like cutting one's hair.

The basis of this conviction, I believe, is the realization that a fetus is not a person, and thus does not have a full-fledged right to life. Perhaps the reason why this claim has been so inadequately defended is that it seems self-evident to those who accept it. And so it is, insofar as it follows from what I take to be perfectly obvious claims about the nature of personhood, and about the proper grounds for ascribing moral rights, claims which ought, indeed, to be obvious to both the friends and foes of abortion. Nevertheless, it is worth examining these claims, and showing how they demonstrate the moral innocuousness of abortion, since this apparently has not been adequately done before.

II

The question which we must answer in order to produce a satisfactory solution to the problem of the moral status of abortion is this: How are we to define the moral community, the set of beings with full and equal moral rights, such that we can decide whether a human fetus is a member of this community or not? What sort of entity, exactly, has the inalienable rights to life, liberty, and the pursuit of happiness? . . . What reason is there for identifying the moral community with the set of all human beings, in whatever way we have chosen to define that term?

1. On the Definition of 'Human'

One reason why this vital . . . question is so frequently overlooked in the debate over the moral status of abortion is that the term 'human' has two distinct, but not often distinguished, senses. This fact results in a slide of meaning, which serves to conceal the fallaciousness of the traditional argument that since (1) it is wrong to kill innocent human beings, and (2) fetuses are innocent human beings, then (3) it is wrong to kill fetuses. For if 'human' is used in the same sense in both (1) and (2) then, whichever of the two senses is meant, one of these premises is question-begging. And if it is used in two different senses then of course the conclusion doesn't follow.

Thus, (1) is a self-evident moral truth,[3] and avoids begging the question about abortion, only if 'human being' is used to mean something like "a full-fledged member of the moral community." (It may or may not also be meant to refer exclusively to members of the species *Homo sapiens*.) We may call this the *moral* sense of 'human'. It is not to be confused with what we will call the *genetic* sense, i.e., the sense in which *any* member of the species is a human being, and no member of any other species could be. If (1) is acceptable only if the moral sense is intended, (2) is non-question-begging only if what is intended is the genetic sense.

In "Deciding Who is Human," [John] Noonan argues for the classification of fetuses with human beings by pointing to the presence of the full genetic code, and the potential capacity for rational thought.[4] It is clear that what he needs to show, for his version of the traditional argument to be valid, is that fetuses are human in the moral sense, the sense in which it is analytically true that all human beings have full moral rights. But, in the absence of any argument showing that whatever is genetically human is also morally human, and he gives none, nothing more than genetic humanity can be demonstrated by the presence of the human genetic code. And, as we will see, the *potential* capacity for rational thought can at most show that an entity has the potential for *becoming* human in the moral sense.

2. Defining the Moral Community

Can it be established that genetic humanity is sufficient for moral humanity? I think that there are very good reasons for not defining the moral community in this way. I would like to suggest an alternative way of defining the moral community, which I will argue for only to the extent of explaining why it is, or should be, self-evident. The suggestion is simply that the moral community consists of all and only *people*, rather than all and only human beings;[5] and probably the best way of demonstrating its self-evidence is by considering the concept of personhood, to see what sorts of entity are and are not persons, and what the decision that a being is or is not a person implies about its moral rights.

What characteristics entitle an entity to be considered a person? This is obviously not the place to attempt a complete analysis of the concept of personhood, but we do not need such a fully adequate analysis just to determine whether and why a fetus is or isn't a person. All we need is a rough and approximate list of the most basic criteria of personhood, and some idea of which, or how many, of these an entity must satisfy in order to properly be considered a person.

In searching for such criteria, it is useful to look beyond the set of people with whom we are acquainted, and ask how we would decide whether a totally alien being was a person or not. (For we have no right to assume that genetic humanity is necessary for personhood.) Imagine a space traveler who lands on an unknown planet and encounters a race of beings utterly unlike any he has ever seen or heard of. If he wants to be sure of behaving morally toward these beings, he has to somehow decide whether they are people, and hence have full moral rights, or whether they are the sort of thing which he need not feel guilty about treating as, for example, a source of food.

How should he go about making this decision? If he has some anthropological background, he might look for such things as religion, art, and the manufacturing of tools, weapons, or shelters, since these factors have been used to distinguish our human from our prehuman ancestors, in what seems to be closer to the moral than the genetic sense of 'human'. And no doubt he would be right to consider the presence of such factors as good evidence that the alien beings were people, and morally human. It would, however, be overly anthropocentric of him to take the absence of these things as adequate evidence that they were not, since we can imagine people who have progressed beyond, or evolved without ever developing, these cultural characteristics.

I suggest that the traits which are most central to the concept of personhood, or humanity in the moral sense, are, very roughly, the following:

1. consciousness (of objects and events external and/or internal to the being), and in particular the capacity to feel pain;
2. reasoning (the *developed* capacity to solve new and relatively complex problems);
3. self-motivated activity (activity which is relatively independent of either genetic or direct external control);
4. the capacity to communicate, by whatever means, messages of an indefinite variety of types, that is, not just with an indefinite number of possible contents, but on indefinitely many possible topics;
5. the presence of self-concepts, and self-awareness, either individual or racial, or both.

Admittedly, there are apt to be a great many problems involved in formulating precise definitions of these criteria, let alone in developing universally valid behavioral criteria for deciding when they apply. But I will assume that both we and our explorer know approximately what (1)–(5) mean, and that he is also able to determine whether or not they apply. How, then should he use his findings to decide whether or not the alien beings are people? We needn't suppose that an entity must have *all* of these attributes to be properly considered a person; (1) and (2) alone may well be sufficient for personhood, and quite probably (1)–(3) are sufficient. Neither do we need to insist that any one of these criteria is *necessary* for personhood, although once again (1) and (2) look like fairly good candidates for necessary conditions, as does (3), if 'activity' is construed so as to include the activity of reasoning.

All we need to claim, to demonstrate that a fetus is not a person, is that any being which satisfies *none* of (1)–(5) is certainly not a person. I consider this claim to be so obvious that I think anyone who denied it, and claimed that a being which satisfied none of (1)–(5) was a person all the same, would thereby demonstrate that he had no notion at all of what a person is—perhaps because he had confused the concept of a person with that of genetic humanity. If the opponents of abortion were to deny the appropriateness of these five criteria, I do not know what further arguments would convince them. We would probably have to admit that our conceptual schemes were indeed irreconcilably different, and that our dispute could not be settled objectively.

I do not expect this to happen, however, since I think that the concept of a person is one which is very nearly universal (to people), and that it is common to both proabortionists and antiabortionists, even though neither group has fully realized the relevance of this concept to the resolution of their dispute. Furthermore, I think that on reflection even the antiabortionists ought to agree not only that (1)–(5) are central to the concept of personhood, but also that it is a part of this concept that all and only people have full moral rights. The concept of a person is in part a moral concept; once we have admitted that *x* is a person we have recognized, even if we have not agreed to respect, *x*'s right to be treated as a member of the moral community. It is true that the claim that *x* is a *human being* is more commonly voiced as part of an appeal to treat *x* decently than is the claim that *x* is a person, but this is either because 'human being' is here used in the sense which implies personhood, or because the genetic and moral senses of 'human' have been confused.

Now if (1)–(5) are indeed the primary criteria of personhood, then it is clear that genetic humanity is neither necessary nor sufficient for establishing that an entity is a person. Some human beings are not people, and there may well be people who are not human beings. A man or woman whose consciousness has been permanently obliterated but who remains alive is a human being which is no longer a person; defective human beings, with no appreciable mental capacity, are not and presumably never will be people; and a fetus is a human being which is not yet a person, and which therefore cannot coherently be said to have full moral rights. Citizens of the next century should be prepared to recognize highly advanced, self-aware robots or computers, should such be developed, and intelligent inhabitants of other worlds, should such be found, as people in the fullest sense, and to respect their moral rights. But to ascribe full moral rights to an entity which is not a person is as absurd as to ascribe moral obligations and responsibilities to such an entity.

3. Fetal Development and the Right to Life

Two problems arise in the application of these suggestions for the definition of the moral community to the determination of the precise moral status of a human fetus. Given that the paradigm example of a person is a normal adult human being, then (1) How like this paradigm, in particular how far advanced since conception, does a human being need to be before it begins to have a right to life by virtue, not of being fully a person as of yet, but of being *like* a person? and (2) To what extent, if any, does the fact that a fetus has the *potential* for becoming a person endow it with some of the same rights? Each of these questions requires some comment.

In answering the first question, we need not attempt a detailed consideration of the moral rights of organisms which are not developed enough, aware enough, intelligent enough, etc., to be considered people, but which resemble people in some respects. It does seem reasonable to suggest that the more like a person, in the relevant respects, a being is, the stronger is the case for regarding it as having a right to life, and indeed the stronger its right to life is. Thus we ought to take seriously the suggestion that, insofar as "the human individual develops biologically in a continuous fashion . . . the rights of a human person might develop in the same way."[6] But we must keep in mind that the attributes which are relevant in determining whether or not an entity is enough like a person to be regarded as having some of the same moral rights are no different from those which are relevant to determining whether or not it is fully a person—i.e., are no different from (1)–(5)—and that being genetically human, or having recognizably human facial and other physical features, or detectable brain activity, or the capacity to survive outside the uterus, are simply not among these relevant attributes.

Thus it is clear that even though a seven- or eight-month fetus has features which make it apt to arouse in us almost the same powerful protective instinct as is commonly aroused by a small infant, nevertheless it is not significantly more personlike than is a very small embryo. It is *somewhat* more personlike; it can apparently feel and respond to pain, and it may even have a rudimentary form of consciousness, insofar as its brain is quite active. Nevertheless, it seems safe to say that it is not fully conscious, in the way that an infant of a few months is, and that it cannot reason, or communicate messages of indefinitely many sorts, does not engage in self-motivated activity, and has no self-awareness. Thus, in the *relevant* respects, a fetus, even a fully developed one, is considerably less personlike than is the average mature mammal, indeed the average fish. And I think that a rational person must conclude that if the right to life of a fetus is to be based upon its resemblance to a person, then it cannot be said to have any more right to life than, let us say, a newborn guppy (which also seems to be capable of feeling pain), and that a right of that magnitude could never override a woman's right to obtain an abortion, at any stage of her pregnancy.

There may, of course, be other arguments in favor of placing legal limits upon the stage of pregnancy in which an abortion may be performed. Given the relative safety of the new techniques of artificially inducing labor during the third trimester, the danger to the woman's life or health is no longer such an argument. Neither is the fact that people tend to respond to the thought of abortion in the later stages of pregnancy with emotional repulsion, since mere emotional responses cannot take the place of moral reasoning in determining what ought to be permitted. Nor, finally, is the frequently heard argument that legalizing abortion, especially late in the pregnancy, may erode the level of respect for human life, leading, perhaps, to an increase in unjustified euthanasia and other crimes. For this threat, if it is a threat, can be better met by educating people to the kinds of moral distinctions which we are making here than by limiting access to abortion (which limitation may, in its disregard for the rights of women, be just as damaging to the level of respect for human rights).

Thus, since the fact that even a fully developed fetus is not personlike enough to have any significant right to life on the basis of its personlikeness shows that no legal restrictions upon the stage of pregnancy in which an abortion may be performed can be justified on the grounds that we should protect the rights of the older fetus; and since there is no other apparent justification for such restrictions, we may conclude that they are entirely unjustified. Whether or not it would be *indecent* (whatever that means) for a woman in her seventh month to obtain an abortion just to avoid having to postpone a trip to Europe, it would not, in itself, be *immoral,* and therefore it ought to be permitted.

4. Potential Personhood and the Right to Life

We have seen that a fetus does not resemble a person in any way which can support the claim that it has even some of the same rights. But what about its *potential*, the fact that if nurtured and allowed to develop naturally it will very probably become a person? Doesn't that alone give it at least some right to life? It is hard to deny that the fact that an entity is a potential person is a strong prima facie reason for not destroying it; but we need not conclude from this that a potential person has a right to life, by virtue of that potential. It may be that our feeling that it is better, other things being equal, not to destroy a potential person is better explained by the fact that potential people are still (felt to be) an invaluable resource, not to be lightly squandered. Surely, if every speck of dust were a potential person, we would be much less apt to conclude that every potential person has a right to become actual.

Still, we do not need to insist that a potential person has no right to life whatever. There may well be something immoral, and not just imprudent, about wantonly destroying potential people, when doing so isn't necessary to protect anyone's rights. But even if a potential person does have some prima facie right to life, such a right could not possibly outweigh the right of a woman to obtain an abortion, since the rights of any actual person invariably outweigh those of any potential person, whenever the two conflict. Since this may not be immediately obvious in the case of a human fetus, let us look at another case.

Suppose that our space explorer falls into the hands of an alien culture, whose scientists decide to create

a few hundred thousand or more human beings, by breaking his body into its component cells, and using these to create fully developed human beings, with, of course, his genetic code. We may imagine that each of these newly created men will have all of the original man's abilities, skills, knowledge, and so on, and also have an individual self-concept, in short that each of them will be a bona fide (though hardly unique) person. Imagine that the whole project will take only seconds, and that its chances of success are extremely high, and that our explorer knows all of this, and also knows that these people will be treated fairly. I maintain that in such a situation he would have every right to escape if he could, and thus to deprive all of these potential people of their potential lives; for his right to life outweighs all of theirs together, in spite of the fact that they are all genetically human, all innocent, and all have a very high probability of becoming people very soon, if only he refrains from acting.

Indeed, I think he would have a right to escape even if it were not his life which the alien scientists planned to take, but only a year of his freedom, or, indeed, only a day. Nor would he be obligated to stay if he had gotten captured (thus bringing all these people-potentials into existence) because of his own carelessness, or even if he had done so deliberately, knowing the consequences. Regardless of how he got captured, he is not morally obligated to remain in captivity for *any* period of time for the sake of permitting any number of potential people to come into actuality, so great is the margin by which one actual person's right to liberty outweighs whatever right to life even a hundred thousand potential people have. And it seems reasonable to conclude that the rights of a woman will outweigh by a similar margin whatever right to life a fetus may have by virtue of its potential personhood.

Thus, neither a fetus's resemblance to a person, nor its potential for becoming a person provides any basis whatever for the claim that it has any significant right to life. Consequently, a woman's right to protect her health, happiness, freedom, and even her life,[7] by terminating an unwanted pregnancy, will always override whatever right to life it may be appropriate to ascribe to a fetus, even a fully developed one. And thus, in the absence of any overwhelming social need for every possible child, the laws which restrict the right to obtain an abortion, or limit the period of pregnancy during which an abortion may be performed, are a wholly unjustified violation of a woman's most basic moral and constitutional rights.

NOTES

1. Judith Thomson, "A Defense of Abortion," *Philosophy & Public Affairs* 1, no. 1 (Fall 1971): 47–66.

2. We may safely ignore the fact that she might have avoided getting raped, e.g., by carrying a gun, since by similar means you might likewise have avoided getting kidnapped, and in neither case does the victim's failure to take all possible precautions against a highly unlikely event (as opposed to reasonable precautions against a rather likely event) mean that he is morally responsible for what happens.

3. Of course, the principle that it is (always) wrong to kill innocent human beings is in need of many other modifications, e.g., that it may be permissible to do so to save a greater number of other innocent human beings, but we may safely ignore these complications here.

4. John Noonan, "Deciding Who Is Human," *Natural Law Forum* 13 (1968): 135.

5. From here on, we will use 'human' to mean genetically human, since the moral sense seems closely connected to, and perhaps derived from, the assumption that genetic humanity is sufficient for membership in the moral community.

6. Thomas L. Hayes, "A Biological View," *Commonweal* 85 (March 17, 1967): 677–78; quoted by Daniel Callahan, in *Abortion: Law, Choice, and Morality* (New York: Macmillan, 1970).

7. That is, insofar as the death rate, for the woman, is higher for childbirth than for early abortion.

Why Abortion Is Immoral

Don Marquis

The view that abortion is, with rare exceptions, seriously immoral has received little support in the recent philosophical literature. No doubt most philosophers affiliated with secular institutions of higher education believe that the anti-abortion position is either a symptom of irrational religious dogma or a conclusion generated by seriously confused philosophical argument. The purpose of this essay is to undermine this general belief. This essay sets out an argument that purports to show, as well as any argument in ethics can show, that abortion is, except possibly in rare cases, seriously immoral, that it is in the same moral category as killing an innocent adult human being.

Don Marquis, "Why Abortion Is Immoral," *The Journal of Philosophy* LXXXVI, 4 (April 1989): 183–202. Reprinted by permission of the publisher and the author.

The argument is based on a major assumption. Many of the most insightful and careful writers on the ethics of abortion . . . believe that whether or not abortion is morally permissible stands or falls on whether or not a fetus is the sort of being whose life it is seriously wrong to end. The argument of this essay will assume, but not argue, that they are correct.

Also, this essay will neglect issues of great importance to a complete ethics of abortion. Some anti-abortionists will allow that certain abortions, such as abortion before implantation or abortion when the life of a woman is threatened by a pregnancy or abortion after rape, may be morally permissible. This essay will not explore the casuistry of these hard cases. The purpose of this essay is to develop a general argument for the claim that the overwhelming majority of deliberate abortions are seriously immoral.

I.

A sketch of standard anti-abortion and pro-choice arguments exhibits how these arguments possess certain symmetries that explain why partisans of those positions are so convinced of the correctness of their own positions, why they are not successful in convincing their opponents, and why, to others, this issue seems to be unresolvable. An analysis of the nature of this standoff suggests a strategy for surmounting it.

Consider the way a typical anti-abortionist argues. She will argue or assert that life is present from the moment of conception or that fetuses look like babies or that fetuses possess a characteristic such as a genetic code that is both necessary and sufficient for being human. Anti-abortionists seem to believe that (1) the truth of all of these claims is quite obvious, and (2) establishing any of these claims is sufficient to show that abortion is morally akin to murder.

A standard pro-choice strategy exhibits similarities. The pro-choicer will argue or assert that fetuses are not persons or that fetuses are not rational agents or that fetuses are not social beings. Pro-choicers seem to believe that (1) the truth of any of these claims is quite obvious, and (2) establishing any of these claims is sufficient to show that an abortion is not a wrongful killing.

In fact, both the pro-choice and the anti-abortion claims do seem to be true, although the "it looks like a baby" claim is more difficult to establish the earlier the pregnancy. We seem to have a standoff. How can it be resolved?

As everyone who has taken a bit of logic knows, if any of these arguments concerning abortion is a good argument, it requires not only some claim characterizing fetuses, but also some general moral principle that ties a characteristic of fetuses to having or not having the right to life or to some other moral characteristic that will generate the obligation or the lack of obligation not to end the life of a fetus. Accordingly, the arguments of the anti-abortionist and the pro-choicer need a bit of filling in to be regarded as adequate.

Note what each partisan will say. The anti-abortionist will claim that her position is supported by such generally accepted moral principles as "It is always prima facie seriously wrong to take a human life" or "It is always prima facie seriously wrong to end the life of a baby." Since these are generally accepted moral principles, her position is certainly not obviously wrong. The pro-choicer will claim that her position is supported by such plausible moral principles as "Being a person is what gives an individual intrinsic moral worth" or "It is only seriously prima facie wrong to take the life of a member of the human community." Since these are generally accepted moral principles, the pro-choice position is certainly not obviously wrong. Unfortunately, we have again arrived at a standoff.

Now, how might one deal with this standoff? The standard approach is to try to show how the moral principles of one's opponent lose their plausibility under analysis. It is easy to see how this is possible. On the one hand, the anti-abortionist will defend a moral principle concerning the wrongness of killing which tends to be broad in scope in order that even fetuses at an early stage of pregnancy will fall under it. The problem with broad principles is that they often embrace too much. In this particular instance, the principle "It is always prima facie wrong to take a human life" seems to entail that it is wrong to end the existence of a living human cancer-cell culture, on the grounds that the culture is both living and human. Therefore, it seems that the anti-abortionist's favored principle is too broad.

On the other hand, the pro-choicer wants to find a moral principle concerning the wrongness of killing which tends to be narrow in scope in order that fetuses will *not* fall under it. The problem with narrow principles is that they often do not embrace enough. Hence, the needed principles such as "It is prima facie seriously wrong to kill only persons" or "It is prima facie wrong to kill only rational agents" do not explain why it is wrong to kill infants or young children or the severely retarded or even perhaps the severely mentally ill. Therefore, we seem again to have a standoff. The anti-abortionist charges, not unreasonably, that pro-choice principles concerning killing are too narrow to be acceptable; the pro-choicer charges, not unreasonably, that anti-abortionist principles concerning killing are too broad to be acceptable.

Attempts by both sides to patch up the difficulties in their positions run into further difficulties. The anti-abortionist will try to remove the problem in her position by reformulating her principle concerning killing in terms of human beings. Now we end up with: "It is always prima facie seriously wrong to end the life of a human being." This principle has the advantage of avoiding the problem of the human cancer-cell culture counterexample. But this advantage is purchased at a high price. For although it is clear that a fetus is both human and alive, it is not at all clear that a fetus is a human *being*. There is at least something to be said for the view that something becomes a human being only after a process of development, and that therefore first trimester fetuses and perhaps all fetuses are not yet human beings. Hence, the anti-abortionist, by this move, has merely exchanged one problem for another.

The pro-choicer fares no better. She may attempt to find reasons why killing infants, young children, and the severely retarded is wrong which are independent of her major principle that is supposed to explain the wrongness of taking human life, but which will not also make abortion immoral. This is no easy task. Appeals to social utility will seem satisfactory only to those who resolve not to think of the enormous difficulties with a utilitarian account of the wrongness of killing and the significant social costs of preserving the lives of the unproductive. A pro-choice strategy that extends the definition of 'person' to infants or even to young children seems just as arbitrary as an anti-abortion strategy that extends the definition of 'human being' to fetuses. Again, we find symmetries in the two positions and we arrive at a standoff.

There are even further problems that reflect symmetries in the two positions. In addition to counterexample problems, or the arbitrary application problems that can be exchanged for them, the standard anti-abortionist principle "It is prima facie seriously wrong to kill a human being," or one of its variants, can be objected to on the grounds of ambiguity. If 'human being' is taken to be a *biological* category, then the anti-abortionist is left with the problem of explaining why a merely biological category should make a moral difference. Why, it is asked, is it any more reasonable to base a moral conclusion on the number of chromosomes in one's cells than on the color of one's skin? If 'human being', on the other hand, is taken to be a *moral* category, then the claim that a fetus is a human being cannot be taken to be a premise in the anti-abortion argument, for it is precisely what needs to be established. Hence, either the anti-abortionist's main category is a morally irrelevant, merely biological category, or it is of no use to the anti-abortionist in establishing (noncircularly, of course) that abortion is wrong.

Although this problem with the anti-abortionist position is often noticed, it is less often noticed that the pro-choice position suffers from an analogous problem. The principle "Only persons have the right to life" also suffers from an ambiguity. The term 'person' is typically defined in terms of psychological characteristics, although there will certainly be disagreement concerning which characteristics are most important. Supposing that this matter can be settled, the pro-choicer is left with the problem of explaining why *psychological* characteristics should make a *moral* difference. If the pro-choicer should attempt to deal with this problem by claiming that an explanation is not necessary, that in fact we do treat such a cluster of psychological properties as having moral significance, the sharp-witted anti-abortionist should have a ready response. We do treat being both living and human as having moral significance. If it is legitimate for the pro-choicer to demand that the anti-abortionist provide an explanation of the connection between the biological character of being a human being and the wrongness of being killed (even though people accept this connection), then it is legitimate for the anti-abortionist to demand that the pro-choicer provide an explanation of the connection between psychological criteria for being a person and the wrongness of being killed (even though that connection is accepted).

[Joel] Feinberg has attempted to meet this objection (he calls psychological personhood "common-sense personhood"):

The characteristics that confer commonsense personhood are not arbitrary bases for rights and duties, such as race, sex or species membership; rather they are traits that make sense out of rights and duties and without which those moral attributes would have no point or function. It is because people are conscious; have a sense of their personal identities; have plans, goals, and projects; experience emotions; are liable to pains, anxieties, and frustrations; can reason and bargain, and so on—it is because of these attributes that people have values and interests, desires and expectations of their own, including a stake in their own futures, and a personal well-being of a sort we cannot ascribe to unconscious or nonrational beings. Because of their developed capacities they can assume duties and responsibilities and can have and make claims on one another. Only because of their sense of self, their life plans, their value hierarchies, and their stakes in their own futures can they be ascribed fundamental rights. There is nothing arbitrary about these linkages.[1]

The plausible aspects of this attempt should not be taken to obscure its implausible features. There is a great deal to be said for the view that being a psychological person under some description is a necessary condition for having duties. One cannot have a duty unless one is capable of behaving morally, and a being's capability of behaving morally will require having a certain psychology. It is far from obvious, however, that having rights entails consciousness or rationality, as Feinberg suggests. We speak of the rights of the severely retarded or the severely mentally ill, yet some of these persons are not rational. We speak of the rights of the temporarily unconscious. The New Jersey Supreme Court based their decision in the Quinlan case on Karen Ann Quinlan's right to privacy, and she was known to be permanently unconscious at that time. Hence, Feinberg's claim that having rights entails being conscious is, on its face, obviously false.

Of course, it might not make sense to attribute rights to a being that would never in its natural history have certain psychological traits. This modest connection between psychological personhood and moral personhood will create a place for Karen Ann Quinlan and the temporarily unconscious. But then it makes a place for fetuses also. Hence, it does not serve Feinberg's pro-choice purposes. Accordingly, it seems that the pro-choicer will have as much difficulty bridging the gap between psychological personhood and personhood in the moral sense as the anti-abortionist has bridging the gap between being a biological human being and being a human being in the moral sense.

Furthermore, the pro-choicer cannot any more escape her problem by making person a purely moral category than the anti-abortionist could escape by the analogous move. For if person is a moral category, then the pro-choicer is left without the recourses for establishing (noncircularly, of course) the claim that a fetus is not a person, which is an essential premise in her argument. Again, we have both a symmetry and a standoff between pro-choice and antiabortion views.

Passions in the abortion debate run high. There are both plausibilities and difficulties with the standard positions. Accordingly, it is hardly surprising that partisans of either side embrace with fervor the moral generalizations that support the conclusions they preanalytically favor, and reject with disdain the moral generalizations of their opponents as being subject to inescapable difficulties. It is easy to believe that the counterexamples to one's own moral principles are merely temporary difficulties that will dissolve in the wake of further philosophical research, and that the counterexamples to the principles of one's opponents are as straightforward as the contradiction between A and O propositions in traditional logic. This might suggest to an impartial observer (if there are any) that the abortion issue is unresolvable.

There is a way out of this apparent dialectical quandary. The moral generalizations of both sides are not quite correct. The generalizations hold for the most part, for the usual cases. This suggests that they are all *accidental* generalizations, that the moral claims made by those on both sides of the dispute do not touch on the *essence* of the matter.

This use of the distinction between essence and accident is not meant to invoke obscure metaphysical categories. Rather, it is intended to reflect the rather atheoretical nature of the abortion discussion. If the generalization a partisan in the abortion dispute adopts were derived from the reason why ending the life of a human being is wrong, then there could not be exceptions to that generalization unless some special case obtains in which there are even more powerful countervailing reasons. Such generalizations would not be merely accidental generalizations; they would point to, or be based upon, the essence of the wrongness of killing, what it is that makes killing wrong. All this suggests that a necessary condition of resolving the abortion controversy is a more theoretical account of the wrongness of killing. After all, if we merely believe, but do not understand, why killing adult human beings such as ourselves is wrong, how could we conceivably show that abortion is either immoral or permissible?

II.

In order to develop such an account, we can start from the following unproblematic assumption concerning our own case: it is wrong to kill *us*. Why is it wrong? Some answers can be easily eliminated. It might be said that what makes killing us wrong is that a killing brutalizes the one who kills. But the brutalization consists of being inured to the performance of an act that is hideously immoral; hence, the brutalization does not explain the immorality. It might be said that what makes killing us wrong is the great loss others would experience due to our absence. Although such hubris is understandable, such an explanation does not account for the wrongness of killing hermits, or those whose lives are relatively independent and whose friends find it easy to make new friends.

A more obvious answer is better. What primarily makes killing wrong is neither its effect on the murderer nor its effect on the victim's friends and relatives, but its effect on the victim. The loss of one's life is one of the greatest losses one can suffer. The loss of one's life deprives one of all the experiences, activities, projects, and enjoyments that would otherwise have constituted one's future. Therefore, killing someone is wrong, primarily because the killing inflicts (one of) the greatest possible losses on the victim. To describe this as the loss of life can be misleading, however. The change in my biological state does not by itself make killing me wrong. The effect of the loss of my biological life is the loss to me of all those activities, projects, experiences, and enjoyments which would otherwise have constituted my future personal life. These activities, projects, experiences, and enjoyments are either valuable for their own sakes or are means to something else that is valuable for its own sake. Some parts of my future are not valued by me now, but will come to be valued by me as I grow older and as my values and capacities change. When I am killed, I am deprived both of what I now value which would have been part of my future personal life, but also what I would come to value. Therefore, when I die, I am deprived of all of the value of my future. Inflicting this loss on me is ultimately what makes killing me wrong. This being the case, it would seem that what makes killing *any* adult human being prima facie seriously wrong is the loss of his or her future.

How should this rudimentary theory of the wrongness of killing be evaluated? It cannot be faulted for deriving an 'ought' from an 'is', for it does not. The analysis assumes that killing me (or you, reader) is prima facie seriously wrong. The point of the analysis is to establish which natural property ultimately explains the wrongness of the killing, given that it is wrong. A natural property will ultimately explain the wrongness of killing, only if (1) the explanation fits with our intuitions about the matter and (2) there is no other natural property that provides the basis for a better explanation of the wrongness of killing. This analysis rests on the intuition that what makes killing a particular human or animal wrong is what it does to that particular human or animal. What makes killing wrong is some natural effect or other of the killing. Some would deny this. For instance, a divine-command theorist in ethics would deny it. Surely this denial is, however, one of those features of divine-command theory which renders it so implausible.

The claim that what makes killing wrong is the loss of the victim's future is directly supported by two considerations. In the first place, this theory explains why we regard killing as one of the worst of crimes. Killing is especially wrong, because it deprives the victim of more than perhaps any other crime. In the second place, people with AIDS or cancer who know they are dying believe, of course, that dying is a very bad thing for them. They believe that the loss of a future to them that they would otherwise have experienced is what makes their premature death a very bad thing for them. A better theory of the wrongness of killing would require a different natural property associated with killing which better fits with the attitudes of the dying. What could it be?

The view that what makes killing wrong is the loss to the victim of the value of the victim's future gains additional support when some of its implications are examined. In the first place, it is incompatible with the view that it is wrong to kill only beings who are biologically human. It is possible that there exists a different species from another planet whose members have a future like ours. Since having a future like that is what makes killing someone wrong, this theory entails that it would be wrong to kill members of such a species. Hence, this theory is opposed to the claim that only life that is biologically human has great moral worth, a claim which many anti-abortionists have seemed to adopt. This opposition, which this theory has in common with personhood theories, seems to be a merit of the theory.

In the second place, the claim that the loss of one's future is the wrong-making feature of one's being killed entails the possibility that the futures of some actual nonhuman mammals on our own planet are sufficiently like ours that it is seriously wrong to kill them also. Whether some animals do have the same right to life as human beings depends on adding to the account of the wrongness of killing some additional account of just what it is about my future or the futures of other adult human beings which makes it wrong to kill us. No such additional account will be offered in this essay. Undoubtedly, the provision of such an account would be a very difficult matter. Undoubtedly, any such account would be quite controversial. Hence, it surely should not reflect badly on this sketch of an elementary theory of the wrongness of killing that it is indeterminate with respect to some very difficult issues regarding animal rights.

In the third place, the claim that the loss of one's future is the wrong-making feature of one's being killed does not entail, as sanctity of human life theories do, that active euthanasia is wrong. Persons who are severely and incurably ill, who face a future of pain and despair, and who wish to die will not have suffered a loss if they are killed. It is, strictly speaking, the value of a human's future which makes killing wrong in this theory. This being so, killing does not necessarily wrong some persons who are sick and dying. Of course, there may be other reasons for a prohibition of active euthanasia, but that is another matter. Sanctity-of-human-life theories seem to hold that active euthanasia is seriously wrong even in an individual case where there seems to be good reason for it independently of public policy considerations. This consequence is most implausible, and it is a plus for the claim that the loss of a future of value is what makes killing wrong that it does not share this consequence.

In the fourth place, the account of the wrongness of killing defended in this essay does straightforwardly entail that it is prima facie seriously wrong to kill children and infants, for we do presume that they have futures of value. Since we do believe that it is wrong to kill defenseless little babies, it is important that a theory of the wrongness of killing easily account for this. Personhood theories of the wrongness of killing, on the other hand, cannot straightforwardly account for the wrongness of killing infants and young children. Hence, such theories must add special ad hoc accounts of the wrongness of killing the young. The plausibility of such ad hoc theories seems to be a function of how desperately one wants such theories to work. The claim that the primary wrong-making feature of a killing is the loss to the victim of the value of its future accounts for the wrongness of killing young children and infants directly; it makes the wrongness of such acts as obvious as we actually think it is. This is a further merit of this theory. Accordingly, it seems that this value of a future-like-ours theory of the wrongness of killing shares strengths of both sanctity-of-life and personhood accounts while avoiding weaknesses of both. In addition, it meshes with a central intuition concerning what makes killing wrong.

The claim that the primary wrong-making feature of a killing is the loss to the victim of the value of its future has obvious consequences for the ethics of abortion. The future of a standard fetus includes a set of experiences, projects, activities, and such which are identical with the futures of adult human beings and are identical with the futures of young children. Since the reason that is sufficient to explain why it is wrong to kill human beings after the time of birth is a reason that also applies to fetuses, it follows that abortion is prima facie seriously morally wrong.

This argument does not rely on the invalid inference that, since it is wrong to kill persons, it is wrong to kill potential persons also. The category that is morally central to this analysis is the category of having a valuable future like ours; it is not the category of personhood. The argument to the conclusion that abortion is prima facie seriously morally wrong proceeded independently of the notion of person or potential person or any equivalent. Someone may wish to start with this analysis in terms of the value of a human future, conclude that abortion is, except perhaps in rare circumstances, seriously morally wrong, infer that fetuses have the right to life, and then call fetuses "persons" as a result of their having the right to life. Clearly, in this case, the category of person is being used to state the *conclusion* of the analysis rather than to generate the *argument* of the analysis.

The structure of this anti-abortion argument can be both illuminated and defended by comparing it to what appears to be the best argument for the wrongness of the wanton infliction of pain on animals. This latter argument is based on the assumption that it is prima facie wrong to inflict pain on me (or you, reader). What is the natural property associated with the infliction of pain which makes such infliction wrong? The obvious answer seems to be that the infliction of pain causes suffering and that suffering is a misfortune. The suffering caused by the infliction of pain is what makes the wanton infliction of pain on me wrong. The wanton infliction of pain on other adult humans causes suffering. The wanton infliction of pain on animals causes suffering. Since causing suffering is what makes the wanton infliction of pain wrong and since the wanton infliction of pain on animals causes suffering, it follows that the wanton infliction of pain on animals is wrong.

This argument for the wrongness of the wanton infliction of pain on animals shares a number of structural features with the argument for the serious prima facie wrongness of abortion. Both arguments start with an obvious assumption concerning what it is wrong to do to me (or you, reader). Both then look for the characteristic or the consequence of the wrong action which makes the action wrong. Both recognize that the wrong-making feature of these immoral actions is a property of actions sometimes directed at individuals other than postnatal human beings. If the structure of the argument for the wrongness of the wanton infliction of pain on animals is sound, then the structure of the argument for the prima facie serious wrongness of abortion is also sound, for the structure of the two arguments is the same. The structure common to both is the key to the explanation of how the wrongness of abortion can be demonstrated without recourse to the category of person. In neither argument is that category crucial.

This defense of an argument for the wrongness of abortion in terms of a structurally similar argument for the wrongness of the wanton infliction of pain on animals succeeds only if the account regarding animals is the correct account. Is it? In the first place, it seems plausible. In the second place, its major competition is Kant's account. Kant believed that we do not have direct duties to animals at all, because they are not persons. Hence, Kant had to explain and justify the wrongness of inflicting pain on animals on the grounds that "he who is hard in his dealings with animals becomes hard also in his dealing with men."[2] The problem with Kant's account is that there seems to be no reason for accepting this latter claim unless Kant's account is rejected. If the alternative to Kant's account is accepted, then it is easy to understand why someone who is indifferent to inflicting pain on animals is also indifferent to inflicting pain on humans, for one is indifferent to what makes inflicting pain wrong in both cases. But, if Kant's account is accepted, there is no intelligible reason why one who is hard in his dealings with animals (or crabgrass or stones) should also be hard in his dealings with men. After all, men are persons: animals are no more persons than crabgrass or stones. Persons are Kant's crucial moral category. Why, in short, should a Kantian accept the basic claim in Kant's argument?

Hence, Kant's argument for the wrongness of inflicting pain on animals rests on a claim that, in a world of Kantian moral agents, is demonstrably false. Therefore, the alternative analysis, being more plausible anyway, should be accepted. Since this alternative analysis has the same structure as the anti-abortion argument being defended here, we have further support for the argument for the immorality of abortion being defended in this essay.

Of course, this value of a future-like-ours argument, if sound, shows only that abortion is prima facie wrong, not that it is wrong in any and all circumstances. Since the loss of the future to a standard fetus, if killed, is, however, at least as great a loss as the loss of the future to a standard adult human being who is killed, abortion, like ordinary killing, could be justified only by the most compelling reasons. The loss of one's life is almost the greatest misfortune that can happen to one. Presumably abortion could be justified in some circumstances, only if the loss consequent on failing to abort would be at least as great. Accordingly, morally permissible abortions will be rare indeed unless, perhaps, they occur so early in pregnancy that a fetus is not yet definitely an individual. Hence, this argument should be taken as showing that abortion is presumptively very seriously wrong, where the presumption is very strong—as strong as the presumption that killing another adult human being is wrong.

III.

How complete an account of the wrongness of killing does the value of a future-like-ours account have to be in order that the wrongness of abortion is a consequence? This account does not have to be an account of the necessary conditions for the wrongness of killing. Some persons in nursing homes may lack valuable human futures, yet it may be wrong to kill them for other reasons. Furthermore, this account does not obviously have to be the sole reason killing is wrong where the victim did have a valuable future. This analysis claims only that, for any killing where the victim did have a valuable future like ours, having that future by itself is sufficient to create the strong presumption that the killing is seriously wrong.

One way to overturn the value of a future-like-ours argument would be to find some account of the wrongness of killing which is at least as intelligible and which has different implications for the ethics of abortion. Two rival accounts possess at least some degree of plausibility. One account is based on the obvious fact that people value the experience of living and wish for that valuable experience to continue. Therefore, it might be said, what makes killing wrong is the discontinuation of that experience for the victim. Let us call this the *discontinuation account.* Another rival account is based upon the obvious fact that people strongly desire to continue to live. This suggests that what makes killing us so wrong is that it interferes with the fulfillment of a strong and fundamental desire, the fulfillment of which is necessary for the fulfillment of any other desires we might have. Let us call this the *desire account.*

Consider first the desire account as a rival account of the ethics of killing which would provide the basis for rejecting the anti-abortion position. Such an account will have to be stronger than the value of a future-like-ours account of the wrongness of abortion if it is to do the job expected of it. To entail the wrongness of abortion, the value of a future-like-ours account has only to provide a sufficient, but not a necessary, condition for the wrongness of killing. The desire account, on the other hand, must provide us also with a necessary condition for the wrongness of killing in order to generate a pro-choice conclusion on abortion. The reason for this is that presumably the argument from the desire account moves from the claim that what makes killing wrong is interference with a very strong desire to the claim that abortion is not wrong because the fetus lacks a strong desire to live. Obviously, this inference fails if someone's having the desire to live is not a necessary condition of its being wrong to kill that individual.

One problem with the desire account is that we do regard it as seriously wrong to kill persons who have little desire to live or who have no desires to live or, indeed, have a desire not to live. We believe it is seriously wrong to kill the unconscious, the sleeping, those who are tired of life, and those who are suicidal. The value-of-a-human-future account renders standard morality intelligible in these cases; these cases appear to be incompatible with the desire account.

The desire account is subject to a deeper difficulty. We desire life, because we value the goods of this life. The goodness of life is not secondary to our desire for it. If this were not so, the pain of one's own premature death could be done away with merely by an appropriate alteration in the configuration of one's desires.

This is absurd. Hence, it would seem that it is the loss of the goods of one's future, not the interference with the fulfillment of a strong desire to live, which accounts ultimately for the wrongness of killing.

It is worth noting that, if the desire account is modified so that it does not provide a necessary, but only a sufficient, condition for the wrongness of killing, the desire account is compatible with the value of a future-like-ours account. The combined accounts will yield an anti-abortion ethic. This suggests that one can retain what is intuitively plausible about the desire account without a challenge to the basic argument of this paper.

It is also worth noting that, if future desires have moral force in a modified desire account of the wrongness of killing, one can find support for an anti-abortion ethic even in the absence of a value of a future-like-ours account. If one decides that a morally relevant property, the possession of which is sufficient to make it wrong to kill some individual, is the desire at some future time to live—one might decide to justify one's refusal to kill suicidal teenagers on these grounds, for example—then, since typical fetuses will have the desire in the future to live, it is wrong to kill typical fetuses. Accordingly, it does not seem that a desire account of the wrongness of killing can provide a justification of a pro-choice ethic of abortion which is nearly as adequate as the value of a human-future justification of an anti-abortion ethic.

The discontinuation account looks more promising as an account of the wrongness of killing. It seems just as intelligible as the value of a future-like-ours account, but it does not justify an anti-abortion position. Obviously, if it is the continuation of one's activities, experiences, and projects, the loss of which makes killing wrong, then it is not wrong to kill fetuses for that reason, for fetuses do not have experiences, activities, and projects to be continued or discontinued. Accordingly, the discontinuation account does not have the anti-abortion consequences that the value of a future-like-ours account has. Yet, it seems as intelligible as the value of a future-like-ours account, for when we think of what would be wrong with our being killed, it does seem as if it is the discontinuation of what makes our lives worthwhile which makes killing us wrong.

Is the discontinuation account just as good an account as the value of a future-like-ours account? The discontinuation account will not be adequate at all, if it does not refer to the *value* of the experience that may be discontinued. One does not want the discontinuation account to make it wrong to kill a patient who begs for death and who is in severe pain that cannot be relieved short of killing. (I leave open the question of whether it is wrong for other reasons.) Accordingly, the discontinuation account must be more than a bare discontinuation account. It must make some reference to the positive value of the patient's experiences. But, by the same token, the value of a future-like-ours account cannot be a bare future account either. Just having a future surely does not itself rule out killing the above patient. This account must make some reference to the value of the patient's future experiences and projects also. Hence, both accounts involve the value of experiences, projects, and activities. So far we still have symmetry between the accounts.

The symmetry fades, however, when we focus on the time period of the value of the experiences, etc., which has moral consequences. Although both accounts leave open the possibility that the patient in our example may be killed, this possibility is left open only in virtue of the utterly bleak future for the patient. It makes no difference whether the patient's immediate past contains intolerable pain, or consists in being in a coma (which we can imagine is a situation of indifference), or consists in a life of value. If the patient's future is a future of value, we want our account to make it wrong to kill the patient. If the patient's future is intolerable, whatever his or her immediate past, we want our account to allow killing the patient. Obviously, then, it is the value of that patient's future which is doing the work in rendering the morality of killing the patient intelligible.

This being the case, it seems clear that whether one has immediate past experiences or not does not work in the explanation of what makes killing wrong. The addition the discontinuation account makes to the value of a human future account is otiose. Its addition to the value-of-a-future account plays no role at all in rendering intelligible the wrongness of killing.

Therefore, it can be discarded with the discontinuation account of which it is a part.

IV.

The analysis of the previous section suggests that alternative general accounts of the wrongness of killing are either inadequate or unsuccessful in getting around the anti-abortion consequences of the value of a future-like-ours argument. A different strategy for avoiding these anti-abortion consequences involves limiting the scope of the value of a future argument. More precisely, the strategy involves arguing that fetuses lack a property that is essential for the value-of-a-future argument (or for any anti-abortion argument) to apply to them.

One move of this sort is based upon the claim that a necessary condition of one's future being valuable is that one values it. Value implies a valuer. Given this one might argue that, since fetuses cannot value their futures, their futures are not valuable to them. Hence, it does not seriously wrong them deliberately to end their lives.

This move fails, however, because of some ambiguities. Let us assume that something cannot be of value unless it is valued by someone. This does not entail that my life is of no value unless it is valued by me. I may think, in a period of despair, that my future is of no worth whatsoever, but I may be wrong because others rightly see value—even great value—in it. Furthermore, my future can be valuable to me even if I do not value it. This is the case when a young person attempts suicide, but is rescued and goes on to significant human achievements. Such young people's futures are ultimately valuable to them, even though such futures do not seem to be valuable to them at the moment of attempted suicide. A fetus's future can be valuable to it in the same way. Accordingly, this attempt to limit the anti-abortion argument fails.

Another similar attempt to reject the anti-abortion position is based on [Michael] Tooley's claim that an entity cannot possess the right to life unless it has the capacity to desire its continued existence. It follows that, since fetuses lack the conceptual capacity to desire to continue to live, they lack the right to life.

Accordingly, Tooley concludes that abortion cannot be seriously prima facie wrong.[3]

What could be the evidence for Tooley's basic claim? Tooley once argued that individuals have a prima facie right to what they desire and that the lack of the capacity to desire something undercuts the basis of one's right to it.[4] This argument plainly will not succeed in the context of the analysis of this essay, however, since the point here is to establish the fetus's right to life on other grounds. Tooley's argument assumes that the right to life cannot be established in general on some basis other than the desire for life. This position was considered and rejected in the preceding section of this paper.

One might attempt to defend Tooley's basic claim on the grounds that, because a fetus cannot apprehend continued life as a benefit, its continued life cannot be a benefit or cannot be something it has a right to or cannot be something that is in its interest. This might be defended in terms of the general proposition that, if an individual is literally incapable of caring about or taking an interest in some X, then one does not have a right to X or X is not a benefit or X is not something that is in one's interest.

Each member of this family of claims seems to be open to objections. As John C. Stevens[5] has pointed out, one may have a right to be treated with a certain medical procedure (because of a health insurance policy one has purchased), even though one cannot conceive of the nature of the procedure. And, as Tooley himself has pointed out, persons who have been indoctrinated, or drugged, or rendered temporarily unconscious may be literally incapable of caring about or taking an interest in something that is in their interest or is something to which they have a right, or is something that benefits them. Hence, the Tooley claim that would restrict the scope of the value of a future-like-ours argument is undermined by counterexamples.

Finally, Paul Bassen[6] has argued that, even though the prospects of an embryo might seem to be a basis for the wrongness of abortion, an embryo cannot be a victim and therefore cannot be wronged. An embryo cannot be a victim, he says, because it lacks sentience. His central argument for this seems to be that, even though plants and the permanently unconscious are alive, they clearly cannot be victims. What is the explanation of this? Bassen claims that the explanation is that their lives consist of mere metabolism and mere metabolism is not enough to ground victimizability. Mentation is required.

The problem with this attempt to establish the absence of victimizability is that both plants and the permanently unconscious clearly lack what Bassen calls "prospects" or what I have called "a future life like ours." Hence, it is surely open to one to argue that the real reason we believe plants and the permanently unconscious cannot be victims is that killing them cannot deprive them of a future life like ours; the real reason is not their absence of present mentation.

Bassen recognizes that his view is subject to this difficulty, and he recognizes that the case of children seems to support this difficulty, for "much of what we do for children is based on prospects." He argues, however, that, in the case of children and in other such cases, "potentially comes into play only where victimizability has been secured on other grounds. . . ."

Bassen's defense of his view is patently question-begging, since what is adequate to secure victimizability is exactly what is at issue. His examples do not support his own view against the thesis of this essay. Of course, embryos can be victims: when their lives are deliberately terminated, they are deprived of their futures of value, their prospects. This makes them victims, for it directly wrongs them.

The seeming plausibility of Bassen's view stems from the fact that paradigmatic cases of imagining someone as a victim involve empathy, and empathy requires mentation of the victim. The victims of flood, famine, rape, or child abuse are all persons with whom we can empathize. That empathy seems to be part of seeing them as victims.

In spite of the strength of these examples, the attractive intuition that a situation in which there is victimization requires the possibility of empathy is subject to counterexamples. Consider a case that Bassen himself offers: "Posthumous obliteration of an author's work constitutes a misfortune for him only if he had wished his work to endure". . . The conditions Bassen wishes to impose upon the possibility of being victimized here seem far too strong. Perhaps this author, due to his unrealistic standards of excellence and his low self-esteem, regarded his work as unworthy of survival, even though it possessed genuine literary merit. Destruction of such work would surely victimize its author. In such a case, empathy with the victim concerning the loss is clearly impossible.

Of course, Bassen does not make the possibility of empathy a necessary condition of victimizability; he requires only mentation. Hence, on Bassen's actual view, this author, as I have described him, can be a victim. The problem is that the basic intuition that renders Bassen's view plausible is missing in the author's case. In order to attempt to avoid counterexamples, Bassen has made his thesis too weak to be supported by the intuitions that suggested it.

Even so, the mentation requirement on victimizability is still subject to counterexamples. Suppose a severe accident renders me totally unconscious for a month, after which I recover. Surely killing me while I am unconscious victimizes me, even though I am incapable of mentation during that time. It follows that Bassen's thesis fails. Apparently, attempts to restrict the value of a future-like-ours argument so that fetuses do not fall within its scope do not succeed.

V.

In this essay, it has been argued that the correct ethic of the wrongness of killing can be extended to fetal life and used to show that there is a strong presumption that any abortion is morally impermissible. If the ethic of killing adopted here entails, however, that contraception is also seriously immoral, then there would appear to be a difficulty with the analysis of this essay.

But this analysis does not entail that contraception is wrong. Of course, contraception prevents the actualization of a possible future of value. Hence, it follows from the claim that futures of value should be maximized that contraception is prima facie immoral. This obligation to maximize does not exist, however; furthermore, nothing in the ethics of killing in this paper entails that it does. The ethics of killing in this essay would entail that contraception is wrong only if something were denied a human future of value by contraception. Nothing at all is denied such a future by contraception, however.

Candidates for a subject of harm by contraception fall into four categories: (1) some sperm or other, (2) some ovum or other, (3) a sperm and an ovum separately, and (4) a sperm and an ovum together. Assigning the harm to some sperm is utterly arbitrary, for no reason can be given for making a sperm the subject of harm rather than an ovum. Assigning the harm to some ovum is utterly arbitrary, for no reason can be given for making an ovum the subject of harm rather than a sperm. One might attempt to avoid these problems by insisting that contraception deprives both the sperm and the ovum separately of a valuable future like ours. On this alternative, too many futures are lost. Contraception was supposed to be wrong, because it deprived us of one future of value, not two. One might attempt to avoid this problem by holding that contraception deprives the combination of sperm and ovum of a valuable future like ours. But here the definite article misleads. At the time of contraception, there are hundreds of millions of sperm, one (released) ovum and millions of possible combinations of all of these. There is no actual combination at all. Is the subject of the loss to be a merely possible combination? Which one? This alternative does not yield an actual subject of harm either. Accordingly, the immorality of contraception is not entailed by the loss of a future-like-ours argument simply because there is no nonarbitrarily identifiable subject of the loss in the case of contraception.

VI.

The purpose of this essay has been to set out an argument for the serious presumptive wrongness of abortion subject to the assumption that the moral permissibility of abortion stands or falls on the moral status of the fetus. Since a fetus possesses a property, the possession of which in adult human beings is sufficient to make killing an adult human being wrong, abortion is wrong. This way of dealing with the problem of abortion seems superior to other approaches to the ethics of abortion, because it rests on an ethics of killing which is close to self-evident, because the crucial morally relevant property clearly applies to fetuses, and because the argument avoids the usual equivocations of 'human life', 'human being', or 'person'. The argument rests neither on religious claims nor on Papal dogma. It is not subject to the objection of "speciesism." Its soundness is compatible with the moral permissibility of euthanasia and contraception. It deals with our intuitions concerning young children.

Finally, this analysis can be viewed as resolving a standard problem—indeed, *the* standard problem—concerning the ethics of abortion. Clearly, it is wrong to kill adult human beings. Clearly, it is not wrong to end the life of some arbitrarily chosen single human cell. Fetuses seem to be like arbitrarily chosen human cells in some respects and like adult humans in other respects. The problem of the ethics of abortion is the problem of determining the fetal property that settles this moral controversy. The thesis of this essay is that the problem of the ethics of abortion, so understood, is solvable.

NOTES

1. Joel Feinberg, "Abortion," in *Matters of Life and Death: New Introductory Essays in Moral Philosophy*, ed. Tom Regan (New York: Random House, 1986), p. 270.

2. "Duties to Animals and Spirits," in *Lectures on Ethics*, trans. Loius Infeld (New York: Harper, 1963), p. 239.

3. Michael Tooley, *Abortion and Infanticide* (New York: Oxford, 1984), pp. 46–47.

4. Tooley, *Abortion and Infanticide*, pp. 44–45.

5. "Must the Bearer of a Right Have the Concept of That to Which He Has a Right?" *Ethics* 95, no. 1 (1984): 68–74.

6. "Present Sakes and Future Prospects: The Status of Early Abortion," *Philosophy and Public Affairs* 11, no. 4 (1982): 314–37.

From *Virtue Theory and Abortion*

Rosalind Hursthouse

* * *

As everyone knows, the morality of abortion is commonly discussed in relation to just two considerations: first, and predominantly, the status of the fetus and whether or not it is the sort of thing that may or may not be innocuously or justifiably killed; and second, and less predominantly (when, that is, the discussion concerns the *morality* of abortion rather than the question of permissible legislation in a just society), women's rights. If one thinks within this familiar framework, one may well be puzzled about what virtue theory, as such, could contribute. Some people assume the discussion will be conducted solely in terms of what the virtuous agent would or would not do . . . Others assume that only justice, or at most justice and charity, will be applied to the issue, generating a discussion very similar to Judith Jarvis Thomson's.[1]

Now if this is the way the virtue theorist's discussion of abortion is imagined to be, no wonder people think little of it. It seems obvious in advance that in any such discussion there must be either a great deal of extremely tendentious application of the virtue terms *just*, *charitable*, and so on or a lot of rhetorical appeal to "this is what only the virtuous agent knows." But these are caricatures; they fail to appreciate the way in which virtue theory quite transforms the discussion of abortion by dismissing the two familiar dominating considerations as, in a way, fundamentally irrelevant. In what way or ways, I hope to make both clear and plausible.

Let us first consider women's rights. Let me emphasize again that we are discussing the *morality* of abortion, not the rights and wrongs of laws prohibiting or permitting it. If we suppose that women do

have a moral right to do as they choose with their own bodies, or, more particularly, to terminate their pregnancies, then it may well follow that a *law* forbidding abortion would be unjust. Indeed, even if they have no such right, such a law might be, as things stand at the moment, unjust, or impractical, or inhumane: on this issue I have nothing to say in this article. But, putting all questions about the justice or injustice of laws to one side, and supposing only that women have such a moral right, *nothing* follows from this supposition about the morality of abortion, according to virtue theory, once it is noted (quite generally, not with particular reference to abortion) that in exercising a moral right I can do something cruel, or callous, or selfish, light-minded, self-righteous, stupid, inconsiderate, disloyal, dishonest—that is, act viciously.[2] Love and friendship do not survive their parties' constantly insisting on their rights, nor do people live well when they think that getting what they have a right to is of preeminent importance; they harm others, and they harm themselves. So whether women have a moral right to terminate their pregnancies is irrelevant within virtue theory, for it is irrelevant to the question "In having an abortion in these circumstances, would the agent be acting virtuously or viciously or neither?"

What about the consideration of the status of the fetus—what can virtue theory say about that? One might say that this issue is not in the province of *any* moral theory; it is a metaphysical question, and an extremely difficult one at that. Must virtue theory then wait upon metaphysics to come up with the answer?

At first sight it might seem so. For virtue is said to involve knowledge, and part of this knowledge consists in having the *right* attitude to things. "Right" here does not just mean "morally right" or "proper" or "nice" in the modern sense; it means "accurate, true." One cannot have the right or correct attitude to something if the attitude is based on or involves false beliefs. And this suggests that if the status of the fetus is relevant to the rightness or wrongness of abortion, its status must be known, as a truth, to the fully wise and virtuous person.

But the sort of wisdom that the fully virtuous person has is not supposed to be recondite; it does not call for fancy philosophical sophistication, and it does not depend upon, let alone wait upon, the discoveries of academic philosophers.[3] And this entails the following, rather startling, conclusion: that the status of the fetus—that issue over which so much ink has been spilt—is, according to virtue theory, simply not relevant to the rightness or wrongness of abortion (within, that is, a secular morality).

Or rather, since that is clearly too radical a conclusion, it is in a sense relevant, but only in the sense that the familiar biological facts are relevant. By "the familiar biological facts" I mean the facts that most human societies are and have been familiar with—that, standardly (but not invariably), pregnancy occurs as the result of sexual intercourse, that it lasts about nine months, during which time the fetus grows and develops, that standardly it terminates in the birth of a living baby, and that this is how we all come to be.

It might be thought that this distinction—between the familiar biological facts and the status of the fetus—is a distinction without a difference. But this is not so. To attach relevance to the status of the fetus, in the sense in which virtue theory claims it is not relevant, is to be gripped by the conviction that we must go beyond the familiar biological facts, deriving some sort of conclusion from them, such as that the fetus has rights, or is not a person, or something similar. It is also to believe that this exhausts the relevance of the familiar biological facts, that all they are relevant to is the status of the fetus and whether or not it is the sort of thing that may or may not be killed.

These convictions, I suspect, are rooted in the desire to solve the problem of abortion by getting it to fall under some general rule such as "You ought not to kill anything with the right to life but may kill anything else." But they have resulted in what should surely strike any nonphilosopher as a most bizarre aspect of nearly all the current philosophical literature on abortion, namely, that, far from treating abortion as a unique moral problem, markedly unlike any

other, nearly everything written on the status of the fetus and its bearing on the abortion issue would be consistent with the human reproductive facts (to say nothing of family life) being totally different from what they are. Imagine that you are an alien extraterrestrial anthropologist who does not know that the human race is roughly 50 percent female and 50 percent male, or that our only (natural) form of reproduction involves heterosexual intercourse, viviparous birth, and the female's (and only the female's) being pregnant for nine months, or that females are capable of childbearing from late childhood to late middle age, or that childbearing is painful, dangerous, and emotionally charged—do you think you would pick up these facts from the hundreds of articles written on the status of the fetus? I am quite sure you would not. And that, I think, shows that the current philosophical literature on abortion has got badly out of touch with reality.

Now if we are using virtue theory, our first question is not "What do the familiar biological facts show—what can be derived from them about the status of the fetus?" but "How do these facts figure in the practical reasoning, actions and passions, thoughts and reactions, of the virtuous and the nonvirtuous? What is the mark of having the right attitude to these facts and what manifests having the wrong attitude to them?" This immediately makes essentially relevant not only all the facts about human reproduction I mentioned above, but a whole range of facts about our emotions in relation to them as well. I mean such facts as that human parents, both male and female, tend to care passionately about their offspring, and that family relationships are among the deepest and strongest in our lives—and, significantly, among the longest-lasting.

These facts make it obvious that pregnancy is not just one among many other physical conditions; and hence that anyone who genuinely believes that an abortion is comparable to a haircut or an appendectomy is mistaken.[4] The fact that the premature termination of a pregnancy is, in some sense, the cutting off of a new human life, and thereby, like the procreation of a new human life, connects with all our thoughts about human life and death, parenthood, and family relationships, must make it a serious matter. To disregard this fact about it, to think of abortion as nothing but the killing of something that does not matter, or as nothing but the exercise of some right or rights one has, or as the incidental means to some desirable state of affairs, is to do something callous and light-minded, the sort of thing that no virtuous and wise person would do. It is to have the wrong attitude not only to fetuses, but more generally to human life and death, parenthood, and family relationships.

Although I say that the facts make this obvious, I know that this is one of my tendentious points. In partial support of it I note that even the most dedicated proponents of the view that deliberate abortion is just like an appendectomy or haircut rarely hold the same view of spontaneous abortion, that is, miscarriage. It is not so tendentious of me to claim that to react to people's grief over miscarriage by saying, or even thinking, "What a fuss about nothing!" would be callous and light-minded, whereas to try to laugh someone out of grief over an appendectomy scar or a botched haircut would not be. It is hard to give this point due prominence within act-centered theories, for the inconsistency is an inconsistency in attitude about the seriousness of loss of life, not in beliefs about which acts are right or wrong. Moreover, an act-centered theorist may say, "Well, there is nothing wrong with *thinking* 'What a fuss about nothing!' as long as you do not say it and hurt the person who is grieving. And besides, we cannot be held responsible for our thoughts, only for the intentional actions they give rise to." But the character traits that virtue theory emphasizes are not simply dispositions to intentional actions, but a seamless disposition to certain actions and passions, thoughts and reactions.

To say that the cutting off of a human life is always a matter of some seriousness, at any stage, is not to deny the relevance of gradual fetal development. Notwithstanding the well-worn point that clear boundary lines cannot be drawn, our emotions and attitudes regarding the fetus do change as it develops, and again when it is born, and indeed further as the baby grows. Abortion for shallow reasons in the later stages is much more shocking than abortion for the same reasons in the early stages in a way that matches the fact that deep grief over miscarriage in the later stages is more appropriate than it is over miscarriage in the earlier stages (when, that is, the grief is solely about the loss of *this* child, not about, as might be the case, the loss of one's only hope of having a child or of having one's husband's child). Imagine (or recall) a woman who already has children; she had not intended to have more, but finds herself unexpectedly pregnant. Though contrary to her plans, the pregnancy, once established as a fact, is welcomed—and then she loses the embryo almost immediately. If this were bemoaned as a tragedy, it would, I think, be a misapplication of the concept of what is tragic. But it may still properly be mourned as a loss. The grief is expressed in such terms as "I shall always wonder how she or he would have turned out" or "When I look at the others, I shall think, 'How different their lives would have been if this other one had been part of them.'" It would, I take it, be callous and light-minded to say, or think, "Well, she has already *got* four children; what's the problem?"; it would be neither, nor arrogantly intrusive in the case of a close friend, to try to correct prolonged mourning by saying, "I know it's sad, but it's not a tragedy; rejoice in the ones you have." The application of *tragic* becomes more appropriate as the fetus grows, for the mere fact that one has lived with it for longer, conscious of its existence, makes a difference. To shrug off an early abortion is understandable just because it is very hard to be fully conscious of the fetus's existence in the early stages and hence hard to appreciate that an early abortion is the destruction of life. It is particularly hard for the young and inexperienced to appreciate this, because appreciation of it usually comes only with experience.

I do not mean "with the experience of having an abortion" (though that may be part of it) but, quite generally, "with the experience of life." Many women who have borne children contrast their later pregnancies with their first successful one, saying that in the later ones they were conscious of a new life growing in them from very early on. And, more generally, as one reaches the age at which the next generation is coming up close behind one, the counterfactuals "If

I, or she, had had an abortion, Alice, or Bob, would not have been born" acquire a significant application, which casts a new light on the conditionals "If I or Alice have an abortion then some Caroline or Bill will not be born."

The fact that pregnancy is not just one among many physical conditions does not mean that one can never regard it in that light without manifesting a vice. When women are in very poor physical health, or worn out from childbearing, or forced to do very physically demanding jobs, then they cannot be described as self-indulgent, callous, irresponsible, or light-minded if they seek abortions mainly with a view to avoiding pregnancy as the physical condition that it is. To go through with a pregnancy when one is utterly exhausted, or when one's job consists of crawling along tunnels hauling coal, as many women in the nineteenth century were obliged to do, is perhaps heroic, but people who do not achieve heroism are not necessarily vicious. That they can view the pregnancy only as eight months of misery, followed by hours if not days of agony and exhaustion, and abortion only as the blessed escape from this prospect, is entirely understandable and does not manifest any lack of serious respect for human life or a shallow attitude to motherhood. What it does show is that something is terribly amiss in the conditions of their lives, which make it so hard to recognize pregnancy and childbearing as the good that they can be.

* * *

The foregoing discussion, insofar as it emphasizes the right attitude to human life and death, parallels to a certain extent those standard discussions of abortion that concentrate on it solely as an issue of killing. But it does not, as those discussions do, gloss over the fact, emphasized by those who discuss the morality of abortion in terms of women's rights, that abortion, wildly unlike any other form of killing, is the termination of a pregnancy, which is a condition of a woman's body and results in *her* having a child if it is not aborted. This fact is given due recognition not by appeal to women's rights but by emphasizing the relevance of the familiar biological and psychological facts and their connection with having the right attitude to parenthood and family relationships. But it may well be thought that failing to bring in women's rights still leaves some important aspects of the problem of abortion untouched.

Speaking in terms of women's rights, people sometimes say things like, "Well, it's her life you're talking about too, you know; she's got a right to her own life, her own happiness." And the discussion stops there. But in the context of virtue theory, given that we are particularly concerned with what constitutes a good human life, with what true happiness or *eudaimonia* is, this is no place to stop. We go on to ask, "And is this life of hers a good one? Is she living well?"

If we are to go on to talk about good human lives, in the context of abortion, we have to bring in our thoughts about the value of love and family life, and our proper emotional development through a natural life cycle. The familiar facts support the view that parenthood in general, and motherhood and childbearing in particular, are intrinsically worthwhile, are among the things that can be correctly thought to be partially constitutive of a flourishing human life. If this is right, then a woman who opts for not being a mother (at all, or again, or now) by opting for abortion may thereby be manifesting a flawed grasp of what her life should be, and be about—a grasp that is childish, or grossly materialistic, or shortsighted, or shallow.

I said "*may* thereby": this *need* not be so. Consider, for instance, a woman who has already had several children and fears that to have another will seriously affect her capacity to be a good mother to the ones she has—she does not show a lack of appreciation of the intrinsic value of being a parent by opting for abortion. Nor does a woman who has been a good mother and is approaching the age at which she may be looking forward to bring a good grandmother. Nor does a woman who discovers that her pregnancy may well kill her, and opts for abortion and adoption. Nor, necessarily, does a woman who has decided to lead a life centered around some other worthwhile activity or activities with which motherhood would compete.

People who are childless by choice are sometimes described as "irresponsible," or "selfish," or "refusing to grow up," or "not knowing what life is about." But one can hold that having children is intrinsically worthwhile without endorsing this, for we are, after all, in the happy position of there being more worthwhile things to do than can be fitted into one lifetime. Parenthood, and motherhood in particular, even if granted to be intrinsically worthwhile, undoubtedly take up a lot of one's adult life, leaving no room for some other worthwhile pursuits. But some women who choose abortion rather than have their first child, and some men who encourage their partners to choose abortion, are not avoiding parenthood for the sake of other worthwhile pursuits, but for the worthless one of "having a good time," or for the pursuit of some false vision of the ideals of freedom or self-realization. And some others who say "I am not ready for parenthood yet" are making some sort of mistake about the extent to which one can manipulate the circumstances of one's life so as to make it fulfill some dream that one has. Perhaps one's dream is to have two perfect children, a girl and a boy, within a perfect marriage, in financially secure circumstances, with an interesting job of one's own. But to care too much about that dream, to demand of life that it give it to one and act accordingly, may be both greedy and foolish, and is to run the risk of missing out on happiness entirely. Not only may fate make the dream impossible, or destroy it, but one's own attachment to it may make it impossible. Good marriages, and the most promising children, can be destroyed by just one adult's excessive demand for perfection.

Once again, this is not to deny that girls may quite properly say "I am not ready for motherhood yet," especially in our society, and, far from manifesting irresponsibility or light-mindedness, show an appropriate modesty or humility, or a fearfulness that does not amount to cowardice. However, even when the decision to have an abortion is the right decision—one that does not itself fall under a vice-related term and thereby one that the perfectly virtuous could recommend—it does not follow that there is no sense in which having the abortion is wrong,

or guilt inappropriate. For, by virtue of the fact that a human life has been cut short, some evil has probably been brought about,[5] and that circumstances make the decision to bring about some evil the right decision will be a ground for guilt if getting into those circumstances in the first place itself manifested a flaw in character.

What "gets one into those circumstances" in the case of abortion is, except in the case of rape, one's sexual activity and one's choices, or the lack of them, about one's sexual partner and about contraception. The virtuous woman (which here of course does not mean simply "chaste woman" but "woman with the virtues") has such character traits as strength, independence, resoluteness, decisiveness, self-confidence, responsibility, serious-mindedness, and self-determination—and no one, I think, could deny that many women become pregnant in circumstances in which they cannot welcome or cannot face the thought of having *this* child precisely because they lack one or some of these character traits. So even in the cases where the decision to have an abortion is the right one, it can still be the reflection of a moral failing—not because the decision itself is weak or cowardly or irresolute or irresponsible or light-minded, but because lack of the requisite opposite of these failings landed one in the circumstances in the first place. Hence the common universalized claim that guilt and remorse are never appropriate emotions about an abortion is denied. They may be appropriate, and appropriately inculcated, even when the decision was the right one.

Another motivation for bringing women's rights into the discussion may be to attempt to correct the implication, carried by the killing-centered approach, that insofar as abortion is wrong, it is a wrong that only women do, or at least (given the preponderance of male doctors) that only women instigate. I do not myself believe that we can thus escape the fact that nature bears harder on women than it does on men, but virtue theory can certainly correct many of the injustices that the emphasis on women's rights is rightly concerned about. With very little amendment, everything that has been said above applies to boys and men too. Although the abortion decision is, in a natural sense, the woman's decision, proper to her, boys and men are often party to it, for well or ill, and even when they are not, they are bound to have been party to the circumstances that brought it up. No less than girls and women, boys and men can, in their actions, manifest self-centeredness, callousness, and light-mindedness about life and parenthood in relation to abortion. They can be self-centered or courageous about the possibility of disability in their offspring; they need to reflect on their sexual activity and their choices, or the lack of them, about their sexual partner and contraception; they need to grow up and take responsibility for their own actions and life in relation to fatherhood. If it is true, as I maintain, that insofar as motherhood is intrinsically worthwhile, being a mother is an important purpose in women's lives, being a father (rather than a mere generator) is an important purpose in men's lives as well, and it is adolescent of men to turn a blind eye to this and pretend that they have many more important things to do.

* * *

NOTES

1. Judith Jarvis Thomson, "A Defense of Abortion," *Philosophy & Public Affairs* 1, no. 1 (Fall 1971): 47–66. One could indeed regard this article as proto-virtue theory (no doubt to the surprise of the author) if the concepts of callousness and kindness were allowed more weight.

2. One possible qualification: if one ties the concept of justice very closely to rights, then if women do have a moral right to terminate their pregnancies it *may* follow that in doing so they do not act unjustly. (Cf. Thomson, "A Defense of Abortion.") But it is debatable whether even that much follows.

3. This is an assumption of virtue theory, and I do not attempt to defend it here. An adequate discussion of it would require a separate article, since, although most moral philosophers would be chary of claiming that intellectual sophistication is a necessary condition of moral wisdom or virtue, most of us, from Plato onward, tend to write as if this were so. Sorting out which claims about moral knowledge are committed to this kind of elitism and which can, albeit with difficulty, be reconciled with the idea that moral knowledge can be acquired by anyone who really wants it would be a major task.

4. Mary Anne Warren, in "On the Moral and Legal Status of Abortion," *Monist* 57 (1973), sec. 1, says of the opponents of restrictive laws governing abortion that "their conviction (for the most part) is that abortion is not a *morally* serious and extremely unfortunate, even though sometimes justified, act, comparable to killing in self-defense or to letting the violinist die, but rather is closer to being a *morally neutral* act, like cutting one's hair" (italics mine). I would like to think that no one *genuinely* believes this. But certainly in discussion, particularly when arguing against restrictive laws or the suggestion that remorse over abortion might be appropriate, I have found that some people *say* they believe it (and often cite Warren's article, albeit inaccurately, despite its age). Those who allow that it is morally serious, and far from morally neutral, have to argue against restrictive laws, or the appropriateness of remorse, on a very different ground from that laid down by the premise "The fetus is just part of the woman's body (and she has a right to determine what happens to her body and should not feel guilty about anything she does to it)."

5. I say "some evil has probably been brought about" on the ground that (human) life is (usually) a good and hence (human) death usually an evil. The exceptions would be (*a*) where death is actually a good or a benefit, because the baby that would come to be if the life were not cut short would be better off dead than alive, and (*b*) where death, though not a good, is not an evil either, because the life that would be led (e.g., in a state of permanent coma) would not be a good.

Abortion Through a Feminist Ethics Lens

Susan Sherwin

Abortion has long been a central issue in the arena of applied ethics, but, the distinctive analysis of feminist ethics is generally overlooked in most philosophic discussions. Authors and readers commonly presume a familiarity with the feminist position and equate it with liberal defences of women's right to choose abortion, but, in fact, feminist ethics yields a different analysis of the moral questions surrounding abortion than that usually offered by the more familiar liberal defenders of abortion rights. Most feminists car agree with some of the conclusions that arise from certain non-feminist arguments on abortion, but they often disagree about the way the issues are formulated and the sorts of reasons that are invoked in the mainstream literature.

Among the many differences found between feminist and non-feminist arguments about abortion, is the fact that most non-feminist discussions of abortion consider the questions of the moral or legal permissibility of abortion in isolation from other questions, ignoring (and thereby obscuring) relevant connections to other social practices that oppress women. They are generally grounded in masculinist conceptions of freedom (e.g., privacy, individual choice, individuals' property rights in their own bodies) that do not meet the needs, interests, and intuitions of many of the women concerned. In contrast, feminists seek to couch their arguments in moral concepts that support their general campaign of overcoming injustice in all its dimensions, including those inherent in moral theory itself.[1] There is even disagreement about how best to understand the moral question at issue: non-feminist arguments focus exclusively on the morality and/or legality of performing abortions, whereas feminists insist that other questions, including ones about accessibility and delivery of abortion services must also be addressed.

Susan Sherwin, "Abortion Through a Feminist Ethics Lens," *Dialogue: Canadian Philosophical Review,* vol. 30, no. 1–2 (1991), © Canadian Philosophical Association 1991, published by Cambridge University Press, reproduced with permission.

Although feminists welcome the support of non-feminists in pursuing policies that will grant women control over abortion decisions, they generally envision very different sorts of policies for this purpose than those considered by non-feminist sympathizers. For example, Kathleen McDonnell (1984) urges feminists to develop an explicitly "'feminist morality' of abortion. . . . At its root it would be characterized by the deep appreciations of the complexities of life, the refusal to polarize and adopt simplistic formulas" (p. 52). Here, I propose one conception of the shape such an analysis should take.

WOMEN AND ABORTION

The most obvious difference between feminist and non-feminist approaches to abortion can be seen in the relative attention each gives to the interests and experiences of women in its analysis. Feminists consider it self-evident that the pregnant woman is a subject of principal concern in abortion decisions. In most non-feminist accounts, however, not only is she not perceived as central, she is rendered virtually invisible. Non-feminist theorists, whether they support or oppose women's right to choose abortion, focus almost all their attention on the moral status of the developing embryo or the fetus.

In pursuing a distinctively feminist ethics, it is appropriate to begin with a look at the role of abortion in women's lives. Clearly, the need for abortion can be very intense: women have pursued abortions under appalling and dangerous conditions, across widely diverse cultures and historical periods. No one denies that if abortion is not made legal, safe, and accessible, women will seek out illegal and life-threatening abortions to terminate pregnancies they cannot accept. Anti-abortion activists seem willing to accept this price, but feminists judge the inevitable loss of women's lives associated with restrictive abortion policies to be a matter of fundamental concern.

Although anti-abortion campaigners imagine that women often make frivolous and irresponsible decisions about abortion, feminists recognize that women have abortions for a wide variety of reasons. Some women, for instance, find themselves seriously ill and incapacitated throughout pregnancy: they cannot continue in their jobs and may face enormous difficulties in fulfilling their responsibilities at home. Many employers and schools will not tolerate pregnancy in their employees or students, and not every woman is able to put her job, career, or studies on hold. Women of limited means may be unable to take adequate care of children they have already borne and they may know that another mouth to feed will reduce their ability to provide for their existing children. Women who suffer from chronic disease, or who feel too young, or too old, or who are unable to maintain lasting relationships may recognize that they will not be able to care properly for a child at this time. Some who are homeless, or addicted to drugs, or who are diagnosed as carrying the AIDS virus may be unwilling to allow a child to enter the world under such circumstances. If the pregnancy is a result of rape or incest, the psychological pain of carrying it to term may be unbearable, and the woman may recognize that her attitude to the child after birth will always be tinged with bitterness. Some women have learned that the fetuses they carry have serious chromosomal anomalies and consider it best to prevent them from being born with a condition bound to cause suffering. Others, knowing the fathers to be brutal and violent, may be unwilling to subject a child to the beatings or incestuous attacks they anticipate: some may have no other realistic way to remove the child (or themselves) from the relationship.

Or a woman may simply believe that bearing a child is incompatible with her life plans at this time, since continuing a pregnancy is likely to have profound repercussions throughout a woman's entire life. If the woman is young, a pregnancy will very likely reduce her chances of education and hence limit her career and life opportunities: "The earlier a woman has a baby, it seems, the more likely she is to drop out of school; the less education she gets, the more likely she is to remain poorly paid, peripheral to the labour market, or unemployed, and the more children

she will have—between one and three more than her working childless counterpart" (Petchesky 1984, p. 150). In many circumstances, having a child will exacerbate the social and economic forces already stacked against her by virtue of her sex (and her race, class, age, sexual orientation, or the effects of some disability, etc.). Access to abortion is a necessary option for many women if they are to escape the oppressive conditions of poverty.

Whatever the reason, most feminists believe that a pregnant woman is in the best position to judge whether abortion is the appropriate response to her circumstances. Since she is usually the only one able to weigh all the relevant factors, most feminists reject attempts to offer any general abstract rules for determining when abortion is morally justified. Women's personal deliberations about abortion include contextually defined considerations reflecting her commitment to the needs and interests of everyone concerned—including herself, the fetus she carries, other members of her household, etc. Because there is no single formula available for balancing these complex factors through all possible cases, it is vital that feminists insist on protecting each woman's right to come to her own conclusions. Abortion decisions are, by their very nature, dependent on specific features of each woman's experience; theoretically dispassionate philosophers and other moralists should not expect to set the agenda for these considerations in any universal way. Women must be acknowledged as full moral agents with the responsibility for making moral decisions about their own pregnancies.[2] Although I think that it is possible for a woman to make a mistake in her moral judgment on this matter (i.e., it is possible that a woman may come to believe that she was wrong about her decision to continue or terminate a pregnancy), the intimate nature of this sort of decision makes it unlikely that anyone else is in a position to arrive at a more reliable conclusion; it is, therefore, improper to grant others the authority to interfere in women's decisions to seek abortions.

Feminist analysis regards the effects of unwanted pregnancies on the lives of women individually and collectively as a central element in the moral evaluation of abortion. Even without patriarchy, bearing a child would be a very important event in a woman's life. It involves significant physical, emotional, social, and (usually) economic changes for her. The ability to exert control over the incidence, timing, and frequency of childbearing is often tied to her ability to control most other things she values. Since we live in a patriarchal society, it is especially important to ensure that women have the authority to control their own reproduction.[3] Despite the diversity of opinion among feminists on most other matters, virtually all feminists seem to agree that women must gain full control over their own reproductive lives if they are to free themselves from male dominance.[4] Many perceive the commitment of the political right wing to opposing abortion as part of a general strategy to reassert patriarchal control over women in the face of significant feminist influence (Petchesky 1980, p.112).

Women's freedom to choose abortion is also linked with their ability to control their own sexuality. Women's subordinate status often prevents them from refusing men sexual access to their bodies. If women cannot end the unwanted pregnancies that result from male sexual dominance, their sexual vulnerability to particular men can increase, because caring for an(other) infant involves greater financial needs and reduced economic opportunities for women.[5] As a result, pregnancy often forces women to become dependent on men. Since a woman's dependence on a man is assumed to entail that she will remain sexually loyal to him, restriction of abortion serves to channel women's sexuality and further perpetuates the cycle of oppression.

In contrast to most non-feminist accounts, feminist analyses of abortion direct attention to the question of how women get pregnant. Those who reject abortion seem to believe that women can avoid unwanted pregnancies by avoiding sexual intercourse. Such views show little appreciation for the power of sexual politics in a culture that oppresses women. Existing patterns of sexual dominance mean that women often have little control over their sexual lives. They may be subject to rape by strangers, or by their husbands, boyfriends, colleagues, employers, customers, fathers, brothers, uncles, and dates. Often, the sexual coercion is not even recognized as such by the participants, but is the price of continued "good will"—popularity, economic survival, peace, or simple acceptance. Few women have not found themselves in circumstances where they do not feel free to refuse a man's demands for intercourse, either because he is holding a gun to her head or because he threatens to be emotionally hurt if she refuses (or both). Women are socialized to be compliant and accommodating, sensitive to the feelings of others, and frightened of physical power; men are socialized to take advantage of every opportunity to engage in sexual intercourse and to use sex to express dominance and power. Under such circumstances, it is difficult to argue that women could simply "choose" to avoid heterosexual activity if they wish to avoid pregnancy. Catherine MacKinnon neatly sums it up: "the logic by which women are supposed to consent to sex [is]: preclude the alternatives, then call the remaining option 'her choice'" (MacKinnon 1989, p. 192).

Nor can women rely on birth control alone to avoid pregnancy. There simply is no form of reversible contraception available that is fully safe and reliable. The pill and the IUD are the most effective means offered, but both involve significant health hazards to women and are quite dangerous for some. No woman should spend the 30 to 40 years of her reproductive life on either form of birth control. Further, both have been associated with subsequent problems of involuntary infertility, so they are far from optimal for women who seek to control the timing of their pregnancies.

The safest form of birth control involves the use of barrier methods (condoms or diaphragms) in combination with spermicidal foams or jelly. But these methods also pose difficulties for women. They may be socially awkward to use: young women are discouraged from preparing for sexual activity that might never happen and are offered instead romantic models of spontaneous passion. (Few films or novels interrupt scenes of seduction for the fetching of contraceptives.) Many women find their male partners unwilling to use barrier methods of contraception and they do not have the power to insist. Further, cost is a limiting factor for many women. Condoms and spermicides are expensive and are not covered under most health care plans. There is only one contraceptive option which offers women safe and fully effective birth control: barrier methods with the back-up option of abortion.[6]

From a feminist perspective, a central moral feature of pregnancy is that it takes place in *women's bodies* and has profound effects on *women's* lives Gender-neutral accounts of pregnancy are not available; pregnancy is explicitly a condition associated with the female body.[7] Because the need for abortion is experienced only by women, policies about abortion affect women uniquely. Thus, it is important to consider how proposed policies on abortion fit into general patterns of oppression for women. Unlike non-feminist accounts, feminist ethics demands that the effects on the oppression of women be a principal consideration when evaluating abortion policies.

THE FETUS

In contrast, most non-feminist analysts believe that the moral acceptability of abortion turns on the question of the moral status of the fetus. Even those who support women's right to choose abortion tend to accept the central premise of the anti-abortion proponents that abortion can only be tolerated if it can be proved that the fetus is lacking some criterion of full personhood.[8] Opponents of abortion have structured the debate so that it is necessary to define the status of the fetus as either valued the same as other humans (and hence entitled not to be killed) or as lacking in all value. Rather than challenging the logic of this formulation, many defenders of abortion have concentrated on showing that the fetus is indeed without significant value (Tooley 1972, Warren 1973); others, such as Wayne Sumner (1981), offer a more subtle account that reflects the gradual development of fetuses whereby there is some specific criterion that determines the degree of protection to be afforded them which is lacking in the early stages of pregnancy but present in the later stages. Thus, the debate often rages between abortion opponents who describe the fetus as an "innocent," vulnerable, morally important, separate being whose life is threatened and who must be protected at all costs, and abortion supporters who try to establish some sort of deficiency inherent to fetuses which removes them from the scope of the moral community.

The woman on whom the fetus depends for survival is considered as secondary (if she is considered at all) in these debates. The actual experiences and responsibilities of real women are not perceived as morally relevant (unless they, too, can be proved innocent by establishing that their pregnancies are a result of rape or incest). It is a common assumption of both defenders and opponents of women's right to choose abortion that many women will be irresponsible in their choices. The important question, though, is whether fetuses have the sort of status that justifies interfering in women's choices at all. In some contexts, women's role in gestation is literally reduced to that of "fetal containers"; the individual women disappear or are perceived simply as mechanical life-support systems.[9]

The current rhetoric against abortion stresses the fact that the genetic make-up of the fetus is determined at conception and the genetic code is incontestably human. Lest there be any doubt about the humanity of the fetus, we are assailed with photographs of fetuses at various stages of development demonstrating the early appearance of recognizably human characteristics, e.g., eyes, fingers, and toes. The fact that the fetus in its early stages is microscopic, virtually indistinguishable from other primate fetuses to the untrained eye, and lacking in the capacities that make human life meaningful and valuable is not deemed relevant by the self-appointed defenders of fetuses. The anti-abortion campaign is directed at evoking sympathetic attitudes towards this tiny, helpless being whose life is threatened by its own mother; it urges us to see the fetus as entangled in an adversarial relationship with the (presumably irresponsible) woman who carries it. We are encouraged to identify with the "unborn child" and not with the (selfish) woman whose life is also at issue.

Within the non-feminist literature, both defenders and opponents of women's right to choose abortion agree that the difference between a late-term fetus and a newborn infant is "merely geographical" and cannot be considered morally significant. But a fetus inhabits a woman's body and is wholly dependent on her unique contribution to its maintenance while a newborn is physically separate though still in need of a lot of care. One can only view the distinction between being in or out of a woman's womb as morally irrelevant if one discounts the perspective of the pregnant woman: feminists seem to be alone in recognizing her perspective as morally important.[10]

Within anti-abortion arguments, fetuses are identified as individuals: in our culture which views the (abstract) individual as sacred, fetuses *qua* individuals should be honoured and preserved. Extraordinary claims are made to try to establish the individuality and moral agency of fetuses. At the same time, the women who carry these fetal individuals are viewed as passive hosts whose only significant role is to refrain from aborting or harming their fetuses. Since it is widely believed that the woman does not actually have to *do* anything to protect the life of the fetus, pregnancy is often considered (abstractly) to be a tolerable burden to protect the life of an individual so like us.[11]

Medicine has played its part in supporting these sorts of attitudes. Fetal medicine is a rapidly expanding specialty, and it is commonplace in professional medical journals to find references to pregnant women as "fetal environments." Fetal surgeons now have at their disposal a repertory of sophisticated technology that can save the lives of dangerously ill fetuses; in light of such heroic successes, it is perhaps understandable that women have disappeared from their view. These specialists see fetuses as their patients, not the women who nurture them. Doctors perceive themselves as the *active* agents in saving fetal lives and, hence, believe that they are the ones in direct relationship with the fetuses they treat.

Perhaps even more distressing than the tendency to ignore the woman's agency altogether and view her as a purely passive participant in the medically controlled events of pregnancy and childbirth is the growing practice of viewing women as genuine threats to the well-being of the fetus. Increasingly, women are viewed as irresponsible or hostile towards their fetuses, and the relationship between them is characterized as adversarial (Overall 1987, p. 60). Concern for the well-being of the fetus is taken as licence for doctors to intervene to ensure that women comply with medical "advice." Courts are called upon to enforce the doctors' orders when moral pressure alone proves inadequate, and

women are being coerced into undergoing unwanted Caesarean deliveries and technologically monitored hospital births. Some states have begun to imprison women for endangering their fetuses through drug abuse and other socially unacceptable behaviours. An Australian state recently introduced a bill that makes women liable to criminal prosecution "if they are found to have smoked during pregnancy, eaten unhealthful foods, or taken any other action which can be shown to have adversely affected the development of the fetus" (Warren 1989, p. 60).

In other words, physicians have joined with anti-abortionist activists in fostering a cultural acceptance of the view that fetuses are distinct individuals, who are physically, ontologically, and socially separate from the women whose bodies they inhabit, and who have their own distinct interests. In this picture, pregnant women are either ignored altogether or are viewed as deficient in some crucial respect and hence subject to coercion for the sake of their fetuses. In the former case, the interests of the women concerned are assumed to be identical with those of the fetus: in the latter, the women's interests are irrelevant because they are perceived as immoral, unimportant, or unnatural. Focus on the fetus as an independent entity has led to presumptions which deny pregnant women their roles as active, independent, moral agents with a primary interest in what becomes of the fetuses they carry. Emphasis on the fetus's status has led to an assumed licence to interfere with women's reproductive freedom.

A FEMINIST VIEW OF THE FETUS

Because the public debate has been set up as a competition between the rights of women and those of fetuses, feminists have often felt pushed to reject claims of fetal value in order to protect women's claims. Yet, as Addelson (1987) has argued, viewing abortion in this way "tears [it] out of the context of women's lives" (p.107). There are other accounts of fetal value that are more plausible and less oppressive to women.

On a feminist account, fetal development is examined in the context in which it occurs, within women's bodies rather than in the imagined isolation implicit in many theoretical accounts. Fetuses develop in specific pregnancies which occur in the lives of particular women. They are not individuals housed in generic female wombs, nor are they full persons at risk only because they are small and subject to the whims of women. Their very existence is relational, developing as they do within particular women's bodies, and their principal relationship is to the women who carry them.

On this view, fetuses are morally significant, but their status is relational rather than absolute. Unlike other human beings, fetuses do not have any independent existence; their existence is uniquely tied to the support of a specific other. Most non-feminist commentators have ignored the relational dimension of fetal development and have presumed that the moral status of fetuses could be resolved solely in terms of abstract metaphysical criteria of personhood. They imagine that there is some set of properties (such as genetic heritage, moral agency, self-consciousness, language use, or self-determination) which will entitle all who possess them to be granted the moral status of persons (Warren 1973, Tooley 1972). They seek some particular feature by which we can neatly divide the world into the dichotomy of moral persons (who are to be valued and protected) and others (who are not entitled to the same group privileges); it follows that it is a merely empirical question whether or not fetuses possess the relevant properties.

But this vision misinterprets what is involved in personhood and what it is that is especially valued about persons. Personhood is a social category, not an isolated state. Persons are members of a community; they develop as concrete, discrete, and specific individuals. To be a morally significant category, personhood must involve personality as well as biological integrity.[12] It is not sufficient to consider persons simply as Kantian atoms of rationality: persons are all embodied, conscious beings with particular social histories. Annette Baier (1985) has developed a concept of persons as "second persons" which helps explain the sort of social dimension that seems fundamental to any moral notion of personhood:

A person, perhaps, is best seen as one who was long enough dependent upon other persons to acquire the essential arts of personhood. Persons essentially are *second* persons, who grow up with other persons. . . . The fact that a person has a life *history*, and that a people collectively have a history depends upon the humbler fact that each person has a childhood in which a cultural heritage is transmitted, ready for adolescent rejection and adult discriminating selection and contribution. Persons come after and before other persons. (P. 84–85; her emphasis.)

Persons, in other words, are members of a social community which shapes and values them, and personhood is a relational concept that must be defined in terms of interactions and relationships with others.

A fetus is a unique sort of being in that it cannot form relationships freely with others, nor can others readily form relationships with it. A fetus has a primary and particularly intimate relationship with the woman in whose womb it develops; any other relationship it may have is indirect, and must be mediated through the pregnant woman. The relationship that exists between a woman and her fetus is clearly asymmetrical, since she is the only party to the relationship who is capable of making a decision about whether the interaction should continue and since the fetus is wholly dependent on the woman who sustains it while she is quite capable of surviving without it.

However much some might prefer it to be otherwise, no one else can do anything to support or harm a fetus without doing something to the woman who nurtures it. Because of this inexorable biological reality, she bears a unique responsibility and privilege in determining her fetus's place in the social scheme of things. Clearly, many pregnancies occur to women who place very high value on the lives of the particular fetuses they carry, and choose to see their pregnancies through to term despite the possible risks and costs involved; hence, it would be wrong of anyone to force such a woman to terminate her pregnancy under these circumstances. Other women, or some of these same women at other times, value other things more highly (e.g., their freedom, their health, or previous responsibilities which conflict with those generated by the pregnancies), and choose not to continue their pregnancies. The value that women ascribe to individual fetuses varies dramatically from case to case, and may well change over the course of any particular pregnancy. There is no absolute value that attaches to fetuses apart from their relational status determined in the context of their particular development.

Since human beings are fundamentally relational beings, it is important to remember that fetuses are characteristically limited in the relationships in which they can participate; within those relationships, they can make only the most restricted "contributions."[13] After birth, human beings are capable of a much wider range of roles in relationships with an infinite variety of partners: it is that very diversity of possibility and experience that leads us to focus on the abstraction of the individual as a constant through all her/his relationships. But until birth, no such variety is possible, and the fetus is defined as an entity within a woman who will almost certainly be principally responsible for it for many years to come.

No human, and especially no fetus, can exist apart from relationships; feminist views of what is valuable about persons must reflect the social nature of their existence. Fetal lives can neither be sustained nor destroyed without affecting the women who support them. Because of a fetus's unique physical status—*within* and dependent on a particular woman—the responsibility and privilege of determining its specific social status and value must rest with the woman carrying it. Fetuses are not persons because they have not developed sufficiently in social relationships to be persons in any morally significant sense (i.e., they are not yet second persons). Newborns, although just beginning their development into persons, are immediately subject to social relationships, for they are capable of communication and response in interaction with a variety of other persons. Thus, feminist accounts of abortion stress the importance of protecting women's right to continue as well as to terminate pregnancies as each sees fit.

FEMINIST POLITICS AND ABORTION

Feminist ethics directs us to look at abortion in the context of other issues of power and not to limit discussion to the standard questions about its moral and legal acceptability. Because coerced pregnancy has repercussions for women's oppressed status generally, it is important to ensure that abortion not only be made legal but that adequate services be made accessible to all women who seek them. This means that within Canada, where medically approved abortion is technically recognized as legal (at least for the moment), we must protest the fact that it is not made available to many of the women who have the greatest need for abortions; vast geographical areas offer no abortion services at all, but unless the women of those regions can afford to travel to urban clinics, they have no meaningful right to abortion. Because women depend on access to abortion in their pursuit of social equality, it is a matter of moral as well as political responsibility that provincial health plans should cover the cost of transport and service in the abortion facilities women choose. Ethical study of abortion involves understanding and critiquing the economic, age, and social barriers that currently restrict access to medically acceptable abortion services.[14]

Moreover, it is also important that abortion services be provided in an atmosphere that fosters women's health and well-being; hence the care offered should be in a context that is supportive of the choices women make. Abortions should be seen as part of women's overall reproductive health and could be included within centres that deal with all matters of reproductive health in an open, patient-centred manner where effective counselling is offered for a wide range of reproductive decisions.[15] Providers need to recognize that abortion is a legitimate option so that services will be delivered with respect and concern for the physical, psychological, and emotional effects on a patient. All too frequently, hospital-based abortions are provided by practitioners who are uneasy about their role and treat the women involved with hostility and resentment. Increasingly, many anti-abortion activists have personalized their attacks and focussed their attention on harassing the women who enter and leave abortion clinics. Surely requiring a woman to pass a gauntlet of hostile protesters on her way to and from an abortion is not conducive to effective health care. Ethical exploration of abortion raises questions about how women are treated when they seek abortions;[16] achieving legal permission for women to dispose of their fetuses if they are determined enough to manage the struggle should not be accepted as the sole moral consideration.

Nonetheless, feminists must formulate their distinctive response to legislative initiatives on abortion. The tendency of Canadian politicians confronted by vocal activists on both sides of the abortion issue has been to seek "compromises" that seem to give something to each (and, thereby, also deprives each of important features sought in policy formation). Thus, the House of Commons recently passed a law (Bill C-43) that allows a woman to have an abortion only if a doctor certifies that her physical, mental, or emotional health will be otherwise threatened. Many non-feminist supporters of women's right to choose consider this a victory and urge feminists to be satisfied with it, but feminists have good reason to object. Besides their obvious objection to having abortion returned to the Criminal Code, feminists also object that this policy considers doctors and not women the best judges of a woman's need for abortion; feminists have little reason to trust doctors to appreciate the political dimension of abortion or to respond adequately to women's needs. Abortion must be a woman's decision, and not one controlled by her doctor. Further, experience shows that doctors are already reluctant to provide abortions to women; the opportunity this law presents for criminal persecution of doctors by anti-abortion campaigners is a sufficient worry to inhibit their participation.[17] Feminists want women's decision-making to be recognized as legitimate, and cannot be satisfied with a law that makes abortion a medical choice.

Feminists support abortion on demand because they know that women must have control over their reproduction. For the same reason, they actively oppose forced abortion and coerced sterilization, practices that are sometimes inflicted on the most powerless women, especially those in the Third World. Feminist ethics demands that access to voluntary, safe, effective birth control be part of any abortion discussion, so that women have access to other means of avoiding pregnancy.[18]

Feminist analysis addresses the context as well as the practice of abortion decisions. Thus, feminists

also object to the conditions which lead women to abort wanted fetuses because there are not adequate financial and social supports available to care for a child. Because feminist accounts value fetuses that are wanted by the women who carry them, they oppose practices which force women to abort because of poverty or intimidation. Yet, the sorts of social changes necessary if we are to free women from having abortions out of economic necessity are vast; they include changes not only in legal and health-care policy, but also in housing, child care, employment, etc. (Petchesky 1980, p. 112). Nonetheless, feminist ethics defines reproductive freedom as the condition under which women are able to make truly voluntary choices about their reproductive lives, and these many dimensions are implicit in the ideal.

Clearly, feminists are not "pro-abortion," for they are concerned to ensure the safety of each pregnancy to the greatest degree possible; wanted fetuses should not be harmed or lost. Therefore, adequate pre- and postnatal care and nutrition are also important elements of any feminist position on reproductive freedom. Where anti-abortionists direct their energies to trying to prevent women from obtaining abortions, feminists seek to protect the health of wanted fetuses. They recognize that far more could be done to protect and care for fetuses if the state directed its resources at supporting women who continue their pregnancies, rather than draining away resources in order to police women who find that they must interrupt their pregnancies. Caring for the women who carry fetuses is not only a more legitimate policy than is regulating them; it is probably also more effective at ensuring the health and well-being of more fetuses.

Feminist ethics also explores how abortion policies fit within the politics of sexual domination. Most feminists are sensitive to the fact that many men support women's right to abortion out of the belief that women will be more willing sexual partners if they believe that they can readily terminate an unwanted pregnancy. Some men coerce their partners into obtaining abortions the women may not want.[19] Feminists understand that many women oppose abortion for this very reason, being unwilling to support a practice that increases women's sexual vulnerability (Luker 1984, p. 209–15). Thus, it is important that feminists develop a coherent analysis of reproductive freedom that includes sexual freedom (as women choose to define it). That requires an analysis of sexual freedom that includes women's right to refuse sex: such a right can only be assured if women have equal power to men and are not subject to domination by virtue of their sex.[20]

In sum, then, feminist ethics demands that moral discussions of abortion be more broadly defined than they have been in most philosophic discussions. Only by reflecting on the meaning of ethical pronouncements on actual women's lives and the connections between judgments on abortion and the conditions of domination and subordination can we come to an adequate understanding of the moral status of abortion in our society. As Rosalind Petchesky (1980) argues, feminist discussion of abortion "must be moved beyond the framework of a 'woman's right to choose' and connected to a much broader revolutionary movement that addresses all of the conditions of women's liberation" (p. 113).

NOTES

1. For some idea of the ways in which traditional moral theory oppresses women, see Morgan (1987) and Hoagland (1988).

2. Critics continue to want to structure the debate around the *possibility* of women making frivolous abortion decisions and hence want feminists to agree to setting boundaries on acceptable grounds for choosing abortion. Feminists ought to resist this injunction, though. There is no practical way of drawing a line fairly in the abstract; cases that may appear "frivolous" at a distance, often turn out to be substantive when the details are revealed, i.e., frivolity is in the eyes of the beholder. There is no evidence to suggest that women actually make the sorts of choices worried critics hypothesize about: e.g., a woman eight months pregnant who chooses to abort because she wants to take a trip or gets in "a tiff" with her partner. These sorts of fantasies, on which demands to distinguish between legitimate and illegitimate personal reasons for choosing abortion chiefly rest, reflect an offensive conception of women as

irresponsible; they ought not to be perpetuated. Women, seeking moral guidance in their own deliberations about choosing abortion, do not find such hypothetical discussions of much use.

3. In her monumental historical analysis of the early roots of Western patriarchy, Gerda Lerner (1986) determined that patriarchy began in the period from 3100 to 600 B.C. when men appropriated women's sexual and reproductive capacity; the earliest states entrenched patriarchy by institutionalizing the sexual and procreative subordination of women to men.

4. There are some women who claim to be feminists against choice in abortion. See, for instance, Callahan (1987), though few spell out their full feminist program. For reasons I develop in this paper, I do not think this is a consistent position.

5. There is a lot the state could do to ameliorate this condition. If it provided women with adequate financial support, removed the inequities in the labour market, and provided affordable and reliable childcare, pregnancy need not so often lead to a woman's dependence on a particular man. The fact that it does not do so is evidence of the state's complicity in maintaining women's subordinate position with respect to men.

6. See Petchesky (1984), especially Chapter 5, "Considering the Alternatives: The Problems of Contraception," where she documents the risks and discomforts associated with pill use and IUDs and the increasing rate at which women are choosing the option of diaphragm or condom with the option of early legal abortions as backup.

7. See Zillah Eisenstein (1988) for a comprehensive theory of the role of the pregnant body as the central element in the cultural subordination of women.

8. Thomson (1971) is a notable exception to this trend.

9. This seems reminiscent of Aristotle's view of women as "flower pots" where men implant the seed with all the important genetic information and the movement necessary for development and women's job is that of passive gestation, like the flower pot. For exploration of the flower pot picture of pregnancy, see Whitbeck (1973) and Lange (1983).

10. Contrast Warren (1989) with Tooley (1972).

11. The definition of pregnancy as a purely passive activity reaches its ghoulish conclusion in the increasing acceptability of sustaining brain-dead women on life support systems to continue their functions as incubators until the fetus can

be safely delivered. For a discussion of this new trend, see Murphy (1989).

12. This apt phrasing is taken from Petchesky (1986), p. 342.

13. Fetuses are almost wholly individuated by the women who bear them. The fetal "contributions" to the relationship are defined by the projections and interpretations of the pregnant woman in the latter stages of pregnancy if she chooses to perceive fetal movements in purposeful ways (e.g., "it likes classical music, wine, exercise").

14. Some feminists suggest we seek recognition of the legitimacy of non-medical abortion services. This would reduce costs and increase access dramatically, with no apparent increase in risk, provided that services were offered by trained, responsible practitioners concerned with the well-being of their clients. It would also allow the possibility of increasing women's control over abortion. See, for example McDonnell (1984), chap. 8.

15. For a useful model of such a centre, see Wagner and Lee (1989).

16. See CARAL/Halifax (1990) for women's stories about their experiences with hospitals and free-standing abortion clinics.

17. The Canadian Medical Association has confirmed those fears. In testimony before the House of Commons committee reviewing the bill, the CMA reported that over half the doctors surveyed who now perform abortions expect to stop offering them if the legislation goes through. Since the Commons passed the bill, the threats of withdrawal of service have increased. Many doctors plan to abandon their abortion service once the law is introduced, because they are unwilling to accept the harassment they anticipate from anti-abortion zealots. Even those who believe that they will eventually win any court case that arises, fear the expense and anxiety involved as the case plays itself out.

18. Therefore, the Soviet model, where women have access to multiple abortions but where there is no other birth control available, must also be opposed.

19. See CARAL/Halifax (1990), p. 20–21, for examples of this sort of abuse.

20. It also requires that discussions of reproductive and sexual freedom not be confined to "the language of control and sexuality characteristic of a technology of sex" (Diamond and Quinby 1988, p. 197), for such language is alienating and constrains women's experiences of their own sexuality.

REFERENCES

Addelson, Kathryn Pyne, 1987. "Moral Passages." In *Women and Moral Theory*. Edited by Eva Feder Kittay and Diana T. Meyers. Totowa, NJ: Rowman & Littlefield.

Baier, Annette, 1985. *Postures of the Mind: Essays on Mind and Morals*. Minneapolis: University of Minnesota Press.

Callahan, Sidney, 1987. "A Pro-life Feminist Makes Her Case." *Utne Reader* (March/April): 104–14.

CARAL/Halifax, 1990. *Telling Our Stories: Abortion Stories from Nova Scotia*. Halifax: CARAL/Halifax (Canadian Abortion Rights Action League).

Daly, Mary, 1973. *Beyond God the Father: Toward a Philosophy of Women's Liberation*. Boston: Beacon Press.

Diamond, Irene, and Lee Quinby, 1988. "American Feminism and the Language of Control." In *Feminism and Foucault: Reflections on Resistance*. Edited by Irene Diamond and Lee Quinby. Boston: Northeastern University Press.

Eisenstein, Zillah R, 1988. *The Female Body and the Law*. Berkeley: University of California Press.

Hoagland, Sara Lucia, 1988. *Lesbian Ethics: Toward New Value*. Palo Alto, CA: Institute of Lesbian Studies.

Lange, Lynda, 1983. "Woman Is Not a Rational Animal: On Aristotle's Biology of Reproduction." In *Discovering Reality: Feminist Perspectives on Epistemology, Metaphysics, Methodology, and Philosophy of Science*. Edited by Sandra Harding and Merill B. Hintickka. Dordrecht, Holland: D. Reidel.

Lerner, Gerda, 1986. *The Creation of Patriarchy*. New York Oxford.

Luker, Kristin, 1984. *Abortion and the Politics of Motherhood*. Berkeley: University of California Press.

MacKinnon, Catherine, 1989. *Toward a Feminist Theory of the State*. Cambridge, MA: Harvard University Press.

McDonnell, Kathleen, 1984. *Not an Easy Choice: A Feminist Re-examines Abortion*. Toronto: The Women's Press.

McLaren, Angus, and Arlene Tigar McLaren, 1986. The Bedroom and the State: The Changing Practices and Politics of Contraception and Abortion in Canada, 1880–1980. Toronto: McClelland and Stewart.

Morgan, Kathryn Pauly, 1987. "Women and Moral Madness." In *Science, Morality and Feminist Theory*. Edited by

Marsha Hanen and Kai Nielsen. *Canadian Journal of Philosophy*, Supplementary Volume 13:201–26.

Murphy, Julien S., 1989. "Should Pregnancies Be Sustained in Brain-dead Women?: A Philosophical Discussion of Postmortem Pregnancy." In *Healing Technology: Feminist Perspectives*. Edited by Kathryn Srother Ratcliff et al. Ann Arbor: The University of Michigan Press.

Overall, Christine, 1987. *Ethics and Human Reproduction: A Feminist Analysis*. Winchester, MA: Allen & Unwin.

Petchesky, Rosalind Pollack, 1980. "Reproductive Freedom: Beyond 'A Woman's Right to Choose." In *Women: Sex and Sexuality*. Edited by Catherine R. Stimpson and Ethel Spector Person. Chicago: University of Chicago Press.

_____. 1984. *Abortion and Woman's Choice: The State, Sexuality, and Reproductive Freedom*. Boston: Northeastern University Press.

Sumner, L. W., 1981. *Abortion and Moral Theory*. Princeton: Princeton University Press.

Thomson, Judith Jarvis, 1971. "A Defense of Abortion." *Philosophy and Public Affairs*, 1:47–66.

Tooley, Michael, 1972. "Abortion and Infanticide." *Philosophy and Public Affairs*, 2,1 (Fall): 37–65.

Van Wagner, Vicki, and Bob Lee, 1989. "Principles into Practice: An Activist Vision of Feminist Reproductive Health Care." In *The Future of Human Reproduction*. Edited by Christine Overall. Toronto: The Women's Press.

CHAPTER 10

Euthanasia and Physician-Assisted Suicide

For fifteen years, Terri Schiavo existed between life and death in that shadow land called a persistent vegetative state, a place where she was wakeful but without awareness or any purposeful behavior. Severe brain damage had left her there, with virtually no chance of recovery. And all the while, a storm of caustic debate swirled around her, reaching its greatest strength in the last few days before her death on March 31, 2005. In 1990 her heart had stopped briefly because of a chemical imbalance, leaving her in that twilight state, kept alive by a feeding tube. She had left no living will, no written record of her wishes should she become indefinitely incapacitated. Her husband, Michael Schiavo, insisted that Terri had told him once that she would prefer death to being kept alive with machines. Her parents rejected his claim and demanded that Terri be kept alive, holding out hope that with proper care she might recover.

The battle between Michael Schiavo and Terri's parents raged on in the courts for years. Again and again, state and federal courts sided with the husband, while the U.S. Supreme Court repeatedly refused to hear the case. In the final days before Terri died, President George W. Bush, the U.S. Congress, the governor of Florida (where she lived), and Florida legislators weighed in on the controversy, supporting Terri's parents.

Finally, a judge allowed the feeding tube to be removed, and Terri Schiavo, age forty-one, died thirteen days later. The parents called the removal "judicial homicide." A Vatican official called it "an attack against God."[1]

So it goes with all public debates on the moral permissibility of euthanasia. Passions rise, claims and counterclaims collide, and stakes are high. In the balance are issues of life and death, science and religion, murder and mercy. The tragic end of Terri Schiavo is only the most dramatic (and dramatized) case in a series of tragic ends that turned into widely publicized moral battlegrounds (see the box "The Death of Karen Ann Quinlan"). The moral questions it incited are typical of such cases: Was removing Terri Schiavo's feeding tube really a case of murder? Or was it a morally permissible act allowing her to die with dignity and escape her bleak condition? What if instead of stopping the tube feeding, her doctors had never started it because they deemed her situation hopeless? Would *that* have been murder—or a permissible act of mercy? Or suppose that soon after Schiavo collapsed, her doctors had decided to give her a lethal injection? Would such an act have been morally wrong? What if Schiavo had left a living will that clearly specified that she did *not* want to be kept alive by any means if she fell into a persistent vegetative state? Would withdrawing the feeding tube or giving her a lethal injection then have been morally acceptable?

Of course, in every instance of euthanasia there are plenty of nonmoral questions too—primarily legal, judicial, medical, scientific, and political. (In the Schiavo case, for example, the moral questions arose side by side with what most informed observers saw as the *real* issue: Who, if anyone, had the legal right to decide for Schiavo what was to become of her?) But these nonmoral concerns

The Death of Karen Ann Quinlan

Like nothing else before it, the case of Karen Ann Quinlan focused the world's attention on the medical truths, the legal complexities, and the moral problems of euthanasia. She was just twenty-one years old when she sustained acute brain damage after imbibing alcohol along with a tranquilizer. She was left in a persistent vegetative state, kept alive by a feeding tube and a respirator, a machine that maintained her breathing mechanically. After several months, members of her family came to accept that her recovery was hopeless and sought permission from the courts to unplug the respirator to allow her to die. Finally in 1976 the New Jersey Supreme Court granted their request. But to everyone's surprise, she continued to breathe without the respirator until 1985, ten years after she slipped into the vegetative state. She died on June 11.*

*See "Famous Cases: Karen Ann Quinlan," *CBC News Online,* March 22, 2005, http://www.cbc.ca/news2 /background/schiavo/vegetative_state.html (January 20, 2015); Barran H. Lerner, "Planning for the Long Goodbye," *New York Times,* June 18, 2004.

are intertwined with the moral concerns. Our task here is to apply moral reasoning to try to unravel the knot.

ISSUE FILE: BACKGROUND

Euthanasia is directly or indirectly bringing about the death of another person for that person's sake.[2] It is thought to provide a benefit or a good for the person by ending a life deemed no longer worth living—a situation that typically arises when someone has an incurable or terminal disease that causes great suffering or when someone experiences an irreversible loss of consciousness (as in the Schiavo case). This notion of dying as a kind of blessing is

preserved in the Greek roots of *euthanasia,* which literally means "easy death." Euthanasia makes sense to many people because they believe that a quick and painless death would be preferable to a slow and painful dying (such as the kind that some terminal cancer patients endure) or a long, vegetative sleep without a chance for a meaningful life.

As you might expect, the moral permissibility of euthanasia depends heavily on the consent of the patient (the person whose death is being considered). Moral philosophers therefore distinguish between euthanasia that is voluntary, nonvoluntary, and involuntary. In **voluntary euthanasia**, the patient requests or agrees to the act. She may make the request in person or leave instructions to be followed in case she becomes incapacitated. Such instructions are usually in the form of an **advance directive** (for example, a living will), a legal document allowing physicians to withhold or withdraw treatments if a patient becomes terminally ill and unable to express her wishes. For any voluntary euthanasia request to be valid, the patient at the time of the request must be competent—that is, capable of making an informed, rational choice. In **nonvoluntary euthanasia**, others besides the patient (family or physicians, for example) choose euthanasia for her because she is not competent (due to illness or injury) and has left no instructions regarding her end-of-life preferences. Euthanasia performed on infants and small children is, of course, nonvoluntary. In **involuntary euthanasia**, the act is carried out against the wishes of the patient and is therefore illegal and widely regarded as immoral.

People also draw a distinction between active and passive euthanasia. **Active euthanasia** is taking a direct action to kill someone, to carry out a "mercy killing." A doctor who gives a patient a lethal injection is performing active euthanasia, and so is a man who suffocates his dying brother to spare him from an unbearably painful passing. **Passive euthanasia** is allowing someone to die by *not* doing something—by withholding or withdrawing measures necessary for sustaining life. A doctor, then, would be performing passive euthanasia if she removed a patient's respirator, did not administer antibiotics to halt a life-threatening infection, or withdrew hydration and nutrition (fluids and nutrients).

Many believe that this active-passive distinction is essential to understanding the moral permissibility of euthanasia. It allows them to maintain that whereas active euthanasia is always wrong, in some cases passive euthanasia may be permissible. This view is widespread among physicians and fits with the popular notion that killing people is morally worse than letting them die. Others, however, argue that there is no moral difference between killing and letting die: in both active and passive euthanasia the patient's death is caused, and they are therefore morally equivalent.

Taking into account the categories of *voluntary*, *nonvoluntary*, *active*, and *passive* (and disregarding *involuntary*), we can identify four kinds of euthanasia: (1) *active voluntary* (mercy killing at the patient's request), (2) *active nonvoluntary* (mercy killing without the patient's consent or request), (3) *passive voluntary* (letting the patient die at her request), and (4) *passive nonvoluntary* (letting the patient die without his consent or request). Generally, the law forbids active euthanasia (either voluntary or nonvoluntary), and the medical profession is officially opposed to it (though the views of individual physicians vary). Passive voluntary euthanasia is legal; by law, competent patients have the right to refuse any kind of medical treatment. Passive nonvoluntary euthanasia may be legal provided that someone (a family member, for example) can be designated to make decisions on behalf of the patient.

Related to, but distinct from, active voluntary euthanasia is **physician-assisted suicide**—the killing of a person by the person's own hand with the help of a physician. Like active voluntary euthanasia, physician-assisted suicide is requested by the patient, and the intended outcome is the patient's death for the relief of pain and suffering. But

the agent who ultimately causes the death in active voluntary euthanasia is the physician, whereas the ultimate causal agent in physician-assisted suicide is the patient. In the former, the physician is primarily responsible for the killing; in the latter, the patient is. In most cases, the physician provides help by prescribing a lethal dose of drugs, which the patient then administers to himself.

In the United States, physician-assisted suicide is legal in six states—Oregon, Washington, Montana, Colorado, Vermont, and California—and in the District of Columbia. U.S. Supreme Court rulings allow each state to decide for itself whether to legalize assisted suicide. The official position of the American Medical Association (AMA), the main professional group for American physicians, is that "physician-assisted suicide is fundamentally incompatible with the physician's role as healer, would be difficult or impossible to control, and would pose serious societal risks."[3]

A factor that can complicate all the foregoing issues is the concept of death itself. One problem is that thanks to modern medical technology, determining when a person is dead is not so straightforward as it once seemed. Death has become more difficult to define. Years ago the prevailing notion was that a person is dead when his breathing and blood flow stop (no respiration and no heartbeat). But nowadays machines can keep an individual's heart and lungs functioning long after the brain permanently and completely shuts down. Thus we can have an individual whose organs are mechanically operated while he is in a coma or persistent vegetative state—*for years*. By the traditional definition of death, such an individual would still be alive, but many people would insist that he is no longer there: he is dead. So the conventional notion of death seems to be inadequate.

Why does correctly defining death matter at all? Say an individual is in the kind of state just described. If we judge him to be dead and thus no longer a person, then perhaps it would be morally

Landmark Court Rulings

In the past five decades, U.S. courts have several times weighed in on the controversial issues of euthanasia and physician-assisted suicide. The following are some of the more far-reaching rulings:

- **1976** The New Jersey Supreme Court ruled that a life-sustaining respirator could be legally disconnected from Karen Ann Quinlan, a young woman who had lapsed into a persistent vegetative state. After it was removed, she remained comatose and lived for another ten years, finally dying in June 1985.

- **1990** The U.S. Supreme Court (in *Cruzan v. Director, Missouri Department of Health*) ruled that a feeding tube could be removed from Nancy Cruzan, a woman in a persistent vegetative state due to an automobile accident, if "clear and convincing evidence" shows that she would have approved of the withdrawal. The ruling recognized the legitimacy of living wills, surrogates to act for incapacitated individuals, and a qualified "right to die."

- **1997** The U.S. Supreme Court (in *Washington v. Glucksberg*) ruled that a Washington State prohibition of physician-assisted suicide did not violate the due process clause of the Fourteenth Amendment.

- **1997** The U.S. Supreme Court (in *Vacco v. Quill*) ruled that a New York State prohibition of physician-assisted suicide did not violate the equal protection clause of the Fourteenth Amendment. The Court acknowledged a crucial distinction between withdrawing life-sustaining treatment and assisted suicide. People may refuse life-sustaining treatment, but assisted suicide is prohibited.

- **2006** In a 6–3 decision in *Gonzales v. Oregon*, the U.S. Supreme Court ruled that the U.S. attorney general is not authorized to ban controlled substances used in physician-assisted suicide. The decision had the effect of upholding Oregon's Death with Dignity Act.

- **2009** In a 4–3 decision in *Baxter v. State of Montana*, the Montana Supreme Court ruled that physician-assisted suicide is not "against public policy." The decision applied only to Montana. The court also ruled that doctors who help terminally ill patients commit suicide cannot be prosecuted under Montana state law.

- **2015** In a 2–1 ruling, the New Mexico Court of Appeals struck down a lower court ruling legalizing physician-assisted suicide, concluding that "aid in dying is not a fundamental liberty interest under the New Mexico Constitution."

---

permissible to disconnect him from the machines, or administer a fatal drug overdose, or remove his feeding tube, or even harvest his organs for transplant into another person. Or would it? If we deem him alive and still a person, perhaps we are not justified in doing *any* of the above. Maybe taking any one of these actions is to commit murder. Depending on the concept of death accepted by the legal system, killing him or allowing him to die could have serious legal consequences.

To overcome the drawbacks of the traditional definition of death, alternative definitions have

been suggested. According to the *whole-brain* definition of death, an individual is dead when all brain functions (including those performed in the brain stem) permanently stop. It has become the primary standard in both medicine and the law for determining death. Critics of the whole-brain standard, though, have pointed out that it is based on a faulty assumption: that the brain is the control center for all physiological functions. Yet some functions (such as respiration) are partially independent of brain activity. In addition, by the whole-brain standard, individuals in an irreversible persistent vegetative state (who have some detectable brain activity) are thought to be alive—a result that some regard as counterintuitive or puzzling.

The *higher-brain* definition of death says that an individual is dead when higher brain functions—those that give rise to consciousness—permanently stop. Some have maintained that because consciousness is necessary for personhood, an individual whose higher brain functions have disappeared is no longer a person and is therefore rightly considered dead. By the higher-brain standard, individuals in a persistent vegetative state (who continue to breathe and have a heartbeat) but whose higher brain functions have ceased are thought to be dead—also a result that some people find counterintuitive.

MORAL THEORIES

Utilitarianism, Kant's ethics, and natural law theory lead to divergent conclusions on the issue of euthanasia. An act-utilitarian would certainly try to take into account how much overall happiness various possible actions could bring about, everyone considered. But she could make this calculation in different ways. The basic approach would be to consider the patient's suffering (as well as that of others involved, such as family members) and the likely success of any treatments and try to determine how much overall happiness would be generated by different actions, including bringing about the patient's death. If the patient's situation were hopeless and his suffering great, an act-utilitarian could decide that the greatest net happiness would result from killing the patient or letting him die. The patient's consent to euthanasia might or might not be a primary concern, depending on how his consent would affect overall happiness. On the other hand, the act-utilitarian might say that euthanasia is contrary to the goal of maximizing happiness because killing a person rules out any possibility of his experiencing happiness in the future. Happiness does not occur in a vacuum; it exists only when persons experience it. So eliminating a person eliminates potential happiness.

Some people—even those who are not thoroughgoing utilitarians—argue against euthanasia on what amounts to rule-utilitarian grounds or something close to it. They contend that regardless of the moral permissibility of euthanasia in specific cases, a general rule (that is, a social policy or law) permitting some types of euthanasia would cause more harm than good. They offer slippery slope arguments such as the following: Passing a law (making a rule) permitting active voluntary euthanasia would inevitably lead to abuses such as more frequent use of nonvoluntary euthanasia and unnecessary killing; therefore, no such law should be passed. Similarly, some argue that a general rule allowing physician-assisted suicide would destroy the "moral center" of the medical profession; if physicians are allowed to kill patients, they will violate their pledge to protect life and to heal, causing patients to distrust them. Of course, it is also possible to argue *for* euthanasia on rule-utilitarian grounds. (Whether such arguments are sound is another matter.) A rule-utilitarian could devise a rule that he thinks would result in a maximization of happiness for everyone if the rule were consistently followed.

Like the utilitarian, the Kantian theorist could also take several different positions on euthanasia, consistent with Kantian principles. She could argue that euthanasia is never permissible because it would entail treating persons as mere disposable things. Kant underscores this view in his discussion of suicide. He maintains that "suicide is in no circumstances permissible" because it robs individuals of their personhood, which is the very foundation of all moral values. Furthermore, it treats persons as if they had no more value than a beast. As Kant puts it, "But the rule of morality does not admit of [suicide] under any condition because it degrades human nature below the level of animal nature and so destroys it."[4] This stern prohibition against suicide may or may not apply equally well to euthanasia—depending on whether those considered for euthanasia are to be regarded as persons. Certainly those who are competent (coherent and rational) are persons and therefore should not be killed or allowed to die. But what would Kant say about individuals who have slipped from waking life into a coma or a vegetative state? Are they still persons with full moral rights? If they are persons, then performing euthanasia on them would be immoral. If they are not persons, then euthanasia might be morally acceptable. In fact, a Kantian might argue that performing euthanasia on individuals in comas or vegetative states may be morally permissible precisely because persons have intrinsic worth and dignity. The bioethicist Ronald Munson explains this view well:

> It may be more in keeping with our freedom and dignity for us to instruct others either to put us to death or to take no steps to keep us alive should we ever be in such a state. Voluntary euthanasia may be compatible with (if not required by) Kant's ethics.
>
> By a similar line of reasoning, it may be that nonvoluntary euthanasia might be seen as a duty that we have to others. We might argue that by putting to death a comatose and hopeless person we are recognizing the dignity that person possessed in his or her previous state.[5]

According to the dominant reading of natural law theory, euthanasia is wrong in almost every instance. It is wrong because we have a moral duty to preserve life. So intentionally performing any kind of euthanasia, active or passive, is impermissible. The doctrine of double effect, however, allows one exception to this rule. Recall that this doctrine makes a distinction between (1) performing a good action that happens to have a bad effect and (2) performing a bad action to achieve a good effect. The former may be permissible, but the latter is not. In the case of euthanasia, the doctrine implies that giving a pain-racked patient a large dose of morphine to end her life (a practice known as *terminal sedation*) is never morally acceptable. But giving her a large dose of morphine with the intention of easing her pain—an act that has the side effect of expediting her death—is permissible. The hastening of the patient's death is permissible because even though it was foreseen, it was not intended.

CRITICAL THOUGHT: Dr. Kevorkian and Physician-Assisted Suicide

Dr. Jack Kevorkian was known as a champion of the right-to-die movement, having helped many incurably ill people commit suicide. He was also known as "Dr. Death," the physician who helped desperate people kill themselves. After many unsuccessful tries, prosecutors finally won a conviction against him for murder: in 1999, he was sentenced to ten to twenty-five years in prison. The *New York Times* reported that the sentence was handed down "despite emotional courtroom pleas on his behalf from the widow and brother of the terminally ill man he was convicted of killing."*

Do you agree with the verdict in this case? Why or why not? If you do not agree, would your opinion change if you knew that many of Dr. Kevorkian's suicide patients were not mentally competent at the time of their deaths (because of depression), as some people allege? If so, why? If you were terminally ill and in horrendous pain with no hope of relief, might you think it morally permissible to use the services of someone like Dr. Kevorkian? If not, why not?

*Dirk Johnson, "Kevorkian Sentenced to 10 to 25 Years in Prison," *New York Times,* April 14, 1999.

In the doctrine of double effect, intention makes all the difference.

MORAL ARGUMENTS

Most plausible euthanasia arguments are about *active* euthanasia (mercy killing, as opposed to letting the patient die). As suggested earlier, passive euthanasia (both voluntary and nonvoluntary) is legal, provided certain conditions are met, and both forms of it are widely believed to be morally acceptable. So let us confine our evaluation here to moral arguments for and against *active voluntary euthanasia* (mercy killing at the patient's request). The question these arguments address, then, is straightforward: *Is active voluntary euthanasia morally permissible?*

As we proceed, we must keep an important distinction in mind: moral permissibility is not the same thing as legal permissibility. Whether euthanasia is morally acceptable is a separate issue from whether it should be legalized. It is possible that we could be justified in believing both that euthanasia

is morally permissible *and* that it should not be legalized—or vice versa. We might plausibly argue that in some cases, performing active voluntary euthanasia is the right thing to do but that legalizing it would have terrible consequences. Legalization could, say, lead doctors to practice active *nonvoluntary* euthanasia or encourage them to care less about preserving life or cause patients to fear or mistrust doctors. To mix up these two kinds of issues—moral and legal—is to invite confusion.

We begin by examining arguments *for* active voluntary euthanasia. The strongest of these are built on two fundamental moral principles: persons have (1) a right of self-determination and (2) an obligation to help someone in serious distress or peril (if they are in a position to help without great risk to themselves). Principle 1 refers to the patient's right of self-determination, and Principle 2 to other persons who might be able to benefit her. Principle 1 assumes that persons have autonomy—the capacity, as Kant would have it, to use reason to guide their own actions and make their own decisions. It asserts that persons have the right to exercise this power to direct their lives as they see fit (with the proviso that their actions not violate the rights of others). Many who appeal to this principle argue that if it applies to how persons live, then it surely applies to how they die, because their dying is part of their life. This is how the bio-ethicist Dan W. Brock explains the importance of this end-of-life self-determination:

> Most people are very concerned about the nature of the last stage of their lives. This reflects not just a fear of experiencing substantial suffering when dying, but also a desire to retain dignity and control during this last period of life. Death is today increasingly preceded by a long period of significant physical and mental decline, due in part to the technological interventions of modern medicine. Many people adjust to these disabilities and find meaning and value in new activities and ways. Others find the impairments and burdens in the last stage of their lives at some point sufficiently great to make life no longer worth living. For many patients near death, maintaining the quality of one's life, avoiding great suffering, maintaining one's dignity, and insuring that others remember us as we wish them to become of paramount importance and outweigh merely extending one's life. But there is no single, objectively correct answer for everyone as to when, if at all, one's life becomes all things considered a burden and unwanted. If self-determination is a fundamental value, then the great variability among people on this question makes it especially important that individuals control the manner, circumstances, and timing of their dying and death.[6]

Principle 2 is a duty of beneficence (a duty to benefit others). Applied to euthanasia, it says that if we are in a position to ease the agony of another, and we can do so without excessive cost to ourselves, we should try to render aid. This tenet applies to persons generally, but it carries extra weight for people with a special relationship with the suffering person, such as family members, close friends, and doctors. Physicians have an explicit obligation to try to relieve the misery of their patients—especially dying patients who often must endure horrific pain and suffering. Many advocates of euthanasia contend that if a competent dying

patient is in agony and asks to be put out of her misery (active voluntary euthanasia), rejecting her plea for mercy would be both cruel and wicked. They also insist that merely withholding treatment from her to hasten her death (passive euthanasia) would only prolong her suffering.

Here is one way to incorporate both Principles 1 and 2 into a single argument for active voluntary euthanasia:

1. Competent persons have a right of self-determination (as long as exercising this right does not violate others' rights).

2. The right of self-determination includes the right of competent persons to decide the manner of their dying and to choose active (voluntary) euthanasia.

3. We have an obligation to help others in serious distress or peril (if we are in a position to help without great risk to ourselves).

4. This duty of beneficence includes the duty, under appropriate conditions, to ease the pain and suffering of competent dying persons by performing active (voluntary) euthanasia.

5. Therefore, active voluntary euthanasia for competent dying persons is permissible.

The central idea behind this argument is that if competent dying persons have a right to choose active euthanasia, and if the duty of beneficence includes performing active voluntary euthanasia, then active voluntary euthanasia is morally permissible. But does the conclusion follow from the premises, and are the premises true? The answer to the first part of this question is yes. The answer to the second part is more complicated. Look at Premises 1 and 3; they articulate the two basic moral principles we began with. These principles qualify as considered moral judgments and are accepted by virtually all parties to the euthanasia debate. We have good reason, then, to say that Premises 1 and 3 are true.

Premises 2 and 4, however, are controversial. Critics of Premise 2 would say that we do indeed have a right of self-determination but that this right *does not* include the right to opt for active voluntary euthanasia. The reason is that active euthanasia is killing, and killing is always wrong. We may have all sorts of rights, but killing is still killing.

This reply, though, is based on a superficial understanding of prohibitions against killing. Some kinds of killing are considered by most people to be morally permissible—for example, killing in self-defense and killing in war. These are regarded as justified killings; unjustified killings are known as *murder*. So even though all killing may be regrettable, not all killing is immoral. Active euthanasia may in fact be a form of acceptable killing.

The opponent of active euthanasia can make a stronger reply along the same lines. He can say that the problem with active euthanasia is not that it is a type of killing, but that it is a type of *unwarranted* killing. A dying patient in the grip of unimaginable pain, for example, does not have to be killed to

escape her agony. Modern medicine is better than ever at alleviating pain—even very intense pain. Spinal blocks, drug combinations, new ways to deliver powerful analgesics (drugs that ease pain)—these options and others can offer dying patients unprecedented levels of pain relief. So euthanasia is uncalled for. If this claim is correct, then opponents can argue that contrary to Premise 4, active euthanasia will actually harm patients by cutting their lives short unnecessarily and thus depriving them of the benefits that may accrue in their remaining days—benefits such as profoundly meaningful moments spent with their families, the chance to come to terms with their dying, and even the possibility of a newfound cure for their disease.[7] Proponents of active euthanasia, however, charge that this upbeat view of pain management is not accurate. They point to several unpleasant facts: though it is *possible* to manage even severe pain well, too often pain is not well managed (for a variety of reasons, including the reluctance of health care workers to administer large doses of pain-relieving drugs); the side effects of the best pain medications (especially when used over the long term) often add to the suffering of the patient; and many dying patients endure not physical pain, but psychological suffering that is unbearable and untreatable by any medication.

Proponents can put forth another kind of argument for active voluntary euthanasia, this one based on the moral significance of killing (active euthanasia) and letting die (passive euthanasia). As we saw earlier, active euthanasia is taking a direct action to kill someone, while passive euthanasia is allowing someone to die by withholding or withdrawing measures necessary for sustaining life. Passive euthanasia is legal (competent patients have the right to refuse treatment) and widely believed to be morally permissible. Active euthanasia is generally illegal, and debate continues over its moral permissibility. Opponents of active euthanasia generally think that there is a profound *moral* difference between killing and letting die: killing is far worse than letting die; in fact, killing is morally wrong while letting die is permissible. But proponents of active voluntary euthanasia assert that the two are morally equivalent. Using this alleged moral equivalence, proponents can construct an argument like this:

1. Passive euthanasia is morally permissible.

2. If passive euthanasia is morally equivalent to active euthanasia, active euthanasia is also morally permissible.

3. Passive euthanasia is morally equivalent to active euthanasia.

4. Therefore, active (voluntary) euthanasia is morally permissible.

The conclusion follows from the premises, and Premises 1 and 2 are uncontroversial. The crux of the matter is Premise 3. What reasons are there for thinking that it is true? Here is an argument for Premise 3 in the form of a classic thought experiment. Suppose Smith will inherit a fortune if his six-year-old cousin dies. So he decides to take matters into his own hands. He slips into the bathroom while his little cousin is taking a bath and drowns him. He makes the whole thing look like an accident and leaves undetected. Now consider Jones, who also will inherit a fortune if his six-year-old cousin dies. He too decides to kill the child, and he too slips into the bathroom while the boy is bathing. But before Jones has a chance to commit the deed, the boy slips in the tub, gets knocked unconscious, and will surely drown unless Jones rescues him. Jones is happy to do nothing and lets the boy drown on his own—a simple "accident." Now which man behaves better morally? If there is a significant moral difference between killing and letting die, we would want to say that Jones's actions are less blameworthy than Smith's. But this distinction doesn't seem correct. The motives and aims of both men are the same.[8]

The line taken here is that if the difference between killing and letting die really is important

morally, then we would judge one man's action (either Smith's or Jones's) to be more blameworthy than that of the other. But our judgment is the same for both, so there must be no moral difference.

Some reject this argument and insist that there is in fact a moral difference between killing and letting die but that the distinction is often obscured in thought experiments like the Smith-Jones story. One critic claims, for example, that in this scenario the two men are equally reprehensible and the two actions appear to be morally equivalent simply because both men *were prepared to kill*. Remove this common factor, and the moral difference between killing and letting die will be apparent.[9]

Some of the strongest arguments *against* active voluntary euthanasia take a slippery slope approach. The gist of most of them is that lifting a moral or legal prohibition against this kind of mercy killing will dilute respect for life and encourage a slow slide from active voluntary euthanasia to active *nonvoluntary* euthanasia and then perhaps to *involuntary* euthanasia. This argument is therefore consequentialist: active voluntary euthanasia is wrong because it leads to bad consequences. (The argument is also sometimes lodged against legalizing this form of euthanasia.) Here is how one bioethicist describes the descent down the slope:

> A person apparently hopelessly ill may be allowed to take his own life. Then he may be permitted to deputize others to do it for him should he no longer be able to act. The judgment of others then becomes the ruling factor. Already at this point euthanasia is not personal and voluntary, for others are acting "on behalf of" the patient as they see fit. This may well incline them to act on behalf of other patients who have not authorized them to exercise their judgment. It is only a short step, then, from voluntary euthanasia (self-inflicted or authorized), to directed euthanasia administered to a patient who has given no authorization, to involuntary euthanasia conducted as part of a social policy.[10]

We can formulate a version of the argument thus:

1. If the general acceptance or approval of active voluntary euthanasia leads to widespread abuses (unjustified killing), then the practice is morally wrong.

2. The general acceptance or approval of active voluntary euthanasia will lead to widespread abuses (unjustified killing).

3. Therefore, active voluntary euthanasia is morally wrong.

This is a valid argument, an instance of *modus ponens*, so we need to focus only on the truth or falsity of the premises. Probably most people who have thought carefully about this kind of argument accept Premise 1 or a variation of it. Premise 2 is the sticking point. Because of a lack of solid evidence on the subject, the social consequences of a general acceptance of active euthanasia are difficult to ascertain. For example, to prove their case, some opponents of euthanasia cite reports on the Dutch experience with physician-assisted suicide. Proponents point to the same reports to undermine that case. The difficulty is that the research is not robust enough to lend unequivocal support to one side or the other. It therefore does not show that Premise 2 is true. Many of the arguments for Premise 2 are arguments by analogy or inferences based on observations concerning human behavior. Generally, these arguments, too, are weak and conjectural.

Those who are skeptical of Premise 2 often simply point out that no good reasons have been provided to support it. At best, they say, arguments for Premise 2 show only that dreadful consequences from widespread use of active euthanasia are possible. As one skeptic puts it,

> Now it cannot be denied that it is *possible* that permitting euthanasia could have these fateful consequences, but that cannot be enough to warrant prohibiting it if it is otherwise justified. A similar *possible* slippery slope worry could have been raised to securing competent patients' rights to decide about life support, but recent history shows such a worry would have been unfounded.[11]

CHAPTER REVIEW

SUMMARY

Euthanasia is directly or indirectly bringing about the death of another person for that person's sake. Its moral status depends in large measure on the consent of the patient. In voluntary euthanasia, the patient agrees to the act. In nonvoluntary euthanasia, others besides the patient decide on euthanasia because he or she is incompetent and has left no statement about end-of-life preferences. In involuntary euthanasia, the act is performed against the patient's wishes. Active euthanasia is taking direct action to kill someone (administering a lethal injection, for example); passive euthanasia is allowing the patient to die by withholding or withdrawing life-sustaining measures.

The traditional notion of death as the cessation of breathing and heartbeat has been revised in light of new developments in medical technology. According to the whole-brain view of death, the individual is dead when all brain functions permanently stop. The higher-brain view of death says that an individual is dead when higher brain functions permanently stop.

An act-utilitarian might see euthanasia as morally permissible because it results in the greatest happiness for all concerned. She could also consistently say that euthanasia is contrary to the goal of maximizing happiness because killing an individual rules out any possibility of that person's future happiness. A rule-utilitarian might say that a general rule permitting some kinds of euthanasia would do more harm than good—or that such a rule would maximize happiness in the long run. A Kantian theorist could consistently reject euthanasia because it entails treating persons as disposable things. Or he could consistently maintain that individuals in comas or persistent vegetative states are no longer persons, and therefore euthanasia is morally acceptable.

Arguments in favor of active voluntary euthanasia are often based on a right of self-determination and a duty to help others in distress. Some arguments for euthanasia, however, depend on the alleged equivalence between active and passive euthanasia. Some of the strongest arguments against euthanasia are of the slippery slope type: active voluntary euthanasia is wrong because it leads to bad consequences, such as an increased risk of unjustified killings.

KEY TERMS
euthanasia (p. 286)
voluntary euthanasia (p. 286)
advance directive (p. 286)
nonvoluntary euthanasia (p. 286)
involuntary euthanasia (p. 286)
active euthanasia (p. 286)
passive euthanasia (p. 286)
physician-assisted suicide (p. 287)

EXERCISES

Review Questions

1. What is euthanasia? What is physician-assisted suicide? (p. 286)
2. What is the difference between voluntary euthanasia and nonvoluntary euthanasia? (p. 286)
3. What is the difference between active and passive euthanasia? (p. 286)
4. Who was Terri Schiavo and what are the main medical and legal facts of her case? (p. 285)
5. Who was Dr. Kevorkian and what role did he play in the debate over physician-assisted suicide? (p. 291)
6. What percentage of American adults think physician-assisted suicide is morally permissible? (p. 293)
7. In what states is physician-assisted suicide legal? (p. 287)

8. What is the American Medical Association's official view of physician-assisted suicide? (p. 287)
9. What is an advance directive? (p. 286)
10. What is the higher-brain definition of death? (p. 289)

Discussion Questions

1. Do you think voluntary active euthanasia is morally permissible in some cases? Why or why not?
2. Critique the Terri Schiavo case. Who was right in their view of what should be done for Terri? Was the participation of politicians in the case helpful? Distracting? Wrong?
3. Was removing Terri Schiavo's feeding tube a case of murder? If not, what was it?
4. What actions (or lack of actions) *should* have been performed in her case?
5. Would you consider her a person in her brain-damaged state? Why or why not?
6. Do you consider Dr. Kevorkian's practice of physician-assisted suicide morally acceptable? Why or why not?
7. Is there a moral difference between killing and letting die? Give reasons for your answer.
8. How might an act-utilitarian argue for physician-assisted suicide? Critique this argument.
9. How might a Kantian argue against physician-assisted suicide?
10. Is the use of terminal sedation ever morally permissible? If so, in what situations?

FURTHER READING

Tom L. Beauchamp, ed., *Intending Death: The Ethics of Assisted Suicide and Euthanasia* (Englewood Cliffs, NJ: Prentice Hall, 1995).

R. B. Brandt, "The Morality and Rationality of Suicide," in *A Handbook for the Study of Suicide,* ed. Seymour Perlin (New York: Oxford University Press, 1975).

Lonnie R. Bristow, President of the American Medical Association, statement on physician-assisted suicide to the U.S. House of Representatives Committee on the

Judiciary, Subcommittee on the Constitution, 104th Cong., 2nd sess., *Congressional Record* 142 (April 29, 1996).

Dan W. Brock, "Medical Decisions at the End of Life," in *A Companion to Bioethics,* ed. Helga Kuhse and Peter Singer (1998; reprint, Malden, MA: Blackwell, 2001).

Daniel Callahan, "When Self-Determination Runs Amok," *Hastings Center Report* 22, no. 2 (March/April 1992): 52–55.

Philippa Foot, "Euthanasia," *Philosophy & Public Affairs* 6, no. 2 (1977): 85–112.

Walter Glannon, "Medical Decisions at the End of Life," in *Biomedical Ethics* (New York: Oxford University Press, 2005).

John Lachs, "When Abstract Moralizing Runs Amok," *Journal of Clinical Ethics* 5, no. 1 (1994): 10–13.

Ronald Munson, "Euthanasia and Physician-Assisted Suicide," in *Intervention and Reflection: Basic Issues in Medical Ethics,* ed. Ronald Munson, 7th ed. (Belmont, CA: Wadsworth, 2004).

Jeffrey Olen and Vincent Barry, "Euthanasia," in *Applying Ethics: A Text with Readings,* 6th ed. (Belmont, CA: Wadsworth, 1999).

The President's Commission for the Study of Ethical Problems in Medicine and Biomedical and Behavioral Research (Washington, DC: Government Printing Office, 1983).

Bonnie Steinbock and Alastair Norcross, eds., *Killing and Letting Die,* 2nd ed. (New York: Fordham University Press, 1994).

Thomas D. Sullivan, "Active and Passive Euthanasia: An Impertinent Distinction?" *Human Life Review* 3, no. 3 (1977): 40–46.

Robert Young, "Voluntary Euthanasia," in *Stanford Encyclopedia of Philosophy,* Summer 2005 ed., ed. Edward N. Zalta, http://plato.stanford.edu/archives/sum2005/entries/euthanasia-voluntary/ (March 1, 2015).

ETHICAL DILEMMAS

1. Assisted Suicide or Murder?

One of the more bizarre cases of assisted suicide in recent times came to its conclusion on September 29, 2014, when New Yorker Kenneth Minor was convicted of manslaughter after stabbing a Long Island motivational speaker. Minor claimed that the man wished to die and had paid him to help him do so.

Minor received a sentence of twelve years when he accepted the prosecutors' plea deal and pled guilty to first-degree manslaughter.

However, Minor's lawyer claims, "We will be back again . . . Our hope is the appellate division will once again reverse this case."

Minor's lawyer, Daniel J. Gotlin, hopes to overturn the conviction by bringing the case to an appeals court. Gotlin argues that the verdict should be thrown out based on procedural grounds. Minor's indictment includes murder charges and assisted suicide charges, which Gotlin claims are mutually exclusive.

Minor has been incarcerated for more than five years, and, according to Gotlin, accepted the plea deal because "he wants finality; he wants this to be over." If Minor is unsuccessful in his appeal, he will have to serve five more years before he is eligible to be released.

Moments before Minor entered his plea, Justice Laura A. Ward of the New York Supreme Court in Manhattan denied Gotlin's request to dismiss the case, stating that a man can be charged for both murder and assisted suicide. However, she did not refute that Minor had a right to appeal her ruling, and said, "Perhaps we will get a definite ruling from the appellate division."

The man who Minor admits to killing, Jeffrey Locker, was found tied up in his car in East Harlem in July 2009. Multiple stab wounds were found on his chest.

Minor claims that Locker, a middle-aged father who had fallen deeply into debt, had hired him to assist in his suicide plan. Minor says he held a knife to a steering wheel while Locker flung himself against it multiple times. Minor's prosecutors found his story incredible and brought a murder charge against him instead of a charge of assisting suicide.

In 2011, Minor was tried and convicted of second-degree murder by a jury. The judge gave him twenty years to life in prison, but the verdict was invalidated two years later by an appellate panel. They concluded that the trial judge had given the jury an incorrect definition of assisted suicide.

Minor was given another trial in January. This time, a charge of assisting suicide was added to his indictment at the request of Cyrus R. Vance Jr., Manhattan district attorney. A jury could now convict him of a lesser charge.

During Minor's first trial, the defense and the prosecution agreed that Minor had participated in Locker's suicide at the request of the deceased, who wished to make his death look like a murder so that his family could claim life insurance.

However, prosecutors argued that it was a case of murder for hire, not assisted suicide, as Minor was still the cause of Locker's death. According to a medical expert, Minor did not simply hold a knife to a steering wheel, but stabbed Locker as he lay in his car. He then used Locker's credit card to withdraw money from an ATM.*

Suppose Minor killed Locker at Locker's request. Would the killing then be morally permissible? Is there a moral difference between physician-assisted suicide and Locker's murder when both actions are taken at the victim's request? What is the difference, if any, between murder and assisted suicide?

Suppose Locker's motive for asking Minor for aid in dying, and for making the death look like murder, was that Locker's life insurance money would pay for the only medical treatment that could save his daughter's life. How would these facts change your moral judgment about the killing?

*Based on James C. McKinley Jr., "Harlem Man Pleads Guilty to Assisting 2009 Death," *New York Times*, September 29, 2014, http://www.nytimes.com/2014/09/30/nyregion/-harlem-man-pleads-guilty-to-assisting-2009-death. html?_r=0 (March 23, 2015).

2. Euthanasia for Newborns

Imagine the unimaginable: Your newborn baby is born with a severe, deadly birth defect or contracts a fatal illness. The baby will die and is in tremendous pain. In this case, is it justified, perhaps even humane, to euthanize the child?

In Holland, some doctors and parents say the answer is yes. Back in 2005, the Netherlands adopted the Groningen Protocol, which is designed to help doctors end the suffering of very sick newborns through euthanasia. The rule requires that five criteria must be met before taking the decision to end the child's life: beyond-a-doubt diagnosis; presence of unbearable suffering; a second expert medical opinion to verify the child's condition; consent of both parents; and compliance with medical standards.

Some critics feared that this would create a "slippery slope" of infanticide, but new research published in the *Journal of Medical Ethics* contends that that has not been the case. The authors reviewed all reported cases of infant euthanasia between 2001 and 2010 (doctors sometimes covertly practiced infanticide before the protocol was passed) and found that in 95 percent of cases the mode of euthanasia was withholding or withdrawing treatment. In 60 percent of those cases, this was because the infant would soon die from an incurable disease. For the remaining 40 percent, quality of life prompted the decision.

However, since 2007, doctors reported euthanizing just two babies. The authors of the new paper suspect that an increase in abortions when fatal problems are detected in the womb may explain this. Alternatively, doctors may be confused about what constitutes euthanasia–such as withholding treatment, food or water—and may be underreporting it. Either way, the authors write, there has not been a detectable snowballing of euthanized babies in Holland as a result of the new protocol.[†]

Provide reasons for your answers to the following questions. Under the circumstances described (severe pain, terminal illness), would child euthanasia ever be morally permissible? Would child euthanasia be permissible if the newborn was not terminal, but in an unalterable vegetative state? Would it be permissible if the newborn suffered from a severe birth defect such as Down syndrome, which causes severe disabilities but does not rule out a worthwhile life?

[†] Rachel Nuwer, "Is It Ever OK to Euthanize a Baby?" Smithsonianmag.com, May 3, 2013. Copyright 2013 Smithsonian Institution. Reprinted with permission from Smithsonian Enterprises. All rights reserved. Reproduction in any medium is strictly prohibited without permission from Smithsonian Institution.

3. The Suicide of Admiral Nimitz

The name of Chester W. Nimitz is legendary in the annals of naval warfare. In June 1942, Admiral Nimitz commanded the U.S. forces assigned to block a Japanese invasion of Midway.

In the Battle of Midway, Nimitz's fighter-bombers caught the Japanese fleet off guard, as its carrier aircraft were being refueled on deck. His pilots swooped in and sent to the bottom four of the Japanese carriers—*Hiryu, Soryu, Akagi and Kaga*—that had led the attack on Pearl Harbor. Midway broke the back of Japanese naval power and was among the most decisive battles in all of history.

Nimitz's son and namesake, Chester W. Nimitz Jr., would rise to the same rank of admiral and become a hero of the Pacific war—a submarine commander who would sink a Japanese destroyer bearing down on his boat by firing torpedoes directly into its bow.

But Chester W. Nimitz Jr. achieved another kind of fame on Jan. 2. In a suicide pact with his 89-year-old wife, the 86-year-old hero ended his life with an overdose of sleeping pills.

Having lost 30 pounds from a stomach disorder, suffering from congestive heart failure and in constant back pain, the admiral had been determined to dictate the hour of his death. His wife, who suffered from osteoporosis so severe her bones were breaking, had gone blind. She had no desire to live without her husband.

So, as the devoted couple had spent their lives together, they decided to end their lives together. The admiral's final order read: "Our decision was made over a considerable period of time and was not carried out in acute desperation. Nor is it the expression of a mental illness. We have consciously, rationally, deliberately and of our own free will taken measures to end our lives today because of the physical limitations on our quality of life placed upon us by age, failing vision, osteoporosis, back and painful orthopedic problems."

According to *The New York Times* obituary, "The Nimitzes did not believe in any afterlife or God, and embraced no religion. But one of Mr. Nimitz's three surviving sisters, Mary Aquinas, 70, is a Catholic nun. . . . Sister Mary said that she could not condone her brother's decision to end his life, but that she felt sympathetic. 'If you cannot see any value to suffering for yourself or others,' she said, 'Then maybe it does make sense to end your life.'"‡

Provide reasons for your answers: Was Admiral Nimitz justified in his decision to commit suicide? Is suicide morally wrong in all circumstances? Is suicide a matter of personal choice, morally permissible if a person freely opts to end her life for whatever reason?

‡Patrick J. Buchanan, "The Sad Suicide of Admiral Nimitz," *World Net Daily*, January 18, 2002. Reprinted by permission of Patrick J. Buchanan and Creators Syndicate, Inc.

READINGS

Active and Passive Euthanasia

JAMES RACHELS

The distinction between active and passive euthanasia is thought to be crucial for medical ethics. The idea is that it is permissible, at least in some cases, to withhold treatment and allow a patient to die, but it

James Rachels, excerpts from "Active and Passive Euthanasia," from *The New England Journal of Medicine*, Vol. 292, No. 2, pp. 78–80. Copyright © 1975 Massachusetts Medical Society. Reprinted with permission from Massachusetts Medical Society.

is never permissible to take any direct action designed to kill the patient. This doctrine seems to be accepted by most doctors, and it is endorsed in a statement adopted by the House of Delegates of the American Medical Association on December 4, 1973:

The intentional termination of the life of one human being by another—mercy killing—is contrary to that for which the medical profession stands and is contrary to the policy of the American Medical Association.

The cessation of the employment of extraordinary means to prolong the life of the body when there is irrefutable evidence that biological death is imminent is the decision of the patient and/or his immediate family. The advice and judgment of the physician should be freely available to the patient and/or his immediate family.

However, a strong case can be made against this doctrine. In what follows I will set out some of the relevant arguments, and urge doctors to reconsider their views on this matter.

To begin with a familiar type of situation, a patient who is dying of incurable cancer of the throat is in terrible pain, which can no longer be satisfactorily alleviated. He is certain to die within a few days, even if present treatment is continued, but he does not want to go on living for those days since the pain is unbearable. So he asks the doctor for an end to it, and his family joins in the request.

Suppose the doctor agrees to withhold treatment, as the conventional doctrine says he may. The justification for his doing so is that the patient is in terrible agony, and since he is going to die anyway, it would be wrong to prolong his suffering needlessly. But now notice this. If one simply withholds treatment, it may take the patient longer to die, and so he may suffer more than he would if more direct action were taken and a lethal injection given. This fact provides strong reason for thinking that, once the initial decision not to prolong his agony has been made, active euthanasia is actually preferable to passive euthanasia, rather than the reverse. To say otherwise is to endorse the option that leads to more suffering rather than less, and is contrary to the humanitarian impulse that prompts the decision not to prolong his life in the first place.

Part of my point is that the process of being "allowed to die" can be relatively slow and painful, whereas being given a lethal injection is relatively quick and painless. Let me give a different sort of example. In the United States about one in 600 babies is born with [Down] syndrome. Most of these babies are otherwise healthy—that is, with only the usual pediatric care, they will proceed to an otherwise normal infancy. Some, however, are born with congenital defects such as intestinal obstructions that require

operations if they are to live. Sometimes, the parents and the doctor will decide not to operate, and let the infant die. Anthony Shaw describes what happens then:

. . . When surgery is denied [the doctor] must try to keep the infant from suffering while natural forces sap the baby's life away. As a surgeon whose natural inclination is to use the scalpel to fight off death, standing by and watching a salvageable baby die is the most emotionally exhausting experience I know. It is easy at a conference, in a theoretical discussion, to decide that such infants should be allowed to die. It is altogether different to stand by in the nursery and watch as dehydration and infection wither a tiny being over hours and days. This is a terrible ordeal for me and the hospital staff—much more so than for the parents who never set foot in the nursery.[1]

I can understand why some people are opposed to all euthanasia, and insist that such infants must be allowed to live. I think I can also understand why other people favor destroying these babies quickly and painlessly. But why should anyone favor letting "dehydration and infection wither a tiny being over hours and days"? The doctrine that says that a baby may be allowed to dehydrate and wither, but may not be given an injection that would end its life without suffering, seems so patently cruel as to require no further refutation. The strong language is not intended to offend, but only to put the point in the clearest possible way.

My second argument is that the conventional doctrine leads to decisions concerning life and death made on irrelevant grounds.

Consider again the case of the infants with [Down] syndrome who need operations for congenital defects unrelated to the syndrome to live. Sometimes, there is no operation, and the baby dies, but when there is no such defect, the baby lives on. Now, an operation such as that to remove an intestinal obstruction is not prohibitively difficult. The reason why such operations are not performed in these cases is, clearly, that the child has [Down] syndrome and the parents and doctor judge that because of that fact it is better for the child to die.

But notice that this situation is absurd, no matter what view one takes of the lives and potentials of such babies. If the life of such an infant is worth preserving, what does it matter if it needs a simple operation? Or, if one thinks it better that such a baby should not live on, what difference does it make that it happens to have an unobstructed intestinal tract? In either case, the matter of life and death is being decided on irrelevant grounds. It is the [Down] syndrome, and not the intestines, that is the issue. The matter should be decided, if at all, on that basis, and not be allowed to depend on the essentially irrelevant question of whether the intestinal tract is blocked.

What makes this situation possible, of course, is the idea that when there is an intestinal blockage, one can "let the baby die," but when there is no such defect there is nothing that can be done, for one must not "kill" it. The fact that this idea leads to such results as deciding life or death on irrelevant grounds is another good reason why the doctrine should be rejected.

One reason why so many people think that there is an important moral difference between active and passive euthanasia is that they think killing someone is morally worse than letting someone die. But is it? Is killing, in itself, worse than letting die? To investigate this issue, two cases may be considered that are exactly alike except that one involves killing whereas the other involves letting someone die. Then, it can be asked whether this difference makes any difference to the moral assessments. It is important that the cases be exactly alike, except for this one difference, since otherwise one cannot be confident that it is this difference and not some other that accounts for any variation in the assessments of the two cases. So, let us consider this pair of cases:

In the first, Smith stands to gain a large inheritance if anything should happen to his six-year-old cousin. One evening while the child is taking his bath, Smith sneaks into the bathroom and drowns the child, and then arranges things so that it will look like an accident.

In the second, Jones also stands to gain if anything should happen to his six-year-old cousin. Like Smith, Jones sneaks in planning to drown the child in his bath. However, just as he enters the bathroom Jones sees the child slip and hit his head, and fall face down in the water. Jones is delighted; he stands by, ready to

push the child's head back under if it is necessary, but it is not necessary. With only a little thrashing about, the child drowns all by himself, "accidentally," as Jones watches and does nothing.

Now Smith killed the child, whereas Jones "merely" let the child die. That is the only difference between them. Did either man behave better, from a moral point of view? If the difference between killing and letting die were in itself a morally important matter, one should say that Jones's behavior was less reprehensible than Smith's. But does one really want to say that? I think not. In the first place, both men acted from the same motive, personal gain, and both had exactly the same end in view when they acted. It may be inferred from Smith's conduct that he is a bad man, although that judgment may be withdrawn or modified if certain further facts are learned about him—for example, that he is mentally deranged. But would not the very same thing be inferred about Jones from his conduct? And would not the same further considerations also be relevant to any modification of this judgment? Moreover, suppose Jones pleaded, in his own defense, "After all, I didn't do anything except just stand there and watch the child drown. I didn't kill him: I only let him die." Again, if letting die were in itself less bad than killing, this defense should have at least some weight. But it does not. Such a "defense" can only be regarded as a grotesque perversion of moral reasoning. Morally speaking, it is no defense at all.

Now, it may be pointed out, quite properly, that the cases of euthanasia with which doctors are concerned are not like this at all. They do not involve personal gain or the destruction of normal healthy children. Doctors are concerned only with cases in which the patient's life is of no further use to him, or in which the patient's life has become or will soon become a terrible burden. However, the point is the same in these cases: the bare difference between killing and letting die does not, in itself, make a moral difference. If a doctor lets a patient die, for humane reasons, he is in the same moral position as if he had given the patient a lethal injection for humane reasons. If his decision was wrong—if, for example, the patient's illness was in fact curable—the decision would be equally regrettable no matter which method was used to carry it out. And if the doctor's decision was the right one, the method used is not in itself important.

The AMA policy statement isolates the crucial issue very well: the crucial issue is "the intentional termination of the life of one human being by another." But after identifying this issue, and forbidding "mercy killing," the statement goes on to deny that the cessation of treatment is the intentional termination of a life. This is where the mistake comes in, for what is the cessation of treatment, in these circumstances, if it is not "the intentional termination of the life of one human being by another"? Of course it is exactly that, and if it were not, there would be no point to it.

Many people will find this judgment hard to accept. One reason, I think, is that it is very easy to conflate the question of whether killing is, in itself, worse than letting die, with the very different question of whether most actual cases of killing are more reprehensible than most actual cases of letting die. Most actual cases of killing are clearly terrible (think, for example, of all the murders reported in the newspapers), and one hears of such cases every day. On the other hand, one hardly ever hears of a case of letting die, except for the actions of doctors who are motivated by humanitarian reasons. So one learns to think of killing in a much worse light than of letting die. But this does not mean that there is something about killing that makes it in itself worse than letting die, for it is not the bare difference between killing and letting die that makes the difference in these cases. Rather, the other factors—the murderer's motive of personal gain, for example, contrasted with the doctor's humanitarian motivation—account for different reactions to the different cases.

I have argued that killing is not in itself any worse than letting die: if my contention is right, it follows that active euthanasia is not any worse than passive euthanasia. What arguments can be given on the other side? The most common, I believe, is the following:

"The important difference between active and passive euthanasia is that, in passive euthanasia, the doctor does not do anything to bring about the patient's death. The doctor does nothing, and the patient dies of whatever ills already afflict him. In active euthanasia,

however, the doctor does something to bring about the patient's death: he kills him. The doctor who gives the patient with cancer a lethal injection has himself caused his patient's death: whereas if he merely ceases treatment, the cancer is the cause of the death."

A number of points need to be made here. The first is that it is not exactly correct to say that in passive euthanasia the doctor does nothing, for he does do one thing that is very important: he lets the patient die. "Letting someone die" is certainly different, in some respects, from other types of action—mainly in that it is a kind of action that one may perform by way of not performing certain other actions. For example, one may let a patient die by way of not giving medication, just as one may insult someone by way of not shaking his hand. But for any purpose of moral assessment, it is a type of action nonetheless. The decision to let a patient die is subject to moral appraisal in the same way that a decision to kill him would be subject to moral appraisal: it may be assessed as wise or unwise, compassionate or sadistic, right or wrong. If a doctor deliberately let a patient die who was suffering from a routinely curable illness, the doctor would certainly be to blame for what he had done, just as he would be to blame if he had needlessly killed the patient. Charges against him would then be appropriate. If so, it would be no defense at all for him to insist that he didn't "do anything." He would have done something very serious indeed, for he let his patient die.

Fixing the cause of death may be very important from a legal point of view, for it may determine whether criminal charges are brought against the doctor. But I do not think that this notion can be used to show a moral difference between active and passive euthanasia. The reason why it is considered bad to be the cause of someone's death is that death is regarded as a great evil—and so it is. However, if it has been decided that euthanasia—even passive euthanasia—is desirable in a given case, it has also been decided that in this instance death is no greater an evil than the patient's continued existence. And if this is true, the usual reason for not wanting to be the cause of someone's death simply does not apply.

Finally, doctors may think that all of this is only of academic interest—the sort of thing that philosophers may worry about but that has no practical bearing on their own work. After all, doctors must be concerned about the legal consequences of what they do, and active euthanasia is clearly forbidden by the law. But even so, doctors should also be concerned with the fact that the law is forcing upon them a moral doctrine that may well be indefensible, and has a considerable effect on their practices. Of course, most doctors are not now in the position of being coerced in this matter, for they do not regard themselves as merely going along with what the law requires. Rather, in statements such as the AMA policy statement that I have quoted, they are endorsing this doctrine as a central point of medical ethics. In that statement, active euthanasia is condemned not merely as illegal but as "contrary to that for which the medical profession stands," whereas passive euthanasia is approved.

However, the preceding considerations suggest that there is really no moral difference between the two, considered in themselves (there may be important moral differences in some cases in their *consequences,* but, as I pointed out, these differences may make active euthanasia, and not passive euthanasia, the morally preferable option). So, whereas doctors may have to discriminate between active and passive euthanasia to satisfy the law, they should not do any more than that. In particular, they should not give the distinction any added authority and weight by writing it into official statements of medical ethics.

NOTE

1. Anthony Shaw, "Doctor, Do We Have a Choice?" *New York Times Magazine,* 30 January 1972, 54.

The Wrongfulness of Euthanasia

J. Gay-Williams

My impression is that euthanasia—the idea, if not the practice—is slowly gaining acceptance within our society. Cynics might attribute this to an increasing tendency to devalue human life, but I do not believe this is the major factor. The acceptance is much more likely to be the result of unthinking sympathy and benevolence. Well-publicized, tragic stories like that of Karen Quinlan elicit from us deep feelings of compassion. We think to ourselves, "She and her family would be better off if she were dead." It is an easy step from this very human response to the view that if someone (and others) would be better off dead, then it might be all right to kill that person. Although I respect the compassion that leads to this conclusion, I believe the

conclusion is wrong. I want to show that euthanasia is wrong. It is inherently wrong, but it is also wrong judged from the standpoints of self-interest and of practical effects.

Before presenting my arguments to support this claim, it would be well to define "euthanasia." An essential aspect of euthanasia is that it involves taking a human life, either one's own or that of another. Also, the person whose life is taken must be someone who is believed to be suffering from some disease or injury from which recovery cannot reasonably be expected. Finally, the action must be deliberate and intentional. Thus, euthanasia is intentionally taking the life of a presumably hopeless person. Whether the life is one's own or that of another, the taking of it is still euthanasia.

It is important to be clear about the deliberate and intentional aspect of the killing. If a hopeless person is given an injection of the wrong drug by mistake and this causes his death, this is wrongful killing but not euthanasia. The killing cannot be the result of accident. Furthermore, if the person is given an injection of a drug that is believed to be necessary to treat his disease or better his condition and the person dies as a result, then this is neither wrongful killing nor euthanasia. The intention was to make the patient well, not kill him. Similarly, when a patient's condition is such that it is not reasonable to hope that any medical procedures or treatments will save his life, a failure to implement the procedures or treatments is not euthanasia. If the person dies, this will be as a result of his injuries or disease and not because of his failure to receive treatment.

The failure to continue treatment after it has been realized that the patient has little chance of benefiting from it has been characterized by some as "passive euthanasia." This phrase is misleading and mistaken. In such cases, the person involved is not killed (the first essential aspect of euthanasia), nor is the death of the person intended by the withholding of additional treatment (the third essential aspect of euthanasia). The aim may be to spare the person additional and unjustifiable pain, to save him from the indignities of hopeless manipulations, and to avoid increasing the financial and emotional burden on his family. When I buy a pencil it is so that I can use it to write, not to contribute to an increase in the gross national product. This may be the unintended consequence of my action, but it is not the aim of my action. So it is with failing to continue the treatment of a dying person. I intend his death no more than I intend to reduce the GNP by not using medical supplies. His is an unintended dying, and so-called "passive euthanasia" is not euthanasia at all.

1. THE ARGUMENT FROM NATURE

Every human being has a natural inclination to continue living. Our reflexes and responses fit us to fight attackers, flee wild animals, and dodge out of the way of trucks. In our daily lives we exercise the caution and care necessary to protect ourselves. Our bodies are similarly structured for survival right down to the molecular level. When we are cut, our capillaries seal shut, our blood clots, and fibrogen is produced to start the process of healing the wound. When we are invaded by

bacteria, antibodies are produced to fight against the alien organisms, and their remains are swept out of the body by special cells designed for clean-up work.

Euthanasia does violence to this natural goal of survival. It is literally acting against nature because all the processes of nature are bent towards the end of bodily survival. Euthanasia defeats these subtle mechanisms in a way that, in a particular case, disease and injury might not.

It is possible, but not necessary, to make an appeal to revealed religion in this connection. Man as trustee of his body acts against God, its rightful possessor, when he takes his own life. He also violates the commandment to hold life sacred and never to take it without just and compelling cause. But since this appeal will persuade only those who are prepared to accept that religion has access to revealed truths, I shall not employ this line of argument.

It is enough, I believe, to recognize that the organization of the human body and our patterns of behavioral responses make the continuation of life a natural goal. By reason alone, then, we can recognize that euthanasia sets us against our own nature. Furthermore, in doing so, euthanasia does violence to our dignity. Our dignity comes from seeking our ends. When one of our goals is survival, and actions are taken that eliminate that goal, then our natural dignity suffers. Unlike animals, we are conscious through reason of our nature and our ends. Euthanasia involves acting as if this dual nature—inclination towards survival and awareness of this as an end—did not exist. Thus, euthanasia denies our basic human character and requires that we regard ourselves or others as something less than fully human.

2. THE ARGUMENT FROM SELF-INTEREST

The above arguments are, I believe, sufficient to show that euthanasia is inherently wrong. But there are reasons for considering it wrong when judged by standards other than reason. Because death is final and irreversible, euthanasia contains within it the possibility that we will work against our own interest if we practice it or allow it to be practiced on us.

Contemporary medicine has high standards of excellence and a proven record of accomplishment, but it does not possess perfect and complete knowledge. A mistaken diagnosis is possible, and so is a mistaken prognosis. Consequently, we may believe that we are dying of a disease when, as a matter of fact, we may not be. We may think that we have no hope of recovery when, as a matter of fact, our chances are quite good. In such circumstances, if euthanasia were permitted, we would die needlessly. Death is final and the chance of error too great to approve the practice of euthanasia.

Also, there is always the possibility that an experimental procedure or a hitherto untried technique will pull us through. We should at least keep this option open, but euthanasia closes it off. Furthermore, spontaneous remission does occur in many cases. For no apparent reason, a patient simply recovers when those all around him, including his physicians, expected him to die. Euthanasia would just guarantee their expectations and leave no room for the "miraculous" recoveries that frequently occur.

Finally, knowing that we can take our life at any time (or ask another to take it) might well incline us to give up too easily. The will to live is strong in all of us, but it can be weakened by pain and suffering and feelings of hopelessness. If during a bad time we allow ourselves to be killed, we never have a chance to reconsider. Recovery from a serious illness requires that we fight for it, and anything that weakens our determination by suggesting that there is an easy way out is ultimately against our own interest. Also, we may be inclined towards euthanasia because of our concern for others. If we see our sickness and suffering as an emotional and financial burden on our family, we may feel that to leave our life is to make their lives easier. The very presence of the possibility of euthanasia may keep us from surviving when we might.

3. THE ARGUMENT FROM PRACTICAL EFFECTS

Doctors and nurses are, for the most part, totally committed to saving lives. A life lost is, for them, almost a personal failure, an insult to their skills and knowledge. Euthanasia as a practice might well alter this. It could have a corrupting influence so that in any case that is severe doctors and nurses might not try hard enough to save the patient. They might decide that the patient would simply be "better off dead" and take the steps necessary to make that come about. This attitude could then carry over to their dealings with patients less seriously ill. The result would be an overall decline in the quality of medical care.

Finally, euthanasia as a policy is a slippery slope. A person apparently hopelessly ill may be allowed to take his own life. Then he may be permitted to deputize others to do it for him should he no longer be able to act. The judgment of others then becomes the ruling factor. Already at this point euthanasia is not personal and voluntary, for others are acting "on behalf of" the patient as they see fit. This may well incline them to act on behalf of other patients who have not authorized them to exercise their judgment. It is only a short step, then, from voluntary euthanasia (self-inflicted or authorized), to directed euthanasia administered to a patient who has given no authorization, to involuntary euthanasia conducted as part of a social policy. Recently many psychiatrists and sociologists have argued that we define as "mental illness" those forms of behavior that we disapprove of. This gives us license then to lock up those who display the behavior. The category of the "hopelessly ill" provides the possibility of even worse abuse. Embedded in a social policy, it would give society or its representatives the authority to eliminate all those who might be considered too "ill" to function normally any longer. The dangers of euthanasia are too great to all to run the risk of approving it in any form. The first slippery step may well lead to a serious and harmful fall.

I hope that I have succeeded in showing why the benevolence that inclines us to give approval of euthanasia is misplaced. Euthanasia is inherently wrong because it violates the nature and dignity of human beings. But even those who are not convinced by this must be persuaded that the potential personal and social dangers inherent in euthanasia are sufficient to forbid our approving it either as a personal practice or as a public policy.

Suffering is surely a terrible thing, and we have a clear duty to comfort those in need and to ease their suffering when we can. But suffering is also a natural part of life with values for the individual and for others that we should not overlook. We may legitimately seek for others and for ourselves an easeful death, as Arthur Dyck has pointed out.[1] Euthanasia, however, is not just an easeful death. It is a wrongful death. Euthanasia is not just dying. It is killing.

NOTE

1. Arthur Dyck, "Beneficent Euthanasia and Benemortasia," in *Beneficent Euthanasia,* ed. Marvin Kohl (Buffalo, NY: Prometheus Books, 1975), 117–29.

From *Voluntary Active Euthanasia*

Dan W. Brock

* * *

THE CENTRAL ETHICAL ARGUMENT FOR VOLUNTARY ACTIVE EUTHANASIA

The central ethical argument for euthanasia is familiar. It is that the very same two fundamental ethical values supporting the consensus on patient's rights to decide about life-sustaining treatment also support the ethical permissibility of euthanasia. These values are individual self-determination or autonomy and individual well-being. By self-determination as it bears on euthanasia, I mean people's interest in making important decisions about their lives for themselves according to their own values or conceptions of a good life, and in being left free to act on those decisions. Self-determination is valuable because it permits people to form and live in accordance with their own conception of a good life, at least within the bounds of justice and consistent with others doing so as well. In exercising self-determination people take responsibility for their lives and for the kinds of persons they become. A central aspect of human dignity lies in people's capacity to direct their lives in this way. The value of exercising self-determination presupposes some minimum of decision making capacities or competence, which thus limits the scope of euthanasia supported by self-determination; it cannot justifiably be

Dan W. Brock, excerpts from "Voluntary Active Euthanasia" from *Hastings Center Report* 22(2): 10–22. Copyright © 1992 The Hastings Center. Reproduced with permission of John Wiley & Sons, Inc.

administered, for example, in cases of serious dementia or treatable clinical depression.

Does the value of individual self-determination extend to the time and manner of one's death? Most people are very concerned about the nature of the last stage of their lives. This reflects not just a fear of experiencing substantial suffering when dying, but also a desire to retain dignity and control during this last period of life. Death is today increasingly preceded by a long period of significant physical and mental decline, due in part to the technological interventions of modern medicine. Many people adjust to these disabilities and find meaning and value in new activities and ways. Others find the impairments and burdens in the last stage of their lives at some point sufficiently great to make life no longer worth living. For many patients near death, maintaining the quality of one's life, avoiding great suffering, maintaining one's dignity, and insuring that others remember us as we wish them to become of paramount importance and outweigh merely extending one's life. But there is no single, objectively correct answer for everyone as to when, if at all, one's life becomes all things considered a burden and unwanted. If self-determination is a fundamental value, then the great variability among people on this question makes it especially important that individuals control the manner, circumstances, and timing of their dying and death.

The other main value that supports euthanasia is individual well-being. It might seem that individual well-being conflicts with a person's self-determination when the person requests euthanasia. Life itself is commonly taken to be a central good for persons, often valued for its own sake, as well as necessary for pursuit of all other goods within a life. But when a competent patient decides to forgo all further life-sustaining treatment then the patient, either explicitly or implicitly, commonly decides that the best life possible for him or her with treatment is of sufficiently poor quality that it is worse than no further life at all. Life is no longer considered a benefit by the patient, but has now become a burden. The same judgment underlies a request for euthanasia: continued life is seen by the patient as no longer a benefit, but now a burden. Especially in the often severely compromised and debilitated states of many critically ill or dying patients, there is no objective standard, but only the competent patient's judgment of whether continued life is no longer a benefit.

Of course, sometimes there are conditions, such as clinical depression, that call into question whether the patient has made a competent choice, either to forgo life-sustaining treatment or to seek euthanasia, and then the patient's choice need not be evidence that continued life is no longer a benefit for him or her. Just as with decisions about treatment, a determination of incompetence can warrant not honoring the patient's choice: in the case of treatment, we then transfer decisional authority to a surrogate, though in the case of voluntary active euthanasia a determination that the patient is incompetent means that choice is not possible.

The value or right of self-determination does not entitle patients to compel physicians to act contrary to their own moral or professional values. Physicians are moral and professional agents whose own self-determination or integrity should be respected as well. If performing euthanasia became legally permissible, but conflicted with a particular physician's reasonable understanding of his or her moral or professional responsibilities, the care of a patient who requested euthanasia should be transferred to another.

Most opponents do not deny that there are some cases in which the values of patient self-determination and well-being support euthanasia. Instead, they commonly offer two kinds of arguments against it that on their view outweigh or override this support. The first kind of argument is that in any individual case where considerations of the patient's self-determination and well-being do support euthanasia, it is nevertheless always ethically wrong or impermissible. The second kind of argument grants that in some individual cases euthanasia may not be ethically wrong, but maintains nonetheless that public and legal policy should never permit it. The first kind of argument focuses on features of any individual case of euthanasia, while the second kind focuses on social or legal policy. In the next section I consider the first kind of argument.

* * *

WOULD THE BAD CONSEQUENCES OF EUTHANASIA OUTWEIGH THE GOOD?

The argument against euthanasia at the policy level is stronger than at the level of individual cases, though even here I believe the case is ultimately unpersuasive, or at best indecisive. The policy level is the place where the main issues lie, however, and where moral considerations that might override arguments in favor of euthanasia will be found, if they are found anywhere. It is important to note two kinds of disagreement about the consequences for public policy of permitting euthanasia. First, there is empirical or factual disagreement about what the consequences would be. This disagreement is greatly exacerbated by the lack of firm data on the issue. Second, since on any reasonable assessment there would be both good and bad consequences, there are moral disagreements about the relative importance of different effects. In addition to these two sources of disagreement, there is also no single, well-specified policy proposal for legalizing euthanasia on which policy assessments can focus. But without such specification, and especially without explicit procedures for protecting against well-intentioned misuse and ill-intentioned abuse, the consequences for policy are largely speculative. Despite these difficulties, a preliminary account of the main likely good and bad consequences is possible. This should help clarify where better data or more moral analysis and argument are needed, as well as where policy safeguards must be developed.

Potential Good Consequences of Permitting Euthanasia

What are the likely good consequences? First, if euthanasia were permitted it would be possible to respect the self-determination of competent patients who want it, but now cannot get it because of its illegality. We simply do not know how many such patients and people there are. In the Netherlands, with a population of about 14.5 million (in 1987), estimates in a recent study were that about 1,900 cases of voluntary active euthanasia or physician-assisted suicide occur annually. No straightforward extrapolation to the United States is possible for many reasons, among them, that we do not know how many people here who want euthanasia now get it, despite its illegality. Even with better data on the number of persons who want euthanasia but cannot get it, significant moral disagreement would remain about how much weight should be given to any instance of failure to respect a person's self-determination in this way.

One important factor substantially affecting the number of persons who would seek euthanasia is the extent to which an alternative is available. The widespread acceptance in the law, social policy, and medical practice of the right of a competent patient to forgo life-sustaining treatment suggests that the number of competent persons in the United States who would want euthanasia if it were permitted is probably relatively small.

A second good consequence of making euthanasia legally permissible benefits a much larger group. Polls have shown that a majority of the American public believes that people should have a right to obtain euthanasia if they want.[1] No doubt the vast majority of those who support this right to euthanasia will never in fact come to want euthanasia for themselves. Nevertheless, making it legally permissible would reassure many people that if they ever do want euthanasia they would be able to obtain it. This reassurance would supplement the broader control over the process of dying given by the right to decide about life-sustaining treatment. Having fire insurance on one's house benefits all who have it, not just those whose houses actually burn down, by reassuring them that in the unlikely event of their house burning down, they will receive the money needed to rebuild it. Likewise, the legalization of euthanasia can be thought of as a kind of insurance policy against being forced to endure a protracted dying process that one has come to find burdensome and unwanted, especially when there is no life-sustaining treatment to forgo. The strong concern about losing control of their care expressed by many people who face serious illness likely to end in death suggests that they give substantial importance to the legalization of euthanasia as a means of maintaining this control.

A third good consequence of the legalization of euthanasia concerns patients whose dying is filled with severe and unrelievable pain or suffering. When there is a life-sustaining treatment that, if forgone, will lead relatively quickly to death, then doing so can bring an end to these patients' suffering without recourse to euthanasia. For patients receiving no such treatment, however, euthanasia may be the only release from their otherwise prolonged suffering and agony. This argument from mercy has always been the strongest argument for euthanasia in those cases to which it applies.

The importance of relieving pain and suffering is less controversial than is the frequency with which patients are forced to undergo untreatable agony that only euthanasia could relieve. If we focus first on suffering caused by physical pain, it is crucial to distinguish pain that could be adequately relieved with modern methods of pain control, though it in fact is not, from pain that is relievable only by death. For a variety of reasons, including some physicians' fear of hastening the patient's death, as well as the lack of a publicly accessible means for assessing the amount of the patient's pain, many patients suffer pain that could be, but is not, relieved.

Specialists in pain control, as for example the pain of terminally ill cancer patients, argue that there are very few patients whose pain could not be adequately controlled, though sometimes at the cost of so sedating them that they are effectively unable to interact with other people or their environment. Thus, the argument from mercy in cases of physical pain can probably be met in a large majority of cases by providing adequate measures of pain relief. This should be a high priority, whatever our legal policy on euthanasia—the relief of pain and suffering has long been, quite properly, one of the central goals of medicine. Those cases in which pain could be effectively relieved, but in fact is not, should only count significantly in favor of legalizing euthanasia if all reasonable efforts to change pain management techniques have been tried and have failed.

Dying patients often undergo substantial psychological suffering that is not fully or even principally the result of physical pain. The knowledge about how to relieve this suffering is much more limited than in the case of relieving pain, and efforts to do so are probably more often unsuccessful. If the argument from mercy is extended to patients experiencing great and unrelievable psychological suffering, the numbers of patients to which it applies are much greater.

One last good consequence of legalizing euthanasia is that once death has been accepted, it is often more humane to end life quickly and peacefully, when that is what the patient wants. Such a death will often be seen as better than a more prolonged one. People who suffer a sudden and unexpected death, for example by dying quickly or in their sleep from a heart attack or stroke, are often considered lucky to have died in this way. We care about how we die in part because we care about how others remember us, and we hope they will remember us as we were in "good times" with them and not as we might be when disease has robbed us of our dignity as human beings. As with much in the treatment and care of the dying, people's concerns differ in this respect, but for at least some people, euthanasia will be a more humane death than what they have often experienced with other loved ones and might otherwise expect for themselves.

Some opponents of euthanasia challenge how much importance should be given to any of these good consequences of permitting it, or even whether some would be good consequences at all. But more frequently, opponents cite a number of bad consequences that permitting euthanasia would or could produce, and it is to their assessment that I now turn.

Potential Bad Consequences of Permitting Euthanasia

Some of the arguments against permitting euthanasia are aimed specifically against physicians, while others are aimed against anyone being permitted to perform it. I shall first consider one argument of the former sort. Permitting physicians to perform euthanasia, it is said, would be incompatible with their fundamental moral and professional commitment as healers to care for patients and to protect life. Moreover, if euthanasia by physicians became common, patients would come to fear that a medication was intended not to treat or care, but instead to kill, and would thus lose trust in their physicians. This position was forcefully stated in a paper by Willard Gaylin and his colleagues:

> The very soul of medicine is on trial. . . . This issue touches medicine at its moral center; if this moral center collapses, if physicians become killers or are even licensed to kill, the profession—and, therewith, each physician—will never again be worthy of trust and respect as healer and comforter and protector of life in all its frailty.

These authors go on to make clear that, while they oppose permitting anyone to perform euthanasia, their special concern is with physicians doing so:

> We call on fellow physicians to say that they will not deliberately kill. We must also say to each of our fellow physicians that we will not tolerate killing of patients and that we shall take disciplinary action against doctors who kill. And we must say to the broader community that if it insists on tolerating or legalizing active euthanasia, it will have to find nonphysicians to do its killing.[2]

If permitting physicians to kill would undermine the very "moral center" of medicine, then almost certainly physicians should not be permitted to perform euthanasia. But how persuasive is this claim? Patients should not fear, as a consequence of permitting voluntary active euthanasia, that their physicians will substitute a lethal injection for what patients want and believe is part of their care. If active euthanasia is restricted to cases in which it is truly voluntary, then no patient should fear getting it unless she or he has voluntarily requested it. (The fear that we might in time also come to accept nonvoluntary, or even involuntary, active euthanasia is a slippery slope worry

I address below.) Patients' trust of their physicians could be increased, not eroded, by knowledge that physicians will provide aid in dying when patients seek it.

. . . In spelling out above what I called the positive argument for voluntary active euthanasia, I suggested that two principal values—respective patients' self-determination and promoting their well-being—underlie the consensus that competent patients, or the surrogates of incompetent patients, are entitled to refuse any life-sustaining treatment and to choose from among available alternative treatments. It is the commitment to these two values in guiding physicians' actions as healers, comforters, and protectors of their patients' lives that should be at the "moral center" of medicine, and these two values support physicians' administering euthanasia when their patients make competent requests for it.

What should not be at that moral center is a commitment to preserving patients' lives as such, without regard to whether those patients want their lives preserved or judge their preservation a benefit to them. . . .

A second bad consequence that some foresee is that permitting euthanasia would weaken society's commitment to provide optimal care for dying patients. We live at a time in which the control of health care costs has become, and is likely to continue to be, the dominant focus of health care policy. If euthanasia is seen as a cheaper alternative to adequate care and treatment, then we might become less scrupulous about providing sometimes costly support and other services to dying patients. Particularly if our society comes to embrace deeper and more explicit rationing of health care, frail, elderly, and dying patients will need to be strong and effective advocates for their own health care and other needs, although they are hardly in a position to do this. We should do nothing to weaken their ability to obtain adequate care and services.

This second worry is difficult to assess because there is little firm evidence about the likelihood of the feared erosion in the care of dying patients. There are at least two reasons, however, for skepticism about this argument. The first is that the same worry could have been directed at recognizing patients' or surrogates' rights to forgo life-sustaining treatment, yet there is no persuasive evidence that recognizing the right to refuse treatment has caused a serious erosion in the quality of care of dying patients. The second reason for skepticism about this worry is that only a very small proportion of deaths would occur from euthanasia if it were permitted. In the Netherlands, where euthanasia under specified circumstances is permitted by the courts, though not authorized by statute, the best estimate of the proportion of overall deaths that result from it is about 2 percent.[3] Thus, the vast majority of critically ill and dying patients will not request it, and so will still have to be cared for by physicians, families, and others. Permitting euthanasia should not diminish people's commitment and concern to maintain and improve the care of these patients.

A third possible bad consequence of permitting euthanasia (or even a public discourse in which strong support for euthanasia is evident) is to threaten the progress made in securing the rights of patients or their surrogates to decide about and to refuse life-sustaining treatment. This progress has been made against the backdrop of a clear and firm legal prohibition of euthanasia, which has provided a relatively bright line limiting the dominion of others over patients' lives. It has therefore been an important reassurance to concerns about how the authority to take steps ending life might be misused, abused, or wrongly extended.

Many supporters of the right of patients or their surrogates to refuse treatment strongly oppose euthanasia, and if forced to choose might well withdraw their support of the right to refuse treatment rather than accept euthanasia. Public policy in the last fifteen years has generally let life-sustaining treatment decisions be made in health care settings between physicians and patients or their surrogates, and without the involvement of the courts. However, if euthanasia is made legally permissible greater involvement of the courts is likely, which could in turn extend to a greater court involvement in life-sustaining treatment decisions. Most agree, however, that increased involvement of the courts in these decisions would be undesirable, as it would make sound decisionmaking more cumbersome and difficult without sufficient compensating benefits.

As with the second potential bad consequence of permitting euthanasia, this third consideration too is speculative and difficult to assess. The feared erosion of patients' or surrogates' rights to decide about life-sustaining treatment, together with greater court involvement in those decisions, are both possible. However, I believe there is reason to discount this generally worry. The legal rights of competent patients and, to a lesser degree, surrogates of incompetent patients to decide about treatment are very firmly embedded in a long line of informed consent and life-sustaining treatment cases, and are not likely to be eroded by a debate over, or even acceptance of, euthanasia. It will not be accepted without safeguards that reassure the public about abuse, and if that debate shows the need for similar safeguards for some life-sustaining treatment decisions they should be adopted there as well. In neither case are the only possible safeguards greater court involvement, as the recent growth of institutional ethics committees shows.

The fourth potential bad consequence of permitting euthanasia . . . turns on the subtle point that making a new option or choice available to people can sometimes make them worse off, even if once they have the choice they go on to choose what is best for them. Ordinarily, people's continued existence is viewed by them as given, a fixed condition with which they must cope. Making euthanasia available to people as an option denies them the alternative of staying alive by default. If people are offered the option of euthanasia, their continued existence is now a choice for which they can be held responsible and which they can be asked by others to justify. We care, and are right to care, about being able to justify ourselves to others. To the extent that our society is unsympathetic to justifying a severely dependent or impaired existence, a heavy psychological burden of proof may be placed on patients who think their terminal illness or chronic infirmity is not a sufficient reason for dying. Even if they otherwise view their life as worth living, the opinion of others around them that it is not can threaten their reason for living and make euthanasia a rational choice. Thus the existence of the option becomes a subtle pressure to request it.

This argument correctly identifies the reason why offering some patients the option of euthanasia would not benefit them. [David] Velleman takes it not as a reason for opposing all euthanasia, but for restricting it to circumstances where there are "unmistakable and overpowering reasons for persons to want the option of euthanasia,"[4] and for denying the option in all other cases. But there are at least three reasons why such restriction may not be warranted. First, polls and other evidence support that most Americans believe euthanasia should be permitted (though the recent defeat of the referendum to permit it in the state of Washington raises some doubt about this support). Thus, many more people seem to want the choice than would be made worse off by getting it. Second, if giving people the option of ending their life really makes them worse off, then we should not only prohibit euthanasia, but also take back from people the right they now have to decide about life-sustaining treatment. The feared harmful effect should already have occurred from securing people's right to refuse life-sustaining treatment, yet there is no evidence of any such widespread harm or any broad public desire to rescind that right. Third, since there is a wide range of conditions in which reasonable people can and do disagree about whether they would want continued life, it is not possible to restrict the permissibility of euthanasia as narrowly as Velleman suggests without thereby denying it to most persons who would want it; to permit it only in cases in which virtually everyone would want it would be to deny it to most who would want it.

A fifth potential bad consequence of making euthanasia legally permissible is that it might weaken the general legal prohibition of homicide. This prohibition is so fundamental to civilized society, it is argued, that we should do nothing that erodes it. If most cases of stopping life support are killing, as I have already argued, then the court cases permitting such killing have already in effect weakened this prohibition. However, neither the courts nor most people have seen these cases as killing and so as challenging the prohibition of homicide. The courts have usually grounded patients' or their surrogates' rights to refuse life-sustaining treatment in rights to privacy, liberty, self-determination, or bodily integrity, not in exceptions to homicide laws.

Legal permission for physicians or others to perform euthanasia could not be grounded in patients' rights to decide about medical treatment. Permitting euthanasia would require qualifying, at least in effect, the legal prohibition against homicide, a prohibition that in general does not allow the consent of the victim to justify or excuse the act. Nevertheless, the very same fundamental basis of the right to decide about life-sustaining treatment—respecting a person's self-determination—does support euthanasia as well. Individual self-determination has long been a well-entrenched and fundamental value in the law, and so extending it to euthanasia would not require appeal to novel legal values or principles. That suicide or attempted suicide is no longer a criminal offense in virtually all states indicates an acceptance of individual self-determination in the taking of one's own life analogous to that required for voluntary active euthanasia. The legal prohibition (in most states) of assisting in suicide and the refusal in the law to accept the consent of the victim as a possible justification of homicide are both arguably a result of difficulties in the legal process of establishing the consent of the victim after the fact. If procedures can be designed that clearly establish the voluntariness of the person's request for euthanasia it would under those procedures represent a carefully circumscribed qualification on the legal prohibition of homicide. Nevertheless, some remaining worries about this weakening can be captured in the final potential bad consequence, to which I will now turn.

This final potential bad consequence is the central concern of many opponents of euthanasia and, I believe, is the most serious objection to a legal policy permitting it. According to this "slippery slope" worry, although active euthanasia may be morally permissible in cases in which it is unequivocally voluntary and the patient finds his or her condition unbearable, a legal policy permitting euthanasia would inevitably lead to active euthanasia being performed in many other cases in which it would be morally wrong. To prevent those other wrongful cases of euthanasia we should not permit even morally justified performance of it.

Slippery slope arguments of this form are problematic and difficult to evaluate. From one perspective, they are the last refuge of conservative defenders of the status quo. When all the opponent's objections to the wrongness of euthanasia itself have been met, the opponent then shifts ground and acknowledges both that it is not in itself wrong and that a legal policy which resulted only in its being performed would not be bad. Nevertheless, the opponent maintains, it should still not be permitted because doing so would result in its being performed in other cases in which it is not voluntary and would be wrong. In this argument's most extreme form, permitting euthanasia is the first and fateful step down the slippery slope to Nazism. Once on the slope we will be unable to get off.

Now it cannot be denied that it is *possible* that permitting euthanasia could have these fateful consequences, but that cannot be enough to warrant prohibiting it if it is otherwise justified. A similar *possible* slippery slope worry could have been raised to securing competent patients' rights to decide about life support, but recent history shows such a worry would have been unfounded. It must be relevant how likely it is that we will end with horrendous consequences and an unjustified practice of euthanasia. How *like*, and *widespread* would the abuses and unwarranted extensions of permitting it be? By abuses, I mean the performance of euthanasia that fails to satisfy the conditions required for voluntary active euthanasia, for example, if the patient has been subtly pressured to accept it. By unwarranted extensions of policy, I mean later changes in legal policy to permit not just voluntary euthanasia, but also euthanasia in cases in which, for example, it need not be fully voluntary. Opponents of voluntary euthanasia on slippery slope grounds have not provided the data or evidence necessary to turn their speculative concerns into well-grounded likelihoods.

It is at least clear, however, that both the character and likelihood of abuses of a legal policy permitting euthanasia depend in significant part on the procedures put in place to protect against them. I will not try to detail fully what such procedures might be, but will just give some examples of what they might include:

1. The patient should be provided with all relevant information about his or her medical condition, current prognosis, available alternative treatments, and the prognosis of each.
2. Procedures should ensure that the patient's request for euthanasia is stable or enduring (a brief waiting period could be required) and fully voluntary (an advocate for the patient might be appointed to ensure this).
3. All reasonable alternatives must have been explored for improving the patient's quality of life and relieving any pain or suffering.
4. A psychiatric evaluation should ensure that the patient's request is not the result of a treatable psychological impairment such as depression.

These examples of procedural safeguards are all designed to ensure that the patient's choice is fully informed, voluntary, and competent, and so a true exercise of self-determination. Other proposals for euthanasia would restrict its permissibility further—for example, to the terminally ill—a restriction that cannot be supported by self-determination. Such additional restrictions might, however, be justified by concern for limiting potential harms from abuse. At the same time, it is important not to impose procedural or substantive safeguards so restrictive as to make euthanasia impermissible or practically infeasible in a wide range of justified cases.

These examples of procedural safeguards make clear that it is possible to substantially reduce, though not to eliminate, the potential for abuse of a policy permitting voluntary active euthanasia. Any legalization of the practice should be accompanied by a well-considered set of procedural safeguards together with an ongoing evaluation of its use. Introducing euthanasia into only a few states could be a form of carefully limited and controlled social experiment that would give us evidence about the benefits and harms of the practice. Even then firm and uncontroversial data may remain elusive, as the continuing controversy over what has taken place in the Netherlands in recent years indicates.[5]

* * *

THE ROLE OF PHYSICIANS

If euthanasia is made legally permissible, should physicians take part in it? Should only physicians be permitted to perform it, as is the case in the Netherlands? In discussing whether euthanasia is incompatible with medicine's commitment to curing, caring for, and comforting patients, I argued that it is not at odds with a proper understanding of the aims of medicine, and so need not undermine patients' trust in their physicians. If that argument is correct, then physicians probably should not be prohibited, either by law or by professional norms, from taking part in a legally permissible practice of euthanasia (nor, of course, should they be compelled to do so if their personal or professional scruples forbid it). Most physicians in the Netherlands appear not to understand euthanasia to be incompatible with their professional commitments.

Sometimes patients who would be able to end their lives on their own nevertheless seek the assistance of physicians. Physician involvement in such cases may have important benefits to patients and others beyond simply assuring the use of effective means. Historically, in the United States suicide has carried a strong negative stigma that many today believe unwarranted. Seeking a physician's assistance, or what can almost seem a physician's blessing, may be a way of trying to remove that stigma and show others that the decision for suicide was made with due seriousness and was justified under the circumstances. The physician's involvement provides a kind of social approval, or more accurately helps counter what would otherwise be unwarranted social disapproval.

There are also at least two reasons for restricting the practice of euthanasia to physicians only. First, physicians would inevitably be involved in some of the important procedural safeguards necessary to a defensible practice, such as seeing to it that the patient is well-informed about his or her condition, prognosis, and possible treatments, and ensuring that all reasonable means have been taken to improve the quality of the patient's life. Second, and probably more important, one necessary protection against abuse of the practice is to limit the persons given authority to perform it, so that they can be held accountable for their exercise of that authority. Physicians, whose training and professional norms give some assurance that they would perform euthanasia responsibly, are an appropriate group of persons to whom the practice may be restricted.

* * *

NOTES

1. P. Painton and E. Taylor, "Love or Let Die," *Time,* 19 March 1990, 62–71; Boston Globe/Harvard University Poll, *Boston Globe,* 3 November 1991.

2. Willard Gaylin, Leon R. Kass, Edmund D. Pellegrino, and Mark Siegler, "Doctors Must Not Kill," *Journal of the American Medical Association* 259 (1988): 2139–40.

3. Paul J. Van der Maas et al., "Euthanasia and Other Medical Decisions Concerning the End of Life," *Lancet* 338 (1991): 669–74.

4. David Velleman commented on an earlier version of the paper delivered at the American Philosophical Association Central Division meetings.

5. Richard Fenigsen, "A Case against Dutch Euthanasia," *Special Supplement, Hastings Center Report* 19, no. 1 (1989): 22–30.

Euthanasia

Philippa Foot

The widely used *Shorter Oxford English Dictionary* gives three meanings for the word "euthanasia": the first, "a quiet and easy death"; the second, "the means of procuring this"; and the third, "the action of inducing a quiet and easy death." It is a curious fact that no one of the three gives an adequate definition of the word as it is usually understood. For "euthanasia" means much more than a quiet and easy death, or the means of procuring it, or the action of inducing it. The definition species only the manner of the death, and if this were all that was implied a murderer, careful to drug his victim, could claim that his act was an act of euthanasia. We find this ridiculous because we take it for granted that in euthanasia it is death itself, not just the manner of death, that must be kind to the one who dies.

To see how important it is that "euthanasia" should not be used as the dictionary definition allows it to be used, merely to signify that a death was quiet and easy, one has only to remember that Hitler's "euthanasia" program traded on this ambiguity.

Under this program, planned before the War but brought into full operation by a decree of 1 September 1939, some 275,000 people were gassed in centers which were to be a model for those in which Jews were later exterminated. Anyone in a state institution could be sent to the gas chambers if it was considered that he could not be "rehabilitated" for useful work. As Dr. Leo Alexander reports, relying on the testimony of a neuropathologist who received 500 brains from one of the killing centers,

> In Germany the exterminations included the mentally defective, psychotics (particularly schizophrenics), epileptics and patients suffering from infirmities of old age and from various organic neurological disorders such as infantile paralysis, Parkinsonism, multiple sclerosis and brain tumors. . . . In truth, all those unable to work and considered nonrehabilitable were killed.[1]

These people were killed because they were "useless" and "a burden on society"; only the manner of their deaths could be thought of as relatively easy and quiet.

Let us insist, then, that when we talk about euthanasia we are talking about a death understood as a good or happy event for the one who dies. This stipulation follows etymology, but is itself not exactly in line with current usage, which would be captured by the condition that the death should *not* be an evil rather than that it *should* be a good. That this is how people talk is shown by the fact that the case of Karen Ann Quinlan and others in a state of permanent coma is often discussed under the heading of "euthanasia." Perhaps it is not too late to object to the use of the word "euthanasia" in this sense. Apart from the break with the Greek origins of the word there are other unfortunate aspects of this extension of the term. For if we say that the death must be supposed to be a good to the subject we can also specify that it shall be for his sake that an act of euthanasia is performed. If we say merely that death shall not be an evil to him, we cannot stipulate that benefiting him shall be the motive where euthanasia is in question. Given the importance of the question, For whose sake are we acting? it is good to have a definition of euthanasia which brings under this heading only cases of opting for death for the sake of the one who dies. Perhaps what is most important is to say either that euthanasia is to be for the good of the subject or at least that death is to be no evil to him, thus refusing to talk Hitler's language. However, in this paper it is the first condition that will be understood, with the additional proviso that by an act of euthanasia we mean one of inducing or otherwise opting for death for the sake of the one who is to die.

A few lesser points need to be cleared up. In the first place it must be said that the word "act" is not to be taken to exclude omission: we shall speak of an act of euthanasia when someone is deliberately allowed to die, for his own good, and not only when positive measures are taken to see that he does. The very general idea we want is that of a choice of action or inaction directed at another man's death and causally effective in the sense that, in conjunction with actual circumstances, it is a sufficient condition of death. Of complications such as overdetermination, it will not be necessary to speak.

A second, and definitely minor, point about the definition of an act of euthanasia concerns the question of fact versus belief. It has already been implied that one who performs an act of euthanasia thinks that death will be merciful for the subject since we have said that it is on account of this thought that the act is done.

But is it enough that he acts with this thought, or must things actually be as he thinks them to be? If one man kills another, or allows him to die, thinking that he is in the last stages of a terrible disease, though in fact he could have been cured, is this an act of euthanasia or not? Nothing much seems to hang on our decision about this. The same condition has got to enter into the definition whether as an element in reality or only as an element in the agent's belief. And however we define an act of euthanasia culpability or justifiability will be the same: if a man acts through ignorance his ignorance may be culpable or it may not.[2]

These are relatively easy problems to solve, but one that is dauntingly difficult has been passed over in this discussion of the definition, and must now be faced. It is easy to say, as if this raised no problems, that an act of euthanasia is by definition one aiming at the *good* of the one whose death is in question, and that it is *for his sake* that his death is desired. But how is this to be explained? Presumably we are thinking of some evil already with him or to come on him if he continues to live, and death is thought of as a release from this evil. But this cannot be enough. Most people's lives contain evils such as grief or pain, but we do not therefore think that death would be a blessing to them. On the contrary life is generally supposed to be a good even for someone who is unusually unhappy or frustrated. How is it that one can ever wish for death for the sake of the one who is to die? This difficult question is central to the discussion of euthanasia, and we shall literally not know what we are talking about if we ask whether acts of euthanasia defined as we have defined them are ever morally permissible without first understanding better the reason for saying that life is a good, and the possibility that it is not always so.

If a man should save my life he would be my benefactor. In normal circumstances this is plainly true; but does one always benefit another in saving his life? It seems certain that he does not. Suppose, for instance, that a man were being tortured to death and was given a drug that lengthened his sufferings; this would not be a benefit but the reverse. Or suppose that in a ghetto in Nazi Germany a doctor saved the life of someone threatened by disease, but that the man once cured was transported to an extermination camp; the doctor might wish for the sake of the patient that he had died of the disease. Nor would a longer stretch of life always be a benefit to the person who was given it. Comparing Hitler's camps with those of Stalin, Dmitri Panin observes that in the latter the method of extermination was made worse by agonies that could stretch out over months.

> Death from a bullet would have been bliss compared with what many millions had to endure while dying of hunger. The kind of death to which they were condemned has nothing to equal it in treachery and sadism.[3]

These examples show that to save or prolong a man's life is not always to do him a service: it may be better for him if he dies earlier rather than later. It must therefore be agreed that while life is normally a benefit to the one who has it, this is not always so.

The judgment is often fairly easy to make—that life is or is not a good to someone—but the basis for it is very hard to find. When life is said to be a benefit or a good, on what grounds is the assertion made?

The difficulty is underestimated if it is supposed that the problem arises from the fact that one who is dead has nothing, so that the good someone gets from being alive cannot be compared with the amount he would otherwise have had. For why should this particular comparison be necessary? Surely it would be enough if one could say whether or not someone whose life was prolonged had more good than evil in the extra stretch of time. Such estimates are not always possible, but frequently they are; we say, for example, "He was very happy in those last years," or, "He had little but unhappiness then." If the balance of good and evil determined whether life was a good to someone we would expect to find a correlation in the judgments. In fact, of course, we find nothing of the kind. First, a man who has no doubt that existence is a good to him may have no idea about the balance of happiness and unhappiness in his life, or of any other positive and negative factors that may be suggested. So the supposed criteria are not always operating where the judgment is made. And secondly the application of the criteria gives an answer that is often wrong. Many

people have more evil than good in their lives; we do not, however, conclude that we would do these people no service by rescuing them from death.

To get around this last difficulty Thomas Nagel has suggested that experience itself is a good which must be brought in to balance accounts.

> . . . life is worth living even when the bad elements of experience are plentiful, and the good ones too meager to outweigh the bad ones on their own. The additional positive weight is supplied by experience itself, rather than by any of its contents.[4]

This seems implausible because if experience itself is a good it must be so even when what we experience is wholly bad, as in being tortured to death. How should one decide how much to count for this experiencing; and why count anything at all?

Others have tried to solve the problem by arguing that it is a man's desire for life that makes us call life a good: if he wants to live then anyone who prolongs his life does him a benefit. Yet someone may cling to life where we would say confidently that it would be better for him if he died, and he may admit it too. Speaking of those same conditions in which, as he said, a bullet would have been merciful, Panin writes,

> I should like to pass on my observations concerning the absence of suicides under the extremely severe conditions of our concentration camps. The more that life became desperate, the more a prisoner seemed determined to hold onto it.[5]

One might try to explain this by saying that hope was the ground of this wish to survive for further days and months in the camp. But there is nothing unintelligible in the idea that a man might cling to life though he knew those facts about his future which would make any charitable man wish that he might die.

The problem remains, and it is hard to know where to look for a solution. Is there a conceptual connection between *life* and *good*? Because life is not always a good we are apt to reject this idea, and to think that it must be a contingent fact that life is usually a good, as it is a contingent matter that legacies are usually a benefit, if they are. Yet it seems not to be a contingent matter that to save someone's life is ordinarily to benefit him. The problem is to find where the conceptual connection lies.

It may be good tactics to forget for a time that it is euthanasia we are discussing and to see how *life* and *good* are connected in the case of living beings other than men. Even plants have things done to them that are harmful or beneficial, and what does them good must be related in some way to their living and dying. Let us therefore consider plants and animals, and then come back to human beings. At least we shall get away from the temptation to think that the connection between life and benefit must everywhere be a matter of happiness and unhappiness or of pleasure and pain; the idea being absurd in the case of animals and impossible even to formulate for plants.

In case anyone thinks that the concept of the beneficial applies only in a secondary or analogical way to plants, he should be reminded that we speak quite straightforwardly in saying, for instance, that a certain amount of sunlight is beneficial to most plants. What is in question here is the habitat in which plants of particular species flourish, but we can also talk, in a slightly different way, of what does them good, where there is some suggestion of improvement or remedy. What has the beneficial to do with sustaining life? It is tempting to answer, "everything," thinking that a healthy condition just is the one apt to secure survival. In fact, however, what is beneficial to a plant may have to do with reproduction rather than the survival of the individual member of the species. Nevertheless there is a plain connection between the beneficial and the life-sustaining even for the individual plant; if something makes it better able to survive in conditions normal for that species it is ipso facto good for it. We need go no further, and could go no further, in explaining why a certain environment or treatment is good for a plant than to show how it helps this plant to survive.[6]

This connection between the life-sustaining and the beneficial is reasonably unproblematic, and there is nothing fanciful or zoomorphic in speaking of benefiting or doing good to plants. A connection with its survival can make something beneficial to a plant. But this is not, of course, to say that we count life as a good to a plant. We may save its life by giving it what is beneficial; we do not benefit it by saving its life.

A more ramified concept of benefit is used in speaking of animal life. New things can be said, such as that an animal is better or worse off for something that happened, or that it was a good or bad thing for it that it did happen. And new things count as benefit. In the first place, there is comfort, which often is, but need not be, related to health. When loosening a collar which is too tight for a dog we can say, "That will be better for it." So we see that the words "better for it" have two different meanings which we mark when necessary by a difference of emphasis, saying "better *for* it" when health is involved. And secondly an animal can be benefited by having its life saved. "Could you do anything for it?" can be answered by, "Yes, I managed to save its life." Sometimes we may understand this, just as we would for a plant, to mean that we had checked some disease. But we can also do something for an animal by scaring away its predator. If we do this, it is a good thing for the animal that we did, unless of course it immediately meets a more unpleasant end by some other means. Similarly, on the bad side, an animal may be worse off for our intervention, and this not because it pines or suffers but simply because it gets killed.

The problem that vexes us when we think about euthanasia comes on the scene at this point. For if we can do something for an animal—can benefit it—by relieving its suffering but also by saving its life, where does the greater benefit come when only death will end pain? It seemed that life was a good in its own right; yet pain seemed to be an evil with equal status and could therefore make life not a good after all. Is it only life without pain that is a good when animals are concerned? This does not seem a crazy suggestion when we are thinking of animals, since unlike human beings they do not have suffering as part of their normal life. But it is perhaps the idea of ordinary life that matters here. We would not say that we had done anything for an animal if we had merely kept it alive, either in an unconscious state or in a condition where, though conscious, it was unable to operate in an ordinary way; and the fact is that animals in severe and continuous pain simply do not operate normally. So we do not, on the whole, have the option of doing the animal good by saving its life though the life would be a life of pain. No doubt there are borderline cases, but that is no problem. We are not trying to make new judgments possible, but rather to find the principle of the ones we do make.

When we reach human life the problems seem even more troublesome. For now we must take quite new things into account, such as the subject's own view of his life. It is arguable that this places extra constraints on the solution: might it not be counted as a necessary condition of life's being a good to a man that he should see it as such? Is there not some difficulty about the idea that a benefit might be done to him by the saving or prolonging of his life even though he himself wished for death? Of course he might have a quite mistaken view of his own prospects, but let us ignore this and think only of cases where it is life as he knows it that is in question. Can we think that the prolonging of his life would be a benefit to him even though he would rather have it end than continue? It seems that this cannot be ruled out. That there is no simple incompatibility between life as a good and the wish for death is shown by the possibility that a man should wish himself dead, not for his own sake, but for the sake of someone else. And if we try to amend the thesis to say that life cannot be a good to one who wishes *for his own sake* that he should die, we find the crucial concept slipping through our fingers. As Bishop Butler pointed out long ago not all ends are either benevolent or self-interested. Does a man wish for death for his own sake in the relevant sense if, for instance, he wishes to revenge himself on another by his death? Or what if he is proud and refuses to stomach dependence or incapacity even though there are many good things left in life for him? The truth seems to be that the wish for death is sometimes compatible with life's being a good and sometimes not, which is possible because the description "wishing for death" is one covering diverse states of mind from that of the determined suicide, pathologically depressed, to that of one who is surprised to find that the thought of a fatal accident is viewed with relief. On the one hand, a man may see his life as a burden but go about his business in a more or less ordinary way; on the other hand, the wish for death may take the form of a rejection of everything that is in life, as it does in severe depression. It seems reasonable to say that life is not

a good to one permanently in the latter state, and we must return to this topic later on.

When are we to say that life is a good or a benefit to a man? The dilemma that faces us is this. If we say that life as such is a good we find ourselves refuted by the examples given at the beginning of this discussion. We therefore incline to think that it is as bringing good things that life is a good, where it is a good. But if life is a good only because it is the condition of good things why is it not equally an evil when it brings bad things? And how can it be a good even when it brings more evil than good?

It should be noted that the problem has here been formulated in terms of the balance of good and evil, not that of happiness and unhappiness, and that it is not to be solved by the denial (which may be reasonable enough) that unhappiness is the only evil or happiness the only good. In this paper no view has been expressed about the nature of goods other than life itself. The point is that on any view of the goods and evils that life can contain, it seems that a life with more evil than good could still itself be a good.

It may be useful to review the judgments with which our theory must square. Do we think that life can be a good to one who suffers a lot of pain? Clearly we do. What about severely handicapped people; can life be a good to them? Clearly it can be, for even if someone is almost completely paralyzed, perhaps living in an iron lung, perhaps able to move things only by means of a tube held between his lips, we do not rule him out of order if he says that some benefactor saved his life. Nor is it different with mental handicap. There are many fairly severely handicapped people—such as those with [Down] Syndrome (Mongolism)—for whom a simple affectionate life is possible. What about senility? Does this break the normal connection between life and good? Here we must surely distinguish between forms of senility. Some forms leave a life which we count someone as better off having than not having, so that a doctor who prolonged it would benefit the person concerned. With some kinds of senility this is however no longer true. There are some in geriatric wards who are barely conscious, though they can move a little and swallow food put into their mouths. To prolong such a state, whether in the old or in the very severely mentally handicapped is not to do them a service or confer a benefit. But of course it need not be the reverse: only if there is suffering would one wish for the sake of the patient that he should die.

It seems, therefore, that merely being alive even without suffering is not a good, and that we must make a distinction similar to that which we made when animals were our topic. But how is the line to be drawn in the case of men? What is to count as ordinary human life in the relevant sense? If it were only the very senile or very ill who were to be said not to have this life it might seem right to describe it in terms of *operation*. But it will be hard to find the sense in which the men described by Panin were not operating, given that they dragged themselves out to the forest to work. What is it about the life that the prisoners were living that makes us put it on the other side of the dividing line from that of some severely ill or suffering patients, and from most of the physically or mentally handicapped? It is not that they were in captivity, for life in captivity can certainly be a good. Nor is it merely the unusual nature of their life. In some ways the prisoners were living more as other men do than the patient in an iron lung.

The suggested solution to the problem is, then, that there is a certain conceptual connection between *life* and *good* in the case of human beings as in that of animals and even plants. Here, as there, however, it is not the mere state of being alive that can determine, or itself count as, a good, but rather life coming up to some standard of normality. It was argued that it is as part of ordinary life that the elements of good that a man may have are relevant to the question of whether saving his life counts as benefiting him. Ordinary human lives, even very hard lives, contain a minimum of basic goods, but when these are absent the idea of life is no longer linked to that of good. And since it is in this way that the elements of good contained in a man's life are relevant to the question of whether he is benefited if his life is preserved, there is no reason why it should be the balance of good and evil that counts.

It should be added that evils are relevant in one way when, as in the examples discussed above, they destroy the possibility of ordinary goods, but in a different way when they invade a life from which the goods are already absent for a different reason. So, for instance, the connection between *life* and *good* may be broken because consciousness has sunk to a very low level, as in extreme senility or severe brain damage. In itself this kind of life seems to be neither good nor evil, but if suffering sets in one would hope for a speedy end.

The idea we need seems to be that of life which is ordinary human life in the following respect—that it contains a minimum of basic human goods. What is ordinary in human life—even in very hard lives—is that a man is not driven to work far beyond his capacity; that he has the support of a family or community; that he can more or less satisfy his hunger; that he has hopes for the future; that he can lie down to rest at night. Such things were denied to the men in the Vyatlag camps described by Panin; not even rest at night was allowed them when they were tormented by bed-bugs, by noise and stench, and by routines such as body-searches and bath-parades—arranged for the night time so that work norms would not be reduced. Disease too can so take over a man's life that the normal human goods disappear. When a patient is so overwhelmed by pain or nausea that he cannot eat with pleasure, if he can eat at all, and is out of the reach of even the most loving voice, he no longer has ordinary human life in the sense in which the words are used here. And we may now pick up a thread from an earlier part of the discussion by remarking that crippling depression can destroy the enjoyment of ordinary goods as effectively as external circumstances can remove them.

This, admittedly inadequate, discussion of the sense in which life is normally a good, and of the reasons why it may not be so in some particular case, completes the account of what euthanasia is here taken to be. An act of euthanasia, whether literally act or rather omission, is attributed to an agent who opts for the death of another because in his case life seems to be an evil rather than a good. The question now to be asked is whether acts of euthanasia are ever justifiable. But there are two topics here rather than one. For it is one thing to say that some acts of euthanasia considered only in themselves and their results are morally unobjectionable, and another to say that it would be all right to legalize them. Perhaps the practice of euthanasia would allow too many abuses, and perhaps there would be too many mistakes. Moreover the practice might have very important and highly undesirable side effects, because it is unlikely that we could change our principles about the treatment of the old and the ill without changing fundamental emotional attitudes and social relations. The topics must, therefore, be treated separately. In the next part of the discussion, nothing will be said about the social consequences and possible abuses of the practice of euthanasia, but only about acts of euthanasia considered in themselves.

What we want to know is whether acts of euthanasia, defined as we have defined them, are ever morally permissible. To be more accurate, we want to know whether it is ever sufficient justification of the choice of death for another that death can be counted a benefit rather than harm, and that this is why the choice is made.

It will be impossible to get a clear view of the area to which this topic belongs without first marking the distinct grounds on which objection may lie when one man ops for the death of another. There are two different virtues whose requirements are, in general, contrary to such actions. An unjustified act of killing, or allowing to die, is contrary to justice or to charity, or to both virtues, and the moral failings are distinct. Justice has to do with what men *owe* each other in the way of noninterference and positive service. When used in this wide sense, which has its history in the doctrine of the cardinal virtues, justice is not especially connected with, for instance, law courts but with the whole area of rights, and duties corresponding to rights. Thus murder is one form of injustice, dishonesty another, and wrongful failure to keep contracts a third; chicanery in a law court or defrauding someone of his inheritance are simply other cases of injustice. Justice as such is not directly linked to the good of another, and may require that something be rendered to him even where it will do him harm, as Hume pointed out when he remarked that a debt must be paid even to a profligate debauchee who "would rather receive harm than benefit from large possessions."[7] Charity, on the other hand, is the virtue which attaches us to the good of others. An act of charity is in question only where something is not demanded by justice, but a lack of charity and of justice can be shown where a man is denied something which he both needs and has a right to; both charity and justice demand that widows and orphans are not defrauded, and the man who cheats them is neither charitable nor just.

It is easy to see that the two grounds of objection to inducing death are distinct. A murder is an act of injustice. A culpable failure to come to the aid of someone whose life is threatened is normally contrary, not to justice, but to charity. But where one man is under contract, explicit or implicit, to come to the aid of another injustice too will be shown. Thus injustice may be involved either in an act or an omission, and the same is true of a lack of charity; charity may demand that someone be aided, but also that an unkind word not be spoken.

The distinction between charity and justice will turn out to be of the first importance when voluntary and nonvoluntary euthanasia are distinguished later on. This is because of the connection between justice and rights, and something should now be said about this. I believe it is true to say that wherever a man acts unjustly he has infringed a right, since justice has to do with whatever a man is owed, and whatever he is owed is his as a matter of right. Something should therefore be said about the different kinds of rights. The distinction commonly made is between having a right in the sense of having a liberty, and having a "claim-right" or "right of recipience." The best way to understand such a distinction seems to be as follows. To say that a man has a right in the sense of liberty is to say that no one can demand that he do not do the thing which he has a right to do. The fact that he has a right to do it consists in the fact that a certain kind of objection does not lie against his doing it. Thus a man has a right in this sense to walk down a public street or park his car in a public parking space. It does not follow that no one else may prevent him from doing so. If for some reason I want a certain man not to park in a certain place I may lawfully park there myself or get my friends to do so, thus preventing him from doing what he has a right (in the sense of a liberty) to do. It is different, however, with a claim-right. This is the kind of right which I have in addition to a liberty when, for example, I have a private parking space; now others have duties in the way of noninterference, as in this case, or of service, as in the case where my claim-right is to goods or services promised to me. Sometimes one of these rights gives other people the duty of securing to me that to which I have a right, but at other times their duty is merely to refrain from interference. If a fall of snow blocks my private parking space there is normally no obligation for anyone else to clear it away. Claim-rights generate duties; sometimes these duties are duties of noninterference; sometimes they are duties of service. If your right gives me the duty not to interfere with you I have "no right" to do it; similarly, if your right gives me the duty to provide something for you I have "no right" to refuse to do it. What *I* lack is the right which is a liberty; I am not "at liberty" to interfere with you or to refuse the service.

Where in this picture does the right to life belong? No doubt people have the right to live in the sense of a liberty, but what is important is the cluster of claim-rights brought together under the title of the right to life. The chief of these is, of course, the right to be free from interferences that threaten life. If other people aim their guns at us or try to pour poison into our drink we can, to put it mildly, demand that they desist. And then there are the services we can claim from doctors, health officers, bodyguards, and firemen; the rights that depend on contract or public arrangement. Perhaps there is no particular point in saying that the duties these people owe us belong to the right to life; we might as well say that all the services owed to anyone by tailors, dressmakers, and couturiers belong to a right called the right to be elegant. But contracts such as those understood in the patient-doctor relationship come in an important way when we are discussing the rights and wrongs of euthanasia, and are therefore mentioned here.

Do people have the right to what they need in order to survive, apart from the right conferred by special contracts into which other people have entered for the supplying of these necessities? Do people in the underdeveloped countries in which starvation is rife have the right to the food they so evidently lack? Joel Feinberg, discussing this question, suggests that they

should be said to have "a claim," distinguishing this from a "valid claim," which gives a claim-right.

The manifesto writers on the other side who seem to identify needs, or at least basic needs, with what they call "human rights," are more properly described, I think, as urging upon the world community the moral principle that *all* basic human needs ought to be recognized as *claims* (in the customary *prima facie* sense) worthy of sympathy and serious consideration right now, even though, in many cases, they cannot yet plausibly be treated as *valid* claims, that is, as grounds of any other people's duties. This way of talking avoids the anomaly of ascribing to all human beings now, even those in pre-industrial societies, such "economic and social rights" as "periodic holidays with pay."[8]

This seems reasonable, though we notice that there are some actual rights to service which are not based on anything like a contract, as for instance the right that children have to support from their parents and parents to support from their children in old age, though both sets of rights are to some extent dependent on existing social arrangements.

Let us now ask how the right to life affects the morality of acts of euthanasia. Are such acts sometimes or always ruled out by the right to life? This is certainly a possibility; for although an act of euthanasia is, by our definition, a matter of opting for death for the good of the one who is to die, there is, as we noted earlier, no direct connection between that to which a man has a right and that which is for his good. It is true that men have the right only to the kind of thing that is, in general, a good: we do not think that people have the right to garbage or polluted air. Nevertheless, a man may have the right to something which he himself would be better off without; where rights exist it is a man's will that counts not his or anyone else's estimate of benefit or harm. So the duties complementary to the right to life—the general duty of noninterference and the duty of service incurred by certain persons—are not affected by the quality of a man's life or by his prospects. Even if it is true that he would be, as we say, "better off dead," so long as he wants to live this does not justify us in killing him and may not justify us in deliberately allowing him to die. All of us have the duty of noninterference, and some of us may have the duty to sustain his life. Suppose, for example, that a retreating army has to leave behind wounded or exhausted soldiers in the wastes of an arid or snowbound land where the only prospect is death by starvation or at the hands of an enemy notoriously cruel. It has often been the practice to accord a merciful bullet to men in such desperate straits. But suppose that one of them demands that he should be left alive? It seems clear that his comrades have no right to kill him, though it is a quite different question as to whether they should give him a life-prolonging drug. The right to life can sometimes give a duty of positive service, but does not do so here. What it does give is the right to be left alone.

Interestingly enough we have arrived by way of a consideration of the right to life at the distinction normally labeled "active" versus "passive" euthanasia, and often thought to be irrelevant to the moral issue. Once it is seen that the right to life is a distinct ground of objection to certain acts of euthanasia, and that this right creates a duty of noninterference more widespread than the duties of care there can be no doubt about the relevance of the distinction between passive and active euthanasia. Where everyone may have the duty to leave someone alone, it may be that no one has the duty to maintain his life, or that only some people do.

Where then do the boundaries of the "active" and "passive" lie? In some ways the words are themselves misleading, because they suggest the difference between act and omission which is not quite what we want. Certainly the act of shooting someone is the kind of thing we were talking about under the heading of "interference," and omitting to give him a drug a case of refusing care. But the act of turning off a respirator should surely be thought of as no different from the decision not to start it; if doctors had decided that a patient should be allowed to die, either course of action might follow, and both should be counted as passive rather than active euthanasia if euthanasia were in question. The point seems to be that interference in a course of treatment is not the same as other interference in a man's life, and particularly if the same body of people are responsible for the treatment and for its discontinuance. In such a case we could speak of the disconnecting of the apparatus as killing the man, or of the hospital as allowing him to die. By and large, it is the act of killing that is ruled out under the heading of noninterference, but not in every case.

Doctors commonly recognize this distinction, and the grounds on which some philosophers have denied it seem untenable. James Rachels, for instance, believes that if the difference between active and passive is relevant anywhere, it should be relevant everywhere, and he has pointed to an example in which it seems to make no difference which is done. If someone saw a child drowning in a bath it would seem just as bad to let it drown as to push its head under water. If "it makes no difference" means that one act would be as iniquitous as the other this is true. It is not that killing is *worse* than allowing to die, but that the two are contrary to distinct virtues, which gives the possibility that in some circumstances one is impermissible and the other permissible. In the circumstances invented by Rachels, both are wicked: it is contrary to justice to push the child's head under the water—something one has no right to do. To leave it to drown is not contrary to justice, but it is a particularly glaring example of lack of charity. Here it makes no practical difference because the requirements of justice and charity coincide; but in the case of the retreating army they did not: charity would have required that the wounded soldier be killed had not justice required that he be left alive.[9] In such a case it makes all the difference whether a man opts for the death of another in a positive action, or whether he allows him to die. An analogy with the right to property will make the point clear. If a man owns something he has the right to it even when its possession does him harm, and we have no right to take it from him. But if one day it should blow away, maybe nothing requires us to get it back for him; we could not deprive him of it, but we may allow it to go. This is not to deny that it will often be an unfriendly act or one based on an arrogant judgment when we refuse to do what he wants. Nevertheless, we would be within our rights, and it might be that no moral objection of any kind would lie against our refusal.

It is important to emphasize that a man's rights may stand between us and the action we would dearly like to take for his sake. They may, of course, also prevent action which we would like to take for the sake of others, as when it might be tempting to kill one man to save several. But it is interesting that the limits of allowable interference, however uncertain, seem stricter in the first case than the second. Perhaps there are no cases in which it would be all right to kill a man against his will *for his own sake* unless they could equally well be described as cases of allowing him to die, as in the example of turning off the respirator. However, there are circumstances, even if these are very rare, in which one man's life would justifiably be sacrificed to save others, and "killing" would be the only description of what was being done. For instance, a vehicle which had gone out of control might be steered from a path on which it would kill more than one man to a path on which it would kill one. But it would not be permissible to steer a vehicle towards someone in order to kill him, against his will, for his own good. An analogy with property rights illustrates the point. One may not destroy a man's property against his will on the grounds that he would be better off without it; there are however circumstances in which it could be destroyed for the sake of others. If his house is liable to fall and kill him that is his affair; it might, however, without injustice be destroyed to stop the spread of a fire.

We see then that the distinction between active and passive, important as it is elsewhere, has a special importance in the area of euthanasia. It should also be clear why James Rachels' other argument, that it is often "more humane" to kill than to allow to die, does not show that the distinction between active and passive euthanasia is morally irrelevant. It might be "more humane" in this sense to deprive a man of the property that brings evils on him, or to refuse to pay what is owed to Hume's profligate debauchee; but if we say this we must admit that an act which is "more humane" than its alternative may be morally objectionable because it infringes rights.

So far we have said very little about the right to service as opposed to the right to noninterference, though it was agreed that both might be brought under the heading of "the right to life." What about the duty to preserve life that may belong to special classes of persons such as bodyguards, firemen, or doctors? Unlike the general public they are not within their rights if they merely refrain from interfering and do not try to sustain life. The subject's claim-rights are two-fold as far as they are concerned and passive as well as active euthanasia may be ruled out here if it is against his will. This is not to say that he has the right to any and every service needed to save or prolong his life; the rights of other people set limits to what may be demanded, both because they have the right not to be interfered with and because they may have a competing right to services. Furthermore one must enquire just what the contract or implicit agreement amounts to in each case. Firemen and bodyguards presumably have a duty which is simply to preserve life, within the limits of justice to others and of reasonableness to themselves. With doctors it may however be different, since their duty relates not only to preserving life but also to the relief of suffering. It is not clear what a doctor's duties are to his patient if life can be prolonged only at the cost of suffering or suffering relieved only by measures that shorten life. George Fletcher has argued that what the doctor is under contract to do depends on what is generally done, because this is what a patient will reasonably expect.[10] This seems right. If procedures are part of normal medical practice then it seems that the patient can demand them however much it may be against his interest to do so. Once again it is not a matter of what is "most humane."

That the patient's right to life may set limits to permissible acts of euthanasia seems undeniable. If he does not want to die no one has the right to practice active euthanasia on him, and passive euthanasia may also be ruled out where he has a right to the services of doctors or others.

Perhaps few will deny what has so far been said about the impermissibility of acts of euthanasia simply because we have so far spoken about the case of one who positively wants to live, and about his rights, whereas those who advocate euthanasia are usually thinking either about those who wish to die or about those whose wishes cannot be ascertained either because they cannot properly be said to have wishes or because, for one reason or another, we are unable to form a reliable estimate of what they are. The question that must now be asked is whether the latter type of case, where euthanasia though not involuntary would again be nonvoluntary, is different from the one discussed so far. Would we have the right to kill someone for his own good so long as we had no idea that he positively wished to live? And what about the life-prolonging duties of doctors in the same circumstances? This is a very difficult problem. On the one hand, it seems ridiculous to suppose that a man's right to life is something which generates duties only where he has signaled that he wants to live; as a borrower does indeed have a duty to return something lent on indefinite loan only if the lender indicates that he wants it back. On the other hand, it might be argued that there is something illogical about the idea that a right has been infringed if someone incapable of saying whether he wants it or not is deprived of something that is doing him harm rather than good. Yet on the analogy of property we would say that a right has been infringed. Only if someone had earlier told us that in such circumstances he would not want to keep the thing could we think that his right had been waived. Perhaps if we could make confident judgments about what anyone in such circumstances would wish, or what he would have wished beforehand had he considered the matter, we could agree to consider the right to life as "dormant," needing to be asserted if the normal duties were to remain. But as things are we cannot make any such assumption; we simply do not know what most people would want, or would have wanted, us to do unless they tell us. This is certainly the case so far as active measures to end life are concerned. Possibly it is different, or will become different, in the matter of being kept alive, so general is the feeling against using sophisticated procedures on moribund patients, and so much is this dreaded by people who are old or terminally ill. Once again the distinction between active and passive euthanasia has come on the scene, but this time because most people's attitudes to the two are so different. It is just possible that we might presume, in the absence of specific evidence, that someone would not wish, beyond a certain point, to be kept alive; it is certainly not possible to assume that he would wish to be killed.

In the last paragraph we have begun to broach the topic of voluntary euthanasia, and this we must now discuss. What is to be said about the case in which there is no doubt about someone's wish to die: either he has told us beforehand that he would wish it in circumstances such as he is now in, and has shown no sign of a change of mind, or else he tells us now, being in possession of his faculties and of a steady mind. We should surely say that the objections previously urged against acts of euthanasia, which it must be remembered were all on the ground of rights, had disappeared. It does not seem that one would infringe someone's right to life in killing him with his permission and in fact at his request. Why should someone not be able to waive his right to life, or rather, as would be more likely to happen, to cancel some of the duties of noninterference that this right entails? (He is more likely to say that he should be killed by this man at this time in this manner, than to say that anyone may kill him at any time and in any way.) Similarly someone may give permission for the destruction of his property, and request it. The important thing is that he gives a critical permission, and it seems that this is enough to cancel the duty normally associated with the right. If someone gives you permission to destroy his property it can no longer be said that you have no right to do so, and I do not see why it should not be the case with taking a man's life. An objection might be made on the ground that only God has the right to take life, but in this paper religious as opposed to moral arguments are being left aside. Religion apart, there seems to be no case to be made out for an infringement of rights if a man who wishes to die is allowed to die or even killed. But of course it does not follow that there is no moral objection to it. Even with property, which is after all a relatively small matter, one might be wrong to destroy what one had the right to destroy. For, apart from its value to other people, it might be valuable to the man who wanted it destroyed, and charity might require us to hold our hand where justice did not.

Let us review the conclusion of this part of the argument, which has been about euthanasia and the right to life. It has been argued that from this side come stringent restrictions on the acts of euthanasia that could be morally permissible. Active nonvoluntary euthanasia is ruled out by that part of the right to life which creates the duty of noninterference though passive nonvoluntary euthanasia is not ruled out, except where the right to life-preserving action has been created by some special condition such as a contract between a man and his doctor, and it is not always certain just what such a contract involves. Voluntary euthanasia is another matter: as the preceding paragraph suggested, no right is infringed if a man is allowed to die or even killed at his own request.

Turning now to the other objection that normally holds against inducing the death of another, that it is against charity, or benevolence, we must tell a very different story. Charity is the virtue that gives attachment to the good of others, and because life is normally a good, charity normally demands that it should be saved or prolonged. But as we so defined an act of euthanasia that it seeks a man's death for his own sake—for his good—charity will normally speak in favor of it. This is not, of course, to say that charity can require an act of euthanasia which justice forbids, but if an act of euthanasia is not contrary to justice—that is, it does not infringe rights—charity will rather be in its favor than against.

Once more the distinction between nonvoluntary and voluntary euthanasia must be considered. Could it ever be compatible with charity to seek a man's death although he wanted to live, or at least had not let us know that he wanted to die? It has been argued that in such circumstances active euthanasia would infringe his right to life, but passive euthanasia would not do so, unless he had some special right to life-preserving service from the one who allowed him to die. What would charity dictate? Obviously when a man wants to live there is a presumption that he will be benefited if his life is prolonged, and if it is so the question of euthanasia does not arise. But it is, on the other hand, possible that he wants to live where it would be better for him to die: perhaps he does not realize the desperate situation he is in, or perhaps he is afraid of dying. So, in spite of a very proper resistance to refusing to go along with a man's own wishes in the matter of life and death, someone might justifiably refuse to prolong the life even of someone who asked him to prolong it, as in the case of refusing to give the wounded soldier a drug that would keep him alive to meet a terrible end. And it is even more obvious that charity does not always dictate that life should be prolonged where a man's own wishes, hypothetical or actual, are not known.

So much for the relation of charity to nonvoluntary passive euthanasia, which was not, like nonvoluntary active euthanasia, ruled out by the right to life. Let us now ask what charity has to say about voluntary euthanasia both active and passive. It was suggested in the discussion of justice that if of sound mind and steady desire a man might give others the *right* to allow him to die or even to kill him, where otherwise this would be ruled out. But it was pointed out that this would not settle the question of whether the act was morally permissible, and it is this that we must now consider. Could not charity speak against what justice allowed? Indeed it might do so. For while the fact that a man wants to die suggests that his life is wretched, and while his rejection of life may itself tend to take the good out of the things he might have enjoyed, nevertheless his wish to die might here be opposed for his own sake just as it might be if suicide were in question. Perhaps there is hope that his mental condition will improve. Perhaps he is mistaken in thinking his disease incurable. Perhaps he wants to die for the sake of someone else on whom he feels he is a burden, and we are not ready to accept this sacrifice whether for ourselves or others. In such cases, and there will surely be many of them, it could not be for his own sake that we kill him or allow him to die, and therefore euthanasia as defined in this paper would not be in question. But this is not to deny that there could be acts of voluntary euthanasia both passive and active against which neither justice nor charity would speak.

We have now considered the morality of euthanasia both voluntary and nonvoluntary, and active and passive. The conclusion has been that nonvoluntary active euthanasia (roughly, killing a man against his will or without his consent) is never justified; that is to say, that a man's being killed for his own good never justifies the act unless he himself has consented to it. A man's rights are infringed by such an action, and it is therefore contrary to justice. However, all the other combinations, nonvoluntary passive euthanasia, voluntary active euthanasia, and voluntary passive euthanasia are sometimes compatible with both justice and charity. But the strong condition carried in the definition of euthanasia adopted in this paper must not be forgotten; an act of euthanasia as here understood is one whose purpose is to benefit the one who dies.

In the light of this discussion let us look at our present practices. Are they good or are they bad? And what changes might be made, thinking now not only of the morality of particular acts of euthanasia but also of the indirect effects of instituting different practices, of the abuses to which they might be subject and of the changes that might come about if euthanasia became a recognized part of the social scene.

The first thing to notice is that it is wrong to ask whether we should introduce the practice of euthanasia as if it were not something we already had. In fact we do have it. For instance it is common, where the medical prognosis is very bad, for doctors to recommend against measures to prolong life, and particularly where a process of degeneration producing one medical emergency after another has already set in. If these doctors are not certainly within their legal rights this is something that is apt to come as a surprise to them as to the general public. It is also obvious that euthanasia is often practiced where old people are concerned. If someone very old and soon to die is attacked by a disease that makes his life wretched, doctors do not always come in with life-prolonging drugs. Perhaps poor patients are more fortunate in this respect than rich patients, being more often left to die in peace; but it is in any case a well recognized piece of medical practice, which is a form of euthanasia.

No doubt the case of infants with mental or physical defects will be suggested as another example of the practice of euthanasia as we already have it, since such infants are sometimes deliberately allowed to die. That they are deliberately allowed to die is certain; children with severe spina bifida malformations are not always operated on even where it is thought that without the operation they will die; and even in the case of children with [Down] Syndrome who have intestinal obstructions the relatively simple operation that would make it possible to feed them is sometimes not performed.[11] Whether this is euthanasia

in our sense or only as the Nazis understood it is another matter. We must ask the crucial question, "Is it for the sake of the child himself that the doctors and parents choose his death?" In some cases the answer may really be yes, and what is more important it may really be true that the kind of life which is a good is not possible or likely for this child, and that there is little but suffering and frustration in store for him.[12] But this must presuppose that the medical prognosis is wretchedly bad, as it maybe for some spina bifida children. With children who are born with [Down] Syndrome it is, however, quite different. Most of these are able to live on for quite a time in a reasonably contented way, remaining like children all their lives but capable of affectionate relationships and able to play games and perform simple tasks. The fact is, of course, that the doctors who recommend against life-saving procedures for handicapped infants are usually thinking not of them but rather of their parents and of other children in the family or of the "burden on society" if the children survive. So it is not for their sake but to avoid trouble to others that they are allowed to die. When brought out into the open this seems unacceptable: at least we do not easily accept the principle that adults who need special care should be counted too burdensome to be kept alive. It must in any case be insisted that if children with [Down] Syndrome are deliberately allowed to die this is not a matter of euthanasia except in Hitler's sense. And for our children, since we scruple to gas them, not even the manner of their death is "quiet and easy"; when not treated for an intestinal obstruction a baby simply starves to death. Perhaps some will take this as an argument for allowing active euthanasia, in which case they will be in the company of an S.S. man stationed in the Warthgenau who sent Eichmann a memorandum telling him that "Jews in the coming winter could no longer be fed" and submitting for his consideration a proposal as to whether "it would not be the most humane solution to kill those Jews who were incapable of work through some quicker means."[13] If we say we are *unable* to look after children with handicaps we are no more telling the truth than was the S.S. man who said that the Jews could not be fed.

Nevertheless if it is ever right to allow deformed children to die because life will be a misery to them, or not to take measures to prolong for a little the life of a newborn baby whose life cannot extend beyond a few months of intense medical intervention, there is a genuine problem about active as opposed to passive euthanasia. There are well-known cases in which the medical staff has looked on wretchedly while an infant died slowly from starvation and dehydration because they did not feel able to give a lethal injection. According to the principles discussed in the earlier part of this paper they would indeed have had no right to give it, since an infant cannot ask that it should be done. The only possible solution—supposing that voluntary active euthanasia were to be legalized—would be to appoint guardians to act on the infant's behalf. In a different climate of opinion this might not be dangerous, but at present, when people so readily assume that the life of a handicapped baby is of no value, one would be loath to support it.

Finally, on the subject of handicapped children, another word should be said about those with severe mental defects. For them too it might sometimes be right to say that one would wish for death for their sake. But not even severe mental handicap automatically brings a child within the scope even of a possible act of euthanasia. If the level of consciousness is low enough it could not be said that life is a good to them, any more than in the case of those suffering from extreme senility. Nevertheless if they do not suffer it will not be an act of euthanasia by which someone opts for their death. Perhaps charity does not demand that strenuous measures are taken to keep people in this state alive, but euthanasia does not come into the matter, any more than it does when someone is, like Karen Ann Quinlan, in a state of permanent coma. Much could be said about this last case. It might even be suggested that in the case of unconsciousness this "life" is not the life to which "the right to life" refers. But that is not our topic here.

What we must consider, even if only briefly, is the possibility that euthanasia, genuine euthanasia, and not contrary to the requirements of justice or charity, should be legalized over a wider area. Here we are up against the really serious problem of abuse. Many people want, and want very badly, to be rid of their elderly relatives and even of their ailing husbands or wives. Would any safeguards ever be able to stop them describing as euthanasia what was really for their own benefit? And would it be possible to prevent the occurrence of acts which were genuinely acts of euthanasia but morally impermissible because infringing the rights of a patient who wished to live?

Perhaps the furthest we should go is to encourage patients to make their own contracts with a doctor by making it known whether they wish him to prolong their life in case of painful terminal illness or of incapacity. A document such as the Living Will seems eminently sensible, and should surely be allowed to give a doctor following the previously expressed wishes of the patient immunity from legal proceedings by relatives.[14] Legalizing active euthanasia is, however, another matter. Apart from the special repugnance doctors feel towards the idea of a lethal injection, it may be of the very greatest importance to keep a psychological barrier up against killing. Moreover it is active euthanasia which is the most liable to abuse. Hitler would not have been able to kill 275,000 people in his "euthanasia" program if he had had to wait for them to need life-saving treatment. But there are other objections to active euthanasia, even voluntary active euthanasia. In the first place it would be hard to devise procedures that would protect people from being persuaded into giving their consent. And secondly the possibility of active voluntary euthanasia might change the social scene in ways that would be very bad. As things are, people do, by and large, expect to be looked after if they are old or ill. This is one of the good things that we have, but we might lose it, and be much worse off without it. It might come to be expected that someone likely to need a lot of looking after should call for the doctor and demand his own death. Something comparable could be good in an extremely poverty-stricken community where the children genuinely suffered from lack of food; but in rich societies such as ours it would surely be a spiritual disaster. Such possibilities should make us very wary of supporting large measures of euthanasia, even where moral principle applied to the individual act does not rule it out.

NOTES

1. Leo Alexander, "Medical Science under Dictatorship," *New England Journal of Medicine,* 14 July 1949, p. 40.

2. For a discussion of culpable and nonculpable ignorance see Thomas Aquinas, *Summa Theologica,* First Part of the Second Part, Question 6, article 8, and Question 19, articles 5 and 6.

3. Dmitri Panin, *The Notebooks of Sologdin* (London, 1976), pp. 66–67.

4. Thomas Nagel, "Death," in James Rachels, ed., *Moral Problems* (New York, 1971), p. 362.

5. Panin, *Sologdin,* p. 85.

6. Yet some detail needs to be filled in to explain why we should not say that a scarecrow is beneficial to the plants it protects. Perhaps what is beneficial must either be a feature of the plant itself, such as protective prickles, or else must work on the plant directly, such as a line of trees which give it shade.

7. David Hume, *Treatise,* Book III, Part II, Section 1.

8. Feinberg, "Human Rights," *Moral Problems in Medicine,* p. 465.

9. It is not, however, that justice and charity conflict. A man does not lack charity because he refrains from an act of injustice which would have been for someone's good.

10. George Fletcher, "Legal Aspects of the Decision not to Prolong Life," *Journal of the American Medical Association* 203, no. 1 (1 Jan. 1968): 119–122. Reprinted in Gorovitz.

11. I have been told this by a pediatrician in a well-known medical center in the United States. It is confirmed by Anthony M. Shaw and Iris A. Shaw, "Dilemma of Informed Consent in Children," *The New England Journal of Medicine* 289, no. 17 (25 Oct. 1973): 885–890. Reprinted in Gorovitz.

12. It must be remembered, however, that many of the social miseries of spina bifida children could be avoided. Professor R.B. Zachary is surely right to insist on this. See, for example, "Ethical and Social Aspects of Spina Bifida," *The Lancet,* 3 Aug. 1968, pp. 274–276. Reprinted in Gorovitz.

13. Quoted by Hannah Arendt, *Eichmann in Jerusalem* (London, 1963), p. 90.

14. Details of this document are to be found in J.A. Behnke and Sissela Bok, eds., *The Dilemmas of Euthanasia* (New York, 1975), and in A.B. Downing, ed., *Euthanasia and the Right to Life: The Case for Voluntary Euthanasia* (London, 1969).

Killing and Allowing to Die

DANIEL CALLAHAN

* * *

If a lessened worry about the consequences of legal euthanasia has been gaining ground, there has been an even more powerful threat to the traditional prohibition against it. No valid distinction, many now argue, can be made between killing and allowing to die, or between an act of commission and one of omission. The standard distinction being challenged rests on the commonplace observation that lives can come to an end as the result of: (a) the direct action of another who becomes the cause of death (as in shooting a person), and (b) the result of impersonal forces where no human agent has acted (death by lightning, or by disease). The purpose of the distinction has been to separate those deaths caused by human action, and those caused by nonhuman events. It is, as a distinction, meant to say something about human beings and their relationship to the world. It is a way of articulating the difference between those actions for which human beings can be held rightly responsible, or blamed, and those of which they are innocent. At

Daniel Callahan, "Can We Return Death to Disease?" from *Hastings Center Report* 19(1): 4–6. Copyright © 1989 The Hastings Center. Reproduced with permission of John Wiley & Sons, Inc.

issue is the difference between physical causality, the realm of impersonal events, and moral culpability, the realm of human responsibility.

The challenges encompass two points. The first is that people can become equally dead by our omissions as well as our commissions. We can refrain from saving them when it is possible to do so, and they will be just as dead as if we shot them. It is our decision itself that is the reason for their death, not necessarily how we effectuate that decision. That fact establishes the basis of the second point: if we *intend* their death, it can be brought about as well by omitted acts as by those we commit. The crucial moral point is not how they die, but our intention about their death. We can, then, be responsible for the death of another by intending that they die and accomplish that end by standing aside and allowing them to die.

Despite these criticisms—resting upon ambiguities that can readily be acknowledged—the distinction between killing and allowing to die remains, I contend, perfectly valid. It not only has a logical validity but, no less importantly, a social validity whose place must be central in moral judgments. As a way of putting the distinction into perspective, I want to suggest that it is best understood as expressing three different, though overlapping, perspectives on nature and human action. I will call them the metaphysical, the moral, and the medical perspectives.

Metaphysical. The first and most fundamental premise of the distinction between killing and allowing to die is that there is a sharp difference between the self and the external world. Unlike the childish fantasy that the world is nothing more than a projection of the self, or the neurotic person's fear that he or she is responsible for everything that goes wrong, the distinction is meant to uphold a simple notion: there is a world external to the self that has its own, and independent, causal dynamism. The mistake behind a conflation of killing and allowing to die is to assume that the self has become master of everything within and outside of the self. It is as if the conceit that modern man might ultimately control nature has been internalized: that, if the self might be able to influence nature by its actions, then the self and nature must be one.

Of course that is a fantasy. The fact that we can intervene in nature, and cure or control many diseases, does not erase the difference between the self and the external world. It is as "out there" as ever, even if more under our sway. That sway, however great, is always limited. We can cure disease, but not always the chronic illness that comes with the cure. We can forestall death with modern medicine, but death always wins in the long run because of the innate limitations of the body, inherently and stubbornly beyond final human control. And we can distinguish between a diseased body and an aging body, but in the end if we wait long enough they always become one and the same body. To attempt to deny the distinction between killing and allowing to die is, then, mistakenly to impute more power to human action than it actually has and to accept the conceit that nature has now fallen wholly within the realm of human control. Not so.

Moral. At the center of the distinction between killing and allowing to die is the difference between physical causality and moral culpability. To bring the life of another to an end by an injection kills the other directly; our action is the physical cause of the death. To allow someone to die from a disease we cannot cure (and that we did not cause) is to permit the disease to act as the cause of death. The notion of physical causality in both cases rests on the difference between human agency and the action of external nature. The ambiguity arises precisely because we can be morally culpable for killing someone (if we have no moral right to do so, as we would in self-defense) and no less culpable for allowing someone to die (if we have both the possibility and the obligation of keeping that person alive). Thus there are cases where, morally speaking, it makes no difference whether we killed or allowed to die; we are equally responsible. In those instances, the lines of physical causality and moral culpability happen to cross. Yet the fact that they can cross in some cases in no way shows that they are always, or even usually, one and the same. We can normally find the difference in all but the most obscure cases. We should not, then, use the ambiguity of such cases to do away altogether with the distinction between killing and allowing to die. The ambiguity may obscure, but does not erase, the line between the two.

There is one group of ambiguous cases that is especially troublesome. Even if we grant the ordinary validity between killing and allowing to die, what about those cases that combine (a) an illness that renders a patient unable to carry out an ordinary biological function (to breathe or eat on his own, for example), and (b) our turning off a respirator or removing an artificial feeding tube? On the level of physical causality, have we killed the patient or allowed him to die? In one sense, it is our action that shortens his life, and yet in another sense his underlying disease brings his life to an end. I believe it reasonable to say that, since his life was being sustained by artificial means (respirator or feeding tube) made necessary because of the fact that he had an incapacitating disease, his disease is the ultimate reality behind his death. But for its reality, there would be no need for artificial sustenance in the first place and no moral issue at all. To lose sight of the paramount reality of the disease is to lose sight of the difference between our selves and the outer world.

I quickly add, and underscore, a moral point: the person who, without good moral reason, turns off a respirator or pulls a feeding tube, can be morally culpable; that the patient has been allowed to die of his underlying condition does not morally excuse him. The moral question is whether we are obliged to continue treating a life that is being artificially sustained. To cease treatment may or may not be morally acceptable; but it should be understood, in either case, that the physical cause of death was the underlying disease.

Medical. An important social purpose of the distinction between killing and allowing to die has been that of protecting the historical role of the physician as one who tries to cure or comfort patients rather than to kill patients. Physicians have been given special knowledge about the body, knowledge that can be used to kill or to cure. They are also given great privileges in making use of that knowledge. It is thus all the more important that physicians' social role and power

be, and be seen to be, a limited power. It may be used only to cure or comfort, never to kill. They have not been given, nor should they be given, the power to use their knowledge and skills to bring life to an end. It would open the way for powerful misuse and, no less importantly, represent an intrinsic violation of what it has meant to be a physician.

Yet if it is possible for physicians to misuse their knowledge and power to kill people directly, are they thereby required to use that same knowledge always to keep people alive, always to resist a disease that can itself kill the patient? The traditional answer has been: not necessarily. For the physician's ultimate obligation is to the welfare of the patient, and excessive treatment can be as detrimental to that welfare as inadequate treatment. Put another way, the obligation to resist the lethal power of disease is limited—it ceases when the patient is unwilling to have it resisted, or where the resistance no longer serves the patient's welfare. Behind this moral premise is the recognition that disease (of some kind) ultimately triumphs and that death is both inevitable sooner or later and not, in any case, always the greatest human evil. To demand of the physician that he always struggle against disease, as if it was in his power always to conquer it, would be to fall into the same metaphysical trap mentioned above: that of assuming that no distinction can be drawn between natural and human agency.

A final word. I suggested earlier that the most potent motive for active euthanasia and assisted suicide stems from a dread of the power of medicine. That power then seems to take on a drive of its own regardless of the welfare or wishes of patients. No one can easily say no—not physicians, not patients, not families. My guess is that happens because too many have already come to believe that it is their choice, and their choice alone, which brings about death; and they do not want to exercise that kind of authority. The solution is not to erase the distinction between killing and allowing to die, but to underscore its validity and importance. We can bring disease as a cause of death back into the care of the dying.

Euthanasia for Disabled People?

LIZ CARR

If I said I wanted to die, the press, celebrities and the public would support my choice, seeing it as rational and understandable. Hell, they would probably set up a GoFundMe campaign to help me make it happen.

Yet when a healthy, non-disabled person wants to kill themself it's seen as a tragedy, and support and prevention tools are provided. If nothing else convinces me that to legalise assisted suicide is not a safe option for many of us, then this does. Suicide is not seen as socially desirable—so why is assisted suicide seen as compassionate when it's for ill or disabled people?

Marieke Vervoort, the 38-year-old Belgian Paralympian gold medallist, is only the most recent disabled person to announce that she is considering euthanasia, saying her "body is exhausted". She is not imminently dying. Yet no one seems to be trying to persuade her that life is worthwhile. Would Usain Bolt be met with the same reaction if he announced his decision to end it all after his last Olympics?

Although proponents of assisted suicide legislation say it's only for those with six months or less to live, they propagandise with cases like that of Daniel James, the 23-year-old man paralysed (but not dying) following a rugby accident, who killed himself at the Swiss clinic Dignitas after he said he did not want to live a "second-class" (that is, disabled) life. Jeffrey Spector, a 54-year-old man also not imminently dying, also killed himself at Dignitas.

The Netherlands, which legalised euthanasia to provide relief for the terminally ill, now regularly provides euthanasia for disabled people who can demonstrate "unbearable suffering". Canada, the most recent nation to legalise euthanasia and assisted suicide, allows it for "serious and incurable illness, disease or disability".

Usually, the two sides of the argument are characterised as "religious" (opposed to legalisation) or "secular" (in favour). But it's not that simple.

Frustrated by the lack of opportunity to have the voices of people like me—of disabled people—heard on this issue, I have decided to combine my activism with my career as a performer.

I've never seen a piece of art or theatre which expresses opposition to legalising assisted suicide from a disabled person's perspective—so I decided to try to rectify that. The result is *Assisted Suicide: The Musical*—a show which premieres this weekend at the Royal Festival Hall, London, and marks the first anniversary of the defeat of the assisted dying bill in parliament.

There were of course religious people there with me and many others outside Westminster on Friday 11 September 2015. But MPs who glanced out the window would have seen more Not Dead Yet (NDY) T-shirts and banners than religious ones. NDY is made up of disabled people opposed to a change in the law. Every major disabled group in the UK, it should be stressed, is opposed to this legislation.

Suicide is, of course, an individual choice. Disabled people who are determined to take their lives may even find it easier to do so than abled people, given the often precarious nature of their existences. But that does not mean that when a fellow human being—disabled or abled—expresses the wish to die because their life is shit, that we should agree with them. The value of a life is not just in its physicality but in our relationships with those around us.

The bill, had it passed, would have licensed doctors to assist in the deaths of terminally ill people who had less than six months to live, were mentally competent and requested such assistance. But the direction legislation has taken in other countries shows that the sympathy we disabled people evoke can be used to justify support for us to kill ourselves while non-disabled people are told they have "everything to live for". How many times has someone come up to me and said how much they admired me just for existing because they could not, in my condition?

There is a fine line between those who are terminally ill and those who are disabled in public perception, and the emotional power behind the campaign for assisted suicide is based on misplaced pity. Rather than telling us we have everything to live for—and we do—we are helped to the proverbial cliff edge and offered a push.

People—disabled and not, with many years or only a few months ahead of them—become suicidal for many, many reasons. We know from surveys in Oregon, one of just four states in the US where assisted suicide is legal, that the reasons people choose this option have little to do with pain, although this is always the emphasis of supporters of assisted dying.

In fact, loss of dignity, loss of autonomy, loss of ability to do daily activities, and fear of being a burden—reasons which are essentially more about the realities of living with a disability in our society—are all more important than pain.

It is worth keeping in mind, too, that, in the context of economic arguments about a health service overly concerned with "waste" of resources, disabled people may be seen as a drain, just like the elderly. We

also know from the US that some people have been denied life-extending treatments because they are too costly while the cheaper assisted suicide option has been offered as an alternative. Think this won't happen here? Medical rationing is the reality of our overstretched NHS.

No one wants us, those we love, or even those we don't to suffer and die in pain. But shouldn't we try to get end-of-life care right before we throw physician-assisted killing into the mix? Currently hospices and palliative care are only available to the few, and hospices continue to rely on donations for their survival.

Please, don't wish death upon us because you feel pity for our condition. It is demoralising when disabled people like Vervoort express—understandably—exhaustion with the everyday struggle of existence and discouragement with life and are met with sad, understanding nods. On Saturday, it is world suicide prevention day. Can we be included in suicide prevention efforts, too, please?

CHAPTER 11

Delivering Health Care

At the burning center of debates about health care in the United States—debates that rage in the U.S. Congress, in the media, at kitchen tables, and in medical and health organizations of all kinds— are a few seemingly simple moral questions: Who should get health care, who should supply it, and who should pay for it? (*Health care,* in this context, includes medical treatment, disease prevention, emergency care, and public health measures.) This debate is not about the morality of individual actions and decisions; it's about the morality of the policies and programs of a society as a whole. It arises from disturbing facts about the citizens of such a prosperous nation: millions afflicted with disease and disability have no access to health care, and many suffer and die as a result. Reality forces society to confront a host of related questions: What do we owe, if anything, to these millions? Are the more fortunate obligated to help those in need? Are citizens entitled only to the health care they can pay for out of their own pockets? Or should everyone—rich and poor—have access to health care? If they should, what level of health care should they have—the best that medical science can offer, the same care that rich people can buy, a bare minimum package of health care? Does everyone have a *right* to health care— such that a society's failure to provide it would be morally wrong?

The fundamental moral issue involved in the health care debate is *justice*, which is about persons getting what is fair or what is their due. With an eye to justice, we condemn racial discrimination and unequal punishments for the same crime because justice demands impartiality—that is, it requires that equals be treated equally unless there is a morally relevant reason for treating them differently. Based on this understanding of justice, many who have thought carefully about the U.S. system of distributing health care think it is unjust. This judgment sits uneasily alongside an even more common criticism: the system is ineffective and unworkable.

ISSUE FILE: BACKGROUND

Health care is expensive, which is why so many Americans do not have access to it: they cannot afford it. Health insurance exists to help people cover the expense of health care, but health insurance itself is expensive, which is why millions lack coverage. Here is a nonpartisan report on the problem:

> In the past, gaps in the public insurance system and lack of access to affordable private coverage left millions without health insurance, and the number of uninsured Americans grew over time, particularly during economic downturns. By 2013, the year before the major coverage provisions of the Affordable Care Act (ACA) ["Obamacare"] went into effect, more than 44 million nonelderly individuals lacked coverage. . . .
>
> Under the ACA, as of 2014, Medicaid coverage has expanded to nearly all adults with incomes at or below 138% of poverty in states that have adopted the expansion, and tax credits are available for people with incomes up to 400% of poverty who purchase coverage through a health insurance marketplace. Millions of people have enrolled in these new coverage options, and the uninsured rate has

dropped to a historic low. Coverage gains were particularly large among low-income people living in states that expanded Medicaid.

Still, millions of people—27.6 million nonelderly individuals as of 2016—remain without coverage. Those most at risk of being uninsured include low-income individuals, adults, and people of color. Cost continues to pose a major barrier to coverage with nearly half (45%) of nonelderly uninsured adults in 2016 saying that they remained uninsured because the cost of coverage was too high.[1]

Uninsured people pay a price for being without health insurance. They often have to forgo or delay treatment, skip medical tests that can detect disease early, go without prescription drugs, and pass on life-saving surgery. They are forced to seek treatment at hospital emergency departments and community clinics, but these options cannot entirely make up for the more comprehensive health care provided through adequate insurance coverage. According to researchers, not having health insurance can be deadly: each year a lack of coverage is responsible for 45,000 deaths.[2]

In 1999, 67 percent of people under 65 (the "nonelderly") got their health coverage through their employer. But in 2014, only 56 percent of the nonelderly got their coverage this way.[3] Fewer employers provided health insurance as a benefit to their employees, and many employees could not afford it or were ineligible for it.

For some, **Medicare** is a source of basic coverage. It's a federally funded insurance program that covers people 65 and older, some adults under 65 with disabilities, and people with end-stage kidney disease. The program is supported by payroll taxes paid by workers during their years of employment. It insures elderly people regardless of health or income, covering hospital care, short-term nursing home services, physicians' bills, outpatient care, and prescription drugs. **Medicaid** is an insurance program supported jointly by the federal government and the states, with the former providing matching funds to the latter. It covers some

low-income families, pregnant women, families and children, and people with disabilities. States may cover additional groups, including individuals receiving home-based care and children in foster care. But because of certain eligibility rules, Medicaid does not cover many who are below the poverty line.

In the U.S. health care system, a troubling contradiction hides in plain sight: while the United States spends an impressively large amount of money on health care, the country earns shockingly low scores on standard assessments of national health. In 2016, the United States spent more on health care than any other country in the world: $9,892 per capita.[4] Yet the United States scored worse on fundamental measures of health than most other developed countries. In 2015, the average life expectancy in the United States was 78.8 years—below that in Australia, Germany, the United Kingdom, Sweden, France, and Japan. The infant mortality rate in the United States was 5.8 deaths per 1,000, which was higher than those in most other developed countries—including the United Kingdom, Japan, Korea, Switzerland, Poland, and Estonia.[5]

The United States has a reputation for offering "the best health care in the world," and in some ways, its care really is the best. The U.S. system outperforms comparable countries in the development and use of medical technologies, and it has shorter wait times for specialist visits, lower in-hospital mortality rates for heart attack and ischemic stroke, and higher five-year survival rates for some cancers. But at the same time, the United States has the highest rate of deaths that could have been prevented through better health care, and it has more frequent hospital admissions for preventable diseases, fewer physicians per capita, higher rates of errors in care (medical, medication, and laboratory errors), and longer wait times to see a doctor.[6]

A 2014 study of the strengths and weaknesses of advanced health care systems around the world

Health Care by Country

Country	Health care spend-ing (per capita)	Avg. life expec-tancy	Infant mor-tality (deaths per 1,000)	% of Pop. cov-ered by insur-ance
United States	$9,892	78.8	5.8	90.9
Canada	$4,753	79.6	4.8	100
United Kingdom	$4,192	81.0	3.9	100
Germany	$5,551	80.7	3.3	100
Switzerland	$7,919	80.8	3.9	100
Australia	$4,708	82.5	3.2	100
Sweden	$5,488	82.3	2.5	100
France	$4,600	82.4	3.7	99.9
Japan	$4,519	83.9	2.1	100

Data from OECD, "Health at a Glance 2017: OECD Indicators," November 10, 2017; OECD.org, OECD Data, "Health Spending," 2016, https://data.oecd.org/healthres/health-spending.htm; Melissa Etehad and Kyle Kim, "The U.S. Spends More on Healthcare Than Any Other Country—but Not with Better Health Outcomes," *Los Angeles Times*, July 18, 2017.

reinforced the idea that the U.S. system was in trouble. The study findings were summarized like this:

> Despite having the most expensive health care system, the United States ranks last overall among 11 industrialized countries on measures of health system quality, efficiency, access to care, equity, and healthy lives, according to a new Commonwealth Fund report. The other countries included in the study were Australia, Canada, France, Germany, the Netherlands, New Zealand, Norway, Sweden, Switzerland, and the United Kingdom. While there is room for improvement in every country, the U.S. stands out for having the highest costs and lowest performance. . . . [7]

Much of the health care in the United States is delivered through **managed care**, a type of

health insurance in which providers (doctors and hospitals, for example) contract with a managed care plan (an HMO, PPO, or POS) to offer health care to a group of patients (members of the plan) at discounted costs. The managed care plan agrees to pay the providers a fixed fee; the providers agree to reduce the price of their services in exchange for the plan's pool of patients; and, to keep costs down, the patients may be restricted to certain medical services and to only those providers that are part of the plan ("in the network").

Managed care plans get credit for trying to contain costs and improve efficiency, but some critics charge that the emphasis on these business values could ultimately degrade the quality of care. They say that physicians in these plans may spend less time with patients, forgo necessary tests and treatments, avoid treating serious health problems, and engender distrust in patients. Physicians, for their part, may worry that their managed care organization will expect them to practice a less compassionate, less conscientious form of medicine. In any case, physicians are expected to try to serve the needs of patients while meeting the demands of a cost-conscious business.

The Affordable Care Act ("Obamacare"), enacted in 2010, was an attempt by the administration of President Barack Obama to solve two of the most intractable problems of the U.S. health care system: the lack of health insurance coverage among millions of Americans and the seemingly unstoppable rise in health care costs. The administration believed that the best way to achieve these ends was to expand both private and public health insurance. Here's a brief summary of the ACA's major provisions:

- It required employers to cover their workers or pay penalties, with exceptions for small employers.

- It provided tax credits to certain small businesses that cover specified costs of health insurance for their employees.

- It required individuals to have basic health insurance, with some exceptions, such as for financial hardship or religious belief (this provision is known as the *individual mandate*).

- It required the creation of state-based (or multi-state) insurance exchanges to help individuals and small businesses purchase insurance. Federal subsidies were established to limit premium costs to between 2 percent of income, for those with incomes at 133 percent of the federal poverty level, and 9.5 percent of income, for those who earn between 300 percent and 400 percent of the federal poverty level.

- It expanded Medicaid to cover people with incomes below [138] percent of federal poverty level.

- It required the creation of temporary high-risk pools for those who cannot purchase health insurance on the private market due to preexisting health conditions.

- It required health insurance plans to cover young adults on their parents' policies.

- It required health insurance plans to cover certain preventive care, such as immunizations, preventive care for children, and specified health screening tests for adults.[8]

The ACA has been controversial since its debut, with political parties lining up for and against it, supporters and detractors arguing over key components, and repeated challenges to the law in federal courts. Supporters have embraced it because it has increased access to health insurance, made

CRITICAL THOUGHT: Comparing Health Care Systems

Consider the features of these four health care systems:

- *Canada.* A single-payer, universal system in which the national government pays for health care through taxes while the private sector provides the care. Private health insurance is available to cover people who choose not to participate in the national plan.

- *Germany.* A universal health care system in which the government pays for care with mandatory contributions, based on income, from employers and employees. The private sector delivers the care. Most Germans obtain coverage through the public system, but some can opt for private health insurance.

- *United Kingdom.* A universal single-payer system of socialized medicine. The government not only

pays for health care through taxes, but also delivers care through state-owned medical facilities. Some private health insurance is also available.

- *United States.* A less-than-universal mixed system of health care consisting of private health insurance obtained through employers, private health insurance acquired through ACA exchanges, single-payer Medicare, and state-financed and state-run Medicaid.

Based on the information above and in the rest of this chapter, which health care system do you think is best? Which system covers the most people, at the lowest cost, with the best health outcomes? Why? Consider the U.S. system. What are its advantages and disadvantages? Would you like to see it move closer to a system like the one in the United Kingdom? Why or why not?

that insurance more affordable, addressed concerns about fairness, and seems to fit well with the notion of a right to health care. Critics complain about increases in premiums and out-of-pocket costs, object to the individual mandate, and insist that providing health insurance is not a legitimate role for the government. In late 2017, the U.S. Congress eliminated the individual mandate; the loss of this key provision of the ACA is likely to add millions of people to the uninsured rolls.[9]

MORAL THEORIES

In Chapter 21 (Global Economic Justice), we discuss justice as it applies to nations and their obligations to the impoverished people of the world. Here we delve into theories of justice as they apply to health care systems.

Broad questions about who should get health care, who should provide it, and who should pay for it are ultimately questions about justice—in particular, about *distributive justice*. This kind of justice concerns the fair distribution of a society's benefits and burdens, such as taxes, jobs, income, government services, social obligations, property, and rights. The idea of distributive justice is that in any society, morality demands that people receive what they are due, what is fair. Debates about the distribution of health care are often, at their most fundamental level, clashes between rival theories of distributive justice. If you ask people why they think a particular allocation of health care resources is good or right, they may give you a variety of reasons—and these reasons can often be traced back logically to a supporting theory of justice. Two types of theories have been especially prominent in moral arguments about health care: libertarian and egalitarian theories.

Libertarian theories of justice say that the advantages and disadvantages of society must be allotted in a way that does not curtail personal liberty. People are entitled only to what they can freely acquire through their own legitimate efforts in a free market. To compel someone to help others—say, to tax a person to pay for someone else's health care—is a violation of personal liberty. In other words, for the libertarian, there are no positive rights—rights that obligate others to help a person obtain something. There are only negative rights—rights that obligate others not to interfere with a person's obtaining something. The state should use coercion only to protect these negative rights and to ensure that the economic marketplace is free of fraud, theft, and contract breaches.

Critics of the libertarian view of health care reject the theory's fundamental premise. For example:

> The problem is, [the fundamental libertarian assumption] leads directly to the conclusion that "if you don't have any money, you shouldn't be entitled to any medicine." This is not a quibble. It's a very basic point about the trouble libertarians have with arguments about fairness in health-care distribution.
>
> Essentially, libertarians don't believe in positive rights. They believe that no matter how rich a society may be, no member of that society has a right to demand a minimal share of basic goods from that society. People have the right not to be interfered with, but they don't have the right to actually get anything. One can think of the position in terms of a desert-island castaway analogy. Let's say two castaways wash up on a desert island, along with their trunks. One is fantastically rich, and he has several trunks full of tinned meat, a water filter, and so on. The other guy just has a carry-on bag with a toothbrush. The question is: is the rich guy morally obliged to share his water filter with the poor guy? Does the poor guy have a *right* to potable water, given that the filter makes adequate water available for everyone? Or would it just be a nice thing, but not a rights-based moral obligation, for the rich guy to share his water?
>
> Libertarians believe the poor guy doesn't have a right to the water. Liberals believe he does. If there's enough water to ensure nobody goes thirsty, then the poor guy has a fundamental right to get a decent share. There may be arguments over how large that decent share is, but fundamentally, people have the right to adequate water in a society where there's enough water to go around.[10]

Egalitarian theories of justice maintain that because every person is of equal value and is worthy of equal moral consideration, the only just way to distribute society's benefits and burdens is *equally*. People are entitled to equal portions, and no person is "more equal" than others. In the case of health care, some egalitarians contend that everyone should get the same basic minimum allotment of health care. Others assert that all health care should be distributed equally, even if this means taking resources away from the wealthy to give to the less well-off. And some say that health care should be divided equally among those most in need. The libertarian, of course, rejects this argument, declaring that economic equality should never take precedence over personal liberties. Liberty trumps equality.

Probably the strongest egalitarian claim is that people have a moral *right* to health care— a guaranteed positive right. As Norman Daniels, an influential advocate for this position, says,

> [A] right to health care imposes an obligation on others to assist the right-bearers in obtaining needed and appropriate services. Specifically, claiming a right to health care includes these other claims: society has the duty to its members to allocate an adequate share of its total resources to health-related needs; society has the duty to provide a just allocation of different types of health care services, taking into account the competing claims of different types of health-care needs; each person is entitled to a fair share of such services, where a "fair share" includes an answer to the question, who should pay for the services? Health-care rights thus form a part of a broader family of positive "welfare" rights that includes rights to education and to income support.[11]

MORAL ARGUMENTS

One of the more interesting arguments in health care policy is the one Daniels uses to try to establish health care as a moral right. He thinks that a right to health care can be derived from the theory of justice set forth by the philosopher John Rawls. Rawls argues in his book *A Theory of Justice* that people are entitled not to equal shares of the basic goods of society, but to an equal chance to acquire them. A society is just when it ensures "fair equality of opportunity" to obtain available benefits.[12]

Daniels contends that disease and disability impair "normal species functioning" and that this impairment limits people's opportunities, undermining equality of opportunity. But, he says, health care can equalize opportunities:

> [H]ealth care in all its forms, whether public health or medical, preventive or acute or chronic, aims to keep people functioning as close to normally as possible. . . . Health care thus preserves for us the range of opportunities we would have, were we not ill or disabled, given our talents and skills.[13]

We can outline Daniels's argument like this:

1. Everyone is entitled to (has a right to) an equal opportunity to obtain the basic goods of society (but not to an equal share of them).

2. To secure equal opportunity, a just society must ensure the "normal species functioning" of its citizens.

3. Disease and disability weaken people's "normal species functioning," limiting the opportunities open to them.

4. Adequate health care can keep people functioning as close to normally as possible and thus preserve their normal range of opportunities.

5. Therefore, people have a positive right to adequate health care.

This is a valid argument, so someone attacking it must focus on the truth of the premises. Premises 3 and 4 are empirical claims that are very likely true. Premises 1 and 2 may be plausible moral principles, but they would be disputed by libertarians who reject the notion of positive rights and by some utilitarians who reject rights that are weightier than considerations of utility.

But how much health care does this right include? The difficulty of answering this question is a challenge to Daniels's view, but he recognizes the problem:

> How equal must our rights to health care be? Specifically, must everyone receive exactly the same kinds of health-care services and coverage, or is fairness in health care compatible with a "tiered" system? Around the world, even countries that offer universal health insurance differ in their answers to this question. In Canada and Norway, for example, no supplementary insurance is permitted. Everyone is served solely by the national health-insurance schemes; though people who seek additional services or more rapid service may go elsewhere, as some Canadians do by crossing the border. In Britain, supplementary private insurance allows about 10 percent of the population to gain quicker access to services for which there is extensive queuing in the public system. Basing a right to health care on an obligation to protect equality of opportunity is compatible with the sort of tiering the British have, but it does not require it, and it imposes some constraints on the kind of tiering allowed.[14]

It seems implausible that an equal right to health care includes universal equal access to all available health care resources. Such a robust allocation would not be economically possible. A better idea, some argue, is a weaker right to a "decent minimum" of health care. This proposal involves a two-tier system: one tier would offer a universally available guaranteed package of basic health care; another tier would provide additional health care options (such as elective services) to anyone who could afford them.

Specifying what's included in a *decent minimum* is problematic. It might include basics such as immunizations, physical exams, and recommended screening tests. But should it also include hospice care, organ transplants, cosmetic surgery, care for special-needs children or institutionalized mentally impaired persons, and experimental treatments?

QUICK REVIEW

Medicare—A federally funded U.S. health insurance program that covers people 65 and older, some adults under 65 with disabilities, and people with end-stage kidney disease.

Medicaid—A health insurance program supported jointly by the U.S. federal government and the states, with the former providing matching funds to the latter. It covers some low-income families, pregnant women, and people with disabilities.

managed care—A type of health insurance in which providers contract with a managed care plan to offer health care to a particular group of patients (members of the plan) at discounted costs.

CHAPTER REVIEW

SUMMARY

Debates about health care in the United States are mostly about who should get health care, who should supply it, and who should pay for it. The fundamental moral issue involved in these debates is justice. Many who have thought carefully about the U.S. system of distributing health care think it is unjust, and some claim that it is ineffective and unworkable. Even after the passage of the Affordable Care Act ("Obamacare"), millions of people have no access to health care, cannot afford health insurance, and sometimes die as a result.

Medicare is a federally funded U.S. health insurance program that covers people 65 and older, some adults under 65 with disabilities, and people with end-stage kidney disease. The program is supported by payroll taxes paid by workers during their years of employment. Medicaid is a health insurance program supported jointly by the federal government and the states that covers some low-income families, pregnant women, and people with disabilities. But Medicaid does not cover many who are below the poverty line.

The United States spends more money on health care than any other developed country, yet it gets low scores on standard assessments of national health. The average life expectancy in the United States is lower than that of other developed countries, and the infant mortality rate is higher.

The United States has a less-than-universal mixed system of health care consisting of private insurance obtained through employers, private insurance acquired through Affordable Care Act exchanges, single-payer Medicare, and state-run Medicaid. In contrast, Canada has a universal single-payer system in which the government pays for health care and the private sector provides the care.

Two types of justice theories—libertarian and egalitarian—have been especially prominent in moral arguments about health care. Libertarian theories of justice say that the advantages and disadvantages of society must be allotted in a way that does not curtail personal liberty. People are entitled only to what they can freely acquire through their own legitimate efforts in a free market. For the libertarian, there are no positive rights. Egalitarian theories of justice maintain that because every person is of equal value and is worthy of equal moral consideration, the only just way to distribute society's benefits and burdens is equally.

Norman Daniels believes that health care is a moral right. He argues that a society is just when it ensures "fair equality of opportunity," and that disease and disability impair "normal species functioning," undermining equality of opportunity. Because health care can equalize opportunities, he argues, it is a positive right.

KEY TERMS
Medicare (p. 335)
Medicaid (p. 335)
managed care (p. 336)

EXERCISES
Review Questions

1. What is the main reason why so many people in the United States lack access to health care? (p. 334)
2. What is Medicare? What is Medicaid? (p. 335)
3. What is the troubling contradiction in the U.S. health care system? (p. 335)
4. In 2016 which country spent more money on health care per capita than any other? (p. 335)
5. In 2015 which of these countries had the highest average life expectancy: Canada, the United Kingdom, Japan, or the United States? (p. 335)
6. What is managed care? (p. 336)
7. Name three of the Affordable Care Act's major provisions. (pp. 336–337)
8. What kind of health care system does the United States have? What are its main features? Is it a system of socialized medicine? How does it differ from the health care system in the United Kingdom? (p. 337)
9. What is distributive justice? (p. 338)
10. What are the chief characteristics of libertarian theories of justice? Of egalitarian theories of justice? (pp. 338–339)

Discussion Questions

1. Which theory of justice is more plausible— libertarian or egalitarian? Why?
2. Does the United States offer the best care in the world? Why or why not?
3. Do libertarian theories favor positive rights? Why or why not?
4. Do people have a moral right to health care? Explain.
5. What is Daniels's argument for a moral right to health care? Do you think it sound? Why or why not?
6. Do you agree that everyone is entitled to an equal opportunity to obtain the basic goods of society? Explain.

7. Do you agree with the view that if you don't have any money, you shouldn't be entitled to any medicine?

8. Is everyone entitled to a "decent minimum" of health care? Why or why not?

9. Are there any circumstances in which it is reasonable to blame people for getting sick and to therefore judge them to be undeserving of health care financed by others? Explain.

10. What should be done, if anything, for the millions of Americans who lack health care because they cannot afford it?

FURTHER READING

Aaron E. Carroll and Austin Frakt, "The Best Health Care System in theWorld: Which One Would You Pick?" *New York Times*, September 18, 2017, https://www.nytimes.com/interactive/2017/09/18/upshot/best-health-care-systemcountrybracket. html.

Norman Daniels, *Just Health Care* (Cambridge: Cambridge University Press, 1985).

Norman Daniels, "Justice and Access to Health Care," in *Stanford Encyclopedia of Philosophy*, October 20, 2017, https://plato.stanford.edu/entries/justice-health careaccess/.

The Guardian, "How Does the US Healthcare System Compare with Other Countries?" July 25, 2017, https://www.theguardian.com/us-news/ng-interactive/2017/jul/25/us-healthcaresystem-vs-other-countries.

Donna K. Hammaker and Thomas M. Knadig, *Health Care Ethics and the Law* (Burlington, MA: Jones & Bartlett, 2017).

Kaiser Family Foundation, "Understanding Health Insurance," KFF.org, https://www.kff.org/understanding-health-insurance/ (December 24, 2017).

Medline Plus, U.S. National Library of Medicine, "Health Insurance," https://medlineplus.gov/healthinsurance.html (December 24, 2017).

Rosamond Rhodes, Margaret P. Battin, and Anita Silvers, eds., *Medicine and Social Justice* (New York: Oxford University Press, 2002).

Elisabeth Rosenthal, *An American Sickness* (New York: Penguin Press, 2017).

Leiyu Shi and Douglas A. Singh, *Essentials of the U.S. Health Care System* (Burlington, MA: Jones & Bartlett, 2017).

Lewis Vaughn, *Bioethics: Principles, Issues, and Cases* (New York: Oxford University Press, 2017).

ETHICAL DILEMMAS

1. Health Care for Undocumented Immigrants?

The U.S. Affordable Care Act makes no provisions for undocumented (unauthorized) immigrants to that country. Consider the implications of this seldom-publicized aspect of the (ACA):

> [T]he ACA's fundamental changes to the healthcare system exclude undocumented immigrants entirely from any potential for improvement to their current situations, and, arguably, will make their circumstances much worse. . . . The means and the services on which they relied before the ACA—whether the volunteer work of physicians, community health clinics, and/or emergency rooms—will likely undergo policy changes that direct resources away from those without healthcare coverage.*

> *Ken Och, "The Affordable Care Act and Distributive Justice: Is It Ethical to Exclude Undocumented Immigrants?" *Ethics and Society*, February 25, 2014, https://ethicsandsociety.org/2014/02/25/the-affordable-careact- and-distributive-justice-is-it-ethical-to-exclude-undocumented-immigrants/.

Lack of health care is likely to worsen the situation of undocumented immigrants, who may have escaped from horrendous economic and political conditions in their native country. Is it then morally permissible to deny health care to them? In any case, they have human rights. Do these rights require the United States to provide basic health care to them? Why or why not?

2. No Health Coverage for the "Undeserving Sick"?

In debates about health coverage, some have argued that we should distinguish between healthy people who have lived their lives the "right way" and unhealthy people who have not taken proper care of themselves. People in the latter group are the "undeserving sick," and they don't deserve health care. For example:

> In a CNN interview, Representative Mo Brooks, an Alabama Republican, makes the case for Trumpcare in much starker terms: It will free healthy people from having to pay the cost of the sick. "It will allow insurance companies to require people who have higher health care costs to contribute more to the insurance pool that helps offset all these costs, thereby reducing the cost to those people who lead good lives, they're healthy, they've done the things to keep their bodies healthy," explained Brooks. "And right now, those are the people who have done things the right way that are seeing their costs skyrocketing."[†]

Is there a morally relevant difference between deserving and underserving sick people? Is it reasonable to blame people for getting cancer, asthma, heart disease, diabetes, and Parkinson's disease? Many diseases arise because of bad genes—should people be blamed for their genetic deficiencies? Should a smoker who gets cancer be considered undeserving of affordable health care? Is a policy of denying health coverage to people because they have not led the right kind of life morally defensible? If so, how?

[†]Jonathan Chait, "Republican Blurts Out That Sick People Don't Deserve Affordable Care" *New York Magazine*, May 1, 2017, http://nymag.com/daily/intelligencer/2017/05/republican-sick-people-dont-deserve-affordable-care.html/.

3. When People Can't Afford Health Care

Study after study has shown that millions of Americans can afford neither health care nor health insurance. Here's another one:

> In a new survey of 9,200 people across 15 states by my organization, the Texas Medical Center Health Policy Institute, 49% of respondents said they must cut other expenses to pay for health care. And they aren't cutting back on frivolities

like expensive electronics. Most often, they said, they had to cut back on their savings, as well as spending on food and clothing, to pay for health care.[‡]

In the American health care system, those who don't have the money to pay for health care—even people with serious illnesses or injuries—often simply get no medical care at all. Is this a fair system? Should health care be available only to those who can pay for it? Only to the well-off? Why or why not?

[‡]Arthur "Tim" Garson Jr., "Half of America Skimps to Pay for Health Care. The Only Fix Is to Cut Waste," *USA Today*, October 23, 2017, https://www.usatoday.com/story/opinion/2017/10/23/cut-health-costs-put-doctors-onsalaries-arthur-tim-garson-jr-column/777179001/.

READINGS

Autonomy, Equality and a Just Health Care System

KAI NIELSEN

I

Autonomy and equality are both fundamental values in our firmament of values, and they are frequently thought to be in conflict. Indeed the standard liberal view is that we must make difficult and often morally ambiguous trade-offs between them.[1] I shall argue that this common view is mistaken and that autonomy cannot be widespread or secure in a society which is not egalitarian: where, that is, equality is not also a very fundamental value which has an operative role within the society.[2] I shall further argue that, given human needs and a commitment to an autonomy respecting egalitarianism, a very different health care system would come into being than that which exists at present in the United States.

I shall first turn to a discussion of autonomy and equality and then, in terms of those conceptions, to a conception of justice. In modernizing societies of Western Europe, a perfectly just society will be

Kai Nielsen, "Autonomy, Equality and a Just Health Care System," *International Journal of Applied Philosophy*, vol. 4, no. 3 (Spring 1989). Reprinted by permission of Philosophy Documentation Center.

a society of equals and in such societies there will be a belief held across the political spectrum in what has been called *moral* equality. That is to say, when viewed with the impartiality required by morality, the life of everyone matters and matters equally.[3] Individuals will, of course, and rightly so, have their local attachments but they will acknowledge that justice requires that the social institutions of the society should be such that they work on the premiss that the life of everyone matters and matters equally. Some privileged elite or other group cannot be given special treatment simply because they are that group. Moreover, for there to be a society of equals there must be a rough equality of condition in the society. Power must be sufficiently equally shared for it to be securely the case that no group or class or gender can dominate others through the social structures either by means of their frequently thoroughly unacknowledged latent functions or more explicitly and manifestly by institutional arrangements sanctioned by law or custom. Roughly equal material resources or power are not things which are desirable in themselves, but they are essential instrumentalities for the very possibility of equal well-being and for as many people as possible having as thorough and as complete a control over their own lives as is compatible with this being true for everyone alike. Liberty cannot flourish without something approaching this equality of condition, and people without autonomous lives will surely live impoverished lives. These are mere commonplaces. In fine, a commitment to achieving equality of condition, far from undermining liberty and autonomy, is essential for their extensive flourishing.

If we genuinely believe in moral equality, we will want to see come into existence a world in which all people capable of self-direction have, and have as nearly as is feasible equally, control over their own lives and can, as far as the institutional arrangements for it obtaining are concerned, all live flourishing lives where their needs and desires as individuals are met as fully as possible and as fully and extensively as is compatible with that possibility being open to everyone alike. The thing is to provide institutional arrangements that are conducive to that.

People, we need to remind ourselves, plainly have different capacities and sensibilities. However, even in the extreme case of people for whom little in the way of human flourishing is possible, their needs and desires, as far as possible, should still also be satisfied in the way I have just described. Everyone in this respect at least has equal moral standing. No preference or pride of place should be given to those capable, in varying degrees, of rational self-direction. The more rational, or, for that matter, the more loveable, among us should not be given preference. No one should. Our needs should determine what is to be done.

People committed to achieving and sustaining a society of equals will seek to bring into stable existence conditions such that it would be possible for everyone, if they were personally capable of it, to enjoy an equally worthwhile and satisfying life or at least a life in which, for all of them, their needs, starting with and giving priority to their more urgent needs, were met and met as equally and as fully as possible, even where their needs are not entirely the same needs. This, at least, is the heuristic, though we might, to gain something more nearly feasible, have to scale down talk of meeting needs to providing conditions propitious for the equal satisfaction for everyone of their

basic needs. Believers in equality want to see a world in which everyone, as far as this is possible, have equal whole life prospects. This requires an equal consideration of their needs and interests and a refusal to just override anyone's interests: to just regard anyone's interests as something which comes to naught, which can simply be set aside as expendable. Minimally, an egalitarian must believe that taking the moral point of view requires that each person's good is afforded equal consideration. Moreover, this is not just a bit of egalitarian ideology but is a deeply embedded considered judgment in modern Western culture capable of being put into wide reflective equilibrium.[4]

II

What is a need, how do we identify needs and what are our really basic needs, needs that are presumptively universal? Do these basic needs in most circumstances at least trump our other needs and our reflective considered preferences?

Let us start this examination by asking if we can come up with a list of universal needs correctly ascribable to all human beings in all cultures. In doing this we should, as David Braybrooke has, distinguish *adventitious* and *course-of-life* needs.[5] Moreover, it is the latter that it is essential to focus on. Adventitious needs, like the need for a really good fly rod or computer, come and go with particular projects. Course-of-life needs, such as the need for exercise, sleep or food, are such that every human being may be expected to have them all at least at some stage of life.

Still, we need to step back a bit and ask: how do we determine what is a need, course-of-life need or otherwise? We need a relational formula to spot needs. We say, where we are speaking of needs, B needs x in order to y, as in Janet needs milk or some other form of calcium in order to protect her bone structure. With course-of-life needs the relation comes out platitudinously as in 'People need food and water in order to live' or 'People need exercise in order to function normally or well'. This, in the very identification of the need, refers to human flourishing or to human well-being, thereby giving to understand that they are basic needs. Perhaps it is better to say instead that this is to specify in part what it is for something to be a basic need. Be that as it may, there are these basic needs we *must* have to live well. If this is really so, then, where they are things we as individuals can have without jeopardy to others, no further question arises, or can arise, about the desirability of satisfying them. They are just things that in such circumstances ought to be met in our lives if they can. The satisfying of such needs is an unequivocally good thing. The questions 'Does Janet need to live?' and 'Does Sven need to function well?' are at best otiose.

In this context David Braybrooke has quite properly remarked that being "essential to living or to functioning normally may be taken as a criterion for being a basic need. Questions about whether needs are genuine, or well-founded, come to an end of the line when the needs have been connected with life or health."[6] Certainly to flourish we must have these things and in some instances they must be met at least to a certain extent even to survive. This being so, we can quite properly call them basic needs. Where these needs do not clash or the satisfying them by one person does not conflict with the satisfying of the equally basic needs of another no question about justifying the meeting of them arises.

By linking the identification of needs with what we must have to function well and linking course-of-life and basic needs with what all people, or at least almost all people, must have to function well, a list of basic needs can readily be set out. I shall give such a list, though surely the list is incomplete. However, what will be added is the same sort of thing similarly identified. First there are needs connected closely to our physical functioning, namely the need for food and water, the need for excretion, for exercise, for rest (including sleep), for a life supporting relation to the environment, and the need for whatever is indispensable to preserve the body intact. Similarly there are basic needs connected with our function as social beings. We have needs for companionship, education, social acceptance and recognition, for sexual activity, freedom from harassment, freedom from domination, for some meaningful work, for recreation and relaxation and the like.[7]

The list, as I remarked initially, is surely incomplete. But it does catch many of the basic things which are in fact necessary for us to live or to function well. Now an autonomy respecting egalitarian society with an interest in the well-being of its citizens—something moral beings could hardly be without—would (trivially) be a society of equals, and as a society of equals it would be committed to (a) *moral* equality and (b) an equality of *condition* which would, under conditions of moderate abundance, in turn expect the equality of condition to be rough and to be principally understood (cashed in) in terms of providing the conditions (as far as that is possible) for meeting the needs (including most centrally the basic needs) of everyone and meeting them equally, as far as either of these things is feasible.

III

What kind of health care system would such an autonomy respecting egalitarian society have under conditions of moderate abundance such as we find in Canada and the United States?

The following are health care needs which are a so basic needs: being healthy and having conditions treated which impede one's functioning well or which adversely affect one's well-being or cause suffering. These are plainly things we need. Where societies have the economic and technical capacity to do so, as these societies plainly do, without undermining other equally urgent or more urgent needs, these health needs, as basic needs, must be met, and the right to have such medical care is a right for everyone in the society regardless of her capacity to pay. This just follows from a commitment to *moral* equality and to an equality of condition. Where we have the belief, a belief which is very basic in non-fascistic modernizing societies, that each person's good is to be given equal consideration, it is hard not to go in that way, given a plausible conception of needs and reasonable list of needs based on that conception.[8] If there is the need for some particular regime of care and the society has the resources to meet that need, without undermining structures protecting other at least equally urgent needs, then, *ceteris paribus*, the society, if it is a decent society, must do so. The commitment to more equality—the commitment to the belief that the life of each person matters and matters equally—entails, given a few plausible empirical premises, that each person's health needs will be the object of an equal regard. Each has an equal claim, *prima facie,* to have her needs satisfied where this is possible. That does not, of course, mean that people should all be treated alike in the sense of their all getting the same thing. Not everyone needs flu shots, braces, a dialysis machine, a psychiatrist, or a triple bypass. What should be equal is that each person's health needs should be the object of equal societal concern since each person's good should be given equal consideration.[9] This does not mean that equal energy should be directed to Hans's rash as to Frank's cancer. Here one person's need for a cure is much greater than the other, and the greater need clearly takes precedence. Both should be met where possible, but where they both cannot then the greater need has pride of place. But what should not count in the treatment of Hans and Frank is that Hans is wealthy or prestigious or creative and Frank is not. Everyone should have their health needs met where possible. Moreover, where the need is the same, they should have (where possible), and where other at least equally urgent needs are not thereby undermined, the same quality treatment. No differentiation should be made between them on the basis of their ability to pay or on the basis of their being (one more so than the other) important people. There should, in short, where this is possible, be open and free medical treatment of the same quality and extent available to everyone in the society. And no two- or three-tier system should be allowed to obtain, and treatment should only vary (subject to the above qualification) on the basis of variable needs and unavoidable differences in different places in supply and personnel, e.g., differences between town and country. Furthermore, these latter differences should be remedied where technically and economically feasible. The underlying aim should be to meet the health care needs of everyone and meet them, in the sense explicated, equally: everybody's needs here should be met as fully as possible; different treatment is only justified where the need is different or where both needs cannot be met. Special treatment for one person rather than another is only justified where, as I remarked, both needs cannot be met or cannot as adequately be met. Constrained by ought implies can;

where these circumstances obtain, priority should be given to the greater need that can feasibly be met. A moral system or a social policy, plainly, cannot be reasonably asked to do the impossible. But my account does not ask that.

To have such a health care system would, I think, involve taking medicine out of the private sector altogether including, of course, out of private entrepreneurship where the governing rationale has to be profit and where supply and demand rules the roost. Instead there must be a health care system firmly in the public sector (publicly owned and controlled) where the rationale of the system is to meet as efficiently and as fully as possible the health care needs of everyone in the society in question. The health care system should not be viewed as a business anymore than a university should be viewed as a business—compare a university and a large hospital—but as a set of institutions and practices designed to meet urgent human needs.

I do not mean that we should ignore costs or efficiency. The state-run railroad system in Switzerland, to argue by analogy, is very efficient. The state cannot, of course, ignore costs in running it. But the aim is not to make a profit. The aim is to produce the most rapid, safe, efficient and comfortable service meeting travellers's needs within the parameters of the overall socio-economic priorities of the state and the society. Moreover, since the state in question is a democracy, if its citizens do not like the policies of the government here (or elsewhere) they can replace it with a government with different priorities and policies. Indeed the option is there (probably never to be exercised) to shift the railroad into the private sector.

Governments, understandably, worry with aging populations about mounting health care costs. This is slightly ludicrous in the United States, given its military and space exploration budgets, but is also a reality in Canada and even in Iceland where there is no military or space budget at all. There should, of course, be concern about containing health costs, but this can be done effectively with a state-run system. Modern societies need systems of socialized medicine, something that obtains in almost all civilized modernizing societies. The United States and South Africa are, I believe, the only exceptions. But, as is evident from my own country (Canada), socialized health care systems often need altering, and their costs need monitoring. As a cost-cutting and as an efficiency measure that would at the same time improve health care, doctors, like university professors and government bureaucrats, should be put on salaries and they should work in medical units. They should, I hasten to add, have good salaries but salaries all the same; the last vestiges of petty entrepreneurship should be taken from the medical profession. This measure would save the state-run health care system a considerable amount of money, would improve the quality of medical care with greater cooperation and consultation resulting from economies of scale and a more extensive division of labor with larger and better equipped medical units. (There would also be less duplication of equipment.) The overall quality of care would also improve with a better balance between health care in the country and in the large cities, with doctors being systematically and rationally deployed throughout the society. In such a system doctors, no more than university professors or state bureaucrats, could not just set up a practice anywhere. They would no more be free to do this than university professors or state bureaucrats. In the altered system there would be no cultural space for it. Placing doctors on salary, though not at a piece work rate, would also result in its being the case that the financial need to see as many patients as possible as quickly as possible would be removed. This would plainly enhance the quality of medical care. It would also be the case that a different sort of person would go into the medical profession. People would go into it more frequently because they were actually interested in medicine and less frequently because this is a rather good way (though hardly the best way) of building a stock portfolio.

There should also be a rethinking of the respective roles of nurses (in all their variety), paramedics and doctors. Much more of the routine work done in medicine—taking the trout fly out of my ear for example—can be done by nurses or paramedics. Doctors, with their more extensive training, could be freed up for other more demanding tasks worthy of their expertise. This would require somewhat different training for all of these different medical personnel and a rethinking of the authority structure in the health care system. But doing this in a reasonable way would improve the teamwork in hospitals, make morale all around a lot better, improve medical treatment and save a very considerable amount of money. (It is no secret that the relations between doctors and nurses are not good.) Finally, a far greater emphasis should be placed on preventative medicine than is done now. This, if really extensively done, utilizing the considerable educational and fiscal powers of the state, would result in very considerable health care savings and a very much healthier and perhaps even happier population. (Whether with the states we actually have we are likely to get anything like that is—to understate it—questionable. I wouldn't hold my breath in the United States. Still, Finland and Sweden are very different places from the United States and South Africa.)

IV

It is moves of this *general* sort that an egalitarian and autonomy loving society under conditions of moderate scarcity should implement. (I say 'general sort' for I am more likely to be wrong about some of the specifics than about the general thrust of my argument.) It would, if in place, limit the freedom of some people, including some doctors and some patients, to do what they want to do. That is obvious enough. But any society, any society at all, as long as it had norms (legal and otherwise) will limit freedom in some way.[10] There is no living in society without some limitation on the freedom to do some things. Indeed a society without norms and thus without any limitation on freedom is a contradiction in terms. Such a mass of people wouldn't be a society. They, without norms, would just be a mass of people. (If these are 'grammatical remarks,' make the most of them.) In our societies I am not free to go for a spin in your car without your permission, to practice law or medicine without a license, to marry your wife while she is still your wife and the like. Many restrictions on our liberties, because they are so common, so widely accepted and thought by most of us to be so reasonable, hardly *seem* like restrictions on our liberty. But they are all the same. No doubt some members of the medical profession would feel quite reined in if the measures

I propose were adopted. (These measures are not part of conventional wisdom.) But the restrictions on the freedom of the medical profession and on patients I am proposing would make for both a greater liberty all around, everything considered, and, as well, for greater wellbeing in the society. Sometimes we have to restrict certain liberties in order to enhance the overall system of liberty. Not speaking out of turn in parliamentary debate is a familiar example. Many people who now have a rather limited access to medical treatment would come to have it and have it in a more adequate way with such a socialized system in place. Often we have to choose between a greater or lesser liberty in a society, and, at least under conditions of abundance, the answer almost always should be 'Choose the greater liberty'. If we really prize human autonomy, if, that is, we want a world in which as many people as possible have as full as is possible control over their own lives, then we will be egalitarians. Our very egalitarianism will commit us to something like the health care system I described, but so will the realization that, without reasonable health on the part of the population, autonomy can hardly flourish or be very extensive. Without the kind of equitability and increased coverage in health care that goes with a properly administered socialized medicine, the number of healthy people will be far less than could otherwise feasibly be the case. With that being the case, autonomy and well-being as well [will] be neither as extensive nor so thorough as it could otherwise be. Autonomy, like everything else, has its material conditions. And to will the end is to will the necessary means to the end.

To take—to sum up—what since the Enlightenment has come to be seen as the moral point of view, and to take morality seriously, is to take it as axiomatic that each person's good be given equal consideration.[11] I have argued that (a) where that is accepted, and (b) where we are tolerably clear about the facts (including facts about human needs), and (c) where we live under conditions of moderate abundance, a health care system bearing at least a family resemblance to the one I have gestured at will be put in place. It is a health care system befitting an autonomy respecting democracy committed to the democratic and egalitarian belief that the life of everyone matters and matters equally.

NOTES

1. Isaiah Berlin, "On the Pursuit of the Ideal," *The New York Review of Books* XXXV (March 1987), pp. 11–18. See also his "Equality" in his *Concepts and Categories* (Oxford, England: Oxford University Press, 1980), pp. 81–102. I have criticized that latter paper in my "Formulating Egalitarianism: Animadversions on Berlin," *Philosophia* 13:3–4 (October 1983), pp. 299–315.

2. For three defenses of such a view see Kai Nielsen, *Equality and Liberty* (Totowa, New Jersey: Rowman and Allanheld, 1985), Richard Norman, *Free and Equal* (Oxford, England: Oxford University Press, 1987), and John Baker, *Arguing for Equality* (London: Verso Press, 1987).

3. Will Kymlicka, "Rawls on Teleology and Deontology," *Philosophy and Public Affairs* 17:3 (Summer 1988), pp. 173–190 and John Rawls, "The Priority of Right and Ideas of the Good," *Philosophy and Public Affairs* 17:4 (Fall 1988), pp. 251–276.

4. Kai Nielsen, "Searching for an Emancipatory Perspective: Wide Reflective Equilibrium and the Hermeneutical Circle" in Evan Simpson (ed.), Anti-*Foundationalism and Practical Reasoning* (Edmonton, Alberta: Academic Printing and Publishing, 1987), pp. 143–164 and Kai Nielsen, "In Defense of Wide Reflective Equilibrium" in Douglas Odegard (ed.) *Ethics and Justification* (Edmonton, Alberta: Academic Printing and Publishing, 1988), pp. 19–37.

5. David Braybrooke, *Meeting Needs* (Princeton, New Jersey: Princeton University Press, 1987), p. 29.

6. *Ibid.*, p. 31.

7. *Ibid.*, p. 37.

8. Will Kymlicka, *op cit.*, p. 190.

9. *Ibid.*

10. Ralf Dahrendorf, *Essays in the Theory of Society* (Stanford, California: Stanford University Press, 1968), pp. 151–78 and G.A. Cohen, "The Structure of Proletarian Unfreedom," *Philosophy and Public Affairs* 12 (1983), pp. 2–33.

11. Will Kymlicka, *op cit.*, p. 190.

The Right to a Decent Minimum of Health Care

ALLEN E. BUCHANAN

THE ASSUMPTION THAT THERE IS A RIGHT TO A DECENT MINIMUM

A consensus that there is (at least) a right to a decent minimum of health care pervades recent policy debates and much of the philosophical literature on health care. Disagreement centers on two issues. Is there a more extensive right than the right to a decent minimum of health care? What is included in the decent minimum to which there is a right?

PRELIMINARY CLARIFICATION OF THE CONCEPT

Different theories of distributive justice may yield different answers both to the question 'Is there a right to a decent minimum?' and to the question 'What comprises the decent minimum?' The justification a particular theory provides for the claim that there is a right to a decent minimum must at least cohere with the justifications it provides for other right-claims. Moreover, the character of this justification will determine, at least in part, the way in which the decent minimum is specified, since it will include an account of the nature and significance of health-care needs. To the extent that the concept of a decent minimum is theory-dependent, then, it would be native to assume that a mere analysis of the concept of a decent minimum would tell us whether there is such a right and what its content is. Nonetheless, before we proceed to an examination of various theoretical attempts to ground and specify a right to a decent minimum, a preliminary analysis will be helpful.

Sometimes the notion of a decent minimum is applied not to health care but to health itself, the claim being that everyone is entitled to some minimal

level, or welfare floor, of health. I shall not explore this variant of the decent minimum idea because I think its implausibility is obvious. The main difficulty is that assuring any significant level of health for all is simply not within the domain of social control. If the alleged right is understood instead as the right to everything which can be done to achieve some significant level of health for all, then the claim that there is such a right becomes implausible simply because it ignores the fact that in circumstances of scarcity the total social expenditure on health must be constrained by the need to allocate resources for other goods.

Though the concept of a right is complex and controversial, for our purpose a partial sketch will do. To say that a person A has a right to something, X, is first of all to say that A is entitled to X, that X is due to him or her. This is not equivalent to saying that if A were granted X it would be a good thing, even a morally good thing, or that X is desired by or desirable for A. Second, it is usually held that valid right-claims, at least in the case of basic rights, may be backed by sanctions, including coercion if necessary (unless doing so would produce extremely great disutility or grave moral evil), and that (except in such highly exceptional circumstances) failure of an appropriate authority to apply the needed sanctions is itself an injustice. Recent rights-theorists have also emphasized a third feature of rights, or at least of basic rights or rights in the strict sense: valid right-claims 'trump' appeals to what would maximize utility, whether it be the utility of the right-holder, or social utility. In other words, if A has a right to X, then the mere fact that infringing A's right would maximize overall utility or even A's utility is not itself a sufficient reason for infringing it.[1] Finally, a universal (or general) right is one which applies to all persons, not just to certain individuals or classes because of their involvement in special actions, relationships, or agreements.

The second feature—enforceability—is of crucial importance for those who assume or argue that there is a universal right to a decent minimum of health care. For, once it is granted that there is such a right and that such a right may be enforced (absent any extremely weighty reason against enforcement), the claim that there is a universal right provides the moral basis for using the coercive power of the state to assure a decent minimum for all. Indeed, the surprising absence of attempts to justify a coercively backed decent minimum policy by arguments that do *not* aim at establishing a universal right suggests the following hypothesis: advocates of a coercively backed decent minimum have operated on the assumption that such a policy must be based on a universal right to a decent minimum. The chief aim of this article is to show that this assumption is false.

I think it is fair to say that many who confidently assume there is a (universal) right to a decent minimum of health care have failed to appreciate the significance of the first feature of our sketch of the concept of a right. It is crucial to observe that the claim that there is a right to a decent minimum is much stronger than the claim that everyone *ought* to have access to such a minimum, or that if they did it would be a good thing, or that any society which is capable, without great sacrifice, of providing a decent minimum but fails to do so is deeply morally defective. None of the latter assertions implies the existence of a right, if this is understood as a moral entitlement which ought to be established by the coercive power of the state if necessary. This simple point finds expression in traditional ethical theories and in our ordinary moral discourse, for a distinction is made between both 'ought'-judgments that express claims of right and those that express imperatives founded on moral virtues other than justice. In particular, a distinction is drawn between imperatives of justice and imperatives of charity or beneficence or generosity, the assumption usually being that only the former may be enforced.

Further, the difference between 'we ought to provide X to A' and 'A has a right to X' is *not* a difference between different degrees of strength or constancy in our moral convictions. To the morally virtuous person the imperatives of charity may be as urgent as those of justice. This point has troubling implications for

attempts to establish right-claims by the use of what Rawls calls the method of reflective equilibrium. According to this method, we are to appeal to our particular considered moral judgments as provisional data to be accounted for and organized by a smaller set of more general moral principles. The difficulty is that we may be much surer that someone ought not to lack a certain form of health care than we are about whether the ground of this judgment is a principle that structures our sense of justice or our sense of charity or beneficence or generosity. And even if we can show what makes health care, or certain kinds of health care, morally important, this in itself will not show that there is a right to health care, unless the appropriate connection with principles of justice can be made.

THE ATTRACTIONS OF THE IDEA OF A DECENT MINIMUM

There are at least three features widely associated with the idea of a right to a decent minimum which, together with the facile consensus that vagueness promotes, help explain its popularity over competing conceptions of the right to health care. First, it is usually, and quite reasonably, assumed that the idea of a decent minimum is to be understood in a society-relative sense. Surely it is plausible to assume that, as with other rights to goods or services, the content of the right must depend upon the resources available in a given society and perhaps also upon a certain consensus of expectations among its members. So the first advantage of the idea of a decent minimum, as it is usually understood, is that it allows us to adjust the level of services to be provided as a matter of right to relevant social conditions and also allows for the possibility that as a society becomes more affluent the floor provided by the decent minimum should be raised.

Second, the idea of a decent minimum avoids the excesses of what has been called the strong equal access principle, while still acknowledging a substantive universal right. According to the strong equal access principle, everyone has an equal right to the best health-care services available. Aside from the weakness of the justifications offered in support of it, the most implausible feature of the strong equal access principle is that it forces us to choose between two unpalatable alternatives. We can either set the publicly guaranteed level of health care lower than the level that is technically possible or we can set it as high as is technically possible. In the former case, we shall be committed to the uncomfortable conclusion that no matter how many resources have been expended to guarantee equal access to that level, individuals are forbidden to spend any of their resources for services not available to all. Granted that individuals are allowed to spend their after-tax incomes on more frivolous items, why shouldn't they be allowed to spend it on health? If the answer is that they should be so allowed, as long as this does not interfere with the provision of an adequate package of health-care services for everyone, then we have retreated from the strong equal access principle to something very like the principle of a decent minimum. If, on the other hand, we set the level of services guaranteed for all so high as to eliminate the problem of persons seeking extra care beyond this level, this would produce a huge drain on total resources, foreclosing opportunities for producing important goods other than health care.

So both the recognition that health care must compete with other goods and the conviction that beyond some less than maximal level of publicly guaranteed services individuals should be free to purchase additional services point toward a more limited right than the strong access principle asserts. Thus, the endorsement of a right to a decent minimum may be more of a recognition of the implausibility of the stronger right to equal access than a sign of any definite position on the content of the right to health care.[2]

A third attraction of the idea of a decent minimum is that since the right to health care must be limited in scope (to avoid the consequences of a strong equal access right), it should be limited to the 'most basic' services, those normally 'adequate' for health, or for a 'decent' or 'tolerable' life. However, although this aspect of the idea of a decent minimum is useful because it calls attention to the fact that health-care needs are heterogeneous and must be assigned some order of priority, it does not itself provide any basis for determining which are most important.

THE NEED FOR A SUPPORTING THEORY

In spite of these attractions, the concept of a right to a decent minimum of health care is inadequate as a moral basis for a coercively backed decent minimum policy in the absence of a coherent and defensible theory of justice. Indeed, when taken together they do not even imply that there is a right to a decent minimum. Rather, they only support the weaker conditional claim that if there is a right to health care, then it is one that is more limited than a right of strong equal access, and is one whose content depends upon available resources and some scheme of priorities which shows certain health services to be more basic than others. It appears, then, that a theoretical grounding for the right to a decent minimum of health care is indispensable.

ARGUMENTS FOR A UNIVERSAL RIGHT TO A DECENT MINIMUM

Elsewhere I have explored what I believe to be the main approaches to justifying and specifying a (universal) right to a decent minimum of health care: utilitarian arguments (for a derivative right), Rawlsian ideal contract arguments, and an argument from equality of opportunity developed by Norman Daniels.[3] Here I can only briefly summarize my reasons for concluding that none of these approaches is adequate.

Utilitarian Arguments

The chief difficulty with utilitarian arguments is that they are not capable of providing a secure foundation for a right to a decent minimum for *everyone*. Consider, for example, the class of [Down] syndrome newborns. These retarded individuals, who often suffer from various physical defects as well, require a large expenditure of social resources over a lifetime. And relative to these costs the contribution these individuals make to social utility is not large, at least as far as we must work with a conception of contribution that is in some way quantifiable. If this is so, then Utilitarianism will justify excluding these infants from even the most minimal health care provided to others as a matter of right.

It is important to see that individuals in this class are capable of various enjoyments and would greatly benefit from the services from which they are excluded. Thus Utilitarianism may require that, even for the most basic services, what is guaranteed for one individual may not be available to another, even though their needs are equal and both would benefit greatly from the service.

My purpose in developing this example is not to show conclusively that there are no circumstances or no likely circumstances in which Utilitarianism would support a (derivative) universal right to a decent minimum of health care. Instead I have only shown that, granted certain plausible factual assumptions which may in fact be satisfied in our society at this time, there is good reason to doubt that Utilitarianism provides a secure foundation for such a right.

Rawls's Ideal Contract Theory

There are well-known objections to Rawls's ideal contract view as a general theory of rights. It has often been noted that the parties' choice of the difference principle depends upon the implausible assumption that they are extremely, indeed infinitely, averse to risk. Further, Nozick and others have challenged the intuitions about fairness on the basis of which Rawls constructs the original position and have also offered examples to show that the difference principle requires redistributions that are intuitively unfair to the better off. Instead of rehearsing these familiar issues, I will concentrate on a different question: Even if these general objections can be met, does Rawls's theory provide the basis for a substantive right to a decent minimum of health care? If Rawls's theory supports a right to health care, it must be derivative upon the basic rights laid down by the principle of greatest equal liberty, the principle of equality of fair opportunity, or the difference principle. And if there is to be such a derivative right to health care, then health care must either be among the primary goods covered by the three principles or it must be importantly connected with some of those goods. Now at least some forms of health care (such as broad services for prevention and health maintenance, including mental health) seem to bear the earmarks of Rawlsian primary goods: they facilitate the effective pursuit of ends in general and may also enhance our ability to criticize

and revise our conceptions of the good. Nonetheless, Rawls does not explicitly list health care among the social primary goods included under the three principles.

Let us suppose that health care is either itself a primary good covered by the difference principle or that health care may be purchased with income or some other form of wealth which is included under the difference principle. In the former case, depending upon various empirical conditions, it might turn out that the best way to satisfy the difference principle is to establish a state-enforced right to health care. But whether maximizing the prospects of the worst off will require such a right and what the content of the right will be depends upon what weight is to be assigned to health care relative to other primary goods included under the difference principle. Similarly, a weighting must also be assigned if we are to determine whether the share of wealth one receives under the difference principle would be sufficient both for health-care needs and for other ends. Until we have some solution to the weighting problem, Rawls's theory can shed only limited light upon the question of priority-relations between health care and other goods and among various forms of health care.

It is important to see that the informational constraints imposed by Rawls's "veil of ignorance" preclude a solution to the problem of weighting health care against other primary goods because the answer will depend upon facts about the particular conditions of the society in which the notions in question are to be applied. At best Rawls's hypothetical contractors would choose a kind of *placeholder* for a principle establishing a right to a decent minimum of health care, on the assumption that the content of the right can only be filled out at later stages of agreement in the light of specific information about their particular society.

However, nothing in Rawls's conception of rational decision suggests that once the relevant, concrete information is available, rational persons will agree on a single assignment of weights to the primary goods. It follows that Rawls's theory does not itself supply content for the notion of a right to a decent minimum of health care: instead, at best, it lays down a very abstract structure within which this content will be worked out through the democratic political processes specified by the list of equal basic liberties. Given this, Rawls's theory advances us very little beyond the broad intuitive consensus that there is a universal right to a decent minimum of health care.

Daniels's Argument from Equality of Opportunity

Partly in response to some of the difficulties noted in the previous section, Norman Daniels has developed an alternative Rawlsian approach to the right to health care. Instead of basing the right to health care on an intuitive but ill-defined notion of a decent minimum, Daniels founds a universal right to health care on a stronger, more inclusive version of Rawls's principle of fair equality of opportunity.

Daniels approaches the right to health care by utilizing the idea of "the normal opportunity range" for a given society. This is "the array of life plans reasonable to pursue within given conditions obtaining in a society. Daniels suggests that we can best understand the distinctive nature and importance of health care if we see that it promotes, restores, or provides surrogates for "normal species functioning," and that normal species functioning is an important contributor to an individual's attainment of the normal opportunity range for his society.[4] The principle from which health-care rights are derived according to Daniels may be stated as follows:

> D. Social resources are to be allocated so as to insure that everyone can attain the normal opportunity range for his or her society.

The success of Daniels's approach depends both upon the plausibility of the overarching principle of equality of opportunity (D) and on the plausibility of the implications of this principle for health-care entitlements. Though he has not yet committed himself unequivocally on this issue, Daniels seems to believe that principle D implies that there is a right to health care that exceeds what is usually thought of as a right to a decent minimum. Daniels emphasizes that the connection between normal species functioning and opportunity and the idea that health care is

to be understood as whatever promotes, restores, or replaces normal species functioning achieves two important goals of a theory of health care: it gives us a way of ranking various health-care services as to their relative importance for normal species functioning and provides a principled way of defining the class of health-care needs which does not limit them to *medical* needs as defined by the current health-care delivery system.

A natural objection to Daniels's view is that even if one reason why health care is important is that it contributes significantly to attainment of the normal opportunity range, this is surely not the only reason, or in many cases not the most basic one. After all, health care often relieves suffering, prevents unwanted death, or enhances one's capacity for enjoying what everyone is able to do, even when it does not extend one's range of opportunities. Though I think this criticism has considerable force, I believe there are other, more telling objections.

The first difficulty is the definition of "normal opportunity range." The phrase "the array of life-plans reasonable to pursue" is ambiguous. For *whom* must a life-plan be reasonable to pursue if it is to be included in the normal opportunity range? If to be included a plan must be reasonable for *everyone* to pursue, regardless of his or her physical abilities, skills, and talents, then the list will be so modest that it is doubtful that it could provide content for a substantive universal right to health care of the sort Daniels wants. If, on the other hand, inclusion in the normal opportunity range requires only that the plan be such that it is reasonable for someone or other to pursue it, then D becomes astonishingly strong, since it will include life-plans requiring exceptional talents and rare characteristics.

On this strong interpretation, Daniels's principle of equality of opportunity is vulnerable to the same objection that leads to the rejection of the strong equal access principle. Granted the gap between most individuals' actual opportunity ranges and the array of plans it is reasonable for some individuals to pursue, and granted the almost limitless possibility for technology and other services which can help narrow the gap, a conscientious commitment to D would create an enormous drain on resources. To say that everyone has a right to whatever arrangements are necessary to insure that it is reasonable for him to aspire to become a neurosurgeon, a first-class logician, an accomplished pianist, or the spouse of a movie star seems excessive to say the least.

It is important to see that this objection cannot be met by replying that the right to health care is only a right to the resources required to achieve normal species functioning for all. For even if it could be shown that this goal is much more modest than that of achieving the normal opportunity range (on the strong interpretation) for all, this would be beside the point. In Daniels's view the basic consideration is the attainment of equality with respect to the normal opportunity range—normal species functioning is only important as one factor among others that contribute to it. So my objection is to the basic principle of justice Daniels proposes.

Finally, if neither the strong nor the weak interpretation is acceptable, Daniels might suggest that the normal opportunity range is that of life-plans which constitute a normal or tolerable or adequate or decent life in the society in question. This strategy, however, is one which Daniels should be reluctant to embrace, since he introduced the notion of a normal opportunity range in the first place to avoid the unilluminating move of 'specifying' the notion of a decent minimum by reference to equally uninformative notions such as that of an adequate or tolerable life.

A second difficulty is that if we eschew the strong interpretation, the attempt to derive a right to health care from the right to enjoy the normal opportunity range for one's own society may involve a sort of circularity which has unfortunately conservative implications for health-care policy. The array of life-plans which all (or most or many) people in a given society can reasonably pursue or that constitute a tolerable or normal or adequate life in that society will be determined in part by the availability and quality of health care in that society. In other words, the normal opportunity range is itself in part a social artifact. Thus in a society with very poor health-care services the normal opportunity range is correspondingly narrow, even if the society were in fact affluent enough to afford a wider range of services which would allow a wider

normal opportunity range. Consequently, a principle which requires only that resources be allocated so as to assure that everyone attains the normal opportunity range would be inadequate in situations in which the normal opportunity range was unacceptably narrow due to a failure to allocate sufficient resources for health care. This suggests that Daniels's principle requiring equal opportunity must be supplemented with a principle requiring equal opportunity must be supplemented with a principle requiring *maximization* of the opportunity range, or at least that the opportunity range is to be maximized up to some limit. After all, the importance of health care on Daniels's account is that it facilitates opportunity, and anyone who is concerned with opportunity rather than with equality for its own sake will desire arrangements which require more than mere equality of opportunity if opportunities are few but can be expanded.

Now a principle requiring equality of opportunity relative to a given opportunity range and a principle requiring maximization of the opportunity range (or maximization up to some limit) may conflict with one another. But if this is so, then some way of balancing the demands of these two principles must be found. In a society in which there were no legal barriers to opportunity and none based on racial or sexual discrimination, it is not obvious that either justice or rational self-interest would require, as Daniels seems to assume, the choice of a system that guarantees equality with respect to the opportunity range rather than a system that allows some inequalities but a wider opportunity range. If the latter alternative is appropriate, then we are again pushed in the direction of the vague but intuitively plausible notion of a decent minimum: this time the notion of a decent minimum opportunity range to which the requirement of equality applies.

A third and somewhat surprising feature of Daniels's position, and one which many will view as objectionable, is that it appears that principle D does *not* guarantee a *universal* right to a decent minimum of health care. For D is silent on how we are to make difficult and basic allocation decisions: it does not tell us whether we are to devote all resources to narrowing the distance between the opportunity ranges of the worst off and the normal opportunity range or to divide resources among all who fall short of the normal opportunity range. Indeed nothing in D even acknowledges that there is a problem of scarcity.

Whether or not D will require some minimal set of health-care services for *all* will depend upon which additional principles we adopt to cope with priority problems in the face of scarcity. If our first priority is to narrow the gap between the worst off and the normal opportunity range, then, depending on how badly off the worst off are and depending upon the total amount of resources available, there may be nothing left for even minimal services for those who do not fall within the worst off class. As in the case of Utilitarianism, whether there is a universal right to a decent minimum will depend upon the facts about the society in question. But in Daniels's scheme it will also depend upon what additional principles of distributive justice are used to supplement the principle of equality of opportunity when the commitment to such a strong principle collides with the realities of scarcity.

If, on the other hand, the commitment to raising the opportunity range of the worst off is to be limited by a principle stating that everyone has a right to some set of services even if there are others who are farther from the normal opportunity range, then, unless this universal right-claim can be nonarbitrarily specified and supported, it appears that we have again ushered in the idea of a decent minimum. And contrary to what Daniels says, his principle of equality of opportunity is a supplement, rather than a replacement for it.

A CHANGE OF STRATEGY

So far I have considered several proposed principles or theories of justice and seen, rather surprisingly, that they do not provide a firm basis for the claim that there is a universal right to a decent minimum of health care or else that they encounter serious difficulties in supplying a practical specification of the content of that right. These deflationary results would be welcomed by a libertarian, who would explain them by the hypothesis that *there is no right to a decent minimum.* Further, a sophisticated libertarian would explain the pervasiveness of the (false) belief that there is a right to a decent minimum by the hypothesis that those who

hold this belief have mistaken the moral imperatives of beneficence or charity for those of justice.

I shall argue, however, that even if the libertarian were right thus far there is still a sound justification for an enforced principle guaranteeing a decent minimum of health care to everyone. The alternative strategy I wish to explore is pluralistic. My suggestion is that the combined weight of arguments from special (as opposed to universal) rights to health care, harm-prevention, prudential arguments of the sort used to justify public health measures, and two arguments that show that effective charity shares features of public goods (in the technical sense) is sufficient to do the work of an alleged universal right to a decent minimum of health care.

Arguments from Special Rights

The right-claim we have been examining (and find unsupported) has been a *universal* right-claim: one that attributes the same right to all persons. *Special* right-claims, in contrast, restrict the right in question to certain individuals or groups.

There are at least three types of arguments that can be given for special rights to health care. First, there are arguments from the requirements of rectifying past or present institutional injustices. It can be argued, for example, that American blacks and native Americans are entitled to a certain core set of health-care services owing to their history of unjust treatment by government or other social institutions, on the grounds that these injustices have directly or indirectly had detrimental effects on the health of the groups in question. Second, there are arguments from the requirements of compensation to those who have suffered unjust harm or who have been unjustly exposed to health risks by the assignable actions of private individuals or corporations—for instance, those who have suffered neurological damage from the effects of chemical pollutants.

Third, a strong moral case can be made for special rights to health care for those who have undergone exceptional sacrifices for the good of society as a whole—in particular those whose health has been adversely affected through military service. The most obvious candidates for such compensatory special rights are soldiers wounded in combat.

Arguments from the Prevention of Harm

The content of the right to a decent minimum is typically understood as being more extensive than those traditional public health services that are usually justified on the grounds that they are required to protect the citizenry from certain harms arising from the interactions of persons living together in large numbers. Yet such services have been a major factor—if not *the* major factor—in reducing morbidity and mortality rates. Examples include sanitation and immunization. The moral justification of such measures, which constitute an important element in a decent minimum of health care, rests upon the widely accepted Harm (Prevention) Principle, not upon a right to health care.

The Harm Prevention argument for traditional public health services, however, may be elaborated in a way that brings them closer to arguments for a universal right to health care. With some plausibility one might contend that once the case has been made for expending public resources on public health measures, there is a moral (and perhaps Constitutional) obligation to achieve some standard of *equal protection* from the harms these measures are designed to prevent. Such an argument, if it could be made out, would imply that the availability of basic public health services should not vary greatly across different racial, ethnic, or geographic groups within the country.

Prudential Arguments

Prudent arguments for health-care services typically emphasize benefits rather than the prevention of harm. It has often been argued, in particular, that the availability of certain basic forms of health care make for a more productive labor force or improve the fitness of the citizenry for national defense. This type of argument, too, does not assume that individuals have moral rights (whether special or universal) to the services in question.

It seems very likely that the combined scope of the various special health-care rights discussed above, when taken together with harm prevention and prudential arguments for basic health services and an argument from equal protection through public health measures, would do a great deal toward satisfying the health-care needs which those who advocate a universal right to a decent minimum are most concerned about. In other words, once the strength of a more pluralistic approach is appreciated, we may come to question the popular dogma that policy initiatives designed to achieve a decent minimum of health care for all must be grounded in a universal moral right to a decent minimum. This suggestion is worth considering because it again brings home the importance of the methodological difficulty encountered earlier. Even if, for instance, there is wide consensus on the considered judgment that the lower health prospects of inner city blacks are not only morally unacceptable but an injustice, it does not follow that this injustice consists of the infringement of a universal right to a decent minimum of health care. Instead, the injustice might lie in the failure to rectify past injustices or in the failure to achieve public health arrangements that meet a reasonable standard of equal protection for all.

Two Arguments for Enforced Beneficence

The pluralistic moral case for a legal entitlement to a decent minimum of health care (in the absence of a universal moral right) may be strengthened further by non-rights-based arguments from the principle of beneficence.[5] The possibility of making out such arguments depends upon the assumption that some principles may be justifiably enforced even if they are not principles specifying valid right-claims. There is at least one widely recognized class of such principles requiring contribution to the production of 'public goods' in the technical sense (for example, tax laws requiring contribution to national defense). It is characteristic of public goods that each individual has an incentive to withhold his contribution to the collective goal even though the net result is that the goal will not be achieved. Enforcement of a principle requiring all individuals to contribute to the goal is necessary to overcome the individual's incentive to withhold contribution by imposing penalties for his own failure to contribute and by assuring him that others will contribute. There is a special subclass of principles whose enforcement is justified not only by the need to overcome the individual's incentive to withhold compliance with the principle but also to ensure that individuals' efforts are appropriately *coordinated*. For example, enforcing the rule of the road to drive only on the right not only ensures a joint effort toward the goal of safe driving but also coordinates individuals' efforts so as to make the attainment of that goal possible. Indeed, in the case of the 'rule of the road' a certain kind of coordinated joint effort is the public good whose attainment justifies enforcement. But regardless of whether the production of a public good requires the solution of a coordination problem or not, there may be no *right* that is the correlative of the coercively backed obligation specified by the principle. There are two arguments for enforced beneficence, and they each depend upon both the idea of coordination and on certain aspects of the concept of a public good.

Both arguments begin with an assumption reasonable libertarians accept: there is a basic moral obligation of charity or beneficence to those in need. In a society that has the resources and technical knowledge to improve health or at least to ameliorate important health defects, the application of this requirement of beneficence includes the provision of resources for at least certain forms of health care. If we are sincere, we will be concerned with the efficacy of our charitable or beneficent impulses. It is all well and good for the libertarian to say that voluntary giving *can* replace the existing array of government entitlement programs, but this *possibility* will be cold comfort to the needy if, for any of several reasons, voluntary giving falters.

Social critics on the left often argue that in a highly competitive acquisitive society such as ours it is native to think that the sense of beneficence will win out over the urgent promptings of self-interest. One need not argue, however, that voluntary giving fails from weakness of the will. Instead one can argue that even if each individual recognizes a moral duty to contribute to the aid of others and is motivationally capable of acting on that duty, some important forms of beneficence will not be forthcoming because each individual will rationally conclude that he should not contribute.

Many important forms of health care, especially those involving large-scale capital investment for technology, cannot be provided except through the contributions of large numbers of persons. This is also true of the most important forms of medical research. But if so, then the beneficent individual will not be able to act effectively, in isolation. What is needed is a coordinated joint effort.

First argument. There are many ways in which I might help others in need. Granted the importance of health, providing a decent minimum of health care for all, through large-scale collective efforts, will be a more important form of beneficence than the various charitable acts A, B, and C, which I might perform *independently*, that is, whose success does not depend upon the contributions of others. Nonetheless, if I am rationally beneficent I will reason as follows: either enough others will contribute to the decent minimum project to achieve this goal, even if I do not contribute to it; or not enough others will contribute to achieve a decent minimum, even if I do contribute. In either case, my contribution will be wasted. In other words, granted the scale of the investment required and the virtually negligible size of my own contribution, I can disregard the minute possibility that my contribution might make the difference between success and failure. But if so, then the rationally beneficent thing for me to do is not to waste my contribution on the project of ensuring a decent minimum but instead to undertake an independent act of beneficence; A, B, or C—where I know my efforts will be needed and efficacious. But if everyone, or even many people, reason in this way, then what we each recognize as the most effective form of beneficence will not come about. Enforcement of a principle requiring contributions to ensuring a decent minimum is needed.

The first argument is of the same form as standard public goods arguments for enforced contributions to national defense, energy conservation, and many other goods, with this exception. In standard public goods arguments, it is usually assumed that the individual's incentive for not contributing is self-interest and that it is in his interest not to contribute because he will be able to partake of the good, if it is produced, even if he does not contribute. In the case at hand, however, the individual's incentive for not contributing to the joint effort is not self-interest, but rather his desire to maximize the good he can do for others with a given amount of his resources. Thus if he contributes but the goal of achieving a decent minimum for all would have been achieved without his contribution, then he has still failed to use his resources in a maximally beneficent way relative to the options of either contributing or not to the joint project, even though the goal of achieving a decent minimum is attained. The rationally beneficent thing to do, then, is not to contribute, even though the result of everyone's acting in a rationally beneficent way will be a relatively ineffective patchwork of small-scale individual acts of beneficence rather than a large-scale, coordinated effort.

Second argument. I believe that ensuring a decent minimum of health care for all is more important than projects A, B, or C, and I am willing to contribute to the decent minimum project, but only if I have assurance that enough others will contribute to achieve the threshold of investment necessary for success. Unless I have this assurance, I will conclude that it is less than rational—and perhaps even morally irresponsible—to contribute my resources to the decent minimum project. For my contribution will be wasted if not enough others contribute. If I lack assurance of sufficient contributions by others, the rationally beneficent thing for me to do is to expend my 'beneficence budget' on some less-than-optimal project A, B, or C, whose success does not depend on the contribution of others. But without enforcement, I cannot be assured that enough others will contribute, and if others reason as I do, then what we all believe to be the most effective form of beneficence will not be forthcoming. Others may fail to contribute either because the promptings of self-interest overpower their sense of beneficence, or because they reason as I did in the First Argument, or for some other reason.

Both arguments conclude that an enforced decent minimum principle is needed to achieve coordinated joint effort. However, there is this difference. The Second Argument focuses on the *assurance problem*, while the first does not. In the Second Argument all that is needed is the assumption that rational beneficence requires assurance that enough others will contribute. In the First Argument the individual's reason for not contributing is not that he lacks assurance that enough others will contribute, but rather that it is

better for him not to contribute regardless of whether other do or not.

Neither argument depends on an assumption of conflict between the individual's moral motivation of beneficence and his inclination of self-interest. Instead the difficulty is that in the absence of enforcement, individuals who strive to make their beneficence most effective will thereby fail to benefit the needy as much as they might.

A standard response to those paradoxes of rationality known as public goods problems is to introduce a coercive mechanism which attaches penalties to noncontribution and thereby provides each individual with the assurance that enough others will reciprocate so that his contribution will not be wasted and an effective incentive for him to contribute even if he has reason to believe that enough others will contribute to achieve the goal without his contribution. My suggestion is that the same type of argument that is widely accepted as a justification for enforced principles requiring contributions toward familiar public goods provides support for a coercively backed principle specifying a certain list of health programs for the needy and requiring those who possess the needed resources to contribute to the establishment of such programs, even if the needy have no *right* to the services those programs provide. Such an arrangement would serve a dual function: it would coordinate charitable efforts by focusing them on one set of services among the indefinitely large constellation of possible expressions of beneficence, and it would ensure that the decision to allocate resources to these services will become effective.

OBJECTIONS AND REPLIES

It might be objected that these two arguments rest upon either of two unacceptable premises: (1) that if something is a moral principle (or at least a basic moral principle) then it may be given the status of a law and enforced by the state, or (2) that it is the role of the state to insure that its citizens are morally virtuous. If the enforced beneficence arguments rested on either of these very general premises they would be implausible, because both (1) and (2) have unacceptable implications for individual liberty. But the enforced beneficence arguments do not assume that any moral principle, or any basic moral principle, may be enforced; nor do they assume that the state is in general the guardian of our morals. Instead, they only contend that one important moral principle may be enforced if, in the absence of enforcement, familiar problems of coordinated joint action would arise. Further, it seems most plausible to regard the conclusion of the enforced beneficence arguments as defeasible: if political conditions were such that the establishment of the required enforcement mechanism would contribute to a dangerous concentration of government power, then the lesser of evils might be to forgo a solution to the coordination and assurance problems.

However, it is unpersuasive to argue that—at least in the United States at this time—a compulsory contribution scheme constitutes an unacceptable threat to liberty by endowing the government with uncontrollable powers. Moreover, some of the most significant dangers which make a general policy of the 'enforcement of morals' unacceptable simply do not apply with any force to the case at hand. In particular, opponents of the enforcement of morals usually rightly point out that such policy would destroy the conditions required for individual autonomy, privacy, and for the flourishing of intimate personal relationship. This is certainly true for the enforcement of many moral principles, especially principles of sexual or religious morality, but it is not at all convincing in the case of arrangements to enforce the moral duty of charity or beneficence. Nor is it obvious that enforced beneficence should be rejected because it will inevitably lead to the enforcement of those moral principles which are more closely connected with autonomy, privacy, and intimate personal relationships.

A more interesting objection is that the enforced beneficence arguments rest on a misunderstanding of the nature of the duty of beneficence: beneficence is traditionally understood as an imperfect duty not just in the sense that the amount of aid one renders is a matter of choice but also in the sense that the choice of recipients is also discretionary. In other words, beneficence only requires that one render aid to some who are needy, not to all. But if so, then the enforced beneficence argument is vulnerable to the same objection I leveled earlier at Utilitarianism: it does not provide a firm moral foundation for a guaranteed minimum for *all*.

At this point, it is important to approach the traditional concept of beneficence more critically than is usually done. Three points must be emphasized. First, some support must be given for the view that beneficence is discretionary with respect to the choice of recipients of aid. It is not enough to offer this assumption as an analytic truth which follows from the concept of the duty of beneficence. Even if the boundaries of the traditional concept could be so clearly delineated, the question of whether it is permissible to choose to aid A and not to aid B (when A's and B's needs are identical) is a moral question. And depending on the answer we arrive at, we may find it appropriate to revise the traditional concept. Second, the more plausible accounts of why the benefactor may be selective seem to be pragmatic rather than conceptual or moral. Third, these pragmatic considerations seem to have less weight when beneficence is viewed—as it is in the enforced beneficence arguments—as a collective, rather than an individual, enterprise.

Even if we could say with confidence that the traditional concept of beneficence includes the idea that the benefactor may be selective, we should ask why this is so. If one examines the *grounds* for the duty of beneficence, either in common-sense morality or in ethical theory, it seems that these are so general that the conclusion they support is that there is a duty to aid the needy—anyone in need, not just some, if one is able to do so.

For example, in the Second Part of *The Foundations of the Metaphysics of Morals*, Kant offers an argument for the conclusion that one ought to help those in need, at least if one can do so without excessive costs to oneself. Kant's claim is that one cannot consistently will the universalization of a maxim of not aiding others in need because to do so would be to deprive oneself of aid from others: a world in which everyone acted on this maxim of nonbeneficence would be one in which one could not count on being helped by others. Now it appears that the same argument would rule out a maxim of helping another in need only if one chooses to: in a world of discretionary benefactors one could not count on aid. Thus one would expect Kant to reject a formulation of the duty of beneficence that allows the benefactor to choose which of the needy he will help (independently of any consideration of the degree or importance of their need). However, Kant does not draw this conclusion. Though he provides an argument that supports the conclusion that we ought to help whoever is in need, Kant does not challenge the traditional view that the duty of beneficence allows the benefactor to exercise discretion in deciding whom to aid.

Similarly, at the level of common-sense morality, the considerations that underlie the duty of beneficence seem very general. One ought to help those in need because they are our fellow human beings in need—not because of any further special characteristics they happen to possess or because of any special preferences we have. Yet here, too, as in Kant's theory, it is usually said that there is much latitude in discharging the duty of beneficence. One may choose to help some and not help others.

How can the very general character of the ground of the duty of beneficence be reconciled with the assumption that the benefactor may exercise discretion? The explanation, I suggest, lies not in moral theory or in an analysis of the concept of beneficence, but in an appreciation of two facts about the circumstances in which individual—opposed to collective—beneficence often occurs. The first is that an individual's resources are so limited that either he will not be able to render significant aid to anyone unless he is selective or he will be able to do so only at excessive cost. The second is that in many cases the individual has more control over his beneficent efforts, and hence more assurance of their success, if he renders aid directly to those close at hand. (One may refrain from contributing to the aid of those far away simply because one is aware that there are numerous opportunities for diverting and diluting one's contribution before it reaches the intended recipient.) It may also be that some of those who accept uncritically the traditional view that beneficence is wholly discretionary as to the choice of beneficiaries do so because of a rather simplistic and overly optimistic assumption: namely,

that if each of us freely chooses some beneficiary or other, everyone, or virtually everyone in need, will receive some aid. This assumption ignores the problem of coordinating individual acts of beneficence emphasized in the two arguments above.

Each of these reasons can, in particular circumstances, justify a policy of selective beneficence. However, in conditions in which a collective effort can provide a minimum of care for all who can need it, without excessive costs to the benefactors, the same very general considerations that ground the duty of beneficence support a nonselective policy.

It is true that two perplexing questions remain unanswered. What counts as excessive costs? And should a guaranteed decent minimum policy aim only at the needy who dwell within the borders of a particular nation-state? Neither of these problems, however, is peculiar to the enforced beneficence arguments; they afflict rights-based approaches as well. Further, while the various moral justifications offered to support the alleged right to a decent minimum are also general in that they apply to human beings as such, the reasons for restricting the enforcement of rights to the national level, when they are good reasons, are as pragmatic as those that explain the assumption that benefactors may be selective. Even if these pragmatic considerations support a restriction of the class of those who are to be aided (or those whose rights are to be protected by our government), they do not justify the much stronger claim that beneficence (or the protection of rights) is essentially discretionary. I conclude, then, that the idea that beneficence allows discretion in the selection of recipients does not itself constitute a telling objection to the enforced beneficence argument for a decent minimum of health care. Instead, it seems more accurate to conclude that the enforced beneficence arguments force us to get clearer about what is central to the concept of beneficence and what is a practical concession to the difficulties of being beneficent in an imperfect world.

A libertarian might raise the potentially more serious objection that the enforced beneficence argument fails to recognize a fundamental qualification. While acknowledging that there may be some rules of social coordination or some principles specifying moral obligations or obligations to contribute to public goods that may be enforced, even in the absence of corresponding rights, the libertarian will point out that enforcing them is permissible *only if* doing so does not violate important moral rights.

I agree wholeheartedly with this qualification. However, if the qualification is to become a sound criticism of the enforced beneficence arguments, the libertartian must discharge two difficult tasks, the second of which no one has yet successfully executed. First, he must clearly specify *which* basic moral rights would be violated by any attempt to enforce the principle of beneficence as it is applied to health care. Second, he must provide a coherent and plausible *justification* for the claim that *these* basic moral rights do exist. To rule out in principle an enforceable duty of beneficence the libertarian would have to specify and justify either a virtually unlimited general right against interference or coercion or a virtually unlimited right to private property. The great obstacle to doing either is that he must avoid begging the question by appealing to intuitions that his nonlibertarian opponent does not share. In the absence of a sound theoretical justification for such rights, the burden of proof is on the libertarian to substantiate the claim that the enforcement in question violates important moral rights.

We have now come full circle. At the outset, I noted that the burden of proof is on those who claim that there is universal right to a decent minimum of health care. I then argued that various attempts to provide theoretical support for the claim that there is such a right are inadequate. If we abandon the quest for a justification for the claim that there is a universal right, however, we should not conclude that the libertarian view triumphs by default. The non-rights-based enforced beneficence arguments shift a similar burden of proof onto the libertarian.

If the approach I have outlined succeeds, it provides a way of avoiding both the burden of justifying the claim that there is a universal right to health care and the equally onerous burden of justifying a virtually unlimited right to private property or against coercion. Surprising as it may seem, an answer to the question of whether society ought to guarantee certain health-care services for all does *not* depend upon our ability to adjudicate decisively between libertarian and welfarist theories of basic rights.

I would like to conclude by observing that the non-rights-based, enforced beneficence approach has interesting implications for the issue of how we are to specify the content of the decent minimum. We have seen that while the type of rights-based argument determines the sorts of considerations which are to guide the specification of content, little can be said about the specification prior to the outcome of political processes or extensive empirical research. This conclusion will be disturbing if one assumes that the guaranteed minimum is a matter of right, since we often tend to think of rights as rather sharply defined. However, the traditional notion of duties of charity or beneficence is that they are 'imperfect duties': by their very nature they are not precisely delineated.

Now those who favor the non-rights-based approach can argue that the difficulty encountered by rights-based approaches in specifying the content of an alleged right to a decent minimum provides indirect support for the position that there is no right to a decent minimum but only an enforceable duty of beneficence or charity to contribute to the attainment of a decent minimum. In other words, the advocate of the enforced beneficence approach can warmly welcome the lack of a principled specification as a vindication of his view rather than accept it begrudgingly as an embarrassing theoretical lacuna. The idea would be that we must frankly acknowledge that the character and scope of the list of services included in the decent minimum is a matter of collective choice. All that is necessary is that there be some fair procedure for reaching a social decision on which set of services to provide.

NOTES

1. Ronald Dworkin, *Taking Rights Seriously* (Cambridge, MA: Harvard University Press, 1977), pp. 184–205.

2. It is not my purpose in this article to articulate the main factors that should determine the content of the decent minimum. For an attempt to do so, see *Securing Access to Health Care*, Report of the President's Commission for the Study of Ethical Problems in Medicine and Biomedical and

Behavioral Research (Washington, D.C., U.S. Government Printing Office, 1983), esp. chap. 1.

3. "Is There a Right to a Decent Minimum of Health Care?" in *Securing Access to Health Care*, Appendix Two.

4. Norman Daniels, "Health-Care Needs and Distributive Justice," *Philosophy & Public Affairs* 10, no. 2 (Spring 1981): 146–79.

5. For an exploration of various arguments for a duty of beneficence and an examination of the relationship between justice and beneficence, in general and in health care, see Allen E. Buchanan, "Philosophical Foundations of Beneficence," *Beneficence and Health Care,* ed. Earl E. Shelp (Dordrecht, Holland: Reidel Publishing Co., 1982).

Is There a Right to Health Care and, If So, What Does It Encompass?

NORMAN DANIELS

IS THERE A RIGHT TO HEALTH CARE?

Legal vs moral rights to health care

One way to answer this question is to adopt the stance of legal positivists, who claim that there are no rights except those that are embodied in actual institutions through law. We would then be able to reply that in nearly every advanced industrial democracy in the world, there is a right to health care, since institutions exist in them that assure everyone access to needed services regardless of ability to pay. The notable exception is the United States, where many poor and near poor people have no insurance coverage for, and thus no assured access to, medically necessary services, although by law they cannot be denied emergency services.

The legal right to health care is embodied in a wide variety of types of health-care systems. These range from national health services, where the government is the provider of services, as in Great Britain, to public insurance schemes, where the government finances services, as in Canada, to mixed public and private insurance schemes, as in Germany and the Netherlands. Despite these differences in the design of systems, there is a broad overlap in the scope or content

of the legal right to health care in these countries. Most cover 'medically necessary' services, including a broad range of preventive, curative, rehabilitative and long-term care for physical and mental diseases, disorders and disabilities. Most exclude uses of medical technologies that enhance otherwise normal functioning or appearance, such as purely cosmetic surgery. The legal rights vary in significant ways, however, for example, in the degree to which they cover new reproductive technologies, or in the types of mental health and long-term care services that are offered.

In the context of rising costs and the rapid dissemination of new technologies, there is growing debate in many countries about how to set limits on the scope of a right to health care. This debate about the scope of rights to health care pushes moral deliberation about such a right into the forefront, even where a legal right is recognized. Legal entitlements, most people believe, should reflect what society is morally obliged to provide by way of medical services. What, then, is the basis and scope of a moral right to health care?

Positive vs negative rights

A right to health care is a *positive* as opposed to a *negative* right. Put quite simply, a positive right requires others to do something beneficial or enabling for right-bearers, whereas a negative right requires others to refrain from doing something, usually harmful or restrictive, to right-bearers. To say that others are required to do something or to refrain from doing something is to say they must so act or refrain even if they could produce more good or improve the world by not doing so (Thomson, 1990). For example, a negative right to free expression requires others to refrain from censuring the expression of the right-bearer even if censuring this speech would make a better world. Some public-health measures that protect people against interference with their health, such as environmental protections that protect people against polluters of air, water and food sources, might be construed as requirements of a negative right. More generally, however, a right to health care imposes an obligation on others to assist the right-bearers in obtaining needed and appropriate services. Specifically, claiming a right to health care includes these other claims: society has the duty to its members to allocate an adequate share of its total resources to health-related needs; society has the duty to provide a just allocation of different types of health care services, taking into account the competing claims of different types of health-care needs; each person is entitled to a fair share of such services, where a 'fair share' includes an answer to the question, who should pay for the services? (Daniels, 1985). Health-care rights thus form a part of a broader family of positive 'welfare' rights that includes rights to education and to income support. Because positive rights require other people to contribute their resources or skills to benefit right-bearers, rather than merely refraining from interfering with them, they have often been thought more difficult to justify than negative rights, and their scope and limits have been harder to characterize.

Theories of justice and rights to health care

If we are to think of a right to health care as a requirement of justice, then we should look to more general theories of justice as a way to specify the scope and limits of that right. On some theories of justice, however, there is little basis for requiring people to assist others by meeting their health care or other needs. Libertarians. for example, believe that fundamental rights to property, including rights to personal assets, such as talents and skills, are violated if society coerces individuals into providing 'needed' resources or skills (Nozick, 1974). Libertarians generally recognize an 'imperfect' duty to act beneficently or charitably, but this duty involves discretion. It can be discharged in different ways that are matters of choice. People denied charity have no right to it and have no complaint against people who act charitably in other ways. Though some have argued that the difficulty of coordinating the delivery of charitable assistance might justify coercive measures (Buchanan, 1984), and others have tried to show that even libertarians must recognize some forms of welfare rights (Sterba, 1985), most libertarians resist any weakening of the property rights at the core of their view (Brennan and Friedman, 1981).

A spectre sometimes raised by libertarians against the idea of a right to health care is that such a right is a 'bottomless pit'. Since new technologies continuously expand the scope of 'medical needs', a right to health care would give rise to unlimited claims on the resources of others (Fried, 1969; Engelhardt, 1986). Protecting such an expansive right to health care would thus not be compatible with the function of a libertarian 'minimal state' to assure the non-violation of rights to liberty and property.

Though there remains controversy about whether utilitarians can provide a basis for recognizing true moral rights, there are strong utilitarian arguments in favour of governments assuring access to at least some broad range of effective medical services. Preventing or curing disease or disability reduces suffering and enables people to function in ways that contribute to aggregate welfare. In addition, knowing that health-care services are available increases personal security and strengthens the ties of community. Utilitarians can also justify redistributing the burden of delivering these benefits to society as a whole, citing the decreasing marginal utility of money to support progressive financing of health-care services (Brandt, 1979).

Beneath these quite general arguments, however, there lies a more specific controversy about the scope of utilitarian entitlements to health care. There seems to be little utilitarian justification for investing resources in health care if those resources would produce more net welfare when invested in other things, yet many people believe they have moral obligations to assist others with their health-care needs even at a net cost in utility. For example, some highly expensive and effective medical treatments that most people believe should be offered to people might not be 'cost beneficial' and thus not defensible on utilitarian grounds. Similarly, many forms of long-term care, especially for those who cannot be restored to productive social activity, are also difficult to defend on utilitarian grounds, yet we insist our health-care systems are obliged to provide such services.

Lack of moral acceptance of the distributive implications of utilitarianism makes many uncomfortable with the use of methods, such as cost-effectiveness analysis, that are intended to guide decisions about resource allocation in health care. For example, an assumption of cost-effectiveness analysis is that a unit of health benefit, such as a quality-adjusted life year (QALY), is of equal value or importance regardless of where it is distributed. But this assumption does not capture the concerns many people have about how much priority to give to the sickest patients, or when aggregating modest benefits to large numbers of people it outweighs the moral importance of delivering more significant benefits to fewer people (Nord, 1993: Daniels, 1993).

Two points about a utilitarian framework for a right to health care are worth noting. Recognizing a right to health care is compatible with recognizing limits on entitlements that result from resource scarcity and the fact that there are competing uses of those resources. Consequently, recognizing a right to health care need not open a bottomless pit. Second, just what entitlements to services follow from a right to health care cannot be specified outside the context of a *system* properly designed to deliver health care in a way that promotes aggregate utility. For the utilitarian, entitlements are *system-relative*. The same two points apply to other accounts of the foundations and limits of a right to health care.

Because many people reject the utilitarian rationales for health care (and other welfare) rights, theorists have explored other ways to ground such rights. Some claim that these rights are presupposed as

enabling conditions for the exercise of other rights or liberties, or as practical presuppositions of all views of justice (Braybrooke, 1987) or as a way of avoiding vulnerability and exploitation (Goodin, 1988). One approach that has been developed in some detail views a right to health care as a special case of a right to equality of opportunity (Daniels, 1985). This approach shows how the most important contractarian theory of justice, Rawls' (1971) account of justice as fairness, can be extended to the problem of health care, since that theory gives prominence to a principle protecting equality of opportunity (Rawls, 1993). Without endorsing that account here, we shall use it to illustrate further the complexity surrounding the concept of a right to health care.

Equal opportunity and a right to health care

The central observation underlying this account of a right to health care is that disease and disability restrict the range of opportunities that would otherwise be open to individuals. This is true whether they shorten our lives or impair our ability to function, including through pain and suffering. Health care in all its forms, whether public health or medical, preventive or acute or chronic, aims to keep people functioning as close to normally as possible. Since we are complex social creatures, our normal functional capabilities include our capabilities for emotional and cognitive functioning and not just physical capabilities. Health care thus preserves for us the range of opportunities we would have, were we not ill or disabled, given our talents and skills.

The significant contribution health care makes to protecting the range of opportunities open to individuals is nevertheless *limited* in two important ways. It is limited because other things, such as the distribution of wealth and income and education, also profoundly affect equality of opportunity. It is also limited because health care, by restricting its aim to protecting normal functioning, leaves the normal distribution of talents and skills unmodified. It aims to help us function as 'normal' competitors, not strictly equal ones.

Some argue that an equal opportunity account of health care should abandon the limit set by a focus on normal functioning (see Arneson, 1988; G. A. Cohen, 1989; Sen, 1992). They claim our concerns about equality, including equality of opportunity, require us to use health-care technologies whenever doing so would equalize opportunity for welfare or equalize capabilities. For example, if through medical intervention we can 'enhance' the otherwise normal capabilities of those who are at a competitive disadvantage, then our commitment to equality of opportunity requires us to do so. Obviously, this version of an equal opportunity account would vastly expand the moral requirements on medicine, yielding a right to health care much more expansive than any now embodied in actual systems and, arguably, one that would make administration of a health-care system unwieldy (Sabin and Daniels, 1994).

This expansive version of the appeal to equal opportunity ignores an important fact about justice: our concern for equality must be reconciled with considerations of liberty and efficiency in arriving at the overall requirements of justice (see Sen, 1992; Cohen, 1995; Daniels, 1996). Such a reconciliation seems to underlie the limits we commonly accept when we appeal to equality of opportunity. We generally believe that rights to equal opportunity are violated only if unfair social practices or preventable or curable diseases or disabilities interfere with the pursuit of reasonable plans of life within our society by making us lose competitive advantage. We accept, however, the fact that the natural distribution of talents and skills, working in an efficient market for them, will both enhance the social product and lead to inequalities in social outcomes. A just society will try to mitigate the effects of these inequalities in competitive advantage in other ways than by eliminating all eliminable differences in capabilities. For example, on Rawls' account, transfers that make the worst off as well off as they can be mitigate the effects on equality of allowing the natural distribution of talents and skills to enhance productivity. In what follows, the account of a right to health care rests on a more limited appeal to equal opportunity, one that takes the maintenance of normal functioning as a reasonable limit.

WHAT DOES A RIGHT TO HEALTH CARE INCLUDE?

System-relative entitlements

By making the right to health care a special case of rights to equality of opportunity, we arrive at a reasonable, albeit incomplete and imperfect, way of restricting its scope while still recognizing its importance. The account does not give individuals a basic right to have all of their health-care needs met. At the same time, there are social obligations to design a health-care system that protects opportunity through an appropriate set of health-care services. If social obligations to provide appropriate health care are not met, then individuals are definitely wronged. For example, if people are denied access—because of discrimination or inability to pay—to a basic tier of services adequate to protect normal functioning, injustice is done to them. If the basic tier available to people omits important categories of services without consideration of their effects on normal functioning, for example, whole categories of mental health or long-term care or preventive services, their rights are violated.

Still, not every medical need gives rise to an entitlement to services. The scope and limits of rights to health care, that is, the entitlements they actually carry with them, will be relative to certain facts about a given system. For example, a health-care system can protect opportunity only within the limits imposed by resource scarcity and technological development within a society. We cannot make a direct inference from the fact that an individual has a right to health care to the conclusion that this person is entitled to some specific health-care service, even if the service would meet a health-care need. Rather the individual is entitled to a specific service only if, in the light of facts about a society's technological capabilities and resource limitations, it should be a part of a system that appropriately protects fair equality of opportunity. The equal opportunity account of a right to health care, like the utilitarian account, makes entitlements to health care system-relative.

Effective treatment of disease and disability

The health care we have strongest claim to is care that effectively promotes normal functioning by reducing the impact of disease and disability, thus protecting the range of opportunities that would otherwise be open to us. Just what counts as 'effective', however? And what should we do about hard cases on the boundary between treatment of disease or disability and enhancement of capabilities?

It is a common feature of public and private insurance systems to limit care to treatments that are not 'experimental' and have some 'proven effectiveness'. Unfortunately, many services that count as standard treatment have little direct evidence about outcomes to support their use (Hadorn, 1992). They are often just customary treatment. Furthermore, it is often controversial just when new treatments or technologies should count as 'safe and efficacious'. What counts as 'reasonably effective' is then a matter of judgement and depends on the kind of condition and the consequences of not correcting it. We might, for example, want to lower our standards for effectiveness when we face a treatment of last resort, or raise them if resource scarcity is very great. On the other hand, we do not owe people a chance to obtain miracles through whatever unproven procedures they prefer to try.

By focusing a right to health care on the maintenance of normal functioning, a line is drawn between uses of medical technologies that count as legitimate 'treatments' and those that we may want but which do not meet our 'health-care needs'. Although we may want medical services that can enhance our appearance, like cosmetic (as opposed to reconstructive) plastic surgery, or that can optimize our otherwise normal functioning, like some forms of counselling or some uses of Prozac, we do not truly need these services to maintain normal functioning. We are obliged to help others achieve normal functioning, but we do not 'owe' each other whatever it takes to make us more beautiful or strong or completely happy (Daniels, 1985).

Though this line is widely used in both public and private insurance practices, it leaves us with hard cases. Some of the hardest issues involve reproductive technologies. Abortion, where there is no preventive or therapeutic need, does not count as 'treatment' because an unwanted pregnancy is not a disease or disability. Some nevertheless insist that requirements of justice, including a right to control one's body, means that non-therapeutic abortion should be included as an entitlement in a health-care system. Some national health-insurance schemes do not cover infertility services. Yet infertility is a departure from normal functioning, even if some people never want to bear children. Controversy may remain about how much social obligation we have to correct this form of impaired opportunity, especially where the costs of some interventions, such as *in vitro* fertilization, are high and their effectiveness is modest. Different societies will judge this question differently, in part because they may place different values on the rearing of biologically related children or on the experience of child-bearing.

Hard cases involve non-reproductive technologies as well. In the United States, for example, many insurers will cover growth hormone treatment only for children deficient in growth hormone, not for those who are equally short but without any pathology. Yet the children denied therapy will suffer just as much as those who are eligible. Similar difficulties are involved in drawing a line between covered and non-covered uses of mental health services (Sabin and Daniels, 1994). As in the cases of reproductive technologies, there is room for different societies to 'construct' the concept of mental disorder somewhat differently, with resulting variation in decisions about insurance coverage.

Rights and limits on effective treatments

Even when some health-care service is reasonably effective at meeting a medical need, not all such needs are equally important. When a disease or disability has little impact on the range of opportunities open to someone, it is not as morally important to treat as other conditions that more seriously impair opportunity. The effect on opportunity thus gives us some guidance in thinking about resource allocation priorities.

Unfortunately, the impact on our range of opportunities gives only a crude and incomplete measure of the importance or priority we should give to a need or service. In making decisions about priorities for purposes of resource allocation in health care, we face difficult questions about distributive fairness that are not answered by this measure of importance. For example, we must sometimes make a choice between investing in a technology that delivers a significant benefit to few people or one that delivers a more modest benefit to a larger number of people. Sometimes we must make a choice between investing in a service that helps the sickest, most impaired patients or one that helps those whose functioning is less impaired. Sometimes we must decide between the fairness of giving a scarce resource to those who derive the largest benefit or giving a broader range of people some chance at getting a benefit. In all of these cases, we lack clear principles for deciding how to make our choices, and the account of a right to health care we are discussing does not provide those principles either (Daniels, 1993). Some methodologies, like cost-effectiveness analysis, are intended to help us make appropriate resource allocation decisions in these kinds of cases. But these methodologies may themselves embody controversial moral assumptions about distributive fairness. This means they cannot serve as decision procedures for making these choices and can at best serve as aids to decision-makers who must be explicit about the moral reasoning that determines the distributive choices they make (Gold et al., 1996).

In any health-care system, then, some choices will have to be made by a fair, publicly accountable, decision-making process. Just what constitutes a fair decision-making procedure for resolving moral disputes about health care entitlements is itself a matter of controversy. It is a problem that has been addressed little in the literature. Our rights are not violated, however, if the choices that are made through fair decision-making procedures turn out to be ones that do not happen to meet our personal needs, but instead meet needs of others that are judged more important (Daniels and Sabin, 1997).

How equal must our rights to health care be?

How equal must our rights to health care be? Specifically, must everyone receive exactly the same kinds of health-care services and coverage, or is fairness in health care compatible with a 'tiered' system? Around the world, even countries that offer universal health insurance differ in their answers to this question. In Canada and Norway, for example, no supplementary insurance *is* permitted. Everyone is served solely by the national health-insurance schemes, though people who seek additional services or more rapid service may go elsewhere, as some Canadians do by crossing the border. In Britain, supplementary private insurance allows about 10 per cent of the population to gain quicker access to services for which there is extensive queuing in the public system. Basing a right to health care on an obligation to protect equality of opportunity is compatible with the sort of tiering the British have, but it does not require it, and it imposes some constraints on the kind of tiering allowed.

The primary social obligation is to assure everyone access to a tier of services that effectively promotes normal functioning and thus protects equality of opportunity. Since health care is not the only important good, resources to be invested in the basic tier are appropriately and reasonably limited, for example, by democratic decisions about how much to invest in education or job training as opposed to health care. Because of their very high 'opportunity costs', there will be some beneficial medical services that it will be reasonable not to provide in the basic tier, or to provide only on a limited basis, for example, with queuing. To say that these services have 'high opportunity costs' means that providing them consumes resources that would produce greater health benefits and protect opportunity more if used in other ways.

In a society that permits significant income and wealth inequalities, some people will want to buy coverage for these additional services. Why not let them? After all, we allow people to use their after-tax income and wealth as they see fit to pursue the 'quality of life' and opportunities they prefer. The rich can buy special security systems for their homes. They can buy safer cars. They can buy private schooling for their children. Why not allow them to buy supplementary health care for their families?

One objection to allowing a supplementary tier is that its existence might undermine the basic tier either economically or politically. It might attract better-quality providers away from the basic tier, or raise costs in the basic tier, reducing the ability of society to meet its social obligations. The supplementary tier might undermine political support for the basic tier, for example, by undercutting the social solidarity needed if people are to remain committed to protecting opportunity for all. These objections are serious, and where a supplementary tier undermines the basic tier in either way, economically or politically, priority must be given to protecting the basic tier. In principle, however, it seems possible to design a system in which the supplementary tier does not undermine the basic one. If that can be done, then a system that permits tiering avoids restricting liberty in ways that some find seriously objectionable.

A second objection is not to tiering itself but to the structure of inequality that results. Compare two scenarios. In one, most people are adequately served by the basic tier and only the best-off groups in society have the means and see the need to purchase supplementary insurance. That is the case in Great Britain. In the other, the basic tier serves only the poorest groups in society and most other people buy supplementary insurance. The Oregon plan to expand Medicaid eligibility partly through rationing the services it covers has aspects of this structure of inequality, since most people are covered by plans that avoid these restrictions (Daniels, 1991). The first scenario seems preferable to the second on grounds of fairness. In the second, the poorest groups can complain that they are left behind by others in society even in the protection of their health. In the first, the majority has less grounds for reasonable resentment or regret.

If the basic tier is not undermined by higher tiers, and if the structure of the inequality that results is not objectionable, then it is difficult to see why some tiering should not be allowed. There is a basic conflict here between concerns about equality and concerns about liberty, between wanting to make sure everyone is treated properly with regard to health care and wanting to give people the liberty to use their resources (after tax) to improve their lives as they see fit. In practice, the crucial constraint on the liberty we allow people seems to depend on the magnitude of the benefit available in the supplementary tier and unavailable in the basic tier. Highly visible forms of saving lives and improving function would be difficult to exclude from the basic tier while we make them available in a supplementary tier. In principle, however, some forms of tiering will not be unfair even when they involve medical benefits not available to everyone.

REFERENCES

Arneson, Richard (1988). Equality and equal opportunity for welfare. *Philosophical Studies,* 54, 79–95.

Brandt, Richard (1979). *A Theory of the Good and the Right.* Oxford: Oxford University Press.

Braybrooke, David (1987). *Meeting Needs.* Princeton, NJ: Princeton University Press.

Brennan, Geoffrey and Friedman, David (1981). A libertarian perspective on welfare. In Peter G. Brown, Conrad Johnson and Paul Vernier (eds), *Income Support: Conceptual and policy issues.* Totowa, NJ: Rowman and Littlefield.

Buchanan, Allen (1984). The right to a decent minimum of health care. *Philosophy and Public Affairs,* 13, 55–78.

Cohen, G. A. (1989). On the currency of egalitarian justice. *Ethics,* 99, 906–44.

Cohen, Joshua (1995). Amartya Sen: *Inequality Reexamined. Journal of Philosophy,* 92/5, 275–88.

Daniels, N. (1985). *Just Health Care.* Cambridge: Cambridge University Press.

—— (1991). Is the Oregon rationing plan fair? *Journal of the American Medical Association,* 265, 2232–5.

—— (1993). Rationing fairly: programmatic considerations. *Bioethics,* 7, 224–33.

—— (1996). *Justice and Justification: reflective equilibrium in theory and practice.* Cambridge: Cambridge University Press.

Daniels, N. and Sabin, J. (1997). Limits to health care: fair procedures, democratic deliberation, and the legitimacy problem for insurers. *Philosophy and Public Affairs,* 26/4, 303–50.

Engelhardt. H. Tristram (1986). *The Foundations of Bioethics*. Oxford: Oxford University Press.

Fried, Charles (1969). *An Anatomy of Value*. Cambridge, MA: Harvard University Press.

Gold, Marthe, Siegel, Joanna, Russell, Louise and Weinstein, Milton (eds) (1996). *Cost-Effectiveness in Health and Medicine: recommendations of the Panel on Cost-Effectiveness in Health and Medicine*. New York: Oxford University Press.

Goodin, Robert (1988). *Reasons for Welfare*. Princeton. NJ: Princeton University Press.

Hadorn, David (ed.) (1992). *Basic Benefits and Clinical Guidelines*. Boulder, CO: Westview Press.

Nord, Eric (1993). The relevance of health state after treatment in prioritizing between different patients. *Journal of Medical Ethics*, 19, 37–42.

Nozick, R. (1974). *Anarchy, State, and Utopia*. New York: Basic Books.

Rawls, J. (1971). *A Theory of Justice*. Cambridge, MA: Harvard University Press.

—— (1993). *Political Liberalism*. New York: Columbia University Press.

Sabin, James and Daniels, Norman (1994). Determining 'medical necessity' in mental health practice. *Hastings Center Report*, 24/6, 5–13.

Sen, Amartya (1992). *Inequality Reexamined*. Cambridge. MA: Harvard University Press.

Sterba, James (1985). From liberty to welfare. *Social Theory and Practice*, 11, 285–305.

Thomson, Judith (1990). *The Realm of Rights*. Cambridge, MA: Harvard University Press.

CHAPTER 12

Animal Welfare

One of philosophy's most important functions is to help us critically examine beliefs that we often simply accept without question. Philosophy seems to have played this role especially well in the issue of animal rights, for it was a philosopher who helped engender the current animal rights movement by arguing that something was very wrong with the traditional attitude toward animals (that is, nonhuman animals) and their treatment. The traditional notion is that an animal is merely a resource that humans may dispose of as they see fit: an animal is food, fuel, or fun—something with instrumental value only. Peter Singer was the philosopher who challenged the received wisdom, declaring in his 1975 book *Animal Liberation* that its subject was the "tyranny of human over nonhuman animals. This tyranny has caused and today is still causing an amount of pain and suffering that can only be compared with that which resulted from the centuries of tyranny by white humans over black humans."[1]

The traditional attitude toward animals has been influential in the West for centuries. It sprang from several sources, including Judeo-Christian thought and the arguments of several distinguished philosophers. The book of Genesis declares that God created humans in his own image, "saying to them, 'Be fruitful, multiply, fill the earth and conquer it. Be masters of the fish of the sea, the birds of heaven and all living animals on the earth'" (Genesis 1:28). Aristotle claims that all of nature exists "specifically for the sake of man," that animals are merely instruments for humankind. Thomas Aquinas is remarkably explicit about humans' proper attitude toward animals:

> Hereby is refuted the error of those who said it is sinful for a man to kill dumb animals: for by divine providence they are intended for man's use in the natural order. Hence it is no wrong for man to make use of them, either by killing them or in any other way whatever.[2]

Aquinas also says that we should avoid being cruel to animals—but only because cruelty to animals might lead to cruelty to humans. Animal cruelty in itself, he explains, is no wrong. Likewise, René Descartes thinks animals are ours to use any way we want. After all, he asserts, animals are not sentient—they are machines, like mechanical clocks, devoid of feelings and incapable of experiencing pleasure or pain. Immanuel Kant, who thinks that people are not means to an end but ends in themselves, contends that animals are means to the end known as man. Today few would agree with Descartes that animals cannot experience pain, but the traditional idea that animals have no (or low) moral standing is widespread.

Those who reject the traditional attitude remind us that beliefs about the moral status of animals influence how animals are treated in the real world—and that treatment, they say, is horrendous on a vast scale. In 2015 and 2016 in the United States alone, more than 18 billion animals were slaughtered for food—cows, poultry, calves, pigs, sheep, and lambs.[3] Critics have charged that the animals are subjected to appalling suffering, including lifelong confinement in spaces so small the animals can hardly move, isolation of veal calves in small crates (and, some say, in almost total darkness), routine mutilation or surgery such as branding and cutting off pigs' tails and chickens' beaks, and the slaughter of chickens and livestock without first stunning them or using any other methods to minimize pain and suffering.[4]

In addition, each year millions of animals—from mice to dogs to primates—are used in laboratory experiments all over the world. Some of this research—no one knows how much—causes significant animal suffering. According to a U.S. government report, in 2007 about 8 percent of larger animals used in experiments (excluding mice and rats) endured "pain or distress" that could not be relieved with medication.

These concerns push us toward the key moral questions that we try to sort out in this chapter: Do animals have instrumental value only? Do they have rights? Do we owe them any moral respect or concern at all? Is it morally permissible to experiment on animals, to raise and kill them for food, to cause them unnecessary pain and suffering? Do animals have the same moral worth as an infant, a mentally incompetent man, a woman with severe senile dementia, or a man in a persistent vegetative state?

ISSUE FILE: BACKGROUND

Fortunately, on these issues there is at least a parcel of common ground. First, almost no one believes, as Descartes did, that animals are equivalent to windup clocks, mechanisms without feelings. Science and common sense suggest that many animals (mostly vertebrates) are *sentient*—that is, that they can have experiences. They can experience bodily sensations such as pain and pleasure as well as emotions such as fear and frustration. Sentient beings are thought to have the capacity to suffer. Second, virtually everyone thinks that being cruel to animals—unnecessarily causing them pain or misery—is wrong. Even when we consider this judgment carefully and critically, it seems inescapable. Third, there

is general agreement, among philosophers at least, that sentient animals are worthy of some degree of moral respect or concern. Most disputes turn on interpretations of this last point: Exactly how much moral concern do we owe animals? Do they deserve the same level of moral consideration that we give to humans? Do they deserve less? How should we treat them?

Such questions are essentially about the **moral status**, or **moral considerability**, of animals. Something has moral status if it is a suitable candidate for moral concern or respect in its own right, regardless of its relationships to humans. Ethically, we cannot treat a being that has moral status just any way we want, as if it were a mere thing. A being with moral status is of moral importance regardless of whether it is a means to something else, and in our dealings with it, we must somehow take this fact into account. Another way of expressing the notion of moral status is to say that any being with moral status is an object of **direct moral consideration** or concern. That is, such a being is worthy of moral concern for its own sake, not because of its relationship to others. A being that is the object of **indirect moral consideration** is granted respect or concern because of its relationship to other individuals. Human beings are objects of direct moral consideration; some say that animals such as dogs, pigs, and rabbits are too. A screwdriver is not the kind of thing that can be the object of direct moral concern, but it may be of indirect moral concern because of its value to a human being. Some people insist that all nonhuman animals are of indirect moral concern, deriving whatever value they have from their usefulness to humans. Many others reject this view, asserting that sentient animals have independent moral status.

Moral status is typically understood to be something that comes in degrees and that can be overridden or discounted in some circumstances. Philosophers speak of varying levels or weights of moral considerability. Some contend that animals have the same moral status as normal adult humans—that, for example, the interests of animals are as morally important as the comparable interests of humans. Some argue that humans deserve more moral respect or concern than animals, that the interests of humans always take precedence over those of animals. Many maintain that moral considerability varies depending on the species (human or nonhuman), with humans enjoying the greatest degree of moral considerability and other species being assigned lower degrees on a sliding scale. But philosophers disagree on the basis for assigning the different rankings. Whatever a being's moral status, it is usually not viewed as absolute; sometimes it may be overridden or canceled by factors thought to be more important. Some people think, for example, that a dog's moral status prohibits humans from beating it just for fun but may allow beatings under some circumstances—say, to prevent it from straying into traffic and causing an accident.

Frequently people use the term **animal rights** as a synonym for *moral status*. When they say that animals have rights, they mean only that animals deserve some degree of direct moral consideration. But often the term is used in a more restricted way to refer to a particularly strong type of moral status. In this stronger sense, for an animal to have rights is for it to be entitled to a kind of moral respect that cannot be overridden (or cannot be overridden easily) by other considerations. Those who accept this notion of animal rights may argue that animals should *never* be condemned to factory farms or used in medical experimentation, even if such treatment would make millions of humans happy. Such rights are analogous to rights that people are supposed to have. People are thought to have a right, for instance, not to be unjustly imprisoned—even if their imprisonment would increase the overall happiness of society as a whole. (We take a closer look at strong animal rights in the next section.)

Before examining arguments that animals have moral status or rights, we should cite a few arguments to the contrary. Some people claim that

only human beings have moral status and that animals, if they matter at all, have only indirect value as resources or tools for people. If cruelty to animals is wrong, it is wrong only because it makes humans callous or upsets people or damages personal property. The usual tack of those who reject moral status for animals is to argue that only beings that possess a particular property have moral status—a property that animals do not possess but humans do. The proposed status-granting properties are numerous and include having a soul, nurturing strong family bonds, using language, being a member of the human species, and being a person or a moral agent.

The notion that animals lack souls and therefore have no moral status is, of course, a traditional religious view defended on traditional religious grounds. Generally, philosophers do not take this path because their focus is on reason and arguments rather than on faith, and because philosophical analysis has rendered the concept of a soul problematic or controversial.

The claim that animals have no moral standing because they do not have the kind of strong family relationships exhibited by humans has been undermined not by philosophy but by science. The same goes for the parallel claim regarding animals' language skills. One philosopher sums up the relevant empirical findings:

> [M]any species of non-humans develop long-lasting kinship ties—orangutan mothers stay with their young for eight to ten years and while they eventually part company, they continue to maintain their relationships. Less solitary animals, such as chimpanzees, baboons, wolves, and elephants maintain extended family units built upon complex individual relationships, for long periods of time. Meerkats in the Kalahari desert are known to sacrifice their own safety by staying with sick or injured family members so that the fatally ill will not die alone. . . . While the lives of many, perhaps most, non-humans in the wild are consumed with struggle for survival, aggression and battle, there are some non-humans whose lives are

CRITICAL THOUGHT: Using Animals to Test Consumer Products

Animals are used not only to test the safety and effectiveness of medical treatments, but also to determine the safety of consumer products such as cosmetics. This practice is fraught with controversy. For example:

> Each year, American doctors inject more than 3 million doses of Botox to temporarily smooth their patients' wrinkles and frown lines. But before each batch is shipped, the manufacturer puts it through one of the oldest and most controversial animal tests available.

> To check the potency of its product under federal safety rules, Allergan Inc. injects mice with Botox until it finds a dose at which half of the animals die—a rough gauge of potential harm to humans.

> Animal protection groups consider this "lethal dose 50 (LD_{50})" test to be "the poster child for everything that's wrong with animal testing," said Martin Stephens, vice president for animal research issues at the Humane Society of the United States. "It's as bad as it gets, poisoning animals to death."

> Allergan officials say they have no choice. Without a federally approved safety test that does not use animals, a company spokeswoman says, LD_{50} "is by default the required test."*

Is this kind of animal testing morally permissible, considering that its purpose is commercial and not medical? Why or why not? Would your using products that have been thoroughly tested using LD_{50} be morally acceptable? Would you change your answer if you knew the testing was done on dogs or horses instead of mice or guinea pigs?

*Gilbert M. Gaul, "In U.S., Few Alternatives to Testing On Animals," *Washington Post*, washingtonpost.com, April 12, 2008.

characterized by expressions of joy, playfulness, and a great deal of sex. Recent studies in cognitive ethology have suggested that some non-humans engage in manipulative and deceptive activity, can construct "cognitive maps" for navigation, and some non-humans appear to understand symbolic representation and are able to use language.[5]

A more common claim is that just *being human*—having the DNA of the human species, in other words—is the property that gives a being moral considerability. If so, then nonhumans do not and cannot have moral status. This view has seemed initially plausible to some, but critics have wondered why simply having human DNA would bestow moral status on a creature.

Perhaps the most telling objection against the human species argument is based on a simple thought experiment. Suppose we humans encounter extraterrestrial creatures who have all the same attributes and capabilities that we have—self-consciousness, intelligence, language skills, reasoning ability, emotions, and more. We would presumably have to admit that these beings have full moral status, just as we do. Yet they are not human. They may not even be carbon-based life forms. Physically they may be nothing like any member of the human species. This strange (but possible) state of affairs suggests that being human is not a necessary condition for having moral status.

Taking a cue from Kant, some philosophers contend that only persons or moral agents can be candidates for moral considerability—and that animals do not make the cut. Persons are typically regarded as rational beings who are free to choose their own ends and determine their own actions and values. Moral agents are beings who can make moral judgments and act according to moral reasons or principles. So the basic claim is that because all or most animals are not persons or moral agents, they can have no moral standing. They simply lack the necessary property.

As many critics have pointed out, using personhood and moral agency as criteria for determining moral status has a troublesome drawback: it not only excludes animals from moral considerability but some humans as well. This difficulty is common to all lack-of-some-necessary-property arguments, which we will examine more closely in the next section.

In any case, many think that all these standards for moral status are in a sense beside the point. To them it is obvious that regardless of whether an animal possesses these "higher" capacities and characteristics, it can suffer. They reason that if it can suffer, then it can be wronged by deliberately causing it to suffer. If deliberately hurting it is wrong, it must have some level of moral considerability.

MORAL THEORIES

How might a utilitarian assess the treatment of nonhuman animals? What would he or she say about their moral status? The most famous answers to these questions come from the utilitarian philosopher Peter Singer, credited with kindling through his writings what is popularly known as the animal rights movement. His most celebrated book, *Animal Liberation*, helped spark serious debates about the treatment of animals, the meat industry, and vegetarianism—debates that continue to this day. Classic utilitarianism says that the right action is the one that produces the best balance of happiness over unhappiness (or pleasure over pain), *everyone considered*. Singer's approach is to include *both* animals and humans in this "everyone." The pain and pleasure of *all* sentient beings must be considered when we are deciding which action maximizes the good.

This inclusion of *all* animals (human and nonhuman) in utilitarian calculations is not new,

however—it was, in fact, advocated by utilitarianism's founder, Jeremy Bentham (1748–1832):

> The day *may* come when the rest of the animal creation may acquire those rights which never could have been witholden from them but by the hand of tyranny. The French have already discovered that the blackness of the skin is no reason why a human being should be abandoned without redress to the caprice of a tormentor. It may one day come to be recognized that the number of the legs, the villosity of the skin, or the termination of the *os sacrum*, are reasons equally insufficient for abandoning a sensitive being to the same fate. What else is it that should trace the insuperable line? Is it the faculty of reason, or perhaps the faculty of discourse? But a full grown horse or dog is beyond comparison a more rational, as well as a more conversable animal, than an infant of a day, or a week, or even a month, old. But suppose they were otherwise, what would it avail? The question is not, Can they reason? nor Can they *talk?* but, *Can they suffer?*[6]

For both Bentham and Singer, what makes a being worthy of moral concern, what requires us to include it in the moral community, is its ability to experience pain and pleasure—its ability to suffer. Why do humans have moral status? Not, says the utilitarian, because of their capacity for reason, social relationships, and personhood—but because of their capacity for suffering. Likewise, because sentient animals can suffer, they too have moral status. Furthermore, Bentham and Singer argue that because both humans and animals can suffer, they both deserve *equal moral consideration*. As Singer says,

> [T]he interests of every being affected by an action are to be taken into account and given the same weight as the like interests of any other being. . . . If a being suffers, there can be no moral justification for refusing to take that suffering into consideration. No matter what the nature of the being, the principle of equality requires that its suffering be counted equally with the like suffering—in so far as rough comparisons can be made—of any other being. If a being is not capable of suffering, or of experiencing enjoyment or happiness, there is nothing to be taken into account.[7]

According to Singer, those who do not give equal moral consideration to human and nonhuman animals are guilty of **speciesism**—discrimination against nonhuman animals just because of their species. Speciesism, he says, is wrong for the same reason that racism and sexism are wrong: it violates the principle of equal consideration—that is, equal consideration of comparable interests.

Equal consideration of comparable interests, however, does not mean equal treatment. Humans and animals have some interests in common (such as avoiding pain), and they differ dramatically in the possession of other interests (humans are capable of enjoying art and studying philosophy, but animals are not). Singer's utilitarianism demands that when comparable interests are involved, those of humans and those of animals must be given equal weight. A pig's suffering is just as important as a man's or a woman's. If a pig and a man are both experiencing intense pain, we must not assume that the man's pain should be taken more seriously. We should regard the agony of both beings with equal concern. But when interests are not comparable, we need not pretend that they are. We may, for example, give weight to a woman's interest in enjoying a good book, but we would give no weight to this interest in a dog, because a dog has no such interest.

What are the implications of Singer's view for the treatment of animals? For one thing, it implies that our system of meat production is wrong and should be abolished. There is general agreement that the meat industry currently causes immense suffering to millions of sentient creatures. In standard utilitarian calculations, if we weigh this extreme suffering against the moderate pleasures it produces (the gustatory enjoyment of humans), we see that the meat industry generates a net balance of evil over good. The alternative to having a meat industry—vegetarianism—would result in far more good than evil. As Singer puts it,

> Since, as I have said, none of these [meat industry] practices cater for anything more than our pleasures of taste, our practice of rearing and killing other

animals in order to eat them is a clear instance of the sacrifice of the most important interests of other beings in order to satisfy trivial interests of our own. To avoid speciesism we must stop this practice, and each of us has a moral obligation to cease supporting this practice.[8]

Some see a problem in Singer's stance, however, because his call for eliminating meat production and embracing vegetarianism does not seem to be fully warranted by his arguments. By Singer's own lights, a humane form of meat production might be morally permissible. If animals could be raised and killed without suffering—if their lives could be pleasant and their deaths painless—then there might be a net balance of good over evil in the process. Then both meat production and meat eating might be acceptable. It seems that Singer's arguments could be used to support reform of the meat production industry just as easily as its total elimination.

As for scientific experimentation on animals, Singer thinks that it might be permissible if the benefits gained from the research outweigh any suffering involved. "[I]f a single experiment could cure a major disease, that experiment would be justifiable," he says.[9] However, he believes that in practice, animal experimentation usually results in more evil than good because often the benefits to humans are negligible.

How would a nonconsequentialist view the treatment of animals? Probably the most influential example of the nonconsequentialist approach is that of Tom Regan, another philosopher who has helped define and inspire the animal rights movement. He argues for *animal rights* proper—that is, animal rights in the restricted sense of having moral considerability that cannot be easily overridden, not in the weaker, generic sense of simply possessing moral status. According to Regan,

> The genius and the retarded child, the prince and the pauper, the brain surgeon and the fruit vendor, Mother Theresa and the most unscrupulous used car salesman—all have inherent value, all possess it *equally*, and *all have an equal right to be treated with respect*, to be

CRITICAL THOUGHT: Should We Experiment on Orphaned Babies?

Consider this controversial argument against speciesism by Peter Singer:

> In the past, argument about vivisection has often missed the point, because it has been put in absolutist terms: Would the abolitionist be prepared to let thousands die if they could be saved by experimenting on a single animal? The way to reply to this purely hypothetical question is to pose another: would the experimenter be prepared to perform his experiment on an orphaned human infant, if that were the only way to save many lives? (I say "orphan" to avoid the complication of parental feelings, although in doing so I am being overfair to the experimenter, since the nonhuman subjects of experiments are not orphans.) If the experimenter is not prepared to use an orphaned human infant, then his readiness to use nonhumans is simple discrimination, since adult apes, cats, mice, and other mammals are more aware of what is happening to them, more self-directing and, so far as we can tell, at least as sensitive to pain, as any human infant.*

What is Singer's point here? Is he advocating the practice of experimenting on orphaned human infants? Suppose you disagree with Singer. What argument would you make against his position?

*Peter Singer, "All Animals Are Equal," *Philosophic Exchange* 1 (1974). Copyright © Peter Singer 1974. Reprinted by permission of author.

treated in ways that do not reduce them to the status of things, as if they exist as resources for others.[10]

Regan maintains that such equal inherent value and equal rights apply to animals just as much as they do to humans. More specifically, he says, they apply to all mature mammals, human and nonhuman. Creatures with inherent value must be treated, in Kant's famous phrase, as ends in themselves, not merely as means to an end. Their value or their treatment does not depend on some utilitarian calculation of pain and pleasure. According to Regan, humans and animals have equal value and equal rights because they share particular mental capacities; they are sensitive, experiencing beings—or as Regan says, "experiencing subjects of a life":

> [W]e are each of us the experiencing subject of a life, a conscious creature having an individual welfare that has importance to us whatever our usefulness to others. We want and prefer things, believe and feel things, recall and expect things. And all these dimensions of our life, including our pleasure and pain, our enjoyment and suffering, our satisfaction and frustration, our continued existence or our untimely death—all make a difference to the quality of our life as lived, as experienced, by us as individuals. As the same is true of those animals who concern us (those who are eaten and trapped, for example), they too must be viewed as the experiencing subjects of a life, with inherent value of their own.[11]

How should we treat animals, then, if they have such rights and if these rights are equal to our own? Regan's theory (what he calls the rights view) implies that if it would be wrong to dissect, hurt, torture, eat, cage, hunt, or trap a human, then it would also be wrong to do the same to an animal—and that the amount of good that might be produced by such acts is irrelevant. Therefore, Regan concludes, all forms of animal experimentation should be abolished. "Because these animals are treated routinely, systematically as if their value were reducible to their usefulness to others," Regan says, "they are routinely, systematically treated with a lack of respect, and thus are their rights routinely, systematically violated."[12] On the same grounds, he thinks that commercial animal agriculture and commercial and sport hunting and trapping should also be abolished.

MORAL ARGUMENTS

Do animals really have equal rights in the strict sense just mentioned? That is, do nonhuman animals have the same right to respect and moral concern that humans have? Using Tom Regan's rights view as inspiration without sticking strictly to his line of reasoning, let us examine some simple (and simplified) arguments for and against this proposition.

For our purposes, we can state the argument for the rights view like this:

1. Nonhuman animals (normal, fully developed mammals) are experiencing subjects of a life (or "experiencing subjects," for short), just as humans are.

2. All experiencing subjects have equal inherent value.

3. All those with equal inherent value are entitled to equal moral rights (the equal right to be treated with respect).

4. Therefore, nonhuman animals have equal moral rights.

This is a valid argument; the conclusion does follow from the three premises. So we have good reason to accept the conclusion if the premises are true. Are they? Premise 1 is an empirical claim about the mental capacities of animals (again, normal, fully developed mammals). There is scientific evidence suggesting that animals do have at least most of the capacities in question. For simplicity's sake, then, let us assume that Premise 1 is true.

Premises 2 and 3 are much more difficult to sort out. We should not accept them unless there are good reasons for doing so. Good reasons would involve separate arguments that support each of them. Regan has provided such arguments, and several critics have responded to them. Some have said, for example, that the notion of inherent value is obscure and that the link between inherent value and moral rights is unclear. Many others have sidestepped these issues and attacked the conclusion directly, arguing that regardless of whether animals have some moral rights, they surely do not have the *same* moral rights that humans do—that is, the equal right to be treated with respect.

Those who take this latter approach begin with an advantage. Our moral common sense suggests that there must be some sort of difference between the moral status of most humans and that of most animals. We tend to think that accidentally running over a man with our car is morally worse than doing the same to a rabbit. Most of us believe that there is an important moral difference between imprisoning women in cages for later slaughter and doing the same to chickens or hogs—even if we also deem the latter cruel and immoral.

Our intuition about such things can be wrong, of course. So those who reject equal moral rights for animals have offered other considerations. The philosopher Mary Anne Warren, for example, argues that animals do indeed have some moral rights, but that there are reasons for thinking that these rights are weaker or less demanding than the rights of humans. For one thing, she notes, the human right to freedom is stronger or more extensive than the animal right to freedom. This right prohibits the unlawful imprisonment of humans, even if the prison is comfortable and spacious. Human dignity and the satisfaction of human aspirations and desires demand a higher degree of freedom of movement than would be required for the satisfaction of the needs or interests of many nonhuman animals. Imprisonment of animals in areas that allow them to satisfy their needs and pursue their natural inclinations, Warren says, "need not frustrate the needs or interests of animals in any significant way, and thus do not clearly violate their rights." In a similar vein, Warren argues that both humans and animals have a prima facie right to life, but this right is generally weaker for animals than for humans. As she puts it, "Human lives, one might say, have greater intrinsic value, because they are worth more *to their possessors*."[13] Humans have hopes, plans, and purposes that make them value continued existence; animals, apparently, lack this forward-looking perspective. Warren adds that nonhuman animals nevertheless have a right to life because, among other things, their premature demise robs them of any future pleasures they might have had.

Regan has responded to such arguments for unequal rights for animals by offering a common counterargument. In general, the arguments contend that animals have less inherent value (and therefore weaker moral rights) because animals lack something that adult humans have—perhaps the ability to reason, intelligence, autonomy, intellect, or some other valuable property. But, Regan says, if this contention is true, then we must say that some humans who lack these characteristics (retarded children or people with serious mental illness, for example) also have less inherent value than normal adult humans and therefore less robust moral rights. In other words, if these critics of equal rights are correct, we are fully justified in treating these "deficient humans" as we would nonhuman animals. "But it is not true," he says, "that such humans . . . have less inherent value than you or I.

Neither, then, can we rationally sustain the view that animals like them in being experiencing subjects of a life have less inherent value. *All* who have inherent value have it *equally*, whether they be human animals or not."[14]

CHAPTER REVIEW

SUMMARY

The traditional attitude toward animals is that they are merely resources that humans can dispose of as they see fit; that is, that animals have instrumental value only. But many reject the traditional view and put forward reasons for supposing that animals have moral status. Something has moral status if it is a suitable candidate for moral concern or respect in its own right.

Some people claim that only humans have moral status and that animals have only indirect moral considerability. The usual approach of those who reject moral status for animals is to argue that a being is entitled to moral status only if it possesses particular properties—and that animals do not possess them. These status-granting properties include having a soul, having strong family bonds, using language, being a member of the human species, and being a person or a moral agent.

One of the more common claims is that one must be human to have moral status. Critics, however, have asked what it is about being human that gives one moral status. A thought experiment used against this claim asks us to imagine meeting extraterrestrial creatures who are like ourselves in many ways. We would presumably have to admit that the aliens have moral status just as we do, even though they are not human. Being human, then, seems not to be necessary for having moral status.

The most famous utilitarian approach to the treatment of animals is that of the philosopher Peter Singer. He argues that the pain and pleasure of animals as well as that of humans must be included in utilitarian calculations. What makes a being worthy of moral concern, he says, is its capacity for suffering, and because both humans and animals can suffer, they deserve equal moral consideration. Consequently, Singer maintains that our system of meat production is wrong and should be abolished.

The most notable nonconsequentialist approach to the treatment of animals is that of Tom Regan. He argues for strong animal rights on the grounds that all "experiencing subjects of a life" have equal inherent value and therefore an equal right to be treated with respect. Experiencing subjects of a life include healthy, mature mammals (humans and nonhumans). Regan maintains that because such animals have equal rights, all commercial animal agriculture and sport hunting and trapping should be abolished.

KEY TERMS
moral status (or **moral considerability**) (p. 372)
direct moral consideration (p. 372)
indirect moral consideration (p. 372)
animal rights (p. 373)
speciesism (p. 376)

EXERCISES
Review Questions
1. What does it mean for a creature to have moral status? (p. 372)
2. What are the two meanings of "animal rights"? (p. 373)
3. What is Aquinas's view on the treatment of animals? (p. 371)
4. What does Descartes believe about animals' ability to experience pain? (p. 371)
5. What does "sentient" mean in relation to animals and humans? (p. 372)
6. What is Regan's view on animal rights? (pp. 376–377)
7. What is "direct moral consideration"? What is "indirect moral consideration"? (p. 372)
8. Do animals have the kind of strong family relationships exhibited by humans? (p. 373)
9. What is speciesism? (p. 376)
10. What is Peter Singer's view on animal rights? (pp. 375–376)

Discussion Questions
1. How might a utilitarian assess the treatment of nonhuman animals?
2. What reasons do people give for thinking that animals do not have moral status? Do you agree with any of these reasons?
3. Is having human DNA the property that gives a being moral considerability? Why or why not?
4. What is the most telling objection against the human species argument?
5. For Bentham and Mill, what makes a being worthy of moral concern?
6. Which view of animal rights—Singer's or Regan's—do you think is morally reasonable? Why?
7. What is Warren's critique of Regan's view of animal rights? Do you agree with her?
8. What is the traditional attitude toward animals? Is it reasonable? Why or why not?
9. What do you believe it is about being human that gives humans moral status? Why?
10. What conclusion do Bentham and Singer draw from the fact that animals can suffer?

FURTHER READING
Carl Cohen, "The Case for the Use of Animals in Biomedical Research," *New England Journal of Medicine* 315 (October 2, 1986): 865–70.

David DeGrazia, *Animal Rights: A Very Short Introduction* (Oxford: Oxford University Press, 2002).

R. G. Frey, "Animals," in *The Oxford Handbook of Practical Ethics,* ed. Hugh LaFollette (New York: Oxford University Press, 2003).

R. G. Frey, *Interests and Rights: The Case against Animals* (Oxford: Clarendon; New York: Oxford University Press, 1980).

Lori Gruen, "Animals," in *A Companion to Ethics,* ed. Peter Singer, corr. ed. (Oxford: Blackwell, 1993).

Mary Midgley, *Animals and Why They Matter* (Harmondsworth: Penguin, 1983).

James Rachels, *Created from Animals: The Moral Implications of Darwinism* (Oxford: Oxford University Press, 1990).

Tom Regan, *The Case for Animal Rights* (Berkeley: University of California Press, 1983).

Tom Regan and Peter Singer, eds., *Animal Rights and Human Obligations,* 2nd ed. (Englewood Cliffs, NJ: Prentice Hall, 1989).

Peter Singer, *Animal Liberation,* 2nd ed. (New York: New York Review of Books, 1990).

Peter Singer, "Ethics beyond Species and beyond Instincts," in *Animal Rights: Current Debates and New Directions,* ed. Cass R. Sunstein and Martha C. Nussbaum (Oxford: Oxford University Press, 2004).

Bonnie Steinbock, "Speciesism and the Idea of Equality," *Philosophy* 53, no. 204 (April 1978): 247–56.

Cass R. Sunstein and Martha C. Nussbaum, eds., *Animal Rights: Current Debates and New Directions* (Oxford: Oxford University Press, 2004).

Mary Anne Warren, "The Rights of the Nonhuman World," in *Environmental Philosophy: A Collection of Readings,* eds. Robert Elliot and Arran Gare (University Park: Pennsylvania State University Press, 1983).

ETHICAL DILEMMAS

1. Animal Testing

The Guardian—Protesters for and against animal testing have predicted an escalating conflict after the two sides clashed during weekend demonstrations in Oxford. Both groups pledged to step up campaigns which have already resulted in death threats aimed at advocates of animal testing and panic buttons installed at the home of a leading provivisection protester.

Pro-Test, the group which organised the Oxford rally of scientists, students and patients, plans a march in London which it hopes will draw 5,000 supporters. A spokesman for Speak, the animal rights group campaigning against a new animal research laboratory in Oxford, said the Pro-Test demonstration had left it "fired up" to take tougher action.

Spokesman Mel Broughton said: "They should be worried, not because they are in any danger of violence, but because they have fired us up even more against them and the university." . . .

Many researchers stayed away from the march, fearing reprisals against them and their families. Professor Tipu Aziz, a leading neurosurgeon, said: "This country has thousands of researchers paralysed by fear. That's a travesty of democracy." . . .

A spokesman for the Animal Liberation Front, Robin Webb, yesterday described the Pro-Test marchers as "irrelevant."

"The ALF supporters will completely ignore this protest group and will continue targeting institutions and companies which are directly involved in building the proposed facility," he said.

The Medical Research Council's chief executive, Colin Blakemore, described the Pro-Test demonstration as "immensely gratifying. For a long time, we have needed this kind of collective response. The people want this thuggery and nastiness off the streets of Oxford."*

Which side in this conflict do you sympathize with more? Why? Suppose you are a member of Pro-Test. How would you argue in favor of scientific animal testing? Say you are an ALF supporter.

What arguments could you make for the banning of most (or all) animal testing? Is either side justified in using violence or the threat of violence to further its cause? Why or why not?

---

2. Seal Hunting and the Fate of the Inuit

Boston Globe—In the 1980s, postcards were distributed to 12 million United States and United Kingdom households depicting the infamous Canadian Atlantic fisher swinging a bat at a baby seal and eliciting an overwhelming emotional response. Major legislative bodies relented to public pressure with a staggering impact on wildlife management. The collapse of the sealskin market marked a victory for protesters who had waged the most effective, international mass media campaign ever undertaken.

The moral victory for animal rights activists not only hurt Newfoundlanders, it adversely affected thousands of Canadian Inuit living in tiny, remote, Arctic hamlets. Antifur protesters lump all seal-hunting methods together. It is tragic but not surprising that there has been virtually no media coverage of the devastating economic, social, and cultural impact of the collapse of the seal skin market on Inuit. If outsiders had known more about Inuit life, perhaps they would not have so easily dismissed all seal-hunting as unethical and cruel.

Canadian Inuit, who number about 46,000, are part of a circumpolar Inuit community numbering about 150,000 in Greenland, Alaska, and Russia. For Canadian Inuit, the seal is not just a source of cash through fur sales, but the keystone of their culture. Although Inuit harvest and hunt many species that inhabit the desert tundra and ice platforms, the seal is their mainstay. . . .

Inuit no longer use seal oil lamps or kudlik for heating, as did their grandparents. But seal meat, which is extremely high in protein, minerals, and vitamins and very low in fat, is still the most valued meat in many parts of the Arctic. Seal skin mittens and boots continue to provide the greatest protection against the harsh Arctic climate.

Like most people, Inuit respond to structural changes by adapting and innovating. They were already dependent on costly hunting supplies by the 1980s. When fur prices plummeted after the sealskin boycott, their credit and cash flow from furs dried up while the cost of supplies rose. Many families could no longer afford hunting equipment. Their fragile economy was imperiled and their vulnerability increased. Their social order was ruptured as they were deprived of the complex social aspect of sharing seal meat.

Their historical, legal, social, and economic situation already placed them at alarmingly higher risks of poverty and violence than other Canadians even when they live outside the North, as 10,000 Inuit have chosen to do. Life expectancy among the Inuit is 10 years lower than other Canadians. Rates of infant mortality, unemployment, illnesses such as diabetes, violence against women, and overcrowded housing are chillingly high.

One of the most brutal aspects of the lack of cultural continuity is the epidemic of youth suicide striking small communities in clusters where one death rapidly engenders another. But the Inuit, having endured myths and misinformation about their culture for decades, have carried on. . . .

The Inuit are resourceful people who deserve more respectful attention from outsiders.[†]

Would a utilitarian like Peter Singer be likely to support a ban on all seal hunting even though it would devastate the Inuit? Would he be likely to approve of the Inuit's hunting if they could always kill the seals painlessly? Would a nonconsequentialist like Tom Regan disapprove of the hunting of the seals under all circumstances? If the fate of the Inuit and the seals was to be decided by either Singer or Regan, which philosopher do you think the Inuit would prefer? Provide reasons for your answers.

[†]Kirt Ejesiak and Maureen Flynn-Burhoe, "Animal Rights vs. Inuit Rights," *The Boston Globe*, May 8, 2005. Reprinted by permission of the authors.

---

3. Should We Keep Animals in Zoos?

CNN—The judgment and criticism built quickly after a 3-year-old got into the enclosure of a 450-pound gorilla at the Cincinnati Zoo. Where were the child's parents? How could the zoo let this happen? Why did an endangered gorilla have to be shot and killed?

But another question emerged among parents, too: Should we be going to zoos at all?

The animal advocacy group People for the Ethical Treatment of Animals said there's a problem with the larger concept of zoos. It said on Twitter that the tragic episode in Cincinnati was the latest proof that "even under the 'best' circumstances . . . captivity is never acceptable for gorillas or other primates."

Change is already happening around the globe, PETA Senior Vice President Lisa Lange said this year after SeaWorld made the stunning announcement that it's moving away from housing killer whales and ending its breeding program. SeaWorld faced growing pressure about its orca policies and then declining park attendance after the release of "Blackfish," which documented the 2010 death of a trainer pulled underwater by a 12,000-pound orca. The current generation of killer whales will be the last orcas housed in captivity at the park, SeaWorld said.

"What we're seeing is the 'Blackfish' effect," Lange said. "The public has completely changed its opinion on exploiting and killing animals for entertainment."[‡]

Is keeping animals in zoos morally permissible? Does it amount to cruelty? Why or why not? Is using animals for the entertainment of humans wrong? If zoo captivity is morally wrong, is it also wrong to visit animals in zoos?

[‡]Kelly Wallace, "After Gorilla Shooting, Are Zoos Becoming 'Obsolete'?", from CNN.com, May 31, 2016. © 2016 Turner Broadcast Systems. All rights reserved. Used by permission and protected by the Copyright Laws of the United States. The printing, copying, redistribution, or retransmission of this content without express written permission is prohibited.

READINGS

All Animals Are Equal

PETER SINGER

In recent years a number of oppressed groups have campaigned vigorously for equality. The classic instance is the Black Liberation movement, which demands an end to the prejudice and discrimination that has made blacks second-class citizens. The immediate appeal of the black liberation movement and its initial, if limited success made it a model for other oppressed groups to follow. We became familiar with liberation movements for Spanish-Americans, gay people, and a variety of other minorities. When a majority group—women—began their campaign, some thought we had come to the end of the road. Discrimination on the basis of sex, it has been said, is the last universally accepted form of discrimination, practiced without secrecy or pretense even in those liberal circles that have long prided themselves on their freedom from prejudice against racial minorities.

One should always be wary of talking of "the last remaining form of discrimination." If we have learnt anything from the liberation movements, we should have learnt how difficult it is to be aware of latent prejudice in our attitudes to particular groups until this prejudice is forcefully pointed out.

A liberation movement demands an expansion of our moral horizons and an extension or reinterpretation of the basic moral principle of equality. Practices that were previously regarded as natural and inevitable come to be seen as the result of an unjustifiable prejudice. Who can say with confidence that all his or her attitudes and practices are beyond criticism? If we wish to avoid being numbered amongst the oppressors, we must be prepared to re-think even our most fundamental attitudes. We need to consider them from the point of view of those most disadvantaged by our attitudes, and the practices that follow from these

attitudes. If we can make this unaccustomed mental switch we may discover a pattern in our attitudes and practices that consistently operates so as to benefit one group—usually the one to which we ourselves belong—at the expense of another. In this way we may come to see that there is a case for a new liberation movement. My aim is to advocate that we make this mental switch in respect of our attitudes and practices towards a very large group of beings: members of species other than our own—or, as we popularly though misleadingly call them, animals. In other words, I am urging that we extend to other species the basic principle of equality that most of us recognise should be extended to all members of our own species.

All this may sound a little far-fetched, more like a parody of other liberation movements than a serious objective. In fact, in the past the idea of "The Rights of Animals" really has been used to parody the case for women's rights. When Mary Wollstonecraft, a forerunner of later feminists, published her *Vindication of the Rights of Women* in 1792, her ideas were widely regarded as absurd, and they were satirized in an anonymous publication entitled *A Vindication of the Rights of Brutes*. The author of this satire (actually Thomas Taylor, a distinguished Cambridge philosopher) tried to refute Wollstonecraft's reasonings by showing that they could be carried one stage further. If sound when applied to women, why should the arguments not be applied to dogs, cats and horses? They seemed to hold equally well for these "brutes": yet to hold that brutes had rights was manifestly absurd; therefore the reasoning by which this conclusion had been reached must be unsound, and if unsound when applied to brutes, it must also be unsound when applied to women, since the very same arguments had been used in each case.

One way in which we might reply to this argument is by saying that the case for equality between men and women cannot validly be extended to non-human animals. Women have a right to vote, for instance, because they are just as capable of making rational decisions as men are; dogs, on the other hand, are incapable of understanding the significance of voting, so they cannot have the right to vote. There are many other obvious ways in which men and women resemble each other closely, while humans and other animals differ greatly. So, it might be said, men and women are similar beings, and should have equal rights, while humans and non-humans are different and should not have equal rights.

The thought behind this reply to Taylor's analogy is correct up to a point, but it does not go far enough. There *are* important differences between humans and other animals, and these differences must give rise to *some* differences in the rights that each have. Recognizing this obvious fact, however, is no barrier to the case for extending the basic principle of equality to non-human animals. The differences that exist between men and women are equally undeniable, and the supporters of Women's Liberation are aware that these differences may give rise to different rights. Many feminists hold that women have the right to an abortion on request. It does not follow that since these same people are campaigning for equality between men and women they must support the right of men to have abortions too. Since a man cannot have an abortion, it is meaningless to talk of his right to have one. Since a pig can't vote, it is meaningless to talk of its right to vote. There is no reason why either Women's Liberation or Animal Liberation should get involved in such nonsense. The extension of the basic principle of equality from one group to another does not imply that we must treat both groups in exactly the same way, or grant exactly the same rights to both groups. Whether we should do so will depend on the nature of the members of the two groups. The basic principle of equality, I shall argue, is equality of consideration; and equal consideration for different beings may lead to different treatment and different rights.

So there is a different way of replying to Taylor's attempt to parody Wollstonecraft's arguments, a way which does not deny the differences between humans and non-humans, but goes more deeply into the question of equality, and concludes by finding nothing absurd in the idea that the basic principle of equality applies to so-called "brutes." I believe that we reach this conclusion if we examine the basis on which our opposition to discrimination on grounds of race or sex ultimately rests. We will then see that we would be on shaky ground if we were to demand equality for blacks, women, and other groups of oppressed humans while denying equal consideration to non-humans.

When we say that all human beings, whatever their race, creed or sex, are equal, what is it that we are asserting? Those who wish to defend a hierarchical, inegalitarian society have often pointed out that by whatever test we choose, it simply is not true that all humans are equal. Like it or not, we must face the fact that humans come in different shapes and sizes; they come with differing moral capacities, differing intellectual abilities, differing amounts of benevolent feeling and sensitivity to the needs of others, differing abilities to communicate effectively, and differing capacities to experience pleasure and pain. In short, if the demand for equality were based on the actual equality of all human beings, we would have to stop demanding equality. It would be an unjustifiable demand.

Still, one might cling to the view that the demand for equality among human beings is based on the actual equality of the different races and sexes. Although humans differ as individuals in various ways, there are no differences between the races and sexes *as such*. From the mere fact that a person is black, or a woman, we cannot infer anything else about that person. This, it may be said, is what is wrong with racism and sexism. The white racist claims that whites are superior to blacks, but this is false—although there are differences between individuals, some blacks are superior to some whites in all of the capacities and abilities that could conceivably be relevant. The opponent of sexism would say the same: a person's sex is no guide to his or her abilities, and this is why it is unjustifiable to discriminate on the basis of sex.

This is a possible line of objection to racial and sexual discrimination. It is not, however, the way that someone really concerned about equality would choose, because taking this line could, in some circumstances, force one to accept a most inegalitarian society. The fact that humans differ as individuals, rather than as races or sexes, is a valid reply to some-one who defends a hierarchical society like, say, South Africa, in which all whites are superior in status to all blacks. The existence of individual variations that cut across the lines of race or sex, however, provides us with no defence at all against a more sophisticated opponent of equality, one who proposes that, say, the interests of those with I.Q. ratings above 100 be pre-ferred to the interests of those with I.Q.s below 100. Would a hierarchical society of this sort really be so much better than one based on race or sex? I think not. But if we tie the moral principle of equality to the factual equality of the different races or sexes, taken as a whole, our opposition to racism and sexism does not provide us with any basis for objecting to this kind of inegalitarianism.

There is a second important reason why we ought not to base our opposition to racism and sexism on any kind of factual equality, even the limited kind [that] asserts that variations in capacities and abilities are spread evenly between the different races and sexes: we can have no absolute guarantee that these abili-ties and capacities really are distributed evenly, with-out regard to race or sex, among human beings. So far as actual abilities are concerned, there do seem to be certain measurable differences between both races and sexes. These differences do not, of course, appear in each case, but only when averages are taken. More important still, we do not yet know how much of these differences is really due to the different genetic endow-ments of the various races and sexes, and how much is due to environmental differences that are the result of past and continuing discrimination. Perhaps all of the important differences will eventually prove to be environmental rather than genetic. Anyone opposed to racism and sexism will certainly hope that this will be so, for it will make the task of ending discrimina-tion a lot easier; nevertheless it would be dangerous to rest the case against racism and sexism on the belief that all significant differences are environmental in origin. The opponent of, say, racism who takes this line will be unable to avoid conceding that if differ-ences in ability did after all prove to have some genetic connection with race, racism would in some way be defensible.

It would be folly for the opponent of racism to stake his whole case on a dogmatic commitment to one particular outcome of a difficult scientific issue which is still a long way from being settled. While attempts to prove that differences in certain selected abilities between races and sexes are primarily genetic in origin have certainly not been conclusive, the same must be said of attempts to prove that these differences are largely the result of environment. At this stage of the investigation we cannot be certain which view is correct, however much we may hope it is the latter.

Fortunately, there is no need to pin the case for equality to one particular outcome of this scientific investigation. The appropriate response to those who claim to have found evidence of genetically-based dif-ferences in ability between the races or sexes is not to stick to the belief that the genetic explanation must be wrong, whatever evidence to the contrary may turn up: instead we should make it quite clear that the claim to equality does not depend on intelligence, moral capacity, physical strength, or similar matters of fact. Equality is a moral ideal, not a simple assertion of fact. There is no logically compelling reason for assum-ing that a factual difference in ability between two people justifies any difference in the amount of con-sideration we give to satisfying their needs and inter-ests. The principle of the equality of human beings is not a description of an alleged actual equality among humans: it is a prescription of how we should treat humans.

Jeremy Bentham incorporated the essential basis of moral equality into his utilitarian system of eth-ics in the formula: "Each to count for one and none for more than one." In other words, the interests of every being affected by an action are to be taken into account and given the same weight as the like inter-ests of any other being. A later utilitarian, Henry Sidg-wick, put the point in this way: "The good of any one individual is of no more importance, from the point of view (if I may say so) of the Universe, than the good of any other."[1] More recently, the leading figures in con-temporary moral philosophy have shown a great deal of agreement in specifying as a fundamental presup-position of their moral theories some similar require-ment which operates so as to give everyone's interests equal consideration—although they cannot agree on how this requirement is best formulated.

It is an implication of this principle of equality that our concern for others ought not to depend on what they are like, or what abilities they possess—although precisely what this concern requires us to do may vary according to the characteristics of those affected by what we do. It is on this basis that the case against racism and the case against sexism must both ultimately rest; and it is in accordance with this principle that speciesism is also to be condemned. If possessing a higher degree of intelligence does not entitle one human to use another for his own ends, how can it entitle humans to exploit non-humans?

Many philosophers have proposed the principle of equal consideration of interests, in some form or other, as a basic moral principle; but, as we shall see in more detail shortly, not many of them have recognised that this principle applies to members of other species as well as to our own. Bentham was one of the few who did realize this. In a forward-looking passage, written at a time when black slaves in the British dominions were still being treated much as we now treat non-human animals, Bentham wrote:

> The day *may* come when the rest of the animal creation may acquire those rights which never could have been witholden from them but by the hand of tyranny. The French have already discovered that the blackness of the skin is no reason why a human being should be abandoned without redress to the caprice of a tormentor. It may one day come to be recognised that the number of the legs, the villosity of the skin, or the termination of the *os sacrum*, are reasons equally insufficient for abandoning a sensitive being to the same fate. What else is it that should trace the insuperable line? Is it the faculty of reason, or perhaps the faculty of discourse? But a full-grown horse or dog is beyond comparison a more rational, as well as a more conversable animal, than an infant of a day, or a week, or even a month, old. But suppose they were otherwise, what would it avail? The question is not, Can they reason? nor Can they *talk*? but, *Can they suffer?*[2]

In this passage Bentham points to the capacity for suffering as the vital characteristic that gives a being the right to equal consideration. The capacity for suffering—or more strictly, for suffering and/or enjoyment or happiness—is not just another characteristic like the capacity for language, or for higher mathematics. Bentham is not saying that those who try to mark "the insuperable line" that determines whether the interests of a being should be considered happen to have selected the wrong characteristic. The capacity for suffering and enjoying things is a pre-requisite for having interests at all, a condition that must be satisfied before we can speak of interests in any meaningful way. It would be nonsense to say that it was not in the interests of a stone to be kicked along the road by a schoolboy. A stone does not have interests because it cannot suffer. Nothing that we can do to it could possibly make any difference to its welfare. A mouse, on the other hand, does have an interest in not being tormented, because it will suffer if it is.

If a being suffers, there can be no moral justification for refusing to take that suffering into consideration. No matter what the nature of the being, the principle of equality requires that its suffering be counted equally with the like suffering—in so far as rough comparisons can be made—of any other being. If a being is not capable of suffering, or of experiencing enjoyment or happiness, there is nothing to be taken into account. This is why the limit of sentience (using the term as a convenient, if not strictly accurate, shorthand for the capacity to suffer or experience enjoyment or happiness) is the only defensible boundary of concern for the interests of others. To mark this boundary by some characteristic like intelligence or rationality would be to mark it in an arbitrary way. Why not choose some other characteristic, like skin color?

The racist violates the principle of equality by giving greater weight to the interests of members of his own race, when there is a clash between their interests and the interests of those of another race. Similarly the speciesist allows the interests of his own species to override the greater interests of members of other species. The pattern is the same in each case. Most human beings are speciesists. I shall now very briefly describe some of the practices that show this.

For the great majority of human beings, especially in urban, industrialized societies, the most direct form of contact with members of other species is at meal-times: we eat them. In doing so we treat them purely as means to our ends. We regard their life and well-being as subordinate to our taste for a particular kind of dish. I say "taste" deliberately—this is purely a matter of pleasing our palate. There can be no defence of eating flesh in terms of satisfying nutritional needs, since it has been established beyond doubt that we could satisfy our need for protein and other essential nutrients far more efficiently with a diet that replaced animal flesh by soy beans, or products derived from soy beans, and other high-protein vegetable products.[3]

It is not merely the act of killing that indicates what we are ready to do to other species in order to gratify our tastes. The suffering we inflict on the animals while they are alive is perhaps an even clearer indication of our speciesism than the fact that we are prepared to kill them.[4] In order to have meat on the table at a price that people can afford, our society tolerates methods of meat production that confine sentient animals in cramped, unsuitable conditions for the entire durations of their lives. Animals are treated like machines that convert fodder into flesh, and any innovation that results in a higher "conversion ratio" is liable to be adopted. As one authority on the subject has said, "cruelty is acknowledged only when profitability ceases."[5] So hens are crowded four or five to a cage with a floor area of twenty inches by eighteen inches, or around the size of a single page of the *New York Times*. The cages have wire floors, since this reduces cleaning costs, though wire is unsuitable for the hens' feet; the floors slope, since this makes the eggs roll down for easy collection, although this makes it difficult for the hens to rest comfortably. In these conditions all the birds' natural instincts are thwarted: they cannot stretch their wings fully, walk freely, dust-bathe, scratch the ground, or build a nest. Although they have never known other conditions, observers have noticed that the birds vainly try to perform these actions. Frustrated at their inability to do so, they often develop what farmers call "vices," and peck each other to death. To prevent this, the beaks of young birds are often cut off.

This kind of treatment is not limited to poultry. Pigs are now also being reared in cages inside sheds. These animals are comparable to dogs in intelligence, and need a varied, stimulating environment if they are not to suffer from stress and boredom. Anyone who kept a dog in the way in which pigs are frequently kept would be liable to prosecution, in England at least, but because our interest in exploiting pigs is greater than our interest in exploiting dogs, we object to cruelty to dogs while consuming the produce of cruelty to pigs. Of the other animals, the condition of veal calves is perhaps worst of all, since these animals are so closely confined that they cannot even turn around or get up and lie down freely. In this way they do not develop unpalatable muscle. They are also made anaemic and kept short of roughage, to keep their flesh pale, since white veal fetches a higher price; as a result they develop a craving for iron and roughage, and have been observed to gnaw wood off the sides of their stalls, and lick greedily at any rusty hinge that is within reach.

Since, as I have said, none of these practices cater for anything more than our pleasures of taste, our practice of rearing and killing other animals in order to eat them is a clear instance of the sacrifice of the most important interests of other beings in order to satisfy trivial interests of our own. To avoid speciesism we must stop this practice, and each of us has a moral obligation to cease supporting the practice. Our custom is all the support that the meat-industry needs. The decision to cease giving it that support may be difficult, but it is no more difficult than it would have been for a white Southerner to go against the traditions of his society and free his slaves; if we do not change our dietary habits, how can we censure those slaveholders who would not change their own way of living?

The same form of discrimination may be observed in the widespread practice of experimenting on other species in order to see if certain substances are safe for human beings, or to test some psychological theory about the effect of severe punishment on learning, or to try out various new compounds just in case something turns up. People sometimes think that all this experimentation is for vital medical purposes, and so will reduce suffering overall. This comfortable belief is very wide of the mark. Drug companies test new shampoos and cosmetics that they are intending to put on the market by dropping them into the eyes of rabbits, held open by metal clips, in order to observe what damage results. Food additives, like artificial colorings and preservatives, are tested by what is known as the "LD_{50}"—a test designed to find the level of consumption at which 50% of a group of animals will die. In the process, nearly all of the animals are made very sick before some finally die, and others pull through. If the substance is relatively harmless, as it often is, huge doses have to be force-fed to the animals, until in some cases sheer volume or concentration of the substance causes death.

Much of this pointless cruelty goes on in the universities. In many areas of science, non-human animals are regarded as an item of laboratory equipment, to be used and expended as desired. In psychology laboratories experimenters devise endless variations and repetitions of experiments that were of little value in the first place. To quote just one example, from the experimenter's own account in a psychology journal: at the University of Pennsylvania, Perrin S. Cohen hung six dogs in hammocks with electrodes taped to their hind feet. Electric shock of varying intensity was then administered through the electrodes. If the dog learnt to press its head against a panel on the left, the shock was turned off, but otherwise it remained on indefinitely. Three of the dogs, however, were required to wait periods varying from 2 to 7 seconds while being shocked before making the response that turned off the current. If they failed to wait, they received further shocks. Each dog was given from 26 to 46 "sessions" in the hammock, each session consisting of 80 "trials" or shocks, administered at intervals of one minute. The experimenter reported that the dogs, who were unable to move in the hammock, barked or bobbed their heads when the current was applied. The reported findings of the experiment were that there was a delay in the dogs' responses that increased proportionately to the time the dogs were required to endure the shock, but a gradual increase in the intensity of the shock had no systematic effect in the timing of the response. The experiment was funded by the National Institutes of Health, and the United States Public Health Service.

In this example, and countless cases like it, the possible benefits to mankind are either nonexistent or fantastically remote; while the certain losses to members of other species are very real. This is, again, a clear indication of speciesism.

In the past, argument about vivisection has often missed this point, because it has been put in absolutist terms: would the abolitionist be prepared to let thousands die if they could be saved by experimenting on a single animal? The way to reply to this purely hypothetical question is to pose another: would the experimenter be prepared to perform his experiment on an orphaned human infant, if that were the only way to save many lives? (I say "orphan" to avoid the complication of parental feelings, although in doing so I am being overfair to the experimenter, since the nonhuman subjects of experiments are not orphans.) If the experimenter is not prepared to use an orphaned human infant, then his readiness to use nonhumans is simple discrimination, since adult apes, cats, mice and other mammals are more aware of what is happening to them, more self-directing and, so far as we can tell, at least as sensitive to pain, as any human infant. There seems to be no relevant characteristic that human infants possess that adult mammals do not have to the same or a higher degree. (Someone might try to argue that what makes it wrong to experiment on a human infant is that the infant will, in time and if left alone, develop into more than the nonhuman, but one would then, to be consistent, have to oppose abortion, since the fetus has the same potential as the infant—indeed, even contraception and abstinence might be wrong on this ground, since the egg and sperm, considered jointly, also have the same potential. In any case, this argument still gives us no reason for selecting a nonhuman, rather than a human with severe and irreversible brain damage, as the subject for our experiments.)

The experimenter, then, shows a bias in favor of his own species whenever he carries out an experiment on a nonhuman for a purpose that he would not think justified him in using a human being at an equal or lower level of sentience, awareness, ability to be self-directing, etc. No one familiar with the kind of results yielded by most experiments on animals can have the slightest doubt that if this bias were eliminated the number of experiments performed would be a minute fraction of the number performed today.

Experimenting on animals, and eating their flesh, are perhaps the two major forms of speciesism in our society. By comparison, the third and last form of speciesism is so minor as to be insignificant, but it is perhaps of some special interest to those for whom this paper was written. I am referring to speciesism in contemporary philosophy.

Philosophy ought to question the basic assumptions of the age. Thinking through, critically and carefully, what most people take for granted is, I believe, the chief task of philosophy, and it is this task that makes philosophy a worthwhile activity. Regrettably, philosophy does not always live up to its historic role. Philosophers are human beings and they are subject to all the preconceptions of the society to which they belong. Sometimes they succeed in breaking free of the prevailing ideology: more often they become its most sophisticated defenders. So, in this case, philosophy as practiced in the universities today does not challenge anyone's preconceptions about our relations with other species. By their writings, those philosophers who tackle problems that touch upon the issue reveal that they make the same unquestioned assumptions as most other humans, and what they say tends to confirm the reader in his or her comfortable speciesist habits.

I could illustrate this claim by referring to the writings of philosophers in various fields—for instance, the attempts that have been made by those interested in rights to draw the boundary of the sphere of rights so that it runs parallel to the biological boundaries of the species *homo sapiens*, including infants and even mental defectives, but excluding those other beings of equal or greater capacity who are so useful to us at mealtimes and in our laboratories. I think it would be a more appropriate conclusion to this paper, however, if I concentrated on the problem with which we have been centrally concerned, the problem of equality.

It is significant that the problem of equality, in moral and political philosophy, is invariably formulated in terms of human equality. The effect of this is that the question of the equality of other animals does not confront the philosopher, or student, as an issue in itself—and this is already an indication of the failure of philosophy to challenge accepted beliefs. Still, philosophers have found it difficult to discuss the issue of human equality without raising, in a paragraph or two, the question of the status of other animals. The reason for this, which should be apparent from what I have said already, is that if humans are to be regarded as equal to one another, we need some sense of "equal" that does not require any actual, descriptive equality of capacities, talents or other qualities. If equality is to be related to any actual characteristics of humans, these characteristics must be some lowest common denominator, pitched so low that no human lacks them—but then the philosopher comes up against the catch that any such set of characteristics which covers *all* humans will not be possessed *only by humans*. In other words, it turns out that in the only sense in which we can truly say, as an assertion of fact, that all humans are equal, at least some members of other species are also equal— equal, that is, to each other and to humans. If, on the other hand, we regard the statement "All humans are equal" in some non-factual way, perhaps as a prescription, then, as I have already argued, it is even more difficult to exclude non-humans from the sphere of equality.

This result is not what the egalitarian philosopher originally intended to assert. Instead of accepting the radical outcome to which their own reasonings naturally point, however, most philosophers try to reconcile their beliefs in human equality and animal inequality by arguments that can only be described as devious.

As a first example, I take William Frankena's well-known article "The Concept of Social Justice." Frankena opposes the idea of basing justice on merit, because he sees that this could lead to highly inegalitarian results. Instead he proposes the principle that:

> . . . all men are to be treated as equals, not because they are equal, in any respect but simply because they are human. They are human because they have emotions and desires, and are able to think, and hence are capable of enjoying a good life in a sense in which other animals are not.[6]

But what is this capacity to enjoy the good life which all humans have, but no other animals? Other animals have emotions and desires, and appear to be capable of enjoying a good life. We may doubt that they can think—although the behavior of some apes, dolphins and even dogs suggests that some of them can—but what is the relevance of thinking? Frankena goes on to admit that by "the good life" he means "not so much the morally good life as the happy or satisfactory life," so thought would appear to be unnecessary for enjoying the good life; in fact to emphasise the need for thought would make difficulties for the egalitarian since only some people are capable of leading intellectually satisfying lives—or morally good lives. This makes it difficult to see what Frankena's principle of equality has to do with simply being *human*. Surely every sentient being is capable of leading a life that is happier or less miserable than some alternative life, and hence has a claim to be taken into account. In this respect the distinction between humans and non-humans is not a sharp division, but rather a continuum along which we move gradually, and with overlaps between the species, from simple capacities for enjoyment and satisfaction, or pain and suffering, to more complex ones.

Faced with a situation in which they see a need for some basis for the moral gulf that is commonly thought to separate humans and animals, but can find no concrete difference that will do the job without undermining the equality of humans, philosophers tend to waffle. They resort to high-sounding phrases like "the intrinsic dignity of the human individual";[7] they talk of the "intrinsic worth of all men" as if men (humans?) had some worth that other beings did not,[8] or they say that humans, and only humans, are "ends in themselves," while "everything other than a person can only have value for a person."[9]

This idea of a distinctive human dignity and worth has a long history; it can be traced back directly to the Renaissance humanists, for instance to Pico della Mirandola's *Oration on the Dignity of Man*. Pico and other humanists based their estimate of human dignity on the idea that man possessed the central, pivotal position in the "Great Chain of Being" that led from the lowliest forms of matter to God himself; this view of the universe, in turn, goes back to both classical and Judeo-Christian doctrines. Contemporary philosophers have cast off these metaphysical and religious shackles and freely invoke the dignity of mankind without needing to justify the idea at all. Why should we not attribute "intrinsic dignity" or "intrinsic worth" to ourselves? Fellow-humans are unlikely to reject the accolades we so generously bestow on them, and those to whom we deny the honor are unable to object. Indeed, when one thinks only of humans, it can be very liberal, very progressive, to talk of the dignity of all human beings. In so doing, we implicitly condemn slavery, racism, and other violations of human rights. We admit that we ourselves are in some fundamental sense on a par with the poorest, most ignorant members of our own species. It is only when we think of humans as no more than a small sub-group of all the beings that inhabit our planet that we may realize that in elevating our own species we are at the same time lowering the relative status of all other species.

The truth is that the appeal to the intrinsic dignity of human beings appears to solve the egalitarian's problems only as long as it goes unchallenged. Once we ask *why* it should be that all humans—including infants, mental defectives, psychopaths, Hitler, Stalin and the rest—have some kind of dignity or worth that no elephant, pig or chimpanzee can ever achieve, we see that this question is as difficult to answer as our original request for some relevant fact that justifies the inequality of humans and other animals. In fact, these two questions are really one: talk of intrinsic dignity or moral worth only takes the problem back one step, because any satisfactory defence of the claim that all and only humans have intrinsic dignity would need to refer to some relevant capacities or characteristics that all and only humans possess. Philosophers frequently introduce ideas of dignity, respect and worth at the point at which other reasons appear to be lacking, but this is hardly good enough. Fine phrases are the last resource of those who have run out of arguments.

In case there are those who still think it may be possible to find some relevant characteristic that distinguishes all humans from all members of other species, I shall refer again, before I conclude, to the existence of some humans who quite clearly are below the level of awareness, self-consciousness, intelligence, and sentience, of many non-humans. I am thinking of humans with severe and irreparable brain damage, and also of infant humans. To avoid the complication of the relevance of a being's potential, however, I shall henceforth concentrate on permanently retarded humans.

Philosophers who set out to find a characteristic that will distinguish humans from other animals rarely take the course of abandoning these groups of humans by lumping them in with the other animals. It is easy to see why they do not. To take this line without re-thinking our attitudes to other animals would entail that we have the right to perform painful experiments on retarded humans for trivial reasons; similarly it would follow that we had the right to rear and kill these humans for food. To most philosophers these consequences are as unacceptable as the view that we should stop treating non-humans in this way.

Of course, when discussing the problem of equality it is possible to ignore the problem of mental defectives, or brush it aside as if somehow insignificant. This is the easiest way out. What else remains? My final example of speciesism in contemporary philosophy has been selected to show what happens when a writer is prepared to face the question of human equality and animal inequality without ignoring the existence of mental defectives, and without resorting to obscurantist mumbo-jumbo. Stanley Benn's clear and honest article "Egalitarianism and Equal Consideration of Interests"[10] fits this description.

Benn after noting the usual "evident human inequalities" argues, correctly I think, for equality of consideration as the only possible basis for egalitarianism. Yet Benn, like other writers, is thinking only of "equal consideration of human interests." Benn is quite open in his defence of this restriction of equal consideration:

. . . not to possess human shape *is* a disqualifying condition. However faithful or intelligent a dog may be, it would be a monstrous sentimentality to attribute to him interests that could be weighed in an equal balance with those of human beings . . . if, for instance, one had to decide between feeding a hungry baby or a hungry dog, anyone who chose the dog would generally be reckoned morally defective, unable to recognize a fundamental inequality of claims.

This is what distinguishes our attitude to animals from our attitude to imbeciles. It would be odd to say that we ought to respect equally the dignity or personality of the imbecile and of the rational man . . . but there is nothing odd about saying that we should respect their interests equally, that is, that we should give to the interests of each the same serious consideration as claims to considerations necessary for some standard of well-being that we can recognize and endorse.

Benn's statement of the basis of the consideration we should have for imbeciles seems to me correct, but why should there be any fundamental inequality of claims between a dog and a human imbecile? Benn sees that if equal consideration depended on rationality, no reason could be given against using imbeciles for research purposes, as we now use dogs and guinea pigs. This will not do: "But of course we do distinguish imbeciles from animals in this regard," he says. That the common distinction is justifiable is something Benn does not question; his problem is how it is to be justified. The answer he gives is this:

. . . we respect the interests of men and give them priority over dogs not *insofar* as they are rational, but because rationality is the human norm. We say it is *unfair* to exploit the deficiencies of the imbecile who falls short of the norm, just as it would be unfair, and not just ordinarily dishonest, to steal from a blind man. If we do not think in this way about dogs, it is because we do not see the irrationality of the dog as a deficiency or a handicap, but as normal for the species. The characteristics, therefore, that distinguish the normal man from the normal dog make it intelligible for us to talk of other men having interests and capacities, and therefore claims, of precisely the same kind as we make on our own behalf. But although these characteristics may provide the point of the distinction between men and other species, they are not in fact the qualifying conditions for membership, or the distinguishing criteria of the class of morally considerable persons; and this is precisely because a man does not become a member of a different species, with its own standards of normality, by reason of not possessing these characteristics.

The final sentence of this passage gives the argument away. An imbecile, Benn concedes, may have no characteristics superior to those of a dog; nevertheless this does not make the imbecile a member of "a different species" as the dog is. *Therefore* it would be "unfair" to use the imbecile for medical research as we use the dog. But why? That the imbecile is not rational is just the way things have worked out, and the same is true of the dog—neither is any more responsible for their mental level. If it is unfair to take advantage of an isolated defect, why is it fair to take advantage of a more general limitation? I find it hard to see anything in this argument except a defence of preferring the interests of members of our own species because they are members of our own species. To those who think there might be more to it, I suggest the following mental exercise. Assume that it has been proven that there is a difference in the average, or normal, intelligence quotient for two different races, say whites and blacks. Then substitute the term "white" for every occurrence of "men" and "black" for every occurrence of "dog" in the passage quoted; and substitute "high I.Q." for "rationality" and when Benn talks of "imbeciles" replace this term by "dumb whites"—that is, whites who fall well below the normal white I.Q. score. Finally, change "species" to "race." Now re-read the passage. It has become a defence of a rigid, no-exceptions division between whites and blacks, based on I.Q. scores, *not withstanding an admitted overlap* between whites and blacks in this respect. The revised passage is, of course, outrageous, and this not only because we have made fictitious assumptions in our substitutions. The point is that in the original passage Benn was defending a

rigid division in the amount of consideration due to members of different species, despite admitted cases of overlap. If the original did not, at first reading strike us as being as outrageous as the revised version does, this is largely because although we are not racists ourselves, most of us are speciesists. Like the other articles, Benn's stands as a warning of the ease with which the best minds can fall victim to a prevailing ideology.

NOTES

1. *The Methods of Ethics* (7th Ed.) p. 382.

2. *Introduction to the Principles of Morals and Legislation*, ch. XVII.

3. In order to produce 1 lb. of protein in the form of beef or veal, we must feed 21 lbs. of protein to the animal. Other forms of livestock are slightly less inefficient, but the average ratio in the U.S. is still 1:8. It has been estimated that the amount of protein lost to humans in this way is equivalent to 90% of the annual world protein deficit.

4. Although one might think that killing a being is obviously the ultimate wrong one can do to it, I think that the infliction of suffering is a clearer indication of speciesism because it might be argued that at least part of what is wrong with killing a human is that most humans are conscious of their existence over time, and have desires and purposes that extend into the future. Of course, if one took this view one would have to hold that killing a human infant or mental defective is not in itself wrong, and is less serious than killing certain higher mammals that probably do have a sense of their own existence over time.

5. Ruth Harrison, *Animal Machines* (Stuart, London, 1964).

6. In R. Brandt (ed.) *Social Justice* (Prentice Hall, Englewood Cliffs, 1962): the passage quoted appears on p. 19.

7. Frankena, *op. cit.*, p. 23.

8. H. A. Bedau, "Egalitarianism and the Idea of Equality" in *Nomos IX: Equality*, ed. J. R. Pennock and J. W. Chapman, New York, 1967.

9. G. Vlastos, "Justice and Equality" in Brandt. *Social Justice*, p. 48.

10. *Nomos IX: Equality:* the passages quoted are on p. 62ff.

The Case for Animal Rights

TOM REGAN

I regard myself as an advocate of animal rights—as a part of the animal rights movement. That movement, as I conceive it, is committed to a number of goals, including:

- the total abolition of the use of animals in science;
- the total dissolution of commercial animal agriculture;
- the total elimination of commercial and sport hunting and trapping.

There are, I know, people who profess to believe in animal rights but do not avow these goals. Factory farming, they say, is wrong—it violates animals' rights—but traditional animal agriculture is all right. Toxicity tests of cosmetics on animals violates their rights, but important medical research—cancer research, for example—does not. The clubbing of baby seals is abhorrent, but not the harvesting of adult seals. I used to think I understood this reasoning. Not any more. You don't change unjust institutions by tidying them up.

What's wrong—fundamentally wrong—with the way animals are treated isn't the details that vary from case to case. It's the whole system. The forlornness of the veal calf is pathetic, heart wrenching; the pulsing pain of the chimp with electrodes planted deep in her brain is repulsive; the slow, tortuous death of the raccoon caught in the leg-hold trap is agonizing. But what is wrong isn't the pain, isn't the suffering, isn't the deprivation. These compound what's wrong. Sometimes—often—they make it much, much worse. But they are not the fundamental wrong.

The fundamental wrong is the system that allows us to view animals as *our resources*, here for *us*—to be eaten, or surgically manipulated, or exploited for sport or money. Once we accept this view of animals—as

our resources—the rest is as predictable as it is regrettable. Why worry about their loneliness, their pain, their death? Since animals exist for us, to benefit us in one way or another, what harms them really doesn't matter—or matters only if it starts to bother us, makes us feel a trifle uneasy when we eat our veal escalope, for example. So, yes, let us get veal calves out of solitary confinement, give them more space, a little straw, a few companions. But let us keep our veal escalope.

But a little straw, more space and a few companions won't eliminate—won't even touch—the basic wrong that attaches to our viewing and treating these animals as our resources. A veal calf killed to be eaten after living in close confinement is viewed and treated in this way: but so, too, is another who is raised (as they say) 'more humanely'. To right the wrong of our treatment of farm animals requires more than making rearing methods 'more humane'; it requires the total dissolution of commercial animal agriculture.

How we do this, whether we do it or, as in the case of animals in science, whether and how we abolish their use—these are to a large extent political questions. People must change their beliefs before they change their habits. Enough people, especially those elected to public office, must believe in change—must want it—before we will have laws that protect the rights of animals. This process of change is very complicated, very demanding, very exhausting, calling for the efforts of many hands in education, publicity, political organization and activity, down to the licking of envelopes and stamps. As a trained and practising philosopher, the sort of contribution I can make is limited but, I like to think, important. The currency of philosophy is ideas—their meaning and rational foundation—not the nuts and bolts of the legislative process, say, or the mechanics of community organization. That's what I have been exploring over the past ten years or so in my essays and talks and, most recently, in my book, *The Case for Animal Rights*. I believe the major conclusions I reach in the book are true because they are supported by the weight of the best arguments. I believe the idea of animal rights has reason, not just emotion, on its side.

In the space I have at my disposal here I can only sketch, in the barest outline, some of the main features of the book. [Its] main themes—and we should not be surprised by this—involve asking and answering deep, foundational moral questions about what morality is, how it should be understood and what is the best moral theory, all considered. I hope I can convey something of the shape I think this theory takes. The attempt to do this will be (to use a word a friendly critic once used to describe my work) cerebral, perhaps too cerebral. But this is misleading. My feelings about how animals are sometimes treated run just as deep and just as strong as those of my more volatile compatriots. Philosophers do—to use the jargon of the day—have a right side to their brains. If it's the left side we contribute (or mainly should), that's because what talents we have reside there.

How to proceed? We begin by asking how the moral status of animals has been understood by thinkers who deny that animals have rights. Then we test the mettle of their ideas by seeing how well they stand up under the heat of fair criticism. If we start our thinking in this way, we soon find that some people believe that we have no duties directly to animals, that we owe nothing to them, that we can do nothing that wrongs them. Rather, we can do wrong acts that involve animals, and so we have duties regarding them, though none to them. Such views may be called indirect duty views. By way of illustration: suppose your neighbour kicks your dog. Then your neighbour has done something wrong. But not to your dog. The wrong that has been done is a wrong to you. After all, it is wrong to upset people, and your neighbour's kicking your dog upsets you. So you are the one who is wronged, not your dog. Or again: by kicking your dog your neighbour damages your property. And since it is wrong to damage another person's property, your neighbour has done something wrong—to you, of course, not to your dog. Your neighbour no more wrongs your dog than your car would be wronged if the windshield were smashed. Your neighbour's duties involving your dog are indirect duties to you. More generally, all of our duties regarding animals are indirect duties to one another—to humanity.

How could someone try to justify such a view? Someone might say that your dog doesn't feel anything and so isn't hurt by your neighbour's kick, doesn't care about the pain since none is felt, is as unaware of anything as is your windshield. Someone might say this, but no rational person will, since, among other considerations, such a view will commit anyone who holds it to the position that no human being feels pain either—that human beings also don't care about what happens to them. A second possibility is that though both humans and your dog are hurt when kicked, it is only human pain that matters. But, again, no rational person can believe this. Pain is pain wherever it occurs. If your neighbour's causing you pain is wrong because of the pain that is caused, we cannot rationally ignore or dismiss the moral relevance of the pain that your dog feels.

Philosophers who hold indirect duty views—and many still do—have come to understand that they must avoid the two defects just noted: that is, both the view that animals don't feel anything as well as the idea that only human pain can be morally relevant. Among such thinkers the sort of view now favoured is one or other form of what is called *contractarianism.*

Here, very crudely, is the root idea: morality consists of a set of rules that individuals voluntarily agree to abide by, as we do when we sign a contract (hence the name contractrarianism). Those who understand and accept the terms of the contract are covered directly; they have rights created and recognized by, and protected in, the contract. And these contractors can also have protection spelled out for others who, though they lack the ability to understand morality and so cannot sign the contract themselves, are loved or cherished by those who can. Thus young children, for example, are unable to sign contracts and lack rights. But they are protected by the contract none the less because of the sentimental interests of others, most notably their parents. So we have, then, duties involving these children, duties regarding them, but no duties to them. Our duties in their case are indirect duties to other human beings, usually their parents.

As for animals, since they cannot understand contracts, they obviously cannot sign; and since they cannot sign, they have no rights. Like children, however, some animals are the objects of the sentimental interest of others. You, for example, love your dog or cat. So those animals that enough people care about (companion animals, whales, baby seals, the American bald eagle), though they lack rights themselves, will be protected because of the sentimental interests of people. I have, then, according to contractarianism, no duty directly to your dog or any other animal, not even the duty not to cause them pain or suffering; my duty not to hurt them is a duty I have to those people who care about what happens to them. As for other animals, where no or little sentimental interest is present—in the case of farm animals, for example, or laboratory rats—what duties we have grow weaker and weaker, perhaps to vanishing point. The pain and death they endure, though real, are not wrong if no one cares about them.

When it comes to the moral status of animals' contractarianism could be a hard view to refute if it were an adequate theoretical approach to the moral status of human beings. It is not adequate in this latter respect, however, which makes the question of its adequacy in the former case, regarding animals, utterly moot. For consider: morality, according to the (crude) contractarian position before us, consists of rules that people agree to abide by. What people? Well, enough to make a difference—enough, that is, *collectively* to have the power to enforce the rules that are drawn up in the contract. That is very well and good for the signatories but not so good for anyone who is not asked to sign. And there is nothing in contractarianism of the sort we are discussing that guarantees or requires that everyone will have a chance to participate equally in framing the rules of morality. The result is that this approach to ethics could sanction the most blatant forms of social, economic, moral and political injustice, ranging from a repressive caste system to systematic racial or sexual discrimination. Might, according to this theory, does make right. Let those who are the victims of injustice suffer as they will. It matters not so long as no one else—no contractor, or too few of them—cares about it. Such a theory takes one's moral breath away . . . as if, for example, there would be nothing wrong with apartheid in South Africa if few white South Africans were upset by it. A theory with so little to recommend it at the level of the ethics of our treatment of our fellow humans cannot have anything more to recommend it when it comes to the ethics of how we treat our fellow animals.

The version of contractarianism just examined is, as I have noted, a crude variety, and in fairness to those of a contractarian persuasion it must be noted that much more refined, subtle and ingenious varieties are possible. For example, John Rawls, in his *A Theory of Justice*, sets forth a version of contractarianism that forces contractors to ignore the accidental features of being a human being—for example, whether one is white or black, male or female, a genius or of modest intellect. Only by ignoring such features, Rawls believes, can we ensure that the principles of justice that contractors would agree upon are not based on bias or prejudice. Despite the improvement a view such as Rawls's represents over the cruder forms of contractarianism, it remains deficient: it systematically denies that we have direct duties to those human beings who do not have a sense of justice—young children, for instance, and many mentally retarded humans. And yet it seems reasonably certain that, were we to torture a young child or a retarded elder, we would be doing something that wronged him or her, not something that would be wrong if (and only if) other humans with a sense of justice were upset. And since this is true in the case of these humans, we cannot rationally deny the same in the case of animals.

Indirect duty views, then, including the best among them, fail to command our rational assent. Whatever ethical theory we should accept rationally, therefore, it must at least recognize that we have some duties directly to animals, just as we have some duties directly to each other. The next two theories I'll sketch attempt to meet this requirement.

The first I call the cruelty-kindness view. Simply stated, this says that we have a direct duty to be kind to animals and a direct duty not to be cruel to them. Despite the familiar, reassuring ring of these ideas, I do not believe that this view offers an adequate theory. To make this clearer, consider kindness. A kind person acts from a certain kind of motive—compassion or concern, for example. And that is a virtue. But there is no guarantee that a kind act is a right act. If I am a generous racist, for example, I will be inclined to act kindly towards members of my own race, favouring their interests above those of others. My kindness would be real and, so far as it goes, good. But I trust it is too obvious to require argument that my kind acts may not be above moral reproach—may, in fact, be positively wrong because rooted in injustice. So kindness, notwithstanding its status as a virtue to be encouraged, simply will not carry the weight of a theory of right action.

Cruelty fares no better. People or their acts are cruel if they display either a lack of sympathy for or, worse, the presence of enjoyment in another's suffering. Cruelty in all its guises is a bad thing, a tragic human failing. But just as a person's being motivated by kindness does not guarantee that he or she does what is right, so the absence of cruelty does not ensure that he or she avoids doing what is wrong. Many people who perform abortions, for example, are not cruel, sadistic people. But that fact alone does not settle the terribly difficult question of the morality of abortion. The case is no different when we examine the ethics of our treatment of animals. So, yes, let us be for kindness and against cruelty. But let us not suppose that being for the one and against the other answers questions about moral right and wrong.

Some people think that the theory we are looking for is utilitarianism. A utilitarian accepts two moral principles. The first is that of equality: everyone's interests count, and similar interests must be counted as having similar weight or importance. White or black, American or Iranian, human or animal—everyone's pain or frustration matter, and matter just as much as the equivalent pain or frustration of anyone else. The second principle a utilitarian accepts is that of utility: do the act that will bring about the best balance between satisfaction and frustration for everyone affected by the outcome.

As a utilitarian, then, here is how I am to approach the task of deciding what I morally ought to do: I must ask who will be affected if I choose to do one thing rather than another, how much each individual will

be affected, and where the best results are most likely to lie—which option, in other words, is most likely to bring about the best results, the best balance between satisfaction and frustration. That option, whatever it may be, is the one I ought to choose. That is where my moral duty lies.

The great appeal of utilitarianism rests with its uncompromising *egalitarianism:* everyone's interests count and count as much as the like interests of everyone else. The kind of odious discrimination that some forms of contractarianism can justify—discrimination based on race or sex, for example—seems disallowed in principle by utilitarianism, as is speciesism, systematic discrimination based on species membership.

The equality we find in utilitarianism, however, is not the sort an advocate of animal or human rights should have in mind. Utilitarianism has no room for the equal moral rights of different individuals because it has no room for their equal inherent value or worth. What has value for the utilitarian is the satisfaction of an individual's interests, not the individual whose interests they are. A universe in which you satisfy your desire for water, food and warmth is, other things being equal, better than a universe in which these desires are frustrated. And the same is true in the case of an animal with similar desires. But neither you nor the animal have any value in your own right. Only your feelings do.

Here is an analogy to help make the philosophical point clearer: a cup contains different liquids, sometimes sweet, sometimes bitter, sometimes a mix of the two. What has value are the liquids: the sweeter the better, the bitterer the worse. The cup, the container, has no value. It is what goes into it, not what they go into, that has value. For the utilitarian you and I are like the cup; we have no value as individuals and thus no equal value. What has value is what goes into us, what we serve as receptacles for; our feelings of satisfaction have positive value, our feelings of frustration negative value.

Serious problems arise for utilitarianism when we remind ourselves that it enjoins us to bring about the best consequences. What does this mean? It doesn't mean the best consequences for me alone, or for my family or friends, or any other person taken individually. No, what we must do is, roughly, as follows: we must add up (somehow!) the separate satisfactions and frustrations of everyone likely to be affected by our choice, the satisfactions in one column, the frustrations in the other. We must total each column for each of the options before us. That is what it means to say the theory is aggregative. And then we must choose that option which is most likely to bring about the best balance of totalled satisfactions over totalled frustrations. Whatever act would lead to this outcome is the one we ought morally to perform—it is where our moral duty lies. And that act quite clearly might not be the same one that would bring about the best results for me personally, or for my family or friends, or for a lab animal. The best aggregated consequences for everyone concerned are not necessarily the best for each individual.

That utilitarianism is an aggregative theory—different individuals' satisfactions or frustrations are added, or summed, or totalled—is the key objection to their theory. My Aunt Bea is old, inactive, a cranky, sour person, though not physically ill. She prefers to go on living. She is also rather rich. I could make a fortune if I could get my hands on her money, money she intends to give me in any event, after she dies, but which she refuses to give me now. In order to avoid a huge tax bite, I plan to donate a handsome sum of my profits to a local children's hospital. Many, many children will benefit from my generosity, and much joy will be brought to their parents, relatives and friends. If I don't get the money rather soon, all these ambitions will come to naught. The once-in-a-lifetime opportunity to make a real killing will be gone. Why, then, not kill my Aunt Bea? Oh, of course I *might* get caught. But I'm no fool and besides, her doctor can be counted on to co-operate (he has an eye for the same investment and I happen to know a good deal about his shady past). The deed can be done . . . professionally, shall we say. There is *very* little chance of getting caught. And as for my conscience being guilt-ridden, I am a resourceful sort of fellow and will take more than sufficient comfort—as I lie on the beach at Acapulco—in contemplating the joy and health I have brought to so many others.

Suppose Aunt Bea is killed and the rest of the story comes out as told. Would I have done anything wrong? Anything immoral? One would have thought that I had. Not according to utilitarianism. Since what I have done has brought about the best balance between totalled satisfaction and frustration for all those affected by the outcome, my action is not wrong. Indeed, in killing Aunt Bea the physician and I did what duty required.

This same kind of argument can be repeated in all sorts of cases, illustrating, time after time, how the utilitarian's position leads to results that impartial people find morally callous. It *is* wrong to kill my Aunt Bea in the name of bringing about the best results for others. A good end does not justify an evil means. Any adequate moral theory will have to explain why this is so. Utilitarianism fails in this respect and so cannot be the theory we seek.

What to do? Where to begin anew? The place to begin, I think, is with the utilitarian's view of the value of the individual—or, rather, lack of value. In its place, suppose we consider that you and I, for example, do have value as individuals—what we'll call *inherent value*. To say we have such value is to say that we are something more than, something different from, mere receptacles. Moreover, to ensure that we do not pave the way for such injustices as slavery or sexual discrimination, we must believe that all who have inherent value have it equally, regardless of their sex, race, religion, birthplace and so on. Similarly to be discarded as irrelevant are one's talents or skills, intelligence and wealth, personality or pathology, whether one is loved and admired or despised and loathed. The genius and the retarded child, the prince and the pauper, the brain surgeon and the fruit vendor, Mother Teresa and the most unscrupulous used-car salesman—all have inherent value, all possess it equally, and all have an equal right to be treated with respect, to be treated in ways that do not reduce them to the status of things, as if they existed as resources for others. My value as an individual is independent of my usefulness to you. Yours is not dependent on your usefulness to me. For either of us to treat the other in ways that fail to show respect for the other's independent value is to act immorally, to violate the individual's rights.

Some of the rational virtues of this view—what I call the rights view—should be evident. Unlike (crude) contractarianism, for example, the rights view *in principle* denies the moral tolerability of any and all forms of racial, sexual or social discrimination; and unlike utilitarianism, this view *in principle* denies that we can justify good results by using evil means that violate an individual's rights—denies, for example, that it could be moral to kill my Aunt Bea to harvest beneficial consequences for others. That would be to sanction the disrespectful treatment of the individual in the name of the social good, something the rights view will not—categorically will not—ever allow.

The rights view, I believe, is rationally the most satisfactory moral theory. It surpasses all other theories in the degree to which it illuminates and explains the foundation of our duties to one another—the domain of human morality. On this score it has the best reasons, the best arguments, on its side. Of course, if it were possible to show that only human beings are included within its scope, then a person like myself, who believes in animal rights, would be obliged to look elsewhere.

But attempts to limit its scope to humans only can be shown to be rationally defective. Animals, it is true, lack many of the abilities humans possess. They can't read, do higher mathematics, build a bookcase or make *baba ghanoush*. Neither can many human beings, however, and yet we don't (and shouldn't) say that they (these humans) therefore have less inherent value, less of a right to be treated with respect, than do others. It is the *similarities* between those human beings who most clearly, most non-controversially have such value (the people reading this, for example), not our differences, that matter most. And the really crucial, the basic similarity is simply this: we are each of us the experiencing subject of a life, a conscious creature having an individual welfare that has importance to us whatever our usefulness to others. We want and prefer things, believe and feel things, recall and expect things. And all these dimensions of our life, including our pleasure and pain, our enjoyment and suffering, our satisfaction and frustration, our continued existence or our untimely death—all make a difference to the quality of our life as lived, as experienced, by us as

individuals. As the same is true of those animals that concern us (the ones that are eaten and trapped, for example), they too must be viewed as the experiencing subjects of a life, with inherent value of their own.

Some there are who resist the idea that animals have inherent value. 'Only humans have such value,' they profess. How might this narrow view be defended? Shall we say that only humans have the requisite intelligence, or autonomy, or reason? But there are many, many humans who fail to meet these standards and yet are reasonably viewed as having value above and beyond their usefulness to others. Shall we claim that only humans belong to the right species, the species *Homo sapiens*? But this is blatant speciesism. Will it be said, then, that all—and only—humans have immortal souls? Then our opponents have their work cut out for them. I am myself not ill-disposed to the proposition that there are immortal souls. Personally, I profoundly hope I have one. But I would not want to rest my position on a controversial ethical issue on the even more controversial question about who or what has an immortal soul. That is to dig one's hole deeper, not to climb out. Rationally, it is better to resolve moral issues without making more controversial assumptions than are needed. The question of who has inherent value is such a question, one that is resolved more rationally without the introduction of the idea of immortal souls than by its use.

Well, perhaps some will say that animals have some inherent value, only less than we have. Once again, however, attempts to defend this view can be shown to lack rational justification. What could be the basis of our having more inherent value than animals? Their lack of reason, or autonomy, or intellect? Only if we are willing to make the same judgement in the case of humans who are similarly deficient. But it is not true that such humans—the retarded child, for example, or the mentally deranged—have less inherent value than you or I. Neither, then, can we rationally sustain the view that animals like them in being the experiencing subjects of a life have less inherent value. *All* who have inherent value have it *equally*, whether they be human animals or not.

Inherent value, then, belongs equally to those who are the experiencing subjects of a life. Whether it belongs to others—to rocks and rivers, trees and gla-ciers, for example—we do not know and may never know. But neither do we need to know, if we are to make the case for animal rights. We do not need to know, for example, how many people are eligible to vote in the next presidential election before we can know whether I am. Similarly, we do not need to know how many individuals have inherent value before we can know that some do. When it comes to the case for animal rights, then, what we need to know is whether the animals that, in our culture, are routinely eaten, hunted and used in our laboratories, for example, are like us in being subjects of a life. And we do know this. We do know that many—literally, billions and billions—of these animals are the subjects of a life in the sense explained and so have inherent value if we do. And since, in order to arrive at the best theory of our duties to one another, we must recognize our equal inherent value as individuals, reason—not sentiment, not emotion—reason compels us to recognize the equal inherent value of these animals and, with this, their equal right to be treated with respect.

That, *very* roughly, is the shape and feel of the case for animal rights. Most of the details of the support-ing argument are missing. They are to be found in the book to which I alluded earlier. Here, the details go begging, and I must, in closing, limit myself to four final points.

The first is how the theory that underlies the case for animal rights shows that the animal rights move-ment is a part of, not antagonistic to, the human rights movement. The theory that rationally grounds the rights of animals also grounds the rights of humans. Thus those involved in the animal rights movement are partners in the struggle to secure respect for human rights—the rights of women, for example, or minorities, or workers. The animal rights movement is cut from the same moral cloth as these.

Second, having set out the broad outlines of the rights view, I can now say why its implications for farming and science, among other fields, are both clear and uncompromising. In the case of the use of animals in science, the rights view is categorically abolition-ist. Lab animals are not our tasters; we are not their kings. Because these animals are treated routinely,

systematically as if their value were reducible to their usefulness to others, they are routinely, systematically treated with a lack of respect, and thus are their rights routinely, systematically violated. This is just as true when they are used in trivial, duplicative, unnecessary or unwise research as it is when they are used in studies that hold out real promise of human benefits. We can't justify harming or killing a human being (my Aunt Bea, for example) just for these sorts of reason. Neither can we do so even in the case of so lowly a creature as a laboratory rat. It is not just refinement or reduction that is called for, not just larger, cleaner cages, not just more generous use of anaesthetic or the elimination of multiple surgery, not just tidying up the system. It is complete replacement. The best we can do when it comes to using animals in science is—not to use them. That is where our duty lies, according to the rights view.

As for commercial animal agriculture, the rights view takes a similar abolitionist position. The funda-mental moral wrong here is not that animals are kept in stressful close confinement or in isolation, or that their pain and suffering, their needs and preferences are ignored or discounted. All these *are* wrong, of course, but they are not fundamentally wrong. They are symptoms and effects of the deeper, systematic wrong that allows these animals to be viewed and treated as lacking independent value, as resources for us—as, indeed, a renewable resource. Giving farm ani-mals more space, more natural environments, more companions does not right the fundamental wrong, any more than giving lab animals more anaesthesia or bigger, cleaner cages would right the fundamental wrong in their case. Nothing less than the total disso-lution of commercial animal agriculture will do this, just as, for similar reasons I won't develop at length here, morality requires nothing less than the total elimination of hunting and trapping for commercial and sporting ends. The rights view's implications, then, as I have said, are clear and uncompromising.

My last two points are about philosophy, my pro-fession. It is, most obviously, no substitute for politi-cal action. The words I have written here and in other places by themselves don't change a thing. It is what we do with the thoughts that the words express—our acts, our deeds—that changes things. All that philosophy can do, and all I have attempted, is to offer a vision of what our deeds should aim at. And the why. But not the how.

Finally, I am reminded of my thoughtful critic, the one I mentioned earlier, who chastised me for being too cerebral. Well, cerebral I have been: indirect duty views, utilitarianism, contractarianism—hardly the stuff deep passions are made of. I am also reminded, however, of the image another friend once set before me—the image of the ballerina as expressive of disciplined passion. Long hours of sweat and toil, of loneliness and practice, of doubt and fatigue: those are the discipline of her craft. But the passion is there too, the fierce drive to excel, to speak through her body, to do it right, to pierce our minds. That is the image of philosophy I would leave with you, not 'too cerebral' but

disciplined passion. Of the discipline enough has been seen. As for the passion: there are times, and these not infrequent, when tears come to my eyes when I see, or read, or hear of the wretched plight of animals in the hands of humans. Their pain, their suffering, their loneliness, their innocence, their death. Anger. Rage. Pity. Sorrow. Disgust. The whole creation groans under the weight of the evil we humans visit upon these mute, powerless creatures. It *is* our hearts, not just our heads, that call for an end to it all, that demand of us that we overcome, for them, the habits and forces behind their systematic oppression. All great movements, it is written, go through three stages: ridicule, discussion, adoption. It is the realization of this third stage, adoption, that requires both our passion and our discipline, our hearts and our heads. The fate of animals is in our hands. God grant we are equal to the task.

Difficulties with the Strong Animal Rights Position

Mary Anne Warren

Tom Regan has produced what is perhaps the definitive defense of the view that the basic moral rights of at least some non-human animals are in no way inferior to our own. In *The Case for Animal Rights*, he argues that all normal mammals over a year of age have the same basic moral rights.[1] Non-human mammals have essentially the same right not to be harmed or killed as we do. I shall call this "the strong animal rights position," although it is weaker than the claims made by some animal liberationists in that it ascribes rights to only some sentient animals.

I will argue that Regan's case for the strong animal rights position is unpersuasive and that this position entails consequences which a reasonable person cannot accept. I do not deny that some non-human animals have moral rights; indeed, I would extend

the scope of the rights claim to include all sentient animals, that is, all those capable of having experiences, including experiences of pleasure or satisfaction and pain, suffering, or frustration.[2] However, I do not think that the moral rights of most non-human animals are identical in strength to those of persons.[3] The rights of most non-human animals may be overridden in circumstances which would not justify overriding the rights of persons. There are, for instance, compelling realities which sometimes require that we kill animals for reasons which could not justify the killing of persons. I will call this view "the weak animal rights" position, even though it ascribes rights to a wider range of animals than does the strong animal rights position.

I will begin by summarizing Regan's case for the strong animal rights position and noting two problems with it. Next, I will explore some consequences of the strong animal rights position which I think are unacceptable. Finally, I will outline the case for the weak animal rights position.

Mary Anne Warren, "A Critique of Regan's Animal Rights Theory," *Between the Species* Vol. 2, No. 4 (Fall 1987): 433–441. Reprinted with permission from Between the Species.

REGAN'S CASE

Regan's argument moves through three stages. First, he argues that normal, mature mammals are not only sentient but have other mental capacities as well. These include the capacities for emotion, memory, belief, desire, the use of general concepts, intentional action, a sense of the future, and some degree of self-awareness. Creatures with such capacities are said to be subjects-of-a-life. They are not only alive in the biological sense but have a psychological identity over time and an existence which can go better or worse for them. Thus, they can be harmed or benefited. These are plausible claims, and well defended. One of the strongest parts of the book is the rebuttal of philosophers, such as R. G. Frey, who object to the application of such mentalistic terms to creatures that do not use a human-style language. The second and third stages of the argument are more problematic.

In the second stage, Regan argues that subjects-of-a-life have inherent value. His concept of inherent value grows out of his opposition to utilitarianism. Utilitarian moral theory, he says, treats individuals as "mere receptacles" for morally significant value, in that harm to one individual may be justified by the production of a greater net benefit to other individuals. In opposition to this, he holds that subjects-of-a-life have a value independent of both the value they may place upon their lives or experiences and the value others may place upon them.

Inherent value, Regan argues, does not come in degrees. To hold that some individuals have more inherent value than others is to adopt a "perfectionist" theory, i.e., one which assigns different moral worth to individuals according to how well they are thought to exemplify some virtue(s), such as intelligence or moral autonomy. Perfectionist theories have been used, at least since the time of Aristotle, to rationalize such injustices as slavery and male domination, as well as the unrestrained exploitation of animals. Regan argues that if we reject these injustices, then we must also reject perfectionism and conclude that all subjects-of-a-life have equal inherent value. Moral agents have no more inherent value than moral patients, i.e., subjects-of-a-life who are not morally responsible for their actions.

In the third phase of the argument, Regan uses the thesis of equal inherent value to derive strong moral rights for all subjects-of-a-life. This thesis underlies the Respect Principle, which forbids us to treat beings who have inherent value as mere receptacles, i.e., mere means to the production of the greatest overall good. This principle, in turn, underlies the Harm Principle, which says that we have a direct *prima facie* duty not to harm beings who have inherent value. Together, these principles give rise to moral rights. Rights are defined as valid claims, claims to certain goods and against certain beings, i.e., moral agents. Moral rights generate duties not only to refrain from inflicting harm upon beings with inherent value but also to come to their aid when they are threatened by other moral agents. Rights are not absolute but may be overridden in certain circumstances. Just what these circumstances are we will consider later. But first, let's look at some difficulties in the theory as thus far presented.

THE MYSTERY OF INHERENT VALUE

Inherent value is a key concept in Regan's theory. It is the bridge between the plausible claim that all normal, mature mammals—human or otherwise—are subjects-of-a-life and the more debatable claim that they all have basic moral rights of the same strength. But it is a highly obscure concept, and its obscurity makes it ill-suited to play this crucial role.

Inherent value is defined almost entirely in negative terms. It is not dependent upon the value which either the inherently valuable individual or anyone else may place upon that individual's life or experiences. It is not (necessarily) a function of sentience or any other mental capacity, because, Regan says, some entities which are not sentient (e.g., trees, rivers, or rocks) may, nevertheless, have inherent value (p. 246). It cannot attach to anything other than an individual; species, eco-systems, and the like cannot have inherent value.

These are some of the things which inherent value is not. But what is it? Unfortunately, we are not told. Inherent value appears as a mysterious non-natural property which we must take on faith. Regan says that it is a *postulate* that subjects-of-a-life have inherent value, a postulate justified by the fact that it avoids certain absurdities which he thinks follow from a purely utilitarian theory (p. 247). But why is the postulate that *subjects-of-a-life* have inherent value? If the inherent value of a being is completely independent of the value that it or anyone else places upon its experiences, then why does the fact that it has certain sorts of experiences constitute evidence that it has inherent value? If the reason is that subjects-of-a-life have an existence which can go better or worse for them, then why isn't the appropriate conclusion that all sentient beings have inherent value, since they would all seem to meet that condition? Sentient but mentally unsophisticated beings may have a less extensive range of possible satisfactions and frustrations, but why should it follow that they have—or may have—no inherent value at all?

In the absence of a positive account of inherent value, it is also difficult to grasp the connection between being inherently valuable and having moral rights. Intuitively, it seems that value is one thing, and rights are another. It does not seem incoherent to say that some things (e.g., mountains, rivers, redwood trees) are inherently valuable and yet are not the sorts of things which can have moral rights. Nor does it seem incoherent to ascribe inherent value to some things which are not individuals, e.g., plant or animal species, though it may well be incoherent to ascribe moral rights to such things.

In short, the concept of inherent value seems to create at least as many problems as it solves. If inherent value is based on some natural property, then why not try to identify that property and explain its moral significance, without appealing to inherent value? And if it is not based on any natural property, then why should we believe in it? That it may enable us to avoid some of the problems faced by the utilitarian is not a sufficient reason, if it creates other problems which are just as serious.

IS THERE A SHARP LINE?

Perhaps the most serious problems are those that arise when we try to apply the strong animal rights position to animals other than normal, mature mammals.

Regan's theory requires us to divide all living things into two categories: those which have the same inherent value and the same basic moral rights that we do, and those which have no inherent value and presumably no moral rights. But wherever we try to draw the line, such a sharp division is implausible.

It would surely be arbitrary to draw such a sharp line between normal, mature mammals and all other living things. Some birds (e.g., crows, magpies, parrots, mynahs) appear to be just as mentally sophisticated as most mammals and thus are equally strong candidates for inclusion under the subject-of-a-life criterion. Regan is not in fact advocating that we draw the line here. His claim is only that normal mature mammals are clear cases, while other cases are less clear. Yet, on his theory, there must be such a sharp line *somewhere*, since there are no degrees of inherent value. But why should we believe that there is a sharp line between creatures that are subjects-of-a-life and creatures that are not? Isn't it more likely that "subjecthood" comes in degrees, that some creatures have only a little self-awareness, and only a little capacity to anticipate the future, while some have a little more, and some a good deal more?

Should we, for instance, regard fish, amphibians, and reptiles as subjects-of-a-life? A simple yes-or-no answer seems inadequate. On the one hand, some of their behavior is difficult to explain without the assumption that they have sensations, beliefs, desires, emotions, and memories; on the other hand, they do not seem to exhibit very much self-awareness or very much conscious anticipation of future events. Do they have enough mental sophistication to count as subjects-of-a-life? Exactly how much is enough?

It is still more unclear what we should say about insects, spiders, octopi, and other invertebrate animals which have brains and sensory organs but whose minds (if they have minds) are even more alien to us than those of fish or reptiles. Such creatures are probably sentient. Some people doubt that they can feel pain, since they lack certain neurological structures which are crucial to the processing of pain impulses in vertebrate animals. But this argument is inconclusive, since their nervous systems might process pain in ways different from ours. When injured, they sometimes act as if they are in pain. On evolutionary grounds, it seems unlikely that highly mobile creatures with complex sensory systems would not have developed a capacity for pain (and pleasure), since such a capacity has obvious survival value. It must, however, be admitted that we do not *know* whether spiders can feel pain (or something very like it), let alone whether they have emotions, memories, beliefs, desires, self-awareness, or a sense of the future.

Even more mysterious are the mental capacities (if any) of mobile microfauna. The brisk and efficient way that paramecia move about in their incessant search for food *might* indicate some kind of sentience, in spite of their lack of eyes, ears, brains, and other organs associated with sentience in more complex organisms. It is conceivable—though not very probable—that they, too, are subjects-of-a-life.

The existence of a few unclear cases need not pose a serious problem for a moral theory, but in this case, the unclear cases constitute most of those with which an adequate theory of animal rights would need to deal. The subject-of-a-life criterion can provide us with little or no moral guidance in our interactions with the vast majority of animals. That might be acceptable if it could be supplemented with additional principles which would provide such guidance. However, the radical dualism of the theory precludes supplementing it in this way. We are forced to say that either a spider has the same right to life as you and I do, or it has no right to life whatever—and that only the gods know which of these alternatives is true.

Regan's suggestion for dealing with such unclear cases is to apply the "benefit of the doubt" principle. That is, when dealing with beings that may or may not be subjects-of-a-life, we should act as if they are. But if we try to apply this principle to the entire range of doubtful cases, we will find ourselves with moral obligations which we cannot possibly fulfill. In many climates, it is virtually impossible to live without swatting mosquitoes and exterminating cockroaches, and not all of us can afford to hire someone to sweep the path before we walk, in order to make sure that we do not step on ants. Thus, we are still faced with the daunting task of drawing a sharp line somewhere on the continuum of life forms—this time, a line demarcating the limits of the benefit of the doubt principle.

The weak animal rights theory provides a more plausible way of dealing with this range of cases, in that it allows the rights of animals of different kinds to vary in strength. . . .

* * *

WHY ARE ANIMAL RIGHTS WEAKER THAN HUMAN RIGHTS?

How can we justify regarding the rights of persons as generally stronger than those of sentient beings which are not persons? There are a plethora of bad justifications, based on religious premises or false or unprovable claims about the differences between human and non-human nature. But there is one difference which has a clear moral relevance: people are at least sometimes capable of being moved to action or inaction by the force of reasoned argument. Rationality rests upon other mental capacities, notably those which Regan cites as criteria for being a subject-of-a-life. We share these capacities with many other animals. But it is not just because we are subjects-of-a-life that we are both able and morally compelled to recognize one another as beings with equal basic moral rights. It is also because we are able to "listen to reason" in order to settle our conflicts and cooperate in shared projects. This capacity, unlike the others, may require something like a human language.

Why is rationality morally relevant? It does not make us "better" than other animals or more "perfect." It does not even automatically make us more intelligent. (Bad reasoning reduces our effective intelligence rather than increasing it.) But it is morally relevant insofar as it provides greater possibilities for cooperation and for the nonviolent resolution of problems. It also makes us more dangerous than non-rational beings can ever be. Because we are potentially more dangerous and less predictable than wolves, we need an articulated system of morality to regulate our conduct. Any human morality, to be workable in the long run, must recognize the equal moral status of all persons, whether through the postulate of equal basic moral rights or in some other way. The recognition of the moral equality of other persons is the price we must each pay for their recognition of our moral equality. Without this mutual recognition of moral equality, human society can exist only in a state of chronic and bitter conflict. The war between the sexes will persist so long as there is sexism and male domination; racial conflict will never be eliminated so long as there are racist laws and practices. But to the extent that we achieve a mutual recognition of equality, we can hope to live together, perhaps as peacefully as wolves, achieving (in part) through explicit moral principles what they do not seem to need explicit moral principles to achieve.

Why not extend this recognition of moral equality to other creatures, even though they cannot do the same for us? The answer is that we cannot. Because we cannot reason with most non-human animals, we cannot always solve the problems which they may cause without harming them—although we are always obligated to try. We cannot negotiate a treaty with the feral cats and foxes, requiring them to stop preying on endangered native species in return for suitable concessions on our part.

> if rats invade our houses . . . we cannot reason with them, hoping to persuade them of the injustice they do us. We can only attempt to get rid of them.[4]

Aristotle was not wrong in claiming that the capacity to alter one's behavior on the basis of reasoned argument is relevant to the full moral status which he accorded to free men. Of course, he was wrong in his other premise, that women and slaves by their nature cannot reason well enough to function as autonomous moral agents. Had that premise been true, so would his conclusion that women and slaves are not quite the moral equals of free men. In the case of most non-human animals, the corresponding premise is true. If, on the other hand, there are animals with whom we can (learn to) reason, then we are obligated to do this and to regard them as our moral equals.

Thus, to distinguish between the rights of persons and those of most other animals on the grounds that only people can alter their behavior on the basis of reasoned argument does not commit us to a perfectionist theory of the sort Aristotle endorsed. There is no excuse for refusing to recognize the moral equality of some people on the grounds that we don't regard them as quite as rational as we are, since it is perfectly clear that most people can reason well enough to determine how to act so as to respect the basic rights of others (if they choose to), and that is enough for moral equality.

But what about people who are clearly not rational? It is often argued that sophisticated mental capacities such as rationality cannot be essential for the possession of equal basic moral rights, since nearly everyone agrees that human infants and mentally incompetent persons have such rights, even though they may lack those sophisticated mental capacities. But this argument is inconclusive, because there are powerful practical and emotional reasons for protecting non-rational human beings, reasons which are absent in the case of most non-human animals. Infancy and mental incompetence are human conditions which all of us either have experienced or are likely to experience at some time. We also protect babies and mentally incompetent people because we care for them. We don't normally care for animals in the same way, and when we do—e.g., in the case of much-loved pets—we may regard them as having special rights by virtue of their relationship to us. We protect them not only for their sake but also for our own, lest we be hurt by harm done to them. Regan holds that such "side-effects" are irrelevant to moral rights, and perhaps they are. But in ordinary usage, there is no sharp line between moral rights and those moral protections which are not rights. The extension of strong moral protections to infants and the mentally impaired in no way proves that non-human animals have the same basic moral rights as people.

WHY SPEAK OF "ANIMAL RIGHTS" AT ALL?

If, as I have argued, reality precludes our treating all animals as our moral equals, then why should we still ascribe rights to them? Everyone agrees that animals are entitled to some protection against human abuse, but why speak of animal *rights* if we are not prepared to accept most animals as our moral equals? The weak animal rights position may seem an unstable compromise between the bold claim that animals have the same basic moral rights that we do and the more common view that animals have no rights at all.

It is probably impossible to either prove or disprove the thesis that animals have moral rights by producing an analysis of the concept of a moral right and checking to see if some or all animals satisfy the conditions for having rights. The concept of a moral right is complex, and it is not clear which of its strands are essential. Paradigm rights holders, i.e., mature and mentally competent persons, are *both* rational and morally autonomous beings and sentient subjects-of-a-life. Opponents of animal rights claim that rationality and moral autonomy are essential for the possession of rights, while defenders of animal rights claim that they are not. The ordinary concept of a moral right is probably not precise enough to enable us to determine who is right on purely definitional grounds.

If logical analysis will not answer the question of whether animals have moral rights, practical considerations may, nevertheless, incline us to say that they do. The most plausible alternative to the view that animals have moral rights is that, while they do not have *rights*, we are, nevertheless, obligated not to be cruel to them. Regan argues persuasively that the injunction to avoid being cruel to animals is inadequate to express our obligations towards animals, because it focuses on the mental states of those who cause animal suffering, rather than on the harm done to the animals themselves (p. 158). Cruelty is inflicting pain or suffering and either taking pleasure in that pain or suffering or being more or less indifferent to it. Thus, to express the demand for the decent treatment of animals in terms of the rejection of cruelty is to invite the too easy response that those who subject animals to suffering are not being cruel because they regret the suffering they cause but sincerely believe that what they do is justified. The injunction to avoid cruelty is also inadequate in that it does not preclude the killing of animals—for any reason, however trivial—so long as it is done relatively painlessly.

The inadequacy of the anti-cruelty view provides one practical reason for speaking of animal rights. Another practical reason is that this is an age in which nearly all significant moral claims tend to be expressed in terms of rights. Thus, the denial that animals have rights, however carefully qualified, is likely to be taken to mean that we may do whatever we like to them, provided that we do not violate any human rights. In such a context, speaking of the rights of animals may be the only way to persuade many people to take seriously protests against the abuse of animals.

Why not extend this line of argument and speak of the rights of trees, mountains, oceans, or anything else which we may wish to see protected from destruction? Some environmentalists have not hesitated to speak in this way, and, given the importance of protecting such elements of the natural world, they cannot be blamed for using this rhetorical device. But, I would argue that moral rights can meaningfully be ascribed only to entities which have some capacity for sentience. This is because moral rights are protections designed to protect rights holders from harms or to provide them with benefits which matter *to them*. Only beings capable of sentience can be harmed or benefited in ways which matter to them, for only such beings can like or dislike what happened to them or prefer some conditions to others. Thus, sentient animals, unlike mountains, rivers, or species, are at least logically possible candidates for moral rights. This fact, together with the need to end current abuses of animals—e.g., in scientific research . . . provides a plausible case for speaking of animal rights.

CONCLUSION

I have argued that Regan's case for ascribing strong moral rights to all normal, mature mammals is unpersuasive because (1) it rests upon the obscure concept of inherent value, which is defined only in negative terms, and (2) it seems to preclude any plausible answer to questions about the moral status of the vast majority of sentient animals. . . .

The weak animal rights theory asserts that (1) any creature whose natural mode of life includes the pursuit of certain satisfactions has the right not to be forced to exist without the opportunity to pursue those satisfactions; (2) that any creature which is capable of pain, suffering, or frustration has the right that such experiences not be deliberately inflicted upon it without some compelling reason; and (3) that no sentient being should be killed without good reason. However, moral rights are not an all-or-nothing affair. The strength of the reasons required to override the rights of a non-human organism varies, depending upon—among other things—the probability that it is sentient and (if it is clearly sentient) its probable degree of mental sophistication.

NOTES

1. Tom Regan, *The Case for Animal Rights* (Berkeley: University of California Press, 1983). All page references are to this edition.

2. The capacity for sentience, like all of the mental capacities mentioned in what follows, is a disposition. Dispositions do not disappear whenever they are not currently manifested. Thus, sleeping or temporarily unconscious persons or non-human animals are still sentient in the relevant sense (i.e., still capable of sentience), so long as they still have the neurological mechanisms necessary for the occurrence of experiences.

3. It is possible, perhaps probable, that some non-human animals—such as cetaceans and anthropoid apes—should be regarded as persons. If so, then the weak animal rights position holds that these animals have the same basic moral rights as human persons.

4. Bonnie Steinbock, "Speciesism and the Idea of Equality," *Philosophy* 53 (1978): 253.

The Case for the Use of Animals in Biomedical Research

CARL COHEN

Using animals as research subjects in medical investigations is widely condemned on two grounds: first, because it wrongly violates the *rights* of animals,[1] and second, because it wrongly imposes on sentient creatures much avoidable *suffering*.[2] Neither of these arguments is sound. The first relies on a mistaken understanding of rights; the second relies on a mistaken calculation of consequences. Both deserve definitive dismissal.

WHY ANIMALS HAVE NO RIGHTS

A right, properly understood, is a claim, or potential claim, that one party may exercise against another. The target against whom such a claim may be registered can be a single person, a group, a community, or (perhaps) all humankind. The content of rights claims also varies greatly: repayment of loans, nondiscrimination by employers, noninterference by the state,

Carl Cohen, "The Case for the Use of Animals in Biomedical Research," the *New England Journal of Medicine* 315 (October 2, 1986): 865–70. Copyright © 1986 Massachusetts Medical Society. Reprinted with permission from Massachusetts Medical Society.

and so on. To comprehend any genuine right fully, therefore, we must know *who* holds the right, *against whom* it is held, and *to what* it is a right.

Alternative sources of rights add complexity. Some rights are grounded in constitution and law (e.g., the right of an accused to trial by jury); some rights are moral but give no legal claims (e.g., my right to your keeping the promise you gave me); and some rights (e.g., against theft or assault) are rooted both in morals and in law.

The differing targets, contents, and sources of rights, and their inevitable conflict, together weave a tangled web. Notwithstanding all such complications, this much is clear about rights in general: they are in every case claims, or potential claims, within a community of moral agents. Rights arise, and can be intelligibly defended, only among beings who actually do, or can, make moral claims against one another. Whatever else rights may be, therefore, they are necessarily human; their possessors are persons, human beings.

The attributes of human beings from which this moral capability arises have been described variously by philosophers, both ancient and modern: the inner consciousness of a free will (Saint Augustine[3]); the grasp, by human reason, of the binding character of moral law (Saint Thomas[4]); the self-conscious participation of human beings in an objective ethical order (Hegel[5]); human membership in an organic moral community (Bradley[6]); the development of the human self through the consciousness of other moral selves (Mead[7]); and the underivative, intuitive cognition of the rightness of an action (Prichard[8]). Most influential has been Immanuel Kant's emphasis on the universal human possession of a uniquely moral will and the autonomy its use entails.[9] Humans confront choices that are purely moral; humans—but certainly not dogs or mice—lay down moral laws, for others and for themselves. Human beings are self-legislative, morally *auto-nomous*.

Animals (that is, nonhuman animals, the ordinary sense of that word) lack this capacity for free moral judgment. They are not beings of a kind capable of exercising or responding to moral claims. Animals therefore have no rights, and they can have none. This is the core of the argument about the alleged rights of animals. The holders of rights must have the capacity to comprehend rules of duty, governing all including themselves. In applying such rules, the holders of rights must recognize possible conflicts between what is in their own interest and what is just. Only in a community of beings capable of self-restricting moral judgments can the concept of a right be correctly invoked.

Humans have such moral capacities. They are in this sense self-legislative, are members of communities governed by moral rules, and do possess rights. Animals do not have such moral capacities. They are not morally self-legislative, cannot possibly be members of a truly moral community, and therefore cannot possess rights. In conducting research on animal subjects, therefore, we do not violate their rights, because they have none to violate.

To animate life, even in its simplest forms, we give a certain natural reverence. But the possession of rights presupposes a moral status not attained by the vast majority of living things. We must not infer, therefore, that a live being has, simply in being alive, a "right" to its life. The assertion that all animals, only because they are alive and have interests, also possess the "right to life"[10] is an abuse of that phrase, and wholly without warrant.

It does not follow from this, however, that we are morally free to do anything we please to animals. Certainly not. In our dealings with animals, as in our dealings with other human beings, we have obligations that do not arise from claims against us based on rights. Rights entail obligations, but many of the things one ought to do are in no way tied to another's entitlement. Rights and obligations are not reciprocals of one another, and it is a serious mistake to suppose that they are.

Illustrations are helpful. Obligations may arise from internal commitments made: physicians have obligations to their patients not grounded merely in their patients' rights. Teachers have such obligations to their students, shepherds to their dogs, and cowboys to their horses. Obligations may arise from differences of status: adults owe special care when playing with young children, and children owe special care when playing with young pets. Obligations may arise from special relationships: the payment of my son's college tuition is something to which he may have no right, although it may be my obligation to bear the burden if I reasonably can; my dog has no right to daily exercise and veterinary care, but I do have the obligation to provide these things for her. Obligations may arise from particular acts or circumstances: one may be obliged to another for a special kindness done, or obliged to put an animal out of its misery in view of its condition—although neither the human benefactor nor the dying animal may have had a claim of right.

Plainly, the grounds of our obligations to humans and to animals are manifold and cannot be formulated simply. Some hold that there is a general obligation to do no gratuitous harm to sentient creatures (the principle of nonmaleficence); some hold that there is a general obligation to do good to sentient creatures when that is reasonably within one's power (the principle of beneficence). In our dealings with animals, few will deny that we are at least obliged to act humanely—that is, to treat them with the decency and concern that we owe, as sensitive human beings, to other sentient creatures. To treat animals humanely, however, is not to treat them as humans or as the holders of rights.

A common objection, which deserves a response, may be paraphrased as follows:

> If having rights requires being able to make moral claims, to grasp and apply moral laws, then many humans— the brain-damaged, the comatose, the senile—who plainly lack those capacities must be without rights. But that is absurd. This proves [the critic concludes] that rights do not depend on the presence of moral capacities.[1,10]

This objection fails; it mistakenly treats an essential feature of humanity as though it were a screen for sorting humans. The capacity for moral judgment that distinguishes humans from animals is not a test to be administered to human beings one by one. Persons who are unable, because of some disability, to perform the full moral functions natural to human beings are certainly not for that reason ejected from the moral community. The issue is one of kind. Humans are of such a kind that they may be the subject of experiments only with their voluntary consent. The choices they make freely must be respected. Animals are of such a kind that it is impossible for them, in principle, to give or withhold voluntary consent or to make a moral choice. What humans retain when disabled, animals have never had.

A second objection, also often made, may be paraphrased as follows:

> Capacities will not succeed in distinguishing humans from the other animals. Animals also reason; animals also communicate with one another; animals also care passionately for their young; animals also exhibit desires and preferences.[11,12] Features of moral relevance—rationality, interdependence, and love— are not exhibited uniquely by human beings. Therefore [this critic concludes], there can be no solid moral distinction between humans and other animals.[10]

This criticism misses the central point. It is not the ability to communicate or to reason, or dependence on one another, or care for the young, or the exhibition of preference, or any such behavior that marks the critical divide. Analogies between human

families and those of monkeys, or between human communities and those of wolves, and the like, are entirely beside the point. Patterns of conduct are not at issue. Animals do indeed exhibit remarkable behavior at times. Conditioning, fear, instinct, and intelligence all contribute to species survival. Membership in a community of moral agents nevertheless remains impossible for them. Actors subject to moral judgment must be capable of grasping the generality of an ethical premise in a practical syllogism. Humans act immorally often enough, but only they—never wolves or monkeys—can discern, by applying some moral rule to the facts of a case, that a given act ought or ought not to be performed. The moral restraints imposed by humans on themselves are thus highly abstract and are often in conflict with the self-interest of the agent. Communal behavior among animals, even when most intelligent and most endearing, does not approach autonomous morality in this fundamental sense.

Genuinely moral acts have an internal as well as an external dimension. Thus, in law, an act can be criminal only when the guilty deed, the actus reus, is done with a guilty mind, mens rea. No animal can ever commit a crime; bringing animals to criminal trial is the mark of primitive ignorance. The claims of moral right are similarly inapplicable to them. Does a lion have a right to eat a baby zebra? Does a baby zebra have a right not to be eaten? Such questions, mistakenly invoking the concept of right where it does not belong, do not make good sense. Those who condemn biomedical research because it violates "animal rights" commit the same blunder.

IN DEFENSE OF "SPECIESISM"

Abandoning reliance on animal rights, some critics resort instead to animal sentience—their feelings of pain and distress. We ought to desist from the imposition of pain insofar as we can. Since all or nearly all experimentation on animals does impose pain and could be readily forgone, say these critics, it should be stopped. The ends sought may be worthy, but those ends do not justify imposing agonies on humans, and by animals the agonies are felt no less. The laboratory use of animals (these critics conclude) must therefore be ended—or at least very sharply curtailed.

Argument of this variety is essentially utilitarian, often expressly so[13]; it is based on the calculation of the net product, in pains and pleasures, resulting from experiments on animals. Jeremy Bentham, comparing horses and dogs with other sentient creatures, is thus commonly quoted: "The question is not, Can they reason? nor Can they talk? but, Can they suffer?" [14]

Animals certainly can suffer and surely ought not to be made to suffer needlessly. But in inferring, from these uncontroversial premises, that biomedical research causing animal distress is largely (or wholly) wrong, the critic commits two serious errors.

The first error is the assumption, often explicitly defended, that all sentient animals have equal moral standing. Between a dog and a human being, according to this view, there is no moral difference; hence the pains suffered by dogs must be weighed no differently from the pains suffered by humans. To deny such equality, according to this critic, is to give unjust preference to one species over another; it is "speciesism." The most influential statement of this moral equality of species was made by Peter Singer:

> The racist violates the principle of equality by giving greater weight to the interests of members of his own race when there is a clash between their interests and the interests of those of another race. The sexist violates the principle of equality by favoring the interests of his own sex. Similarly the speciesist allows the interests of his own species to override the greater interests of members of other species. The pattern is identical in each case.[2]

This argument is worse than unsound; it is atrocious. It draws an offensive moral conclusion from a deliberately devised verbal parallelism that is utterly specious. Racism has no rational ground whatever. Differing degrees of respect or concern for humans for no other reason than that they are members of different races is an injustice totally without foundation in the nature of the races themselves. Racists, even if acting on the basis of mistaken factual beliefs, do grave moral wrong precisely because there is no morally relevant distinction among the races. The supposition of

such differences has led to outright horror. The same is true of the sexes, neither sex being entitled by right to greater respect or concern than the other. No dispute here.

Between species of animate life, however—between (for example) humans on the one hand and cats or rats on the other—the morally relevant differences are enormous, and almost universally appreciated. Humans engage in moral reflection; humans are morally autonomous; humans are members of moral communities, recognizing just claims against their own interest. Human beings do have rights; theirs is a moral status very different from that of cats or rats.

I am a speciesist. Speciesism is not merely plausible: it is essential for right conduct, because those who will not make the morally relevant distinctions among species are almost certain, in consequence, to misapprehend their true obligations. The analogy between speciesism and racism is insidious. Every sensitive moral judgment requires that the differing natures of the beings to whom obligations are owed be considered. If all forms of animate life—or vertebrate animal life?—must be treated equally, and if therefore in evaluating a research program the pains of a rodent count equally with the pains of a human, we are forced to conclude (1) that neither humans nor rodents possess rights, or (2) that rodents possess all the rights that humans possess. Both alternatives are absurd. Yet one or the other must be swallowed if the moral equality of all species is to be defended.

Humans owe to other humans a degree of moral regard that cannot be owed to animals. Some humans take on the obligation to support and heal others, both humans and animals, as a principal duty in their lives; the fulfillment of that duty may require the sacrifice of many animals. If biomedical investigators abandon the effective pursuit of their professional objectives because they are convinced that they may not do to animals what the service of humans requires, they will fail, objectively, to do their duty. Refusing to recognize the moral differences among species is a sure path to calamity. (The largest animal rights group in the country is People for the Ethical Treatment of Animals; its codirector,

Ingrid Newkirk, calls research using animal subjects "fascism" and "supremacism." "Animal liberationists do not separate out the *human* animal," she says, "so there is no rational basis for saying that a human being has special rights. A rat is a pig is a dog is a boy. They're all mammals."[15])

Those who claim to base their objection to the use of animals in biomedical research on their reckoning of the net pleasures and pains produced make a second error, equally grave. Even if it were true—as it is surely not—that the pains of all animate beings must be counted equally, a cogent utilitarian calculation requires that we weigh all the consequences of the use, and of the nonuse, of animals in laboratory research. Critics relying (however mistakenly) on animal rights may claim to ignore the beneficial results of such research, rights being trump cards to which interest and advantage must give way. But an argument that is explicitly framed in terms of interest and benefit for all over the long run must attend also to the disadvantageous consequences of not using animals in research, and to all the achievements attained and attainable only through their use. The sum of the benefits of their use is utterly beyond quantification. The elimination of horrible disease, the increase of longevity, the avoidance of great pain, the saving of lives, and the improvement of the quality of lives (for humans and for animals) achieved through research using animals is so incalculably great that the argument of these critics, systematically pursued, establishes not their conclusion but its reverse: to refrain from using animals in biomedical research is, on utilitarian grounds, morally wrong.

When balancing the pleasures and pains resulting from the use of animals in research, we must not fail to place on the scales the terrible pains that would have resulted, would be suffered now, and would long continue had animals not been used. Every disease eliminated, every vaccine developed, every method of pain relief devised, every surgical procedure invented, every prosthetic device implanted—indeed, virtually every modern medical therapy is due, in part or in whole, to experimentation using animals. Nor may we ignore, in the balancing process, the predictable gains in human (and animal) well-being that are probably achievable in the future but that will not be achieved if the decision is made now to desist from such research or to curtail it.

Medical investigators are seldom insensitive to the distress their work may cause animal subjects. Opponents of research using animals are frequently insensitive to the cruelty of the results of the restrictions they would impose.[2] Untold numbers of human beings—real persons, although not now identifiable—would suffer grievously as the consequence of this well-meaning but shortsighted tenderness. If the morally relevant differences between humans and animals are borne in mind, and if all relevant considerations are weighed, the calculation of long-term consequences must give overwhelming support for biomedical research using animals.

CONCLUDING REMARKS

Substitution

The humane treatment of animals requires that we desist from experimenting on them if we can accomplish the same result using alternative methods—in vitro experimentation, computer simulation, or others. Critics of some experiments using animals rightly make this point.

It would be a serious error to suppose, however, that alternative techniques could soon be used in most research now using live animal subjects. No other methods now on the horizon—or perhaps ever to be available—can fully replace the testing of a drug, a procedure, or a vaccine, in live organisms. The flood of new medical possibilities being opened by the successes of recombinant DNA technology will turn to a trickle if testing on live animals is forbidden. When initial trials entail great risks, there may be no forward movement whatever without the use of live animal subjects. In seeking knowledge that may prove critical in later clinical applications, the unavailability of animals for inquiry may spell complete stymie. In the United States, federal regulations require the testing of new drugs and other products on animals, for efficacy and safety, before human beings are exposed to them.[16,17] We would not want it otherwise.

Every advance in medicine—every new drug, new operation, new therapy of any kind—must sooner or later be tried on a living being for the first time. That trial, controlled or uncontrolled, will be an experiment. The subject of that experiment, if it is not an animal, will be a human being. Prohibiting the use of live animals in biomedical research, therefore, or sharply restricting it, must result either in the blockage of much valuable research or in the replacement of animal subjects with human subjects. These are the consequences—unacceptable to most reasonable persons—of not using animals in research.

Reduction

Should we not at least reduce the use of animals in biomedical research? No, we should increase it, to avoid when feasible the use of humans as experimental subjects. Medical investigations putting human subjects at some risk are numerous and greatly varied. The risks run in such experiments are usually unavoidable, and (thanks to earlier experiments on animals) most such risks are minimal or moderate. But some experimental risks are substantial.

When an experimental protocol that entails substantial risk to humans comes before an institutional review board, what response is appropriate? The investigation, we may suppose, is promising and deserves support, so long as its human subjects are protected against unnecessary dangers. May not the investigators be fairly asked, Have you done all that you can to eliminate risk to humans by the extensive testing of that drug, that procedure, or that device on animals? To achieve maximal safety for humans we are right to require thorough experimentation on animal subjects before humans are involved.

Opportunities to increase human safety in this way are commonly missed; trials in which risks may be shifted from humans to animals are often not devised, sometimes not even considered. Why? For the investigator, the use of animals as subjects is often more expensive, in money and time, than the use of human subjects. Access to suitable human subjects is often quick and convenient, whereas access to appropriate animal subjects may be awkward, costly, and burdened with red tape. Physician-investigators have often had more experience working with human beings and know precisely where the needed pool of subjects is to be found and how they may be enlisted. Animals, and the procedures for their use, are often less familiar to these investigators. Moreover, the use of animals in place of humans is now more likely to be the target of zealous protests from without. The upshot is that humans are sometimes subjected to risks that animals could have borne, and should have borne, in their place. To maximize the protection of human subjects, I conclude, the wide and imaginative use of live animal subjects should be encouraged rather than discouraged. This enlargement in the use of animals is our obligation.

Consistency

Finally, inconsistency between the profession and the practice of many who oppose research using animals deserves comment. This frankly ad hominem observation aims chiefly to show that a coherent position rejecting the use of animals in medical research imposes costs so high as to be intolerable even to the critics themselves.

One cannot coherently object to the killing of animals in biomedical investigations while continuing to eat them. Anesthetics and thoughtful animal husbandry render the level of actual animal distress in the laboratory generally lower than that in the abattoir. So long as death and discomfort do not substantially differ in the two contexts, the consistent objector must not only refrain from all eating of animals but also protest as vehemently against others eating them as against others experimenting on them. No less vigorously must the critic object to the wearing of animal hides in coats and shoes, to employment in any industrial enterprise that uses animal parts, and to any commercial development that will cause death or distress to animals.

Killing animals to meet human needs for food, clothing, and shelter is judged entirely reasonable by most persons. The ubiquity of these uses and the virtual universality of moral support for them confront the opponent of research using animals with an inescapable difficulty. How can the many common uses of animals be judged morally worthy, while their use in scientific investigation is judged unworthy?

The number of animals used in research is but the tiniest fraction of the total used to satisfy assorted human appetites. That these appetites, often base and satisfiable in other ways, morally justify the far larger consumption of animals, whereas the quest for improved human health and understanding cannot justify the far smaller, is wholly implausible. Aside from the numbers of animals involved, the distinction in terms of worthiness of use, drawn with regard to any single animal, is not defensible. A given sheep is surely not more justifiably used to put lamb chops on the supermarket counter than to serve in testing a new contraceptive or a new prosthetic device. The needless killing of animals is wrong; if the common killing of them for our food or convenience is right, the less common but more humane uses of animals in the service of medical science are certainly not less right.

Scrupulous vegetarianism, in matters of food, clothing, shelter, commerce, and recreation, and in all other spheres, is the only fully coherent position the critic may adopt. At great human cost, the lives of fish and crustaceans must also be protected, with equal vigor, if speciesism has been forsworn. A very few consistent critics adopt this position. It is the reductio ad absurdum of the rejection of moral distinctions between animals and human beings.

Opposition to the use of animals in research is based on arguments of two different kinds—those relying on the alleged rights of animals and those relying on the consequences for animals. I have argued that arguments of both kinds must fail. We surely do have obligations to animals, but they have, and can have, no rights against us on which research can infringe. In calculating the consequences of animal research, we must weigh all the long-term benefits of the results achieved—to animals and to humans—and in that calculation we must not assume the moral equality of all animate species.

NOTES

1. Regan T. The case for animal rights. Berkeley, Calif.: University of California Press, 1983.

2. Singer P. Animal liberation. New York: Avon Books, 1977.

3. St. Augustine. Confessions. Book Seven, 397 A.D. New York: Pocket-books, 1957: 104–26.

4. St. Thomas Aquinas. Summa theologica. 127, A.D. Philosophic texts. New York: Oxford University Press, 1960:353–66.

5. Hegel GWF. Philosophy of right. 1821. London: Oxford University Press, 1952:105–10.

6. Bradley FH. Why should I be moral? 1876. In: Melden Al. ed. Ethical theories. New York: Prentice-Hall, 1950:345–59.

7. Mead GH. The genesis of the self and social control. 1925. In: Reck AJ. ed. Selected writings. Indianapolis: Bobbs-Merrill, 1964:264–93.

8. Prichard HA. Does moral philosophy rest on a mistake? 1912. In: Cellars W. Hospers J.eds. Readings in ethical theory. New York: Appleton-Century-Crofts, 1952:149–63.

9. Kant I. Fundamental principles of the metaphysic of morals. 1785. New York: Liberal Arts Press, 1949.

10. Rollin BE. Animal rights and human morality. New York: Prometheus Books, 1981.

11. Hoff C. Immoral and moral uses of animals. N Engl J Med 1980; 302:115–8.

12. Jamieson D. Killing persons and other beings. In: Miller HB. Williams WH, eds. Ethics and animals. Clifton, N.J.: Humana Press, 1983:135–46.

13. Singer P. Ten years of animal liberation. New York Review of Books, 1985: 31:46–52.

14. Bentham J. Introduction to the principles of morals and legislation. London: Athlone Press, 1970.

15. McCabe K. Who will live, who will die? Washingtonian Magazine, August 1986:115.

16. U.S. Code of Federal Regulations, Title 21, Sect. 505(i). Food, drug, and cosmetic regulations.

17. U.S. Code of Federal Regulations. Title 16, Sect. 1500. 40–2. Consumer product regulations.

How to Argue for (and Against) Ethical Veganism

Tristram McPherson

This paper has two goals. The first is to offer a carefully reasoned argument for *ethical veganism*: the view that it is (at least typically) wrong to eat or otherwise use animal products. The second goal is to give you, the reader, some important tools for developing, evaluating, and replying to reasoned arguments for ethical conclusions. I begin by offering you a brief essay, arguing that it is wrong to eat meat. This essay both introduces central elements of my case for veganism, and serves as one helpful model of a short ethics essay. In the remainder of this paper, I use the model essay as a target, to illustrate important strategies for developing objections to ethical arguments. I will also illustrate a range of important ways for the vegan to reply to these objections. You can use the models and skills I illustrate here in your own essays, and in your reasoned evaluation of ethical arguments. I conclude that the arguments and replies offered in this paper add up to a powerful reasoned case for ethical veganism. You can practice the skills I illustrate here to deciding for yourself—in a reasoned way—whether my conclusion is correct.

I begin with the promised model essay:

IT IS WRONG TO EAT MEAT

Most of us think that it would be wrong to adopt a puppy from a shelter, in order to take it home and torture it until it dies. However, we do not think it is wrong to eat a steak for dinner. In this essay, I will argue that these views are hard to square with each other, and that the second view is false: it is wrong to eat meat. My argument has the following structure:

1. It is wrong to make animals suffer
2. If it is wrong to make animals suffer, then it is wrong to kill animals

Tristam McPherson, "How to Argue for (and Against) Ethical Veganism," in Anne Barnhill, Mark Budolfson, and Tyler Doggett, ed., *Food, Ethics, and Ethical Veganism* (New York: Oxford University Press, 2016). Reprinted by permission of the author.

3. If it is wrong to kill animals, then it is wrong to eat meat

   C. It is wrong to eat meat.

This argument is *valid*. This means that the conclusion must be true if all of the premises are true. I will defend each of these premises in turn.

First, why think that it is wrong to make animals suffer? To begin, think about why it is wrong to make another person suffer. Part of the most plausible explanation is that because suffering is awful to experience, it is wrong to inflict suffering. Because an animal's suffering is awful for it, this explanation entails that it is wrong to make an animal suffer.

This premise of my argument assumes that animals *can* suffer, which is mildly controversial. For example, René Descartes suggested that animals are just complicated machines with no inner lives (1991 [1640], 148). However, Descartes' views are scientifically indefensible (see Allen and Trestman 2014, §7.1), so I set them aside.

You might object to my case for my first premise that it is only wrong to make a creature suffer if that creature is an ethical agent: the sort of being who can be morally responsible for its actions. But this is false. It is wrong to make babies suffer, and they are not ethical agents. You might object that it is only wrong to make *human beings* suffer. This is implausible for several reasons. First, think about torturing a baby: what is wrong with this is surely the nature of the suffering inflicted, not the fact that the baby has a human genetic code. Second, imagine a non-human animal with a miraculous mutation, which has the ability to speak, reason, and feel as much as you or I do. Surely the mere fact that such an animal is not genetically human does not make it okay to torture it (compare Peter Singer's argument against such "speciesism" in his 1977). And, finally, think again about the case I began this essay with: it is wrong to torture a puppy. But surely the central explanation here is just the same as with a human victim: torture will inflict horrible suffering on the puppy, and it is wrong to inflict such suffering.

Some authors, like Carl Cohen (1986, 867), insist that all suffering is not equal: human suffering is much more ethically important than animal suffering. My argument is compatible with this thesis. I am not arguing that torturing a puppy is just as bad as torturing a human being. I think the latter is typically much worse. My claim is only that making the puppy suffer is wrong, and that the pleasure a human being might take from torturing it does not justify inflicting that suffering.

Next, I argue that if it is wrong to make animals suffer, it is wrong to kill them. Some people find the idea that it is wrong to kill animals much less intuitive than the idea that it is wrong to make them suffer. However, an example shows that this combination of views—that it is wrong to make animals suffer, but not to kill them—is difficult to defend. Suppose that there is a cow that has a disease that will be fatal unless treated by giving the cow a painful medical operation. If the cow would go on to have a long and pleasant life after the operation, performing this operation seems good, not wrong. This shows that an ordinarily wrongful act—inflicting suffering on a cow—can be permissible if it is necessary to save the cow's life. But if *saving* an animal's life can justify inflicting suffering that would otherwise be wrong, it is hard to understand how *taking* that animal's life could be a matter of ethical indifference.

We can bolster this initial argument by combining it with a plausible explanation of why it is wrong to kill animals. One important reason why killing a *person* is typically wrong is that killing typically deprives the victim of an objectively valuable future. That is, killing someone deprives them of the valuable experiences activities, projects, etc. that they would otherwise have had (compare Marquis 1989, §II; I do not claim, with Marquis, that this is the "primary" thing wrong with killing). This principle applies to animals as well: just as suffering can make an animal's life go badly, pleasant experiences can make it go well. So, just as with humans, it is plausible that it is (typically) wrong to kill animals because doing so deprives them of a valuable future.

Finally, I argue that if it is wrong to kill animals, it is wrong to eat meat. Killing and eating are, obviously, not the same thing: in our economically specialized society, many meat-eaters never even see the animals they eat alive, let alone make them suffer or kill them. However, this doesn't mean that eating meat is okay. To see why, consider an analogy.

There is a new restaurant in town: the food is sensational, and the prices are very low. How do they do it? Here's how: the owner kidnaps world-class chefs, and enslaves them at the restaurant. Suppose that the owner is connected with the mob, and going to the police would just get you killed. Your patronizing the restaurant does not enslave anyone, but it still seems wrong. The explanation for why it is wrong is roughly that by patronizing the restaurant, you would be *complicit* in wrongdoing: you would be benefiting from a wrongful act (enslavement), while economically supporting the wrongdoer (the slaver).

Making animals suffer may be less awful than enslaving another human being. But the same form of explanation applies to eating meat. The raising of animals for food causes those animals a horrifying amount of suffering, and early death (see Mason and Singer 1990 for some of the literally grisly details). If it is wrong to kill animals and to cause them to suffer, then the industry that produces our meat acts wrongly on a massive scale. It is wrong to eat meat because in doing so you are complicit with that massive and systematic wrongdoing.

In this essay I have argued that it is wrong to eat meat. One clarification of this conclusion is in order: like many ethical claims, it should be read as a claim about what is *typically* true. It is typically wrong for you to break all of my fingers, but if doing so is the only way to prevent nuclear catastrophe, break away! Similarly, there may be unusual circumstances in which it is permissible or even required to eat meat. Nonetheless, if my argument is sound, each of us does wrong almost every time we sit down to a meal that contains meat.

I have written "It is Wrong to Eat Meat" as a model short philosophy essay. Unless your professor tells you otherwise, you would do well to emulate several of the stylistic features of this essay:

• The introduction offers a brief clear motive for the question addressed, states the essay's thesis, and previews the argument to come;

- The argument of the paper is summarized in valid premise/conclusion form;
- The essay does not waste words: every sentence is dedicated to developing the central argument, explaining a concept, introducing an objection or replying to it, or doing other important work. Even the conclusion does important work, introducing a crucial clarification of the argument.
- The essay does not use lengthy quotes from its sources: instead, it cites those sources after stating (in my own words) key claims that I take from them.

The argument of this essay is also an excellent target for reasoned objections. I now discuss how to offer such objections.

First, let's back up a bit and think about the activity that we are engaged in. We are seeking to make and to evaluate reasoned arguments about ethics. For example, the model essay did not just disagree with the claim that it is okay to eat meat; it offered reasons for thinking that claim is incorrect, and it organized those reasons into an argument. Making an argument does not simply aim to persuade your reader. I know, for example, that no reasoned argument is as likely to change eating habits as grisly video footage of life inside the animal factories that produce our meat. If philosophers aimed simply to persuade, we would write clever advertising, rather than carefully argued essays. Instead, my aim as a philosopher is to seek the truth together with my audience, in a way that respects the ability of each person involved to find the truth herself, using her own ability to reason. My aim now is to offer you some tools to enable you to skillfully engage in this sort of respectful argumentation.

For many of you, the conclusion of the model essay is a challenge to your ethical views. You may be tempted to reply to this sort of challenge by simply disagreeing with the conclusion. Resist this temptation: if an author offers you an argument, and you ignore the argument, and you ignore the argument and simply reject their conclusion, it is very difficult to seek the truth together with you. So, when you are presented with an argument, your central question should be: does this argument give me good reason to accept its conclusion? The model argument appears to be *valid*: the truth of its premises would logically ensure the truth of the conclusion. When you object to a valid argument, you should focus on objecting to its premises, not the conclusion. This is because the argument purports to offer you reasons to accept its conclusion, and if you cannot explain why you should reject those reasons, you aren't providing a compelling reply to the argument.[1] On the other hand, if you can identify a good reason to reject one of the premises of an argument, you have made an important and constructive contribution, by explaining why a reasonable person should not be persuaded by the argument. This is why it is important to learn how to offer reasoned objections to the premises of an argument.

Developing reasoned objections is in part a creative task, and there is no recipe for doing it well. However, there are several useful general strategies for finding good objections. Taking the model essay as a target, I will introduce some of these strategies, and illustrate them with exemplary objections to the model essay. Another important philosophical skill is to assess the import of potential objections. Because of this, when I consider each objection I will discuss whether the objections can be answered, whether it calls for some amendment to the model essay's argument, or whether it constitutes a promising line of objection to the overall strategy of the model argument. The point of carefully exploring objections and replies is to arrive ultimately at the best arguments that can be made on each side of an ethical issue, like the issue of whether it is wrong to eat meat. Because objections should target the premises of an argument (as I have emphasized), I will organize my discussion by focusing on each premise in turn.

PREMISE ONE: INFLICTING SUFFERING

Premise One of the model argument says:

1. It is wrong to make animals suffer

In this section, I consider objections to this principle that are instances of three general strategies for identifying objections: looking to extreme cases, appealing to an obscured distinction, and appealing to a competing ethical principle.

One excellent way to find objections to ethical principles is to look to extreme cases (Hájek forthcoming-b, §4; this and Hájek forthcoming-a are excellent sources of heuristics for doing philosophy, although they are most suited for somewhat advanced philosophy students). There are several relevant *types* of extreme cases. One type of extreme case involves *raising the stakes*. Suppose, for example, that some generic supervillain will incinerate the earth unless you torture this puppy. It is surely required (and not wrong) to torture the puppy in that case. So it is not *always* wrong to cause animals to suffer.

It is not enough to find an objection: you should also think about how someone sympathetic to the argument that you are objecting to should reply to your objection. In this case, there is a decisive reply to this objection: the conclusion of the model essay already granted that it is only *typically* wrong to eat meat. Because scenarios involving comic-book supervillains are extremely atypical, this is not an effective objection to the argument of the model essay. There is an important lesson here: make sure that you interpret the argument you are objecting to accurately and fairly. Failure to do this is so common it has its own name: the *straw man* fallacy.

A different sort of extreme case is more potent. If we arranged animals on a continuum of cognitive sophistication, we would notice that puppies (which featured in the model argument) are relatively close to us on that continuum. So: what happens to the model argument as we move to animals farther away from us on that continuum? Here is one salient example: oysters and other bivalves lack brains, and so are almost certainly incapable of suffering. Because one cannot make an oyster suffer, it cannot be wrong to eat an oyster for the reasons suggested in the model essay.[2] Because there is nothing atypical about eating oysters, this case is an important objection to the argument in the model essay.

One important way to reply to an objection is to concede that it requires one to modify one's argument. This objection to the model argument is powerful, and the best reply is thus concessive. I grant that the model argument does not explain why it is wrong to eat oysters, and so I conclude that the conclusion of

the model argument should be restricted to apply only to eating animals that can suffer.

This in turn raises a further question: *which* animals, exactly, can suffer? Here there are formidable methodological barriers to investigation (Allen and Trestman 2014, §4). The core problem is that we have no direct access to animals' experiential states, so we must reason about their inner lives on the basis of behavioral, functional, neurobiological and evolutionary considerations. Unsurprisingly, the strongest case for suffering can be made for mammals, where the evolutionary and neurobiological parallels with humans are closest. However, we should not assume that only mammals can experience pain; some have argued that there is evidence for pain experience in all vertebrates (Varner 2003), and in many cases we may simply lack adequate empirical knowledge to be able to assess the issue. Especially hard cases include cephalopods such as squid, which are behaviorally very sophisticated but evolutionarily distant from us. My approach to this issue invokes a modest sort of precautionary principle: Because we are not in a position to be confident about whether birds, fish, and cephalopods can suffer, we are not in a position to know whether we act wrongly when we eat them. Indifference to the possibility that we act wrongly is a vice, and we should avoid eating these animals on that basis.

A second powerful way to find objections to a premise is to identify an important distinction that the argument for that premise ignores. For example, one could argue that Premise One of the model essay becomes less plausible once we make the distinction between *being in pain* and *suffering*. Some philosophers grant that many animals can be in pain. However, they suggest that suffering requires something in addition to being in pain that most non-human animals lack. For example, perhaps it requires a conscious belief: that *I am having this pain* (for discussion, see Akhtar 2011, 496–499). An objector might argue that it is suffering in this sense—and not merely being in pain—that is ethically significant. If this were true, then my argument would at very least be incomplete: I would need to discuss the nature of suffering more carefully, and then explore which animals can experience it.

The best reply to this objection begins by emphasizing that the important issue here is not how we should use the word *suffering* (in philosophy you should usually avoid fighting about how to use words). It is rather whether conscious belief (or something like it) is required for pain to be ethically significant. If we are clear on this point, another extreme case shows why this objection fails. The most intense pains tend to fully occupy us: one is unlikely to be thinking anything—let alone *this pain is happening to me*—when in utter agony. But surely it is wrong to inflict utter agony on someone, because of how awful it feels (compare Rachels 2011, 898). This shows that it can be wrong to inflict pain that does not count as suffering in the objector's stipulated sense. If this is true of agonizing pains, it should be true of less intense pains. And if it is true for our own case, it should be true for animals as well. I thus conclude that this objection fails.

A third way to object to an ethical premise is to identify and defend an independently plausible ethical principle that conflicts with it. You may have encountered such a principle in your previous study of ethics, or you might be able to develop one yourself. One example of this strategy is to argue against Premise One of the model argument by appealing to contractualism, which is one of the most influential contemporary approaches to ethics and political philosophy. The basic idea of contractualism is that moral (or political) principles are principles that reasonable persons would agree to as rules to govern their lives together. So understood, contractualism can seem to cast serious doubt on the ethical significance of animals. As Peter Carruthers notes, according to the contractualist, "Morality is viewed as constructed *by* human beings, in order to facilitate interactions *between* human beings . . ." (1992, 102, emphasis his). Because it is hard to see how a principle like Premise One would help to facilitate such interactions, contractualism may seem to give us good reasons to reject this premise.

I have two interlocking replies to this objection. First, the most plausible forms of contractualism do not have the implications that the objector claims. Exemplary here is T.M. Scanlon's extremely influential contractualist ethical theory. Scanlon is careful to argue that his theory can be extended to protect animals (1998, 177–84). Further, Scanlon is clear that we have strong reasons that are not based in the contractual principle, so his view is compatible with the idea that we might have such reasons not to harm animals. Other philosophers have been more ambitious, offering contractualist arguments on behalf of animals (Rowlands 2002, Ch. 3; Talbert 2006).

Of course, there are some contractualist theories that have the implications that Carruthers suggests. But these are controversial views among contractualists, and contractualism itself is only one of a number of controversial and competing general ethical theories. Because of this controversy, however, it is unlikely that we should be confident in the truth of these contractualist theories. Without such confidence, however, it is hard to see how these theories could give us good reasons to reject Premise One. Further, the case of animals is exactly one where these theories appear implausible. Because it is obviously wrong for me to torture puppies just for fun, it counts against a moral theory that implies otherwise. This sort of case is part of a deep and more general challenge. As Martha Nussbaum (2006) and others have argued, many of our most important moral concerns address the interests of distinctively vulnerable parties (such as children, the severely mentally handicapped, and animals), and not simply the interactions between equally capable adult humans. A contractualism that ignores these interests is indefensible. In light of these considerations, it will be very difficult to mount a compelling case against Premise One of my argument that appeals to contractualism.

In this section I have considered three kinds of objections to Premise One of my argument. An important part of my reply has been concessive, refining the premise that I want to defend: so refined, the thesis states that it is typically wrong to inflict pain on a range of animals, including at least all mammals. So refined, I have suggested that it is very difficult to reasonably reject this premise.

PREMISE TWO: KILLING ANIMALS

Premise Two of the model argument says:

2. If it is wrong to make animals suffer, then it is wrong to kill animals

This premise is *conditional*. In order to successfully object to a conditional, one would need to find a reasonable way to accept the *antecedent* (i.e. the first part) of the conditional, while rejecting the *consequent* (i.e. the second part). Here, this would mean granting that it is wrong to make animals suffer, and arguing that it is nonetheless okay to kill them. I will consider three strategies for objecting to this premise. These strategies all target my explanation of why we should accept this premise. This was the idea that the wrongness of killing is well-explained by the fact that killing deprives the victim of a valuable future. The first strategy appeals to a competing explanation, the second strategy objects that my explanation is incomplete, and the third objects that my explanation has a false presupposition.

Just as a promising objection can be based in a competing ethical principle, so we can base an objection in a competing ethical explanation. In arguing for Premise Two, I offered a general explanation of the wrongness of killing: that killing can be wrong because it deprives the victim of a valuable future. One seemingly competing explanation is that killing you would be wrong because it would violate your autonomy. *Violation* here includes two important and separable ideas. First, killing you would interfere with your exercise of your autonomy. You cannot live your life in the way you choose if you are dead. Second, killing you would be a way of failing to respect your autonomy: if I take myself to be licensed to kill you, I take myself to have the right to ride roughshod over your own view of how your life should go.

In certain cases, this explanation of the wrongness of killing may seem markedly superior to the "valuable future" explanation offered in the model essay. For example, suppose that Alice is near death and in pain, but wishes to continue living. If I inject her with a lethal does of morphine, I wrongly kill her. (Notice that this is another instance of using an extreme case to make a point.) The best explanation here is that I have wrongly failed to respect her right to autonomously determine whether she continues to live. By contrast, it is not clear that I deprive her of a valuable future at all. Because most non-human animals are not autonomous agents (there may be borderline cases of

non-human agency, such as chimpanzees), this competing explanation suggests that Premise Two is false.

To see why this objection is not promising, notice that the autonomy-violation explanation also clearly fails in some cases. Because you are an autonomous agent, I should not force you to go to bed at a certain time, even if it is good for you to do so. By contrast, I act *rightly* when I paternalistically force my three-year-old son to go to bed at an appropriate time. This is because he is not an autonomous agent. It would obviously be very wrong to kill my son, but since he is not an autonomous agent, this cannot be explained in terms of autonomy violation.

You might think that this leaves us at an impasse: we have two candidate explanations of the wrongness of killing (valuable future-deprivation and autonomy-violation) and counter-examples to each. Does this show that both must be bad explanations? No. A better diagnosis is that each of these accounts provides a *typically sufficient but not necessary* explanation of the wrongness of killing. That is: killing can be wrong *either* because it violates autonomy, *or* because it deprives the victim of a valuable future (or both). On this account, one of the reasons why it is uncontroversial that it is wrong to kill an adult human in a range of ordinary circumstances is that there are several different things wrong with such killing. Because Premise Two of the model argument requires only that the valuable future-deprivation explanation is typically sufficient, this reply vindicates that premise.

Another important way to object to an ethical principle or explanation is to argue that it is *incomplete*. Whenever someone offers a principle or explanation, it is always a good idea to ask: is that *all* that is doing the important explanatory work here? Or have I only been given a part of the best ethical principle that applies to this sort of case? For example, one might think that a future's merely *being valuable* is not sufficient to explain why we must not eliminate it. Suppose that my wife and I were debating whether to have another child. If we did, that child would almost certainly have a valuable future. But it seems clear that I do no wrong simply by preventing that future: my having had a vasectomy does not make me akin to a murderer. Michael Tooley (1972) proposes an explanation of this fact: in order for it to be wrong to deprive an entity of a valuable future, that entity needs to have the capacity to care about its own continued existence. Because the child I do not conceive does not currently exist, it cannot care about its future existence, and hence I do not wrong it by preventing its future, on Tooley's view. One might appeal to Tooley's view to argue that it is not wrong to kill most animals because they are not cognitively sophisticated enough to care about their continued existence.

It is not obvious whether some animals can care about their futures in the relevant way. However, I set this aside, and instead focus on arguing against Tooley's explanatory claim (notice that I do so by appealing to extreme cases reasoning). Suppose that artificial intelligence research advances to the point that we are capable of creating intelligent and autonomous androids, capable of almost everything humans are: sophisticated reasoning, love, physical and emotional pain, etc. Suppose this type of android is programmed to be simply incapable of caring about its own continued existence, although it can and typically does care deeply about particular others. In light of this programming, such androids would be predictably prone to certain tragic behavior: they would sometimes lay down their lives to save others from inconsequential harms. It would be obviously wrong to kill such an android—even with its consent—to save yourself from a splinter. The android's inability to care about its future is a rational imperfection, but not one that licenses killing it.

We can square our judgments about the nonexistent child and the android if we suggest that the android is (imagined to be) an ethically significant being that now exists, while the non-existent child is a merely possible entity. We can then amend our ethical explanation as follows: it is wrong to deprive existing creatures of valuable futures, but it is not wrong to prevent non-existing entities from coming into existence. This explanation implies that it is wrong to kill existing animals, and so supports Premise Two.

A third way to object to an explanation is to argue that it has a false presupposition. That is: it works only by implicitly assuming some false claim. One crucial presupposition of my explanation of the wrongness of killing animals is that if I refrain from killing a cow today, there is a single moral patient—the cow—that will enjoy various pleasant cow experiences in the future. The objector suggests that we have reason to doubt this, if we think carefully about the conditions for the continued existence of a given moral patient.

The objection can be initially motivated by another extreme case: suppose that a mad scientist was able to map the neural structure of our brains, and then *swap* those structures: your brain is "wiped" and then rebuilt in accordance with the map of my brain, so that your body is now the home of beliefs, desires, and "memories" near identical to mine (pre-operation), and vice-versa. Suppose that the mad scientist performs this swap shortly after I injected my own heart with a slow-acting but lethal poison. Arguably, thanks to the mad scientist's intervention, I will have survived, and succeeded in killing you, rather than myself.

Some philosophers use cases like these to argue that *psychological continuity* is required for personal identity or ethically significant survival. In the case above, the idea is that I survive the operation because the surviving body houses a psychology that is continuous with my pre-operation psychology. This sort of case matters to my argument for the following reason. Suppose that the psychological connections across the life of a cow are not very rich. Then, in killing the cow now, I may be depriving *it* of only an inconsequential amount of valuable future. I will also be preventing a series of future "cows" from coming into existence and enjoying life. But as we saw from the nonexistent child case, it appears not to be wrong to refrain from bringing into existence beings with valuable futures.

This leads us to the central issue: do animals have rich enough psychological connections to underwrite the intuitive thought that a given cow (e.g.) is the same moral patient over time? I am cautiously optimistic that they do, in at least many cases. For example, many animals appear capable of various forms of memory (Allen and Trestman 2014, §7.4). However, as with questions about animal pain and suffering, answers here are likely to vary substantially across species in ways that require careful empirical work to tease out.

It is worth making two further points. First, theories of personal identity—and related claims about the persistence of a given moral patient—are extremely difficult to assess. The view that psychological continuity is the criterion of ethically significant survival is controversial. And on many competing views—on which organism continuity, or brain continuity can underwrite ethically significant survival, for example—the objection will fail immediately. Second, the precautionary approach to practical ethics that I advocated in the preceding section is again relevant here. This objection certainly reveals deep complexities ignored by the argument of the model essay. However, we should only be content to reject that argument if these complexities lead us to be confident that it is not wrong to kill animals.

In this section I have argued that the appeal to autonomy-violation complements—rather than competes with—the valuable future-deprivation account of the wrongness of killing. I also argued that it can be wrong to kill a being that is incapable of caring about its own continued existence. In discussing this issue, I amended the ethical principle I endorse to claim that it is wrong to deprive an *existing* moral patient of the valuable future that it would otherwise have. And I argued that many animals are probably the same moral patient across time (although I granted that the issues here are quite complex).

PREMISE THREE: USING ANIMAL PRODUCTS

Premise Three of the model argument is the claim that:

3. If it is wrong to kill animals, then it is wrong to eat meat

I argued for this claim by defending another ethical principle: that it is wrong to be complicit in wrongdoing: to benefit from that wrongdoing, and to support it. Here we can ask two questions: should we accept this principle, and does it really support Premise Three? In this section I begin by considering an objection to the idea that this principle supports Premise Three, before considering whether this principle is objectionably incomplete.

It is always wise to consider whether an ethical principle really supports the conclusion it is intended to. Consider a case that illustrates this sort of objection to Premise Three. Suppose Alice is driving carefully on a country road, when a deer jumps in front of her truck without warning. The deer is killed instantly, and Alice moves its carcass to the side of the road and leaves. Zoe, who lives nearby, sees all of this. Zoe knows how to dress a deer carcass and has a taste for venison. She takes the carcass home, dresses it, cooks some, and eats it (compare Bruckner 2016 for further discussion of cases like this one). In this scenario, Zoe knowingly prepared and ate meat. But in doing so, Zoe is not complicit in any wrongdoing: Alice's killing of the deer was neither malicious nor negligent, so it is hard to see how it could be wrong. This is a case where eating meat is not complicit in wrongful killing, so it is a case where Premise Three fails to hold, even if the principle I offer is true.

I am happy to grant the objector this case. Recall that my conclusion is that eating meat is *typically* wrong. This case helpfully brings out another atypical exception. The objection lacks more general force exactly because in the overwhelming majority of cases, the meat that we eat *is* wrongfully produced (at least if the arguments for Premises One and Two are sound).

We saw in the previous section that a good strategy for finding objections to an explanation is to challenge its completeness. The same is true for ethical principles like my complicity principle. We can challenge the completeness of my principle by arguing that complicity with the wrongful treatment of animals could only be wrong if it tended to make a difference to how much wrongful treatment there was (see Appiah 1986–7 for a version of this view about complicity). I will call this the *efficacy objection*. This objection has significant force: one might wonder what the point of avoiding complicity is, if it makes no difference to how much animal suffering occurs.

Because I take this to be the single most important challenge to the argument of the model paper, I will offer three potentially complementary replies. (Please note that I offer multiple replies to help illustrate the issues here. In general you should focus on developing the single strongest reply to an objection as clearly as you can, rather than offering multiple replies.)

The first reply accepts the objection, and claims that it is wrong to eat meat because doing so *does* tend to make a difference to the amount of mistreatment of animals. This might seem absurd: by the time I buy a chicken at the store (for example) it is already dead. And the idea that every chicken bought will cause another one to be raised, made to suffer, and then killed, is plainly false. Peter Singer (1980, 335–6, and following him, Norcross 2004, Kagan 2011, and Rachels 2011) has replied to this challenge in the following way: There must be some change in demand for chicken that the market would notice. For example, Singer imagines that for every 10,000 vegetarians, there would be one fewer 20,000-bird broiler factory, harming and killing 100,000 chickens a year. He imagines further that if we were just below the threshold—if, for example, 1,009,999 people were vegetarians—the last 9,999 vegetarians would save no chickens, because demand for chicken would be just above the threshold that triggers a change in supply. Given these assumptions, and given that we do not know exactly how many other vegetarians there are, someone becoming vegetarian has only a 1/10,000 chance of making any difference to the number of chickens made to suffer and die.

That sounds depressing. But Singer argues that we should pay attention to the other numbers: if one *is* that 1/10,000, one will save 100,000 chickens a year. In light of this, the *expected* effect of becoming vegetarian is the effect you would have if you make a difference divided by your chance of making that difference; in the example, saving 100,000/10,000 = 10 chickens a year from short but awful lives. Of course, these precise numbers are merely illustrative; Singer grants that we do not know where exactly the thresholds are. But he suggests that the structure of probable effects will be similar on any reasonable hypothesis about these thresholds. So, according to Singer, while any reduction or increase in one's meat consumption has a tiny chance of making a difference to the amount of wrongful animal suffering and death, the difference you will make if you do make a difference will be correspondingly huge. And this, it might be claimed, is what makes it wrong to eat meat. If Singer's reasoning is sound, it answers the efficacy objection: complicity is wrong in part because it has an ethically significant chance of making an ethically significant difference. While Singer's reply is promising, his argument is somewhat complex, and relies on some controversial

assumptions (see Budolfson *forthcoming* for an important reply). In light of this, I will explore alternative ways of replying to the efficacy objection.

Singer's argument illustrates two important ideas worth keeping in mind in your ethical reasoning. First, sometimes the *expected* effects of your actions are ethically significant, and not just their actual effects. (In this case, the alleged expected effect of being a vegetarian is sparing ten chickens a year from short and awful lives, even if for most vegetarians, there is no actual effect on chicken well-being.) Second, in thinking about the effects of an action, it is sometimes important to step back from focusing on the particular act, and think about how that act fits into overall patterns.

A second response to the efficacy objection appeals to these patterns in another way, by focusing on the ethical significance of what groups of people do together. One advantage of this approach is that it is uncontroversial that meat-eaters as a group *do* make a difference to the amount of animal suffering: if there were no omnivores there would be no factory farms.

I will introduce the key idea with another example. Suppose that there are two small cities, Upstream and Downstream, along the same river. The river is the only available source of water for the households in each city draws its water from the river as the river comes into the city, and dumps its sewage in the river as it flows out of the city. The sewage dumped in the river in Upstream flows down the river and pollutes the drinking water drawn from the river in Downstream. As a result, the people in Downstream are constantly getting seriously ill and dying. Suppose that each household in Upstream could, at small cost, bury their sewage instead of dumping it in the river. If everyone in Upstream did this, it would end the health catastrophe in Downstream. However, given the number of other households that are actually polluting, a single person in Upstream burying his sewage would not save anyone in Downstream from illness or death.

It seems plausible that the sewage-dumpers in Upstream *together* wrongfully cause massive amounts of suffering and death in Downstream. Anyone in Upstream who dumps her sewage in the river is thus part of a group that acts wrongly. It is easy to cease to be part of that group, however: one need only bury one's sewage. It seems plausible that one should bury one's sewage in this situation, rather than dump it into the river. We could explain this by appealing to the following ethical principle: if one can avoid being part of a group that together does serious wrong, then one acts wrongly by continuing to be a member of that group. This principle applies neatly to eating meat. Together, the meat-eaters make a tremendous difference: without their demand for meat, no one would cause animals to suffer and die in order to produce it. So the meat-eaters together make vast amounts of wrongful pain and death happen to animals. So, by the ethical principle just proposed, one acts wrongly by continuing to be a member of that group.

This reply answers the efficacy objection by appealing to group efficacy. However, the issue of when exactly it is wrong to remain a part of an ethically objectionable group is very complicated. (Sometimes, for example, it is only by being part of such a group that one can mitigate the bad things the group does.) So I will explore another alternative response to the efficacy objection, which is the one I find most promising.

This response directly rejects the efficacy objection, and defends the claim that complicity with wrongdoing can be a sufficient explanation for wrongdoing, even if it has no expected bad effects. I will defend this response in three ways: by appealing to a plausibly analogous ethical principle, by clarifying the anti-complicity principle, and by appealing to a variant on an earlier case that helps to distinctively motivate it.

The first thing to notice is that there are other plausible ethical principles that require us to act even when our doing so will not make a difference. For example, the duty of *fair play* requires that one not benefit from successful cooperative institutions without making a fair contribution to them; i.e., that one not *freeride* (see e.g. Klosko 2004). Consider, as an example, sneaking onto a public bus without paying the fare.

Second, it may be useful to more precisely state the principle that I endorse (see McPherson *2016-b* for more detailed discussion):

Anti-Complicity It is typically wrong to aim to benefit by cooperating with the wrongful elements of others' plans

When introducing a principle, it is often useful to briefly explain each of the elements of that principle. I now do this for Anti-Complicity. My talk of "plans" here should not be taken to apply only to patterns of explicit reasoning; rather it should include the pattern of goals that explain an individual's or institution's behavior. If my unconscious desire to humiliate my rival explains all of my behavior, humiliating my rival counts as my plan, even if I would never consciously admit this is what I am up to. My talk of "benefit" should similarly be read in an expansive way: smoking does more harm than good, but if one seeks the enjoyment of a cigarette, one is aiming at benefit in the sense I am interested in. We should understand "cooperating" in the following way: our plans often call for others to act in certain ways. For example, if I make widgets for sale, my plan includes others' buying those widgets. Of course, it is not crucial that any particular person buys my widgets. So anyone who buys a widget counts as cooperating with my plan. Finally plans can be disjunctive: someone can plan to read the newspaper, buy some tools at the store, and then use the tools to torture a puppy. The clearly wrongful part here is the puppy torturing. Buying the tools is instrumental to the wrongful behavior, and is arguably wrongful for that reason, and reading the newspaper is not a wrongful part of the plan. It is most clear that we should not cooperate with the wrongful part of the plan.

Anti-Complicity is plausible in part because it can explain the wrongness of certain acts that cannot be explained by either the group or individual efficacy explanations. Return to the example in the model essay: the restaurant that kidnaps and enslaves chefs to make its food. Suppose the restaurant is *demand-insensitive*: it's partly a money-laundering operation, and so it will remain in business even if no one ever patronizes it. This means that neither an individual, nor the whole group of patrons, have any chance of reducing the amount of slavery in the restaurant by refusing to patronize it. Still, it seems wrong to go to the restaurant and enjoy the fruits of the slave chefs' unwilling labors. Anti-Complicity can explain why, while principles that demand that the individual or group make a difference cannot.

If the arguments earlier in the paper are correct, the meat industry has a wrongful plan: to produce meat in a way that involves egregious amounts of pain and early death, and then to sell that meat. They do not, of course, typically sell it directly to consumers. But consumers buying meat is clearly part of their plan: for if consumers do not buy, then wholesalers will not either, and the meat industry's plan would not be economically viable. (This is why meat-industry groups sometimes advertise directly to consumers: to increase consumer-level demand for their goods.) So, in buying meat, one is cooperating with their wrongful plan. And Anti-Complicity suggests that doing so is typically wrong.

Of the three explanations that I have discussed here (individual efficacy, group efficacy, and Anti-Complicity), I prefer the last. However, it is worth emphasizing that, as with explanation of the wrongness of killing, it is not clear that these explanations compete. Rather, if each is sound, they could be complementary explanations of the wrongness of eating meat. This means that the objector has her work cut out for her. For each of the three explanations that I have discussed, she must either debunk the relevant explanatory principle, or argue that the principle does not entail that it is wrong to eat meat. For example, one might insist that individual efficacy is required for wrongdoing in these cases, and then argue against the Singer-style reasoning. I take this to be the most promising way to reject the argument, but to nonetheless be a very difficult task.

THE IMPLICATIONS OF THE ARGUMENT: VEGANISM

In the previous three sections, I have considered several objections to each of the three premises of the model argument, and refined that argument in light of those objections. I now want to consider the broader implications of the argument, as refined. I will begin by considering two objections to the argument that target gaps between the premises and my overall thesis: ethical veganism.

An obvious but important objection at this stage notes that my aim in this paper is to argue for ethical veganism: the view that it is (at least typically) wrong to eat or otherwise use animal products. However, the model argument concludes only that it is wrong to eat *meat*. The model argument itself thus fails to establish ethical veganism. I grant this objection. However, the argument I have developed in this paper naturally extends to support ethical veganism.

The first point to notice is that it is possible to imagine farming with animals in a way that does not involve shortening their lives or making them suffer. My argument does not suggest any objection to using animal products made on such farms. However, when we turn from possible to actual animal farming, we find that my case against killing animals and making them suffer applies to almost all of the institutions that produce animal products (with the exceptions of some shellfish farms). The reasons lie in the interaction between biology and economics. Consider a single example: even the most humane dairy farm will typically produce as many male calves as female, and almost all of the males will be killed early, so as not to be an economic burden. That means that the central plan of almost any economically viable dairy farming operation involves raising cows to be killed (or to be sold to another operation, knowing the latter operation will kill them), a practice that I have argued above is typically wrong. And this in turn means that the overall argument I have proposed applies here: the core plan of economically viable dairy farms involves systematic wrongdoing, and I have argued that it is wrong to be complicit with such wrongdoing. But one would be complicit with such wrongdoing if one were to buy and consume the milk (e.g.) produced on such farms, and hence buying and consuming such milk would be wrong. This example generalizes to the institutions that produce almost all of our animal products: eggs, cheese, leather, etc. And for this reason I think that my argument supports ethical veganism as opposed to a requirement to be a vegetarian who merely refrains from eating meat.

A second worry about my overall argument is that the initial simple statement of the argument in premise and conclusion from in the model essay is misleading. In the preceding sections, I have emphasized various ways that this argument should be refined, but there is a general worry that should be explored. The conclusion of the model argument emphasized that it is only *typically* wrong to eat meat. And as I explained in my initial discussion of Premise One, this qualifier should be read back into the premises. So the argument should look like this:

1. It is typically wrong to make animals suffer
2. If it is typically wrong to make animals suffer, then it is typically wrong to kill animals
3. If it is typically wrong to kill animals, then it is typically wrong to eat meat
   C. It is typically wrong to eat meat.

The first thing to do is to verify that this statement of the argument, like the statement in the model essay, is valid. It is: the addition of the word "typically" does not alter the logical form of the argument, which is: *P, if P then Q, if Q then R, so R,* which is a slightly more complex variant of the classic *modus ponens* argument form. However, there are two connected worries about the argument as given. First, the reference to typicality points us at a range of ordinary cases, but every sort of exception that we have identified for each premise is an exception that must hold for the argument as a whole. The discussion has identified a raft of "atypical" exception cases: cases of making animals suffer to avoid ethically awful alternatives, cases of eating oysters and other animals incapable of experiencing pain, and cases of eating meat (like some roadkill) that was not wrongfully produced.

These cases do not exhaust the set of potential exceptions that the argument permits. And one might worry that as a result, the argument might be far too weak to support anything resembling veganism. To begin to see the force of this worry, notice that I have granted that human suffering and death may tend to be substantially more ethically significant than the suffering and death of non-human animals. This is because, as we saw above, killing you or making you suffer would be wrong for multiple reasons: some have to do with the awfulness of suffering, and the deprivation of your future, and others have to do with the ethical significance of your autonomy.

In light of this, my argument at least suggests that the most central and pressing human interests should typically take priority over the welfare of non-human animals. For example, my conclusion is compatible with the idea that we should typically harm or kill a non-human animal if doing so is needed to prevent suffering or death to a human being. This is practically relevant: in various times and places, animal products have been an essential element of the only feasible nutritionally adequate human diets. For example, in many parts of the world, owning a cow—or even a handful of chickens—can offer crucial protection against certain forms of malnutrition. I take it to be a virtue of my argument that it is compatible with cases like these counting as legitimate exceptions to the vegan principle.

At this point, however, one may wonder whether the case for veganism has any practical bite at all. After all, becoming a vegan involves a non-trivial sacrifice of real goods. Consider three sorts of examples. First, there is a sea of delicious animal-involving food, so as a vegan one sacrifices access to a range of interesting aesthetic goods. Second, food is deeply meaningful to many people, and animal products are centrally involved in many important cultural traditions and occasions. To be a vegan is thus to complicate one's relationship to those traditions and meanings. Finally, because shared values are central to many personal and professional relationships, veganism could be an impediment to such relationships, especially in cultural contexts where veganism is seen as threatening.

If the fact that veganism required one to sacrifice goods like these typically rendered omnivorism permissible, then veganism would not typically be ethically required, as I claim. Instead, it would be an admirable but non-obligatory ideal. However, I do not think that the sorts of sacrifices just mentioned suffice to make omnivorism permissible. The core issue here is how weighty the considerations in favor of veganism that I have developed in this paper are. The issue is complex, but I think that a reasonable heuristic can be derived from the initial example in the model paper: *some circumstances* would warrant torturing the stray puppy imagined in that example. But those circumstances would be comparatively dire. I contend that only similarly dire circumstances would warrant ordering the sirloin steak for dinner. And the sacrifices typically involved in becoming vegan, while significant, fall well below this threshold.

Challenging this heuristic would be yet another natural way to object to the argument of this paper. However, I think the heuristic is basically sound. And if it is, the argument of the paper suggests that we ought to eschew almost all animal products in almost all ordinary circumstances. We ought, in other words, to be vegan.

PEDAGOGICAL CODA

I conclude this paper by returning to my pedagogical aims: to aid you in thinking about how to make (and critically examine) philosophical arguments in ethics. In order to do so, I will review the basic elements of philosophical argument that I have sought to explain and illustrate in this paper.

The argument of the model essay began with a vivid *example*: the claim that it would be wrong to torture a puppy in a specific scenario. This case supported a *general principle*: that it is wrong to make animals suffer. The case supported the principle in part because the case seems *representative* of the principle. It does not seem that there is some unique feature of puppies that explains why it is wrong to torture them, for example. This principle was also supported by an underlying *ethical explanation*: it is wrong to cause animals to suffer, *because of how awful it is to experience suffering*. Although general principles themselves appear explanatorily illuminating, explanations and general principles can be different. One way to see this is to notice that there can be multiple good explanations of a single ethical principle, as in the case of the future-deprivation and autonomy-violation explanations of the wrongness of killing. In making arguments, cases, general principles, and explanations are likely to be the most important elements to develop. These elements should fit together in a rationally compelling way, and one good way to do that is to put these elements together into a valid argument, as I again did in the model essay.

In critically examining an argument, you might in principle target the structure of the argument itself: for example, showing that the argument contains some fallacious reasoning. Or you might challenge the ethical claims the argument makes about specific cases: for example, you could try to argue that there is nothing wrong with torturing puppies. (But I dearly hope you don't do that!) It is far more common for it to be useful to challenge the general principles and explanations offered in an argument. I have discussed several important ways of executing these challenges. First, it can be useful to look to extreme cases, to see if principles are really generally applicable. For example, the model argument appeals to suffering to explain why it is wrong to eat meat. But some animals (such as oysters) cannot suffer. So the model argument cannot explain why it is wrong to eat them. Second, it can be useful to see if an argument only works because it obscures an ethically important distinction. I discussed this issue using the example of the contrast between being in pain and suffering. Third, it is always a good idea to ask if there is a superior competitor to the general principle or ethical explanation offered in an argument. Examples of this strategy discussed above were the objection from contractualism, and the objection that autonomy violation is the best explanation of why killing is typically wrong. Fourth, a very natural objection to an explanation or principle is that it is *incomplete*. For example, I considered the idea that it is only wrong to deprive a creature of its valuable future *if* that creature is capable of caring about that future. And I discussed the idea that complicity with wrongdoing is only morally objectionable if such complicity can make a difference to the extent of the underlying wrongdoing. Fifth, another important type of objection to some explanations is that those explanations rest on false presuppositions. For example, I considered the possibility that most animals do not have valuable futures in the ethically relevant sense, because most animals lack rich enough psychological connections to remain the same moral patient from one day to the next. Finally, another important way to challenge an argument is to show that there is a gap between an explanation offered in support of an ethical principle, and the principle itself. For example, the case of eating blamelessly produced roadkill suggests that there is a gap between its being wrong to kill animals, and its being wrong to eat meat, because some meat does not come from animals that were wrongfully killed.

I take these to be some of the most important tools for critically analyzing philosophical arguments. However, there are many more to be discovered. One very good habit to get into when reading philosophical papers is to ask: what kind of argument is this? How is this author objecting to that argument? If you do that consistently, you will soon have a very rich repertoire of tools for evaluating others' arguments, and making your own. One final note about how to use these tools. Probably the most important place to use the tools I have discussed in this paper is in revising your own paper. Once you have a draft of your paper in hand, you should be merciless in carefully reading through it, asking: how compelling is this argument? How could someone reasonably object to it? Are their objections sound? In my view, it is most important to use these tools to examine arguments for the conclusions that you most care about. Only by doing so can you determine whether these conclusions are reasonable, or whether you are guilty of wishful thinking, only accepting them *because* you care about them.[3]

NOTES

1. This paragraph simplifies in several ways. First, in some arguments the premises (even if true) simply fail to support the conclusion, even given a charitable interpretation. Clearly demonstrating that fact can be a powerful way of objecting to such an argument. Second, some philosophers have argued that it can be legitimate to object to certain arguments as a whole, without criticizing either specific premises or the logical structure of the argument. For discussion relevant to our topic, see McPherson 2014 and *2016-a*.

2. There might, however, be other arguments that count against eating animals that cannot suffer: for example, one could offer environmental objections to how some such animals are raised or harvested, or appeal to the idea that simply being a fellow animal is morally significant.

3. One final bit of guidance: you should always recognize help you have received in writing a paper! I am indebted to many people for helpful comments and discussion of ideas related to this paper. These include Mark Budolfson, David Plunkett, Tyler Doggett, Andrew Chignell, Sean Walsh, Derek Baker, Tom Dougherty, Gideon Rosen, and Katie Batterman, to audiences at Rhodes College, Bowling Green State University, Charles Sturt University, and Virginia Commonwealth University, and to many of my students for discussion. I am also indebted to Liz Harman, whose talk about ethical vegetarianism first started me thinking systematically about it. Parts of this paper draw significantly on my 2014, and especially my *2016-b*.

WORKS CITED

Akhtar, Sahar. "Animal Pain and Welfare: Can Pain Sometimes Be Worse for Them Than for Us?" *Oxford Handbook of Animal Ethics.* Eds. Tom Beauchamp and R.G. Frey. Oxford University Press, 2011. 495–518.

Allen, Colin, and Michael Trestman. "Animal Consciousness." *The Stanford Encyclopedia of Philosophy* (Summer 2014 Edition). Ed. Edward N. Zalta. <http://plato.stanford.edu/archives/sum2014/entries/consciousness-animal/>.

Appiah, Kwame Anthony. "Racism and Moral Pollution." *Philosophical Forum* 18.2–3 (1986). 185–202.

Bruckner, Donald W. "Strict Vegetarianism is Immoral" in *The Moral Complexities of Eating Meat*, Eds. Robert Fischer and Ben Bramble. Oxford University Press: 2016. 30–47.

Budolfson, Mark. "The Inefficacy Objection and the Problem with the Expected Consequences Response", *Philosophical Studies, forthcoming.*

Carruthers, Peter. *The Animals Issue.* Cambridge: Cambridge University Press, 1992.

Cohen, Carl. "The Case for the Use of Animals in Biomedical Research." *The New England Journal of Medicine* 315, 1986. 865–869.

Descartes, Rene. *The Philosophical Writings of Descartes Vol. III.* Ed. and Tr. John Cottingham, Robert Stoothoff, Dugald Murdoch, and Anthony Kenny. Cambridge, Cambridge University Press, 1991.

Hájek, Alan. "Heuristics for Philosophical Creativity." *forthcoming* in *The Philosophy of Creativity.* Eds. Elliot Samuel Paul and Scott Barry Kaufman. Oxford: Oxford University Press. *Cited as forthcoming-a.*

——. "Philosophical Heuristics and Philosophical Methodology." *forthcoming* in *The Oxford Handbook of Philosophical Methodology.* Eds. Herman Cappelen, Tamar Gendler, and John Hawthorne. Oxford: Oxford University Press. *Cited as forthcoming-b.*

Kagan, Shelly. "Do I Make a Difference?" *Philosophy and Public Affairs* 39.2 (2011). 105–141.

Klosko, George. *The Principle of Fairness and Political Obligation* (New Edition). Rowman and Littlefield, 2004.

McPherson, Tristram. "A Case for Ethical Veganism." *Journal of Moral Philosophy* 11(6), 2014. 677–703.

——. "A Moorean Defense of the Omnivore?" in *The Moral Complexities of Eating Meat*, Eds. Robert Fischer and Ben Bramble. Oxford University Press: 2016. 118–134. *Cited as 2016–a.*

——. "Why I am a Vegan (and You Should be One Too)." in *Philosophy Comes to Dinner*, Eds. Andrew Chignell, Terence Cuneo, and Matthew Halterman. Routledge: 2016. 73–91. Cited as *2016–b.*

Marquis, Don. "Why Abortion is Immoral." *Journal of Philosophy* 86.4, April 1989. 183–202.

Mason, Jim and Peter Singer. *Animal Factories* Revised and Updated Edition. Harmony: 1990.

Norcross, Alasdair. "Puppies, Pigs, and People: Eating Meat and Marginal Cases." *Philosophical Perspectives* 18 (Ethics), 2004. 229–245.

Nussbaum, Martha. *Frontiers of Justice*. Harvard: Belknap, 2006.

Rachels, Stuart. "Vegetarianism." *Oxford Handbook of Animal Ethics*. Eds. Tom Beauchamp and R. G. Frey. Oxford: Oxford University Press, 2011. 877–905.

Rowlands, Mark. *Animals Like Us*. Verso: 2002.

Scanlon, T. M. *What We Owe to Each Other*. Cambridge, MA: Belknap: 1998.

Singer, Peter. *Animal Liberation*. New York: Avon, 1977.

——. "Utilitarianism and Vegetarianism." *Philosophy and Public Affairs*. 9.4 (Summer 1980), 325–337.

Talbert, Matthew. "Contractualism and Our Duties to Nonhuman Animals." *Environmental Ethics* 28 (Summer 2006). 202–215.

Tooley, Michael. "Abortion and Infanticide." *Philosophy and Public Affairs* 2.1 (August 1972). 37–65.

Varner, Gary. *In Nature's Interests*. Oxford: Oxford University Press, 1998.

CHAPTER 13

Environmental Ethics

For most of its history, Western ethics has focused on the moral values, rights, and obligations of *humans*. The relevant questions have been, What is the good for *humans*? What value should we place on a *human* life or person? What obligations or duties do we have to our fellow *humans*? What moral rights, if any, do *humans* have? In large part, the rest of the planet seems to have been left out of our moral equations. The nonhuman animals, the plants, the waters, the land—these have mattered, if at all, largely because they affect the well-being of humankind.

But the planet is not what it used to be. The world's natural resources are being depleted. Human technology, culture, and avarice are devouring forests and meadows, poisoning water and air, wiping out ecosystems and species—and threatening the interests of the very beings who have wielded so much technological and cultural power. Some observers predict doom. They say that humans have gone too far and that the world as we know it will end not with a bang or a whimper, but a gasp: a gasp for uncontaminated air, water, or food. But whether the situation is or is not this dire, the profound environmental changes that humans have produced on earth have inspired many to see the proper purview of ethics as encompassing not just humans but the whole natural world. Consequently a new set of ethical questions is demanding our attention: Is the environment valuable in its own right, regardless of its usefulness for people? Do animals or plants have moral rights? Are they somehow intrinsically valuable? If they are intrinsically valuable or worthy of moral consideration, what makes them

so? Does a dolphin have more moral value than a rat? or a rat more than a redwood? or an individual mongoose more than its species? What obligations, if any, do humans have to the natural world? Should the interests of people take precedence over the interests or needs of the environment? Is it morally permissible, for example, to halt the construction of a dam that will bring prosperity to thousands of poor people but will also destroy a species of crayfish?

Then there are the questions that arise from the largest, most calamitous, most intractable environmental threat of all: climate change. It is the one environmental problem that is entangled with all the others, the one that humans are causing globally while suffering from it locally. The science behind it, at least in broad outlines, is well understood:

Greenhouse gases such as carbon dioxide (CO_2) absorb heat (infrared radiation) emitted from Earth's surface. Increases in the atmospheric concentrations of these gases cause Earth to warm by trapping more of this heat. Human activities—especially the burning of fossil fuels since the start of the Industrial Revolution—have increased atmospheric CO_2 concentrations by about 40%, with more than half the increase occurring since 1970. Since 1900, the global average surface temperature has increased by about 0.8°C (1.4°F). This has been accompanied by warming of the ocean, a rise in sea level, a strong decline in Arctic sea ice, and many other associated climate effects. Much of this warming has occurred in the last four decades. Detailed analyses have shown that the warming during this period is mainly a result of the increased concentrations of CO_2 and other greenhouse gases. Continued emissions of these gases will cause further climate change, including substantial increases in global average surface temperature and important changes in regional climate.[1]

Scientists say the worldwide consequences of this process are alarming and ominous: a global rise in sea level, ocean warming, the retreat of glaciers everywhere, severe droughts, coastal flooding, the receding of Arctic ice, increased acidity in the oceans, frequent heat waves, heavy rainfalls, and increased species extinction.

Given this runaway train of global warming, the moral questions hit home hard: What is an individual morally obligated to do about it? What are countries duty-bound to do about it? Should we do something even if our efforts cause widespread economic hardship, loss of jobs, social upheaval, and the demise of whole industries? Should we do something now even though the only people who will benefit from our sacrifices will be future generations? What, after all, do we owe the future? Do we have a moral obligation *not* to act in ways that might contribute, even slightly, to global warming? For example, are we obligated not to drive a gas guzzler, use an inefficient heating system, run the air conditioner nonstop, avoid recycling, or waste water?

Trying to answer such questions through critical reasoning is the main business of *environmental ethics,* a branch of applied ethics. Let us explore how these questions arise, determine whether traditional moral theories can shed any light on them, and evaluate arguments that are frequently used to address important environmental issues.

ISSUE FILE: BACKGROUND

Environmental issues can emerge from a variety of real-world challenges besides climate change: endangered species, pollution, wilderness preservation, treatment of animals, ecosystem protection, waste disposal, global population, resource allocation, energy use, economics, food production, world hunger, social justice, and the welfare of future generations.

As you would expect, serious disputes about environmental issues involve both the nonmoral and the moral—nonmoral facts (often scientific or technical) and moral principles or judgments. More often than not, there is substantial agreement on the former but serious divergence on the latter. All parties may agree, for instance, that building a road through a forest would help a struggling town prosper and that the project would wipe out a rare species of butterfly, but the debate rages over whether prosperity is more valuable than the butterfly.

Moral arguments in environmental ethics depend heavily on notions of *value* and *moral status.* The distinction between *instrumental* and *intrinsic* value is especially important. Recall that something with instrumental (or extrinsic) value is valuable as a means to something else; something with intrinsic value is valuable in itself, for its own sake. For many people, nature possesses instrumental value (some think it has instrumental value *only*). They may therefore believe that a forest has value because of its economic worth, because it provides the raw materials for making houses, furniture, and paper. Or because it helps make the environment livable for humans by cleaning the air as it absorbs carbon dioxide and releases oxygen. Or because it adds to the quality of human life simply by being beautiful, inspiring, or impressive. Or because it provides a home to many animal and plant species that are themselves instrumentally valuable to humans. In all these cases, the value of the forest is measured by its positive effects on human well-being. The forest is good because it is good for human beings. On the other hand, for many other people, nature has intrinsic value—it is valuable regardless of its usefulness to humanity. (Keep in mind that nature or objects in nature can have both instrumental and intrinsic value.) So they might say that the forest should be cherished for what it is, for its own sake, regardless of whether it can contribute to the welfare or happiness of humankind. The forest has intrinsic value because of its aesthetic qualities, its organizational complexity, its status as a living thing, or some other value-granting property. Even without utility, it can have great intrinsic worth.

Many debates in environmental ethics revolve around the concept of *moral status,* or *moral considerability*. As we saw in the previous chapter, something has moral status if it is a suitable candidate for moral concern or respect in its own right. Everyone agrees that humans have moral status; many believe that nonhuman animals also have moral status; some insist that *all* living things have moral status (including plants and even one-celled creatures); some think that the natural environment generally—mountains, oceans, rivers, and all—has moral status; and a few believe Planet Earth as a whole has moral status. A fundamental issue in environmental ethics is precisely what sorts of entities have moral status—and why.

Many things can have instrumental or intrinsic value yet have no moral status—that is, they may not deserve our direct moral concern. A bicycle can have instrumental value as a mode of transportation, but it is not the kind of thing that can have moral status. Michelangelo's magnificent sculpture *David* is generally thought to have intrinsic aesthetic value, but few philosophers would think that it has moral status. Some theorists draw such a distinction as follows: "We can have obligations *regarding* a painting, but not *to* a painting. We ought to treat beautiful paintings with respect, but not because we have obligations to the paintings. We ought to respect them because they are beautiful (or because their owners have rights), not because they have rights."[2]

Often the question at issue in environmental debates is not whether something has moral status, but whether it has greater or lesser moral status than something else. Does an ape have the same moral status as a domestic cow? Do animals (human and nonhuman) deserve the same level of moral concern as plants? Do humans and nonhuman animals have the same moral status? Is a cat as morally important as a cabbage? Does a species have a stronger claim on our moral concern than any individual of a species? As we will soon see, many people, on various grounds, give priority to one or more species over others, some think all living things equal, and some rank species over individuals.

In light of these considerations, we should not be surprised that a central question in environmental ethics is, What entities have moral status and to what degree do they have it? The answer that has been assumed in the Western world for much of its history is known as **anthropocentrism**, the notion that only humans have moral standing. By anthropocentric (human-centered) lights, the rest of nature has only instrumental value—that is, nonhuman animals, plants, mountains, and streams have value only because they are valuable in some way to humans. An anthropocentrist sees animals, plants, and ecosystems as means to enhance the well-being of humankind, to serve the ends of human beings. This stance, however, does not imply a disregard for the environment. He may be genuinely concerned about the destruction of rain forests, the extinction of species, river and lake pollution, the destruction of wetlands, animal cruelty, and global warming—but only because these calamities might lead to a less livable environment for humans, or their loss of enjoyable aesthetic or spiritual experiences of nature, or their feelings of distress at the thought of animal suffering, or dramatic climate changes that could endanger human lives. On what grounds should humans be granted this exclusive moral status? The traditional justification has been along Kantian lines: that humans are moral agents or persons—they are capable of making free, rational moral choices.

Another influential answer to our question is what could be called **zoocentrism**, the notion that animals—both human and nonhuman—have moral status. As we saw in the previous chapter, advocates for animal rights, notably the philosophers Peter Singer and Tom Regan, take this view, insisting that human and nonhuman animals are equally deserving of moral considerability or respect. Singer

CLIMATE CHANGE: How We Know It's Real

If global warming and climate change are actually happening (and have been happening), then humans are faced with a dreadful moral decision: to take action now to help save the future, or to do nothing and suffer through an uncertain present. But deciding rationally requires knowing the facts—knowing whether climate change is real. Ninety-seven percent of all climate scientists and most of the world's leading scientific organizations affirm that it is. But *how* do they know this? Here's the answer from NASA, one of the world's leading climate research agencies.

> The overwhelming majority of climate scientists agree that human activities, especially the burning of fossil fuels (coal, oil, and gas), are responsible for most of the climate change currently being observed.
>
> But how has this conclusion been reached? Climate science, like all science, is a process of collective learning that relies on the careful gathering and analyses of data, the formulation of hypotheses, the development of models to study key processes and make testable predictions, and the combined use of observations and models to test scientific understanding. Scientific knowledge builds over time as new observations and data become available. . . . In the case of climate change, scientists have understood for more than a century that emissions from the burning of fossil fuels could lead to increases in the Earth's average surface temperature. Decades of research have confirmed and extended this understanding.

How do we know that Earth has warmed?

Scientists have been taking widespread measurements of Earth's surface temperature since around 1880. These data have steadily improved and, today, temperatures are recorded by thermometers at many thousands of locations, both on the land and over the oceans. Different research groups, including the NASA Goddard Institute for Space Studies, Britain's Hadley Centre for Climate Change, the Japan Meteorological Agency, and NOAA's National Climatic Data Center have used these raw measurements to produce records of long-term global surface temperature change. These groups work carefully to make sure the data aren't skewed by such things as changes in the instruments taking the measurements or by other factors that affect local temperature, such as additional heat that has come from the gradual growth of cities.

These analyses all show that Earth's average surface temperature has increased by more than 1.4°F (0.8°C) over the past 100 years, with much of this increase taking place over the past 35 years. A temperature change of 1.4°F may not seem like much if you're thinking about a daily or seasonal fluctuation, but it is a significant change when you think about a permanent increase averaged across the entire planet. . . .

How do we know that greenhouse gases lead to warming?

As early as the 1820s, scientists began to appreciate the importance of certain gases in regulating the temperature of the Earth. Greenhouse gases—which include carbon dioxide (CO_2), methane, nitrous oxide, and water vapor—act like a blanket in the atmosphere, keeping heat in the lower atmosphere. Although greenhouse gases comprise only a tiny fraction of Earth's atmosphere, they are critical for keeping the planet warm enough to support life as we know it.

Here's how the "greenhouse effect" works: as the Sun's energy hits Earth, some of it is reflected back to space, but most of it is absorbed by the land and oceans. This absorbed energy is then radiated upward from Earth's surface in the form of heat. In the absence of greenhouse gases, this heat would simply escape to space, and the planet's average surface temperature would be well below freezing. But greenhouse gases absorb and redirect some of this energy downward, keeping heat near Earth's surface. As concentrations of heat-trapping greenhouse gases increase in the atmosphere, Earth's natural greenhouse effect is enhanced (like a thicker blanket), causing surface temperatures to rise. Reducing the levels of greenhouse gases in the atmosphere would cause a decrease in surface temperatures.

How do we know that humans are causing greenhouse gas concentrations to increase?

[O]nce humans began digging up long-buried forms of carbon such as coal and oil and burning them for energy, additional CO_2 began to be released into the atmosphere much more rapidly than in the natural carbon cycle. Other human activities, such as cement production and cutting down and burning of forests (deforestation), also add CO_2 to the atmosphere. . . .

To determine how CO_2 concentrations varied prior to such modern measurements, scientists have studied the composition of air bubbles trapped in ice cores extracted from Greenland and Antarctica. These data show that, for at least 2,000 years before the Industrial Revolution, atmospheric CO_2 concentrations were steady and then began to rise sharply beginning in the late 1800s. Today, atmospheric CO_2 concentrations exceed 390 parts per million—nearly 40% higher than preindustrial levels, and, according to ice core data, higher than at any point in the past 800,000 years.

Human activities have increased the atmospheric concentrations of other important greenhouse gases as well. Methane, which is produced by the burning of fossil fuels, the raising of livestock, the decay of landfill wastes, the production and transport of natural gas, and other activities, increased sharply through the 1980s before starting to level off at about two-and-a-half times its preindustrial level. Nitrous oxide has increased by roughly 15% since 1750, mainly as a result of agricultural fertilizer use, but also from fossil fuel burning and certain industrial processes. Certain industrial chemicals, such as chlorofluorocarbons (CFCs), act as potent greenhouse gases and are long-lived in the atmosphere. Because CFCs do not have natural sources, their increases can be attributed unambiguously to human activities. . . .

In addition to direct measurements of CO_2 concentrations in the atmosphere, scientists have amassed detailed records of how much coal, oil, and natural gas is burned each year. They also estimate how much CO_2 is being absorbed, on average, by the oceans and the land surface. These analyses show that about 45% of the CO_2 emitted by human activities remains in the atmosphere. Just as a sink will fill up if water is entering it faster than it can drain, human production of CO_2 is outstripping Earth's natural ability to remove it from the air. As a result, atmospheric CO_2 levels are increasing and will remain elevated for many centuries. Furthermore, a forensic-style analysis of the CO_2 in the atmosphere reveals the chemical "fingerprint" of carbon from fossil fuels. Together, these lines of evidence prove conclusively that the elevated CO_2 concentration in the atmosphere is the result of human activities.*

*NASA Science, *Climate Change: How Do We Know?*, January 2, 2018, https://climate.nasa.gov/evidence/.

contends that moral status is justified for nonhuman animals when they, like humans, possess the psychological property of sentience. Sentient nonhuman animals can experience pain and pleasure, just as humans can; therefore, he says, they are entitled to the same level of moral respect. Some critics, however, object to this kind of animal egalitarianism, affirming that all sentient animals do have moral status but that humans have greater moral considerability than nonhuman animals.

Some theorists want to expand the sphere of moral status to include more than just animals.

They hold to **biocentrism**, or life-centered eth-ics, the view that all living entities have moral status, whether sentient or not. People, cats, trees, weeds, algae, amoebas, germs—all these are worthy of some sort of moral concern simply because they are alive. This moral concern, many biocentrists say, is justified by the teleological nature of liv-ing things (*telos* is Greek for "goal"). Living things are goal-directed, striving consciously or uncon-sciously toward some good. They therefore have moral status. But biocentrists differ on how much respect to grant living things. Some assert that all living things have *equal* moral status: exactly the same moral considerability is accorded to human beings, dogs, redwood trees, and amoebas. These biocentrists are therefore **species egalitarians**. Other biocentrists, **species nonegalitarians**, think that not all living beings are created equal— some have more moral worth than others. A none-galitarian might argue that a human deserves more respect than an elk, an elk more than a rat, and a rat more than a cactus.

In either form, biocentrism implies that in our moral deliberations we cannot ignore how our actions might affect both sentient and nonsentient living beings, as some forms of anthropocentrism might have us do. If we want to build a shopping mall on wetlands, we must consider all the plants and animals that the project would destroy—and judge whether their deaths would outweigh any benefits that the mall would provide to humans and other living things.

In both zoocentrism and biocentrism, the fundamental unit of moral consideration is the *individual*—the individual animal or plant. Only individuals have moral status. This perspective, then, is *individualistic,* its advocates being called **ecological individualists**. In contrast, some theorists say that the proper focus of moral concern is not the individual but the entire biosphere and its ecosystems—what has been called the "biotic community." This view, then, is *holistic;* its propo-nents are **ecological holists**. It implies that in

considering our moral obligations to the environ-ment, the good of the whole will always outweigh the good of an individual. An elk, for example, may be killed to preserve a species of plant or to ensure the health of its ecosystem. As one theorist expressed it, "A thing is right when it tends to pre-serve the integrity, stability, and beauty of the biotic community. It is wrong when it tends otherwise."[3] What properties might confer moral considerabil-ity on the biotic community or an ecosystem? A holist might say that such an environmental whole deserves our respect because it is a unity of beauti-fully integrated parts, or it is a self-regulating sys-tem, or its destruction would diminish the world's genetic possibilities.

MORAL THEORIES

On environmental issues, some traditional moral theories have been strongly anthropocentric. Kant's theory is a good example, mandating duties to people because they are ends in themselves but establishing no direct duties to animals. For Kant, animals have instrumental value only. As he puts it, "Animals . . . are there merely as means to an end. That end is man."[4] Thomas Aquinas, author of the most famous version of natural law theory, also thinks animals are tools to be employed at the discretion of humans. In addition, the Bible has seemed to many to suggest an anthropocentric attitude toward nature, commanding that humans "subdue" the earth and "have dominion over the fish of the sea and over the birds of the air and over every living thing that moves upon the earth" (Genesis 1:28). But traditional theories can also be—and have been—construed in various ways to support nonanthropocentric approaches to envi-ronmental ethics.

As we have seen, some theorists adopt a non-consequentialist or Kantian perspective on nature. They reject instrumentalist views in favor of the notion that the environment or its constituents have intrinsic value, just as persons are thought to be intrinsically valuable. Probably the most overtly Kantian theorist is the philosopher Paul Taylor, a biocentrist who argues that "it is the good (well-being, welfare) of individual organisms, considered as entities having inherent worth, that determines our moral relations with the Earth's wild communities of life" and that "[their] well-being, as well as human well-being, is something to be realized *as an end in itself.*"[5] Some zoocentrists also have a Kantian bent. For example, Tom Regan argues that sentient animals, human and nonhuman, possess equal intrinsic worth and therefore have an equal moral right not to be treated as mere things.[6] In this account, just as there are certain things that we should not do to humans regardless of the resulting utilitarian benefits, so there are ways of treating nonhuman animals that are wrong regardless of the advantages to humans. According to Regan, the result of applying this outlook to the treatment of

animals would be the eradication of factory farming, animal experimentation, and hunting.

Utilitarianism has also been put to use in defense of nonhuman animals. Following the lead of the philosopher Jeremy Bentham, utilitarianism's founder, Peter Singer maintains that in calculating which action will produce the greatest overall satisfaction of interests (for example, an interest in avoiding pain), we must include the interests of all sentient creatures and give their interests equal weight. The pain suffered by a human is no more important than that experienced by a nonhuman animal. This view seems to imply that any factory farming in which animals suffer greatly before being slaughtered is wrong. But it also seems to suggest that if the animals could be raised without such suffering, factory farming may be morally permissible, even if they are killed in the end.

Our moral obligations regarding climate change can be derived from any of the moral theories just mentioned. A nonconsequentialist, for example, might argue that we have a duty to protect or save the earth because the planet as a whole has intrinsic value. A utilitarian could make a strong case that we should try to reverse climate change because the consequences of not doing so would be apocalyptic.

MORAL ARGUMENTS

Serious environmental issues and the arguments that surround them are numerous, varied, and complex, so for the purposes of evaluation, let us focus on arguments pertaining to the one question that has concerned us most throughout this chapter: *When, if ever, do environmental entities or beings have moral status?* As we have seen, environmental philosophers and other thinkers have argued for and against different kinds of entities having moral considerability and for and against various justifications for that status. The entities thought to be worthy of such moral concern include human beings exclusively (anthropocentrism), human and nonhuman animals (zoocentrism), living things (biocentrism),

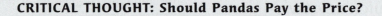

CRITICAL THOUGHT: Should Pandas Pay the Price?

Some of the most controversial disputes in environmental ethics involve conflicts between concern for endangered species and the economic needs and demands of humans. Here is just one of many recent examples:

> (*China Daily*)—The more than 100 wild giant pandas in Northwest China's Gansu Province are now stepping onto the verge of extinction because of a decline in their ability to reproduce, according to Xinhua reports.
>
> Researchers from the Gansu Baishuijiang Giant Panda Nature Reserve said the giant pandas in the province now live in five separate habitats, making mating among the groups almost impossible.
>
> According to basic principles of genetics and the pandas' reproduction habits, a group of less than 50 giant pandas are predicted to become extinct at some point as a result of a weakening reproductive ability caused by inbreeding.
>
> Wang Hao, a giant panda expert of Peking University, said the fragmentation of wild pandas' habitats had become the biggest threat to the survival of the species.
>
> Wang said that the construction of highways is cutting large panda habitats into smaller and

> smaller ones, increasing the risk of degeneration of the species. . . .
>
> Wang estimated that the annual cost to protect one wild panda exceeds 5 million yuan (US$617,000).*

Which should be given more moral weight—the people or the pandas? What are your reasons for preferring one over the other? If you agree that we should try to save endangered species like the panda, how much should we be willing to pay to do so? Is $617,000 per panda an acceptable price? How about $1 million? Suppose saving one panda would put one thousand people out of a job, forcing scores of families into poverty. Would saving the pandas be worth that cost? Why or why not? What moral principle would you devise to help you answer these questions (and similar questions regarding any endangered species)?

*Guo Nei, reprinted with permission of SydiGate Media Inc. from "Road Construction Segregates Giant Pandas' Habitats in Gansu," *China Daily*, December 5, 2006; permission conveyed through Copyright Clearance Center, Inc.

and collections or systems of living things such as species or ecosystems (ecological holism). The properties that are supposed to validate their claim to moral worth range across a broad spectrum of possibilities—from moral agency or sentience to complexity to self-regulation to beauty.

To begin, let us examine a simple argument containing a premise that offers a common answer to our question—the answer that entities in the environment have moral status because they are *natural* (lacking human interference or contrivance).

1. All natural entities have moral status (intrinsic value or rights, for example).

2. Old-growth forests are natural entities.

3. Therefore, old-growth forests have moral status.

We can see right away that this is a valid argument, but—as is so often the case in moral arguments—the moral premise (Premise 1) is not obviously true (though the other premise definitely is). What reasons might someone give to support the statement that objects in nature deserve our respect just because their properties are due solely to natural processes?

One reason that could be put forth is that Premise 1 is supported by our moral intuitions (our considered moral judgments, for example). To test this idea, mull over this thought experiment:

Imagine that a certain mine requires the destruction of a group of trees on a rocky outcrop and of the outcrop itself. Environmentalists protest that such destruction involves an uncompensated loss of value. The mining company promises to reconstruct the outcrop from synthetic parts and to replace the trees with plastic models. This bit of artificial environment will be indistinguishable, except by laboratory analysis, from what was originally there. It will be exactly as appealing to look at, no animals will be harmed as a consequence, and no ecosystem will be disrupted.[7]

What, if anything, would be wrong with replacing these natural entities with synthetic ones? A few trees would be destroyed, and thus there is a loss of living things, but let us mentally discount the loss. Would this substitution of nonnatural for natural make a moral difference? Would the mining company be guilty of wrongdoing? If this scenario suggests to us that the property of naturalness does confer some kind of moral standing on objects, then perhaps our moral intuitions do support Premise 1.

The obvious move for a critic is to assert that it is not at all clear whether moral intuitions offer such support. Perhaps we are merely confused, actually worrying not about unnaturalness but about harm to ecosystems or extermination of wildlife.[8]

A defender of Premise 1 could try another tack. She could attempt to take our moral intuitions in a different direction, declaring that just as fake works of art seem to have less value for us than the originals, so synthetic objects in the environment have less intrinsic value than their natural counterparts or originals. We simply do not appreciate replicas of fine sculptures as much as we do the originals, and we do not respect artificial trees as much as we do natural ones. The property of being natural, then, appears to confer some value on objects—and thus some level of moral standing.[9]

A detractor could cast doubt on this line by pointing out that there seem to be instances in which we do in fact value the artificial more than the natural. For example, Niagara Falls on the American side of the border with Canada is undeniably beautiful and majestic, exemplifying the ideal waterfall in its natural state. But oddly enough, the majestic, "natural" state of the falls is largely a product of human ingenuity. Because of natural erosion, the falls deteriorate over time and—without human intervention—would suffer so much damage that they would no longer look much like the falls people have come to expect. Through reconstruction and control of water flow, engineers have saved Niagara Falls, a now largely artificial phenomenon that people would almost certainly prefer over the natural but less impressive version.[10]

Let us now consider a "higher-level" sort of argument, one that tries to establish the truth of a particular environmental theory, in this case biocentric egalitarianism. Recall that this doctrine asserts that all living things possess equal moral status—no being is superior to any other in moral considerability. Humans, then, are not entitled to more respect than apes or redwoods or elk. Here is how the philosopher Paul Taylor argues for this position:[11]

1. Humans are members of earth's community of life in exactly the same way that all other living things are members.

2. Human beings and all other living things constitute a dynamic system of interlinked and interdependent parts.

3. Each living thing is a "teleological center of life, pursuing its own good in its own way."

4. Human beings are not superior to other species.

5. Therefore, all living things have equal moral status.

This argument is complex and deserves far more close analysis than we can provide here. But we can home in on a few interesting elements.

Consider Premise 4. At the outset, note that the argument is not valid: the conclusion does not follow from the first four premises. Taylor acknowledges this fact but suggests that if we accept Premises 1–4, then it would at least be more reasonable than not to accept the conclusion. He says the same thing about Premise 4: if we accept Premises 1–3, it would not be unreasonable to accept the fourth premise. But some argue that Premise 4 does not follow from Premises 1–3. More to the point, it could be argued that even if we accept that humans are part of an interdependent community of life in which all members are teleological centers pursuing their own good, we are not necessarily being unreasonable if we then reject the idea that humans are on a par with all other species. Even if Premises 1–3 are true, we are not obliged to accept Premise 4.

Some philosophers have argued directly against Taylor's conclusion (Statement 5) by drawing out its implications. If all species are morally equal, what would that imply about how we treat various species? One critic gives this answer:

> What seems far more problematic for species egalitarianism is that it seems to suggest that it makes no difference *what* we kill. Vegetarians typically think it worse to kill a cow than to kill a carrot. Are they wrong? Yes they are, according to species egalitarianism. In this respect, species egalitarianism cannot be right. I believe we have reason to respect nature. But we fail to give nature due respect if we say we should have no more respect for a cow than for a potato.[12]

This counterargument is, of course, another appeal to our moral intuitions. We are asked to reflect on whether it would be morally permissible to treat a cow as if it had the same moral status as a potato. If they do deserve the same level of respect, then if we must kill one of them, we should not care which. They are moral equals. But if we think that it does matter which one we kill, we have reason to reject the notion that they are moral equals—and thus deny biocentric egalitarianism.

CHAPTER REVIEW

SUMMARY

Environmental ethics, a branch of applied ethics, explores questions about the value of nature and its constituents, the relationship between the environment and humans, and the moral obligations that humans have toward the environment. Logical arguments in the field rely on several key concepts, including instrumental value, intrinsic value, and moral status or considerability. Something with instrumental value is valuable as a means to something else; something with intrinsic value is valuable in itself. An entity has moral status if it is a suitable candidate for moral concern or respect in its own right.

Several positions have been staked out regarding the proper attitude of humans toward nature. Anthropocentrism is the view that only humans have moral standing; zoocentrism, that animals do; and biocentrism, that all living things do. Species egalitarians believe that all living things have equal moral status; species nonegalitarians, that they do not. Ecological individualists think that only individuals have moral status; ecological holists, that only the biosphere and its ecosystems do.

Some theorists have adopted a Kantian perspective on the environment. Paul Taylor insists that organisms have inherent worth and should not be treated merely as means to ends. Tom Regan asserts that sentient beings possess equal intrinsic worth and should not be considered mere things. A utilitarian stance is also possible, as Peter Singer has demonstrated in his position on animal rights.

KEY TERMS
anthropocentrism (p. 431)
zoocentrism (p. 431)
biocentrism (p. 434)
species egalitarian (p. 434)
species nonegalitarian (p. 434)
ecological individualist (p. 434)
ecological holist (p. 434)

EXERCISES

Review Questions

1. What is moral status? (p. 431)
2. What is anthropocentrism? (p. 431)
3. Define zoocentrism and biocentrism. (p. 431, 434)
4. What is a species egalitarian? (p. 434)
5. What is the difference between instrumental and intrinsic value? (p. 430)
6. On what grounds might someone believe that nature has intrinsic value? (p. 430)
7. What is the difference between species egalitarianism and species nonegalitarianism? (p. 434)
8. What is an ecological holist? An ecological individualist? (p. 434)
9. What was Kant's attitude toward animals? (p. 434)
10. What pieces of evidence have convinced scientists that climate change is happening? (p. 432–433)

Discussion Questions

1. Who or what has moral status—humans, nonhuman animals, trees? Explain.
2. Do you believe that all living things have equal moral status? Why or why not?
3. Are you an anthropocentrist? Are you a zoocentrist?
4. Do you think that humans and animals have equal moral status? Why or why not?
5. Does a human baby have the same moral status as a dog or horse? Explain.
6. Do you think Kant was wrong about animals having only instrumental value? Why or why not?
7. Do entities in the environment have moral status because they are natural? Explain.
8. Critique Paul Taylor's argument for biocentric egalitarianism.
9. Critique the claim that climate change is not a real phenomenon.
10. Do you believe that you have a moral obligation to try to help counteract global warming? Explain.

FURTHER READING

Jeffrey Bennett, *A Global Warming Primer* (Boulder, CO: Big Kid Science, 2016).

Andrew Brennan and Yeuk-Sze Lo, "Environmental Ethics," in *Stanford Encyclopedia of Philosophy*, Summer 2002 ed., ed. Edward N. Zalta, http://plato.stanford .edu/archives/sum2002/entries/ethics-environmental / (March 1, 2015).

J. Baird Callicott, "The Search for an Environmental Ethic," in *Matters of Life and Death: New Introductory Essays in Moral Philosophy,* ed. Tom Regan, 2nd ed. (New York: Random House, 1986).

Andrew Dessler, *Introduction to Climate Change* (Cambridge: Cambridge University Press, 2016).

Robert Elliot, "Environmental Ethics," in *A Companion to Ethics,* ed. Peter Singer, corr. ed. (Oxford: Blackwell, 1993).

Garrett Hardin, "The Tragedy of the Commons," *Science* 162 (December 13, 1968): 1243–48.

Robert Heilbroner, "What Has Posterity Ever Done for Me?" *New York Times Magazine,* January 19, 1975, 14–15.

Aldo Leopold, "The Land Ethic," in *A Sand County Almanac: And Sketches Here and There* (1949; reprint, New York: Oxford University Press, 1981).

Jennifer Marohasy, ed., *Climate Change: The Facts 2017* (Melbourne, VIC: Connor Court, 2017).

Arne Naess, "The Shallow and the Deep: Long-Range Ecological Movement," *Inquiry* 16 (Spring 1973): 95–100.

Holmes Rolston III, "Values in and Duties to the Natural World," in *Ecology, Economics, Ethics: The Broken Circle,* ed. F. Herbert Bormann and Stephen R. Kellert (New Haven: Yale University Press, 1991).

Albert Schweitzer, "Reverence for Life," in *Civilization and Ethics,* trans. John Naish (London: Black, 1923).

Walter Sinnot-Armstrong and Richard B. Howarth, ed., *Perspectives on Climate Change: Science, Economics, Politics, Ethics* (Amsterdam: Elsevier, 2005).

Christopher D. Stone, "Should Trees Have Standing? Toward Legal Rights for Natural Objects" in *Should Trees Have Standing? Toward Legal Rights for Natural Objects* (Los Altos, CA: William Kaufman, 1974).

Lynn White Jr., "The Historical Roots of Our Ecological Crisis," *Science* 155 (March 1967): 1203–7.

ETHICAL DILEMMAS

1. The Moral Dilemma of Climate Change

Climate change presents us with a moral dilemma that we cannot escape. The problem presented by climate change and our attempts to solve it will affect not only us but also our children and grandchildren. Climate change is no ordinary puzzle: it's a serious intergenerational challenge. Here's one way of expressing it:

> It boils down to this: We benefit mightily from burning cheap coal and will shoulder most of the expense associated with switching the global economy to low-carbon fuel sources. But our grandchildren and great-grandchildren will pay the price for our profligate energy ways and will reap the majority of the benefit of our shift to cleaner-burning fuels.*

Should we pay now to try to rein in global warming and its awful effects, or should we let our kids pay? Do we have moral obligations to future generations, to people who don't yet exist? If we do have obligations to them, how much should we sacrifice now to do our duty?

*Nicole Heller and Douglas Fischer, "Ethical Dilemma Profoundly Sways Economics of Climate Change," Climate Central, January 27, 2011, http://www.climatecentral.org/news/ethical-dilemma-profoundly -sways-economics-of-climate-change.

2. Saving the Glaciers

The glaciers have been disappearing from Glacier National Park in Montana and adjoining Waterton National Park in Canada. In 1850, Glacier is said to have had 150 glaciers; in 2006, there were 27. In response to this trend, various organizations petitioned for the parks to be designated endangered by being placed on the danger list of the World Heritage Committee. As one report says,

> Endangered status would require the World Heritage Committee to find ways to mitigate how climate change affects the park, [the law professor who wrote the petition] said. . . Better fuel efficiency for automobiles and stronger energy efficiency standards for buildings and appliances are among the ways to reduce greenhouse pollution that contributes to warming, the petition [said].
>
> But some denounced the petition as unnecessary and unsupported by scientific data, while one group of scientists estimated that if climate trends continue, Glacier Park's glaciers will disappear completely by 2030.[†]

Suppose the glaciers' melting would have no appreciable effect on the environment except that they would no longer exist. Would conservationists still be justified in trying to save the glaciers?

If so, how could they justify their efforts? If not, why not? Suppose the glaciers could be saved only if the government spends $10 billion on pollution controls—money that would have to be taken away from social programs. Would this cost be worth it? Why or why not? Justify your answers.

[†]Associated Press, "Endangered Status for Glacier National Park?" NBCNEWS.com, February 16, 2006, http://www.nbcnews.com/id/11389665/ns/us_news-environment/t/endangered-status-glacier-national -park/#.VOj_I1PF9RY (February 21, 2015).

3. Ivory-Billed Woodpecker v. Irrigation

While ornithologists continue to debate whether the ivory-billed woodpecker still lingers in the bayous of Arkansas, the rare bird, once presumed extinct, is now being used by conservationists in their fight against a federally funded and potentially devastating irrigation project.

A Little Rock federal court will hear a case against the U.S. Army Corps of Engineers' Grand Prairie Area Demonstration Project. Plaintiffs ask that all work be halted on the project until appropriate environmental studies can be performed to evaluate its effect on the woodpecker.

Lisa Swann of the National Wildlife Federation states that the Grand Prairie project would be "a recipe for disaster" for the near extinct bird, though the U.S. Army Corps maintains that the $319 million project, which would replenish exhausted groundwater aquifers in a 242,000-acre agricultural region, is completely safe.

The corps biologist, Ed Lambert, argues that their "biological assessment" performed last spring has proven that the Grand Prairie project will bring no harm to the woodpecker.

Plans for Grand Prairie have been underway since the 1980s, when studies found that the groundwater aquifers of east-central Arkansas were in danger of depletion by rice growers. The corps has been working with area farmers to build reservoirs that will eventually be filled with water pumped from the White River.

According to the corps, Grand Prairie will not only aid farmers, but also create new wetland habitat for waterfowl and shorebirds. The water piped in from the White River could also replenish the slowly shrinking hardwood forests of Arkansas and reintroduce thousands of acres of native grassland.

However, Swann's group and other environmentalists see the project differently. They argue that the project will waste huge amounts of tax dollars and benefit only farmers. The National Wildlife Federation stated in one publication that the "mammoth sucking machine" will damage wetlands and pollute the water, threatening ducks, mussels, and a variety of other species in the region that rely on clean and safe water.

The celebrity among these species is the ivory-billed woodpecker, long believed to be extinct. Sightings since the 1940s were given little credit by experts, as the smaller pileated woodpecker, which has similar coloring, is commonly mistaken for the ivory-bill.

One expert, however, began to investigate these sightings. Tim Gallagher, of the Cornell Lab of Ornithology and editor of *Living Bird* magazine, began to study the mysterious ivory-bill in the 1970s. Eventually, his research led him to Gene Sparling, who claimed to have seen a red-crested male while kayaking in the wetlands of eastern Arkansas.

During the winter of 2004, Gallagher set out to catch a glimpse of the elusive bird himself, accompanied by Sparling and a fellow birder, and on February 27, Gallagher succeeded in spotting a male ivory-bill. Further expeditions ensued, and on April 28, 2005, an article in *Science* was published proclaiming that the ivory-bill was no longer extinct.[‡]

Assume that the woodpecker does exist and that the water project would wipe it out. Should the project proceed or be cancelled? Why? How might a species egalitarian (biocentrist) answer this? A species nonegalitarian? An ecological holist?

[‡]Based on Mike Stuckey, "New Star of the Bird World Stars in Lawsuit, Too," MSNBC.com, January 25, 2006, www.nbcnews.com/id/10929337/ (January 20, 2012).

READINGS

People or Penguins

William F. Baxter

I start with the modest proposition that, in dealing with pollution, or indeed with any problem, it is helpful to know what one is attempting to accomplish. Agreement on how and whether to pursue a particular objective, such as pollution control, is not possible unless some more general objective has been identified and stated with reasonable precision. We talk loosely of having clean air and clean water, of preserving our wilderness areas, and so forth. But none of these is a sufficiently general objective: each is more accurately viewed as a means rather than as an end.

With regard to clean air, for example, one may ask, "how clean?" and "what does clean mean?" It is even reasonable to ask, "why have clean air?" Each of these questions is an implicit demand that a more general community goal be stated—a goal sufficiently general in its scope and enjoying sufficiently general assent among the community of actors that such "why" questions no longer seem admissible with respect to that goal.

If, for example, one states as a goal the proposition that "every person should be free to do whatever he wishes in contexts where his actions do not interfere with the interests of other human beings," the speaker is unlikely to be met with a response of "why." The goal may be criticized as uncertain in its implications or difficult to implement, but it is so basic a tenet of our civilization—it reflects a cultural value so broadly shared, at least in the abstract—that the question "why" is seen as impertinent or imponderable or both.

I do not mean to suggest that everyone would agree with the "spheres of freedom" objective just stated. Still less do I mean to suggest that a society could subscribe to four or five such general objectives that would be adequate in their coverage to serve as testing criteria by which all other disagreements might be measured. One difficulty in the attempt to construct such a list is that each new goal added will conflict, in certain applications, with each prior goal listed; and thus each goal serves as a limited qualification on prior goals.

Without any expectation of obtaining unanimous consent to them, let me set forth four goals that I generally use as ultimate testing criteria in attempting to frame solutions to problems of human organization. My position regarding pollution stems from these four criteria. If the criteria appeal to you and any part of what appears hereafter does not, our disagreement will have a helpful focus: which of us is correct, analytically, in supposing that his position on pollution would better serve these general goals. If the criteria do not seem acceptable to you, then it is to be expected that our more particular judgments will differ, and the task will then be yours to identify the basic set of criteria upon which your particular judgments rest.

My criteria are as follows:

1. The spheres of freedom criterion stated above.
2. Waste is a bad thing. The dominant feature of human existence is scarcity—our available resources, our aggregate labors, and our skill in employing both have always been, and will continue for some time to be, inadequate to yield to every man all the tangible and intangible satisfactions he would like to have. Hence, none of those resources, or labors, or skills, should be wasted—that is, employed so as to yield less than they might yield in human satisfactions.
3. Every human being should be regarded as an end rather than as a means to be used for the betterment of another. Each should be afforded dignity and regarded as having an absolute claim to an evenhanded application of such rules as the community may adopt for its governance.

4. Both the incentive and the opportunity to improve his share of satisfactions should be preserved to every individual. Preservation of incentive is dictated by the "no-waste" criterion and enjoins against the continuous, totally egalitarian redistribution of satisfactions, or wealth; but subject to that constraint, everyone should receive, by continuous redistribution if necessary, some minimal share of aggregate wealth so as to avoid a level of privation from which the opportunity to improve his situation becomes illusory.

The relationship of these highly general goals to the more specific environmental issues at hand may not be readily apparent, and I am not yet ready to demonstrate their pervasive implications. But let me give one indication of their implications. Recently scientists have informed us that use of DDT in food production is causing damage to the penguin population. For the present purposes let us accept that assertion as an indisputable scientific fact. The scientific fact is often asserted as if the correct implication—that we must stop agricultural use of DDT—followed from the mere statement of the fact of penguin damage. But plainly it does not follow if my criteria are employed.

My criteria are oriented to people, not penguins. Damage to penguins, or sugar pines, or geological marvels is, without more, simply irrelevant. One must go further, by my criteria, and say: Penguins are important because people enjoy seeing them walk about rocks; and furthermore, the well-being of people would be less impaired by halting use of DDT than by giving up penguins. In short, my observations about environmental problems will be people-oriented, as are my criteria. I have no interest in preserving penguins for their own sake.

It may be said by way of objection to this position, that it is very selfish of people to act as if each person represented one unit of importance and nothing else was of any importance. It is undeniably selfish. Nevertheless I think it is the only tenable starting place for analysis for several reasons. First, no other position corresponds to the way most people really think and act—i.e., corresponds to reality.

Second, this attitude does not portend any massive destruction of nonhuman flora and fauna, for people depend on them in many obvious ways, and they will be preserved because and to the degree that humans do depend on them.

Third, what is good for humans is, in many respects, good for penguins and pine trees—clean air for example. So that humans are, in these respects, surrogates for plant and animal life.

Fourth, I do not know how we could administer any other system. Our decisions are either private or collective. Insofar as Mr. Jones is free to act privately, he may give such preferences as he wishes to other forms of life: he may feed birds in winter and do with less himself, and he may even decline to resist an advancing polar bear on the ground that the bear's appetite is more important than those portions of himself that the bear may choose to eat. In short my basic premise does not rule out private altruism to competing life-forms. It does rule out, however, Mr. Jones's inclination to feed Mr. Smith to the bear, however hungry the bear, however despicable Mr. Smith.

Insofar as we act collectively on the other hand, only humans can be afforded an opportunity to participate in the collective decisions. Penguins cannot vote now and are unlikely subjects for the franchise—pine trees more unlikely still. Again each individual is free to cast his vote so as to benefit sugar pines if that is his inclination. But many of the more extreme assertions that one hears from some conservationists amount to tacit assertions that they are specially appointed representatives of sugar pines, and hence that their preferences should be weighted more heavily than the preferences of other humans who do not enjoy equal rapport with "nature." The simplistic assertion that agricultural use of DDT must stop at once because it is harmful to penguins is of that type.

Fifth, if polar bears or pine trees or penguins, like men, are to be regarded as ends rather than means, if they are to count in our calculus of social organization, someone must tell me how much each one counts, and someone must tell me how these life-forms are to be permitted to express their preferences, for I do not know either answer. If the answer is that certain people are to hold their proxies, then I want to know how those proxy-holders are to be selected: self-appointment does not seem workable to me.

Sixth, and by way of summary of all the foregoing, let me point out that the set of environmental issues under discussion—although they raise very complex technical questions of how to achieve any objective—ultimately raise a normative question: what *ought* we to do. Questions of *ought* are unique to the human mind and world—they are meaningless as applied to a nonhuman situation.

I reject the proposition that we *ought* to respect the "balance of nature" or to "preserve the environment" unless the reason for doing so, express or implied, is the benefit of man.

I reject the idea that there is a "right" or "morally correct" state of nature to which we should return. The word "nature" has no normative connotation. Was it "right" or "wrong" for the earth's crust to heave in contortion and create mountains and seas? Was it "right" for the first amphibian to crawl up out of the primordial ooze? Was it "wrong" for plants to reproduce themselves and alter the atmospheric composition in favor of oxygen? For animals to alter the atmosphere in favor of carbon dioxide both by breathing oxygen and eating plants? No answers can be given to these questions because they are meaningless questions.

All this may seem obvious to the point of being tedious, but much of the present controversy over environment and pollution rests on tacit normative assumptions about just such nonnormative phenomena: that it is "wrong" to impair penguins with DDT, but not to slaughter cattle for prime rib roasts. That it is wrong to kill stands of sugar pines with industrial fumes, but not to cut sugar pines and build housing for the poor. Every man is entitled to his own preferred definition of Walden Pond, but there is no definition that has any moral superiority over another, except by reference to the selfish needs of the human race.

From the fact that there is no normative definition of the natural state, it follows that there is no normative definition of clean air or pure water—hence no definition of polluted air—or of pollution—except by reference to the needs of man. The "right" composition of the atmosphere is one which has some dust in it and some lead in it and some hydrogen sulfide in it—just those amounts that attend a sensibly organized society thoughtfully and knowledgeably pursuing the greatest possible satisfaction for its human members.

The first and most fundamental step toward solution of our environmental problems is a clear recognition that our objective is not pure air or water but rather some optimal state of pollution. That step immediately suggests the question: How do we define and attain the level of pollution that will yield the maximum possible amount of human satisfaction?

Low levels of pollution contribute to human satisfaction but so do food and shelter and education and music. To attain ever lower levels of pollution, we must pay the cost of having less of these other things. I contrast that view of the cost of pollution control with the more popular statement that pollution control will "cost" very large numbers of dollars. The popular statement is true in some senses, false in others; sorting out the true and false senses is of some importance. The first step in that sorting process is to achieve a clear understanding of the difference between dollars and resources. Resources are the wealth of our nation; dollars are merely claim checks upon those resources. Resources are of vital importance; dollars are comparatively trivial.

Four categories of resources are sufficient for our purposes: At any given time a nation, or a planet if you prefer, has a stock of labor, of technological skill, of capital goods, and of natural resources (such as mineral deposits, timber, water, land, etc.). These resources can be used in various combinations to yield goods and services of all kinds—in some limited quantity. The quantity will be larger if they are combined efficiently, smaller if combined inefficiently. But in either event the resource stock is limited, the goods and services that they can be made to yield are limited; even the most efficient use of them will yield less than our population, in the aggregate, would like to have.

If one considers building a new dam, it is appropriate to say that it will be costly in the sense that it will require x hours of labor, y tons of steel and concrete, and z amount of capital goods. If these resources are devoted to the dam, then they cannot be used to build hospitals, fishing rods, schools, or electric can openers. That is the meaningful sense in which the dam is costly.

Quite apart from the very important question of how wisely we can combine our resources to produce goods and services, is the very different question of how they get distributed—who gets how many goods? Dollars constitute the claim checks which are distributed among people and which control their share of national output. Dollars are nearly valueless pieces of paper except to the extent that they do represent claim checks to some fraction of the output of goods and services. Viewed as claim checks, all the dollars outstanding during any period of time are worth, in the aggregate, the goods and services that are available to be claimed with them during that period—neither more nor less.

It is far easier to increase the supply of dollars than to increase the production of goods and services—printing dollars is easy. But printing more dollars doesn't help because each dollar then simply becomes a claim to fewer goods, i.e., becomes worth less.

The point is this: many people fall into error upon hearing the statement that the decision to build a dam, or to clean up a river, will cost $X million. It is regrettably easy to say: "It's only money. This is a wealthy country, and we have lots of money." But you cannot build a dam or clean a river with $X million—unless you also have a match, you can't even make a fire. One builds a dam or cleans a river by diverting labor and steel and trucks and factories from making one kind of goods to making another. The cost in dollars is merely a shorthand way of describing the extent of the diversion necessary. If we build a dam for $X million, then we must recognize that we will have $X million less housing and food and medical care and electric can openers as a result.

Similarly, the costs of controlling pollution are best expressed in terms of the other goods we will have to give up to do the job. This is not to say the job should not be done. Badly as we need more housing, more medical care, and more can openers, and more symphony orchestras, we could do with somewhat less of them, in my judgment at least, in exchange for somewhat cleaner air and rivers. But that is the nature of the trade-off, and analysis of the problem is advanced if that unpleasant reality is kept in mind. Once the trade-off relationship is clearly perceived, it is possible to state in a very general way what the optimal level of pollution is. I would state it as follows:

People enjoy watching penguins. They enjoy relatively clean air and smog-free vistas. Their health is improved by relatively clean water and air. Each of these benefits is a type of good or service. As a society we would be well advised to give up one washing machine if the resources that would have gone into that washing machine can yield greater human satisfaction when diverted into pollution control. We should give up one hospital if the resources thereby freed would yield more human satisfaction when devoted to elimination of noise in our cities. And so on, trade-off by trade-off, we should divert our productive capacities from the production of existing goods and services to the production of a cleaner, quieter, more pastoral nation up to—and no further than—the point at which we value more highly the next washing machine or hospital that we would have to do without than we value the next unit of environmental improvement that the diverted resources would create.

Now this proposition seems to me unassailable but so general and abstract as to be unhelpful—at least unadministerable in the form stated. It assumes we can measure in some way the incremental units of human satisfaction yielded by very different types of goods. The proposition must remain a pious abstraction until I can explain how this measurement process can occur. . . . But I insist that the proposition stated describes the result for which we should be striving—and again, that it is always useful to know what your target is even if your weapons are too crude to score a bull's eye.

It's Not My Fault: Global Warming and Individual Moral Obligations
WALTER SINNOTT-ARMSTRONG

Previous [essays] have focused on scientific research, economic projections, and government policies. However, even if scientists establish that global warming is occurring, even if economists confirm that its costs will be staggering, and even if political theorists agree that governments must do something about it, it is still not clear what moral obligations regarding global warming devolve upon individuals like you and me. That is the question to be addressed in this essay.

1. ASSUMPTIONS

To make the issue stark, let us begin with a few assumptions. I believe that these assumptions are probably

Walter Sinnott-Armstrong, "It's Not My Fault: Global Warming and Individual Moral Obligations" in Perspectives on Climate Change: Science, Economics, Politics, Ethics, ed. Walter Sinnott-Armstrong and Richard B. Howarth (Amsterdam: Elsevier, 2005), 285–307. © 2005 Emerald Publishing Limited. All rights reserved. Reprinted with permission.

roughly accurate, but none is certain, and I will not try to justify them here. Instead, I will simply take them for granted for the sake of argument.

First, global warming has begun and is likely to increase over the next century. We cannot be sure exactly how much or how fast, but hot times are coming.

Second, a significant amount of global warming is due to human activities. The main culprit is fossil fuels.

Third, global warming will create serious problems for many people over the long term by causing climate changes, including violent storms, floods from sea level rises, droughts, heat waves, and so on. Millions of people will probably be displaced or die.

Fourth, the poor will be hurt most of all. The rich countries are causing most of the global warming, but they will be able to adapt to climate changes more easily. Poor countries that are close to sea level might be devastated.

Fifth, governments, especially the biggest and richest ones, are able to mitigate global warming. They can impose limits on emissions. They can require or give incentives for increased energy efficiency. They can stop deforestation and fund reforestation. They can develop ways to sequester carbon dioxide in oceans or underground. These steps will help, but the only long-run solution lies in alternatives to fossil fuels. These alternatives can be found soon if governments start massive research projects now.

Sixth, it is too late to stop global warming. Because there is so much carbon dioxide in the atmosphere already, because carbon dioxide remains in the atmosphere for so long, and because we will remain dependent on fossil fuels in the near future, governments can slow down global warming or reduce its severity, but they cannot prevent it. Hence, governments need to adapt. They need to build seawalls. They need to reinforce houses that cannot withstand storms. They need to move populations from low-lying areas.

Seventh, these steps will be costly. Increased energy efficiency can reduce expenses, adaptation will create some jobs, and money will be made in the research and production of alternatives to fossil fuels. Still, any steps that mitigate or adapt to global warming will slow down our economies, at least in the short run. That will hurt many people, especially many poor people.

Eighth, despite these costs, the major governments throughout the world still morally ought to take some of these steps. The clearest moral obligation falls on the United States. The United States caused and continues to cause more of the problem than any other country. The United States can spend more resources on a solution without sacrificing basic necessities. This country has the scientific expertise to solve technical problems. Other countries follow its lead (sometimes!). So the United States has a special moral obligation to help mitigate and adapt to global warming.

2. THE PROBLEM

Even assuming all of this, it is still not clear what I as an individual morally ought to do about global warming. That issue is not as simple as many people assume.

I want to bring out some of its complications.

It should be clear from the start that "individual" moral obligations do not always follow directly from "collective" moral obligations. The fact that your government morally ought to do something does not prove that "you" ought to do it, even if your government fails. Suppose that a bridge is dangerous because so much traffic has gone over it and continues to go over it. The government has a moral obligation to make the bridge safe. If the government fails to do its duty, it does not follow that I personally have a moral obligation to fix the bridge. It does not even follow that I have a moral obligation to fill in one crack in the bridge, even if the bridge would be fixed if everyone filled in one crack, even if I drove over the bridge many times, and even if I still drive over it every day. Fixing the bridge is the government's job, not mine. While I ought to encourage the government to fulfill its obligations, I do not have to take on those obligations myself.

All that this shows is that government obligations do not "always" imply parallel individual obligations. Still, maybe "sometimes" they do. My government has a moral obligation to teach arithmetic to the children in my town, including my own children. If the government fails in this obligation, then I do take on a moral obligation to teach arithmetic to my children. Thus, when the government fails in its obligations, sometimes I have to fill in, and sometimes I do not.

What about global warming? If the government fails to do anything about global warming, what am I supposed to do about it? There are lots of ways for me as an individual to fight global warming. I can protest against bad government policies and vote for candidates who will make the government fulfill its moral obligations. I can support private organizations that fight global warming, such as the Pew Foundation, or boycott companies that contribute too much to global warming, such as most oil companies. Each of these cases is interesting, but they all differ. To simplify our discussion, we need to pick one act as our focus.

My example will be wasteful driving. Some people drive to their jobs or to the store because they have no other reasonable way to work and eat. I want to avoid issues about whether these goals justify driving, so I will focus on a case where nothing so important is gained. I will consider driving for fun on a beautiful Sunday afternoon. My drive is not necessary to cure depression or calm aggressive impulses. All that is gained is pleasure: Ah, the feel of wind in your hair! The views! How spectacular! Of course, you could drive a fuel-efficient hybrid car. But fuel-efficient cars have less "get up and go." So let us consider a gas-guzzling sport utility vehicle. Ah, the feeling of power! The excitement! Maybe you do not like to go for drives in sport utility vehicles on sunny Sunday afternoons, but many people do.

Do we have a moral obligation not to drive in such circumstances? This question concerns driving, not "buying" cars. To make this clear, let us assume that I borrow the gas-guzzler from a friend. This question is also not about "legal" obligations. So let us assume that it is perfectly legal to go for such drives. Perhaps it ought to be illegal, but it is not. Note also that my question is not about what would be "best." Maybe it would be better, even morally better, for me not to drive a gas-guzzler just for fun. But that is not the issue I want to address here. My question is whether I have a "moral" obligation not to drive a gas-guzzler just for fun on this particular sunny Sunday afternoon.

One final complication must be removed. I am interested in global warming, but there might be other moral reasons not to drive unnecessarily. I risk causing an accident, since I am not a perfect driver. I also will likely spew exhaust into the breathing space of pedestrians, bicyclists, or animals on the side of the road as I drive by. Perhaps these harms and risks give me a moral obligation not to go for my joyride. That is not clear. After all, these reasons also apply if I drive the most efficient car available, and even if I am driving to work with no other way to keep my job. Indeed, I might scare or injure bystanders even if my car gave off no greenhouse gases or pollution. In any case, I want to focus on global warming. So my real question is whether the facts about global warming give me any moral obligation not to drive a gas-guzzler just for fun on this sunny Sunday afternoon.

I admit that I am "inclined" to answer, "Yes." To me, global warming does "seem" to make such wasteful driving morally wrong.

Still, I do not feel confident in this judgment. I know that other people disagree (even though they are also concerned about the environment). I would probably have different moral intuitions about this case if I had been raised differently or if I now lived in a different culture. My moral intuition might be distorted by overgeneralization from the other cases where I think that other entities (large governments) do have moral obligations to fight global warming. I also worry that my moral intuition might be distorted by my desire to avoid conflicts with my environmentalist friends. The issue of global warming generates strong emotions because of its political implications and because of how scary its effects are. It is also a peculiarly modern case, especially because it operates on a much grander scale than my moral intuitions evolved to handle long ago when acts did not have such long-term effects on future generations (or at least people were not aware of such effects). In such circumstances, I doubt that we are justified in trusting our moral intuitions alone. We need some kind of confirmation.

One way to confirm the truth of my moral intuitions would be to derive them from a general moral principle. A principle could tell us why wasteful driving is morally wrong, so we would not have to depend on bare assertion. And a principle might be supported by more trustworthy moral beliefs. The problem is "which" principle?

3. ACTUAL ACT PRINCIPLES

One plausible principle refers to causing harm. If one person had to inhale all of the exhaust from my car, this would harm him and give me a moral obligation not to drive my car just for fun. Such cases suggest:

The harm principle: We have a moral obligation not to perform an act that causes harm to others.

This principle implies that I have a moral obligation not to drive my gas-guzzler just for fun "if" such driving causes harm.

The problem is that such driving does "not" cause harm in normal cases. If one person were in a position to inhale all of my exhaust, then he would get sick if I did drive, and he would not get sick if I did not drive (under normal circumstances). In contrast, global warming will still occur even if I do not drive just for fun. Moreover, even if I do drive a gas-guzzler just for fun for a long time, global warming will not occur unless lots of other people also expel greenhouse gases. So my individual act is neither necessary nor sufficient for global warming.

There are, admittedly, special circumstances in which an act causes harm without being either necessary or sufficient for that harm. Imagine that it takes three people to push a car off a cliff with a passenger locked inside, and five people are already pushing. If I join and help them push, then my act of pushing is neither necessary nor sufficient to make the car go off the cliff. Nonetheless, my act of pushing is a cause (or part of the cause) of the harm to the passenger. Why? Because I intend to cause harm to the passenger, and because my act is unusual. When I intend a harm to occur, my intention provides a reason to pick my act out of all the other background circumstances and identify it as a cause. Similarly, when my act is unusual in the sense that most people would not act that way, that also provides a reason to pick out my act and call it a cause.

Why does it matter what is usual? Compare matches. For a match to light up, we need to strike it so as to create friction. There also has to be oxygen. We do not call the oxygen the cause of the fire, since oxygen is usually present. Instead, we say that the friction causes the match to light, since it is unusual for that friction to occur. It happens only once in the life of each match. Thus, what is usual affects ascriptions of causation even in purely physical cases.

In moral cases, there are additional reasons not to call something a cause when it is usual. Labeling an act a cause of harm and, on this basis, holding its agent responsible for that harm by blaming the agent or condemning his act is normally counterproductive when that agent is acting no worse than most other people. If people who are doing "no" worse than average are condemned, then people who are doing "much" worse than average will suspect that they will still be subject to condemnation even if they start doing better, and even if they improve enough to bring themselves up to the average. We should distribute blame (and praise) so as to give incentives for the worst offenders to get better. The most efficient and effective way to do this is to reserve our condemnation for those who are well below average. This means that we should not hold people responsible for harms by calling their acts causes of harms when their acts are not at all unusual, assuming that they did not intend the harm.

The application to global warming should be clear. It is not unusual to go for joyrides. Such drivers do not intend any harm. Hence, we should not see my act of driving on a sunny Sunday afternoon as a cause of global warming or its harms.

Another argument leads to the same conclusion: the harms of global warming result from the massive quantities of greenhouse gases in the atmosphere. Greenhouse gases (such as carbon dioxide and water vapor) are perfectly fine in small quantities. They help plants grow. The problem emerges only when there is too much of them. But my joyride by itself does not cause the massive quantities that are harmful.

Contrast someone who pours cyanide poison into a river. Later someone drinking from the river downstream ingests some molecules of the poison. Those molecules cause the person to get ill and die. This is very different from the causal chain in global warming, because no particular molecules from my car cause global warming in the direct way that particular molecules of the poison do cause the drinker's death. Global warming is more like a river that is going to flood downstream because of torrential rains. I pour a quart of water into the river upstream (maybe just because I do not want to carry it). My act of pouring the quart into the river is not a cause of the flood. Analogously, my act of driving for fun is not a cause of global warming.

Contrast also another large-scale moral problem: famine relief. Some people say that I have no moral obligation to contribute to famine relief because the famine will continue and people will die whether or not I donate my money to a relief agency. However, I could help a certain individual if I gave my donation directly to that individual. In contrast, if I refrain from driving for fun on this one Sunday, there is no individual who will be helped in the least. I cannot help anyone by depriving myself of this joyride.

The point becomes clearer if we distinguish global warming from climate change. You might think that my driving on Sunday raises the temperature of the globe by an infinitesimal amount. I doubt that, but, even if it does, my exhaust on that Sunday does not cause any climate change at all. No storms or floods or droughts or heat waves can be traced to my individual act of driving. It is these climate changes that cause harms to people. Global warming by itself causes no harm without climate change. Hence, since my individual act of driving on that one Sunday does not cause any climate change, it causes no harm to anyone.

The point is not that harms do not occur from global warming. I have already admitted that they do. The point is also not that my exhaust is overkill, like poisoning someone who is already dying from poison. My exhaust is not sufficient for the harms of global warming, and I do not intend those harms. Nor is it the point that the harms from global warming occur much later in time. If I place a time bomb in a building, I can cause harm many years later. And the point is not that the harm I cause is imperceptible. I admit that some harms can be imperceptible because they are too small or for other reasons. Instead, the point is simply that my individual joyride does not cause global warming, climate change, or any of their resulting harms, at least directly.

Admittedly, my acts can lead to other acts by me or by other people. Maybe one case of wasteful driving creates a bad habit that will lead me to do it again and again. Or maybe a lot of other people look up to me and would follow my example of wasteful driving. Or maybe my wasteful driving will undermine my commitment to environmentalism and lead me to stop supporting important green causes or to harm the environment in more serious ways. If so, we could apply:

The indirect harm principle: We have a moral obligation not to perform an act that causes harm to others indirectly by causing someone to carry out acts that cause harm to others.

This principle would explain why it is morally wrong to drive a gas-guzzler just for fun if this act led to other harmful acts.

One problem here is that my acts are not that influential. People like to see themselves as more influential than they really are. On a realistic view, however, it is unlikely that anyone would drive wastefully if I did and would not if I did not. Moreover, wasteful driving is not that habit forming. My act of driving this Sunday does not make me drive next Sunday. I do not get addicted. Driving the next Sunday is a separate decision. And my wasteful driving will not undermine my devotion to environmentalism. If my argument in this chapter is correct, then my belief that the government has a moral obligation to fight global warming is perfectly compatible with a belief that I as an individual have no moral obligation not to drive a gas-guzzler for fun. If I keep this compatibility in mind, then my driving my gas-guzzler for fun will not undermine my devotion to the cause of getting the government to do something about global warming.

Besides, the indirect harm principle is misleading. To see why, consider David. David is no environmentalist. He already has a habit of driving his gas-guzzler for fun on Sundays. Nobody likes him, so nobody follows his example. But David still has a moral obligation not to drive his gas-guzzler just for fun this Sunday, and his obligation has the same basis as mine, if I have one. So my moral obligation cannot depend on the factors cited by the indirect harm principle.

The most important problem for supposed indirect harms is the same as for direct harms: even if I create a bad habit and undermine my personal environmentalism and set a bad example that others follow, all of this would still not be enough to cause climate change if other people stopped expelling greenhouse gases. So, as long as I neither intend harm nor do anything unusual, my act cannot cause climate change even if I do create bad habits and followers. The scale of climate change is just too big for me to cause it, even "with a little help from my friends."

Of course, even if I do not cause climate change, I still might seem to contribute to climate change in the sense that I make it worse. If so, another principle applies:

The contribution principle: We have a moral obligation not to make problems worse.

This principle applies if climate change will be worse if I drive than it will be if I do not drive.

The problem with this argument is that my act of driving does not even make climate change worse. Climate change would be just as bad if I did not drive. The reason is that climate change becomes worse only if more people (and animals) are hurt or if they are hurt worse. There is nothing bad about global warming or climate change in itself if no people (or animals) are harmed. But there is no individual person or animal who will be worse off if I drive than if I do not drive my gas-guzzler just for fun. Global warming and climate change occur on such a massive scale that my individual driving makes no difference to the welfare of anyone.

Some might complain that this is not what they mean by "contribute." All it takes for me to contribute to global warming in their view is for me to expel greenhouse gases into the atmosphere. I do "that" when I drive, so we can apply:

The gas principle: We have a moral obligation not to expel greenhouse gases into the atmosphere.

If this principle were true, it would explain why I have a moral obligation not to drive my gas-guzzler just for fun.

Unfortunately, it is hard to see any reason to accept this principle. There is nothing immoral about greenhouse gases in themselves when they cause no harm. Greenhouse gases include carbon dioxide and water vapor, which occur naturally and help plants grow. The problem of global warming occurs because of the high quantities of greenhouse gases, not because of anything bad about smaller quantities of the same gases. So it is hard to see why I would have a moral obligation not to expel harmless quantities of greenhouse gases. And that is all I do by myself.

Furthermore, if the gas principle were true, it would be unbelievably restrictive. It implies that I have a moral obligation not to boil water (since water vapor is a greenhouse gas) or to exercise (since I expel carbon dioxide when I breathe heavily). When you think it through, an amazing array of seemingly morally acceptable activities would be ruled out by the gas principle. These implications suggest that we had better look elsewhere for a reason why I have a moral obligation not to drive a gas-guzzler just for fun.

Maybe the reason is risk. It is sometimes morally wrong to create a risk of a harm even if that harm does not occur. I grant that drunk driving is immoral, because it risks harm to others, even if the drunk driver gets home safely without hurting anyone. Thus, we get another principle:

The risk principle: We have a moral obligation not to increase the risk of harms to other people.

The problem here is that global warming is not like drunk driving. When drunk driving causes harm, it is easy to identify the victim of this particular drunk driver. There is no way to identify any particular victim of my wasteful driving in normal circumstances.

In addition, my earlier point applies here again. If the risk principle were true, it would be unbelievably restrictive. Exercising and boiling water also expel greenhouse gases, so they also increase the risk of global warming if my driving does. This principle implies that almost everything we do violates a moral obligation.

Defenders of such principles sometimes respond by distinguishing significant from insignificant risks or increases in risks. That distinction is problematic, at least here. A risk is called significant when it is "too" much. But then we need to ask what makes this risk too much when other risks are not too much. The reasons for counting a risk as significant are then the real reasons for thinking that there is a moral obligation not to drive wastefully. So we need to specify those reasons directly instead of hiding them under a waffle-term like "significant."

4. INTERNAL PRINCIPLES

None of the principles discussed so far is both defensible and strong enough to yield a moral obligation not to drive a gas-guzzler just for fun. Maybe we can do better by looking inward.

Kantians claim that the moral status of acts depends on their agents' maxims or "subjective principles of volition"—roughly what we would call motives or intentions or plans. This internal focus is evident in Kant's first formulation of the categorical imperative:

The universalizability principle: We have a moral obligation not to act on any maxim that we cannot will to be a universal law.

The idea is not that universally acting on that maxim would have bad consequences. (We will consider that kind of principle below.) Instead, the claim is that some maxims "cannot even be thought as a universal law of nature without contradiction." However, my maxim when I drive a gas-guzzler just for fun on this sunny Sunday afternoon is simply to have harmless fun. There is no way to derive a contradiction from a universal law that people do or may have harmless fun. Kantians might respond that my maxim is, instead, to expel greenhouse gases. I still see no way to derive a literal contradiction from a universal law that people do or may expel greenhouse gases. There would be bad consequences, but that is not a contradiction, as Kant requires. In any case, my maxim (or intention or motive) is not to expel greenhouse gases. My goals would be reached completely if I went for my drive and had my fun without expelling any greenhouse gases. This leaves no ground for claiming that my driving violates Kant's first formula of the categorical imperative.

Kant does supply a second formulation, which is really a different principle:

The means principle: We have a moral obligation not to treat any other person as a means only.

It is not clear exactly how to understand this formulation, but the most natural interpretation is that for me to treat someone as a means implies my using harm to that person as part of my plan to achieve my goals. Driving for fun does not do that. I would have just as much fun if nobody were ever harmed by global warming. Harm to others is no part of my plans. So Kant's principle cannot explain why I have a moral obligation not to drive just for fun on this sunny Sunday afternoon.

A similar point applies to a traditional principle that focuses on intention:

The doctrine of double effect: We have a moral obligation not to harm anyone intentionally (either as an end or as a means).

This principle fails to apply to my Sunday driving both because my driving does not cause harm to anyone and because I do not intend harm to anyone. I would succeed in doing everything I intended to do if I enjoyed my drive but magically my car gave off no greenhouse gases and no global warming occurred.

Another inner-directed theory is virtue ethics. This approach focuses on general character traits rather than particular acts or intentions. It is not clear how to derive a principle regarding obligations from virtue ethics, but here is a common attempt:

The virtue principle: We have a moral obligation not to perform an act that expresses a vice or is contrary to virtue.

This principle solves our problem if driving a gas-guzzler expresses a vice, or if no virtuous person would drive a gas-guzzler just for fun.

How can we tell whether this principle applies? How can we tell whether driving a gas-guzzler for fun "expresses a vice"? On the face of it, it expresses a desire for fun. There is nothing vicious about having fun. Having fun becomes vicious only if it is harmful or risky. But I have already responded to the principles of harm and risk. Moreover, driving a gas-guzzler for fun does not always express a vice. If other people did not produce so much greenhouse gas, I could drive my gas-guzzler just for fun without anyone being harmed by global warming. Then I could do it without being vicious. This situation is not realistic, but it does show that wasteful driving is not essentially vicious or contrary to virtue.

Some will disagree. Maybe your notions of virtue and vice make it essentially vicious to drive wastefully. But why? To apply this principle, we need some antecedent test of when an act expresses a vice. You cannot just say, "I know vice when I see it," because other people look at the same act and do not see vice, just fun. It begs the question to appeal to what you see when others do not see it, and you have no reason to believe that your vision is any clearer than theirs. But that means that this virtue principle cannot be applied without begging the question. We need to find some reason why such driving is vicious. Once we have this reason, we can appeal to it directly as a reason why I have a moral obligation not to drive wastefully. The side step through virtue does not help and only obscures the issue.

Some virtue theorists might respond that life would be better if more people were to focus on general character traits, including green virtues, such as moderation and love of nature. One reason is that it is so hard to determine obligations in particular cases. Another reason is that focusing on particular obligations leaves no way to escape problems like global warming. This might be correct. Maybe we should spend more time thinking about whether we have green virtues rather than about whether we have specific obligations. But that does not show that we do have a moral obligation not to drive gas-guzzlers just for fun. Changing our focus will not bring any moral obligation into existence. There are other important moral issues besides moral obligation, but this does not show that moral obligations are not important as well.

5. COLLECTIVE PRINCIPLES

Maybe our mistake is to focus on individual persons. We could instead, focus on institutions. One institution is the legal system, so we might adopt:

The ideal law principle: We have a moral obligation not to perform an action if it ought to be illegal.

I already said that the government ought to fight global warming. One way to do so is to make it illegal to drive wastefully or to buy (or sell) inefficient gas-guzzlers. If the government ought to pass such laws, then, even before such laws are passed, I have a moral obligation not to drive a gas-guzzler just for fun, according to the ideal law principle.

The first weakness in this argument lies in its assumption that wasteful driving or gas-guzzlers ought to be illegal. That is dubious. The enforcement costs of a law against joyrides would be enormous. A law against gas-guzzlers would be easier to enforce, but inducements to efficiency (such as higher taxes on gas and gas-guzzlers, or tax breaks for buying fuel-efficient cars) might accomplish the same goals with less loss of individual freedom. Governments ought to accomplish their goals with less loss of freedom, if they can. Note the "if." I do not claim that these other laws would work as well as an outright prohibition of gas-guzzlers. I do not know. Still, the point is that such alternative laws would not make it illegal (only expensive) to drive a gas-guzzler for fun. If those alternative laws are better than outright prohibitions (because they allow more freedom), then the ideal law

principle cannot yield a moral obligation not to drive a gas-guzzler now.

Moreover, the connection between law and morality cannot be so simple. Suppose that the government morally ought to raise taxes on fossil fuels in order to reduce usage and to help pay for adaptation to global warming. It still seems morally permissible for me and for you not to pay that tax now. We do not have any moral obligation to send a check to the government for the amount that we would have to pay if taxes were raised to the ideal level. One reason is that our checks would not help to solve the problem, since others would continue to conduct business as usual. What would help to solve the problem is for the taxes to be increased. Maybe we all have moral obligations to try to get the taxes increased. Still, until they are increased, we as individuals have no moral obligations to abide by the ideal tax law instead of the actual tax law.

Analogously, it is actually legal to buy and drive gas-guzzlers. Maybe these vehicles should be illegal. I am not sure. If gas-guzzlers morally ought to be illegal, then maybe we morally ought to work to get them outlawed. But that still would not show that now, while they are legal, we have a moral obligation not to drive them just for fun on a sunny Sunday afternoon.

Which laws are best depends on side effects of formal institutions, such as enforcement costs and loss of freedom (resulting from the coercion of laws). Maybe we can do better by looking at informal groups.

Different groups involve different relations between members. Orchestras and political parties, for example, plan to do what they do and adjust their actions to other members of the group in order to achieve a common goal. Such groups can be held responsible for their joint acts, even when no individual alone performs those acts. However, gas-guzzler drivers do not form this kind of group. Gas-guzzler drivers do not share goals, do not make plans together, and do not adjust their acts to each other (at least usually).

There is an abstract set of gas-guzzler drivers, but membership in a set is too arbitrary to create moral responsibility. I am also in a set of all terrorists plus me, but my membership in that abstract set does not make me responsible for the harms that terrorists cause.

The only feature that holds together the group of people who drive gas-guzzlers is simply that they all perform the same kind of act. The fact that so many people carry out acts of that kind does create or worsen global warming. That collective bad effect is supposed to make it morally wrong to perform any act of that kind, according to the following:

The group principle: We have a moral obligation not to perform an action if this action makes us a member of a group whose actions together cause harm.

Why? It begs the question here merely to assume that, if it is bad for everyone in a group to perform acts of a kind, then it is morally wrong for an individual to perform an act of that kind. Besides, this principle is implausible or at least questionable in many cases. Suppose that everyone in an airport is talking loudly. If only a few people were talking, there would be no problem. But the collective effect of so many people talking makes it hard to hear announcements, so some people miss their flights. Suppose, in these circumstances, I say loudly (but not too loudly), "I wish everyone would be quiet." My speech does not seem immoral, since it alone does not harm anyone. Maybe there should be a rule (or law) against such loud speech in this setting (as in a library), but if there is not (as I am assuming), then it does not seem immoral to do what others do, as long as they are going to do it anyway, so the harm is going to occur anyway.

Again, suppose that the president sends everyone (or at least most taxpayers) a check for $600. If all recipients cash their checks, the government deficit will grow, government programs will have to be slashed, and severe economic and social problems will result. You know that enough other people will cash their checks to make these results to a great degree inevitable. You also know that it is perfectly legal to cash your check, although you think it should be illegal, because the checks should not have been issued in the first place. In these circumstances, is it morally wrong for you to cash your check? I doubt it. Your act of cashing your check causes no harm by itself, and you have no intention to cause harm. Your act of cashing your check does make you a member of a group that collectively causes harm, but that still does not seem to give you a

moral obligation not to join the group by cashing your check, since you cannot change what the group does. It might be morally good or ideal to protest by tearing up your check, but it does not seem morally obligatory.

Thus, the group principle fails. Perhaps it might be saved by adding some kind of qualification, but I do not see how.

6. COUNTERFACTUAL PRINCIPLES

Maybe our mistake is to focus on actual circumstances. So let us try some counterfactuals about what would happen in possible worlds that are not actual. Different counterfactuals are used by different versions of rule-consequentialism.

One counterfactual is built into the common question, "What would happen if everybody did that?" This question suggests a principle:

The general action principle: I have a moral obligation not to perform an act when it would be worse for everyone to perform an act of the same kind.

It does seem likely that, if everyone in the world drove a gas-guzzler often enough, global warming would increase intolerably. We would also quickly run out of fossil fuels. The general action principle is, thus, supposed to explain why it is morally wrong to drive a gas-guzzler.

Unfortunately, that popular principle is indefensible. It would be disastrous if every human had no children. But that does not make it morally wrong for a particular individual to choose to have no children. There is no moral obligation to have at least one child.

The reason is that so few people "want" to remain childless. Most people would not go without children even if they were allowed to. This suggests a different principle:

The general permission principle: I have a moral obligation not to perform an act whenever it would be worse for everyone to be permitted to perform an act of that kind.

This principle seems better because it would not be disastrous for everyone to be permitted to remain childless. This principle is supposed to be able to explain why it is morally wrong to steal (or lie, cheat, rape, or murder), because it would be disastrous for everyone to be permitted to steal (or lie, cheat, rape, or murder) whenever (if ever) they wanted to.

Not quite. An agent is permitted or allowed in the relevant sense when she will not be liable to punishment, condemnation (by others), or feelings of guilt for carrying out the act. It is possible for someone to be permitted in this sense without knowing that she is permitted and, indeed, without anyone knowing that she is permitted. But it would not be disastrous for everyone to be permitted to steal if nobody knew that they were permitted to steal, since then they would still be deterred by fear of punishment, condemnation, or guilt. Similarly for lying, rape, and so on. So the general permission principle cannot quite explain why such acts are morally wrong.

Still, it would be disastrous if everyone knew that they were permitted to steal (or lie, rape, etc.). So we simply need to add one qualification:

The public permission principle: I have a moral obligation not to perform an act whenever it would be worse for everyone to know that everyone is permitted to perform an act of that kind.

Now this principle seems to explain the moral wrongness of many of the acts we take to be morally wrong, since it would be disastrous if everyone knew that everyone was permitted to steal, lie, cheat, and so on.

Unfortunately, this revised principle runs into trouble in other cases. Imagine that 1000 people want to take Flight 38 to Amsterdam on October 13, 2003, but the plane is not large enough to carry that many people. If all 1,000 took that particular flight, then it would crash. But these people are all stupid and stubborn enough that, if they knew that they were all allowed to take the flight, they all would pack themselves in, despite warnings, and the flight would crash. Luckily, this counterfactual does not reflect what actually happens. In the actual world, the airline is not stupid. Since the plane can safely carry only 300 people, the airline sells only 300 tickets and does not allow anyone on the flight without a ticket. If I have a ticket for that flight, then there is nothing morally wrong with me taking the flight along with the other 299 who have tickets. This shows that an act is not always morally wrong when it would (counterfactually) be disastrous for everyone to know that everyone is allowed to do it.

The lesson of this example applies directly to my case of driving a gas-guzzler. Disaster occurs in the airplane case when too many people do what is harmless by itself. Similarly, disaster occurs when too many people burn too much fossil fuel. But that does not make it wrong in either case for one individual to perform an individual act that is harmless by itself. It only creates an obligation on the part of the government (or airline) to pass regulations to keep too many people from acting that way.

Another example brings out another weakness in the public permission principle. Consider open marriage. Max and Minnie get married because each loves the other and values the other person's love. Still, they think of sexual intercourse as a fun activity that they separate from love. After careful discussion before they got married, each happily agreed that each may have sex after marriage with whomever he or she wants. They value honesty, so they did add one condition: every sexual encounter must be reported to the other spouse. As long as they keep no secrets from each other and still love each other, they see no problem with their having sex with other people. They do not broadcast this feature of their marriage, but they do know (after years of experience) that it works for them.

Nonetheless, the society in which Max and Minnie live might be filled with people who are very different from them. If everyone knew that everyone is permitted to have sex during marriage with other people as long as the other spouse is informed and agreed to the arrangement, then various problems would arise. Merely asking a spouse whether he or she would be willing to enter into such an agreement would be enough to create suspicions and doubts in the other spouse's mind that would undermine many marriages or keep many couples from getting married, when they would have gotten or remained happily married if they had not been offered such an agreement. As a result, the society will have less love, fewer stable marriages, and more unhappy children of unnecessary divorce. Things would be much better if everyone believed that such agree-ments were not permitted in the first place, so they condemned them and felt guilty for even consider-ing them. I think that this result is not unrealistic, but here I am merely postulating these facts in my example.

The point is that, even if other people are like this, so that it would be worse for everyone to know that everyone is permitted to have sex outside of marriage with spousal knowledge and consent, Max and Min-nie are not like this, and they know that they are not like this, so it is hard to believe that they as individuals have a moral obligation to abide by a restriction that is justified by other people's dispositions. If Max and Minnie have a joint agreement that works for them, but they keep it secret from others, then there is noth-ing immoral about them having sex outside of their marriage (whether or not this counts as adultery). If this is correct, then the general permission principle fails again.

As before, the lesson of this example applies directly to my case of driving a gas-guzzler. The rea-son why Max and Minnie are not immoral is that they have a right to their own private relationship as long as they do not harm others (such as by spread-ing disease or discord). But I have already argued that my driving a gas-guzzler on this Sunday afternoon does not cause harm. I seem to have a right to have fun in the way I want as long as I do not hurt anybody else, just like Max and Minnie. So the public permis-sion principle cannot explain why it is morally wrong to drive a gas-guzzler for fun on this sunny Sunday afternoon.

One final counterfactual approach is contractu-alism, whose most forceful recent proponent is Tim Scanlon. Scanlon proposes:

The contractualist principle: I have a moral obligation not to perform an act whenever it violates a general rule that nobody could reasonably reject as a public rule for governing action in society.

Let us try to apply this principle to the case of Max and Minnie. Consider a general rule against adultery, that is, against voluntary sex between a married person and someone other than his or her spouse, even if the spouse knows and consents. It might seem that Max and Minnie could not reason-ably reject this rule as a public social rule, because they want to avoid problems for their own society. If so, Scanlon's principle leads to the same question-able results as the public permission principle. If Scanlon replies that Max and Minnie "can" reason-ably reject the anti-adultery rule, then why? The most plausible answer is that it is their own business how they have fun as long as they do not hurt any-body. But this answer is available also to people who drive gas-guzzlers just for fun. So this principle can-not explain why that act is morally wrong.

More generally, the test of what can be rejected "reasonably" depends on moral intuitions. Envi-ronmentalists might think it unreasonable to reject a principle that prohibits me from driving my gas-guzzler just for fun, but others will think it reasonable to reject such a principle, because it restricts my free-dom to perform an act that harms nobody. The appeal to reasonable rejection itself begs the question in the absence of an account of why such rejection is unrea-sonable. Environmentalists might be able to specify reasons why it is unreasonable, but then it is those rea-sons that explain why this act is morally wrong. The framework of reasonable rejection becomes a distract-ing and unnecessary side step.

7. WHAT IS LEFT?

We are left with no defensible principle to support the claim that I have a moral obligation not to drive a gas-guzzler just for fun. Does this result show that this claim is false? Not necessarily.

Some audiences have suggested that my journey through various principles teaches us that we should not look for general moral principles to back up our moral intuitions. They see my arguments as a "reduc-tio ad absurdum" of principlism, which is the view that moral obligations (or our beliefs in them) depend on principles. Principles are unavailable, so we should focus instead on particular cases, according to the opposing view called particularism.

However, the fact that we cannot find any principle does not show that we do not need one.

I already gave my reasons why we need a moral principle to back up our intuitions in this case. This case is controversial, emotional, peculiarly modern, and likely to be distorted by overgeneralization and partiality. These factors suggest that we need confirmation for our moral intuitions at least in this case, even if we do not need any confirmation in other cases.

For such reasons, we seem to need a moral principle, but we have none. This fact still does not show that such wasteful driving is not morally wrong. It only shows that we do not "know" whether it is morally wrong. Our ignorance might be temporary. If someone comes up with a defensible principle that does rule out wasteful driving, then I will be happy to listen and happy if it works. However, until some such principle is found, we cannot claim to know that it is morally wrong to drive a gas-guzzler just for fun.

The demand for a principle in this case does not lead to general moral skepticism. We still might know that acts and omissions that cause harm are morally wrong because of the harm principle. Still, since that principle and others do not apply to my wasteful driving, and since moral intuitions are unreliable in cases like this, we cannot know that my wasteful driving is morally wrong.

This conclusion will still upset many environmentalists. They think that they know that wasteful driving is immoral. They want to be able to condemn those who drive gas-guzzlers just for fun on sunny Sunday afternoons.

My conclusion should not be so disappointing. Even if individuals have no such moral obligations, it is still morally better or morally ideal for individuals not to waste gas. We can and should praise those who save fuel. We can express our personal dislike for wasting gas and for people who do it. We might even be justified in publicly condemning wasteful driving and drivers who waste a lot, in circumstances where such public rebuke is appropriate. Perhaps people who drive wastefully should feel guilty for their acts and ashamed of themselves, at least if they perform such acts regularly; and we should bring up our children so that they will feel these emotions. All of these reactions are available even if we cannot truthfully say that such driving violates a moral "obligation." And these approaches might be more constructive in the long run than accusing someone of violating a moral obligation.

Moreover, even if individuals have no moral obligations not to waste gas by taking unnecessary Sunday drives just for fun, governments still have moral obligations to fight global warming, because they can make a difference. My fundamental point has been that global warming is such a large problem that it is not individuals who cause it or who need to fix it. Instead, governments need to fix it, and quickly. Finding and implementing a real solution is the task of governments. Environmentalists should focus their efforts on those who are not doing their job rather than on those who take Sunday afternoon drives just for fun.

This focus will also avoid a common mistake. Some environmentalists keep their hands clean by withdrawing into a simple life where they use very little fossil fuels. That is great. I encourage it. But some of these escapees then think that they have done their duty, so they rarely come down out of the hills to work for political candidates who could and would change government policies. This attitude helps nobody. We should not think that we can do enough simply by buying fuel-efficient cars, insulating our houses, and setting up a windmill to make our own electricity. That is all wonderful, but it neither does little or nothing to stop global warming, nor does this focus fulfill our real moral obligations, which are to get governments to do their job to prevent the disaster of excessive global warming. It is better to enjoy your Sunday driving while working to change the law so as to make it illegal for you to enjoy your Sunday driving.

Are All Species Equal?

DAVID SCHMIDTZ

I. RESPECT FOR NATURE

Species egalitarianism is the view that all species have equal moral standing.[1] To have moral standing is, at a minimum, to command respect, to be something more than a mere thing. Is there any reason to believe that all species have moral standing in even this most minimal sense? If so—that is, if all species command respect—is there any reason to believe they all command *equal* respect?

The following sections summarise critical responses to the most famous philosophical argument for species egalitarianism. I then try to explain why other species command our respect but also why they do not command equal respect. The intuition that we should have respect for nature is part of what motivates people to embrace species egalitarianism, but one need not be a species egalitarian to have respect for nature. I close by questioning whether species egalitarianism is even compatible with respect for nature.

II. THE GROUNDING OF SPECIES EGALITARIANISM

According to Paul Taylor, anthropocentrism 'gives either exclusive or primary consideration to human interests above the good of other species.'[2] The alternative to anthropocentrism is biocentrism, and it is biocentrism that, in Taylor's view, grounds species egalitarianism:

The beliefs that form the core of the biocentric outlook are four in number:

(a) The belief that humans are members of the Earth's Community of life in the same sense and on the same terms in which other living things are members of that community.

(b) The belief that the human species, along with all other species, are integral elements in a system of interdependence.

(c) The belief that all organisms are teleological centres of life in the sense that each is a unique individual pursuing its own good in its own way.

(d) The belief that humans are not inherently superior to other living beings.

Taylor concludes, 'Rejecting the notion of human superiority entails its positive counterpart: the doctrine of species impartiality. One who accepts that doctrine regards all living things as possessing inherent worth—the *same* inherent worth, since no one species has been shown to be either higher or lower than any other.'[3]

Taylor does not claim that this is a valid argument, but he thinks that if we concede (a), (b), and (c), it would be unreasonable not to move to (d), and then to his egalitarian conclusion. Is he right? For those who accept Taylor's three premises (and who thus interpret those premises in terms innocuous enough to render them acceptable), there are two responses. First, we may go on to accept (d), following Taylor, but then still deny that there is any warrant for moving from there to Taylor's egalitarian conclusion. Having accepted that our form of life is not superior, we might choose instead to regard it as inferior. More plausibly, we might view our form of life as noncomparable. We simply do not have the same kind of value as nonhumans. The question of how we compare to nonhumans has a simple answer: we do not compare to them.

Alternatively, we may reject (d) and say humans are indeed inherently superior but our superiority is a moot point. Whether we are inherently superior (that is, superior as a form of life) does not matter much. Even if we are superior, the fact remains that within the web of ecological interdependence mentioned in premises (a) and (b), it would be a mistake to ignore the needs and the telos of the other species referred to in premise (c). Thus, there are two ways of rejecting

Taylor's argument for species egalitarianism. Each, on its face, is compatible with the respect for nature that motivates Taylor's egalitarianism in the first place.

Taylor's critics, such as James Anderson and William French, have taken the second route. They reject (d). After discussing their arguments, and building on some while rejecting others, I explore some of our reasons to have respect for nature and ask whether they translate into reasons to be species egalitarians.

III. IS SPECIES EGALITARIANISM HYPOCRITICAL?

Paul Taylor and Arne Naess are among the most intransigent of species egalitarians, yet they allow that human needs override the needs of nonhumans.[4] William C. French argues that they cannot have it both ways.[5] French perceives a contradiction between the egalitarian principles that Taylor and Naess officially endorse and the unofficial principles they offer as the real principles by which we should live. Having proclaimed that we are all equal, French asks, what licenses Taylor and Naess to say that, in cases of conflict, nonhuman interests can legitimately be sacrificed to vital human interests?

French has a point. James C. Anderson makes a similar point.[6] Yet, somehow the inconsistency of Taylor and Naess is too obvious. Perhaps their position is not as blatantly inconsistent as it appears. Let me suggest how Taylor and Naess could respond to French. Suppose I find myself in a situation of mortal combat with an enemy soldier. If I kill my enemy to save my life, that does not entail that I regard my enemy as inherently inferior (i.e., as an inferior form of life). Likewise, if I kill a bear to save my life, that does not entail that I regard the bear as inherently inferior. Therefore, Taylor and Naess can, without hypocrisy, deny that species egalitarianism requires a radically self-effacing pacifism.

What, then, does species egalitarianism require? It requires us to avoid mortal combat whenever we can, not just with other humans but with living things in general. On this view, we ought to regret finding ourselves in kill-or-be-killed situations that we could have avoided. There is no point in regretting the fact

that we must kill in order to eat, though, for there is no avoiding that. Species egalitarianism is compatible with our having a limited license to kill.

What seems far more problematic for species egalitarianism is that it seems to suggest that it makes no difference *what* we kill. Vegetarians typically think it is worse to kill a cow than to kill a potato. Are they wrong? Yes they are, according to species egalitarianism. In this respect, species egalitarianism cannot be right. I do believe we have reason to respect nature. But we fail to give nature due respect if we say we should have no more respect for a cow than for a potato.

IV. IS SPECIES EGALITARIANISM ARBITRARY?

Suppose interspecies comparisons are possible. Suppose the capacities of different species, and whatever else gives species moral standing, are commensurable. In that case, it could turn out that all species are equal, but that would be quite a fluke.

Taylor says a being has intrinsic worth if and only if it has a good of its own. Anderson does not disagree, but he points out that if we accept Taylor's idea of a thing having a good of its own, then that licenses us to notice differences among the various kinds of 'good of its own.' (We can notice differences without being committed to ranking them.) For example, we can distinguish, along Aristotelian lines, vegetative, animal, and cognitive goods of one's own. To have a vegetative nature is to be what Taylor, in premise (c), calls a teleological centre of life. A being with an animal nature is a teleological centre of life, and more. A being with a cognitive as well as animal nature is a teleological centre of life, and more still. Cognitive nature may be something we share with whales, dolphins, and higher primates. It is an empirical question. Anderson's view is that so long as we do not assume away this possibility, valuing cognitive capacity is not anthropocentric. The question is what would make *any* species superior to another (p. 348).

As mentioned earlier, Taylor defines anthropocentrism as giving exclusive or primary consideration to human interests above the good of other species. So, when we acknowledge that cognitive capacity is one valuable capacity among others, are we giving exclusive or primary considerations to human interests? Anderson thinks not, and surely he is right. Put it this way: if biocentrism involves resolving to ignore the fact that cognitive capacity is something we value—if biocentrism amounts to a resolution to value only those capacities that all living things share—then biocentrism is at least as arbitrary and question-begging as anthropocentrism.

It will not do to defend species egalitarianism by singling out a property that all species possess, arguing that this property is morally important, and then concluding that all species are therefore of equal moral importance. The problem with this sort of argument is that, where there is one property that provides a basis for moral standing, there might be others. Other properties might be possessed by some but not all species, and might provide bases for different kinds or degrees of moral standing.

V. THE MULTIPLE BASES OF MORAL STANDING

Taylor is aware of the Aristotelian classification scheme, but considers its hierarchy of capacities to be question-begging. Taylor himself assumes that human rationality is on a par with a cheetah's foot-speed. In this case, though, perhaps it is Taylor who begs the question. It hardly seems unreasonable to see the difference between the foot-speed of chimpanzees and cheetahs as a difference of degree, while seeing the difference between the sentience of a chimpanzee and the nonsentience of a tree as a difference in kind.

Anthropocentrists might argue that the good associated with cognitive capacity is superior to the good associated with vegetative capacity. Could they be wrong? Let us suppose they are wrong. For argument's sake, let us suppose *vegetative* capacity is the superior good. Even so, the exact nature of the good associated with an organism's vegetative capacity will depend upon the organism's other capacities. For example, Anderson (p. 358) points out that even if health in a human and health in a tree are instances of the same thing, they need not have the same moral standing. Why not? Because health in a human has an instrumental value that health in a tree lacks. John Stuart Mill's swine can take pleasure in its health but trees cannot. Animals have a plant's capacities plus more. In turn, humans (and possibly dolphins, apes, and so on) have an animal's capacities plus more. The comparison between Socrates and swine therefore is less a matter of comparing swine to non-swine and more a matter of comparing swine to 'swine-plus' (Anderson, p. 361). Crucially, Anderson's argument for the superiority of Socrates over swine does not presume that one capacity is higher than another. We do not need to make any assumptions about the respective merits of animal or vegetative versus cognitive capacities in order to conclude that the capacities of 'swine-plus' are superior to those of swine.

We may of course conclude that *one* of the grounds of our moral standing (i.e., our vegetative natures) is something we share with all living things. Beyond that, nothing about equality even suggests itself. In particular, it begs no questions to notice that there are grounds for moral standing that we do not share with all living things.

VI. IN PRAISE OF SPECIESISM

William French invites us to see species rankings not 'as an assessment of some inherent superiority, but rather as a considered moral recognition of the fact that greater ranges of vulnerability are generated by broader ranges of complexity and capacities' (p. 56). One species outranks another not because it is a superior form of life but rather because it is a more vulnerable form of life. French, if I understand correctly, interprets vulnerability as a matter of having *more* to lose. This interpretation is problematic. It implies that a millionaire, having more to lose than a pauper, is by that fact more vulnerable than the pauper. Perhaps this interpretation is forced upon French, though. If French had instead chosen a more natural interpretation—if he had chosen to interpret vulnerability as a matter of *probability* of loss—then a ranking by vulnerability would not be correlated to complex capacities in the way he wants. Ranking by probability of loss would change on a daily basis, and the top-ranked species often would be an amphibian.

If we set aside questions about how to interpret vulnerability, there remains a problem with French's proposal. If having complex capacities is not itself morally important, then being in danger of losing them is not morally important either. Vulnerability, on any interpretation, is essentially of derivative importance; any role it could play in ranking species must already be played by the capacities themselves.

Yet, although I reject French's argument, I do not reject his inegalitarian conclusion. The conclusion that mice are the moral equals of chimpanzees is about as insupportable as a conclusion can be. Suppose that, for some reason, we take an interest in how chimpanzees rank compared to mice. Perhaps we wonder what we would do in an emergency where we could save a drowning chimpanzee or a drowning mouse but not both. More realistically, we might wonder whether, other things equal, we have any reason to use mice in our medical experiments rather than chimpanzees. Species egalitarianism seems to say not.

Suppose we decide upon reflection that, from our human perspective, chimpanzees are superior to mice and humans are superior to chimpanzees. Would the perceived superiority of our form of life give us reason to think we have no obligations whatsoever to mice, or to chimpanzees? Those who believe we have fewer obligations to inferior species might be pressed to say whether they also would allow that we have fewer obligations to inferior human beings. Lawrence Johnson, for example, rhetorically asks whether it is worse to cause a person pain if the person is a Nobel Prize winner.[7] Well, why not? Echoing Peter Singer, Johnson argues that if medical researchers had to choose between harvesting the organs of a chimpanzee or a brain-damaged human baby, 'one thing we cannot justify is trying to have it both ways. If rationality is what makes the basic moral difference, then we cannot maintain that the brain-damaged infant ought to be exempt from utilisation just because it is human while at the same time allowing that the animal can be used if utility warrants' (p. 52).

Does this seem obvious? It should not. Johnson presumes that rationality is relevant to justification at the *token* level when speciesists (i.e., those who believe some species, the human species in particular, are superior to others) presumably would invoke rationality as a justification at the *type* level. One can say rationality makes a moral difference at the type level without thereby taking any position on whether rationality makes a moral difference at the token level. A speciesist could say humanity's characteristic rationality mandates respect for humanity, not merely for particular humans who exemplify human rationality. Similarly, once we note that chimpanzees have characteristic cognitive capacities that mice lack, we do not need to compare individual chimpanzees and mice on a case by case basis in order to have a moral justification for planning to use a mouse rather than a chimpanzee in an experiment.

Of course, some chimpanzees lack the characteristic features in virtue of which chimpanzees command respect as a species, just as some humans lack the characteristic features in virtue of which humans command respect as a species. It is equally obvious that some chimpanzees have cognitive capacities (for example) that are superior to the cognitive capacities of some humans. But whether every human being is superior to every chimpanzee is beside the point. The point is that we can, we do, and we should make decisions on the basis of our recognition that mice, chimpanzees, and humans are relevantly different types. We can have it both ways after all. Or so a speciesist could argue.

VII. EQUALITY AND TRANSCENDENCE

Even if speciesists are right to see a nonarbitrary distinction between humans and other species, though, the fact remains that, as Anderson (p. 362) points out, claims of superiority do not easily translate into justifications of domination. We can have reasons to treat nonhuman species with respect, regardless of whether we consider them to be on a moral par with *homo [sic] sapiens*.

What kind of reasons do we have for treating other species with respect? We might have respect for chimpanzees or even mice on the grounds that they are sentient. Even mice have a rudimentary point of view and rudimentary hopes and dreams, and we might well respect them for that. But what about plants? Plants, unlike mice and chimpanzees, do not care what happens to them. It is literally true that they could not care less. So, why should we care? Is it even possible for us to have any good reason, other than a purely instrumental reason, to care what happens to plants?

When we are alone in a forest wondering whether it would be fine to chop down a tree for fun, our perspective on what happens to the tree is, so far as we know, the only perspective there is. The tree does not have its own. Thus, explaining why we have reason to care about trees requires us to explain caring from our point of view, since that (we are supposing) is all there is. In that case, we do not have to satisfy *trees* that we are treating them properly; rather, we have to satisfy *ourselves*. So, again, can we have noninstrumental reasons for caring about trees—for treating them with respect?

One reason to care (not the only one) is that gratuitous destruction is a failure of self-respect. It is a repudiation of the kind of self-awareness and self-respect that we can achieve by repudiating wantonness. So far as I know, no one finds anything puzzling in the idea that we have reason to treat our lawns or living rooms with respect. Lawns and living rooms have instrumental value, but there is more to it than that. Most of us have the sense that taking reasonable care of our lawns and living rooms is somehow a matter of self-respect, not merely a matter of preserving their instrumental value. Do we have similar reasons to treat forests with respect? I think we do. There is an aesthetic involved, the repudiation of which would be a failure of self-respect. (Obviously, not everyone feels the same way about forests. Not everyone feels the same way about lawns and living rooms, either. But the point here is to make sense of respect for nature, not to argue that respect for nature is in fact universal or that failing to respect nature is irrational.)[8] If and when we identify with a Redwood, in the sense of being inspired by it, having respect for its size and age and so on, then as a psychological fact, we really do face moral questions about how we ought to treat it. If and when we come to see a Redwood in that light, subsequently turning our backs on it becomes a kind of self-effacement. The values that we thereby fail to take seriously are *our* values, not the tree's.

A related way of grounding respect for nature is suggested by Jim Cheney's remark that 'moral regard is appropriate wherever we are *able* to manage it—in light of our sensibilities, knowledge, and cultural/personal histories. . . . The limits of moral regard are set only by the limitations of one's own (or one's species' or one's community's) ability to respond in a caring manner.'[9] Should we believe Cheney's rather startling proposal that moral regard is appropriate whenever we can manage it? One reason to take it very seriously is that exercising our capacity for moral regard is a way of expressing respect for that capacity. Developing that capacity is a form of self-realization.

Put it this way. I am arguing that the attitude we take toward gazelles (for example) raises issues of self-respect insofar as we see ourselves as relevantly like gazelles. My reading of Cheney suggests a different and complementary way of looking at the issue. Consider that lions owe nothing to gazelles. Therefore, if we owe it to gazelles not to hunt them, it must be because we are *unlike* lions, not (or not only) because we are *like* gazelles.

Unlike lions, we have a choice about whether to hunt gazelles, and we are capable of deliberating about that choice in a reflective way. We are capable of caring about the gazelle's pain, the gazelle's beauty, the gazelle's hopes and dreams (such as they are), and so forth. And if we do care, then in a more or less literal way, something is wrong with us—we are less than fully human—if we cannot adjust our behaviour in the light of what we care about. If we do not care, then we are missing something. For a human being, to lack a broad respect for living things and beautiful things and well-functioning things is to be stunted in a way.

Our coming to see other species as commanding respect is itself a way of transcending our animal natures. It is ennobling. It is part of our animal natures unthinkingly to see ourselves as superior, and to try to dominate accordingly; our capacity to see ourselves as equal is one of the things that makes us different. Thus, our capacity to see ourselves as equal may be one of the things that makes us superior. Coming to see all species as equal may not be the best way of transcending our animal natures—it does not work for me—but it is one way. Another way of transcending our animal natures and expressing due respect for nature is simply to not worry so much about ranking species. This latter way is, I think, better. It is more respectful of our own reflective natures. It does not dwell on rankings. It does not insist on seeing equality where a more reflective being simply would see what is there to be seen and would not shy away from respecting the differences as well as the commonalities. The whole idea of ranking species, even as equals, sometimes seems like a child's game. It seems beneath us.

VIII. RESPECT FOR EVERYTHING

Thus, a broad respect for living or beautiful or well-functioning things need not translate into equal respect. It need not translate into universal respect, either. I can appreciate mosquitoes to a degree. My wife (a biochemist who studies mosquito immune systems) even finds them beautiful, or so she says. My own appreciation, by contrast, is thin and grudging and purely intellectual. In neither degree nor kind is it anything like the appreciation I have for my wife, or for human beings in general, or even for the rabbits I sometimes find eating my flowers in the morning. Part of our responsibility as moral agents is to be somewhat choosy about what we respect and how we respect it. I can see why people shy away from openly accepting that responsibility, but they still have it.

Johnson says speciesism is as arbitrary as racism unless we can show that the differences are morally relevant (p. 51). This is, to be sure, a popular sentiment among radical environmentalists and animal liberationists. But are we really like racists when we think it is worse to kill a dolphin than to kill a tuna? The person who says there is a relevant similarity between speciesism and racism has the burden of proof: go ahead and identify the similarity. Is seeing moral significance in biological differences between chimpanzees and potatoes anything like seeing moral significance in biological differences between races? I think not.

Is it true that we need good reason to *exclude* plants and animals from the realm of things we regard as commanding respect? Or do we need reason to *include* them? Should we be trying to identify properties in virtue of which a thing forfeits presumptive moral standing? Or does it make more sense to be trying to identify properties in virtue of which a thing commands respect? The latter seems more natural

to me, which suggests the burden of proof lies with those who claim we should have respect for other species.

I would not say, though, that this burden is unbearable. One reason to have regard for other species has to do with self-respect. (As I said earlier, when we mistreat a tree that we admire, the values we fail to respect are our values, not the tree's.) A second reason has to do with self-realisation. (As I said, exercising our capacity for moral regard is a form of self-realisation.) Finally, at least some species seem to share with human beings precisely those cognitive and affective characteristics that lead us to see human life as especially worthy of esteem. Johnson describes experiments in which rhesus monkeys show extreme reluctance to obtain food by means that would subject monkeys in neighbouring cages to electric shock (p. 64n). He describes the case of Washoe, a chimpanzee who learned sign language. Anyone who has tried to learn a foreign language ought to be able to appreciate how astonishing an intellectual feat it is that an essentially nonlinguistic creature could learn a language—a language that is not merely foreign but the language of another species.

Johnson believes Washoe has moral standing (pp. 27–31), but he does not believe that the moral standing of chimpanzees, and indeed of all living creatures, implies that we must resolve never to kill (p. 136). Thus, Johnson supports killing introduced animal species (feral dogs, rabbits, and so forth) to prevent the extermination of Australia's native species, including native plant species (p. 174).

Is Johnson guilty of advocating the speciesist equivalent of ethnic cleansing? Has he shown himself to be no better than a racist? I think not. Johnson is right to want to take drastic measures to protect Australia's native flora, and the idea of respecting trees is intelligible. Certainly one thing I feel in the presence of Redwoods is something like a feeling of respect. But I doubt that what underlies Johnson's willingness to kill feral dogs is mere respect for Australia's native plants. I suspect that his approval of such killings turns on the needs and aesthetic sensibilities of human beings, not just the interests of plants.[10] For example, if the endangered native species happened to be a malaria-carrying mosquito, I doubt that Johnson would advocate wiping out an exotic but minimally intrusive species of amphibian in order to save the mosquitoes.

Aldo Leopold urged us to see ourselves as plain citizens of, rather than conquerors of the biotic community, but there are some species with whom we can never be fellow citizens.[11] The rabbits eating my flowers in the back yard are neighbours, and I cherish their company, minor frictions notwithstanding. I feel no sense of community with mosquitoes, though, and not merely because they are not warm and furry. Some mosquito species are so adapted to making human beings miserable that moral combat is not accidental; rather, combat is a natural state. It is how such creatures live. Recall Cheney's remark that the limits of moral regard are set by the limits of our ability to respond in a caring manner. I think it is fair to say human beings are not able to respond to malaria-carrying mosquitoes in a caring manner. At very least, most of us would think less of a person who did respond to them in a caring manner. We would regard the person's caring as a parody of respect for nature.

The conclusion that *all* species have moral standing is unmotivated. For human beings, viewing apes as having moral standing is a form of self-respect. Viewing viruses as having moral standing is not. It is good to have a sense of how amazing living things are, but being able to marvel at living things is not the same as thinking all species have moral standing. Life as such commands respect only in the limited but nonetheless important sense that for self-aware and reflective creatures who want to act in ways that make sense, deliberately killing something is an act that does not make sense unless we have good reason to do it. Destroying something for no good reason is (at best) the moral equivalent of vandalism.

IX. THE HISTORY OF THE DEBATE

There is an odd project in the history of philosophy that equates what seem to be three distinct projects:

1. determining our essence;
2. specifying how we are different from all other species;
3. specifying what makes us morally important.

Equating these three projects has important ramifications. Suppose for the sake of argument that what makes us morally important is that we are capable of suffering. If what makes us morally important is necessarily the same property that constitutes our essence, then our essence is that we are capable of suffering. And if our essence necessarily is what makes us different from all other species, then we can deduce that dogs are not capable of suffering.

Likewise with rationality. If rationality is our essence, then rationality is what makes us morally important and also what makes us unique. Therefore, we can deduce that chimpanzees are not rational. Alternatively, if some other animal becomes rational, does that mean our essence will change? Is that why some people find Washoe, the talking chimpanzee, threatening?

The three projects, needless to say, should not be conflated in the way philosophy seems historically to have conflated them, but we can reject species equality without conflating them. If we like, we can select a property with respect to which all species are the same, then argue that that property confers moral standing, then say all species have moral standing. To infer that all species have the same standing, though, would be to ignore the possibility that there are other morally important properties with respect to which not all species are equal.

There is room to wonder whether species egalitarianism is even compatible with respect for nature. Is it true that we should have no more regard for dolphins than for tuna? Is it true that the moral standing of chimpanzees is no higher than that of mosquitoes? I worry that these things are not only untrue, but also disrespectful. Dolphins and chimpanzees command more respect than species egalitarianism allows.

There is no denying that it demeans us to destroy species we find beautiful or otherwise beneficial. What about species in which we find neither beauty nor benefit? It is, upon reflection, obviously in our interest to enrich our lives by finding them beautiful or beneficial, if we can. By and large, we must agree with Leopold that it is too late for conquering the biotic community. Our most pressing task now is to find ways of fitting in. Species egalitarianism is one way of trying to understand how we fit in. In the end, it is not an acceptable way. Having respect for nature and being a species egalitarian are two different things.

NOTES

1. A species egalitarian may or may not believe that individual living things all have equal moral standing. A species egalitarian may think a given whooping crane matters more than a given bald eagle because the cranes are endangered, despite believing that the differences between the two species qua species are not morally important.

2. Paul W. Taylor (1983) In defense of biocentrism, *Environmental Ethics*, 5: 237–43, here p. 240.

3. Taylor (1994), [*Respect for Nature* (Princeton, NJ: Princeton University Press)], p. 35.

4. Arne Naess (1973) The shallow and the deep, long-range ecology movement: a summary, *Inquiry*, 16: 95–100.

5. William C. French (1995) Against biospherical egalitarianism, *Environmental Ethics*, 17: 39–57, here pp. 44ff.

6. James C. Anderson (1993) Species equality and the foundations of moral theory, *Environmental Values,* 2: 347–65, here p. 350.

7. Lawrence Johnson (1991) *A Morally Deep World* (New York, Cambridge University Press), p. 52.

8. Thus, the objective is to explain how a rational agent could have respect for trees, not to argue that a rational agent could not fail to have respect. In utilitarian terms, a person whose utility function leaves no room to derive pleasure from respecting trees is not irrational for failing to respect trees, but people whose utility functions include a potential for deriving pleasure from respecting trees have reason (other things equal) to enrich their lives by realising that potential.

9. Jim Cheney (1987) Eco-feminism and deep ecology, *Environmental Ethics* 9: 115–45, here p. 144.

10. Johnson believes ecosystems as such have moral standing and that, consequently, 'we should always stop short of entirely destroying or irreparably degrading any ecosystem' (p. 276). 'Chopping some trees is one thing, then, but destroying a forest is something else' (p. 276). But this is impossible to square with his remark that there 'is an ecosystem in a tiny puddle of water in a rotting stump' (p. 265). Thus, when Johnson says ecosystems should never be destroyed, he does not mean ecosystems per se. Rather he means forests, deserts, marshes, and so on—ecosystems that are recognisable as habitat either for humans or for species that humans care about.

11. Aldo Leopold (1966, first published in 1949) *Sand County Almanac* (New York, Oxford University Press) p. 240.

From *The Land Ethic*

ALDO LEOPOLD

When god-like Odysseus returned from the wars in Troy, he hanged all on one rope a dozen slave-girls of his household whom he suspected of misbehavior during his absence.

This hanging involved no question of propriety. The girls were property. The disposal of property was then, as now, a matter of expediency, not of right and wrong.

Concepts of right and wrong were not lacking from Odysseus' Greece: witness the fidelity of his wife through the long years before at last his black-prowed galleys clove the wine-dark seas for home. The ethical

structure of that day covered wives, but had not yet been extended to human chattels. During the three thousand years which have since elapsed, ethical criteria have been extended to many fields of conduct, with corresponding shrinkages in those judged by expediency only.

This extension of ethics, so far studied only by philosophers, is actually a process in ecological evolution. Its sequences may be described in ecological as well as in philosophical terms. An ethic, ecologically, is a limitation on freedom of action in the struggle for existence. An ethic, philosophically, is a differentiation of social from anti-social conduct. These are two definitions of one thing. The thing has its origin in the tendency of interdependent individuals or groups to evolve modes of co-operation. The ecologist calls these symbioses. Politics and economics are advanced symbioses in which the original free-for-all competition has been replaced, in part, by co-operative mechanisms with an ethical content.

The complexity of co-operative mechanisms has increased with population density, and with the efficiency of tools. It was simpler, for example, to define the anti-social uses of sticks and stones in the days of the mastodons than of bullets and billboards in the age of motors.

The first ethics dealt with the relation between individuals; the Mosaic Decalogue is an example. Later accretions dealt with the relation between the individual and society. The Golden Rule tries to integrate the individual to society; democracy to integrate social organization to the individual.

There is as yet no ethic dealing with man's relation to land and to the animals and plants which grow upon it. Land, like Odysseus' slave-girls, is still property. The land-relation is still strictly economic, entailing privileges but not obligations.

The extension of ethics to this third element in human environment is, if I read the evidence correctly, an evolutionary possibility and an ecological necessity. It is the third step in a sequence. The first two have already been taken. Individual thinkers since the days of Ezekiel and Isaiah have asserted that the despoliation of land is not only inexpedient but wrong. Society, however, has not yet affirmed their belief. I regard the present conservation movement as the embryo of such an affirmation.

An ethic may be regarded as a mode of guidance for meeting ecological situations so new or intricate, or involving such deferred reactions, that the path of social expediency is not discernible to the average individual. Animal instincts are modes of guidance for the individual in meeting such situations. Ethics are possibly a kind of community instinct in-the-making.

THE COMMUNITY CONCEPT

All ethics so far evolved rest upon a single premise: that the individual is a member of a community of interdependent parts. His instincts prompt him to compete for his place in the community, but his ethics prompt him also to co-operate (perhaps in order that there may be a place to compete for).

The land ethic simply enlarges the boundaries of the community to include soils, waters, plants, and animals, or collectively: the land.

This sounds simple: do we not already sing our love for and obligation to the land of the free and the home of the brave? Yes, but just what and whom do we love? Certainly not the soil, which we are sending helter-skelter downriver. Certainly not the waters, which we assume have no function except to turn turbines, float barges, and carry off sewage. Certainly not the plants, of which we exterminate whole communities without batting an eye. Certainly not the animals, of which we have already extirpated many of the largest and most beautiful species. A land ethic of course cannot prevent the alteration, management, and use of these 'resources,' but it does affirm their right to continued existence, and, at least in spots, their continued existence in a natural state.

In short, a land ethic changes the role of *Homo sapiens* from conquerer of the land-community to plain member and citizen of it. It implies respect for his fellow-members, and also respect for the community as such.

In human history, we have learned (I hope) that the conquerer role is eventually self-defeating. Why? Because it is implicit in such a role that the conqueror knows, *ex cathedra,* just what makes the community clock tick, and just what and who is valuable, and what and who is worthless, in community life. It always turns out that he knows neither, and this is why his conquests eventually defeat themselves.

In the biotic community, a parallel situation exists. Abraham knew exactly what the land was for: it was to drop milk and honey into Abraham's mouth. At the present moment, the assurance with which we regard this assumption is inverse to the degree of our education.

The ordinary citizen today assumes that science knows what makes the community clock tick; the scientist is equally sure that he does not. He knows that the biotic mechanism is so complex that its workings may never be fully understood.

* * *

SUBSTITUTES FOR A LAND ETHIC

When the logic of history hungers for bread and we hand out a stone, we are at pains to explain how much the stone resembles bread. I now describe some of the stones which serve in lieu of a land ethic.

One basic weakness in a conservation system based wholly on economic motives is that most members of the land community have no economic value. Wildflowers and songbirds are examples. Of the 22,000 higher plants and animals native to Wisconsin, it is doubtful whether more than 5 per cent can be sold, fed, eaten, or otherwise put to economic use. Yet these creatures are members of the biotic community, and if (as I believe) its stability depends on its integrity, they are entitled to continuance.

When one of these non-economic categories is threatened, and if we happen to love it, we invent subterfuges to give it economic importance. At the beginning of the century songbirds were supposed to be disappearing. Ornithologists jumped to the rescue with some distinctly shaky evidence to the effect that insects would eat us up if birds failed to control them. The evidence had to be economic in order to be valid.

It is painful to read these circumlocutions today. We have no land ethic yet, but we have at least drawn nearer the point of admitting that birds should continue as a matter of biotic right, regardless of the presence or absence of economic advantage to us.

A parallel situation exists in respect of predatory mammals, raptorial birds, and fish-eating birds. Time was when biologists somewhat overworked the evidence that these creatures preserve the health of game by killing weaklings, or that they control rodents for the farmer, or that they prey only on 'worthless' species. Here again, the evidence had to be economic in order to be valid. It is only in recent years that we hear the more honest argument that predators are members of the community, and that no special interest has the right to exterminate them for the sake of a benefit, real or fancied, to itself. Unfortunately this enlightened view is still in the talk stage. In the field the determination of predators goes merrily on: witness the impending erasure of the timber wolf by fiat of Congress, the Conservation Bureaus, and many state legislatures.

Some species of trees have been 'read out of the party' by economics-minded foresters because they grow too slowly, or have too low a sale value to pay as timber crops: white cedar, tamarack, cypress, beech, and hemlock are examples. In Europe, where forestry is ecologically more advanced, the non-commercial tree species are recognized as members of the native forest community, to be preserved as such, within reason. Moreover some (like beech) have been found to have a valuable function in building up soil fertility. The interdependence of the forest and its constituent tree species, ground flora, and fauna is taken for granted.

Lack of economic value is sometimes a character not only of species or groups, but of entire biotic communities: marshes, bogs, dunes, and 'deserts' are examples. Our formula in such cases is to relegate their conservation to government as refuges, monuments, or parks. The difficulty is that these communities are usually interspersed with more valuable private lands; the government cannot possibly own or control such scattered parcels. The net effect is that we have relegated some of them to ultimate extinction over large areas. If the private owner were ecologically minded, he would be proud to be the custodian of a reasonable proportion of such areas, which add diversity and beauty to his farm and to his community.

* * *

To sum up: a system of conservation based solely on economic self-interest is hopelessly lopsided. It tends to ignore, and thus eventually to eliminate, many elements in the land community that lack commercial value, but that are (as far as we know) essential to its healthy functioning. It assumes, falsely, I think, that the economic parts of the biotic clock will function without the uneconomic parts. It tends to relegate to government many functions eventually too large, too complex, or too widely dispersed to be performed by government.

* * *

THE LAND PYRAMID

An ethic to supplement and guide the economic relation to land presupposes the existence of some mental image of land as a biotic mechanism. We can be ethical only in relation in something we can see, feel, understand, love, or otherwise have faith in.

The image commonly employed in conservation education is 'the balance of nature.' For reasons too lengthy to detail here, this figure of speech fails to describe accurately what little we know about the land mechanism. A much truer image is the one employed in ecology: the biotic pyramid.

* * *

Plants absorb energy from the sun. This energy flows through a circuit called the biota, which may be represented by a pyramid consisting of layers. The bottom layer is the soil. A plant layer rests on the soil, an insect layer on the plants, a bird and rodent layer on the insects, and so on up through various animal groups to the apex layer, which consists of the larger carnivores.

The species of a layer are alike not in where they came from, or in what they look like, but rather in what they eat. Each successive layer depends on those below it for food and often for other services, and each in turn furnishes food and services to those above. Proceeding upward, each successive layer decreases in numerical abundance. Thus, for every carnivore there are hundreds of his prey, thousands of their prey, millions of insects, uncountable plants. The pyramidal form of the system reflects this numerical progression from apex to base. Man shares an intermediate layer with the bears, raccoons, and squirrels which eat both meat and vegetables.

The lines of dependency for food and other services are called food chains. Thus soil-oak-deer-Indian is a chain that has now been largely converted to soil-corn-cow-farmer. Each species, including ourselves, is a link in many chains. The deer eats a hundred plants other than oak, and the cow a hundred plants other than corn. Both, then, are links in a hundred chains. The pyramid is a tangle of chains so complex as to seem disorderly, yet the stability of the system proves it to be a highly organized structure. Its functioning depends on the co-operation and competition of its diverse parts.

In the beginning, the pyramid of life was low and squat; the food chains short and simple. Evolution has added layer after layer, link after link. Man is one of thousands of accretions to the height and complexity of the pyramid. Science has given us many doubts, but it has given us at least one certainty: the trend of evolution is to elaborate and diversify the biota.

Land, then, is not merely soil; it is a fountain of energy flowing through a circuit of soils, plants, and animals. Food chains are the living channels which conduct energy upward; death and decay return it to the soil. The circuit is not closed; some energy is dissipated in decay, some is added by absorption from the air, some is stored in soils, peats, and long-lived forests; but it is a sustained circuit, like a slowly augmented revolving fund of life. There is always a net loss by downhill wash, but this is normally small and offset by the decay of rocks. It is deposited in the ocean and, in the course of geological time, raised to form new lands and new pyramids.

The velocity and character of the upward flow of energy depend on the complex structure of the plant and animal community, much as the upward flow of sap in a tree depends on its complex cellular organization. Without this complexity, normal circulation would presumably not occur. Structure means the characteristic numbers, as well as the characteristic kinds and functions, of the component species. This interdependence between the complex structure of the land and its smooth functioning as an energy unit is one of its basic attributes.

When a change occurs in one part of the circuit, many other parts must adjust themselves to it. Change does not necessarily obstruct or divert the flow of energy; evolution is a long series of self-induced changes, the net result of which has been to elaborate the flow mechanism and to lengthen the circuit. Evolutionary changes, however, are usually slow and local. Man's invention of tools has enabled him to make changes of unprecedented violence, rapidity, and scope.

* * *

THE OUTLOOK

It is inconceivable to me that an ethical relation to land can exist without love, respect, and admiration for land, and a high regard for its value. By value, I of course mean something far broader than mere economic value; I mean value in the philosophical sense.

* * *

The 'key-log' which must be moved to release the evolutionary process for an ethic is simply this: quit thinking about decent land-use as solely an economic problem. Examine each question in terms of what is ethically and esthetically right, as well as what is economically expedient. A thing is right when it tends to preserve the integrity, stability, and beauty of the biotic community. It is wrong when it tends otherwise.

It of course goes without saying that economic feasibility limits the tether of what can or cannot be done for land. It always has and it always will. The fallacy the economic determinists have tied around our collective neck, and which we now need to cast off, is the belief that economics determines *all* land use. This is simply not true. An innumerable host of actions and attitudes, comprising perhaps the bulk of all land relations, is determined by the land-users' tastes and predilections, rather than by his purse. The bulk of all land relations hinges on investments of time, forethought, skill, and faith rather than on investments of cash. As a land-user thinketh, so is he.

I have purposely presented the land ethic as a product of social evolution because nothing so important as an ethic is ever 'written.' Only the most superficial student of history supposes that Moses 'wrote' the Decalogue; it evolved in the minds of a thinking community, and Moses wrote a tentative summary of it for a 'seminar.' I say tentative because evolution never stops.

The evolution of a land ethic is an intellectual as well as emotional process. Conservation is paved with good intentions which prove to be futile, or even dangerous, because they are devoid of critical understanding either of the land, or of economic land-use. I think it is a truism that as the ethical frontier advances from the individual to the community, its intellectual content increases.

The mechanism of operation is the same for any ethic: social approbation for right actions: social disapproval for wrong actions.

By and large, our present problem is one of attitudes and implements. We are remodeling the Alhambra with a steam-shovel, and we are proud of our yardage. We shall hardly relinquish the shovel, which after all has many good points, but we are in need of gentler and more objective criteria for its successful use.

CHAPTER 14

Racism, Equality, and Discrimination

On Friday night, August 11, 2017, in Charlottesville, Virginia—beloved city of Thomas Jefferson, site of the university he founded, and bastion of the Confederacy—white supremacists marched on the campus of the University of Virginia, carrying torches and chanting Nazi slogans. On Saturday they rallied again in Charlottesville, yelling racial slurs and displaying swastikas, Confederate flags, and Ku Klux Klan symbols. They were accompanied by militiamen toting assault rifles. The ostensible purpose of the gathering was to protest the removal of a statue dedicated to the memory of Robert E. Lee, the famous Confederate general. Counterprotestors shouted progressive slogans, carried anti-racist signs, and sang civil rights–era songs. Skirmishes broke out between the two sides, and a woman was killed and several others injured when a 20-year-old man from Ohio drove his car into a crowd of counterprotestors. Two Virginia State Police troopers who had been monitoring the conflict also died when their helicopter crashed near Charlottesville.

These heartrending events are among the latest in America's long history of racial conflict and prejudice. Such incidents seem all the more painful because they afflict a nation whose professed ideals include liberty, justice, and equality. If because of these ideals, the United States has been a shining city on a hill, beaming hope to the world, the light seems to many to have dimmed. From the Charlottesville tragedy (and other contemporary episodes of racial conflict), scholars can trace a clear line of race-related tragedies and racist violence back through colonial and U.S. history. Here are a few of the most notable moments:

- **1619** English colonists bring the first African slaves to the colony of Jamestown.

- **1660s** "Slave codes" are enacted to outlaw interracial marriage and the freeing of slaves by their masters (manumission). Slavery becomes a life sentence.

- **Late 1700s** The United States' founding document, the Constitution, establishes a new nation but grants no rights to slaves. Almost half of the men who craft the Constitution own slaves. Thomas Jefferson insists that Africans and their descendants are less than human.

- **1863** President Abraham Lincoln (1809–1865) delivers the Emancipation Proclamation, which declares that slaves in the states of the Confederacy shall be free. Two years later, after the Civil War, slavery is officially abolished, but racist doctrines that justify slavery and the lower status of blacks are widespread.

- **1866–1870s** The Ku Klux Klan, a terrorist organization known as "The Invisible Empire of the South," beats, tortures, and hangs black Americans for asserting their rights or for simply being black. The Klan has thousands of members and survives well into the twenty-first century.

- **1870** The 15th Amendment is adopted into the U.S. Constitution, granting the right to vote to African American men (but not women).

- **1880s** Former Confederacy states enact Jim Crow laws—legislation designed to deny black citizens the right to vote and to ensure unequal segregation in virtually every area of public life. Jim Crow laws do not exist in Northern states, but widespread racial discrimination does.

- **1896** The Supreme Court's ruling in *Plessy v. Ferguson* permits increased segregation and Jim Crow practices.

- **1875–1950** Over 4,000 black men, women, and children are murdered in racial terror lynchings. They are hanged, burned alive, and hacked to death.

- **1955** Rosa Parks is arrested for not relinquishing her bus seat to a white man, helping to launch the Montgomery bus boycott.

- **1958** Twenty-four states throughout the country have laws that ban marriage between people of different races. Some people are arrested and jailed for violating the prohibitions. Intermarriage laws stand until 1967, when the Supreme Court rules them unconstitutional.

- **1960s** Blacks are discriminated against in restaurants, restrooms, classrooms, lunch counters, hospitals, theaters, train cars, at cemeteries, and on buses. Killings and beatings of peaceful black protestors and their white supporters shock the nation with their brutality and frequency.

- **1965** The Voting Rights Act passes, allowing the federal government to intervene to help blacks vote.

- **1968** In Memphis, James Earl Ray assassinates Martin Luther King Jr., the leader of the civil rights movement and a tireless advocate of change through nonviolence.

To make sense of the issues that have emerged from this history, we have to start at the beginning with an understanding of the moral implications of race and racism and our responses to them.

ISSUE FILE: BACKGROUND

What is race? Who is a racist? For many people, these questions seem to pose no conceptual difficulties at all. They think it is perfectly obvious what race is, for they can point to people who seem to belong to one race, and they can point to others who seem to belong to a different race. And even though there is less agreement about what *racism* or *racist* means, many believe they know a racist when they see one. At the same time, unless they are resolute bigots, most people want never to be guilty of racism, however it's defined, and never to be called a racist, whether or not they are guilty of the charge. But after a hundred years of studying race and racism, scholars (mostly sociologists and philosophers) have concluded that our understanding of these ideas may be simplistic or even morally suspect.

The core idea of race—that is, the notion of discrete groups of people who share distinct biological and cultural traits—is actually relatively new, arising in different forms over time beginning around the sixteenth century and changing in the Americas and Europe in response to colonization and slavery. As Europeans subjugated and enslaved Africans and native peoples in the Americas, the idea of superior and inferior races took hold and was used to justify inhumane treatment of whole cultures. But in ancient times, no one thought to categorize humans into exclusive racial groups. To the ancients, cultures might differ in various ways, but dividing the world into races the way you might sort jellybeans into separate piles by color was not done. For example, the philosopher Lawrence Blum says that

> [I]n the ancient Greco-Roman world, Africans were identified primarily by skin color, nose shape and hair texture. . . . The Greeks were quite interested in the dark skin of Ethiopians, which they attributed to climatic conditions; but they did not homogenize all darker-skinned persons into a single social grouping. They were clearly aware of distinct shades of dark skin.

The Greeks were respectful of dark-skinned Africans, whom they encountered in war, as both allies and adversaries, and in commerce. Nubia, an African civilization south of Egypt inhabited by persons of "Negroid" features, was respected as a military power. Dark-skinned Africans were identified generally as "human beings with the capacity for freedom and justice, piety, and wisdom."[1]

In the late eighteenth century, science was establishing itself as a relatively new way of acquiring reliable knowledge about the world. In the nineteenth and early twentieth centuries, several thinkers tried to apply its principles to the study of race. The result was what is now known as *scientific racism*. Several scientifically minded investigators examined the physical characteristics of people from different cultures and parts of the world and concluded that (1) humanity can indeed be divided into separate and distinct races, (2) race enables us to explain the most basic differences among people, and (3) some races are superior to others—and the white European race is superior to all. Using suspect assumptions, skull and brain measurements, "intelligence" tests, and travel accounts, these men argued that white European men were more biologically advanced and more intelligent than any other racial group—and that this superiority explained their dominance in the world. Later scientists, however, uncovered a host of errors and biases in this research and debunked the claim of European superiority.

In the twenty-first century, science still has not firmly established that there are such things as races that differ in certain essential, inherent characteristics. The traditional idea is that race consists of heritable biological features common to all members of a racial group, features that explain the character and cultural traits of those members. But the consensus among scientists and philosophers is that this view is false. As the sociologist Tanya Maria Golash-Boza explains:

Race is a social construction, an idea we endow with meaning through daily interactions. It has no biological basis. This might seem odd to read, as the physical differences between a Kenyan, a Swede, and a Han Chinese, for example, are obvious. However, these physical differences do not necessarily mean that the world can be divided into discrete racial groups. If you were to walk from Kenya to Sweden to China, you would note incremental gradations in physical differences between people across space, and it would be difficult to decide where to draw the line between Africa and Europe and between Europe and Asia. There may be genetic differences between Kenyans and Swedes, but the genetic variations within the Kenyan population are actually greater than those between Swedes and Kenyans. Although race is a social, as opposed to a biological, construction, it has a wide range of consequences in our society, especially when used as a sorting and stratifying mechanism.[2]

According to Blum, popular thinking about race generally dispenses with the biological component, but not with the idea of *inherency*—the notion that "certain traits of mind, character, and temperament are inescapably part of a racial group's 'nature' and hence define its racial fate."[3] A group's nature is thought to be fixed and unalterable. This view of race says that whites are naturally this way; Asians are naturally that way; blacks have this inherent character trait; Jews exhibit this inherent disposition.

Some philosophers, known as race skeptics, who accept that race has no physical scientific basis argue that the concept of race should be discarded entirely. Blum maintains that

the contemporary American conception of race contains certain morally troubling features independent of its use in specifically racist contexts: exaggerated difference and moral distance between those of different races, which discourages an experienced sense of common humanity; an overdrawn and falsely grounded sense of commonality among members of the same race; a notion of being trapped in one's racial fate; encouragement of stereotyping racial others rather than seeing them as individuals; and an implication that, because of their racial membership, some persons have greater worth or ability than others.[4]

But other philosophers, called race constructivists, agree that biological race is a myth but are reluctant to jettison the social construct. As the political scientist Michael James explains:

Race constructivists accept the skeptics' dismissal of biological race but argue that the term still meaningfully refers to the widespread grouping of individuals into certain categories by society, indeed often by the very members of such racial ascriptions. Normatively, race constructivists argue that since society labels people according to racial categories, and since such labeling often leads to race-based differences in resources, opportunities, and well-being, the concept of race must be conserved, in order to facilitate race-based social movements or policies, such as affirmative action, that compensate for socially constructed but socially relevant racial differences.[5]

The view of many researchers and scholars is that races (in the biological sense) don't exist, but "racialized groups"—groups that people *believe* are discrete and immutable races and treat as such—do. Throughout American history, people have believed (and still believe) that there are identifiable races called "whites" and "blacks," and society has treated these groups accordingly.[6]

In any case, a commitment to either the traditional (biological) or the inherency view of race is a presupposition of racism. Racism is based on the belief that distinct races exist and that significant differences (such as moral, intellectual, or cultural differences) among races can be distinguished. What pushes this view about race into **racism** is the additional belief that some races are inferior in these significant respects or otherwise deserving of dislike or hostility.

The key concepts in this definition are what Blum calls *inferiorization* and *antipathy*. He suggests that all forms of racism can be related to these two themes:

Inferiorization is linked to historical racist doctrine and racist social systems. Slavery, segregation, imperialism, apartheid, and Nazism all treated certain groups as inferior to other groups . . .

Though race-based antipathy is less related to the original concept of "racism," today the term unequivocally encompasses racial bigotry, hostility, and hatred. Indeed, the racial bigot is many people's paradigm image of a "racist.". . .

Historical systems of racism did of course inevitably involve racial antipathy as well as inferiorization. Hatred of Jews was central to Nazi philosophy; and it is impossible to understand American racism without seeing hostility to blacks and Native Americans as integral to the nexus of attitudes and emotions that shored up slavery and segregation.[7]

Blum hopes that an understanding of racism as defined by these two concepts will help stanch what has been called the "conceptual inflation" of the words *racist* and *racism*. He and other scholars see the terms losing their moral import and ability to shame because they are overused and misapplied. People, words, symbols, policies, practices, institutions—such things are clearly racist if they involve inferiorization and antipathy directed at racial groups. But many other things labeled racist, according to the definition above, are not racist. As Blum says,

Some feel that the word [racist] is thrown around so much that anything involving "race" that someone does not like is liable to castigation as "racist.". . . A local newspaper called certain blacks "racist" for criticizing other blacks who supported a white over a black candidate for mayor. A white girl in Virginia said that it was "racist" for an African American teacher in her school to wear African attire. . . . Merely mentioning someone's race (or racial designation), using the word "Oriental" for Asians without recognizing its origins and its capacity for insult, or socializing only with members of one's own racial group are called "racist.". . .

Not every instance of racial conflict, insensitivity, discomfort, miscommunication, exclusion, injustice, or ignorance should be called "racist." Not all *racial* incidents are *racist* incidents. We need a more varied and nuanced moral vocabulary for talking about the domain of race. . . . All forms of racial ills should elicit concern from responsible individuals. If someone displays racial insensitivity, but not racism, people should be able to see that for what it is.[8]

CRITICAL THOUGHT: White Privilege

What is white privilege, and what does it have to do with racism? *White privilege* refers to the advantages or benefits that whites enjoy simply because they are white. The philosopher Lawrence Blum says that there are two distinct forms of white privilege:

> One is simply that of being spared racial discrimination, stigmatizing, indignities, stereotyping, and other race-based wrongs. . . . A second, however, consists in material benefits accruing to whites because of discrimination against racial minorities. When a black is denied a job because of discrimination, there is one more job available to a non-black (usually a white). When poor schooling leaves many blacks and Latinos inadequately prepared for higher education or the job market, jobs and places in colleges become more available to whites (and to others, such as some Asian groups, positioned to take advantage of these opportunities).*

To whites, racial privilege can seem almost invisible. Tanya Maria Golash-Boza explains:

> If you are white, it can be difficult to notice that you are not being followed around the store [by security]; that people are smiling at you on the street instead of clutching their purses; that no one asks you if you speak English; that you are not asked for identification when paying with a credit card. Instead, you are likely to think that these things are normal—that this is simply how things are.†

Some define racism as a *system* of privilege and believe that being part of such a system makes you a racist, which of course makes all whites racist. But Blum thinks it's a mistake to conflate white privilege with personal racism:

> The whole point of the idea of white privilege is that it does *not* depend on the attitudes of its beneficiaries toward disadvantaged racial groups; nonracists still partake of white privilege. . . . What is so disturbing about white privilege is that you need not be in any way personally blameworthy for having it, but it is still unfair that you do. It is not personally racist to have white privilege. . . . [W]hite privilege is a different sort of racial ill than personal racism. But it is morally wrong to be complacent about or accepting of racial privileges once one knows one possesses them; one is (often) thereby being complicit with injustice.‡

The eminent philosopher of race Naomi Zack argues that white privilege is real and pervasive, but that how we talk about white privilege is problematic:

> [White privilege discourse] goes too far in blaming all whites for all forms of racism and it does not go far enough in directly addressing injustice against nonwhites. . . . [W]hite privilege discourse may miss the importance of racial injustice and degenerate into just another display of the advantages that white people have of not being required to respond to racial injustice against their racial group. . . . Yes, whites are privileged, but no amount of exhortation to "check" their privilege or confessional discourse in response will correct the legal injustice of police homicide based on racial profiling.**

*Lawrence Blum, *I'm Not a Racist But* (Ithaca, NY: Cornell University Press, 2002), 72.
†Tanya Maria Golash-Boza, *Race and Racisms* (New York: Oxford University Press, 2016), 52.
‡Blum, 73, 76.
**Naomi Zack, "Uses and Abuses of the Discourse of White Privilege," Philosopher (blog), June 24, 2016, https://politicalphilosopher.net/2016/06/24/featured-philosopher-naomi-zack/. Reprinted with permission.

We should not, however, infer from any of this that the magnitude of racism and inequality in society has been exaggerated. In fact, it's likely that indirect or veiled racism and inequality are more serious than we might imagine. Here's a sketch of a few of the more egregious problems, from the social scientist and race scholar Eduardo Bonilla-Silva:

> Blacks and dark-skinned racial minorities lag well behind whites in virtually every area of social life; they are about three times more likely to be poor than whites, earn about 40 percent less than whites, and have about an eighth of the net worth that whites have. They also receive an inferior education compared to whites, even when they attend integrated institutions. In terms of housing, black-owned units comparable to white-owned ones are valued at 35 percent less. Blacks and Latinos also have less access to the entire housing market because whites, through a variety of exclusionary practices by white realtors and homeowners, have been successful in effectively limiting their entrance into many neighborhoods. Blacks receive impolite treatment in stores, in restaurants, and in a host of other commercial transactions. Researchers have also documented that blacks pay more for goods such as cars and houses than do whites. Finally, blacks and dark-skinned Latinos are the targets of racial profiling by the police, which, combined with the highly racialized criminal court system, guarantees their overrepresentation among those arrested, prosecuted, incarcerated, and if charged for a capital crime, executed. Racial profiling on the highways has become such a prevalent phenomenon that a term has emerged to describe it: driving while black. In short, blacks and most minorities are "at the bottom of the well."[9]

Racism often involves **racial prejudice**—racially biased opinions based on incomplete or erroneous information. Racial prejudice can be either the result of racism or a pretext for it. **Racial discrimination** is unfavorable treatment of people because of their race. Prejudice and discrimination can be directed at traits other than race, including sexual orientation, age, gender, ethnicity, religion, and national origins. Discrimination based on any of these can be a violation of law or policy. Many people probably think that racism is essentially **individual racism**, person-to-person acts of intolerance or discrimination. But as Bonilla-Silva points out, a prevalent, almost invisible kind of racism is **institutional** or **structural racism**, unequal treatment that arises from the way organizations, institutions, and social systems operate. The people who work within such systems may or may not be racially prejudiced, but the systems themselves cause racial discrimination and inequality. Consider this example:

> Another practice . . . is employers' recruiting by word of mouth among current workers in the company rather than advertising in job listings. There is a nonracial business rationale for doing so: it saves publicity costs, and it garners job applicants for whom a reliable worker has vouched, thus saving on the costs of assessing job suitability in a larger group of unknown applicants. Nevertheless, such recruiting has a disparate racial impact . . . in many occupations blacks and Latinos constitute a smaller proportion of the workforce than their percentage in the population, and workers' networks are generally race-specific. Thus word-of-mouth recruiting perpetuates racial injustice and sustains the legacy of racial discrimination. . . . Hence, in the service of racial justice, [word-of-mouth recruiting] should generally be abandoned; employers should seek qualified black and Latino applicants, or at least not employ practices that discourage them.[10]

Many race scholars (and many whites of all professions) believe that individual racism and discrimination have declined markedly since the 1960s. And the more obvious signs of racism have indeed diminished, which is perhaps why most whites believe that racism is no longer a significant problem. Other social scientists, however, argue that racism in less overt forms is widespread. Bonilla-Silva explains:

> Nowadays, except for members of white supremacist organizations, few whites in the United States claim to be "racist." Most whites assert they "don't see any color, just people"; that although the ugly face of discrimination is still with us, it is no longer the central factor determining minorities' life chances; and, finally, that, like Dr. Martin Luther King Jr., they aspire to live in a society where "people are judged by the content of their character, not by the color of their skin." More poignantly, most

whites insist that minorities (especially blacks) are the ones responsible for what "race problem" we have in this country. . . . Most whites believe that if blacks and other minorities would just stop thinking about the past, work hard, and complain less (particularly about racial discrimination), then Americans of all hues could "all get along."[11]

If whites do see contemporary racial inequality, says Bonilla-Silva, they are likely to blame it on nonracial factors:

[W]hites rationalize minorities' contemporary status as the product of market dynamics, naturally occurring phenomena, and blacks' imputed cultural limitations. For instance, whites can attribute Latinos' high poverty rate to a relaxed work ethic ("the Hispanics are manana, manana, manana—tomorrow, tomorrow, tomorrow") or residential segregation as the result of natural tendencies among groups ("Does a cat and dog mix? I can't see it. You can't drink milk and scotch. Certain mixes don't mix.").[12]

Like many other scholars, Bonilla-Silva also maintains that today the forces that create racial inequality are often nearly invisible:

[C]ontemporary racial inequality is reproduced through "new racism" practices that are subtle, institutional, and apparently nonracial. In contrast to the Jim Crow era, where racial inequality was enforced through overt means (e.g., signs saying "No Niggers Welcomed Here" or shotgun diplomacy at the voting booth), today racial practices operate in a "now you see it, now you don't" fashion. For example, residential segregation, which is almost as high today as it was in the past, is no longer accomplished through overtly discriminatory practices. Instead, covert behaviors such as not showing all the available units, steering minorities and whites into certain neighborhoods, quoting higher rents or prices to minority applicants, or not advertising units at all are the weapons of choice to maintain separate communities. In the economic field, "smiling face" discrimination ("We don't have jobs now, but please check later"), advertising job openings in mostly white networks and ethnic newspapers, and steering highly educated people of color into poorly remunerated jobs or

jobs with limited opportunities for mobility are the new ways of keeping minorities in a secondary position. Politically, although the civil rights struggles have helped remove many of the obstacles for the electoral participation of people of color, racial gerrymandering, multimember legislative districts, election runoffs, annexation of predominately white areas, at-large district elections, and anti-single-shot devices (disallowing concentrating votes [on] one or two candidates in cities using at-large elections) have become standard practices to disenfranchise people of color.[13]

All these indirect, institutional, covert means of creating racial inequality are what Bonilla-Silva calls "racism without racists." With this form of racism, blacks and other minorities can be disadvantaged while the individuals responsible for the injustice may be difficult to identify—or may not exist at all.

The most elementary moral question we can ask about racism and discrimination is, Why are they wrong? To the consequentialist, the answer is easy: they are wrong because they hurt people. It is difficult to imagine a racist belief or action resulting in a favorable balance of good over bad. The nonconsequentialist answer is also straightforward. It is likely to appeal to two fundamental moral principles: *respect for persons* and *justice*. The principle of respect for persons is the cornerstone of Kantian ethics and several other moral theories. It says that each person has equal inherent value, regardless of social status, power, prestige, and racial or ethnic identity. We fail to respect persons if we inhibit their freedom of choice, speech, or action; violate their rights; coerce or enslave them; disadvantage or harm them; discriminate against them; or use them to achieve an end that is not their own. The principle of *justice* says that equals must be treated equally and fairly; that is, persons must be treated the same unless there is a morally relevant difference between them, and they must get what is due them. Racial discrimination is contrary to justice because it treats one group differently than it does another, even though no morally relevant differences exist between them.

A painful and divisive issue that illustrates the many conflicts about race, racism (especially institutional racism), and discrimination that can arise is affirmative action. **Affirmative action** is a way of making amends for, or eradicating, discrimination based on race, ethnicity, and gender. It takes the form of policies and programs (usually mandated by government) designed to bring about the necessary changes in businesses, colleges, and other organizations. Consider this famous case: A white man named Alan Bakke applies for admission to the School of Medicine at the University of California, Davis. Only one hundred slots are available, and there are many other applicants. His grades and admissions test scores, however, are good. The medical school denies him admission anyway—and grants admission to several others whose grades and scores are lower than his. As it turns out, the school has reserved sixteen of the available slots for minority students, and many of the students who fill those slots have lower grades and test scores than Bakke. He sues, claiming that he has been denied admission solely because of his race. His case goes all the way to the U.S. Supreme Court, which is strongly divided but eventually decides in his favor. The majority opinion says that preferring members of a group solely on account of their race or ethnic origin is a clear-cut instance of discrimination. The court finds that quota systems like the one used at the School of Medicine at UC Davis are unconstitutional, but that in some situations the use of race or minority status in admissions decisions may be permissible.

This famous Supreme Court case—*Regents of the University of California v. Bakke* (1978)—is one of many to grapple with the issue of affirmative action, a social policy that is still being ferociously debated almost forty years after the *Bakke* decision was handed down. It illustrates why this issue is so explosive, so complicated, and so important: disputes over affirmative action invariably involve complex collisions of beliefs and values about racism, sexism, discrimination, civil rights, justice,

equality, desert, opportunity, and social utility. Little wonder, then, that disagreements flare where agreement would be expected, and that people often presumed to have different perspectives on the issue—liberals and conservatives, blacks and whites, men and women—may be just as likely to take the same side.

Affirmative action is notorious for touching off strong feelings that evoke simplistic, knee-jerk answers—precisely the kind of answers we want to avoid here. Only reflective, well-reasoned responses will do for moral questions like these: Are quota systems such as the one cited in the Bakke case morally permissible? Should people be given preference in college admissions or employment because they are members of a particular minority group? Should members of a minority group that was discriminated against in the past be given preferential treatment as compensation for that earlier discrimination? Is preferential treatment for minorities and women permissible even though it deprives white males of equal opportunities? Can affirmative action help create a more just and diverse society—or does it lead to a less just one, divided by race and culture?

The ideal that spawned affirmative action is that all persons deserve equal respect and equal opportunity in employment and education. It is an expression of the principle of justice that equals should be treated equally.

Affirmative action in the United States evolved over the past half century from several groundbreaking laws, executive orders, and court cases. Most notable among these is the Civil Rights Act of 1964, enacted at a time when racial discrimination in the United States was a deeply implanted infection—painful, injurious, and widespread. Discrimination against minorities and women was rampant in the workplace, in college admissions offices, in government contracting, and in countless places of business, from barbershops to factories. Amounting to a direct assault on unequal treatment, the act outlawed discrimination in public accommodations (such as restaurants and hotels), public schools and universities, and business organizations of all kinds. Regarding the latter, the act declares:

It shall be an unlawful employment practice for an employer—

(1) to fail or refuse to hire or discharge any individual or otherwise to discriminate against any individual with respect to his compensation, terms, conditions, or privileges of employment, because of such individual's race, color, religion, sex, or national origin; or

(2) to limit, segregate, or classify his employees or applicants for employment in any way which would deprive or tend to deprive any individual of employment opportunities or otherwise adversely affect his status as an employee, because of such individual's race, color, religion, sex, or national origin.[14]

Later, as the executive branch and the courts tried to interpret or implement antidiscrimination policies, affirmative action took on a broader meaning. Many U.S. companies and universities have gone beyond simply banning discriminatory practices. With prompting from the federal government, they have tried to institute equal opportunity ("to level the playing field") by ensuring that minority groups and women are represented in fair numbers (that is, numbers reflecting the proportion of such individuals in the whole community or the total workforce). But achieving fair or proportional representation has often required preferential treatment for the designated groups. Through the use of quotas or other means, members of the preferred groups have been favored over nonmembers, who are typically white males.

Thus we can say that there are actually two kinds of affirmative action—weak and strong.[15] **Weak affirmative action** is the use of policies and procedures to end discriminatory practices and ensure equal opportunity. It hews close to the spirit and the letter of the Civil Rights Act of 1964, which decrees in Title VI that "[no] person in the United States shall, on the ground of race, color, or national origin, be excluded from participation in, denied the benefits of, or be subjected to discrimination under any program or activity receiving Federal financial assistance." Weak affirmative action can involve many strategies for expanding equal opportunity, but it stops short of preferential treatment. As the philosopher Louis P. Pojman explains it,

[Weak affirmative action] includes such things as dismantling of segregated institutions, widespread advertisement to groups not previously represented in certain privileged positions, special scholarships for the disadvantaged classes (e.g., the poor, regardless of race or gender), and even using diversity or under-representation of groups with a history of past discrimination as a tie breaker when candidates for these goods and offices are relatively equal. The goal of *Weak Affirmative Action* is equal opportunity to compete, not equal results. We seek to provide each citizen regardless of race or gender a fair chance to the most favored positions in society. There is no more moral requirement to guarantee that 12% of professors are Black than to guarantee that 85% of the players in the National Basketball Association are White.[16]

Weak affirmative action, then, is hardly controversial. Probably few people nowadays would object to efforts to end discrimination against minorities and women and to give people an equal chance to get ahead. But strong affirmative action is a different matter.

Strong affirmative action is the use of policies and procedures to favor particular individuals because of their race, gender, or ethnic background. It is a kind of preferential treatment that is usually implemented through favoring plans, quota systems, or other approaches. The point of a quota system is to ensure that an organization has a predetermined number or percentage of minority or women members. Typically, a proportion of available positions or slots are reserved for the preferred

CRITICAL THOUGHT: Are Legacy Admissions Racist?

Take a look at this excerpt from a report on college "legacy" admissions published in the *Christian Science Monitor*:

> WASHINGTON, D.C.—At Penn, they "take it very seriously." At Michigan, it "gets you extra points." At Harvard, it "is not ignored," and at Notre Dame, they are "very open" to it. "It" is "legacy": an admissions designation used by most private and some public universities for applicants whose relatives attended the school, and who, as such, get some degree of preferential treatment. It's a practice as old as colleges themselves, and is intended to boost alumni support and donations and foster a sense of community.
>
> It's also racist, argue its critics.
>
> Following fast on the footsteps of last year's Supreme Court entry into the delicate area of affirmative-action admissions, lawmakers are taking a hard look at this so-called reverse affirmative

action, which gives an edge to those whose parents and grandparents went to selective colleges at a time when most minorities there were few and far between[.]*

Are legacies indeed racist? If you think so, what are your reasons? If you think not, what argument would you put forth to support your belief? If you were the president of a state college, what policy toward legacies would you try to establish? Do legacies violate the Civil Rights Act of 1964? Why or why not?

*Danna Harman, "Family Ties: An Unfair Advantage?" *Christian Science Monitor,* February 6, 2004. © 2004 Christian Science Monitor. All rights reserved. Used by permission and protected by the Copyright Laws of the United States. The printing, copying, redistribution, or retransmission of this content without express written permission is prohibited.

people, as was the arrangement at the School of Medicine at UC Davis in the Bakke case. Sometimes the result of using a quota system is that less qualified people are hired or accepted while equally or more qualified people are not—with the difference being only that the preferred ones are women or members of a minority group.

Defenders of strong affirmative action have offered several justifications for it. A leading argument is that because in generations past minorities were treated cruelly and unjustly, they now deserve compensation for those terrible wrongs. Giving minorities preferential treatment in employment and education is the best way to make amends. As one philosopher puts it, "Racism was directed against Blacks whether they were talented, average, or mediocre, and attenuating the effects of racism requires distributing remedies similarly. Affirmative action policies compensate for the harms of racism (overt and institutional)

through antidiscrimination laws and preferential policies."[17]

Another argument is that strong affirmative action is necessary to foster *diversity* in a population—diversity of race, ethnicity, gender, culture, and outlook. Diversity is rightly thought to be an extremely valuable commodity for any free society. It promotes understanding of cultures and viewpoints different from one's own, which in turn encourages tolerance and cooperation in an increasingly heterogeneous world. Some think it valuable enough to use strong affirmative action to achieve it.

As you would expect, diversity is thought to be critical to education—especially in universities, where the issue of promoting diversity through admission preferences has been vigorously debated. Many universities have tested the use of preferences for diversity's sake, encouraged by the majority opinion in the Bakke case, which states that "[t]he atmosphere of 'speculation, experiment and creation'—so essential to the quality of higher education—is widely believed to be promoted by a diverse student body."[18]

But strong affirmative action is strongly opposed by many who see it as *reverse discrimination*—unequal, preferential treatment of some people (mostly white males) to advance the interests of others (minorities and women). The main charge is that preferential treatment on the basis of race, gender, or minority status is *always* wrong. It is just as immoral when used against white males as it is when used against blacks or women. Speaking specifically of racial preferences, the philosopher Carl Cohen provides a succinct statement of this claim:

> It uses categories that *must not* be used to distinguish among persons with respect to their entitlements in the community. Blacks and whites are equals, as blondes and brunettes are equals, as Catholics and Jews are equals, as Americans of every ancestry are equal. No matter who the beneficiaries may be or who the victims, preference on the basis of race is morally wrong. It was wrong in the distant past and in the recent past; it is wrong now; and it will always be wrong. Race preference violates the principle of human equality.[19]

MORAL THEORIES

In the debates over strong affirmative action, those who oppose it as well as those who endorse it appeal to conventional moral theories—both consequentialist and nonconsequentialist. Many who support strong affirmative action make the utilitarian argument that these policies can have enormous benefits for minorities and women as well as for society as a whole. They contend, as suggested earlier, that preferential programs can increase racial and cultural diversity, which helps promote tolerance, mutual understanding, and better use of people's talents, and—in higher education—enhances learning. They also argue

that preferential policies can have great social utility by creating role models for minorities and women whose self-esteem and hopes for success have been dimmed by generations of discrimination. They assert that role models are essential for demonstrating to young people that significant achievement is possible. Finally, some think the best argument is that strong affirmative action may be able to eradicate racism and transform our race-conscious society. A proponent of this view outlines the argument as follows:

> [Affirmative action programs] rest on two judgments. The first is a judgment of social theory: that the United States will continue to be pervaded by racial divisions as long as the most lucrative, satisfying, and important careers remain mainly the prerogative of members of the white race, while others feel themselves systematically excluded from a professional and social elite. The second is a calculation of strategy: that increasing the number of blacks who are at work in the professions will, in the long run, reduce the sense of frustration and injustice and racial self-consciousness in the black community to the point at which blacks may begin to think of themselves as individuals who can succeed like others through talent and initiative. At that future point the consequences of nonracial admissions programs, whatever these consequences might be, could be accepted with no sense of racial barriers or injustice.[20]

Many opponents of strong affirmative action also make utilitarian appeals. Their most straightforward counterargument is that those who favor race or gender preferences are simply wrong about the consequences of the policies: the consequences either are not as beneficial as supposed or are actually injurious. Opponents try to undermine the diversity argument by insisting that racial and ethnic diversity does not necessarily result in diversity of ideas or outlooks, that no scientific evidence supports the notion that diversity policies yield benefits in education or learning, and that giving priority to racial or

CRITICAL THOUGHT: Are Whites-Only Scholarships Unjust?

Keeping in mind what you've read about weak and strong affirmative action in this chapter, consider the following news item:

(CNN)—A whites-only scholarship to be awarded Wednesday by a student Republican organization at Roger Williams University in Bristol, Rhode Island, has drawn both controversy and support.

"It all began two weeks ago as a way for the college Republican groups to express their opposition and tell people they are against race-based scholarships and affirmative action," June Speakman, faculty adviser for the College Republicans told CNN. "We never expected such an overwhelming response of e-mails and media attention."

The scholarship is for $250, but College Republicans president Jason Mattera said he has received donations and pledges totaling $4,000 for future whites-only scholarships.

Mattera is of Puerto Rican descent and was awarded a $5,000 scholarship from the Hispanic College Fund. He said he believes being eligible for such scholarships gives him "an inherent advantage over my white peers." He wants the university to award scholarships based on merit and not ethnicity.

Applicants for the College Republicans' scholarship must be of Caucasian descent, have high honors, write an essay, and show an impressive list of accomplishments, Mattera said. Sixteen people applied.

Roger Williams University does not sponsor or endorse the scholarship, university spokesman Rick Goff told CNN.

"The scholarship is entirely initiated by the College Republicans at the university," he said. . . .

The state Republican Party has criticized the scholarship as having racist overtones.*

Is this whites-only scholarship an example of *weak* or *strong* affirmative action—or neither? Is it racist or discriminatory? If so, are blacks-only scholarships in the same category? If not, what distinguishes the one type of scholarship from the other? That is, what are your reasons for thinking that one is unjust while the other is not? Is there an implicit argument in the student organization's offering a whites-only scholarship? If so, what is it?

*Jennifer Styles, "Whites-Only Scholarship Generates Controversy," CNN.com, February 20, 2004, www.cnn.com/2004/EDUCATION/02/18/whites.only.scholars (February 27, 2015). © 2004 Turner Broadcast Systems. All rights reserved. Used by permission and protected by the Copyright Laws of the United States. The printing, copying, redistribution, or retransmission of this content without express written permission is prohibited.

gender diversity in the workplace would severely undermine competence and efficiency, which are highly valued by society. They reject the role model argument on the grounds that role models selected by race or gender are not necessarily the role models we need. The best role models in education, they say, are people who are the best— the most competent, knowledgeable, inspiring, and decent—*whatever the color of their skin, their background, or their gender.* Many opposed to racial preferences doubt that such treatment can help eliminate racism and promote a color-blind society. In fact, they argue that racial preferences can often have the opposite effect:

Preference puts distinguished minority achievement under a cloud. It imposes upon every member of the preferred minority the demeaning burden of presumed inferiority. Preference *creates* that burden; it *makes* a stigma of the race of those who are preferred by race. An ethnic group given special favor by the community is *marked* as needing special favor—and the mark is borne prominently by every one of its members. Nasty racial stereotypes are reinforced, and the malicious imputation of

> ## QUICK REVIEW
>
> **racism**—The belief that distinct races exist, that significant differences (such as moral, intellectual, or cultural differences) among races can be distinguished, and that some races are inferior in these significant respects or otherwise deserving of dislike or hostility.
>
> **racial prejudice**—Racially biased opinions based on incomplete or erroneous information.
>
> **racial discrimination**—Unfavorable treatment of people because of their race. Prejudice and discrimination can be directed at traits other than race, including sexual traits.
>
> **individual racism**—Person-to-person acts of intolerance or discrimination.
>
> **institutional** or **structural racism**—Unequal treatment that arises from the way organizations, institutions, and social systems operate.
>
> **affirmative action**—A way of making amends for, or eradicating, discrimination based on race, ethnicity, and gender.
>
> **weak affirmative action**—The use of policies and procedures to end discriminatory practices and ensure equal opportunity.
>
> **strong affirmative action**—The use of policies and procedures to favor particular individuals because of their race, gender, or ethnic background.

inferiority is inescapable because it is tied to the color of the skin.[21]

As noted earlier, a common nonconsequentialist argument for strong affirmative action is based on the notion of compensatory justice: historically, minorities (blacks, Native Americans, Hispanics, and others) were the victims of racism by the white majority; justice requires that members of those minorities now be compensated for that past mistreatment; racial preferences in employment and education are appropriate compensation; therefore, racial preferences are morally permissible. As you might guess, many who wish to counter this argument also appeal to justice. They argue that compensation is just only (1) if it is given in proper measure to specific persons who have been harmed, and (2) if the specific persons who caused the harm do the compensating. But with racial preferences, this direct connection that morality seems to require is missing. The result, they contend, is that often the nonminority person who suffers because of compensatory justice (because he is well qualified but denied admission, for example) has had nothing to do with past racism, and the person who benefits from compensatory justice has suffered very little from racism (because, for example, he or she is well educated with above-average income). They conclude that racial preferences are unjust.

MORAL ARGUMENTS

Let us look a little more closely at the argument from compensatory justice, giving particular attention to how a supporter of strong affirmative action might articulate and defend it. Consider this version of the argument, narrowly focused on compensatory claims that blacks might have against whites for historical discrimination:

1. In the past, blacks have been cruelly and systematically discriminated against by whites.

2. Blacks thus are owed just compensation for this ill treatment.

3. Strong affirmative action in the form of racial preferences is the most morally appropriate form of such compensation.

4. Therefore, racial preferences (in employment and education) should be used to compensate blacks for past discrimination.

First, note that this argument is valid and that Premise 1 is true. Both those for and those against racial preferences would be likely to accept this premise, a statement of historical fact that few thoughtful people would dispute. Premises 2 and 3, on the other hand, are very contentious claims.

The most common way to support Premise 2 is to appeal to our moral intuitions about the justice of compensating people who have been wronged. We tend to think that people who have been wronged do in fact deserve reparations, that valid grievances warrant redress. Many argue that blacks have been mistreated and discriminated against for so many generations that today they still suffer the lingering effects—they are disadvantaged before they even begin to compete for jobs, school admissions, and grades. Racial preferences help give them the edge that they need—and that they justly deserve as repayment for cruelties suffered in the past.

Those who reject Premise 2 counter that the principle of just compensation is certainly legitimate, but compensation in the form of racial preferences is not just. Compensation, they argue, should go to the particular persons who have been wronged, and the compensation should be paid by the specific persons who wronged them. But with racial preferences, they contend, the blacks who benefit are not all equally deserving of redress. The ancestors of contemporary blacks were almost certainly not equally wronged, not all wronged in the same fashion, and not all wronged more than some poor white males were wronged. As Carl Cohen says,

> [M]any of Hispanic ancestry now enjoy here, and have long enjoyed, circumstances as decent and as well protected as those enjoyed by Americans of all other ethnicities. The same is true of African Americans, some of whom are impoverished and some of whom are rich and powerful. Rewards distributed on the basis of ethnic membership assume that the damages suffered by some were suffered by all—an assumption that we know to be false.[22]

Advocates of racial preferences can counter this criticism with an analogy. In the United States, military veterans receive preferential treatment when they apply for civil service jobs. Their applications are automatically given extra weight, which means that sometimes veterans may land jobs even when nonveteran applicants are equally qualified. The notion behind this policy is that a grateful nation owes veterans something for their service. The policy assumes that all veterans are owed preferential treatment even though some of them have served longer and more courageously than others. So, the advocate of preferences asks, why should not blacks be treated according to a similar policy? Why should not all blacks be owed preferential treatment because of past discrimination—and owed it in equal measure even though some blacks have been wronged more than others?

Another kind of attack on Premise 2 focuses not on the people compensated, but on those penalized so that the debt can be paid. The claim is that racial preferences are unjust because they punish people who have done nothing to merit punishment. When blacks get preferential treatment in employment, the argument goes, some white males end up losing out—even though these whites had no part in past racism and may have never discriminated against anyone. Clearly, penalizing people for wrongdoing that they did not—and could not—commit is unjust; therefore, racial preferences are unjust.

A frequent reply to this argument is that the white males thought to be innocent victims of reverse discrimination are not as innocent as we might think. According to this response, white males are the recipients of advantages and privileges that have been unjustly extracted from blacks for generations—therefore, strong affirmative action does not take from white males anything that is rightfully theirs. The philosopher Judith Jarvis Thomson, an advocate of racial preferences, makes the point in the following way:

> No doubt few, if any, [young white male applicants] have themselves, individually, done any wrongs to blacks and women. But they have profited from

the wrongs the community did. Many may actually have been direct beneficiaries of policies which excluded or downgraded blacks and women—perhaps in school admissions, perhaps in access to financial aid, perhaps elsewhere; and even those who did not directly benefit in this way had, at any rate, the advantage in the competition which comes of confidence in one's full membership, and of one's rights being recognized as a matter of course.[23]

Critics have tried to rebut this argument by questioning its underlying assumption—the notion that, as one philosopher puts it, "if someone gains from an unjust practice for which he is not responsible and even opposes, the gain is not really his and can be taken from him without injustice."[24] This rebuttal relies on the commonsense moral principle that a person who wrongs others is morally obligated to compensate them for that wrong, but the wrongdoer's descendants are not. The sins of the parents cannot be transferred to the children.

Premise 3—that racial preferences are just and appropriate moral compensation for past discrimination—is defended by many, but probably most ably by Thomson:

> [In] fact the nature of the wrongs done is such as to make jobs the best and most suitable form of compensation. What blacks and women were denied was full membership in the community; and nothing can more appropriately make amends for that wrong than precisely what will make them feel they now finally have it. And that means jobs. Financial compensation (the cost of which could be shared equally) slips through the fingers; having a job, and discovering you do it well, yield—perhaps better than anything else—that very self-respect which blacks and women have had to do without.[25]

Though several arguments can be tried against Premise 3, one in particular goes to the heart of the debate on racial preferences. It says that preferential treatment is not fitting compensation because it ignores the true standard by which jobs and positions should be awarded—competence:

> [T]he normal criterion of competence is a strong prima facie consideration when the most important

positions are at stake. There are three reasons for this: (1) treating people according to their merits respects them as persons, as ends in themselves, rather than as means to social ends (if we believe that individuals possess a dignity that deserves to be respected, then we ought to treat that individual on the basis of his or her merits, not as a mere instrument for social policy); (2) society has given people expectations that if they attain certain levels of excellence they will be awarded appropriately; and (3) filling the most important positions with the best qualified is the best way to ensure efficiency in job-related areas and in society in general.[26]

CHAPTER REVIEW

SUMMARY

The core idea of race—that is, the notion of discrete groups of people who share distinct biological and cultural traits—is relatively new, arising in different forms over time beginning around the sixteenth century and changing in the Americas and Europe in response to colonization and slavery.

In the nineteenth and early twentieth centuries, several thinkers tried to apply scientific principles to the study of race. The result was what is now known as *scientific racism*. Later scientists discredited this body of research.

In the twenty-first century, science still has not firmly established that there are such things as races that differ in certain essential, inherent characteristics. The traditional idea is that race consists of heritable biological features common to all members of a racial group that explain the character and cultural traits of those members. But the consensus among scientists and philosophers is that this view is false.

Racism is based on the belief that distinct races exist and that significant differences (such as moral, intellectual, or cultural differences) among races can be distinguished. What pushes this view about race into racism is the additional belief that some races are inferior in these significant respects or otherwise deserving of dislike or hostility.

Racism often involves racial prejudice—racially biased opinions based on incomplete or erroneous information. Racial prejudice can be either the result of racism or a pretext for it. Racial discrimination is unfavorable treatment of people because of their race. Prejudice and discrimination can be directed at traits other than race, including sexual orientation, age, gender, ethnicity, religion, and national origins. Discrimination based on any of these traits can be a violation of law or policy. Individual racism consists of person-to-person acts of intolerance or discrimination, whereas the prevalent, almost invisible kind of racism known as institutional or structural racism consists of unequal treatment that arises from the way organizations, institutions, and social systems operate.

From a nonconsequentialist perspective, racism is wrong because it violates two important moral principles: respect for persons and justice. The principle of respect for persons says that each person has equal inherent value, regardless of social status, power, prestige, or racial or ethnic identity. The principle of justice says that equals must be treated equally and fairly.

Affirmative action is meant to make up for or eliminate minority and gender discrimination, which is a form of unwarranted mistreatment. Affirmative action seeks to realize the ideal of equal respect and opportunity for all in employment and education. Weak affirmative action is generally not controversial because it uses policies and procedures to ensure equal opportunity without demanding that one group be preferred over another. Strong affirmative action, on the other hand, is controversial because it makes use of minority and gender preferences.

Those who defend strong affirmative action argue that it is needed to compensate certain groups for mistreatment and discrimination of the past. It is also thought to level the playing field—to give minorities and women an edge in the competition for jobs and educational admissions. Some also contend that such preferences are justified because they help promote cultural, ethnic, and intellectual diversity, a beneficial force in free societies. Strong affirmative action is opposed by many who think it is reverse discrimination, unequal treatment that penalizes white males to give advantages to blacks and women. These critics generally reject all forms of preferential treatment whether they favor white males or not.

Arguments for and against strong affirmative action can appeal to both consequentialist and nonconsequentialist theories. Some argue that preferential treatment is justified because it has positive consequences for minorities and for society as a whole. Others argue that such policies do not work as advertised and actually harm the people they are meant to help. Nonconsequentialist arguments appeal to justice, asserting that affirmative action programs are just (doing compensatory justice, for example) or unjust (distorting compensatory justice).

KEY TERMS

racism (p. 473)
racial prejudice (p. 475)
racial discrimination (p. 475)
individual racism (p. 475)
institutional or **structural racism** (p. 475)
affirmative action (p. 477)
weak affirmative action (p. 478)
strong affirmative action (p. 478)

EXERCISES

Review Questions

1. Is racism part of humankind's nature? That is, have people always sorted one another into racial groups and then considered some groups inferior or deserving of malice? (p. 471)
2. What is scientific racism? Has science definitely established that there are such discrete things as races? (p. 472)
3. What is inherency? (p. 472)
4. What is racism? What two key elements does Blum say are contained in the concept of racism? (p. 473)
5. Why does Blum say that not every instance of racial conflict, insensitivity, ignorance, or miscommunication should be called racist? (p. 473)

6. What is racial prejudice? What is racial discrimination? (p. 475)

7. What is institutional racism? Is it always easy to detect? Why or why not? (pp. 475-476)

8. What is white privilege? (p. 474)

9. What is weak affirmative action? What is strong affirmative action? (p. 478)

10. What are racialized groups? (p. 473)

Discussion Questions

1. Name three of the more egregious examples of inequality and racism that Bonilla-Silva mentions. Do you agree that they are racist? Why or why not?

2. What does Bonilla-Silva mean by the phrase "racism without racists"?

3. Why does Naomi Zack think that white privilege discourse is problematic?

4. Do you believe, as Bonilla-Silva does, that covert forms of racism are widespread? Why or why not?

5. Do you believe that strong affirmative action is morally acceptable? Why or why not?

6. Is a white person who benefits from white privilege a racist? Is he a racist if he denies that white privilege exists? Explain.

7. What arguments can be lodged against strong affirmative action?

8. According to Bonilla-Silva, how can racial inequality and its effects be nearly invisible?

9. Is weak affirmative action morally preferable to strong affirmative action? Why or why not?

10. Are there such things as distinct races, and can significant moral and intellectual differences be distinguished among them?

FURTHER READING

Andrew Altman, "Discrimination," in *Stanford Encyclopedia of Philosophy*, Winter 2016 ed., ed. Edward N. Zalta, https://plato.stanford.edu/archives/win2016/entries/discrimination/.

Kwame Anthony Appiah, "Racisms," in *Anatomy of Racism*, ed. David Theo Goldberg (Minneapolis: University of Minnesota Press, 1990).

Lawrence Blum, *"I'm Not a Racist But . . ." : The Moral Quandary of Race* (Ithaca, NY: Cornell University Press, 2002).

Eduardo Bonilla-Silva, *Racism without Racists*, 5th ed. (Lanham, MD: Rowman and Littlefield, 2018).

Tanya Maria Golash-Boza, *Racism and Racisms: A Critical Approach* (New York: Oxford University Press, 2016).

David Theo Goldberg, ed., *Anatomy of Racism* (Minneapolis, MN: University of Minnesota Press, 1990).

Ali Rattansi, *Racism: A Very Short Introduction* (Oxford: Oxford University Press, 2007).

Naomi Zack, *The Ethics and Mores of Race: Equality after the History of Philosophy* (Lanham, MD: Rowman and Littlefield, 2011).

Naomi Zack, ed., *The Oxford Handbook of Philosophy and Race* (New York: Oxford University Press, 2017).

Naomi Zack, *White Privilege and Black Rights: The Injustice of U.S. Police Racial Profiling and Homicide* (Lanham, MD: Rowman and Littlefield, 2015).

ETHICAL DILEMMAS

1. Does Race Matter?

Rachel Dolezal, the white woman who for 10 years pretended she was black before being publicly outed, has called for racial fluidity to be recognised in the same way as transgenderism.

The former National Association for the Advancement of Colored People (NAACP) leader said race is "less biological than gender" and believes the term "transracial" is a useful term to describe how race should be considered in the future.

Ms. Dolezal also claimed "race is a lie, so how can you lie about a lie?" in response to her public shaming in 2015 when she was outed by her parents as "biologically Caucasian."

"Gender is understood—we have progressed, we have evolved into understanding gender is not binary, it is not even biological but what strikes me as so odd is that race is not biological either and actually race has been to some extent less biological than gender," she told *Newsnight's* Emily Maitlis.

The former civil rights activist claims she can no longer work because of the controversy and is "ostracised" in Spokane, Washington, where she is forced to remain due to a custody arrangement with her son's father.

"As a result of me being discredited, called a liar and a fraud, a con—and not just distrusting my work but everything I did, including my resume, was called into question," she said. . . .

"The thing that hurt the worst was from the black community because I still feel like that is home for me and even if I get evicted or get pushed to the fringe or some people don't see me as part of that group, it is still where I feel like I fit and where I feel at home," she said. . . .

Ms. Dolezal was fired as head of the Spokane chapter of the NAACP and kicked off a police ombudsman commission when she was outed. She also lost her job teaching African studies at Eastern Washington University in nearby Cheney and has been accused of cultural appropriation by both the white and black community.*

Is Ms. Dolezal right—is race a lie? Is it "less biological than gender"? Whether race is or isn't biological, did she do anything wrong in assuming a black identity? If so, what is her transgression? Was it pretending to be something she's not—or was it that she challenged society's assumptions about what race is?

*Lucy Pasha-Robinson, "Rachel Dolezal: White Woman Who Identifies as Black Calls for 'Racial Fluidity' to Be Accepted," *The Independent*, March 2017, http://www.independent.co.uk/news/people/rachel-dolezal-white-woman-black-racial-fluidity-accepted-transracial-naacp-a7653131.html. Reprinted by permission of ESI Media.

---

2. Racial Preferences for Whites?

Affirmative action is most often thought of as a racial preference for marginalized peoples—a way to ensure that those who are often discriminated against have places in schools and in the workforce. But some insist that the roots of affirmative action are firmly grounded in a racial preference for whites.

One commentator argues that the abolition of white indentured servitude perfectly encapsulates white racial preference, for though white slavery was no longer legal in the United States as of the nineteenth century, black and indigenous workers remained in bondage. Racial preference for whites was the guiding principle behind the 1790 Naturalization Act, which granted U.S. citizenship to almost any immigrant of European ancestry, but excluded blacks, Asians, and American Indians. Asian exclusion laws, segregation, and the concept of manifest destiny, which led to the annexation of half of Mexico, are also products of affirmative action for whites.

He points out that as recently as the 1960s, the Federal Housing Administration provided loans almost exclusively to white families. From the 1930s to the 1960s, approximately 15 million whites were able to obtain homes with FHA loans, while people of color received no such aid.

He concludes that the group that has benefited most through affirmative action programs is white America. The laws and public policies of the United States have been shaped and molded by white racial preference, and many of the social and economic inequalities we face today are the result of years of affirmative action for whites.[†]

Do you agree with this commentator that racial preferences for whites have always been a major part of U.S. history? If so, do you think that the U.S. government should make amends for such past inequalities? Why or why not? If racial preferences for whites have indeed always been widespread, were they always unjust as well? Suppose they were unjust. Would racial preferences in favor of *nonwhites* now be just? Why or why not?

[†]Based on Tim Wise, "The Mother of All Racial Preferences," Znet, May 24, 2003, https://zcomm.org /zcommentary/the-mother-of-all-racial-preferences-by-tim-wise/. Originally appeared as a ZNet commentary at www.zmag.org.

---

3. Are Racial Preferences Harmful?

Over the past few years, researchers have begun to produce large datasets that make it possible to compare the fortunes of minority students who attend universities that use varying levels of admissions preferences. In many contexts, scholars find that students perform better, both in the short-term and the long-term, when students' credentials are closer to those of their classmates. When students are surrounded by peers who have much higher credentials, they often have more trouble persisting in a difficult major, graduating from college or getting a good job.

This phenomenon is known as the "mismatch effect," and last month I published a study in the *Stanford Law Review,* trying to determine whether the mismatch effect operates in law schools. . . . My study focused on black law students and compared black and white outcomes.

I found that law schools almost universally use very large preferences for blacks to achieve something very close to racial proportionality. The credentials gap between white and black students is about 30 times larger than it would be in a race-blind regime.

Starting a highly competitive curriculum with a large academic disadvantage, blacks wind up clustered in the bottom tenth of the class at nearly all law schools. I estimate the mismatch effect increases the number of black dropouts from law school by 40%, and increases the number of blacks failing their first bar exam by 80%.

The mismatch effect appears to operate in the job market as well. Law firms—once thought to be single-minded in their determination to recruit lawyers from the most elite schools possible—turn out to weigh law school grades more heavily than school prestige. The typical black law graduate, I estimate, loses about $10,000 in annual earnings because large preferences induce her to make a bad trade-off between law school prestige and law school grades.[‡]

Sander's study is controversial, but suppose it shows what he says it does. Would you then favor *dismantling* preferences for black law students? Would you favor *maintaining* law school preference systems if they helped black students rather than harmed them? Why or why not? Some people advocate using preferences in higher education to redress the wrongs of past discrimination. To be logically consistent, should they disregard evidence suggesting that preferences hurt blacks?

[‡] Richard Sander, "Preferences Hurt Black Law Students," UCLA Today, Vol. 25, No. 10 (February 2005). Used by permission of the author.

READINGS

Racisms

KWAME ANTHONY APPIAH

If the people I talk to and the newspapers I read are representative and reliable, there is a good deal of racism about. People and policies in the United States, in Eastern and Western Europe, in Asia and Africa and Latin America are regularly described as "racist." Australia had, until recently, a racist immigration policy; Britain still has one; racism is on the rise in France; many Israelis support Meir Kahane, an anti-Arab racist; many Arabs, according to a leading authority, are anti-Semitic racists;[1] and the movement to establish English as the "official language" of the United States is motivated by racism. Or, at least, so many of the people I talk to and many of the journalists with the newspapers I read believe.

But visitors from Mars—or from Malawi—unfamiliar with the Western concept of racism could be excused if

Kwame Anthony Appiah, "Racisms," in *Anatomy of Racism*, ed. David Theo Goldberg (Minneapolis: University of Minnesota Press, 1970), 3–17. © 1990 University of Minnesota Press. Reprinted by permission of University of Minnesota Press.

they had some difficulty in identifying what exactly racism was. We see it everywhere, but rarely does anyone stop to say what it is, or to explain what is wrong with it. Our visitors from Mars would soon grasp that it had become at least conventional in recent years to express abhorrence for racism. They might even notice that those most often accused of it—members of the South African Nationalist party, for example—may officially abhor it also. But if they sought in the popular media of our day—in newspapers and magazines, on television or radio, in novels or films—for an explicit definition of this thing "we" all abhor, they would very likely be disappointed.

Now, of course, this would be true of many of our most familiar concepts. *Sister, chair, tomato*—none of these gets defined in the course of our daily business. But the concept of racism is in worse shape than these. For much of what we say about it is, on the face of it, inconsistent.

It is, for example, held by many to be racist to refuse entry to a university to an otherwise qualified

"Negro" candidate, but not to be so to refuse entry to an equally qualified "Caucasian" one. But "Negro" and "Caucasian" are both alleged to be names of races, and invidious discrimination on the basis of race is usually held to be a paradigm case of racism. Or, to take another example, it is widely believed to be evidence of an unacceptable racism to exclude people from clubs on the basis of race; yet most people, even those who think of "Jewish" as a racial term, seem to think that there is nothing wrong with Jewish clubs, whose members do not share any particular religious beliefs, or Afro-American societies, whose members share the juridical characteristic of American citizenship and the "racial" characteristic of being black.

I say that these are inconsistencies "on the face of it," because, for example, affirmative action in university admissions is importantly different from the earlier refusal to admit blacks or Jews (or other "Others") that it is meant, in part, to correct. Deep enough analysis may reveal it to be quite consistent with the abhorrence of racism; even a shallow analysis suggests that it is intended to be so. Similarly, justifications can be offered for "racial" associations in a plural society that are not available for the racial exclusivism of the country club. But if we take racism seriously we ought to be concerned about the adequacy of these justifications.

In this essay, then, I propose to take our ordinary ways of thinking about race and racism and point up some of their presuppositions. And since popular concepts are, of course, usually fairly fuzzily and untheoretically conceived, much of what I have to say will seem to be both more theoretically and more precisely committed than the talk of racism and racists in our newspapers and on television. My claim is that these theoretical claims are required to make sense of racism as the practice of reasoning human beings. If anyone were to suggest that much, perhaps most, of what goes under the name "racism" in our world cannot be given such a rationalized foundation, I should not disagree: but to the extent that a practice cannot be rationally reconstructed it ought, surely, to be given up by reasonable people. The right tactic with racism, if you really want to oppose it, is to object to it rationally in the form in which it stands the best chance of meeting objections. The doctrines I want to discuss can be

rationally articulated: and they are worth articulating rationally in order that we can rationally say what we object to in them.

RACIST PROPOSITIONS

There are at least three distinct doctrines that might be held to express the theoretical content of what we call "racism." One is the view—which I shall call *racialism*[2]—that there are heritable characteristics, possessed by members of our species, that allow us to divide them into a small set of races, in such a way that all the members of these races share certain traits and tendencies with each other that they do not share with members of any other race. These traits and tendencies characteristic of a race constitute, on the racialist view, a sort of racial essence; and it is part of the content of racialism that the essential heritable characteristics of what the nineteenth century called the "Races of Man" account for more than the visible morphological characteristics—skin color, hair type, facial features—on the basis of which we make our informal classifications. Racialism is at the heart of nineteenth-century Western attempts to develop a science of racial difference; but it appears to have been believed by others—for example, Hegel, before then, and many in other parts of the non-Western world since—who have had no interest in developing scientific theories.

Racialism is not, in itself, a doctrine that must be dangerous, even if the racial essence is thought to entail moral and intellectual dispositions. Provided positive moral qualities are distributed across the races, each can be respected, can have its "separate but equal" place. Unlike most Western-educated people, I believe—and I have argued elsewhere[3]—that racialism is false; but by itself, it seems to be a cognitive rather than a moral problem. The issue is how the world is, not how we would want it to be.

Racialism is, however, a presupposition of other doctrines that have been called "racism," and these other doctrines have been, in the last few centuries, the basis of a great deal of human suffering and the source of a great deal of moral error.

One such doctrine we might call "extrinsic racism": extrinsic racists make moral distinctions between members of different races because they believe that the racial essence entails certain morally relevant qualities. The basis for the extrinsic racists' discrimination between people is their belief that members of different races differ in respects that *warrant* the differential treatment, respects—such as honesty or courage or intelligence—that are uncontroversially held (at least in most contemporary cultures) to be acceptable as a basis for treating people differently. Evidence that there are no such differences in morally relevant characteristics—that Negroes do not necessarily lack intellectual capacities, that Jews are not especially avaricious—should thus lead people out of their racism if it is purely extrinsic. As we know, such evidence often fails to change an extrinsic racist's attitudes substantially, for some of the extrinsic racist's best friends have always been Jewish. But at this point—if the racist is sincere—what we have is no longer a false doctrine but a cognitive incapacity, one whose significance I shall discuss later in this essay.

I say that the *sincere* extrinsic racist may suffer from a cognitive incapacity. But some who espouse extrinsic racist doctrines are simply insincere intrinsic racists. For *intrinsic racists*, on my definition, are people who differentiate morally between members of different races because they believe that each race has a different moral status, quite independent of the moral characterstics entailed by its racial essence. Just as, for example, many people assume that the fact that they are biologically related to another person—a brother, an aunt, a cousin—gives them a moral interest in that person,[4] so an intrinsic racist holds that the bare fact of being of the same race is a reason for preferring one person to another. (I shall return to this parallel later as well.)

For an intrinsic racist, no amount of evidence that a member of another race is capable of great moral, intellectual, or cultural achievements, or has characteristics that, in members of one's own race, would make them admirable or attractive, offers any ground for treating that person as he or she would treat similarly endowed members of his or her own race. Just so, some sexists are "intrinsic sexists," holding that the bare fact that someone is a woman (or man) is a reason for treating her (or him) in certain ways.

There are interesting possibilities for complicating these distinctions: some racists, for example, claim, as the Mormons once did, that they discriminate between people because they believe that God requires them to do so. Is this an extrinsic racism, predicated on the combination of God's being an intrinsic racist and the belief that it is right to do what God wills? Or is it intrinsic racism because it is based on the belief that God requires these discriminations because they are right? (Is an act pious because the gods love it, or do they love it because it is pious?) Nevertheless, the distinctions between racialism and racism and between two potentially overlapping kinds of racism provide us with the skeleton of an anatomy of the propositional contents of racial attitudes.

RACIST DISPOSITIONS

Most people will want to object already that this discussion of the propositional content of racist moral and factual beliefs misses something absolutely crucial to the character of the psychological and sociological reality of racism, something I touched on when I mentioned that extrinsic racist utterances are often made by people who suffer from what I called a "cognitive incapacity." Part of the standard force of accusations of racism is that their objects are in some way *irrational*. The objection to Professor Shockley's claims about the intelligence of blacks is not just that they are false; it is rather that Professor Shockley seems, like many people we call "racist," to be unable to see that the evidence does not support his factual claims and that the connection between his factual claims and his policy prescriptions involves a series of non sequiturs.

What makes these cognitive incapacities especially troubling—something we should respond to with more than a recommendation that the individual, Professor Shockley, be offered psychotherapy—is that they conform to a certain pattern: namely, that it is especially where beliefs and policies that are to the disadvantage of nonwhite people that he shows the sorts of disturbing failure that have made his views both notorious and notoriously unrealiable. Indeed, Professor Shockley's reasoning works extremely well in some other areas: that he is a Nobel Laureate in physics is part of what makes him so interesting an example.

This cognitive incapacity is not, of course, a rare one. Many of us are unable to give up beliefs that play a part in justifying the special advantages we gain (or hope to gain) from our positions in the social order—in particular, beliefs about the positive characters of the class of people who share that position. Many people who express extrinsic racist beliefs—many white South Africans, for example—are beneficiaries of social orders that deliver advantages to them by virtue of their "race," so that their disinclination to accept evidence that would deprive them of a justification for those advantages is just an instance of this general phenomenon.

So too, evidence that access to higher education is as largely determined by the quality of our earlier educations as by our own innate talents, does not, on the whole, undermine the confidence of college entrants from private schools in England or the United States or Ghana. Many of them continue to believe in the face of this evidence that their acceptance at "good" universities shows them to be intellectually better endowed (and not just better prepared) than those who are rejected. It is facts such as these that give sense to the notion of false consciousness, the idea that an ideology can prevent us from acknowledging facts that would threaten our position.

The most interesting cases of this sort of ideological resistance to the truth are not, perhaps, the ones I have just mentioned. On the whole, it is less surprising, once we accept the admittedly problematic notion of self-deception, that people who think that certain attitudes or beliefs advantage them or those they care about should be able, as we say, to "persuade" themselves to ignore evidence that undermines those beliefs or attitudes. What is more interesting is the existence of people who resist the truth of a proposition while thinking that its wider acceptance would in no way disadvantage them or those individuals about whom they care—this might be thought to describe Professor Shockley; or who resist the truth when they recognize that its acceptance would actually advantage them—this might be the case with some black people who have internalized negative racist stereotypes; or

who fail, by virtue of their ideological attachments, to recognize what is in their own best interests at all.

My business here is not with the psychological or social processes by which these forms of ideological resistance operate, but it is important, I think, to see the refusal on the part of some extrinsic racists to accept evidence against the beliefs as an instance of a widespread phenomenon in human affairs. It is a plain fact, to which theories of ideology must address themselves, that our species is prone both morally and intellectually to such distortions of judgment, in particular to distortions of judgment that reflect partiality. An inability to change your mind in the face of appropriate[5] evidence is a cognitive incapacity; but it is one that all of us surely suffer from in some areas of belief; especially in areas where our own interests or self-images are (or seem to be) at stake.

It is not, however, as some have held, a tendency that we are powerless to resist. No one, no doubt, can be impartial about everything—even about everything to which the notion of partiality applies; but there is no subject matter about which most sane people cannot, in the end, be persuaded to avoid partiality in judgment. And it may help to shake the convictions of those whose incapacity derives from this sort of ideological defense if we show them how their reaction fits into this general pattern. It is, indeed, because it generally *does* fit this pattern that we call such views "racism"—the suffix "-ism" indicating that what we have in mind is not simply a theory but an ideology. It would be odd to call someone brought up in a remote corner of the world with false and demeaning views about white people a "racist" if that person gave up these beliefs quite easily in the face of appropriate evidence.

Real live racists, then, exhibit a systematically distorted rationality, the kind of systematically distorted rationality that we are likely to call "ideological." And it is a distortion that is especially striking in the cognitive domain: extrinsic racists, as I said earlier, however intelligent or otherwise well informed, often fail to treat evidence against the theoretical propositions of extrinsic racism dispassionately. Like extrinsic racism, intrinsic racism can also often be seen as ideological; but since scientific evidence is not going to settle the issue, a failure to see that it is wrong represents a cognitive incapacity only on controversially realist views about morality. What makes intrinsic racism similarly ideological is not so much the failure of inductive or deductive rationality that is so striking in someone like Professor Shockley but rather the connection that it, like extrinsic racism, has with the interests—real or perceived—of the dominant group.[6] Shockley's racism is in a certain sense directed *against* nonwhite people: many believe that his views would, if accepted, operate against their objective interests, and he certainly presents the black "race" in a less than flattering light.

I propose to use the old-fashioned term "racial prejudice" in the rest of this essay to refer to the deformation of rationality in judgment that characterizes those whose racism is more than a theoretical attachment to certain propositions about race.

RACIAL PREJUDICE

It is hardly necessary to raise objections to what I am calling "racial prejudice"; someone who exhibits such deformations of rationality is plainly in trouble. But it is important to remember that propositional racists in a racist culture have false moral beliefs but may not suffer from racial prejudice. Once we show them how society has enforced extrinsic racist stereotypes, once we ask them whether they really believe that race in itself, independently of those extrinsic racist beliefs, justifies differential treatment, many will come to give up racist propositions, although we must remember how powerful a weight of authority our arguments have to overcome. Reasonable people may insist on substantial evidence if they are to give up beliefs that are central to their cultures.

Still, in the end, many will resist such reasoning; and to the extent that their prejudices are really not subject to any kind of rational control, we may wonder whether it is right to treat such people as morally responsible for the acts their racial prejudice motivates, or morally reprehensible for holding the views to which their prejudice leads them. It is a bad thing that such people exist; they are, in a certain sense, bad people. But it is not clear to me that they are responsible for the fact that they are bad. Racial prejudice, like

prejudice generally, may threaten an agent's autonomy, making it appropriate to treat or train rather than to reason with them.

But once someone has been offered evidence both (1) that their reasoning in a certain domain is distorted by prejudice, and (2) that the distortions conform to a pattern that suggests a lack of impartiality, they ought to take special care in articulating views and proposing policies in that domain. They ought to do so because, as I have already said, the phenomenon of partiality in judgment is well attested in human affairs. Even if you are not immediately persuaded that you are yourself a victim of such a distorted rationality in a certain domain, you should keep in mind always that this is the usual position of those who suffer from such prejudices. To the extent that this line of thought is not one that itself falls within the domain in question, one can be held responsible for not subjecting judgments that *are* within that domain to an especially extended scrutiny; and this is a fortiori true if the policies one is recommending are plainly of enormous consequence.

If it is clear that racial prejudice is regrettable, it is also clear in the nature of the case that providing even a superabundance of reasons and evidence will often not be a successful way of removing it. Nevertheless, the racist's prejudice will be articulated through the sorts of theoretical propositions I dubbed extrinsic and intrinsic racism. And we should certainly be able to say something reasonable about why these theoretical propositions should be rejected.

Part of the reason that this is worth doing is precisely the fact that many of those who assent to the propositional content of racism do not suffer from racial prejudice. In a country like the United States, where racist propositions were once part of the national ideology, there will be many who assent to racist propositions simply because they were raised to do so. Rational objection to racist propositions has a fair chance of changing such people's beliefs.

EXTRINSIC AND INTRINSIC RACISM

It is not always clear whether someone's theoretical racism is intrinsic or extrinsic, and there is certainly no reason why we should expect to be able to settle the question. Since the issue probably never occurs to most people in these terms, we cannot suppose that they must have an answer. In fact, given the definition of the terms I offered, there is nothing barring someone from being both an intrinsic and an extrinsic racist, holding both that the bare fact of race provides a basis for treating members of his or her own race differently from others and that there are morally relevant characteristics that are differentially distributed among the races. Indeed, for reasons I shall discuss in a moment, *most* intrinsic racists are likely to express extrinsic racist beliefs, so that we should not be surprised that many people seem, in fact, to be committed to both forms of racism.

The Holocaust made unreservedly clear threat that racism poses to human decency. But it also blurred our thinking because in focusing our attention on the racist character of the Nazi atrocities, it obscured their character as atrocities. What is appalling about Nazi racism is not just that it presupposes, as all racism does, false (racialist) beliefs—not simply that it involves a moral incapacity (the inability to extend our moral sentiments to all our fellow creatures) and a moral failing (the making of moral distinctions without moral differences)—but that it leads, first, to oppression and then to mass slaughter. In recent years, South African racism has had a similar distorting effect. For although South African racism has not led to killings on the scale of the Holocaust—even if it has both left South African judicially executing more (mostly black) people per head of population than most other countries and led to massive differences between the life chances of white and nonwhite South Africans—it *has* led to the systematic oppression and economic exploitation of people who are not classified as "white," and to the infliction of suffering on citizens of all racial classifications, not least by the police state that is required to maintain that exploitation and oppression.

Part of our resistance, therefore, to calling the racial ideas of those, such as the Black Nationalists of the 1960s, who advocate racial solidarity, by the same term that we use to describe the attitudes of Nazis or of members of the South African Nationalist party, surely resides in the fact that they largely did not contemplate using race as a basis for inflicting harm.

Indeed, it seems to me that there is a significant pattern in the modern rhethoric of race, such that the discourse of racial solidarity is usually expressed through the language of *intrinsic* racism, while those who have used race as the basis for oppression and hatred have appealed to *extrinsic* racist ideas. This point is important for understanding the character of contemporary racial attitudes.

The two major uses of race as a basis for moral solidarity that are most familiar in the West are varieties of Pan-Africanism and Zionism. In each case it is presupposed that a "people," Negroes or Jews, has the basis for shared political life in the fact of being of the same race. There are varieties of each form of "nationalism" that make the basis lie in shared traditions; but however plausible this may be in the case of Zionism, which has in Judaism, the religion, a realistic candidate for a common and nonracial focus for nationality, the peoples of Africa have a good deal less in common culturally than is usually assumed. I discuss this issue at length in *In My Father's House: Essays in the Philosophy of African Culture*, but let me say here that I believe the central fact is this: what blacks in the West, like secularized Jews, have mostly in common is that they are perceived—both by themselves and by others—as belonging to the same race, and that this common race is used by others as the basis for discriminating against them. "If you ever forget you're a Jew, a goy will remind you." The Black Nationalists, like some Zionists, responded to their experience of racial discrimination by accepting the racialism it presupposed.[7]

Although race is indeed at the heart of Black Nationalism, however, it seems that it is the fact of a shared race, not the fact of a shared racial character, that provides the basis for solidarity. Where racism is implicated in the basis for national solidarity, it is intrinsic, not (or not only) extrinsic. It is this that makes the idea of fraternity one that is naturally applied in nationalist discourse. For, as I have already observed, the moral status of close family members is not normally thought of in most cultures as depending on qualities of character; we are supposed to love our brothers and sisters in spite of their faults and not because of their virtues. Alexander Crummell, one of the founding fathers of Black Nationalism, literalizes the metaphor of family in these startling words:

> Races, like families, are the organisms and ordinances of God; and race feeling, like family feeling, is of divine origin. The extinction of race feeling is just as possible as the extinction of family feeling. Indeed, a race *is* a family.[8]

It is the assimilation of "race feeling" to "family feeling" that makes intrinsic racism seem so much less objectionable than extrinsic racism. For this metaphorical identification reflects the fact that, in the modern world (unlike the nineteenth century), intrinsic racism is acknowledged almost exclusively as the basis of feelings of community. We can surely, then, share a sense of what Crummell's friend and co-worker Edward Blyden called "the poetry of politics," that is, "the feeling of race," the feeling of "people with whom we are connected."[9] The racism here is the basis of acts of supererogation, the treatment of others better than we otherwise might, better than moral duty demands of us.

This is a contingent fact. There is no logical impossibility in the idea of racialists whose moral beliefs lead them to feelings of hatred for other races while leaving no room for love of members of their own. Nevertheless most racial hatred is in fact expressed through extrinsic racism: most people who have used race as the basis for causing harm to others have felt the need to see the others as independently morally flawed. It is one thing to espouse fraternity without claiming that your brothers and sisters have any special qualities that deserve recognition, and another to espouse hatred of others who have done nothing to deserve it.[10]

Many Afrikaners—like many in the American South until recently—have a long list of extrinsic racist answers to the question why blacks should not have full civil rights. Extrinsic racism has usually been the basis for treating people worse than we otherwise might, for giving them less than their humanity entitles them to. But this too is a contingent fact. Indeed, Crummell's guarded respect for white people derived from a belief in the superior moral qualities of the Anglo-Saxon race.

Intrinsic racism is, in my view, a moral error. Even if racialism were correct, the bare fact that someone was of another race would be no reason to treat them worse—or better—than someone of my race. In our public lives, people are owed treatment independently of their biological characters: if they are to be differently treated there must be some morally relevant difference between them. In our private lives, we are morally free to have aesthetic preferences between people, but once our treatment of people raises moral issues, we may not make arbitrary distinctions. Using race in itself as a morally relevant distinction strikes most of us as obviously arbitrary. Without associated moral characteristics, why should race provide a better basis than hair color or height or timbre of voice? And if two people share all the properties morally relevant to some action we ought to do, it will be an error—a failure to apply the Kantian injunction to universalize our moral judgments—to use the bare facts of race as the basis for treating them differently. No one should deny that a common ancestry might, in particular cases, account for similarities in moral character. But then it would be the moral similarities that justified the different treatment.

It is presumably because most people—outside the South African Nationalist party and the Ku Klux Klan—share the sense that intrinsic racism requires arbitrary distinctions that they are largely unwilling to express it in situations that invite moral criticism. But I do not know how I would argue with someone who was willing to announce an intrinsic racism as a basic moral idea; the best one can do, perhaps, is to provide objections to possible lines of defense of it.

DE GUSTIBUS

It might be thought that intrinsic racism should be regarded not so much as an adherence to a (moral) proposition as the expression of a taste, analogous, say, to the food prejudice that makes most English people unwilling to eat horse meat, and most Westerners unwilling to eat the insect grubs that the !Kung people find so appetizing. The analogy does at least this much for us, namely, to provide a model of the way that *extrinsic* racist propositions can be a reflection of an underlying prejudice. For, of course, in most cultures food prejudices are rationalized: we say insects are unhygienic and cats taste horrible. Yet a cooked insect is no more health-threatening than a cooked carrot, and the unpleasant taste of cat meat, far from justifying our prejudice against it, probably derives from that prejudice.

But there the usefulness of the analogy ends. For intrinsic racism, as I have defined it, is not simply a taste for the company of one's "own kind," but a moral doctrine, one that is supposed to underlie differences in the treatment of people in contexts where moral evaluation is appropriate. And for moral distinctions we cannot accept that "de gustibus non est disputandum." We do not need the full apparatus of Kantian ethics to require that public morality be constrained by reason.

A proper analogy would be with someone who thought that we could continue to kill cattle for beef, even if cattle exercised all the complex cultural skills of human beings. I think it is obvious that creatures that shared our capacity for understanding as well as our capacity for pain should not be treated the way we actually treat cattle—that "intrinsic speciesism" would be as wrong as racism. And the fact that most people think it is worse to be cruel to chimpanzees than to frogs suggests that they may agree with me. The distinction in attitudes surely reflects a belief in the greater richness of the mental life of chimps. Still, I do not know how I would *argue* against someone who could not see this; someone who continued to act on the contrary belief might, in the end, simply have to be locked up.

THE FAMILY MODEL

I have suggested that intrinsic racism is, at least sometimes, a metaphorical extension of the moral priority of one's family; it might, therefore, be suggested that a defense of intrinsic racism could proceed along the same lines as a defense of the family as a center of moral interest. The possibility of a defense of family relations as morally relevant—or, more precisely, of the claim that one may be morally entitled (or even obliged) to make distinctions between two otherwise morally indistinguishable people because one is related to one and not to the other—is theoretically important for

the prospects of a philosophical defense of intrinsic racism. This is because such a defense of the family involves—like intrinsic racism—a denial of the basic claim, expressed so clearly by Kant, that from the perspective of morality, it is as rational agents *simpliciter* that we are to assess and be assessed. For anyone who follows Kant in this, what matters, as we might say, is not who you are but how you try to live. Intrinsic racism denies this fundamental claim also. And, in so doing, as I have argued elsewhere, it runs against the mainstream of the history of Western moral theory.[11]

The importance of drawing attention to the similarities between the defense of the family and the defense of the race, then, is not merely that the metaphor of family is often invoked by racism: it is that each of them offers the same general challenge to the Kantian stream of our moral thought. And the parallel with the defense of the family should be especially appealing to an intrinsic racist, since many of us who have little time for racism would hope that the family is susceptible to some such defense.

The problem in generalizing the defense of the family, however, is that such defense standardly begin at a point that makes the argument for intrinsic racism immediately implausible: namely, with the family as the unit through which we live what is most intimate, as the center of private life. If we distinguish, with Bernard Williams, between ethical thought, which takes seriously "the demands, needs, claims, desires, and generally, the lives of other people,"[12] and morality, which focuses more narrowly on obligation, it may well be that private life matters to us precisely because it is altogether unsuited to the universalizing tendencies of morality.

The functioning family unit has contracted substantially with industrialization, the disappearance of the family as the unit of production, and the increasing mobility of labor, but there remains that irreducible minimum: the parent or parents with the child or children. In this "nuclear" family, there is, of course, a substantial body of shared experience, shared attitudes, shared knowledge and beliefs; and the mutual psychological investment that exists within this group is, for most of us, one of the things that gives meaning to our lives. It is a natural enough confusion—which we find again and again in discussions of adoption in the popular media—that identifies the relevant group with the biological unit of *genitor, genetrix,* and *offspring* rather than with the social unit of those who share a common domestic life.

The relations of parents and their biological children are of moral importance, of course, in part because children are standardly the product of behavior voluntarily undertaken by their biological parents. But the moral relations between biological siblings and half-siblings cannot, as I have already pointed out, be accounted for in such terms. A rational defense of the family ought to appeal to the causal responsibility of the biological parent and the common life of the domestic unit, and not to the brute fact of biological relatedness, even if the former pair of considerations defines groups that are often coextensive with the groups generated by the latter. For brute biological relatedness bears no necessary connection to the sorts of human purposes that seem likely to be relevant at the most basic level of ethical thought.

An argument that such a central group is bound to be crucially important in the lives of most human beings in societies like ours is not, of course, an argument for any specific mode of organization of the "family": feminism and the gay liberation movement have offered candidate groups that could (and sometimes do) occupy the same sort of role in the lives of those whose sexualities or whose dispositions otherwise make the nuclear family uncongenial; and these candidates have been offered specifically in the course of defenses of a move toward societies that are agreeably beyond patriarchy and homophobia. The central thought of these feminist and gay critiques of the nuclear family is that we cannot continue to view any one organization of private life as "natural," once we have seen even the broadest outlines of the archaeology of the family concept.

If that is right, then the argument for the family must be an argument for a mode of organization of life and feeling that subserves certain positive functions; and however the details of such an argument would proceed it is highly unlikely that the same functions could be served by groups on the scale of races, simply because, as I say, the family is attractive in part exactly for reasons of its personal scale.

I need hardly say that rational defense of intrinsic racism along the lines I have been considering are not easily found. In the absence of detailed defenses to consider, I can only offer these general reasons for doubting that they can succeed: the generally Kantian tenor of much of our moral thought threatens the project from the start; and the essentially unintimate nature of relations within "races" suggests that there is little prospect that the defense of the family—which seems an attractive and plausible project that extends ethical life beyond the narrow range of a universalizing morality—can be applied to a defense of races.

CONCLUSIONS

I have suggested that what we call "racism" involves both propositions and dispositions.

The propositions were, first, that there are races (this was *racialism*) and, second, that these races are morally significant either (a) because they are contingently correlated with morally relevant properties (this was *extrinsic racism*) or (b) because they are intrinsically morally significant (this was *intrinsic racism*).

The disposition was a tendency to assent to false propositions, both moral and theoretical, about races—propositions that support policies or beliefs that are to the disadvantage of some race (or races) as opposed to others, and to do so even in the face of evidence and argument that should appropriately lead to giving those propositions up. This disposition I called "racial prejudice."

I suggested that intrinsic racism had tended in our own time to be the natural expression of feelings of community, and this is, of course, one of the reasons why we are not inclined to call it racist. For, to the extent that a theoretical position is not associated with irrationally held beliefs that tend to the *dis*advantage of some group, it fails to display the *directedness* of the distortions of rationality characteristic of racial prejudice. Intrinsic racism may be as irrationally held as any other view, but it does not *have* to be directed *against* anyone.

So far as theory is concerned I believe racialism to be false: since theoretical racism of both kinds presupposes racialism, I could not logically support racism of either variety. But even if racialism were true, both forms of theoretical racism would be incorrect. Extrinsic racism is false because the genes that account for the gross morphological differences that underlie our standard racial categories are not linked to those genes that determine, to whatever degree such matters are determined genetically, our moral and intellectual characters. Intrinsic racism is mistaken because it breaches the Kantian imperative to make moral distinctions only on morally relevant grounds—granted that there is no reason to believe that race, *in se*, is morally relevant, and also no reason to suppose that races are like families in providing a sphere of ethical life that legitimately escapes the demands of a universalizing morality.

NOTES

1. Bernard Lewis, *Semites and Anti-Semites* (New York: Norton, 1986).

2. I shall be using the words "racism" and "racialism" with the meanings I stipulate: in some dialects of English they are synonyms, and in most dialects their definition is less than precise. For discussion of recent biological evidence see M. Nei and A. K. Roychoudhury, "Genetic Relationship and Evolution of Human Races," *Evolutionary Biology,* vol. 14 (New York: Plenum, 1983), pp. 1–59; for useful background see also M. Nei and A. K. Roychoudhury, "Gene Differences between Caucasian, Negro, and Japanese Populations, " *Science,* 177 (August 1972), pp. 434–35.

3. See my "The Uncompleted Argument: Du Bois and the Illusion of Race," *Critical Inquiry,* 12 (Autumn 1985); reprinted in Henry Louis Gates (eds.), *"Race," Writing, and Difference* (Chicago: University of Chicago Press, 1986), pp. 21–37.

4. This fact shows up most obviously in the assumption that adopted children intelligibly make claims against their natural siblings: natural parents are, of course, causally responsible for their child's existence and that could be the basis of moral claims, without any sense that biological relatedness entailed rights or responsibilities. But no such basis exists for an interest in natural *siblings*; my sisters are not causally responsible for my existence. See "The Family Model," later in this essay.

5. Obviously what evidence should *appropriately* change your beliefs is not independent of your social or historical situa-

tion. In mid-nineteenth-century America, in New England quite as much as in the heart of Dixie, the pervasiveness of the institutional support for the prevailing system of racist belief—the fact that it was reinforced by religion and state, and defended by people in the universities and colleges, who had the greatest cognitive authority—meant that it would have been appropriate to insist on a substantial body of evidence and argument before giving up assent to racist propositions. In California in the 1980s, of course, matters stand rather differently. To acknowledge this is not to admit to a cognitive relativism; rather, it is to hold that, at least in some domains, the fact that a belief is widely held—and especially by people in positions of cognitive authority—may be a good prima facie reason for believing it.

6. Ideologies, as most theorists of ideology have admitted, standardly outlive the period in which they conform to the objective interests of the dominant group in a society; so even someone who thinks that the dominant group in our society no longer needs racism to buttress its position can see racism as the persisting ideology of an earlier phase of society. (I say "group" to keep the claim appropriately general; it seems to me a substantial further claim that the dominant group whose interests an ideology serves is always a class.) I have argued, however, in "The Conservation of 'Race' " that racism continues to serve the interests of the ruling classes in the West; in *Black American Literature Forum,* 23 (Spring 1989), pp. 37–60.

7. As I argued in "The Uncompleted Argument: Du Bois and the Illusion of Race." The reactive (or dialectical) character of this move explains why Sartre calls its manifestations in Négritude an "antiracist racism"; see "Orphée Noir," his preface to Senghor's *Anthologie de la nonvelle poésie négre et malagache de langue francaise* (Paris: PUF, 1948). Sartre believed, of course, that the synthesis of this dialectic would be the transcendence of racism; and it was his view of it as a stage—the antithesis—in that process that allowed him to see it as a positive advance over the original "thesis" of European racism. I suspect that the reactive character of antiracist racism accounts for the tolerance that is regularly extended to it in liberal circles; but this tolerance is surely hard to justify unless one shares Sartre's optimistic interpretation of it as a stage in a process that leads to the end of all racisms. (And unless your view of this dialectic is deterministic, you should in any case want to play an argumentative role in moving to this next stage.)

For a similar Zionist response see Horace Kallen's "The Ethics of Zionism," *Maccabaean,* August 1906.

8. "The Race Problem in America," in Brotz's *Negro Social and Political Thought* (New York: Basic Books, 1966), p. 184.

9. *Christianity, Islam and the Negro Race* (1887; reprinted Edinburgh: Edinburgh University Press, 1967), p. 197.

10. This is in part a reflection of an important asymmetry: loathing, unlike love, needs justifying; and this, I would argue, is because loathing usually leads to acts that are *in se* undesirable, whereas love leads to acts that are largely *in se* desirable—indeed, supererogatorily so.

11. See my "Racism and Moral Pollution," *Philosophical Forum*, 18 (Winter-Spring 1986–87), pp. 185–202.

12. *Ethics and the Limits of Philosophy* (Cambridge, Mass: Harvard University Press, 1985), p. 12. I do not, as is obvious, share William's skepticism about morality.

Racism: What It Is and What It Isn't

Lawrence Blum

We in the United States are notoriously poor at communicating about racial matters. David Shipler, in his informative and insightful book *A Nation of Strangers*, rightly says, "Blacks and Whites do not listen well to each other (Shipler, 1997, p. 447). Native Americans, Latinos, Chicanos, and Asian-Americans are not all that much better. We find honest discussion about race across racial lines especially difficult. Ironically, race is the subject of scores of books and articles. And one often hears impatience expressed about race. "Race is talked to death," it is said.

There may be a lot of words written about race. But there is a good deal less honest, open, and productive conversation about it among persons of different races than there needs to be. For the past several years I have taught courses on race and racism to undergraduates, graduate students in education, and high school students. Most of my classes are quite racially and ethnically diverse. In my experience a range of reasons accounts for the lack of productive conversation. People are afraid of giving offense. They are afraid of revealing prejudices they know are not socially acceptable. They are afraid of *appearing* prejudiced, even if they are actually not. They feel ignorant of groups other than their own and are afraid to risk revealing their ignorance and trying to remedy it. The whole idea of "race" just

carries unpleasant associations with them, and they would rather avoid it. They may think we should all be "color-blind," that it is somehow wrong even to take notice of or make reference to other people's racial identity. This idea of color-blindness is both particularly strong, yet also particularly misplaced, among teachers, especially at the pre-college level. Teachers can not serve their students fully unless they are aware of the full range of factors affecting their lives, and race is very likely to be one of those factors (Schofield, 1989).

Some reasons for reluctance to engage in race discussions are more race-specific. Blacks, and to a lesser extent other people of color, may want to avoid what they assume will be offensive or at least annoying remarks from others. Or they might not want to have to be in a position of correcting others' (especially whites') ignorance. Latinos, Native Americans, and Asian-Americans may not be certain how to insert themselves into a discourse which seems to them dominated by "black/white" issues, or they may feel resentful of this dominance, and assume their specific concerns will not be adequately attended to. Notwithstanding these obstacles, I have also found a great deal of good will among students, and an anxious desire for their teachers to create contexts that facilitate constructive interracial interchange.

Each of the cited obstacles is deserving of further attention. However, I wish in this lecture to focus on a different obstacle, though one that bears on several of those just mentioned. It is the idea of "racism" itself. There is a great deal of confusion surrounding

Lawrence Blum, reprinted by permission from Springer Nature: *Studies in Philosophy and Education*, "Racism: What it is and What it isn't," Vol. 21 (2002), pp. 203–218, Copyright © 2002.

the meaning of "racism" and "racist." Yet one thing is clear—few people wish to be, or to be thought of as, "racists." Fear of being thought racist, together with a good deal of confusion as to "what" being racist consists in, is a potent formula for inhibition regarding discussion racial matters, most especially for whites who are, understandably, in most danger of being thought to be, and indeed of actually being, racists.

Clarifying meanings is the professional task of the philosopher, and I think that if we become clearer about what "racism" actually consists in, and what lies outside of the scope of racism yet may still be morally problematic, we will be better equipped to engage in productive discussions about race. Of course I have no illusions that merely clarifying meanings will bring about either racial justice or racial harmony, or even the more minimal goal of producing helpful conversations about these matters. But it seems an essential first step.

The words "racism" and "racist" have become deeply entrenched in the moral vocabulary of the United States and Western Europe. "Is television a racist institution?" asks an article concerning the NAACP's criticizing the fall 1999 prime-time network shows for having no "minority" actors in lead roles in twenty-seven new series (Weinraub, 1999, pp. A1, A14). Blacks who criticized other blacks for supporting a white over a black candidate in a mayoral race were called racist. A white girl in Virginia said that it was racist for an African-American teacher in her school to wear African attire (Shipler, p. 92). The Milton, Wisconsin, school board voted to retire its "Redmen" name and logo depicting a Native American wearing a headdress, because they have been criticized as racist. "Racist" has become the standard way to condemn and deplore people, actions, policies, symbols, and institutions for malfeasance in the racial domain.

In serving as a term of moral reproach, "racism" has joined more time-honored vices such as "dishonesty," "cruelty," "cowardice," and "hypocrisy." Apart from a small number of avowed white supremacists, most Americans wish very much to avoid being called "racist." In this regard, "racist" operates similarly to "cruel." Few admit to being cruel. Persons who are cruel might say the target of their cruelty deserved it,

or they might simply fail to recognize the harm caused by their actions. Similarly, no one admits to being racist. Those who are, or are thought to be, might say their remarks were just a joke; they did not intend any harm; people are just being oversensitive; it was a personal, not a racial, thing; and the like. One expects people who are accused of being racist to deny it and newspapers should stop regarding this as newsworthy.

OVERUSING "RACISM"

Yet the widely-shared reproach carried by "racist" is threatened by a current tendency to overuse the term. Some feel that the word is thrown around so much that anything involving "race" that someone does not like is liable to castigation as "racist"—for example, merely mentioning someone's race (or racial designation),[1] using the word "Oriental" for Asians without recognizing its origins and its capacity for insult, or socializing only with members of one's own racial group. Many people would not agree, or would not be sure, that *any* of the four examples in the paragraph before the previous one constitute "racism." A few observers go even further and suspect that the word has lost all significant meaning. "Racism is . . . what black activists define it to be. . . . When words lose coherent meaning, they also lose the power to shame. 'Racism,' 'sexism,' and 'homophobia' have become such words. Labels that should horrify are simply shrugged off" (Nuechterlein, 1996, p. B9). *Time* columnist Lance Morrow sees social damage in this same development: "The words 'racism' and 'racist' are a feckless indulgence, corrosive to blacks and whites alike and to relations between them" (Morrow, 1996, p. 18).

A major reason for what Robert Miles calls the "conceptual inflation" (Miles, 1989, pp. 41–68), to which the idea of "racism" has been subject is its having become the central or even only notion used to mark morally suspect behavior, attitude, and social practice regarding race. The result—either something is racist, or it is morally in the clear. In Boston a white police officer, as a bizarre joke and apparently with no malice intended, placed a hangman's noose on the motorcycle of a black police officer. "Police probe sees no racism in noose prank," says the headline of an article reporting the findings of an investigation into the incident. Perhaps the white officer was not "a racist," nor operating from racist motives; but, as the victim in the incident said, "You cannot hang a noose like that near any black man who knows his history and say it does not have tremendous significance" (*Boston Globe*, p. B1).[2] If our only choices are to label an act "racist" or "nothing to get too upset about," those who seek to garner moral attention to some racial malfeasance will be tempted to call it "racist." That overuse in turn feeds a diminishing of "racism's" moral force, and thus contributes to weakened concern about racism and other racial ills.

Not all rac*ial* incidents are rac*ist* incidents. Not every instance of racial conflict, insensitivity, discomfort, miscommunication, exclusion, injustice, or ignorance should be called "racist." This more varied and nuanced moral vocabulary needs to be more fully utilized, complementing "racist" and "racism." All forms of racial ills should elicit concern from responsible citizens. If someone displays racial insensitivity, but not racism, people should be able to see that straightforwardly as a matter of moral concern. In a soccer game, a nine-year-old white boy said "Boy, pass the ball over here" to one of his black teammates, and "was virtually accused of being a racist by the father of one of his teammates," says an article on the incident. (That description may itself reflect the loss of an evaluative vocabulary other than "racist" and "racism," rather than what the black boy's father actually said.) In any case, the white boy was almost surely not "a racist" and the article itself goes on to express more accurately the racial ill involved in his remark: "The word 'boy' is a tripwire attached to so much charged racial baggage that it is no longer safely used as a term for a prepubescent male."

If a policy has a racially unjust effect, or unequally affects already unequally placed racial groups, this too should be reason for concern, even if there is no suggestion that it arises from racist motives, or is part of the sort of entrenched pattern strongly rooted in historical racism. For example, school lunch programs have been criticized for relying too strongly on milk, in light of the African-Americans' substantial propensity toward lactose intolerance; but no untoward motives, or failures of sensitivity, need have prompted the original policies favoring milk for them to be of concern. Similarly, it is troubling if prime-time TV fails adequately to reflect its viewers', and the society's, ethnoracial diversity; but it is not necessarily "racist."[3] Someone who exhibits a culpable ignorance about racial matters bearing on an interaction with an acquaintance or co-worker should feel a degree of shame about this, and be motivated to correct that ignorance—without her having to think she has been "racist." We should not be faced with the choice of "racism or nothing."

"Racism's" conceptual inflation and moral overload can arise from a another source as well—designating as "racism" any prejudice, injustice, domination, inferiorizing, bigotry, and the like, against human groups defined in *any* manner, for example, by gender, disability, nationality. In *The Decent Society*, Avishai Margalit, an Israeli philosopher, defines racism as the denying of dignity to *any human group*, and uses as a particular test case "retarded" persons (Margalit, 1996, pp. 80–83). This inflated use of racism pays indirect tribute to the centrality of racism as a form of oppression and denial of dignity in contemporary Western consciousness. That centrality is reflected also in later coinages, such as "sexism," "ableism" (discrimination against the disabled). "racism," and "heterosexism"—all consciously modeled on "racism," and attempting to draw on racism's moral opprobrium to condemn other phenomena seen as in important ways analogous to racism.[4] This "racism"-influenced proliferation of other "isms" at least avoids the confusion wrought by Margalit's conflating all of them with "racism" itself. At least it encourages us to explore the similarities between discrimination, exploitation, and denials of dignity based on race, and those based on other human attributes, such as gender, sexual orientation, disability, national membership, and the like, thereby allowing the possibility of significant *disanalogies*. Margalit's subsuming all these moral ills under "racism" cuts off that inquiry at the starting line, and, in so doing, contributes to a counterproductive inflation of the term "racism."

RACIST JOKES AND RACIST PERSONS

A different source of confusion and moral overload regarding racism concerns what one might call racism's location. Many different kinds of entity can be racist—actions, institutions, practices, symbols, statements, jokes, persons, to name a few. The moral significance of an attribution of racism differs depending on its location. Take racist jokes for instance. A person who tells a racist joke is not necessarily "a racist," in the sense of a person who harbors pervasive racial animosity or inferiorizing attitudes toward a racially defined group. He may tell the joke without sharing the racist sentiments the jokes expresses. People often tell jokes as a way of trying to win acceptance; they might tell whatever they think will bring a laugh. Imagine, for example, someone telling a joke that makes fun of Asian-Americans in a particularly demeaning manner, in order to gain acceptance in a group. (The group could consist of any ethnoracial group, except Asian-Americans. I am not assuming that only whites tell racist jokes [or are racists, for that matter].)[5] This individual does not necessarily hold racist views of Asians or Asian-Americans. The joke is racist, but the teller of the joke is not.

Of course, this does not mean that, as long as one does not share the racist views a joke expresses, it is perfectly fine to tell such a joke. To think that it is all right is to reason in precisely the all-or-nothing manner I have been criticizing. It is a very bad thing to tell a racist joke. One often hears public figures who have been caught out telling a racist joke or making a racist remark defending themselves by saying that did not intend any offense to the group in question, that they are not racist. Often this defense is quite disingenuous, and the individual in fact does hold the racist attitudes implied in the joke. But even when it is not, this is a feeble defense from a moral point of view. It is bad to tell a racist joke, whether one means to offend, or holds racist attitudes, or not.

Jokes, and humor more generally, raise a common locational issue about racism—the difference between intention and effect—illustrated in two examples of racist humor that came to public attention in the late 1990s. One was a fraternity party, in which the fraternity members dressed up in Native American warrior attire and wielded tomahawks. A second, again a fraternity, involved staging a mock slave auction. In both cases, members of the fraternities in question defended themselves by saying that they did not mean to offend anyone. But the moral shortcoming in both cases did not lie in setting out to deliberately demean Native Americans and African-Americans. It lay in their failing to realize that what they were doing *was* demeaning to Native Americans and African-Americans, whether they *intended* this or not. It is not even clear that ignorance of the affront would be morally more acceptable than an intention to affront.

Still, engaging in racist humor does not make one a racist. More generally, clarity and racial understanding would be advanced if people attempted to take greater care in locating the racism they allege in a situation. Is it a practice are racist that is racist, whether the persons who participate in the practice are racist or not? Is it the motive of an act that is racist? Is it an attitude taken to be expressed in a remark, or the remark itself? Is it a person about whom one knows enough to say that he or she is "a racist?"

To help us avoid the first form of confusion about racism—conceptual inflation—I will suggest a core meaning rooted in the history of its use, that confines "racism" to phenomena deserving of the severest moral condemnation (within the appropriately located type, that is, act, statement, joke, person, and so on). Fixing on such a definition should encourage us to make use of the considerable other resources our language affords us for describing and evaluating race-related ills that do not characteristically rise to the level of racism—racial insensitivity, racial conflict, racial injustice, racial ignorance, racial discomfort, and others. Such an agreed-upon meaning for "racism" should facilitate interracial communication, at least in diminishing a free-floating and pervasive fear of the dreaded charge of "racism"—by making clearer what is and what is not to be counted as racism—while at the same time encouraging a wider scope of moral concern to race-related phenomena. In doing so, my suggested definition of racism should stanch the creeping loss of moral cachet of the term "racism" itself, with its attendant undermining of moral concern toward racism and other race-related ills.

DEFINING "RACISM"

In proffering a definition of racism, it would be folly to claim that one was doing no more than articulating "our concept" of racism. Even apart from inflationary usages, it is not likely that all employments of that concept cohere in an overall, self-consistent whole. Nevertheless, especially in light of the history of this concept, I hope my proposal can reasonably be viewed as a plausible candidate for a core meaning.

"Racism" was first used by German social scientists in the 1930s to refer to the ideology of race superiority central to Nazism, and its core historical meaning broadened out to other systems of racial domination and oppression, such as segregation, South African apartheid, and European colonialism. In this light, I want to suggest that all forms of racism can be related to either of two general "themes"—*inferiorization*, and *antipathy*. Inferiorizing is treating the racial other as inferior or lesser value and, secondarily, viewing the racial other as inferior. Racial antipathy is simply a strong dislike, often tinged with hostility, toward individuals or groups because of their race. Of the two modes, inferiorization is more obviously linked to historical racist doctrines and social systems. Slavery, segregation, imperialism, apartheid, and Nazism all involved certain groups being regarded as and treated as inferior to other groups.

But race-based hatred was also central to the ideological and attitudinal components of Nazism, and, for whatever reason, racial bigotry, hostility, and hatred are now securely linked to the contemporary idea of "racism" in both Europe and the United States. Indeed, the racial bigot is many people's paradigm image of "a racist," and few would now deny application of the appellation "racist" to such persons. A disturbing but illuminating example of appellation "racist" to such persons. A disturbing but illuminating example of contemporary antipathy racism occurred in Washington state in 1999. The Makah tribe of the Olympic Peninsula announced its intention to hunt for whales as a way of instilling pride and tradition in the tribe's youth. The hunt was permitted by the government, and the tribe killed a whale in May of that year. Many non-Native American Washington residents were outraged by this act. Amidst arguably reasonable objections to the whale hunting were expressions of outright antipathy racism toward the Makah, and toward Native Americans more generally. One letter to the *Seattle Times*, for example, said, "I have a very real hatred for Native Americans now. It's embarrassing, but I would be lying if I said it wasn't the truth" (Tizon, 1999).

Inferiorizing and antipathy racism are distinct. Some superiority racists do not hate the target of their beliefs. They may have a paternalistic concern and feelings of kindness for persons they regard as their human inferiors. This form of racism was prevalent among slave owners, and characterized many whites' views of blacks during the segregation era in the United States. The concern and kindness are misdirected, and demeaning, because the other is not seen as an equal, or even as a full human being; it is a racist from of concern. Nevertheless such attitudes are distinct from antipathy and hatred.

On the other side, not every race hater regards the target of her hatred as inferior. In the U.S. antipathy toward Asians and Jews often accompanies, and is in part driven by a kind of resentment of those seen as in some ways superior (e.g. more successful). And some whites who hate blacks do not really regard blacks as inferior; they may fear and be hostile to them, but fear and hostility are not the same as contempt and other forms of inferiorizing. (Again, antipathy and contempt may accompany one another). Survey research suggests that pure superiority racism toward blacks has substantially decreased since segregation, more so than hostility-based racism (Schuman et al., pp. 156–157). Nevertheless, the great and persistent racial inequalities in our society provide a standing encouragement to advantaged groups to see disadvantaged groups as somehow deserving their lower status.

However, antipathy and inferiorizing racism are not entirely separate either. The paternalistic inferiorizing racist (e.g., a white segregationist) often hates those members of the racial group who do not accept the inferior social position he regards as appropriate to their inferior natures—for example, blacks who do not engage in the deference behavior the paternalistic racist expects. Emmett Till was lynched in 1955 out of hatred directed toward a young black man who had transgressed the rules of racial deference and constraint defining him as an inferior being. In addition, many racist both hate *and* regard as inferior members of a particular racial group (and not only a particular subcategory of such members, such as those who do not "stay in their place").

RACIAL AND RACIST STEREOTYPES

If we confine racism to manifestations or representations of racial antipathy or racial inferiorizing, we can see that many things can go wrong in the area of race without being racist. Consider two objectionable stereotypes of blacks, for instance—blacks as intellectually deficient, and blacks as good dancers. The first is a straightforwardly racist stereotype; it portrays blacks as inferior in regard to a fundamental human attribute. The second, however, is not racist, on my account. It attributes a positive rather than a negative quality. It is a far less objectionable stereotype than the inferiority stereotype.

Nevertheless, the stereotype of blacks as good dancers is still an objectionable one. Like any stereotype, it wildly overgeneralizes about a group; it blinds us to the internal diversity of the group—some blacks are bad dancers, some are good, some are so-so (and this is so of every racial group). Also, all stereotyping discourages recognizing the individuality of members of the group.

The stereotype of blacks as good dancers is also objectionable in a more specific, historically contextual sense, which can be recognized in the more variegated moral vocabulary revealed by loosening our fixation on "racism" and "racist." This stereotype hearkens back to the slave era, when viewing blacks as good dancers was bound up with their being seen as mentally inferior. While this direct implication is no longer clearly attached to the "good dancer" stereotype, stereotypes must be viewed historically as well as contemporarily, and a given stereotype's resonance with a much more distinctly racist stereotype renders it objectionable in a way that stereotypes without such

historical resonance would not be. Other stereotypes lacking such historical resonance are, for example, Asians as poor drivers, blacks as poor swimmers, and whites as not being able to jump. All are objectionable, racial (race-based) stereotypes. But it is moral overload to call them *racist* stereotypes, and to do so contributes to a cheapening of the moral force of the idea of "racism."

RACIAL DISCOMFORT OR ANXIETY

Another application of the definition of racism is the difference between racial antipathy and what I will call "racial discomfort" or "racial anxiety." Consider the following example.

Ms. Verano is a white fourth grade teacher. She feels comfortable with all the children in her very racially-mixed class. She holds all students to equally high standards of performance. But, though she has never admitted this to herself, she is not really comfortable with most of the black parents. She does not dislike blacks, nor does she think they are inferior. However, she is not particularity familiar with African-American culture, knows very few blacks other than her students, and is not confident about her ability to communicate with blacks other than her students, and is not confident about her ability to communicate with black adults. As a result Ms. Verano is somewhat defensive when speaking with black parents in parent conferences, and is not able to listen to their concerns and viewpoints about their children as well as she does with parents in other racial groups. Because she does not glean as much information from the black parents about their children as she does from the other parents, she is not able to serve these children as well as the other children in her class. Ms. Verano does not have antipathy or inferiorizing attitudes toward blacks. To call her a "racist" would be conceptual inflation. She bears no antipathy towards blacks. I have built this feature into the example. Nor does she regard blacks as inferior.

Ms. Verano's situation is best described by saying that she is uncomfortable with black adults (not children). She has "racial discomfort" or "racial anxiety."

Racial anxiety is quite common in the United States, especially, I believe, among whites, although it can be found in any racial group. Racial anxiety can stem from different sources, and one of them can be anxiety that one's racist prejudices be revealed. In this case racial anxiety would be a manifestation of racism. However, racial anxiety is not always racist in its genesis. We can realize that a group of persons in different from us in some socially important way, and we can feel that we are just not knowledgeable enough about this group to feel comfortable in the presence of its members. We can be anxious that we will embarrass ourselves by saying or doing the "wrong thing." We may worry that the group will dislike or reject us if we attempt to approach it. This social anxiety is perfectly familiar regarding cultural differences; the individual is anxious approaching a culture about which she lacks knowledge. Members of different racial groups are also often quite ignorant of one anothers' modes of life (sometimes but not always because cultural and racial differences correspond), even if they interact in schools and workplaces. In a sense racial anxiety is even *more* likely than mere cultural anxiety, since differences in "race" are more socially charged than are cultural differences. If one is equally ignorant of the other group, there is more reason to be anxious that one will violate some unforeseen norm with regard to a racially different group than a culturally different one.

In itself, racial anxiety or discomfort is not racism. Nor is racial discomfort the sort of thing for which its possessor is subject to moral criticism. It is not morally bad to be racially anxious, as it is morally bad to be racially prejudiced. However, racial discomfort is still a bad thing, and an individual who recognizes her racial anxiety should not rest content with it just because it is not a moral blot on her character. This is so, in part, because, as in Ms. Verano's case, it can lead to acts of a discriminatory character; Ms. Verano is unlikely to be able to educate her black pupils to the same degree as she does her other students, since she will lack information pertinent to them.

In addition racial anxiety reinforces a sense of separateness and "otherness" concerning those of other racial groups. It makes it difficult to recognize internal diversity in such groups, and to appreciate the individuality of members of the group. It feeds into (in addition to drawing on) the homogenizing of racial groups that is a typical pitfall in the racial arena.

Racial discomfort is also inimical to the development of interracial community and other forms of productive interracial relationship. It inhibits a sense of identification across racial lines, and reinforces a sense (particularly found among high school and some college students) that it is somehow more "natural" to socialize with members of one's own racial group than of other groups. We should strive for a society in which people feel as comfortable as possible interacting in all public and private venues with members of ethnic and racial groups other than their own. Such comfort would not only make social existence more pleasant, varied, and interesting for members of all groups, but would serve the purpose of civic attachment and civic engagement as well. Teachers in a position to do so would do well to make an effort to decrease racial discomfort and anxiety in their classes, for example by forming interracial groups for various tasks, encouraging interracial communication, explicitly discussing its importance and pitfalls, and the like.[6] Individuals are well advised to look for signs of racial discomfort in themselves and, if they discover them, do what they can to relieve this discomfort, for example by reaching out to persons of other racial groups or by becoming more familiar with and knowledgeable about the modes of life of those groups.

Furthermore, the fact that it is generally difficult to tell whether reluctance to engage with racial others is a product of antipathy or mere discomfort itself takes a toll on racial minorities who have to worry and wonder about the source of some troubling racial interaction. "In waiting rooms or lobbies . . . I've tried to initiate a conversation [with whites], and I could tell they don't want to talk,' says Sharon Walter, an African-American. 'But when a white person walks in, conversation begins. I don't want to think it's racism . . . The better part of me wants to think otherwise' " (Shipler, p. 448). Merely having such thoughts is itself a psychic cost.

In summary, then, racial anxiety or discomfort is not, in itself, racist (although it *can* be a manifestation of underlying racism). Yet it is still a bad thing, destructive to interracial relationships.

RACE, IDENTITY, AND RECOGNITION

Another race-related ill distinct from racism is illustrated in the following example. A Haitian-American girl is one of two black students in her class. When a race-related issue arises in discussion, the teacher turns to her and asks her what "the black point of view" is on the question at hand.

There seem several distinct though related wrongs this teacher has committed. He has failed to recognize Haitian-Americans as a distinct ethnic group within the larger "black" umbrella. He has treated a racial group in an overly homogeneous manner, implying that there could be something that could coherently be called "the black point of view" on an issue. Finally, he has failed to recognize the student as an individual, with her own individual views.

These three related forms of misrecognition are directed toward an individual or a group of which the individual is a member. The latter two—racial homogenization, and not acknowledging individuality—are particularly serious failings in a teacher. However, that is not to say that they are "racist." The teacher's behavior need not imply that he harbors animus toward blacks, or regards them as inferior.

RACIAL MOTIVES AND RACIAL STEREOTYPES

Confusion about both the location and the meaning of racism infected public understanding of a particularly tragic event that took place in Providence, Rhode Island, in January, 2000. Several women were fighting in a late-night diner. The night manager threw the patrons out of the diner, at which point some male friends got involved, one of whom drew a gun. Inside the diner, an off-duty patrolman, Cornel Young, Jr., an African-American, was waiting for a take-out order. Meanwhile, the police had been called to the scene outside. Officer Young, after warning the patrons to get down, rushed outside to help the two officers on the scene, his gun drawn. (Providence police are required to carry their firearms when off duty.)

The two officers had ordered the male friend to drop his gun, which he did, and they then turned to Officer Young and ordered him to do so as well. It is not clear whether Young heard the order, but in any case he did not comply, and the two officers, who were white, shot and killed him. It emerged that, despite the officers' failing to recognize Officer Young, one of the officers had been a police academy classmate of Young's, and both had graduated in the same class three years earlier.

The killing sparked community outrage and anguish. Charges of racism were made. It was said that the killing was "racially motivated." Eventually a federal civil rights investigation took place, and the two officers were cleared of having intended to deprive Officer Young of his civil rights, or of acting out of racial animosity.

It is impossible to know whether the two officers were racially biased against blacks. However, their behavior is perfectly consistent with their lacking any form of racial prejudice or racial motivation. It is not likely that they shot at Young because they disliked black people. Some people, recognizing this, then felt some relief. The incident turned from one involving racism to a (mere) "tragic accident."

But this response oversimplifies. Racism may be absent in motivations and attitudes but be present elsewhere. In this situation, it is much more plausible to think that it lay in the stereotypes that the officers carried in their minds about blacks. That is why, or part of why, they reacted to a black man with a gun in plainclothes as if he were a perpetrator, even though they actually knew him as a fellow officer. In another widely-reported case around the same time, four white officers in New York City killed an innocent black man whom they wrongly took to be reaching for a gun. Treating blackness as if it were an indicator of suspiciousness or criminality is referred to as "racial profiling" and has come in for a good deal of public criticism as a result of these and similar incidents, not only ones involving fatalities.

The white officers who killed Officer Young were apparently genuinely remorseful and upset by their having unwittingly killed a fellow officer. But this does not mean they were not prey to racial stereotypes linking blackness to criminality. Officer Young's mother was surely correct when she said that her son would be unlikely to have been shot had he been white. But it is important to be careful about what we mean if we say that he was killed "because he was black." If does not necessarily mean "out of hostility or animosity toward black persons." It could mean "because he was seen in the moment as a dangerous person and this was so in part because he was black." I believe it is also plausible to refer to this racial stereotype as "racist." But my point here is not so much to defend that position as to encourage clarity as to the location of what is, or was, racially objectionable in the situation. It was in the stereotype, not in the motives of the white officers. And it shows the tremendous danger that can accompany racist stereotypes even in the absence of racial antipathy; they can be life threatening.

I have given a stripped down version of this complex racial situation, and want to mention only two other points. First, some members of the community placed some of the blame on the Providence police department's failure to educate its police force about the dangers and wrong of racial stereotyping and racial profiling. That is, they have seen the fault in a kind of institutional irresponsibility regarding race, in the context of a recognition that antiblack stereotypes are particularly troubling in a police force that is meant to be protectors of their community.

The second race-related matter is more speculative on my part. Even though the white officers, and especially the one who graduated from the police academy with Office Young, knew him, it is possible that a form of racial homogenization was involved in their failure to recognize him. Perhaps the officer in some sense still saw all blacks, or black men, as "looking alike." Perhaps in the heat of the moment the image of blackness blocked his seeing Officer Young as an individual person. Racial thinking does, in general, inhibit the perception of others as individuals; the case of the teacher asking the black student for "the black point of view" would be another version of this same homogenization. Perhaps—again I am speculating—although the white officer did know Officer Young, whites and blacks did not interact much on or off the job; if so this social segregation might have contributed to the racial homogenization that in turn contributed to his failing to recognize Officer Young.

CONCLUSION

Gaining some clarity about what "racism" means will help us engage in productive conversations about racial matters—conversations that are too infrequent, both inside and outside classroom settings. We have seen three ways by which we might gain that clarity. First, within a given category (actions, jokes, stereotypes, remarks, stereotypes, persons), we should confine "racism" to especially egregious wrongs in that category. Not every stereotype is racist. Not every remark that is racially offensive is racist. Not every racially insensitive action is a racist action. I have suggested that the distinct opprobrium attaching to "racism" and "racist" can be retained and protected if we recognize that racism refers to racial inferiorization or racial antipathy, and that the different categorical forms of racism can all be related to either of those two definitions.

Second, we should not confuse racism in one category with racism in another. A person who is prey to a racist stereotype is not necessarily "a racist;" nor does she necessarily operate from racist motives. A remark can be unquestionably racist without the person making the remark being a racist, or making the remark for a racist reason, or motive.

Finally, in endeavoring to protect the distinct moral opprobrium of the accusation of "racism" from conceptual inflation and moral overload, as well as from categorical drift and confusion, we must at the same time recognize that "racism" by no means captures all of what can go wrong in the domain of race. There is a much larger terrain of moral ills in the racial domain than racism itself, and we should draw on our manifold linguistic resources—racial insensitivity, failure to recognize racial identity, racial ignorance, racial anxiety, racial injustice, racial homogenization, and so on—to express and describe moral disvalue in this domain. Moral concern is appropriately directed toward this wider domain, and should not be confined to racism appropriately so called.

NOTES

1. I do not believe that there are races in the sense in which "races" is generally understood in popular discourse, so I regard it as misleading to say that someone "is of a certain race." It is more accurate to say that someone has, or has been assigned, a racial designation, or that she is a member of a racial group; I will generally use the latter expression.

2. The black officer seemed clearly to be referring to lynching.

3. It is noteworthy that it was the newspaper article, rather than the NAACP itself, that called the networks "racist," or framed the issue as one of racism. Kweisi Mfume, the president of the NAACP, said only that the programming was "a virtual whitewash." *New York Times*, Sept 20, 1999, A1.

4. Of these listed, only "sexism" has fully succeeded in attaching moral condemnation to its referent—discrimination against, or the denial of dignity to, women, or discrimination on the basis of sex in general—in popular thought and speech.

5. In *"I'm Not a Racist, But . . . "* I argue that members of any group can be racist. For instance, I counter the view that only whites can be racist because only whites hold power as a racial group.

6. Stephan 1999 provides a wealth of information about how to improve intergroup relations in schools.

REFERENCES

Black, White Officers Cited in Noose Incident, *Boston Globe*, April 29, 1999, B1.

Blum, L. (2002). *I'm not a racist, but . . . The moral quandary of race.* Ithaca: Cornell University Press.

Margalit, A. (1996). *The decent society.* Cambridge: Harvard University Press.

Miles, R. (1989). *Racism.* London: Routledge.

Morrow, L. (1994). *Time, b*[12/5/94] *cited in Extra!*, vol. 9, #2, March/April 1996.

Nuechterlein, J., in *First things*, August-September, 1996, from *Chronicle of Higher Education*, September 6.

Schofield, J.W. (1989). *Black and white in school: Trust, tension, or tolerance?* New York: Teachers College Press.

Schuman, H., Steeh, C., Bobo, L. & Krysan, M. (1997). *Racial attitudes in America: Trends and interpretation*, revised edn. Cambridge: Harvard University Press.

Shipler, D.K. (1997). *A country of strangers: Blacks and whites in America.* New York: Vintage Books.

Stephan, W. (1999). *Reducing prejudice and stereotyping in schools.* New York: Teachers College Press.

Tizon, A., Whale killing uncovers anti-Indian hatred, *Boston Globe*, May 30, 1999.

Weinraub, B., Stung by criticism of fall shows, TV Networks add minority roles, *New York Times*, 1999.

Dear White America

GEORGE YANCY

I have a weighty request. As you read this letter, I want you to listen with love, a sort of love that demands that you look at parts of yourself that might cause pain and terror, as James Baldwin would say. Did you hear

that? You may have missed it. I repeat: *I want you to listen with love.* Well, at least try.

We don't talk much about the urgency of love these days, especially within the public sphere. Much of our discourses these days is about revenge, name calling, hate, and divisiveness. I have yet to hear it from our presidential hopefuls, or our political pundits. I don't mean the Hollywood type of love, but the scary kind, the kind that risks not being reciprocated, the kind that refuses to flee in the face of danger. To make it a bit easier for you, I've decided to model, as best as I can, what I'm asking of you. Let me demonstrate the vulnerability that I wish you to show. As a child of Socrates, James Baldwin and Audre Lorde, let me speak the truth, refuse to err on the side of caution.

This letter is a gift for you. Bear in mind, though that some gifts can be heavy to bear. You don't have to accept it; there is no obligation. I give it freely, believing that many of you will throw the gift back in my face, saying that I wrongly accuse you, that I am too sensitive, that I'm race hustler, and that I blame white people (you) for everything.

I have read many of your comments. I have even received some hate mail. In this letter, I ask you to look deep, to look into your souls with silence, to quiet that voice that will speak to you of your white "innocence." So, as you read this letter, take a deep breath. Make a space for my voice in the deepest part of your psyche. Try to listen, to practice being silent. There are times when you must quiet your own voice to hear from or about those who suffer in ways that you do not.

What if I told you that I'm sexist? Well, I am. Yes. I said it and I mean just that. I have watched my male students squirm in their seats when I've asked them to identify and talk about their sexism. There are few men, I suspect, who would say that they are sexists, and even fewer would admit that their sexism actually oppresses women. Certainly not publicly, as I've just done. No taking it back now.

To make things worse, I'm an academic, a philosopher. I'm supposed to be one of the "enlightened" ones. Surely, we are beyond being sexists. Some, who may genuinely care about my career, will say that I'm being too risky, that I am jeopardizing my academic livelihood. Some might even say that as a black male, who has already been stereotyped as a "crotch-grabbing, sexual fiend," that I'm at risk of reinforcing that stereotype. (Let's be real, that racist stereotype has been around for centuries; it is already part of white America's imaginary landscape.)

Yet, I refuse to remain a prisoner of the lies that we men like to tell ourselves—that we are beyond the messiness of sexism and male patriarchy, that we don't oppress women. Let me clarify. This doesn't mean that I intentionally hate women or that I desire to oppress them. It means that despite my best intentions, I perpetuate sexism every day of my life. Please don't take this as a confession for which I'm seeking forgiveness. Confessions can be easy, especially when we know that forgiveness is immediately forthcoming.

As a sexist, I have failed women. I have failed to speak out when I should have. I have failed to engage critically and extensively their pain and suffering in my writing. I have failed to transcend the rigidity of gender roles in my own life. I have failed to challenge those poisonous assumptions that women are "inferior" to men or to speak out loudly in the company of male philosophers who believe that feminist philosophy is just a nonphilosophical fad. I have been complicit with, and have allowed myself to be seduced by, a country that makes billions of dollars from sexually objectifying women, from pornography, commercials, video games, to Hollywood movies. I am not innocent.

I have been fed a poisonous diet of images that fragment women into mere body parts. I have also been complicit with a dominant male narrative that says that women enjoy being treated like sexual toys. In our collective male imagination, women are "things" to be used for our visual and physical titillation. And even as I know how poisonous and false these sexist assumptions are, I am often ambushed by my own hidden sexism. I continue to see women through the male gaze that belies my best intentions not to sexually objectify them. Our collective male erotic feelings and fantasies are complicit in the degradation of women. And we must be mindful that not all women endure sexual degradation in the same way.

I recognize how my being a sexist has a differential impact on black women and women of color who are not only victims of racism, but also sexism, *my sexism*. For example, black women and women of color not only suffer from sexual objectification, but the ways in which they are objectified is linked to how they are racially depicted, some as "exotic" and others as "hyper-sexual." You see, the complicity, the responsibility, the pain that I cause runs deep. And, get this. I refuse to seek shelter; I refuse to live a lie. So, every day of my life I fight against the dominant male narrative, choosing to see women as subjects, not objects. But even as I fight, there are moments of failure. Just because I fight against sexism does not give me clean hands, as it were, at the end of the day; I continue to falter, and I continue to oppress. And even though the ways in which I oppress women is unintentional, this does not free me of being responsible.

If you are white, and you are reading this letter, I ask that you don't run to seek shelter from your own racism. Don't hide from your responsibility. Rather, begin, right now, to practice being vulnerable. Being neither a "good" white person nor a liberal white person will get you off the proverbial hook. I consider myself to be a decent human being. Yet, I'm sexist. Take another deep breath. I ask that you try to be "un-sutured." If that term brings to mind a state of pain, open flesh, it is meant to do so. After all, it is painful to let go of your "White innocence," to use this letter as a mirror, one that refuses to show you what you want to see, one that demands that you look at the lies that you tell yourself so that you don't feel the weight of responsibility for those who live under the yoke of whiteness, your whiteness.

I can see your anger. I can see that this letter is being misunderstood. This letter is not asking you to feel bad about yourself, to wallow in guilt. That is too easy. I'm asking for you to tarry, to linger, with the ways in which you perpetuate a racist society, the ways in which you are racist. I'm now daring you to face a racist history which, paraphrasing Baldwin, has placed you where you are and that has formed your own racism. Again, in the sprit of Baldwin, I am asking you to enter into battle with your white self. I'm asking that you open yourself up; to speak to, to admit to, the racist poison that is inside of you.

Again, take a deep breath. Don't tell me about how many black friends you have. Don't tell me that you are married to someone of color. Don't tell me that you voted for Obama. Don't tell me that *I'm* the racist. Don't tell me that you don't see color. Don't tell

me that I'm blaming whites for everything. To do so is to hide yet again. You may have never used the N-word in your life, you may hate the K.K.K., but that does not mean that you don't harbor racism and benefit from racism. After all, you are part of a system that allows you to walk into stores where you are not followed, where you get to go for a bank loan and your skin does not count against you, where you don't need to engage in "the talk" that black people and people of color must tell their children when they are confronted by white police officers.

As you reap comfort from being white, we suffer for being black and people of color. But your comforts is linked to our pain and suffering. Just as my comfort in being male is linked to the suffering of women, which makes me sexist, so, too, you are racist. That is the gift that I want you to accept, to embrace. It is a form of knowledge that is taboo. Imagine the impact that the acceptance of this gift might have on you and the world.

Take another deep breath. I know that there are those who will write to me in the comment section with boiling anger, sarcasm, disbelief, denial. There are those who will say, "Yancy is just an angry black man." There are others who will say, "Why isn't Yancy telling black people to be honest about the violence in their own black neighborhoods?" Or, "How can Yancy say that all white people are racists?" If you are saying these things, then you've already failed to listen. I come with a gift. You're already rejecting the gift that I have to offer. This letter is about *you*. Don't change the conversation. I assure you that so many black people suffering from poverty and joblessness, which is linked to high levels of crime, are painfully aware of the existential toll that they have had to face because they are black and, as Baldwin adds, *"for no other reason."*

Some of your white brothers and sisters have made this leap. The legal scholar Stephanie M. Wildman, has written, "I simply believe that no matter how hard I work at not being racist, I still am. Because part of racism is systemic, I benefit from the privilege that I am struggling to see." And the journalism professor Robert Jensen: "I like to think I have changed, even though I routinely trip over the lingering effects of that internalized racism and the institutional racism around me. Every time I walk into a store at the same times as a black man and the security guard follows him and leaves me alone to shop, I am benefiting from white privilege."

What I'm asking is that you first accept the racism within yourself, accept all of the truth about what it means for you to be white in a society that was created for you. I'm asking for you to trace the blinds that tie you to forms of domination that you would rather not see. When you walk into the world, you can walk with assurance; you have already signed a contract, so to speak, that guarantees you a certain form of social safety.

Baldwin argues for a form of love that is "a state of being, or state of grace–not in the infantile American sense of being made happy but in the tough and universal sense of quest and daring and growth." Most of my days, I'm engaged in a personal and society battle against sexism. So many times, I fail. And so many times, I'm complicit. But I refuse to hide behind that mirror that lies to me about my "non-sexist nobility." Baldwin says, "Love takes off the masks that we fear we cannot live without and know we cannot live within." In my heart, I'm done with the mask of sexism, though I'm tempted every day to wear it. And, there are times when it still gets the better of me.

White America, are you prepared to be at war with yourself, your white identity, your white power, your white privilege? Are you prepared to show me a white self that love has unmasked? I'm asking for love in return for a gift; in fact, I'm hoping that this gift might help you to see yourself in ways that you have not seen before. Of course, the history of white supremacy in American belies this gesture of black gift-giving, this gesture of non-sentimental love. Martin Luther King Jr. was murdered even as he loved.

Perhaps the language of this letter will encourage a split—not a split between black and white, but a fissure in your understanding, a space for loving a Trayvon Martin, Eric Garner, Tamir Rice, Aiyana Jones, Sandra Bland, Laquan McDonald and others. I'm suggesting a form of love that enables you to see the role that you play (even despite your anti-racist actions) in a *system* that continues to value black lives on the cheap.

Take one more deep breath. I have another gift.

If you have young children, before you fall off to sleep tonight, I want you to hold your child. Touch your child's face. Smell your child's hair. Count the fingers on your child's hand. See the miracle that is your child. And then, with as much vision as you can muster, I want you to imagine that your child is black.

In peace,
George Yancy

Uses and Abuses of the Discourse of White Privilege

Naomi Zack

White privilege in real life is something real that exists. White privilege *discourse* is thought, talk, and writing about white privilege—it is not the thing itself.

Our present idea of white privilege was introduced by Peggy McIntosh in 1989: "White privilege is like

Naomi Zack, "Uses and Abuses of the Discourse of White Privilege," Philosopher (blog), June 24, 2016, politicalphilosopher.net. Reprinted with permission.

an invisible weightless knapsack of special provisions, maps, passports, codebooks, visas, clothes, tools and blank checks." The idea lives on in exhortations to *Check your privilege!* on college campuses and through broader public and social media. But the *discourse* of white privilege is problematic from two angles—it goes too far in blaming all whites for all forms of racism and it does not go far enough in directly addressing injustice against nonwhites. Both perspectives are worth consideration but the second is more important because it involves violations of fundamental human rights.

Whites cannot call or email or log onto a Bureau of White Privilege to check their white accounts, draw on their white assets, withdraw white funds, or use white credits to make purchases. But whites are generally better off than nonwhites—in health, wealth, freedom, education, longevity, and a host of other human goods. That is, although overt oppression expressed by an official ideology of white supremacy is largely past in our post-civil rights era of formal equality, racist historical effects persist. White (European and American) "privileges" endure. White privilege is a network of dispositions in society whereby individuals behave differently, that is, better to whites than nonwhites, solely because whites are white. Attitudes, beliefs, and emotions are the internal psychic component of white privilege and they include freedom from worrying about or suffering from racism.

However, not all whites, all of the time, enjoy privileges compared to nonwhites or are responsible for the comparative disadvantages of nonwhites. And even though some whites may be complicit with the racism of others, their expressed non-racist views and cultural contributions should not be dismissed solely on the grounds of their race. That is, to shut down speech just because it is uttered by a white person would be unfair and when racial *ad hominem* is robustly denounced on behalf of people of color, the fallacy should be recognized in an even-handed way. (We continue to be shocked by Kant's, "This fellow was quite black . . . a clear proof that what he said was stupid.") Still, "Check your privilege!" or white privilege discourse has more serious pitfalls than such insults to white people. The discourse seems to be incapable of addressing injustice against people of color.

In progressive, left-liberal society, it is virtuous not to exaggerate one's disadvantage or ignore unfair or unearned advantage. The motivation for white privilege discourse is that the person being asked or told to check her privilege will be ashamed after recognizing that she has unfair or unearned advantages solely due to being white—and that insight will serve social justice. It's as though the discourse of foodies about their abundant culinary choices and self-indulgent practices could correct the problems of world hunger!

White privilege discourse is largely about the facts of white racial advantage and what white people think and feel about that. Building awareness of racial imbalances is progressive. But as a leading response to contemporary injustice, white privilege discourse may miss the importance of racial injustice and degenerate into just another display of the advantages that white people have of not being required to respond to racial injustice against their racial group. After all, and for the most part, whites are treated justly, in wealthy, democratic, capitalistic societies.

Awareness by whites of their privilege, in an ongoing discourse that whites conduct, is neither cognitively nor rhetorically adequate for addressing injustice. If black people can be killed or executed by police officers, without trial or even the appearance of criminal action, while white people are left alone, this is not wholly or solely a matter of white privilege. Yes, white people are better off, but to confine resistance to the injustice done to nonwhites to discourse about how whites are privileged in being left alone (i.e., to only talk about white privilege), minimizes or trivializes the injustice against nonwhites. This injustice could only be wholly or solely a matter of white privilege if we lived in and accepted the norms of a maximally repressive totalitarian society where it was customary for government officials to execute anyone without trial or even the appearance of criminal action. Against that background, we could say that those who were not treated that way were privileged. They would be privileged in enjoying that perk of exceptional leniency. But we do not live in such a system or accept a normative totalitarian description of the system we do live in. We live in a system where everyone, regardless of race is supposed to have the same basic rights. That nonwhites are not recognized as having these rights is not a privilege of whites, but a violation of the rights of nonwhites.

Nevertheless, human rights have only an ideal status. Philosophically they are only posits and morally those who are outraged by the injustice of rights violation have little power. But, the basis for outrage concerning the recent high profile cases of summary execution of unarmed young black men by police officers is a *legal* issue, a matter of positive law in U.S. jurisdictions. U.S. citizens are constitutionally protected by certain rights that most, especially whites, still correctly assume are in force for them: the right to privacy from unjustified government search and seizure (where death is a form of seizure); the right to due process; the right to equal protection by government officials.

The Fourth Amendment states that "the people" have a right "to be secure in their persons, houses, papers, and effects, against unreasonable searches and seizures. . . but upon probable cause." The Fourteenth Amendment reads in part that that no state shall "deny to any person within its jurisdiction the equal protection of the laws." Police racial profiling followed by summary execution violates both amendments. However, these constitutional rights have been steadily eroded by the U.S. Supreme Court in recent decades. In *Graham v. Connor* in 1989, the Justices ruled that claims that police have used excessive force must be analyzed under an "objective reasonableness" standard referring to officer behavior, rather than rules of due process or probable cause. In *Plumhoff et al. v. Richard* (2012), the Court ruled that Fourth Amendment rights must be balanced against the "qualified immunity" of officers. These rulings and similar ones come to bear in cases like the shooting of Michael Brown, where all an officer need do to avoid indictment or conviction for manslaughter or murder is claim that he believed his life was in danger.

To protect the rights of minorities against police—really everyone's rights, but the recent killings of unarmed young men concern minorities—it will likely be necessary to revisit at least *Graham* and *Plumhoff*. The civil rights movement of the 1950s and 60s were led by impassioned and brilliant lawyers, constantly bringing cases before the courts. These days, the legal cases that get the most attention are those aimed at dismantling affirmative action. Yes, whites are privileged, but no amount of exhortation to "check " their privilege or confessional discourse in response, will correct the legal injustice of police homicide based on racial profiling.

Police racial profiling and is attendant violence is not the only form of rights violation that corresponds to nonwhite race in the United States and is neglected by white privilege discourse. Unequal educational resources in materials and teacher skills have persisted after *Brown v. Board of Education* called for integrated education "with all deliberate speed" in 1954. But K-12 schools are funded by local property taxes that are directly related to real estate values. It's been widely publicized since the 1970s that the differences in tax-based educational resources per child are as much as 1000 percent between mainly black and brown neighborhoods, as residential racial segregation has persisted due to differences in wealth and income, along with social preferences regarding the race of neighbors. All modern democracies uphold public education as a fundamental right at this time, but that right cannot be fully implemented in the United States given the disparities in opportunities for children that result from ongoing residential segregation. No amount of positive descriptions of the privileges of white middle class school children mitigates the deprivations of poor nonwhite children who do not have comparable learning opportunities. Needed is egalitarian educational reform to enlarge those opportunities. No amount or intensity of discourse about the privilege of white children a few blocks away could fill in for what poor nonwhite children lack. And again, if equal adequate education is a right, a structure in which nonwhite children are deprived of that right is a problem of injustice in and of itself. And that problem is not addressed by talking about the fact that white children enjoy the right! (That there are structural inequalities that perpetuate rights violations of nonwhites underscores the importance of resistance that attends to rights instead of privileges.)

The Case Against Affirmative Action

Louis P. Pojman

Hardly a week goes by but that the subject of Affirmative Action does not come up. Whether in the form of preferential hiring, nontraditional casting, quotas, "goals and time tables," minority scholarships, race-norming, reverse discrimination, or employment of members of underutilized groups, the issue confronts us as a terribly perplexing problem. Affirmative action was one of the issues that divided the Democratic and Republican parties during the 1996 election, the Democrats supporting it ("Mend it don't end it") and the Republicans opposing it ("affirmative action is reverse racism"). During the last general election (November 7, 1996) California voters by a 55% to 45% vote approved Proposition 209 (called the "California Civil Rights Initiative") which made it illegal to discriminate on the basis of race or gender, hence ending Affirmative Action in public institutions in California. The Supreme Court recently refused to rule on the appeal, thus leaving it to the individual states to decide how they will deal with this issue. Both sides have reorganized for a renewed battle. Meanwhile, on Nov. 11, 1977, the European Union's High Court of Justice in Luxembourg approved Affirmative Action programs giving women preferential treatment in the 15 European Union countries.

Let us agree that despite the evidences of a booming economy, the poor are suffering grievously, with children being born into desperate material and psychological poverty; for them the ideal of "equal opportunity for all" is a cruel joke. Many feel that the federal government has abandoned its guarantee to provide the minimum necessities for each American, so that the pace of this tragedy seems to be worsening daily. In addition to this, African-Americans have a legacy of slavery and unjust discrimination to contend with, and other minorities have also suffered from injustice.

Louis Pojman, "The Case Against Affirmative Action" from *International Journal of Applied Philosophy*, 1998, Vol. 12, No.1, pp. 97–115. Reprinted by permission of Philosophy Documentation Center.

Women have their own peculiar history of being treated unequally in relevant ways. What is the answer to this national problem? Is it increased welfare? More job training? More support for education? Required licensing of parents to have children? Negative income tax? More support for families or for mothers with small children? All of these have merit and should be part of the national debate. But, my thesis is, however tragic the situation may be (and we may disagree on just how tragic it is), one policy is *not* a legitimate part of the solution and that is *reverse, unjust discrimination* against young white males. Strong Affirmative Action, which implicitly advocates reverse discrimination, while no doubt well intentioned, is morally heinous, asserting, by implication, that *two wrongs make a right*.

The *Two Wrongs Make a Right* Thesis goes like this: Because *some* Whites once enslaved some Blacks, the descendants of those slaves (some of whom may now enjoy high incomes and social status) have a right to opportunities and offices over better qualified Whites who had nothing to do with either slavery or the oppression of Blacks (and who may even have suffered hardship comparable to that of poor Blacks). In addition, Strong Affirmative Action creates a new Hierarchy of the Oppressed: Blacks get primary preferential treatment, women second, Native Americans third, Hispanics fourth, Handicapped fifth, and Asians sixth and so on until White males, no matter how needy or well qualified, must accept the leftovers. Naturally, combinations of oppressed classes (e.g., a one-eyed, Black Hispanic female) trump all single classifications. The equal protection clause of the Fourteenth Amendment becomes reinterpreted as "Equal protection for all equals, but some equals are more equal than others."

Before analyzing arguments concerning Affirmative Action, I must define my terms.

By *Weak Affirmative Action* I mean policies that will increase the opportunities of disadvantaged people to attain social goods and offices. It includes such things as dismantling of segregated institutions, widespread advertisement to groups not previously represented in certain privileged positions, special scholarships for the disadvantaged classes (e.g., the poor, regardless of race or gender), and even using diversity or under-representation of groups with a history of past discrimination as a tie breaker when candidates for these goods and offices are relatively equal. The goal of *Weak Affirmative Action* is equal opportunity to compete, not equal results. We seek to provide each citizen regardless of race or gender a fair chance to the most favored positions in society. There is no more moral requirement to guarantee that 12% of professors are Black than to guarantee that 85% of the players in the National Basketball Association are White.

By *Strong Affirmative Action* I mean preferential treatment on the basis of race, ethnicity or gender (or some other morally irrelevant criterion), discriminating in favor of underrepresented groups against overrepresented groups, aiming at roughly equal results. *Strong Affirmative Action* is *reverse discrimination*. It says it is right to do wrong to correct a wrong. This is the policy currently being promoted under the name of *Affirmative Action,* so I will use that term or "AA" for short throughout this essay to stand for this version of affirmative action. I will not argue for or against the principle of *Weak Affirmative Action.* Indeed, I think it has some moral weight. *Strong Affirmative Action* has none, or so I will argue.

This essay concentrates on AA policies with regard to race, but the arguments can be extended to cover ethnicity and gender. I think that if a case for Affirmative Action can be made it will be as a corrective to racial oppression. I will examine [nine] arguments regarding AA. The first six will be *negative,* attempting to show that the best arguments for Affirmative Action fail. The last three will be *positive* arguments for policies opposing Affirmative Action.

I. A CRITIQUE OF ARGUMENTS FOR AFFIRMATIVE ACTION

A. The Need for Role Models

This argument is straightforward. We all have need of role models, and it helps to know that others like us can be successful. We learn and are encouraged to strive for excellence by emulating our heroes and "our kind of people" who have succeeded.

In the first place it's not clear that role models of one's own racial or sexual type are necessary (let alone sufficient) for success. One of my heroes was Gandhi, an Indian Hindu, another was my grade school science teacher, Miss DeVoe, and another Martin Luther King, behind whom I marched in Civil Rights demonstrations. More important than having role models of one's "own type" is having genuinely good people, of whatever race or gender, to emulate. Our common humanity should be a sufficient basis for us to see the possibility of success in people of virtue and merit. To yield to the demand, however tempting it may be, for "role-models-just-like-us" is to treat people like means not ends. It is to elevate morally irrelevant particularity over relevant traits, such as ability and integrity. We don't need people exactly like us to find inspiration. As Steve Allen once quipped, "If I had to follow a role model exactly, I would have become a nun."

Furthermore, even if it is of some help to people with low self-esteem to gain encouragement from seeing others of their particular kind in successful positions, it is doubtful whether this is a sufficient reason to justify preferential hiring or reverse discrimination. What good is a role model who is inferior to other professors or physicians or business personnel? The best way to create role models is to promote people because they are the best qualified for the job. It is the violation of this fact that is largely responsible for the widespread whisper in the medical field (at least in New York), "Never go to a Black physician under 40" (referring to the fact that AA has affected the medical system during the past twenty years). Fight the feeling how I will, I cannot help wondering on seeing a Black or woman in a position of honor, "Is she in this position because she merits it or because of Affirmative Action?" Where Affirmative Action is the policy, the "figment of pigment" creates a stigma of undeservedness, whether or not it is deserved.[1]

Finally, entertain this thought experiment. Suppose we discovered that tall handsome white males somehow made the best role models for the most people, especially poor people. Suppose even large numbers of minority people somehow found inspiration in their sight. Would we be justified in hiring tall handsome white males over better qualified short Hispanic women, who were deemed less role-model worthy?

B. The Compensation Argument

The argument goes like this: blacks have been wronged and severely harmed by whites. Therefore white society should compensate blacks for the injury caused them. Reverse discrimination in terms of preferential hiring, contracts, and scholarships is a fitting way to compensate for the past wrongs.

This argument actually involves a distorted notion of compensation. Normally, we think of compensation as owed by a specific person A to another person B whom A has wronged in a specific way C. For example, if I have made $5,000 and only have $10,000 in assets, it would not be possible for you to collect $20,000 in damages—even though that is the amount of loss you have incurred.

Sometimes compensation is extended to groups of people who have been unjustly harmed by the greater society. For example, the United States government has compensated the Japanese-Americans who were interred during the Second World War, and the West German government has paid reparations to the survivors of Nazi concentration camps. But here a specific people have been identified who were wronged in an identifiable way by the government of the nation in question.

On the face of it, demands by blacks for compensation do not fit the usual pattern. Southern States with Jim Crow laws could be accused of unjustly harming blacks, but it is hard to see that the United States government was involved in doing so. Much of the harm done to blacks was the result of private discrimination, not state action. So the Germany/US analogy doesn't hold. Furthermore, it is not clear that all blacks were harmed in the same way or whether some were *unjustly* harmed or harmed more than poor whites and others (e.g., short people). Finally, even if identifiable blacks were harmed by identifiable social practices, it is not clear that most forms of Affirmative Action are appropriate to restore the situation. The usual practice of a financial payment seems more appropriate than

giving a high level job to someone unqualified or only minimally qualified, who, speculatively, might have been better qualified had he not been subject to racial discrimination. If John is the star tailback of our college team with a promising professional future, and I accidentally (but culpably) drive my pickup truck over his legs, and so cripple him, John may be due compensation, but he is not due the tailback spot on the football team.

Still, there may be something intuitively compelling about compensating members of an oppressed group who are minimally qualified. Suppose that the Hatfields and the McCoys are enemy clans and some youths from the Hatfields go over and steal diamonds and gold from the McCoys, distributing it within the Hatfield economy. Even though we do not know which Hatfield youths did the stealing, we would want to restore the wealth, as far as possible, to the McCoys. One way might be to tax the Hatfields, but another might be to give preferential treatment in terms of scholarships and training programs and hiring to the McCoys.

This is perhaps the strongest argument for Affirmative Action, and it may well justify some weaker versions of AA, but it is doubtful whether it is sufficient to justify strong versions with quotas and goals and time tables in skilled positions. There are at least two reasons for this. First, we have no way of knowing how many people of any given group would have achieved some given level of competence had the world been different. This is especially relevant if my objections to the Equal Results Argument (below) are correct. Secondly, the normal criterion of competence is a strong prima facie consideration when the most important positions are at stake. There are three reasons for this: (1) treating people according to their merits respects them as persons, as ends in them-selves, rather than as means to social ends (if we believe that individuals possess a dignity which deserves to be respected, then we ought to treat that individual on the basis of his or her merits, not as a mere instrument for social policy); (2) society has given people expectations that if they attain certain levels of excellence they will be awarded appropriately; and (3) filling the most important positions with the best qualified is the best way to ensure efficiency in job-related areas and in society in general. These reasons are not absolutes. They can be over-ridden.[2] But there is a strong presumption in their favor, so that a burden of proof rests with those who would override them.

At this point we get into the problem of whether innocent non-blacks should have to pay a penalty in terms of preferential hiring of blacks. We turn to that argument.

C. The Argument for Compensation from Those Who Innocently Benefitted from Past Injustice

Young White males as innocent beneficiaries of unjust discrimination against blacks and women have no grounds for complaint when society seeks to level the tilted field. They may be innocent of oppressing blacks, other minorities, and women, but they have unjustly benefited from that oppression or discrimination. So it is perfectly proper that less qualified women and blacks be hired before them.

The operative principle is: He who knowingly and willingly benefits from a wrong must help pay for the wrong. Judith Jarvis Thomson puts it this way. "Many [white males] have been direct beneficiaries of policies which have downgraded blacks and women . . . and even those who did not directly benefit . . . had, at any rate, the advantage in the competition which comes of the confidence in one's full membership [in the community], and of one's right being recognized as a matter of course."[3] That is, white males obtain advantages in self-respect and self-confidence deriving from a racist/sexist system which denies these to blacks and women.

Here is my response to this argument: As I noted in the previous section, compensation is normally individual and specific. If A harms B regarding x, B has a right to compensation from A in regards to x. If A steals B's car and wrecks it, A has an obligation to compensate B for the stolen car, but A's son has no obligation to compensate B. Furthermore, if A dies or disappears, B has no moral right to claim that society compensate him for the stolen car—though if he has insurance, he can make such a claim to the insurance company. Sometimes a wrong cannot be compensated, and we just have to make the best of an imperfect world.

Suppose my parents, divining that I would grow up to have an unsurpassable desire to be a basketball player, bought an expensive growth hormone for me. Unfortunately, a neighbor stole it and gave it to little Michael, who gained the extra 13 inches—my 13 inches—and shot up to an enviable 6 feet 6 inches. Michael, better known as Michael Jordan, would have been a runt like me but for his luck. As it is he profited from the injustice, and excelled in basketball, as I would have done had I had my proper dose.

Do I have a right to the millions of dollars that Jordan made as a professional basketball player—the unjustly innocent beneficiary of my growth hormone? I have a right to something from the neighbor who stole the hormone and it might be kind of Jordan to give me free tickets to the [Bulls] basketball games, and remember me in his will. As far as I can see, however, he does not *owe* me anything, either legally or morally.

Suppose further that Michael Jordan and I are in high school together and we are both qualified to play basketball, only he is far better than I. Do I deserve to start in his position because I would have been as good as he is had someone not cheated me as a child? Again, I think not. But if being the lucky beneficiary of wrongdoing does not entail that Jordan (or the coach) owes me anything in regards to basketball, why should it be a reason to engage in preferential hiring in academic positions or highly coveted jobs? If minimal qualifications are not adequate to override excellence in basketball, even when the minimality is a consequence of wrongdoing, why should they be adequate in other areas?

D. The Diversity Argument

It is important that we learn to live in a pluralistic world, learning to get along with those of other races, conditions, and cultures, so we should have schools and employment situations as fully integrated as possible. In a shrinking world we need to appreciate each other's culture and specific way of looking at life. Diversity is an important symbol and educative device. Thus, proponents of AA argue, preferential treatment is warranted to perform this role in society.

Once again, there is some truth in these concerns. Diversity of ideas challenges us to scrutinize our own values and beliefs, and diverse customs have aesthetic and moral value, helping us to appreciate the novelty and beauty in life. Diversity may expand our moral horizons. But, again, while we can admit the value of diversity, it hardly seems adequate to over-ride the moral requirement to treat each person with equal respect. *Diversity for diversity's sake is moral promiscuity,* since it obfuscates rational distinctions, undermines treating individuals as ends, treating them, instead, as mere means (to the goals of social engineering), and, furthermore, unless those hired are highly qualified, the diversity factor threatens to become a fetish. At least at the higher levels of business and the professions, *competence* far outweighs considerations of diversity. I do not care whether the group of surgeons operating on me reflect racial or gender balance, but I do care that they are highly qualified. Neither do most football or basketball fans care whether their team reflects ethnic and gender diversity, but demand the best combination of players available. And likewise with airplane pilots, military leaders, business executives, and, may I say it, teachers and university professors. One need not be a white male to teach, let alone appreciate, Shakespeare, nor need one be Black to teach, let alone appreciate, Alice Walker's *Color Purple.*

There may be times when diversity may be seem to be "crucial" to the well-being of a diverse community, such as for a police force. Suppose that White policemen tend to overreact to young Black males and the latter group distrust white policemen. Hiring more less qualified Black policemen, who would relate better to these youth, may have overall utilitarian value. But such a move, while we might take it as a lesser evil, could have serious consequences in allowing the demographic prejudices to dictate social policy. A better strategy would be to hire the best police, that is, those who can perform in disciplined, intelligent manner, regardless of their race. A White policeman must be able to arrest a Black burglar, even as a Black policeman must be able to arrest a White rapist. The quality of the police man or woman, not their race or gender is what counts.

On the other hand, if a Black policeman, though lacking some of the formal skills of the White policeman, really is able to do better job in the Black community, this might constitute a case of merit, not Affirmative Action. As Stephen Kershnar points out, this is similar to the legitimacy of hiring Chinese men to act as undercover agents in Chinatown.[4]

E. The Equal Results Argument

Some philosophers and social scientists hold that human nature is roughly identical, so that on a fair playing field the same proportion from every race and ethnic group and both genders would attain to the highest positions in every area of endeavor. It would follow that any inequality of results itself is evidence for inequality of opportunity.

> History is important when considering governmental rules like Test 21 because low scores by blacks can be traced in large measure to the legacy of slavery and racism: segregation, poor schooling, exclusion from trade unions, malnutrition, and poverty have all played their roles. Unless one assumes that blacks are naturally less able to pass the test, the conclusion must be that the results are themselves socially and legally constructed, not a mere given for which law and society can claim no responsibility.
>
> The conclusion seems to be that genuine equality eventually requires equal results. Obviously blacks have been treated unequally throughout US history, and just as obviously the economic and psychological effects of that inequality linger to this day, showing up in lower income and poorer performance in school and on tests than whites achieve. Since we have no reason to believe that differences in performance can be explained by factors other than history, equal results are a good benchmark by which to measure progress made toward genuine equality. (John Arthur, *The Unfinished Constitution* [Belmont, CA: Wadsworth Publishing Co, 1990], p. 238)

Sterling Harwood seems to support a similar theory when he writes, "When will [AA] end? When will affirmative action stop compensating blacks? As soon as the unfair advantage is gone, affirmative action will stop. The elimination of the unfair advantage can be determined by showing that the percentage of blacks hired and admitted at least roughly equaled the percentage of blacks in the population."[5]

Albert G. Mosley develops a similar argument. "Establishing Blacks' presence at a level commensurate with their proportion in the relevant labor market need not be seen as an attempt to actualize some valid prediction. Rather, given the impossibility of determining what level of representation Blacks would have achieved were it not for racial discrimination, the assumption of proportional representation is the only *fair* assumption to make. This is not to argue that Blacks should be maintained in such positions, but their contrived exclusion merits equally contrived rectification."[6] The result of a just society should be equal numbers in proportion to each group in the work force.

However, Arthur, Mosley, and Harwood fail even to consider studies that suggest that there are innate differences between races, sexes, and groups. If there are genetic differences in intelligence, temperament, and other qualities within families, why should we not expect such differences between racial groups and the two genders? Why should the evidence for this be completely discounted?

Mosley's reasoning is as follows: Since we don't know for certain whether groups proportionately differ in talent, we should presume that they are equal in every respect. So we should presume that if we were living in a just society, there would be roughly proportionate representation in every field (e.g., equal representation of doctors, lawyers, professors, carpenters, airplane pilots, basketball players, and criminals). Hence, it is only fair—productive of justice—to aim at proportionate representation in these fields.

But the logic is flawed. Under a situation of ignorance we should not presume equality or inequality of representation—but conclude that we *don't know* what the results would be in a just society. Ignorance doesn't favor equal group representation any more than it favors unequal representation. It is neutral between them.

Consider this analogy. Suppose that you were the owner of a National Basketball Association team. Suppose that I and other frustrated White basketball players bring a class-action suit against you and all the other team owners, claiming that you have subtly

and systematically discriminated against White and Asian basketball players who make up less than 20% of the NBA players. You reply that you and the other owners are just responding to individual merit, we respond that the discrimination is a function of deep prejudice against White athletes, especially basketball players, who are discouraged in every way from competing on fair terms with Blacks who dominate the NBA. You would probably wish that the matter of unequal results was not brought up in the first place, but once it has been, would you not be in your rights to defend yourself by producing evidence, showing that *average* physiological differences exist between Blacks and Whites and Asians, so that we should not presume unjust discrimination?

Similarly, the proponents of the Doctrine of Equal Results open the door to a debate over average ability in ethnic, racial and gender groups. The proponent of equal or fair opportunity would just as soon downplay this feature in favor of judging people as individuals by their merit (hard though that may be). But if the proponent of AA insists on the Equal Results Thesis, we are obliged to examine the Equal Results Thesis, we are obliged to examine the Equal Abilities Thesis, on which it is based—the thesis that various ethnic and gender groups all have the same distribution of talent on the relevant characteristic. With regard to cognitive skills we must consult the best evidence we have on average group differences. We need to compare average IQ scores, SAT scores, standard personality testing, success in academic and professional areas and the like. If the evidence shows that group differences are nonexistent, the AA proponent may win, but if the evidence turns out to be against the Equal Abilities Thesis, the AA proponent loses. Consider for a start that the average white and Asian scores 195 points higher on the SAT tests and that on virtually all IQ tests for the past seven or eight decades the average Black IQ is 85 as opposed to the average White and Asian IQ at over 100, or that males and females differ significantly on cognitive ability tests. Females outperform males in reading comprehension, perceptual speed, and associative memory (ratios of 1.4 to 2.2), but males typically outnumber females among high scoring individuals in mathematics, science and social science (by a ratio of 7.0 in the top 1% of overall mathematics distribu-tion).[7] The results of average GRE, LSAT, MCAT scores show similar patterns or significant average racial dif-ference. The Black scholar Glenn Loury notes, "In 1990 black high school seniors from families with annual incomes of $70,000 or more scored an average of 855 on the SAT, compared with average scores of 855 and 879 respectively for Asian-American and white seniors whose families had incomes between $10,000 and 20,000 per year."[8] Note, we are speaking about statisti-cal averages. There are brilliant and retarded people in each group.

When such statistics are discussed many people feel uncomfortable and want to drop the subject. Per-haps these statistics are misleading, but then we need to look carefully at the total evidence. The proponent of equal opportunity urges us to get beyond racial and gender criteria in assignment of offices and opportuni-ties and treat each person, not as an *average* White or Black or female or male, but as a *person* judged on his or her own merits.

Furthermore, on the logic of Mosley and com-pany, we should take aggressive AA against Asians and Jews since they are overrepresented in science, tech-nology, and medicine, and we should presume that Asians and Jews are no more talented than average. So that each group receives its fair share, we should ensure that 12% of the philosophers in the United States are Black, reduce the percentage of Jews from an estimated 15% to 2%—thus firing about 1,300 Jew-ish philosophers. The fact that Asians are producing 50% of Ph.D.s in science and math in this country and blacks less than 1% clearly shows, on this reason-ing, that we are providing special secret advantages to Asians. By this logic, we should reduce the quota of Blacks in the NBA to 12%.

But why does society have to enter into this results game in the first place? Why do we have to decide whether all difference is environmental or genetic? Perhaps we should simply admit that we lack suffi-cient evidence to pronounce on these issues with any certainty—but if so, should we not be more modest in insisting on equal results? Here's a thought experi-ment. Take two families of different racial groups, Green and Blue. The Greens decide to have only two children, to spend all their resources on them, and to give them the best possible education. The two Green kids respond well and end up with achievement test scores in the 99th percentile. The Blues fail to prac-tice family planning and have 15 children. They can only afford 2 children, but lack of ability or whatever prevents them from keeping their family size down. Now they need help for their large family. Why does society have to step in and help them? Society did not force them to have 15 children. Suppose that the achievement test scores of the 15 children fall below the 25th percentile. They cannot compete with the Greens. But now enters AA. It says that it is society's fault that the Blue children are not as able as the Greens and that the Greens must pay extra taxes to enable the Blues to compete. No restraints are put on the Blues regarding family size. This seems unfair to the Greens. Should the Green children be made to bear responsibility for the consequences of the Blue's voluntary behavior?

My point is simply that philosophers like Arthur, Harwood, and Mosley need to cast their net wider and recognize that demographics and childbearing and -rearing practices are crucial factors in achieve-ment. People have to take some responsibility for their actions. The equal results argument (or axiom) misses a greater part of the picture.

F. THE "NO ONE DESERVES HIS TALENTS" ARGUMENT AGAINST MERITOCRACY

According to this argument, the competent do not deserve their intelligence, their superior charac-ter, their industriousness, or their discipline; there-fore they have no right to the best positions in society; therefore it is not unjust to give these positions to less (but still minimally) qualified blacks and women. In one form this argument holds that since no one deserves anything, society may use any critertia it pleases to distribute goods. The criterion most often designated is social utility. Versions of this argument are found in the writings of John Arthur, John Rawls, Bernard Boxill, Michael Kinsley, Ronald Dworkin, and Richard Wasserstrom. Rawls writes, "No one deserves his place in the distribution of native endowments, any more than one deserves one's initial starting place in society. The assertion that a man deserves the superior character that enables him to make the effort to cultivate his abilities is equally problematic; for his character depends in large part upon fortunate family and social circumstances for which he can claim no credit. The notion of desert seems not to apply to these cases."[9] Michael Kinsley is even more adamant.

> Opponents of affirmative action are hung up on a distinction that seems more profoundly irrelevant: treating individuals versus treating groups. What is the moral difference between dispensing favors to people on their "merits" as individuals and passing out society's benefits on the basis of group identification?
>
> Group identifications like race and sex are, of course, immutable. They have nothing to do with a person's moral worth. But the same is true of most of what comes under the label "merit." The tools you need for getting ahead in a meritocratic society—not all of them but most: talent, education, instilled cultural values such as ambition—are distributed just as arbitrarily as skin color. They are fate. The notion that people somehow "deserve" the advantages of these characteristics in a way they don't "deserve" the advantage of their race is powerful, but illogical.[10]

It will help to put the argument in outline form.

1. Society may award jobs and positions as it sees fit as long as individuals have no claim to these positions.
2. To have a claim to something means that one has earned it or deserves it.
3. But no one has earned or deserves his intelligence, talent, education or cultural values which produce superior qualifications.
4. If a person does not deserve what produces something, he does not deserve its products.
5. Therefore better qualified people do not deserve their qualifications.
6. Therefore, society may override their qualifications in awarding jobs and positions as it sees fit (for social utility or to compensate for previous wrongs).

So it is permissible if a minimally qualified black or woman is admitted to law or medical school ahead of a white male with excellent credentials or if a less qualified person from an "underutilized" group gets a professorship ahead of an eminently better qualified white male. Sufficiency and underutilization together outweigh excellence.

My response: Premise 4 is false. To see this, reflect that just because I do not deserve the money that I have been given as a gift (for instance) does not mean that I am not entitled to what I get with that money. If you and I both get a gift of $100 and I bury mine in the sand for 5 years while you invest yours wisely and double its value at the end of five years, I cannot complain that you should split the increase 50/50 since neither of us deserved the original gift. If we accept the notion of responsibility at all, we must hold that persons deserve the fruits of their labor and conscious choices. Of course, we might want to distinguish moral from legal desert and argue that, morally speaking, effort is more important than outcome, whereas, legally speaking, outcome may be more important. Nevertheless, there are good reasons in terms of efficiency, motivation, and rough justice for holding a strong prima facie principle of giving scarce high positions to those most competent.

The attack on moral desert is perhaps the most radical move that egalitarians like Rawls and company have made against meritocracy, and the ramifications of their attack are far reaching. Here are some implications: Since I do not deserve my two good eyes or two good kidneys, the social engineers may take one of each from me to give to those needing an eye or a kidney—even if they have damaged their organs by their own voluntary actions. Since no one deserves anything, we do not deserve pay for our labors or praise for a job well done or first prize in the race we win. The notion of moral responsibility vanishes in a system of levelling.

But there is no good reason to accept the argument against desert. We do act freely and, as such, we are responsible for our actions. We deserve the fruits of our labor, reward for our noble feats and punishment for our misbehavior.

We have considered six arguments for Affirmative Action and have found no compelling case for Strong AA and only one plausible argument (a version of the compensation argument) for Weak AA. We must now turn to the arguments against Affirmative Action to see whether they fare any better.

II. ARGUMENTS AGAINST AFFIRMATIVE ACTION

A. Affirmative Action Requires Discrimination Against a Different Group

Weak AA weakly discriminates against new minorities, mostly innocent young white males, and Strong Affirmative Action strongly discriminates against these new minorities. As I argued in I. C, this discrimination is unwarranted, since, even if some compensation to blacks were indicated, it would be unfair to make innocent white males bear the whole brunt of the payments. Recently I had this experience. I knew a brilliant philosopher, with outstanding publications in first level journals, who was having difficulty getting a tenure-track position. For the first time in my life i offered to make a phone call on his behalf to a university to which he had applied. When I got the Chair of the Search Committee, he offered that the committee was under instructions from the Administration to hire a woman or a Black. They had one of each on their short-list, so they weren't even considering the applications of White males. At my urging he retrieved my friend's file, and said, "This fellow looks far superior to the two candidates we're interviewing, but there's nothing I can do about it." Cases like this come to my attention regularly. In fact, it is poor white youth who become the new pariahs on the job market. The children of the wealthy have little trouble getting into the best private grammar schools and, on the basis of superior early education, into the best universities, graduate schools, managerial and professional positions. Affirmative Action simply shifts injustice, setting Blacks, Hispanics, Native Americans, Asians and women against young white males, especially ethnic and poor white males. It makes no more sense to discriminate in favor of a rich Black or female who had the opportunity of the best family and education available against a poor White, then it does to discriminate in favor of White males against Blacks or women. It does little to rectify the goal of providing equal opportunity to all.

At the end of his essay supporting Affirmative Action, Albert Mosley points out that other groups besides Blacks have been benefitted by AA, "women, the disabled, the elderly."[11] He's correct in including the elderly, for through powerful lobbies, such as the AARP, they do get special benefits, including Medicare, and may sue on the grounds of being discriminated against due to *Agism*, prejudice against older people. Might this not be a reason to reconsider Affirmative Action? Consider the sheer rough percentages of those who qualify for AA programs.

GROUP	PERCENTAGE in population
1. Women	52%
2. Blacks	12%
3. Hispanics	9%
4. Native Americans	2%
5. Asians	4%
6. Physically & Mentally Disabled	10%
7. Welfare recipients	6%
8. The Elderly	25% (est. Adults over 60)
9. Italians	3% (in New York City)
Totals	123%

The elderly can sue on the grounds of Agism, receive entitlements in terms of Social Security and Medicare, and have the AARP lobbying on their behalf. Recently, it has been proposed that homosexuals be included in oppressed groups deserving Affirmative Action. At Northeastern University in 1996 the faculty governing body voted to grant homosexuals Affirmative Action status at this university. How many more percentage points would this add? Several authors have advocated putting all poor people on the list. And if we took handicaps seriously would we not add ugly people, obese people, and, especially, short people, for which there is ample evidence of discrimination? How about left-handed people (about 9% of the population)—they can't play short-stop or third base and have to put up with a right-handedly biased world. The only group not on the list is that of White males. Are they, especially healthy, middle class young White males, becoming the new "oppressed class"? Should we add them to our list?

Respect for persons entails that we treat each persons as an end in him or herself, not simply as a means to be used for social purposes. What is wrong about discrimination against Blacks is that it fails to treat Black people as individuals, judging them instead by their skin color, not their merit. What is wrong about discrimination against women is that it fails to treat them as individuals, judging them by their gender, not their merit. What is equally wrong about *Affirmative Action* is that it fails to treat White males with dignity as individuals, judging them by *both their race and gender*, instead of their merit. *Current Strong Affirmative Action is both racist and sexist.*

B. Affirmative Action Encourages Mediocrity and Incompetence

A few years ago Rev. Jesse Jackson joined protesters at Harvard Law School in demanding that the Law School faculty hire black women. Jackson dismissed Dean of the Law School, Robert C. Clark's standard of choosing the best qualified person for the job as "Cultural anemia." "We cannot just define who is qualified in the most narrow vertical academic terms," he said "Most people in the world are yellow, brown, black, poor, non-Christian and don't speak English, and they can't wait for some white males with archaic rules to appraise them."[12] It might be noted that if Jackson is correct about the depth of cultural decadence at Harvard, blacks might be well advised to form and support their own more vital law schools and leave places like Harvard to their archaism.

At several universities, the administration has forced departments to hire members of minorities even when far superior candidates were available. Shortly after obtaining my PhD in the late 70s I was mistakenly identified as a black philosopher (I had a civil rights record and was once a black studies major) and was flown to a major university, only to be rejected for a more qualified candidate when it discovered that I was white.

Stories of the bad effects of Affirmative Action abound. The philosopher Sidney Hook writes that "At one Ivy League university, representatives of the

Regional HEW[13] demanded an explanation of why there were no women or minority students in the Graduate Department of Religious Studies. They were told that a reading knowledge of Hebrew and Greek was presupposed. Whereupon the representatives of HEW advised orally: 'Then end those old fashioned programs that require irrelevant languages. And start up programs on relevant things which minority group students can study without learning languages.'"[14]

Nicholas Capaldi notes that the staff of HEW itself was one-half women, three-fifths members of minorities, and one-half black—a clear case of racial overrepresentation.

In 1972 officials at Stanford University discovered a proposal for the government to monitor curriculum in higher education: the "Summary Statement . . . Sex Discrimination Proposed HEW Regulation to Effectuate Title IX of the Education Amendment of 1972" to "establish and use internal procedure for reviewing curricula, designed both to ensure that they do not reflect discrimination on the basis of sex and to resolve complaints concerning allegations of such discrimination, pursuant to procedural standards to be prescribed by the Director of the office of Civil Rights." Fortunately, Secretary of HEW Caspar Weinberger discovered the intrusion and assured Stanford University that he would never approve of it.

Government programs of enforced preferential treatment tend to appeal to the lowest possible common denominator. Witness the 1974 HEW Revised Order No. 14 on Affirmative Action expectations for preferential hiring: "Neither minorities nor female employees should be required to possess higher qualifications than those of the lowest qualified incumbents."

Furthermore, no test may be given to candidates unless it is *proved* to be relevant to the job.

No standard or criteria which have, by intent or effect, worked to exclude women or minorities as a class can be utilized, unless the institution can demonstrate the necessity of such standard to the performance of the job in question.

Whenever a validity study is called for . . . the user should include . . . an investigation of suitable alternative methods of using the selection procedure which have as little adverse impact as possible . . . Whenever the user is shown an alternative selection procedure with evidence of less adverse impact and substantial evidence of validity for the same job in similar circumstances, the user should investigate it to determine the appropriateness of using or validating it in accord with these guidelines.[15]

At the same time Americans are wondering why standards in our country are falling and the Japanese and Koreans are getting ahead. Affirmative Action with its twin idols, Sufficiency of Qualification and Diversity, is the enemy of excellence. I will develop this thought in the next section.

C. An Argument from the Principle of Merit

Traditionally, we have believed that the highest positions in society should be awarded to those who are best qualified. The Koran states that "A ruler who appoints any man to an office, when there is in his dominion another man better qualified for it, sins against God and against the State." Rewarding excellence both seems just to the individuals in the competition and makes for efficiency. Note that one of the most successful acts of racial integration, the Brooklyn Dodgers' recruitment of Jackie Robinson in the late 40s, was done in just this way, according to merit. If Robinson had been brought into the major league as a mediocre player or had batted .200 he would have been scorned and sent back to the minors where he belonged.

As mentioned earlier, merit is not an absolute value, but there are strong *prima facie* reasons for awarding positions on that basis, and it should enjoy a weighty presumption in our social practices.

In a celebrated article Ronald Dworkin says that "Bakke had no case" because society did not owe Bakke anything. That may be, but then why does it owe anyone anything? Dworkin puts the matter in Utility terms, but if that is the case, society may owe Bakke a place at the University of California/Davis, for it seems a reasonable rule-utilitarian principle that achievement should be awarded in society. We generally want the best to have the best positions, the best qualified candidate to win the political office, the most brilliant and competent scientist to be chosen for the most challenging research project, the best qualified pilots to become commercial pilots, only the best soldiers to become generals. Only when little is at stake do we weaken the standards and content our-selves with sufficiency (rather than excellence)—there are plenty of jobs where "sufficiency" rather than excellence is required. Perhaps we have even come to feel that medicine or law or university professorships are so routine that they can be performed by minimally qualified people—in which case AA has a place.

Note! no one is calling for quotas or proportional representation of *underutilized* groups in the National Basketball Association where blacks make up 80% of the players. But, surely, if merit and merit alone reigns in sports, should it not be valued at least as much in education and industry?

The case for meritocracy has two pillars. One pillar is a deontological argument which holds that we ought to treat people as ends and not merely means. By giving people what they deserve as *individuals*, rather than as members of *groups* we show respect for their inherent worth. If you and I take a test, and you get 95% of the answers correct, and I only get 50% correct, it would be unfair to you for both of us to receive the same grade, say an A, and even more unfair to give me a higher grade A+ than your B+. Although I have heard cases where teachers have been instructed to "race norm" in grading (giving Blacks and Hispanics higher grades for the same numerical scores), most proponents of AA stop short of advocating such a practice. But, I would ask them, what's really the difference between taking the overall average of a White and a Black and "race norming" it? If teachers shouldn't do it, why should administrators?

The second pillar for meritocracy is utilitarian. In the end, we will be better off by honoring excellence. We want the best leaders, teachers, policemen, physicians, generals, lawyers, and airplane pilots that we can possibly produce in society. So our program should be to promote equal opportunity, as much as is feasible in a free market economy, and reward people according to their individual merit.

CONCLUSION

Let me sum up my discussion. The goal of the Civil Rights movement and of moral people everywhere has been justice for all, including equal opportunity. The question is: how best to get there. Civil Rights legislation removed the unjust legal barriers, opening the way towards equal opportunity, but it did not tackle the deeper causes that produce differential results. Weak Affirmative Action aims at encouraging minorities to strive for excellence in all areas of life, without unduly jeopardizing the rights of majorities. The problem of Weak Affirmative Action is that it easily slides into Strong Affirmative Action where quotas, goals and timetables," "equal results"—in a word—*reverse discrimination*—prevail and are forced onto groups, thus promoting mediocrity, inefficiency, and resentment. Furthermore, AA aims at the higher levels of society—universities and skilled jobs, but if we want to improve our society, the best way to do it is to concentrate on families, children, early education, and the like, so all are prepared to avail themselves of opportunity. Affirmative Action, on the one hand, is too much, too soon and on the other hand, too little, too late.

In addition to the arguments I have offered, Affirmative Action, rather than unite people of good will in the common cause of justice, tends to balkanize us into segregation-thinking. Professor Derrick Bell of Harvard Law School recently said that the African American Supreme Court Judge Clarence Thomas, in his opposition to Affirmative Action "doesn't think black." Does Bell really claim that there is a standard and proper "Black" (and presumably a White) way of thinking? Ideologues like Bell, whether radical Blacks like himself, or Nazis who advocate "think Aryan," both represent the same thing: cynicism about rational debate, the very antithesis of the quest for impartial truth and justice. People who believe in reason to resolve our differences will oppose this kind of balkanization of the races.

Martin Luther said that humanity is like a man mounting a horse who always tends to fall off on the other side of the horse. This seems to be the case with Affirmative Action. Attempting to redress the discriminatory iniquities of our history, our well-intentioned social engineers now engage in new forms of discriminatory iniquity and thereby think that they have successfully mounted the horse of racial harmony. They have only fallen off on the other side of the issue.

NOTES

1. This argument is related to *The Need of Breaking Stereotypes Argument*. Society may simply need to know that there are talented Blacks and women, so that it does not automatically assign them lesser respect or status. The right response is that hiring less qualified people is neither fair to those better qualified who are passed over nor an effective way to remove inaccurate stereotypes. If high competence is accepted as the criterion for hiring, then it is unjust to override it for purposes of social engineering. Furthermore, if Blacks and women are known to hold high positions simply because of reverse discrimination, they will still lack the respect due to those of their rank.

2. Merit sometimes may be justifiably overridden by need, as when parents choose to spend extra earnings on special education for their disabled child rather than for their gifted child. Sometimes we may override merit for utilitarian purposes. E.g., suppose you are the best short stop on a baseball team but are also the best catcher. You'd rather play short stop, but the manager decides to put you at catcher because, while your friend can do an adequate job at short, no one else is adequate at catcher. It's permissible for you to be assigned the job of catcher. Probably, some expression of appreciation would be due you.

3. Judith Jarvis Thomson, "Preferential Hiring," in Marshall Cohen, Thomas Nagel and Thomas Scanlon, eds., *Equality and Preferential Treatment* (Princeton: Princeton University Press, 1977).

4. Stephen Kershnar pointed this out in written comments (December 22, 1997).

5. Sterling Harwood, "The Justice of Affirmative Action," in Yeager Hudson and C. Peden, eds., *The Bill of Rights: Bicentennial Reflections* (Lewiston, NY: Edwin Mellen).

6. Albert G. Mosley in his and Nicholas Capaldi's *Affirmative Action: Social Justice or Unfair Preference?* (Rowman and Littlefield, 1996), p. 28.

7. Larry Hedges and Amy Nowell, "Sex Differences in Mental Test Scores, Variability, and Numbers of High-Scoring Individuals," *Science* 269 (July 1995), pp. 41–45.

8. Glen Loury, "'Getting Involved': An Appeal for Greater Community Participation in the Public Schools," *Washington Post Education Review* (August 6, 1995).

9. John Rawls, *A Theory of Justice* (Harvard University Press, 1971), p. 104.

10. Michael Kinsley, "Equal Lack of Opportunity," *Harper's* (June 1983).

11. Albert Mosley, op. cit., p. 53.

12. *New York Times*, May 10, 1990.

13. HEW stands for the Federal Department of "Health, Education & Welfare."

14. Quoted by Nicholas Capaldi, *Out of Order: Affirmative Action and the Crisis of Doctrinaire Liberalism* (Buffalo, NY: Prometheus, 1985).

15. Capaldi, op. cit., p. 95

From *In Defense of Affirmative Action*

Tom L. Beauchamp

Affirmative action policies have had their strongest appeal when discrimination that barred groups from desirable institutions persisted although forbidden by law. Policies that establish target goals, timetables, and quotas were initiated to ensure more equitable opportunities by counterbalancing apparently intractable prejudice and systemic favoritism. The policies that were initiated with such lofty ambitions are now commonly criticized on grounds that they establish quotas that unjustifiably elevate the opportunities of members of targeted groups, discriminate against equally qualified or even more qualified members of majorities, and perpetuate racial and sexual paternalism.

Affirmative action policies favoring *groups* have been controversial since former United States President Lyndon Johnson's 1965 executive order that required federal contractors to develop affirmative action policies.[1] Everyone now agrees that *individuals* who have been injured by past discrimination should be made whole for the inquiry, but it remains controversial whether and how past discrimination against groups

justifies preferential treatment for the group's *current* members. Critics of group preferential policies hold that compensating individuals for unfair discrimination can alone be justified, but it is controversial whether individuals can be harmed merely by virtue of a group membership.[2]

Most who support affirmative action and those who oppose it both seek the best means to the same end: a color-blind, sex-blind society. Their goals do not differ. Nor do they entirely disagree over the means. If a color-blind, sex-blind society can be achieved and maintained by legal guarantees of equal opportunities to all, both parties agree that social policies should be restricted to this means. Here agreement ends. Those who support affirmative action do not believe such guarantees can be fairly and efficiently achieved other than by affirmative action policies. Those who seek an end to affirmative action believe that the goals can be achieved in other ways and that affirmative action policies themselves unjustifiably discriminate. I will be supporting affirmative action policies against this counterposition.

TWO PIVOTAL CONCEPTS

Like virtually all problems in practical ethics, the meaning of a few central terms can powerfully affect one's moral viewpoint. The terms "affirmative

Tom L. Beauchamp, reprinted by permission from Springer Nature: *Journal of Ethics*, "In Defense of Affirmative Action," Vol. 2, No. 2 (1998), pp. 143–158. Copyright © 1998, Kluwer Academic Publishers.

action" and "quotas" have proved particularly troublesome, because they have been defined in both minimal and maximal ways. The original meaning of "affirmative action" was minimalist. It referred to plans to safeguard equal opportunity, to protect against discrimination, to advertise positions openly, and to create scholarship programs to ensure recruitment from specific groups.[3] Few now oppose open advertisement and the like, and if this were all that were meant by "affirmative action," few would oppose it. However, "affirmative action" has assumed new and expanded meanings. Today it is typically associated with quotas and preferential policies that target specific groups, especially women or minority members.

I will not favor either the minimalist or the maximalist sense of "affirmative action." I will use the term to refer to positive steps taken to hire persons from groups previously and presently discriminated against, leaving open what will count as a "positive step" to remove discrimination. I thus adopt a broad meaning.

A number of controversies have also centered on the language of *quotas*.[4] A "quota," as I use the term, does not mean that fixed numbers of a group must be admitted, hired, or promoted—even to the point of including less qualified persons if they are the only available members of a targeted groups. Quotas are target numbers or percentages that an employer, admissions office, recruitment committee, and the like sincerely attempt to meet. Less qualified persons are occasionally hired or promoted under a policy that incorporates quotas; but it is no part of affirmative action or the meaning of "quotas" to hire persons who lack basic qualifications. Quotas are numerically expressible goals pursued in good faith and with due diligence.

The language of "quotas" can be toned down by speaking of hopes, objectives, and guidelines; but cosmetic changes of wording only thinly obscure a policy established to recruit from groups in which the goals are made explicitly by numbers. Thus, when John Sununu—presumably a strong opponent of quotas—told Secretary of Defense Richard Cheney that he "wanted 30 percent of the remaining 42 top jobs in the Defense Department to be filled by women and minorities,"[5] he was using a quota. Likewise, universities sometimes use quotas when the subtleties of faculty and staff hiring and promotion and student admission make no mention of them. For example, if the chair of a department says the department should hire 2 to 3 women in the next 5 available positions, the formula constitutes a quota, or at least a numerical target.

Reasons typically offered in defense of targeted affirmative action, with or without quotas, are the following: "We have many women students who need and do not have an ample number of role models and mentors." "The provost has offered a group of special fellowships to bring more minorities to the university." "More diversity is much needed in this department." "The goals and mission of this university strongly suggest a need for increased representation of women and minorities." In pursuing these objectives, members of departments and committees commonly act in ways that suggest they willingly endorse what either is or has a strong family resemblance to a specific target.

THE PREVALENCE OF DISCRIMINATION AS THE RATIONALE FOR AFFIRMATIVE ACTION

The moral problem of affirmative action is primarily whether specific targets, including quotas in the broad sense, can legitimately be used. To support affirmative action as a weapon against discrimination is not necessarily to endorse it in all institutions. Racial, sexual, and religious forms of discrimination affecting admission, hiring, and promotion have been substantially reduced in various sectors of US society, and perhaps even completely eliminated in some. The problem is that in other social sectors it is common to encounter discrimination in favor of a favored group or discrimination against disliked, distrusted, unattractive, or neglected groups. The pervasive attitudes underlying these phenomena are the most important background conditions of the debate over affirmative action, and we need to understand these pockets of discrimination in order to appreciate the attractions of affirmative action.

Statistics

Statistics constituting at least *prima facie* evidence of discrimination in society are readily available. These data indicate that in sizable parts of US society white males continue to receive the highest entry-level salaries when compared to all other social groups; that women with similar credentials and experience to those of men are commonly hired at lower positions or earn lower starting salaries than men and are promoted at one-half the rate of their male counterparts, with the consequence that the gap between salaries and promotion rates is still growing at an increasing rate; that 70% or more of white-collar positions are held by women, although they hold only about 10% of management positions; that three out of seven US employees occupy white-collar positions, whereas the ratio is but one of seven of African-Americans; and, finally, that a significant racial gap in unemployment statistics is a consistent pattern in the US, with the gap now greatest for college-educated, African-American males.[6] Whether these statistics demonstrate invidious discrimination is controversial, but additional data drawn from empirical studies reinforce the judgment that racial and sexual discrimination are reasons for and perhaps the best explanation of these statistics.

Housing

For example, studies of real estate rentals, housing sales, and home mortgage lending show a disparity in rejection rates—for example, loan rejection rates between white applicants and minority applicants. Wide disparities exist even after statistics are adjusted for economic differences; minority applicants are over 50% more likely to be denied a loan than white applicants of equivalent economic status. Other studies indicate that discrimination in sales of houses is prevalent in the US. Race appears to be as important as socioeconomic status in failing to secure both houses and loans, and studies also show that the approval rate for African-Americans increase in lending institutions with an increase in the proportion of minority employees in that institution.[7]

Jobs

A similar pattern is found in employment. In 1985 the Grier Partnership and the Urban League produced independent studies that reveal striking disparities in the employment levels of college-trained African-Americans and whites in Washington, DC, one of the best markets for African-Americans. Both studies found that college-trained African-Americans have much more difficulty than their white counterparts in securing employment. Both cite discrimination as the major underlying factor.[8]

In a 1991 study by the Urban Institute, employment practices in Washington, DC and Chicago were examined. Equally qualified, identically dressed white and African-American applicants for jobs were used to test for basis in the job market, as presented by newspaper-advertised positions. Whites and African-Americans were matched identically for speech patterns, age, work experience, personal characteristics, and physical build. Investigators found repeated discrimination against African-American male applicants. The higher the position, the higher the level of discrimination. The white men received job offers three times more often than the equally qualified African-Americans who interviewed for the same position. The authors of the study concluded that discrimination against African-American men is "widespread and entrenched."[9]

These statistics and empirical studies help frame racial discrimination in the US. Anyone who believes that only a narrow slice of surface discrimination exists will be unlikely to agree with what I have been and will be arguing, at least if my proposals entail strong affirmative action measures. By contrast, one who believes that discrimination is securely and almost invisibly entrenched in many sectors of society will be more likely to endorse or at least tolerate resolute affirmative action policies.

Although racism and sexism are commonly envisioned as intentional forms of favoritism and exclusion, intent to discriminate is not a necessary condition of discrimination. Institutional networks can unintentionally hold back or exclude persons. Hiring by personal friendships and word of mouth are common instances, as are seniority systems. Numerical targets are important remedies for these camouflaged areas, where it is particularly difficult to shatter patterns of discrimination and reconfigure the environment.[10]

The US Supreme Court has rightly upheld affirmative action programs with numerically expressed hiring formulas when intended to quash the effects of both intentional and unintentional discrimination.[11] The Court has also maintained that such formulas have sometimes been structured so that they unjustifiably exceed proper limits.[12] The particulars of the cases will determine how we are to balance different interests and considerations.

THE JUSTIFICATION OF AFFIRMATIVE ACTION

This balancing strategy is warranted. Numerical goals or quotas are justified if and only if they are necessary to overcome the discriminatory effects that could not otherwise be eliminated with reasonable efficiency. It is the intractable and often deeply hurtful character of racism and sexism that justified aggressive policies to remove their damaging effects. The history of affirmative action in the US, though short, is an impressive history of fulfilling once-failed promises, displacing disillusion, and protecting the most vulnerable members of US society against demeaning abuse. It has delivered the US from what was little more than a caste system and a companion of apartheid.

We have learned in the process that numerical formulas are sometimes essential tools, sometimes excessive tools, and sometimes permissible but optional tools—depending on the subtleties of the case. We can expect each case to be different, and for this reason we should be cautious about general pronouncements regarding the justifiability of numerical formulas—as well as the merit of merit-based systems and blinded systems. The better perspective is that until the facts of particular cases have been carefully assessed, we are not positioned to support or oppose any particular affirmative action policy or its abandonment.

The US Supreme Court has allowed these numerical formulas in plans that are intended to combat a manifest imbalance in traditionally segregated job categories (even if the particular workers drawn from minorities were not victims of past discrimination). In *Local 28 v. Equal Employment Opportunity Commission*, a minority hiring goal of 29.23 percent had been established. The Court held that such specific numbers are justified when dealing with persistent or egregious discrimination. The Court found that the history of Local 28 was one of complete "foot-dragging resistance" to the idea of hiring without discrimination in their apprenticeship training programs from minority groups. The Court argued that "affirmative race-conscious relief" may be the only reasonable means to the end of assuring equality of employment opportunities and to eliminate deeply ingrained discriminatory practices.[13]

In a 1989 opinion, by contrast, the US Supreme Court held in *City of Richmond v. J. A. Croson* that Richmond, Virginia, officials could not require contractors to set aside 30 percent of their budget for subcontractors who owned "minority business enterprises." This particular plan was not written to remedy the effects of prior or present discrimination. The Court found that *this way* of fixing a percentage based on race, in the absence of evidence of identified discrimination, denied citizens an equal opportunity to compete for subcontracts. Parts of the reasoning in this case were reaffirmed in the 1995 case of *Adarand Constructors Inc. v. Pena*.

Some writers have interpreted *Croson, Adarand,* and the 1997 decision of a three-judge panel of the 9th US Circuit Court of Appeals to the effect that California's voter-approved ban on affirmative action (Proposition 209) is constitutional as the dismantling of affirmative action plans that use numerical goals. Perhaps this prediction will turn out to be correct, but the US Supreme Court has consistently adhered to a balancing strategy that I believe captures the fitting way to frame issues of affirmative action.[14] It allows us to use race and sex as relevant bases of policies if and only if it is essential to do so in order to achieve a larger and justified social purpose.

These reasons for using race and sex in policies are far distant from the role of these properties in invidious discrimination. Racial discrimination and sexual discrimination typically spring from feelings of superiority and a sense that other groups deserve lower social status. Affirmative action entails no such attitude or intent. Its purpose is to restore to persons a status they have been unjustifiably denied, to help them escape stigmatization, and to foster relationships of interconnectedness in society.[15]

Affirmative action in pockets of the most vicious and visceral racism will likely be needed for another generation in the US, after which the US should have reached its goals of fair opportunity and equal consideration. Once these goals are achieved, affirmative action will no longer be justified and should be abandoned in the US. The goal to be reached at that point is not proportional representation, which has occasionally been used as a basis for fixing target numbers in affirmative action policies, but as such is merely a means to the end of discrimination, not an end to be pursed for its own sake. The goal is simply fair opportunity and equal consideration.

* * *

TOLERATING REVERSE DISCRIMINATION

It has often been said that reverse discrimination is caused by affirmative action policies and that this discrimination is no better than the racial or sexual discrimination that affirmative actions allegedly frustrates.[16] Some instances of such discriminatory exclusion do occur, of course, and compensation or rectification for an injured party is sometimes the appropriate response. However, some of these setbacks to the interests of those excluded by a policy may be no more objectionable than various burdens produced by social policies that advantage some members of society and disadvantage others. Inheritance laws, for example, favor certain members of society over others, whereas policies of eminent domain disadvantage persons who wish to retain what is legitimately their property in order to advance the public good. Such laws and outcomes are warranted by a larger public benefit and by justice-based considerations that conflict with the interests of the disadvantaged parties. The point is that disadvantages to majorities produced

by affirmative action may be warranted by the promotion of social ideals of equal treatment for groups that were severely mistreated in the past.

In assessing the disadvantages that might be caused to members of majorities (primarily white males), we should remember that there are disadvantages to other parties that operate in the current system, many of which will not be affected by affirmative action or by its absence. For example, just as young white males may now be paying a penalty for wrongs committed by older white males (who will likely never be penalized), so the older members of minority groups and older women who have been most disadvantaged in the past are the least likely to gain an advantage from affirmative action policies. Paradoxically, the younger minority members and women who have suffered least from discrimination now stand to gain the most from affirmative action. Despite these unfairnesses, there is no clear way to remedy them.

Policies of affirmative action may have many other shortcomings as well. For example, they confer economic advantages upon some who do not deserve them and generate court battles, jockeying for favored position by a multiple array of minorities, a lowering of admission and work standards in some institutions, heightened racial hostility, and continued suspicion that well-placed women and minority group members received their positions purely on the basis of quotas, thereby damaging their self-respect and the respect of their colleagues. Affirmative action is not a perfect social tool, but it is the best tool yet created as a way of preventing a recurrence of the far worse imperfections of our past policies of segregation and exclusion.

JUDGING THE PAST AND THE PRESENT

Looking back at this deplorable history and at the unprecedented development of affirmative action policies over the past thirty years in the US, what moral judgments can we reach about persons who either initiated these policies or those who failed to initiate such programs? Can we say that anyone has engaged in moral wrongdoing in implementing these policies, or exhibited moral failure in not implementing them? Addressing these questions should help us better judge the present in light of the past.

I will examine these questions through the classic AT&T affirmative action agreement in the 1970s. The salient facts of this case are as follows: The US Equal Employment Opportunity Commission (EEOC) had investigated AT&T in the 1960s on grounds of alleged discriminatory practices in hiring and promotion. In 1970 the EEOC stated that the firm engaged in "pervasive, system-wide, and blatantly unlawful discrimination in employment against women, African-Americans, Spanish-surnamed Americans, and other minorities."[17] The EEOC argued that the employment practices of AT&T violated several civil rights laws and had excluded women from all job classifications except low paying clerical and operator positions.

AT&T denied all charges and produced a massive array of statistics about women and minorities in the workforce. However, these statistics tended to undermine the corporation's own case. They showed that half the company's 700,000 employees were female, but that the women were all either secretaries or operators. It became apparent that the company categorized virtually all of its jobs in terms of men's work and women's work. The federal government was determined to obliterate this aspect of corporate culture in the belief that no other strategy would break the grip of this form of sexism. Eventually AT&T threw in the towel and entered a Consent Decree, which was accepted by a Philadelphia court in 1973. This agreement resulted in payments of $15 million in back wages to 13,000 women and 2,000 minority-group men and $23 million in raises to 36,000 employees who had been harmed by previous policies.

Out of this settlement came a companywide "model affirmative action plan" that radically changed the character of AT&T hiring and its promotion practices. The company agreed to create an "employee profile" in its job classifications to be achieved faster than would normally occur. It established racial and gender goals and intermediate targets in 15 job categories to be met in quarterly increments. The goals were determined by statistics regarding representative numbers of workers in the relevant labor market. The decree required that under conditions of a target failure, a less qualified (but qualified) person could take precedence over a more qualified person with greater seniority. This condition applied only to promotions, not to layoffs and rehiring, where seniority continued to prevail.

As was inevitable under this arrangement, reverse discrimination cases emerged. The well known McAleer case came before Judge Gerhard A. Gesell, who held in 1976 that McAleer was a faultless employee who became an innocent victim through an unfortunate who became an innocent victim through an unfortunate but justifiable use of the affirmative action process.[18] Judge Gersell ruled that McAleer was entitled to monetary compensation (as damages), but not entitled to the promotion to which he thought he was entitled because the discrimination the Consent Decree had been designed to eliminate might be perpetuated if a qualified woman were not given the promotion.[19]

This AT&T case history, like many affirmative action cases, is a story of changed expectations and changing moral viewpoints. At the core of any framework for the evaluation of such cases is a distinction between *wrongdoing* and *culpability*, which derives from the need to evaluate the moral quality of actions by contrast to agents. For example, we might want to say that AT&T's hiring practices were wrong and that many employees were wronged by them, without judging anyone culpable for the wrongs done.

Virtually everyone is now agreed, including AT&T officials, that AT&T's hiring and promotion practices did involve unjustified discrimination and serious wrongdoing. Even basic moral principles were violated—for example, that one ought to treat persons with equal consideration and respect, that racial and sexual discrimination are impermissible, and the like. Less clear is whether the agents involved should be blamed. Several factors place limits on our ability to make judgments about the blameworthiness of agents—or at least the fairness of doing so. These factors include culturally induced moral ignorance, a changing circumstance in the specification of moral principles, and indeterminacy in an organization's division of labor and designation of responsibility. All were present to some degree in the AT&T case.

Judgments of exculpation depend, at least to some extent, on whether proper moral standards were acknowledged in which the events transpired—for example, in the professional ethics of the period. If we had possessed clear standards regarding the justice of hiring and promotion in the 1950s and 1960s, it would be easier to find AT&T officials culpable. The absence of such standards is a factor in our reflections about culpability and exculpation, but need not be part of our reflection on the wronging that occurred.

The fact of culturally induced moral ignorance does not by itself entail exculpation or a lack of accountability for states of ignorance. The issue is the degree to which persons are accountable for holding and even perpetuating or disseminating the beliefs that they hold when an opportunity to remedy or modify the beliefs exists. If such opportunities are unavailable, a person may have a valid excuse; but the greater the opportunity to eliminate ignorance the less is exculpation appropriate. Persons who permit their culturally induced moral ignorance to persist through a series of opportunities to correct the beliefs thereby increase their culpability.

The more persons are obstinate in not facing issues, and the more they fail to perceive the plight of other persons who may be negatively affected by their failure to act, the more likely are we to find their actions or inactions inexcusable. No doubt culturally induced moral ignorance was a mitigating factor in the 1960s and early 1970s, but I believe US history also shows that it was mixed with a resolute failure to face moral problems when it was widely appreciated that they were serious problems and were being faced by other institutions.

The central issue for my purposes is not whether discriminatory attitudes should be judged harshly in the pre-affirmative action situation at AT&T, but whether the affirmative action policy that was adopted itself involved wrongdoing or constituted, then or now, an activity for which we would blame persons who establish such policies. I do not see how agents could be blamed for maintaining and enforcing this program, despite its toughness. Given AT&T's history as well as the desperate situation of discrimination in US society, under what conditions could agents be culpable even if McAleer-type cases of reverse discrimination occasionally resulted? Even if we assume that

McAleer and others were wronged in the implementation of the policy, it does not follow that the agents were culpable for their support of the policy.

Today, many corporate programs similar to the AT&T policy are in place. We can and should ask both whether persons are wronged by these policies and whether those who use the policies are culpable. The answer seems to me the same in the 1990s as it was in the 1970s: As long as there is persistent, intractable discrimination in society, the policies will be justified and the agents nonculpable, even if some persons are harmed and even wronged by the policies. To say that we should right wrongs done by the policies is not to say that we should abandon the policies themselves.

Indeed, I defend a stronger view: Affirmative action was a noble struggle against a crippling social ill in the 1960s and 1970s, and those who took part in the struggle deserve acknowledgement for their courage and foresight. Those who failed to seize the opportunity to enact affirmative action policies or some functional equivalent such as company-wide enforcement of equal opportunity are culpable for what, in many cases, were truly serious moral failures.

There is no reason to believe that, in this respect, the situation is changed today from the 1970s. Today persons in corporations, universities, and government agencies who are aware or should be aware that a high level of racism or sexism exists are culpable if they fail to move to counteract its invidious effects by affirmative policies or similarly serious interventions such as meaningful enforcement of fair opportunity. To say that we should judge the officers of these institutions culpable for their moral failures is not to say that there are no mitigating conditions for their failures, such as the mixed messages they have received over the past fifteen years from federal officials and the general cultural climate of moral indifference to the problem. At the same time, the mitigating conditions are weaker today than in the 1970s because the excuse of culturally induced moral ignorance is weaker. In general, there are now fewer excuses available for not taking an aggressive posture to combat discrimination than ever before.

All of this is not to say that we are never culpable for the way we formulate or implement affirmative action policies. One aspect of these policies for which we likely will be harshly judged in the future is a failure of truthfulness in publicly disclosing and advertising the commitments of the policies—for example, in advertising for new positions.[20] Once it has been determined that a woman or a minority group member will most likely be hired, institutions now typically place advertisements that include lines such as the following:

> Women and minority-group candidates are especially encouraged to apply. The University of X is an equal opportunity, affirmative action employer.

Advertisements and public statements rarely contain more information about an institution's affirmative action objectives, although often more information might be disclosed that would be of material relevance to applicants. The following are examples of facts or objectives that might be disclosed: A department may have reserved its position for a woman or minority; the chances may be overwhelming that only a minority; group member will be hired; the interview team may have decided in advance that only women will be interviewed; the advertised position may be the result of a university policy that offers an explicit incentive (perhaps a new position) to a department if a minority representative is appointed, etc. Incompleteness in disclosure and advertising sometimes stems from fear of legal liability, but more often from fear of departmental embarrassment and harm either to reputation or to future recruiting efforts.

The greater moral embarrassment, however, is our ambivalence and weak conceptions of what we are doing. Many, including academics, fear making public what they believe to be morally commendable in their recruiting efforts. There is something deeply unsatisfactory about a reluctance to disclose one's real position. This situation is striking, because the justification for the position is presumably that it is a morally praiseworthy endeavor. Here we have a circumstance in which the actions taken may not be wrong, but the agents are culpable for a failure to clearly articulate the basis of their actions and to allow those bases to be openly debated so that their true merits can be assessed by all affected parties.

CONCLUSION

During the course of the last thirty years, the widespread acceptance of racial segregation and sexual dominance in the US has surrendered to a more polite culture that accepts racial integration and sexual equality. This discernible change of attitude and institutional policy has led to an imposing public opposition to preferential treatment on the basis of race and sex in general. In this climate what should happen to affirmative action?

As long as our choices are formulated in terms of the false dilemma of either special preference for groups or individual merit, affirmative action is virtually certain to be overthrown. US citizens are now wary and weary of all forms of group preference, other than the liberty to choose one's preferred groups. I would be pleased to witness the defeat of affirmative action were the choice the simple one of group preference or individual merit. But it is not. Despite the vast changes of attitudes in thirty years of US culture, the underlying realities are naggingly familiar. Perhaps in another thirty years we can rid ourselves of the perils of affirmative action. But at present the public good and our sense of ourselves as a nation will be well served by retaining what would in other circumstances be odious policies. They merit preservation as long as we can say that, on balance, they serve us better than they disserve us.

NOTES

1. Executive Order 11246. C.F.R. 339 (1964–65).

2. See J. Angelo Corlett, "Racism and Affirmative Action," *Journal of Social Philosophy* 24 (1993), pp. 163–175; and Cass R. Sunstein, "The Limits of Compensatory Justice," in John Chapman (ed.), *Nomos XXXIII: Compensatory Justice* (New York: New York University Press, 1991), pp. 281–310.

3. See Thomas Nagel, "A Defense of Affirmative Action," Testimony before the Subcommittee on the Constitution of the Senate Judiciary Committee, June 18, 1981; and Louis Pojman, "The moral Status of Affirmative Action," *Public Affairs Quarterly* 6 (1992), pp. 181–206.

4. See the analyses in Gertrude Ezorsky, *Racism and Justice* (Ithaca, NY: Cornell University Press, 1991); and Robert Fullinwider, *The Reverse Discrimination Controversy* (Totowa, NJ: Rowman and Allanheld, 1980).

5. Bob Woodward, *The Commanders* (New York: Simon and Schuster, 1991), p. 72.

6. Bron Taylor, *Affirmative Action at work: Law, Politics, and Ethics* (Pittsburgh: University of Pittsburgh Press, 1991); Morley Gunderson, "Male-Female Wage Differentials and Policy Responses," *Journal of Economic Literature* 27 (1989), and Morley Gunderson, "Pay and Employment Equity in the United States and Canada," *International Journal of Manpower* 15 (1994), pp. 26–43; Patricia Gaynor and Garey Durden, "Measuring the Extent of Earnings Discrimination: An Update," *Applied Economics* 27 (1995), pp. 669–767; Marjorie L. Baldwin and William G. Johnson, "The Employment Effects of Wage Discrimination Against Black Men," *Industrial & Labor Relations Review* 49 (1996), pp. 302–316; Franklin D. Wilson, Marta Tienda, and Lawrence Wu, "Race and Unemployment: Labor Market Experiences of Black and White Men, 1968-1988," *Work & Occupations* 22 (1995), pp. 245–270; National Center for Educational Statistics, *Faculty in Higher Education Institutions*, 1988, *Contractor Survey Report*,, complied Susan H. Russell et al. (Washington: US Dept. of Education, 1990), pp. 5-13; Betty M. Vetter, ed., *Professional Women and Minorities: A Manpower Data Resource Service,* 8th ed. (Washington: Commission on Science and Technology, 1989); (anonymous) "Less Discrimination for women but Poorer Prospect at Work than Men," *Management Services* 40 (1996), p. 6; Cynthia D. Anderson and Donald Tomaskovic-Devey, "Patriarchal Pressures: An Exploration of Organizational Processes that Exacerbate and Erode Gender Earnings Inequality," *Work & Occupations* 22 (1995), pp. 328–356; Thomas J. Bergman and G. E. Martin, "Tests for Compliance with Phases Plans to Equalize Discriminate Wages," *Journal of Applied Business Research* 11 (1994/1995), pp. 136–143.

7. Brent W. Ambrose, William T. Hughes, Jr., and Patrick Simmons, "Policy Issues concerning Racial and Ethnic Differences in Home Loan Rejection Rates," *Journal of Housing Research* 6 (1995), pp. 115–135; *A Common Destiny; Blacks and American Society*, ed. Gerald D. Jaynes and Robin M. Williams, Jr., Committee on the Status of Black Americans, Commission on Behavioral and Social Sciences and Education, National Research Council (Washington: NAS Press, 1989), pp. 12-13, 138-148; Sunwoong Kim, Gregory D. Squire, "Lender Characteristics and Racial Disparities in Mortgage Lending," *Journal of Housing Research* 6 (1995), pp. 99–113; Glenn B. Canner and Wayne Passmore, "Home Purchase Leading in Low-Income Neighborhoods and to Low-Income Borrowers," *Federal Reserve Bulletin* 81 (1995), pp. 71–103; Constance L. Hays, "Study Says Prejudice in Suburbs Is Aimed Mostly at Blacks," *The New York Times* (November 23,

1988), pp. A16; John R. Walter, "The Fair Lending Laws and their Enforcement," *Economic Quarterly* 81 (1995), pp. 61–77; Stanley D. Longhofer, "Discrimination in Mortgage lending: What have We Learned?" *Economic Commentary* [Federal Reserve Bank of Cleveland] (August 15, 1996), pp. 1–4.

8. As reported by Rudolf A. Pyatt, Jr., "Significant Job Studies," *The Washington Post* (April 30, 1985), pp. D1–D2. See also Paul Burstein, *Discrimination, Jobs and Politics* (Chicago: University of Chicago Press, 1985); Bureau of Labor Statistics, *Employment and Earnings* (Washington: US Dept. of Labor, Jan. 1989); *A Common Destiny*, op. cit., pp. 16–18, 84–88.

9. See Margery Austin Turner, Michael Fix, and Raymond Struyk, *Opportunities Denied, Opportunities Diminished: Discrimination in Hiring* (Washington, DC: The Urban Institute, 1991).

10. See Laura Purdy, "Why Do We Need Affirmative Action?" *Journal of Social Philosophy* 25 (1994), pp. 133–143; Farrell Bloch, *Antidiscrimination Law and Minority Employment: Recruitment Practices and Regulatory Constraints* (Chicago: University of Chicago Press, 1994); Joseph Sartorelli, "Gay Rights and Affirmative Action" in *Gay Ethics*, ed. Timothy F. Murphy (New York: Haworth Press, 1994); Taylor, *Affirmative Action at Work.*

11. *Fullilove v. Klutznick*, 448 U.S. 448 (1980); *United Steelworkers v. Weber*, 443 U.S. 193 (1979); *United States v. Paradise*, 480 U.S. 149 (1987); *Johnson v. Transportation Agency*, 480 U.S. 616 (1987); *Alexander v. Choate*, 469 U.S. 287, at 295.

12. *Firefighters v. Stotts*, 467 U.S. 561 (1984); *City of Richmond v. J. A. Croson Co.*, 109 S.Ct. 706 (1989); *Adarand Constructors Inc. v. Federico Pena*, 63 LW 4523 (1995); *Wygant v. Jackson Bd. of Education*, 476 U.S. 267 (1986); *Wards Cove Packing v. Atonio*, 490 U.S. 642.

13. In 1964 the New York Commission for Human Rights investigated the union and concluded that it excluded nonwhites through an impenetrable barrier of hiring by discriminatory selection. The state Supreme Court concurred and issued a "cease and desist" order. The union ignored it. Eventually, in a 1975 trial, the US District Court found a record "replete with instances of bad faith" and ordered a "remedial racial goal of 29% nonwhite membership" (based on the percentage of nonwhite in the local labor pool). Another court then found that the union had "consistently and egregiously violated" the law of the land (Title 7, in particular). In 1982 and 1983 court fines and civil contempt proceeding were issued. In the early 1980s virtually nothing had been done to modify the discriminatory hiring practices after 22 years of struggle.

14. For a very different view, stressing inconsistency, see Young S. Lee, "Affirmative Action and Judicial Standards of

Review: A Search for the Elusive Consensus," *Review of Public Personnel Administration* 12 (1991), pp. 47–69.

15. See Robert Ladenson, "Ethics in the American Workplace," *Business and Professional Ethics Journal* 14 (1995), pp. 17–31; Ezorsky, *Racism and Justice: The Case for Affirmative Action*, op. cit.; Thomas E. Hill, Jr., "The Message of Affirmative Action," *Social Philosophy and policy* 8 (1991), pp. 108–129; Jorge L. Garcia, "The Heart of Racism," *Journal of Social Philosophy* 27 (1996), pp. 5–46.

16. See Robert Fullinwider, *The Reverse Discrimination Controversy*, op. cit.; Nicholas Capaldi, *Out of Order* (Buffalo, NY, 1985); F. R. Lynch, *Invisible Victims: White Males and the Crisis of Affirmative Action* (Westport, CT: Greenwood Press, 1989); Barry R. Gross, eds., *Reverse Discrimination* (Buffalo: Prometheus Books, 1977).

17. US Equal Employment Opportunity Commission, "Petition to Intervene," Federal Communications Commission Hearings on AT&T Revised Tariff Schedule (December 10, 1970), p. 1.

18. *McAleer v. American Telephone and Telegraph Company*, 416 F. Supp. 435 (1976); "AT&T Denies Job Discrimination Charges, Claims Firm Is Equal Employment Leader," *The Wall Street Journal* (December 14, 1970), p.6; Richard M. Hodgetts, "AT&T versus the Equal Employment Opportunity Commission," in *The Business Enterprise: Social Challenge, Social Response* (Philadelphia, W. B. Saunders Company, 1977), pp. 176–182.

19. According to a representative of the legal staff in AT&T's Washington Office (phone conversation on March 10, 1982).

20. See Steven M. Cahn, "Colleges Should be Explicit about Who Will be Considered for Jobs," *The Chronicle of Higher Education* (April 5, 1989), p. B3.

CHAPTER 15

Sexual Morality

Sex has probably always been controversial, a volatile subject that triggers intense emotions, social angst, and legal and religious sanctions. Fortunately, it has also attracted the interest of moral philosophers who have tried to shed light on its ethical uncertainties. Typically, the moral issues involved are of two kinds: (1) those that focus on the morality of specific types of sexual acts and the context of those acts, and (2) those that concern an individual's free consent to such acts. Regarding the first group of issues, many people commend or condemn oral sex, anal sex, masturbation, homosexual sex, group sex, premarital sex, promiscuous sex, transgenderism, prostitution, contraception, pornography, and whatever is labeled "sexual perversion." The second group of issues involve consent to sexual acts and violations of consent, or sexual assault, now a source of excruciating and passionate conflicts on college and university campuses. Transgender persons do not fit easily into either group, since to some people, their very existence is a moral issue.

Unfortunately, people's positions on these questions usually have more to do with their upbringing, religious traditions, or cultural background than with plausible moral arguments. So let's see what critical thinking can tell us about the ethics of sexuality.

ISSUE FILE: BACKGROUND

Sexual Behavior

The central question in the morality of sexual behavior is, What kind of sexual behavior is morally permissible, and under what circumstances?

People generally give one of three answers: (1) sex is permissible only in a marriage between a man and a woman; (2) sex is permissible between informed, consenting adults; and (3) sex is permissible between informed, consenting adults who are bound by love or commitment.

The first answer is the **conventional view**: sex is morally acceptable only between one man and one woman who are married to each other by legal authority. Sex involving the unmarried or sex in adulterous relationships is impermissible—that is, premarital sex and extramarital sex are wrong. In a religious strain of the conventional view, some sex acts performed by married partners—acts that are incompatible with procreation—are also prohibited. These acts include masturbation, oral sex, anal sex, and sex using contraceptives.

The conventional attitude has been championed by Christianity, Judaism, and Islam, and has been vigorously defended in the natural law teachings of the Roman Catholic Church. For a long time it was the dominant view of sexual ethics in the West, but since the 1960s its influence has faded. In a 2014 public opinion poll, 66 percent of respondents said they believe it morally acceptable for a man and woman to have sex before marriage.[1] And whatever people say they believe about the subject, their actual behavior is a far cry from the conventional standard. Research shows that sex before marriage is almost universal among Americans. By age forty-four, 95 percent have had premarital sexual relations.[2]

The second answer is the **liberal view** (not to be confused with the political outlook with the same name). Directly counter to the conventional stance, it says that as long as basic moral standards are respected (for example, no one is harmed or coerced), any sexual activity engaged in by informed, consenting adults is permissible. Provided that people adhere to the relevant moral principles, all kinds of sexual behavior condemned by the conventionalist would be morally acceptable, including premarital sex, extramarital sex, group sex, masturbation, and homosexuality.

The third answer is the **moderate view**, which says that sex is permissible, whether in marriage or not, if the consenting partners have a serious emotional connection. Moral sex does not require marriage, but it does entail more than just the informed, freely given consent of the people involved. For some, this needed connection is love, affection, or mutual caring; for others it's a commitment to sustaining the relationship. Provided that the necessary element is present, both premarital and extramarital sex could be permitted, but promiscuous sex would probably be disallowed.

As you would expect, the conventionalist and the liberal take opposing views on the rightness of **homosexuality** (sexual relations between people of the same sex). The conventionalist denounces it as abnormal, unnatural, harmful, or dangerous. It is always and everywhere wrong. The liberal sees no morally relevant difference between heterosexual and homosexual sex. The behavior is morally permissible if it conforms to legitimate moral standards and involves consenting adults.

VITAL STATS: Sexual Behavior

- By age 20, 77 percent of adults have had sex, and 75 percent have had premarital sex.

- By age 44, 94 percent of women and 96 percent of men have had premarital sex.

- Among adults aged 25–44, 98 percent of women and 97 percent of men have had vaginal intercourse; 89 percent of women and 90 percent of men have had oral sex with an opposite-sex partner; and 36 percent of women and 44 percent of men have had anal sex with an opposite-sex partner.

- Half or more of women ages 18 to 39 report giving or receiving oral sex in the past 90 days.

- The sexual repertoires of U.S. adults vary dramatically, with more than 40 combinations of sexual activity described at adults' most recent sexual event. Adult men and women rarely engage in just one sex act when they have sex.

- 46 percent of high school students report having sexual intercourse; 14 percent report sexual intercourse with four or more persons.

- Among teenagers and young adults (age 15–21), 11 percent of women and 4 percent of men have reported a same-sex sexual experience.

- On average, men experience first intercourse at 16.9 years; women at 17.4.

Statistic from CBS/*New York Times* Poll, January 11–15, 2009, N = 1,112 adults nationwide, MoE ± 3; The Alan Guttmacher Institute, published and unpublished data, 2002, 2011, www.guttmacher.org (May 3, 2012); Lawrence B. Finer, "Trends in Premarital Sex in the United States, 1954–2003," *Public Health Reports*, 122 (January–February 2007), www.publichealthreports.org/issueopen.cfm?articleID=1784 (February 16, 2015); National Health Statistics Reports, "Sexual Behavior, Sexual Attraction, and Sexual Identity in the United States (2006–2008)," number 36, March 3, 2011; Centers for Disease Control and Prevention, "Trends in the Prevalence of Sexual Behaviors," National YRBS, 1991–2009; compiled data from The Kinsey Institute.

All these diverse views are related to issues involving the sale and use of **pornography**: sexually explicit images or text meant to cause sexual excitement or arousal. Many who take a conventional view of sexual morality are likely to favor censorship of pornographic material on the grounds that it encourages the very behavior they oppose—premarital sex, extramarital sex, and unacceptable sexual behavior. They may oppose pornography because they believe it is bad for people and institutions. Personal and institutional immorality, lowering of moral standards, decay of religious values and traditions, the undermining of personal virtue, the debasement and subordination of women, increases in crime and social disorder, psychological damage—these and other ills are said to be the possible results of producing or using pornography. Those who adopt a liberal view of sexual morality are likely to condone the use of pornography (but oppose child pornography and underage exposure to pornography). They may reject claims about the harm that pornography causes, pointing to a lack of supporting evidence for them. Many who argue against censorship may also appeal to a principle of individual liberty. They may hold that the only legitimate reason for limiting liberty is the prevention of harm to others. We are free to think, believe, say, desire, and choose as we see fit—as long as we do not harm our fellow citizens.

Campus Sexual Assault

Sociologists, psychologists, and journalists who study sexual violence have uncovered an unsettling fact that has for years been hidden in plain sight: sexual assault against college and university women on campus is shockingly common, and often responses to it by both government officials and school administrators have been remarkably ill-informed, naïve, even callous. A statistic that has been regularly misunderstood or misused, but well supported by research is that one in five female undergraduates will be sexually assaulted while attending college.[3]

This level of violence against women has engendered both moral indignation and fervent action. As the author and sociologist Alison E. Hatch says,

> Sexual assault on college campuses is not a new phenomenon. And unfortunately, statistics indicate it happens with alarming frequency. The privilege of attending an institution of higher learning should not, but regrettably does, come with a 1 in 5 chance a woman, or 1 in 20 chance a man, will be sexually assaulted while in pursuit of a degree. Naturally, in light of such statistics, many people are outraged. Contemporary student activists, taking a page out of history from antirape activists in the 1970[s] and 1980s, are fighting for change. They are educating others on the reality of campus sexual assault and rape culture, they are fighting for their schools to be held accountable for their all-too-often poor treatment of survivors, and they are fighting for their schools to take sexual assault seriously and hold perpetrators responsible for their actions. Some contemporary politicians have entered the dialogue, fighting for tougher legislation and demanding that schools cease to turn a blind eye to the assaults occurring on their campuses.[4]

There is also a growing awareness that sexual assault can have serious psychological and physical affects. In addition to physical injuries caused by forcible rape, sexual assault can lead to PTSD (post-traumatic strees disorder), depression, and thoughts of suicide. Incapacitated rape—rape while the victim is unconscious or intoxicated—can induce the same kind of psychological harm.

Part of the difficulty of grappling with this topic is that the terms *sexual assault* and *rape* are frequently misunderstood, and sometimes equated. They are distinct. *Rape* is the penetration of the vagina or anus with any body part or object, or the penetration of the mouth by the sex organ of another person, without the consent (verbal or nonverbal) of the victim. Legally and morally, consent cannot be given when the victim is forced, harmed, threatened, or tricked; neither can consent be assumed when the victim is silent, unconscious, drunk, drugged, underage, or mentally or physically disabled. Sexual intercourse with an unconscious victim is rape.

Sexual assault is a broader term, which includes rape as well as nonpenetrative sexual acts such as attempted rape, forced kissing, and unwanted groping of sexual parts. Sexual assault, then, is not a synonym for rape, although some people assume that it is.

Research has identified many of the factors associated with college life that increase the likelihood of sexual assault. The journalist Vanessa Grigoriadis says that the chief cause is college life itself:

We're better off focusing on what is largely causing sexual assault: the number of times that one comes into contact with acquaintances or, in particular, what sociologists call "in-network strangers," often at a party or at an off-campus apartment. An in-network stranger is the friend of a friend from the next dorm over, someone's brother visiting for the weekend, a guy who strikes up a conversation with you in the library stacks. . . . [A]t college, although students perceive themselves as being among peers, they are actually surrounded by strangers. The risk is college itself, as defined in the popular imagination, those heavenly expanses of pretty quads, homecoming games, and rowdy frats.[5]

One part of college life that is strongly linked to sexual assault is partying. As Grigoriadis explains,

A small cohort of students used to spend their college years in a YOLO haze; sociologists now think many undergrads do so. Given this environment, the term *acquaintance rape*, which replaced *date rape* in colloquial language long ago—*date rape* sounded too romantic—has been shifted to the side by some experts by another, more specific phrase: *party rape*. This means the assault comes after a social, sexualized atmosphere, even if it doesn't happen between a girl and a guy she likes.[6]

Some observers think that a lot of the blame for the sexual assault phenomenon should be laid on campus *hookup culture*. Today's college students seldom have traditional dates as their parents did; instead, they hookup—they have no-strings-attached sexual encounters disconnected from the messiness of romantic commitments. One worry is that hookups naturally seem to involve alcohol, and alcohol is a risk factor for sexual assault. And some are concerned that hookup culture dilutes a sense of personal responsibility for any negative ramifications of sex and shields perpetrators of assault from blame for the harm they cause. On the other hand, campus sexual assaults have been happening for decades without the help of hookup culture.

Research shows that the perpetrators of sexual assault are almost all male, whether the gender of their victims is male or female. As Hatch says,

The vast majority, approximately 90 percent, of campus sexual assaults are perpetrated by someone a victim knows. Typically, assailants are boyfriends, exboyfriends, classmates, acquaintances, coworkers, or friends. For some survivors, knowing their perpetrator complicates their decisions to report the assault to officials and likely plays a role in the overall low report rates. Other possible risk factors for assailants include men who hold negative attitudes toward women, accept rape myths, consume violent/degrading pornography, are controlling, lack empathy, and/or perceive a lack of sanctions for abusive behavior.[7]

Aside from the activities of activists and survivors, the single most powerful influence on how sexual assault is handled at U.S. colleges and universities has been Title IX, a federal law that forbids discrimination based on gender in any educational institution receiving federal funds. If a school violates Title IX, it could lose that funding. Sexual assault is considered a form of discrimination that interferes with the victim's equal right to an education, so Title IX applies. The statute, as interpreted by the U.S. Department of Education, requires schools to stop campus sexual assault, prevent future occurrences, adjudicate the competing claims of supposed victim and assailant, and mete out justice for both.

Under this system, survivors of sexual assault who think their school's response is inadequate or unjust can file a complaint with the U.S. Department of Education's Office of Civil Rights (OCR), which then must investigate the school's handling of the allegations. An alternative is to sue their school under Title IX.

But there is considerable skepticism among survivors and activists about the ability of colleges and universities to deal effectively with charges of sexual assault. As Hatch says,

> Many campus sexual assault survivors believe that their college or university failed to take their sexual assault seriously. Survivors have reported all kinds of institutional mismanagement, at a range of different colleges and universities across the nation, including experiencing the following from campus officials: callousness, disbelief, defamation, retribution for reporting, failure to provide support and protection, failure to hold perpetrators responsible, and efforts to cover up allegations. . . .
>
> The existing research on school responses largely supports the criticisms that universities and colleges are not holding perpetrators accountable.[8]

Moral questions surface at every turn in these cases, but mostly concern (1) whether and how justice is served after a sexual assault occurs and (2) whether the requirement of consent is met in any kind of sexual encounter. The first concern focuses on how the college or university handles an allegation of assault and how it treats the person claiming assault as well as the accused. One flash point here is how the evidence for assault is weighed, a question that often arises in an atmosphere in which complainants demand to be believed and defendants charge that procedures are biased against them (see the box Critical Thought: Proving Sexual Assault.)

The second concern is crucial because without clear consent by both individuals, a hookup is, by definition, sexual assault. The requirement of consent is that in sexual activity, mutual consent (permission to engage in sex) must be clear and freely granted (without coercion, violence, or threats) by

CRITICAL THOUGHT: Proving Sexual Assault

Sexual assault is maddeningly difficult to prove. Most campus sexual assaults are not reported; when they are, few of the accused are judged guilty (responsible); and of the few judged guilty, even fewer are ever punished. A victim's suffering is often compounded because she believes she has been denied justice. But many of the accused make the same claim; they, too, think they have been treated unjustly. They believe that at least part of this injustice stems from the rules of evidence that the OCR has required schools to follow. The rules are based on a "preponderance of evidence" standard. By this criterion, a school hearing or panel can find the accused responsible even if it is only slightly more likely than not that he has committed a wrongful act—that is, a likelihood of only 50.1 percent. The alternative standard, one used in many court cases

and formerly at some schools, is the "clear and convincing" rule, which requires a much higher likelihood (perhaps as high as 70 percent) that the accused did in fact commit sexual assault. Critics argue that the preponderance standard introduces considerable doubt about the verdict and denies the accused a fair and just hearing. Many victims believe that the higher standard would allow only a tiny percentage of guilty verdicts. (Recently, the Department of Education has sought to weaken the requirement to use the preponderance standard.)

Which standard of evidence is more just in campus sexual assault cases? Why? Does the preponderance of evidence standard presume that false allegations are rare? Does the fact that sexual assault is hard to prove justify the use of the preponderance standard?

individuals capable of giving consent (not drunk, drugged, or underage, for example).

The long-standing policy on college campuses regarding consent has been "no means no," which says essentially that sexual activity can proceed until one partner says no. Sexual activity that takes place beyond that point is assault. The problem with this standard is that silence alone or lack of resistance does not necessarily mean yes, and when people are intimidated, fearful, or threatened, they may feel that they cannot say no. A better standard, some experts say, is "yes means yes," or what is called "affirmative consent." In this approach, sexual activity must begin with a crystal-clear verbal *yes* or an equally unambiguous nonverbal *yes* (such as sounds of pleasure or removal of clothing). This yes must precede each phase of action, from kissing to fondling to penetration and beyond. Some interpret affirmative consent as a series of awkward interruptions and step-by-step formalities, but others think it can be practiced in a smoother, less burdensome way. In any case, affirmative consent is now standard policy in hundreds of schools, and it has been signed into law in New York, California, and Illinois.

"Yes means yes," however, does have critics. They object to what some regard as its mood-killing awkwardness, and they worry about the inherent fuzziness of nonverbal cues; the risk of misinterpretation is high. They must admit, though, that there is more clarity in "yes means yes" than "no means no."

MORAL THEORIES

Major moral theories have important implications for the morality of sexual behavior. As we have seen (in Chapter 6), natural law theory holds that right actions are those directed toward the aims revealed in nature. According to the Roman Catholic account of the theory, because procreation is foremost among these aims, actions consistent with it are permissible and actions incompatible with it are

forbidden. Sexual intercourse between a man and a woman is the supreme act of procreation, and marriage provides the necessary stable context to nurture the fruits of procreation—children. Thus, only sex between a man and a woman joined by marriage can be morally legitimate. The Vatican declares:

> Experience teaches us that love must find its safeguard in the stability of marriage, if sexual intercourse is truly to respond to the requirements of its own finality and to those of human dignity. These requirements call for a conjugal contract sanctioned and guaranteed by society—a contract which establishes a state of life of capital importance both for the exclusive union of the man and the woman and for the good of their family and of the human community.[9]

Premarital sex is, therefore, proscribed, as is contraception and sexual activity not directed at procreation, such as oral sex, masturbation, and homosexuality.

Although Immanuel Kant favored a conventional approach to sex and marriage, some thinkers have derived from his theory a liberal view of sexual ethics. Recall Kant's dictum that we must always treat people as ends in themselves, never merely as a means to an end. Thomas Mappes says that to treat someone merely, or solely, as a means is to *use* that person, to treat that person without the respect that she deserves. He defines *using another person* as violating the requirement that interactions with that person be based on her voluntary informed consent. This implies that "using another person (in the morally significant sense) can arise in at least two ways: via *coercion*, which is antithetical to voluntary consent, and via *deception*, which undermines the informed character of voluntary consent."[10]

According to these guidelines, any sexual activity in which one person deceives or coerces another is wrong. But when the principle of voluntary informed consent is respected, a broad range of sexual practices is permissible.

A utilitarian is likely to sanction many kinds of sexual activity on the grounds that they produce the greatest overall happiness or good for all concerned. Sexual behavior that results in the greatest net good (the greatest utility) is morally right regardless of whether it is unconventional, "unnatural," deviant, marital, extramarital, procreative, or recreational.

Maximizing utility in sexual matters, however, requires weighing many possible harms and benefits. Those involved in a sexual relationship may risk sexually transmitted disease, pregnancy, emotional distress (such as humiliation, disappointment, or guilt), disruptions in family life (as a result of adultery, for example), and social or legal censure. But they may also experience a great deal of sexual pleasure, attain a sense of well-being and psychological satisfaction, and forge strong bonds of affection and mutual caring.

On the issue of sexual assault, it's easy to see how both consequentialist and nonconsequentialist theories would condemn any such act. By virtually any calculation of utility, sexual violence would be counted as an instance of seriously immoral action. And as an action against a person without his or her consent, sexual assault is, on almost any nonconsequentialist view, a violation of the rights of personhood.

MORAL ARGUMENTS

The key difference between the conventional and the liberal view of sexuality is that the former insists that sexual behavior has a morally significant goal, and the latter assumes that sex has no goal at all. This, anyway, is the central premise in an argument for sexual liberalism put forth by Alan Goldman. He says that several faulty theories of sexuality are based on the idea that sex's rightful goal is procreation, communication, or the expression of love and that "sex which does not fit one of these models or fulfill one of these functions is in some way deviant or incomplete."[11] The Roman Catholic view, for example, is that homosexuality, masturbation, and oral or anal sex are not aimed at the prescribed goal of procreation and are therefore immoral or perverted. Goldman, however, rejects this goal-directed (or, as he says, "means-end") analysis of sex. He maintains instead that sex is not a means to some other goal—sex is just "plain sex." Sexual desire, he says, is "desire for contact with another person's body and for the pleasure which such contact produces. . . ."

> The desire for physical contact with another person is a minimal criterion for (normal) sexual desire, but is both necessary and sufficient to qualify normal desire as sexual. Of course, we may want to express other feelings through sexual acts in various contexts; but without the desire for the physical contact in and for itself, or when it is sought for other reasons, activities in which contact is involved are not predominantly sexual. Furthermore, the desire for physical contact in itself, without the wish to express affection or other feelings through it, is sufficient to render sexual the activity of the agent which fulfills it.[12]

Sexual pleasure, he says, is what is most valuable about sex, and pleasure is intrinsically valuable. So sex does not need to be assigned some larger goal or purpose. On this point, Igor Primoratz agrees:

> We have no reason to believe that there is only one morally acceptable aim or purpose of human sexual experience and behavior, whether prescribed by nature or enjoined by society...Sex has no special moral significance; it is morally neutral. No act is either morally good or bad, right or wrong, merely in virtue of being a sexual act....Accordingly, there is neither need nor room for a set of moral considerations that apply only to sex and constitute sexual morality in the strict sense of the terms. What does apply to choices, acts, and practices in the field of sex are the same moral rules and principles that apply in nonsexual matters.[13]

Goldman and Primoratz do not affirm that sexual behavior can never be immoral, only that it cannot be immoral merely because it is sexual. If sexual behavior is immoral, it is so because it violates moral principles or rules that apply to any other kinds of actions. "Our first conclusion regarding morality and sex," Goldman says, "is therefore that no conduct otherwise immoral should be excused because it is sexual conduct, and nothing in sex is immoral unless condemned by rules which apply elsewhere as well."[14]

According to Goldman, the views that posit a proper goal for sex (the means-end analyses) inevitably fall into inconsistency. For example, the sex-as-procreation theory condemns oral-genital sex (because it is not a reproductive function) yet fails to denounce kissing or handholding, which are also sexual but not reproductive.

As you would expect, those who champion conventional sexual morality reject "plain sex" arguments. They hold that sexual encounters have a deeper, more significant meaning than sexual liberals would admit. Sexual experiences are not just physical events; they involve the commingling of persons' spiritual and moral selves. As such, they express and affirm moral values, and the right kind of sex expresses and affirms the right kind of values (specifically, the conventional values of mutual commitment through marriage). Sex that is devoid of these values is morally deficient or perverse.

One of the more contentious—and divisive—issues in sexual ethics is homosexuality. The most heated arguments concern whether homosexual behavior is immoral, and many of these arguments center around the charge that homosexuality is unnatural or abnormal.

Some people take *unnatural* to mean something like "not commonly done by animals." If homosexual behavior is not found among animals in nature, then it is unnatural and, therefore, morally unacceptable. But biologists and others dispute this contention. For example:

> We know that in species after species, right through the animal kingdom, students of animal behavior report unambiguous evidence of homosexual attachments and behavior—in insects, fish, birds, and lower and higher mammals. . . . Whatever the moral implications of homosexuality and naturalness may be, it is false that homosexuality is immoral because it does not exist amongst animals.[15]

For many who denounce homosexuality, *unnatural* means "out of the norm," "a deviation from the usual pattern," and this unnaturalness is reason enough to call homosexual behavior immoral. A common counterargument is that it does not follow from an action's statistical abnormality that it is immoral. Many acts are statistically out of the norm—skydiving, composing operas, eating snails—but we do not necessarily think them morally wrong.

While acknowledging the weaknesses of the foregoing definitions, some conventionalists offer more sophisticated abnormality arguments. Consider this line of reasoning:

> This paper defends the view that homosexuality is abnormal and hence undesirable—not because it is immoral or sinful, or because it weakens society or hampers evolutionary development, but for a purely mechanical reason. It is a misuse of bodily parts. Clear empirical sense attaches to the idea of *the use* of such bodily parts as genitals, the idea that they are *for* something, and consequently to the idea of their misuse. I argue on grounds involving natural selection that misuse of bodily parts can with high probability be connected to unhappiness. . . . I . . . draw a seemingly evident corollary from my view that homosexuality is abnormal and likely to lead to unhappiness.[16]

The argument here is that homosexuality is a misuse of a bodily part—specifically, the penis, which is for injecting sperm into the vagina, not for the abnormal functions that gay men prefer. This misuse leads to unhappiness because it frustrates "an innately rewarding desire." Society has an interest in promoting happiness; and since homosexuality makes for unhappiness, society ought to discourage it by not legalizing it.

A typical rejoinder to this argument is that evolutionary adaptations, whatever their form, tell us nothing about how people *ought* to behave.

QUICK REVIEW

conventional view (of sexuality)—The idea that sex is morally acceptable only between a man and a woman who are legally married to each other.

liberal view (of sexuality)—The idea that as long as basic moral standards are respected, any sexual activity engaged in by informed, consenting adults is permissible.

moderate view (of sexuality)—The idea that sex is permissible, whether in marriage or not, if the consenting partners have a serious emotional connection.

homosexuality—Sexual relations between people of the same sex.

pornography—Sexually explicit images or text meant to cause sexual excitement or arousal.

Just because blind accidents of nature have shaped humans in a particular way, that doesn't mean people are obligated to stay as they are. As one philosopher puts it, "Human beings are completely at liberty to dispose of their work, their behavior, and even such things as their anatomy and physiology as they see fit."[17] Contrary to natural law theory, knowing how nature *is* tells us nothing about how we *ought to be*.

CHAPTER REVIEW

SUMMARY

The moral issues relating to sexuality are of two kinds: (1) those that focus on the morality of specific types of sexual acts and the context of those acts,

and (2) those that concern an individual's free consent to such acts. Regarding the first kind of issue, the key question is, What kind of sexual behavior is morally permissible, and under what circumstances? The most common answers are: (1) sex is permissible only in a marriage between a man and a woman (the conventional view); (2) sex is permissible between informed, consenting adults (the liberal view); and (3) sex is permissible between informed, consenting adults who are bound by love or commitment (the moderate view).

Natural law theory offers a conventional account of sexual morality, exemplified by Roman Catholic teachings on the subject. Premarital and extramarital sex are forbidden, as well as contraception, oral and anal sex, masturbation, and homosexuality. A liberal view of sexual ethics can be derived from Kantian theory; this view says that any sexual activity in which one person deceives or coerces another is wrong, but when the principle of voluntary informed consent is respected, a broad range of sexual practices is permissible. Utilitarianism is likely to endorse many kinds of sexual activity on the grounds that they maximize utility.

Some philosophers reject the idea that sex's rightful goal is procreation, communication, or the expression of love. This goal-oriented view implies that sex that does not aim at one of these objectives is deviant or incomplete. But for many sexual liberals, sex does not have a lofty goal; its value is simply the sexual pleasure that comes from physical contact. Pleasure is intrinsically valuable, so a further goal for sexual acts is not needed.

A common charge against homosexuality is that it is unnatural or abnormal. People rebut these claims by trying to show that they are unfounded or confused, or by arguing that abnormality does not imply immorality.

The second kind of moral issue involves consent to sexual acts and violations of consent, or sexual assault, a topic of major interest on college and university campuses. Rape is the penetration of the vagina or anus with any body part or object, or the penetration of the mouth by the sex organ of another person, without the consent (verbal or nonverbal) of the victim. Sexual assault is a broader term, which includes rape as well as nonpenetrative sexual acts such as attempted rape, forced kissing, and unwanted groping of sexual parts.

The moral questions mostly concern (1) whether and how justice is served after a sexual assault occurs and (2) whether the requirement of consent is met in any kind of sexual encounter. The first question applies to how a college or university handles an allegation of assault and how it treats the person claiming assault as well as the accused. One flash point here is how the evidence for assault is weighed, a question that often arises in an atmosphere in which complainants demand to be believed and defendants charge that procedures are biased against them.

KEY TERMS
conventional view (of sexuality) (p. 536)
liberal view (of sexuality) (p. 536)
moderate view (of sexuality) (p. 537)
homosexuality (p. 537)
pornography (p. 538)

EXERCISES
Review Questions
1. What is the conventional moral view of sex? (p. 536)
2. What is the difference between the liberal view and the moderate view of sexual behavior? (pp. 536–537)
3. What is homosexuality, and what is the conventionalist view of it? (p. 537)
4. What is sexual assault? What is rape? (pp. 538–539)
5. Is campus sexual assault a rare occurrence or a common one? (p. 538)
6. Typically, what are the characteristics of a perpetrator of campus sexual assault? (p. 539)
7. What is the campus policy known as "yes means yes"? (p. 541)
8. What is the view of sexuality according to the Catholic version of natural law theory? (p. 541)

9. What is the argument that Goldman offers against the goal-directed view of sex? (pp. 542–543)
10. What are the arguments for and against the claim that homosexuality is unnatural and therefore immoral? (p. 543)

Discussion Questions
1. What is the difference between the conventional and the moderate view of sexual behavior? Which approach seems more plausible?
2. On what grounds would a utilitarian sanction or condemn particular kinds of sexual activity? Do you ever use the utilitarian perspective to assess the morality of sexual acts? If so, how?
3. What is goal-directed sexual activity? Why do Goldman and Primoratz reject this view of sex?
4. On the conventional view of sex, sexual behavior has a morally significant goal. What does this statement mean? Do you agree? Why or why not?
5. Which view of sexual behavior (conventional, liberal, or moderate) comes closest to your own perspective? What are your reasons for favoring it?
6. What does consent have to do with determining whether sexual assault has occurred?
7. What factors do you think most influence the incidence of sexual assault on campus? Do you think hookup or partying culture has an effect? Explain.
8. How has Title IX influenced the way colleges and universities deal with sexual assault?
9. Research shows that most campus sexual assaults happen early in the first year of college. Does this fact suggest any particular precautions or behavior changes that freshmen should take into account?
10. Do you think that the "yes means yes" standard for ensuring consensual sex is reasonable? Does following this standard make sex awkward or less enjoyable? Is it superior to the "no means no" approach?

FURTHER READING

C. Bohmer, *Sexual Assault on Campus: The Problem and the Solution* (Lanham, MD: Lexington Books, 1993).

A. Clark and A. Pino, *We Believe You: Survivors of Campus Sexual Assault Speak Out* (New York: Henry Holt and Company, 2016).

K. Dick and A. Ziering, *The Hunting Ground: The Inside Story of Sexual Assault on American College Campuses* (New York: Skyhorse, 2016).

Vanessa Grigoriadis, *Blurred Lines: Rethinking Sex, Power, and Consent* (Boston: Houghton Mifflin, 2017).

Alison E. Hatch, *Campus Sexual Assault* (Santa Barbara, CA: ABC-CLIO, 2017).

Catherine Kaukinen, Michelle Hughes Miller, and Rachael A. Powers, ed., *Addressing Violence against Women on College Campuses* (Philadelphia: Temple University Press, 2017).

R. Mairuo, ed., *Perspectives on College Sexual Assault* (New York: Springer Publishing, 2015).

ETHICAL DILEMMAS

1. Avoiding Morality in Sex Lessons

London (*The Sunday Times*)—Parents should avoid trying to convince their teenage children of the difference between right and wrong when talking to them about sex, a new government leaflet is to advise.

Instead, any discussion of values should be kept "light" to encourage teenagers to form their own views, according to the brochure, which one critic has called "amoral."

"Talking to Your Teenager About Sex and Relationships" will be distributed in pharmacies from next month as part of an initiative led by Beverley Hughes, the children's minister.

The leaflet comes in the wake of the case of Alfie Patten, the 13-year-old boy from East Sussex who fathered a child with a 15-year-old girl and sparked a debate about how to cut rates of teenage parenthood.

It advises: "Discussing your values with your teenagers will help them to form their own. Remember, though, that trying to convince them of what's right and wrong may discourage them from being open."*

Should parents keep issues of right and wrong out of discussions about sex with their children? Should parents convey the idea that right and wrong has nothing to do with sex? Why or why not? In school sex education, should discussions of ethics be forbidden? Is ethics irrelevant to contemporary sexual behavior?

*Jack Grimston, "Parents Told: Avoid Morality in Sex Lessons," *Times Online*, February 22, 2009. Reprinted by permission of News Licensing.

2. Premarital Abstinence Pledges

(*Washington Post*)—Teenagers who pledge to remain virgins until marriage are just as likely to have premarital sex as those who do not promise abstinence and are significantly less likely to use condoms and other forms of birth control when they do, according to a study released today.

The new analysis of data from a large federal survey found that more than half of youths became sexually active before marriage regardless of whether they had taken a "virginity pledge," but that the percentage who took precautions against pregnancy or sexually transmitted diseases was 10 points lower for pledgers than for non-pledgers.

"Taking a pledge doesn't seem to make any difference at all in any sexual behavior," said Janet E. Rosenbaum of the Johns Hopkins Bloomberg School of Public Health, whose report appears in the January issue of the journal *Pediatrics*. "But it does seem to make a difference in condom use and other forms of birth control that is quite striking."

The study is the latest in a series that have raised questions about programs that focus on encouraging abstinence until marriage, including those that specifically ask students to publicly declare their intention to remain virgins. The new analysis, however, goes beyond earlier analyses by focusing on teens who had similar values about sex and other issues before they took a virginity pledge.[†]

Suppose, as this report suggests, abstinence pledges are ineffective and can reduce condom use and increase the risk of teen pregnancy. Would it be immoral to promote the pledges among teens? Should the effectiveness of the pledges in reducing teen pregnancy or STDs have any bearing on the morality of promoting the pledges? Is premarital sex among teens morally wrong regardless of its physical and social risks? Give reasons for your answers.

3. Evidence of Sexual Assault

An intense debate is under way about what level of evidence should be required in campus adjudication hearings to find a student guilty of campus sexual assault. Putative victims of sexual assault want a minimal standard (a "preponderance of evidence") that requires only slightly more than 50 percent likelihood of guilt. Because sexual assault is so hard to prove, they argue, the lower standard is the most reasonable and just; otherwise, very few alleged rapists would ever be found guilty. But the secretary of the U.S. Department of Education wants a higher standard—"clear and convincing" evidence, which amounts to approximately 70 percent likelihood of guilt.

(*New York Times*)—Education Secretary Betsy DeVos on Friday scrapped a key part of government policy on campus sexual assault, saying she was giving colleges more freedom to balance the rights of accused students with the need to crack down on serious misconduct.

The move, which involved rescinding two sets of guidelines several years old, was part of one of the fiercest battles in higher education today, over whether the Obama administration, in trying to get colleges to take sexual assault more seriously, had gone too far and created a system that treated the accused unfairly.

The most controversial portion of the Obama-era guidelines had demanded colleges use the lowest standard of proof, "preponderance of the evidence," in deciding whether a student is responsible for sexual assault, a verdict that can lead to discipline and even expulsion. On Friday, the Education Department said colleges were free to abandon that standard and raise it to a higher standard known as "clear and convincing evidence."

In announcing the change, the latest in a widespread rollback of Obama-era rules by the Trump administration, the department issued a statement saying that the old rules "lacked basic elements of fairness."[‡]

If the lower standard of evidence makes it easier to prove the culpability of accused students, would it also implicate many blameless students? If the higher standard is more just or fair, would it also allow many blameworthy students to escape blame? Which approach is fairer? Are they both bad? Explain.

[‡]Stephanie Saul and Kate Taylor, "Betsy DeVos Reverses Obama-Era Policy on Campus Sexual Assault Investigations," September 22, 2017, https://www.nytimes.com/2017/09/22/us/devos-colleges-sex-assault.html. © 2017 The New York Times. All rights reserved. Used by permission and protected by the Copyright Laws of the United States. The printing, copying, redistribution, or retransmission of this content without express written permission is prohibited.

READINGS

From *Plain Sex*

ALAN H. GOLDMAN

I

* * *

I shall suggest here that sex continues to be misrepresented in recent writings, at least in philosophical writings, and I shall criticize the predominant form of analysis which I term "means-end analysis." Such

conceptions attribute a necessary external goal or purpose to sexual activity, whether it be reproduction, the expression of love, simple communication, or interpersonal awareness. They analyze sexual activity as a means to one of these ends, implying that sexual desire is a desire to reproduce, to love or be loved, or to communicate with others. All definitions of this type suggest false views of the relation of sex to perversion and morality by implying that sex which does not fit one of these models or fulfill one of these functions is in some way deviant or incomplete.

The alternative, simpler analysis with which I will begin is that sexual desire is desire for contact with another person's body and for the pleasure which such contact produces; sexual activity is activity which tends to fulfill such desire of the agent. Whereas Aristotle and Butler were correct in holding that pleasure is normally a byproduct rather than a goal of purposeful action, in the case of sex this is not so clear. The desire for another's body is, principally among other things, the desire for the pleasure that physical contact brings. On the other hand, it is not a desire for a particular sensation detachable from its causal context, a sensation which can be derived in other ways. This definition in terms of the general goal of sexual desire appears preferable to an attempt to more explicitly list or define specific sexual activities, for many activities such as kissing, embracing, massaging, or holding hands may or may not be sexual, depending upon the context and more specifically upon the purposes, needs, or desires into which such activities fit. The generality of the definition also represents a refusal (common in recent psychological texts) to overemphasize orgasm as the goal of sexual desire or genital sex as the only norm of sexual activity (this will be hedged slightly in the discussion of perversion below).

Central to the definition is the fact that the goal of sexual desire and activity is the physical contact itself, rather than something else which this contact might express. By contrast, what I term "means-end analyses" posit ends which I take to be extraneous to plain sex, and they view sex as a means to these ends. Their fault lies not in defining sex in terms of its general goal, but in seeing plain sex as merely a means to other separable ends. I term these "means-end analyses" for convenience, although "means-separable-end analyses," while too cumbersome, might be more fully explanatory. The desire for physical contact with another person is a minimal criterion for (normal) sexual desire, but is both necessary and sufficient to qualify normal desire as sexual. Of course, we may want to express other feelings through sexual acts in various contexts; but without the desire for the physical contact in and for itself, or when it is sought for other reasons, activities in which contact is involved are not predominantly sexual. Furthermore, the desire

for physical contact in itself, without the wish to express affection or other feelings through it, is sufficient to render sexual the activity of the agent which fulfills it. Various activities with this goal alone, such as kissing and caressing in certain contexts, qualify as sexual even without the presence of genital symptoms of sexual excitement. The latter are not therefore necessary criteria for sexual activity.

This initial analysis may seem to some either over- or underinclusive. It might seem too broad in leading us to interpret physical contact as sexual desire in activities such as football and other contact sports. In these cases, however, the desire is not for contact with another body per se, it is not directed toward a particular person for that purpose, and it is not the goal of the activity—the goal is winning or exercising or knocking someone down or displaying one's prowess. If the desire is purely for contact with another specific person's body, then to interpret it as sexual does not seem an exaggeration. A slightly more difficult case is that of a baby's desire to be cuddled and our natural response in wanting to cuddle it. In the case of the baby, the desire may be simply for the physical contact, for the pleasure of the caresses. If so, we may characterize this desire, especially in keeping with Freudian theory, as sexual or protosexual. It will differ nevertheless from full-fledged sexual desire in being more amorphous, not directed outward toward another specific person's body. It may also be that what the infant unconsciously desires is not physical contact per se but signs of affection, tenderness, or security, in which case we have further reason for hesitating to characterize its wants as clearly sexual. The intent of our response to the baby is often the showing of affection, not the pure physical contact, so that our definition in terms of action which fulfils sexual desire *on the part of the agent* does not capture such actions, whatever we say of the baby. (If it is intuitive to characterize our response as sexual as well, there is clearly no problem here for my analysis.) The same can be said of signs of affection (or in some cultures polite greeting) among men or women: these certainly need not be homosexual when the intent is only to show friendship, something extrinsic to plain sex although valuable when added to it.

Our definition of sex in terms of the desire for physical contact may appear too narrow in that a person's personality, not merely her or his body, may be sexually attractive to another, and in that looking or conversing in a certain way can be sexual in a given context without bodily contact. Nevertheless, it is not the contents of one's thoughts per se that are sexually appealing, but one's personality as embodied in certain manners of behavior. Furthermore, if a person is sexually attracted by another's personality, he or she will desire not just further conversation, but actual sexual contact. While looking at or conversing with someone can be interpreted as sexual in given contexts it is so when intended as preliminary to, and hence parasitic upon, elemental sexual interest. Voyeurism or viewing a pornographic movie qualifies as a sexual activity, but only as an imaginative substitute for the real thing (otherwise a deviation from the norm as expressed in our definition). The same is true of masturbation as a sexual activity without a partner.

That the initial definition indicates at least an ingredient of sexual desire and activity is too obvious to argue. We all know what sex is, at least in obvious cases, and do not need philosophers to tell us. My preliminary analysis is meant to serve as a contrast to what sex is not, at least, not necessarily. I concentrate upon the physically manifested desire for another's body, and I take as central the immersion in the physical aspect of one's own existence and attention to the physical embodiment of the other. One may derive pleasure in a sex act from expressing certain feelings to one's partner or from awareness of the attitude of one's partner, but sexual desire is essentially desire for physical contact itself: it is a bodily desire for the body of another that dominates our mental life for more or less brief periods. Traditional writings were correct to emphasize the purely physical or animal aspect of sex; they were wrong only in condemning it. This characterization of sex as an intensely pleasurable physical activity and acute physical desire may seem to some to capture only its barest level. But it is worth distinguishing and focusing upon this least common denominator in order to avoid the false views of sexual morality and perversion which emerge from thinking that sex is essentially something else.

II

We may turn then to what sex is not, to the arguments regarding supposed conceptual connections between sex and other activities which it is necessary to conceptually distinguish. The more comprehensible attempt to build an extraneous purpose into the sex act identifies that purpose as reproduction, its primary biological function. While this may be "nature's" purpose, it certainly need not be ours (the analogy with eating, while sometimes overworked, is pertinent here). While this identification may once have had a rational basis which also grounded the identification of the value and morality of sex with that applicable to reproduction and childrearing, the development of contraception rendered the connection weak. Methods of contraception are by now so familiar and so widely used that it is not necessary to dwell upon the changes wrought by these developments in the concept of sex itself and in a rational sexual ethic dependent upon that concept. In the past, the ever present possibility of children rendered the concepts of sex and sexual morality different from those required at present. There may be good reasons, if the presence and care of both mother and father are beneficial to children, for restricting reproduction to marriage. Insofar as society has a legitimate role in protecting children's interests, it may be justified in giving marriage a legal status, although this question is complicated by the fact (among others) that children born to single mothers deserve no penalties. In any case, the point here is simply that these questions are irrelevant at the present time to those regarding the morality of sex and its potential social regulation. . . .

It is obvious that the desire for sex is not necessarily a desire to reproduce, that the psychological manifestation has become, if it were not always, distinct from its biological roots. There are many parallels, as previously mentioned, with other natural functions. The pleasures of eating and exercising are to a large extent independent of their roles in nourishment or health (as the junk-food industry discovered with a vengeance). Despite the obvious parallel with sex, there is still a tendency for many to think that sex acts which can be reproductive are, if not more moral or less immoral, at least more natural. These categories of morality and "naturalness," or normality, are not to be identified with each other, as will be argued below, and neither is applicable to sex by virtue of its connection to reproduction. The tendency to identify reproduction as the conceptually connected end of sex is most prevalent now in the pronouncements of the Catholic church. There the assumed analysis is clearly tied to a restrictive sexual morality according to which acts become immoral and unnatural when they are not oriented towards reproduction, a morality which has independent roots in the Christian sexual ethic as it derives from Paul. However, the means-end analysis fails to generate a consistent sexual ethic: homosexual and oral-genital sex is condemned while kissing or caressing, acts equally unlikely to lead in themselves to fertilization, even when properly characterized as sexual according to our definition, are not.

III

Before discussing further relations of means-end analyses to false or inconsistent sexual ethics and concepts of perversion, I turn to other examples of these analyses. One common position views sex as essentially an expression of love or affection between the partners. It is generally recognized that there are other types of love besides sexual, but sex itself is taken as an expression of one type, sometimes termed "romantic" love.[1] Various factors again ought to weaken this identification. First, there are other types of love besides that which it is appropriate to express sexually, and "romantic" love itself can be expressed in many other ways. I am not denying that sex can take on heightened value and meaning when it becomes a vehicle for the expression of feelings of love or tenderness, but so can many other usually mundane activities such as getting up early to make breakfast on Sunday, cleaning the house, and so on. Second, sex itself can be used to communicate many other emotions besides love, and, as I will argue below, can communicate nothing in particular and still be good sex.

On a deeper level, an internal tension is bound to result from an identification of sex, which I have described as a physical-psychological desire, with love as a long-term, deep emotional relationship between two individuals. As this type of relationship, love is

permanent, at least in intent, and more or less exclusive. A normal person cannot deeply love more than a few individuals even in a lifetime. We may be suspicious that those who attempt or claim to love many love them weakly if at all. Yet, fleeting sexual desire can arise in relation to a variety of other individuals one finds sexually attractive. It may even be, as some have claimed, that sexual desire in humans naturally seeks variety, while this is obviously false of love. For this reason, monogamous sex, even if justified, almost always represents a sacrifice or the exercise of self-control on the part of the spouses, while monogamous love generally does not. There is no such thing as casual love in the sense in which I intend the term "love." It may occasionally happen that a spouse falls deeply in love with someone else (especially when sex is conceived in terms of love), but this is relatively rare in comparison to passing sexual desires for others; and while the former often indicates a weakness or fault in the marriage relation, the latter does not.

If love is indeed more exclusive in its objects than is sexual desire, this explains why those who view sex as essentially an expression of love would again tend to hold a repressive or restrictive sexual ethic. As in the case of reproduction, there may be good reasons for reserving the total commitment of deep love to the context of marriage and family—the normal personality may not withstand additional divisions of ultimate commitment and allegiance. There is no question that marriage itself is best sustained by a deep relation of love and affection; and even if love is not naturally monogamous, the benefits of family units to children provide additional reason to avoid serious commitments elsewhere which weaken family ties. It can be argued similarly that monogamous sex strengthens families by restricting and at the same time guaranteeing an outlet for sexual desire in marriage. But there is more force to the argument that recognition of a clear distinction between sex and love in society would help avoid disastrous marriages which result from adolescent confusion of the two when sexual desire is mistaken for permanent love, and would weaken damaging jealousies which arise in marriages in relation to passing sexual desires. The love and affection of a sound marriage certainly differs from the adolescent romantic variety, which is often a mere substitute for sex in the context of a repressive sexual ethic.

In fact, the restrictive sexual ethic tied to the means-end analysis in terms of love again has failed to be consistent. At least, it has not been applied consistently, but forms part of the double standard which has curtailed the freedom of women. It is predictable in light of this history that some women would now advocate using sex as another kind of means, as a political weapon or as a way to increase unjustly denied power and freedom. The inconsistency in the sexual ethic typically attached to the sex-love analysis, according to which it has generally been taken with a grain of salt when applied to men, is simply another example of the impossibility of tailoring a plausible moral theory in this area to a conception of sex which builds in conceptually extraneous factors.

I am not suggesting here that sex ought never to be connected with love or that it is not a more significant and valuable activity when it is. Nor am I denying that individuals need love as much as sex and perhaps emotionally need at least one complete relationship which encompasses both. Just as sex can express love and take on heightened significance when it does, so love is often naturally accompanied by an intermittent desire for sex. But again love is accompanied appropriately by desires for other shared activities as well. What makes the desire for sex seem more intimately connected with love is the intimacy which is seen to be a natural feature of mutual sex acts. Like love, sex is held to lay one bare psychologically as well as physically. Sex is unquestionably intimate, but beyond that the psychological toll often attached may be a function of the restrictive sexual ethic itself, rather than a legitimate apology for it. The intimacy involved in love is psychologically consuming in a generally healthy way, while the psychological tolls of sexual relations, often including embarrassment as a correlate of intimacy, are too often the result of artificial sexual ethics and taboos. The intimacy involved in both love and sex is insufficient in any case in light of previous points to render a means-end analysis in these terms appropriate.

* * *

V

I have now criticized various types of analysis sharing or suggesting a common means-end form. I have suggested that analyses of this form relate to attempts to limit moral or natural sex to that which fulfills some purpose or function extraneous to basic sexual desire. The attempts to brand forms of sex outside the idealized models as immoral or perverted fail to achieve consistency with intuitions that they themselves do not directly question. The reproductive model brands oral-genital sex a deviation, but cannot account for kissing or holding hands; the communication account holds voyeurism to be perverted but cannot accommodate sex acts without much conscious thought or seductive nonphysical foreplay; the sex-love model makes most sexual desire seem degrading or base. The first and last condemn extramarital sex on the sound but irrelevant grounds that reproduction and deep commitment are best confined to family contexts. The romanticization of sex and the confusion of sexual desire with love operate in both directions: sex outside the context of romantic love is repressed; once it is repressed, partners become more difficult to find and sex becomes romanticized further, out of proportion to its real value for the individual.

What all these analyses share in addition to a common form is accordance with and perhaps derivation from the Platonic-Christian moral tradition, according to which the animal or purely physical element of humans is the source of immorality, and plain sex in the sense I defined it is an expression of this element, hence in itself to be condemned. All the analyses examined seem to seek a distance from sexual desire itself in attempting to extend it conceptually beyond the physical. The love and communications analyses seek refinement or intellectualization of the desire; plain physical sex becomes vulgar, and too straightforward sexual encounters without an aura of respectable cerebral communicative content are to be avoided. [Robert] Solomon explicitly argues that sex cannot be a "mere" appetite, his argument being that if it were, subway exhibitionism and other vulgar forms would be pleasing.[2] This fails to recognize that sexual desire can be focused or selective at the same time as being physical. Lower animals are not attracted by every other member of their species, either. Rancid food forced down one's throat is not pleasing, but that certainly fails to show that hunger is not a physical appetite. Sexual desire lets us know that we are physical beings and, indeed, animals; this is why traditional Platonic morality is so thorough in its condemnation. Means-end analyses continue to reflect this tradition, sometimes unwittingly. They show that in conceptualizing sex it is still difficult, despite years of so-called revolution in this area, to free ourselves from the lingering suspicion that plain sex as physical desire is an expression of our "lower selves," that yielding to our animal natures is subhuman or vulgar.

VI

Having criticized these analyses for the sexual ethics and concepts of perversion they imply, it remains to contrast my account along these lines. To the question of what morality might be implied by my analysis, the answer is that there are no moral implications whatever. Any analysis of sex which imputes a moral character to sex acts in themselves is wrong for that reason. There is no morality intrinsic to sex, although general moral rules apply to the treatment of others in sex acts as they apply to all human relations. We can speak of a sexual ethic as we can speak of a business ethic, without implying that business in itself is either moral or immoral or that special rules are required to judge business practice which are not derived from rules that apply elsewhere as well. Sex is not in itself a moral category, although like business it invariably places us into relations with others in which moral rules apply. It gives us opportunity to do what is otherwise recognized as wrong, to harm others, deceive them or manipulate them against their wills. Just as the fact that an act is sexual in itself never renders it wrong or adds to its wrongness if it is wrong on other grounds (sexual acts towards minors are wrong on other grounds, as will be argued below), so no wrong act is to be excused because done from a sexual motive. If a "crime of passion" is to be excused, it would have to be on grounds of temporary insanity rather than sexual context (whether insanity does constitute a legitimate excuse for certain actions is too big a topic to argue here). Sexual motives are among others which may

become deranged, and the fact that they are sexual has no bearing in itself on the moral character, whether negative or exculpatory, of the actions deriving from them. Whatever might be true of war, it is certainly not the case that all's fair in love or sex.

Our first conclusion regarding morality and sex is therefore that no conduct otherwise immoral should be excused because it is sexual conduct, and nothing in sex is immoral unless condemned by rules which apply elsewhere as well. The last clause requires further clarification. Sexual conduct can be governed by particular rules relating only to sex itself. But these precepts must be implied by general moral rules when these are applied to specific sexual relations or types of conduct. The same is true of rules of fair business, ethical medicine, or courtesy in driving a car. In the latter case, particular acts on the road may be reprehensible, such as tailgating or passing on the right, which seem to bear no resemblance as actions to any outside the context of highway safety. Nevertheless their immorality derives from the fact that they place others in danger, a circumstance which, when avoidable, is to be condemned in any context. This structure of general and specifically applicable rules describes a reasonable sexual ethic as well. To take an extreme case, rape is always a sexual act and it is always immoral. A rule against rape can therefore be considered an obvious part of sexual morality which has no bearing on nonsexual conduct. But the immorality of rape derives from its being an extreme violation of a person's body, of the right not to be humiliated, and of the general moral prohibition against using other persons against their wills, not from the fact that it is a sexual act.

The application elsewhere of general moral rules to sexual conduct is further complicated by the fact that it will be relative to the particular desires and preferences of one's partner (these may be influenced by and hence in some sense include misguided beliefs about sexual morality itself). This means that there will be fewer specific rules in the area of sexual ethics than in other areas of conduct, such as driving cars, where the relativity of preference is irrelevant to the prohibition of objectively dangerous conduct. More reliance will have to be placed upon the general moral rule, which in this area holds simply that the preferences, desires, and interests of one's partner or potential partner ought to be taken into account. This rule is certainly not specifically formulated to govern sexual relations; it is a form of the central principle of morality itself. But when applied to sex, it prohibits certain actions, such as molestation of children, which cannot be categorized as violations of the rule without at the same time being classified as sexual. I believe this last case is the closest we can come to an action which is wrong *because* it is sexual, but even here its wrongness is better characterized as deriving from the detrimental effects such behavior can have on the future emotional and sexual life of the naive victims, and from the fact that such behavior therefore involves manipulation of innocent persons without regard for their interests. Hence, this case also involves violation of a general moral rule which applies elsewhere as well.

Aside from faulty conceptual analyses of sex and the influence of the Platonic moral tradition, there are two more plausible reasons for thinking that there are moral dimensions intrinsic to sex acts per se. The first is that such acts are normally intensely pleasurable. According to a hedonistic, utilitarian moral theory they therefore should be at least prima facie morally right, rather than morally neutral in themselves. To me this seems incorrect and reflects unfavorably on the ethical theory in question. The pleasure intrinsic to sex acts is a good, but not, it seems to me, a good with much positive moral significance. Certainly I can have no duty to pursue such pleasure myself, and while it may be nice to give pleasure of any form to others, there is no ethical requirement to do so, given my right over my own body. The exception relates to the context of sex acts themselves, when one partner derives pleasure from the other and ought to return the favor. This duty to reciprocate takes us out of the domain of hedonistic utilitarianism, however, and into a Kantian moral framework, the central principles of which call for just such reciprocity in human relations. Since independent moral judgments regarding sexual activities constitute one area in which ethical theories are to be tested, these observations indicate here, as I believe others indicate elsewhere, the fertility of the Kantian, as opposed to the utilitarian, principles in reconstructing reasoned moral consciousness.

It may appear from this alternative Kantian viewpoint that sexual acts must be at least prima facie wrong in themselves. This is because they invariably involve at different stages the manipulation of one's partner for one's own pleasure, which might appear to be prohibited on the formulation of Kant's principle which holds that one ought not to treat another as a means to such private ends. A more realistic rendering of this formulation, however, one which recognizes its intended equivalence to the first universalizability principle, admits no such absolute prohibition. Many human relations, most economic transactions for example, involve using other individuals for personal benefit. These relations are immoral only when they are one-sided, when the benefits are not mutual, or when the transactions are not freely and rationally endorsed by all parties. The same holds true of sexual acts. The central principle governing them is the Kantian demand for reciprocity in sexual relations. In order to comply with the second formulation of the categorical imperative, one must recognize the subjectivity of one's partner (not merely by being aroused by her or his desire, as [Thomas] Nagel describes). Even in an act which by its nature "objectifies" the other, one recognizes a partner as a subject with demands and desires by yielding to those desires, by allowing oneself to be a sexual object as well, by giving pleasure or ensuring that the pleasures of the acts are mutual. It is this kind of reciprocity which forms the basis for morality in sex, which distinguishes right acts from wrong in this area as in others. (Of course, prior to sex acts one must gauge their effects upon potential partners and take these longer range interests into account.)

VII

I suggested earlier that in addition to generating confusion regarding the rightness or wrongness of sex acts, false conceptual analyses of the means-end form cause confusion about the value of sex to the individual. My account recognizes the satisfaction of desire and the pleasure this brings as the central psychological function of the sex act for the individual. Sex affords us a paradigm of pleasure, but not a cornerstone of value. For most of us it is not only a needed outlet for desire but also the most enjoyable form of recreation we know. Its value is nevertheless easily mistaken by being confused with that of love, when it is taken as essentially an expression of that emotion. Although intense, the pleasures of sex are brief and repetitive rather than cumulative. They give value to the specific acts which generate them, but not the lasting kind of value which enhances one's whole life. The briefness of these pleasures contributes to their intensity (or perhaps their intensity makes them necessarily brief), but it also relegates them to the periphery of most rational plans for the good life.

By contrast, love typically develops over a long term relation; while its pleasures may be less intense and physical, they are of more cumulative value. The importance of love to the individual may well be central in a rational system of value. And it has perhaps an even deeper moral significance relating to the identification with the interests of another person, which broadens one's possible relationships with others as well. Marriage is again important in preserving this relation between adults and children, which seems as important to the adults as it is to the children in broadening concerns which have a tendency to become selfish. Sexual desire, by contrast, is desire for another which is nevertheless essentially self-regarding. Sexual pleasure is certainly a good for the individual, and for many it may be necessary in order for them to function in a reasonably cheerful way. But it bears little relation to those other values just discussed, to which some analyses falsely suggest a conceptual connection.

VIII

While my initial analysis lacks moral implications in itself, as it should, it does suggest by contrast a concept of sexual perversion. Since the concept of perversion is itself a sexual concept, it will always be defined relative to some definition of normal sex; and any conception of the norm will imply a contrary notion of perverse forms. The concept suggested by my account again differs sharply from those implied by the means-end analyses examined above. Perversion does not represent a deviation from the reproductive function

(or kissing would be perverted), from a loving relationship (or most sexual desire and many heterosexual acts would be perverted), or from efficiency in communicating (or unsuccessful seduction attempts would be perverted). It is a deviation from a norm, but the norm in question is merely statistical. Of course, not all sexual acts that are statistically unusual are perverted—a three-hour continuous sexual act would be unusual but not necessarily abnormal in the requisite sense. The abnormality in question must relate to the *form of the desire* itself in order to constitute sexual perversion; for example, desire, not for contact with another, but for merely looking, for harming or being harmed, for contact with items of clothing. This concept of sexual abnormality is that suggested by my definition of normal sex in terms of its typical desire. However not all unusual desires qualify either, only those with the typical physical sexual effects upon the individual who satisfies them. These effects, such as erection in males, were not built into the original definition of sex in terms of sexual desire, for they do not always occur in activities that are properly characterized as sexual, say, kissing for the pleasure of it. But they do seem to bear a closer relation to the definition of activities as perverted. (For those who consider only genital sex sexual, we could build such symptoms into a narrower definition, then speaking of sex in a broad sense as well as "proper" sex.)

Solomon and Nagel disagree with this statistical notion of perversion. For them the concept is evaluative rather than statistical. I do not deny that the term "perverted" is often used evaluatively (and purely emotively for that matter), or that it has a negative connotation for the average speaker. I do deny that we can find a norm, other than that of statistically usual desire, against which all and only activities that properly count as sexual perversions can be contrasted. Perverted sex is simply abnormal sex, and if the norm is not to be an idealized or romanticized extraneous end or purpose, it must express the way human sexual desires usually manifest themselves. Of course not all norms in other areas of discourse need be statistical in this way. Physical health is an example of a relatively clear norm which does not seem to depend upon the numbers of healthy people. But the concept in this case achieves its clarity through the connection of physical health with other clearly desirable physical functions and characteristics, for example, living longer. In the case of sex, that which is statistically abnormal is not necessarily incapacitating in other ways, and yet these abnormal desires with sexual effects upon their subject do count as perverted to the degree to which their objects deviate from usual ones. The connotations of the concept of perversion beyond those connected with abnormality or statistical deviation derive more from the attitudes of those likely to call certain acts perverted than from specifiable features of the acts themselves. These connotations add to the concept of abnormality that of *sub*normality, but there is no norm against which the latter can be measured intelligibly in accord with all and only acts intuitively called perverted.

The only proper evaluative norms relating to sex involve degrees of pleasure in the acts and moral norms, but neither of these scales coincides with statistical degrees of abnormality, according to which perversion is to be measured. The three parameters operate independently (this was implied for the first two when it was held above that the pleasure of sex is a good, but not necessarily a moral good). Perverted sex may be more or less enjoyable to particular individuals than normal sex, and more or less moral, depending upon the particular relations involved. Raping a sheep may be more perverted than raping a woman, but certainly not more condemnable morally.[3] It is nevertheless true that the evaluative connotations attaching to the term "perverted" derive partly from the fact that most people consider perverted sex highly immoral. Many such acts are forbidden by long standing taboos, and it is sometimes difficult to distinguish what is forbidden from what is immoral. Others, such as sadistic acts, are genuinely immoral, but again not at all because of their connection with sex or abnormality. The principles which condemn these acts would condemn them equally if they were common and nonsexual. It is not true that we properly could continue to consider acts perverted which were found to be very common practice across societies. Such acts, if harmful, might continue to be condemned properly as immoral, but it was just shown that the immorality

of an act does not vary with its degree of perversion. If not harmful, common acts previously considered abnormal might continue to be called perverted for a time by the moralistic minority; but the term when applied to such cases would retain only its emotive negative connotation without consistent logical criteria for application. It would represent merely prejudiced moral judgments.

To adequately explain why there is a tendency to so deeply condemn perverted acts would require a treatise in psychology beyond the scope of this paper. Part of the reason undoubtedly relates to the tradition of repressive sexual ethics and false conceptions of sex; another part to the fact that all abnormality seems to disturb and fascinate us at the same time. The former explains why sexual perversion is more abhorrent to many than other forms of abnormality; the latter indicates why we tend to have an emotive and evaluative reaction to perversion in the first place. It may be, as has been suggested according to a Freudian line,[4] that our uneasiness derives from latent desires we are loathe to admit, but this thesis takes us into psychological issues I am not competent to judge. Whatever the psychological explanation, it suffices to point out here that the conceptual connection between perversion and genuine or consistent moral evaluation is spurious and again suggested by misleading means-end idealizations of the concept of sex.

The position I have taken in this paper against those concepts is not totally new. Something similar to it is found in Freud's view of sex, which of course was genuinely revolutionary, and in the body of writings deriving from Freud to the present time. But in his revolt against romanticized and repressive conceptions, Freud went too far—from a refusal to view sex as merely a means to a view of it as the end of all human behavior, although sometimes an elaborately disguised end. This pansexualism led to the thesis (among others) that repression was indeed an inevitable and necessary part of social regulation of any form, a strange consequence of a position that began by opposing the repressive aspects of the means-end view. Perhaps the time finally has arrived when we can achieve a reasonable middle ground in this area, at least in philosophy if not in society.

NOTES

1. Even Bertrand Russell, whose writing in this area was a model of rationality, at least for its period, tends to make this identification and to condemn plain sex in the absence of love: "sex intercourse apart from love has little value, and is to be regarded primarily as experimentation with a view to love." *Marriage and Morals* (New York: Bantam, 1959), p. 87.

2. [Robert] Solomon, "Sex and Perversion," *Philosophy and Sex,* ed. R. Baker and F. Elliston (Buffalo: Prometheus, 1975), p. 285.

3. The example is like one from Sara Ruddick, "Better Sex," *Philosophy and Sex,* p. 96.

4. See Michael Slote, "Inapplicable Concepts and Sexual Perversion," *Philosophy and Sex.*

From *Sexual Morality*

ROGER SCRUTON

* * *

We must now attempt to apply the Aristotelian strategy to the subject-matter of this book, and ask whether there is such a thing as sexual virtue, and, if so, what is it, and how is it acquired? Clearly, sexual desire, which is an interpersonal attitude with the most far-reaching consequences for those who are joined by it, cannot be morally neutral. On the contrary, it is in the experience of sexual desire that we are most vividly conscious of the distinction between virtuous and vicious impulses, and most vividly aware that, in the choice between them, our happiness is at stake.

The Aristotelian strategy enjoins us to ignore the actual conditions of any particular person's life, and to look only at the permanent features of human nature. We know that people feel sexual desire; that they feel erotic love, which may grow from desire; that they may avoid both these feelings, by dissipation or self-restraint. Is there anything to be said about desire, other than that it falls within the general scope of the virtue of temperance, which enjoins us to desire only what reason approves?

The first, and most important, observation to be made is that the capacity for love in general, and for

erotic love in particular, is a virtue. . . . [E]rotic love involves an element of mutual self-enhancement; it generates a sense of the irreplaceable value, both of the other and of the self, and of the activities which bind them. To receive and to give this love is to achieve something of incomparable value in the process of self-fulfilment. It is to gain the most powerful of all interpersonal *guarantees*; in erotic love the subject becomes conscious of the full reality of his personal existence, not only in his own eyes, but in the eyes of another. Everything that he is and values gains sustenance from his love, and every project receives a meaning beyond the moment. All that exists for us as mere hope and hypothesis—the attachment to life and to the body—achieves under the rule of *erōs* the aspect of a radiant certainty. Unlike the cold glances of approval, admiration and pride, the glance of love sees value precisely in that which is the course of anxiety and doubt: in the merely contingent, merely 'empirical', existence of the flesh, the existence which we did not choose, but to which we are condemned. It is the answer to man's fallen condition—to his *Geworfenheit*.

To receive erotic love, however, a person must be able to give it: or if he cannot, the love of others will be a torment to him, seeking from him that which he cannot provide, and directing against him the fury of a disappointed right. It is therefore unquestionable that we have reason to acquire the capacity for erotic love, and, if this means bending our sexual impulses in a certain direction, that will be the direction of sexual virtue. Indeed, . . . the development of the sexual impulse towards love may be impeded: there are sexual habits which are vicious, precisely in neutralising the capacity for love. The first thing that can be said, therefore, is that we all have reason to avoid those habits and to educate our children not to possess them.

Here it may be objected that not every love is happy, that there are many—Anna Karenina, for example, or Phaedra—whose capacity for love was the cause of their downfall. But we must remind ourselves of the Aristotelian strategy. In establishing that courage or wisdom is a virtue, the Aristotelian does not argue that the possession of these virtues is in every particular circumstance bound to be advantageous. A parable of Derek Parfit's, adapted from T. C. Schelling, adequately shows what is a stake: Suppose a man breaks into my house and commands me to open the safe for him, saying that, if I do not comply, he will begin to shoot my children. He has heard me telephone the police, and knows that, if he leaves any of us alive, we will be able to give information sufficient to arrest him if he takes what the safe contains. Clearly it is irrational in these circumstances to open the safe—since that will not protect any of us—and also not to open it, since that would cause the robber to kill my children one by one in order to persuade me of his sincerity. Suppose, however, I possess a drug that causes me to become completely irrational. I swallow the pill, and cry out: 'I love my children, therefore kill them'; the man tortures me and I beg him to continue; and so on. In these changed circumstances, my assailant is powerless to obtain what he wants and can only flee before the police arrive. In other words, in such a case, it is actually in the interests of the subject to be irrational: he has overwhelming circumstantial *reason* to be irrational, just as Anna Karenina had an overwhelming circumstantial *reason* to be without the capacity for love. Clearly, however, it would be absurd, on these grounds, to inculcate a habit of irrationality in our children; indeed no *reason* could be given, in the absence of detailed knowledge of a person's future, for acquiring such a habit. In so far as reasons can be given now, for the cultivation of this or that state of character, they must justify the cultivation of rationality

before all else—for how can I flourish according to my nature as a rational agent if I am not at least rational?

In like manner, it is not the particular personal tragedy but the generality of the human condition that determines the basis of sexual morality. Tragedy and loss are the rare but necessary outcomes of a process which we all have reason to undergo. (Indeed, it is part of the point of tragedy that it divorces in our imagination the right and the good from the merely prudential: that it sets the value of life against the value of mere survival.) We wish to know, in advance of any particular experience, which dispositions a person must have if he is successfully to express himself in sexual desire and to be fulfilled in his sexual endeavours. Love is the fulfilment of desire, and therefore love is its *telos*. A life of celibacy may also be fulfilled; but, assuming the general truth that most of us have a powerful, and perhaps overwhelming, urge to make love, it is in our interests to ensure that love—and not some other thing—is made.

Love, I have argued, is prone to jealousy, and the object of jealousy is defined by the thought of the beloved's desire. Because jealousy is one of the greatest of psychical catastrophes, involving the possible ruin of both partners, a morality based in the need for erotic love must forestall and eliminate jealousy. It is in the deepest human interest, therefore, that we form the habit of fidelity. This habit is natural and normal; but it is also easily broken, and the temptation to break it is contained in desire itself—in the element of generality which tempts us always to experiment, to verify, to detach ourselves from that which is too familiar in the interest of excitement and risk. Virtuous desire is faithful; but virtuous desire is also an artefact, made possible by a process of moral education which we do not, in truth, understand in its complexity.

If that observation is correct, a whole section of traditional sexual morality must be upheld. The fulfilment of sexual desire defines the nature of desire: *to telos phuseis estin*. And the nature of desire gives us our standard of normality. There are enormous varieties of human sexual conduct, and of 'common-sense' morality: some societies permit or encourage polygamy, others look with indifference upon premarital intercourse, or regard marriage itself as no more than an episode in a relation that pre-exists and perhaps survives it. But no society, and no 'common-sense' morality—not even, it seems, the morality of Samoa—looks with favour upon promiscuity or infidelity, unless influenced by a doctrine of 'emancipation' or 'liberation' which is dependent for its sense upon the very conventions which it defies. Whatever the institutional forms of human sexual union, and whatever the range of permitted partners, sexual desire is itself inherently 'nuptial': it involves concentration upon the embodied existence of the other, leading through tenderness to the 'vow' of erotic love. It is a telling observation that the civilisation which has most tolerated the institution of polygamy—the Islamic—has also, in its erotic literature, produced what are perhaps the intensest and most poignant celebrations of monogamous love, precisely through the attempt to capture, not the institution of marriage, but the human datum of desire.

The nuptiality of desire suggests, in its turn, a natural history of desire: a principle of development which defines the 'normal course' of sexual education. 'Sexual maturity' involves incorporating the sexual impulse into the personality, and so making sexual desire into an expression of the subject himself, even though it is, in the heat of action, a force which also overcomes him. If the Aristotetlian approach to these things is as plausible as I think it is, the virtuous habit will also have the character of a 'mean': it will involve the disposition to desire what is desirable, despite the competing impulses of animal lust (in which the intentionality of desire may be demolished) and timorous frigidity (in which the sexual impulse is impeded altogether). Education is directed towards the special kind of temperance which shows itself, sometimes as chastity, sometimes as fidelity, sometimes as passionate desire, according to the 'right judgement' of the subject. In wanting what is judged to be desirable, the virtuous person wants what may also be loved, and what may therefore be obtained without hurt or humiliation.

Virtue is a matter of degree, rarely attained in its completion, but always admired. Because traditional sexual education has pursued sexual virtue, it is worthwhile summarising its most important features, in order to see the power of the idea that underlies and justifies it.

The most important feature of traditional sexual education is summarised in anthropological language as the 'ethic of pollution and taboo'. The child was taught to regard his body as sacred, and as subject to pollution by misperception or misuse. The sense of pollution is by no means a trivial side-effect of the 'bad sexual encounter': it may involve a penetrating disgust, at oneself, one's body and one's situation, such as is experienced by the victim of rape. Those sentiments—which arise from our 'fear of the obscene'—express the tension contained within the experience of embodiment. At any moment we can become 'mere body', the self driven from its incarnation, and its habitation ransacked. The most important root idea of personal morality is that I am *in* my body, not (to borrow Descartes' image) as a pilot in a ship, but as an incarnate self. My body is identical with me, and sexual purity is the precious guarantee of this.

Sexual purity does not forbid desire: it simply ensures the status of desire as an interpersonal feeling. The child who learns 'dirty habits' detaches his sex from himself, sets it outside himself as something curious and alien. His fascinated enslavement to the body is also a withering of desire, a scattering of erotic energy and a loss of union with the other. Sexual purity sustains the *subject* of desire, making him present as a self in the very act which overcomes him.

The extraordinary spiritual significance accorded to sexual 'purity' has, of course, its sociobiological and its psychoanalytical explanations. But what, exactly, is its *meaning*, and have people been right to value it? In Wagner's *Parsifal*, the 'pure fool' is uniquely credited with the power to heal the terrible wound which is the physical sign of Amfortas's sexual 'pollution'. He alone can redeem Kundry, the 'fallen' woman, whose sexual licence is so resistant to her penitent personality, that it must be confined to another world, of which she retains only a dim and horrified consciousness. That other world is a world of pleasure and opportunity, a world of the 'permitted'. It is governed, however, by the impure eunuch Klingsor, whose rule is a kind of slavery. Wagner finds the meaning of Christian redemption in the fool's chastity, which leads him to renounce the rewards of an impure desire for the sake of another's salvation. Parsifal releases Amfortas from the hold of 'magic', from the 'charm' which tempts Szymanowski's King Roger towards a vain apotheosis. Parsifal is the harbinger of peace and freedom, in a world that has been enslaved by the magic of desire.

The haunting symbols of this opera owe their power to feelings that are too deep to be lightly dismissed as aesthetic artefacts. But what is their meaning for people who live unsheltered by religion? The answer is to be found, not in religious, but in sexual, feeling. The purely human redemption which is offered to us in love is dependent, in the last analysis, upon public recognition of the value of chastity, and of the sacrilege involved in a sexual impulse that wanders free from the controlling impulse of respect. The 'pollution' of the prostitute is not that she gives herself for money, but that she gives herself to those whom she hates or despises. This is the 'wound' of unchastity, which cannot be healed in solitude by the one who suffers it, but only by his acceptance into a social order which confines the sexual impulse to the realm of intimate relations. The chaste person sustains the ideal of sexual innocence, by giving honourable form to chastity as a way of life. Through his example, it becomes not foolish but admirable to ignore the promptings of a desire that brings no intimacy or fulfilment. Chastity is not a private policy, followed by one individual alone for the sake of his peace of mind. It has a wider and more generous significance: it attempts to draw others into complicity, and to sustain a social order that confines the sexual impulse to the personal sphere.

Chastity exists in two forms: as a publicly declared and publicly recognised role or policy (the chastity of the monk, priest or nun); or as a private resolution, a recognition of the morality that lies dormant in desire. Thus Hans Sachs, in *Die Meistersinger*, who has the opportunity to fulfil his desire, chooses rather to renounce it, knowing that it will not be reciprocated. Sachs is loved and admired for the irreproachable aloneness which makes him the property of all. He is the buttress of Nuremberg, whose satisfactions are public satisfactions, precisely because his own seed has not been sown. His melancholy and bookish

contemplation of the trivialities of progenerative man are in one sense a sigh from the genetic depth: the species is alive in this sigh, just as the individual dies in it. In another sense, however, his melancholy is the supreme affirmation of the reality of others' joys: the recognition that desire must be silenced, in order that others may thrive in their desire.

The child was traditionally brought up to achieve sexual fulfilment only *through* chastity, which is the condition which surrounds him on his first entering the adult world—the world of commitments and obligations. At the same time, he was encouraged to ponder certain 'ideal objects' of desire. These, presented to him under the aspect of an idealised physical beauty, were never *merely* beautiful, but also endowed with the moral attributes that fitted them for love. This dual inculcation of 'pure' habits and 'ideal' love might seem, on the face of it, to be unworthy of the name of education. Is it not, rather, like the mere *training* of a horse or a dog, which arbitrarily forbids some things and fosters others, without offering the first hint of a reason why? And is it not the distinguishing mark of education that it engages with the rational nature of its recipient, and does not merely mould him indifferently to his own understanding of the process? Why, in short, is this moral education, rather than a transference into the sexual sphere—as Freud would have it—of those same processes of interdiction that train us to defecate, not in our nappies, but in a porcelain pot?

The answer is clear. The cult of innocence is an attempt to generate rational conduct, by incorporating the sexual impulse into the self-activity of the subject. It is an attempt to impede the impulse, until such a time as it may attach itself to the interpersonal project that leads to its fulfilment: the project of union with another person, who is wanted not merely for his body, but for the person who *is* this body. Innocence is the disposition to avoid sexual encounter, except with the person whom one may fully desire. Children who have lost their innocence have acquired the habit of gratification through the body alone, in a state of partial or truncated desire. Their gratification is detached from the conditions of personal fulfilment and wanders from object to object with no settled tendency to attach itself to any, pursued all the while by a sense of the body's obscene dominion. 'Debauching of the innocent' was traditionally regarded as a most serious offence, and one that offered genuine *harm* to the victim. The harm in question was not physical, but moral: the undermining of the process which prepares the child to enter the world of *erōs*. (Thus Nabokov's Lolita, who passes with such rapidity from childish provocativeness to a knowing interest in the sexual act, finds, in the end, a marriage devoid of passion, and dies without knowledge of desire.)

The personal and the sexual can become divorced in many ways. The task of sexual morality is to unite them, to sustain thereby the intentionality of desire, and to prepare the individual for erotic love. Sexual morality is the morality of embodiment: the posture which strives to unite us with our bodies, precisely in those situations when our bodies are foremost in our thoughts. Without such a morality the human world is subject to a dangerous divide, a gulf between self and body, at the verge of which all our attempts at personal union falter and withdraw. Hence the prime focus of sexual morality is not the attitude to others, but the attitude to one's own body and its uses. Its aim is to safeguard the integrity of our embodiment. Only on that condition, it is thought, can we inculcate either innocence in the young or fidelity in the adult. Such habits are, however, only one part of sexual virtue. Traditional morality has combined its praise of them with a condemnation of other things—in particular of the habits of lust and perversion. And it is not hard to find the reason for these condemnations.

Perversion consists precisely in a diverting of the sexual impulse from its interpersonal goal, or towards some act that is intrinsically destructive of personal relations and of the values that we find in them. The 'dissolution' of the flesh, which the Marquis de Sade regarded as so important an element in the sexual aim, is in fact that dissolution of the soul; the perversions described by de Sade are not so much attempts to destroy the flesh of the victim as to rid his flesh of its personal meaning, to wring out, with the blood, the rival perspective. That is true in one way or another of all perversion, which can be simply described as the habit of finding a sexual release that avoids or abolishes the *other*, obliterating his embodiment with the

obscene perception of his body. Perversion is narcissistic, often solipsistic, involving strategies of replacement which are intrinsically destructive of personal feeling. Perversion therefore prepares us for a life without personal fulfilment, in which no human relation achieves foundation in the acceptance of the other, as this acceptance is provided by desire.

Lust may be defined as a genuine sexual desire, from which the goal of erotic love has been excluded, and in which whatever tends towards that goal—tenderness, intimacy, fidelity, dependence—is curtailed or obstructed. There need be nothing perverted in this. Indeed the special case of lust which I have discussed under the title of Don Juanism, in which the project of intimacy is constantly abbreviated by the flight towards another sexual object, provides one of our paradigms of desire. Nevertheless, the traditional condemnation of lust is far from arbitrary, and the associated contrast between lust and love far from a matter of convention. Lust is also a habit, involving the disposition to give way to desire, without regard to any personal relation with the object. (Thus perversions are all forms of lust even though lust is not in itself a perversion.) Naturally, we all feel the promptings of lust, but the rapidity with which sexual acts become sexual habits, and the catastrophic effect of a sexual act which cannot be remembered without shame or humiliation, give us strong reasons to resist them, reasons that Shakespeare captured in these words:

Th'expence of Spirit in a waste of shame
Is lust in action, and till action, lust
Is perjur'd, murdrous, blouddy, full of blame,
Savage, extreame, rude, cruell, not to trust,
Injoyd no sooner but dispised straight,
Past reason hunted, and no sooner had,
Past reason hated as a swollowed bayt,
On purpose layd to make the taker mad:
Mad in pursuit and in possession so,
Had, having, and in quest to have, extreame,
A blisse in proofe, and prov'd, a very woe,
Before a joy proposd, behind, a dreame,
　　All this the world well knowes, yet none knowes
　　　　well
　　To shun the heaven that leads men to this hell.

In addition to the condemnation of lust and perversion, however, some part of traditional sexual education can be seen as a kind of sustained war against fantasy. It is undeniable that fantasy can play an important part in all our sexual doings, and even the most passionate and faithful lover may, in the act of love, rehearse to himself other scenes of sexual abandon than the one in which he is engaged. Nevertheless, there is truth in the contrast (familiar, in one version, from the writings of Freud) between fantasy and reality, and in the sense that the first is in some way destructive of the second. Fantasy replaces the real, resistant, objective world with a pliant substitute—and that, indeed, is its purpose. Life in the actual world is difficult and embarrassing. Most of all it is difficult and embarrassing in our confrontation with other people, who, by their very existence, make demands that we may be unable or unwilling to meet. It requires a great force, such as the force of sexual desire, to overcome the embarrassment and self-protection that shield us from the most intimate encounters. It is tempting to take refuge in substitutes, which neither embarrass us nor resist the impulse of our spontaneous cravings. The habit grows, in masturbation, of creating a compliant world of desire, in which unreal objects become the focus of real emotions, and the emotions themselves are rendered incompetent to participate in the building of personal relations. The fantasy blocks the passage to reality, which becomes inaccessible to the will.

Even if the fantasy can be overcome so far as to engage in the act of love with another, a peculiar danger remains. The other becomes veiled in substitutes; he is never fully himself in the act of love; it is never clearly *him* that I desire, or *him* that I possess, but always rather a composite object, a universal body, of which he is but one among a potential infinity of instances. Fantasy fills our thoughts with a sense of the obscene, and the orgasm becomes, not the possession of another, but the expenditure of energy on his depersonalised body. Fantasies are private property, which I can dispose according to my will, with no answerability to the other whom I abuse through them. He, indeed, is of no intrinsic interest to me, and serves merely as my opportunity for self-regarding

pleasure. For the fantasist, the ideal partner is indeed the prostitute, who, because she can be purchased, solves at once the moral problem presented by the presence of another at the scene of sexual release.

The connection between fantasy and prostitution is deep and important. The effect of fantasy is to 'commodify' the object of desire, and to replace the law of sexual relationship between people with the law of the market. Sex itself can then be seen as a commodity: something that we pursue and obtain in quantifiable form, and which comes in a variety of packages: in the form of a woman or a man; in the form of a film or a dream; in the form of a fetish or an animal. In so far as the sexual act is seen in this way, it seems morally neutral—or, at best, impersonal. Such criticism as may be offered will concern merely the dangers for the individual and his partner of this or that sexual package: for some bring diseases and discomforts of which others are free. The most harmless and hygienic act of all, on this view, is the act of masturbation, stimulated by whatever works of pornography are necessary to prompt the desire for it in the unimaginative. This justification for pornography has, indeed, recently been offered.

As I have already argued, however, fantasy does not exist comfortably with reality. It has a natural tendency to realise itself: to remake the world in its own image. The harmless wanker with the video-machine can at any moment turn into the desperate rapist with a gun. The 'reality principle' by which the normal sexual act is regulated is a principle of personal encounter, which enjoins us to respect the other person, and to respect, also, the sanctity of his body, as the tangible expression of another self. The world of fantasy obeys no such rule, and is governed by monstrous myths and illusions which are at war with the human world—the illusions, for example, that women wish to be raped, that children have only to be awakened in order to give and receive the intensest sexual pleasure, that violence is not an affront but an affirmation of a natural right. All such myths, nurtured in fantasy, threaten not merely the consciousness of the man who lives by them, but also the moral structure of his surrounding world. They render the world unsafe for self and other, and cause the subject to look on everyone, not as an end in himself, but as a possible means to his private pleasure. In his world, the sexual encounter has been 'fetishised', to use the apt Marxian term, and every other human reality has been poisoned by the sense of the expendability and replaceability of the other.

It is a small step from the preoccupation with sexual virtue, to a condemnation of obscenity and pornography (which is its published form). Obscenity is a direct assault on the sentiment of desire, and therefore on the social order that is based on desire and which has personal love as its goal and fulfilment. There is no doubt that the normal conscience cannot remain neutral towards obscenity, any more than it can remain neutral towards paedophilia and rape (which is not to say that obscenity must also be treated as a *crime*). It is therefore unsurprising that traditional moral education has involved censorship of obscene material, and a severe emphasis on 'purity in thought, word and deed'—an emphasis which is now greeted with irony or ridicule.

Traditional sexual education was, despite its exaggerations and imbecilities, truer to human nature than the libertarian culture which has succeeded it. Through considering its wisdom and its shortcomings, we may understand how to resuscitate an idea of sexual virtue, in accordance with the broad requirements of the Aristotelian argument that I have . . . been presenting. The ideal of virtue remains one of 'sexual integrity'; of a sexuality that is entirely integrated into the life of personal affection, and in which the self and its responsibility are centrally involved and indissolubly linked to the pleasures and passions of the body.

Traditional sexual morality has therefore been the morality of the body. Libertarian morality, by contrast, has relied almost entirely on a Kantian view of the human subject, as related to his body by no coherent moral tie. Focussing as he does on an idea of purely personal respect, and assigning no distinctive place to the body in our moral endeavour, the Kantian inevitably tends towards permissive morality. No sexual act can be wrong merely by virtue of its physical character, and the ideas of obscenity, pollution and perversion have no obvious application. His attitude to homosexuality is conveniently summarised in this passage from a Quaker pamphlet:

> We see no reason why the physical nature of the sexual act should be the criterion by which the question whether it is moral should be decided. An act which (for example) expresses true affection between two individuals and gives pleasure to them both, does not seem to us to be sinful by reason *alone* of the fact that it is homosexual. The same criteria seem to apply whether a relationship is heterosexual or homosexual.

Such sentiments are the standard offering of the liberal and utilitarian moralities of our time. However much we may sympathise with their conclusions, it is not possible to accept the shallow reasoning that leads up to them, and which bypasses the great metaphysical conundrum to which all sexual morality is addressed: the conundrum of embodiment. [D. H.] Lawrence asserts that 'sex is *you*', and offers some bad but revealing lines on the subject:

> And don't, with the nasty, prying mind, drag it
>   out from its deeps
> And finger it and force it, and shatter the rhythm it
>   keeps
> When it is left alone, as it stirs and rouses and sleeps.

If anything justifies Lawrence's condemnation of the 'nasty, prying mind', it is the opposite of what he supposes. Sex 'sleeps' in the soul precisely because, and to the extent that, it is buried there by education. If sex is you, it is because you are the product of that education, and not just its victim. It has endowed you with what I have called 'sexual integrity': the ability to be *in* your body, in the very moment of desire.

The reader may be reluctant to follow me in believing that traditional morality is largely justified by the ideal of sexual integrity. But if he accepts the main tenor of my argument, he must surely realise that the ethic of 'liberation', far from promising the release of the self from hostile bondage, in fact heralds the dissipation of the self in loveless fantasy: th'expence of Spirit, in a waste of shame.

Why Shouldn't Tommy and Jim Have Sex?
A Defense of Homosexuality

JOHN CORVINO

Tommy and Jim are a homosexual couple I know. Tommy is an accountant; Jim is a botany professor. They are in their forties and have been together fourteen years, the last five of which they've lived in a Victorian house that they've lovingly restored. Although their relationship has had its challenges, each has made sacrifices for the sake of the other's happiness and the relationship's long-term success.

I assume that Tommy and Jim have sex with each other (although I've never bothered to ask). Furthermore, I contend that they probably *should* have sex with each other. For one thing, sex is pleasurable. But it is also much more than that: a sexual relationship can unite two people in a way that virtually nothing else can. It can be an avenue of growth, of communication, and of lasting interpersonal fulfillment. These are reasons why most heterosexual couples have sex even if they don't want children, don't want children yet, or don't want additional children. And if these reasons are good enough for most heterosexual couples, then they should be good enough for Tommy and Jim.

Of course, having a reason to do something does not preclude there being an even better reason for not doing it. Tommy might have a good reason for drinking orange juice (it's tasty and nutritious) but an even better reason for not doing so (he's allergic). The point is that one would need a pretty good reason for denying a sexual relationship to Tommy and Jim, given the intense benefits widely associated with such relationships. The question I shall consider in this paper is thus quite simple: Why shouldn't Tommy and Jim have sex?

HOMOSEXUAL SEX IS "UNNATURAL"

Many contend that homosexual sex is "unnatural." But what does that mean? Many things that people value—clothing, houses, medicine, and government, for example—are unnatural in some sense. On the other hand, many things that people detest—disease, suffering, and death, for example—are "natural" in the sense that they occur "in nature." If the unnaturalness charge is to be more than empty rhetorical flourish, those who levy it must specify what they mean. Borrowing from Burton Leiser, I will examine several possible meanings of "unnatural."

What Is Unusual or Abnormal Is Unnatural

One meaning of "unnatural" refers to that which deviates from the norm, that is, from what most people do. Obviously, most people engage in heterosexual relationships. But does it follow that it is wrong to engage in homosexual relationships? Relatively few people read Sanskrit, pilot ships, play the mandolin, breed goats, or write with both hands, yet none of these activities is immoral simply because it is unusual. As the Ramsey Colloquium, a group of Jewish and Christian scholars who oppose homosexuality, writes, "The statistical frequency of an act does not determine its moral status." So while homosexuality might be unnatural in the sense of being unusual, that fact is morally irrelevant.

What Is Not Practiced by Other Animals Is Unnatural

Some people argue, "Even animals know better than to behave homosexually: homosexuality must be wrong." This argument is doubly flawed. First, it rests on a false premise. Numerous studies—including Anne Perkins's study of "gay" sheep and George and Molly Hunt's study of "lesbian" sea gulls—have shown that some animals do form homosexual pair-bonds. Second, even if animals did not behave homosexually, that fact would not prove that homosexuality is immoral. After all, animals don't cook their food, brush their teeth, participate in religious worship, or attend college; human beings do all of these without moral censure. Indeed, the idea that animals could provide us with our standards—especially our sexual standards—is simply amusing.

What Does Not Proceed from Innate Desires Is Unnatural

Recent studies suggesting a biological basis for homosexuality have resulted in two popular positions. One side proposes that homosexual people are "born that way" and that it is therefore natural (and thus good) for them to form homosexual relationships. The other side maintains that homosexuality is a lifestyle choice, which is therefore unnatural (and thus wrong). Both sides assume a connection between the origin of homosexual orientation, on the one hand, and the moral value of homosexual activity, on the other. And insofar as they share that assumption, both sides are wrong.

Consider first the pro-homosexual side: "They are born that way; therefore it's natural and good." This inference assumes that all innate desires are good ones (i.e., that they should be acted upon). But that assumption is clearly false. Research suggests that some people are born with a predisposition toward violence, but such people have no more right to strangle their neighbors than anyone else. So while people like Tommy and Jim may be born with homosexual tendencies, it doesn't follow that they ought to act on them. Nor does it follow that they ought *not* to act on them, even if the tendencies are not innate. I probably do not have any innate tendency to write with my left hand (since I, like everyone else in my family, have always been right-handed), but it doesn't follow that it would be immoral for me to do so. So simply asserting that homosexuality is a lifestyle choice will not show that it is an immoral lifestyle choice.

Do people "choose" to be homosexual? People certainly don't seem to choose their sexual *feelings*, at least not in any direct or obvious way. (Do you? Think about it.) Rather, they find certain people attractive and certain activities arousing, whether they "decide" to or not. Indeed, most people at some point in their lives wish that they could control their feelings more—for example, in situations of unrequited love—and find it frustrating that they cannot. What they *can* control to a considerable degree is how and when they act upon those feelings. In that sense, both homosexuality and heterosexuality involve lifestyle choices. But in either case, determining the origin of the feelings will not determine whether it is moral to act on them.

What Violates an Organ's Principal Purpose Is Unnatural

Perhaps when people claim that homosexual sex is unnatural they mean that it cannot result in procreation. The idea behind the argument is that human organs have various natural purposes: eyes are for seeing, ears are for hearing, genitals are for procreating. According to this argument, it is immoral to use an organ in a way that violates its particular purpose.

Many of our organs, however, have multiple purposes. Tommy can use his mouth for talking, eating, breathing, licking stamps, chewing gum, kissing women, or kissing Jim; and it seems rather arbitrary to claim that all but the last use are "natural." (And if we say that some of the other uses are "unnatural, but not immoral," we have failed to specify a morally relevant sense of the term "natural.")

Just because people can and do use their sexual organs to procreate, it does not follow that they should not use them for other purposes. Sexual organs seem very well suited for expressing love, for giving and receiving pleasure, and for celebrating, replenishing, and enhancing a relationship—even when procreation is not a factor. Unless opponents of homosexuality are prepared to condemn heterosexual couples who use contraception or individuals who masturbate, they must abandon this version of the unnaturalness argument. Indeed, even the Roman Catholic Church, which forbids contraception and masturbation, approves of sex for sterile couples and of sex during pregnancy, neither of which can lead to procreation. The Church concedes here that intimacy and pleasure are morally legitimate purposes for sex, even in cases where procreation is impossible. But since homosexual sex can achieve these purposes as well, it is inconsistent for the Church to condemn it on the grounds that it is not procreative.

One might object that sterile heterosexual couples do not *intentionally* turn away from procreation, whereas homosexual couples do. But this distinction doesn't hold. It is no more possible for Tommy to procreate with a woman whose uterus has been removed than it is for him to procreate with Jim. By having sex with either one, he is intentionally engaging in a non-procreative sexual act.

Yet one might press the objection further and insist that Tommy and the woman *could* produce children if the woman were fertile: whereas homosexual relationships are essentially infertile, heterosexual relationships are only incidentally so. But what does that prove? Granted, it might require less of a miracle for a woman without a uterus to become pregnant than for Jim to become pregnant, but it would require a miracle nonetheless. Thus it seems that the real difference here is not that one couple is fertile and the other not, nor that one couple "could" be fertile (with the help of a miracle) and the other not, but rather that one couple is male-female and the other male-male. In other words, sex between Tommy and Jim is wrong because it's male-male—i.e., because it's homosexual. But that, of course, is no argument at all.

What Is Disgusting or Offensive Is Unnatural

It often seems that when people call homosexuality "unnatural" they really just mean that it's disgusting. But plenty of morally neutral activities—handling snakes, eating snails, performing autopsies, cleaning toilets, and so on—disgust people. Indeed, for centuries, most people found interracial relationships disgusting, yet that feeling—which has by no means disappeared—hardly proves that such relationships are wrong. In sum, the charge that homosexuality is unnatural, at least in its most common forms, is longer on rhetorical flourish than on philosophical cogency. At best it expresses an aesthetic judgment, not a moral judgment.

HOMOSEXUAL SEX IS HARMFUL

One might instead argue that homosexuality is harmful. The Ramsey Colloquium, for instance, argues that homosexuality leads to the breakdown of the family and, ultimately, of human society, and it points to the "alarming rates of sexual promiscuity, depression, and suicide and the ominous presence of AIDS within the homosexual subculture." Thomas Schmidt marshals copious statistics to show that homosexual activity undermines physical and psychological health. Such charges, if correct, would seem to provide strong evidence against homosexuality. But are the charges correct? And do they prove what they purport to prove?

One obvious (and obviously problematic) way to answer the first question is to ask people like Tommy and Jim. It would appear that no one is in a better position to judge the homosexual lifestyle than those who know it firsthand. Yet it is unlikely that critics would trust their testimony. Indeed, the more homosexual people try to explain their lives, the more critics accuse them of deceitfully promoting an agenda. (It's like trying to prove that you're not crazy. The more you object, the more people think, "That's exactly what a crazy person would say.")

One might instead turn to statistics. An obvious problem with this tack is that both sides of the debate bring forth extensive statistics and "expert" testimony, leaving the average observer confused. There is a more subtle problem as well. Because of widespread antigay sentiment, many homosexual people won't acknowledge their romantic feelings to themselves, much less to researchers. I have known a number of gay men who did not "come out" until their forties and fifties, and no amount of professional competence on the part of interviewers would have been likely to open their closets sooner. Such problems compound the usual difficulties of finding representative population samples for statistical study.

Yet even if the statistical claims of gay rights opponents were true, they would not prove what they purport to prove, for several reasons. First, as any good statistician realizes, correlation does not equal cause. Even if homosexual people were more likely to commit suicide, be promiscuous, or contract AIDS than the general population, it would not follow that their homosexuality causes them to do these things. An alternative—and very plausible—explanation is that these phenomena, like the disproportionately high crime rates among African Americans, are at least partly a function of society's treatment of the group in question. Suppose you were told from a very early age that the romantic feelings that you experienced were sick, unnatural, and disgusting. Suppose further that expressing these feelings put you at risk of social ostracism or, worse yet, physical violence. Is it not plausible that you would, for instance, be more inclined to depression than you would be without such obstacles? And that such depression could, in its extreme forms, lead to suicide or other self-destructive behaviors? (It is indeed remarkable that couples like Tommy and Jim continue to flourish in the face of such obstacles.)

A similar explanation can be given for the alleged promiscuity of homosexuals. The denial of legal marriage, the pressure to remain in the closet, and the overt hostility toward homosexual relationships are all more conducive to transient, clandestine encounters than they are to long-term unions. As a result, that which is challenging enough for heterosexual couples—settling down and building a life together—becomes far more challenging for homosexual couples.

Indeed, there is an interesting tension in the critics' position here. Opponents of homosexuality commonly claim that "marriage and the family . . . are fragile institutions in need of careful and continuing support." And they point to the increasing prevalence of divorce and premarital sex among heterosexuals as evidence that such support is declining. Yet they refuse to concede that the complete absence of similar support for homosexual relationships might explain many of the alleged problems of homosexuals. The critics can't have it both ways: if heterosexual marriages are in trouble despite the various social, economic, and legal incentives for keeping them together, society should be little surprised that homosexual relationships—which not only lack such supports, but face overt hostility—are difficult to maintain.

One might object that if social ostracism were the main cause of homosexual people's problems, then homosexual people in more "tolerant" cities like New York and San Francisco should exhibit fewer such problems than their small-town counterparts; yet statistics do not seem to bear this out. This objection underestimates the extent of antigay sentiment in our society. By the time many gay and lesbian people move to urban centers, they have already been exposed to (and may have internalized) considerable hostility toward homosexuality. Moreover, the visibility of homosexuality in urban centers makes gay and lesbian people there more vulnerable to attack (and thus more likely to exhibit certain difficulties). Finally, note that urbanites *in general* (not just homosexual urbanites) tend to exhibit higher rates of promiscuity, depression, and sexually transmitted disease than the rest of the population.

But what about AIDS? Opponents of homosexuality sometimes claim that even if homosexual sex is not, strictly speaking, immoral, it is still a bad idea, since it puts people at risk for AIDS and other sexually transmitted diseases. But that claim is misleading: it is infinitely more risky for Tommy to have sex with a woman who is HIV-positive than with Jim, who is HIV-negative. Obviously, it's not homosexuality that's harmful, it's the virus; and the virus may be carried by both heterosexual and homosexual people.

Now it may be true (in the United States, at least) that homosexual males are statistically more likely to carry the virus than heterosexual females and thus that homosexual sex is *statistically* more risky than heterosexual sex (in cases where the partner's HIV status is unknown). But opponents of homosexuality need something stronger than this statistical claim. For if it is wrong for men to have sex with men because their doing so puts them at a higher AIDS risk than heterosexual sex, then it is also wrong for women to have sex with men because their doing so puts them at a higher AIDS risk than homosexual sex (lesbians as a group have the lowest incidence of AIDS). Purely from the standpoint of AIDS risk, women ought to prefer lesbian sex.

If this response seems silly, it is because there is obviously more to choosing a romantic or sexual partner than determining AIDS risk. And a major part of the decision, one that opponents of homosexuality consistently overlook, is considering whether one can have a mutually fulfilling relationship with the partner. For many people like Tommy and Jim, such fulfillment—which most heterosexuals recognize to be an important component of human flourishing—is only possible with members of the same sex.

Of course, the foregoing argument hinges on the claim that homosexual sex can only cause harm indirectly. Some would object that there are certain activities—anal sex, for instance—that for anatomical reasons are intrinsically harmful. But an argument against anal intercourse is by no means tantamount to an argument against homosexuality: neither all nor only homosexuals engage in anal sex. There are plenty of other things for both gay men and lesbians to do in bed. Indeed, for women, it appears that the most common forms of homosexual activity may be *less* risky than penile-vaginal intercourse, since the latter has been linked to cervical cancer.

In sum, there is nothing *inherently* risky about sex between persons of the same gender. It is only risky under certain conditions: for instance, if they exchange diseased bodily fluids or if they engage in certain "rough" forms of sex that could cause tearing of delicate tissue. Heterosexual sex is equally risky under such conditions. Thus, even if statistical claims like those of Schmidt and the Ramsey Colloquium were true, they would not prove that homosexuality is immoral. At best, they would prove that homosexual people—like everyone else—ought to take great care when deciding to become sexually active.

Of course, there's more to a flourishing life than avoiding harm. One might argue that even if Tommy and Jim are not harming each other by their relationship, they are still failing to achieve the higher level of fulfillment possible in a heterosexual relationship, which is rooted in the complementarity of male and female. But this argument just ignores the facts: Tommy and Jim are homosexual *precisely because* they find relationships with men (and, in particular, with each other) more fulfilling than relationships with women. Even evangelicals (who have long advocated "faith healing" for homosexuals) are beginning to acknowledge that the choice for most homosexual people is not between homosexual relationships and heterosexual relationships, but rather between homosexual

relationships and celibacy. What the critics need to show, therefore, is that no matter how loving, committed, mutual, generous, and fulfilling the relationship may be, Tommy and Jim would flourish more if they were celibate. Given the evidence of their lives (and of others like them), this is a formidable task indeed.

Thus far I have focused on the allegation that homosexuality harms those who engage in it. But what about the allegation that homosexuality harms other, nonconsenting parties? Here I will briefly consider two claims: that homosexuality threatens children and that it threatens society.

Those who argue that homosexuality threatens children may mean one of two things. First, they may mean that homosexual people are child molesters. Statistically, the vast majority of reported cases of child sexual abuse involve young girls and their fathers, stepfathers, or other familiar (and presumably heterosexual) adult males. But opponents of homosexuality argue that when one adjusts for relative percentage in the population, homosexual males appear more likely than heterosexual males to be child molesters. As I argued above, the problems with obtaining reliable statistics on homosexuality render such calculations difficult. Fortunately, they are also unnecessary.

Child abuse is a terrible thing. But when a heterosexual male molests a child (or rapes a woman or commits assault), the act does not reflect upon all heterosexuals. Similarly, when a homosexual male molests a child, there is no reason why that act should reflect upon all homosexuals. Sex with adults of the same sex is one thing; sex with *children* of the same sex is quite another. Conflating the two not only slanders innocent people, it also misdirects resources intended to protect children. Furthermore, many men convicted of molesting young boys are sexually attracted to adult women and report no attraction to adult men. To call such men "homosexual," or even "bisexual," is probably to stretch such terms too far.

Alternatively, those who charge that homosexuality threatens children might mean that the increasing visibility of homosexual relationships makes children more likely to become homosexual. The argument for this view is patently circular. One cannot prove that doing *X* is bad by arguing that it causes other people to do *X*, which is bad. One must first establish independently that *X* is bad. That said, there is not a shred of evidence to demonstrate that exposure to homosexuality leads children to become homosexual.

But doesn't homosexuality threaten society? A Roman Catholic priest once put the argument to me as follows: "Of course homosexuality is bad for society. If everyone were homosexual, there would be no society." Perhaps it is true that if everyone were homosexual, there would be no society. But if everyone were a celibate priest, society would collapse just as surely, and my friend the priest didn't seem to think that he was doing anything wrong simply by failing to procreate. Jeremy Bentham made the point somewhat more acerbically roughly 200 years ago: "If then merely out of regard to population it were right that [homosexuals] should be burnt alive, monks ought to be roasted alive by a slow fire."

From the fact that the continuation of society requires procreation, it does not follow that *everyone* must procreate. Moreover, even if such an obligation existed, it would not preclude homosexuality. At best, it would preclude *exclusive* homosexuality: homosexual people who occasionally have heterosexual sex can procreate just fine. And given artificial insemination, even those who are exclusively homosexual can procreate. In short, the priest's claim—if everyone were homosexual, there would be no society—is false; and even if it were true, it would not establish that homosexuality is immoral.

The Ramsey Colloquium commits a similar fallacy. Noting (correctly) that heterosexual marriage promotes the continuation of human life, it then infers that homosexuality is immoral because it fails to accomplish the same. But from the fact that procreation is good, it does not follow that childlessness is bad—a point that the members of the colloquium, several of whom are Roman Catholic priests, should readily concede.

I have argued that Tommy and Jim's sexual relationship harms neither them nor society. On the contrary, it benefits both. It benefits them because it makes them happier—not merely in a short-term, hedonistic sense, but in a long-term, "big picture" sort of way. And, in turn, it benefits society, since it makes Tommy and Jim more stable, more productive, and

more generous than they would otherwise be. In short, their relationship—including its sexual component—provides the same kinds of benefits that infertile heterosexual relationships provide (and perhaps other benefits as well). Nor should we fear that accepting their relationship and others like it will cause people to flee in droves from the institution of heterosexual marriage. After all, as Thomas Williams points out, the usual response to a gay person is not "How come *he* gets to be gay and I don't?"

HOMOSEXUALITY VIOLATES BIBLICAL TEACHING

At this point in the discussion, many people turn to religion. "If the secular arguments fail to prove that homosexuality is wrong," they say, "so much the worse for secular ethics. This failure only proves that we need God for morality." Since people often justify their moral beliefs by appeal to religion, I will briefly consider the biblical position.

At first glance, the Bible's condemnation of homosexual activity seems unequivocal. Consider, for example, the following two passages, one from the "Old" Testament and one from the "New":

> You shall not lie with a male as with a woman; it is an abomination. (Lev. 18:22)

> For this reason God gave them up to degrading passions. Their women exchanged natural intercourse for unnatural, and in the same way also the men, giving up natural intercourse with women, were consumed with passion for one another. Men committed shameless acts with men and received in their own persons the due penalty for their error. (Rom. 1:26–27)

Note, however, that these passages are surrounded by other passages that relatively few people consider binding. For example, Leviticus also declares,

> The pig . . . is unclean for you. Of their flesh you shall not eat, and their carcasses you shall not touch; they are unclean for you. (11:7–8)

Taken literally, this passage not only prohibits eating pork, but also playing football, since footballs are made of pigskin. (Can you believe that the University of Notre Dame so flagrantly violates Levitical teaching?)

Similarly, St. Paul, author of the Romans passage, also writes, "Slaves, obey your earthly masters with fear and trembling, in singleness of heart, as you obey Christ" (Eph. 6:5)—morally problematic advice if there ever were any. Should we interpret this passage (as Southern plantation owners once did) as implying that it is immoral for slaves to escape? After all, God himself says in Leviticus,

> [Y]ou may acquire male and female slaves . . . from among the aliens residing with you, and from their families that are with you, who have been born in your land; and they may be your property. You may keep them as a possession for your children after you, for them to inherit as property. (25:44–46)

How can people maintain the inerrancy of the Bible in light of such passages? The answer, I think, is that they learn to interpret the passages *in their historical context.*

Consider the Bible's position on usury, the lending of money for interest (for *any* interest, not just excessive interest). The Bible condemns this practicle in no uncertain terms. In Exodus God says that "if you lend money to my people, to the poor among you, you shall not exact interest from them" (22:25). Psalm 15 says that those who lend at interest may not abide in the Lord's tent or dwell on his holy hill (1–5). Ezekiel calls usury "abominable"; compares it to adultery, robbery, idolatry, and bribery; and states that anyone who "takes advanced or accrued interest . . . shall surely die; his blood shall be upon himself" (18:13).

Should believers therefore close their savings accounts? Not necessarily. According to orthodox Christian teaching, the biblical prohibition against usury no longer applies. The reason is that economic conditions have changed substantially since biblical times, such that usury no longer has the same negative consequences it had when the prohibitions were issued. Thus, the practice that was condemned by the Bible differs from contemporary interest banking in morally relevant ways.

Yet are we not in a similar position regarding homosexuality? Virtually all scholars agree that homosexual relations during biblical times were vastly different from relationships like Tommy and Jim's. Often such relations were integral to pagan practices. In Greek society,

they typically involved older men and younger boys. If those are the kinds of features that the biblical authors had in mind when they issued their condemnations, and such features are no longer typical, then the biblical condemnations no longer apply. As with usury, substantial changes in cultural context have altered the meaning and consequences—and thus the moral value—of the practice in question. Put another way, using the Bible's condemnations of homosexuality against contemporary homosexuality is like using its condemnations of usury against contemporary banking.

Let me be clear about what I am *not* claiming here. First, I am not claiming that the Bible has been wrong before and therefore may be wrong this time. The Bible may indeed be wrong on some matters, but for the purpose of this argument I am assuming its infallibility. Nor am I claiming that the Bible's age renders it entirely inapplicable to today's issues. Rather, I am claiming that when we do apply it, *we must pay attention to morally relevant cultural differences between biblical times and today.* Such attention will help us distinguish between specific time-bound prohibitions (for example, laws against usury or homosexual relations) and the enduring moral values they represent (for example, generosity or respect for persons). And as the above argument shows, my claim is not very controversial. Indeed, to deny it is to commit oneself to some rather strange views on slavery, usury, women's roles, astronomy, evolution, and the like.

Here, one might also make an appeal to religious pluralism. Given the wide variety of religious beliefs (e.g., the Muslim belief that women should cover their faces, the Orthodox Jewish belief against working on Saturday, the Hindu belief that cows are sacred and should not be eaten), each of us inevitably violates the religious belief of others. But we normally don't view such violations as occasions for moral censure, since we distinguish between beliefs that depend on particular revelations and beliefs that can be justified independently (e.g., that stealing is wrong). Without an independent justification for condemning homosexuality, the best one can say is, "My religion says so." But in a society that cherishes religious freedom, that reason alone does not normally provide grounds for moral or legal sanctions. That people still fall back on that reason in discussions of homosexuality suggests that they may not have much of a case otherwise.

CONCLUSION

As a last resort, opponents of homosexuality typically change the subject: "But what about incest, polygamy, and bestiality? If we accept Tommy and Jim's sexual relationship, why shouldn't we accept those as well?" Opponents of interracial marriage used a similar slippery-slope argument in the 1960s when the Supreme Court struck down antimiscegenation laws. It was a bad argument then, and it is a bad argument now.

Just because there are no good reasons to oppose interracial or homosexual relationships, it does not follow that there are no good reasons to oppose incestuous, polygamous, or bestial relationships. One might argue, for instance, that incestuous relationships threaten delicate familial bonds, or that polygamous relationships result in unhealthy jealousies (and sexism), or that bestial relationships—do I need to say it?—aren't really "relationships' at all, at least not in the sense we've been discussing. Perhaps even better arguments could be offered (given much more space than I have here). The point is that there is no logical

connection between homosexuality, on the one hand, and incest, polygamy, and bestiality, on the other:

Why, then, do critics continue to push this objection? Perhaps it's because accepting homosexuality requires them to give up one of their favorite arguments: "It's wrong because we've always been taught that it's wrong." This argument—call it the argument from tradition—has an obvious appeal: people reasonably favor tried-and-true ideas over unfamiliar ones, and they recognize the foolishness of trying to invent morality from scratch. But the argument from tradition is also a dangerous argument, as any honest look at history will reveal.

I conclude that Tommy and Jim's relationship, far from being a moral abomination, is exactly what it appears to be to those who know them: a morally positive influence on their lives and on others. Accepting this conclusion takes courage, since it entails that our moral traditions are fallible. But when these traditions interfere with people's happiness for no sound reason, they defeat what is arguably the very point of morality: promoting individual and communal well-being. To put the argument simply, Tommy and Jim's relationship makes them better people. And that's not just good for Tommy and Jim: that's good for everyone.

From Seduction, Rape, and Coercion

Sarah Conly

* * *

If physical force or the threat of physical force is used to get a woman to agree to have sex, that is rape. If psychological force is used, can that also be rape?

1. VERBAL COERCION

What is at issue here? The question is about what is sometimes called verbal coercion, but the issue is not merely about the use of words rather than actual

From Sarah Conly, "Seduction, Rape, and Coercion," *Ethics* 115 (October 2004): 96–121. © 2004 by The University of Chicago. Reprinted by permission of The University of Chicago Press.

physical violence. Of course words alone can result in rape, if the words threaten physical violence. The issue here is distinct. Proponents of an expansion of our definition of rape argue that, just as physical force is a form of coercion which invalidates consent so that ensuing sex is rape, it is "verbal coercion" if a person agrees to have sex because of the use of words which cause or threaten to cause (only) emotional duress.

* * *

The question is whether such pressure, if it results in a person having sex who would not otherwise have wanted to, is indeed coercive; that is, whether it is truly sufficiently harmful and sufficiently wrongful that we may say that the person who changes her mind as a result of such pressure has been raped. What if the motivation to have sex comes not from fear of physical violence but from fear of emotional harm? What if the force used to overcome a woman's resistance is not physical force but emotional pressure? Can this be rape? The answer, I think, is that it may or may not be. Infliction of emotional harm can invalidate consent, and sex that arises as a result of this can thus be rape. Other emotional harms (even if perhaps more painful) can be consistent with valid consent. What we need to do is differentiate between the different circumstances of harm to understand when consent is and is not valid.

* * *

[T]here is controversy about what (if any) kind of emotional pressure should count as coercive. Campus behavior codes, freed from the evidentiary requirements of a court of law (and freed from the responsibility of sending the perpetrator to prison), have recently seen more prosecutions for what once would have been considered consensual sex, precisely because some have adopted standards of assault which include overbearing of the other's will through emotional pressure. In such cases, the charge of rape seems to stem from the fact that, while the victims were not physically constrained to have sex, they were in some sense browbeaten into having intercourse they would not otherwise have chosen to have. Thus, it is argued, the sex was not truly voluntary. Even the widely accepted admonition that "No Means No" has been the subject of controversy for this reason: what follows from a woman's saying "no" to sex? To proceed immediately to penetration would clearly be wrong, but what about trying to talk her into sex, to press with blandishments or tears, to harangue; in short, to refuse to give up? Opinion is divided: some feel that "no" means simply that you should not advance physically on someone who has told you to stop, but others feel that spirit of the rule is violated by continuing to verbally press the issue after one person has stated her desire. Especially in the conditions in which such pressure is likely to occur (when it is late and we are tired and/or to some degree inebriated) the pursuit of the sexual goal in the face of opposition has seemed to some to constitute a force which, while not violent, nullifies consent in the same way physical force does.[1]

Proponents of such changes, and corresponding changes in the law, worry about the susceptibility of one person to certain sorts of psychological force brought to bear by another. The psychological forces brought to bear may be various and may be used singly, or . . . conjointly. The aggressor may implore and wheedle until the other feels guilt; he may tease her with jealousy, berate her for her coldness and immaturity, chastise her for the harm she does him, refute her reasoning when she tries to articulate her position, and subject her to a barrage of angry words. Ultimately she may find herself in a state of psychological exhaustion, feeling unable to resist in the face of what seems an implacable will. In these cases, it is argued, the woman has been forced against her will as surely as if the aggressor had used physical violence.

To some, then, the recognition of the potency of some sorts of speech, of the psychological pressure it can convey, is a long-delayed recognition of the true dynamics of (some, many, or all, depending on whom you talk to) sexual encounters. To others this sort of interpretation of a sexual encounter represents a deviation from good sense. It may be unjust in that it castigates as rapists those who simply are persuasive at getting what they want. It may also be harmful to those who concede to such pressure, in particular to women, since they are most often thought of as the victims of such verbal coercion. If we accept that (some) women are unable to withstand the psychological force brought to bear upon them, this makes them seem like less than autonomous agents. If these women had sex when they didn't want to, why then did they have sex?[2] Physical force or the threat of it makes sense of having sex against one's will, it is thought, but absent physical force, how are we to make sense of someone who does something she really doesn't want to do? For some, accepting that psychological pressure could be a means to rape wrongly suggests that women are weak minded, prone to collapse under "emotional pressure" and to concede to the desires of the stronger-minded male.[3] . . .

This is a dilemma. It seems intuitively right to many (and certainly to me) that we should hold the delinquent fathers and foster fathers who threatened their children into sex responsible for being rapists and that the man who had intercourse with the eight-year-old girl was clearly forcing himself upon an innocent victim, whether or not he threatened to hit her if she wouldn't have sex. Yet, it seems implausible to say that whenever someone gives into irrational suasion to have sex, or has sex only out of fear of displeasing someone she cares for, or out of a desire to please, a rape has occurred.

Deciding to Have Sex

The differing notions of choice and rape turn in part on different accounts of the psychology involved—on how the decision about having sex is made. One central issue seems to be whether or not the woman wanted to do what she did, but this is a complex question. What is it not to want to have sex? We are seldom univocal as to reasons for doing anything. A woman may want to have sex to express love, even if she is not physically aroused. Perhaps she is tired, but her husband is leaving for a two-week trip, and she wants to have sex to feel closer to him. Perhaps she even wants to do it just because he wants to do it. He has read a lot of feminist literature, however, and is a sensitive guy and won't sulk or become angry if she doesn't have sex; he just won't feel as happy as he would if she did. She loves him, however, and wants him to feel loved. Even in the latter case, where his attitude contributes to her decision—where indeed, were it not for his desire she wouldn't want to have sex—her having sex doesn't plausibly seem to be rape, any more than my buying Girl Scout cookies only to avoid hurting the feelings of the little girl selling them means I've been robbed. Having a reason to oppose having sex as well as positive reasons to have sex doesn't mean that when she does have sex at another's behest it must be rape. Similarly, however, we cannot say that if a woman had some positive motivation to have sex that means any ensuing sex must have been consensual. Anyone might have a desire to have sex (she was physically aroused, she wants to please the man she is in love with) and have lots of reasons not to have sex—she's afraid of sexually transmitted diseases, she has contrary religious convictions, and so forth. Saying that she wanted to have sex in some ways does not determine whether the ensuing sex is consensual.

What seems to determine the question, then, is not simply whether or not the person had some desire to have or not have sex, or even whether the desire to have sex is a function of another person's antecedent desire, but whether the motivation which decides her to have sex is a result of coercive pressure. If she weighs the religious conviction against her physical arousal and decides that all things considered, she prefers to have sex, she has not been raped. If she weighs her desire not to have sex against the threat of violence by a knife-wielding rapist and decides that, given the choice of sex or death, she, all things considered, prefers to have sex, she has been raped. If her desire to have sex is a result of coercive pressure, then the fact that she did what she wanted to do is neither here nor there, because the options from which she had to choose were illegitimately narrow. The question here, then, is when is psychological pressure coercive?

II. BUT WHAT IS COERCION?

We need to examine when the criteria we generally feel are required for coercion to be present are also present in cases of psychological pressure. None of these is seen as sufficient for coercion, but all are seen as necessary, and when psychological pressure doesn't meet these criteria, it is not coercive.

Intent. One requirement for coercion is that the coercer is doing what he does intentionally. Accidentally doing something which causes another to decide to have sex with you can't be considered coercive. The question of *mens rea* has long played a role in the legal determination of rape. While our discussion is not of what constitutes legal rape but of what constitutes rape from the moral perspective, it may still be held that there can be no wrongdoing unless there is a perpetrator who has acted with a blameworthy frame of mind. In the case of legal rape, the idea is that the perpetrator either knows that the woman has given no valid consent, or should have known, in that he would have known with a reasonable amount of perspicacity or concern. Can the person who has placed psychological pressure be in a sufficiently culpable frame of mind to be held a rapist when he has sex with someone who, without threat of violence, has said that she would, given the circumstances, prefer to have sex?

It seems possible. The culpable frame of mind required for the legal designation of rape is not one where the perpetrator recognizes that he is morally or legally in the wrong. Rather, the perpetrator has simply to know that the victim did not consent or to be in a situation where he should have known. The fact that he may sincerely believe himself to be in the right (because the woman owed him sex, or whatever) does not excuse him. Similarly, while the person who places psychological pressure may believe himself to be in the right in having achieved the other's consent by threatening (mere) psychological pain, this does not suffice to excuse him from the charge of rape. If he knows that the other's consent was obtained only through the pressure he has brought to bear, he is aware of the relevant facts. The question is whether what he has done invalidates consent in the way physical force does, so that the ensuing sex is rape.

Choice. Some may argue that psychological pressure cannot be properly coercive because in typical cases of psychological pressure one has a choice of whether or not to yield, whereas in cases of physical force no such decision is possible. It is possible that, in some cases of psychological pressure, the victim of pressure is so demoralized as to literally lose the ability to choose—and this may be true [of young incest victims]—but we cannot assume that this is typical, at least among adults. More normally, in the case of psychological pressure, the victim is not forced to have sex, but rather chooses to have sex in order to prevent losing a relationship, to avoid an angry confrontation, or to avoid other pain. In cases of physical force, it is argued, no such choice is possible.

This looks like a distinction initially, but it does not reflect our modern beliefs about rape. While at one point in time it was true that, both culturally and legally, sex was only considered rape if the woman was literally physically overwhelmed such that she could not stop the assailant in any way, this narrow concept of rape is outmoded. A woman confronted with an armed rapist may yield to the mere threat of force, without our saying she consented to have sex. There is a sense, no doubt, in which she chooses to have sex when she chooses to have sex rather than to be beaten or killed. She was nonetheless raped because the choice is not free, and to say that the choice is not free is to say that she is placed under coercive pressure and made to choose between illegitimate options.[4] Choice under psychological pressure might, then, be equally unfree: the mere ability to choose the better of two alternatives doesn't mean that there was insufficient force for sex to count as rape. That she can choose whether or not to have sex or suffer psychological harm does not in itself mean she has not been raped, any more than the fact that a woman might choose to have sex rather than be violently abused means she hasn't been raped.

Harm. For a choice to be coerced, however, it is necessary that the person doing the choosing has no reasonable choice between doing what the coercer wants and the bad option which the coercer has introduced.[5] Not every threat constitutes coercion, because some threats don't introduce harms great enough to affect my decision procedure. My neighbor can't say he was coerced into supporting my bid for election because I told him I would make terribly unfriendly faces at him if he didn't do so; while I shouldn't be making faces at people who don't support me, it's not so bad that he can claim that he had no other option than to vote my way. Can psychological pain be sufficient to say that the person subjected to threats of psychological harm has no reasonable choice but to succumb to the will of the coercer?

Why not? Clearly, psychological pain can be extreme. A person might recover more quickly from a physical beating than an emotional breakup; indeed, it may be the emotional component of a beating that makes it so bad—the same amount of harm suffered from falling down the stairs would be far less traumatic. The picture the critic has here seems to be of someone who agrees to have sex to avoid some slight loss, say, so her boyfriend won't break a date with her in order to go watch football, and such critics think not having a date just doesn't seem so awful an option as to constrain a person's choice. This is true: one may agree to have sex for foolish reasons, like wanting to brag to friends that her boyfriend has never left her alone on Saturday night. To say the choice to have sex for such slight goods should not count as coerced does not, however, show that psychological pressure generally can't be coercive. The same slippery slope can occur with physical force. What if someone threatens that he will pinch the woman if she does not have sex with him? If she agrees, has she been coerced? Assuming that the woman has the normal capacity for pain, has no peculiar traumas associated with pinching, and so forth, then the threat of a slight pain would probably not count as coercive, whatever the intent of the threatener, because being pinched is a reasonable option to choose over having sex with someone you don't want to have sex with. If she concedes to his wishes, we will probably think she didn't really mind having sex to begin with, even given the uncouthness of his advance. We won't think she was raped.

The point is that, with both physical and psychological threats, there will be greater and lesser pains. Precisely what degree of pain constitutes coercive force will be difficult to say, but there is no reason to think that psychological pain cannot be awful, so awful that it makes unwanted sex the more reasonable option.[6]

Legitimacy. For an offer to be coercive, however, it must do more than constrain the options of the chooser. It must do this illegitimately.[7] Whether or not I coerce my son in telling him he cannot go to the Rollerworld dance unless he does his homework depends on whether I have the right to control his activities in this particular way.[8] Sometimes a pressure may be brought to bear to make someone do something that he or she doesn't want to do and that pressure is entirely within the rights of the individual doing the pressuring. If I tell an employee I will fire him if he doesn't do a better job, I may cause him great distress and overbear his will to play computer games at work, but I haven't done anything wrong. If, on the other hand, I tell him that I will shoot him or even that I will ridicule his appearance around the office, then I have proffered a sanction which is not legitimate, even though my goal may be a reasonable one. Or, if I threaten to fire him, not because he is doing a bad job but because he refuses to enter the basketball pool, I extend my control into realms

where I have no right of control. I have a right of sanction, but only in certain ways and only on certain grounds. There are ways we can bend others to our will and ways we can't, and what these are seem to be determined by the nature of the specific relationship. Is it legitimate to pressure someone to have sex? This will depend on the kind of pressure brought to bear and the legitimate parameters of the relationship in which it is brought to bear.

Clearly, in some relationships it is not legitimate to pressure someone to have sex. The cases of [fathers and daughters] are ones where the authority of fatherhood does not extend into the realm of sex, and using it is clearly an abuse. Demands for sex in such relationships are illegitimate. In the realm of merely social relationships, though, where there is no personal or institutional authority being extended to a use beyond its justified parameters, the issue is not so clear. Can a person legitimately threaten to break off with someone if she refuses to have sex, intending that this threat will make her have sex where normally she would choose not to? Can he legitimately do this knowing that her pain at his prospective departure will be the determining factor in her decision to have sex with him? There are two cases: he threatens to break off because that is his sincere intent if no sex is included in the relationship and he feels he should let her know this. Or, he may threaten to break off, sincerely intending to leave this unsatisfactory relationship but also hoping that his threat will motivate her to have sex, even if her other desires not to have sex remain in place. That is, in the second case he hopes to manipulate her into doing what he wants. Reflection shows that, while the second of these may be less than admirable, neither case constitutes rape.

Clearly, as the boss may fire the employee, one person may break up with another. Clearly, as the boss may threaten the employee with firing in order to improve his performance, one may threaten the other person in a relationship with a break-up if things don't improve. Can the specific area of improvement be sexual? It is not that a romantic partner has a duty, explicit or implicit, to provide sex, in the way that an employee does have a duty to do the work associated with the job. At the same time, the absence of this duty in a romantic relationship is a function of the fact that such relationships are open ended. Just as being in a relationship does not, per se, give one any duties, it is also the case that one can, without stepping out of bounds, make the relationship dependent on various conditions that suit one's own needs. Often the things which are asked are those we are so familiar with we may think of them as simply constitutive of there being a relationship, but they may in fact be conditions set by one partner for another. Person A may say she wants Person B to communicate more if they are to stay together. Person B may insist that Person A remain faithful and that, without this condition being met, person B will leave. We don't look upon these demands as being coercive, but rather as the sorts of conditions most people set on relationships, as a legitimate attempt to craft the relationship they want, even if that requires finding a different partner. This may be manipulative, in that the intent is to make someone do something she wouldn't otherwise want, but it seems manipulative in a way which we accept in dealing with others, where introducing systems of rewards and sanctions to get others to do what you want, in this less than ideal world, is sometimes necessary and often goes by the name of compromise. We may say that, if you will do the dishes, I will do the cooking; if you won't do the dishes, I won't do the cooking. It would be much nicer if we didn't pressure one another to change behaviors, as it would be nicer if we never even wanted the other to change. In the real world, though, this happens, and we recognize that this sort of trade-off is an unfortunate need when people of different desires try to stay together. Relationships are founded on odd precepts, and if one of the partners is unilaterally responsible for making the continuance of the relationship conditional on the relationship including some particular activity, that is in itself legitimate.

* * *

Are such conditions always legitimate? No. As with employer-employee relationships, there are limits to what you may demand and limits to what sanctions you may threaten if even your legitimate demands are not met. Demands placed within a relationship

should have reasonable bearing on the health of the relationship, and should not be inherently immoral, and sanctions offered for failure to meet even reasonable demands are limited. I am assuming, however, that engaging in sex, all things being equal, is not immoral and has reasonable bearing on the relationship is, as argued above, a justified response.[9]

So, it does seem within a person's rights to want sex to be a part of a romantic relationship and also within that person's rights to tell the partner that, if there is no sex, he will decamp. This does amount to a demand, indeed a threat, insofar as the fear of losing the relationship is an incentive to have sex and the one intends this fear to motivate the other to have sex, just as the wife who says she'll divorce if her husband is unfaithful again intends this fear to motivate him to change his ways. When you enter into a relationship, however, you lay yourself open to the possibility of being hurt in various ways. One is that the other person may tell you you'll be dumped if you don't change, and that may place you in a painful dilemma, that is, doing something you don't want to do or losing the relationship. This can be true if you are asked to be faithful, and it can be true if you are asked to have sex. Just as the one person has the right to ask, the other has the right to decide not to do any of the things she is asked. But no one has the right to insist that a relationship cause no pain, and no one can claim to have been coerced just because the prospect of pain changes behavior.

III. DECIDING TO HAVE SEX, REDUX

Not every case of deciding to have sex is so clear, however. It would be nice if every person who decided to have sex weighed all the advantages and disadvantages of doing so, decided correctly which considerations have the most weight for her or him, and acted accordingly. In such cases we may say the person did what he or she wanted to do. What do we say, though, when we confront an agent whose actions do not accurately reflect her strongest desire? Many persons engage in sex in a way which they later regret, not just because of unforeseen consequences but because the act was, even at that time, contrary to their overall motivational structure; it was in some sense not what they truly wanted at the time. Some people have sex out of weakness of will

* * *

Not surprisingly, this happens frequently in the realm of sexuality, where on the one hand there is a strong motivation to engage in sexual activity and on the other hand there are many desires and values which mitigate against it. This in itself, however, may have nothing to do with coercion. Two people can weakly and mutually succumb to the lure of romance (or whatever) without their roles being that of victim and villain. While weakness is no doubt morally problematic in terms of each person's assessment of his or her own character, neither has anything to blame the other for, any more than the dieter can blame the whipped cream. The problem arises when one feels that one's weakness has somehow been induced by another.

A. Seduction

Weakness induced by another is what we've come to know as seduction. In seduction, a person does not simply act weakly because she finds the prospect of sex overwhelmingly tempting; she is brought to this weakness by the interference of someone else. There are two ways this can happen: the victim of seduction can be brought to do something that she in many way likes but which she is trying to resist. She can be led to succumb to temptation so that desire overcomes conviction. Or, she may be importuned to do something that she is not attracted to, and distracted by grief or fear, she may give in, without fully rational consideration. It is this which might lead one to see seduction as a species of rape, because pressure is brought to bear on the woman to act in a way that runs counter not just to what she would not want without that pressure but also to what she really wants even given that pressure. . . .

The proximity of the lure causes her to see it most vividly and to feel its attractions most poignantly, and this causes her to choose weakly, to give in to temptation. The important thing is that these appeals do not contribute to any rational decision-making process,

but rather undercut it. The seducer does not allow the other time to collect herself, to think about what it really would be best to do. Thus, the circumstances may be as relevant as the content of the appeal in determining whether or not this is seduction: what in midafternoon over coffee in the student union might be a rational discussion about the desirability of including sex in the relationship may well be productive of an emotional maelstrom at 2:00 A.M. in the dark of his room. Were she in control of herself, she might resist, or she might, upon reflection, have a change of heart and decide that, if having sex is the only way to continue the relationship, then that is worth it. But in this circumstance reflection is not an option, and no exertion of self-control is forthcoming. She gives in, unable to resist the pressure of the moment, unable to act on the decision she would make if the circumstances of his demands did not induce weakness.

Weakness and positive temptation. If a man consciously tries to undercut a woman's decision-making process by arousing emotion and is successful in this, is the ensuing sex rape? Consider, first, an analogous case, where the seduced is already attracted to whatever it is that she is trying to resist and where the seducer increase her desires while trying to undercut her appreciation of the reasons to resist. You go into a store, where your eye is caught by the attractive but expensive item you've always wanted but know to be a luxury you can't afford. As you stand contemplating it, you are approached by the High Pressure Salesman, who is paid by commission and who is not going to be dissuaded from trying to sell you this piece by considerations of your welfare. It's him against you, and he does everything he can to overcome your defenses. Well, not everything he can—he doesn't pull a gun and threaten you with death if you don't buy the item; he doesn't tell you that your safety or the security of your children is at stake. He doesn't use violence as a threat in any sense nor induce terror. Rather, he tries to subvert your reasoning process. When you tell him, weakening, that you can't afford the a. but e. item, he tells you that in the long run the item isn't really that expensive; if, for example, you calculate how much you will be paying per hour, the amount is negligible. He argues that, in certain cases, the item may even be construed as saving you money—you'll be using the a. but e. item so much that you won't spend on all those other less attractive items and, anyway, when it's time for resale you might well get rid of the a. but e. item for more than you paid for it. He astutely perceives whom you are likely to admire and tells you that this is the sort of item Michael Jordan/Hillary Rodham Clinton/ Eminem is bound to have around the house. And most of all, whatever he says, he doesn't let you think. He looks for a point of vulnerability, a weakness through which he can corrupt the solid reasoning process with which you came in and convince you that what he wants is really what you want.

Would this work? It depends, of course, on the person. For one thing, you've got to be tempted by the a. but e. item to begin with and to have a sufficiently ingenuous character not to recognize that this is essentially an adversarial relationship. As with seduction, only some people are vulnerable to the pressure. But, as with seduction, some people are vulnerable, and they give in, only to rue an action which was expressive neither of their heartfelt desires nor their considered principles. This is bad. We look down on high pressure salesmen as being manipulative and self-interested. But while this is true, such a sales technique is not assault. The salesman does not rob you. He does not even misrepresent issues of fact. He aids you to pursue something you want by increasing your desire for it and decreasing your recognition of the reasons against it. This is like a person who wants you off your diet and wafts fresh bread under your nose while telling you that just this once won't hurt. It wouldn't work if you weren't enticed by the smell of fresh bread. It might not work if they weren't also talking to you to reduce your resistance. Combining the two things, though, sometimes does work. In the realm of sexuality, it is like someone who increases the other's already existing desire to have sex, perhaps by touch, perhaps by words, while trying to dispose of their reasons not to have sex.

Such a person is not admirable, but just as the high pressure salesman is not a robber and the bread-wafter is not guilty of assault by force-feeding, the seducer who persuades you to do something you are attracted to but might otherwise have been able to resist is not guilty of rape. If he touches you when you have told him to stop, he is guilty of assault, but if you don't try to stop him from touching you and you let him talk to you about why it is okay to have sex, changing your mind is ultimately a decision for which you are responsible.

Weakness and negative sanctions. What if you are led to act weakly, though, not because of a positive attraction but because of a threat of emotional pain? And what if the other has induced this emotional pain just in order to subvert your thinking processes and get you to do what they want? This is not so much temptation as anxiety and as such it looks much more like coercion. Again, let us take a (putative) analogy which has been defused by avoiding sexual content. Let us imagine your sleazy Cousin Beau. Beau is a charming ne'er do well. He's always had a kind word for you, his little cousin, and when you were young, he would take you for piggy-back rides when your more sober relatives engaged in boring conversations and imitate their irritable admonitions at the dinner table. Now, though, you are a young adult, with a good job and a disposable income, and Beau approaches you with dollar signs in his eyes. His proposition is vague but urgent—that you should invest your savings in a business opportunity directed by Beau himself. You are not so blinded by affection as to think that this looks like a golden opportunity, but you don't know how to handle the situation. Beau has always been so funny and kind, and he looks so sincere, and the imagined prospect of your refusal seems to cut him, a member of your own family with whom you've enjoyed so many youthful hours, to the quick. If you had time you could think more clearly, but giving you time to think is just what he doesn't want. He stresses his own suffering, hearkens back to the many times he's helped you, and suggests that he can't possibly feel the same in the future if you won't do this little thing, which can't possibly hurt you and which could help him so much. You feel guilty, you feel sorry, you feel Beau may turn against you if you fail him, and, most of all, you feel confused. The more Beau sees this, the harder he pushes. And, suppose that he is joined in the pursuit of your money by Cousin Flo. Flo has never been a buddy. She has spent both your youths making you feel inferior for your poor sense of fashion, your inability to attract boyfriends, your ugly nose. As such things often happen, instead of rejecting Flo as unworthy of your attention, you tried all the harder to live up to her standards—after all, she was older, prettier, and obviously cooler. The one thing you want to do is avoid that sneer. When Cousin Flo castigates you for once again failing to make the grade by investing in this great opportunity, when she says she'd hoped that you would finally have caught up to her in taste and acumen and would thus take the cousins up on this proposition, you quail. You've been worn down by a youth of inferiority, and it's as hard to muster the strength to withstand her judgment now as it was then.

Cousin Beau is a sleaze. Cousin Flo has a despicable character. But for all this, I don't think we can say that they are thieves, nor even that they are extortionists. It isn't that you haven't reasonable alternatives to giving them money. It is rather that you don't, as Beau gazes at you appealingly, or as Flo curls her lip, see your way clearly as to what your choice should be. The cousins have placed pressure of a sort an honorable person wouldn't, and we evaluate their character accordingly, but they have not forced your compliance. . . .

Are these analogous to seduction? They have in common that they feature people who coax, cajole, wheedle, importune, harangue, berate, and browbeat another into doing their bidding. Certainly there are differences. Strangely, women may be more vulnerable when it comes to giving up their bodies than to giving up money. On the one hand, we recognize the body to be the locus of autonomy, not to be interfered with, but on the other hand we romanticize a man's pursuit of a hesitant woman in a way that may make a woman feel unnaturally cold, inferior, and guilty if she doesn't yield to his passion.[10] Furthermore, the use of the body by another can be much more of a loss than the loss of money; few things hit as close to home as having one's very body taken over by another. But the fact that seduction is worse than having money wormed out of you, just as rape is worse than theft, doesn't mean the analogy is not apt. The point is that the difference between

seduction and rape is the same as finagled money loss and robbery. The seducer tries to suborn the person's thought process just the way Cousin Beau does. The thief and the rapist don't try to undercut the victim's ability to decide what she should do: they don't need to, because they present her with a choice—her money or her life, sex or being beaten—that she can make quite rationally.

The question, then, is not so much whether a person is acting weakly or fully in accordance with her own judgment, or whether she is acting in a way she would not were it not for the pressures of another, rather than acting uniquely on her own desires. The question is whether these pressures placed on her, and which may make her decide against her own most considered desires, are placed on her appropriately.

But, one might ask, can it ever be proper to place pressure on adults to do what they really don't want to do, either by increasing a desire they are trying to fight or by diminishing or outweighing a desire which is really in accord with their overall motivational structure?

* * *

When it comes to sex, there is no doubt that, in some cases, the lover who tries to sell sex to his reluctant partner truly thinks that she will be better off once she sees how great sex with him is. In others, the effort is surely not so disinterested, but it is again within the normal scope of relationships that we try to persuade others to do what we want and that that persuasion is not purely rational. We need perhaps a more general recognition of the fact that, when it comes to sex, the two parties involved may have a conflict of interests and that cultural stereotypes and ideologies have been invented which try to hide this fact.[11] We cannot assume that even the most romantic of encounters is not at heart adversarial. But adversarial interests may not make an action immoral. It is often fair enough that we want different things and that we try to get the other person to do what we want.

And where such actions are immoral, where we go beyond the normal degree of dishonesty or manipulation implicit in human relationships, the resulting intercourse may not be rape. It is not rape if the person asking for sex stays within what he has a right to ask for. This is not to say that there are conditions where one has a right to have sex even if the other person does not consent: there aren't. Rather, one has a right to ask for the other's consent and to try to persuade the other to give consent as long as one does this within legitimate parameters: the other should be a competent adult, capable of making a decision; sanctions should only be those one has a right to impose, like ending the relationship, not violence; there should be no use of authority derived from extraneous positions (as father, employer, etc.). No one has a right to control our bodies or to touch us when we do not want to be touched, but it is a part of our lives as moral agents that people close to us have the right to talk to us about things we may not want to hear, even when that means they are being downright nasty. We can go away if we want and not see the person any more but, if we want to be involved in a relationship, we cannot reasonably insist that we never hear anything we don't want to hear. It is part of our life as moral agents that we need to learn to negotiate through others' desires.

* * *

CONCLUSION

We need to expand our conceptual framework and our terminology so that we can capture greater differences than we typically do. There is a cultural tradition which has divided sexual intercourse into either morally unacceptable rape or morally acceptable nonrape. The truth is that there are many finer distinctions which we need to recognize and to which we need to develop a sensitivity. We do this in other areas, where we recognize actions of deceit, hurtfulness, and damage which are not the worst of transgressions and yet which are not morally neutral. We know generally that there is a difference between actions which (*a*) infringe others' rights (say, stealing), (*b*) don't infringe others' rights but are nonetheless wrong (like failing to give to someone in need), (*c*) are not wrong but which nonetheless evince bad character (giving to the needy but only to feel your own superiority), and (*d*)

are none of these yet may nonetheless be regrettable for their repercussions. What we need to understand is that sex is at least as complex as other areas of human interaction and has just as many varieties of wrong as well as of good, and as we have been accustomed to differentiate within other areas of human interaction so should we here.

To subsume all areas of sexual wrong under the heading of rape does a disservice to all concerned. It hurts those whose laudable goal is just to show that sex can be dark and hurtful; they lose credibility when they are perceived as exaggerating, and their perfectly appropriate criticisms of sexual practice may be dismissed. It is bad for those who are the aggressors in any sexual situation, who may feel that, as long as they have not committed rape, their actions are morally neutral: they need to learn that actions outside of rape can be despicable and to cultivate awareness as to which are and which are not morally acceptable forms of suasion. To call all sexual wrongdoing rape also does a disservice to those who have suffered the absolute terror of violent assault and whose suffering can't, I think, be compared to that of the person who has reluctantly agreed to have sex to avoid emotional distress. This may be a case where analytical philosophy, with its conceptual distinctions and semantic precision, can indeed explain something to our sense of order and can actually be useful.

NOTES

1. One well-known example of a college sexual offense policy which deviates greatly from the law is the Antioch College Sexual Offense policy. While the Antioch policy does not specifically address verbal coercion, it articulates two common concerns: first, it says that rape can occur even where there is no physical force or threat of physical force; second, it introduces a far more stringent standard of what real consent is than that in use in rape law. At Bates College, where I was teaching when writing this article, the description of rape in the sexual offense policy includes acts of intercourse which have been consented to because of emotional pressure. When asked, an administrator gave as an example of emotional pressure a person repeatedly telling his girlfriend he would break up

with her if she would not have sex. See also an interesting exchange on the use of Pineau's article "Date Rape: A Feminist Analysis" in the training of the student judicial board at Pomona College in its student paper, *The Student Life*, October 12 and November 2, 2001.

2. Of course, some will immediately answer this question by pointing to the inculcation of cultural mores, specifically those which make women feel they have an obligation to have sex, as mentioned earlier in this article. Some of those who propose holding women entirely responsible for their choices in these conditions, however, seem to believe that pointing to the acceptance of cultural mores in explaining these actions again denigrates these women's claim to autonomy. Perhaps the idea is that a truly autonomous being should be able to rise above cultural influence when it comes to decisions about sex.

3. See Katie Roiphe's popular *The Morning After: Sex, Fear, and Feminism on Campus* (New York: Little, Brown, 1993). A more balanced assessment of widening the scope of what is considered rape may be found in Linda Lemoncheck's "When Good Sex Turns Bad: Rethinking a Continuum Model of Sexual Violence against Women," in *A Most Detestable Crime*, ed. Keith Burgess-Jackson (Oxford: Oxford University Press, 1999), pp. 159–82.

4. Here, and generally, I am following Alan Wertheimer's account of coercion, as presented in *Coercion* (Princeton, N.J.: Princeton University Press, 1987). Wertheimer explicates and defends what he calls a two-pronged account of coercion, where for A's threat to be coercive (1) A leaves B with no reasonable choice and (2) A's proposal is wrongful, where the wrongfulness relies on more than just the fact that A leaves B no reasonable choice (pp. 30–31 ff.). One way in which A's proposal can be wrongful is that it may be a proposal A has no right to make. Naturally, not everyone accepts this account of coercion. In particular, there are those who think coercion is a morally neutral term, so that to say an act is coercive is not to say that it is (even prima facie) morally wrong. Samuel Dubois Cook in "Coercion and Social Change," in *Coercion*, ed. Roland Pennock and John Chapman (Chicago: Aldine Atherton, 1972), pp. 107–43, argues, e.g., that a legitimate government can rightfully coerce its citizens in some cases. For my purposes, this difference is simply one of word use. Those who think coercion is in itself a morally neutral term can look at the question I address as whether coercion in the case of sex is legitimate.

5. Again, I am following Wertheimer.

6. The degree of harm required to make the choice of sex the only reasonable one open to the victim is naturally an issue of debate. If a boss threatens to fire an employee if she does not have sex, some will argue that, while the use of power is clearly illegitimate here, the harm is not sufficient to say the woman has no reasonable choice. Those who agree with such a low estimate of harm will argue that this is rather merely sexual harassment. In the case of the young daughters threatened with the anger of their parent, I think such a harm is sufficiently great to make the pressure to have sex genuinely coercive, and the ensuing sex rape. It may also be that, in the case of children and parents, the children have less than a complete ability to judge the degree of harm the parent may be able to do them, since the parent's authority interferes with their own ability to use their judgment. In such a case the pressure to have sex may be seen as not only coercive but also as what I call seductive, in that it interferes with the reasoning process of the victim. I discuss seduction in Sec. III.

7. This follows Wertheimer's account.

8. We may assume here that not going to the dance would cause my son great pain.

9. Marcia Baron has influenced my views here on the parameters of demands that may be made within relationships.

10. Remember what an insult it has been for a woman to be called "frigid."

11. Just as culture has veiled the conflict of interest which may rise within romantic encounters, it has perhaps exaggerated the danger to women from strangers. The idea that predators lie in wait for women has been used to convince women that they need protectors, which, in turn, may make them more vulnerable to the men whom they see as close to them: boyfriends, family members, even dates. See Susan Griffin's seminal "Rape: The All American Crime," first published in *Ramparts* (10 [September 1971]: 23–36), and Claudia Card's "Rape as a Terrorist Institution," in *Violence, Terrorism, and Justice*, ed. R. G. Frey and Christopher W. Morris (Cambridge: Cambridge University Press, 1991), pp. 296–319.

Sex under Pressure: Jerks, Boorish Behavior, and Gender Hierarchy
Scott A. Anderson

Seduction is not always a matter of charms, flatteries, and sparks; sometimes it is less like runaway passion and more like sexual assault. But even when it is not criminal, it can be ethically suspect. Seducers often use plain and not-so-plain pressure to get the objects of their desires to acquiesce to sexual proposals. Further problems stem from the way background forces and injustices—systematic gender hierarchy, for instance—empower some seducers and weaken their targets. How are we to evaluate the ethics of such pressuring? And in particular, how useful is it to ask whether such pressure amounts to a kind of coercion, or to ask whether the person seduced consents under such pressure? . . .

A recent essay by Sarah Conly throws a useful light on this question.[1] She explores the issues in sexual pressuring by investigating the ethics of similar techniques as they are used in non-sexual contexts. Although Conly's approach manifests good sense . . . there are problems with some of its central insights. We cannot fully appraise the pressures seducers use without attending to the wider context in which they occur. This context includes our hierarchical gender system, as well as the many other sources of pressure to have (or sometimes not to have) sex that come from friends, peers, parents, and the social organization of many spheres of (especially young) adulthood.

One might suppose that as long as the pressures involved in seduction do not undermine or disregard the target's consent, then such pressures are ethically unexceptional.[2] But a proper appreciation of the place of consent requires us to attend to certain structural aspects of human interaction, especially sexual interaction, which may affect consent's value. I will argue that Conly, like some others who have recently tackled the topic, overlooks these deeper structural matters.[3] Male seducers, unlike women, are able to draw upon advantages conferred by male dominance within a gender hierarchy. If we fail to attend to such contextual features of gender relations, it will be difficult to see why ordinary sexual pressuring ("seduction") by men is ethically more serious than many other ways one might be a jerk; conversely, attending to this context may indicate ways to undercut these advantages, and thereby to promote women's autonomy and satisfaction in their sexual relationships with men.

CONSENT TO SEX UNDER PRESSURE

Our laws, social norms, religious views, and personal values give us numerous, sometimes conflicting directions for what is good or bad, permissible or impermissible, in the pursuit of sexual relationships with others. Some methods are ruled out entirely, while others are at least ethically suspect. Philosophers have taken to investigating the relationship between sex and laws, norms and values in part because we want to protect the autonomy of people in making decisions about whom to have sex with, when, how, and so on. Among the suspect methods of starting or furthering a sexual relationship is the use of psychological pressure aimed to overcome the hesitation or resistance of a prospective sexual partner. The difficulty in evaluating the use of pressure techniques can be brought out by comparing them to rape or sexual assault. These latter violations are accomplished by direct physical force or by using the threat of such force, or by use of disabling drugs, or when someone is physically unable to consent. These uses of power against a person allow an aggressor to proceed to have sex with his victim regardless of what she wants, thus manifesting complete disregard for her consent, and undercutting her autonomy. We have no difficulty, we may presume, in agreeing that any such conduct is wrong and should be illegal. Using pressure techniques to achieve a seduction, however, seems trivial by comparison.[4]

Hence there is an opening and use for a dedicated philosophical account of the ethics of pressuring someone into having sex.

In Conly's essay we find . . . guidance on a variety of cases where one person uses various forms of psychological pressure or manipulation in order to get another to acquiesce to sex. . . . Conly focuses the heart of her essay on less extreme cases of seduction involving ordinary, competent adults. She analyzes common seduction as a kind of intentionally induced "weakness of the will." The seduced party is brought to engage in or consent to activity that she would reject if allowed a cool moment and time to reflect. The seduced party yields because the seducer has applied various forms of pressure to her that breaks down or circumvents her ability to follow her best interests, rightly viewed. The pressures of interest here are limited to those of ordinary, if not laudable, social or familial interaction—e.g., wheedling, whining, emotional manipulation, mild intimidation, petty deceits, and threats to alter or end one's relationship with someone who refuses to bend to one's will. (I will refer to the lot of these as "pressures" or "boorishness" where these terms will then exclude more objectionable means. Those who engage in such activities I will call "jerks.") Seducers intentionally use these pressure techniques precisely because they tend to induce people to acquiesce to the wishes of seducers, even though doing so is against what the seduced person (at least initially) regarded as her best interests.

There are a number of ways one might evaluate the ethics of pressure techniques in sexual pursuits, but any such evaluation must be wary of condemning activity which, even if not ideal, is in the interests of the parties involved, and carries no serious external costs. Conly holds that the key issue in evaluating a jerk's use of pressure is whether the jerk *coerces* the target of attention into sexual activity the target does not want . . . [T]he critical elements of the test for coercion are whether a particular threatened sanction is sufficiently harmful or painful to leave the target "no choice" but to avoid it; and whether the threatener acts illegitimately in threatening to impose such a sanction. When a use of pressure satisfies both of these conditions, it counts as coercive; otherwise, the

pressure is non-coercive, and its use to obtain sexual favors is, if not benign, at least of lesser moral concern than rape or the extreme forms of seduction from which Conly begins.[5]

Conly argues that less egregious forms of sexual pressuring are non-coercive, and thus lack the legal and moral implications that rape or sexual assault have. She notes, "it seems implausible to say that whenever someone gives into irrational suasion to have sex, or has sex only out of fear of displeasing someone she cares for, or out of a desire to please, a rape has occurred." Although the boorish behavior of a seducer may be problematic, within the context of a romantic relationship, the use of emotional pressures is not, she thinks, illegitimate. . . .

Conly then turns to the question of whether playing on the weaknesses or emotions of one's desired partner makes one's use of pressure illegitimate. She stacks such cases up against ones in which salespeople or relatives use similar techniques to close a sale or to cajole someone into investing in their schemes. However unpleasant or inappropriate such measures are, they fall short of criminal: if you submit to the high-pressure salesman's pitch, or invest in a good-for-nothing relative's scheme, you have nonetheless not been robbed. Similarly, she holds, if one succumbs to the temptations, badgering, or guilt-trips of a (would-be) lover, one cannot reasonably accuse him or her of rape:

> It is not rape if the person asking for sex stays within what he has a right to ask for. . . . We can go away if we want and not see the person any more but, if we want to be involved in a relationship, we cannot reasonably insist that we never hear anything we don't want to hear. It is part of our life as moral agents that we need to learn to negotiate through others' desires.[6]

Based on these considerations, Conly . . . reasonably opposes dichotomizing sexual intercourse into either rape or nonrape. "The truth is that there are many finer distinctions which we need to recognize and to which we need to develop a sensitivity". She further denies that all uses of pressure to have sex are on a par; for instance, she holds that it is illegitimate for employers to use their economic leverage to pressure employees into having sex, or for parents and teachers to use their authority to seduce. . . .

CONSENT TO SEX IN CONTEXT

It is uncontroversial that coercing someone into sex is condemnable, and thus that all permissible means of inducing another to have sex must be non-coercive. Our question is whether and how to draw ethical distinctions among the various non-coercive means, and what then to do with those distinctions. One might, for instance, see Conly's aim as limited to expounding the proper limits of the definition of rape in criminal law, and denying that boorishness in the pursuit of sexual relations is at all comparable to rape. With this conclusion I have no complaints. . . . Some, however, have linked seduction with rape, not so much to urge that the law treat seducers and rapists alike, but rather to point out the similarity of the powers and impositions frequently manifested in both. Conly appears to object equally to this linkage, seeing it as a sort of exaggeration of the wrongs involved in pressuring into sex.[7] My aim here is not so much to defend the rhetoric connecting seduction to rape, but to argue that there is something valuable in looking for connections here. This value is easily overlooked by an account of seduction like Conly's, which analyzes it in terms of coercion, understood pressures on the will, and consent. Her account, I will suggest, fails to make sense of the reasons that have led feminists to try to forge this connection. By narrowing our analysis of seduction to the individual's use of pressure and its effects on the seducee's will, she tends to ignore background factors that are crucial to understanding the ethics of the seducer's behavior and the problems of seduction for the seduced.

We can see reason to worry about this in the generic way Conly treats ethical judgments about sex, which is insensitive to the special context of sex and sexuality that give sexual pressuring its particular urgency. She writes, for instance, that,

[T]he fact that seduction is worse than having money wormed out of you, just as rape is worse than theft, doesn't mean the analogy is not apt. The point is that the difference between seduction and rape is the same as finagled money loss and robbery.

Regarding the criminality of the conduct involved, Conly may be correct; but insofar as she is drawing a deeper lesson about how these behaviors compare as social ills, her analysis misses the deep difference that context makes in these disparate fields of ethical concern. While robberies and finagling may both point up the evils of greed and the importance we attach to money, robbing and finagling are not connected in the way that raping and pressuring into sex are. The fact that there are robbers about, and that one must take precautions against them does not greatly affect the viability of finagling or the harm involved in it. Nor do finaglers exacerbate the damages caused by robbers. By contrast, the existence and pervasiveness of violence used as a means to obtain sex is integrally connected to the hierachical structure of gender relations. This structure in turn greatly alters the viability of a man's pressuring a woman into sex, and the harm such pressuring causes—even if she does not relent, and especially if she does.

Conly's analysis leaves no room for these contextual matters, in that it treats seduction as strictly a matter of one individual's questionable ethical conduct impacting another individual who is potentially afflicted by weakness of the will. Both of these characters suffer from what amount to internal defects of character, which apparently have nothing to do with each other.

* * *

So, if one limits one's evaluations of sex under pressure to a choice between *consensual* versus *coerced*, one is left with little to say about what is wrong or problematic with the behavior of men who pressure women into having sex with them. In this light, we may regard those feminists who have linked such pressuring to rape as attempting to bring into view the problematic role that gender hierarchy plays in framing the situation faced by a woman targeted by a male seducer. Despite denying this connection, Conly does apparently think there is something problematic about the pressuring conduct of jerks, and not just in the cases where it oversteps the line between boorishness and assault. The question is how to explain the nature of this problem.

* * *

EVALUATING SEXUAL PRESSURE IN A CONTEXT OF SEXUAL INEQUALITY

In explaining why a woman submits to sex with a man, it will often suffice to say that he threatened her with violence if she refused. We rarely feel we need to press further and ask why she assumed that he was capable of violence, why she assumed the threat was in earnest, or why she assumed that if she denied him that he would have gone ahead, against his own interests, and executed his threat. Even if he is a relative stranger to her, we do not usually press for answers to such questions. Why? Because we know what men, or at least some men, are like. That is, we know such things as that it is not uncommon for men to harm women awfully, that men often do so even against their own best interests, and that demonstrating an inclination to do so can alter the ground-rules for their interactions with women to their advantage. In other words, our understanding of how men can coerce women into unwanted sex depends upon our understanding of the kinds of powers men possess over women, when they are likely to use them, and so forth.

To understand the ethical significance of pressuring into sex, we need to have a similar understanding of how and why such pressure works. It is not wholly obvious why pressuring someone to have sex is at all likely to succeed, or work better than thoughtfulness and charm, say, or why using pressure appears to some a reasonable strategy with respect to their ends. The idea that one person could put pressure on another to do something antecedently unwanted is straightforward enough; in some sense, just asking another to do something is a form of pressure. Yet this does not explain why anyone would yield to such pressure. It is helpful here to bear in mind that all pressurings, whether towards sex or any other end, take place in a particular context that likely provides us with various facilities and obstacles concerning our ability to resist external pressure. In some contexts (say, parent-child relations), the use of pressure works largely because children have no choice but to rely on their parents. Such pressure is also entirely expected and reasonable because of the need to sway the behaviors and values of people not yet fully formed or competent to judge independently.[8]

In other contexts (say, strangers passing on the street), the use of pressure to alter personal choices is not just unexpected and culturally inappropriate, it is also fairly easy to dismiss without loss. One can walk away, and the pressurer usually has no useful avenue by which to continue or increase his pressuring.

Thus the ability of one person to pressure another into unwanted sex needs to be explained by reference to the factors that make such pressure relevant to one's ends, predictably effective in altering behavior, and socially viable (i.e., not quickly and strongly discouraged).[9] My suggestion is that an investigation into the workings of pressuring into sex will reveal real differences in its significance when used by men as opposed to when used by women. So, for example, when a fraternity man pressures a sorority woman into sex, we would do well to notice how institutional, social, and relational factors combine to make such pressure viable. On the (relatively) more benign side are included factors such as the interest sorority women have in fitting in with their sisters and in finding dates for social functions. More problematically, there are pressures associated with proving one's physical attractiveness, attracting a steady boyfriend as a protector/shield against unwanted aggression, and in avoiding an escalation of aggression that could lead to rape . . . .

Furthermore, men pressuring women into having sex takes place against a background in which men and women differ in their ability to use or to resist violent attack. . . . Thus, we should not divorce our analysis of pressuring techniques in intimate encounters from the wider range of techniques a party has at his or her disposal. While men and women may be equally likely to resort to boorish behavior to achieve their sexual ends, men are known to turn sometimes to much more potent and dangerous techniques than women typically are, and men are generally able to fend off the relatively few women who might be inclined to use such techniques themselves. Hence the ability to apply pressure to have unwanted sex may differ markedly between men and women on average. Men are able to pressure women more effectively because their pressure is backed by their much greater ability to escalate that pressure into the range of the very dangerous.

Of course, when a man pressures a woman to have sex with him, he may well be unwilling to engage in such escalation; that is, he may be willing to pressure or manipulate her, but not to lay a hand without consent. But once he demonstrates that he is willing to violate norms of proper respect for his intended in the first way, it may be much harder for her to tell that he is not willing to resort to more potent means. Whether he likes it or not, his ability to apply pressure is augmented by the background common knowledge that men have the ability and a non-trivial likelihood to use force and violence against women. Unless, that is, he makes special provisions to defeat this augmentation. To do so, he would have to indicate that even though he is willing to violate certain lesser ethical norms, he would refuse to violate the more vital ones . . . . [I]t is a rather tricky matter to communicate such principles, and it would also work against one's advantage to do so. So a man might need to be subtle, unfussy and explicit—all at once—to employ boorish means to pressure a woman to have sex, while refraining from drawing upon the strength conferred by his access to more deeply unethical ones.

* * *

The advantages that male jerks have compared to female jerks might also help explain the fact that the reported effects of being subjected to such techniques appear to differ significantly along gender lines. Some researchers have reported that sexual aggressiveness by women against men is more acceptable than analogous aggression by men against women would be. When women are aggressive, it is often reconceived as "romance" or "expressing her sexuality" or being "seductive."[10] Some studies have also found that men's reactions to being aggressed against by a woman differ markedly depending upon the attractiveness of the aggressor.[11] By contrast, women frequently report much more negative responses to being subjected to sexual pressure from men. . . .[12]

[T]his understanding of how pressuring into unwanted sex works, and the context in which it occurs, suggests our question is more complex than choosing between allowing women the right to have sex with jerks vs. denying the validity of their consent to

such sex. In the context of gender hierarchy enforced by violence (among other forms of power), the ethical defects in a man's pressuring a woman to have sex reach beyond its boorishness, and may encompass a kind of unfair advantage-taking, among other things. As the microcosm of undergraduate Greek life in the U.S. suggests, a wide range of pressures fall on individuals making decisions about sex, and many of these pressures derive from the hierarchical (and heterosexist) nature of contemporary gender relations.[13] When a man goes ahead and violates such norms as exist to protect women's sexual autonomy, he may at the same time be availing himself of the disparity in power between men and women more generally. Hence, whether or not we should deny the possibility of a woman's consenting to sex in such conditions, we can certainly criticize the boorishness of a male jerk's sexual conduct for reasons that may not apply to analogous conduct in non-sexual matters, or even to women's sexual boorishness, for that matter.

As for positive suggestions arising from this analysis, we can agree with Conly's reluctance to equate sexual pressuring and rape, either ethically or legally, but we need not suppose that such equations exhaust the range of our potential ethical responses. It may be an advance simply to be able to say why pressuring someone to have sex she does not want is bad: for instance, by pointing out how such pressure frequently relies on a background of violence and inequality, or how such pressure tends to ally with other pressures which additively may give women many fewer opportunities for social or other fulfillment than they might have otherwise. It may also be the case that some institutions, such as fraternities, sororities, and the like, and the campuses that house them, may be in a position to develop codes or norms of sexual conduct that give individuals defenses against unwanted sexual pressure, short of charging someone with rape or assault. Given that these places are currently the sites of norms that add to the pressures to have sex, perhaps they can instead develop norms that work to neutralize at least some pressures to have sex. Taking away at least some of the advantages that male jerks employ in pressuring women to have unwanted sex would almost certainly add to women's overall happiness and autonomy with respect to sex.

NOTES

1. S. Conly, "Seduction, Rape, and Coercion", *Ethics* 115/1 (2004), 96–121.

2. The topic of consent, especially regarding sexual relations, has been much discussed in the philosophical and legal literature. The most important books include S. Schulhofer, *Unwanted Sex* (Cambridge: Harvard, 1998); D. Archard, *Sexual Consent* (Oxford: Westview, 1998); and A. Wertheimer, *Consent to Sexual Relations* (Cambridge: Cambridge University Press, 2004). Also of interest are the essays published in two special issues of *Legal Theory*, 2/2 and 2/3 (1996).

3. In particular, I mean to demonstrate a problem that affects, e.g., Wertheimer's *Consent* and his work on coercion more generally (e.g., A. Wertheimer, *Coercion* (Princeton: Princeton University Press, 1987)), from which Conly takes her guidance on coercion. Conly's deep reliance on Wertheimer is one example of the profound influence his work has had. There is much to like and respect in his work, and its influence is justified by his careful scholarship. But his failure to attend to the power relations between coercer and coercee, or between (male) sexual aggressor and (female) sexual object, weakens his analysis in the same ways that the difficulties in Conly's paper exhibit.

4. This claim must be understood in a modern context; historically, matters of "seduction" were extremely serious ones for women, since it often amounted to both rape and the ruination of her prospects for a decent marriage. . . . For a useful overview of the legal history of the sexual predation called seduction, see L. VanderVelde, "The Legal Ways of Seduction", *Stanford Law Review* 48/4 (1996), 817–901.

5. Conly actually parses Wertheimer's "two-pronged" test into four separate conditions: the coercer's intent, the coercee's constrained choice, the harm imposed on the coercee, and the illegitimacy of the coercer's offer. "Choice" and "legitimacy" become the key factors since Conly would admit, it seems, that jerks use pressure with intent, and that the harms they cause are at least sometimes non-trivial.

6. One might be bothered here . . . about Conly's framing the issues in the passages here and above in terms of rights. Indeed it sounds strange to speak about a "right to want sex to be a part of a romantic relationship." Still, Conly's point here seems reasonable enough, I think, even if one is wary of rights talk. Her claim might be restated as holding simply that there are some kinds of relationships of which sex is a constitutive activity and in which sexual fulfillment is part of the point of the relationship. If so, then one might sometimes reasonably negotiate with another about what sort of relationship (if any) they wish to be part of, and what part sex will play in it. Just as one person cannot rightly impose participation in a sexual relationship on another, so one party cannot unilaterally impose a non-sexual relationship on another (especially if the relationship were originally a sexual one) without allowing the other some say about this. That is, unless one accepts that sex must be confined to something like the traditional Roman Catholic institution of marriage, which would not dissolve just because one partner stopped agreeing to sex within it. Barring this sort of restriction on acceptable sexual relationships, there will be a need to reach mutual agreement over the part that sex will play in relationships in which sex is a permissible or even constitutive part, and these terms will in some respects always be open for renegotiation.

7. "To subsume all areas of sexual wrong under the heading of rape does a disservice to all concerned. It hurts those whose laudable goal is just to show that sex can be dark and hurtful; they lose credibility when they are perceived as exaggerating, and their perfectly appropriate criticisms of sexual practice may be dismissed".

8. Given the whole of the dynamic between parent and child, it can be very difficult to dismiss such pressure, even long after the aspect of dependency has lapsed or even reversed.

9. I should also mention that the viability of using pressure will depend also on the particular psychological characteristics of the people involved, but it is important not to overemphasize their role: while some are better able or more willing to use pressure than others, and some more susceptible to it, discovering these facts about oneself or others requires experience and practice in contexts where such pressures are (likely) already a feature of how some people interact with others.

10. The authors discussing this research note that equivalent conduct by a man could be criminally prosecuted. See C. Struckman-Johnson and P. B. Anderson, "Men Do and Women Don't": Difficulties in Researching Sexually Aggressive Women," in P. B. Anderson and C. Struckman-Johnson, 1998, 9-18, pp. 14–15.

11. C. Struckman-Johnson and D. Struckman-Johnson, "The Dynamics and Impact of Sexual Coercion of Men by Women", in P. B. Anderson and C. Struckman-Johnson, 121–143; and C. Struckman-Johnson and D. Struckman-Johnson, "Men's Reactions to

Hypothetical Forceful Sexual Advances from Women: The Role of Sexual Standards, Relationship Availability, and the Beauty Bias", *Sex Roles* 37/5-6 (1997), 319–333. At a recent talk, this sentence generated an understandable laugh from the audience. But the serious underlying point is that if the perceived "attractiveness" of the aggressor is the main concern of the aggressed-upon, then it is likely that the aggression itself constitutes a different sort of worry for men so targeted than it does for women.

12. See, e.g., the essays by C. Struckman-Johnson and P. B. Anderson; C. L. Muehlenhard; E. S. Byers and L. F. O'Sullivan; and W. Stock, in P. B. Anderson and C. Struckman-Johnson, *Sexually Aggressive Women.*

13. Several readers of this paper . . . have expressed the view that the sexual playing field for women may be getting more even, at least in Europe, perhaps in the West more generally. While this may be so, and we can hope so, I see no evidence that any large society has truly reached parity in social power between men and women.

CHAPTER 16

Free Speech on Campus

In 2017, at Middlebury College in Vermont, student protesters disrupted a speech by a controversial scholar, shouting him down, turning their backs to him, shoving him, pulling fire alarms, and injuring a faculty member in the melee. The speaker was Charles Murray, the author of *The Bell Curve* and *Coming Apart*, who argues that race and intelligence determine social and economic status. Many have charged him with racism, and scholars have denounced his work as pseudoscience and bigotry. A conservative student group had invited Murray to Middlebury, but hundreds of students and alumni opposed the invitation. The protesters chanted, "Racist, sexist, anti-gay, Charles Murray go away!"

Earlier in the year, an even more violent protest against an invited speaker occurred at the University of California, Berkeley. A group of student Republicans had invited the right-wing provocateur and writer Milo Yiannopoulos to speak on campus. They billed the speech as a way to rattle the liberal campus with a seldom-heard conservative viewpoint. But the speech was canceled when a large group of student protesters gathered and activists exploded fireworks, hurled bricks, set fires, and smashed windows.

The same kind of scenario has played out at other institutions of higher learning across the United States. Speakers have been disinvited or prevented from speaking by loud or violent protests. In most cases, protesting students were objecting to speech that they thought demeaned, subordinated, or marginalized vulnerable groups such as African Americans, women, and the LGBTQ community.

In their view, free speech must not be used as an excuse to harm already disadvantaged groups.

In many other instances, speech on campus has been censored or punished because it was deemed harmful or offensive. For example:

> [S]ome students in the United States [have been motivated] to demand that universities sanction people for writing "I'm with Trump" or "Build That Wall" in chalk on college campuses, to force university administrators to cancel an appearance by the conservative writer Ben Shapiro (who was to speak on how diversity initiatives can hamper free speech), to demand the resignation of a student leader who posted an "All Lives Matter" Twitter message in the wake of the assassination of five police officers in Dallas, or to demand a federal investigation after professor Laura Kipnis wrote a scholarly essay questioning campus attitudes about sexual relations.[1]

In all such cases, students believe that the moral evil to be avoided or defeated is **hate speech**, spoken or written words used to insult, disparage, or attack people based on their social or ethnic group. Hate speech, they insist, should be banned, censored, or punished because it harms those who are its victims. It can harm people, some say, by causing emotional and physical distress, insulting the dignity of individuals, subordinating members of minority groups, and "assaulting" vulnerable groups through offensive speech that many consider a form of violence.

The response of many colleges and universities to hate speech has been to enact **speech codes**, campus regulations that ban the use of language or symbols thought to embody hate speech. The free speech scholars Erwin Chemerinsky and Howard Gillman provide this illustration:

> One of the most prominent examples involved the University of Michigan, which was motivated to devise a hate speech code after some truly horrendous events on campus. In 1987, flyers were distributed that declared "open season" on blacks. Blacks were referred to as "saucer lips," "porch monkeys," and "jigaboos." A student disc jockey allowed racist jokes to be broadcast on the campus radio station, and student demonstrations were interrupted by the display of a KKK uniform from a nearby dorm window. Another flyer proclaimed, "Niggers get off campus" and "Darkies don't belong in classrooms—they belong hanging from trees." The university had to respond to such horrific expression.[2]

The perceived harm of offensive speech has also prompted calls for "trigger warnings" on course materials that are considered demeaning or traumatic; the resignations of editors after campus newspapers publish provocative articles; the dismissal of administrators when their views contradict those held by some campus organizations; and "safe spaces" for students who wish to retreat from exposure to offensive or unwelcome speech.

The central conflict in campus free speech controversies is between two moral goods that are crucial to higher education: (1) free speech that enables the expression of all ideas and the unfettered search for truth, and (2) a campus environment that protects and respects the learning experiences of all students. Many who are caught up in free speech debates seem to accept that there is no way to accommodate both moral ideals. A large number of students believe that offensive speech, especially hate speech, should be suppressed or punished. Protecting minorities from verbal harm, they insist, is more important than freedom of speech. Others favor the unimpeded exercise of free speech—regardless of its effects on others. Their view is that for the sake of democracy and the search for knowledge, speech—even if offensive, racist, politically incorrect, or divisive—must not be restricted.

Some see a middle path between these opposing positions where both values can be accommodated. The author and education scholar Sigal R. Ben-Porath, for example, argues for what she calls

> inclusive freedom—an approach to free speech on campus that takes into account the necessity of protecting free speech in order to protect democracy and the pursuit of knowledge while recognizing the equal necessity of making sure that all are included in the ensuing conversation.[3]

Part of the difficulty in reaching well-reasoned conclusions about free speech is the lack of understanding of what free speech is, what the U.S. Constitution and the U.S. Supreme Court say about protected (allowed) and unprotected speech, what the historical connection has been between free speech and struggles for social justice, and what reasons people have for their views on free speech.

There is no remedy for such misunderstandings other than solid moral reasoning and a good grasp of the nonmoral facts. This chapter should help on both counts.

ISSUE FILE: BACKGROUND

Free speech—the right to express your opinions or ideas without burdensome restraints from government or society—is both a moral and a legal/political value. It is enshrined in the U.S. Constitution's First Amendment, which guarantees freedom of expression by barring Congress from restricting what the press can disseminate and what individuals can say. Under the First Amendment, a vast range of speech—most of the speech we encounter every day—is protected. Most liberal democracies recognize their citizens' right to free expression, and several international bodies have declared freedom of expression a human right. Here, "speech" or "expression" refers to a variety of actions, not just speaking, but writing, yelling, acting, painting, burning flags, carrying signs, singing, and more.

The first point to understand about free speech is that it is not an absolute right. Every society

CRITICAL THOUGHT: Who Can Say the N-word?

Why can't white people use the n-word? Black people use it, rap songs use it, movies use it. This is an uncomfortable question that seems to flare up in private and public discussions (or arguments) every day. One of the clearer answers has been offered by the author and commentator on African American issues Ta-Nehisi Coates. During a panel discussion, he said the words we use depend on context, and it's normal in our culture to restrict our use of specific words to some contexts with certain people. So even though his wife calls him "honey," it would not be appropriate for a strange woman to call him that. And even though his dad was called Billy by his family, it would not be acceptable for his son to call him that. Coates said a white friend had a cabin in upstate New York and referred to it as "the white trash cabin." But Coates insisted, "I would never refer to that cabin" like that. "I would never tell him, 'I'm coming to your white trash cabin.'"

Coates declared, "The question one must ask is why so many white people have difficulty extending things that are basic laws of how human beings interact to black people."*

Is Coates right that white people should not use the n-word? Why or why not? Is his reason for thinking such use is impermissible plausible? Explain.

*German Lopez, "Ta-Nehisi Coates Has an Incredibly Clear Explanation for Why White People Shouldn't Use the N-word," Vox, November 9, 2017, https://www.vox.com/identities/2017/11/9/16627900/ta-nehisi-coates-n-word.

places limits on free speech; speech must be limited when it conflicts with other values that society holds dear. Under U.S. law, the reasons for limiting speech are few and narrowly defined, and prohibited speech includes such things as libel, threats, and obscenity.

Much of American history is the story of free speech—how the Founders wove it into the fabric of our democratic ideals, how it was challenged and strengthened through the years, how it gave dissenters and reformers the means to fight for social justice, how the courts came to see it as the fundamental right that supported all the others, and how it made social and intellectual progress possible. The protections that the United States affords free speech are the strongest in the world.

Many free speech historians remind citizens of how much depends on their right to speak and write freely. John Arthur explains:

First, as J. S. Mill argued long ago, free and unfettered debate is vital for the pursuit of truth. If knowledge is to grow, people must be free to put forth ideas and theories they deem worthy of consideration, and others must be left equally free to criticize them. Even false ideas should be protected, Mill argued, so that the truth will not become mere dogma, unchallenged and little understood. "However true [an opinion] may be," he wrote, "if it is not fully, frequently, and fearlessly discussed, it will be held as a dead dogma, not a living truth.". . .

Free speech is also an essential feature of democratic government. Fair, democratic elections cannot occur unless candidates are free to debate and criticize each other's policies, nor can government be run efficiently unless corruption and abuses can be exposed by a free press. . . .

A third value, individual autonomy, is also served by free speech. In chapter III of *On Liberty*, "Of Individuality, as One of the Elements of Well Being," Mill writes that "He who lets the world, or his own portion of it, choose his plan of life for him, has no need of any other faculty than the ape-like one of imitation." . . . Mill's suggestion is that the best life does not result from being forced to live a certain way, but instead is freely chosen without coercion from outside. But if Mill is right, then freedom of speech as well as action are important to achieve a worthwhile life. Free and open discussion helps people exercise their capacity of reasoning and judgment, capacities that are essential for autonomous and informed choices.[4]

But what of offensive speech, racist speech, hate speech? Should they be censored—or given First Amendment protection? A 2015 survey suggests that the current generation of students would opt for censorship. It showed that almost three-quarters of students favor disciplinary action for "any student or faculty member on campus who uses language that is considered racist, sexist, homophobic or otherwise offensive."[5]

Chemerinsky and Gillman offer a plausible explanation for this attitude:

This generation [of students] has a strong and persistent urge to protect others against hateful, discriminatory, or intolerant speech, especially in educational settings.

This is the first generation of students educated, from a young age, not to bully. For as long as they can remember, their schools have organized "tolerance weeks." Our students often told stories of how bullying at school and on social media had affected people they cared about. They are deeply sensitized to the psychological harm associated with hateful or intolerant speech. . . .

Arguments about the social value of freedom of speech are very abstract to them, because they did not grow up at a time when the act of punishing speech was associated with undermining other worthwhile values.

Our students knew little about the history of free speech in the United States and had no awareness of how important free speech had been to vulnerable political minorities. The two of us grew up in the time of the civil rights movement and anti-Vietnam War protests. We saw first hand how officials attempted to stifle or punish protestors in the name of defending values or protecting the public peace. We also saw how free speech assisted the drive for desegregation, the push to end the war, and the efforts of historically marginalized people to challenge convention and express their identities in new ways. In our experience, speech that was sometimes considered offensive, or that made

people uncomfortable, was a good and necessary thing. We have an instinctive distrust of efforts by authorities to suppress speech.[6]

In the twentieth century, especially during the 1950s and 1960s, the Supreme Court gradually, case by case, extended First Amendment protection to a wider range of controversial, offensive, and dissenting speech. Court rulings made it clear, for example, that the speech of civil rights protesters could not be banned or punished just because segregationists (and others) found their dissenting words deeply offensive. The court also ruled that protected speech includes anti-war protests, anti-government rhetoric, blasphemy, (some) obscene speech, and "offensive utterances" of all kinds. In fact, the court has concluded that the government cannot forbid or punish any speech unless it is an instance of libel, incitement to lawlessness, obscenity, harassment, serious threats, or "fighting words" (epithets or insults spoken face to face and likely to injure or provoke an immediate, violent action). The upshot is that, as far as the court is concerned, offensive speech and hate speech are protected speech.

It should not be surprising, then, that over the years, the courts have repeatedly ruled against speech codes at colleges and universities. (State schools are bound by the First Amendment; private schools are not, but generally try to honor it in practice anyway.) Hundreds of schools have adopted such codes, many of which have been challenged in court—and all of the challenged codes have been ruled unconstitutional. Despite the schools' laudable motive of ridding their campuses of foul racist slurs and hateful stigmatizing messages, their efforts to craft codes that would condemn offensive speech while not infringing on protected speech seem to have failed. Often the courts found that the codes were too vague to be useful and so broad that they identified obviously protected speech as banned speech. Worse, in too many instances, the codes were used not to punish hate speech, but to criticize opinions and political views that people disliked.

Microaggressions

Examining free speech issues will eventually bring you to the idea of microaggression. Microaggressions are defined as commonplace slights or insults conveyed intentionally or unintentionally by words or actions to disadvantaged groups. Each instance of microaggression may by itself amount to only a minor irritation, but cumulatively, such occurrences can be seriously detrimental to those affected. Microaggressions can be subtle, ambiguous, hardly noticed—but injurious over time. White people are said to be guilty of microaggression, for example, when they ask an Asian American classmate in what country he was born. Or when they ask an African American what the black view of rap music is. Or when they say "You're really pretty for a dark-skinned girl." Or they ask a black friend why she sounds white. Some even contend that people are guilty of microaggression whey they claim to be color-blind, claim to favor affirmative action, or use the term "politically correct."

But critics representing a variety of racial and social backgrounds have found fault with the concept. While acknowledging that cumulative slights or insults can be harmful, and that even subtle forms of prejudice should be addressed, they argue that using the concept of microaggression can itself be harmful and counterproductive.

Conor Friedersdorf, for example, says that the term "microaggression" is inapt:

To be sure, there are minor, objectionable, cumulatively burdensome actions that can accurately be called "aggressive." Catcalling is a familiar example. A man who crowds alongside a woman for a half-block while trying to get her phone number is behaving aggressively. . . . But a well-intentioned white or black student asking an Asian American classmate, "What country are you from?" is unfortunate even as it is unaggressive.

Aggression is "hostility" or "violent behavior" or "the forceful pursuit of one's interests." If there's going to be a term for behavior that is burdensome partly because the often well-intentioned people who do it are blind to its wrongness and cumulative effect, baking "aggression" into that term is hugely confusing. What's more, the confusion seems likely to needlessly increase the tension between the person experiencing the grievance and the person who is ostensibly responsible.*

Nick Haslam also questions the usefulness of viewing social bias or hostility through the "microaggression" lens:

The challenge in responding to criticisms of the microaggression concept is not to throw the baby out with the bathwater. Subtle prejudice and unconscious bias are real and consequential. It is also beyond question that the general decline in overt expressions of bigotry in recent decades does not signal the end of prejudice. People who claim to be free of it may harbour troubling attitudes and behave in discriminating ways.

However, "microaggression" is not the best way to think about subtle prejudice. Its definition is amorphous and elastic. It fails to appreciate the ambiguity of social interaction, relies too exclusively on subjective perceptions, and too readily ascribes hostile intent. By doing so, the idea of microaggression contributes to a punitive and accusatory environment that is more likely to create backlash than social progress.†

*Conor Friedersdorf, "Why Critics of the 'Microaggression' Framework Are Skeptical," *Atlantic*, September 14, 2015, https://www.theatlantic.com/politics/archive/2015/09/why-critics-of-the-microaggressions-framework-are-skeptical/405106/.

†Nick Haslam, "The Trouble with 'Microaggressions,'" *The Conversation*, January 16, 2017, https://theconversation.com/the-trouble-with-microaggressions-71364.

The courts may have more or less agreed that speech codes are unconstitutional or unworkable, but the bigger question is whether the codes are *morally* acceptable. Should colleges and universities use them to stamp out verbal harm to minorities?

Many on both sides of this debate agree that hate speech can indeed cause harm. Richard Delgado and Jean Stefancic argue that hate speech can do damage to targeted groups in several ways:

> Hate speech is not merely unpleasant or offensive. It may leave physical impacts on those it visits, particularly when uttered in one-on-one situations accompanied by at least an implicit threat. . . .
>
> The immediate, short-term harms of hate speech include rapid breathing, headaches, raised blood pressure, dizziness, rapid pulse rate, drug-taking, risk-taking behavior, and even suicide. The stresses of repeated racial abuse may have long-term consequences, including damaged self-esteem, lower aspiration level, and depression. . . .
>
> In addition to the immediate physical harms . . . hate speech can cause mental and psychological effects. These include fear, nightmares, and withdrawal from society. . . .
>
> The harms of hate speech go beyond damage to the psyches and bodies of its victims. It can also affect their pecuniary prospects and life chances.[7]

To these harms, some would add another: the damage done when hate speech increases hatred (racial or otherwise) in others, which can lead to violence and discrimination.

Thus the most frequently heard arguments about campus free speech concern whether hate speech should be regulated to prevent harm to vulnerable groups. Those who support speech regulation maintain that the harms caused by hate speech are substantial, that this fact is reason enough to ban it, and that any harms caused by speech codes are minimal. On the other side, those who reject speech regulation maintain that speech codes cause far more harm than they prevent. Chemerinsky and Gillman argue that speech codes are so inherently vague and overly broad that the codes

often end up punishing people for their political views, that the codes punish people other than their intended targets, and that speech codes inescapably "ban the expression of unpopular ideas and views, which never is tolerable in colleges and universities."[8]

Some critics of speech codes insist that it's possible to have unfettered free speech on campus while protecting students from hate and bigotry. According to Ben-Porath:

> Both those committed to pure free speech and those favoring the protection of vulnerable groups often assume that one needs to choose, that there is an inherent tension between the two principles. . . .
>
> But in fact this tension can be alleviated by an ongoing, clear commitment by college leadership and members to create and sustain an environment conducive to open expression. While such an environment must operate within the boundaries of legal requirements, a more nuanced, responsive, and relational approach can often accomplish what a hundred regulations cannot.[9]

Chemerinsky and Gillman concur:

> [Campuses] cannot and should not punish speech because it is offensive. But certain speech can be punished: true threats, harassment, destruction of property, and disruptions of classes and campus activities. Campuses can create time, place, and manner restrictions that protect the learning environment while also protecting free expression. Moreover—and this is too often forgotten—campus leaders can engage in more speech, proclaiming the type of community they seek and condemning speech that is inconsistent with it.[10]

MORAL THEORIES

A nonconsequentialist could take a strong stand for free speech, arguing that to respect people's right of free speech is, as Kant would say, to treat them as ends in themselves rather than merely as means to ends. A nonconsequentialist perspective on free speech is embedded in the First Amendment: free speech is a moral right that is not justified by

CRITICAL THOUGHT: Is Hate Speech Violence?

Hate speech can cause psychological and physiological distress in some who hear it (or read it), and some speech, such as serious threats and "fighting words," can provoke violence. But can speech *be* violence? Can words be equivalent to physically violent acts?

Many have thought so, and some have used this belief as a pretext for committing violence against those who utter offensive speech. Speaking of the uproar over Milo Yiannopoulos at UC Berkeley, one woman said, "His words are violent, or a form of violence."

Several commentators have echoed this speech-equals-violence view, but many others disagree. Catherine Rampell, a columnist for the *Washington Post*, says,

> Here's the problem with suggesting that upsetting speech warrants "safe spaces," or otherwise conflating mere words with physical assault: If speech is violence, then violence becomes a justifiable response to speech.
>
> Just ask college students. A fifth of undergrads now say it's acceptable to use physical force to silence a speaker who makes "offensive and hurtful statements."*

According to Suzanne Nossel, executive director of PEN America, an international organization that defends free expression,

> It's true that insults or slurs or incitement can lead to confrontation. (Hutu broadcasts during the 1994 Rwanda genocide and Hitler's entreaties to German national pride, for instance, coaxed violence on a mass scale.) But while there is a continuum of acceptable speech, language and violence should not be confused. The way to preserve our freedom of expression is to insist that speech, no matter how offensive, cannot justify violent reprisal. Otherwise we risk becoming like China, Turkey, Iran and other autocracies, where brutality against journalists and draconian punishments for dissenting ideas are normal. . . .
>
> [T]he power that speech holds to visit serious harm does not make it, in itself, violent. It is risky even to make this comparison, because it helps give cover to the idea that noxious speech may be answered with brute force.[†]

Is violence ever a justified response to offensive speech? If so, in what circumstances? If you use violence against someone who demeans a racial group, is he then justified in using violence against you if he considers your speech offensive? How do you think society would change if violence were widely considered an appropriate response to any speech perceived to be offensive or harmful?

*Catherine Rampell, "A Chilling Study Shows How Hostile Students Are toward Free Speech," *Washington Post*, September 18, 2017, https://www.washingtonpost.com/opinions/a-chilling-study-shows-how-hostile-college-students-are-toward-free-speech/2017/09/18/cbb1a234-9ca8-11e7-9083-fbfddf6804c2_story.html?utm_term=.ea6296c00091.
[†]Suzanne Nossel, "No, Speech Is Not the Same Thing as Violence," *Washington Post*, June 22, 2017, https://www.washingtonpost.com/outlook/no-hateful-speech-is-not-the-same-thing-as-violence/2017/06/22/63c2c07a-5137-11e7-be25-3a519335381c_story.html?utm_term=.ae80288dc545.

its good consequences (even though the Founders did recognize the power of free speech to undergird a young democracy). This does not mean, however, that the right of free speech is necessarily absolute. Typically, free speech must be balanced against competing values such as justice, equality, security, and the right to privacy.

If free speech is viewed as a universal, nonconsequentialist right, then certain norms follow. First, the right of free speech is so central to morality that

College Students and Free Speech

A new study reveals trends that free speech advocates might find alarming. Almost 20 percent of undergraduates at U.S. colleges and universities say that using violence to silence a controversial speaker is acceptable. Four in ten think (incorrectly) that hate speech is not protected by the First Amendment. And a majority of undergraduates agree that shouting down controversial speakers so they can't be heard would be appropriate. Here are more details:*

Does the First Amendment protect hate speech?

	Yes	No	Don't Know
All	39%	44%	16%
Female	31%	49%	21%
Male	51%	38%	11%

A student group opposed to the speaker disrupts the speech by loudly and repeatedly shouting so that the audience cannot hear the speaker. Do you agree or disagree that the student group's actions are acceptable?

	Agree	Disagree
All	51%	49%
Democrat	62%	38%
Republican	39%	61%
Independent	45%	55%

A student group opposed to the speaker uses violence to prevent the speaker from speaking. Do you agree or disagree that the student group's actions are acceptable?

	Agree	Disagree
All	19%	81%
Democrat	20%	80%
Republican	22%	78%
Independent	16%	84%
Male	30%	70%
Female	10%	90%

*John Villasenor, Brookings Institute, "Views Among College Students Regarding the First Amendment: Results from a New Survey"; national survey, 1500 current undergraduates, September 18, 2017, https://www.brookings.edu/blog/fixgov/2017/09/18/views-among-college-students-regarding-the-first-amendment-results-from-a-new-survey/.

very strong reasons (such as conflicts with other important rights) are required to overrule it. Second, the right of free speech does not allow exercising that right if doing so interferes with someone else's free speech rights. Free speech rights cannot justify shouting down or physically attacking a speaker because his views are deemed offensive or upsetting. If free speech can be banned simply because someone is offended, *any* speech can be banned, and the right of free speech is no right at all. Third, it is wrong to censor or punish some speakers and not others based solely on the views or ideas expressed.

Both those who seek to restrict free speech and those who reject restrictions argue from a consequentialist perspective. Delgado and Stefancic argue for the banning of hate speech on the grounds that it causes great harm (which is not counterbalanced by the possible benefits):

The harms of hate speech include its adverse impacts—sometimes devastating ones—on the victim, the speaker, and society at large. The harms vary, of course, according to the type of hate speech. The more diffuse kind—for example, "All n*****s are inferior and should go back to Africa"—is apt to be more harmful to society in general. The more targeted

---

variety—"You goddamn n*****, go back to Africa"—harms society as well, particularly cumulatively, but its principal impact is felt by the individual victim.[11]

Some have argued that speech critical of an identity group or speech that upsets people in such a group is in fact a form of violence. If so, they contend, such speech is definitely harmful (and has no counterweight of sufficient benefits) and, on those grounds, should be banned.

As we have seen, some who reject censorship recognize the harms of hate speech but argue that censoring it causes even more harm, and that the benefits of free speech outweigh by far any supposed disadvantages. As Chemerinsky and Gillman say,

[P]rotecting hate speech is necessary because the alternative—granting governments the power to punish speakers they don't like—creates even more harm. The argument in favor of hate speech laws is essentially an argument for granting people in authority the power to censor or punish individuals who insult, stigmatize, or demean others, and it is inevitable that such vague and broad authority will be abused or used in ways that were not contemplated by censorship advocates.[12]

MORAL ARGUMENTS

One way to argue against speech codes is to try to show that they do more harm than good.

1. If, on balance, speech codes do more harm than good, they should be eliminated.

2. Speech codes do harm (by impeding the search for knowledge, undermining democracy, banning the expression of unpopular ideas and views, and hampering free and open dialogue).

3. Speech codes may do good by preventing some harm to vulnerable groups, but the good does not outweigh the harm the codes cause.

4. Therefore, speech codes should be eliminated.

This is a valid argument, so we must focus on the truth of the premises. Premise 1 would be accepted by many on both sides of the debate. It is the least controversial premise. Premises 2 and 3 are the heart of the argument. What evidence or reasoning supports Premise 2? The history of speech codes shows that they have indeed been used to censor political views, unwelcome opinions, protected speech, and ideas expressed by people other than those for whom the codes were intended.

Premise 3 is likewise open to question. Those who reject speech codes accept it; those who favor them tend to deny it. The disagreement is about the extent of harm and good involved. The pro-code side contends that the damage done to vulnerable groups by hate speech is immense and that this kind of harm is much more serious than any caused by censorship. The anti-code side maintains that, while the harm caused by censorship is clear, there is no evidence that speech codes have lessened hate speech on campus.

CHAPTER REVIEW

SUMMARY

Recently, speech on college campuses has been censored or punished, and invited speakers have been disinvited or shouted down. Many students believe these actions are needed to curtail hate speech: spoken or written words used to insult or disparage people because of their social or racial group. Hate speech, they contend, can harm people by causing emotional and physical distress, insulting the dignity of individuals, subordinating minorities, and "assaulting" vulnerable groups through offensive language. In response to what they consider hate speech, colleges and universities have enacted speech codes, campus regulations that ban the use of symbols or language thought to embody hate speech.

The central conflict in campus free speech controversies is between two moral goods crucial to higher education: (1) free speech that enables the expression of all ideas and the unfettered search for truth, and (2) a campus environment that protects and respects the learning experiences of all students. Some free speech scholars believe that both these values can be accommodated, while many students think they cannot be.

Under the U.S. Constitution's First Amendment, a vast range of speech is protected, including offensive language or ideas and hate speech. Unprotected speech includes serious threats, libel, and "fighting words."

The most frequently heard arguments about campus free speech concern whether hate speech should be regulated to prevent harm to minorities and other vulnerable groups. Those against speech codes argue that they undermine democracy and the search for knowledge and that they violate free speech rights. Those who favor speech codes insist that they are needed to protect blacks and other minorities from harmful speech.

KEY TERMS

hate speech (p. 589)
speech codes (p. 589)

EXERCISES

Review Questions

1. What is hate speech? What are speech codes? (pp. 589–590)
2. What is the central conflict in campus free speech controversies? (p. 590)
3. What are the reasons free speech advocates give for not censoring offensive speech? (p. 591)
4. Does the First Amendment protect hate speech? (p. 592)
5. Why is the right of free speech not absolute? (pp. 590–591)
6. According to John Arthur, what are three important benefits of having the right to speak and write freely? (p. 591)
7. What are four kinds of speech that the First Amendment does *not* protect? (p. 591)
8. What has been the courts' prevailing attitude toward speech codes at colleges and universities? (p. 592)
9. How can hate speech harm a member of a minority group? (p. 594)
10. What argument could a nonconsequentialist make for free speech? (pp. 594–596)

Discussion Questions

1. Do you believe that shouting down a controversial speaker so he or she can't be heard is morally permissible? Why or why not? If your silencing a controversial speaker is morally permissible, would it be morally permissible for others to shout down a speaker you like but they disdain?
2. Do you think hate speech should be banned? Why or why not?
3. Is free speech (including the right to use hate speech) necessary for the search for knowledge? Explain.
4. How could speech codes be used not to ban hate speech but to censor political views that are unpopular or unwelcome?
5. What criticisms have been lodged against the concept of microaggression? Do you agree with them? Why or why not?
6. Why does Friedersdorf say that calling certain behavior a "microaggression" is "hugely confusing"?
7. The U.S. Supreme Court has ruled that hate speech is protected speech. Do you agree with this decision? Explain.
8. Why does Catherine Rampell say that equating speech with violence is a problem? Do you agree?
9. Suzanne Nossel says that the way to preserve our freedom of expression is to insist that speech, no matter how offensive, cannot justify

violent reprisal. How could you argue against this view? How could you argue for it?

10. In what ways can a college or university foster tolerance and an inclusive learning environment—without banning offensive speech?

FURTHER READING

American Civil Liberties Union (ACLU), https://www.aclu.org/.

Sigal R. Ben-Porath, *Free Speech on Campus* (Philadelphia: University of Pennsylvania Press, 2017).

Erwin Chemerinsky and Howard Gillman, *Free Speech on Campus* (New Haven, CT: Yale University Press, 2017).

Stanley Fish, *There's No Such Thing as Free Speech . . . and It's a Good Thing Too* (New York: Oxford University Press, 1994).

David van Mill, "Freedom of Speech," in *Stanford Encyclopedia of Philosophy*, Summer 2017 ed., ed. Edward N. Zalta, https://plato.stanford.edu/archives/sum2017/entries/freedom-speech/.

Tom Slater, ed., *Unsafe Space: The Crisis of Free Speech on Campus* (London: Palgrave Macmillan, 2016).

Jeremy Waldron, *The Harm in Hate Speech* (Cambridge: Harvard University Press, 2012).

ETHICAL DILEMMAS

1. Free Speech and the Hangman's Noose

One way to express hatred and bias toward blacks and other minorities is to display objects that represent such attitudes. Consider this report from the Southern Poverty Law Center about nooses found on academic campuses:

> Since the day after the 2016 presidential election through March 31, the Southern Poverty Law Center has documented 1,863 bias incidents. Of these, 292, or 15.67%, were anti-black motivated incidents. One of the most pervasive manifestations of these happenings is the display of nooses.
>
> Several examples have surfaced on academic campuses in the past month. In May, bananas with odious messages were found hanging from nooses on American University's campus in Washington, D.C. Just over a week later, two Maryland men were arrested for hanging a noose outside Crofton Middle School. Similarly, four students were recently identified as being involved with hanging a black teddy bear from a noose at Wakefield High School in North Carolina.*

Displaying certain recognizable symbols in public or private space is thought to be a form of speech. To blacks, nooses are offensive symbols that represent the crime of lynching and the horrific history of lynchings during and after the Jim Crow era. Should students have the right to display nooses on campus? That is, should such displays be allowed on the grounds of free speech? Serious threats are not protected by law. Can the display of a noose on campus be construed as a threat and therefore be banned and punished?

*Southern Poverty Law Center, "Frequency of Noose Hate Crime Incidents Surges," by Hatewatch Staff, Hatewatch Blog. June 5, 2017, https://www.splcenter.org/hatewatch/2017/06/05/frequency-noose-hate-crime-incidents-surges. Reprinted with permission.

2. Hate Speech Online

(The Guardian)—Matthew Prince had the power to kill the white supremacist hate site the Daily Stormer for years, but he didn't choose to pull the trigger until 16 August. That's when the chief executive of website security company Cloudflare "woke up . . . in a bad mood and decided to kick them off the Internet", as he told his employees in an internal email. Without Cloudflare's protection, the Daily Stormer was forced to retreat to the darknet, where it is inaccessible to the majority of internet users.

Cloudflare is just one of many internet companies that cleaned house amid a wave of public outrage following a deadly white supremacist rally in Charlottesville. Critics charge that technology platforms have enabled a disparate network of racist extremists to seek one another out, raise funds, and plan and execute such rallies. But unlike consumer facing companies such as Facebook, YouTube, PayPal and Discord, and even as liberal voices—including the *Guardian* editorial board—applaud it, Cloudflare won't defend its actions.[†]

Should hate speech websites be allowed to freely spread their offensive white supremacist message online? Why or why not? If internet companies shut them down, is that a violation of their free speech rights? If hate websites are to be regulated, who should do the regulating? The government? Internet companies?

[†]Julia Carrie Wong, "The Far Right Is Losing Its Ability to Speak Freely Online. Should the Left Defend It?" *The Guardian*, August 28, 2017, https://www.theguardian.com/technology/2017/aug/28/daily-stormer-alt-right -cloudflare-breitbart.

3. Offensive Speech and Racial Violence

Is uttering a racial slur—even in an attempt to explain its use in literature—an act of racial violence or discrimination? Consider this example:

(HuffPost)—Colleges and universities have long been considered places where one can challenge dominant ideas in order to provoke a robust intellectual discussion. But with what some say is a growing push for political correctness, critics contend academia has lost the ability to have a free-flowing scholarly discourse.

Lawyer and author Wendy Kaminer found herself at the center of that heated debate this year when she joined a free speech panel discussion at Smith College and used a racial slur while discussing its use in literature and academia. Kaminer joined *HuffPost Live* on Wednesday and explained what transpired on the panel.

"I was accused of committing an explicit act of racial violence because I questioned our growing list of words we can only know by their initials," Kaminer said. "I questioned the value and the uses of euphemisms and in doing so, I uttered

CHAPTER 16: FREE SPEECH ON CAMPUS ☼ 601

a few forbidden words, including a racially charged word. And by doing so, I was accused of committing an act of racial violence."

Kaminer, whose position on the issue has been critiqued, took issue with the idea that "offensive words" could be considered "the same as discrimination." In her conversation with *HuffPost Live's* Marc Lamont Hill, a Morehouse College professor, she defended her use of the word in the context of the discussion and spoke out against the so-called "censorship" to which academics have been subjected.[‡]

Do you think that even in an academic setting, using a racial slur to explain its function in literature is an instance of racial violence? If so, would using the term to explain its offensiveness and hurtfulness also be unacceptable? If not, why not?

[‡]Rahel Gebreyes, "Author Wendy Kaminer Defends Her Use of a Racial Slur During a Free Speech Panel," *HuffPost*, June 5, 2015, https://www.huffingtonpost.com/entry/wendy-kaminer-racial-slur-free-speech_n_7521858.html. © 2015 Oath Inc. All rights reserved. Used by permission and protected by the Copyright Laws of the United States. The printing, copying, redistribution, or retransmission of this content without express written permission is prohibited.

READINGS

Why It's a Bad Idea to Tell Students Words Are Violence
Jonathan Haidt and Greg Lukianoff

Of all the ideas percolating on college campuses these days, the most dangerous one might be that speech is sometimes violence. We're not talking about verbal threats of violence, which are used to coerce and intimidate, and which are illegal and not protected by the First Amendment. We're talking about speech that is deemed by members of an identity group to be critical of the group, or speech that is otherwise upsetting to members of the group. This is the kind of speech that many students today refer to as a form of violence. If Milo Yiannopoulos speaks on the University of California, Berkeley, campus, is that an act of violence?

Recently, the psychologist Lisa Feldman Barrett, a highly respected emotion researcher at Northeastern University, published an essay in *The New York Times* titled, "When is speech violence?" She offered support from neuroscience and health-psychology research

Jonathan Haidt and Greg Lukianoff, "Why It's a Bad Idea to Tell Students Words Are Violence," *The Atlantic*, July 18, 2017. © 2017 The Atlantic Media Co., as first published in The Atlantic Magazine. All rights reserved. Distributed by Tribune Content Agency, LLC.

for students who want to use the word "violence" in this expansive way. The essay made two points that we think are valid and important, but it drew two inferences from those points that we think are invalid.

First valid point: Chronic stress can cause physical damage. Feldman Barrett cited research on the ways that chronic (not short-term) stressors "can make you sick, alter your brain—even kill neurons—and shorten your life." The research here is indeed clear.

First invalid inference: Feldman Barrett used these empirical findings to advance a syllogism: "If words can cause stress, and if prolonged stress can cause physical harm, then it seems that speech—at least certain types of speech—can be a form of violence." It is logically true that if A can cause B and B can cause C, then A can cause C. But following this logic, the resulting inference should be merely that words can cause physical harm, not that words are violence. If you're not convinced, just re-run the syllogism starting with "gossiping about a rival," for example, or "giving one's students a lot of homework." Both practices can cause prolonged stress to others, but that doesn't turn them into forms of violence.

Feldman Barrett's second valid point lies in her argument that young people are antifragile—they grow from facing and overcoming adversity:

> Offensiveness is not bad for your body and brain. Your nervous system evolved to withstand periodic bouts of stress, such as fleeing from a tiger, taking a punch or encountering an odious idea in a university lecture. Entertaining someone else's distasteful perspective can be educational. . . . When you're forced to engage a position you strongly disagree with, you learn something about the other perspective as well as your own. The process feels unpleasant, but it's a good kind of stress—temporary and not harmful to your body—and you reap the longer-term benefits of learning.

Feldman Barrett could have gone a step further: This "good kind of stress" isn't just "not harmful," it also sometimes makes an individual stronger and more resilient. The next time that person faces a similar situation, she'll experience a milder stress response because it is no longer novel, and because her coping repertoire has grown. This was the argument at the heart of our 2015 essay in *The Atlantic*, "The Coddling of the American Mind." We worried that colleges were making students more fragile—more easily harmed—by trying to protect them from the sorts of small and brief offensive experiences that Feldman Barrett is talking about.

Feldman Barrett then contrasted brief experiences of offensiveness with chronic stressors:

> What's bad for your nervous system, in contrast, are long stretches of simmering stress. If you spend a lot of time in a harsh environment worrying about your safety, that's the kind of stress that brings on illness and remodels your brain. That's also true of a political climate in which groups of people endlessly hurl hateful words at one another, and of rampant bullying in school or on social media. A culture of constant, casual brutality is toxic to the body, and we suffer for it.

We agree. But what, then, are the implications for college campuses?

In Feldman Barrett's second invalid inference, she writes:

> That's why it's reasonable, scientifically speaking, not to allow a provocateur and hatemonger like Milo

Yiannopoulos to speak at your school. He is part of something noxious, a campaign of abuse. There is nothing to be gained from debating him, for debate is not what he is offering.

But wait, wasn't Feldman Barrett's key point the contrast between short- and long-term stressors? What would have happened had Yiannopoulos been allowed to speak at Berkeley? He would have faced a gigantic crowd of peaceful protesters, inside and outside the venue. The event would have been over in two hours. Any students who thought his words would cause them trauma could have avoided the talk and left the protesting to others. Anyone who joined the protests would have left with a strong sense of campus solidarity. And most importantly, all Berkeley students would have learned an essential lesson for life in 2017: How to encounter a troll without losing one's cool. (The goal of a troll, after all, is to make people lose their cool.)

Feldman Barrett's argument only makes sense if Yiannopoulos's speech is interpreted as one brief episode in a long stretch of "simmering stress" on campus. The argument works only if Berkeley students experience their school as a "harsh environment," a "culture of constant, casual brutality" in which they are chronically "worrying about [their] safety." Maybe that is the perception of some students. But if so, is the solution to change the school or to change the perception?

Aggressive and even violent protests have erupted at some of the country's most progressive schools, such as Berkeley, Middlebury College, and Evergreen State College. Are these schools brutal and toxic environments for members of various identity groups? Or has a set of new ideas on campus taught students to see oppression and violence wherever they look? If students are repeatedly told that *numerical disparities are proof of systemic discrimination*, and *a clumsy or insensitive question is an act of aggression (a "microaggression")*, and *words are sometimes acts of violence that will shorten your life*, then it begins to make sense that they would worry about their safety, chronically, even within some of America's most welcoming and protective institutions.

We are not denying that college students encounter racism and other forms of discrimination on campus, from individuals or from institutional systems. We are, rather, pointing out a fact that is crucial in any discussion of stress and its effects: People do not react to the world as it is; they react to the world as they interpret it, and those interpretations are major determinants of success and failure in life. As we said in our *Atlantic* article:

> Rather than trying to protect students from words and ideas that they will inevitably encounter, colleges should do all they can to equip students to thrive in a world full of words and ideas that they cannot control. One of the great truths taught by Buddhism (and Stoicism, Hinduism, and many other traditions) is that you can never achieve happiness by making the world conform to your desires. But you can master your desires and habits of thought. This, of course, is the goal of cognitive behavioral therapy.

We wrote those words in early 2015. We were responding to stories from across the country about new demands that students were making for protection from the kinds of offensiveness that Feldman Barrett says are "not bad for your body or brain." We explained why we thought that widespread adoption of trigger warnings, safe spaces, and microaggression training would backfire. Rather than keeping students safe from harm, a culture of "safety" teaches students to engage in some of the same cognitive distortions that cognitive-behavioral therapy tries to eliminate. Distortions such as "emotional reasoning," "catastrophizing," and "dichotomous thinking," we noted, are associated with anxiety, depression, and difficulty coping. We think our argument is much stronger today, for two reasons.

First, our article was published in August of 2015, a few months before a wave of campus protests began at Missouri, Yale, and dozens of other schools. Those protesters usually demanded that their universities implement an array of policies designed to keep students "safer" from offense—policies such as microaggression training supplemented by the creation of systems for reporting and punishing microaggressors, along with the creation of more ethnic- or identity-based centers. We expect that these policies—whose effectiveness is not supported by empirical evidence—will, in the long run, lead students to feel even less

"safe" on campus than they did in 2015, because they may increase the number of offenses perceived while heightening feelings of identity-based division and victimization. Some evidence also suggests that diversity training, when not carefully and sensitively implemented, can create a backlash, which amplifies tensions.

Second, we wrote our article at a time that saw hints of a mental-health crisis on campuses, but no conclusive survey evidence. Two years later, the evidence is overwhelming. The social psychologist Jean Twenge has just written a book, titled *iGen* (which is short for "internet generation"), in which she analyzes four large national datasets that track the mental health of teenagers and college students. When the book is released in August, Americans will likely be stunned by her findings. Graph after graph shows the same pattern: Lines drift mildly up or down across the decades as baby boomers are followed by Gen-X, which is followed by the millennials. But as soon as the data includes iGen—those born after roughly 1994—the rates of anxiety, depression, loneliness, and suicide spike upward.

Is iGen so different from the millennials because the former faces more chronic, long-term stress? Have the country's colleges suddenly become brutal, toxic places, increasingly hostile to members of various identity groups? Some would argue, as Twenge does, that social media changed the nature of iGen's social interactions. But if social media is the biggest cause of the mental-health crisis then the solution lies in changing the nature or availability of social media for teenagers. Making the offline world "safer" by banning the occasional stress-inducing speaker will not help.

We think the mental-health crisis on campus is better understood as a crisis of resilience. Since 2012, when members of iGen first began entering college, growing numbers of college students have become less able to cope with the challenges of campus life, including offensive ideas, insensitive professors, and rude or even racist and sexist peers. Previous generations of college students learned to live with such challenges in preparation for success in the far more offense-filled world beyond the college gates. As Van Jones put it in response to a question by David Axelrod about how progressive students should react to ideologically offensive speakers on campus:

> I don't want you to be safe, ideologically. I don't want you to be safe, emotionally. I want you to be strong. That's different. I'm not going to pave the jungle for you. Put on some boots, and learn how to deal with adversity. I'm not going to take all the weights out of the gym; that's the whole point of the gym. This is the gym.

This is why the idea that speech is violence is so dangerous. It tells the members of a generation already beset by anxiety and depression that the world is a far more violent and threatening place than it really is. It tells them that words, ideas, and speakers can literally kill them. Even worse: At a time of rapidly rising political polarization in America, it helps a small subset of that generation justify political violence. A few days after the riot that shut down Yiannopoulos's talk at Berkeley, in which many people were punched, beaten, and pepper sprayed by masked protesters, the main campus newspaper ran five op-ed essays by students and recent alumni under the series title "Violence as self defense." One excerpt: "Asking people to maintain peaceful dialogue with those who legitimately do not think their lives matter is a violent act."

The implication of this expansive use of the word "violence" is that "we" are justified in punching and pepper-spraying "them," even if all they did was say words. We're just defending ourselves against their "violence." But if this way of thinking leads to actual violence, and if that violence triggers counter-violence from the other side (as happened a few weeks later at Berkeley), then where does it end? In the country's polarized democracy, telling young people that "words are violence" may in fact lead to a rise in real, physical violence.

Free speech, properly understood, is not violence. It is a cure for violence.

In his 1993 book *Kindly Inquisitors*, the author Jonathan Rauch explains that freedom of speech is part of a system he calls "Liberal Science"—an intellectual system that arose with the Enlightenment and made the movement so successful. The rules of Liberal Science include: No argument is ever truly over, anyone can participate in the debate, and no one gets to claim special authority to end a question once and for all. Central to this idea is the role of evidence, debate, discussion, and persuasion. Rauch contrasts Liberal Science with the system that dominated before it—the "Fundamentalist" system—in which kings, priests, oligarchs, and others with power decide what is true, and then get to enforce orthodoxy using violence.

Liberal Science led to the radical social invention of a strong distinction between words and actions, and though some on campus question that distinction today, it has been one of the most valuable inventions in the service of peace, progress, and innovation that human civilization ever came up with. Freedom of speech is the eternally radical idea that individuals will try to settle their differences through debate and discussion, through evidence and attempts at persuasion, rather than through the coercive power of administrative authorities—or violence.

To be clear, when we refer to "free speech," we are not talking about things like threats, intimidation, and incitement. The First Amendment provides categorical exceptions for those because such words are linked to actual physical violence. The First Amendment also excludes harassment—when words are used in a directed pattern of discriminatory behavior.

But the extraordinary body of legal reasoning that has developed around the First Amendment also recognizes that universities are different from other settings. In a 2010 decision by the U.S. Court of Appeals for the Ninth Circuit—*Rodriguez v. Maricopa County Community College District*—Chief Judge Alex Kozinski noted " . . . the urge to censor is greatest where debate is most disquieting and orthodoxy most entrenched . . ." then explained the special nature of universities, using terms that illustrate Rauch's Liberal Science:

> The right to provoke, offend, and shock lies at the core of the First Amendment. This is particularly so on college campuses. Intellectual advancement has traditionally progressed through discord and dissent, as a diversity of views ensures that ideas survive because they are correct, not because they are popular. Colleges and universities—sheltered from the currents of popular opinion by tradition, geography, tenure and

monetary endowments—have historically fostered that exchange. But that role in our society will not survive if certain points of view may be declared beyond the pale.

In sum, it was a radical enlightenment idea to tolerate the existence of dissenters, and an even more radical idea to actually engage with them. Universities are—or should be—the preeminent centers of Liberal Science. They have a duty to foster an intellectual climate that separates true ideas from popular but fallacious ones.

The conflation of words with violence is not a new or progressive idea invented on college campuses in the last two years. It is an ancient and regressive idea. Americans should all be troubled that it is becoming popular again—especially on college campuses, where it least belongs.

Restoring Free Speech on Campus

Geoffrey R. Stone and Will Creeley

Censorship in the academic community is commonplace. Students and faculty are increasingly being investigated and punished for controversial, dissenting or simply discomforting speech. It is time for colleges and universities to take a deep breath, remember who they are and reaffirm their fundamental commitment to freedom of expression.

The past academic year offers a depressing number of examples of institutions of higher education failing to live up to their core mission. At Northwestern University, for example, Professor Laura Kipnis endured a months-long Title IX investigation for publishing an essay in the Chronicle of Higher Education in which she discussed a high-profile sexual assault case. Just a few months later, her fellow professor, Alice Dreger, courageously resigned in protest over Northwestern's censorship of a faculty-edited medical journal.

In a similar vein, Louisiana State University fired Professor Teresa Buchanan after nearly two decades of service for her occasional use of profanity, which the university suddenly deemed "sexual harassment," and Chicago State University enacted a new cyberbullying policy to silence a blog that was critical of university leadership.

At Iowa State University, administrators censored T-shirts created by the university's student chapter of the National Organization for the Reform of Marijuana

Geoffrey R. Stone and Will Creeley, "Restoring Free Speech on Campus," *Washington Post*, September 25, 2015. Reprinted by permission of the author.

Laws. The Regents of the University of California are considering adopting a "Statement of Principles Against Intolerance" that would ban "derogatory language reflecting stereotypes or prejudice." Other institutions are considering banning so-called "microaggressions" or requiring "trigger warnings" to protect students from having to confront potentially upsetting ideas and subjects. Still others have withdrawn invitations to speakers who have taken positions that some members of the community find unpleasant, offensive or wrong-headed—a practice President Obama criticized this month, saying that leaving students "coddled and protected from different points of view" is "not the way we learn."

Restrictions on free expression on college campuses are incompatible with the fundamental values of higher education. At public institutions, they violate the First Amendment; at most private institutions, they break faith with stated commitments to academic freedom. And these restrictions are widespread: The Foundation for Individual Rights in Education's most recent survey of college and university policies found that more than 55 percent of institutions maintain illiberal speech codes that prohibit what should be protected speech. For students and faculty, the message is clear: Speaking your mind means putting your education or your career at risk.

Enough is enough. Our colleges and universities should redeem the promise of the new academic year by reaffirming their commitments to freedom of expression.

Last year, the University of Chicago convened a Committee on Freedom of Expression to do exactly that. The committee issued a statement identifying the principles that must guide institutions committed to attaining knowledge through free and open discourse. Guaranteeing members of the academic community "the broadest possible latitude to speak, write, listen, challenge, and learn," the statement guarantees students and faculty the right "to discuss any problem that presents itself."

How should students and scholars respond when challenged by speech with which they disagree, or that they even loathe? The Chicago statement sets forth the answer: "by openly and vigorously contesting the ideas that they oppose." Anticipating the push and pull of passionate debate, the statement sets forth important ground rules: "Debate or deliberation may not be suppressed because the ideas put forth are thought by some or even by most members of the University community to be offensive, unwise, immoral, or wrong-headed."

Perhaps most important, the Chicago statement makes clear that "it is not the proper role of the University to attempt to shield individuals from ideas and opinions they find unwelcome, disagreeable, or even deeply offensive." Laura Kipnis, Alice Dreger and Teresa Buchanan would have benefited from this frank and necessary recognition.

Encouragingly, Princeton University, American University and Purdue University have already adopted the core of the Chicago statement as their own. If colleges and universities nationwide were to follow their example—either by adopting the Chicago statement or forging one of their own—academic censorship would face a powerful new challenge.

Backed by a strong commitment to freedom of expression and academic freedom, faculty could challenge one another, their students and the public to consider new possibilities, without fear of reprisal. Students would no longer face punishment for exercising their right to speak out freely about the issues most important to them. Instead of learning that voicing one's opinions invites silencing, students would be taught that spirited debate is a vital necessity for the advancement of knowledge. And they would be taught that the proper response to ideas they oppose is not censorship, but argument on the merits. That, after all, is what a university is for.

Free speech and academic freedom will not protect themselves. With public reaffirmation of the necessity of free speech on campus, the current wave of censorship that threatens the continuing excellence of U.S. higher education can be repudiated, as it should be, as a transitory moment of weakness that disrespects what our institutions of higher learning must represent.

Speech Codes and Expressive Harm

Andrew Altman

I   INTRODUCTION

During the 1980s and early 1990s, many American colleges and universities adopted rules prohibiting speech that denigrates individuals on the basis of race, gender, ethnicity, religion, sexual orientation and similar categories of social identity. An apparent rash of racist

and sexist incidents on campuses across the nation had led to the adoption of these 'speech codes'.[1] For example, at the University of Michigan, someone had written on a blackboard "A mind is a terrible thing to waste—especially on a nigger." (Lawrence, 1993: 55). The bigotry exhibited in such incidents was widely condemned. Yet, the codes designed to respond to this bigotry generated considerable controversy.

Critics argued that the codes violated the principle of free speech. They did not claim that all rules regulating speech on campus would be objectionable. Rules against rallies or demonstrations in the library

Andrew Altman, "Speech Codes and Expressive Harm," in *Ethics in Practice*, ed. Hugh La Follatte, (Oxford: Blockwell, 2007), 411–20. Copyright © 2007 by Blackwell Publishing Ltd. Reproduced with permission of John Wiley & Sons, Inc.

would be unobjectionable. The aim of such rules would simply be to allow all students to use the library facilities without disruption, and no particular political beliefs or social attitudes would be singled out for suppression. But speech codes were entirely different, as the critics saw it: the codes aimed to suppress the expression of certain beliefs and attitudes. And such an aim, the critics argued, was incompatible with any adequate understanding of free speech.

Advocates of the codes pointed to the harm caused to those targeted by "hate speech": generalized psychic distress, feelings of anger and alienation, a sense of physical insecurity, and the various academic and social difficulties that naturally flow from such psychological disturbances. Treating the interests of all students with equal consideration, argued the advocates, required rules punishing hate speech. Code advocates also argued that restrictions on campus hate speech could help combat bigoted attitudes and practices in society at large.

American courts have uniformly sided with the critics of campus speech codes (Shiell, 1998, pp. 73–97). In a series of cases, courts struck down a variety of codes as unconstitutional. It might seem that these legal rulings would have put the controversy to rest. But that has not happened. Discussion and debate over the legitimacy of speech codes continues.

Because the US Supreme Court has not taken up a speech code case, there is some room to argue that the legal door has not been shut entirely on the question of the constitutionality of the codes. But the continuation of the controversy does not depend on expectations about future court action. It continues because the codes raise crucial ethical and political questions in a society committed both to freedom of speech and to equality under the law. What is the best way to understand the principle of free speech? Are there special aspects of the university context that must be taken into account by that understanding? Are there special aspects of American history and society that make a difference to the speech code debate? Legal cases can help shed light on such questions, but no court ruling can decisively settle them.[2]

In my view, it is difficult to justify speech codes solely on the basis of the harmful causal effects of hate speech. But I think that there is another type of harm to consider, what has been called "expressive harm" (Pildes and Niemi, 1993; Anderson and Pildes, 2000). Expressive harm is not a causal consequence of hate speech. Rather, it is a harm that derives from the kind of attitude expressed in the very act of hate speech, and it is independent of the causal effects of such a speech act.

In the next section, I explain why the causally harmful results of hate speech provide an insufficient basis on which to justify speech codes. Section III then gives an account of the nature of expressive harm, focusing on how symbolic speech by public officials can do expressive harm to an individual's right to be treated by government with equal respect and consideration. Section IV compares and contrasts private individuals with public officials when it comes to speech that does expressive harm. That section also formulates two main obstacles to justifying speech codes. In Sections V and VI, I seek to surmount those obstacles and present the case for speech codes. Section VII examines several campus speech policies, arguing for the superiority of a certain type of speech code.

II CAUSAL HARM

In an influential essay, Mari Matsuda writes: "When racist propaganda appears on campus, target-group students experience debilitated access to the full university experience. This is so even when it is directed at groups rather than at individuals" (1993, p. 45). And to those speech-code skeptics inclined to dismiss the harm of hate speech as merely psychological, Charles Lawrence points out: "Psychic injury is no less an injury than being struck in the face, and it often is far more severe. Racial epithets and harassment often cause deep emotional scarring and feeling of anxiety and fear that pervade every aspect of a victim's life" (1993, p. 74).

There is little doubt that hate speech can have psychologically debilitating effects and those effects in turn can interfere with a student's opportunities to enjoy the educational and social benefits of campus life. Black students who walk into a classroom in which the blackboard has written on it a vicious racial epithet directed against them will likely—and reasonably—respond with anger and even rage. Moreover, additional psychological injury is certainly possible: the students may come to think that they are unwelcome and even unsafe on campus. As Matsuda notes, hate speech often uses symbols, such as a burning crosses and swastikas, which are associated with violence against minorities.

Advocates of speech codes also argue that hate speech reinforces and perpetuates bigoted attitudes and practices in society at large. Thus Lawrence writes that "racist speech . . . distorts the marketplace of ideas by muting or devaluing the speech of Blacks and other despised minorities" (1993, p. 78). He contends that racist speech defames Blacks as a group: it causes a reputational injury to all Blacks, not simply to the immediate targets. Delgado and Stefancic also point to the general social effects of hate speech: "the racist insult remains one of the most pervasive channels through which discriminatory attitudes are imparted" (1997, p. 4).

The harms cited by the advocates of speech codes are real and serious. Undoubtedly, the members of society have a moral obligation to combat those harms. The issue is whether university speech codes are a justifiable way to proceed.

Some critics of speech codes argue that other means of combating the harms of hate speech should be pursued. Such means include "counterspeech," i.e., speaking out against the bigoted attitudes of hate speakers. Also included are educational programs aimed at promoting equality and highlighting the harm caused by bigotry. Thomas Simon doubts that speech codes or educational programs make any significant impact on racism but suggests that universities can exert some substantial leverage in society's fight for racial equality by "carefully examining their employment practices, investment decisions, and community service" (1994, p. 186).

Advocates of speech codes claim that the remedies suggested by Simon and others should be pursued in addition to speech codes, not in place of them. But that claim is persuasive only if speech codes are a justifiable way to regulate speech. The prima facie plausibility of the claim that the codes seek to suppress the expression of certain viewpoints places a substantial burden of argument on those who contend that they are justifiable. That burden is only increased by the availability of other ways of combating the causal harms of hate speech.

The arguments that we have canvassed thus far have little chance of meeting that burden because they appear to license restrictions on speech that sweep too broadly. The arguments would not only license speech codes banning the use of racial epithets and slurs. Philosophical, literary, religious, and scientific works conveying racist, sexist or heterosexist ideas would be subject to prohibition. As Martin Golding says in his critique of speech codes, racist and anti-Semitic beliefs that are "sanitized" and presented in the form of scholarly work [are] potentially more harmful that the slurs and epithets that students may hurl at one another (2000, p. 54). Such sanitized bigotry, e.g., the notorious anti-Semitic tract, "Protocols of the Elders of Zion," has the appearance of a work of scholarship and so may well have a greater psychological and reputational impact on the group it targets than the vulgar racist rant of a student.

Yet, a university is precisely where any work that purports to have objective validity should be available for critical assessment. As Golding has argued, the university is "a form of institutionalized rationality" that subjects knowledge-claims to the test of "critical examination . . . by competent inquirers" (2000, pp. 18, 22). The function of the university requires "communal discussion" and "the *organized* pursuit of knowledge," and it would be seriously compromised by the prohibition of works that convey bigoted ideas and views (Golding, 2000, pp. 17–18).

Moreover, there is a body of literature that is not the fraudulent work of vicious bigots but is regarded as racist by many and would be subject to prohibition under the arguments of Lawrence and Matsuda. Consider the work on race of the psychologist J.P. Rushton, who summarizes it this way:

In new studies and reviews of the world literature, I consistently find that East Asians and their descendants average a larger brain size, greater intelligence, more sexual restraint, slower rates of maturation, and greater law abidingness and social organization than do Europeans and their descendants who average higher scores on these dimensions than do Africans and their descendants. I proposed a gene-based evolutionary origin for this pattern. (2000)

Rushton's views have the potential to cause much more reputational damage to Blacks than an undergraduate's drunken utterance of a racial slur. Moreover, regardless of Rushton's intent, it is reasonable to think that his views would reinforce the bigoted attitudes of those inclined to treat Blacks as moral inferiors. And the views would obviously provoke anger among Black students.

Yet, Rushton's work may not be legitimately banned from libraries, classrooms, and other campus forums by a speech code. The institutional rationality of the university demands that the work be available for the critical analysis of scholarly experts and for the study of interested students.

The university's role as a testing ground for claims to knowledge makes it difficult for advocates of speech codes to meet their burden of justification solely by pointing to the harmful causal consequences of hate speech. But this does not necessarily doom all efforts to justify the codes. There is another form of harm associated with hate speech—expressive harm. A justification that takes account of both causal and expressive harm has better prospects for success. Let us turn to some examples to illustrate the existence and nature of expressive harm.

III EXPRESSIVE HARM: PUBLIC ACTORS

In the recent past, there was considerable controversy sparked by southern states that flew the Confederate flag over their capitols. On July 1, 2000, South Carolina became the last state to remove the flag from its site over the seat of the state government. Blacks and many others take the flag to be a symbol of slavery and racism, and they construed the display of the flag to be an expression of racist attitudes. Some southern whites rejected that interpretation and argued that the flag was a legitimate expression of reverence for the valor of their ancestors who suffered and died during the Civil War. But in the wake of protests, state legislators voted to take the flag down.

What was the harm of flying the flag over state capitols? In *NAACP* v. *Hunt* (1990), a federal appeals court rejected the claim that Alabama was violating the Equal Protection Clause of the Fourteenth Amendment by flying the Confederate flag over its capitol. The court reasoned that the only harm done by the flying of the flag was the emotional distress of the plaintiffs and that such harm did not amount to a violation of the constitutional principle of equality.

However, the court's reasoning was flawed by its failure to see that there is another form of harm done by the flying of the flag, which did violate the equality principle. The flying of the flag did expressive harm to Blacks: aside from its causal consequences, the act of flying the flag was the expression of a racist attitude hostile, or at least grossly indifferent, to the interests of Blacks (Forman, 1991, p. 508). The official expression of such an attitude constituted a violation of the right to be treated by government with equal respect and consideration.

There are undoubtedly well-meaning individuals who take pride in the display of the Confederate flag. But they fail to realize that the nation is not sufficiently removed from its history of racial oppression for the flag to be a benign cultural symbol. The debilitating effects of past racism still severely hamper the life chances of Blacks, and current racism aggravates the wounds left by this history (Bobo, 1997). The meaning of the flag is still freighted with the history and legacy of racial oppression.

In such a context, flying the flag over the seat of government is, at best, an expression of a callous indifference toward the state's racial minorities and counts as an expressive harm to them. As Anderson and Pildes explain it, "a person suffers expressive harm when she is treated according to principles that express negative or inappropriate attitudes toward her" (2000, p. 1528). And Alabama was treating its Black citizens in exactly that way.

Another example of expressive harm is found in Amar's hypothetical variation of the Hunt case: suppose that Alabama adopted as its official motto the slogan "The White Supremacy State" (1998, 254). It would be strained to argue that non-White plaintiffs seeking a ruling that the state had violated the Equal Protection Clause would need to prove that the adoption of the motto had causal effects harmful to racial equality. Indeed, under certain scenarios, the motto might produce political backlash promoting equality. The fact is that the very adoption of the motto, apart from its causal consequences, is a harm to racial minorities. It is an expressive harm.

IV EXPRESSIVE HARM: PRIVATE ACTORS

In the Confederate flag and state motto cases, public officials were the ones whose actions did expressive harm. Their status as officials made the harms ascribable to the state and so—the circuit court's ruling notwithstanding—a constitutional violation. But the expressive harm they did was independent of their official status. State officials can typically exert much more casual power in the world than private citizens. And what they express through their acts might well have much more widespread causal effects than the expressive activities of a private individual. Those causal effects may result in harms that most private individuals simply do not have the causal capacity to produce, for example, widespread loss of employment opportunities. But the private individual is capable of doing expressive harm. Just as a state official can express callous indifference or hostility to racial minorities, so can a private citizen. And expression of such an attitude can amount to a harm in both sorts of cases.

On the other hand, there is a big difference between the expressive harm to racial equality committed by a state official and the same sort of harm done by a private individual. When the expressive harm is done by the communicative act of a private individual, it is protected by free speech principles. It is unjustifiable for the law to allow state officials to fly the Confederate Flag above their capitols, but the law should protect private individuals who wish to display the flag outside their homes or on their car antennas. Such private actions can express indifference or

hostility to racial equality, but it should be not subject to legal sanction.

Private hate speakers thus have a free-speech shield that protects them from liability for the expressive harm they may do, just as that same shield usually protects them from liability for the harmful causal effects of their speech. So it may seem that we have not really advanced the argument for speech codes. Moreover, one can claim that the argument has been made even more difficult by the difference between official and private speech.

When a university punishes a student for a speech code violation, it seems to be committing an expressive harm against him. Aside from any bad causal effects the punishment may have on the student, it is an expression of the emphatic moral condemnation of his social attitudes. And critics of restrictions on hate speech might contend that such condemnation by government violates the rights of hate speakers to equal consideration. Everyone should be permitted to express their views, without discrimination on the basis of what those views are (Dworkin, 1995, pp. 200–1). Accordingly, we appear to have two strong reasons against speech codes. The campus hate speaker may do expressive harm, but that form of harm is no less protected by free speech principles that the causal harm he may do. And the university's punitive response to the hate speaker is a form of official moral condemnation that expressively harms the speaker. The challenge of justifying speech codes depends upon a cogent response to these two reasons. The next two sections seek to develop such a response.

V MORAL CONTEMPT

The expressive harm of hate speech plays two related roles in the justification of speech codes. First, it helps explain why certain forms of hate speech should be regarded as "low value" speech in the university context. Second, it serves to distinguish those forms of hate speech that ought to be subject to official restriction from those that ought to be protected against such restriction. Let us begin with a look at how the meaning and use of racial epithets can be understood in terms of the idea of expressive harm.

Racial epithets and similar terms of abuse are communicative tools for expressing an extreme form of moral contempt.[3] Such contempt involves the attitude that the person targeted by the epithet belongs to a group whose members have a lower moral status than those in the group to which the speaker belongs. For those who think in such terms, it is appropriate to express such contempt when members of the morally subordinate groups seek to be treated as equals. The expression of extreme contempt is thought to be fitting because those who are moral inferiors are trying to act as equals: they are impostors who need to be treated as such. Racial epithets and similar terms of abuse are words whose use is to treat someone in a morally degrading way by expressing a certain form of moral contempt toward them. Racist or sexist speech in the form of scientific or philosophical discourse might also convey contempt, but that is not the principal purpose of those forms of discourse. Rather, the vocabulary of such discourse is for formulating and expressing ideas that claim to have objective validity. Any such validity-claim is subject to critical scrutiny and challenge by anyone who can raise such a challenge, even by those persons whom the claim might assert to be moral inferiors to the speaker. "Scientific racism" might explicitly assert that a certain racial group is inherently less intelligent or more prone to crime than other racial groups, but in making such claims it implicitly invites anyone to produce arguments and evidence to refute them.

It is true that the use of epithets can be part of assertions that claim objective validity. Anti–Semites can say "Kikes are all thieves." But hate speech couched in scientific or philosophical discourse does not employ such epithets because the discourse is meant to convey objective claims unadorned by the subjective feelings of the speaker. In contrast, the point of epithets is precisely to express the feelings of the speaker.

The contrast explains why hate speech couched in the discourse of science, philosophy, theology or other scholarly vocabularies should be protected. The claims that such speech makes are subject to the scrutiny, challenge and refutation of those operating within the institutional rationality of the university. As Golding has stressed, that rationality requires protection even for speech that claims or suggests some groups of humans are inherently inferior to others.

In contrast, speech using racist epithets and similarly abusive terms is "low value" speech in the university context because it contributes virtually nothing to the operation of the institutional rationality of the university at the same time that it is used to degrade members of the university community. The exercise of that rationality involves the critical assessment of claims to objective validity. It is difficult to see what role is played in that process by the use of epithets to express contempt for and degrade persons who are members of the university community on the basis of their race, gender, and other categories of social identity.

My argument might be rejected on the basis of the reasoning in the case of *Cohen* v. *California*. Writing for the Court, Justice Harlan said that the words on the jacket Cohen wore into a courthouse, "Fuck the Draft," conveyed a message in which the emotional and cognitive elements were inseparable. Protecting Cohen's message against the Vietnam War draft meant protecting the expletive in terms of which the message was expressed. And the Court held that the message must be protected as the expression of Cohen's political viewpoint.

It may be argued that Harlan's reasoning applies to the use of racist or sexist epithets. Such epithets convey a message in which emotional and cognitive elements are mixed and the message must be protected as the expression of certain viewpoint. However, there is an important difference between campus hate-speech cases and Cohen's case: the campus cases—but not Cohen's—are closely analogous to cases of verbal racial harassment in the workplace. And restrictions on such harassment at work are unobjectionable.

Cohen was not acting in an employment context but rather as a member of the general public, expressing his views in a building open to the public. And he caused no disturbance in courthouse operations. But imagine that he were an employee at a business with Black employees and that he wore a jacket in the workplace saying "Fuck niggers." Such expression could be justifiably prohibited on grounds of equal employment opportunity.

Campus speech cases are more like such an employment case than they are like the actual Cohen case. Students are not employees. But they do have a defined role within the university, and they should not be materially disadvantaged in their role on account of their race, gender, or sexual orientation. The use of racial epithets and similar terms of abuse in the campus context is reasonably thought to interfere with equal educational opportunity, just as the use of such terms can interfere with equal employment opportunity in the workplace.

It is also true that the principle of equal educational opportunity must be construed in a way that is responsive to the special role of the university in critically examining all ideas claiming objective validity. Hate speech in the mode of scientific or philosophical discourse can cause psychological distress sufficient to interfere with a student's ability to enjoy the opportunities of campus life. But in that case, it is the ideas expressed that are the grounds for the distress. And, unlike other institutions, the role of the university in critically assessing ideas requires that distress caused by the assertion of ideas be excluded as a reason for adopting a speech policy. However, that role does not require the university to ignore the causal effects of racist epithets on the student.

Sadurski has claimed that "insensitivity to many psychic harms is the price of a broadened scope for individual autonomy" (1999, 224). It is also true that a certain degree of such insensitivity is the price of a university's commitment to the free expression and critical testing of ideas claiming objective validity. But the causal harm of racial epithets is not the result of putting forth propositions that claim objective validity. Rather, the causal harm is the product of the extreme moral contempt that the epithets express. Thus, a university speech policy that takes account of the causal harms of such epithets is not subject to

the same objection as a policy that takes account of the causal harm of statements that claim objective validity.

VI   OFFICIAL CONDEMNATION

Let us now turn to the matter of whether a speech code treats hate speakers with less than equal consideration. After all, such a code makes them liable to punitive measures for the expression of their social and political attitudes, and "the significance of punishment is moral condemnation" (Kahan, 1996, p. 598). There is no circumventing the fact that a speech policy that employs punishment to express such condemnation seeks to suppress speech for the viewpoint it expresses. And in so doing, the policy violates the equal expressive rights of those who hold the disfavored viewpoints.

Any viewpoint-biased speech restriction should be troubling to those who value strong protections for freedom of speech. But it is important to place the speech code debate in its broader social and historical context in order to understand how a limited departure from viewpoint neutrality can be justifiable.

Consider again the Confederate flag dispute. Blacks and many others reasonably took the flag as symbolic of the state's indifference, or even antagonism, to racial equality. Removal of the flag was reasonably construed as an expressive affirmation of that value. The removal was hardly viewpoint-neutral and could not have been in the situation. But the expressive affirmation of racial equality was justifiable, and even mandatory, under the circumstances.

The flag was reasonably construed as standing for a set of values associated with the Confederacy, including white supremacy. In theory, the flag can stand for such virtues as courage and honor without the taint of the white supremacist regime those virtues in fact served. But in contemporary American society the display of the flag cannot be purified of such a taint. There is no way for a state to display the flag over its capitol without it being reasonably interpreted as callous indifference to interests of its black citizens.

Many advocates of speech codes appear to see the code controversy in similar terms: adopting a speech code is a way of symbolically affirming the value of racial equality but not adopting one amounts to the expressive repudiation of that value (Shiffrin, 1999, pp. 78–80). But the analogy is not quite right. The failure to have a code is not analogous to displaying a symbol whose meaning is still inextricably intertwined with racism. For that reason, it is wrong to think that it is morally, even if not legally, mandatory for any university to have a speech code. But having such a code still may be a justifiable option.

A speech code is an expressive affirmation of racial equality. So are other aspects of university life, such as the observance of the Martin Luther King holiday. Hate speakers may object to the holiday as a departure from viewpoint neutrality and a denigration of their right to equality. They don't get to have an official holiday for their favorite opponent of the civil rights movement. But the nation's commitment to racial equality means that hate speakers and advocates of racial equality simply are not treated in an absolutely evenhanded way, nor should they be. The history of racial injustice is so egregious, and its lingering effects still so troublesome, that some tilt away from strict expressive neutrality and in the direction of racial equality is entirely justifiable. The question is the degree and nature of the tilt.

Critics of speech codes may concede that symbolically affirming racial equality and condemning bigotry through official holidays is fine but then argue that it is an entirely different matter when it comes to using punitive measures for strictly symbolic purposes. But speech codes can be reasonably understood as more than a strictly symbolic gesture. Their condemnation of bigotry sends a strong educational message to the university community and arguably deters forms of verbal degradation that interfere with a student's opportunity to enjoy benefits of campus life.

It may be true that speech codes are not indispensable for providing equal educational opportunity: counterspeech that condemns instances of campus bigotry and other alternatives might work. But it is not unreasonable for a school to judge that a speech code would be of sufficient value to warrant its adoption. The question is how to formulate a code that serves equal opportunity while respecting the centrality of free expression to the role of the university.

VII SPEECH CODES

Some advocates of speech codes defend bans on hate speech that sweep more broadly than the use of epithets (Matsuda, 1993, pp. 44–5; Lawrence, 1993, p. 70). Such broad codes would prohibit hate speech formulated in scientific, philosophical, or theological terms. It should be clear that my analysis rejects codes of that kind as inconsistent with the central place that free speech must play in the life of the university. A speech code must be narrowly drawn in order to be justifiable (Weinstein, 1999, pp. 52, 127; Cohen, 1996, pp. 212–14).

A typical version of a narrow code prohibits hate speech only when (a) it uses racial epithets or analogously abusive terms based on sex, sexual orientation, and similar categories of social identity, (b) the speaker intends to degrade persons through his use of such terms, and (c) the terms are addressed directly to a specific person or small group of persons.

In criticizing narrow speech codes, some legal theorists have suggested that general rules against verbal harassment would be preferable to codes formulated in terms of race, gender, and so on (Golding, 2000, p. 60). Such general rules would not select out particular categories of verbal harassment, but would rather prohibit any verbal abuse that materially interfered with a (reasonable) student's ability to learn and enjoy the other benefits of campus life and that was intended to cause such interference. General harassment rules certainly have much to be said for them as an alternative to narrow speech codes. A student's opportunities to take advantage of the benefits of the university should not be materially interfered with by any form of verbal harassment. And if the speech policy of a university were restricted to racial epithets and the like, then students who were harassed for other reasons, e.g., their political affiliation, could rightly complain that the university was not adequately protecting their interest in equal educational opportunity. Accordingly, it is reasonable to think that general rules against all forms of verbal harassment would be preferable to a speech code limited to categories such as race and gender. Nonetheless, it is possible to give due recognition to the special expressive and causal harm of racial epithets within a set of general rules prohibiting any verbal harassment that interferes with a student's equal educational opportunity.

The capacity of racial epithets to express extreme moral contempt gives them an unusual power to interfere with a student's efforts to take advantage of her educational opportunities. General rules against verbal harassment can be interpreted and applied in a way that takes account of that fact. For instance, the use of anti-Semitic epithets could be judged a violation of the rules even in the case of just a single incident, while other forms of abusive speech, e.g., those targeting a person's political affiliation, would need to involve repeated episodes before they would rise to the level of a violation. Or the use of a racist epithet might be judged a violation when it is reasonably foreseeable that an individual in the targeted group would be exposed to the abusive term, even if the epithet were not specifically directed at her.[4] For other forms of verbal harassment, directly addressing the targeted individual might be required.

The basic standard for a violation would be the same in all cases of verbal harassment: Did the abusive speech materially interfere with a student's opportunity to take advantage of the benefits of campus life?[5] But in the interpretation and application of that standard, the distinctive expressive power of racist epithets and similar terms of abuse would be taken into account.[6]

A campus speech policy that took account of that special expressive power could do a better job of protecting equal opportunity than general rules against verbal harassment that failed to be responsive to expressive harm of hate speech. And the policy could also do a better job than speech codes limited to the prohibition of verbal abuse based on race, gender, sexual orientation, and similar categories of social identity. Taking account of the expressive power of racial epithets and analogous terms of abuse involves some departure from the principle that restrictions on speech should be viewpoint-neutral. But the departure is relatively minor and the value served—equal educational opportunity in our institutions of higher education—is an important one.

REFERENCES

Amar, Akhil (1998). *The Bill of Rights*. New Haven, CT: Yale University Press.

Anderson, Elizabeth and Richard Pildes (2000). "Expressive Theories of Law: A General Restatement," *University of Pennsylvania Law Review* 148: 1503–75.

Bobo, Lawrence (1997). "Laissez-Faire Racism: The Crystallization of a Kinder, Gentler, Antiblack Ideology." In Steven Tuch and Jack Martin (eds.), *Racial Attitudes in the 1990s*. Westport: Praeger.

Cohen v. *California*. 1971. 403 U.S. 15.

Cohen, Joshua (1996). "Freedom of Expression." In David Heyd (ed.), *Toleration*. Princeton, NJ: Princeton University Press, pp. 173–225.

Delgado, Richard and Jean Stefancic (1997). *Must We Defend Nazis?* New York: New York University Press.

Dworkin, Ronald (1995). *Freedom's Law*. Cambridge, MA: Harvard University Press.

Forman, James (1991). "Driving Dixie Down: Removing the Confederate Flag from Southern State Capitols," *Yale Lam Journal* 101: 505–26.

Golding, Martin (2000). *Free Speech on Campus*. Lanham, MD: Rowman and Littlefield.

Kahan, Daniel, (1996) "What Do Alternative Sanctions Mean?" *University of Chicago Lam Review* 62: 591–653.

Lawrence, Charles (1993). "If He Hollers Let Him Go: Regulating Racist Speech on Campus." In Mari Masuda et al. (eds.), *Words that Wound.* Boulder. CO: Westview, pp. 53–88.

Matsuda, Mari (1993). "Public Response to Hate Speech: Considering The Victim's Story." In Mari Matsuda et al. (eds.), *Words that Wound.* Boulder, CO: Westview, pp. 17–51.

NAACP v. *Hunt.* 1990. 891 F.2d 1555 (11th Cir). Pildes, Richard and Richard Niemi (1993). "Expressive Harms, 'Bizarre Districts' and Voting Rights," *Michigan Law Review* 92: 483–587.

Rushton, J. P. (2000). *http://www.sscl.uwo.cal psychology/faculty/rushton.html*

Sadurski, Wojcieck (1999). *Freedom of Expression and Its Limits.* Dordrecht: Kluwer.

Shiell, Timothy (1998). *Campus Hate Speech on Trial.* Lawrence: University Press of Kansas.

Shiffrin, Steven (1999). *Dissent, Injustice, and the Meanings of America.* Princeton NJ: Princeton University Press.

Simon, Thomas (1994) "Fighting Racism: Hate Speech Detours." In M. N. S. Sellers (ed.), *An Ethical Education.* Providence, RI: Berg, pp. 171–86.

Weinstein, James (1999) *Hate Speech, Pornography, and the Radical Attack on Free Speech Doctrine.* Boulder, CO: Westview.

Wisconsin v. *Mitchell.* 1993. 113 S.Ct. 2194.

NOTES

1. In this essay, I use the term "speech code" to refer to rules that punish individuals for speech that degrades or demeans others on the basis of race or the other listed features.

2. Under US constitutional law, there is an important distinction between state and private universities: the former, but not the latter, are subject to the free speech clause of the Constitution. For this essay, I will assume that most, if not all, private institutions of higher education place a high value on free speech and desire to respect free-speech principles.

3. My analysis of epithets is meant to capture a standard use of such terms. There are other uses.

4. Consider the case from the University of Michigan, cited in section I.

5. There should also be requirements that the speech intentionally interfere with the student's opportunities and that the response of the affected student be reasonable.

6. Delgado and Stefancic (1997) propose general rules against verbal harassment combined with provisions for extra punishment in cases where the harassment is based on race, gender, and the like. They point out that their proposal appears to be consistent with the Supreme Court ruling in *Wisconsin* v. *Mitchell* (1993), which permitted a state to enhance criminal penalties for crimes committed from racially discriminatory motives. It is unclear, though, whether the Court would extend that ruling to cases where the underlying "crime" is a speech offense. My proposal is not that extra punishment be given for hate speech, but rather that the expressive harm of such speech be factored into the question of whether an incident rises to the level of an offense. The two proposals are not incompatible, although I think that, aside from truly egregious cases, a university's punitive response to hate speech episodes should be relatively mild and mainly symbolic.

What "Snowflakes" Get Right About Free Speech

Ulrich Baer

At one of the premieres of his landmark Holocaust documentary, "Shoah" (1985), the filmmaker Claude Lanzmann was challenged by a member of the

audience, a woman who identified herself as a Holocaust survivor. Lanzmann listened politely as the woman recounted her harrowing personal account of the Holocaust to make the point that the film failed to fully represent the recollections of survivors. When she finished, Lanzmann waited a bit, and then said, "Madame, you are an experience, but not an argument."

This exchange, conveyed to me by the Russian literature scholar Victor Erlich some years ago, has stayed with me, and it has taken on renewed significance as the struggles on American campuses to negotiate issues of free speech have intensified—most recently in protests at Auburn University against a visit by the white nationalist Richard Spencer.

Lanzmann's blunt reply favored reasoned analysis over personal memory. In light of his painstaking research into the Holocaust, his comment must have seemed insensitive but necessary at the time. Ironically, "Shoah" eventually helped usher in an era of testimony that elevated stories of trauma to a new level of importance, especially in cultural production and universities.

During the 1980s and '90s, a shift occurred in American culture; personal experience and testimony, especially of suffering and oppression, began to challenge the primacy of argument. Freedom of expression became a flash point in this shift. Then as now, both liberals and conservatives were wary of the privileging of personal experience, with its powerful emotional impact, over reason and argument, which some fear will bring an end to civilization, or at least to freedom of speech.

My view (and, like all the views expressed here, it does not represent the views or policies of my employer, New York University) is that we should resist the temptation to rehash these debates. Doing so would overlook the fact that a thorough generational shift has occurred. Widespread caricatures of students as overly sensitive, vulnerable and entitled "snowflakes" fail to acknowledge the philosophical work that was carried out, especially in the 1980s and '90s, to legitimate experience—especially traumatic experience—which had been dismissed for decades as unreliable, untrustworthy and inaccessible to understanding.

The philosopher Jean-François Lyotard, best known for his prescient analysis in "The Postmodern Condition" of how public discourse discards the categories of true/false and just/unjust in favor of valuing the mere fact that something is being communicated, examined the tension between experience and argument in a different way.

Instead of defining freedom of expression as guaranteeing the robust debate from which the truth emerges, Lyotard focused on the asymmetry of different positions when personal experience is challenged by abstract arguments. His extreme example was Holocaust denial, where invidious but often well-publicized cranks confronted survivors with the absurd challenge to produce incontrovertible eyewitness evidence of their experience of the killing machines set up by the Nazis to exterminate the Jews of Europe. Not only was such evidence unavailable, but it also challenged the Jewish survivors to produce evidence of their own legitimacy in a discourse that had systematically denied their humanity.

Lyotard shifted attention away from the content of free speech to the way certain topics restrict speech as a public good. Some things are unmentionable and undebatable, but not because they offend the sensibilities of the sheltered young. Some topics, such as claims that some human beings are by definition inferior to others, or illegal or unworthy of legal standing, are not open to debate because such people cannot debate them on the same terms.

The recent student demonstrations at Auburn against Spencer's visit—as well as protests on other campuses against Charles Murray, Milo Yiannopoulos and others—should be understood as an attempt to ensure the conditions of free speech for a greater group of people, rather than censorship. Liberal free-speech advocates rush to point out that the views of these individuals must be heard first to be rejected. But this is not the case. Universities invite speakers not chiefly to present otherwise unavailable discoveries, but to present to the public views they have presented elsewhere. When those views invalidate the humanity of some people, they restrict speech as a public good.

In such cases there is no inherent value to be gained from debating them in public. In today's age, we also have a simple solution that should appease all those concerned that students are insufficiently exposed to controversial views. It is called the internet, where all kinds of offensive expression flourish unfettered on a vast platform available to nearly all.

The great value and importance of freedom of expression, for higher education and for democracy, is hard to overestimate. But it has been regrettably easy for commentators to create a simple dichotomy between a younger generation's oversensitivity and free speech as an absolute good that leads to the truth. We would do better to focus on a more sophisticated understanding, such as the one provided by Lyotard, of the necessary conditions for speech to be a common, public good. This requires the realization that in politics, the parameters of public speech must be continually redrawn to accommodate those who previously had no standing.

The rights of transgender people for legal equality and protection against discrimination are a current example in a long history of such redefinitions. It is only when trans people are recognized as fully human, rather than as men and women in disguise, as Ben Carson, the current secretary of housing and urban development claims, that their rights can be fully recognized in policy decisions.

The idea of freedom of speech does not mean a blanket permission to say anything anybody thinks. It means balancing the inherent value of a given view with the obligation to ensure that other members of a given community can participate in discourse as fully recognized members of that community. Free-speech protections—not only but especially in universities, which aim to educate students in how to belong to various communities—should not mean that someone's humanity, or their right to participate in political speech as political agents, can be freely attacked, demeaned or questioned.

The student activism that has roiled campuses—at Auburn, Missouri, Yale, Berkeley, Middlebury and elsewhere—is an opportunity to take stock of free speech issues in a changed world. It is also an opportunity to take into account the past few decades of scholarship that has honed our understanding of the rights to expression in higher education, which maintains particularly high standards of what is worthy of debate.

The recent controversies over the conflict between freedom of expression and granting everyone access to speech hark back to another telling moment. In 1963, Yale University had rescinded an invitation to Alabama's segregationist governor, George C. Wallace. In 1974, after unruly protests prevented William Shockley from debating his recommendation for voluntary sterilization of people with low I.Q.s, and other related incidents, Yale issued a report on how best to uphold the value of free speech on campus that remains the gold standard for many other institutions.

Unlike today's somewhat reflexive defenders of free speech, the Yale report situated the issue of free speech on campus within the context of an increasingly inclusive university and the changing demographics of society at large. While Yale bemoaned the occasional "paranoid intolerance" of student protesters, the university also criticized the "arrogant insensitivity" of free speech advocates who failed to acknowledge that requiring of someone in public debate to defend their human worth conflicts with the community's obligation to assure all of its members equal access to public speech.

It is perhaps telling that in the 1980s and '90s, while I was also a doctoral student there, Yale ultimately became the hotbed of philosophical thinking that acknowledged the claims of people who had not been granted full participation in public discourse. Their accounts, previously dismissed as "unspeakable" or "unimaginable," now gained legitimacy in redefining the rules of what counts as public speech. Lyotard taught at Yale in early 1990s, and his and others' thoughts on how to resolve the asymmetry in discussions between perpetrators and victims of systemic or personal violence, without curtailing speech too much, seeped into other disciplines.

Lyotard and others were interested in expanding the frames of discourse, as they had been before, when married women were granted full legal status after centuries of having their very being legally suspended upon marriage.

When Yale issued its guidelines about free speech, it did so to account for a new reality, in the early 1970s, when increasing numbers of minority students and women enrolled at elite college campuses. We live in a new reality as well. We should recognize that the current generation of students, roundly ridiculed by an unholy alliance of so-called alt-right demagogues and campus liberals as coddled snowflakes, realized something important about this country before the pundits and professors figured it out.

What is under severe attack, in the name of an absolute notion of free speech, are the rights, both legal and cultural, of minorities to participate in public discourse.

The snowflakes sensed, a good year before the election of President Trump, that insults and direct threats could once again become sanctioned by the most powerful office in the land. They grasped that racial and sexual equality is not so deep in the DNA of the American public that even some of its legal safeguards could not be undone.

The issues to which the students are so sensitive might be benign when they occur within the ivory tower. Coming from the campaign trail and now the White House, the threats are not meant to merely offend. Like President Trump's attacks on the liberal

media as the "enemies of the American people," his insults are meant to discredit and delegitimize whole groups as less worthy of participation in the public exchange of ideas.

As a college professor and university administrator with over two decades of direct experience of campus politics, I am not overly worried that even the shrillest heckler's vetoes will end free speech in America. As a scholar of literature, history and politics, I am especially attuned to the next generation's demands to revise existing definitions of free speech to accommodate previously delegitimized experiences. Freedom of expression is not an unchanging absolute. When its proponents forget that it requires the vigilant and continuing examination of its parameters, and instead invoke a pure model of free speech that has never existed, the dangers to our democracy are clear and present.

We should thank the student protestors, the activists in Black Lives Matter and other "overly sensitive" souls for keeping watch over the soul of our republic.

The Progressive Ideas behind the Lack of Free Speech on Campus
WENDY KAMINER

Is an academic discussion of free speech potentially traumatic? A recent panel for Smith College alumnae aimed at "challenging the ideological echo chamber" elicited this ominous "trigger/content warning" when a transcript appeared in the campus newspaper: "Racism/racial slurs, ableist slurs, antisemitic language, anti-Muslim/Islamophobic language, anti-immigrant language, sexist/misogynistic slurs, references to race-based violence, references to antisemitic violence."

No one on this panel, in which I participated, trafficked in slurs. So what prompted the warning?

Wendy Kaminer, "The Progressive Ideas behind the Lack of Free Speech on Campus," *Washington Post*, February 20, 2015. Copyright Wendy Kaminer. Reprinted by permission.

Smith President Kathleen McCartney had joked, "We're just wild and crazy, aren't we?" In the transcript, "crazy" was replaced by the notation: "[ableist slur]."

One of my fellow panelists mentioned that the State Department had for a time banned the words "jihad," "Islamist" and "caliphate"—which the transcript flagged as "anti-Muslim/Islamophobic language."

I described the case of a Brandeis professor disciplined for saying "wetback" while explaining its use as a pejorative. The word was replaced in the transcript by "[anti-Latin@/anti-immigrant slur]." Discussing the teaching of "Huckleberry Finn," I questioned the use of euphemisms such as "the n-word" and, in doing so, uttered that forbidden word. I described what I thought was the obvious difference between quoting a word in the context of discussing language, literature or prejudice and hurling it as an epithet.

Two of the panelists challenged me. The audience of 300 to 400 people listened to our spirited, friendly debate—and didn't appear angry or shocked. But back on campus, I was quickly branded a racist, and I was charged in the Huffington Post with committing "an explicit act of racial violence." McCartney subsequently apologized that "some students and faculty were hurt" and made to "feel unsafe" by my remarks.

Unsafe? These days, when students talk about threats to their safety and demand access to "safe spaces," they're often talking about the threat of unwelcome speech and demanding protection from the emotional disturbances sparked by unsettling ideas. It's not just rape that some women on campus fear: It's discussions of rape. At Brown University, a scheduled debate between two feminists about rape culture was criticized for, as the Brown Daily Herald put it, undermining "the University's mission to create a safe and supportive environment for survivors." In a school-wide e-mail, Brown President Christina Paxon emphasized her belief in the existence of rape culture and invited students to an alternative lecture, to be given at the same time as the debate. And the Daily Herald reported that students who feared being "attacked by the viewpoints" offered at the debate could instead "find a safe space" among "sexual assault peer educators, women peer counselors and staff" during the same time slot. Presumably they all shared the same viewpoints and could be trusted not to "attack" anyone with their ideas.

How did we get here? How did a verbal defense of free speech become tantamount to a hate crime and offensive words become the equivalent of physical assaults?

You can credit—or blame—progressives for this enthusiastic embrace of censorship. It reflects, in part, the influence of three popular movements dating back decades: the feminist anti-porn crusades, the pop-psychology recovery movement and the emergence of multiculturalism on college campuses.

In the 1980s, law professor Catharine MacKinnon and writer Andrea Dworkin showed the way, popularizing a view of free speech as a barrier to equality. These two impassioned feminists framed pornography—its production, distribution and consumption—as an assault on women. They devised a novel definition of pornography as a violation of women's civil rights, and championed a model anti-porn ordinance that would authorize civil actions by any woman "aggrieved" by pornography. In 1984, the city of Indianapolis adopted the measure, defining pornography as a "discriminatory practice," but it was quickly struck down in federal court as unconstitutional. "Indianapolis justifies the ordinance on the ground that pornography affects thoughts," the court noted. "This is thought control."

So MacKinnnon and Dworkin lost that battle, but their successors are winning the war. Their view of allegedly offensive or demeaning speech as a civil rights violation, and their conflation of words and actions, have helped shape campus speech and harassment codes and nurtured progressive hostility toward free speech.

The recovery movement, which flourished in the late '80s and early '90s, adopted a similarly dire view of unwelcome speech. Words wound, anti-porn feminists and recovering co-dependents agreed. Self-appointed recovery experts, such as the best-selling author John Bradshaw, promoted the belief that most of us are victims of abuse, in one form or another. They broadened the definition of abuse to include a range of common, normal childhood experiences, including being chastised or ignored by your parents on occasion. From this perspective, we are all fragile and easily damaged by presumptively hurtful speech, and censorship looks like a moral necessity.

These ideas were readily absorbed on college campuses embarking on a commendable drive for diversity. Multiculturalists sought to protect historically disadvantaged students from speech considered racist, sexist, homophobic or otherwise discriminatory. Like abuse, oppression was defined broadly. I remember the first time, in the early '90s, that I heard a Harvard student describe herself as oppressed, as a woman of color. She hadn't been systematically deprived of fundamental rights and liberties. After all, she'd been admitted to Harvard. But she had been offended and unsettled by certain attitudes and remarks. Did she have good reason to take offense? That was an irrelevant question. Popular therapeutic culture defined verbal "assaults" and other forms of discrimination by the subjective, emotional responses of self-proclaimed victims.

This reliance on subjectivity, in the interest of equality, is a recipe for arbitrary, discriminatory enforcement practices, with far-reaching effects on individual liberty. The tendency to take subjective allegations of victimization at face value—instrumental in contemporary censorship campaigns—also leads to the presumption of guilt and disregard for due process in the progressive approach to alleged sexual assaults on campus.

This is a dangerously misguided approach to justice. "Feeling realities" belong in a therapist's office. Incorporated into laws and regulations, they lead to the soft authoritarianism that now governs many American campuses. Instead of advancing equality, it's teaching future generations of leaders the "virtues" of autocracy.

CHAPTER 17

Drugs, Guns, and Personal Liberty

In our personal lives, in society, and in morality itself, few values are counted more precious than individual liberty, our right of self-governance or self-determination. Countless moral conflicts that cause both personal anguish and social strife begin with perceived threats to individual freedom. Often the heart of the matter is someone's claiming a right to exercise personal freedom by doing something—using drugs, owning a gun, having an abortion, marrying a same-sex partner—while others declare that no such right exists. No such right exists, the argument usually goes, because exercising it causes harm to persons or society at large. Debates about drug use and gun ownership thus have much in common. They also seem to be blazing as hot as ever on social media, in the news, and anywhere ethics and arguments are taken seriously.

ISSUE FILE: BACKGROUND

Drugs: Social Harms versus Personal Freedom

No matter how drug use and its accompanying harms are measured, the conclusion to be drawn is the same: the damage to society's institutions and people's lives has been both pervasive and tragic. In 2016, over 64,000 Americans died from overdoses of illicit drugs and prescription opioids. Between 2006 and 2010, excessive alcohol use led to 88,000 deaths. Cigarette smoking and exposure to tobacco smoke cause almost a half million deaths per year. In 2015, over 27 million Americans (aged twelve and older) were users of illegal drugs. That's 12.5 percent of males in this age group, and 7.9 percent

of females.[1] Marijuana was the illicit drug most commonly used (19.8 million users), followed by the nonmedical use of prescription drugs (4.5 million), cocaine (1.5 million), hallucinogens (1.3 million), inhalants (496,000), and heroin (289,000).[2] The resulting injury to the heart, liver, kidneys, lungs, brain, and many other systems is well documented, and annual drug-related deaths number in the tens of thousands. The National Institute on Drug Abuse sums up the effects of drug abuse like this:

> Drug-related deaths have more than doubled since the early 1980s. There are more deaths, illnesses, and disabilities from substance abuse than from any other preventable health condition. Today, one in four deaths is attributable to alcohol, tobacco, and illicit drug use.[3]

Some commentators say the war on drugs has caused more misery than the actual use of drugs. Violence has always accompanied drug trafficking by dealers and cartels, and death and injury are unavoidable in efforts to enforce drug laws. Thousands have been killed in drug-related violence, including many innocents who had nothing to do with illegal drugs. In 2016, there were 1,572,579 arrests for violating drug laws. The great majority of these were for possession; only 15.3 percent were for selling or producing drugs.[4]

State and federal prisons have been filled to capacity with people arrested for drug violations, many of them sentenced to long prison terms for possessing small amounts of marijuana. Thousands of lengthy prison terms for breaking drug laws have been handed down because many statutes—often enacted as part of zero-tolerance drug policies—require

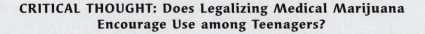

CRITICAL THOUGHT: Does Legalizing Medical Marijuana Encourage Use among Teenagers?

Between 1999 and 2006, ten states legalized medical marijuana: Alaska, California, Colorado, Hawaii, Maine, Montana, Nevada, Oregon, Vermont, and Washington. How did these changes affect recreational marijuana use among teenagers? Existing data show that during this period there was no statistically significant rise in teen marijuana use in any of these states. There was, however, a statistically significant drop in four of the states: Alaska, California, Hawaii, and Montana.*

What do these data suggest about teen marijuana use? Do they show that marijuana use is harmless? Do they prove that medical marijuana should be legalized in every state? What claim about medical marijuana do they disprove?

*Substance Abuse and Mental Health Services Administration (SAMHSA), National Household Surveys on Drug Abuse (NHSDA), 1999–2006; Statistical Assessment Service (STATS).

mandatory minimum sentences. Some states, however, have repealed laws that mandate tough sentences for nonviolent drug offenses, and two-thirds of Americans agree with these changes.[5]

In the United States, attitudes toward drug use and drug law enforcement are changing. Two-thirds of Americans now think the government should pay more attention to treatment for users of hard drugs (cocaine and heroin, for example) than to prosecution of these users. Some states are abandoning mandatory prison sentences for those guilty of nonviolent drug offenses. In 2001, only 47 percent thought such a move was a good idea; in 2014, 63 percent thought so.

The legalization of marijuana is receiving much more support from the public than it did a few years ago. In 2004, 60 percent of Americans were against legalization; 32 percent were for it. In 2016, only 37 percent were against legalization; 57 percent were for legalization.[6]

The term **drug** has been surprisingly difficult to define to everyone's satisfaction. A general definition that can aid our discussions is "a nonfood chemical substance that can affect the functions or makeup of the body." Thus, cocaine and marijuana are drugs, but so are nicotine, alcohol, and caffeine. When doctors, nurses, and medical researchers use

the word *drugs*, they mean substances designed to treat or prevent disease. In this category are all prescription drugs and nonfood over-the-counter (OTC) medicines (not including vitamins, which are considered food substances). *Drug abuse* and *drug habit* usually refer to the nonmedical, proscribed use of psychotropic (mind-altering) substances. Marijuana, prescription medicines (used nonmedically), alcohol, nicotine, and cocaine are all drugs in this sense.

Several terms prominent in discussions of drugs are important but are often misused and misunderstood. **Drug addiction**, like *drug*, is a term whose definition is debated by experts and nonexperts alike. An authoritative medical manual says that drug addiction is

> an intense craving for the drug and compulsive, uncontrolled use of the drug despite harm done to the user or other people. People who are addicted spend more and more time obtaining the drug, using the drug, or recovering from its effects. Thus, addiction usually interferes with the ability to work, study, or interact normally with family and friends.[7]

Drug dependence is a condition in which discontinuing the use of a drug is extremely difficult, involving psychological or physical symptoms. In *physical* dependence, discontinuing the drug leads to uncomfortable physical symptoms of withdrawal—symptoms that can be physically painful, even life threatening. In *psychological* dependence, there is both a strong craving (an acute desire to repeat taking the drug) and an unpleasant experience of withdrawal (an intense distress when not taking the drug).

> The intense desire and compulsion to use a drug lead to using it in larger amounts, more frequently, or over a longer period than at first intended. People who are psychologically dependent on a drug give up social and other activities because of drug use. They also continue to use the drug even though they know that the drug is physically harmful or interferes with other aspects of their life, including family and work.[8]

Debates about the morality of producing, selling, or using illicit drugs are often muddied by misunderstandings of the terms *legalization*, *criminalization*, and *decriminalization*. **Legalization** is the making of the production and sale of drugs legal—that is, making their sale and production no longer a punishable crime. Drugs could be legalized by giving the government the exclusive right to regulate and sell them to the public, much as states now regulate and sell alcohol. Or they could be legalized by allowing individuals to freely buy and sell them without incurring criminal punishment. **Criminalization** is making the *use* (and possession) of drugs a criminal offense. Under a criminalized system, merely possessing drugs in a specified amount can be punished by fines or prison. **Decriminalization** is allowing people to use drugs without being liable to criminal prosecution and punishment.

How different states apply these policies can vary. They can criminalize the use of particular drugs or virtually all of them. They can punish the production and sale of drugs while decriminalizing their use. (Even in full decriminalization, drug use under particular circumstances—while driving a car or flying an airplane, for example—would likely remain a crime.) Or they can opt for a strict zero-tolerance policy and outlaw their use, production, and sale.

A much-debated alternative to punishing people for drug offenses is what experts call **harm reduction**. The idea is to concentrate not on

---

DIVERSE VIEWS ON LEGALIZING MARIJUANA

Percentage of U.S. adults saying use of marijuana should be . . .

	Legal (%)	Illegal (%)
Total	57	37
Men	60	34
Women	55	40
White	59	36
Black	59	37
Millennial (18–35)	71	25
Generation X (36–51)	57	38
Baby Boomer (52–70)	56	40
Republican	41	55
Democrat	66	30
Independent	63	33

Pew Research Center, survey conducted August 23–September 2, 2016, http://www.pewresearch.org/fact-tank/2016/10/12/support-for-marijuana-legalization-continues-to-rise/.

---

decreasing the number of users or the quantity of available drugs in society, but on reducing the harm that arises from drugs and drug laws. Douglas Husak explains this option:

> Many sensible and enlightened commentators propose that the best drug policy is whatever will minimize harm. Their basic insight is that current drug policy initiatives are almost always evaluated by a criterion we should reject: the test of *use-reduction* (or *prevalence-reduction*). In other words, at the present time, no suggestion about how to improve our policy will be accepted unless it offers the potential to reduce the numbers of persons who use drugs. Theorists who favor a standard of harm-reduction point out that the total amount of harm that drugs cause in our society might actually decrease, even though the number of drug users would increase. If the average harm caused per user were reduced, total social harm might go down while the number of users went up.
>
> The most promising harm-reduction programs are needle exchange programs for heroin addicts and medical programs for patients whose symptoms are alleviated by smoking marijuana. Both of these ideas can effectively reduce harm in society.[9]

From whatever perspective we wish to view the issue of drug use and abuse, there are moral questions that demand our attention. These questions fall into two broad categories: (1) the moral permissibility of using drugs; and (2) the morality of legal and social policies that address the use of drugs. Questions of the first type are concerned with personal autonomy, individual liberty, moral and legal rights, harm to oneself, and harm to others. Questions of the second type are about the ethics of drug laws and policies, and the prosecution and punishment of drug users.

Gun Ownership: Security versus Individual Rights

Stubborn realities make debates about guns and gun control in the United States disconcertingly complex, uninformative, and exasperating. Gun violence in the nation is shockingly prevalent, more so than in any other developed country. In 2014, there were 33,736 firearm deaths (suicides, homicides, and accidental shootings). This is a death rate of 10.6 deaths per 100,000 population; the country with the next highest rate is Finland with 3.6 deaths; the United Kingdom's rate is 0.2.[10] And the rate of gun ownership in the United States is among the highest in the world—in 2007, the U.S. rate was 89 guns per 100 people. Yemen had the next highest, at 55 guns per 100 people. It's estimated that there is a gun in 35 percent of American households.[11] About 8 million people have a license or permit to carry a concealed handgun, and an unknown number of people carry concealed handguns without legal permission.[12]

Another factor is that in the United States, obtaining a gun is not difficult. Weak or nonexistent gun regulations make it so. As firearms scholar David Degrazia points out,

> High ownership rates are presumably related, in part, to gun regulations that make it very easy to purchase and possess firearms in this country. American adults who lack any specific disqualifying criminal or psychiatric history are eligible buyers. While state laws vary, federal exclusionary criteria—such as having a felony conviction or having been committed to a psychiatric institution—leave eligible many people

with troubling histories that suggest a degree of dangerousness. Eligible buyers include persons convicted of violent misdemeanors (except domestic violence), individuals with substantial records of alcohol abuse, and many people who have significant psychiatric problems but have not been hospitalized for them: stalkers under temporary restraining orders are not required to surrender firearms they already own.[13]

Debates about gun control may seem intractable, in part because each side appeals implicitly to different basic moral values and fails to appreciate the other side's moral commitment. Lester H. Hunt describes an aspect of this conflict:

> One side focuses on the [Western] liberal value of empathy for injury and suffering, while the other emphasizes the equally liberal ideas of dignity and autonomy. I am tempted to call the former tradition "compassion-based," but for the fact that both are based on compassion of a sort. What each has compassion *for* is somewhat different, though. For the former, what is important is rescuing human beings from pain, while the latter places importance on repairing individual dignity and self-respect. I, personally, have a good deal of sympathy for the dignity and self-respect side of this divide, but for the moment that is not my point. Rather, I urge the reader to understand that the gun debate is separated by contrasting ethical ideas, and that unless we keep this in mind we are apt to seriously miss the point of the debate.[14]

Gun control refers to laws and policies designed to restrict the possession, use, and availability of firearms.[15] Gun control supporters stake out a range of positions, from an absolute ban on all firearms (except those used by the police and military) to a variety of restrictions that are generally tougher than what exists now. Pro-gun (gun rights) advocates are committed to opposing almost all restrictions on the ownership and use of guns. Existing federal gun laws limit the government's role in firearm control to licensing and inspecting gun dealers, regulating the sale and transfer of guns across state and international borders, preventing the ownership of guns by high-risk groups (such as felons), and limiting the availability of machine guns and armor-piercing bullets. States and cities have

VITAL STATS: Guns in the United States

- In 2014, there were 33,736 firearm deaths (suicides, homicides, and accidental shootings), which is a death rate of 10.6 deaths per 100,000 population, the highest rate in the world. The death rate for the United Kingdom is 0.2 per 100,000.
- The United States has six times as many gun homicides as Canada, and almost sixteen times as many as Germany.
- Since the Sandy Hook Elementary School shooting (in which twenty children and six adults were killed), over 1,500 mass shootings have occurred. (A mass shooting is defined as an incident in which four or more people are shot, not including the shooter.)
- In 2007, the U.S. rate of gun ownership was among the highest in the world—89 guns per 100 people.
- Americans own almost half of the world's 650 million privately owned guns.
- 22 percent of Americans own one or more guns.

- About 8 million people have a license or permit to carry a concealed handgun, and an unknown number of people carry concealed handguns without legal permission.
- Three-quarters of teenage homicides are related to the use of firearms.
- In 2010, emergency rooms treated 73,505 non-fatal gunshot injuries.*

*National Center for Health Statistics, "Suicide and Self-Inflicted Injury," "Assault or Homicide," 2013, https://www.cdc.gov/nchs/fastats/suicide.htm (December 31, 2017); National Center for Health Statistics, "All Injuries," 2014, https://www.cdc.gov/nchs/fastats/injury.htm (December 31, 2017); *American Journal of Medicine*, March 2016, vol. 129, iss. 3, 266–73; Philip J. Cook and Kristina A. Goss, *The Gun Debate: What Everyone Needs to Know* (New York: Oxford University Press, 2014), 22; American Academy of Pediatrics, "Firearms and Adolescents," *Pediatrics* 89 (April 1992), 784–87; Congressional Research Service 2012, "Small Arms Survey," 2007; UNODC, "Small Arms Survey," 2012; Gun Violence Archive, 2013–2017.

their own regulations, which may reinforce or augment federal laws.

Degrazia says the United States currently has a "very minimal level of gun control" and should enact more rigorous measures—what he calls a "moderately extensive set of gun regulations." His list of policy recommendations includes the following:

1. Purchase of a gun should be legally permitted only upon obtaining a license, and the first step in acquiring a license should be demonstration of special need for a firearm.

2. Those who demonstrate special need for a firearm should have to pass a rigorous training course on firearm use and safety before obtaining a license.

3. No one should be legally permitted to purchase, own, or use a gun prior to age twenty-one.

4. Laws should stipulate that only properly licensed adults may use a gun, and that one may not use someone else's gun except in a life-threatening emergency calling for forceful defense.

5. Guns should be acquirable only from federally licensed dealers while private sales and the gifting of guns should be illegal.

6. Federally licensed dealers should be permitted to sell a firearm to a given individual only after completing a criminal and psychiatric background check (no exceptions).[16]

Probably very few extended debates about guns proceed without at least a mention of the Second Amendment to the U.S. Constitution. Pro-gun advocates consider it the lynchpin of their case for the right to own and use firearms. It reads: "A well

SURVEY: VIEWS OF U.S. ADULTS ON GUN POLICY

View	Percentage of U.S. adults
Gun laws should be more strict.	52
Gun laws are about right.	30
Gun laws should be less strict.	18
Strongly favor preventing people with mental illnesses from purchasing guns.	73
Strongly favor creating a federal government database to track all gun sales.	50
Strongly favor allowing people to carry concealed guns in more places.	19
Strongly favor banning assault style weapons.	53
Strongly favor barring gun purchases by people on no-fly or watch lists.	66

Pew Research Center, "America's Complex Relationship with Guns," Survey of U.S. Adults conducted March 13–17 and April 4–18, 2017.

regulated Militia, being necessary to the security of a free State, the right of the people to keep and bear Arms, shall not be infringed." As generations of legal scholars and judges have pointed out, and as contemporary disputants in gun control debates have discovered, this wording is peculiar and ambiguous, and disagreements about its meaning abound. As firearms scholars Glenn H. Utter and Robert J. Spitzer, however, point out:

> Although the issues arising over the interpretation of the Amendment have been many, two tend to predominate. First, does it protect a collective (in other words, state) right related to militia service, or an individual right, and second, assuming that it does in fact protect the right of individuals to keep and bear arms, does it apply to the states as well as the national government?[17]

In past decades, the U.S. Supreme Court has weighed in only occasionally on the issue of individual vs. collective rights. Early rulings on the matter suggested that the right to keep and bear arms was a collective right connected to militia service. But in 2008, in the case of *District of Columbia v. Heller*, the court overturned Washington, DC's 1976 ban on individual handgun possession. The ruling affirmed an individual's right to keep and bear arms for self-defense. *Heller* and a similar ruling issued two years later in *McDonald v. City of Chicago* did not invalidate all gun control laws, but they did crush the old gun control dream of banning all handguns.

No matter what interpretation of the Second Amendment we prefer, the moral questions about gun rights and gun control remain, and we must seek answers through moral philosophy. The central moral questions are: Is there a moral right to own firearms, and do individuals have a moral right to use them in self-defense? The law cannot provide answers here, but we have a good chance of finding some through moral theories and moral arguments.

MORAL THEORIES

Traditional moral theories have interesting implications for drug use. A utilitarian would judge the moral permissibility of using illicit drugs by how well that choice maximizes happiness, everyone considered. So she might reason like this: On the positive side, using drugs (nonmedically or recreationally) could provide the user with pleasure, euphoria, a respite from stress, a break from the mundane, or some other desirable experience. She might then balance these benefits with several alleged negatives (depending on the kind of drug): addiction, dependence, withdrawal, physical disability, psychological impairment, loss of employment, damage done to personal relationships, and harm to other people. On the list of negatives she must also include the legal ramifications of drug use: the possibility of arrest, prosecution, imprisonment, and having a criminal record. She would have to make a judgment about the extent and likelihood of all these legal and nonlegal problems, difficult calculations about which experts disagree. She might finally conclude that the cost of using a particular drug far outweighs the benefits. Or she might assess the evidence differently and decide that the negatives for all concerned are not as bad as some people suggest.

These considerations of course pertain to the morality of personal drug use, but our utilitarian could also make a similar calculation about drug laws and policy generally. For example, based on her assessment of the overall effects of an antidrug law, she might conclude that enforcement of the law causes more unhappiness than the drug itself does, or that using the drug does more harm to more people than the law does.

Kantian ethics is likely to condemn the use of illicit drugs on the grounds that it violates a version of the categorical imperative: never use persons merely as a means to an end but always as an end in themselves. Kant would have us include ourselves in this formula. When we use illicit drugs, he might say, we use ourselves merely as a means to the end of drug-induced pleasure, stress reduction, or altered consciousness. What's more, we impair the very thing that constitutes our personhood—our autonomy, our capacity for reasoned self-determination. Some commentators argue that in full-blown drug addiction, our autonomy is destroyed altogether. In addiction, they say, the addict's freedom to choose is lost, for he is a slave to his chemical master. Others contend, however, that free will is not diminished as much as some critics say, especially if the drug addict freely chooses to use drugs in the first place.

It's hard to see how natural law theory could ever condone hard drug use. Recall that in this theory, the morally right action is one that follows the dictates of nature. Whatever people do, they must fulfill their God-given, natural purpose. Lying is immoral, for example, because it goes against human nature, which naturally inclines toward social living where truth contributes to peaceful coexistence. Using mind-altering drugs, however, can lead to addiction, which forces the mind into an unnatural state in which autonomy is weakened and the moral law is obscured.

Historically, the moral implications of gun control have been explored using both consequentialist and nonconsequentialist theories. But for many people, the most straightforward way to argue for or against guns is through some form of utilitarianism: judging a gun policy by its balance of good and bad effects, everyone considered. A gun control advocate might point to a long list of possible tragic consequences of not having appropriate gun laws in place and conclude that the argument against guns (and for gun control) is extremely strong. Here's one way to make this case:

> Gun control supporters offer empirical evidence of a positive correlation between murder rates and the availability of guns (especially handguns). Availability of guns is also positively correlated with suicide and accident rates. This empirical evidence is best understood against the background of the following armchair argument: (1) Guns (and especially handguns) are the easiest way to kill others or oneself. People can stand at a relatively safe distance and pull the trigger. (2) When people are angry, they act in ways they do not normally act. They may strike out at others. If they have a gun, they are more likely to use that gun. Although they could resort to a knife or a baseball bat, they are less likely to do so, and, even if they do, those weapons are less likely to cause a serious or fatal injury. (3) When people are depressed, they act in ways they would not act normally. If they have a gun close to hand, they are more likely to kill themselves. Although they might slit their wrists or take pills, they are less likely to do so, and, even if they do, they are less likely to kill themselves. (4) When people handle guns, even for a legitimate purpose, the probability of serious or fatal injury to themselves or others increases. When children have access to guns, the likelihood of an accident increases still more.

> The conclusion of the armchair argument is clear: the more widely available guns are, the more people will be murdered, will commit suicide, and will die of accidents.[18]

A gun rights advocate could argue in similar fashion:

> Gun control laws do not deter crime; gun ownership deters crime. A Nov. 26, 2013 study found that,

between 1980 and 2009, "assault weapons bans did not significantly affect murder rates at the state level" and "states with restrictions on the carrying of concealed weapons had higher gun-related murders." While gun ownership doubled in the twentieth century, the murder rate decreased. John R. Lott, Jr., PhD, author of *More Guns, Less Crime: Understanding Crime and Gun Control Laws*, stated, "States with the largest increases in gun ownership also have the largest drops in violent crimes . . . The effect on 'shall-issue' [concealed gun] laws on these crimes [where two or more people were killed] has been dramatic. When states passed these laws, the number of multiple-victim shootings declined by 84 percent. Deaths from these shootings plummeted on average by 90 percent and injuries by 82 percent." A Dec. 10, 2014 Pew survey found that 57% of people believe that owning a gun protects them from being victimized. Journalist John Stossel explained, "Criminals don't obey the law . . . Without the fear of retaliation from victims who might be packing heat, criminals in possession of these [illegal] weapons now have a much easier job . . . As the saying goes, 'If guns are outlawed, only outlaws will have guns.'"[19]

As with any utilitarian argument, much depends on the empirical support for the premises. In the gun control debate, the nonmoral facts aren't always clear. One reason for this is that solid evidence for various claims is often lacking because of the difficulty of establishing cause and effect relationships. (Does the availability of guns cause more crime or diminish it? Does carrying concealed guns deter crime?) Another reason is that partisans in the verbal conflicts are susceptible to the usual biases that plague arguments in any emotionally charged debate—and disputes about gun control can be especially vehement. In the supercharged atmosphere, evidence is frequently ignored, downplayed, misconstrued, and exaggerated.

MORAL ARGUMENTS

Some of the more compelling arguments for and against drug use involve questions of the second type, those concerning the morality of legal restrictions or bans on the use of drugs. The essential query is, Under what circumstances is the government justified in preventing or stopping people from using drugs recreationally? The answers, or justifications, are usually derived from three principles: (1) the harm principle; (2) the paternalism principle; or (3) the legal moralism principle. When people try to explain their reasons for advocating a "war on drugs" or any other kind of interference with drug use, they almost always appeal to one or more of these fundamental ideas.

The **harm principle** says that authorities are justified in restricting some people's freedom to prevent harm to others. The government claims for itself the right to arrest, subdue, punish, or quarantine anyone if doing so will prevent harm to the public. Numerous civil laws, criminal laws, and judicial rulings rest firmly on the harm principle. The great utilitarian John Stuart Mill articulated this principle best when he said, "The only purpose for which power can be rightfully exercised over any member of a civilized community, against his will, is to prevent harm to others."[20]

Many who are opposed to recreational drug use assert that drug users hurt plenty of people. Users, they say, are more likely to neglect their children, abuse their spouses, cheat their employers by doing poor work, steal to support their drug habit, and hurt other people through accidents and negligence. In addition, drug users burden society with the costs of drug-law enforcement, drug treatment, legal prosecution, and imprisonment. As James Q. Wilson says, "The notion that abusing drugs such as cocaine is a 'victimless crime' is not only absurd but dangerous."[21]

Proponents of decriminalization counter that the harms of illicit drug use are exaggerated, are based on worst-case scenarios, and lack supporting evidence. Furthermore, they maintain that most of the harms that accompany drug use are not the direct result of drug use but of antidrug laws and policies. Douglas Husak itemizes some of these alleged harms:

> In the first place, prohibition [of drugs and drug use] has always been aimed—or selectively

enforced—against minorities. . . . In addition, drug prohibition is destructive of public health. Since the vast majority of illicit drugs taken for recreational purposes are purchased on the street from unlicensed sellers, consumers can have no confidence about what they are buying. . . . Street drugs may contain deadly impurities, and unknown potencies can contribute to deaths from overdose. . . . Truth is among the foremost casualties of our misguided drug policy. The demonization of illicit drugs is so pervasive that frank and honest discourse is all but impossible. . . . There may be no greater threat to the rule of law than corruption and abuse of authority among government officials. Prohibition and the huge amounts of money in the illicit drug trade create irresistible temptations for law-enforcement agents to place themselves above the law. . . . Our punitive drug policies cost exorbitant amounts of money. . . . Most of this money has been wasted. If we stopped punishing drug users, taxpayers would reap enormous savings.[22]

For some who favor decriminalization, trying to judge the issue by some utilitarian standard—that is, by weighing harms and benefits—is entirely wrongheaded. The real issue, they say, is not harms but justice. The decision to punish someone for breaching a law should be decided according to *what is just*. If Jones commits a crime, we don't decide his fate by balancing the good and bad effects of his actions. The utilitarian calculus is useless here. We try instead to determine what a just treatment of him would be, what his rights are, and what he deserves. Underlying this view is the idea that people are rational, autonomous beings whose freedom to choose and act should not be constrained without strong justification.

The **paternalism principle** asserts that authorities are sometimes justified in limiting people's freedom to prevent them from harming themselves. To act paternally is to curtail a person's liberty for her own good, regardless of what her preferences are. A paternalistic drug law would, say, criminalize a drug user's actions to prevent him from doing something that might injure or impair

him. One paternalistic argument concludes that people must be protected from freely and knowingly choosing to take addictive drugs that can undermine their autonomy.

Peter de Marneffe takes a paternalistic view. He declares that there is only one good reason for drug prohibition—that some people will be worse off if drugs are legalized. He argues:

> Drug prohibition is justified, in my view, as reducing the independent harms of drug abuse [harms besides those caused by drug-law enforcement]. But it is commonly objected that drug laws "don't work." If so, it is no argument for drug legalization. In this sense laws against murder and theft do not work either, but this does not mean that we should abolish them.[23]

As you might expect, those who condemn paternalistic drug laws usually base their arguments on the supreme value of autonomy. Whatever the form of such laws, they say, they are still unacceptable assaults on individual liberty, even if they are intended to somehow protect autonomy.

The **legal moralism** principle is the doctrine that the government is justified in curbing people's freedom in order to force them to obey moral rules. For the legal moralist, if an act is immoral, that's reason enough to make it a crime and prosecute those who violate the law. Estimations of harm need not be involved. The principle of course can be applied not just to drug use but to any action thought to breach moral standards. Wilson's attitude toward antidrug laws is decidedly moralistic:

> Even now, when the dangers of drug use are well-understood, many educated people still discuss the drug problem in almost every way except the right way. They talk about the "costs" of drug use and the "socioeconomic factors" that shape that use. They rarely speak plainly—drug use is wrong because it is immoral and it is immoral because it enslaves the mind and destroys the soul.[24]

A common reply to the doctrine of legal moralism is that it conflicts with other commonsense moral beliefs or policies we have. Decriminalization

---

> ## QUICK REVIEW
>
> **drug**—A nonfood chemical substance that can affect the functions and makeup of the body.
>
> **drug addiction**—An intense craving for a drug and compulsive, uncontrolled use of the drug despite harm done to the user or other people.
>
> **drug dependence**—A condition in which discontinuing the use of a drug is extremely difficult, involving psychological or physical symptoms.
>
> **legalization**—Making the production and sale of drugs legal.
>
> **criminalization**—Making the use (and possession) of drugs a criminal offense.
>
> **decriminalization**—Allowing the use of drugs without criminal penalties.
>
> **harm reduction**—A drug policy aimed at reducing the harm that arises from drugs and drug laws.
>
> **gun control**—Laws and policies designed to restrict the possession, use, and availability of firearms.
>
> **harm principle**—The view that authorities are justified in restricting some people's freedom to prevent harm to others.
>
> **paternalism principle**—The view that authorities are sometimes justified in limiting people's freedom to prevent them from harming themselves.
>
> **legal moralism**—The doctrine that the government is justified in curbing people's freedom in order to force them to obey moral rules.

supporters ask why drug use, and not other kinds of behavior, should be outlawed simply because it is deemed immoral. Many actions are thought to be immoral—cheating at golf, plagiarizing, lying to a spouse, breaking a solemn vow, betraying a confidence—but few think these actions should be regarded as crimes and prosecuted as such. Critics of legal moralism say that legal moralists must explain why drug use should be a crime just because it's immoral, but not other presumably immoral acts like betraying a confidence. Why is drug use a crime and not cheating at golf or lying to a spouse? Decriminalization proponents say legal

moralists have yet to explain this inconsistency, so the doctrine of legal moralism is an inadequate justification for making drug use illegal.

A common pro-gun argument appeals not to consequences but to rights. The idea is that the right to own a gun derives from a more fundamental right: the right of self-defense. The Second Amendment scholar Nelson Lund says, "The right to self-defense and to the means of defending oneself is a basic natural right that grows out of the right to life," and that "many [gun control laws] interfere with the ability of law-abiding citizens to defend themselves against violent criminals."[25]

David Degrazia, an advocate for moderate gun control, lays out what he believes is a plausible self-defense argument for gun ownership and then critiques it. Here's a shortened version of the argument:

1. People have a basic right to physical security.

2. This right is violated by (unjustified) assaults and is threatened by burglaries.

3. People have a moral right to take necessary measures to prevent their basic rights from being violated.

4. The right to take such measures supports a moral right to self-defense.

5. The right to self-defense includes the freedom to use adequate means to defend oneself.

6. In present-day circumstances in the United States, adequate self-defense requires that competent adults have the option of gun ownership.

7. Thus, competent adults in the United States today have a moral right to gun ownership.[26]

Degrazia finds fault with several parts of the argument, but focuses mostly on Premise 6. He asks, "Does the option of owning firearms enable more adequate self-defense and physical security than would be possible if this option were unavailable?" His answer is "no":

An even-handed examination of available evidence suggests that, in the United States today, possession of guns *does not*, generally speaking, enable more adequate self-defense and physical security. First, the evidence suggests that owning guns tends to be self-defeating in the sense of making household members, on balance, less safe than they would be if the house were free of firearms. Second, the evidence casts doubt on the proposition that, in the event of a break-in while one is at home, having a gun, on balance, promotes the goal of self-defense.[27]

CHAPTER REVIEW

SUMMARY

A *drug* is a nonfood chemical substance that can affect the functions or makeup of the body. *Drug addiction* is "an intense craving for the drug and compulsive, uncontrolled use of the drug despite harm done to the user or other people." *Drug dependence* is a condition in which discontinuing the use of a drug is extremely difficult, involving psychological or physical symptoms. *Drug legalization* refers to making the production and sale of drugs legal—that is, making their sale and production no longer a punishable crime. *Criminalization* makes the use (and possession) of drugs a criminal offense. *Decriminalization* allows people to use drugs without being liable to criminal prosecution and punishment.

A utilitarian would judge the moral permissibility of using illicit drugs by how well that choice maximizes happiness, everyone considered. Kantian ethics is likely to condemn the use of illicit drugs on the grounds that it violates a version of the categorical imperative: never use persons merely as a means to an end but always as an end in themselves. Natural law theorists condemn hard drug use on the grounds that mind-altering drugs can lead to addiction, which forces the mind into an unnatural state in which autonomy is weakened and the moral law is obscured.

Arguments against decriminalization are often derived from three principles: (1) the harm principle; (2) the paternalism principle; or (3) the legal moralism principle. When people try to explain their reasons for advocating a "war on drugs" or any other kind of interference with drug use, they almost always appeal to one or more of these fundamental ideas.

Gun control refers to laws and policies designed to restrict the possession, use, and availability of firearms. Gun control supporters stake out a range of positions, from an absolute ban on all firearms (except those used by the police and military) to a variety of restrictions that are generally tougher than what exists now. Pro-gun (gun rights) advocates are committed to opposing almost all restrictions on the ownership and use of guns. Existing federal gun laws limit the government's role in firearm control to licensing and inspecting gun dealers, regulating the sale and transfer of guns across state and international borders, preventing the ownership of guns by high-risk groups (such as felons), and limiting the availability of machine guns and armor-piercing bullets.

Pro-gun advocates consider the Second Amendment the lynchpin of their case for the right to own and use firearms. But its wording is ambiguous, and disagreements about its meaning abound. The central moral questions in gun control are: Is there a moral right to own firearms, and do individuals have a moral right to use them in self-defense?

KEY TERMS

drug (p. 622)
drug addiction (p. 622)
drug dependence (p. 622)
legalization (p. 623)
criminalization (p. 623)
decriminalization (p. 623)
harm reduction (p. 623)
gun control (p. 624)
harm principle (p. 628)
paternalism principle (p. 629)
legal moralism (p. 629)

EXERCISES

Review Questions

1. What is the difference between drug addiction and drug dependence? (p. 622)
2. What is the difference between legalization and criminalization? (p. 623)

3. What is the drug policy known as harm reduction? (p. 623)

4. What is the harm principle? How is the harm principle used to justify government interference with drug use? (p. 628)

5. What is the paternalism principle? (p. 629)

6. What is legal moralism? (p. 629)

7. What is gun control? (p. 624)

8. What is the Second Amendment? How is it related to debates about gun control? (pp. 625–626)

9. What is the rate of gun ownership in the United States? (p. 625)

10. How many firearms deaths occurred in 2014? How does this death rate compare to that of other developed countries? (p. 625)

Discussion Questions

1. Is legal moralism ever justified? Why or why not?

2. How might a utilitarian argue for or against drug criminalization?

3. Should hard drugs like cocaine be legalized? Give reasons for your answer.

4. Is harm reduction a better response to drug use than criminalization? Why or why not?

5. In general, are paternalistic drug laws justified? That is, is it ever morally permissible to curtail people's freedom to prevent them from harming themselves?

6. How can gun ownership be justified by an appeal to a right of self-defense?

7. Should gun control laws be stricter than they are now? Why or why not?

8. Should gun purchases be allowed only after purchasers obtain a license? Explain.

9. Should there be an absolute legal ban on all guns? Why or why not?

10. Evaluate the self-defense argument that Degrazia sets forth. Is it sound? Are its premises true?

FURTHER READING

Jonathan P. Caulkins, Angela Hawken, Beau Kilmer, and Mark Kleiman, *Marijuana Legalization: What Everyone Needs to Know* (New York: Oxford University Press, 2012).

Philip J. Cook and Kristina A. Goss, *The Gun Debate: What Everyone Needs to Know* (New York: Oxford University Press, 2014).

David Degrazia and Lester H. Hunt, *Debating Gun Control: How Much Regulation Do We Need?* (New York: Oxford University Press, 2016).

Douglas Husak and Peter de Marneffe, *The Legalization of Drugs: For and Against* (Cambridge: Cambridge University Press, 2005).

National Institute of Drug Abuse, "Medical Consequences of Drug Abuse," December 2012, http://www.drugabuse.gov/related-topics/medical-consequences-drug-abuse/mortality.

Pew Research Center, "America's New Drug Policy Landscape," April 2, 2014, http://www.people-press.org/2014/04/02/.

Substance Abuse and Mental Health Services Administration, Center for Behavioral Health Statistics and Quality, September 4, 2014, "The NSDUH Report: Substance Use and Mental Health Estimates from the 2013 National Survey on Drug Use and Health: Overview of Findings," Rockville, MD.

Glen H. Utter and Robert J. Spitzer, *The Gun Debate: An Encyclopedia of Gun Rights & Gun Control in the United States* (Amenia, NY: Grey House, 2016).

James Q. Wilson, "Against the Legalization of Drugs," *Commentary*, February 1990.

ETHICAL DILEMMAS

1. Mass Shootings and Gun Laws

Politico.com—A majority of Americans support passing new gun control legislation, according to a new Gallup poll released on Thursday—marking the first time a majority of those surveyed has expressed such a view since Gallup started tracking the issue in 2000.

The poll—taken in the month between the deadly mass shootings in Las Vegas on Oct. 1 and in Sutherland Springs, Texas, on Nov. 5—found that 51 percent of Americans were in favor of increased gun legislation.*

Mass shootings often increase support for gun control laws to deter such violence. But how likely is it that gun regulations will prevent mass shootings? Is the government morally obligated to find out what policies can and cannot prevent these shootings? Do citizens have a duty to press the government for action?

*Christiano Lima, "Gallup Poll: Majority of Americans Now Favor More Gun Laws," *Politico*, November 9, 2017, https://www.politico.com/story/2017/11/09/gun-control-gallup-poll-244759.

---

2. Against Legalization or Decriminalization of Drugs

Position Statement from Drug Watch International: The legalization or decriminalization of drugs would make harmful, psychoactive, and addictive substances affordable, available, convenient, and marketable. It would expand the use of drugs. It would remove the social stigma attached to illicit drug use, and would send a message of tolerance for drug use, especially to youth. . . .

The use of illicit drugs is illegal because of their intoxicating effects on the brain, damaging impact on the body, adverse impact on behavior, and potential for abuse. Their use threatens the health, welfare, and safety of all people, of users and non-users alike.[†]

Do you agree with this position statement? Is the description of the effects of drug use accurate or exaggerated? Does legalization or decriminalization imply that the government approves of drug use? Explain your answers.

[†]Drug Watch International, "Position Statement," August 1, 1994, http://www.drugwatch.org/resources/publications/position-statements-and-resolutions/ (February 15, 2015).

---

3. Is Marijuana Medicine?

The marijuana plant contains several chemicals that may prove useful for treating a range of illnesses or symptoms, leading many people to argue that it should be made legally available for medical purposes. In fact, a growing number of states (29 as of March 2018) have legalized marijuana's use for certain medical conditions.

The term "medical marijuana" is generally used to refer to the whole unprocessed marijuana plant or its crude extracts, which are not recognized or approved as medicine by the U.S. Food and Drug Administration (FDA). But scientific study of the active chemicals in marijuana, called *cannabinoids*, has led to the development of two FDA-approved medications already, and is leading to the development of new pharmaceuticals that harness the therapeutic benefits of cannabinoids while minimizing or eliminating the harmful side effects (including the "high") produced by eating or smoking marijuana leaves.[‡]

Should marijuana be made available to people for medical reasons? It is not legal in most states; should it stay that way, or should all states legalize it? Why or why not? Suppose you think using marijuana for medical or recreational purposes is immoral or harmful to society. Would you change your mind about its use if it were found to be a cure for hard-to-treat cancers? Explain.

[‡]National Institute on Drug Abuse, "DrugFacts: Is Marijuana Medicine?" December 2014, http://www.drugabuse.gov/publications /drugfacts/marijuana-medicine (February 15, 2015).

READINGS

The Ethics of Addiction
THOMAS SZASZ

Lest we take for granted that we know what drug addiction is, let us begin with some definitions.

According to the World Health Organization's Expert Committee on Drugs Liable to Produce Addiction,

Drug addiction is a state of periodic or chronic intoxication detrimental to the individual and to society, produced by the repeated consumption of a drug (natural or synthetic). Its characteristics include: (1) an overpowering desire or need (compulsion) to continue taking the drug and to obtain it by any means, (2) a tendency to increase the dosage, and (3) a psychic (psychological) and sometimes physical dependence on the effects of the drug.[1]

Since this definition hinges on the harm done to the individual and to society by the consumption of the drug, it is clearly an ethical one. Moreover, by not specifying what is "detrimental" or who shall ascertain it and on what grounds, this definition immediately assimilates the problem of addiction with other

Thomas Szasz, "The Ethics of Addiction," from *The Theology of Medicine* (1977). Reprinted with permission from the Estate of Thomas Szasz.

psychiatric problems in which psychiatrists define the patient's dangerousness to himself and others. Actually, physicians regard as detrimental what people do to themselves but not what they do to people. For example, when college students smoke marijuana, that is detrimental; but when psychiatrists administer psychotropic drugs to involuntary mental patients, that is not detrimental.

The rest of the definition proposed by the World Health Organization is of even more dubious value. It speaks of an "overpowering desire" or "compulsion" to take the drug and of efforts to obtain it "by any means." Here again, we sink into the conceptual and semantic morass of psychiatric jargon. What is an "overpowering desire" if not simply a desire by which we choose to let ourselves be overpowered? And what is a "compulsion" if not simply an unresisted inclination to do something, and keep on doing it, even though someone thinks we should not be doing it?

Next, we come to the effort to obtain the addictive substance "by any means." That suggests that the substance is prohibited, or is very expensive for some other reason, and is hence difficult to obtain for the ordinary person rather than that the person who wants it has an inordinate craving for it. If there were an abundant and inexpensive supply of what the "addict" wants, there would be no reason for him to go to "any means" to obtain it. Does the World Health Organization's definition mean that one can be addicted only to a substance that is illegal or otherwise difficult to obtain? If so—and there is obviously some truth to the view that forbidden fruit tastes sweeter, although it cannot be denied that some things are sweet regardless of how the law treats them—then that surely removes the problem of addiction from the sphere of medicine and psychiatry and puts it squarely into that of morals and law.

The definition of addiction offered in *Webster's Third New International Dictionary of the English Language, Unabridged* exhibits the same difficulties. It defines addiction as "the compulsory uncontrolled use of habit-forming drugs beyond the period of medical need or under conditions harmful to society." This definition imputes lack of self-control to the addict over his taking or not taking a drug, a dubious proposition at best; at the same time, by qualifying an act as an addiction depending on whether or not it harms society, it offers a moral definition of an ostensibly medical condition.

Likewise, the currently popular term *drug abuse* places this behavior squarely in the category of ethics. For it is ethics that deals with the right and wrong uses of man's powers and possessions.

Clearly, drug addiction and drug abuse cannot be defined without specifying the proper and improper uses of certain pharmacologically active agents. The regular administration of morphine by a physician to a patient dying of cancer is the paradigm of the proper use of a narcotic, whereas even its occasional self-administration by a physically healthy person for the purpose of pharmacological pleasure is the paradigm of drug abuse.

I submit that these judgments have nothing whatever to do with medicine, pharmacology, or psychiatry. They are moral judgments. Indeed, our present views on addiction are astonishingly similar to some of our former views on sex. Intercourse in marriage with the aim of procreation used to be the paradigm of the proper use of one's sexual organs, whereas intercourse outside of marriage with the aim of carnal pleasure used to be the paradigm of their improper use.

Until recently, masturbation—or self-abuse, as it was called—was professionally declared and popularly accepted as both the cause and the symptom of a variety of illnesses.[2]

To be sure, it is now virtually impossible to cite a contemporary American (or foreign) medical authority to support the concept of self-abuse. Medical opinion now holds that there is simply no such thing, that whether a person masturbates or not is medically irrelevant, and that engaging in the practice or refraining from it is a matter of personal morals or life-style. On the other hand, it is now virtually impossible to cite a contemporary American (or foreign) medical authority to oppose the concept of drug abuse. Medical opinion now holds that drug abuse is a major medical, psychiatric, and public-health problem; that drug addiction is a disease similar to diabetes, requiring prolonged (or lifelong) and carefully supervised medical treatment; and that taking or not taking drugs is primarily, if not solely, a matter of medical concern and responsibility.

Like any social policy, our drug laws may be examined from two entirely different points of view—technical and moral. Our present inclination is either to ignore the moral perspective or to mistake the technical for the moral.

An example of our misplaced overreliance on a technical approach to the so-called drug problem is the professionalized mendacity about the dangerousness of certain types of drugs. Since most of the propagandists against drug abuse seek to justify certain repressive policies by appeals to the alleged dangerousness of various drugs, they often falsify the facts about the true pharmacological properties of the drugs they seek to prohibit. They do so for two reasons: first, because many substances in daily use are just as harmful as the substances they want to prohibit; second, because they realize that dangerousness alone is never a sufficiently persuasive argument to justify the prohibition of any drug, substance, or artifact. Accordingly, the more the "addiction-mongers" ignore the moral dimensions of the problem, the more they must escalate their fraudulent claims about the dangers of drugs.

To be sure, some drugs are more dangerous than others. It is easier to kill oneself with heroin than with aspirin. But it is also easier to kill oneself by jumping off a high building than a low one. In the case of drugs, we regard their potentiality for self-injury as justification for their prohibition; in the case of buildings, we do not.

Furthermore, we systematically blur and confuse the two quite different ways in which narcotics may cause death—by a deliberate act of suicide and by accidental overdosage.

As I have suggested elsewhere, we ought to consider suicide a basic human right. If so, it is absurd to deprive an adult of a drug (or of anything else) because he might use it to kill himself. To do so is to treat everyone the way institutional psychiatrists treat the so-called suicidal mental patient: they not only imprison such a person but take everything away from him—shoelaces, belts, razor blades, eating utensils, and so forth—until the "patient" lies naked on a mattress in a padded cell, lest he kill himself. The result is the most degrading tyrannization in the annals of human history.

Death by accidental overdose is an altogether different matter. But can anyone doubt that this danger now looms so large precisely because the sale of narcotics and many other drugs is illegal? People who buy illicit drugs cannot be sure what drug they are getting or how much of it. Free trade in drugs, with governmental action limited to safeguarding the purity of the product and the veracity of the labeling, would reduce the risk of accidental overdose with "dangerous drugs" to the same levels that prevail, and that we find acceptable, with respect to other chemical agents and physical artifacts that abound in our complex technological society.

Although this essay is not intended as an exposition on the pharmacological properties of narcotics and other mind-affecting drugs, it might be well to say something more about the medical and social dangers they pose. Before proceeding to that task, I want to make clear, however, that in my view, regardless of their dangerousness, all drugs should be legalized (a misleading term I employ reluctantly as a concession to common usage). Although I recognize that some drugs—notably heroin, the amphetamines, and LSD among those now in vogue—may have undesirable personal or social consequences, I favor free trade in drugs for the same reason the Founding Fathers favored free trade in ideas: in an open society, it is none of the government's business what idea a man puts into his mind; likewise, it should be none of the government's business what drug he puts into his body.

It is a fundamental characteristic of human beings that they get used to things: one becomes habituated, or addicted, not only to narcotics, but to cigarettes, cocktails before dinner, orange juice for breakfast, comic strips, sex, and so forth. It is similarly a fundamental characteristic of living organisms that they acquire increasing tolerance to various chemical agents and physical stimuli: the first cigarette may cause nothing but nausea and headache; a year later, smoking three packs a day may be pure joy. Both alcohol and opiates are addictive, then, in the sense that the more regularly they are used, the more the user craves them and the greater his tolerance for them becomes. However, there is no mysterious process of "getting hooked" involved in any of this. It is simply an aspect of the universal biological propensity for learning, which is especially well-developed in man. The opiate habit, like the cigarette habit or the food habit, can be broken—usually without any medical assistance—provided the person wants to break it. Often he doesn't. And why indeed should he if he has nothing better to do with his life? Or as happens to be the case with morphine, if he can live an essentially normal life while under its influence? That, of course, sounds completely unbelievable, or worse—testimony to our "addiction" to half a century of systematic official mendacity about opiates, which we can break only by suffering the intellectual withdrawal symptoms that go with giving up treasured falsehoods.

Actually, opium is much less toxic than alcohol. Moreover, just as it is possible to be an alcoholic and work and be productive, so it is (or rather, it used to be) possible to be an opium addict and work and be productive. Thomas De Quincey and Samuel Taylor Coleridge were both opium takers, and "Kubla Khan," considered one of the most beautiful poems in the English language, was written while Coleridge was under the influence of opium.[3] According to a definitive study by Light and others published by the American Medical Association in 1929, "morphine addiction is not characterized by physical deterioration or impairment of physical fitness. . . . There is no evidence of change in the circulatory, hepatic, renal, or endocrine functions. When it is considered that these subjects had been addicted for at least five years, some of them as long as twenty years, these negative observations are highly significant."[4] In a 1928 study, Lawrence Kolb, an assistant surgeon general of the United States Public Health Service, found that of 119 persons addicted to opiates through medical practice, 90 had good industrial records and only 29 had poor ones. . . .

I am not citing this evidence to recommend the opium habit. The point is that we must, in plain honesty, distinguish between pharmacological effects and personal inclinations. Some people take drugs to cope—to help them function and conform to social expectations. Others take them to cop out—to ritualize their refusal to function and conform to social expectations. Much of the drug abuse we now witness—perhaps nearly all of it—is of the second type. But instead of acknowledging that addicts are unable or unfit or unwilling to work and be normal, we prefer to believe that they act as they do because certain drugs—especially heroin, LSD, and the amphetamines—make them sick. If only we could get them well, so runs this comfortable and comforting view, they would become productive and useful citizens. To believe that is like believing that if an illiterate cigarette smoker would only stop smoking, he would become an Einstein. With a falsehood like that, one can go far. No wonder that politicians and psychiatrists love it.

The idea of free trade in drugs runs counter to another cherished notion of ours—namely, that everyone must work and that idleness is acceptable only under special conditions. In general, the obligation to work is greatest for healthy adult white males. We tolerate idleness on the part of children, women, blacks, the aged, and the sick, and we even accept the responsibility of supporting them. But the new wave of drug abuse affects mainly young adults, often white

males who are, in principle at least, capable of working and supporting themselves. But they refuse: they drop out, adopting a life-style in which *not* working, *not* supporting oneself, *not* being useful to others, are positive values. These people challenge some of the most basic values of our society. It is hardly surprising, then, that society wants to retaliate, to strike back. Even though it would be cheaper to support addicts on welfare than to "treat" them, doing so would be legitimizing their life-style. That, "normal" society refuses to do. Instead, the majority acts as if it felt that, so long as it is going to spend its money on addicts, it is going to get something out of it. What society gets out of its war on addiction is what every persecutory movement provides for the persecutors: by defining a minority as evil (or sick), the majority confirms itself as good (or healthy). (If that can be done for the victim's own good, so much the better.) In short, the war on addiction is a part of that vast modern enterprise which I have named the "manufacture of madness." It is indeed a therapeutic enterprise, but with this grotesque twist: its beneficiaries are the therapists, and its victims are the patients.

Most of all perhaps, the idea of free trade in narcotics frightens people because they believe that vast masses of our population would spend their days and nights smoking opium or mainlining heroin instead of working and shouldering their responsibilities as citizens. But that is a bugaboo that does not deserve to be taken seriously. Habits of work and idleness are deep-seated cultural patterns; I doubt that free trade in drugs would convert industrious people from hustlers into hippies at the stroke of a legislative pen.

The other side of the economic coin regarding drugs and drug controls is actually far more important. The government is now spending millions of dollars—the hard-earned wages of hard-working Americans—to support a vast and astronomically expensive bureaucracy whose efforts not only drain our economic resources and damage our civil liberties but create ever more addicts and, indirectly, the crime associated with the traffic in illicit drugs. Although my argument about drug taking is moral and political and does not depend upon showing that free trade in drugs would also have fiscal advantages over our present policies, let me indicate briefly some of the economic aspects of the drug-control problem.

On April 1, 1967, New York State's narcotics addiction-control program, hailed as "the most massive ever tried in the nation," went into effect. "The program, which may cost up to $400 million in three years," reported *The New York Times*, "was hailed by Governor Rockefeller as 'the start of an unending war.'"[5] Three years later, it was conservatively estimated that the number of addicts in the state had tripled or quadrupled. New York State Senator John Hughes reported that the cost of caring for each addict during that time was $12,000 per year (as against $4,000 per year for patients in state mental hospitals).[6] It was a great time, though, for some of the ex-addicts themselves. In New York City's Addiction Services Agency, one ex-addict started at $6,500 a year on November 27, 1967, and was making $16,000 seven months later. Another started at $6,500 on September 12, 1967, and went up to $18,100 by July 1, 1969.[7] The salaries of the medical bureaucrats in charge of the programs are similarly attractive. In short, the detection and rehabilitation of addicts is good business; and so was, in former days, the detection and rehabilitation of witches. We now know that the spread of witchcraft in the late Middle Ages was due more to the work of witchmongers than to the lure of witchcraft. Is it not possible that, similarly, the spread of addiction in our day is due more to the work of addictmongers than to the lure of narcotics?. . .

* * *

Clearly, the argument that marijuana—or heroin, or methadone, or morphine—is prohibited because it is addictive or dangerous cannot be supported by facts. For one thing, there are many drugs—from insulin to penicillin—that are neither addictive nor dangerous but are nevertheless also prohibited—they can be obtained only through a physician's prescription. For another, there are many things—from dynamite to guns—that are much more dangerous than narcotics (especially to others) but are not prohibited. As everyone knows, it is still possible in the United States to walk into a store and walk out with a shotgun. We enjoy that right not because we do not believe that guns are dangerous, but because we believe even more

strongly that civil liberties are precious. At the same time, it is not possible in the United States to walk into a store and walk out with a bottle of barbiturates, codeine, or other drugs. We are now deprived of that right because we have come to value medical paternalism more highly than the right to obtain and use drugs without recourse to medical intermediaries.

I submit, therefore, that our so-called drug-abuse problem is an integral part of our present social ethic, which accepts "protections" and repressions justified by appeals to health similar to those that medieval societies accepted when they were justified by appeals to faith.[8] Drug abuse (as we now know it) is one of the inevitable consequences of the medical monopoly over drugs—a monopoly whose value is daily acclaimed by science and law, state and church, the professions and the laity. As the Church formerly regulated man's relations to God, so Medicine now regulates his relations to his body. Deviation from the rules set forth by the Church was then considered to be heresy and was punished by appropriate theological sanctions, called *penance*; deviation from the rules set forth by Medicine is now considered to be drug abuse (or some sort of mental illness) and is punished by appropriate medical sanctions, called *treatment*.

The problem of drug abuse will thus be with us so long as we live under medical tutelage. This is not to say that if all access to drugs were free, some people would not medicate themselves in ways that might upset us or harm them. That of course is precisely what happened when religious practices became free.

What I am suggesting is that although addiction is ostensibly a medical and pharmacological problem, actually it is a moral and political problem. We talk as if we were trying to ascertain which drugs *are* toxic, but we act as if we were trying to decide which drugs *ought to be* prohibited.

We ought to know, however, that there is no necessary connection between facts and values, between what is and what ought to be. Thus, objectively quite harmful acts, objects, or persons may be accepted and tolerated—by minimizing their dangerousness. Conversely, objectively quite harmless acts, objects, or persons may be prohibited and persecuted—by exaggerating their dangerousness. It is always necessary to distinguish—and especially so when dealing with social policy—between description and prescription, fact and rhetoric, truth and falsehood.

To command adherence, social policy must be respected; and to be respected, it must be considered legitimate. In our society, there are two principal methods of legitimizing policy—social tradition and scientific judgment. More than anything else, time is the supreme ethical arbiter. Whatever a social practice might be, if people engage in it generation after generation, then that practice becomes acceptable.

Many opponents of illegal drugs admit that nicotine may be more harmful to health than marijuana; nevertheless, they argue that smoking cigarettes should be legal but smoking marijuana should not be, because the former habit is socially accepted while the latter is not. That is a perfectly reasonable argument. But let us understand it for what it is—a plea for legitimizing old and accepted practices and illegitimizing novel and unaccepted ones. It is a justification that rests on precedence, not on evidence.

The other method of legitimizing policy, increasingly more important in the modern world, is through the authority of science. In matters of health, a vast and increasingly elastic category, physicians thus play important roles as legitimizers and illegitimizers. One result is that, regardless of the pharmacological effects of a drug on the person who takes it, if he obtains it through a physician and uses it under medical supervision, that use is, ipso facto, legitimate and proper; but if he obtains it through nonmedical channels and uses it without medical supervision (and especially if the drug is illegal and the individual uses it solely for the purpose of altering his mental state), then that use is, ipso facto, illegitimate and improper. In short, being medicated by a doctor is drug use, while self-medication (especially with certain classes of drugs) is drug abuse.

That too is a perfectly reasonable arrangement. But let us understand it for what it is—a plea for legitimizing what doctors do, because they do it with good, therapeutic intent; and for illegitimizing what laymen do, because they do it with bad, self-abusive (masturbatory) intent. It is a justification that rests on the principles of professionalism, not of pharmacology.

That is why we applaud the systematic medical use of methadone and call it "treatment for heroin addiction," but decry the occasional nonmedical use of marijuana and call it "dangerous drug abuse."

Our present concept of drug abuse thus articulates and symbolizes a fundamental policy of scientific medicine—namely, that a layman should not medicate his own body but should place its medical care under the supervision of a duly accredited physician. Before the Reformation, the practice of true Christianity rested on a similar policy—namely, that a layman should not himself commune with God but should place his spiritual care under the supervision of a duly accredited priest. The self-interests of the Church and of Medicine in such policies are obvious enough. What might be less obvious is the interest of the laity in them: by delegating responsibility for the spiritual and medical welfare of the people to a class of authoritatively accredited specialists, those policies—and the practices they ensure—relieve individuals from assuming the burdens of those responsibilities for themselves. As I see it, our present problems with drug use and drug abuse are just one of the consequences of our pervasive ambivalence about personal autonomy and responsibility.

* * *

I propose a medical reformation analogous to the Protestant Reformation—specifically, a "protest" against the systematic mystification of man's relationship to his body and his professionalized separation from it. The immediate aim of the reform would be to remove the physician as intermediary between man and his body and to give the layman direct access to the language and contents of the pharmacopoeia. It is significant that until recently physicians wrote prescriptions in Latin and that medical diagnoses and treatments are still couched in a jargon whose chief aim is to awe and mystify the laity. If man had unencumbered access to his own body and the means of chemically altering it, it would spell the end of Medicine, at least as we now know it. That is why, with faith in Medicine so strong, there is little interest in this kind of medical reform: physicians fear the loss of their privileges; laymen, the loss of their protections.

Our present policies with respect to drug use and drug abuse thus constitute a covert plea for legitimizing certain privileges on the part of physicians and illegitimizing certain practices on the part of everyone else. The upshot is that we act as if we believed that only doctors should be allowed to dispense narcotics, just as we used to believe that only priests should be allowed to dispense holy water.

Finally, since luckily we still do not live in the utopian perfection of one world, our technical approach to the drug problem has led, and will undoubtedly continue to lead, to some curious attempts to combat it.

* * *

I believe that just as we regard freedom of speech and religion as fundamental rights, so we should also regard freedom of self-medication as a fundamental right; and that instead of mendaciously opposing or mindlessly promoting illicit drugs, we should, paraphrasing Voltaire, make this maxim our rule: I disapprove of what you take, but I will defend to the death your right to take it!

To be sure, like most rights, the right of self-medication should apply only to adults; and it should not be an unqualified right. Since these are important qualifications, it is necessary to specify their precise range.

John Stuart Mill said (approximately) that a person's right to swing his arm ends where his neighbor's nose begins. Similarly, the limiting condition with respect to self-medication should be the inflicting of actual (as against symbolic) harm on others.

Our present practices with respect to alcohol embody and reflect this individualistic ethic. We have the right to buy, possess, and consume alcoholic beverages. Regardless of how offensive drunkenness might be to a person, he cannot interfere with another person's right to become inebriated so long as that person drinks in the privacy of his own home or at some other appropriate location and so long as he conducts himself in an otherwise law-abiding manner. In short, we have a right to be intoxicated—in private. Public intoxication is considered to be an offense against others and is therefore a violation of the criminal law.

The same principle applies to sexual conduct. Sexual intercourse, especially between husband and wife, is surely a right. But it is a right that must be exercised at home or at some other appropriate location; it is not a right in a public park or on a downtown street. It makes sense that what is a right in one place may become, by virtue of its disruptive or disturbing effect on others, an offense somewhere else.

The right to self-medication should be hedged in by similar limits. Public intoxication, not only with alcohol but with any drug, should be an offense punishable by the criminal law. Furthermore, acts that may injure others—such as driving a car—should, when carried out in a drug-intoxicated state, be punished especially strictly and severely. The habitual use of certain drugs, such as alcohol and opiates, may also harm others indirectly by rendering the subject unmotivated for working and thus unemployed. In a society that supports the unemployed, such a person would, as a consequence of his own conduct, place a burden on the shoulders of his working neighbors. How society might best guard itself against that sort of hazard I cannot discuss here. However, it is obvious that prohibiting the use of habit-forming drugs offers no protection against that risk, but only adds to the tax burdens laid upon the productive members of society.

The right to self-medication must thus entail unqualified responsibility for the effects of one's drug-intoxicated behavior on others. For unless we are willing to hold ourselves responsible for our own behavior and hold others responsible for theirs, the liberty to ingest or inject drugs degenerates into a license to injure others. But here is the catch: we are exceedingly reluctant to hold people responsible for their misbehavior. That is why we prefer diminishing rights to increasing responsibilities. The former requires only the passing of laws, which can then be more or less freely violated or circumvented; whereas the latter requires prosecuting and punishing offenders, which can be accomplished only by just laws justly enforced. The upshot is that we increasingly substitute tenderhearted tyranny for tough-spirited liberty.

Such then would be the situation of adults were we to regard the freedom to take drugs as a fundamental right similar to the freedom to read and to worship.

What would be the situation of children? Since many people who are now said to be drug addicts or drug abusers are minors, it is especially important that we think clearly about this aspect of the problem.

I do not believe, and I do not advocate, that children should have a right to ingest, inject, or otherwise use any drug or substance they want. Children do not have the right to drive, drink, vote, marry, or make binding contracts. They acquire those rights at various ages, coming into their full possession at maturity, usually between the ages of eighteen and twenty-one. The right to self-medication should similarly be withheld until maturity.

* * *

In short, I suggest that "dangerous" drugs be treated more or less as alcohol and tobacco are treated now. (That does not mean that I believe the state should make their use a source of tax revenue.) Neither the use of narcotics nor their possession should be prohibited, but only their sale to minors. Of course, that would result in the ready availability of all kinds of drugs among minors—though perhaps their availability would be no greater than it is now but only more visible and hence more easily subject to proper controls. That arrangement would place responsibility for the use of all drugs by children where it belongs: on parents and their children. That is where the major responsibility rests for the use of alcohol and tobacco. It is a tragic symptom of our refusal to take personal liberty and responsibility seriously that there appears to be no public desire to assume a similar stance toward other dangerous drugs.

* * *

Sooner or later, we shall have to confront the basic moral dilemma underlying our drug problem: does a person have the right to take a drug—any drug—not because he needs it to cure an illness, but because he wants to take it?

The Declaration of Independence speaks of our inalienable right to "life, liberty, and the pursuit of happiness." How are we to interpret that phrase? By asserting that we ought to be free to pursue happiness by playing golf or watching television but not by drinking alcohol, or smoking marijuana, or ingesting amphetamines?

The Constitution and the Bill of Rights are silent on the subject of drugs. Their silence would seem to imply that the adult citizen has, or ought to have, the right to medicate his own body as he sees fit. Were that not the case, why should there have been a need for a constitutional amendment to outlaw drinking? But if ingesting alcohol was, and is now again, a constitutional right, is ingesting opium, or heroin, or barbiturates, or anything else not also such a right? If it is, then the Harrison Narcotic Act is not only a bad law but unconstitutional as well, because it prescribes in a legislative act what ought to be promulgated in a constitutional amendment.

The nagging questions remain. As American citizens, do we and should we have the right to take narcotics or other drugs? Further, if we take drugs and conduct ourselves as responsible and law-abiding citizens, do we and should we have a right to remain unmolested by the government? Lastly, if we take drugs and break the law, do we and should we have a right to be treated as persons accused of a crime rather than as patients accused of being mentally ill?

These are fundamental questions that are conspicuous by their absence from all contemporary discussions of problems of drug addiction and drug abuse. In this area as in so many others, we have allowed a moral problem to be disguised as a medical question and have then engaged in shadowboxing with metaphorical diseases and medical attempts, ranging from the absurd to the appalling, to combat them.

The result is that instead of debating the use of drugs in moral and political terms, we define our task as the ostensibly narrow technical problem of protecting people from poisoning themselves with substances for whose use they cannot possibly assume responsibility. That, I think, best explains the frightening national consensus against personal responsibility for taking drugs and for one's conduct while under their influence. In 1965, for example, when President Johnson sought a bill imposing tight federal controls over "pep pills" and "goof balls," the bill cleared the House by a unanimous vote, 402 to 0.

* * *

Finally, those repeated unanimous votes on far-reaching measures to combat drug abuse are bitter reminders that when the chips are really down, that is, when democratic lawmakers can preserve their intellectual and moral integrity only by going against certain popular myths, they prove to be either mindless or spineless. They prefer running with the herd to courting unpopularity and risking reelection.

After all is said and done—after millions of words are written, thousands of laws are enacted, and countless numbers of people are "treated" for "drug abuse"—it all comes down to whether we accept or reject the ethical principle John Stuart Mill so clearly enunciated in 1859:

> The only purpose for which power can be rightfully exercised over any member of a civilized community, against his will, is to prevent harm to others. His own good, either physical or moral, is not a sufficient warrant. He cannot rightfully be compelled to do or forebear because it will make him happier, because, in the opinions of others, to do so would be wise, or even right. . . . In the part [of his conduct] which merely concerns himself, his independence is, of right, absolute. Over himself, over his own body and mind, the individual is sovereign.[9]

The basic issue underlying the problem of addiction—and many other problems, such as sexual activity between consenting adults, pornography, contraception, gambling, and suicide—is simple but vexing: in a conflict between the individual and the state, where should the former's autonomy end and the latter's right to intervene begin?

One way out of the dilemma lies through concealment: by disguising the moral and political question as a medical and therapeutic problem, we can, to protect the physical and mental health of patients, exalt the state, oppress the individual, and claim benefits for both.

The other way out of it lies through confrontation: by recognizing the problem for what it is, we can choose to maximize the sphere of action of the state at the expense of the individual or of the individual at the expense of the state. In other words, we can commit ourselves to the view that the state, the representative of many, is more important than the individual and that it therefore has the right, indeed the duty, to regulate the life of the individual in the best interests of the group. Or we can commit ourselves to the view that individual dignity and liberty are the supreme values of life and that the foremost duty of the state is to protect and promote those values.

In short, we must choose between the ethic of collectivism and the ethic of individualism and pay the price of either—or of both.

NOTES

1. Quoted in L. C. Kolb, *Noyes' Modern Clinical Psychiatry*, 7th ed. (Philadelphia: Saunders, 1968), p. 516.

2. See my *The Manufacture of Madness: A Comparative Study of the Inquisition and the Mental Health Movement* (New York: Harper & Row, 1970), pp. 180–206.

3. A. Montagu, "The Long Search for Euphoria," *Reflections* 1 (May–June 1966): 65.

4. A. B. Light et al., *Opium Addiction* (Chicago: American Medical Association, 1929), p. 115; quoted in Alfred R. Lindesmith, *Addiction and Opiates* (Chicago: Aldine, 1968), p. 40.

5. *The New York Times*, April 1, 1967.

6. Editorial, "About Narcotics," *Syracuse Herald-Journal*, March 6, 1969.

7. *The New York Times*, June 29, 1970.

8. See my *Ideology and Insanity: Essays on the Psychiatric Dehumanization of Man* (Garden City, N.Y.: Doubleday, Anchor Press, 1970).

9. J. S. Mill, *On Liberty* (Chicago: Regnery, 1955), p. 13.

Against the Legalization of Drugs

JAMES Q. WILSON

In 1972, the President appointed me chairman of the National Advisory Council for Drug Abuse Prevention. Created by Congress, the Council was charged with providing guidance on how best to coordinate the national war on drugs. (Yes, we called it a war then, too.) In those days, the drug we were chiefly concerned with was heroin. When I took office, heroin use had been increasing dramatically. Everybody was worried that this increase would continue. Such phrases as "heroin epidemic" were commonplace.

That same year, the eminent economist Milton Friedman published an essay in *Newsweek* in which he called for legalizing heroin. His argument was on two grounds: as a matter of ethics, the government has no right to tell people not to use heroin (or to drink or to commit suicide); as a matter of economics, the prohibition of drug use imposes costs on society that far exceed the benefits. Others, such as the psychoanalyst Thomas Szasz, made the same argument.

We did not take Friedman's advice. (Government commissions rarely do.) I do not recall that we even discussed legalizing heroin, though we did discuss (but did not take action on) legalizing a drug, cocaine, that many people then argued was benign. Our marching orders were to figure out how to win the war on heroin, not to run up the white flag of surrender.

That was 1972. Today, we have the same number of heroin addicts that we had then—half a million, give or take a few thousand. Having that many heroin addicts is no trivial matter; these people deserve our attention. But not having had an increase in that number for over fifteen years is also something that deserves our attention. What happened to the "heroin epidemic" that many people once thought would overwhelm us?

The facts are clear: a more or less stable pool of heroin addicts has been getting older, with relatively few new recruits. In 1976 the average age of heroin users who appeared in hospital emergency rooms was about twenty-seven; ten years later it was thirty-two. More than two-thirds of all heroin users appearing in emergency rooms are now over the age of thirty. Back in the early 1970's, when heroin got onto the national political agenda, the typical heroin addict was much younger, often a teenager. Household surveys show the same thing—the rate of opiate use (which includes heroin) has been flat for the better part of two decades. More fine-grained studies of inner-city neighborhoods confirm this. John Boyle and Ann Brunswick found that the percentage of young blacks in Harlem who used heroin fell from 8 percent in 1970–71 to about 3 percent in 1975–76.

Why did heroin lose its appeal for young people? When the young blacks in Harlem were asked why they stopped, more than half mentioned "trouble with the law" or "high cost" (and high cost is, of course, directly the result of law enforcement). Two-thirds said that heroin hurt their health; nearly all said they had had a bad experience with it. We need not rely, however, simply on what they said. In New York City in 1973–75, the street price of heroin rose dramatically and its purity sharply declined, probably as a result of the heroin shortage caused by the success of the Turkish government in reducing the supply of opium base and of the French government in closing down heroin-processing laboratories located in and around Marseilles. These were short-lived gains for, just as Friedman predicted, alternative sources of supply—mostly in Mexico—quickly emerged. But the three-year heroin shortage interrupted the easy recruitment of new users.

Health and related problems were no doubt part of the reason for the reduced flow of recruits. Over the preceding years, Harlem youth had watched as more and more heroin users died of overdoses, were poisoned by adulterated doses, or acquired hepatitis from dirty needles. The word got around: heroin can kill you. By 1974 new hepatitis cases and drug-overdose deaths had dropped to a fraction of what they had been in 1970.

Alas, treatment did not seem to explain much of the cessation in drug use. Treatment programs can and do help heroin addicts, but treatment did not explain the drop in the number of *new* users (who by definition had never been in treatment) nor even much of the reduction in the number of experienced users.

No one knows how much of the decline to attribute to personal observation as opposed to high prices or reduced supply. But other evidence suggests strongly that price and supply played a large role. In 1972 the National Advisory Council was especially worried by the prospect that U.S. servicemen returning to this country from Vietnam would bring their heroin habits with them. Fortunately, a brilliant study by Lee Robins of Washington University in St. Louis put that fear to rest. She measured drug use of Vietnam veterans shortly after they had returned home. Though many had used heroin regularly while in Southeast Asia, most gave up the habit when back in the United States. The reason: here, heroin was less available and sanctions on its use were more pronounced. Of course, if a veteran had been willing to pay enough—which might have meant traveling to another city and would certainly have meant making an illegal contact with a disreputable dealer in a threatening neighborhood in order to acquire a (possibly) dangerous dose—he could have sustained his drug habit. Most veterans were unwilling to pay this price, and so their drug use declined or disappeared.

RELIVING THE PAST

Suppose we had taken Friedman's advice in 1972. What would have happened? We cannot be entirely certain, but at a minimum we would have placed the young heroin addicts (and, above all, the prospective addicts) in a very different position from the one in which they actually found themselves. Heroin would have been legal. Its price would have been reduced by 95 percent (minus whatever we chose to recover in taxes.) Now that it could be sold by the same people who make aspirin, its quality would have been assured—no poisons, no adulterants. Sterile hypodermic needles would have been readily available at the neighborhood drugstore, probably at the same counter where the heroin was sold. No need to travel to big cities or unfamiliar neighborhoods—heroin could have been purchased anywhere, perhaps by mail order.

There would no longer have been any financial or medical reason to avoid heroin use. Anybody could have afforded it. We might have tried to prevent children from buying it, but as we have learned from our efforts to prevent minors from buying alcohol and tobacco, young people have a way of penetrating markets theoretically reserved for adults. Returning Vietnam veterans would have discovered that Omaha and Raleigh had been converted into the pharmaceutical equivalent of Saigon.

Under these circumstances, can we doubt for a moment that heroin use would have grown exponentially? Or that a vastly larger supply of new users would have been recruited? Professor Friedman is a Nobel Prize-winning economist whose understanding of market forces is profound. What did he think would happen to consumption under his legalized regime? Here are his words: "Legalizing drugs might increase the number of addicts, but it is not clear that it would. Forbidden fruit is attractive, particularly to the young."

Really? I suppose that we should expect no increase in Porsche sales if we cut the price by 95 percent, no increase in whiskey sales if we cut the price by a comparable amount—because young people only want fast cars and strong liquor when they are "forbidden." Perhaps Friedman's uncharacteristic lapse from the obvious implications of price theory can be explained by a misunderstanding of how drug users are recruited. In his 1972 essay he said that "drug addicts are deliberately made by pushers, who give likely prospects their first few doses free." If drugs were legal it would not pay anybody to produce addicts, because everybody would buy from the cheapest source. But as every drug expert knows, pushers do not produce addicts. Friends or acquaintances do. In fact, pushers are usually reluctant to deal with non-users because a non-user could be an undercover cop. Drug use spreads in the same way any fad or fashion spreads: somebody who is already a user urges his friends to try, or simply shows already-eager friends how to do it.

But we need not rely on speculation, however plausible, that lowered prices and more abundant supplies would have increased heroin usage. Great Britain once followed such a policy and with almost exactly those results. Until the mid-1960's, British physicians were allowed to prescribe heroin to certain classes of addicts. (Possessing these drugs without a doctor's prescription remained a criminal offense.) For many years this policy worked well enough because the addict patients were typically middle-class people who had become dependent on opiate painkillers while undergoing hospital treatment. There was no drug culture. The British system worked for many years, not because it prevented drug abuse, but because there was no problem of drug abuse that would test the system.

All that changed in the 1960's. A few unscrupulous doctors began passing out heroin in wholesale amounts. One doctor prescribed almost 600,000 heroin tablets—that is, over thirteen pounds—in just one year. A youthful drug culture emerged with a demand for drugs far different from that of the older addicts. As a result, the British government required doctors to refer users to government-run clinics to receive their heroin.

But the shift to clinics did not curtail the growth in heroin use. Throughout the 1960's the number of addicts increased—the late John Kaplan of Stanford estimated by fivefold—in part as a result of the diversion of heroin from clinic patients to new users on the streets. An addict would bargain with the clinic doctor over how big a dose he would receive. The patient wanted as much as he could get, the doctor wanted to give as little as was needed. The patient had an advantage in this conflict because the doctor could not be certain how much was really needed. Many patients would use some of their "maintenance" dose and sell the remaining part to friends, thereby recruiting new addicts. As the clinics learned of this, they began to shift their treatment away from heroin and toward methadone, an addictive drug that, when taken orally, does not produce a "high" but will block the withdrawal pains associated with heroin abstinence.

Whether what happened in England in the 1960's was a mini-epidemic or an epidemic depends on whether one looks at numbers or at rates of change.

Compared to the United States, the numbers were small. In 1960 there were 68 heroin addicts known to the British government; by 1968 there were 2,000 in treatment and many more who refused treatment. (They would refuse in part because they did not want to get methadone at a clinic if they could get heroin on the street.) Richard Hartnoll estimates that the actual number of addicts in England is five times the number officially registered. At a minimum, the number of British addicts increased by thirtyfold in ten years; the actual increase may have been much larger.

In the early 1980's the numbers began to rise again, and this time nobody doubted that a real epidemic was at hand. The increase was estimated to be 40 percent a year. By 1982 there were thought to be 20,000 heroin users in London alone. Geoffrey Pearson reports that many cities—Glasgow, Liverpool, Manchester, and Sheffield among them—were now experiencing a drug problem that once had been largely confined to London. The problem, again, was supply. The country was being flooded with cheap, high-quality heroin, first from Iran and then from Southeast Asia.

The United States began the 1960's with a much larger number of heroin addicts and probably a bigger at-risk population than was the case in Great Britain. Even though it would be foolhardy to suppose that the British system, if installed here, would have worked the same way or with the same results, it would be equally foolhardy to suppose that a combination of heroin available from leaky clinics and from street dealers who faced only minimal law-enforcement risks would not have produced a much greater increase in heroin use than we actually experienced. My guess is that if we had allowed either doctors or clinics to prescribe heroin, we would have had far worse results than were produced in Britain, if for no other reason than the vastly larger number of addicts with which we began. We would have had to find some way to police thousands (not scores) of physicians and hundreds (not dozens) of clinics. If the British civil service found it difficult to keep heroin in the hands of addicts and out of the hands of recruits when it was dealing with a few hundred people, how well would the American civil service have accomplished the same tasks when dealing with tens of thousands of people?

BACK TO THE FUTURE

Now cocaine, especially in its potent form, crack, is the focus of attention. Now as in 1972 the government is trying to reduce its use. Now as then some people are advocating legalization. Is there any more reason to yield to those arguments today than there was almost two decades ago?

I think not. If we had yielded in 1972 we almost certainly would have had today a permanent population of several million, not several hundred thousand, heroin addicts. If we yield now we will have a far more serious problem with cocaine.

Crack is worse than heroin by almost any measure. Heroin produces a pleasant drowsiness and, if hygienically administered, has only the physical side effects of constipation and sexual impotence. Regular heroin use incapacitates many users, especially poor ones, for any productive work or social responsibility. They will sit nodding on a street corner, helpless but at least harmless. By contrast, regular cocaine use leaves the user neither helpless nor harmless. When smoked (as with crack) or injected, cocaine produces instant, intense, and short-lived euphoria. The experience generates a powerful desire to repeat it. If the drug is readily available, repeat use will occur. Those people who progress to "bingeing" on cocaine become devoted to the drug and its effects to the exclusion of almost all other considerations—job, family, children, sleep, food, even sex. Dr. Frank Gawin at Yale and Dr. Everett Ellinwood at Duke report that a substantial percentage of all high-dose, binge users become uninhibited, impulsive, hypersexual, compulsive, irritable, and hyperactive. Their moods vacillate dramatically, leading at times to violence and homicide.

Women are much more likely to use crack than heroin, and if they are pregnant, the effects on their babies are tragic. Douglas Besharov, who has been following the effects of drugs on infants for twenty years, writes that nothing he learned about heroin prepared him for the devastation of cocaine. Cocaine harms the fetus and can lead to physical deformities or neurological damage. Some crack babies have for all practical purposes suffered a disabling stroke while still in the womb. The long-term consequences of this brain damage are lowered cognitive ability and the onset of mood disorders. Besharov estimates that about 30,000 to 50,000 such babies are born every year, about 7,000 in New York City alone. There may be ways to treat such infants, but from everything we now know the treatment will be long, difficult, and expensive. Worse, the mothers who are most likely to produce crack babies are precisely the ones who, because of poverty or temperament, are least able and willing to obtain such treatment. In fact, anecdotal evidence suggests that crack mothers are likely to abuse their infants.

The notion that abusing drugs such as cocaine is a "victimless crime" is not only absurd but dangerous. Even ignoring the fetal drug syndrome, crack-dependent people are, like heroin addicts, individuals who regularly victimize their children by neglect, their spouses by improvidence, their employers by lethargy, and their co-workers by carelessness. Society is not and could never be a collection of autonomous individuals. We all have a stake in ensuring that each of us displays a minimal level of dignity, responsibility, and empathy. We cannot, of course, coerce people into goodness, but we can and should insist that some standards must be met if society itself—on which the very existence of the human personality depends—is to persist. Drawing the line that defines those standards is difficult and contentious, but if crack and heroin use do not fall below it, what does?

The advocates of legalization will respond by suggesting that my picture is overdrawn. Ethan Nadelmann of Princeton argues that the risk of legalization is less than most people suppose. Over 20 million Americans between the ages of eighteen and twenty-five have tried cocaine (according to a government survey), but only a quarter million use it daily. From this Nadelmann concludes that at most 3 percent of all young people who try cocaine develop a problem with it. The implication is clear: make the drug legal and we only have to worry about 3 percent of our youth.

The implication rests on a logical fallacy and a factual error. The fallacy is this: the percentage of occasional cocaine users who become binge users *when the drug is illegal* (and thus expensive and hard to find) tells us nothing about the percentage who will become dependent when the drug is legal (and thus cheap and abundant). Drs. Gawin and Ellinwood report, in common with several other researchers, that controlled or occasional use of cocaine changes to compulsive and frequent use "when access to the drug increases" or when the user switches from snorting to smoking. More cocaine more potently administered alters, perhaps sharply, the proportion of "controlled" users who become heavy users.

The factual error is this: the federal survey Nadelmann quotes was done in 1985, *before* crack had become common. Thus the probability of becoming dependent on cocaine was derived from the responses of users who snorted the drug. The speed and potency of cocaine's action increases dramatically when it is smoked. We do not yet know how greatly the advent of crack increases the risk of dependency, but all the clinical evidence suggests that the increase is likely to be large.

It is possible that some people will not become heavy users even when the drug is readily available in its most potent form. So far there are no scientific grounds for predicting who will and who will not become dependent. Neither socioeconomic background nor personality traits differentiate between casual and intensive users. Thus, the only way to settle the question of who is correct about the effect of easy availability on drug use, Nadelmann or Gawin and Ellinwood, is to try it and see. But that social experiment is so risky as to be no experiment at all, for if cocaine is legalized and if the rate of its abusive use increases dramatically, there is no way to put the genie back in the bottle, and it is not a kindly genie.

HAVE WE LOST?

Many people who agree that there are risks in legalizing cocaine or heroin still favor it because, they think, we have lost the war on drugs. "Nothing we have done has worked" and the current federal policy is just "more of the same." Whatever the costs of greater drug use, surely they would be less than the costs of our present, failed efforts.

That is exactly what I was told in 1972—and heroin is not quite as bad a drug as cocaine. We did not surrender and we did not lose. We did not win, either.

What the nation accomplished then was what most efforts to save people from themselves accomplish: the problem was contained and the number of victims minimized, all at a considerable cost in law enforcement and increased crime. Was the cost worth it? I think so, but others may disagree. What are the lives of would-be addicts worth? I recall some people saying to me then, "Let them kill themselves." I was appalled. Happily, such views did not prevail.

Have we lost today? Not at all. High-rate cocaine use is not commonplace. The National Institute of Drug Abuse (NIDA) reports that less than 5 percent of high-school seniors used cocaine within the last thirty days. Of course this survey misses young people who have dropped out of school and miscounts those who lie on the questionnaire, but even if we inflate the NIDA estimate by some plausible percentage, it is still not much above 5 percent. Medical examiners reported in 1987 that about 1,500 died from cocaine use; hospital emergency rooms reported about 30,000 admissions related to cocaine abuse.

These are not small numbers, but neither are they evidence of a nationwide plague that threatens to engulf us all. Moreover, cities vary greatly in the proportion of people who are involved with cocaine. To get city-level data we need to turn to drug tests carried out on arrested persons, who obviously are more likely to be drug users than the average citizen. The National Institute of Justice, through its Drug Use Forecasting (DUF) project, collects urinalysis data on arrestees in 22 cities. As we have already seen, opiate (chiefly heroin) use has been flat or declining in most of these cities over the last decade. Cocaine use has gone up sharply, but with great variation among cities. New York, Philadelphia, and Washington, D.C., all report that two-thirds or more of their arrestees tested positive for cocaine, but in Portland, San Antonio, and Indianapolis the percentage was one-third or less.

In some neighborhoods, of course, matters have reached crisis proportions. Gangs control the streets, shootings terrorize residents, and drug-dealing occurs in plain view. The police seem barely able to contain matters. But in these neighborhoods—unlike at Palo Alto cocktail parties—the people are not calling for legalization, they are calling for help. And often not much help has come. Many cities are willing to do almost anything about the drug problem except spend more money on it. The federal government cannot change that; only local voters and politicians can. It is not clear that they will.

It took about ten years to contain heroin. We have had experience with crack for only about three or four years. Each year we spend perhaps $11 billion on law enforcement (and some of that goes to deal with marijuana) and perhaps $2 billion on treatment. Large sums, but not sums that should lead anyone to say, "We just can't afford this any more."

The illegality of drugs increases crime, partly because some users turn to crime to pay for their habits, partly because some users are stimulated by certain drugs (such as crack or PCP) to act more violently or ruthlessly than they otherwise would, and partly because criminal organizations seeking to control drug supplies use force to manage their markets. These also are serious costs, but no one knows how much they would be reduced if drugs were legalized. Addicts would no longer steal to pay black-market prices for drugs, a real gain. But some, perhaps a great deal, of that gain would be offset by the great increase in the number of addicts. These people, nodding on heroin or living in the delusion-ridden high of cocaine, would hardly be ideal employees. Many would steal simply to support themselves, since snatch-and-grab, opportunistic crime can be manged [*sic*] even by people unable to hold a regular job or plan an elaborate crime. Those British addicts who get their supplies from government clinics are not models of law-abiding decency. Most are in crime, and though their per-capita rate of criminality may be lower thanks to the cheapness of their drugs, the total volume of crime they produce may be quite large. Of course, society could decide to support all unemployable addicts on welfare, but that would mean that gains from lowered rates of crime would have to be offset by large increases in welfare budgets.

Proponents of legalization claim that the costs of having more addicts around would be largely if not entirely offset by having more money available with which to treat and care for them. The money would come from taxes levied on the sale of heroin and cocaine.

To obtain this fiscal dividend, however, legalization's supporters must first solve an economic dilemma. If they want to raise a lot of money to pay for welfare and treatment, the tax rate on the drugs will have to be quite high. Even if they themselves do not want a high rate, the politicians' love of "sin taxes" would probably guarantee that it would be high anyway. But the higher the tax, the higher the price of the drug, and the higher the price the greater the likelihood that addicts will turn to crime to find the money for it and that criminal organizations will be formed to sell tax-free drugs at below-market rates. If we managed to keep taxes (and thus prices) low, we would get that much less money to pay for welfare and treatment and more people could afford to become addicts. There may be an optimal tax rate for drugs that maximizes revenue while minimizing crime, bootlegging, and the recruitment of new addicts, but our experience with alcohol does not suggest that we know how to find it.

THE BENEFITS OF ILLEGALITY

The advocates of legalization find nothing to be said in favor of the current system except, possibly, that it keeps the number of addicts smaller than it would otherwise be. In fact, the benefits are more substantial than that.

First, treatment. All the talk about providing "treatment on demand" implies that there is a demand for treatment. That is not quite right. There are some drug-dependent people who genuinely want treatment and will remain in it if offered; they should receive it. But there are far more who want only short-term help after a bad crash; once stabilized and bathed, they are back on the street again, hustling. And even many of the addicts who enroll in a program honestly wanting help drop out after a short while when they discover that help takes time and commitment. Drug-dependent people have very short time horizons and a weak capacity for commitment. These two groups—those looking for a quick fix and those unable to stick with a long-term fix—are not easily helped. Even if we increase the number of treatment slots—as we should—we would have to do something to make treatment more effective.

One thing that can often make it more effective is compulsion. Douglas Anglin of UCLA, in common with many other researchers, has found that the longer one stays in a treatment program, the better the chances of a reduction in drug dependency. But he, again like most other researchers, has found that drop-out rates are high. He has also found, however, that patients who enter treatment under legal compulsion stay in the program longer than those not subject to such pressure. His research on the California civil-commitment program, for example, found that heroin users involved with its required drug-testing program had over the long term a lower rate of heroin use than similar addicts who were free of such constraints. If for many addicts compulsion is a useful component of treatment, it is not clear how compulsion could be achieved in a society in which purchasing, possessing, and using the drug were legal. It could be managed, I suppose, but I would not want to have to answer the challenge from the American Civil Liberties Union that it is wrong to compel a person to undergo treatment for consuming a legal commodity.

Next, education. We are now investing substantially in drug-education programs in the schools. Though we do not yet know for certain what will work, there are some promising leads. But I wonder how credible such programs would be if they were aimed at dissuading children from doing something perfectly legal. We could, of course, treat drug education like smoking education: inhaling crack and inhaling tobacco are both legal, but you should not do it because it is bad for you. That tobacco is bad for you is easily shown; the Surgeon General has seen to that. But what do we say about crack? It is pleasurable, but devoting yourself to so much pleasure is not a good idea (though perfectly legal)? Unlike tobacco, cocaine will not give you cancer or emphysema, but it will lead you to neglect your duties to family, job, and neighborhood? Everybody is doing cocaine, but you should not?

Again, it might be possible under a legalized regime to have effective drug-prevention programs, but their effectiveness would depend heavily, I think, on first having decided that cocaine use, like tobacco use, is purely a matter of practical consequences; no

fundamental moral significance attaches to either. But if we believe—as I do—that dependency on certain mind-altering drugs *is* a moral issue and that their illegality rests in part on their immorality, then legalizing them undercuts, if it does not eliminate altogether, the moral message.

That message is at the root of the distinction we now make between nicotine and cocaine. Both are highly addictive; both have harmful physical effects. But we treat the two drugs differently, not simply because nicotine is so widely used as to be beyond the reach of effective prohibition, but because its use does not destroy the user's essential humanity. Tobacco shortens one's life, cocaine debases it. Nicotine alters one's habits, cocaine alters one's soul. The heavy use of crack, unlike the heavy use of tobacco, corrodes those natural sentiments of sympathy and duty that constitute our human nature and make possible our social life. To say, as does Nadelmann, that distinguishing morally between tobacco and cocaine is "little more than a transient prejudice" is close to saying that morality itself is but a prejudice.

THE ALCOHOL PROBLEM

Now we have arrived where many arguments about legalizing drugs begin: is there any reason to treat heroin and cocaine differently from the way we treat alcohol?

There is no easy answer to that question because, as with so many human problems, one cannot decide simply on the basis either of moral principles or of individual consequences; one has to temper any policy by a common-sense judgment of what is possible. Alcohol, like heroin, cocaine, PCP, and marijuana, is a drug—that is, a mood-altering substance—and consumed to excess it certainly has harmful consequences: auto accidents, barroom fights, bedroom shootings. It is also, for some people, addictive. We cannot confidently compare the addictive powers of these drugs, but the best evidence suggests that crack and heroin are much more addictive than alcohol.

Many people, Nadelmann included, argue that since the health and financial costs of alcohol abuse are so much higher than those of cocaine or heroin abuse, it is hypocritical folly to devote our efforts to preventing cocaine or drug use. But as Mark Kleiman of Harvard has pointed out, this comparison is quite misleading. What Nadelmann is doing is showing that a *legalized* drug (alcohol) produces greater social harm than *illegal* ones (cocaine and heroin). But of course. Suppose that in the 1920's we had made heroin and cocaine legal and alcohol illegal. Can anyone doubt that Nadelmann would now be writing that it is folly to continue our ban on alcohol because cocaine and heroin are so much more harmful?

And let there be no doubt about it—widespread heroin and cocaine use are associated with all manner of ills. Thomas Bewley found that the mortality rate of British heroin addicts in 1968 was 28 times as high as the death rate of the same age group of non-addicts, even though in England at the time an addict could obtain free or low-cost heroin and clean needles from British clinics. Perform the following mental experiment: suppose we legalized heroin and cocaine in this country. In what proportion of auto fatalities would the state police report that the driver was nodding off on heroin or recklessly driving on a coke high? In what proportion of spouse-assault and child-abuse cases would the local police report that crack was involved? In what proportion of industrial accidents would safety investigators report that the forklift or drill-press operator was in a drug-induced stupor or frenzy? We do not know exactly what the proportion would be, but anyone who asserts that it would not be much higher than it is now would have to believe that these drugs have little appeal except when they are illegal. And that is nonsense.

An advocate of legalization might concede that social harm—perhaps harm equivalent to that already produced by alcohol—would follow from making cocaine and heroin generally available. But at least, he might add, we would have the problem "out in the open" where it could be treated as a matter of "public health." That is well and good, *if* we knew how to treat—that is, cure—heroin and cocaine abuse. But we do not know how to do it for all the people who would need such help. We are having only limited success in coping with chronic alcoholics. Addictive behavior is immensely difficult to change, and the best methods

for changing it—living in drug-free therapeutic communities, becoming faithful members of Alcoholics Anonymous or Narcotics Anonymous—require great personal commitment, a quality that is, alas, in short supply among the very persons—young people, disadvantaged people—who are often most at risk for addiction.

Suppose that today we had, not 15 million alcohol abusers, but half a million. Suppose that we already knew what we have learned from our long experience with the widespread use of alcohol. Would we make whiskey legal? I do not know, but I suspect there would be a lively debate. The Surgeon General would remind us of the risks alcohol poses to pregnant women. The National Highway Traffic Safety Administration would point to the likelihood of more highway fatalities caused by drunk drivers. The Food and Drug Administration might find that there is a nontrivial increase in cancer associated with alcohol consumption. At the same time the police would report great difficulty in keeping illegal whiskey out of our cities, officers being corrupted by bootleggers, and alcohol addicts often resorting to crime to feed their habit. Libertarians, for their part, would argue that every citizen has a right to drink anything he wishes and that drinking is, in any event, a "victimless crime."

However the debate might turn out, the central fact would be that the problem was still, at that point, a small one. The government cannot legislate away the addictive tendencies in all of us, nor can it remove completely even the most dangerous addictive substances. But it can cope with harms when the harms are still manageable.

SCIENCE AND ADDICTION

One advantage of containing a problem while it is still containable is that it buys time for science to learn more about it and perhaps to discover a cure. Almost unnoticed in the current debate over legalizing drugs is that basic science has made rapid strides in identifying the underlying neurological processes involved in some forms of addiction. Stimulants such as cocaine and amphetamines alter the way certain brain cells communicate with one another. That alteration is complex and not entirely understood, but in simplified form it involves modifying the way in which a neurotransmitter called dopamine sends signals from one cell to another.

When dopamine crosses the synapse between two cells, it is in effect carrying a message from the first cell to activate the second one. In certain parts of the brain that message is experienced as pleasure. After the message is delivered, the dopamine returns to the first cell. Cocaine apparently blocks this return, or "reuptake," so that the excited cell and others nearby continue to send pleasure messages. When the exaggerated high produced by cocaine-influenced dopamine finally ends, the brain cells may (in ways that are still a matter of dispute) suffer from an extreme lack of dopamine, thereby making the individual unable to experience any pleasure at all. This would explain why cocaine users often feel so depressed after enjoying the drug. Stimulants may also affect the way in which other neurotransmitters, such as serotonin and noradrenaline, operate.

Whatever the exact mechanism may be, once it is identified it becomes possible to use drugs to block either the effect of cocaine or its tendency to produce dependency. There have already been experiments using desipramine, imipramine, bromocriptine, carbamazepine, and other chemicals. There are some promising results.

Tragically, we spend very little on such research, and the agencies funding it have not in the past occupied very influential or visible posts in the federal bureaucracy. If there is one aspect of the "war on drugs" metaphor that I dislike, it is its tendency to focus attention almost exclusively on the troops in the trenches, whether engaged in enforcement or treatment, and away from the research-and-development efforts back on the home front where the war may ultimately be decided.

I believe that the prospects of scientists in controlling addiction will be strongly influenced by the size and character of the problem they face. If the problem is a few hundred thousand chronic, high-dose users of an illegal product, the chances of making a difference at a reasonable cost will be much greater than if the problem is a few million chronic users of legal substances. Once a drug is legal, not only will its use increase but many of those who then use it will prefer the drug to the treatment: they will want the pleasure, whatever the cost to themselves or their families, and they will resist—probably successfully—any effort to wean them away from experiencing the high that comes from inhaling a legal substance.

IF I AM WRONG . . .

No one can know what our society would be like if we changed the law to make access to cocaine, heroin, and PCP easier. I believe, for reasons given, that the result would be a sharp increase in use, a more widespread degradation of the human personality, and a greater rate of accidents and violence.

I may be wrong. If I am, then we will needlessly have incurred heavy costs in law enforcement and some forms of criminality. But if I am right, and the legalizers prevail anyway, then we will have consigned millions of people, hundreds of thousands of infants, and hundreds of neighborhoods to a life of oblivion and disease. To the lives and families destroyed by alcohol we will have added countless more destroyed by cocaine, heroin, PCP, and whatever else a basement scientist can invent.

Human character is formed by society; indeed, human character is inconceivable without society, and good character is less likely in a bad society. Will we, in the name of an abstract doctrine of radical individualism, and with the false comfort of suspect predictions, decide to take the chance that somehow individual decency can survive amid a more general level of degradation?

I think not. The American people are too wise for that, whatever the academic essayists and cocktail-party pundits may say. But if Americans today are less wise than I suppose, then Americans at some future time will look back on us now and wonder, what kind of people were they that they could have done such a thing?

Gun Control

HUGH LaFOLLETTE

Many of us assume that we must either oppose or support gun control. Not so. We have a range of alternatives. Even this way of speaking oversimplifies our choices since there are two distinct scales on which to place alternatives. One scale concerns the degree (if at all) to which guns should be abolished. This scale moves from those who want no abolition (NA) of any guns, through those who want moderate abolition (MA)— that is, to forbid access to some subclasses of guns—to those who want absolute abolition (AA). The second scale concerns the restrictions (if any) on those guns that are available to private citizens. This scale moves from those who want absolute restrictions (AR) through those who want moderate restrictions (MR) to those who want no restrictions (NR) at all. Restrictions vary not only in strength but also in content. We could restrict who owns guns, how they obtain them, where and how they store them, and where and how they carry them.

Our options are further complicated by the union of these scales. On one extreme no private citizen can own any guns (AA, which is functionally equivalent to AR), while at the other extreme, every private citizen can own any gun with no restrictions (NA+NR). But once we leave those extremes, which few people hold, the options are defined by a pair of coordinates along these distinct scales. While most people embrace positions on the "same" end of both scales, others embrace more exotic mixtures: some will want few weapons available to private citizens but virtually no restrictions on those guns that are available (MA+NR), while others may prefer making most guns available but want to seriously restrict them (NA+MR).

So our choice is not merely to support or oppose gun control but to decide *who* can own *which* guns under *what conditions.* Although I cannot pretend to provide a definitive account here, I can isolate the central issues

and offer the broad outline of an appropriate solution. To simplify discussion, I adopt the following locutions: those opposed to most abolition and most restrictions advocate a "serious right to bear arms," while those supporting more widespread abolition and more substantial restrictions are "gun control advocates." This simplification, of course, masks significant disagreements among advocates of each position.

I. JUSTIFYING PRIVATE OWNERSHIP OF GUNS

A. A Moral Question

Do citizens have a "serious right to bear arms"? This is a moral question, not a constitutional one. For even if the Constitution did grant this right, we should determine if there are sufficiently compelling arguments against private gun ownership to warrant changing the Constitution. By contrast, if this were not a constitutional right, we should determine if there are strong reasons why the state should not ban or control guns and if these reasons are sufficiently compelling to make this a constitutional right. Most defenders of private gun ownership claim we do have a moral right—as well as a constitutional one—and that this right is not an ordinary right but a fundamental one.

1. A fundamental right.—If they are correct, they would have the justificatory upper hand. Were this a fundamental right, it would not be enough to show that society would benefit from controlling access to guns.[1] The arguments for gun control would have to be overwhelming. Yet there is also a hefty cost in claiming that this is a fundamental right: the evidence for the right must meet especially rigorous standards.

What makes a right fundamental? A fundamental right is a non-derivative right protecting a *fundamental* interest. Not every interest we individually cherish is fundamental. Since most interests are prized by someone, such a notion of "fundamental interest" would be anemic, serving no special justificatory role. Fundamental interests are special; they are integrally related to a

Hugh LaFollette, "Gun Control," *Ethics* 110 (January 2000): 263–81, © 2000 by The University of Chicago. Reprinted by permission of The University of Chicago Press.

person's chance of living a good life, *whatever her particular interests, desires, and beliefs happen to be.* For example, living in a society that protects speech creates an environment within which each of us can pursue our particular interests, goals, needs, and development, whatever our interests happen to be. Is the purported right to bear arms like this paradigmatic fundamental right?

Even if it were, that would not establish straightforwardly that it is impermissible to abolish or restrict private ownership of guns. After all, fundamental rights standardly have conditions, boundaries, or restrictions on them. Some rights, like the right to vote, are *conditional* upon reaching a specified age, and they can be *forfeited* by emigrants and imprisoned felons. In addition, most right tokens can be *restricted* or *overridden* when the exercise of that right harms others. For example, my right to free religious expression gives me wide discretion in how I exercise my religion. I can remove my kids from high school and exclude them from selected school activities (*Wisconsin v. Yoder*, 406 U.S. 205 [1972]; *Moody v. Cronin*, 484 F. Supp. 270 [1979]). I can sacrifice animals (*Church of the Lukumi Babalu Aye v. City of Hialeah*, 508 U.S. 520 [1993]). Nonetheless, it does not permit me to sacrifice humans. Nor does my right to free speech permit me to slander someone or to preach outside her window at 2:00 A.M. Tokens of fundamental rights may be restricted to protect others from serious harms arising from the exercise of those rights.

Of course rights would not be worth much if they were subject straightforwardly to the wishes of the majority. We fiercely defend fundamental right types although their tokens sometimes undercut society's interests. We cannot restrict or put conditions on fundamental rights except for compelling reasons, and individuals cannot forfeit their fundamental rights (if they can forfeit them at all) except for overwhelming reasons. Still, although tokens of a right sometimes run counter to the majority's wishes, we should not infer that rights standardly undermine the public interest.[2] Fundamental rights (freedom of speech, freedom of association, etc.) benefit society as well as individuals. Permitting free speech, religion, and association is the best—and arguably the only—way for society to uncover the truth.[3] Of course, not every right has such a significant social payoff—although most fundamental rights do. Still, we minimally assume fundamental rights (right types) do not harm society.

This provides a framework for evaluating people's claims that a right is fundamental. Advocates must show that and how granting the right protects individuals' fundamental interests, and they must be prepared to respond to objections that granting that right type will harm society. These are serious obstacles for gun advocates. It is difficult to see that a serious right to bear arms satisfies either of these requirements, let alone both.

First, I see no compelling reason to think that owning a gun is a fundamental interest. Other fundamental interests are necessary to one's flourishing no matter what her particular desires, interests, and beliefs. It is difficult to see how this is true of guns. Moreover, the interests protected by paradigmatic fundamental rights—our interests in unfettered speech, freedom of religion, and freedom of association—are not merely means to my flourishing, they are elements constituting it. By contrast, having a gun in my bed stand, in my closet, or on my person might be a means for me to achieve my ends, but they are not constitutive elements of my flourishing. Hence, owning guns is not a fundamental interest.

Wheeler disagrees. He argues that the right to bear arms is fundamental since guns are the best way to protect our fundamental interest in self-defense.[4] However, on his view, guns are not inherently valuable; they are valuable only as a means of self-defense.[5] I fail to see how this could make the right to bear arms fundamental. Not every means to a fundamental interest is a fundamental right. That would arguably make most actions protected by fundamental rights. Nonetheless, the connection between owning guns and self-defense is an important issue that I address later.

Others might claim that gun ownership is an essential element for the flourishing of a proper citizen. A proper citizen, on this view, is one capable of providing for and defending his family. Although each citizen can (generally) fend for himself, citizens come together to form a limited government to provide those few needs they cannot easily satisfy on their own. However, this vision of the citizen is very controversial, more controversial than the interest in gun ownership it seeks to justify. It assumes each of us has far more control over our lives than we arguably do have. Furthermore, even if this conception were defensible, it would not establish a fundamental right to bear arms since guns are mere means to independent citizenship. They are not constitutive of that citizenship. Hence, it is doubtful that the purported right to bear arms satisfies the first requirement of a fundamental right.

Second, we have evidence that granting this right type does harm society. If this evidence is at all credible, then granting this purported right would not satisfy the second requirement either. But this does not resolve the issue. Although people do not have a fundamental right to own guns, gun control might be wrong because it violates some derivative right or simply because it is bad public policy.

2. A derivative right.—Suppose we determined that the right to bear arms is not a fundamental right but a derivative right. This would still be a significant finding since derivative rights, like fundamental ones, cannot be restricted without good evidence. Prima facie, I think we have such a derivative right. Each of us has a fundamental right of noninterference: we should be allowed to live our lives as we wish so long as we do not thereby harm others. This is a right each of us needs no matter what our particular interests. That general right derivatively protects personally important activities.

For instance, I would be furious if the state forbade me from sharing a pint with a friend. Nonetheless, although consuming alcohol is a particular interest and enjoyment I have, it is not a constitutive element of the good life in the way that the freedoms of speech, religion, and association are. That is why I do not have a fundamental right to consume alcohol. Consequently, the conditions under which my consumption of alcohol can be legitimately restricted are more lax than they would be if the activity were a fundamental interest.

Nonetheless, since I have a prima facie derivative right to consume alcohol, the state can legitimately abolish or restrict alcohol consumption only if it can show that doing so is an effective means of protecting the public from harm. They can do that in some cases: people who consume substantial amounts of alcohol are dangerous drivers. Since this behavior is unacceptably risky to others, the state can legitimately restrict drinking while driving. Whether privately owning guns is similarly risky is something we must discover.

B. Bad Public Policy

If private gun ownership were not a derivative right, it might still be bad policy to substantially restrict or abolish guns. There are always costs of enforcing a law. Sometimes these costs are prohibitive, especially when the public does not support that law. If the public will not voluntarily comply with the law, then the state must try to force compliance. In their efforts to do so, they invariably employ excessively intrusive methods. Such methods never entirely succeed, and, to the extent that they do, they undermine public confidence in and support for all law. Consider America's experience with Prohibition. Although one of Prohibition's aims—to protect innocents from harm caused by those under the influence—was laudable, the law was unenforceable and excessively costly. Consequently, less than two decades after Prohibition was passed via constitutional amendment, it was repealed.

The cost of enforcing any law—and especially an unpopular law—weighs against making any behavior illegal unless we have solid evidence that the behavior is seriously harmful. If we adopt a weaker standard—if we criminalize every action type whose tokens occasionally lead to some harm—then we would criminalize most behavior. As a result, even if there were no right to bear arms, we should still not seek to substantially limit private ownership of guns unless we had good reason to think that would prevent serious harm.

C. Summing Up: Justifying the Private Ownership of Guns

The preceding analysis isolates three questions we must answer in deciding whether people should be permitted to own guns: (1) How important is owning a gun to some people? (2) What are the consequences of private gun ownership? and (3) Is abolishing or restricting private ownership of guns bad policy? Although gun ownership is not a fundamental interest, many people want to own guns and think they have good reason to do so. That is sufficient to show that serious gun control would undermine gun owners' interests. Moreover, there is some reason to think that serious gun control in countries with a strong tradition of gun ownership would be bad policy. Therefore, we should certainly not abolish, and arguably should not restrict, private ownership of guns without good reason. Are there good reasons? To answer this question, we must determine the effects of private gun ownership: (*a*) How likely is it that private gun ownership seriously harms others? and (*b*) Are there substantial benefits of gun ownership that might counterbalance any harm?

II. HARM, DANGER, AND RISK

We must be careful when we say that guns cause harm. Guns kill people because agents use them to kill people (or misuse them in ways that cause people to be killed). As the National Rifle Association (NRA) puts it: "Guns don't kill people, people do." In one sense their claim is uncontroversial: murder is the act of an agent, and guns are not agents. In another way, their claim is irrelevant. No gun control advocate claims, hints, or suggests that guns are moral agents. Guns are objects, and objects do no evil. But not all objects are created equal. Imagine the NNWA (National Nuclear Weapons Association) claiming that "tactical nuclear weapons don't kill people, people do." While in one sense their claim would be true, in a more profound way, it would be ludicrous.

Of course guns are not nuclear weapons. Guns are not as dangerous as nuclear weapons, and some guns have seemingly legitimate uses. The question is whether the character of guns makes them especially harmful. We know that some objects—tactical nuclear weapons, biochemical weapons, live grenades, and so forth, are much more dangerous than feathers, ice cream, and butter knives. Where do guns fall along this continuum?

There are two distinct but related questions: (1) Are guns inherently dangerous? and (2) What is the empirical probability that guns cause serious harm? "Inherently dangerous" objects are those whose nature or design is sufficient to justify our prediction that they will cause harm independent of any empirical evidence. We do not need double-blind empirical studies to know that nuclear weapons are inherently dangerous: they were designed to cause harm, and their nature

is such that we can confidently predict they will cause harm. The two questions are intricately related since inherently dangerous objects are more likely to cause serious harm. Yet they are separable because some dangerous objects are not inherently so. Automobiles, alcohol, and cigarettes were not designed to cause harm, but all are causally implicated in many people's deaths. Other things being equal, we are more prone to control inherently dangerous objects than objects that merely have harm as an unwanted side effect.

Guns, unlike autos, are inherently dangerous. Guns were invented for the military; they were designed to cause (and threaten) harm.[6] The same aims determine the ways in which guns are redesigned: they are changed to make them more efficient at causing harm. In contrast, a significant aim of redesigning automobiles is to make them less dangerous. To some extent these efforts have succeeded. Although the absolute number of annual traffic fatalities has not noticeably declined, the number of fatalities per mile traveled has declined 75 percent since the 1950s.[7] We have enhanced the auto's original aim of efficient transportation while lessening harmful side effects. That is why we can sensibly say that the automobile is not inherently dangerous despite the fact that it causes harm. We cannot say the same for guns.

The literature of gun advocates supports my contention that guns are inherently dangerous. They advocate the private ownership of guns to prevent crime and to arm the militia. Guns can serve these purposes only because they are an effective means of inflicting and threatening harm. Even guns normally not used to harm humans have purposes that ride piggyback on this fundamental purpose. Shotguns are used to kill animals, and target guns are designed to be especially accurate. Taken together, this evidence supports the common view that guns are inherently dangerous. That is why we have special reasons to regulate them.

Although inherently dangerous, guns are far less dangerous than weapons of mass destruction, and they do have seemingly legitimate uses. That is why we must show just how risky they are before we can legitimately abolish or seriously restrict them. We must also determine if they have sufficient benefits such that we should permit them, even if risky.

A. An Intermediate Conclusion

We have shown that owning guns is not a fundamental interest and that guns are inherently dangerous. That is why we cannot categorically dismiss all forms of gun control. However, this is a weak conclusion. For although guns are inherently dangerous, they may not be so dangerous as to justify more than a system of minimal registration. What seems clear is that their inherent dangerousness precludes the idea that guns cannot be subject to governmental control. Some form of gun control cannot be categorically dismissed. Before determining the actual danger that guns present, we should first determine how risky an action must be before we can justifiably restrict it.

B. Risk

Humans are notoriously bad at judging risk. Often we are unaware of, or are inattentive to, the seriousness of risks. For instance, we may drive while inebriated. At other times we overestimate the risks. For instance, we may refuse to fly because we think it is too dangerous. A proper determination of risk would be based on a careful accounting of the action's costs and benefits. We should determine (1) the probability of harm, (2) the seriousness of harm (the product of the gravity and extent of the harm), (3) the probability of achieving the benefits, (4) the significance of the benefits (the product of the importance and extent of the benefit), and then act accordingly. Of course even if we reach the same determination to the above questions, we might still disagree about whether to act: we might disagree about what risks are worth which benefits. Nonetheless, we can all agree that (*a*) as the likelihood and seriousness of harm increase, we have increased reason to refrain from acting, while (*b*) as the likelihood and importance of the benefits increase, we have increased reasons to act. We can import these lessons into the law.

C. Legal Rules

But not straightforwardly. The issue is not whether we should own guns if they are legal, although that is a fascinating question. The question is whether the state should curtail private gun ownership. The foregoing considerations are relevant but not decisive. The decision to permit private ownership of guns is shaped by two factors pulling in opposite directions. First, even if we think Roger (an adult) stupidly engages in a dangerous activity (sky diving or boxing or racing), we might think Roger's autonomy requires that we permit it. Our commitment to individual liberty weighs against the government's abolishing or restricting the private ownership of guns as a way of limiting harm.[8] Second, some actions (smoking in public places) that are acceptably risky to Roger might be unacceptably risky to others. Are guns also unacceptably risky to others?

Put differently, gun control does not concern what private individuals should do but what governments should allow private individuals to do. We must determine the risk of permitting the private ownership of guns, constrained by these complicating considerations. To illustrate how this might work, consider the following example. We have evidence that a number of wrecks are caused by drivers using cellular phones. Roger wants to use his cellular phone while commuting to work. He decides the inconvenience of not using the cellular phone is worse than the small probability of personal harm. He might overestimate the inconvenience of not being able to use his cellular phone or insufficiently appreciate the seriousness of the risk. However, since he is an adult, we might think we should not interfere with his decision to use a cellular phone while driving. That is what autonomy requires. Yet Roger is not the only person at risk. Passengers in his or other cars may also be harmed. The seriousness of harm to them must also be considered in deciding to permit or restrict drivers' use of cellular phones.

These judgments of risk must be further tempered by the costs of enforcement mentioned earlier. Although we know that using cellular phones while driving may lead to accidents, we also know other activities may do the same—drinking coffee while driving, eating a donut, looking at a map, talking to a passenger, driving more than two hours without stopping, driving on less than six hours of sleep, driving home after a bad day at the office, and so forth. We can reasonably presume that we should not make all these activities illegal. The probabilities of serious harm are small, and enforcing such laws would require far-reaching intrusions into everyone's life. When the risks of an activity's causing grave harm to many others are small and the costs of interference are significant, then we should not criminalize the action. But as the probability of grave and widespread harm increases, then, other things being equal, we should criminalize the action.

For instance, when people are released from prison (and not just on parole) they have "paid their debt to society." Yet we do not permit them to own a gun. We judge that they are more likely to harm others. Of course not all of them—and likely not a majority of them—would harm others if they were permitted to own a gun. They are prevented from owning guns because they are members of a group statistically more likely to cause harm: we judge that allowing former felons to own guns is unacceptably risky. The NRA and most other gun advocates agree.

Someone might counter, though, that we deny felons the right to own guns not because we judge that permitting them to own guns is risky but that they, by their actions, have *forfeited* the right to own guns. But that is not the best justification for our action. Why should felons forfeit their right after they have served their time and are free of all obligations to the state? For instance, while imprisoned in the United States, felons do forfeit their right against unlawful searches and seizures. But once they are released from prison (and are no longer on parole or probation), a former felon has an unconditional right against unlawful searches and seizures—the same as every other United States resident.

At first glance, there is some reason to think that felons who use guns in the commission of a crime could forfeit their right to own a gun in the same way that drunk drivers lose their licenses. However, drunk drivers do not lose their license forever, while in most jurisdictions felons are *never* permitted to own guns. Moreover, the prohibition against former felons' owning guns is not limited to those who use guns in the commission of a crime. Hence, it is more plausible to think that we can prevent released felons from owning guns because we judge that they are more likely to commit crimes with guns.

This is our rationale for all laws proscribing risky actions. Every drunk driver does not cause an accident. Most do not. Yet we do not flinch at laws forbidding drunk driving. For it is not merely that drunk drivers are statistically more likely to cause harm; they are more likely to cause harm *because* they are inebriated. We can arguably use the same rationale to justify restricting access to guns. We restrict access not only because guns

are inherently dangerous but because—if gun-control advocates are right—permitting private ownership of guns is very risky.

III. WHAT WE NEED TO KNOW

We can now specify what we must know in order to intelligently decide whether to prohibit or restrict gun ownership (or any other risky action): (1) Is there a statistically significant correlation between the action (private ownership of guns) and harm (homicides, accidental deaths, suicides, armed robbery, etc.)? (2) Do we have good reason to think this correlation indicates that the purportedly risky action causes the harm? (3) How serious are these resultant harms? and (4) How important is the activity that the state wishes to control (*a*) to the individual agent and (*b*) to the society?

In deciding whether to restrict the behavior, we must balance these considerations using the following general guidelines: (1) If we have evidence that the behavior causes harm, then we have some reason to limit the behavior. As the evidence increases, the reasons for prohibiting the behavior increase. As the probability that the behavior will lead to *serious* harm (the product of the gravity and extent of the harm) approaches certainty, then the reasons for forbidding the behavior become very strong. (2) The more grave and widespread the potential harm, the more reason we have to constrain the behavior. If the gravity and extent of the harm are substantial, we might constrain the behavior even if our evidence that the behavior causes the harm is moderate. (3) The higher the probability that allowing the action will have important benefits, the stronger the reason to permit it. The greater the benefits, the greater the reason to permit it.

Libertarians might claim that individuals' rights are so strong that the state cannot justifiably intervene even to constrain those who put others at extreme risk. The state should not proscribe risky actions, although they can intervene after harm has occurred. This use of "risk" is misleading. If on one occasion I drive while inebriated, I engage in a risky action: there is some probability that I and others will be harmed. However, permitting people to drive while inebriated will definitely cause harm, although we cannot specify in advance who will be harmed. A personal decision to own a gun is risky in the former sense. A decision to permit citizens to privately own guns is—depending on the evidence—risky in the latter sense. If gun control advocates are right about the evidence, then we have good grounds to constrain private gun use. The question is, are they right?

IV. ASSESSING THE EVIDENCE

A. Armchair Arguments

Debates over gun control typically begin, and sometimes end, with armchair arguments. Both sides offer armchair explanations of why (and how) the presence (or absence) of guns will increase (or decrease) violent crime. It is tempting to categorically dismiss armchair arguments since they seem to be poor substitutes for empirical evidence. However, it would be a mistake to assume we could devise sound empirical studies or understand their results without armchair arguments. In a study to discover if widespread availability of guns increases the number of homicides or decreases crime, we need armchair arguments to tell us which variables we should control.[9] Without them we would not know that we should control for the extent of poverty, the incidence of drug use, increases in the number of police officers, or the introduction of tougher (or more lax) penalties. Without them we would not know that we do not need to control for the price of mayonnaise, the criminal's eye color, or who won the World Series.

Armchair arguments also take center stage in evaluating empirical studies, in criticizing experimental design, and in reinterpreting the reported findings.[10] So before I discuss the empirical evidence, I summarize some significant armchair arguments employed by gun advocates and gun-control advocates.

1. More weapons, more violence.—Gun control supporters offer empirical evidence of a positive correlation between murder rates and the availability of guns (especially handguns). Availability of guns is also positively correlated with suicide and accident rates. This empirical evidence is best understood against the background of the following armchair arguments. (1) Guns (and especially handguns) are the easiest way to kill others or oneself. People can stand at a relatively safe distance and pull the trigger. (2) When people are angry, they can act in ways they would not act normally. They may strike out at others. If they had a gun close to hand, they

would be more likely to use that gun. Although they could resort to a knife or a baseball bat, they would be less likely to do so, and, even if they did, those weapons are less likely to cause a serious or fatal injury. (3) When people are depressed, they can act in ways they would not act normally. If they had a gun close to hand, they would be more likely to kill themselves. Although they might slit their wrists or take pills, they would be less likely to do so, and, even if they did, they would be less likely to kill themselves. (4) When people handle guns, even for a legitimate purpose, the probability of serious or fatal injury to themselves or others increases. When children have access to guns, the likelihood of an accident increases still more.

The conclusion of the armchair argument is clear: the more widely available guns are, the more people will be murdered, will commit suicide, and will die of accidents. This is a plausible armchair prediction. Perhaps it is wrong. Maybe it is reasonable but overinflated. Or it might be that the prediction is well founded but that the widespread availability of guns is nonetheless justified. What is apparent is that the claim that widespread availability of guns increases the number of homicides, suicides, and accidental deaths is highly plausible. It is difficult to imagine that it is false.

2. Availability of guns prevents or stops crimes.—Gun advocates offer empirical evidence supporting the claim that guns prevent crime; their armchair arguments undergird and explain those studies. The motivating idea is simple: most criminals want to minimize their risks when committing a crime. If they know that someone in a house is armed, they will be less likely to enter that house, at least when the person is home and awake. Potential criminals are also less likely to assault or rob someone whom they believe is carrying a weapon. Finally, when criminals try to rob or assault an armed person, the person is more likely to foil the crime. This, too, is a plausible armchair prediction. Perhaps it is wrong. Maybe the claim is overinflated. Perhaps guns have these benefits, but there are other effects of owning guns—for example, those mentioned above—which outweigh them. What is apparent is that the claim that the widespread availability of guns would prevent or thwart some crimes is highly plausible. It is difficult to imagine that it is false. Of course we cannot stop with these armchair arguments. We must assess the empirical evidence.

B. The Data

The empirical evidence is difficult to assess, and, to the extent that we can, it does not univocally support either side. You might not know this from listening to the public policy debate. Some gun-control advocates imply that strict gun laws would all but eliminate murder, while some gun advocates imply that having a gun in every home would virtually end crime. Both claims are unfounded. Gun control will not virtually eliminate murder. Arming all citizens will not virtually eliminate crime. About that we can be confident. The problem is determining the precise effects of permitting or restricting guns. The available evidence is less than compelling But we must make a judgment based on the best evidence we have.

1. The connection between availability of guns and murder.—Perhaps the most well-established statistic is this: the more widely available guns (especially handguns) are, the more people are murdered. The figures are duplicated time and again in country after country. Here is the bottom line: "The correlation between any gun-prevalence and the overall murder rate is .67, while it is .84 between handgun prevalence and overall murder rate."[11] These figures are significant to the .01 level; that is, the chance that these correlations could occur merely by chance is less than one out of 100. This correlation meets the statisticians' gold standard.

But this does not resolve the issue, for it does not establish what gun control advocates claim it shows, namely, that gun control is an effective way of substantially lessening the murder rate. First, a statistical correlation shows that two things are linked, but it does not tell us if the first caused the second, the second caused the first, or if there is some third factor which caused both. Second, even if the items are causally related, we do not know that changing the cause will straightforwardly change the effect since another factor might intervene to sustain the effect.

Gun advocates proffer their own armchair explanation for the correlations: these correlations reflect the character of the respective social and political systems. The European countries where murder rates are lower have more social solidarity and are more heterogeneous than the United States. Whether these social factors explain all of the correlation is debatable, but I am confident they explain some of it. Were the United States to

regulate guns as tightly as most European countries, our murder rates arguably would fall, but they would not plummet immediately to European levels.

We might settle the issue if we could conduct controlled experiments, randomly dividing our population in half, giving half of them guns, removing all the guns from the other half, and then monitoring the murder rate. Of course, that would be morally unacceptable, politically unrealistic, and probably even scientifically unachievable. Before we had enough time to exclude all possible intervening causes, sufficient time might have elapsed so that new intervening causes could have emerged. But we are not left in the dark. We have empirical evidence that helps adjudicate between competing explanations of the correlation.

First, we have empirical evidence, bolstered by armchair arguments, that guns are more lethal than other weapons. Some claim the ratio is 5:1; no estimates are lower than 2:1.[12] This partly explains the strong correlation between guns and homicides. If people get angry the same number of times, those using the most lethal weapons are more likely to kill their victims.

Second, the nature of secondary gun markets helps explain how the widespread availability of guns increases crime in general and homicides in particular. Various opponents of gun control claim that "If we outlaw guns, only outlaws will have guns." Armchair arguments suggest why this is a silly claim. Where, one might ask, do criminals get their guns? They often steal them or buy them from those who purchased them legally. Even guns obtained from other criminals are usually traceable to people who purchased them legally. Empirical evidence supports this armchair supposition. Most criminals report having stolen their guns, received them from a friend or family member, or purchased them from someone who had stolen it. At least half a million guns are stolen each year, and these swell the numbers of guns available illegally.[13]

Not only does the primary (legal) market affect the availability of guns on secondary markets, it also affects the price of guns on those markets, much "like the analogous markets for motor vehicles or prescription drugs."[14] As we restrict the availability of guns in the primary market, the supply of guns in the secondary markets decreases and their cost increases.[15] This increase in cost will diminish teenagers' ability to obtain guns since they are least able to afford hefty prices. Since teenagers commit most deadly crimes, decreasing the availability of legal guns will thereby decrease the number of homicides. The converse is true as well: having huge numbers of legally available guns increases the number of guns on secondary markets and typically lowers their price. This makes it easier for prospective criminals, including teenagers, to obtain guns.

Third, having a gun around the house (or on the person)—even for self-protection—apparently increases the chance that someone in the family will kill themselves with the gun or will be the victim of a homicide or an accident. One study found that "for every time a gun in the home was involved in a self-protection homicide, they noted 1.3 unintentional deaths, 4.5 criminal homicides, and 37 firearm suicides."[16] This implies that for every case where someone in a gun-owning household uses a gun to successfully stop a life-threatening attack, nearly forty-three people in similar households will die from a gunshot. Taken together the evidence does not prove that widespread availability of guns increases the number of homicides. However, that empirical evidence, bolstered by earlier armchair arguments, makes the claim highly plausible.

2. The use of guns to prevent crime.—The biggest "gun" in the anti-gun-control lobby is the claim that having (and perhaps carrying) a gun prevents crime. As I noted earlier, this is a sensible armchair claim. Someone contemplating a robbery is more likely to proceed if they think they can succeed with little risk to themselves. So if a prospective robber believes the tenants are at home and have a gun they know how to use, then he likely will seek another target. Two surveys support this belief. According to one survey, 4 percent of all Americans have used a handgun in the past five years to avert a crime. Given those figures, researchers estimate that there are at least 600,000 defensive uses of guns per year. Kleck uses these results, in conjunction with another survey, to claim that the number might be as high as 2.5 million.[17] Given the number of violent crimes using guns, "the best evidence indicates that guns are used about as often for defensive purposes as for criminal purposes."[18] If true, that is a powerful reason to resist attempts to limit availability of guns.[19] Such statistics, particularly when bolstered by moving anecdotes of

those who have saved their lives by having a gun, cannot be cavalierly dismissed by gun control advocates.

However, these figures are inflated, likely dramatically so. First, Kleck's methodology is flawed. Surveys have an inherent tendency to overestimate rare events. Kleck made his estimates based on phone interviews with people in 5,000 dwelling units. One percent of those units claimed to have used a gun defensively in the past year. Kleck inferred from these responses that there are 2.5 million defensive handgun uses per year. However, since this inference is based on an affirmative answer by one person out of a hundred, that means that for every chance for a false negative (someone who falsely denies using a gun defensively) there are ninety-nine chances for a false positive (someone who falsely claims to have used a gun defensively).[20] The probability that this or some other bias skews the findings is substantial.

Second, Kleck's findings are inconsistent with findings by the National Crime Victimization Survey (NCVS), which interviewed far more people and interviewed them more regularly.[21] Kleck's estimates even clash with the findings of the NCVS on the incidence and circumstances of robberies (which seems less subject to reporting bias). If Kleck's figures were correct, then "Kleck asks us to believe that burglary victims in gun owning households use their guns in self-defense more than 100% of the time, even though most were initially asleep."[22]

Finally, if there were 2.5 million defensive gun uses each year, how many of those were necessary? Given the negative results of private gun ownership, gun advocates should show not only that guns deter crime but that they are the best way of doing so. Some people plausibly claim that owning a dog is an effective deterrent. If true, then a not insignificant percentage of those who used a gun defensively could have achieved the same results without the accompanying danger. In summary, there is no doubt that guns deter some crime and stop the completion of other crimes, just not in the numbers that Kleck claims.

John Lott supplements Kleck's argument by claiming that the widespread use of concealed weapons would decrease the annual number of homicides by 1,400; rapes by 4,200; aggravated assaults by 60,000; and robberies by 12,000.[23] If true, and if there were no countervailing costs, this would be a powerful reason not only to permit guns but to encourage people to have and carry them. However, Lott's conclusions have also come under severe criticism: "The central problem is that crime moves in waves, yet Lott's analysis does not include variables that can explain these cycles. For example, he used no variables on gangs, on drug consumption, or community policing. As a result, many of Lott's findings make no sense. He finds for instance, that both increasing the rate of unemployment and reducing income reduces the rate of violent crimes."[24] Perhaps the most compelling critique comes from Jens Ludwig, who compares the rate of violent crime toward youths and adults in states that passed shall-issue carrying permits. Most of these states issue gun permits only to people over twenty-one. Armchair considerations predict that younger people, who cannot legally carry, will not receive the full benefits from the purported deterrent effect of shall-issue laws. Thus, those under twenty-one years of age are a natural control group to track general swings in crime. Once we include this factor, we find that shall-issue laws lead to higher—not lower—homicide and robbery rates.[25]

I also have an overarching worry about Lott's conclusions. The one correlation in the gun control debate that seemingly is beyond dispute is the high correlation between the presence of guns—especially handguns—and homicide rates. Gun advocates offer explanations for the correlation, but no one I have seen seriously challenges it. I find it difficult to square this correlation with Kleck's and Lott's claims that having more guns—and toting them—will lower crime.

C. An Overall Assessment of the Empirical Evidence

The strong correlation between the presence of guns and a higher murder rate is compelling. Since the correlation is statistically significant to a .01 level, it is difficult to believe that limiting private gun ownership will not have a noticeable effect on the numbers of murders. Gun advocates disagree: they claim that cultural factors explain the correlation. Although I think they are partly correct, they draw the wrong inference. For one crucial difference between European and American cultures is the widespread presence of guns. Each culture is the way it is, at least in part, because of the role guns (or their absence) played in its creation and maintenance. Therefore, curtailing the private possession of guns might well change the American culture so that it would be less violent. Consequently,

it is not only that fewer guns would directly cause some decline in violent crimes—which it should. It is also likely to reshape the cultural values which, along with the ready availability of deadly weapons, led to such an extraordinarily high murder rate in America.

However, the statistical evidence that guns prevent or thwart crimes is suggestive and cannot be ignored despite its identified weaknesses. In summary, the overall statistical evidence tilts in favor of gun control advocates, although the evidence is disputable. But we should not expect nor do we need indisputable evidence. We can act on the best evidence we have while being open to new evidence. If widespread availability of guns were responsible for even one-fourth of the increase in the number of murders, that would be a significant harm that the state should prevent if it could do so in a relatively unintrusive and morally acceptable way.

There is little doubt that we could do that, at least to some degree. If nothing else, we could control some types of guns and ammunition. To take one obvious example, teflon-coated bullets are designed to pierce protective vests. People do not use these bullets to pierce the vests on a deer or a squirrel, on a target or a clay pigeon. They use them to pierce the vests on people, usually law-enforcement officers. This ammunition has no purpose except to cause harm. Hence, we are justified in abolishing teflon bullets and in establishing severe criminal penalties for those possessing them. This would not save large numbers of lives. But, assuming the enforcement of this ban is not impractical, then, if it saved even a few lives, that would be a compelling reason to outlaw such bullets.

Some guns, however, have a much wider use, even if they occasionally are used for ill. People have seemingly legitimate uses for shotguns and single-shot rifles. Consequently, barring strong evidence to the contrary, we should not abolish them. We should, however, study their contributory role in causing harm and explore ways we might reduce this harm in a relatively unintrusive way.

The central debate concerns handguns. The evidence we have shows that handguns are disproportionately used in homicides and in robberies. Although "there are approximately three times as many long guns as handguns in the US, more than 80 percent of gun homicides and 90 percent of gun robberies involve handguns."[26] The experience in Canada suggests that criminals will not switch to long guns if handguns are unavailable. Given the special role handguns play in causing harm, we have compelling reasons to extensively control, or perhaps even abolish, handguns. But policy considerations, mentioned earlier, should give us pause.

V. A THIRD WAY

In the past we not only assumed that we must either support or oppose gun control, we assumed that the only way to control guns is to legally proscribe access to them. We should consider other options. Although I find the idea of a world without handguns immensely appealing, there are reasons to seek alternatives, especially in countries like the United States with a deeply entrenched gun culture. In the present political climate, the abolition or serious control of guns in the United States is unlikely to work and unlikely to happen. There are far too many people who desperately want guns. There are far too many people who own guns. Any attempt to disarm the society would be beset with problems like those that plagued Prohibition. We have other possibilities.

We could employ elements of a policy that we use to control another inherently dangerous object: dynamite. Dynamite has many beneficial uses. That is why we permit people to own it under specifiable conditions, for example, to build a road. But it is also inherently dangerous. That is why we heavily restrict its purchase, storage, and use. I cannot own dynamite for recreation (I like the flash), for hunting (I am a lousy shot), or for protection (I would not hear an intruder). Owning dynamite is rarely a significant interest and never a fundamental one. More important to the present point, even when we do permit people to own dynamite, we subject them to strict legal liability. The owner is financially liable for any harm caused by his dynamite, even if he was not negligent.

I propose we make handgun owners (and perhaps ultimately all gun owners) strictly liable for harm caused by the use of their guns. If Jones's child takes his gun and kills someone while committing a crime, then Jones will be financially responsible to those harmed. If Jones's child accidentally kills a neighbor's child, Jones will be financially responsible to the child's family. If someone steals Jones's gun and kills someone while robbing them, then Jones will owe the victim compensatory damages. And if Jones were negligent in the storing of the gun, he could be subject to punitive damages as well. Perhaps if he were grossly negligent in storing the gun (he left it lying in his front yard, next to a school playground), we might even bring criminal charges against him.

This procedure is justified since guns are inherently dangerous, and it is only reasonable to expect people to take responsibility for their risky actions. The benefits are notable: many people would be disinclined to own guns, while those owning guns would likely take greater care in storing, handling, and using them. This arguably could achieve the central aims of gun control without direct government intervention. Doubtless that means that some people will be forced to pay for the misdeeds or mistakes of others in ways we might dislike. However, that is a more attractive policy than continuing the current scheme in which guns are easily obtained in the United States or completely denying individuals' interest in owning guns.

To make this option more palatable, we could let gun owners purchase liability insurance to cover potential losses. We might even require them to purchase insurance. After all, most states require drivers to have automobile insurance. This insurance-based system of strict liability would make people take more care with any guns they own while providing financial remuneration to those harmed by the use of those guns.

Perhaps this will not work. Other proposals might work better. What seems clear to me is that we need to do something: we cannot continue with the status quo.

NOTES

1. Todd C. Hughes and Lester H. Hunt, "The Liberal Basis of the Right to Bear Arms," *Public Affairs Quarterly* (in press).

2. R. Dworkin, *Taking Rights Seriously* (London: Duckworth, 1977).

3. John Stuart Mill, *On Liberty* (Indianapolis: Hackett, 1978).

4. Samual C. Wheeler, Jr., "Self-Defense: Rights and Coerced Risk Acceptance," *Public Affairs Quarterly* 11 (1997): 431–43.

5. Ibid., pp. 433–38.

6. Charles Singer, E. J. Holmyard, A. R. Hall, and Treavor Williams, *A History of Technology*, 7 vols. (Oxford: Oxford University Press, 1956), vol. 2, p. 367.

7. David Hemenway, "Guns, Public Health, and Public Safety," in *Guns and the Constitution,* ed. Dennis A. Henigan, E. Bruce Nicholson, and David Hemenway (Northampton, Mass.: Aletheia Press, 1995), pp. 49–82, p. 52.

8. Hughes and Hunt.

9. John R. Lott, *More Guns, Less Crime: Understanding Crime and Gun-Control Laws* (Chicago: University of Chicago Press, 1998), pp. 21–24.

10. Dan Black and Daniel Nagin, "Do Right-to-Carry Laws Deter Violent Crime?" *Journal of Legal Studies* 27 (1998): 209–20; Philip J. Cook, Stephanie Mollinoni, and Thomas B. Cole, "Regulating Gun Markets," *Journal of Criminal Law and Criminology* 86 (1995): 59–92; Phillip J. Cook, Jens Ludwig, and David Hemenway, "The Gun Debate's New Mythical Number: *How* Many Defensive Uses Per Year?" *Journal of Policy Analysis and Management* 16 (1997): 463–69; David Hemenway, "The Myth of Millions of Annual Self-Defense Gun Uses: A Case Study of Survey Overestimates of Rare Events," *Chance* 10 (1997): 6–10, "Review of *More Guns, Less Crime,*" *New England Journal of Medicine* 339 (1998): 2029–30; Lott; Wheeler.

11. Gregg Lee Carter, *The Gun Control Movement* (New York: Twayne Publishers, 1997), p. 3.

12. Albert J. Reiss, Jr., and Jeffrey A. Roth, eds., *Understanding and Preventing Violence* (Washington, D.C.: National Academy Press, 1993), p. 260.

13. Cook, Mollinoni, and Cole, p. 81.

14. Ibid., p. 71.

15. Ibid., p. 73.

16. Reiss and Roth, eds., p. 267.

17. Gary Kleck, *Point Blank: Guns and Violence in America* (New York: Aldine De Gruyter, 1991), pp. 105–6.

18. Ibid., p. 107.

19. Gary Kleck, *Targeting Guns: Firearms and Their Control* (New York: Aldine de Gruyter, 1997).

20. David Hemenway, "Survey Research and Self-Defense Gun Use: An Explanation of Extreme Overestimates," *Journal of Criminal Law and Criminology* 87 (1997): 1430–45.

21. U.S. Department of Justice, *Criminal Victimization in the United States, 1993: A National Crime Victimization Survey* (Washington, D.C.: Government Printing Office, 1996).

22. Hemenway, "Survey Research and Self-Defense Gun Use: An Explanation of Extreme Overestimates," p. 1442.

23. Lott, p. 54.

24. Hemenway, "Review of *More Guns, Less Crime,*" p. 2029.

25. Jens Ludwig, "Concealed Gun-Carrying Laws and Violent Crime: Evidence from State Panel Data," *International Review of Law and Economics* 18 (1998): 239–54.

26. Hemenway, "Guns, Public Health, and Public Safety," p. 60.

Political Philosophy and the Gun Control Debate: What Would Bentham, Mills, and Nozick Have to Say?

STACEY NGUYEN

Last Monday, in a press release that marked the one-year anniversary of the shooting at Aurora, House Minority Leader Nancy Pelosi (D) said: "We must uphold our oath to 'protect and defend' the Constitution and all Americans by expanding background

Stacey Nguyen, "Political Philosophy and the Gun Control Debate: What Would Bentham, Mills, and Nozick Have to Say?" *Berkeley Political Review,* August 5, 2013, https://bpr .berkeley.edu/2013/08/05/political-philosophy-and-the-gun -control-debatewhat-would-bentham-mills-and-nozick-have -to-say/. Reprinted with permission.

checks and keeping dangerous firearms out of the wrong hands." After this press release, several parties proceeded to criticize Pelosi's comments.

For example, CNS News pointed out that Pelosi's oath does not include the phrase "to protect and defend the Constitution," which is found in the President's oath. Part of her oath reads: "I do solemnly swear that I will support and defend the Constitution of the United States against all enemies, foreign and domestic."

Moreover, Erich Pratt, director of communications for Gun Owners of America, claimed that the American constitution makes no allowances for gun control. "If Pelosi really wants to apply the lessons from Aurora, Colorado in order to save lives," Pratt said, "she will work to repeal gun laws that discourage good people from carrying firearms."

These trivial arguments lead one to wonder how useful rhetorical and philosophical approaches are for public policy—or in this case, toothless nitpicking. While gun rights advocates claim that we just need to better enforce current laws, it is the loopholes and weak policies, coupled with gun lobbying, that make it more difficult to do so and much easier to illegally acquire guns. In April, new gun measures considered by the Senate failed miserably, with only two out of nine amendments passing. Some of the measures that failed included comprehensive background checks, bans and limits on assault weapons, and crackdown strategies on gun trafficking. With recent mass shootings and the tens of thousands of gun-related deaths that occur each year in the United States, the lack of gun regulation is absolutely unacceptable.

But while I can't argue against policy being more tangible than philosophizing, I believe that there is value in understanding the micro-foundations of legal policies. Through understanding and applying different philosophical approaches to justice, we can expand our appreciation for the significance and complexity of political issues. And more importantly, we can learn to rigorously question our fundamental beliefs and stray a bit further from the traditional left-right dichotomy.

First, let's talk about the contentious document itself—the one and only, Second Amendment. Many politicians and scholars have argued over the philosophy of the Second Amendment, imposing a historical analysis of the Constitution and regarding it as either an original, inviolable piece or a living document. In 2008, the Supreme Court decided in District of Columbia vs. Heller that the Second Amendment provides an individual right to bear arms independent of any collective right. So while people cannot have tanks or missiles, they have an individual right to handguns, because as Justice Scalia puts it, "handguns are the most popular weapon chosen by Americans for self-defense in the home, and a complete prohibition of their use is invalid."

The originalist argument is self-explanatory—the Constitution was set in stone when it was ratified in 1787 and it is not an evolving document. On the other hand, the "living document" approach finds that the Second Amendment was written in a different context. Firstly, people still used guns to hunt for food and ward off frequent foreign invasions two hundred years ago. Back then, guns were also used to suppress slave rebellions and fight Native Americans. This is not to say that gun rights advocates are racists, but rather that the Founders' intents were geared towards state protection, not individual rights. Moreover, major advances in gun technology mean that semi-automatic weapons with enhanced magazine capacities are more lethal. Today' semi-automatic weapons, like the Colt AR-15, resemble military-style firearms and are a far cry from colonial-era muskets and rifles. Advanced technology calls for advanced safety precautions. In short, gun policies should not reflect a blind adherence to the Constitution, but instead grow with human and technological advancements.

Now, I would like to argue for the necessity for gun legislation on the grounds of social welfare and individual liberty, using the two political philosophies of utilitarianism and possessive libertarianism. Ultimately, there's no *correct* way to approach this complex and contentious issue, but exploring different philosophical approaches invites greater insight. I don't claim to have a complete analysis or even the solutions to the problem—at most, just some food for thought.

BENTHAMITE AND MILLIAN UTILITARIANISM

Many arguments for gun control are grounded in utilitarian thought. Jeremy Bentham, the founder of modern utilitarian thought, held that the morality of an action was determined by its contribution to overall happiness—an act should be done if it produces the greatest amount of happiness over unhappiness. Articulated by J. S. Mill, the Harm Principle, one of the tenets of modern utilitarianism, states that individuals are free to do as they please unless their actions harm other individuals. Applying the Harm Principle, the general stance is that guns produce more harm than happiness or social utility. First, and foremost, guns cost lives. Two out of three homicides, half of all suicides, and a third of all robberies are committed with guns. In the United States, the total number of handgun deaths from 1980 to 2006 exceeds 32,000 per year, according to UPenn's Health System. Additionally, the fiscal costs of gun injuries are disadvantageous in the utilitarian calculus. According to the CDC, firearm related deaths cost the United States health care system $37 billion, and nonfatal gunshot wounds cost another $3.7 billion in 2005 alone. This means that the taxpayer money that has gone toward healthcare for firearm injuries could have been invested in more socially beneficial causes, such as education and mental health care.

One might say that having less gun regulation is more utilitarian, because having access to guns may save lives. The research reflects otherwise. Firstly, the Harvard Injury Control Research Center (HICRC) showed that across states and high-income nations, more guns mean more homicides. Secondly, research shows that guns are used more often for intimidation than as weapons of self-defense. For example, a survey found that nearly 1% of Americans reported using guns to defend themselves or their property while 50% used guns in an aggressive manner, such as in escalating an argument. Additionally, another survey found that if an assault victim is carrying a gun, they are 4.5 times more likely to be shot and 4.2 times more likely to be killed. The self-defense argument may ostensibly appear utilitarian, but it is not backed up by the evidence at hand.

POSSESSIVE LIBERTARIANISM

In contrast to utilitarianism, possessive libertarianism is the main philosophical approach for reducing gun regulation. In *Anarchy, State, and Utopia*, political philosopher Robert Nozick fleshed out the baseline for modern American libertarian thought. A proponent of the inviolability of individuals, Nozick supported a minimal state that would only protect negative rights like individuals' right to privacy and right to not be killed, but not promote positive rights such as social welfare programs or education. A Nozickian thinker would supposedly be opposed to gun control because of choice-based liberty and individual autonomy.

But for the same reasons, libertarian philosophy can be used to support the necessity for gun control. Firstly, the idea that individuals should be held accountable for their actions complements libertarian philosophy. As Dr. Jack Russell, professor of philosophy at the University of North Dakota School of Law, puts it: "Nothing is more consistent with the libertarian point of view than registering guns and including serial numbers on every bullet. It is only when a person's property is traceable, when we can figure out who shot whom, that we can live in a libertarian world." Members of the NRA themselves care about the responsibility that comes with gun ownership—roughly 75% of the NRA believes in background checks, that concealed carry permits shouldn't be granted to individuals with violent misdemeanors or assaults under their belts, that permits should only be granted to those who have gone through gun safety training, and that being arrested for domestic violence disqualifies individuals from gun ownership. Moreover, government interference with gun acquisition reflects not a hoarding of power, but rather a responsibility for protecting its citizens' negative rights. All in all, it appears that stronger gun regulation is consistent with libertarian philosophy.

Utilitarianism and possessive libertarianism are two fundamental philosophies of justice, but neither is right nor wrong. This particular interpretation of both theories reflects a strong need for more rigorous gun policies and constructive conversations on the basis of individual responsibility and greater social concerns. Undoubtedly, there remain many more philosophical questions to ponder. Should there be borders for gun control? Is bearing arms even a fundamental human right like the freedom of speech or the right to assembly?

Ultimately, the problem is not whether the individual is an end or a means to an end; the problem is simply gun violence, which hurts both society and the individual. The solution is not simple, and will also have to take into consideration structural issues of poverty, education, and health care. But the solution, in any case, will have to start with stronger federal gun policies and more effective leadership from our elected representatives.

CHAPTER 18

Capital Punishment

Few moral issues provoke the kind of fiery emotions and fervent debate that capital punishment does. In some circles, the very mention of the words *death penalty* is enough to set off a cross fire of opinions from all sides of the subject—as well as an onslaught of zealotry and moral confusion. At the center of all the commotion is a clash of fundamental moral values, a conflict heightened by the realization that weighing in the balance is, ultimately and tragically, the life or death of a human being.

In this controversy, the **abolitionists** (those who wish to abolish capital punishment) most often appeal to basic moral principles such as "Do not kill," "Honor the sanctity of life," or "Respect human dignity." The **retentionists** (those who wish to retain the death penalty) are likely to appeal to other principles: "Punish the guilty," "Give murderers the punishment they deserve," "A life for a life," or "Deter the ultimate crime (murder) with the ultimate punishment." On the most general and fundamental of these principles—not killing, respecting human dignity, and punishing the guilty—almost all parties to the dispute agree. But retentionists and abolitionists are usually at odds over how these principles should be interpreted.

Retentionists like to remind us of murderers whose crimes are so horrific that the death penalty may seem the only fitting punishment. Thus they bring up such moral monsters as Timothy McVeigh (who used a bomb to kill 168 men, women, and children), Ted Bundy (who murdered, by his own count, more than 100 women), John Wayne Gacy (who raped and murdered 33 boys and men), and

Adolf Eichmann (who facilitated the murder of millions during the Holocaust). Abolitionists, on the other hand, tell of the horrors that often accompany the death penalty: innocent people who are wrongly convicted and executed, executions that go wrong and cause excruciating pain to those executed, and the suspiciously high percentage of poor and minority people who are executed in the United States. Commonplace in the capital punishment debate, such facts may move us to anger, pity, disgust, or sadness, and they may inform our thinking in important ways. But we should not allow our emotional reaction to them to interfere with the vital task that we begin in this chapter—the careful evaluation of arguments for and against capital punishment.

ISSUE FILE: BACKGROUND

In the legal sense, **punishment** is the deliberate and authorized causing of pain or harm to someone thought to have broken a law. It is a legal sanction imposed by society on offenders for violating society's official norms. The justification for punishment—the reason why society uses it—generally takes one of two forms. As we will see later, many believe that the sole reason we should punish the wrongdoer is because he morally *deserves* punishment. His desert is the only justification required, and meting out punishment to those who deserve it is morally obligatory and a morally good thing. Others believe that the only proper justification is the good consequences for society that the punishment of offenders will bring—most notably, the prevention of future crimes and the maintenance of an orderly society.

Capital punishment is punishment by execution of someone officially judged to have committed a serious, or capital, crime. For thousands of years, this extreme sanction has been used countless times in the Western world for a variety of offenses—rape, murder, horse theft, kidnapping, treason, sodomy, spying, blasphemy, witchcraft, and many others. A wide assortment of execution methods have also been employed, ranging from the ancient and medieval (crucifixion, drawing and quartering, burning alive, impalement, etc.) to the handful of standard techniques of the past two centuries (hanging, firing squad, lethal gas, electrocution, and lethal injection). In twenty-first-century America, most death penalty states (thirty-one in 2016) reserve capital punishment for the crime of murder, and lethal injection is authorized in all of them. Seventeen states authorize other modes of execution, including lethal gas, hanging, and firing squad.[1]

As of April 2017, there were 2,843 prisoners on death row in the United States, and in 2016, five states carried out a total of twenty executions. In 2017, 42 percent of death row inmates were white, 42 percent were black, and 13 percent were Latino. In 2016, Georgia executed nine inmates, more than any other state, and Texas executed seven. Alabama executed two, and Florida and Missouri executed one inmate each. By mid-2017, nineteen states and the District of Columbia were without the death penalty: Alaska, Connecticut, Delaware, Hawaii, Illinois, Iowa, Maine, Maryland, Massachusetts, Michigan, Minnesota, New Jersey, New Mexico, New York, North Dakota, Rhode Island, Vermont, West Virginia, and Wisconsin.[2]

The trend in executions in the United States has varied over the past few decades. The number of executions carried out each year between the mid-1930s and the 1970s gradually declined, from a high of 200 down to 0 in 1976. But from 1977 to 1999, the annual toll ramped up again,

from 1 in 1977 to 98 in 1999. Since this high point, another downward trend has set in, with the number of executions in 2004 dropping to 59, and in 2013 to 39.[3] The gradual decrease in executions has coincided with significant public support for the death penalty for convicted murderers. Gallup polls show that between 1994 and 2014, the percentage of American adults in favor of capital punishment for murder has fluctuated annually but always stayed within the 60 to 80 percent range. In the last seven years, however, the range has been 60 to 64 percent. These numbers decreased significantly when people were asked to consider life in prison without parole as an option.[4]

Most other countries have officially abolished the death penalty or simply stopped using it. One hundred four nations—including Canada, Mexico, and all the Western European countries—are in this category. In 2016, twenty-three countries carried out executions. Most executions took place in China, Iran, Saudi Arabia, Iraq, and Pakistan. Not counting China, 87 percent of executions took place in just four countries—Iran, Saudi Arabia, Iraq, and Pakistan.[5]

The use of capital punishment in the United States has been shaped by several landmark Supreme Court decisions. In 1972, in *Furman v. Georgia*, the court ruled that capital punishment as it was then being applied in certain states was unconstitutional. The ruling put a halt to executions across the country. Yet the court did not declare that the death penalty itself was unconstitutional. The majority on the court thought that its usual administration—which allowed juries to impose the death penalty arbitrarily without any legal guidance—constituted "cruel and unusual punishment," a violation of the Eighth Amendment of the Constitution.

Many states then promptly rewrote their death penalty statutes to try to minimize administrative arbitrariness. A few states passed laws decreeing that the death penalty would be mandatory for particular capital crimes. But in *Woodson v. North*

Carolina (1976), the Supreme Court declared mandatory death sentences unconstitutional. Some states instituted sentencing guidelines to provide standards for the judge or jury deliberating about whether to impose the death penalty. In *Gregg v. Georgia* (1976), the court ruled that such death penalty laws prescribing proper guidelines were constitutional, at least in cases of murder. This ruling in effect reinstated capital punishment in the country, and executions resumed in the following year. Since 1976, few state statutes have allowed the death penalty for anything but homicide cases.

More recently the court has banned the use of the death penalty for particular kinds of offenders. In *Atkins v. Virginia* (2002), the court held that the execution of mentally disabled persons is cruel and unusual punishment and is therefore unconstitutional. In *Roper v. Simmons* (2005), the court held that executing those who were under the age of eighteen when they committed their crimes is also a violation of Eighth Amendment protection against cruel and unusual punishment. Before *Roper*, seven states had no minimum age for execution, and fifteen states had set the minimum at between fourteen and seventeen years old. In *Kennedy v. Louisiana* (2008), the court ruled a Louisiana statute unconstitutional. The law permitted the death penalty for child rape in cases in which the child did not die.

An important tradition in law that bears on capital punishment is the distinction between types of punishable killing: namely, between first-degree murder, second-degree murder, and manslaughter. Statutes vary by jurisdiction, but generally first-degree murder is killing (1) with premeditation; (2) while performing a major crime (felony) such as armed robbery, kidnapping, or rape; or (3) involving particular egregious circumstances such as the deaths of several people or of a child or police officer. Second-degree murder is killing without premeditation but with some degree of intent ("malice aforethought"). Manslaughter is killing without premeditation or intent, as when one person kills

another in "the heat of passion" or by driving drunk. Usually, only first-degree murder makes a defendant eligible for the death penalty.

MORAL THEORIES

Both retentionists and abolitionists appeal to consequentialist and nonconsequentialist moral theories. Retentionist arguments are often thoroughly utilitarian, contending that use of capital punishment can create a favorable balance of happiness over unhappiness for society. One common argument is that the death penalty achieves such utility through *prevention*—by preventing the criminal from striking again. Better than any other form of punishment, the retentionist says, the death penalty protects society from repeat criminals, those violent and dangerous offenders who cannot be reformed. The retentionist claims that life in prison without parole—the usual alternative to the death penalty—is an inadequate substitute. Violent lifers can kill other inmates and prison guards, or they can escape to terrorize society again. By also appealing to utility, the abolitionist may object to this line of argument by insisting that the retentionist produce empirical evidence showing that executing violent criminals does indeed protect society better than the use of life sentences. After all, such premises about deterrence are empirical claims, and empirical claims require supporting evidence.

A related retentionist argument asserts that the death penalty, more than any other form of punishment (including life in prison), can achieve great overall utility through *deterrence*—the dissuading of possible offenders from committing capital crimes. This utilitarian argument is thought by many to be the retentionists' strongest. The utilitarian philosopher John Stuart Mill claims that for a particular kind of would-be criminal, capital punishment is the most effective deterrent of all:

> But the influence of punishment is not to be estimated by its effect on hardened criminals. Those whose habitual way of life keeps them, so to speak,

at all times within sight of the gallows, do grow to care less about it; as, to compare good things with bad, an old soldier is not much affected by the chance of dying in battle. I can afford to admit all that is often said about the indifference of the professional criminals to the gallows. Though of that indifference one-third is probably bravado and another third confidence that they shall have the luck to escape, it is quite probable that the remaining third is real. But the efficacy of a punishment which acts principally through the imagination, is chiefly to be measured by the impression it makes on those who are still innocent; by the horror with which it surrounds the first promptings of guilt; the restraining influence it exercises over the beginning of the thought which, if indulged, would become a temptation; the check which it exerts over the graded declension towards the state—never suddenly attained—in which crime no longer revolts, and punishment no longer terrifies.[6]

Like the prevention appeal, the deterrence argument requires supporting evidence—specifically, evidence showing that the execution of criminals really does deter serious criminal behavior better than lesser punishments such as imprisonment. Abolitionists, however, are quick to question any such evidence. In fact, even many retentionists agree that the relevant scientific studies on the deterrence question are conflicting or otherwise inconclusive.

The central difficulty in conducting these studies is the number of variables that must be controlled to get reliable results. A social scientist, for example, could select two very similar jurisdictions, one with the death penalty and one without, and compare the murder rates in each. Presumably, if capital punishment deters murderers, then the jurisdiction using the death penalty should have a lower murder rate than the jurisdiction without it. But it is virtually impossible to rule out the influence of extraneous factors on the study results. Besides being influenced by the penal system, murder rates may be affected by many variables—unemployment, cultural conventions, moral beliefs, political climate, media influence, availability of lethal weapons, incidence of illegal drug use, history of violence, income level, and on and on. No two jurisdictions are exactly alike, and many differences (both known and unknown) could contribute to the rise or fall of serious crime rates.

Despite these research problems, many retentionists still consider the case for deterrence strong. They argue that even if science does not yet offer unequivocal support for the death penalty's power to deter capital crimes, common sense does. The philosopher Louis Pojman takes this tack. He contends that it is obvious that most people want to avoid jail and that long sentences will deter most potential criminals better than short ones—and that there are good reasons to believe that the death penalty deters better still. One reason, he says, is that a large proportion of crimes are committed by criminals who weigh the risks and benefits of their criminal activity and become more attracted to particular crimes the milder the punishments are. And there are good indications that the death penalty would exert maximum deterrence in these cases: "The fact that those who are condemned to death do everything in their power to get their sentences postponed or reduced to long-term prison sentences, in the way *lifers* do not, shows that they fear death more than life in prison."[7]

The abolitionist can offer a couple of responses to this argument from common sense. First, even if the death penalty is a more severe punishment than life in prison, it does not follow that the death penalty deters murderers better. The prospect of life in prison may very well deter future murderers just as effectively as the death penalty can. Second, it is possible that the threat of capital punishment motivates potential killers not to avoid killing but to try harder not to get caught.

Recognizing the uncertainties in trying to assess levels of deterrence, some retentionists argue that despite the unknowns, our wisest and most morally responsible move is to bet that capital punishment does deter murderers. The reasoning that leads to

CRITICAL THOUGHT: The Morality Of Botched Executions

In recent years, controversy has surrounded executions by lethal injection because in a disconcerting number of cases, the executions have gone horribly wrong. In 2014, for example, in at least three executions, instead of dying within ten or fifteen minutes, the prisoners writhed or gasped for much longer, up to nearly two hours in one instance. Consider this more recent report on the problem:

> WASHINGTON–A deeply divided U.S. Supreme Court upheld the use of a controversial drug in lethal-injection executions Monday, even as two dissenting justices said for the first time they think it's "highly likely" the death penalty itself is unconstitutional.
>
> The justices voted 5–4 in a case from the state of Oklahoma that the sedative midazolam can be used in executions without violating a constitutional prohibition on cruel and unusual punishment.
>
> The drug that was used in executions in Arizona, Ohio and Oklahoma in 2014 took longer than usual and raised concerns that it did not perform its intended task of putting inmates into a coma-like sleep.
>
> In Oklahoma, state officials tried to halt the lethal injection after the inmate writhed on the

gurney and moaned. He died 43 minutes after the process began.

> Executions have been on hold in Ohio since a troubling 26-minute execution in 2014 during which a prisoner getting a first-ever two-drug combo repeatedly gasped and snorted. In Arizona, officials were cleared of any wrongdoing in an execution that lasted nearly two hours, but they nevertheless changed the drugs they use to put inmates to death.*

Do you think botched executions like these constitute "cruel and unusual punishment" that is prohibited by the Constitution? Are executions morally permissible (or impermissible) regardless of their cruelty? Why or why not? Do you believe botched executions offer good reasons to do away with the death penalty? Or do they merely suggest there should be a ban on lethal injections but not other forms of execution? Why or why not?

*Mark Sherman, "U.S. Court Oks Use of Drug Implicated in Botched Executions," Associated Press, June 29, 2015, http://globalnews.ca/news/2081474/u-s-court-oks-use-of-drug-implicated-in-botched-executions/ (August 22, 2015). © The Associated Press. Reprinted by permission.

this conclusion is essentially a utilitarian calculation. The philosopher Ernest van den Haag was the first to articulate this argument. The choice we are faced with, he says, is either to use the death penalty or not to use it—and we must choose while not knowing for sure whether it is a superior deterrent. If we use the penalty, we risk killing convicted murderers (and saving innocent lives). If we abolish the penalty, we risk bringing about the deaths of innocent victims (and saving the lives of murderers). If we must risk something, he says, it is better to risk the lives of convicted murderers than those of innocent people. Thus, our best bet is to retain the death

penalty. "I believe we have no right to risk additional future victims of murder for the sake of sparing convicted murderers," van den Haag asserts, "on the contrary, our moral obligation is to risk the possible ineffectiveness of executions."[8]

A common abolitionist reply to this argument is that the utilitarian calculation is incomplete. The assessment of net happiness, says the abolitionist, fails to take into account the possibility that the death penalty could *encourage* violent crime instead of just deterring it. How? Some argue that violent criminals who know they are likely to get the death penalty may commit murder to avoid being captured. In addition, some abolitionists maintain that capital punishment has a brutalizing effect on society—it makes killing human beings seem more morally and psychologically acceptable. If so, executing people could cause more harm than good and be a very poor bet for society.

On utilitarian grounds, abolitionists can attack capital punishment directly (as opposed to simply countering retentionist arguments). In perhaps the most common of such approaches, the abolitionist argues that more net happiness is created in society by sentencing murderers to life in prison without parole than by executing them. Life sentences promote the welfare of society by preventing murderers from killing again—and they do so without generating the disadvantages and pain inherent in a system of capital punishment.

Another utilitarian argument against the death penalty is that this form of punishment is simply too costly:

> The death penalty is much more expensive than its closest alternative—life imprisonment with no parole. Capital trials are longer and more expensive at every step than other murder trials. Pretrial motions, expert witness investigations, jury selection, and the necessity for two trials—one on guilt and one on sentencing—make capital cases extremely costly, even before the appeals process begins. Guilty pleas are almost unheard of when the punishment is death. In addition, many of these trials result in a life sentence rather than the death penalty, so the state pays the cost of life imprisonment on top of the expensive trial.[9]

Retentionists often respond to this argument by questioning whether the costs have been calculated accurately and fairly. Perhaps more often, they offer a nonconsequentialist reply: if the death penalty is a just punishment, then the costs involved are irrelevant.

In the death penalty debate, appeals to nonconsequentialist theories are common on both sides of the issue. Abolitionists devise arguments against capital punishment using what they take to be fundamental moral principles regarding the value or dignity of human life. For them, regardless of its social utility, the death penalty is wrong because it violates these principles. For example, they may argue that everyone has a right to life (a basic moral principle), even hardened criminals, and that the death penalty is a violation of this right—therefore, executing criminals is wrong. To this argument, retentionists usually reply along these lines: people do indeed have a right to life, but this right is not absolute. That is, a person's right to life can sometimes be overridden for good reasons. For example, if your life is being threatened, it is morally permissible to kill an attacker in self-defense. So the right to life does not hold in every situation no matter what. It may be morally permissible, then, to sometimes set this right aside.

To make their case, abolitionists often appeal to notions of fairness or justice. One prevalent argument is based on the assertion that our penal system is inherently unjust, sometimes executing innocent people (numerous cases have come to light in which people who had been executed or who were on death row were later found to be innocent). Because the death penalty is irrevocable—that is, there is no way to "undo" an execution or to compensate the executed—the execution of the innocent is an especially egregious miscarriage of justice. Therefore, we should get rid of the death penalty, since abolition is the only way to avoid such tragedies. Retentionists are generally unmoved by this argument, offering counterarguments like this one:

> Miscarriages of justice result in innocent people being sentenced to death and executed, even in criminal-law systems in which greatest care is taken to ensure that it never comes to that. But this does not stem from the intrinsic nature of the institution of capital punishment; it results from deficiencies, limitations, and imperfections of the criminal law procedures in which this punishment is meted out. Errors of justice do not demonstrate the need to do away with capital punishment; they simply make it incumbent on us to do everything possible to improve even further procedures of meting it out.[10]

The main nonconsequentialist argument for the death penalty is based on the theory of punishment known as **retributivism**—the view that offenders deserve to be punished, or "paid back," for their crimes and to be punished in proportion to the severity of their offenses. Retributivism says that offenders should be punished because *they deserve to be punished.* Punishment is a matter of justice, not social utility. If offenders are not punished, justice is not done. Kant, probably the most influential retributivist, declares that there is only one reason to punish someone for his offenses:

> Juridical punishment can never be administered merely as a means for promoting another good either with regard to the criminal himself or to civil society, but must in all cases be imposed only because the individual on whom it is inflicted has committed a crime.[11]

We can distinguish two kinds of retributivism according to the nature of the penal payback required. Kant accepts retributivism based on the doctrine of *lex talionis*—the idea that the punishment should match the crime in kind, that justice demands "an eye for an eye, a life for a life." He thinks that whatever harm the criminal does to the innocent, that same kind of harm should be done to the criminal. Thus, the only just punishment for a man who wrongfully and deliberately takes someone's life is the taking of *his* life. Other retributivists are uncomfortable with the notion of punishing in kind (should rapists be raped? should torturers be tortured?). They favor *proportional retributivism*, in which punishment reflects the seriousness of the crime but does not necessarily *resemble* the crime. For these retributivists, murder is the worst possible crime and deserves the worst possible punishment—the death of the offender.

Underpinning many retributive views of capital punishment is a Kantian emphasis on respect for persons. Persons have dignity and inherent worth and are ends in themselves. Deliberately killing an innocent person, says the retributivist, is so heinous a crime, such an intolerable evil, that it merits the ultimate punishment—the death of the murderer. So when the killer takes a life, she must forfeit her own. As Kant says,

> Even if a civil society resolved to dissolve itself with the consent of all its members . . . the last murderer lying in prison ought to be executed before the resolution was carried out. This ought to be done in order that every one may realize the desert of his deeds, and that blood-guiltiness may not remain on the people; for otherwise they will all be regarded as participants in the murder as a public violation of justice.[12]

Perhaps surprisingly, often the retributivist also appeals to the dignity and worth of the murderer. As Kant notes, treating persons with respect means treating them as rational agents who make free choices and are responsible for their actions. To justly punish persons—to give them what they deserve—is to acknowledge their status as responsible agents deserving of respect. He asserts, then, that executing

---

QUICK REVIEW

abolitionist—One who wishes to abolish capital punishment.

retentionst—One who wishes to retain the death penalty.

punishment—The deliberate and authorized causing of pain or harm to someone though to have broken a law.

capital punishment—Punishment by execution of someone officially judged to have committed a serious, or capital, crime.

retributivism—The view that offenders deserve to be punished, or "paid back," for their crimes and to be punished in proportion to the severity of their offenses.

a murderer is not an affront to human dignity but a recognition of it.

A frequent reaction to the retributivist view is that penal retribution is not justice but revenge. The retributivist replies that this charge is muddled: vengeance refers to making the offender suffer because of one's sense of outrage, grief, or frustration toward her and her crime; retribution involves moral deliberation about an offender's just deserts.

MORAL ARGUMENTS

Is the death penalty a morally permissible form of punishment? As you know by now, many arguments have been put forth on both sides of this issue—too many for any single book to tackle, let alone a single chapter. But we can dissect one of the more widely used (and interesting) examples. Let us begin with a popular argument *against* the death penalty:

1. If the death penalty discriminates against blacks, it is unjust.

2. If the death penalty is unjust, it should be abolished.

3. The death penalty discriminates against blacks.

4. Therefore, the death penalty should be abolished.

This argument is valid, so our evaluation of it should focus on the truth of the premises. Premises 1 and 2 are moral statements; Premise 3 is an empirical statement about the use of the death penalty against African Americans. (Arguments like this are used with equal force when focusing on other minority groups as well as the poor and uneducated; for simplicity's sake we focus on blacks, who make up the largest segment of minority death row inmates.)

Let us examine the empirical claim first: is Premise 3 true? We can give it more precision by recasting it like this: The administration of the death penalty is biased against blacks. Many abolitionists insist that this claim is indeed accurate. They say,

for example, that blacks convicted of murder are more likely to be sentenced to death than whites convicted of murder. How is this claim supported? Here is one way:

> [T]he Reverend Jesse Jackson, in his book *Legal Lynching*, argues that "[n]umerous researchers have shown conclusively that African American defendants are far more likely to receive the death penalty than are white defendants charged with the same crime." The support for this claim is said to be the undisputed fact that when compared to their percentage in the overall population African Americans are overrepresented on death row. For example, while 12 percent of the population is African American, about 43 percent of death row inmates are African American, and 38 percent of prisoners executed since 1977 are African American.[13]

But such statistical comparisons can be misleading, say some retentionists:

> The relevant population for comparison is not the general population, but rather the population of murderers. If the death penalty is administered without regard to race, the percentage of African American death row inmates found at the end of the process should not exceed the percentage of African American defendants charged with murder at the beginning. The available statistics indicate that is precisely what happens. The Department of Justice found that while African Americans constituted 48 percent of adults charged with homicide, they were only 41 percent of those admitted to prison under sentence of death. In other words, once arrested for murder, blacks are actually less likely to receive a capital sentence than are whites.[14]

Needless to say, Premise 3 (in the form examined here and in several other variations) is controversial. That does not mean, of course, that its truth or falsity is unknowable. New research or conscientious examination of existing research may provide the support that Premise 3 requires. In any event, the support must come in the form of solid statistical data carefully interpreted. Anecdotal evidence—for example, news stories

CRITICAL THOUGHT: Different Cases, Same Punishment

Consider the contrasts in the description of two men executed on the same day for a capital crime:

> One is Troy Davis, a black man who was convicted of killing a white off-duty police officer in Savannah, Georgia, in 1989. The other is Lawrence Brewer, a white man who in 1998 participated in the grisly murder of James Byrd Jr., a black man whom Brewer and two other men attacked.*

> Davis said to the last that he was innocent, no physical evidence or weapon tied him to the crime, and many witnesses against him at the trial later recanted their testimony. Millions of people, including the pope, pleaded for mercy for Davis. Brewer admitted his crime, in which he and two other men chained a black man to a pickup truck and dragged him until his body was torn into pieces. Later, in letters he wrote in jail, Brewer bragged about the murder and touted the thrill it gave him. Few asked for mercy for Brewer.

What do these very different cases suggest about the system of capital punishment in the United States? Despite the contrast between these two men—one despicable and clearly guilty, the other a sympathetic character whose guilt was in doubt—they were both executed by the state. Does this outcome suggest that an injustice was perpetrated? Should the nature of the crime, the character of the accused, or the degree of certainty about guilt affect the penalty for a crime? Based on the information given here, would you say that justice was done?

*Trymaine Lee, "Troy Davis and Lawrence Brewer, a Tale of Two Executions," *Huffington Post*, September 21, 2011, http://www.huffingtonpost.com/2011/09/21/troy-davis-and-lawrence-b_n_974293.html.

of apparent unequal treatment of whites and blacks—cannot help us much.

As we did with Premise 3, we can restate Premise 1 to make it more specific: If the administration of the death penalty is biased against blacks, it is unjust. On a straightforward reading, this assertion would seem to be acceptable to both retentionists and abolitionists. Few would deny that applying the death penalty in a discriminatory fashion is unjust, for equals must be treated equally. On this reading, the premise is almost certainly true. But many abolitionists would interpret the statement differently. They would contend that if the administration of the death penalty is biased against blacks, then the death penalty itself is unjust. Some abolitionists accept this view because they believe there is no way to apply the death penalty fairly; the administration of capital punishment is inherently unjust. Others would say that there is no way to separate the "death penalty itself" from the way it is administered. In the real world, there is only the death-penalty-as-actually-applied, which is inescapably unfair.

A common reply to the abolitionist understanding of Premise 1 is that it misses an important distinction: the unjust administration of a punishment does not entail the injustice of the punishment itself. As one retentionist says,

> [This charge of unfairness] is not an argument, either against the death penalty or against any other form of punishment. It is an argument against unjust and inequitable distribution of penalties. If the trials of wealthy men are less likely to result in convictions than those of poor men, then something must be done to reform the procedure in criminal courts. . . . But the maldistribution of penalties is no argument against any particular form of penalty.[15]

It seems that we cannot decide the truth of Premise 1 without a much more thorough examination of the arguments for and against it, a task beyond the scope of this discussion. So let us move to our revised Premise 2: If the administration of the death penalty is unjust, it should be abolished. As you can see, this premise has the same kind of ambiguity that we see in Premise 1. Again the abolitionist reading is that an unjust application of the death penalty is an indictment against capital punishment itself, so capital punishment should be abolished. Thus the same arguments and counterarguments surrounding Premise 1 also apply here.

At this point, we have not determined whether this abolitionist argument is a good one. But we have gained insight into this part of the capital punishment debate. Look again at the argument in its revised form:

1. If the administration of the death penalty is biased against blacks, it is unjust.

2. If the administration of the death penalty is unjust, it should be abolished.

3. The administration of the death penalty is biased against blacks.

4. Therefore, the death penalty should be abolished.

We have seen how difficult it can be to make this argument work. If any one of the premises is false, the conclusion is not supported and the argument fails. (Also, the argument is now valid only on the reading preferred by abolitionists.) But we have also found that the lynchpin of the argument is the abolitionist view that injustice in the system of capital punishment is the same as injustice in capital punishment itself. If abolitionists can establish this equivalence, the argument is much more likely to succeed. The other links in the chain of reasoning—the injustice of discrimination and the need to abolish unjust punishments—are generally accepted by all parties to the dispute.

We have also learned something about the retentionist position. We have discovered how retentionists can readily agree that the application

of the death penalty discriminates against blacks, that this biased treatment is unconscionable and unjust, and that such a discriminatory system should be reformed or abolished—and still consistently believe that it can be morally permissible for the state to put a convicted murderer to death.

CHAPTER REVIEW

SUMMARY

Capital punishment is a form of legal punishment—execution—reserved for someone convicted of committing a capital crime, usually some form of murder. Abolitionists wish to abolish capital punishment; retentionists want to retain it. In several decisions, the U.S. Supreme court has sanctioned and circumscribed the use of the death penalty. In *Gregg v. Georgia*, the court ruled that administration of the death penalty—if used according to proper guidelines—is constitutional in cases of murder. Other rulings banned the execution of disabled persons and of those who were under eighteen when they committed their crimes.

Both retentionists and abolitionists appeal to utilitarianism and nonconsequentialist moral theories to make their case. Retentionists often argue that the death penalty maximizes the welfare of society by preventing repeat crimes or deterring future crimes. Retributivists argue on nonconsequentialist grounds that capital punishment is morally permissible because it accords with the demands of justice. Abolitionists, on the other hand, often contend that the death penalty does more harm than good to society and that life in prison without parole results in more net happiness than executions do. Many abolitionists also take the nonconsequentialist route by insisting that the death penalty violates some fundamental moral principles—the right to life, the dignity of human beings, and the injustice of executing the innocent.

KEY TERMS

abolitionist (p. 666)
retentionist (p. 666)
punishment (p. 666)
capital punishment (p. 667)
retributivism (p. 672)

EXERCISES

Review Questions

1. What is an abolitionist? A retentionist? (p. 666)
2. What moral principles do abolitionists generally appeal to? (p. 666)
3. What moral principles do retentionists appeal to? (p. 666)
4. What fundamental moral principles do both abolitionists and retentionists accept? (p. 666)
5. For what crime is the death penalty usually reserved? (p. 666)
6. How many states now use capital punishment in their criminal justice system? (p. 667)
7. In 1972, what Supreme Court case temporarily halted executions in the United States? (p. 667)
8. For what kinds of offenders has the Supreme Court banned the use of the death penalty? (p. 668)
9. What is the deterrence argument against capital punishment? (pp. 668–669)
10. What is the difference between first-degree murder, second-degree murder, and manslaughter? (p. 668)

Discussion Questions

1. What consequentialist arguments can retentionists use to support their case? Do you accept any of these arguments? Why or why not?
2. What is the retentionist's main non-consequentialist argument? Do you accept it?
3. What moral theories can the abolitionist appeal to? Which one do you think provides the strongest reasons for abolishing capital punishment?
4. What evidence is needed to shore up the deterrence argument? Is this evidence obviously strong? What counterargument can the abolitionist make?
5. The abolitionist argues that more net happiness is created in society by sentencing murderers to life in prison without parole than by executing them. How would you counter this argument?
6. How does Pojman frame the deterrence argument? Is his argument sound or strong? Explain.
7. What is van den Haag's retention argument? How would you respond to it?
8. What is the *lex talionis* doctrine of retributivism? Do you accept it? Why or why not?
9. How can a Kantian respect for persons underpin a retributive view of capital punishment?
10. Is capital punishment ever a just punishment for murder? Why or why not?

FURTHER READING

Hugo Adam Bedau, "Capital Punishment and Social Defense," in *Matters of Life and Death: New Introductory Essays in Moral Philosophy*, ed. Tom Regan, 2nd ed. (New York: Random House, 1986).

Hugo Adam Bedau and Paul Cassell, eds., *Debating the Death Penalty: Should America Have Capital Punishment? The Experts on Both Sides Make Their Best Case* (Oxford: Oxford University Press, 2004).

Gregg v. Georgia, 428 U.S. 153, 153–207 (1976). Justice Potter Stewart et al., Opinion of the Court.

Gregg v. Georgia, 428 U.S. 153, 231–41 (1976). Justice Thurgood Marshall, Dissenting Opinion.

Sidney Hook, "The Death Sentence," *New Leader*, April 3, 1961.

Alex Kozinski, "Tinkering with Death," *New Yorker*, February 10, 1997, 48–52.

Burton Leiser, "The Death Penalty Is Permissible," in *Liberty, Justice and Morals: Contemporary Value Conflicts*, 3rd ed. (New York: Macmillan, 1986).

John Stuart Mill, "Speech in Favor of Capital Punishment," 1868, http://ethics.sandiego.edu/books/Mill/Punishment/ (March 1, 2015).

Stephen Nathanson, "An Eye for an Eye?" in *An Eye for an Eye? The Morality of Punishing by Death* (Totowa, NJ: Rowman and Littlefield, 1987).

Louis P. Pojman, "Why the Death Penalty Is Morally Permissible," in *Debating the Death Penalty: Should America Have Capital Punishment? The Experts on Both Sides Make Their Best Case*, eds. Hugo Bedau and Paul Cassell (Oxford: Oxford University Press, 2004).

William H. Shaw, "Punishment and the Criminal Justice System," in *Contemporary Ethics: Taking Account of Utilitarianism* (Malden, MA: Blackwell, 1999).

Ernest van den Haag, "On Deterrence and the Death Penalty," *Journal of Criminal Law, Criminology, and Police Science* 60, no. 2 (1969): 141–47.

ETHICAL DILEMMAS

1. Redemption and Capital Punishment

In 2005, 51-year-old Stanley Tookie Williams, convicted murderer and Crips gang co-founder, was executed by the State of California. His many supporters—including celebrities such as Jamie Foxx and Snoop Dogg—denounced the execution as unjust because while in prison he had sought and found redemption. As one report says,

> The case became the state's highest-profile execution in decades. Hollywood stars and capital punishment foes argued that Williams' sentence should be commuted to life in prison because he had made amends by writing children's books about the dangers of gangs and violence.

> Gov. Arnold Schwarzenegger rejected Williams' plea for clemency on the grounds that Williams was not genuinely remorseful about the Crips' killings. Williams was convicted of murdering four people—a 26-year-old store clerk and a couple and their 43-year-old daughter. At the trial, witnesses said he bragged and laughed about the murders.

> The Associated Press quoted Williams saying, "There is no part of me that existed then that exists now."*

Suppose Williams was guilty of the murders for which he was convicted, and suppose he had a genuine change of heart and performed many commendable deeds while in prison. Should Williams's sentence then have been commuted to life in prison? Why or why not? Is redemption compatible with justice? If a murderer mends his ways, should this change have an effect on his punishment? Is mercy (giving someone a break) compatible with justice (giving someone what he deserves)?

*"Tookie Williams Is Executed," CBSNews.com, 13 December 2005, http://www.cbsnews.com/news/tookie-williams-is-executed-13-12-2005/ (January 27, 2015).

2. Poor Representation

Delma Banks, Jr. was charged in the 1980 murder of Richard Whitehead of Texas. The only evidence against Banks was the testimony of an informant who in exchange for his testimony received $200 and the dismissal of an arson charge that could have resulted in his [sic] life sentence as a habitual offender. Banks' lawyer did not vigorously cross-examine the informant, nor did he investigate the case. Had he done so, he would have learned of strong evidence that Banks was in another city at the time of the crime. Banks received such poor representation that former FBI director and United States District Court Judge William Sessions weighed in to urge the Supreme Court to temporarily stay his execution. On April 21, 2003 the U.S. Supreme Court accepted Banks' case for review.[†]

Do you think Banks should have gotten a new trial? Assuming capital punishment is morally permissible, would it ever be right to put someone to death who had not received adequate legal representation? Why or why not? What do you think would constitute adequate legal representation? Suppose someone who is duly sentenced to die got excellent legal representation except for one minor point—her lawyer dozed off for fifteen seconds during her trial. Should this small lapse be a good enough reason to throw out her conviction and demand a new trial?

[†]American Civil Liberties Union, "Inadequate Representation," from ACLU.org, October 8, 2003. Copyright © 2003 American Civil Liberties Union, www.aclu.org/capital-punishment/inadequate-representation. Reprinted with permission.

3. The Morality of Criminal Exonerations

How many are sentenced to death in the United States for crimes they did not commit?

A new study believes the figure is 1 in every 25—or 4.1 percent.

The study, released Monday in the *Proceedings of the National Academy of Sciences*, "tells you that a surprising number of innocent people are sentenced to death," Samuel R. Gross, the lead author, said in an interview with *Newsweek*. "It tells you that a lot of them haven't been exonerated. Some of them no doubt have been executed."

Since 1973, 144 people on death row have been exonerated. As a percentage of all death sentences, that's just 1.6 percent. But if the innocence rate is 4.1 percent, more than twice the rate of exoneration, the study suggests what most people assumed but dreaded: An untold number of innocent people have been executed. Further, the majority of those wrongfully sentenced to death are likely to languish in prison and never be freed.

"I'm a little surprised it's this high," said Richard Dieter, executive director of the Death Penalty Information Center, a nonprofit that works to educate the public about capital punishment. "I did not think the number would point to more than twice as high" as the number of cases that end in exonerations.

In all, the study, "Rate of False Conviction of Criminal Defendants Who Are Sentenced to Death," shows that more than half of the innocent people sentenced to death in the past 41 years are unaccounted for. . . .

The study seeks to put to rest the conventional wisdom that wrongful criminal convictions are extremely rare. "[T]here is no shortage of lawyers and judges who assert confidently that the number of wrongful convictions is negligible," the authors write. Supreme Court Justice Antonin Scalia, for example, quoted a *New York Times*

op-ed in a 2006 concurring opinion to claim that felony convictions have an "error rate
.027 percent—or, to put it another way, a success rate of 99.973 percent."[‡]

If a significant number of innocent people are being sentenced to death, and many of these people are wrongly executed, is this an argument against capital punishment? That is, if there is a real possibility of mistakenly executing the innocent, should the death penalty be abolished? Why or why not? Does the possibility of fatal errors in our system of justice suggest that the whole system should be scrapped? If we decide to retain capital punishment, shouldn't we at the same time try hard to eliminate mistakes? How hard? To what lengths should we go to ensure a just system of punishment?

[‡]Pema Levy, "One in 25 Sentenced to Death in the U.S. Is Innocent, Study Claims," *Newsweek*, April 28, 2014, http://www.newsweek.com/one-25-executed-us-innocent-study-claims-248889 (August 22, 2017). © 2014 Newsweek Media Group. All rights reserved. Used by permission and protected by the Copyright Laws of the United States. The printing, copying, redistribution, or retransmission of this content without express written permission is prohibited.

READINGS

The Ultimate Punishment: A Defense

ERNEST VAN DEN HAAG

In an average year about 20,000 homicides occur in the United States. Fewer than 300 convicted murderers are sentenced to death. But because no more than thirty murderers have been executed in any recent year, most convicts sentenced to death are likely to die of old age.[1] Nonetheless, the death penalty looms large in discussions: it raises important moral questions independent of the number of executions.[2]

The death penalty is our harshest punishment.[3] It is irrevocable: it ends the existence of those punished, instead of temporarily imprisoning them. Further, although not intended to cause physical pain, execution is the only corporal punishment still applied to adults. These singular characteristics contribute to the perennial, impassioned controversy about capital punishment.

Ernest van den Haag, republished with permission of Harvard Law Review Association, from "The Ultimate Punishment: A Defense," *Harvard Law Review* 99: 1662–69. Copyright © 1986 by Harvard Law Review Association.

I. DISTRIBUTION

Consideration of the justice, morality, or usefulness, of capital punishment is often conflated with objections to its alleged discriminatory or capricious distribution among the guilty. Wrongly so. If capital punishment is immoral *in se*, no distribution among the guilty could make it moral. If capital punishment is moral, no distribution would make it immoral. Improper distribution cannot affect the quality of what is distributed, be it punishment or rewards. Discriminatory or capricious distribution thus could not justify abolition of the death penalty. Further, maldistribution inheres no more in capital punishment than in any other punishment.

Maldistribution between the guilty and the innocent is, by definition, unjust. But the injustice does not lie in the nature of the punishment. Because of the finality of the death penalty, the most grievous maldistribution occurs when it is imposed upon the innocent. However, the frequent allegations of discrimination and capriciousness refer to maldistribution among the guilty and not to the punishment of the innocent.

Maldistribution of any punishment among those who deserve it is irrelevant to its justice or morality. Even if poor or black convicts guilty of capital offenses suffer capital punishment, and other convicts equally guilty of the same crimes do not, a more equal distribution, however desirable, would merely be more equal. It would not be more just to the convicts under sentence of death.

Punishments are imposed on persons, not on racial or economic groups. Guilt is personal. The only relevant question is: does the person to be executed deserve the punishment? Whether or not others who deserved the same punishment, whatever their economic or racial group, have avoided execution is irrelevant. If they have, the guilt of the executed convicts would not be diminished, nor would their punishment be less deserved. To put the issue starkly, if the death penalty were imposed on guilty blacks, but not on guilty whites, or, if it were imposed by a lottery among the guilty, this irrationally discriminatory or capricious distribution would neither make the penalty unjust, nor cause anyone to be unjustly punished, despite the undue impunity bestowed on others.

Equality, in short, seems morally less important than justice. And justice is independent of distributional inequalities. The ideal of equal justice demands that justice be equally distributed, not that it be replaced by equality. Justice requires that as many of the guilty as possible be punished, regardless of whether others have avoided punishment. To let these others escape the deserved punishment does not do justice to them, or to society. But it is not unjust to those who could not escape.

These moral considerations are not meant to deny that irrational discrimination, or capriciousness, would be inconsistent with constitutional requirements. But I am satisfied that the Supreme Court has in fact provided for adherence to the constitutional requirement of equality as much as is possible. Some inequality is indeed unavoidable as a practical matter in any system.[4] But, *ultra posse nemo obligatur.* (Nobody is bound beyond ability.)

Recent data reveal little direct racial discrimination in the sentencing of those arrested and convicted of murder.[5] The abrogation of death penalty for rape has eliminated a major source of racial discrimination. Concededly, some discrimination based on the race of murder victims may exist; yet, this discrimination affects criminal victimizers in an unexpected way. Murderers of whites are thought more likely to be executed than murderers of blacks. Black victims, then, are less fully vindicated than white ones. However, because most black murderers kill blacks, black murderers are spared the death penalty more often than are white murderers. They fare better than most white murderers.[6] The motivation behind unequal distribution of the death penalty may well have been to discriminate against blacks, but the result has favored them. Maldistribution is thus a straw man for empirical as well as analytical reasons.

II. MISCARRIAGES OF JUSTICE

In a recent survey Professors Hugo Adam Bedau and Michael Radelet found that 7000 persons were executed in the United States between 1900 and 1985 and that 25 were innocent of capital crimes.[7] Among the innocents they list Sacco and Vanzetti as well as Ethel and Julius Rosenberg. Although their data may be questionable, I do not doubt that, over a long enough period, miscarriages of justice will occur even in capital cases.

Despite precautions, nearly all human activities, such as trucking, lighting, or construction, cost the lives of some innocent bystanders. We do not give up these activities, because the advantages, moral or material, outweigh the unintended losses.[8] Analogously, for those who think the death penalty just, miscarriages of justice are offset by the moral benefits and the usefulness of doing justice. For those who think the death penalty unjust even when it does not miscarry, miscarriages can hardly be decisive.

III. DETERRENCE

Despite much recent work, there has been no conclusive statistical demonstration that the death penalty is a better deterrent than are alternative punishments. However, deterrence is less than decisive for either side. Most abolitionists acknowledge that they would continue to favor abolition even if the death penalty were shown to deter more murders than alternatives could deter.[9] Abolitionists appear to value the life of a convicted murderer or, at least, his non-execution, more highly than they value the lives of the innocent victims who might be spared by deterring prospective murderers.

Deterrence is not altogether decisive for me either. I would favor retention of the death penalty as retribution even if it were shown that the threat of execution could not deter prospective murderers not already deterred by the threat of imprisonment.[10] Still, I believe the death penalty, because of its finality, is more feared than imprisonment, and deters some prospective murderers not deterred by the threat of imprisonment. Sparing the lives of even a few prospective victims by deterring their murderers is more important than preserving the lives of convicted murderers because of the possibility, or even the probability, that executing them would not deter others. Whereas the lives of the victims who might be saved are valuable, that of the murderer has only negative value, because of his crime. Surely the criminal law is meant to protect the lives of potential victims in preference to those of actual murderers.

Murder rates are determined by many factors; neither the severity nor the probability of the threatened sanction is always decisive. However, for the long run, I share the view of Sir James Fitzjames Stephen: "Some men, probably, abstain from murder because they fear that if they committed murder they would be hanged. Hundreds of thousands abstain from it because they regard it with horror. One great reason why they regard it with horror is that murderers are hanged."[11] Penal sanctions are useful in the long run for the formation of the internal restraints so necessary to control crime. The severity and finality of the death penalty is appropriate to the seriousness and the finality of murder.[12]

IV. INCIDENTAL ISSUES: COST, RELATIVE SUFFERING, BRUTALIZATION

Many nondecisive issues are associated with capital punishment. Some believe that the monetary cost of appealing a capital sentence is excessive. Yet most comparisons of the cost of life imprisonment with the cost of execution, apart from their dubious relevance, are flawed at least by the implied assumption that life prisoners will generate no judicial costs during their imprisonment. At any rate, the actual monetary costs are trumped by the importance of doing justice.

Others insist that a person sentenced to death suffers more than his victim suffered, and that this (excess) suffering is undue according to the *lex talionis* (rule of retaliation). We cannot know whether the murderer on death row suffers more than his victim suffered; however, unlike the murderer, the victim deserved none of the suffering inflicted. Further, the limitations of the *lex talionis* were meant to restrain private vengeance, not the social retribution that has taken its place. Punishment—regardless of the motivation—is not intended to revenge, offset, or compensate for the victim's suffering, or to be measured by it. Punishment is to vindicate the law and the social order undermined by the crime. This is why a kidnapper's penal confinement is not limited to the period for which he imprisoned his victim; nor is a burglar's confinement meant merely to offset the suffering or the harm he caused his victim; nor is it meant only to offset the advantage he gained.[13]

Another argument heard . . . is that, by killing a murderer, we encourage, endorse, or legitimize unlawful killing. Yet, although all punishments are meant to be unpleasant, it is seldom argued that they legitimize the unlawful imposition of identical unpleasantness. Imprisonment is not thought to legitimize kidnapping; neither are fines thought to legitimize robbery. The difference between murder and execution, or between kidnapping and imprisonment, is that the first is unlawful and undeserved, the second a lawful and deserved punishment for an unlawful act. The physical similarities of the punishment to the crime are irrelevant. The relevant difference is not physical, but social.[14]

V. JUSTICE, EXCESS, DEGRADATION

We threaten punishments in order to deter crime. We impose them not only to make the threats credible but also as retribution (justice) for the crimes that were not deterred. Threats and punishments are necessary to deter and deterrence is a sufficient practical justification for them. Retribution is an independent moral justification. Although penalties can be unwise, repulsive, or inappropriate, and those punished can be pitiable, in a sense the infliction of legal punishment on a guilty person cannot be unjust. By committing the crime, the criminal volunteered to assume the risk of receiving a legal punishment that he could have avoided by not committing the crime. The punishment he suffers is the punishment he voluntarily risked suffering and, therefore, it is no more unjust to him than any other event for which one knowingly volunteers to assume the risk. Thus, the death penalty cannot be unjust to the guilty criminal.[15]

There remain, however, two moral objections. The penalty may be regarded as always excessive as retribution and always morally degrading. To regard the death penalty as always excessive, one must believe that no crime—no matter how heinous—could possibly justify capital punishment. Such a belief can be neither corroborated nor refuted; it is an article of faith.

Alternatively, or concurrently, one may believe that everybody, the murderer no less than the victim, has an imprescriptible (natural?) right to life. The law therefore should not deprive anyone of life. I share Jeremy Bentham's view that any such "natural and imprescriptible rights" are "nonsense upon stilts."[16]

Justice Brennan has insisted that the death penalty is "uncivilized," "inhuman," inconsistent with "human dignity" and with "the sanctity of life," that it "treats members of the human race as nonhumans, as objects to be toyed with and discarded," that it is "uniquely degrading to human dignity" and "by its very nature, [involves] a denial of the executed person's humanity." Justice Brennan does not say why he thinks execution "uncivilized." Hitherto most civilizations have had the death penalty, although it has been discarded in Western Europe, where it is currently unfashionable probably because of its abuse by totalitarian regimes.

By "degrading," Justice Brennan seems to mean that execution degrades the executed convicts. Yet philosophers, such as Immanuel Kant and G. W. F. Hegel, have insisted that, when deserved, execution, far from degrading the executed convict, affirms his humanity by affirming his rationality and his responsibility for his actions. They thought that execution, when deserved, is required for the sake of the convict's dignity. (Does not life imprisonment violate human dignity more than execution, by keeping alive a prisoner deprived of all autonomy?)

Common sense indicates that it cannot be death—our common fate—that is inhuman. Therefore, Justice Brennan must mean that death degrades when it comes not as a natural or accidental event, but as a deliberate social imposition. The murderer learns through his punishment that his fellow men have found him unworthy of living; that because he has murdered, he is being expelled from the community of the living. This degradation is self-inflicted. By murdering, the murderer has so dehumanized himself that he cannot remain among the living. The social recognition of his self-degradation is the punitive essence of execution. To believe, as Justice Brennan appears to, that the degradation is inflicted by the execution reverses the direction of causality.

Execution of those who have committed heinous murders may deter only one murder per year. If it does, it seems quite warranted. It is also the only fitting retribution for murder I can think of.

NOTES

1. Death row as a semipermanent residence is cruel, because convicts are denied the normal amenities of prison life. Thus, unless death row residents are integrated into the prison population, the continuing accumulation of convicts on death row should lead us to accelerate either the rate of executions or the rate of communications. I find little objection to integration.

2. The debate about the insanity defense is important for analogous reasons.

3. Some writers, for example, Cesare Bonesana, Marchese di Beccaria, have thought that life imprisonment is more severe. However, the overwhelming majority of both abolitionists and of convicts under death sentence prefer life imprisonment to execution.

4. The ideal of equality, unlike the ideal of retributive justice (which can be approximated separately in each instance), is clearly unattainable unless all guilty persons are apprehended, and therefore tried, convicted and sentenced by the same court, at the same time. Unequal justice is the best we can do; it is still better than the injustice, equal or unequal, which occurs if, for the sake of equality, we deliberately allow some who could be punished to escape.

5. *See* BUREAU OF JUSTICE STATISTICS, U.S. DEP'T OF JUSTICE, BULLETIN No. NJC-98,399, CAPITAL PUNISHMENT 1984, at 9 (1985); Johnson, *The Executioner's Bias*, NAT'L REV., Nov. 15, 1985, at 44.

6. It barely need be said that any discrimination *against* (for example, black murderers of whites) must also be discrimination *for* (for example, black murderers of blacks).

7. Bedau & Radelet, *Miscarriages of Justice in Potentially Capital Cases* (1st draft, Oct. 1985) (on file at Harvard Law School Library).

8. An excessive number of trucking accidents or of miscarriages of justice could offset the benefits gained by trucking or the practice of doing justice. We are, however, far from this situation.

9. For most abolitionists, the discrimination argument, *see supra* pp. 1662–64, is similarly nondecisive: they would favor abolition even if there could be no racial discrimination.

10. If executions were shown to increase the murder rate in the long run, I would favor abolition. Sparing the innocent victims who would be spared by the nonexecution of murderers would be more important to me than the execution, however just, of murderers. But although there is a lively discussion of the subject, no serious evidence exists to support the hypothesis that executions produce a higher murder rate.

11. H. GROSS, A THEORY OF CRIMINAL JUSTICE 489 (1979) (attributing this passage to Sir James Fitzjames Stephen).

12. Weems v. United States, 217 U.S. 349 (1910), suggests that penalties be proportionate to the seriousness of the crime—a common theme of the criminal law. Murder, therefore, demands more than life imprisonment, if, as I believe, it is a more serious crime than other crimes punished by life imprisonment. In modern times, our sensibility requires that the range of punishments be narrower than the range of crimes—but not so narrow as to exclude the death penalty.

13. Thus restitution (a civil liability) cannot satisfy the punitive purpose of penal sanctions, whether the purpose be retributive or deterrent.

14. Some abolitionists challenge: if the death penalty is just and serves as a deterrent, why not televise executions? The answer is simple. The death even of a murderer, however well-deserved, should not serve as public entertainment. It so served in earlier centuries. But in this respect our sensibility has changed for the better, I believe. Further, television unavoidably would trivialize executions, wedged in, as they would be, between game shows, situation comedies and the like. Finally, because televised executions would focus on the physical aspects of the punishment, rather than the nature of the crime and the suffering of the victim, a televised execution would present the murderer as the victim of the state. Far from communicating the moral significance of the execution, television would shift the focus to the pitiable fear of the murderer. We no longer place in cages those sentenced to imprisonment to expose them to public view. Why should we so expose those sentenced to execution?

15. An explicit threat of punitive action is necessary to the justification of any legal punishment: *nulla poena sine lege* (no punishment without [preexisting] law). To be sufficiently justified, the threat must in turn have a rational and legitimate purpose. "Your money or your life" does not qualify; nor does the threat of an unjust law; nor, finally, does a threat that is altogether disproportionate to the importance of its purpose. In short, preannouncement legitimizes the threatened punishment only if the threat is warranted. But this leaves a very wide range of justified threats. Furthermore, the punished person is aware of the penalty for his actions and thus volunteers to take the risk even of an unjust punishment. His victim, however, did not volunteer to risk anything. The question whether any self-inflicted injury—such as a legal punishment—ever can be unjust to a person who knowingly risked it is a matter that requires more analysis than is possible here.

16. THE WORKS OF JEREMY BENTHAM 105 (J. Bowring ed. 1972).

From *Justice, Civilization, and the Death Penalty: Answering van den Haag*

Jeffrey H. Reiman

On the issue of capital punishment, there is as clear a clash of moral intuitions as we are likely to see. Some (now a majority of Americans) feel deeply that justice requires payment in kind and thus that murderers should die; and others (once, but no longer, nearly a majority of Americans) feel deeply that the state ought not be in the business of putting people to death.[1] Arguments for either side that do not do justice to the intuitions of the other are unlikely to persuade anyone not already convinced. And, since, as I shall suggest, there is truth on both sides, such arguments are easily refutable, leaving us with nothing but conflicting intuitions and no guidance from reason in distinguishing the better from the worse. In this context, I shall try to make an argument for the abolition of the death penalty that does justice to the intuitions on both sides. I shall sketch out a conception of retributive justice that accounts for the justice of executing murderers, and then I shall argue that *though the death penalty is a just punishment for murder*, abolition of the death penalty is part of the civilizing mission of modern states.

* * *

[I.] JUST DESERTS AND JUST PUNISHMENTS

In my view, the death penalty is a just punishment for murder because the *lex talionis*, an eye for an eye, and so on, is just, although, as I shall suggest at the end of this section, it can only be rightly applied when its implied preconditions are satisfied. The *lex talionis* is a version of retributivism. Retributivism—as the word itself suggests—is the doctrine that the offender should be *paid back* with suffering he deserves because of the evil he has done, and the *lex talionis* asserts that injury equivalent to that he imposed is what the offender deserves.[2] But the *lex talionis* is not the only version of retributivism. Another, which I shall call "proportional retributivism," holds that what retribution requires is not equality of injury between crimes and punishments, but "fit" or proportionality, such that the worst crime is punished with the society's worst penalty, and so on, though the society's worst punishment need not duplicate the injury of the worst crime.[3] Later, I shall try to show how a form of proportional retributivism is compatible with acknowledging the justice of the *lex talionis*. Indeed, since I shall defend the justice of the *lex talionis*, I take such compatibility as a necessary condition of the validity of any form of retributivism.

There is nothing self-evident about the justice of the *lex talionis* nor, for that matter, of retributivism. The standard problem confronting those who would justify retributivism is that of overcoming the suspicion that it does no more than sanctify the victim's desire to hurt the offender back. Since serving that desire amounts to hurting the offender simply for the satisfaction that the victim derives from seeing the offender suffer, and since deriving satisfaction from the suffering of others seems primitive, the policy of imposing suffering on the offender for no other purpose than giving satisfaction to his victim seems primitive as well. Consequently, defending retributivism requires showing that the suffering imposed on the wrongdoer has some worthy point beyond the satisfaction of victims. In what follows, I shall try to identify a proposition—which I call the *retributivist principle*—that I take to be the nerve of retributivism. I think this principle accounts for the justice of the *lex talionis* and indicates the point of the suffering demanded by retributivism. Not to do too much of the work of the death penalty advocate, I shall make no extended argument for the principle beyond suggesting the considerations that make it plausible. I shall identify these considerations by drawing, with considerable license, on Hegel and Kant.

I think that we can see the justice of the *lex talionis* by focusing on the striking affinity between it and the *golden rule*. The *golden rule* mandates "Do unto others as you would have others do unto you," while the *lex talionis* counsels "Do unto others as they have done unto you." It would not be too far-fetched to say that the *lex talionis* is the law enforcement arm of the golden rule, at least in the sense that if people were actually treated as they treated others, then everyone would necessarily follow the golden rule because then people could only willingly act toward others as they were willing to have others act toward them. This is not to suggest that the *lex talionis* follows from the golden rule, but rather that the two share a common moral inspiration: the equality of persons. Treating others as you *would* have them treat you means treating others as equal to you, because adopting the golden rule as one's guiding principle implies that one counts the suffering of others to be as great a calamity as one's own suffering, that one counts one's right to impose suffering on others as no greater than their right to impose suffering on one, and so on. This leads to the *lex talionis* by two approaches that start from different points and converge.

I call the first approach "Hegelian" because Hegel held (roughly) that crime upsets the equality between persons and retributive punishment restores that equality by "annulling" the crime.[4] As we have seen, acting according to the golden rule implies treating others as your equals. Conversely, violating the golden rule implies the reverse: Doing to another what you would *not* have that other do to you violates the equality of persons by asserting a right toward the other that the other does not possess toward you. Doing back to you what you did "annuls" your violation by reasserting that the other has the same right toward you that you assert toward him. Punishment according to the *lex talionis* cannot heal the injury that the other has suffered at your hands, rather it rectifies the indignity he has suffered, by restoring him to equality with you.

"Equality of persons" here does not mean equality of concern for their happiness, as it might for a utilitarian. On such a (roughly) utilitarian understanding of equality, imposing suffering on the wrongdoer equivalent to the suffering he has imposed would have little

point. Rather, equality of concern for people's happiness would lead us to impose as little suffering on the wrongdoer as was compatible with maintaining the happiness of others. This is enough to show that retributivism (at least in this "Hegelian" form) reflects a conception of morality quite different from that envisioned by utilitarianism. Instead of seeing morality as administering doses of happiness to individual recipients, the retributivist envisions morality as maintaining the relations appropriate to equally sovereign individuals. A crime, rather than representing a unit of suffering added to the already considerable suffering in the world, is an assault on the sovereignty of an individual that temporarily places one person (the criminal) in a position of illegitimate sovereignty over another (the victim). The victim (or his representative, the state) then has the right to rectify this loss of standing relative to the criminal by meting out a punishment that reduces the criminal's sovereignty in the degree to which he vaunted it above his victim's. It might be thought that this is a duty, not just a right, but that is surely too much. The victim has the right to forgive the violator without punishment, which suggests that it is by virtue of having the right to punish the violator (rather than the duty), that the victim's equality with the violator is restored.

I call the second approach "Kantian" since Kant held (roughly) that, since reason (like justice) is no respecter of the sheer difference between individuals, when a rational being decides to act in a certain way toward his fellows, he implicitly authorizes similar action by his fellows toward him.[5] A version of the golden rule, then, is a requirement of reason: acting rationally, one always acts as he would have others act toward him. Consequently, to act toward a person as he has acted toward others is to treat him as a rational being, that is, as if his act were the product of a rational decision. From this, it may be concluded that we have a duty to do to offenders what they have done, since this amounts to according them the respect due rational beings.[6] Here too, however, the assertion of a duty to punish seems excessive, since, if this duty arises because doing to people what they have done to others is necessary to accord them the respect due rational beings, then we would have a duty to do to all rational persons *everything*—good, bad, or indifferent—that they do to others. The point rather is that, by his acts, a rational being *authorizes* others to do the same to him, he doesn't *compel* them to. Here too, then, the argument leads to a right, rather than a duty, to exact the *lex talionis*. And this is supported by the fact that we can conclude from Kant's argument that a rational being cannot validly complain of being treated in the way he has treated others, and where there is no valid complaint, there is no injustice, and where there is no injustice, others have acted within their rights.[7] It should be clear that the Kantian argument also rests on the equality of persons, because a rational agent only implicitly authorizes having done to him action similar to what he has done to another, if he and the other are similar in the relevant ways.

The "Hegelian" and "Kantian" approaches arrive at the same destination from opposite sides. The "Hegelian" approach starts from the victim's equality with the criminal, and infers from it the victim's right to do to the criminal what the criminal has done to the victim. The "Kantian" approach starts from the criminal's rationality, and infers from it the criminal's authorization of the victim's right to do to the criminal what the criminal has done to the victim. Taken together, these approaches support the following proposition: The equality and rationality of persons implies that an offender deserves and his victim has the right to impose suffering on the offender equal to that which he imposed on the victim. This is the proposition I call the *retributivist principle*, and I shall assume henceforth that it is true. This principle provides that the *lex talionis* is the criminal's just desert and the victim's (or as his representative, the state's) right. Moreover, the principle also indicates the point of retributive punishment, namely, it affirms the equality and rationality of persons, victims and offenders alike. And the point of this affirmation is, like any moral affirmation, to make a statement, to the criminal, to impress upon him his equality with his victim (which earns him a like fate) and his rationality (by which his actions are held to authorize his fate), and to the society, so that recognition of the equality and rationality of persons becomes a visible part of our shared moral environment that none can ignore in justifying their actions to one another.

* * *

The truth of the retributivist principle establishes the justice of the *lex talionis*, but, since it establishes this as a right of the victim rather than a duty, it does not settle the question of whether or to what extent the victim or the state should exercise this right and exact the *lex talionis*. This is a separate moral question because strict adherence to the *lex talionis* amounts to allowing criminals, even the most barbaric of them, to dictate our punishing behavior. It seems certain that there are at least some crimes, such as rape or torture, that we ought not try to match. And this is not merely a matter of imposing an alternative punishment that produces an equivalent amount of suffering, as, say, some number of years in prison that might "add up" to the harm caused by a rapist or a torturer. Even if no amount of time in prison would add up to the harm caused by a torturer, it still seems that we ought not torture him even if this were the only way of making him suffer as much as he has made his victim suffer. Or, consider someone who has committed several murders in cold blood. On the *lex talionis*, it would seem that such a criminal might justly be brought to within an inch of death and then revived (or to within a moment of execution and then reprieved) as many times as he has killed (minus one), and then finally executed. But surely this is a degree of cruelty that would be monstrous.

Since the retributivist principle establishes the *lex talionis* as the victim's right, it might seem that the question of how far this right should be exercised is "up to the victim." And indeed, this would be the case in the state of nature. But once, for all the good reasons familiar to readers of John Locke, the state comes into existence, public punishment replaces private, and the victim's right to punish reposes in the state. With this, the decision as to how far to exercise this right goes to the state as well. To be sure, since (at least with respect to retributive punishment) the victim's right is the source of the state's right to punish, the state must exercise its right in ways that are faithful to the victim's right. Later, when I try to spell out the upper and lower limits of just punishment, these may be taken as indicating the range within which the state can punish and remain faithful to the victim's right.

I suspect that it will be widely agreed that the state ought not administer punishments of the sort described above even if required by the letter of the *lex talionis*, and thus, even granting the justice of *lex talionis*, there are occasions on which it is morally appropriate to diverge from its requirements. We must, of course, distinguish such morally based divergence from that which is based on practicality. Like any moral principle, the *lex talionis* is subject to "ought implies can." It will usually be impossible to do to an offender exactly what he has done—for example, his offense will normally have had an element of surprise that is not possible for a judicially imposed punishment, but this fact can hardly free him from having to bear the suffering he has imposed on another. Thus, for reasons of practicality, the *lex talionis* must necessarily be qualified to call for doing to the offender *as nearly as possible* what he has done to his victim. When, however, we refrain from raping rapists or torturing torturers, we do so for reasons of morality, not of practicality. And, given the justice of the *lex talionis*, these moral reasons cannot amount to claiming that it would be *unjust* to rape rapists or torture torturers. Rather the claim must be that, even though it would be just to rape rapists and torture torturers, other moral considerations weigh against doing so.

* * *

This way of understanding just punishment enables us to formulate proportional retributivism so that it is compatible with acknowledging the justice of the *lex talionis*: If we take the *lex talionis* as spelling out the offender's just deserts, and if other moral considerations require us to refrain from matching the injury caused by the offender while still allowing us to punish justly, then surely we impose just punishment if we impose the closest morally acceptable approximation to the *lex talionis*. Proportional retributivism, then, in requiring that the worst crime be punished by the society's worst punishment and so on, could

be understood as translating the offender's just desert into its nearest equivalent in the society's table of morally acceptable punishments. Then the two versions of retributivism (*lex talionis* and proportional) are related in that the first states what just punishment would be if nothing but the offender's just desert mattered, and the second locates just punishment at the meeting point of the offender's just deserts and the society's moral scruples. And since this second version only modifies the requirements of the *lex talionis* in light of other moral considerations, it is compatible with believing that the *lex talionis* spells out the offender's just deserts, much in the way that modifying the obligations of promisers in light of other moral considerations is compatible with believing in the binding nature of promises.

* * *

[II.] CIVILIZATION, PAIN, AND JUSTICE

As I have already suggested, from the fact that something is justly deserved, it does not automatically follow that it should be done, since there may be other moral reasons for not doing it such that, all told, the weight of moral reasons swings the balance against proceeding. The same argument that I have given for the justice of the death penalty for murderers proves the justice of beating assaulters, raping rapists, and torturing torturers. Nonetheless, I believe, and suspect that most would agree, that it would not be right for us to beat assaulters, rape rapists, or torture torturers, *even though it were their just deserts*—and even if this were the only way to make them suffer as much as they had made their victims suffer. Calling for the abolition of the death penalty, though it be just, then, amounts to urging that as a society we place execution in the same category of sanction as beating, raping, and torturing, and treat it as something it would also not be right for us to do to offenders, *even if it were their just deserts*.

To argue for placing execution in this category, I must show what would be gained therefrom; and to show that, I shall indicate what we gain from placing torture in this category and argue that a similar gain is to be had from doing the same with execution.

I select torture because I think the reasons for placing it in this category are, due to the extremity of torture, most easily seen—but what I say here applies with appropriate modification to other severe physical punishments, such as beating and raping. First, and most evidently, placing torture in this category broadcasts the message that we as a society judge torturing so horrible a thing to do to a person that we refuse to do it even when it is deserved. Note that such a judgment does not commit us to an absolute prohibition on torturing. No matter how horrible we judge something to be, we may still be justified in doing it if it is necessary to prevent something even worse. Leaving this aside for the moment, what is gained by broadcasting the public judgment that torture is too horrible to inflict even if deserved?

I think the answer to this lies in what we understand as civilization. In *The Genealogy of Morals*, Nietzsche says that in early times "pain did not hurt as much as it does today."[8] The truth in this puzzling remark is that progress in civilization is characterized by a lower tolerance for one's own pain and that suffered by others. And this is appropriate, since, via growth in knowledge, civilization brings increased power to prevent or reduce pain and, via growth in the ability to communicate and interact with more and more people, civilization extends the circle of people with whom we empathize. If civilization is characterized by lower tolerance for our own pain and that of others, then publicly refusing to do horrible things to our fellows both signals the level of our civilization *and, by our example, continues the work of civilizing*. And this gesture is all the more powerful if we refuse to do horrible things to those who deserve them. I contend then that the more things we are able to include in this category, the more civilized we are and the more civil*izing*. Thus we gain from including torture in this category, and if execution is especially horrible, we gain still more by including it.

* * *

Thus far, by analogy with torture, I have argued that execution should be avoided because of how horrible it is to the one executed. But there are reasons of another sort that follow from the analogy with torture. Torture is to be avoided not only because of what it says about *what* we are willing to do to our fellows, but also because of what it says about *us* who are willing to do it. To torture someone is an awful spectacle not only because of the intensity of pain imposed, but because of what is required to be able to impose such pain on one's fellows. The tortured body cringes, using its full exertion to escape the pain imposed upon it—it literally begs for relief with its muscles as it does with its cries. To torture someone is to demonstrate a capacity to resist this begging, and that in turn demonstrates a kind of hardheartedness that a society ought not parade.

And this is true not only of torture, but of all severe corporal punishment. Indeed, I think this constitutes part of the answer to the puzzling question of why we refrain from punishments like whipping, even when the alternative (some months in jail versus some lashes) seems more costly to the offender. Imprisonment is painful to be sure, but it is a reflective pain, one that comes with comparing what is to what might have been, and that can be temporarily ignored by thinking about other things. But physical pain has an urgency that holds body and mind in a fierce grip. Of physical pain, as Orwell's Winston Smith recognized, "you could only wish one thing: that it should stop."[9] Refraining from torture in particular and corporal punishment in general, we both refuse to put a fellow human being in this grip *and* refuse to show our ability to resist this wish. The death penalty is the last corporal punishment used officially in the modern world. And it is corporal not only because administered via the body, but because the pain of foreseen, humanly administered death strikes us with the urgency that characterizes intense physical pain, causing grown men to cry, faint, and lose control of their bodily functions. There is something to be gained by refusing to endorse the hardness of heart necessary to impose such a fate.

By placing execution alongside torture in the category of things we will not do to our fellow human beings even when they deserve them, we broadcast the message that totally subjugating a person to the power of others *and* confronting him with the advent of his own humanly administered demise is too horrible to be done by civilized human beings to their fellows even when they have earned it: too horrible to do, and too horrible to be capable of doing. And I contend that broadcasting this message loud and clear would in the long run contribute to the general detestation of murder and be, to the extent to which it worked itself into the hearts and minds of the populace, a deterrent. In short, refusing to execute murderers though they deserve it both reflects and continues the taming of the human species that we call civilization. Thus, I take it that the abolition of the death penalty, though it is a just punishment for murder, is part of the civilizing mission of modern states.

* * *

NOTES

1. Asked, in a 1981 Gallup Poll, "Are you in favor of the death penalty for persons convicted of murder?" 66.25% were in favor, 25% were opposed, and 8.75% had no opinion. Asked the same question in 1966, 47.5% were opposed, 41.25% were in favor, and 11.25% had no opinion (Timothy J. Flanagan, David J. van Alstyne, and Michael R. Gottfredson, eds., *Sourcebook of Criminal Justice Statistics—1981*, U.S. Department of Justice, Bureau of Justice Statistics [Washington, D.C.: U.S. Government Printing Office, 1982], p. 209).

2. I shall speak throughout of retribution as paying back for "harm caused," but this is shorthand for "harm intentionally attempted or caused"; likewise when I speak of the death penalty as punishment for murder, I have in mind premeditated, first-degree murder. Note also that the harm caused by an offender, for which he is to be paid back, is not necessarily limited to the harm done to his immediate victim. It may include as well the suffering of the victim's relatives or the fear produced in the general populace, and the like. For simplicity's sake, however, I shall continue to speak as if the harm for which retributivism would have us pay the offender back is the harm (intentionally attempted or done) to his immediate victim. Also, retribution is not to be confused with *restitution*. Restitution involves restoring the *status quo ante*, the condition prior to the offense. Since it was in this condition that the criminal's offense was committed, it is this condition that constitutes the baseline against which retribution is exacted. Thus retribution involves imposing a loss on the offender measured from the status quo ante. For example, returning a thief's loot to his victim so that thief and victim now own what they did before the offense is *restitution*. Taking

enough from the thief so that what he is left with is less than what he had before the offense is *retribution*, since this is just what he did to his victim.

3. "The most extreme form of retributivism is the law of retaliation: 'an eye for an eye'" (Stanley I. Benn, "Punishment," *The Encyclopedia of Philosophy* 7, ed. Paul Edwards [New York: Macmillan, 1967], p. 32). Hugo Bedau writes: "retributive justice need not be thought to consist of *lex talionis*. One may reject that principle as too crude and still embrace the retributive principle that the severity of punishments should be graded according to the gravity of the offense" (Hugo Bedau, "Capital Punishment," in *Matters of Life and Death*, ed. Tom Regan [New York: Random House, 1980], p. 177).

4. Hegel writes that "The sole positive existence which the injury [i.e., the crime] possesses is that it is the particular will of the criminal [i.e., it is the criminal's intention that distinguishes criminal injury from, say, injury due to an accident]. Hence to injure (or penalize) this particular will as a will determinately existent is to annul the crime, which otherwise would have been held valid, and to restore the right" (G. W. F. Hegel, *The Philosophy of Right*, trans. by T. M. Knox [Oxford: Clarendon Press, 1962; originally published in German in 1821], p. 69, see also p. 331n). I take this to mean that the right is a certain equality of sovereignty between the wills of individuals, crime disrupts that equality by placing one will above others, and punishment restores the equality by annulling the illegitimate ascendance. On these grounds, as I shall suggest below, the desire for revenge (strictly limited to the desire "to even the score") is more respectable than philosophers have generally allowed. And so Hegel writes that "The annulling of crime in this sphere where right is immediate [i.e., the condition prior to conscious morality] is principally revenge, which is just in its content in so far as it is retributive" (ibid., p. 73).

5. Kant writes that "any undeserved evil that you inflict on someone else among the people is one that you do to yourself. If you vilify him, you vilify yourself; if you steal from him, you steal from yourself; if you kill him, you kill yourself." Since Kant holds that "If what happens to someone is also willed by him, it cannot be a punishment," he takes pains to distance himself from the view that the offender *wills* his punishment. "The chief error contained in this sophistry," Kant writes, "consists in the confusion of the criminal's [that is, the murderer's] own judgment (which one must necessarily attribute to his reason) that he must forfeit his life with a resolution of the will to take his own life" (Immanuel Kant, *The Metaphysical Elements of Justice, Part I of The Metaphysics of Morals*, trans. by J. Ladd [Indianapolis: Bobbs-Merrill, 1965; originally

published in 1797], pp. 101, 105–106). I have tried to capture this notion of attributing a judgment to the offender rather than a resolution of his will with the term 'authorizes.'

6. "Even if a civil society were to dissolve itself by common agreement of all its members. . . , the last murderer remaining in prison must first be executed, so that everyone will duly receive what his actions are worth" (Kant, ibid., p. 102).

7. "It may also be pointed out that no one has ever heard of anyone condemned to death on account of murder who complained that he was getting too much [punishment] and therefore was being treated unjustly; everyone would laugh in his face if he were to make such a statement" (Kant, *Metaphysical Elements of Justice*, p. 104; see also p. 133).

8. Friedrich Nietzsche, *The Birth of Tragedy and The Genealogy of Morals*, trans. Francis Golffing (New York: Doubleday, 1956), pp. 199–200.

9. George Orwell, *1984* (New York: New American Library, 1983; originally published in 1949), p. 197.

The Case Against the Death Penalty
Hugo Adam Bedau

CAPITAL PUNISHMENT AND SOCIAL DEFENSE

The Analogy with Self-Defense

Capital punishment, it is sometimes said, is to the body politic what self-defense is to the individual. If the latter is not morally wrong, how can the former be? To assess the strength of this analogy, we need first to inspect the morality of self-defense.

Except for absolute pacifists, who believe it is morally wrong to use violence even to defend themselves or others from undeserved aggression, most of us believe that it is not morally wrong and may even be our moral duty to use violence to prevent aggression directed against either ourselves or innocent third parties. The law has long granted persons the right to defend themselves against the unjust aggressions of others, even to the extent of using lethal force to kill an assailant. It is very difficult to think of any convincing argument that would show it is never rational to risk the death of another to prevent death or grave injury to oneself. Certainly self-interest dictates the legitimacy of self-defense. So does concern for the well-being of others. So also does justice. If it is unfair for one person to inflict undeserved violence

on another, then it is hard to see how morality could require the victim to acquiesce in the attempt by another to do so, even if resistance involves risks or injury to the assailant.

The foregoing account assumes that the person acting in self-defense is innocent of any provocation of the assailant. It also assumes that there is no alternative to victimization except resistance. In actual life, both assumptions—especially the second—are often false, because there may be a third alternative: escape, or removing oneself from the scene of imminent aggression. Hence, the law imposes on us the "duty to retreat." Before we use violence to resist aggression, we must try to get out of the way, lest unnecessary violence be used to resist aggression. Now suppose that unjust aggression is imminent, and there is no path open for escape. How much violence may justifiably be used to ward off aggression? The answer is: No more violence than is necessary to prevent the aggressive assault. Violence beyond that is unnecessary and therefore unjustified. We may restate the principle governing the use of violence in self-defense by reference to the concept of "deadly force" by the police in the discharge of their duties. The rule is this: Use of deadly force is justified only to prevent loss of life in immediate jeopardy where a lesser use of force cannot reasonably be expected to save the life that is threatened.

From Hugo Adam Bedau, "Capital Punishment," in *Matters of Life and Death*, ed. Tom Regan (New York: McGraw-Hill, 1993), 177–79, 181–91. Copyright © 1993 McGraw-Hill Education. Reprinted by permission.

In real life, violence in self-defense in excess of the minimum necessary to prevent aggression, even though it is not justifiable, is often excusable. One cannot always tell what will suffice to deter an aggressor and avoid becoming a victim; thus the law looks with a certain tolerance upon the frightened and innocent would-be victim who in self-protection turns upon a vicious assailant and inflicts a fatal injury even though a lesser injury would have been sufficient. What is not justified is deliberately using more violence than is necessary to avoid becoming a victim. It is the deliberate, not the impulsive or the unintentional, use of violence that is relevant to the death-penalty controversy, since the death penalty is enacted into law and carried out in each case deliberately—with ample time to weigh alternatives. Notice that we are assuming that the act of self-defense is to protect oneself or a third party. The reasoning outlined here does not extend to the defense of one's property. Shooting a thief to prevent one's automobile from being stolen cannot be excused or justified in the way that shooting an assailant charging with a knife pointed at one's face can be. Our criterion must be that deadly force is never justified to prevent crimes against property or other violent crimes not immediately threatening the life of an innocent person.

The rationale for self-defense as set out above illustrates two moral principles of great importance to our discussion. . . . One is that if a life is to be risked, then it is better that it be the life of someone who is guilty (in this context, the initial assailant) rather than the life of someone who is not (the innocent potential victim). It is not fair to expect the innocent prospective victim to run the added risk of severe injury or death in order to avoid using violence in self-defense to the extent of possibly killing his or her assailant. Rather, fairness dictates that the guilty aggressor ought to be the one to run the risk.

The other principle is that taking life deliberately is not justified so long as there is any feasible alternative. One does not expect miracles, of course, but in theory, if shooting a burglar through the foot will stop the burglary and enable one to call the police for help, then there is no reason to shoot to kill. Likewise, if the burglar is unarmed, there is no reason to shoot at all. In actual life, of course, a burglar is likely to be shot at by an aroused householder who does not know whether the burglar is armed, and prudence may seem to dictate the assumption that he or she is. Even so, although the burglar has no right to commit a felony against a person or a person's property, the attempt does not give the victims the right to respond in whatever way they please, and then to excuse or justify such conduct on the ground that they were "only acting in self-defense." In these ways the law shows a tacit regard for the life even of a felon and discourages the use of unnecessary violence even by the innocent; morality can hardly do less.

* * *

The Death Penalty and Deterrence

Determining whether the death penalty is an effective deterrent is even more difficult than determining its effectiveness as a crime preventive. In general, our knowledge about how penalties deter crimes and whether in fact they do—whom they deter, from which crimes, and under what conditions—is distressingly inexact. Most people nevertheless are convinced that punishments do deter, and that the more severe a punishment is the better it will deter. For half a century, social scientists have studied the questions whether the death penalty is a deterrent and whether it is a better deterrent than the alternative of imprisonment. Their verdict, while not unanimous, is nearly so. Whatever may be true about the deterrence of lesser crimes by other penalties, the deterrence achieved by the death penalty for murder is not measurably any greater than the deterrence achieved by long-term imprisonment. In the nature of the case, the evidence is quite indirect. No one can identify for certain any crimes that did not occur because the would-be offender was deterred by the threat of the death penalty and could not have been deterred by a less severe threat. Likewise, no one can identify any crimes that did occur because the offender was not deterred by the threat of prison even though he or she could have been deterred by the threat of death. Nevertheless, such evidence as we have fails to show that the more severe penalty (death) is really a better deterrent than the less severe penalty (imprisonment) for such crimes as murder.

If the death penalty and long-term imprisonment are equally effective (or ineffective) as deterrents to murder, then the argument for the death penalty on grounds of deterrence is seriously weakened. One of the moral principles identified earlier now comes into play: Unless there is a good reason for choosing a more rather than a less severe punishment for a crime, the less severe penalty is to be preferred. This principle obviously commends itself to anyone who values human life and who concedes that, all other things being equal, less pain and suffering is always better than more. Human life is valued in part to the degree that it is free of such experiences when they serve no known purpose. If the death penalty is not a more effective deterrent than imprisonment, then its greater severity amounts to nothing less than gratuitous suffering and deprivation. Accordingly, we must reject it in favor of some less severe alternative, unless we can identify some more weighty moral principle that the death penalty serves better and that any less severe mode of punishment ignores. Whether there is any such principle is unclear.

A Cost/Benefit Analysis of the Death Penalty

A full study of the costs and benefits involved in the practice of capital punishment would not be confined solely to the question of whether it is a better deterrent or preventive of murder than imprisonment. Any thoroughgoing utilitarian approach to the death-penalty controversy would need to examine carefully other costs and benefits as well, because maximizing the balance of all the social benefits over all the social costs is the sole criterion of right and wrong according to utilitarianism. . . . Let us consider, therefore, some of the other costs and benefits to be calculated. Clinical psychologists have presented evidence to suggest that the death penalty actually incites some persons of unstable mind to murder others, either because they are afraid to take their own lives and hope that society will punish them for murder by putting them to death, or because they fancy that they, too, are killing with justification analogously to the lawful and presumably justified killing involved in capital punishment. If such evidence is sound, capital punishment can serve as a counter-preventive or even an incitement to murder; such

incited murders become part of its social cost. Imprisonment, however, has not been known to incite any murders or other crimes of violence in a comparable fashion. (A possible exception might be found in the imprisonment of terrorists, which has inspired other terrorists to take hostages as part of a scheme to force the authorities to release their imprisoned comrades.) The risks of executing the innocent are also part of the social cost. The historical record is replete with innocent persons arrested, indicted, convicted, sentenced, and occasionally legally executed for crimes they did not commit. This is quite apart from the guilty persons unfairly convicted, sentenced to death, and executed on the strength of perjured testimony, fraudulent evidence, subornation of jurors, and other violations of the civil rights and liberties of the accused. Nor is this all. The high costs of a capital trial and of the inevitable appeals, the costly methods of custody most prisons adopt for convicts on "death row," are among the straightforward economic costs that the death penalty incurs. Conducting a valid cost/benefit analysis of capital punishment would be extremely difficult; nevertheless, on the basis of the evidence we have, it is quite possible that such a study would show that abolition of all death penalties is much less costly than their retention.

What If Executions Did Deter?

From the moral point of view, it is quite important to determine what one should think about capital punishment if the evidence were clearly to show that the death penalty is a distinctly superior method of social defense by comparison with less severe alternatives. Kantian moralists, as we have seen, . . . would have no use for such knowledge, because their entire case for the morality of the death penalty rests on the way it is thought to provide just retribution, not on the way it is thought to provide superior social defense. For a utilitarian, however, such knowledge would be conclusive. Those who follow Locke's reasoning would also be gratified, because they defend the morality of the death penalty both on the ground that it is retributively just and on the ground that it provides needed social defense.

What about the opponents of the death penalty, however? To oppose the death penalty in the face of incontestable evidence that it is an effective method of social defense violates the moral principle that where grave risks are to be run, it is better that they be run by the guilty than by the innocent. Consider in this connection an imaginary world in which executing the murderer would invariably restore the murder victim to life, whole and intact, as though no murder had ever occurred. In such a miraculous world, it is hard to see how anyone could oppose the death penalty on moral grounds. Why shouldn't a murderer die if that will infallibly bring the innocent victim back to life? What could possibly be morally wrong with taking the murderer's life under such conditions? The death penalty would be an instrument of perfect restitution, and it would give a new and better meaning to *lex talionis*, "a life for a life." The whole idea is fanciful, of course, but it shows as nothing else can how opposition to the death penalty cannot be both moral and wholly unconditional. If opposition to the death penalty is to be morally responsible, then it must be conceded that there are conditions (however unlikely) under which that opposition should cease.

But even if the death penalty were known to be a uniquely effective social defense, we could still imagine conditions under which it would be reasonable to oppose it. Suppose that in addition to being a slightly better preventive and deterrent than imprisonment, executions also have a slight incitive effect (so that for every ten murders an execution prevented or deterred, another murder was incited). Suppose also that the administration of criminal justice in capital cases was inefficient and unequal, and tended to secure convictions and death sentences only for murderers who least "deserved" to be sentenced to death (including some death sentences and a few executions of the innocent). Under such conditions, it would be reasonable to oppose the death penalty, because on the facts supposed more (or not fewer) innocent lives would be threatened and lost by using the death penalty than would be risked by abolishing it. It is important to remember throughout our evaluation of the deterrence controversy that we cannot ever apply the principle . . . that advises us to risk the lives of the guilty to save the lives of the innocent. Instead, we must rely on a weaker principle: Weigh the risk for the general public against

the execution of those who are *found* guilty by an imperfect system of criminal justice. These hypothetical factual assumptions illustrate the contingencies upon which the morality of opposition to the death penalty rests. And not only the morality of opposition; the morality of any defense of the death penalty rests on the same contingencies. This should help us understand why, in resolving the morality of capital punishment one way or the other, it is so important to know, as well as we can, whether the death penalty really does prevent or incite crime, whether the innocent really are ever executed, and how likely is the occurrence of these things in the future.

How Many Guilty Lives Is One Innocent Life Worth?

The great unanswered question that utilitarians must face concerns the level of social defense that executions should be expected to achieve before it is justifiable to carry them out. Consider three possible situations: (1) At the level of a hundred executions per year, each additional execution of a convicted murderer reduces the number of murder victims by ten. (2) Executing every convicted murderer reduces the number of murders to 5,000 victims annually, whereas executing only one out of ten reduces the number to 5,001. (3) Executing every convicted murderer reduces the murder rate no more than does executing one in a hundred and no more than does a random pattern of executions.

Many people contemplating situation (1) would regard this as a reasonable trade-off: The execution of each additional guilty person saves the lives of ten innocent ones. (In fact, situation (1) or something like it may be taken as a description of what most of those who defend the death penalty on grounds of social defense believe is true.) But suppose that, instead of saving 10 lives, the number dropped to 0.5, i.e., one victim avoided for each two additional executions. Would that be a reasonable price to pay? We are on the road toward the situation described in (2), where a drastic 90 percent reduction in the number of persons executed causes the level of social defense to drop by only 0.0002 percent. Would it be worth it to execute so many more murderers to obtain such a slight increase in social defense? How many guilty lives is one innocent life worth? (Only those who think that guilty lives are worthless—or of worth equal to that of the innocent—can avoid facing this problem.) In situation (3), of course, there is no basis for executing all convicted murderers, since there is no gain in social defense to show for each additional execution after the first out of each hundred has been executed. How, then, should we determine which out of each hundred convicted murderers is the unlucky one to be put to death?

If a complete and thoroughgoing cost/benefit analysis of the death penalty were possible, we might be able to answer such questions. But an appeal merely to the moral principle that if lives are to be risked then let it be the lives of the guilty rather than of the innocent will not suffice. (We have already noticed . . . that this abstract principle is of little use in the actual administration of criminal justice, because the police and the courts do not deal with the guilty as such but only with those *judged* guilty.) Nor will it suffice to agree that society deserves all the crime prevention and deterrence it can get as a result of inflicting severe punishments. These principles are consistent with too many different policies. They are too vague by themselves to resolve the choice on grounds of social defense when one is confronted with hypothetical situations like those proposed above.

Since no adequate cost/benefit analysis of the death penalty exists, there is no way to resolve these questions from that standpoint at this time. Moreover, it can be argued that we cannot have such an analysis without already establishing in some way or other the relative value of innocent lives versus guilty lives. Far from being a product of cost/benefit analysis, a comparative evaluation of lives would have to be available to us before we undertook any such analysis. Without it, no cost/benefit analysis of this problem can get off the ground. Finally, it must be noted that our knowledge at present does not indicate that we are in anything like the situation described above in (1). On the contrary, from the evidence we do have it seems we achieve about the same deterrent and preventive effects whether we punish murder by death or by imprisonment. . . . Something like the situation in (2) or in (3) may therefore be correct. If so, this shows that the choice between the two policies of capital punishment and life imprisonment for murder will probably have to be made on some basis

other than social defense; on that basis alone, the two policies are equivalent and therefore equally acceptable.

CAPITAL PUNISHMENT AND RETRIBUTIVE JUSTICE

No discussion of the morality of punishment would be complete without taking into account the two leading principles of retributive justice relevant to the capital punishment controversy. One is the principle that crimes ought to be punished. The other is the principle that the severity of a punishment ought to be proportional to the gravity of the offense. These are moral principles of recognized weight. Leaving aside all questions of social defense, how strong a case for capital punishment can be made on their basis? How reliable and persuasive are these principles themselves?

Crime Must Be Punished

Given the general rationale for punishment sketched earlier, . . . there cannot be any dispute over the principle that crime ought to be punished. In embracing it, of course, we are not automatically making a fetish of "law and order," in the sense that we would be if we thought that the most important single thing to do with social resources is to punish crimes. Fortunately, this principle need not be in dispute between proponents and opponents of the death penalty. Even defenders of the death penalty must admit that putting a convicted murderer in prison for years is a punishment of that criminal. The principle that crime must be punished is neutral to our controversy, because both sides acknowledge it.

The other principle of retributive justice is the one that seems to be decisive. Under *lex talionis*, it must always have seemed that murderers ought to be put to death. Proponents of the death penalty, with rare exceptions, have insisted on this point, and even opponents of the death penalty must give grudging assent to the seeming fittingness of demanding capital punishment for murder. The strategy for opponents of the death penalty is to argue either that (1) this principle is not really a principle of justice after all, or that (2) to the extent it is, it does not require death for murderers, or that (3) in any case it is not the only principle of punitive justice. As we shall see, all these objections have merit.

Is Murder Alone to Be Punished by Death?

Let us recall, first, that not even the biblical world limited the death penalty to the punishment of murder. Many other nonhomicidal crimes also carried this penalty (e.g., kidnapping, witchcraft, cursing one's parents). In our own nation's recent history, persons have been executed for aggravated assault, rape, kidnapping, armed robbery, sabotage, and espionage. It is not possible to defend *any* of these executions (not to mention some of the more bizarre capital statutes, like the one in Georgia that used to provide an optional death penalty for desecration of a grave) on grounds of just retribution. Either such executions are not justified or they are justified on some ground other than retribution. In actual practice, few if any defenders of the death penalty have ever been willing to rest their case entirely on the moral principle of just retribution as formulated in terms of "a life for a life." (Kant was a conspicuous exception.) Most defenders of the death penalty have implied by their willingness to use executions to defend not only life but limb and property as well, that they did not place much value on the lives of criminals when compared with the value of both lives and things belonging to innocent citizens.

Are All Murders to Be Punished by Death?

European civilization for several centuries has tended to limit the variety of criminal homicides punishable by death. Even Kant took a casual attitude toward a mother's killing of her illegitimate child. ("A child born into the world outside marriage is outside the law . . . , and consequently it is also outside the protection of the law."[1]) In the United States, the development two hundred years ago of the distinction between first- and second-degree murder was an attempt to narrow the class of criminal homicides deserving the death penalty. (First-degree murder has been variously defined. Typically it consists of (a) any willful, deliberate, premeditated homicide or (b) any homicide during the commission of another felony, e.g., armed robbery, rape, burglary. Second-degree murder is any other intentional homicide.) Yet those

dead owing to manslaughter, or to any kind of unintentional, accidental, unpremeditated, unavoidable, unmalicious killing are just as dead as the victims of the most ghastly murder. Both the law in practice and moral reflection show how difficult it is to identify all and only the criminal homicides that are appropriately punished by death (assuming that any are). Individual judges and juries differ in the conclusions they reach. The history of capital punishment for homicides reveals continual efforts, uniformly unsuccessful, to specify the criteria defining those homicides for which the slayer should die. Sixty years ago, Justice Benjamin Cardozo of the United States Supreme Court said of the distinction between degrees of murder that it was

> . . . so obscure that no jury hearing it for the first time can fairly be expected to assimilate and understand it. I am not at all sure that I understand it myself after trying to apply it for many years and after diligent study of what has been written in the books. Upon the basis of this fine distinction with its obscure and mystifying psychology, scores of men have gone to their death.[2]

Similar skepticism has been expressed on the reliability and rationality of death-penalty statutes that give the trial court the discretion to sentence to prison or to death. As Justice John Marshall Harlan of the Supreme Court observed some two decades ago,

> Those who have come to grips with the hard task of actually attempting to draft means of channeling capital sentencing discretion have confirmed the lesson taught by history. . . . To identify before the fact those characteristics of criminal homicide and their perpetrators which call for the death penalty, and to express these characteristics in language which can be fairly understood and applied by the sentencing authority, appear to be tasks which are beyond present human ability.[3]

The abstract principle that the punishment of death best fits the crime of murder turns out to be extremely difficult to interpret and apply.

If we look at the matter from the standpoint of the actual practice of criminal justice, we can only conclude that "a life for a life" plays little or no role whatever. Plea bargaining (in which a person charged with a crime pleads guilty in exchange for a less severe sentence than he might have received if his case went to trial and he was found guilty), even where murder is concerned, is widespread. Studies of criminal justice reveal that what the courts (trial or appellate) in a given jurisdiction decide on a given day is first-degree murder suitably punished by death could just as well have been decided in a neighboring jurisdiction on another day either as second-degree murder or as first-degree murder but without the death penalty. The factors that influence prosecutors in determining the charge under which they will prosecute go far beyond the simple principle of "a life for a life." Cynics, of course, will say that these facts show that our society does not care about justice. One might also reply that either justice in punishment does not consist of retribution, because there are other principles of justice; or there are other moral considerations besides justice that must be honored; or retributive justice is not adequately expressed in the idea of "a life for a life"; or justice in the criminal justice system is beyond our reach.

Is Death Sufficiently Retributive?

Those who advocate capital punishment for murder on retributive grounds must face the objection that, on their own principles, the death penalty in some cases is morally inadequate. How could death in the electric chair or the gas chamber or before a firing squad or by lethal injection suffice as just retribution, given the savage, brutal, wanton character of so many murders? How can retributive justice be served by anything less than equally savage methods of execution? From a retributive point of view, the oft-heard exclamation, "Death is too good for him!," has a certain truth. Are defenders of the death penalty willing to embrace this consequence of their own doctrine?

If they were, they would be stooping to the squalor of the murderer. Where the quality of the crime sets the limits of just methods of punishment, as it will if we attempt to give exact and literal implementation to *lex talionis*, society will find itself descending to the cruelties and savagery that criminals employ. What is worse, society would be deliberately authorizing such acts, in the cool light of reason, and not (as is usually true of vicious criminals) impulsively or in hatred and

anger or with an insane or unbalanced mind. Moral constraints, in short, prohibit us from trying to make executions perfectly retributive. Once we grant that such constraints are proper, it is unreasonable to insist that the principle of "a life for a life" nevertheless by itself justifies the execution of murderers.

Other considerations take us in a different direction. Few murders, outside television and movie scripts, involve anything like an execution. An execution, after all, begins with a solemn pronouncement of the death sentence from a judge; this is followed by detention of the convicted person in maximum security awaiting the date of execution, during which various complex and protracted appeals will be pursued; after this there is a clemency hearing before the governor, and then "the last mile" to the execution chamber itself. As the French writer Albert Camus once remarked,

> For there to be an equivalence, the death penalty would have to punish a criminal who had warned his victim of the date at which he would inflict a horrible death on him and who, from that moment onward, had confined him at his mercy for months. Such a monster is not encountered in private life.[4]

Differential Severity Does Not Require Executions

What, then, emerges from our examination of retributive justice and the death penalty? If retributive justice is thought to consist in *lex talionis*, all one can say is that this principle has never exercised more than a crude and indirect effect on the actual punishments meted out by society. Other moral principles interfere with a literal and single-minded application of this one. Some homicides seem improperly punished by death at all; others would require methods of execution too horrible to inflict. In any case, proponents of the death penalty rarely confine themselves to reliance on nothing but this principle of just retribution, since they rarely confine themselves to supporting the death penalty only for murder.

But retributive justice need not be identified with *lex talionis*. One may reject that principle as too crude and still embrace the retributive principle that the severity of punishments should be graded according to the gravity of the offense. Even though one need not claim that life imprisonment (or any kind of punishment other than death) "fits" the crime of murder, one can claim that this punishment is the proper one for murder. To do this, the schedule of punishments accepted by society must be arranged so that this mode of imprisonment is the most severe penalty used. Opponents of the death penalty can embrace this principle of retributive justice, even though they must reject a literal *lex talionis*.

Equal Justice and Capital Punishment

During the past generation, the strongest practical objection to the death penalty has been the inequity with which it has been applied. As the late Supreme Court Justice William O. Douglas once observed, "One searches our chronicles in vain for the execution of any member of the affluent strain of the society.[5] One does not search our chronicles in vain for the crime of murder committed by the affluent. All the sociological evidence points to the conclusion that the death penalty is the poor man's justice; hence the slogan, "Those without the capital get the punishment." The death penalty is also racially sensitive. Every study of the death penalty for rape (unconstitutional only since 1977) has confirmed that black rapists (especially where the victim is white) are far more likely to be sentenced to death and executed than white rapists. Convicted black murderers are more likely to end up on "death row" than are others, and the killers of whites (whether white or nonwhite) are more likely to be sentenced to death than are the killers of nonwhites.

Let us suppose that the factual basis for such a criticism is sound. What follows for the morality of capital punishment? Many defenders of the death penalty have been quick to point out that since there is nothing intrinsic about the crime of murder or rape dictating that only the poor or only racial-minority males will commit it, and since there is nothing overtly racist about the statutes that authorize the death penalty for murder or rape, capital punishment itself is hardly at fault if in practice it falls with unfair impact on the poor and the black. There is, in short, nothing in the death penalty that requires it to be applied unfairly and with arbitrary or discriminatory results. At worst such results stem from defects in the system of administering criminal justice. (Some, who dispute the facts cited above, would deny even this.) There is an adequate remedy—execute more whites, women, and affluent murderers.

Presumably, both proponents and opponents of capital punishment would concede that it is a fundamental dictate of justice that a punishment should not be unfairly—inequitably or unevenly—enforced and applied. They should also be able to agree that when the punishment in question is the extremely severe one of death, then the requirement to be fair in using such a punishment becomes even more stringent. There should be no dispute in the death penalty controversy over these principles of justice. The dispute should begin only when one attempts to connect the principles with the actual use of this punishment.

In this country, many critics of the death penalty have argued, we would long ago have got rid of it entirely if equal and fair application had been a condition of its use. In the words of the attorneys who argued against the death penalty before the Supreme Court during 1972, "It is a freakish aberration, a random extreme act of violence, visibly arbitrary and discriminatory—a penalty reserved for unusual application because, if it were usually used, it would affront universally shared standards of public decency."[6] It is difficult to dispute this judgment, when one considers that there have been in the United States during the past fifty years about half a million criminal homicides, about a third of a million persons arrested for these crimes, but fewer than four thousand executions (all but three dozen of which were of men).

We can look at these statistics in another way to illustrate the same point. If we could be assured that the nearly four thousand persons executed were the worst of the bad, repeated offenders impossible to incarcerate safely (much less to rehabilitate), the most dangerous murderers in captivity—the ones who had killed more than once and were likely to kill again, and the least likely to be confined in prison without chronic danger to other inmates and the staff—then one might accept half a million murders and a few thousand executions with a sense that rough justice had been done. But the truth is otherwise. Persons are sentenced to death and executed not because they have been found to be uncontrollably violent or hopelessly poor risks for safe confinement and release. Instead, they are executed because at trial they had a poor defense (inexperienced or overworked counsel); they had no funds to bring sympathetic witnesses to court; they are transients or strangers in the community where they are tried; the prosecuting attorney wanted the publicity that goes with "sending a killer to the chair"; there were no funds for an appeal or for a transcript of the trial record; they are members of a despised racial or political minority. In short, the actual study of why particular persons have been sentenced to death and executed does not show any careful winnowing of the worst from the bad. It shows that those executed were usually the unlucky victims of prejudice and discrimination, the losers in an arbitrary lottery that could just as well have spared them, the victims of the disadvantages that almost always go with poverty. A system like this does not enhance human life; it cheapens and degrades it. However heinous murder and other crimes are, the system of capital punishment does not compensate for or erase those crimes. It tends only to add new injuries of its own to the catalogue of human brutality.

* * *

NOTES

1. Immanuel Kant, *The Metaphysical Elements of Justice* (1797), Indianapolis, Ind.: Bobbs-Merrill (1965), translated by John Ladd, p. 106.

2. Benjamin Cardozo, "What Medicine Can Do for Law" (1928), reprinted in Margaret E. Hall, ed., *Selected Writings of Benjamin Nathan Cardozo*. New York: Fallon, 1947, p. 384.

3. *McGautha v. California*, 402 U.S. 183 (1971), at p. 204.

4. Albert Camus, *Resistance, Rebellion, and Death*. New York: Knopf, 1961, p. 199.

5. *Furman v. Georgia*, 408 U.S. 238 (1972), at pp. 251–252.

6. NAACP Legal Defense and Educational Fund, Brief for Petitioner in *Aikens v. California*, O.T. 1971, No. 68-5027, reprinted in Philip English Mackey, ed., *Voices Against Death: American Opposition to Capital Punishment*, 1787–1975. New York: Burt Franklin, 1976, p. 288.

A Life for a Life

IGOR PRIMORATZ

According to the retributive theory, consequences of punishment, however important from the practical point of view, are irrelevant when it comes to its justification; *the* moral consideration is its justice. Punishment is morally justified insofar as it is meted out as retribution for the offense committed. When someone has committed an offense, he deserves to be punished: it is just, and consequently justified, that he be punished. The offense is the sole ground of the state's right and duty to punish. It is also the measure of legitimate punishment: the two ought to be proportionate. So the issue of capital punishment within the retributive approach comes down

to the question, Is this punishment ever proportionate retribution for the offense committed, and thus deserved, just, and justified?

The classic representatives of retributivism believed that it was, and that it was the only proportionate and hence appropriate punishment, if the offense was *murder*—that is, criminal homicide perpetrated voluntarily and intentionally. In other cases, the demand for proportionality between offense and punishment can be satisfied by fines or prison terms; the crime of murder, however, is an exception in this respect, and calls for the literal interpretation of the *lex talionis*. The uniqueness of this crime has to do with the uniqueness of the value which has been deliberately destroyed. We come across this idea as early as the original formulation of the retributive view—the biblical teaching on punishment: "You shall accept no ransom for the life of a murderer who is guilty of death; but he shall be put to death."[1] The rationale of this command—one that clearly distinguishes the biblical conception of the criminal law from contemporaneous criminal law systems in the Middle East—is that man was not only created *by* God, like every other creature, but also, alone among all the creatures, *in the image of God*:

> That man was made in the image of God . . . is expressive of the peculiar and supreme worth of man. Of all creatures, Genesis 1 relates, he alone possesses this attribute, bringing him into closer relation to God than all the rest and conferring upon him the highest value. . . . This view of the uniqueness and supremacy of human life . . . places life beyond the reach of other values. The idea that life may be measured in terms of money or other property . . . is excluded. Compensation of any kind is ruled out. The guilt of the murderer is infinite because the murdered life is invaluable; the kinsmen of the slain man are not competent to say when he has been paid for. An absolute wrong has been committed, a sin against God which is not subject to human discussion. . . . Because human life is invaluable, to take it entails the death penalty.[2]

This view that the value of human life is not commensurable with other values, and that consequently there is only truly equivalent punishment for murder, namely death, does not necessarily presuppose a theistic outlook. It can be claimed that, simply because we have to be alive if we are to experience and realize any other value at all, there is nothing equivalent to the murderous destruction of a human life except the destruction of the life of the murderer. Any other retribution, no matter how severe, would still be less than what is proportionate, deserved, and just. As long as the murderer is alive, no matter how bad the conditions of his life may be, there are always at least *some* values he can experience and realize. This provides a plausible interpretation of what the classical representatives of retributivism as a philosophical theory of punishment, such as Kant and Hegel, had to say on the subject.[3]

It seems to me that this is essentially correct. With respect to the larger question of the justification of punishment in general, it is the retributive theory that gives the right answer. Accordingly, capital punishment ought to be retained where it obtains, and reintroduced

in those jurisdictions that have abolished it, although we have no reason to believe that, as a means of deterrence, it is any better than a very long prison term. It ought to be retained, or reintroduced, for one simple reason: that justice be done in cases of murder, that murderers be punished according to their deserts.

There are a number of arguments that have been advanced against this rationale of capital punishment.

Two of these arguments have to do, in different ways, with the idea of the right to life. The first is the famous argument of Beccaria that the state cannot have the right to take away the life of its citizen, because its rights in relation to him are based on the social contract, and it cannot be assumed that he has transferred his right to life to the state and consented to be executed.

> By what right can men presume to slaughter their fellows? Certainly not that right which is the foundation of sovereignty and the laws. For these are nothing but the sum of the smallest portions of each man's own freedom; they represent the general will which is the aggregate of the individual wills. Who has ever willingly given up to others the authority to kill him? How on earth can the minimum sacrifice of each individual's freedom involve handing over the greatest of all goods, life itself? And even if that were so, how can it be reconciled with the other principle which denies that a man is free to commit suicide, which he must be, if he is able to transfer that right to others or to society as a whole?[4]

The most obvious way of attacking Beccaria's argument would be to call into question its philosophical basis, the social contract theory of political obligation. This is what Hegel does, for instance; he conceives of the nature and grounds of political obligation in a completely different manner, so he can do away with Beccaria with a single sentence: "The state is not a contract at all."[5] I shall not argue along these lines, however. This is not the place to take up the problem of political obligation and to assess the social contract theory as a solution to it. What Beccaria is saying here can in any case be refuted even within the framework of that theory.

Both steps in his argument are wrong, and for the same reason. The act of consenting to be executed if one commits murder is presented as a kind of suicide.

Against the background of this conflation, it seems convincing to claim that it would be utterly unreasonable to do that, and the case appears to be strengthened even further by the appeal to the moral prohibition of suicide. This latter prohibition is, of course, rather controversial, to say the least; it was controversial in Beccaria's time as well. But his argument fails even if we grant him this point. For by consenting to be executed if I murder someone, I do not commit a kind of suicide—I do not "sacrifice the greatest of all goods" I have, my own life. My consent could be described in these terms if it were unconditional, if it implied that others were entitled to do with my life whatever they chose, quite independently of my own choices and actions. In order to show that capital punishment is legitimate from the standpoint of the contract theory of political obligation, however, we need not assume that citizens have agreed to *that*. All that is needed is the assumption of a conditional consent—consent to be executed *if* one commits murder; and it is, of course, up to everyone to choose whether to commit such a crime or not. To agree to this, obviously, is not the same as to sacrifice one's life, to commit a suicide of sorts. And it is not so unreasonable to assume that citizens have agreed to this if, against the background of the social contract theory, we grant, first, that the laws, including criminal laws, ought to be just, and second, that the only proportionate and hence just punishment for murder is capital punishment.[6]

The second abolitionist argument makes use of the idea of a right to life in a more straightforward manner: it simply says that capital punishment is illegitimate because it violates the right to life, which is a fundamental, absolute, sacred right belonging to each and every human being, and therefore ought to be respected even in a murderer.[7]

If any rights are fundamental, the right to life is certainly one of them; but to claim that it is absolute, inviolable under any circumstances and for any reason, is a different matter. If an abolitionist wants to argue her case by asserting an absolute right to life, she will also have to deny moral legitimacy to taking human life in war, revolution, and self-defense. This kind of pacifism is a consistent but farfetched and hence implausible position.

I do not believe that the right to life (nor, for that matter, any other right) is absolute. I have no general theory of rights to fall back upon here; instead, let me pose a question. Would we take seriously the claim to an absolute, sacred, inviolable right to life—coming from the mouth of a *confessed murderer*? I submit that we would not, for the obvious reason that it is being put forward by the person who confessedly denied another human being this very right. But if the murderer cannot plausibly claim such a right for himself, neither can *anyone else* do that in his behalf. This suggests that there is an element of reciprocity in our general rights, such as the right to life or property. I can convincingly claim these rights only so long as I acknowledge and respect the same rights of others. If I violate the rights of others, I thereby lose the same rights. If I am a murderer, I have no *right* to live.

Some opponents of capital punishment claim that a criminal law system which includes this punishment is contradictory: "It seems absurd to me," says Beccaria, "that the laws, which are the expression of the public will, and which hate and punish murder, should themselves commit one, and that to deter citizens from murder, they should decree a public murder."[8]

This seems to be one of the more popular arguments against the death penalty, but it is not a good one. If it were valid, it would prove too much. Exactly the same might be claimed of other kinds of punishment: of prison terms, that they are "contradictory" to the legal protection of liberty; of fines, that they are "contradictory" to the legal protection of property. Fortunately enough, it is not valid, for it begs the question at issue. In order to be able to talk of the state as "murdering" the person it executes, one has to use the word "murder" in the very same sense—that is, in the usual sense, which implies the idea of the *wrongful* taking the life of another—both when speaking of what the murderer has done to the victim and of what the state is doing to him by way of punishment. But this is precisely the question at issue: whether capital punishment *is* "murder," whether it is wrongful or morally justified and right.

The next two arguments attack the retributive rationale of capital punishment by questioning the claim that it is only this punishment that satisfies the demand for proportion between offense and punishment in the case of murder. The first points out that any two human lives are different in many important respects, such as age, health, physical and mental capability, so that it does not make much sense to consider them equally valuable. What if the murdered person was very old, practically at the very end of her natural life, while the murderer is young, with most of his life still ahead of him, for instance? Or if the victim was gravely and incurably ill, and thus doomed to live her life in suffering and hopelessness, without being able to experience almost anything that makes a human life worth living, while the murderer is in every respect capable of experiencing and enjoying things life has to offer? Or the other way round? Would not the death penalty in such cases amount either to taking a more valuable life as a punishment for destroying a less valuable one, or *vice versa*? Would it not be either too much, or too little, and in both cases disproportionate, and thus unjust and wrong, from the standpoint of the retributive theory itself?[9]

Any plausibility this argument might appear to have is the result of a conflation of differences between, and value of, human lives. No doubt, any two human lives are *different* in innumerable ways, but this does not entail that they are not *equally valuable*. I have no worked-out general theory of equality to refer to here, but I do not think that one is necessary in order to do away with this argument. The modern humanistic and democratic tradition in ethical, social, and political thought is based on the idea that all human beings are equal. This finds its legal expression in the principle of equality of people under the law. If we are not willing to give up this principle, we have to stick to the assumption that, all differences notwithstanding, any two human lives, *qua* human lives, are equally valuable. If, on the other hand, we allow that, on the basis of such criteria as age, health, or mental or physical ability, it can be claimed that the life of one person is more or less valuable than the life of another, and we admit such claims in the sphere of law, including criminal law, we shall thereby give up the principle of equality of people under the law. In all consistency, we shall not

be able to demand that property, physical and personal integrity, and all other rights and interests of individuals be given equal consideration in courts of law either—that is, we shall have to accept systematic discrimination between individuals on the basis of the same criteria across the whole field. I do not think anyone would seriously contemplate an overhaul of the whole legal system along these lines.

The second argument having to do with the issue of proportionality between murder and capital punishment draws our attention to the fact that the law normally provides for a certain period of time to elapse between the passing of a death sentence and its execution. It is a period of several weeks or months; in some cases it extends to years. This period is bound to be one of constant mental anguish for the condemned. And thus, all things considered, what is inflicted on him is disproportionately hard and hence unjust. It would be proportionate and just only in the case of "a criminal who had warned his victim of the date at which he would inflict a horrible death on him and who, from that moment onward, had confined him at his mercy for months."[10]

The first thing to note about this argument is that it does not support a full-fledged abolitionist stand; if it were valid, it would not show that capital punishment is *never* proportionate and just, but only that it is *very rarely* so. Consequently, the conclusion would not be that it ought to be abolished outright, but only that it ought to be restricted to those cases that would satisfy the condition cited above. Such cases do happen, although, to be sure, not very often; the murder of Aldo Moro, for instance, was of this kind. But this is not the main point. The main point is that the argument actually does not hit at capital punishment itself, although it is presented with that aim in view. It hits at something else: a particular way of carrying out this punishment, which is widely adopted in our time. Some hundred years ago and more, in the Wild West, they frequently hanged the man convicted to die almost immediately after pronouncing the sentence. I am not arguing here that we should follow this example today; I mention this piece of historical fact only in order to show that the interval between sentencing someone to death and carrying out the sentence is not a *part* of capital punishment itself. However unpalatable we might find those Wild West hangings, whatever objections we might want to voice against the speed with which they followed the sentencing, surely we shall not deny them the *description* of "executions." So the implication of the argument is not that we ought to do away with capital punishment altogether, nor that we ought to restrict it to those cases of murder where the murderer had warned the victim weeks or months in advance of what he was going to do to her, but that we ought to reexamine the procedure of carrying out this kind of punishment. We ought to weigh the reasons for having this interval between the sentencing and executing, against the moral and human significance of the repercussions such an interval inevitably carries with it.

These reasons, in part, have to do with the possibility of miscarriages of justice and the need to rectify them. Thus we come to the argument against capital punishment which, historically, has been the most effective of all: many advances of the abolitionist movement have been connected with discoveries of cases of judicial errors. Judges and jurors are only human, and consequently some of their beliefs and decisions are bound to be mistaken. Some of their mistakes can be corrected upon discovery; but precisely those with most disastrous repercussions—those which result in innocent people being executed—can never be rectified. In all other cases of mistaken sentencing we can revoke the punishment, either completely or in part, or at least extend compensation. In addition, by exonerating the accused we give moral satisfaction. None of this is possible after an innocent person has been executed; capital punishment is essentially different from all other penalties by being completely irrevocable and irreparable.[11] Therefore, it ought to be abolished.

A part of my reply to this argument goes along the same lines as what I had to say on the previous one. It is not so far-reaching as abolitionists assume; for it would be quite implausible, even fanciful, to claim that there have *never* been cases of murder which left no room whatever for reasonable doubt as to the guilt and full responsibility of the accused. Such cases may

not be more frequent than those others, but they do happen. Why not retain the death penalty at least for them?

Actually, this argument, just as the preceding one, does not tell against capital punishment itself, but against the existing procedures for trying capital cases. Miscarriages of justice result in innocent people being sentenced to death and executed, even in the criminal-law systems in which the greatest care is taken to ensure that it never comes to that. But this does not stem from the intrinsic nature of the institution of capital punishment; it results from deficiencies, limitations, and imperfections of the criminal law procedures in which this punishment is meted out. Errors of justice do not demonstrate the need to do away with capital punishment; they simply make it incumbent on us to do everything possible to improve even further procedures of meting it out.

To be sure, this conclusion will not find favor with a diehard abolitionist. "I shall ask for the abolition of Capital Punishment until I have the infallibility of human judgement demonstrated to me," that is, as long as there is even the slightest possibility that innocent people may be executed because of judicial errors, Lafayette said in his day.[12] Many an opponent of this kind of punishment will say the same today. The demand to do away with capital punishment altogether, so as to eliminate even the smallest chance of that ever happening—the chance which, admittedly, would remain even after everything humanly possible has been done to perfect the procedure, although then it would be very slight indeed—is actually a demand to give a privileged position to murderers as against all other offenders, big and small. For if we acted on this demand, we would bring about a situation in which proportionate penalties would be meted out for all offenses, *except* for murder. Murderers would not be receiving the only punishment truly proportionate to their crimes, the punishment of death, but some other, lighter, and thus disproportionate penalty. All other offenders would be punished according to their deserts; only murderers would be receiving less than *they* deserve. In all other cases justice would be done in full; only in cases of the gravest of offenses, the crime of murder, justice would not be carried out in full measure. It is a great and tragic miscarriage of justice when an innocent person is mistakenly sentenced to death and executed, but systematically giving murderers advantage over all other offenders would also be a grave injustice. Is the fact that, as long as capital punishment is retained, there is a possibility that over a number of years, or even decades, an injustice of the first kind may be committed, unintentionally and unconsciously, reason enough to abolish it altogether, and thus end up with a system of punishments in which injustices of the second kind are perpetrated daily, consciously, and inevitably?[13]

There is still another abolitionist argument that actually does not tell against capital punishment itself, but against something else. Figures are sometimes quoted which show that this punishment is much more often meted out to the uneducated and poor than to the educated, rich, and influential people; in the United States, much more often to African Americans than to whites. These figures are adduced as a proof of the inherent injustice of this kind of punishment. On account of them, it is claimed that capital punishment is not a way of doing justice by meting out deserved punishment to murderers, but rather a means of social discrimination and perpetuation of social injustice.

I shall not question these findings, which are quite convincing, and anyway, there is no need to do that in order to defend the institution of capital punishment. For there seems to be a certain amount of discrimination and injustice not only in sentencing people to death and executing them, but also in meting out other penalties. The social structure of the death rows in American prisons, for instance, does not seem to be basically different from the general social structure of American penitentiaries. If this argument were valid, it would call not only for abolition of the penalty of death, but for doing away with other penalties as well.

But it is not valid; as Burton Leiser has pointed out,

this is not an argument, either against the death penalty or against any other form of punishment. It is an argument against the unjust and inequitable distribution of penalties. If the trials of wealthy men are less likely to result in convictions than those of poor men, then something must be done to reform the procedure

in criminal courts. If those who have money and standing in the community are less likely to be charged with serious offenses than their less affluent fellow citizens, then there should be a major overhaul of the entire system of criminal justice . . . But the maldistribution of penalties is no argument against any particular form of penalty.[14]

There is, finally, the argument that the moral illegitimacy of capital punishment is obvious from the widespread contempt for those who carry it out: "Logically, if the Death Penalty *were* morally justified, the executioner's calling would be considered an honourable one. The fact that even its keenest supporters shrink from such a man with loathing and exclude him from their circle, is in itself an indication that capital Punishment stands morally condemned."[15]

This is also a poor argument, for several reasons. The contempt for the executioner and the accompanying social ostracism is by no means a universal phenomenon in history; on the contrary, it is a comparatively modern one. In earlier ages, the person who carried out capital punishment—whether the professional executioner or, before this became an occupation in its own right, the judge, or some other high-ranking official, sometimes even the ruler himself, or a relative of the murdered person—was always regarded with respect.[16] Quite apart from this, the so-called common moral consciousness to which the argument appeals is not to be seen as some kind of supreme tribunal in moral matters. Among reasons of general nature for this is that it would be an unreliable, inconsistent, confused, and confusing tribunal. On the one hand, when viewed historically, it hardly seems a very good guide to the moral status of various occupations, for in earlier ages it used to condemn very resolutely and strongly the merchant, the banker, the actor, which no one would think of disparaging today, abolitionists included. On the other hand, it has proved itself quite inconsistent on the issue of the moral basis of punishment in general, voicing incompatible views, now retributive, now utilitarian.[17] It is not at all surprising that both advocates and opponents of capital punishment have claimed its support for their views.[18] But if it supports both sides in this more restricted dispute as well, then it actually supports neither.

There is still another facet of this illogical, irrational streak inherent to the common moral consciousness that comes to the fore in connection with this dispute. If the contempt for the executioner is really rooted in the belief that what he carries out is morally reprehensible, then it is surely heaped upon the wrong person. For he merely carries out decisions on which he has no say whatsoever. Those who are responsible are, in the first instance, the judge and members of the jury. They, on their part, act as they do against the background of criminal laws for which responsibility lies at a further remove still—with the legislators. These, again, legislate in the name of the people, if the political system is a representative one. But for some reason the common moral consciousness has never evinced contempt of any of these.

NOTES

1. Numbers 35.31 (R.S.V.).

2. M. Greenberg, "Some Postulates of Biblical Criminal Law," in J. Goldin (ed.), *The Jewish Expression* (New York: Bantam, 1970), pp. 25–26. (Post-biblical Jewish law evolved toward the virtual abolition of the death penalty, but that is of no concern here.)

3. "There is no *parallel* between death and even the most miserable life, so that there is no equality of crime and retribution [in the case of murder] unless the perpetrator is judicially put to death" (I. Kant, "The Metaphysics of Morals," *Kant's Political Writings*, ed. H. Reiss, trans. H.B. Nisbet [Cambridge: Cambridge University Press, 1970], p. 156). "Since life is the full compass of a man's existence, the punishment [for murder] cannot simply consist in a 'value', for none is great enough, but can consist only in taking away a second life" (G.W.F. Hegel, *Philosophy of Right*, trans. T.M. Knox [Oxford: Oxford University Press, 1965], p. 247).

4. C. Beccaria, *On Crimes and Punishments*, trans. R. Davies, ed. R. Bellamy (Cambridge: Cambridge University Press, 1995), p. 66.

5. G.W.F. Hegel, *Philosophy of Right*, p. 71.

6. For critical comments on my analysis and refutation of Beccaria's argument, developed in the paper on "Kant and Beccaria," *Kant-Studien* 69 (1978) and summarized here in the briefest way possible, see M. A. Cattaneo, *Beccaria e Kant. Il valore dell'uomo nel diritto penale* (Sassari: Università di Sassari, 1981), pp. 20–30.

7. For an example of this view, see L.N. Tolstoy, *Smertnaya kazn i hristianstvo* (Berlin: I.P. Ladizhnikov, n.d.), pp. 40–41.

8. C. Beccaria, *Crimes and Punishments*, p. 70.

9. Cf. W. Blackstone, *Commentaries on the Laws of England*, 4th ed., ed. J. DeWitt Andrews (Chicago: Callaghan & Co., 1899), p. 1224.

10. A. Camus, "Reflections on the Guillotine," *Resistance, Rebellion and Death*, trans. J. O'Brien (London: Hamish Hamilton, 1961), p. 143.

11. For an interesting critical discussion of this point, see M. Davis, "Is the Death Penalty Irrevocable?," *Social Theory and Practice* 10 (1984).

12. Quoted in E.R. Calvert, *Capital Punishment in the Twentieth Century* (London: G.P. Putnam's Sons, 1927), p. 132.

13. For a criticism of this argument, see L. Sebba, "On Capital Punishment—A Comment," *Israel Law Review* 17 (1982), pp. 392–395.

14. B.M. Leiser, *Liberty, Justice and Morals: Contemporary Value Conflicts* (New York: Macmillan, 1973), p. 225.

15. E.R. Calvert, *Capital Punishment*, p. 172.

16. For a good review of the relevant historical data, see A.F. Kistyakovsky, *Izsledovanie o smertnoy kazni*, 2nd ed. (St. Petersburg: L.F. Panteleev, 1896), pp. 260–267.

17. See *supra*, pp. 55–56.

18. Cf. I. Kant, "Metaphysics of Morals," p. 157, and C. Beccaria, *Crimes and Punishments*, p. 50.

CHAPTER 19

Political Violence: War, Terrorism, and Torture

When has *Homo sapiens* ever been nonviolent? Probably never. The evolution of humans parallels the evolution of their instruments for killing each other. Violence seems as much a part of human life as it ever was, except that the efficiency of our violent methods has improved. Spears can dispatch one person at a time, but smart bombs can kill by the dozens, and nuclear weapons can eliminate the human race altogether.

Fortunately, while human beings have been inflicting violence, they have also been raising moral questions about its use. The central concern is this: When, if ever, are we morally justified in resorting to it? Is *every* use of violence wrong, as Buddhist and Christian doctrines have insisted? To just about everyone, violence is inherently bad, an evil in itself. If so, how can perpetrating it ever be morally permissible? If we condemn an aggressor for his assault on the innocent, what should we say when the innocent rise up and kill him in self-defense? Should we condemn them too? Is violence ever justified to protect something less valuable than your life—your property, your rights, your reputation, your income?

All these questions apply with double force to *political* violence, the resort to violence for political ends. War, terrorism, torture, revolution, assassination, civil war, and violent demonstrations—these are all paradigm cases of violence with political aims. Unlike personal violence (for example, muggings, shootings, and rapes), political violence is large in its scale and its effects. A war can involve millions; terrorism can terrify thousands.

In recent years, philosophers have paid a lot of attention to the morality of violence, especially to

issues arising from political violence in the form of war, terrorism, and torture. They have clarified concepts, sharpened the focus of moral debate, and arrived at some well-argued answers to the major questions. In this chapter, we examine some of this important philosophical work.

ISSUE FILE: BACKGROUND

We all know what violence is. Or do we? In fact, the term *violence* in common usage has multiple meanings and is difficult to pin down. Consider: we often refer to the violence of a storm, or to a violent mood, or to the violence of social injustice, or to the violence done by anything we disapprove of (as in "censorship is violence against the human spirit" or "your remarks are violent acts against minorities"). But if we are to make sense of moral arguments regarding violence, we must be clear about the meaning of the term. For the purposes of this discussion, we can define violence (against people) as some philosophers have: the physical or psychological attack on, or the vigorous abuse of, persons, causing their suffering, injury, or death. (Violence can also involve the destroying or damaging of property.) By this definition, striking, shoving, stabbing, raping, and shooting someone are clear instances of violence, and so are political acts such as wars, terrorism, torture, and the like. We would also count as violence the severe harming of a person psychologically through verbal abuse or humiliation. Denying people the right to vote, perpetuating social inequalities, and defaming a person may be immoral or illegal, but these actions are not examples of violence as just defined.

Most people hold that because violence is inherently bad, it should be used only if there is strong moral justification for it. In other words, violence is prima facie wrong—wrong unless there are good reasons for thinking it morally permissible. Thus people often speak of war and other modes of violence as things to be *resorted to*, actions to be taken only after other options are exhausted.

But why is violence wrong? One answer often given is that it constitutes a violation of people's rights—their right to life, self-determination, respect as a person, or immunity from harm. Another view is that violence is prima facie wrong because it runs afoul of the moral principles of justice, freedom, and utility (human welfare). Some argue that the wrongness of violence arises from its detrimental effects on society: it's wrong because it makes society worse off than if no violence were present. This is one way to articulate a consequentialist notion of violence, but there are others, all based on the premise that violence is (generally) wrong because its bad consequences (usually) outweigh the good.

The most destructive, horrifying violence known to humans is practiced in war. War is a form of political violence because its essence is violent conflict between political communities, usually for the purpose of deciding who gets to effect political changes. Ever since philosophers began examining the ethics of war over two millennia ago, the main moral questions have been (1) How—if at all—can war be justified? and (2) Assuming it can be justified, how should it be conducted? Most serious responses to these questions have fallen into three major categories, traditionally labeled *realism, pacifism,* and *just war theory*.

Realism (as applied to warfare) is the view that moral standards are not applicable to war, which must be judged only on prudence, on how well war serves state interests. War cannot be immoral, only more or less advantageous for the state. Eminent realists of the past include the philosophers

Niccolò Machiavelli (1469–1527) and Thomas Hobbes (1588–1679); modern realists include Reinhold Niebuhr and Henry Kissinger, former U.S. secretary of state for the Nixon administration.

Realists may argue that morality has no part to play in warfare because all moral statements are meaningless or unknowable or because moral norms do not apply to states, just to persons. The former claim denies that there can be appeals to any moral standards at all and is therefore vulnerable to the usual arguments that philosophers make against such moral skepticism (see Chapter 2). To the latter view, some nonrealists may reply that there is no good reason to think that states are exempt from moral judgments. Nonrealists may also insist that despite the seemingly unrestrained brutality of war, common sense suggests that sometimes moral norms do apply to warfare. According to this position, even when people favor a war of extreme, indeed savage, measures, they tend to believe that there are at least some moral limits to what can be done. Most would probably balk at the use of nuclear weapons, or the deliberate killing of children, or the mass rape of all noncombatant women.

Pacifism is the view that war is never morally permissible. (The term is also often used to refer to the broader idea that all violence is wrong or that all killing is wrong.) Pacifists in this sense are opposed to all wars regardless of the reasons behind them. They may or may not, however, be against all uses of personal violence, or violence between individuals. They may believe, for example, that personal violence in self-defense or in law enforcement may be justified. To make their case, pacifists may argue in a consequentialist vein that war is never justified, because it always produces more bad than good. The catastrophic loss of life and the widespread destruction of war can never offset whatever political or material gains are achieved; riches, land, oil, or power cannot outweigh the carnage. Pacifists may also rely on a nonconsequentialist argument like this: War is always wrong, because in the deliberate killing of human beings it violates a fundamental right—the right to life. This right—which may have either a religious or a secular basis—is absolute, admitting no exceptions.

The usual objection to the consequentialist approach is that though war is horrific and often (perhaps usually) produces more bad than good, at least sometimes the results may be good overall. It is possible, this argument goes, that waging a war could save the lives of many more people than are killed in the conflict or that fighting one small war could prevent a much larger one. A common objection to the pacifist's nonconsequentialist line is that even though a person has a right to life, we may be morally justified in killing him or her in self-defense if there is no other way to save our own lives. Thus sometimes killing in war is regrettable but necessary—and therefore morally permissible.

Just war theory is the doctrine that war may be morally permissible under stipulated conditions. It is a centuries-old attempt to understand how war—an enduring form of systematic killing—can be reconciled with our moral presumptions *against* killing. It specifies when resorting to war may be morally justified and how armed conflict should be conducted to meet the minimal demands of morality. Thomas Aquinas produced the most influential discourse on the doctrine, which has been evolving ever since as both religious and secular thinkers have tried to improve it. Just war theory has become the most widely used lens through which the ethics of war is viewed these days. As one theorist points out,

> To be sure, this tradition has often found expression in church law and theological reflection; yet it also appears in codifications and theories of international law, in military manuals on how rightly to conduct war, and—as Michael Walzer has shown in *Just and Unjust Wars*—in the judgments and reactions of common people.[1]

Just war theory is concerned with two main issues: (1) the justification for resorting to war (traditionally labeled *jus ad bellum*, or "the justice of war")

and (2) the moral permissibility of acts in war (*jus in bello*, or "justice in war").

Theorists have addressed *jus ad bellum* by specifying that going to war can be morally permissible only if certain requirements are met. Aquinas urged the first three requirements in the following list, and later thinkers embraced them and added several more. According to the theory, only if all the requirements are met can a war be considered just.

1. *The cause must be just.* War is such a horrifying business that only a just cause—a morally legitimate reason—can justify going to war. The most commonly cited just cause is self-defense against attack. The usual thinking is that precisely as individuals are entitled to use violence to defend themselves against violent personal attacks, so states have the right to defend against unjust attacks from another state. The implication here is that states have no right to *instigate* a war.

Many theorists define a just cause broadly: a just cause is resistance to substantial aggression, which has been defined as "the type of aggression that violates people's most fundamental rights."[2] This resistance includes self-defense against external threat, of course. But it also may encompass defending the innocent from deadly attack (as in genocide or "ethnic cleansing," for example), defending people whose basic human rights are being violated by a brutal regime, or defending other states from unjust external attack. Some early theorists thought that wars could be justifiably fought to convert or punish those of a different religion—a view now rejected by Western philosophers and theologians but still strongly supported in some parts of the world.

Some people argue that war in self-defense is justified only in response to an actual attack; others maintain that an attack need not be actual but only feared—that is, a "preventive war" may be justified. But many contend that to start a war on such grounds is to act on a mere fear of the unknown and to invite other states to launch attacks for no good reason (or for ulterior motives). In response to this worry, a number of theorists maintain that a war is justified only if the threat of attack from another state is "immediate and imminent," which means something like "clearly about to happen." Such a war is properly called preemptive. Much of the debate about the United States' launching a preemptive strike against Iraq in 2003 has been about whether this "immediate and imminent" standard was met as well as about whether the standard is relevant when there might be a danger from weapons of mass destruction.

2. *The war must be sanctioned by proper authority.* The resort to war must be approved by a state's rightful government. As Aquinas says, a just war requires "the authority of the sovereign by whose command the war is to be waged. For it is not the business of a private individual to declare war."[3]

3. *The war should be fought with the right intentions.* Wars must be waged for the sake of the just cause, not moved by some illegitimate motive such as bloodlust, greed, empire expansion, or ethnic hatred. Aquinas continues,

> [I]t is necessary that the belligerents should have a rightful intention, so that they intend the advancement of good, or the avoidance of evil. . . . For it may happen that the war is declared by the legitimate authority, and for a just cause, and yet be rendered unlawful through a wicked intention.

CRITICAL THOUGHT: Preemptive War on Iraq

According to most forms of just war theory, a preemptive attack against a state is justified only if that state presents a substantial danger that is "immediate and imminent." As some commentators on just war theory explain, "To establish this condition [of immediate and imminent threat], evidence of planning that is virtually completed needs to be shown."* Now consider this description of the run-up to the U.S. preemptive strike on Iraq in 2003.

> [President George W. Bush] claimed that he was justified [in going to war with Iraq] so as to prevent (really to preempt) Iraq from attacking the United States. But such talk of prevention is imprecise, for it may refer either to a necessary preemption of an impending attack or merely to an unjustified fear as a pretext for war based on other motivations. In his 2003 State of the Union speech, Bush said that "The British government has learned that Saddam Hussein recently sought significant quantities of uranium from Africa." Such a claim was meant to show that Iraq posed

an imminent, not merely a speculative threat to the United States. In addition, Bush said that he was not required to wait for the United States to be attacked, or even to wait for all of the evidence needed to show that Iraq might attack.[†]

Assume this passage is an accurate depiction of the pre-war situation and is the only relevant information available to you. Would you judge the threat from Iraq to be "immediate and imminent"? Why or why not? Based on what you have learned about just war theory in this chapter, do you think a fair-minded just war theorist would say the attack on Iraq was justified or unjustified? Why? Do *you* believe that starting the war was just? What are your reasons?

*Larry May, Eric Rovie, and Steven Viner, introduction to *The Morality of War: Classical and Contemporary Readings,* eds. May, Rovie, and Viner (Upper Saddle River, NJ: Pearson/Prentice Hall, 2006), xi.
†Ibid.

4. *Armed conflict should be a last resort.* For a war to be just, all peaceful means of sorting out differences between adversaries should be tried first. Diplomacy, economic pressure, world opinion—all these avenues and others should be exhausted before employing guns and bombs.

5. *The good resulting from war must be proportional to the bad.* The good expected to come from fighting for a just cause must be weighed against the tremendous evils that will inevitably accompany war—death, destruction, pain, and loss on a mass scale.

6. *There must be a reasonable chance of success.* Futile wars should not be waged. Mass killing with no likelihood of achieving anything is unjust. So only if success is reasonably probable should a state resort to war.

Just war theorists believe that it is possible for a resort to war to be morally permissible while the conduct of that war is morally abhorrent. They therefore are concerned not only with *jus ad bellum* but also with *jus in bello,* right action during the meting out of the violence. They explicitly reject the popular notion that once war commences, there are no moral restraints whatsoever on what can be done to anyone or anything during the conflict. Michael Walzer, the leading contemporary advocate for just war theory, asserts that the popular view is "profoundly wrong":

> War is indeed ugly, but there are degrees of ugliness and humane men must, as always, be concerned with degrees. . . . Surely there is a point at which the means employed for the sake of this or that political goal come into conflict with a more general human purpose: the maintenance of moral standards and the survival of some sort of international society. At that point, political arguments against the use of such means are overshadowed, or ought to be, by moral arguments. At that point, war is not merely ugly but criminal.[4]

Traditionally, requirements for *jus in bello*—the so-called rules of war—have included the following:

1. *Discrimination.* Those fighting a war must distinguish between combatants and noncombatants,

never deliberately targeting the latter. People who should not be intentionally attacked are said to have **noncombatant immunity**, a status traditionally reserved for women, children, the elderly, and the sick and injured. Though some noncombatants are almost certain to be killed or harmed in any war, such tragedies are supposed to be unavoidable or unintended and therefore pardonable.

The distinction between combatant and noncombatant is often not very clear, especially when a conflict involves fighters wearing civilian clothes and operating among peaceful inhabitants. Michael Walzer offers a helpful distinction by saying that noncombatants are those who are not "engaged in harm." But some thinkers have tended to blur the line between people usually thought to have immunity and those who do not. They ask, Should people be given immunity if they cheer on their combatants, give them food, and shelter them? Are they really to be regarded as "innocent civilians"?

In any case, the prohibition against intentionally attacking noncombatants is enshrined in international law and widely regarded as the most fundamental "rule of war."

2. *Proportionality.* The use of force should be proportional to the rightful aims of the war—"overkill" is disallowed. Even in bitter conflict, combatants should not kill or destroy more than necessary to achieve the just ends for which the war is waged.

3. *No evil means.* Many just war theorists maintain that certain tactics and weapons in war are "evil in themselves" and thus should never be used regardless of a war's aims. Such evil means are said to include genocide, biological or chemical warfare (use of anthrax and nerve gas, for example), nuclear attack, and rape.

4. *Benevolent quarantine.* Soldiers who surrender to their enemies have rights and should be treated accordingly. They must be given "benevolent quarantine" as prisoners of war (POWs)—humane captivity in safe confines removed from the battlefield. In that environment they must not be subjected

to execution, torture, starvation, or other forms of serious abuse.

Blood brother to war is the grisly phenomenon of terrorism, an old scourge that has persisted into the twenty-first century. The ethical questions it evokes are thornier than they might seem at first glance: What is terrorism? Is terrorism ever justified? Who commits terrorist acts? Can states commit terrorist acts? Is the United States or any other country guilty of terrorism? For example, was the Allied bombing of German cities in World War II (in which hundreds of thousands of civilians died) a case of state terrorism? How should we treat terrorists? How should we respond to terrorist violence? How much, if at all, should we curtail civil liberties to protect ourselves against terrorism? Can we evaluate the morality of terrorism in the same way we assess the morality of war (by using, for example, just war theory)?

Most people probably think they know what terrorism is, yet it is notoriously difficult to define. One of the main challenges is to differentiate terrorism from acts of war and violent crimes. In the definition adopted by the U.S. Department of State, terrorism is "premeditated, politically motivated violence perpetrated against noncombatant targets by subnational groups or clandestine agents, usually intended to influence an audience."[5] According to a 1974 British government definition, terrorism is "the use of violence for political ends, and includes any use of violence for the purpose of putting the public, or any section of the public, in fear."[6] For our discussion we can use a definition that comprises key elements in common usage or philosophical writing: **terrorism** is violence against noncombatants for political, religious, or ideological ends.

Some think terrorism is a recent phenomenon. But scholars who define terrorism broadly maintain that its history is long and bloody. The term *terrorism* sprang from the French Revolution's Reign of Terror, in which the new state sanctioned the use of terror against its enemies, real or imagined,

executing thousands of mostly ordinary citizens. In the nineteenth century, anarchists aimed to inspire the masses to revolution with terrifying deeds against established regimes. They achieved worldwide attention and spread public alarm—but no revolution—by assassinating several state leaders, including President William McKinley in the United States and Tsar Alexander II in Russia.

The twentieth century had a shockingly large share of terrorism, in both old and new forms driven by familiar and unfamiliar motives. Terrorism in the first half of the century was mostly nationalist (as were terrorist groups in Ireland, Palestine, Algeria, and the Balkans), state-sponsored (by, for example, the Serbian and Bulgarian governments), and state-administered (as in Nazi Germany, Stalinist Russia, and several South American dictatorships). Its preferred form was assassination and mass killing. The second half witnessed more state-sponsored terrorism as well as the predominance of terrorism, which was ideological or religious. Terrorism in this period was distinguished by its heavy reliance on the horrors of airline hijackings, kidnappings, and suicide bombings. According to the Center for Defense Information,

> Through the 1960s and 1970s, the numbers of those groups that might be described as terrorist swelled to include not only nationalists, but those motivated by ethnic and ideological considerations. The former included groups such as the Palestinian Liberation Organization (and its many affiliates), the Basque ETA, and the Provisional Irish Republican Army, while the latter comprised organizations such as the Red Army Faction (in what was then West Germany) and the Italian Red Brigades. As with the emergence of modern terrorism almost a century earlier, the United States was not immune from this latest wave, although there the identity-crisis-driven motivations of the white middle-class Weathermen starkly contrasted with the ghetto-bred malcontent [sic] of the Black Panther movement.[7]

Since around the mid-1990s, the threat of religiously inspired terrorism has expanded dramatically. In 1998, there were 37 incidents of religious terrorism worldwide resulting in 758 deaths. In 2001, there were 99 incidents and 3,275 deaths, most of which occurred in the September 11 attacks on the United States. In 2005, religious terrorists killed 2,061 people throughout the world in 606 incidents.[8] In 2009, there were nearly 15,000 deaths from terrorist attacks of all kinds; 9,280 of these were caused by Sunni Islamic extremists, while 1,052 were committed by Christian extremists.[9] As the Council on Foreign Affairs reported,

> Religious terrorists seek to use violence to further what they see as divinely commanded purposes, often targeting broad categories of foes in an attempt to bring about sweeping changes. Religious terrorists come from many faiths, as well as from small cults. . . . Because religious terrorists are concerned not with rallying a constituency of fellow nationalists or ideologues but with pursuing their own vision of divine will, they lack one of the major constraints that historically has limited the scope of terror attacks, experts say. As [the terrorism expert Bruce] Hoffman puts it, the most extreme religious terrorists can sanction "almost limitless violence against a virtually open-ended category of targets: that is, anyone who is not a member of the terrorists' religion or religious sect."[10]

Among the more infamous terrorist incidents of the past forty-plus years are the following, as described by the U.S. Department of State:

Munich Olympic Massacre, September 5, 1972: Eight Palestinian "Black September" terrorists seized eleven Israeli athletes in the Olympic Village in Munich, West Germany. In a bungled rescue attempt by West German authorities, nine of the hostages and five terrorists were killed.

Iran Hostage Crisis, November 4, 1979: After President Carter agreed to admit the Shah of Iran into the United States, Iranian radicals seized the U.S. Embassy in Tehran and took 66 American diplomats hostage. Thirteen hostages were soon released, but the remaining 53 were held until their release on January 20, 1981.

Grand Mosque Seizure, November 20, 1979: 200 Islamic terrorists seized the Grand Mosque in Mecca, Saudi Arabia, taking hundreds of pilgrims hostage.

Saudi and French security forces retook the shrine after an intense battle in which some 250 people were killed and 600 wounded.

Pan Am 103 Bombing, December 21, 1988: Pan American Airlines Flight 103 was blown up over Lockerbie, Scotland, by a bomb believed to have been placed on the aircraft by Libyan terrorists in Frankfurt, West Germany. All 259 people on board were killed.

World Trade Center Bombing, February 26, 1993: The World Trade Center in New York City was badly damaged when a car bomb planted by Islamic terrorists exploded in an underground garage. The bomb left 6 people dead and 1,000 injured. The men carrying out the attack were followers of Umar Abd al-Rahman, an Egyptian cleric who preached in the New York City area.

Bombing of the Federal Building in Oklahoma City, April 19, 1995: Right-wing extremists Timothy McVeigh and Terry Nichols destroyed the Federal Building in Oklahoma City with a massive truck bomb that killed 166 and injured hundreds more in what was up to then the largest terrorist attack on American soil.

Terrorist Attacks on U.S. Homeland, September 11, 2001: Two hijacked airliners crashed into the twin towers of the World Trade Center. Soon thereafter, the Pentagon was struck by a third hijacked plane. A fourth hijacked plane, suspected to be bound for a high-profile target in Washington, crashed into a field in southern Pennsylvania. The attacks killed 3,025 U.S. citizens and other nationals. President Bush and Cabinet officials indicated that Osama bin Laden was the prime suspect and that they considered the United States in a state of war with international terrorism. . . .

Car Bomb Explosion in Bali, October 12, 2002: A car bomb exploded outside the Sari Club Discotheque in Denpasar, Bali, Indonesia, killing 202 persons and wounding 300 more. Most of the casualties, including 88 of the dead, were Australian tourists. Seven Americans were among the dead. Al-Qaeda claimed responsibility. Two suspects were later arrested and convicted. Iman Samudra, who had trained in Afghanistan with al-Qaeda and was suspected of belonging to Jemaah Islamiya, was sentenced to death on September 10, 2003.[11]

To this list we could add many more incidents, and probably most shocking among them would be the March 11, 2004, attacks in Madrid and the July 7, 2005, bombings in London. In Madrid a coordinated series of bombs exploded on four commuter trains, killing 191 people and injuring more than 1,500. Investigators blamed Islamic militants connected to cells in Europe. In London, four jihadists set off bombs almost simultaneously on a double-decker bus and three subway trains, killing themselves and fifty-two other people and injuring hundreds. In 2008, in Mumbai, India, Pakistan-based militants killed 174 people in a shooting rampage. And in 2011, a man described as a Christian right-wing extremist set off a large bomb in Oslo, Norway, killing 8 people, then systematically murdered 69 others at an island youth camp.

The most recent events in global terrorism are also the most frightening. In 2014, large swaths of Iraqi and Syrian territory were taken over by a group known as the Islamic State of Iraq and Syria (ISIS). It is made up of thousands of Islamist militants drawn from the Syrian civil war, jihadist elements in Iraq, and volunteers from Europe, the United States, and elsewhere. ISIS aspires to be a caliphate, an Islamic nation, calling itself the Islamic State, but its methods are terrorist on a mass scale:

> The stories, the videos, the acts of unfathomable brutality have become a defining aspect of ISIS, which controls a nation-size tract of land and has now pushed Iraq to the precipice of dissolution. Its adherents kill with such abandon that even the leader of al-Qaeda has disavowed them. . . .
>
> [I]n terms of impact, the acts of terror have been wildly successful. From beheadings to summary executions to amputations to crucifixions, the terrorist group has become the most feared organization in the Middle East. That fear, evidenced in fleeing Iraqi soldiers and 500,000 Mosul residents, has played a vital role in the group's march toward Baghdad. In many cases, police and soldiers literally ran, shedding their uniforms as they went, abandoning large caches of weapons.[12]

ISIS as an occupying power in Iraq and Syria has now been crushed by the United States and its allies. But it is still a transnational movement with the ability to inspire followers around the world. In the West, several individuals acting alone have launched terrorist attacks in the name of ISIS, killing dozens of innocent people.

The question that all terrorism provokes is, What should be our moral response to it? Many argue that a violent response is the wrong response, that a "war on terror" is misguided and morally impermissible. The proper response, they say, is dialogue with aggressors, a criminal justice approach instead of military force, and the eradication of the true causes of terrorism—poverty, oppression, suffering, and injustice. As one observer has said,

> In my view, the most effective counterterrorism approach would arise from a foreign policy that took the sufferings of people in other countries seriously. A progressive orientation would stand in contrast to today's official counterterrorism, which views suffering as irrelevant, or even as a reason to inflate the terrorist danger.[13]

The opposing view is that violence may in fact be a morally justified reaction to terrorism—that is, morally justified by the lights of just war theory. As noted earlier, just war theory is the timeworn doctrine that war may be morally permissible if particular requirements are met. It lays out the conditions under which resorting to war would be morally justified and specifies the criteria for judging the morality of how it is fought. Some contend that all the criteria can sometimes be met, justifying a carefully measured military response to terrorist attacks. Thus one observer argues that

> according to just war theory, defending against this sort of terrorism is a just cause; that within significant constraints sovereign political authorities can have authority to undertake military actions for the sake of this just cause, notwithstanding the nature of organization of the terrorists; and that a political community can pursue such a cause with right intention, even though in the world as it is military efforts to defend against terrorism may well not meet this condition.[14]

Others say that government antiterrorism activities and policies (what has been called the "war on terror") have gone too far by undermining civil liberties in the name of security. A prime concern is that some overreaching antiterrorism laws meant to be temporary can easily become permanent. Critics have also charged that repressive governments have used the war on terror as an excuse to violate the human rights and civil liberties of innocent people deemed undesirable by the state.

A more fundamental—and controversial—moral issue is whether terrorist actions can ever be morally justified. Many argue on various grounds that terrorism is never morally permissible, regardless of the merits of the terrorists' cause. The philosopher Haig Khatchadourian, for example, argues that acts of terrorism are always wrong because (1) they violate basic principles of just war theory and (2), except in rare cases in which other overriding moral principles apply, they violate their victims' right to be treated as moral persons. Regarding reason (1), Khatchadourian claims that terrorism in all forms violates the just war principles of discrimination and proportionality. Concerning reason (2), he says that

> [t]reating people as moral persons means treating them with consideration in two closely related ways. First, it means respecting their autonomy as individuals with their own desires and interests, plans and projects, commitments and goals. That autonomy is clearly violated if they are humiliated, coerced and terrorized, taken hostage or kidnapped, and above all, killed. Second, consideration . . . includes sensitivity to and consideration of their feelings and desires, aspirations, projects, and goals. That in turn is an integral part of treating their life as a whole—including their relationships and memories—as a thing of value. Finally, it includes respecting their "culture or ethnic, religious or racial identity or heritage." These things are the very antithesis of what terrorism does to its victims and the victimized.[15]

Similarly, the just war theorist Michael Walzer asserts that terrorism is wrong because it is an indiscriminate attack on the innocent. He thinks that a terrorist attack is worse than rape or murder because these crimes are at least directed at specific persons for particular reasons, even if those reasons are perverse. But terrorist violence is aimed at no one in particular for no purpose that could be linked to a specific person. For the terrorist, any innocent person who happens to fit into a broad category is as good a target as any other. "Terrorists are like killers on a rampage," says Walzer, "except that their rampage is not just expressive of rage or madness; the rage is purposeful and programmatic. It aims at a general vulnerability: Kill these people in order to terrify those."[16]

Not everyone agrees, however. A few thinkers, while deploring terrorist violence, argue that in some cases terrorism may be morally permissible. In fact, some maintain that particular instances of terrorism can even meet the requirements of just war theory and can therefore be justified in the same way that acts of war are justified. For example, one proponent of this view argues that when a stateless group has its right of self-determination thwarted, it may have a just cause—and an organization representing the group can be "a morally legitimate authority to carry out violence as a last resort to defend the group's rights."[17]

Disputes about the moral permissibility of terrorist actions can quickly bring us back to arguments about a plausible definition of terrorism. Suppose, for instance, that the preferred definition of terrorism is a variation on the one proposed earlier: deliberate use of violence against noncombatants for political or ideological purposes. This definition would apply to many acts that seem to be unambiguous examples of terrorism—the September 11 attacks, the Munich Olympics massacre, the Bali car bombing of October 2002, and many others. But what about the following cases in which noncombatants were also deliberately killed for political reasons: the Allied bombings of Dresden and other German cities in World War II and the atomic obliteration of Hiroshima and Nagasaki? According to our revised definition, aren't these also terrorist acts? And if so, could not the United States and Britain be classified as terrorist states?

Some are willing to accept such implications of our definition (or similar ones). They think that deliberately targeting noncombatants for political or ideological purposes is never morally acceptable—no matter who does the targeting. So for them, the World War II city bombings were indeed instances of terrorism, and the states doing the bombing were acting as terrorists. Others avoid these repugnant implications by working from a definition that confines terrorism to **nonstate actors**—that is, to individuals or groups that are not sovereign states. (Recall the definition of terrorism offered by the U.S. Department of State—"premeditated, politically motivated violence perpetrated against noncombatant targets by subnational groups or clandestine agents[.]") Terrorism then would be the killing of innocents by al-Qaeda or the Red Brigades, but not by a sovereign polity like the United States. Walzer, however, takes the line that terrorism is never morally justified, but that some of the city bombings in World War II *were* justified (and therefore were not terrorism) because they were done in a "supreme emergency"—circumstances in which civilization itself is threatened with imminent destruction.

Often where there is war or terrorism, there is also torture. As with other forms of political violence, the vexing question is whether torture is ever morally justified. And the most challenging version of this question is whether it is permissible to use torture to prevent terrorist carnage.

Torture is the intentional inflicting of severe pain or suffering on people to punish or intimidate them or to extract information from them. It has been used by both secular and religious authorities for centuries and continues to this day to be applied to hapless victims throughout the world—despite worldwide condemnation of the practice and its absolute prohibition in international law, including by United Nations treaties and the Geneva Conventions.

For generations the United States officially opposed torture and prosecuted both American soldiers and the nation's enemies for using harsh methods against captives. But the administration of President George W. Bush was accused of authorizing and employing interrogation tactics that had long been regarded as torture. The subjects were suspected terrorists, and the purpose of the severe approach was to wrest from them some information that might help authorities crush terrorist groups or prevent future terrorist attacks. Reports show that "waterboarding" (simulated drowning) and other extreme techniques were used against detainees in U.S.-run facilities overseas.

Three issues dominate the debates over the morality of torture: (1) Does torture work? (2) Is torture ever morally acceptable? and (3) What should be the state's policy regarding the use of torture?

As usually understood, question 1 is about whether torture is effective in getting reliable information from suspects. Science has yet to definitively answer this question, and the views of expert interrogators conflict. Many intelligence officers claim that torture rarely, if ever, yields useful information; other experts assert that torture occasionally produces valuable data. People in both camps worry about the indirect effect of using harsh methods: the damage to American prestige and influence, the increased likelihood of our enemies using torture against us, and the slide down the slippery slope toward the wider use of more brutal means.

For many nonconsequentialists, the answer to question 2 is an absolutist "no"—torture is the use of a person merely as a means, a clear instance of a lack of respect for a human being. Torture is therefore always wrong. But most people are probably not absolutists; they think that in rare cases there could be exceptions to a no-torture rule. (We consider a popular argument for this view in the "Moral Arguments" section.)

Question 3 is a separate issue entirely. Whether or not we believe that torture would be morally justified in a particular instance, we might take a very different view about legalizing or institutionalizing it. On this matter, there are three main positions: (1) torture should be illegal and never sanctioned in any circumstances; (2) torture should be illegal and officially condemned but unofficially (and secretly) used when necessary; and (3) torture should be a legal instrument of the state, although administered under strict guidelines and oversight.

Those taking the first approach insist that legalizing torture would have devastating consequences. It would corrupt democratic institutions, diminish our moral authority in the world, cause torture to become routine and widespread in society, and arouse worldwide resentment and anger toward us.

Those who prefer the second approach believe that torture may sometimes be necessary, but that acknowledging its use could cause many of the problems that worry those in the first group. Their critics accuse them of hypocrisy, but they see no good alternative to this clandestine, "under the radar" strategy.

The third approach is preferred by many who deplore the hypocrisy of the second group but are convinced that the use of torture is inevitable. They hold that if torture is legalized, its use can be better controlled than in any unofficial arrangement, and its abuses and proliferation can be limited. Alan Dershowitz advocates this third way, recommending a system in which official interrogators may use torture only after they acquire permission—"torture warrants"—from a judge.

MORAL THEORIES

Both consequentialist and nonconsequentialist perspectives have been given major roles in the ethics of war and peace. On the consequentialist side, utilitarianism has been used both to support and to undermine pacifism. Some have argued, for example, that by utilitarian lights, antiwar pacifism must be true. The philosopher Thomas Nagel provides some examples of such pacifist arguments:

It may even be argued that war involves violence on such a scale that it is never justified on utilitarian grounds—the consequences of refusing to go to war will never be as bad as the war itself would be, even if atrocities were not committed. Or in a more sophisticated vein it might be claimed that a uniform policy of never resorting to military force would do less harm in the long run, if followed consistently, than a policy of deciding each case on utilitarian grounds (even though on occasion particular applications of the pacifist policy might have worse results than a specific utilitarian decision).[18]

Whether good consequences produced by a pacifist stance would always in fact outweigh the bad of war making is, of course, a question of nonmoral fact—and some utilitarians assert that the facts do not help the pacifist's case. These critics say there is no evidence to support the notion that a policy of pacifism always results in less death and suffering. As one philosopher says,

[I]t is worthwhile to point out that the general history of the human race certainly offers no support for the supposition that turning the other cheek always produces good effects on the aggressor. Some aggressors, such as the Nazis, were apparently "egged on" by the "pacifist" attitude of their victims.[19]

Utilitarians can push this kind of argument even further and say that resorting to war is sometimes justified because it results in a better balance of good over bad, everyone considered, than not going to war. (Obviously, they too would need to back up such an empirical claim.) To be consistent, they would also want to base the moral rightness of military actions in war (*jus in bello*) on utilitarian considerations.

As we saw earlier, utilitarian elements are built into just war theory, which is a coherent system of both consequentialist and nonconsequentialist requirements. In our previous list of *jus ad bellum* conditions, the last three requirements are usually taken as consequentialist: (4) last resort, (5) good proportional to the bad, and (6) reasonable chance of success. And the *jus in bello* conditions of discrimination and proportionality are often viewed as rules for maximizing the good for both combatants and noncombatants.

When justifying views on the resort to war, both pacifists and nonpacifists may take a nonconsequentialist approach, appealing to fundamental moral principles rather than to the results of actions. As we have seen, pacifists typically rest their case on the right to life; nonpacifists, on the right of self-defense or the defense of basic human rights generally. The former regard their moral principle as absolute—it allows no exceptions—but the latter may not.

As you would expect, there can be stark differences on many critical matters between the consequentialist and nonconsequentialist. One such issue is the treatment of noncombatants. Absolutist nonconsequentialists maintain that the intentional killing of noncombatants is always morally wrong regardless of the circumstances, but consequentialists insist that sometimes there are exceptions:

> Regarding the absolute prohibition on intentional killing of noncombatants, absolutists have been termed "immunity theorists." Immunity theorists hold that it is always morally impermissible to intentionally kill noncombatants in war. Noncombatants are "innocent" and thus immune from attack. . . .
>
> . . . Consequentialists believe that actions in war can be morally justified depending on the end or aim of the action. If it is morally sufficient, the end can justify the means. . . . From this perspective, consequentialists, unlike absolutists, can morally justify the intentional killing of noncombatants or "innocents" in war. A controversial example addressed in this debate is the bombing of Hiroshima and Nagasaki in World War II. Consequentialists can morally justify these bombings. Absolutists, however, contend that these bombings were immoral because these bombings targeted noncombatants.[20]

How would traditional moral theories have us view the moral justification of terrorism? It seems that act-utilitarianism would have to sanction at least some terrorist attacks. The act-utilitarian must admit that it is possible for a terrorist action to yield the best overall results in a situation—and "best overall results" is the overriding factor here. But a utilitarian could not consistently condone terrorist actions that served only the interests of a particular group, for the theory demands that right actions produce the greatest overall happiness, *everyone considered*. Many (or perhaps most) acts of terrorism are clearly meant to exclusively favor a specific segment of a population; everyone is deliberately *not* considered.

Some writers contend that even though consequentialist moral theories can justify terrorism, the theories can do so "only under conditions that terrorists in the flesh will find it difficult to satisfy."[21] Consider: Consequentialism would demand that the terrorist acts be effective and efficient and that there be no nonterrorist actions likely to yield better or equal results. Such theories would require that the aim to be achieved be worth the horrific damage that a terrorist act can produce.

Terrorists themselves sometimes justify their actions on consequentialist grounds: they assert that only terrorism can help them achieve their objectives. But many observers are skeptical of terrorism's power to attain *any* political ends, especially the goal of liberation from an oppressive regime. Walzer observes, "I doubt that terrorism has ever achieved national liberation—no nation that I know of owes its freedom to a campaign of random murder."[22] Certainly terrorism can frighten the public and increase the terrorists' notoriety, but winning a political struggle is a much rougher road. If terrorism is indeed an ineffective strategy, then this fact could form the backbone of a consequentialist argument *against* terrorist acts.

Nonconsequentialist moral theories (or nonconsequentialist moral principles) often yield condemnations of terrorism in all forms. A traditional natural law theorist would insist that terrorism is always wrong because it violates the prohibition against intentionally killing the innocent. Natural law's doctrine of double effect—which disallows intentional bad actions even if they achieve good results—would lead to this conclusion (assuming the definition of terrorism given earlier). Some people, of course, could try to counter this view by rejecting the doctrine of double effect or by questioning the concept of moral innocence. A Kantian theorist or other nonconsequentialist could argue that terrorism is not morally permissible because it violates innocent persons' human rights, their right to life, or their autonomy or because terrorism uses people merely as a means to an end.

Many philosophers view terrorism from the perspective of just war theory. Some of them argue that terrorism is wrong because it violates key conditions of just war theory—in particular, discrimination, proportionality (both *jus ad bellum* and *jus in bello*), last resort, and just cause. As we saw earlier, some reject this claim and maintain that just war theory, rightly interpreted, shows that in some instances terrorism may be justified because it meets all the conditions.

A nonconsequentialist is likely to consider torture wrong in all circumstances—wrong because it violates the rights of persons, primarily by severely diminishing their autonomy as individuals. A consequentialist could either accept or reject the use of torture, depending on her assessment of the likely effects. She could decide that torture is justified in rare cases in which it could prevent a massive terrorist attack or lead to the destruction of a terrorist cell involved in the killing of hundreds or thousands of people. She could also argue that when all the consequences of torturing someone are carefully weighed, torture is never the best option. Its negative ramifications always outweigh the positive.

MORAL ARGUMENTS

Perhaps the simplest argument against political violence is based on the commonsense presumption that violence of any kind is inherently (prima facie) wrong and therefore requires very strong reasons for believing that in a particular case it is justified. One form this argument could take is this:

Violence is inherently wrong; there are no good reasons to suppose that it is ever justified; therefore, violence (including political violence) is always wrong. This argument puts the burden of proof on those who allege that sometimes violence is permissible.

But the problem for anyone who relies on this line is that many people have been happy to take up this burden, arguing in the case of war, terrorism, or torture that there are indeed strong reasons why violence is occasionally justified. Likewise, many who insist on nonviolence have not been content to rest their case on this burden-of-proof argument. They have tried to show that strong arguments can independently support their position.

As we have seen, it's possible to argue for and against the resort to war using either a consequentialist or nonconsequentialist tack. Just war theory is a mix of both these approaches, and it has probably been the focus of most of the philosophical disputes concerning war and peace.

One set of arguments about war that continues to provoke intense debate is **humanitarian intervention**. The conventional model of a justified resort to war is one sovereign state defending itself against another's aggression. A state's self-defense is thought to be just cause for unleashing the dogs of war. But humanitarian intervention is a different sort of scenario, for it involves a state (or states) going to war to defend people of another state against the murderous aggression of their own regime. The aggression may appear in the form of genocide, ethnic cleansing, forced starvation, and mass imprisonment or slavery—the kinds of atrocities that occurred forty years ago in Cambodia and Uganda, and more recently in Somalia, East Timor, Kosovo, Rwanda, and Libya. The situations that are said to cry out for humanitarian intervention are both compelling and alien to early just war theory:

> The standard cases have a standard form: a government, an army, a police force, tyrannically controlled, attacks its own people or some subset of its own people, a vulnerable minority, say, territorially based or dispersed throughout the country. . . . The

attack takes place within the country's borders; it doesn't require any boundary crossings; it is an exercise of sovereign power. There is no aggression, no invading army to resist and beat back. Instead, the rescuing forces are the invaders; they are the ones who, in the strict sense of international law, begin the war. But they come into a situation where the moral stakes are clear: the oppressors or, better, the state agents of oppression are readily identifiable; their victims are plain to see.[23]

To get to the heart of these matters, we want to ask, Is humanitarian intervention ever morally permissible? Those who say yes—the interventionists—might offer an argument like this:

1. An individual has a duty to try to stop an unjust and potentially fatal attack against someone (to intervene), even if defending the victim requires using violence against the attacker (assuming that the defender is capable of acting without too much personal risk, and there is no other way to stop the attack).

2. Humanitarian intervention by a state (or states) is exactly analogous to this type of personal intervention on behalf of seriously threatened victims.

3. Therefore, states have a duty of humanitarian intervention (under the right circumstances).

This argument is, of course, inductive—an argument by analogy. Probably few people would balk at Premise 1: it is a simple moral principle drawn from commonsense morality. Some might insist that a principle declaring that we have a *duty* to intervene is too strong—better to say that in the right circumstances, intervening is *morally permissible*, not obligatory. Though this complaint may have merit, let us stay with the original wording for simplicity's sake.

Premise 2 is the weak link here. For an argument by analogy to be strong, the two things being compared must be sufficiently similar in relevant ways. In this case, the intervention of an individual to halt an attack on another person must be relevantly similar to an intervention by sovereign states to stop aggression by another state against people

within the state's borders. But noninterventionists might claim that the argument is weak because the personal and national circumstances are different in important respects. One difference is the well-established doctrine of international conduct that one sovereign state may not meddle in the internal affairs of another. This noninterference principle, says the noninterventionist, seems much stronger than any analogous rule on the personal level. Even interfering in a family conflict in which one family member is being brutally assaulted by the others may seem morally permissible sometimes, while analogous interference in a state's internal conflicts seems less morally clear cut.

There is much more that can be said both for and against Premise 2, but let us turn to another interventionist argument:

1. All persons have certain supremely important, basic rights—for example, rights to life, to self-determination, and to freedom from harm—rights that must not be violated by either people or states.

2. People who have these basic rights violated are entitled to use force to defend them, and it is morally permissible for other people or states to use force to help in that defense (humanitarian intervention).

3. People or states that violate others' basic rights forfeit their own right not to have force used against them.

4. Therefore, humanitarian intervention in defense of basic rights is morally permissible.

Interventionists are likely to get very little disagreement about either Premise 1 or Premise 3. For a majority of moral philosophers, the concepts of moral rights and their forfeiture are plausible elements in most of the major moral traditions. But Premise 2 is controversial. The idea of people using force in self-defense (to protect their lives or property, for example) is part of commonsense morality, but noninterventionists have questioned the defense of others' rights that involves crossing borders and violating state sovereignty. A critical problem, they would argue, is that the principle embodied in Premise 2 would have us ignore the rights of sovereign states to defend human rights—yet state sovereignty is itself a well-established principle of international relations. So we have a conflict of moral principles. In a utilitarian vein, noninterventionists may also argue that a policy of humanitarian intervention that ignores state sovereignty and attends to the countless violations of rights by a state could lead to perpetual wars everywhere. Some noninterventionists allow that intervention may indeed be necessary in certain extraordinary cases involving genocide, massacres, and other extreme horrors. But they think that intervention should be reserved for these horrors; otherwise, perpetual war will in fact be the norm.

In this era of the "war on terror" and the worldwide threat of terrorist acts, moral arguments on terrorism are both extremely important and often controversial. Probably the liveliest—and, to some, the most disturbing—disputes have to do with the moral permissibility of terrorist acts. Consider the tragic events of September 11, 2001. Many people the world over assume without question that those who caused that horrific loss of life committed acts of terrorism that were morally wrong and monstrously evil. And many careful thinkers have come to the same conclusions, albeit by a more reflective, reasoned route. Plenty of people in both groups believe that terrorism is always morally wrong. But some equally reflective observers who are just as horrified by September 11 argue that terrorism may sometimes be permissible (and that many who disagree are being inconsistent, perhaps even hypocritical). We may even hear arguments for the permissibility of terrorism from people sympathetic to certain terrorist causes. Let us look more closely at some of these disputes. First, consider this argument:

1. If the killing of innocents is sometimes morally permissible in war, then it is morally permissible in terrorism (defined here as the intentional killing of innocents for political purposes).

2. The killing of innocents is sometimes morally permissible in war.

3. Therefore, the killing of innocents is sometimes morally permissible in terrorism.

This conclusion asserts that we cannot condemn all acts of terrorism out of hand, for some may be morally justified. The argument is that, as most people believe, killing innocents in wartime is sometimes permissible. Noncombatants are usually killed and maimed in war because combat so often happens near or among them. Still, most people are willing to accept this "collateral damage" as the inevitable—but regrettable—consequence of waging war. Some civilian deaths are unavoidable but morally permissible. Yet if they are morally acceptable in war, they must be morally acceptable aspects of terrorism. After all, both kinds of violence involve the death of innocents during hostilities directed at political ends.

Many critics of this argument would accept Premise 2 but reject Premise 1, insisting that there is a morally significant difference between the killing of innocents in war and in terrorist attacks. They would say that the killing of noncombatants in war is morally permissible because it is unintended; noncombatant deaths happen inadvertently as combatants are targeted. Terrorist killings, however, are wrong because they are intentional. The deliberate slaughter of innocents is never morally acceptable. Obviously, this response is an appeal to the doctrine of double effect.

But some would not accept this appeal, reasoning along the following lines:

> While the principle of double effect is plausible in some cases, it is severely defective. To see this, suppose that the September 11 attackers had only intended to destroy the Pentagon and the World Trade Center and had no desire to kill anyone. Suppose that they knew, however, that thousands would die in the attack on the buildings. And suppose, following the attack, they said "We are not murderers. We did not mean to kill these people."
>
> What would be our reaction? I very much doubt that we would think them less culpable. They could

not successfully justify or excuse their actions by saying that although they foresaw the deaths of many people, these deaths were not part of their aim. We would certainly reject this defense. But if we would reject the appeal to double effect in this case, then we should do so in others.[24]

Not everyone would agree with this reasoning, but let us move on to a related argument:

1. Deliberately killing innocents for political or ideological reasons is morally wrong.

2. Deliberately killing noninnocents for such reasons may be morally permissible (as in war or revolution, for example).

3. Some people commonly thought to be innocents are actually noninnocents (they are pseudo-innocents).

4. Therefore, deliberately killing pseudo-innocents for political or ideological reasons may in some cases be morally permissible.

This argument states formally what is often alleged more casually: that some actions usually condemned as instances of terrorism (involving the deliberate killing of innocents) are *not* terrorist acts at all because the "innocents" are not really innocent. This claim (common in some cultures and often uttered by terrorists themselves) is that some people should be judged noninnocents if they, for example, indirectly aid or sympathize with a hated regime, or happen to belong to the same race or religion as those presumed guilty of committing some acts of injustice or oppression, or are simply part of a system or enterprise that adversely affects a favored group. Such an attitude has been held by many, most infamously by Osama bin Laden:

> The ruling to kill the Americans and their allies—civilian and military—is an individual duty for every Muslim who can do it in any country in which it is possible to do, in order to liberate the Al Aksa Mosque and the holy mosque from their grip, and in order for their families to move out of all the lands of Islam, defeated and unable to threaten any Muslim.[25]

The precise distinction between innocents and noninnocents (or combatants and noncombatants) in war is controversial among philosophers. But most of these thinkers do acknowledge a clear difference between the two concepts, and many reject the sort of blurring of the distinctions common among those who wish to justify terrorism. A typical argument against such justifications is that if the distinctions are discarded, then anyone and everyone could be deemed guilty and therefore a legitimate target of terrorism. For example, if ordinary individuals who buy bananas and thereby contribute to an economy run by a bloodthirsty dictatorship somehow share the blame for the regime's crimes, then any man, woman, or child could share the guilt—and deserve the terrorist's justice. Attributing guilt to people because of such remote connections to wrongdoing, critics say, seems to reduce the notions of guilt and innocence to absurdity.

Probably the strongest—and most controversial—argument for the political use of torture is based on the so-called ticking-bomb scenario. Suppose a bomb will soon detonate in a major American city, killing a hundred thousand innocent people. The only way to prevent this massive loss of life is to torture the terrorist who planted the bomb until he reveals its location. Would it be morally permissible to waterboard or electrocute him until he talks? (Note that this is a separate question from torture's legality.) Many think the obvious answer is yes and that there is strong moral justification for using torture in this case. What considerations could lead to this conclusion? Here is one philosopher's answer (referring to a similar version of the ticking-bomb situation):

> Consider the following points: (1) The police reasonably believe that torturing the terrorist will probably save thousands of lives; (2) the police know that there is no other way to save those lives; (3) the threat to life is more or less imminent; (4) the thousands about to be murdered are innocent—the terrorist has no good, let alone decisive, justificatory moral reason for murdering them; (5) the terrorist is known to be

(jointly with other terrorists) morally responsible for planning, transporting, and arming the nuclear device and, if it explodes, he will be (jointly with other terrorists) morally responsible for the murder of thousands.[26]

QUICK REVIEW

realism (as applied to warfare)—The view that moral standards are not applicable to war, and that war instead must be judged on how well it serves state interests.

pacifism—The view that war is never morally permissible.

just war theory—The doctrine that war may be morally permissible under stipulated conditions.

jus ad bellum—The justification for resorting to war; the justice of war.

jus in bello—The moral permissibility of acts in war; justice in war.

noncombatant immunity—The status of a person who should not be intentionally attacked in war.

terrorism (as defined in this chapter)—Violence against noncombatants for political, religious, or ideological ends.

terrorism (the definition preferred by the U.S. Department of State)—Premeditated, politically motivated violence perpetrated against noncombatant targets by subnational groups or clandestine agents, usually intended to influence an audience.

nonstate actors—Individuals or groups that are not sovereign states.

torture—The intentional inflicting of severe pain or suffering on people to punish or intimidate them or extract information from them.

humanitarian intervention—The act of a state (or states) going to war to defend people of another state against the murderous aggression of their own regime.

Some take a deontological approach to this issue and declare that torture is always wrong in all circumstances (a common absolutist position). Critics of this view say that it is suspect because torturing people usually seems to be morally not as bad as killing them. If so, it would be implausible to assert that torturing the terrorist is absolutely forbidden but that not torturing him and letting thousands die would be morally permissible.

Others who are opposed to torture believe that ticking-bomb scenarios are too contrived to be taken seriously; such states of affairs simply don't happen in the real world. The usual response to this is that in light of what we know about terrorist tactics and aims (and about police cases that resemble ticking-bomb scenarios), we have good reasons to believe the opposite—ticking-bomb situations are indeed possible.

CHAPTER REVIEW

SUMMARY

Political violence is the resort to violence for political ends. War, terrorism, torture, revolution, assassination, civil war, and violent demonstrations are examples. Violence is the physical or psychological attack on, or the vigorous abuse of, persons, causing their suffering, injury, or death. (Violence can also involve the destroying or damaging of property.) Violence is considered prima facie wrong—wrong unless there are good reasons for thinking it morally permissible. Thus people often speak of war and other modes of violence as things to be *resorted to*, actions to be taken only after other options are exhausted.

Violence is thought to be wrong for several reasons. Some argue that violence constitutes a violation of people's rights—their right to life, self-determination, respect as a person, or immunity from harm. Another view is that violence is wrong because it runs afoul of the moral principles of justice, freedom, and utility (human welfare). The consequentialist position is that

violence is (generally) wrong because its bad consequences (usually) outweigh the good.

The main ethical questions regarding war and
peace are (1) how—if at all—the resort to war can be
justified, and (2) assuming it can be justified, how it
should be conducted. Most serious answers to such
questions come from three distinct perspectives. Realism is the view that moral standards are not applicable to war, though considerations of prudence are.
Pacifism is the view that war is never morally permissible. Just war theory is the doctrine that war may be
morally permissible under stipulated conditions.

Depending on how they judge the empirical evidence, utilitarians may with logical consistency take
either a pacifist or a nonpacifist stance on war. Nonconsequentialists may also consistently support or
reject pacifism. Pacifists typically rest their case on
the nonconsequentialist principle of the right to life.
Nonpacifists may back their case with the nonconsequentialist principles of the right to self-defense or of
human rights generally.

Terrorism is violence against noncombatants
for political, religious, or ideological ends. The key
question that terrorism provokes is what our moral
response to it should be. Should it always and everywhere be condemned? Or is terrorism sometimes justified? One way to grapple with terrorism is to try to
apply the requirements of just war theory to terrorist
acts. Many philosophers argue that by the lights of
just war theory, terrorism is never morally permissible.
Others contend that it is possible for terrorism to meet
just war criteria and thereby prove itself justified. Even
without reference to just war theory, some argue that
terrorism is always wrong because it violates the victims' right to be treated as moral persons, or because it
is an indiscriminate attack on the innocent.

A consequentialist moral theory would probably
condone terrorism if it maximized happiness or welfare for all concerned, but in actual cases this requirement may make terrorism very difficult to justify.

Torture is the intentional inflicting of severe pain
or suffering on people to punish or intimidate them or
to extract information from them. Three issues dominate the debates over the morality of torture: (1) Does
torture work? (2) Is torture ever morally acceptable?

and (3) What should be the state's policy regarding the
use of torture?

KEY TERMS

realism (as applied to warfare) (p. 706)
pacifism (p. 706)
just war theory (p. 707)
jus ad bellum (p. 707)
jus in bello (p.707)
noncombatant immunity (p. 709)
terrorism (as defined in this chapter) (p. 710)
terrorism (the definition preferred by the U.S.
Department of State) (p. 710)
nonstate actors (p. 714)
torture (p. 714)
humanitarian intervention (p. 717)

EXERCISES

Review Questions

1. What is violence, as some philosophers have
   defined it? (p. 705)
2. What is realism as it applies to warfare? (p. 706)
3. What is pacifism? (p. 706)
4. What is just war theory? (p. 707)
5. What are the two main moral issues addressed
   in just war theory? (p. 707)
6. Identify three requirements in just war theory
   that must be met to justify war. (pp. 707–709)
7. What are the *jus in bello* requirements for moral
   conduct in war? (p. 709)
8. What is noncombatant immunity? (p. 709)
9. How is terrorism defined in this text? How does
   the U.S. Department of State define it? (p. 710)
10. What is torture? What reasons have torturers given
    to explain or justify their use of torture? (p. 714)

Discussion Questions

1. If violence is wrong, why is it wrong? Is it that
   violence is a violation of people's rights? Or is
   there some other reason?
2. Are you a realist regarding war? Are there any
   moral restraints on the use of political violence?
3. Can war ever be morally justified? If so, how? If
   not, why not?

4. Do you believe there are circumstances in which torturing a suspected terrorist is morally permissible? Explain.

5. How might someone use just war theory to justify the Allied participation in World War II?

6. Can terrorism ever be morally justified? Why or why not?

7. Was the atomic obliteration of Hiroshima and Nagasaki in World War II an act of terrorism? Explain.

8. How might pacifists (who argue that all wars are wrong) justify their position? How might someone argue against it?

9. What is the difference between a preventive and a preemptive war? Can a preventive war ever be justified? Why or why not?

10. Is a pacifist being consistent if she opposes all wars but condones personal violence used in self-defense or in law enforcement? Why or why not?

FURTHER READING

G. E. M. Anscombe, "War and Murder," in *Nuclear Weapons: A Catholic Response,* ed. Walter Stein (New York: Sheed and Ward, 1961).

Thomas Aquinas, *Summa Theologica,* Second Part of the Second Part, Questions 40, 64, and 69.

Joseph M. Boyle Jr., "Just War Doctrine and the Military Response to Terrorism," *Journal of Political Philosophy* 11, no. 2 (2003): 153–70.

R. G. Frey and Christopher W. Morris, eds., *Violence, Terrorism, and Justice* (Cambridge: Cambridge University Press, 1991).

Robert Fullinwider, "Terrorism, Innocence, and War," in *War After September 11,* ed. Verna V. Gehring (Lanham, MD: Rowman and Littlefield, 2003).

David Luban, "The War on Terrorism and the End of Human Rights," *Philosophy & Public Policy Quarterly* 22, no. 3 (Summer 2002): 9–14.

Larry May, Eric Rovie, and Steve Viner, eds., *The Morality of War: Classical and Contemporary Readings* (Upper Saddle River, NJ: Pearson/Prentice Hall, 2006).

Thomas Nagel, "War and Massacre," *Philosophy & Public Affairs* 1, no. 2 (Winter 1972): 123–43.

Jan Narveson, "Pacifism: A Philosophical Analysis," *Ethics* 75, no. 4 (1965): 259–71.

Brian Orend, "War," in *Stanford Encyclopedia of Philosophy*, Winter 2005 ed., ed. Edward N. Zalta, http://plato.stanford.edu/archives/win2005/entries /war/ (March 1, 2015).

Louis P. Pojman, "The Moral Response to Terrorism and the Cosmopolitan Imperative," in *Terrorism and International Justice,* ed. James P. Sterba (New York: Oxford University Press, 2003).

Henry Shue, "War," in *The Oxford Handbook of Practical Ethics,* ed. Hugh LaFollette (Oxford: Oxford University Press, 2003).

Charles Townshend, *Terrorism: A Very Short Introduction* (Oxford: Oxford University Press, 2002).

Andrew Valls, "Can Terrorism Be Justified?" in *Ethics in International Affairs,* ed. Valls (Lanham, MD: Rowman and Littlefield, 2000).

Michael Walzer, *Just and Unjust Wars: A Moral Argument with Historical Illustrations,* 2nd ed. (New York: Basic Books, 1992).

John Howard Yoder, *When War Is Unjust: Being Honest in Just-War Thinking,* 2nd ed. (Maryknoll, NY: Orbis Books, 1996).

ETHICAL DILEMMAS

1. Intervention to Stop ISIS

In 2014, President Barack Obama authorized U.S. air strikes against a group of militant Islamists known as the Islamic State of Iraq and Syria (ISIS) to prevent them from possibly committing genocide against members of the Yezidi sect, a religious minority trapped on a mountaintop in northwest Iraq. In a speech, the president sought to justify the intervention:

> [A]t the request of the Iraqi government—we've begun operations to help save Iraqi civilians stranded on the mountain. As ISIL [ISIS] has marched across Iraq, it has

waged a ruthless campaign against innocent Iraqis. And these terrorists have been especially barbaric towards religious minorities, including Christian and Yezidis, a small and ancient religious sect. Countless Iraqis have been displaced. And chilling reports describe ISIL militants rounding up families, conducting mass executions, and enslaving Yezidi women.

In recent days, Yezidi women, men and children from the area of Sinjar have fled for their lives. And thousands—perhaps tens of thousands—are now hiding high up on the mountain, with little but the clothes on their backs. They're without food, they're without water. People are starving. And children are dying of thirst. Meanwhile, ISIL forces below have called for the systematic destruction of the entire Yezidi people, which would constitute genocide. So these innocent families are faced with a horrible choice: descend the mountain and be slaughtered, or stay and slowly die of thirst and hunger.

I've said before, the United States cannot and should not intervene every time there's a crisis in the world. So let me be clear about why we must act, and act now. When we face a situation like we do on that mountain—with innocent people facing the prospect of violence on a horrific scale, when we have a mandate to help—in this case, a request from the Iraqi government—and when we have the unique capabilities to help avert a massacre, then I believe the United States of America cannot turn a blind eye. We can act, carefully and responsibly, to prevent a potential act of genocide. That's what we're doing on that mountain.*

Was President Obama justified in ordering the armed intervention? What if the Iraqi government had not requested military action from the United States? Would the intervention be justified then? Why or why not? How would just war theory apply? How might a utilitarian evaluate the permissibility of the United States' military action? What might a nonconsequentialist say about it?

*Barack Obama, "Statement by the President," August 7, 2014, http://www.whitehouse.gov/the-press-office/2014/08/07/statement-president (February 27, 2015).

---

2. War in Afghanistan

Consider this time line detailing the run-up to the U.S. invasion of Afghanistan in 2001.

September 11—Hijacked airliners are flown into the twin towers of the World Trade Center in New York and the Pentagon, outside Washington DC. A fourth plane crashes in Pennsylvania. In an address to the nation, President Bush describes the attacks as "deliberate and deadly terrorist acts." He says he has directed the U.S. intelligence and law enforcement communities "to find those responsible and bring them to justice," adding that the U.S. "will make no distinction between the terrorists who committed these acts and those who harbor them."

September 12—President Bush declares that the attacks were "acts of war." The United Nations Security Council passes Resolution 1368, recognizing "the inherent right of individual and collective self-defense" and calling on all states to work together to bring the perpetrators of the attacks to justice. The North Atlantic Council for the first time invokes Article 5 of NATO's founding treaty, stating that an armed attack against any member state shall be considered as an attack against all.

September 18—Congress passes a resolution giving the President authorization for the use of force "against those nations, organizations, or persons he determines planned, authorized, committed, or aided the terrorist attacks that occurred on September 11, 2001, or harbored such organizations or persons."

September 20—In an address to a joint session of Congress, President Bush says all the evidence suggests al-Qaeda was responsible for the attacks, and warns the Taliban regime that they must "hand over the terrorists, or they will share in their fate." The Department of Justice issues an Interim Rule stating that non-citizens can be detained for 48 hours without charge, or in the event of an "emergency or other extraordinary circumstance" for "an additional reasonable period of time.". . .

October 4—The British government issues a statement saying it is confident that Osama bin Laden and the al-Qaeda network "planned and carried out the atrocities of 11 September," and setting out the evidence for their conclusion.

October 7—U.S. military forces launch 'Operation Enduring Freedom' against Taliban and al-Qaeda facilities in Afghanistan. In a televised address, President Bush says U.S. actions "are designed to disrupt the use of Afghanistan as a terrorist base of operations, and to attack the military capability of the Taliban regime."[†]

Was the U.S. response to the September 11 attacks a legitimate act of self-defense? Why or why not? According to just war theory, was the U.S. invasion of Afghanistan justified? If so, how does the resort to warfare square with each of the just war conditions? If not, why not? How does the decision to go to war fail any just war requirements?

[†]Anthony Dworkin and Ariel Meyerstein, "A Defining Moment—International Law Since September 11: A Timeline," Crimes of War Project, February 18, 2006. Reprinted with permission of the Crimes of War Project and the authors.

---

3. Terrorism and Torture

WASHINGTON—Most Americans and a majority of people in Britain, France and South Korea say torturing terrorism suspects is justified at least in rare instances, according to AP-Ipsos polling.

The United States has drawn criticism from human rights groups and many governments, especially in Europe, for its treatment of terror suspects. President Bush and other top officials have said the U.S. does not torture, but some suspects in American custody have alleged they were victims of severe mistreatment.

The polling, in the United States and eight of its closest allies, found that in Canada, Mexico and Germany people are divided on whether torture is ever justified. Most people opposed torture under any circumstances in Spain and Italy.

"I don't think we should go out and string everybody up by their thumbs until somebody talks. But if there is definitely a good reason to get an answer, we should do whatever it takes," said Billy Adams, a retiree from Tomball, Texas.

In America, 61 percent of those surveyed agreed torture is justified at least on rare occasions. Almost nine in 10 in South Korea and just over half in France and Britain felt that way.[‡]

Do you agree with most Americans that the use of torture is sometimes morally permissible in fighting terrorism? If so, what circumstances do you think would justify torture? If not, why not? How might a utilitarian justify (or oppose) torture? How might a Kantian theorist argue against torturing suspected terrorists?

[‡]Associated Press, "Poll Finds Broad Approval of Terrorist Torture," published on MSNBC.com, December 9, 2005. © The Associated Press. Reprinted by permission.

READINGS

Reconciling Pacifists and Just War Theorists

JAMES P. STERBA

Traditionally pacifism and just war theory have represented radically opposed responses to aggression. Pacifism has been interpreted to rule out any use of violence in response to aggression. Just war theory has been interpreted to permit a measured use of violence in response to aggression. It has been thought that the two views might sometimes agree in particular cases—for example, that pacifists and just war theorists might unconditionally oppose nuclear war, but beyond that it has been generally held that the two views lead to radically opposed recommendations. In this paper, I hope to show that this is not the case. I will argue that pacifism and just war theory, in their most morally defensible interpretations, can be substantially reconciled both in theory and practice.

In traditional just war theory there are two basic elements: an account of just cause and an account of just means. Just cause is usually specified as follows:

1) There must be substantial aggression;
2) Nonbelligerent correctives must be either hopeless or too costly; and
3) Belligerent correctives must be neither hopeless nor too costly.

Needless to say, the notion of substantial aggression is a bit fuzzy, but it is generally understood to be the type of aggression that violates people's most fundamental rights. To suggest some specific examples of what is and is not substantial aggression, usually the taking of hostages is regarded as substantial

James P. Sterba, excerpts from "Reconciling Pacifists and Just War Theorists," *Social Theory and Practice* Vol. 18, No. 1 (Spring 1992): 21–38. Reprinted with permission of Social Theory and Practice.

aggression while the nationalization of particular firms owned by foreigners is not so regarded. But even when substantial aggression occurs, frequently nonbelligerent correctives are neither hopeless nor too costly. And even when nonbelligerent correctives are either hopeless or too costly, in order for there to be a just cause, belligerent correctives must be neither hopeless nor too costly.

Traditional just war theory assumes, however, that there are just causes and goes on to specify just means as imposing two requirements:

1) Harm to innocents should not be directly intended as an end or a means.
2) The harm resulting from the belligerent means should not be disproportionate to the particular defensive objective to be attained.

While the just means conditions apply to each defensive action, the just cause conditions must be met by the conflict as a whole.

It is important to note that these requirements of just cause and just means are not essentially about war at all. Essentially, they constitute a theory of just defense that can apply to war but can also apply to a wide range of defensive actions short of war. Of course, what needs to be determined is whether these requirements can be justified. Since just war theory is usually opposed to pacifism, to secure a non-question-begging justification for the theory and its requirements we need to proceed as much as possible from premises that are common to pacifists and just war theorists alike. The difficulty here is that there is not just one form of pacifism but many. So we need to determine which form of pacifism is most morally defensible.

Now when most people think of pacifism they tend to identify it with a theory of nonviolence. We can call this view "nonviolent pacifism." It maintains that:

> Any use of violence against other human beings is morally prohibited.

It has been plausibly argued, however, that this form of pacifism is incoherent. In a well-known article, Jan Narveson rejects nonviolent pacifism as incoherent because it recognizes a right to life yet rules out any use of force in defense of that right.[1] The view is incoherent, Narveson claims, because having a right entails the legitimacy of using force in defense of that right at least on some occasions.

Given the cogency of objections of this sort, some have opted for a form of pacifism that does not rule out all violence but only lethal violence. We can call this view "nonlethal pacifism." It maintains that

> Any lethal use of force against other human beings is morally prohibited.

In defense of nonlethal pacifism, Cheyney Ryan has argued that there is a substantial issue between the pacifist and the nonpacifist concerning whether we can or should create the necessary distance between ourselves and other human beings in order to make the act of killing possible.[2] To illustrate, Ryan cites George Orwell's reluctance to shoot at an enemy soldier who jumped out of a trench and ran along the top of a parapet half-dressed and holding up his trousers with both hands. Ryan contends that what kept Orwell from shooting was that he couldn't think of the soldier as a thing rather than a fellow human being.

However, it is not clear that Orwell's encounter supports nonlethal pacifism. For it may be that what kept Orwell from shooting the enemy soldier was not his inability to think of the soldier as a thing rather than a fellow human being but rather his inability to think of the soldier who was holding up his trousers with both hands as a threat or a combatant. Under this interpretation, Orwell's decision not to shoot would accord well with the requirements of just war theory.

Let us suppose, however, that someone is attempting to take your life. Why does that permit you, the defender of nonlethal pacifism might ask, to kill the person making the attempt? The most cogent response, it seems to me, is that killing in such a case is not evil, or at least not morally evil, because anyone who is wrongfully engaged in an attempt upon your life has already forfeited his or her right to life by engaging in such aggression.[3] So, provided that you are reasonably certain that the aggressor is wrongfully engaged in an attempt upon your life, you would be morally justified in killing, assuming that it is the only way of saving your own life.

There is, however, a form of pacifism that remains untouched by the criticisms I have raised against both nonviolent pacifism and nonlethal pacifism. This form of pacifism neither prohibits all violence nor even all uses of lethal force. We can call the view "anti-war pacifism" because it holds that

> Any participation in the massive use of lethal force in warfare is morally prohibited.

In defense of anti-war pacifism, it is undeniable that wars have brought enormous amounts of death and destruction in their wake and that many of those who have perished in them are noncombatants or innocents. In fact, the tendency of modern wars has been to produce higher and higher proportions of noncombatant casualties, making it more and more difficult to justify participation in such wars. At the same time, strategies for nonbelligerent conflict resolution are rarely intensively developed and explored before nations choose to go to war, making it all but impossible to justify participation in such wars.

To determine whether the requirements of just war theory can be reconciled with those of anti-war pacifism, however, we need to consider whether we should distinguish between harm intentionally inflicted upon innocents and harm whose infliction on innocents is merely foreseen. On the one hand, we could favor a uniform restriction against the infliction of harm upon innocents that ignores the intended/foreseen distinction. On the other hand, we could favor a differential restriction which is more severe against the intentional infliction of harm upon innocents but is less severe against the infliction of harm that is merely foreseen. What needs to be determined, therefore, is whether there is any rationale for favoring this differential restriction on harm over a uniform restriction. But this presupposes that we can, in practice, distinguish between what is foreseen and what is intended, and some have challenged whether this can be done. So first we need to address this challenge.

Now the practical test that is frequently appealed to in order to distinguish between foreseen and intended elements of an action is the Counterfactual Test. According to this test, two questions are relevant:

1) Would you have performed the action if only the good consequences would have resulted and not the evil consequences?
2) Would you have performed the action if only the evil consequences resulted and not the good consequences?

If an agent answers "Yes" to the first question and "No" to the second, some would conclude that (1) the action is an intended means to the good consequences; (2) the good consequences are an intended end; and (3) the evil consequences are merely foreseen.

But how well does this Counterfactual Test work? Douglas Lackey has argued that the test gives the wrong result in any case where the "act that produces an evil effect produces a larger good effect."[4] Lackey cites the bombing of Hiroshima as an example. That bombing is generally thought to have had two effects: the killing of Japanese civilians and the shortening of the war. Now suppose we were to ask:

1) Would Truman have dropped the bomb if only the shortening of the war would have resulted but not the killing of the Japanese civilians?
2) Would Truman have dropped the bomb if only the Japanese civilians would have been killed and the war not shortened?

And suppose that the answer to the first question is that Truman would have dropped the bomb if only the shortening of the war would have resulted but not the killing of the Japanese civilians, and the answer to the second question is that Truman would not have dropped the bomb if only the Japanese civilians would have been killed and the war not shortened. Lackey concludes from this that the killing of civilians at Hiroshima, self-evidently a means for shortening the war, is by the Counterfactual Test classified not as a means but as a mere foreseen consequence. On these grounds, Lackey rejects the Counterfactual Test as an effective device for distinguishing between the foreseen and the intended consequences of an action.

Unfortunately, this is to reject the Counterfactual Test only because one expects too much from it. It is to expect the test to determine all of the following:

1) Whether the action is an intended means to the good consequences;
2) Whether the good consequences are an intended end of the action; and
3) Whether the evil consequences are simply foreseen consequences.

In fact, this test is only capable of meeting the first two of these expectations. And the test clearly succeeds in doing this for Lackey's own example, where the test shows the bombing of Hiroshima to be an intended means to shortening the war, and shortening the war an intended consequence of the action.

To determine whether the evil consequences are simply foreseen consequences, however, an additional test is needed, which I shall call the Nonexplanation Test. According to this test, the relevant question is:

> Does the bringing about of the evil consequences help explain why the agent undertook the action as a means to the good consequences?

If the answer is "No," that is, if the bringing about of the evil consequences does not help explain why the agent undertook the action as a means to the good consequences, the evil consequences are merely foreseen. But if the answer is "Yes," the evil consequences are an intended means to the good consequences.

Of course, there is no guaranteed procedure for arriving at an answer to the Nonexplanation Test. Nevertheless, when we are in doubt concerning whether the evil consequences of an act are simply foreseen, seeking an answer to the Nonexplanation Test will tend to be the best way of reasonably resolving that doubt. For example, applied to Lackey's example, the Nonexplanation Test comes up with a "Yes," since the evil consequences in this example do help explain why the bombing was undertaken to shorten the war. For according to the usual account, Truman ordered the bombing to bring about the civilian deaths which by their impact upon Japanese morale were expected to shorten the war. So, by the Nonexplanation Test, the civilian deaths were an

intended means to the good consequences of shortening the war.

Assuming then that we can distinguish in practice between harm intentionally inflicted upon innocents and harm whose infliction on innocents is merely foreseen, we need to determine whether there is any rationale for favoring a differential restriction that is more severe against the intentional infliction of harm upon innocents but is less severe against the infliction of harm that is merely foreseen over a uniform restriction against the infliction of harm upon innocents that ignores the intended/foreseen distinction.

Let us first examine the question from the perspective of those suffering the harm. Initially, it might appear to matter little whether the harm would be intended or just foreseen by those who cause it. From the perspective of those suffering harm, it might appear that what matters is simply that the overall amount of harm be restricted irrespective of whether it is foreseen or intended. But consider—don't those who suffer harm have more reason to protest when the harm is done to them by agents who are directly engaged in causing harm to them than when the harm is done incidentally by agents whose ends and means are good? Don't we have more reason to protest when we are being used by others than when we are affected by them only incidentally?

Moreover, if we examine the question from the perspective of those causing harm, additional support for this line of reasoning can be found. For it would seem that we have more reason to protest a restriction against foreseen harm than we have reason to protest a comparable restriction against intended harm. This is because a restriction against foreseen harm limits our actions when our ends and means are good whereas a restriction against intended harm only limits our actions when our ends or means are evil or harmful, and it would seem that we have greater grounds for acting when both our ends and means are good than when they are not. Consequently, because we have more reason to protest when we are being used by others than when we are being affected by them only incidentally, and because we have more reason to act when both our ends and means are good than when they are not, we should favor the foreseen/intended distinction that is incorporated into just means.

It might be objected, however, that at least sometimes we could produce greater good overall by violating the foreseen/intended distinction of just means and acting with the evil means of intentionally harming innocents. On this account, it might be argued that it should be permissible at least sometimes to intentionally harm innocents in order to achieve greater good overall.

Now it seems to me that this objection is well-taken in so far as it is directed against an absolute restriction upon intentional harm to innocents. It seems clear that there are expectations to such a restriction when intentional harm to innocents is

1) trivial (for example, as in the case of stepping on someone's foot to get out of a crowded subway);
2) easily repairable (for example, as in the case of lying to a temporarily depressed friend to keep him from committing suicide); or
3) greatly outweighed by the consequences of the action, especially to innocent people (for example, as in the case of shooting one of two hundred civilian hostages to prevent in the only way possible the execution of all two hundred).

Yet while we need to recognize these executions to an absolute restriction upon intentional harm to innocents, there is good reason not to permit simply maximizing good consequences overall because that would place unacceptable burdens upon particular individuals. More specifically, it would be an unacceptable burden on innocents to allow them to be intentionally harmed in cases other than the exceptions we have just enumerated. And, allowing for these exceptions, we would still have reason to favor a differential restriction against harming innocents that is more severe against the intentional infliction of harm upon innocents but is less severe against the infliction of harm upon innocents that is merely foreseen. Again, the main grounds for this preference is that we would have more reason to protest when we are being used by others than when we are being affected by them only incidentally, and more reason to act when both our ends and means are good than when they are not.

So far, I have argued that there are grounds for favoring a differential restriction on harm to innocents that is more severe against intended harm and less severe against foreseen harm. I have further argued that this restriction is not absolute so that when the evil intended is trivial, easily repairable or greatly outweighed by the consequences, intentional harm to innocents can be justified. Moreover, there is no reason to think that anti-war pacifists would reject either of these conclusions. Anti-war pacifists are opposed to any participation in the massive use of lethal force in warfare, yet this need not conflict with the commitment of just war theorists to a differential but nonabsolute restriction on harm to innocents as a requirement of just means.[5] Where just war theory goes wrong, according to anti-war pacifists, is not in its restriction on harming innocents but rather in its failure to adequately determine when belligerent correctives are too costly to constitute a just cause or lacking in the proportionality required by just means. According to anti-war pacifists, just war theory provides insufficient restraint in both of these areas. Now to evaluate this criticism, we need to consider a wide range of cases where killing or inflicting serious harm on others in defense of oneself or others might be thought to be justified, beginning with the easiest cases to assess from the perspectives of anti-war pacifism and the just war theory and then moving on to cases that are more difficult to assess from those perspectives.

Case 1 where only the intentional or foreseen killing of an unjust aggressor would prevent one's own death.[6] This case clearly presents no problems. In the first place, anti-war pacifists adopted their view because they were convinced that there were instances of justified killing. And, in this case, the only person killed is an unjust aggressor. So surely anti-war pacifists would have to agree with just war theorists that one justifiably kill an unjust aggressor if it is the only way to save one's life.

Case 2 where only the intentional or foreseen killing of an unjust aggressor and the foreseen killing of one innocent bystander would prevent one's own death and that of five other innocent people.[7] In this case, we have the foreseen killing of an innocent person as well as the killing of the unjust aggressor, but since it is the only way to save one's own life and the lives of five other innocent people, anti-war pacifists and just war theorists alike would have reason to judge it morally permissible. In this case, the intended life-saving benefits to six innocent people is judged to outweigh the foreseen death of one innocent person and the intended or foreseen death of the unjust aggressor.

Case 3 where only the intentional or foreseen killing of an unjust aggressor and the foreseen killing of one innocent bystander would prevent the death of five other innocent people. In this case, despite the fact that we lack the justification of self-defense, saving the lives of five innocent people in the only way possible should still provide anti-war pacifists and just war theorists with sufficient grounds for granting the moral permissibility of killing an unjust aggressor, even when the killing of an innocent bystander is a foreseen consequence. In this case, the intended lifesaving benefits to five innocent people would still outweigh the foreseen death of one innocent person and the intended or foreseen death of the unjust aggressor.

Case 4 where only the intentional or foreseen killing of an unjust aggressor and the foreseen killing of five innocent people would prevent the death of two innocent people. In this case, neither anti-war pacifists nor just war theorists would find the cost and proportionality requirements of just war theory to be met. Too many innocent people would have to be killed to save too few. Here the fact that the deaths of the innocents would be merely foreseen does not outweigh the fact that we would have to accept the deaths of five innocents and the death of the unjust aggressor in order to be able to save two innocents.

Notice that up to this point in interpreting these cases, we have simply been counting the number of innocent deaths involved in each case and opting for whichever solution minimized the loss of innocent lives that would result. Suppose, however, that an unjust aggressor is not threatening the lives of innocents but only their welfare or property. Would the taking of the unjust aggressor's life in defense of the welfare and property of innocents be judged proportionate? Consider the following case.

Case 5 where only the intentional or foreseen killing of an unjust aggressor would prevent serious injury to oneself

and five other innocent people. Since in this case the intentional or foreseen killing of the unjust aggressor is the only way of preventing serious injury to oneself and five other innocent people, then, by analogy with Cases 1–3, both anti-war pacifists and just war theorists alike would have reason to affirm its moral permissibility. Of course, if there were any other way of stopping unjust aggressors in such cases short of killing them, that course of action would clearly be required. Yet if there is no alternative, the intentional or foreseen killing of the unjust aggressor to prevent serious injury to oneself and/or five other innocent people would be justified.

In such cases, the serious injury could be bodily injury, as when an aggressor threatens to break one's limbs, or it could be serious psychological injury, as when an aggressor threatens to inject mind-altering drugs, or it could be a serious threat to property. Of course, in most cases where serious injury is threatened, there will be ways of stopping aggressors short of killing them. Unfortunately, this is not always possible.

In still other kinds of cases, stopping an unjust aggressor would require indirectly inflicting serious harm, but not death, upon innocent bystanders. Consider the following cases.

Case 6 where only the intentional or foreseen infliction of serious harm upon an unjust aggressor and the foreseen infliction of serious harm upon one innocent bystander would prevent serious harm to oneself and five other innocent people.

Case 7 where only the intentional or foreseen infliction of serious harm upon an unjust aggressor and the foreseen infliction of serious harm upon one innocent bystander would prevent serious harm to five other innocent people.

In both of these cases, serious harm is indirectly inflicted upon one innocent bystander in order to prevent greater harm from being inflicted by an unjust aggressor upon other innocent people. In Case 6, we also have the justification of self-defense, which is lacking in Case 7. Nevertheless, with regard to both cases, anti-war pacifists and just war theorists should agree that preventing serious injury to five or six innocent people in the only way possible renders it morally permissible to inflict serious injury upon an unjust aggressor, even when the serious injury of one innocent person is a foreseen consequence. In these cases, by analogy with Cases 2 and 3, the foreseen serious injury of one innocent person and the intended or foreseen injury of the unjust aggressor should be judged proportionate given the intended injury-preventing benefits to five or six other innocent people.

Up to this point there has been the basis for general agreement among anti-war pacifists and just war theorists as to how to interpret the proportionality requirement of just means, but in the following case this no longer obtains.

Case 8 where only the intentional or foreseen killing of an unjust aggressor and the foreseen killing of one innocent bystander would prevent serious injuries to the members of a much larger group of people.

The interpretation of this case is crucial. In this case, we are asked to sanction the loss of an innocent life in order to prevent serious injuries to the members of a much larger group of people. Unfortunately, neither anti-war pacifists nor just war theorists have explicitly considered this case. Both anti-war pacifists and just war theorists agree that we can inflict serious injury upon an unjust aggressor and an innocent bystander to prevent greater injury to other innocent people, as in Cases 6 and 7, and that one can even intentionally or indirectly kill an unjust aggressor to prevent serious injury to oneself or other innocent people as in Case 5. Yet neither anti-war pacifists nor just war theorists have explicitly addressed the question of whether we can indirectly kill an innocent bystander in order to prevent serious injuries to the members of a much larger group of innocent people. Rather they have tended to confuse Case 8 with Case 5 where it is agreed that one can justifiably kill an unjust aggressor in order to prevent serious injury to oneself or five other innocent people. In Case 8, however, one is doing something quite different: one is killing an innocent bystander in order to prevent serious injury to oneself and five other innocent people.

Now this kind of trade-off is not accepted in standard police practice. Police officers are regularly instructed not to risk innocent lives simply to prevent serious injury to other innocents. Nor is there any reason to think that a trade-off that is unacceptable in standard police practice would be acceptable in larger scale conflicts. Thus, for example, even if the Baltic republics could have effectively freed themselves from the Soviet Union by infiltrating into Moscow several bands of saboteurs who would then attack several military and government installations in Moscow, causing an enormous loss of innocent lives, such trade-offs would not have been justified. Accordingly, it follows that if the proportionality requirement of just war theory is to be met, we must save more innocent lives than we cause to be lost, we must prevent more injuries than we bring about, and we must not kill innocents, even indirectly, simply to prevent serious injuries to ourselves and others.

Of course, sometimes our lives and well-being are threatened together. Or better, if we are unwilling to sacrifice our well-being then our lives are threatened as well. Nevertheless, if we are justified in our use of lethal force to defend ourselves in cases where we will indirectly kill innocents, it is because our lives are also threatened, not simply our well-being. And the same holds for when we are defending others.

What this shows is that the constraints imposed by just war theory on the use of belligerent correctives are actually much more severe than anti-war pacifists have tended to recognize. In determining when belligerent correctives are too costly to constitute a just cause or lacking in the proportionality required by just means, just war theory under its most morally defensible interpretation

1) allows the use of belligerent means against unjust aggressors only when such means minimize the loss and injury to innocent lives overall;
2) allows the use of belligerent means against unjust aggressors to indirectly threaten innocent lives only to prevent the loss of innocent lives, not simply to prevent injury to innocents; and
3) allows the use of belligerent means to directly or indirectly threaten or even take the lives of unjust aggressors when it is the only way to prevent serious injury to innocents.

Now it might be objected that all that I have shown through the analysis of the above eight cases is that killing in defense of oneself or others is morally permissible, not that it is morally required or morally obligatory. That is true. I have not established any obligation to respond to aggression with lethal force in these cases, but only that it is morally permissible to do so. For one thing, it is difficult to ground an obligation to use lethal force on self-defense alone, as would be required in Case 1 or in one version of Case 5. Obligations to oneself appear to have an optional quality that is absent from obligations to others. In Cases 2–3 and 5–7, however, the use of force would prevent serious harm or death to innocents, and here I contend it would be morally obligatory if either the proposed use of force required only a relatively small personal sacrifice from us or if we were fairly bound by convention or a mutual defense agreement to come to the aid of others. In such cases, I think we can justifiably speak of a moral obligation to kill or seriously harm in defense of others.

Another aspect of Cases 1–3 and 5–7 to which someone might object is that it is the wrongful actions of others that put us into situations where I am claiming that we are morally justified in seriously harming or killing others. But for the actions of unjust aggressors, we would not be in situations where I am claiming that we are morally permitted or required to seriously harm or kill.

Yet doesn't something like this happen in a wide range of cases when wrongful actions are performed? Suppose I am on the way to the bank to deposit money from a fund-raiser, and someone accosts me and threatens to shoot me if I don't hand over the money. If I do hand over the money, I would be forced to do something I don't want to do, something that involves a loss to myself and others. But surely it is morally permissible for me to hand over the money in this case. And it may even be morally required for me to do so if resistance would lead to the shooting of others in addition to myself. So it does seem that bad people, by altering the consequences of our actions, can alter our obligations as well. What our obligations are under nonideal conditions are different from what they would be under ideal conditions. If a group of thugs comes into this room and make it very clear that they intend to shoot me if each of you doesn't

give them one dollar, I think, and I would hope that you would also think, that each of you now has an obligation to give the thugs one dollar when before you had no such obligation. Likewise, I think that the actions of unjust aggressors can put us into situations where it is morally permissible or even morally required for us to seriously harm or kill when before it was not.

Now it might be contended that anti-war pacifists would concede the moral permissibility of Cases 1–3 and 5–7 but still maintain that any participation in the massive use of lethal force in warfare is morally prohibited. The scale of the conflict, anti-war pacifists might contend, makes all the difference. Of course, if this simply means that many large-scale conflicts will have effects that bear no resemblance to Cases 1–3 or 5–7, this can hardly be denied. Still, it is possible for some large-scale conflicts to bear a proportionate resemblance to the above cases. For example, it can be argued plausibly that India's military action against Pakistan in Bangladesh and the Tanzanian incursion into Uganda during the rule of Idi Amin resemble Cases 3, 5, or 7 in their effects upon innocents.[8] What this shows is that anti-war pacifists are not justified in regarding every participation in the massive use of lethal force in warfare as morally prohibited. Instead, anti-war pacifists must allow that at least in some real-life cases, wars and other large-scale military operations both have been and will be morally permissible.

This concession from anti-war pacifists, however, needs to be matched by a comparable concession from just war theorists themselves, because too frequently they have interpreted their theory in morally indefensible ways. When just war theory is given a morally defensible interpretation, I have argued that the theory favors a strong just means prohibition against intentionally harming innocents. I have also argued that the theory favors the use of belligerent means only when such means 1) minimize the loss and injury to innocent lives overall; 2) threaten innocent lives only to prevent the loss of innocent lives, not simply to prevent injury to innocents; and 3) threaten or even take the lives of unjust aggressors when it is the only way to prevent serious injury to innocents.

Obviously, just war theory, so understood, is going to place severe restrictions on the use of belligerent means in warfare. In fact, most of the actual uses of belligerent means in warfare that have occurred turn out to be unjustified. For example, the U.S. involvement in Nicaragua, El Salvador, and Panama, Soviet involvement in Afghanistan, Israeli involvement in the West Bank and the Gaza Strip all violate the just cause and just means provisions of just war theory as I have defended them. Even the recent U.S.-led war against Iraq violated both the just cause and just means provisions of just war theory.[9] In fact, one strains to find examples of justified applications of just war theory in recent history. Two examples I have already referred to are India's military action against Pakistan in Bangladesh and the Tanzanian incursion into Uganda during the rule of Idi Amin. But after mentioning these two examples it is difficult to go on. What this shows is that when just war theory and anti-war pacifism are given their most morally defensible interpretations, both views can be reconciled. In this reconciliation, the few wars and large-scale conflicts that meet the stringent requirements of just war theory are the only wars and large-scale conflicts to which anti-war pacifists cannot justifiably object.[10] We can call the view that emerges from this reconciliation "just war pacifism." It is the view which claims that due to the stringent requirements of just war theory, only very rarely will participation in a massive use of lethal force in warfare be morally justified. It is the view on which I rest my case for the reconciliation of pacifism and just war theory.[11]

NOTES

1. Jan Narveson, "Pacifism: A Philosophical Analysis," *Ethics* 75 (1965): 259–71.

2. Cheyney Ryan, "Self-Defense, Pacifism and the Possibility of Killing," *Ethics* 93 (1983): 514–24.

3. Alternatively, one might concede that even in this case killing is morally evil, but still contend that it is morally justified because it is the lesser of two evils.

4. Douglas P. Lackey, "The Moral Irrelevance of the Counterforce/Countervalue Distinction," *The Monist* 70 (1987): 255–76.

5. This is because the just means restrictions protect innocents quite well against the infliction of intentional harm.

6. By an "unjust aggressor" I mean someone who the defender is reasonably certain is wrongfully engaged in an attempt upon her life or the lives of other innocent people.

7. What is relevant in this case is that the foreseen deaths are a relatively small number (one in this case) compared to the number of innocents whose lives are saved (six in this case). The primary reason for using particular numbers in this case and those that follow is to make it clear that at this stage of the argument no attempt is being made to justify the large-scale killing that occurs in warfare.

8. Although there is a strong case for India's military action against Pakistan in Bangladesh and the Tanzanian incursion into Uganda during the rule of Idi Amin, there are questions that can be raised about the behavior of Indian troops in Bangladesh following the defeat of the Pakistanian forces and about the regime Tanzania put in power in Uganda.

9. The just cause provision was violated because the extremely effective economic sanctions were not given enough time to work. It was estimated that when compared to past economic blockades, the blockade against Iraq had a near 100% chance of success if given about a year to work. (See *The New York Times*, January 14, 1991.) The just means provision was violated because the number of combatant and noncombatant deaths was disproportionate. As many as 120,000 Iraqi soldiers were killed, according to U.S. intelligence sources.

10. Of course, anti-war pacifists are right to point out that virtually all wars that have been fought have led to unforeseen harms and have been fought with less and less discrimination as the wars progressed. Obviously, these are considerations that in just war theory must weigh heavily against going to war.

11. Of course, more needs to be done to specify the requirements of just war pacifism. One fruitful way to further specify these requirements is to appeal to a hypothetical social contract decision procedure as has been done with respect to other practical problems. Here I have simply tried to establish the defensibility of just war pacifism without appealing to any such procedure. Yet once the defensibility of just war pacifism has been established, such a decision procedure will prove quite useful in working out its particular requirements.

Drones, Ethics, and the Armchair Soldier

JOHN KAAG

Ten years ago, I watched the Iraq invasion unfold on TV. It was for me, like most Americans, a remote-control event, the type that you tuned into occasionally to see how it was going before changing the channel, like the Olympics. And, as often happens in the Olympics, we crushed the opposition. But we Americans at home were not the only ones with remote controls. Many of our soldiers also had them, and used them to direct one of the most devastating military assaults in the history of modern warfare. The technological superiority of the United States—its ability to strike with precision from a distance—produced something like the "shock and awe" the media had relentlessly advertised. And it inspired a similar reaction in moral and legal theorists who were concerned about the relationship between advanced military technologies and the legitimation of warfare.

Ten years later, I'm a philosopher writing a book about the ethics of drone warfare. Some days I fear that I will have either to give up the book or to give up philosophy. I worry that I can't have both. Some of my colleagues would like me to provide decision procedures for military planners and soldiers, the type that could guide them, automatically, unthinkingly, mechanically, to the right decision about drone use. I try to tell them that this is not how ethics, or philosophy, or humans, work.

I try to tell them that the difference between humans and robots is precisely the ability to think and reflect, in Immanuel Kant's words, to set and pursue ends for themselves. And these ends cannot be set beforehand in some hard and fast way—even if Kant sometimes thought they could.

What disturbs me is the idea that a book about the moral hazard of military technologies should be written as if it was going to be read by robots: input decision procedure, output decision and correlated

action. I know that effective military operations have traditionally been based on the chain of command and that this looks a little like the command and control structure of robots. When someone is shooting at you, I can only imagine that you need to follow orders mechanically. The heat of battle is neither the time nor the place for cool ethical reflection.

Warfare, unlike philosophy, could never be conducted from an armchair. Until now. For the first time in history, some soldiers have this in common with philosophers: they can do their jobs sitting down. They now have what I've always enjoyed, namely "leisure," in the Hobbesian sense of the word, meaning they are not constantly afraid of being killed. Hobbes thought that there are certain not-so-obvious perks to leisure (not being killed is the obvious one). For one, you get to think. This is what he means when he says that "leisure is the mother of philosophy." I tend to agree with Hobbes: only those who enjoy a certain amount of leisure can be philosophers.

Ethics has long been taught—at least in passing—to officer candidates and battlefield soldiers. But this new breed of remote control soldier will have the time and the space to think through unprecedentedly complex moral quandaries, like the question of using a drone to kill an unarmed human being who may be in the early planning stages of a terrorist attack. A 2011 Pentagon study (which anticipated the results of the psychological examination of pilots earlier this year) showed that nearly 30 percent of drone pilots experience what the military calls "burnout," defined by what the military describes, in unusually sophisticated language, as "an existential crisis."

You might be under the impression that philosophy is in the business of causing rather than alleviating existential crises. And so you may think that acquainting soldiers with the Gordian knots of philosophy will do little to increase their job satisfaction.

But this is only partially correct.

Working one's way through the complexities of "just war" and moral theory makes it perfectly clear that ethics is not about arriving easily at a single right answer, but rather coming to understand the profound difficulty of doing so. Experiencing this difficulty is what philosophers call existential responsibility. One of the jobs of philosophy, at least as I understand it, is neither to help people to avoid these difficulties nor to exaggerate them, but rather to face them in resolute and creative ways. In short, the job of philosophy is not to create existential crises, but to handle or work through existential responsibility.

In the past, the leaders and military strategists who initiated and oversaw military operations were supposed to shoulder the brunt of existential responsibility. This was appropriate, since they did so from the relative safety of their fortified bunkers or, at the very least, from behind a row of protective ground troops. These ground troops, unfortunately, had more pressing concerns than existential responsibility. They did not have leisure, unlike their commanders, who also often had the philosophical training to think through the complexities of their jobs.

Here we could think about President Obama's being schooled in Aquinas and Augustine or, even better, Alexander the Great's studying under Aristotle. This training was not simply a degree requirement at Officer Candidate School or one of the United States military academies, but a sustained, ongoing, and rigorous engagement with a philosophical tradition. Alexander lived with Aristotle. This type of training, I would like to think, helped commanders face the challenge of moral responsibility (if it did not necessarily lead them to the right moral choice). To be clear, studying philosophy does not hard-wire a student to be moral or to always do the right thing. Once again, this is the way that robots, not humans, work. Humans cannot be fully hard-wired. But it does give a student some practice at shouldering the responsibility of being a moral agent. And if we give our soldiers the tools to make informed moral decisions, then we should think about giving them the freedom to do so by making more legal space for selective conscientious objection or for disobeying orders on moral grounds.

In a recent post in *The Stone*, Jeff McMahan argued that traditional "just war theory" should be reworked

in several important ways. He suggested that the tenets of a revised theory apply not only to governments, traditionally represented by commanders and heads of state, but also to individual soldiers. This is a significant revision since it broadens the scope of responsibility for warfare beyond political institutions to include the men and women who engage in combat. This has always been the case with the principles of jus in bello (the conventions or rules that govern military conduct) but McMahan intends individuals to be held responsible for the additional standards of jus ad bellum, those guidelines that describe the permissibility of initiating military operations. Specifically, McMahan believes that individuals are to bear at least some responsibility in upholding "just cause" requirements. McMahan expects more of soldiers and, in this age of drones and leisure, he is right to do so.

I suspect many armchair soldiers would welcome some new intellectual tools to handle this newfound responsibility. As it turns out, some of these "new" tools have been around since Plato and Augustine (fathers of Western moral theory and the just war tradition, respectively), but some are in fact new, or at least newer, and have yet to be introduced in the training of armchair soldiers. Warfare, until this point, had been too brutal, too immediate, too threatening, for soldiers to spend much time on the theoretical matters of ethics. But as technology makes warfare more leisurely it has, for the first time, the chance to be genuinely—and complexly—philosophical. My point here is not that these new armchair soldiers are to be criticized for failing in their moral responsibilities. My point is rather that while drones are to be applauded for keeping these soldiers out of harm's way physically, we would do well to remember that they do not keep them out of harm's way morally or psychologically. The high rates of "burnout" should drive this home. Supporting our troops requires ensuring that they are provided not just with training and physical armor, but with the intellectual tools to navigate these new difficulties.

To be sure, the question of what new responsibilities soldiers have is not the only, nor even the most important, ethical question concerning the use of drones. Hannah Arendt claimed, in her analysis of World War II, that "in general, the degree of responsibility increases as we draw further away from the man who uses the fatal instrument with his own hands." Just as was the case in the invasion of Iraq 10 years ago, the most important questions we should be asking should not be directed to armchair soldiers but to those of us in armchairs at home: What wars are being fought in our name? On what grounds are they being fought?

Can Terrorism Be Morally Justified?

STEPHEN NATHANSON

Can terrorism be morally justified?

Even asking this question can seem like an insult—both to victims of terrorist actions and to moral common sense. One wants to say: if the murder of innocent people by terrorists is not clearly wrong, what is?

But the question is more complicated than it looks. We can see this by broadening our focus and considering some of the other beliefs held by people who condemn terrorism. Very few of us accept the pacifist view that all violence is wrong. Most of us believe that some acts of killing and injuring people are morally justified. Indeed, most of us think that war is sometimes justified, even though it involves organized, large-scale killing, injuring, and destruction and even though innocent civilians are usually among the victims of war. So, most of us believe that even the killing of innocent people is sometimes morally justified. It is this fact that makes the condemnation of terrorism morally problematic. We pick out terrorism for special condemnation because its victims are civilian noncombatants rather than military or governmental officials, but we also believe that such killings are sometimes morally permissible.

Seen in a broader context, moral judgments of terrorism often seem hypocritical. They often presuppose self-serving definitions of "terrorism" that allow people to avoid labeling actions that they approve as instances of terrorism, even though these actions are indistinguishable from other acts that are branded with this negative label. On other occasions, moral judgments of terrorism rest on biased, uneven applications of moral principles to the actions of friends and foes. Principles that are cited to condemn the actions of foes are ignored when similar actions are committed by friends.

We need to ask then: Can people who believe that war is sometimes morally permissible consistently condemn terrorist violence? Or are such condemnations necessarily hypocritical and self-serving?

If we are to avoid hypocrisy, then we need both (a) a definition of terrorism that is neutral with respect to who commits the actions, and (b) moral judgments of terrorism that derive from the consistent, even-handed applications of moral criteria.

This paper aims to achieve both of these things. First, I begin with a definition of terrorism and then discuss why terrorism is always wrong. In addition, I want to show that the condemnation of terrorism does not come without other costs. A consistent approach to terrorism requires us to revise some common judgments about historical events and forces us to reconsider actions in which civilians are killed as "collateral damage" (i.e., side effects) of military attacks.

My aim, then, is to criticize both terrorist actions and a cluster of widespread moral views about violence and war. This cluster includes the following beliefs:

1. Terrorism is always immoral.
2. The Allied bombing of cities in World War II was morally justified because of the importance of defeating Nazi Germany and Japan.

Stephen Nathanson, from "Can Terrorism Be Morally Justified?" in *Morality in Practice*, ed. James P. Sterba, 7th ed. (Belmont, CA: Wadsworth/Thomson, 2004), 602–10. Reprinted with permission from Stephen Nathanson.

3. It is morally permissible to kill civilians in war if these killings are not intended.

The trouble with this cluster is that the first belief expresses an absolute prohibition of acts that kill innocent people while the last two are rather permissive. If we are to avoid inconsistency and hypocrisy, we must revise our views either (a) by accepting that terrorism is sometimes morally permissible, or (b) by judging that city bombings and many collateral damage killings are morally wrong. I will defend the second of these options.

DEFINING TERRORISM

I offer the following definition of terrorism to launch my discussion of the moral issues. Terrorist acts have the following features:

1. They are acts of serious, deliberate violence or destruction.
2. They are generally committed by groups as part of a campaign to promote a political or social agenda.
3. They generally target limited numbers of people but aim to influence a larger group and/or the leaders who make decisions for the group.
4. They either kill or injure innocent people or pose a serious threat of such harms to them.

This definition helps in a number of ways. First, it helps us to distinguish acts of terrorism from other acts of violence. Nonviolent acts are not terrorist acts; nor are violent actions that are unrelated to a political or social agenda. Ironically, some terrible kinds of actions are not terrorist because they are too destructive. As condition 3 tells us, terrorism generally targets limited numbers of people in order to influence a larger group. Acts of genocide that aim to destroy a whole group are not acts of terrorism, but the reason why makes them only worse, not better.

Second, the definition helps us to identify the moral crux of the problem with terrorism. Condition 1 is not the problem because most of us believe that some acts of violence are morally justified. Condition 2 can't be the problem because anyone who believes in just causes of war must accept that some causes are so important that violence may be a legitimate way to promote them. Condition 3 is frequently met by permissible actions, as when we punish some criminals to deter other people from committing crimes. Condition 4 seems closer to what is essentially wrong with terrorism. If terrorism is always immoral, it is because it kills and injures innocent people.

As I have already noted, however, morally conscientious people sometimes want to justify acts that kill innocent people. If a blanket condemnation of terrorism is to be sustained, then we must either condemn all killings of innocent people, or we must find morally relevant differences between the killing of innocents by terrorists and the killing of innocents by others whose actions we find morally acceptable.

TERRORISM AND CITY BOMBING: THE SAME OR DIFFERENT?

Many people who condemn terrorism believe that city bombing in the war against Nazism was justified, even though the World War II bombing campaigns intentionally targeted cities and their inhabitants. This view is defended by some philosophical theorists, including Michael Walzer, in his book *Just and Unjust Wars,* and G. Wallace in "Terrorism and the Argument from Analogy."[1] By considering these theorists, we can see if there are relevant differences that allow us to say that terrorism is always wrong but that the World War II bombings were morally justified.

One of the central aims of Michael Walzer's *Just and Unjust Wars* is to defend what he calls the "war convention," the principles that prohibit attacks on civilians in wartime. Walzer strongly affirms the principle of noncombatant immunity, calling it a "fundamental principle [that] underlies and shapes the judgments we make of wartime conduct." He writes:

> A legitimate act of war is one that does not violate the rights of the people against whom it is directed. . . . [N]o one can be threatened with war or warred against, unless through some act of his own he has surrendered or lost his rights.[2]

Unlike members of the military, civilians have not surrendered their rights in any way, and therefore, Walzer says, they may not be attacked.

Given Walzer's strong support for noncombatant immunity and his definition of terrorism as the "method of random murder of innocent people," it is no surprise that he condemns terrorism. At one point, after describing a terrorist attack on an Algerian milk bar frequented by teenagers, he writes:

> Certainly, there are historical moments when armed struggle is necessary for the sake of human freedom. But if dignity and self-respect are to be the outcomes of that struggle, it cannot consist of terrorist attacks against children.[3]

Here and elsewhere, Walzer denounces terrorism because it targets innocent people.

Nonetheless, he claims that the aerial attacks on civilians by the British early in World War II were justified. In order to show why, he develops the concept of a "supreme emergency." Nazi Germany, he tells us, was no ordinary enemy; it was an "ultimate threat to everything decent in our lives."[4] Moreover, in 1940, the Nazi threat to Britain was imminent. German armies dominated Europe and sought to control the seas. Britain feared an imminent invasion by a country that threatened the basic values of civilization.

According to Walzer, the combination of the enormity and the imminence of the threat posed by Nazi Germany produced a supreme emergency, a situation in which the rules prohibiting attacks on civilians no longer held. If killing innocents was the only way to ward off this dreadful threat, then it was permissible. Since air attacks on German cities were the only means Britain had for inflicting harm on Germany, it was morally permissible for them to launch these attacks.

Walzer does not approve all of the city bombing that occurred in World War II. The emergency lasted, he thinks, only through 1942. After that, the threat diminished, and the constraints of the war convention should once again have been honored. In fact, the bombing of cities continued throughout the war, climaxing in massive attacks that killed hundreds of thousands of civilians: the bombing of Dresden, the fire bombings of Japanese cities by the United States, and the atomic bombings of Hiroshima and Nagasaki. According to Walzer, none of these later attacks were justified because the supreme emergency had passed.

While Walzer's discussion begins with the special threat posed by Nazism, he believes that supreme emergencies can exist in more ordinary situations. In the end, he supports the view that if a single nation is faced by "a threat of enslavement or extermination[,]" then its "soldiers and statesmen [may] override the rights of innocent people for the sake of their own political community. . . ."[5] While he expresses this view with "hesitation and worry," he nevertheless broadens the reach of the concept of "supreme emergency" to include circumstances that arise in many wars.

The problem for Walzer is that his acceptance of the broad "supreme emergency" exception threatens to completely undermine the principle of noncombatant immunity that lies at the heart of his own view of the ethics of warfare. How can the principle of noncombatant immunity be fundamental if it can be overridden in some cases? Moreover, his condemnation of terrorism is weakened because it seems to be possible that people might resort to terrorism in cases that qualify as supreme emergencies, as when their own people are threatened by extermination or enslavement. Walzer's defense of the bombing of cities, then, seems to be inconsistent with his sweeping denunciation of terrorism.

WALLACE'S ARGUMENT FROM ANALOGY

While Walzer does not directly address the tension between the two parts of his view, G. Wallace explicitly tries to defend the view that terrorism is wrong and that the bombing of cities was justified. According to Wallace, the bombing campaign was justified because it satisfied all four of the following criteria:

1. It was a measure of last resort.
2. It was an act of collective self-defense.
3. It was a reply in kind against a genocidal, racist aggressor.
4. It had some chances of success.

He then asks whether acts of terrorism might be justified by appeal to these very same criteria.

Wallace's answer is that the [acts of] terrorism cannot meet these criteria. Or, more specifically, he says that while any one of the criteria might be met by a terrorist act, all four of them cannot be satisfied. Why not? The problem is not with criteria 2 and 3; a community might well be oppressed by a brutal regime and might well be acting in its own defense. In these respects, its situation would be like that of Britain in 1940.

But, Wallace claims, conditions 1 and 4 cannot both be satisfied in this case. If the community has a good chance of success through the use of terrorism (thus satisfying condition 4), then other means of opposition might work as well, and terrorism will fail to be a last resort. Hence it will not meet condition 1. At the same time, if terrorist tactics are a last resort because all other means of opposition will fail, then the terrorist tactics are also likely to fail, in which case condition 4 is not met.

What Wallace has tried to show is that there are morally relevant differences between terrorism and the city bombings by Britain. Even if some of the criteria for justified attacks on civilians can be met by would-be terrorists, all of them cannot be. He concludes that "[E]ven if we allow that conditions (1) and (4) can be met separately, their joint satisfaction is impossible."[6]

Unfortunately, this comforting conclusion—that the British city bombing was justified but that terrorism cannot be—is extremely implausible. Both terrorism and city bombing involve the intentional killing of innocent human beings in order to promote an important political goal. Wallace acknowledges this but claims that the set of circumstances that justified city bombing could not possibly occur again so as to justify terrorism.

There is no basis for this claim, however. Wallace accepts that the right circumstances occurred in the past, and so he should acknowledge that it is at least possible for them to occur in the future. His conclusion ought to be that if city bombing was justifiable, then terrorism is in principle justifiable as well. For these reasons, I believe that Wallace, like Walzer, is logically committed to acknowledging the possibility of morally justified terrorism.

This is not a problem simply for these two authors. Since the historical memory of city bombing in the United States and Britain sees [such tactics] as justifiable means of war, the dilemma facing these authors

faces our own society. We condemn terrorists for intentionally killing innocent people while we think it was right to use tactics in our own wars that did the same. Either we must accept the view that terrorism can sometimes be justified, or we must come to see our own bombings of cities as violations of the prohibitions on killing civilians in wartime.

TERRORISM, COLLATERAL DAMAGE, AND THE PRINCIPLE OF DOUBLE EFFECT

Many of us believe that wars are sometimes justified, but we also know that even if civilians are not intentionally killed, the deaths of civilians is a common feature of warfare. Indeed, during the twentieth century, civilian deaths became a larger and larger proportion of the total deaths caused by war. A person who believes that wars may be justified but that terrorism cannot be must explain how this can be.

One common approach focuses on the difference between intentionally killing civilians, as terrorists do, and unintentionally killing civilians, as sometimes happens in what we regard as legitimate acts of war. According to this approach, terrorism is wrong because it is intentional while so-called "collateral damage" killings and injuries are morally permissible because they are not intended.

This type of view is developed by Igor Primoratz in "The Morality of Terrorism."[7] Primoratz attempts to show why terrorism is morally wrong and how it differs from other acts of wartime killing that are morally permissible.

First, he makes it clear that, by definition, terrorism always involves the intentional killing of innocent people. He then offers a number of arguments to show why such killings are wrong. The first two have to do with the idea that persons are moral agents who are due a high level of respect and concern. He writes:

> [E]very human being is an individual, a person separate from other persons, with a unique, irreproducible thread of life and a value that is not commensurate with anything else.[8]

Given the incommensurable value of individual persons, it is wrong to try to calculate the worth of some hoped-for goal by comparison with the lives and deaths of individual people. This kind of calculation violates the ideal of giving individual lives our utmost respect and concern. Terrorists ignore this central moral ideal. They treat innocent people as political pawns, ignoring their individual worth and seeing their deaths simply as means toward achieving their goals.

In addition, Primoratz argues, terrorists ignore the moral relevance of guilt and innocence in their treatment of individuals. They attack people who have no responsibility for the alleged evils that the terrorists oppose and thus violate the principle that people should be treated in accord with what they deserve.

Terrorists, Pirmoratz tells us, also forsake the ideal of moral dialogue amongst equals. They not only decide who will live and who will die, but they feel no burden to justify their actions in ways that the victims might understand and accept. People who take moral ideas seriously engage in open discussion in order to justify their actions. They engage others in moral debate. Ideally, according to Primoratz, a moral person who harms others should try to act on reasons that are so compelling that they could be acknowledged by their victims. Terrorist acts cannot be justified to their victims, and terrorists are not even interested in trying to do so.

Though these ideas are sketched out rather than fully developed, Primoratz successfully expresses some important moral values. Drawing on these values, he concludes that terrorism is incompatible with "some of the most basic moral beliefs many of us hold."[9]

Primoratz vs. Trotsky

Having tried to show why terrorism is wrong, Primoratz considers an objection put forward by Leon Trotsky, who defended terrorism as a revolutionary tactic. Trotsky claims that people who approve traditional war but condemn revolutionary violence are in a weak position because the differences between these are morally arbitrary. If wars that kill innocent people can be justified, Trotsky claims, then so can revolutions that kill innocent people.

Primoratz replies by arguing that there is an important moral difference between terrorism and

some acts of war that kill innocent people. While he acknowledges that the "suffering of civilians . . . is surely inevitable not only in modern, but in almost all wars," Primoratz stresses that the moral evaluation of acts of killing requires that we "attend not only to the suffering inflicted, but also to the way it is inflicted."[10] By this, he means that we need, among other things, to see what the person who did the act intended.

To illustrate his point, he contrasts two cases of artillery attacks on a village. In the first case, the artillery attack is launched with the explicit goal of killing the civilian inhabitants of the village. The civilians are the target of the attack. This attack is the equivalent of terrorism since both intentionally target innocent people, and just like terrorism, it is immoral.

In a second case, the artillery attack is aimed at "soldiers stationed in the village." While the soldiers know that innocent people will be killed, that is not their aim.

> Had it been possible to attack the enemy unit without endangering the civilians in any way, they would certainly have done so. This was not possible, so they attacked although they knew that the attack would cause civilian casualties too; but they did their best to reduce those inevitable, but undesired consequences as much as possible.[11]

In this second case, the civilian deaths and injuries are collateral damage produced by an attack on a legitimate military target. That is the key difference between terrorism and legitimate acts of war. Terrorism is intentionally directed at civilians, while legitimate acts of war do not aim to kill or injure civilians, even when this is their effect.

Primoratz concludes that Trotsky and other defenders of terrorism are wrong when they equate war and terrorism. No doubt, the intentional killing of civilians does occur in war, and when it does Primoratz would condemn it for the same reason he condemns terrorism. But if soldiers avoid the intentional killing of civilians, then their actions can be morally justified, even when civilians die as a result of what they do. As long as soldiers and revolutionaries avoid the intentional killing of innocent people, they will not be guilty of terrorist acts.

Problems with Primoratz's View

Primoratz's view has several attractive features. Nonetheless, it has serious weaknesses.

In stressing the role of intentions, Primoratz appeals to the same ideas expressed by what is called the "principle of double effect." According to this principle, we should evaluate actions by their intended goals rather than their actual consequences. An act that produces collateral damage deaths is an unintentional killing and hence is not wrong in the way that the same act would be if the civilians' deaths were intended.

While the principle of double effects is plausible in some cases, it is actually severely defective. To see this, suppose that the September 11 attackers had only intended to destroy the Pentagon and the World Trade Center and had no desire to kill anyone. Suppose that they knew, however, that thousands would die in the attack on the buildings. And suppose, following the attack, they said "We are not murderers. We did not mean to kill these people."

What would be our reaction? I very much doubt that we would think them less culpable. They could not successfully justify or excuse their actions by saying that although they foresaw the deaths of many people, these deaths were not part of their aim. We would certainly reject this defense. But if we would reject the appeal to double effect in this case, then we should do so in others.

In Primoratz's example, the artillery gunners attack the village with full knowledge of the high probability of civilian deaths. The artillery gunners know they will kill innocent people, perhaps even in large numbers, and they go ahead with the attack anyway. If it would not be enough for my imagined September 11 attackers to say that they did not intend to kill people, then it is not enough for Primoratz's imagined soldiers to say that they did not mean to kill the villagers when they knew full well that this would result from their actions.

If we accept Primoratz's defense of collateral damage killings, his argument against terrorism is in danger of collapsing because terrorists can use Primoratz's language to show that their actions, too, may be justifiable. If Primoratz succeeds in justifying the collateral damage killings and if the distinction between these killings and terrorism cannot rest solely on whether the killings are intentional, then the criteria that he uses may justify at least some terrorist acts. Like the soldiers in his example, the terrorists may believe that the need for a particular attack is "so strong and urgent that it prevailed over the prohibition of killing or maiming a comparatively small number of civilians." Consistency would require Primoratz to agree that the terrorist act was justified in this case.

Recall, too, Primoratz's claim that actions need to be capable of being justified to the victims themselves. Would the victims of the artillery attack accept the claim that the military urgency justified "killing or maiming a comparatively small number of civilians?"[12] Why should they accept the sacrifice of their own lives on the basis of this reasoning?

In the end, then, Primoratz does not succeed in showing why terrorism is immoral while collateral damage killing can be morally justified. Like Wallace and Walzer, he has trouble squaring the principles that he uses to condemn terrorism with his own approval of attacks that produce foreseeable collateral damage deaths.

The problem revealed here is not merely a problem for a particular author. The view that collateral damage killings are permissible because they are unintended is a very widespread view. It is the view that United States officials appealed to when our bombings in Afghanistan produced thousands of civilian casualties. Our government asserted that we did not intend these deaths to occur, that we were aiming at legitimate targets, and that the civilian deaths were merely collateral damage. Similar excuses are offered when civilians are killed by cluster bombs and land mines, weapons whose delayed detonations injure and kill people indiscriminately, often long after a particular attack is over.

There are many cases in which people are morally responsible for harms that they do not intend to bring about, but if these harms can be foreseen, their claims that they "did not mean to do it" are not taken seriously. We use labels like "reckless disregard" for human life or "gross negligence" to signify that wrongs have been done, even though they were not deliberate. When such actions lead to serious injury and death, we condemn such actions from a moral point of view, just as we condemn terrorism. The principle of double effect does not show that these condemnations are mistaken. If we want to differentiate collateral damage killings from terrorism so as to be consistent in our moral judgments, we will need something better than the principle of double effect and the distinction between intended and unintended effects.

A SKETCH OF A DEFENSE

I want to conclude by sketching a better rationale for the view that terrorist attacks on civilians are always wrong but that some attacks that cause civilian deaths and injuries as unintended consequences are morally justified.

I have argued that a central problem with standard defenses of collateral damage killings is that they lean too heavily on the distinction between what is intended and what is foreseen. This distinction, when used with the doctrine of double effect, is too slippery and too permissive. As I noted above, it might provide an excuse for the September 11 attacks if (contrary to fact) the attacks were only targeting the World Trade Center *building* and the Pentagon *building* and did not actually aim to kill innocent civilians.

Michael Walzer makes a similar criticism of the double effect principle. "Simply not to intend the death of civilians is too easy," he writes. "What we look for in such cases is some sign of a positive commitment to save civilian lives."[13] Walzer calls his revised version the principle of "double intention." It requires military planners and soldiers to take positive steps to avoid or minimize these evils, even if these precautions increase the danger to military forces.

Walzer's rule is a step in the right direction, but we need to emphasize that the positive steps must be significant. They cannot be *pro forma* or minimal efforts. In order to show a proper respect for the victims of these attacks, serious efforts must be made to avoid death and injury to them. I suggest the following set of requirements for just, discriminate fighting, offering them as a sketch rather than a full account. The

specifics might have to be amended, but the key point is that serious efforts must be made to avoid harm to civilians. Not intending harm is not enough. In addition, military planners must really exert themselves. They must, as we say, *bend over backwards* to avoid harm to civilians. For example, they must:

1. Target attacks as narrowly as possible on military resources;
2. Avoid targets where civilian deaths are extremely likely;
3. Avoid the use of inherently indiscriminate weapons (such as land mines and cluster bombs) and inherently indiscriminate strategies (such as high-altitude bombing of areas containing both civilian enclaves and military targets); and
4. Accept that when there are choices between damage to civilian lives and damage to military personnel, priority should be given to saving civilian lives.

If a group has a just cause for being at war and adheres to principles like these, then it could be said to be acknowledging the humanity and value of those who are harmed by its actions. While its attacks might expose innocent people to danger, its adherence to these principles would show that it was not indifferent to their well-being. In this way, it would show that its actions lack the features that make terrorism morally objectionable.

Why is this? Because the group is combining its legitimate effort to defend itself or others with serious efforts to avoid civilian casualties. The spirit of their effort is captured in the phrase I have already used: "bending over backwards." The "bend over backwards" ideal is superior to the principle of double effect in many ways. First, it goes beyond the weak rule of merely requiring that one not intend to kill civilians. Second, while the double effect rule's distinction between intended and unintended results permits all sorts of fudges and verbal tricks, the "bend over backwards" rule can be applied in a more objective and realistic way. It would be less likely to approve sham compliance than is the doctrine of double effect.

The "bend over backwards" rule might even satisfy Primoratz's requirement that acts of violence be justifiable to their victims. Of course, no actual victim is likely to look favorably on attacks by others that will result in the victim's death or serious injury. But suppose we could present the following situation to people who might be victims of an attack (a condition that most of us inhabit) and have them consider it from something like Rawls's veil of ignorance. We would ask them to consider the following situation:

- Group A is facing an attack by group B; if successful, the attack will lead to death or the severest oppression of group A.
- The only way that group A can defend itself is by using means that will cause death and injury to innocent members of group B.
- You are a member of one of the groups, but you do not know which one.

Would you approve of means of self-defense that will kill and injure innocent members of B in order to defend group A?

In this situation, people would not know whether they would be victims or beneficiaries of whatever policy is adopted. In this circumstance, I believe that they would reject a rule permitting either intentional or indiscriminate attacks on civilians. Thus, they would reject terrorism as a legitimate tactic, just as they would reject indiscriminate attacks that kill and injure civilians.

At the same time, I believe that they would approve a rule that combined a right of countries to defend themselves against aggression with the restrictions on means of fighting contained in the "bend over backwards" rule. This would have the following benefits. If one were a member of a group that had been attacked, one's group would have a right of self-defense. At the same time, if one were an innocent citizen in the aggressor country, the defenders would be required to take serious steps to avoid injury or death to you and other civilians.

If people generally could accept such a rule, then actions that adhere to that rule would be justifiable to potential victims as well as potential attackers. This would include actions that cause civilian casualties but that adhere to the "bend over backwards" principle.

I believe that this sort of approach achieves what nonpacifist critics of terrorism want to achieve. I provide a principled basis for condemning terrorism, no matter who it is carried out by, and a principled justification of warfare that is genuinely defensive. Moreover, the perspective is unified in a desirable way. Terrorist actions cannot be morally justified because the *intentional* targeting of civilians is the most obvious kind of violation of the "bend over backwards" rule.

At the same time that these principles allow for the condemnation of terrorism, they are immune to charges of hypocrisy because they provide a basis for criticizing not only terrorist acts but also the acts of any group that violates the "bend over backwards" rule, either by attacking civilians directly or by failing to take steps to avoid civilian deaths.

CONCLUSION

Can terrorism be morally justified? Of course not. But if condemnations of terrorism are to have moral credibility, they must rest on principles that constrain our own actions and determine our judgments of what we ourselves do and have done. To have moral credibility, opponents of terrorism must stand by the principles underlying their condemnations, apply their principles in an evenhanded way, and bend over backwards to avoid unintended harms to civilians. Only in this way can we begin inching back to a world in which those at war honor the moral rules that prohibit the taking of innocent human lives. As long as condemnations of terrorism are tainted by hypocrisy, moral judgments will only serve to inflame people's hostilities rather than reminding them to limit and avoid serious harms to one another.

NOTES

1. Michael Walzer, *Just and Unjust Wars* (New York: Basic Books, 1977); Gerry Wallace, "Terrorism and the Argument from Analogy," *Journal of Moral and Social Studies*, vol. 6 (1991), 149–160.

2. Walzer, 135.

3. Walzer, 205.

4. Walzer, 253.

5. Walzer, 254.

6. Wallace, 155–156.

7. Igor Primoratz, "The Morality of Terrorism?" *Journal of Applied Philosophy*, vol. 14 (1997), 222.

8. Primoratz, 224.

9. Primoratz, 225.

10. Primoratz, 227.

11. Primoratz, 227.

12. Primoratz, 228.

13. Walzer, 155–156.

The Case for Torturing the Ticking Bomb Terrorist

ALAN M. DERSHOWITZ

The arguments in favor of using torture as a last resort to prevent a ticking bomb from exploding and killing many people are both simple and simple-minded. Bentham constructed a compelling hypothetical case to support his utilitarian argument against an absolute prohibition on torture:

> Suppose an occasion were to arise, in which a suspicion is entertained, as strong as that which would be received as a sufficient ground for arrest and commitment as for felony—a suspicion that at this very time a considerable number of individuals are actually suffering, by illegal violence inflictions equal in intensity to those which if inflicted by the hand of justice, would universally be spoken of under the name of torture. For the purpose of rescuing from torture these hundred innocents, should any scruple be made of applying equal or superior torture, to extract the requisite information from the mouth of one criminal, who having it in his power to make known the place where at this time the enormity was practising or about to be practised, should refuse to do so? To say nothing of wisdom, could any pretence be made so much as to the praise of blind and vulgar humanity, by the man who to save one criminal, should determine to abandon 100 innocent persons to the same fate?

If the torture of one guilty person would be justified to prevent the torture of a hundred innocent persons, it would seem to follow—certainly to Bentham—that it would also be justified to prevent the murder of thousands of civilians in the ticking bomb case. Consider two hypothetical situations that are not, unfortunately, beyond the realm of possibility. In fact, they are both extrapolations on actual situations we have faced.

Several weeks before September 11, 2001, the Immigration and Naturalization Service detained Zacarias Moussaoui after flight instructors reported suspicious statements he had made while taking flying lessons and paying for them with large amounts of cash. The government decided not to seek a warrant to search his computer. Now imagine that they had, and that they discovered he was part of a plan to destroy large occupied buildings, but without any further details. They interrogated him, gave him immunity from prosecution, and offered him large cash rewards and a new identity. He refused to talk. They then threatened him, tried to trick him, and employed every lawful technique available. He still refused. They even injected him with sodium [pentothal] and other truth serums, but to no avail. The attack now appeared to be imminent, but the FBI still had no idea what the target was or what means would be used to attack it. We could not simply evacuate all buildings indefinitely. An FBI agent proposes the use of nonlethal torture—say, a sterilized needle inserted under the fingernails to produce unbearable pain without any threat to health or life, or the method used in the film *Marathon Man*, a dental drill through an unanesthetized tooth.

The simple cost-benefit analysis for employing such nonlethal torture seems overwhelming: it is surely better to inflict nonlethal pain on one guilty terrorist who is illegally withholding information needed to prevent an act of terrorism than to permit a large number of innocent victims to die. Pain is a lesser and more remediable harm than death; and the lives of a thousand innocent people should be valued more than the bodily integrity of one guilty person. If the variation on the Moussaoui case is not sufficiently compelling to make this point, we can always raise the stakes. Several weeks after September 11, our government received reports that a ten-kiloton nuclear weapon may have been stolen from Russia and was on its way to New York City, where it would be detonated and kill hundreds of thousands of people. The reliability of the source, code named Dragonfire, was uncertain, but assume for purposes of this hypothetical extension of the actual case that the source was a captured terrorist—like the one tortured by the Philippine authorities—who knew precisely how and where the weapon was being brought into New York and was to be detonated. Again, everything short of torture is tried, but to no avail. It is not absolutely certain torture will work, but it is our last, best hope for preventing a cataclysmic nuclear devastation in a city too large to evacuate in time. Should nonlethal torture be tried? Bentham would certainly have said yes.

The strongest argument against any resort to torture, even in the ticking bomb case, also derives from Bentham's utilitarian calculus. Experience has shown that if torture, which has been deemed illegitimate by the civilized world for more than a century, were now to be legitimated—even for limited use in one extraordinary type of situation—such legitimation would constitute an important symbolic setback in the worldwide campaign against human rights abuses. Inevitably, the legitimation of torture by the world's leading democracy would provide a welcome justification for its more widespread use in other parts of the world. Two Bentham scholars, W. L. Twining and

P. E. Twining, have argued that torture is unacceptable even if it is restricted to an extremely limited category of cases:

> There is at least one good practical reason for drawing a distinction between justifying an isolated act of torture in an extreme emergency of the kind postulated above and justifying the *institutionalisation* of torture as a regular practice. The circumstances are so extreme in which most of us would be prepared to justify resort to torture, if at all, the conditions we would impose would be so stringent, the practical problems of devising and enforcing adequate safeguards so difficult and the risks of abuse so great that it would be unwise and dangerous to entrust any government, however enlightened, with such a power. Even an out-and-out utilitarian can support an absolute prohibition against institutionalised torture on the ground that no government in the world can be trusted not to abuse the power and to satisfy in practice the conditions he would impose.

Bentham's own justification was based on *case* or *act* utilitarianism—a demonstration that in a *particular case*, the benefits that would flow from the limited use of torture would outweigh its costs. The argument against any use of torture would derive from *rule* utilitarianism—which considers the implications of establishing a precedent that would inevitably be extended beyond its limited case utilitarian justification to other possible evils of lesser magnitude. Even terrorism itself could be justified by a case utilitarian approach. Surely one could come up with a singular situation in which the targeting of a small number of civilians—blowing up a German kindergarten by the relatives of inmates in a Nazi death camp, for example, and threatening to repeat the targeting of German children unless the death camps were shut down.

The reason this kind of single-case utilitarian justification is simple-minded is that it has no inherent limiting principle. If nonlethal torture of one person is justified to prevent the killing of many important people, then what if it were necessary to use lethal torture—or at least torture that posed a substantial risk of death? What if it were necessary to torture the suspect's mother or children to get him to divulge the information? What if it took threatening to kill his family, his friends, his entire village? Under a simple-minded quantitative case utilitarianism, any-thing goes as long as the number of people tortured or killed does not exceed the number that would be saved. This is morality by numbers, unless there are other constraints on what we can properly do. These other constraints can come from rule utilitari-anisms or other principles of morality, such as the pro-hibition against deliberately punishing the innocent. Unless we are prepared to impose some limits on the use of torture or other barbaric tactics that might be of some use in preventing terrorism, we risk hurtling down a slippery slope into the abyss of amorality and ultimately tyranny. Dostoevsky captured the com-plexity of this dilemma in *The Brothers Karamazov* when he had Ivan pose the following question to Alyo-sha: "Imagine that you are creating a fabric of human destiny with the object of making men happy in the end, giving them peace at last, but that it was essen-tial and inevitable to torture to death only one tiny creature—that baby beating its breast with its fist, for instance—and to found that edifice on its unavenged tears, would you consent to be the architect on those conditions? Tell me the truth."

A willingness to kill an innocent child suggests a willingness to do anything to achieve a necessary result. Hence the slippery slope.

It does not necessarily follow from this under-standable fear of the slippery slope that we can never consider the use of nonlethal infliction of pain, if its use were to be limited by acceptable principles of morality. After all, imprisoning a witness who refuses to testify after being given immunity is designed to be punitive—that is painful. Such imprisonment can, on occasion, produce more pain and greater risk of death than nonlethal torture. Yet we continue to threaten and use the pain of imprisonment to loosen the tongues of reluctant witnesses.

It is commonplace for police and prosecutors to threaten recalcitrant suspects with prison rape. As one prosecutor put it: "You're going to be the boyfriend of a very bad man." The slippery slope is an argument of caution, not a debate stopper, since virtually every compromise with an absolutist approach to rights carries the risk of slipping further. An appropriate response to the slippery slope is to build in a principled

break. For example, if nonlethal torture were legally limited to convicted terrorists who had knowledge of future massive terrorist acts, were given immunity, and still refused to provide the information, there might still be objections to the use of torture, but they would have to go beyond the slippery slope argument.

The case utilitarian argument for torturing a tick-ing bomb terrorist is bolstered by an argument from analogy—an *a fortiori* argument. What moral principle could justify the death penalty for past individual mur-ders and at the same time condemn nonlethal torture to prevent future mass murders? Bentham posed this rhetorical question as support for his argument. The death penalty is, of course, reserved for convicted mur-derers. But again, what if torture was limited to con-victed terrorists who refused to divulge information about future terrorism? Consider as well the analogy to the use of deadly force against suspects fleeing from arrest for dangerous felonies of which they have not yet been convicted. Or military retaliations that pro-duce the predictable and inevitable collateral killing of some innocent civilians. The case against torture, if made by a Quaker who opposes the death penalty, war, self-defense, and the use of lethal force against fleeing felons, is understandable. But for anyone who justifies killing on the basis of a cost-benefit analysis, the case against the use of nonlethal torture to save multiple lives is more difficult to make. In the end, absolute opposition to torture—even nonlethal torture in the ticking bomb case—may rest more on historical and aesthetic considerations than on moral or logical ones.

In debating the issue of torture, the first question I am often asked is, "Do you want to take us back to the Middle Ages?" The association between any form of torture and gruesome death is powerful in the minds of most people knowledgeable of the history of its abuses. This understandable association makes it diffi-cult for many people to think about nonlethal torture as a technique for *saving* lives.

The second question I am asked is, "What kind of torture do you have in mind?" When I respond by describing the sterilized needle being shoved under the fingernails, the reaction is visceral and often visible—a shudder coupled with a facial gesture of disgust. Discussions of the death penalty on the other hand can be conducted without these kinds of reactions, especially now that we literally put the condemned prisoner "to sleep" by laying him out on a gurney and injecting a lethal substance into his body. There is no breaking of the neck, burning of the brain, bursting of internal organs, or gasping for breath that used to accompany hanging, electrocution, shooting, and gassing. The executioner has been replaced by a paramedical technician, as the aesthetics of death have become more acceptable. All this tends to cover up the reality that death is forever while nonlethal pain is temporary. In our modern age death is underrated, while pain is overrated.

I observed a similar phenomenon several years ago during the debate over corporal punishment that was generated by the decision of a court in Singapore to sentence a young American to medically supervised lashing with a cane. Americans who support the death penalty and who express little concern about inner-city prison conditions were outraged by the specter of a few welts on the buttocks of an American. It was an utterly irrational display of hypocrisy and double standards. Given a choice between a medically administered whipping and one month in a typical state lockup or prison, any rational and knowledgeable person would choose the lash. No one dies of welts or pain, but many inmates are raped, beaten, knifed, and otherwise mutilated and tortured in American prisons. The difference is that we don't see—and we don't want to see—what goes on behind their high walls. Nor do we want to think about it. Raising the issue of torture makes Americans think about a brutalizing and unaesthetic phenomenon that has been out of our consciousness for many years.

THE THREE—OR FOUR—WAYS

The debate over the use of torture goes back many years, with Bentham supporting it in a limited category of cases, Kant opposing it as part of his categorical imperative against improperly using people as means for achieving noble ends, and Voltaire's views on the matter being "hopelessly confused." The modern resort to terrorism has renewed the debate over how a rights-based society should respond to the prospect of using nonlethal torture in the ticking bomb situation. In the late 1980s the Israeli government appointed a commission headed by a retired Supreme Court justice to look into precisely that situation. The commission concluded that there are "three ways for solving this grave dilemma between the vital need to preserve the very existence of the state and its citizens, and maintain its character as a law-abiding state." The first is to allow the security service to continue to fight terrorism in "a twilight zone which is outside the realm of law." The second is "the way of the hypocrites: they declare that they abide by the rule of law, but turn a blind eye to what goes on beneath the surface." And the third, "the truthful road of the rule of law," is that the "law itself must insure a proper framework for the activity" of the security services in seeking to prevent terrorist acts.

There is of course a fourth road: namely to forgo any use of torture and simply allow the preventable terrorist act to occur. After the Supreme Court of Israel outlawed the use of physical pressure, the Israeli security services claimed that, as a result of the Supreme Court's decision, at least one preventable act of terrorism had been allowed to take place, one that killed several people when a bus was bombed. Whether this claim is true, false, or somewhere in between is difficult to assess. But it is clear that if the preventable act of terrorism was of the magnitude of the attacks of September 11, there would be a great outcry in any democracy that had deliberately refused to take available preventive action, even if it required the use of torture. During numerous public appearances since September 11, 2001, I have asked audiences for a show of hands as to how many would support the use of nonlethal torture in a ticking bomb case. Virtually every hand is raised. The few that remain down go up when I ask how many believe that torture would actually be used in such a case.

Law enforcement personnel give similar responses. This can be seen in reports of physical abuse directed against some suspects that have been detained following September 11, reports that have been taken quite seriously by at least one federal judge. It is confirmed by the willingness of U.S. law enforcement officials to facilitate the torture of terrorist suspects by repressive regimes allied with our intelligence agencies. As one former CIA operative with thirty years of experience reported: "A lot of people are saying we need someone at the agency who can pull fingernails out. Others are saying, 'Let others use interrogation methods that we don't use.' The only question then is, do you want to have CIA people in the room?" The real issue, therefore, is not whether some torture would or would not be used in the ticking bomb case—it would. The question is whether it would be done openly, pursuant to a previously established legal procedure, or whether it would be done secretly, in violation of existing law.

Several important values are pitted against each other in this conflict. The first is the safety and security of a nation's citizens. Under the ticking bomb scenario this value may require the use of torture, if that is the only way to prevent the bomb from exploding and killing large numbers of civilians. The second value is the preservation of civil liberties and human rights. This value requires that we not accept torture as a legitimate part of our legal system. In my debates with two prominent civil libertarians, Floyd Abrams and Harvey Silverglate, both have acknowledged that they would want nonlethal torture to be used if it could prevent thousands of deaths, but they did not want torture to be officially recognized by our legal system. As Abrams put it: "In a democracy sometimes it is necessary to do things off the books and below the radar screen." Former presidential candidate Alan Keyes took the position that although torture might be *necessary* in a given situation it could never be *right*. He suggested that a president *should* authorize the torturing of a ticking bomb terrorist, but that this act should not be legitimated by the courts or incorporated into our legal system. He argued that wrongful and indeed unlawful acts might sometimes be necessary to preserve the nation, but that no aura of legitimacy should be placed on these actions by judicial imprimatur.

This understandable approach is in conflict with the third important value: namely, open accountability and visibility in a democracy. "Off-the-book actions below the radar screen" are antithetical to the theory and practice of democracy. Citizens cannot approve or disapprove of governmental actions of which they are unaware. We have learned the lesson of history that off-the-book actions can produce terrible consequences. Richard Nixon's creation of a group of "plumbers" led to Watergate, and Ronald Reagan's authorization of an off-the-books foreign policy in Central America led to the Iran-Contra scandal. And these are only the ones we know about!

Perhaps the most extreme example of such a hypocritical approach to torture comes—not surprisingly—from the French experience in Algeria. The French army used torture extensively in seeking to prevent terrorism during a brutal colonial war from 1955 to 1957. An officer who supervised this torture, General Paul Aussaresses, wrote a book recounting what he had done and seen, including the torture of dozens of Algerians. "The best way to make a terrorist talk when he refused to say what he knew was to torture him," he boasted. Although the book was published decades after the war was over, the general was prosecuted—but not for what he had done to the Algerians. Instead, he was prosecuted for *revealing* what he had done, and seeking to justify it.

In a democracy governed by the rule of law, we should never want our soldiers or our president to take any action that we deem wrong or illegal. A good test of whether an action should or should not be done is whether we are prepared to have it disclosed—perhaps not immediately, but certainly after some time has passed. No legal system operating under the rule of law should ever tolerate an "off-the-books" approach to necessity. Even the defense of necessity must be justified lawfully. The road to tyranny has always been paved with claims of necessity made by those responsible for the security of a nation. Our system of checks and balances requires that all presidential actions, like all legislative or military actions, be consistent with governing law. If it is necessary to torture in the ticking bomb case, then our governing laws must accommodate this practice. If we refuse to change our law to accommodate any particular action, then our government should not take that action.

Only in a democracy committed to civil liberties would a triangular conflict of this kind exist. Totalitarian and authoritarian regimes experience no such conflict, because they subscribe to neither the civil libertarian nor the democratic values that come in conflict with the value of security. The hard question is: which value is to be preferred when an inevitable clash occurs? One or more of these values must inevitably be compromised in making the tragic choice presented by the ticking bomb case. If we do not torture, we compromise the security and safety of our citizens. If we tolerate torture, but keep it off the books and below the radar screen, we compromise principles of democratic accountability. If we create a legal structure for limiting and controlling torture, we compromise our principled opposition to torture in all circumstances and create a potentially dangerous and expandable situation.

In 1678, the French writer François de La Rochefoucauld said that "hypocrisy is the homage that vice renders to virtue." In this case we have two vices: terrorism and torture. We also have two virtues: civil liberties and democratic accountability. Most civil libertarians I know prefer hypocrisy, precisely because it appears to avoid the conflict between security and civil liberties, but by choosing the way of the hypocrite these civil libertarians compromise the value of democratic accountability. Such is the nature of tragic choices in a complex world. As Bentham put it more than two centuries ago: "Government throughout is but a choice of evils." In a democracy, such choices must be made, whenever possible, with openness and democratic accountability, and subject to the rule of law.

Consider another terrible choice of evils that could easily have been presented on September 11, 2001—and may well be presented in the future: a hijacked passenger jet is on a collision course with a densely occupied office building; the only way to prevent the destruction of the building and the killing of its occupants is to shoot down the jet, thereby killing its innocent passengers. This choice now seems easy, because the passengers are certain to die anyway and their somewhat earlier deaths will save numerous lives. The passenger jet must be shot down. But what if it were only *probable*, not certain, that the jet would crash into the building? Say, for example, we know from cell phone transmissions that passengers are struggling to regain control of the hijacked jet, but it

is unlikely they will succeed in time. Or say we have no communication with the jet and all we know is that it is off course and heading toward Washington, D.C., or some other densely populated city. Under these more questionable circumstances, the question becomes *who* should make this life and death choice between evils—a decision that may turn out tragically wrong?

No reasonable person would allocate this decision to a fighter jet pilot who happened to be in the area or to a local airbase commander—unless of course there was no time for the matter to be passed up the chain of command to the president or the secretary of defense. A decision of this kind should be made at the highest level possible, with visibility and accountability.

Why is this not also true of the decision to torture a ticking bomb terrorist? Why should that choice of evils be relegated to a local policeman, FBI agent, or CIA operative, rather than to a judge, the attorney general, or the president?

There are, of course, important differences between the decision to shoot down the plane and the decision to torture the ticking bomb terrorist. Having to shoot down an airplane, though tragic, is not likely to be a recurring issue. There is no slope down which to slip. Moreover, the jet to be shot down is filled with our fellow citizens—people with whom we can identify. The suspected terrorist we may choose to torture is a "they"—an enemy with whom we do not identify but with whose potential victims we do identify. The risk of making the wrong decision, or of overdoing the torture, is far greater, since we do not care as much what happens to "them" as to "us." Finally, there is something different about torture—even nonlethal torture—that sets it apart from a quick death. In addition to the horrible history associated with torture, there is also the aesthetic of torture. The very idea of deliberately subjecting a captive human being to excruciating pain violates our sense of what is acceptable. On a purely rational basis, it is far worse to shoot a fleeing felon in the back and kill him, yet every civilized society authorizes shooting such a suspect who poses dangers of committing violent crimes against the police or others. In the United States we execute convicted murderers, despite compelling evidence of the unfairness and ineffectiveness of capital punishment.

Yet many of us recoil at the prospect of shoving a sterilized needle under the finger of a suspect who is refusing to divulge information that might prevent multiple deaths. Despite the irrationality of these distinctions, they are understandable, especially in light of the sordid history of torture.

We associate torture with the Inquisition, the Gestapo, the Stalinist purges, and the Argentine colonels responsible for the "dirty war." We recall it as a prelude to death, an integral part of a regime of gratuitous pain leading to a painful demise. We find it difficult to imagine a benign use of nonlethal torture to save lives.

Yet there was a time in the history of Anglo-Saxon law when torture was used to save life, rather than to take it, and when the limited administration of nonlethal torture was supervised by judges, including some who are well remembered in history. This fascinating story has been recounted by Professor John Langbein of Yale Law School, and it is worth summarizing here because it helps inform the debate over whether, if torture would in fact be used in a ticking bomb case, it would be worse to make it part of the legal system, or worse to have it done off the books and below the radar screen.

In his book on legalized torture during the sixteenth and seventeenth centuries, *Torture and the Law of Proof*, Langbein demonstrates the trade-off between torture and other important values. Torture was employed for several purposes. First, it was used to secure the evidence necessary to obtain a guilty verdict under the rigorous criteria for conviction required at the time—either the testimony of two eyewitnesses or the confession of the accused himself. Circumstantial evidence, no matter how compelling, would not do. As Langbein concludes, "no society will long tolerate a legal system in which there is no prospect in convicting unrepentant persons who commit clandestine crimes. Something had to be done to extend the system to those cases. The two-eyewitness rule was hard to compromise or evade, but the confession invited 'subterfuge.'" The subterfuge that was adopted permitted the use of torture to obtain confessions from suspects against whom there was compelling circumstantial evidence of guilt. The circumstantial evidence,

alone, could not be used to convict, but it was used to obtain a torture warrant. That torture warrant was in turn used to obtain a confession, which then had to be independently corroborated—at least in most cases (witchcraft and other such cases were exempted from the requirement of corroboration).

Torture was also used against persons already convicted of capital crimes, such as high treason, who were thought to have information necessary to prevent attacks on the state.

Langbein studied eighty-one torture warrants, issued between 1540 and 1640, and found that in many of them, especially in "the higher cases of treasons, torture is used for discovery, and not for evidence." Torture was "used to protect the state": and "mostly that meant preventive torture to identify and forestall plots and plotters." It was only when the legal system loosened its requirement of proof (or introduced the "black box" of the jury system) and when perceived threats against the state diminished that torture was no longer deemed necessary to convict guilty defendants against whom there had previously been insufficient evidence, or to secure preventive information.

The ancient Jewish system of jurisprudence came up with yet another solution to the conundrum of convicting the guilty and preventing harms to the community in the face of difficult evidentiary barriers. Jewish law required two witnesses and a specific advance warning before a guilty person could be convicted. Because confessions were disfavored, torture was not an available option. Instead, the defendant who had been seen killing by one reliable witness, or whose guilt was obvious from the circumstantial evidence, was formally acquitted, but he was then taken to a secure location and fed a concoction of barley and water until his stomach burst and he died. Moreover, Jewish law permitted more flexible forms of self-help against those who were believed to endanger the community.

Every society has insisted on the incapacitation of dangerous criminals regardless of strictures in the formal legal rules. Some use torture, others use informal sanctions, while yet others create the black box of a jury, which need not explain its commonsense verdicts. Similarly, every society insists that, if there are steps that can be taken to prevent effective acts of terrorism, these steps should be taken, even if they require some compromise with other important principles.

In deciding whether the ticking bomb terrorist should be tortured, one important question is whether there would be less torture if it were done as part of the legal system, as it was in sixteenth- and seventeenth-century England, or off the books, as it is in many countries today. The Langbein study does not definitively answer this question, but it does provide some suggestive insights. The English system of torture was more visible and thus more subject to public accountability, and it is likely that torture was employed less frequently in England than in France. "During these years when it appears that torture might have become routinized in English criminal procedure, the Privy Council kept the torture power under careful control and never allowed it to fall into the hands of the regular law enforcement officers," as it had in France. In England "no law enforcement officer . . . acquired the power to use torture without special warrant." Moreover, when torture warrants were abolished, "the English experiment with torture left no traces." Because it was under centralized control, it was easier to abolish than it was in France, where it persisted for many years.

It is always difficult to extrapolate from history, but it seems logical that a formal, visible, accountable, and centralized system is somewhat easier to control than an ad hoc, off-the-books, and under-the-radar-screen nonsystem. I believe, though I certainly cannot prove, that a formal requirement of a judicial warrant as a prerequisite to nonlethal torture would decrease the amount of physical violence directed against suspects. At the most obvious level, a double check is always more protective than a single check. In every instance in which a warrant is requested, a field officer has already decided that torture is justified and, in the absence of a warrant requirement, would simply proceed with the torture. Requiring that decision to be approved by a judicial officer will result in fewer instances of torture even if the judge rarely turns down a request. Moreover, I

believe that most judges would require compelling evidence before they would authorize so extraordinary a departure from our constitutional norms, and law enforcement officials would be reluctant to seek a warrant unless they had compelling evidence that the suspect had information needed to prevent an imminent terrorist attack. A record would be kept of every warrant granted, and although it is certainly possible that some individual agents might torture without a warrant, they would have no excuse, since a warrant procedure would be available. They could not claim "necessity," because the decision as to whether the torture is indeed necessary has been taken out of their hands and placed in the hands of a judge. In addition, even if torture were deemed totally illegal without any exception, it would still occur, though the public would be less aware of its existence.

I also believe that the rights of the suspect would be better protected with a warrant requirement. He would be granted immunity, told that he was now compelled to testify, threatened with imprisonment if he refused to do so, and given the option of providing the requested information. Only if he refused to do what he was legally compelled to do—provide necessary information, which could not incriminate him because of the immunity—would he be threatened with torture. Knowing that such a threat was authorized by the law, he might well provide the information. If he still refused to, he would be subjected to judicially monitored physical measures designed to cause excruciating pain without leaving any lasting damage.

Let me cite two examples to demonstrate why I think there would be less torture with a warrant requirement than without one. Recall the case of the alleged national security wiretap placed on the phones of Martin Luther King by the Kennedy administration in the early 1960s. This was in the days when the attorney general could authorize a national security wiretap without a warrant. Today no judge would issue a warrant in a case as flimsy as that one. When Zacarias Moussaoui was detained after raising suspicions while trying to learn how to fly an airplane, the government did not seek a national security wiretap because its lawyers believed that a judge would not have granted one. If Moussaoui's computer could have been searched without a warrant, it almost certainly would have been.

It should be recalled that in the context of searches, our Supreme Court opted for a judicial check on the discretion of the police, by requiring a search warrant in most cases. The Court has explained the reason for the warrant requirement as follows: "The informed and deliberate determinations of magistrates . . . are to be preferred over the hurried action of officers." Justice Robert Jackson elaborated:

> The point of the Fourth Amendment, which often is not grasped by zealous officers, is not that it denies law enforcement the support of the usual inferences which reasonable men draw from evidence. Its protection consists in requiring that those inferences be drawn by a neutral and detached magistrate instead of being judged by the officer engaged in the often competitive enterprise of ferreting out crime. Any assumption that evidence sufficient to support a magistrate's disinterested determination to issue a search warrant will justify the officers in making a search without a warrant would reduce the Amendment to nullity and leave the people's homes secure only in the discretion of police officers.

Although torture is very different from a search, the policies underlying the warrant requirement are relevant to the question whether there is likely to be more torture or less if the decision is left entirely to field officers, or if a judicial officer has to approve a request for a torture warrant. As Abraham Maslow once observed, to a man with a hammer, everything looks like a nail. If the man with the hammer must get judicial approval before he can use it, he will probably use it less often and more carefully.

There are other, somewhat more subtle, considerations that should be factored into any decision regarding torture. There are some who see silence as a virtue when it comes to the choice among such horrible evils as torture and terrorism. It is far better, they argue, not to discuss or write about issues of this sort, lest they become legitimated. And legitimation is an appropriate concern. Justice Jackson, in his opinion in one of the cases concerning the detention of Japanese-Americans during World War II, made the following relevant observation:

Much is said of the danger to liberty from the Army program for deporting and detaining these citizens of Japanese extraction. But a judicial construction of the due process clause that will sustain this order is a far more subtle blow to liberty than the promulgation of the order itself. A military order, however unconstitutional, is not apt to last longer than the military emergency. Even during that period a succeeding commander may revoke it all. But once a judicial opinion rationalizes such an order to show that it conforms to the Constitution, or rather rationalizes the Constitution to show that the Constitution sanctions such an order, the Court for all time has validated the principle of racial discrimination in criminal procedure and of transplanting American citizens. The principle then lies about like a loaded weapon ready for the hand of any authority that can bring forward a plausible claim of an urgent need. Every repetition imbeds that principle more deeply in our law and thinking and expands it to new purposes. All who observe the work of courts are familiar with what Judge Cardozo described as "the tendency of a principle to expand itself to the limit of its logic." A military commander may overstep the bounds of constitutionality, and it is an incident. But if we review and approve, that passing incident becomes the doctrine of the Constitution. There it has a generative power of its own, and all that it creates will be in its own image.

A similar argument can be made regarding torture: if an agent tortures, that is "an incident," but if the courts authorize it, it becomes a precedent. There is, however, an important difference between the detention of Japanese-American citizens and torture. The detentions were done openly and with presidential accountability; torture would be done secretly, with official deniability. Tolerating an off-the-book system of secret torture can also establish a dangerous precedent.

A variation on this "legitimation" argument would postpone consideration of the choice between authorizing torture and forgoing a possible tactic necessary to prevent an imminent act of terrorism until after the choice—presumably the choice to torture—has been made. In that way, the discussion would not, in itself, encourage the use of torture. If it were employed, then we could decide whether it was justified, excusable, condemnable, or something in between. The problem with that argument is that no FBI agent who tortured a suspect into disclosing information that prevented an act of mass terrorism would be prosecuted—as the policemen who tortured the kidnapper into disclosing the whereabouts of his victim were not prosecuted. In the absence of a prosecution, there would be no occasion to judge the appropriateness of the torture.

I disagree with these more passive approaches and believe that in a democracy it is always preferable to decide controversial issues in advance, rather than in the heat of battle. I would apply this rule to other tragic choices as well, including the possible use of a nuclear first strike, or retaliatory strikes—so long as the discussion was sufficiently general to avoid giving our potential enemies a strategic advantage by their knowledge of our policy.

Even if government officials decline to discuss such issues, academics have a duty to raise them and submit them to the marketplace of ideas. There may be danger in open discussion, but there is far greater danger in actions based on secret discussion, or no discussion at all.

Whatever option our nation eventually adopts—no torture even to prevent massive terrorism, no torture except with a warrant authorizing nonlethal torture, or no "officially" approved torture but its selective use beneath the radar screen—the choice is ours to make in a democracy. We do have a choice, and we should make it—before local FBI agents make it for us on the basis of a false assumption that we do not really "have a choice."

* * *

My Tortured Decision

Ali Soufan

For seven years I have remained silent about the false claims magnifying the effectiveness of the so-called enhanced interrogation techniques like waterboarding. I have spoken only in closed government hearings, as these matters were classified. But the release last week of four Justice Department memos on interrogations allows me to shed light on the story, and on some of the lessons to be learned.

One of the most striking parts of the memos is the false premises on which they are based. The first, dated August 2002, grants authorization to use harsh interrogation techniques on a high-ranking terrorist, Abu Zubaydah, on the grounds that previous methods hadn't been working. The next three memos cite the successes of those methods as a justification for their continued use.

It is inaccurate, however, to say that Abu Zubaydah had been uncooperative. Along with another F.B.I.

agent, and with several C.I.A. officers present, I questioned him from March to June 2002, before the harsh techniques were introduced later in August. Under traditional interrogation methods, he provided us with important actionable intelligence.

We discovered, for example, that Khalid Shaikh Mohammed was the mastermind of the 9/11 attacks. Abu Zubaydah also told us about Jose Padilla, the so-called dirty bomber. This experience fit what I had found throughout my counterterrorism career: traditional interrogation techniques are successful in identifying operatives, uncovering plots and saving lives.

There was no actionable intelligence gained from using enhanced interrogation techniques on Abu Zubaydah that wasn't, or couldn't have been, gained from regular tactics. In addition, I saw that using these alternative methods on other terrorists backfired on more than a few occasions—all of which are still classified. The short sightedness behind the use of these techniques ignored the unreliability of the methods, the nature of the threat, the mentality and modus operandi of the terrorists, and due process.

Defenders of these techniques have claimed that they got Abu Zubaydah to give up information leading to the capture of Ramzi bin al-Shibh, a top aide to Khalid Shaikh Mohammed, and Mr. Padilla. This is false. The information that led to Mr. Shibh's capture came primarily from a different terrorist operative who was interviewed using traditional methods. As for Mr. Padilla, the dates just don't add up: the harsh techniques were approved in the memo of August 2002, Mr. Padilla had been arrested that May.

One of the worst consequences of the use of these harsh techniques was that it reintroduced the so-called Chinese wall between the C.I.A. and F.B.I., similar to the communications obstacles that prevented us from working together to stop the 9/11 attacks. Because the bureau would not employ these problematic techniques, our agents who knew the most about the terrorists could have no part in the investigation. An F.B.I. colleague of mine who knew more about Khalid Shaikh Mohammed than anyone in the government was not allowed to speak to him.

It was the right decision to release these memos, as we need the truth to come out. This should not be a partisan matter, because it is in our national security interest to regain our position as the world's foremost defenders of human rights. Just as important, releasing these memos enables us to begin the tricky process of finally bringing these terrorists to justice.

The debate after the release of these memos has centered on whether C.I.A. officials should be prosecuted for their role in harsh interrogation techniques.

That would be a mistake. Almost all the agency officials I worked with on these issues were good people who felt as I did about the use of enhanced techniques: it is un-American, ineffective and harmful to our national security.

Fortunately for me, after I objected to the enhanced techniques, the message came through from Pat D'Amuro, an F.B.I. assistant director, that "we don't do that," and I was pulled out of the interrogations by the F.B.I. director, Robert Mueller (this was documented in the report released last year by the Justice Department's inspector general).

My C.I.A. colleagues who balked at the techniques, on the other hand, were instructed to continue. (It's worth nothing that when reading between the lines of the newly released memos, it seems clear that it was contractors, not C.I.A. officers, who requested the use of these techniques.)

As we move forward, it's important to not allow the torture issue to harm the reputation, and thus the effectiveness, of the C.I.A. The agency is essential to our national security. We must ensure that the mistakes behind the use of these techniques are never repeated. We're making a good start: President Obama has limited interrogation techniques to the guidelines set in the Army Field Manual, and Leon Panetta, the C.I.A. director, says he has banned the use of contractors and secret overseas prisons for terrorism suspects (the so-called black sites). Just as important, we need to ensure that no new mistakes are made in the process of moving forward—a real danger right now.

CHAPTER 20

The Ethics of Immigration

The history of U.S. immigration is long; the nation's immigration policy has always been controversial (and variable); and debates about the morality of immigration have been rumbling since its founding. The moral issues are many and complex: Are nations morally obligated to accept all immigrants (to have more or less open borders)? Do nations have the moral right to reject all immigrants (to have more or less closed borders)? If a nation admits immigrants, what are the selection criteria it can use to decide which immigrants to accept? Is it morally right, for example, to accept all white Christians but turn away all dark-skinned Pakistanis? Do rich nations have a moral obligation to accept refugees—the poor, oppressed, or persecuted? What rights, if any, do undocumented ("illegal" or "unauthorized") immigrants have? Are countries obligated to grant citizenship to undocumented immigrants who have for years lived peacefully within their borders, paid taxes, contributed to the economy, supported their community, and never broken a law?

As with any moral questions, intelligent answers about immigration must rest on moral principles or reasons and nonmoral facts. The moral reasoning involved is straightforward, and the moral principles appealed to are familiar. The nonmoral facts, however, have too often been hard to come by. It is likely that a great deal of what you think you know about immigration is false. Perhaps this chapter can remedy some of this confusion.

ISSUE FILE: BACKGROUND

From the beginning of the republic, Americans have often viewed immigrants with suspicion or fear, even while admiring the contributions they made to the nation. And immigration policies have reflected this ambivalence. In 1790, a law was passed to spell out who could be naturalized (made a citizen). The applicant had to be a resident for two years, a person of "good moral character," and a "free white person." From 1875 to 1917, new restrictions limited or banned immigration from many parts of the world, especially Asia. Immigrants with contagious diseases were banned, as were criminals, "lunatics," epileptics, polygamists, anarchists, political extremists, beggars, and others. In the early 1920s, laws were passed to limit the number of immigrants from southern and eastern Europe (who were thought to be detrimental to American society) and to favor immigrants from northern and western Europe.

Throughout U.S. history, anti-immigration feelings have always run strong, even though America itself is a land of immigrants. For example,

> Benjamin Franklin warned about the damaging effects of the Germans on U.S. society (1753). During the Civil War General Ulysses S. Grant issued an expulsion order for all Jews within the parts of the territory he controlled (1862). The largest single mass lynching in U.S. history took place in New Orleans in 1891 when 11 Sicilians (who had been accused of murder but had been found *not* guilty) were attacked by an angry mob of 10,000 people. New immigrants from many racial or ethnic groups often struggled to make a place for themselves in

America amid public sentiment that portrayed them as dirty, criminally inclined, unhealthy, or otherwise undesirable.[1]

In 1965, Congress passed the Immigration and Nationality Act, which radically changed immigration policy. Before that time, immigration had been driven by a quota system that gave preference to immigrants from Western Europe. But the new policy favored skilled immigrants and those who, by immigrating, could help reunite families. Since the law took effect, most immigrants have arrived from Latin America, South Asia, and East Asia, while a smaller number have come from Western Europe. In 2015, 27 percent of immigrants living in the United States came from Mexico; 27 percent from Asia (mostly China and India); 14 percent from Europe and Canada; and 4 percent from the Middle East.[2]

In 2015, the number of foreign-born individuals in the United States (both legal and unauthorized) rose to 43.2 million, or 13.4 percent of the total population. This percentage of immigrants is actually much lower than that of many other developed nations, including Canada (21.8 percent), Switzerland (29.4 percent), and Australia (28.2 percent). (The immigrant portion of the overall U.S. population was actually larger in 1890, when it was 14.8 percent, the highest in U.S. history.[3]) Americans tend to overestimate immigrants' share of the population, believing that it is over twice as large (33 percent) as it actually is (less than 14 percent).[4]

Many people—including many politicians and commentators—also overestimate the number of unauthorized immigrants living in the United States. In 2015, the number was about 11 million, making up one-quarter of all immigrants and 3.4 percent of the country's overall population. The other immigrants were lawful residents (temporary or permanent) and naturalized citizens—nearly 34 million.[5]

Each year, about a million immigrants enter the United States, while over a million immigrants become lawful permanent residents—that is, they get a green card, which means they are on their way to becoming full-fledged citizens. In general, green-card immigrants can apply for citizenship after living continuously in the country for five years. Most of them are sponsored by family members who are already U.S. citizens.[6]

As immigrants are entering the United States, others are leaving via **deportation**, defined by the U.S. government as the formal removal of a foreign national from the United States for violating an immigration law. About 344,000 immigrants were deported in 2016. Between 2001 and 2008, the Bush administration deported 2 million immigrants; between 2009 and 2016, the Obama administration deported about 3 million. Most deportees are not criminals, but are deported for other reasons.[7]

The federal government defines a **refugee** as "someone who has fled from his or her home country and cannot return because he or she has a well-founded fear of persecution based on religion, race, nationality, political opinion or membership in a particular social group." From 1975 to 2017, the United States resettled about 3 million refugees within its borders. In 2016 alone, the United States resettled almost 85,000 refugees, most of them from the Democratic Republic of the Congo, but also many from Syria, Myanmar, Iraq, and Somalia. Nearly 39,000 of them were Muslims, and over 37,000 were Christians.[8] Refugees are allowed to remain indefinitely in the United States as legal permanent residents, although they may apply for citizenship after being a resident for five years.

Americans have several worrying misconceptions about immigration. Here's a sketch of some of them.

- **In a few years, Hispanics will be the majority in the United States, and whites will be a minority.** This assumption is false.

According to the U.S. Census Bureau, no population group is projected to be in the majority (more than 50 percent of the whole population) in 2044 or even in 2060. Non-Hispanic whites will still be the largest population group.[9]

- **Immigrants commit more crimes than native-born people do.** Experts reject this claim. Immigration scholar and author Cari Lee Skogberg Eastman summarizes the evidence: "Scholarship on the topic spanning decades has overwhelmingly found that immigrants actually show less propensity toward crime than native-born citizens and that immigration can even be considered a factor in the decrease of violent crime in the United States."[10]

- **Immigrants are taking jobs away from American citizens.** Available evidence suggests that this assertion is unfounded. As Eastman says, "There are specific segments of the U.S. labor force in which unauthorized immigrants may compete with native labor pools, but because employment is not a zero-sum game, most immigrants don't compete directly with U.S. citizens for jobs. Research shows that immigration actually helps create jobs and sometimes boosts wages for native workers, and that immigrant labor is particularly necessary for STEM (science, technology, engineering, mathematics) jobs because there are not enough U.S.-born applicants to fill those positions."[11]

- **Undocumented immigrants pay no taxes.** Evidence from a variety of sources shows that undocumented immigrants do in fact pay taxes. The U.S. Chamber of Commerce explains: "Undocumented immigrants pay sales taxes, just like every other consumer in the United States. Undocumented immigrants also pay property taxes—even if they rent housing. More than half of undocumented immigrants have federal and state income, Social Security, and Medicare taxes automatically deducted from their paychecks. However, undocumented immigrants working 'on the books' are not eligible for

any of the federal or state benefits that their tax dollars help to fund. As a result, undocumented immigrants provide an enormous subsidy to the Social Security system in particular. Each year, Social Security taxes are withheld from billions of dollars in wages earned by workers whose names and Social Security numbers do not match the records of the Social Security Administration (SSA). According to the SSA, undocumented immigrants paid $13 billion in payroll taxes into the Social Security Trust Funds in 2010 alone."

- **Immigration harms the economy.** Many people insist that immigration has an adverse effect on the U.S. economy, but if it does, the impact is minimal. Most research on the subject shows that immigration generally benefits the economy. As the economic writer Eduardo Porter says, "[T]he proposition that immigration weighs on productivity is in tension with many studies that show that immigration tends to raise productivity and increase economic output, mostly by multiplying the earnings of immigrants themselves. Immigration to the United States increases innovation, slows the aging of the work force and opens new opportunities for some domestic workers."[12]

- **Unauthorized immigration is getting worse.** Despite widespread belief in this claim, there are plenty of reasons to doubt it. Unauthorized immigration (which includes both illegal border crossings and people who overstay their visas) has been generally declining since 2007, when the total unauthorized population was 12.2 million. There has also been a decrease in the number of arrests of unauthorized immigrants, an upsurge in the number of U.S. Border Patrol agents, and a rise in the number of immigrants leaving the United States to go back to their home countries.[13]

Political opposition to granting undocumented immigrants amnesty or a "path to citizenship" is often expressed like this: "Why don't they just get in line and wait their turn?" The answer, as immigration experts point out, is "There is no line."

As the America Immigration Council puts it,

Immigration to the United States on a temporary or permanent basis is generally limited to three different routes: employment, family reunification, or humanitarian protection. While the U.S. immigration system is generous, each of these possibilities is highly regulated and subject to numerical limitations and eligibility requirements. Most unauthorized immigrants do not have the necessary family or employment relationships and often cannot access humanitarian protection, such as refugee or asylum status.[14]

Eastman says:

[M]ost of the unauthorized persons currently living in the United States would not qualify to come legally under [U.S. immigration laws]. Many do not have family members already living legally in the United States. Even for those who do, the visa backlogs for certain categories of family members (especially siblings or children of U.S. citizens) can be decades long. In November 2015, the wait time to bring a sibling from the Philippines was 23 years; for Mexico it was 17 years. On top of that, annual caps are established for most visa categories, and there is a 7 percent per-county limit on the number of visas issued. Overwhelmingly, demand exceeds supply in the majority of those categories. In 2015, for example, the per-country visa limit was 25,900, but there were 1,323,978 applicants from Mexico alone. . . . Legal immigration to the United States today is a very complicated process that requires specific resources or requirements for eligible applicants. For many of the poor or disadvantaged who come seeking economic opportunities, there simply is no legal way to enter the United States.[15]

Two general perspectives on the morality of immigration dominate serious debate. **Cosmopolitanism** is the view that wealthy nations able to ease the suffering of the world's poor and oppressed have a moral obligation to do so, and that this obligation is as strong concerning a nation's own citizens as it is concerning foreigners. (This outlook is a kind of *moral* cosmopolitanism,

which should be distinguished from political or economic cosmopolitanism.) Cosmopolitanism, then, inclines toward open borders.

Anticosmopolitanism is the contrary position: wealthy nations able to ease the suffering of the world's poor and oppressed have a moral obligation to do so, but they also have moral obligations to their own citizens that may be weightier than those concerning foreigners. According to anticosmopolitanism, closed borders can be justified. Stephen Macedo sums up his brand of anticosmopolitanism like this:

I argue that if high levels of immigration have detrimental impact on our least well-off citizens, that is a reason to limit immigration, even if those who seek admission seem to be poorer than our own poor whose condition is worsened by their entry.[16]

Thinkers have made their case for cosmopolitanism in different ways. Those who appeal to equality and freedom (*cosmopolitan egalitarians*) contend that everyone—both compatriots and noncitizens—is entitled to equal moral rights and consideration and that allowing open borders is the key to eliminating the vast economic inequalities in the world. A *libertarian* perspective appeals to property rights and a person's right to freedom of movement. Libertarians argue that restricted immigration (1) interferes with citizens' right to allow foreigners to enter their property and (2) impedes foreigners' right to freedom of movement. Those who appeal to *utilitarian* considerations argue that restricting immigration has adverse consequences, especially economically. Closed borders restrict trade, waste talents, and impede prosperity.

The reasons given for restricting immigration are varied—and usually controversial:

- **Security.** Nations are obligated to protect their citizens from external threats (such as terrorism), and many people regard limitations on immigration as an obvious way to do this. But there is substantial disagreement over whether immigration limitations would be effective.

CRITICAL THOUGHT: Deporting Children

WASHINGTON—President Trump on Tuesday ordered an end to the Obama-era program that shields young undocumented immigrants from deportation, calling it an "amnesty-first approach" and urging Congress to pass a replacement before he begins phasing out its protections in six months.

As early as March, officials said, some of the 800,000 young adults brought to the United States illegally as children who qualify for the program, Deferred Action for Childhood Arrivals [DACA], will become eligible for deportation. The five-year-old policy allows them to remain without fear of immediate removal from the country and gives them the right to work legally.*

The children protected by the DACA program were not responsible for their immigration into the United States and for their being undocumented. Should they still be deported? Should they be permitted to stay and work? Does this situation seem like punishing children for the actions of their parents? What would be a just resolution of this predicament?

*Michael D. Shear and Julie Hirschfeld Davis, "Trump Moves to End DACA and Calls on Congress to Act," *New York Times*, September 5, 2017.

- **Culture.** Many favor closed borders to preserve what they perceive as their nation's distinctive culture. Critics, however, ask whether the empirical assumptions about cultural identity and change are actually true, and whether citizens have a moral right either to resist or to impose changes to their culture.

- **Economy.** A very common assumption is that allowing immigrants into a country will wreck its economy. Critics often reject this view, admitting that open borders may harm certain workers but benefit many other workers and the economy as a whole. If this is the case, they ask—if a minority of workers want to maintain closed borders while the majority would benefit greatly from opening them—is it morally permissible to keep things as they are for the sake of the minority?

- **Welfare.** Some argue that a wealthy nation that offers substantial welfare benefits to its citizens (such as Sweden and other Scandinavian countries) cannot afford to have open

QUICK REVIEW

deportation—The formal removal of a foreign national from a country for violating an immigration law.

refugee—Someone who has fled from his or her home country and cannot return because he or she has a well-founded fear of persecution based on religion, race, nationality, political opinion or membership in a particular social group.

cosmopolitanism—The view that wealthy nations able to ease the suffering of the world's poor and oppressed have a moral obligation to do so and that this obligation is as strong concerning a nation's own citizens as it is concerning foreigners.

anticosmopolitanism—The view that wealthy nations able to ease the suffering of the world's poor and oppressed have a moral obligation to do so, but they also have moral obligations to their own citizens that may be weightier than those concerning foreigners.

borders. If such a welfare state placed no limits on immigration, it would be inundated by poor and needy people from impoverished countries seeking benefits. The welfare system would collapse, and the nation would no longer be a welfare state. Some argue, however, that this predicament of the welfare state does not provide a justification for closing borders. There may be ways to distribute benefits, they say, while keeping borders open—by, for example, delaying welfare benefits to new immigrants until after a few years of residency.

MORAL THEORIES

Both consequentialist and nonconsequentialist theories have been used to formulate arguments and claims about immigration. Those who think nations should restrict or forbid immigration (that is, anticosmopolitans) often argue in a utilitarian vein, pointing out that open borders would have objectionable consequences. They contend, for example, that immigration must be limited or halted to protect the nation's distinctive culture. Allowing immigrants to pour in through open borders, they argue, will irrevocably alter the culture or destroy it altogether. This nonmoral assertion would have to be supported by empirical facts, and they may or may not be at hand. Cultural change—whether caused by immigration or by internal factors—is often difficult to predict, and identifying objectively the features of a culture worth preserving can be tricky. Citizens can also argue that borders should be closed for other utilitarian reasons: because immigration will disrupt the economy, break the welfare system, turn control of the country over to foreigners, or unacceptably change the nature of the political system. These claims, of course, would also require empirical support.

CRITICAL THOUGHT: Accepting or Rejecting Refugees

Consider how U.S. policy regarding refugees is changing:

> Since World War II, the United States has been the world's leader in resettling refugees. Most refugees never got the chance to come to a new country and start a new life, but if they did, there was a substantial chance—even a 50 percent chance—that the country that welcomed them was the United States.
>
> After less than a year in office, Donald Trump has not only officially drawn the era of global refugee leadership to a close. He's withdrawn the US from the global community for refugee protection.
>
> Domestically, the Trump administration has declared that it will allow no more than 45,000 refugees into the US during the current fiscal year (which began on October 1 and continues through September 30, 2018). That number is less than half the total of the last years of the Obama administration, when the government set its refugee "ceiling" to at least 100,000 refugees in the last two years. The Trump administration's newly announced levels are, in fact, the most restrictive limit the United States has set in the 70-year history of refugee resettlement.*

Does the United States have a moral obligation to resettle refugees? If so, why? If not, why not? If the United States has such an obligation, what proportion of the world's refugees must the country resettle? What would constitute a legitimate reason for turning away some refugees and accepting others?

*Dara Lind, "The Trump Administration Doesn't Believe in the Global Refugee Crisis," *Vox*, December 4, 2017, https://www.vox.com/policy-and-politics/2017/10/3/16379016/trump-refugees.

Some arguments for and against immigration are based not on utility, but on one or more moral principles. Christopher Heath Wellman, for example, argues that nations have a right to close their borders, a right derived from the more fundamental right to freedom of association. People, he says, clearly have a right to associate with particular individuals and to disassociate from others. As he puts it,

> we take for granted that each individual has a right to choose his or her marital partner and the associates with whom he or she practices his or her religion. . . . [J]ust as an individual has a right to determine whom (if anyone) he or she would like to marry, a group of fellow-citizens has a right to determine whom (if anyone) it would like to invite into its political community. And just as an individual's freedom of association entitles one to remain single, a state's freedom of association entitles it to exclude all foreigners from its political community.[17]

MORAL ARGUMENTS

It's not possible here to examine all the arguments that have been marshaled in the battles over immigration, but we can look closely at one of them. Stephen Macedo argues for his position in a nonconsequentialist vein—specifically, he appeals to a particular concept of justice. He asks, "How should we think about the apparent ethical conflict between, on the one hand, the cosmopolitan humanitarian impulse to admit less well-off persons from abroad who wish to immigrate to the United States and, on the other hand, the special obligation we have to less well-off Americans, including or especially African Americans?"[18] His answer is that seeing to the needs of one's own citizens is generally a weightier obligation than helping noncitizens:

> Citizens have special obligations to one another: we have special reasons to be concerned with the distribution of wealth and opportunities among citizens. The comparative standing of citizens matters in some ways that the comparative standing of citizens and noncitizens does not. . . . I argue against what is sometimes characterized as a "cosmopolitan" position with respect to distributive justice and defend the idea that distributive justice is an obligation that holds among citizens . . . What is the basis of these special obligations among citizens? I argue that it is as members or co-participants in self-governing political communities that we have special obligations to our fellow members.[19]

Macedo says that in aiding our fellow citizens, we should give priority to those compatriots who need our help the most:

> We must consider the justifiability of policies from the standpoint of the least well-off among our citizens. John Rawls's theory of justice stands for the proposition that the political equality of citizens requires this sort of "distributive" justification among citizens: it is not reasonable to expect our less-well-off fellow citizens to accede to a policy on the grounds that it makes those with the luck of superior endowment by nature and birth even better off. Immigration policy—as part of the basic structure of social institutions—ought to be answerable to the interests of the poorest Americans.

Here's one way of using Macedo's justice principle in a simple argument:

1. If high levels of immigration by low-skilled workers make it unlikely that we will fulfill our moral obligations to the poorest Americans, then we should reduce or stop such immigration.

2. Currently high levels of immigration by low-skilled workers do make it unlikely that we will fulfill our moral obligations to the poorest Americans.

3. Therefore, we should reduce or stop high levels of immigration by low-skilled workers.

This is a valid argument. Premise 1 is a moral statement derived from Macedo's distributive justice principle, which he defends at length. Premise 2 is a nonmoral statement that must be supported by empirical evidence.

CHAPTER REVIEW

SUMMARY

Immigration policies have changed repeatedly through-out American history and have often embodied anti-immigrant outlooks. The immigration system for the past several decades has favored skilled workers and family reunification. Misconceptions that Americans have about immigration include the notions that immi-grants commit more crimes than native-born people do, that undocumented immigrants pay no taxes, and that immigrants are taking jobs away from American citizens.

Two general perspectives dominate serious debate about immigration. Cosmopolitanism is the view that wealthy nations able to ease the suffering of the world's poor and oppressed have a moral obligation to do so and that this obligation is as strong con-cerning foreigners as it is concerning a nation's own citizens. Anticosmopolitanism is the contrary posi-tion: wealthy nations able to ease the suffering of the world's poor and oppressed have a moral obligation to do so, but they also have moral obligations to their own citizens that may be weightier than those con-cerning foreigners. Both consequentialist and non-consequentialist theories have been used to formulate arguments and claims about immigration.

KEY TERMS

deportation (p. 757)
refugee (p. 757)
cosmopolitanism (p. 759)
anticosmopolitanism (p. 759)

EXERCISES

Review Questions

1. What is a refugee? What is deportation? (p. 757)
2. What is cosmopolitanism? Is cosmopolitanism now the immigration policy of the United States? (p. 759)
3. What is anticosmopolitanism? How does it differ from cosmopolitanism? (p. 759)

4. Have immigrants coming to America always been welcomed with open arms? (To answer this question, provide examples.) (pp. 756–757)
5. In 2015, how many foreign-born individuals were living in the United States? (p. 757)
6. In 2015, what percentage of the entire U.S. population was foreign-born? (p. 757)
7. How many immigrants were deported during the George W. Bush presidency? The Obama presidency? (p. 757)
8. Do immigrants commit more crimes than native-born people do? (p. 758)
9. Is it true that immigrants pay no taxes? (p. 758)
10. Why don't all immigrants "get in line" to wait their turn to become citizens instead of entering the country illegally? (p. 759)

Discussion Questions

1. Which view makes the most sense to you—cosmopolitanism or anticosmopolitanism? Why?
2. Should children brought into a country illegally ever be deported? Why or why not?
3. Is "preserving the culture" a good reason to restrict immigration? Why or why not?
4. Does the United States have a moral obligation to resettle refugees? Under what circumstances would the country *not* have such an obligation?
5. Does a country have the right to close its borders? Explain.
6. Is seeing to the needs of one's own citizens generally a weightier obligation than helping noncitizens? Why or why not?
7. How does Macedo justify his anticosmopolitanism?
8. What is Wellman's justification for his view that nations have a right to close their borders?
9. Is there anything wrong in offering unauthorized immigrants "a path to citizenship"? Explain.
10. Would it ever be just to ban the immigration of people because they profess a particular religion? Is so, why? If not, why not?

FURTHER READING

G. Brock, *Global Justice* (Oxford: Oxford University Press, 2009).

Joseph H. Carens, *The Ethics of Immigration* (New York: Oxford University Press, 2013).

Phillip Cole and C. Wellman, *Debating the Ethics of Immigration: Is There a Right to Exclude?* (New York: Oxford University Press, 2011).

Cari Lee Skogberg Eastman, *Immigration: Examining the Facts* (Santa Barbara, CA: ABC-CLIO, 2017).

C. Kukathas, "Immigration," in *The Oxford Handbook of Practical Ethics* (New York: Oxford University Press, 2002), 567–90.

Pew Research Center, "Immigration," http://www.pewresearch.org/topics/immigration/ (November 29, 2017).

Alex Sager, ed., *The Ethics and Politics of Immigration* (London: Rowman and Littlefield, 2016).

Peter Singer, *Practical Ethics* (Cambridge: Cambridge University Press, 1993).

Christopher Heath Wellman, "Immigration," in *Stanford Encyclopedia of Philosophy*, Summer 2015 ed., ed. Edward N. Zalta, https://plato.stanford.edu/entries/immigration/ (March 23, 2015).

ETHICAL DILEMMAS

1. Rejecting Jewish Refugees

The modern refugee policy of the United States was shaped partly in response to the nation's callous treatment of refugees during Nazi rule in Europe. As one observer says,

> The US (and other countries in the Western Hemisphere) could have saved thousands of Jews from the Nazis. They didn't. At one point, the US literally turned away a ship of 900 German Jews. Shortly afterward, it rejected a proposal to allow 20,000 Jewish children to come to the US for safety.*

The name of the ship was the *St. Louis*, which set sail from Hamburg, Germany, in May 1939. It eventually ended up in waters off the coast of Miami, Florida, waiting for permission to land. But the United States, which could have easily accommodated the passengers, wouldn't allow it. The *St. Louis* was forced to sail back across the Atlantic, and most of the passengers were divvied up among a handful of European countries, all of which were eventually taken over by the Nazis. Out of the original 900 passengers, 254 perished in the Holocaust.

Was the United States morally obligated to take in the refugees from Nazi-dominated Europe? If so, what moral principle or principles could have justified that action? If not, why not?

*Dara Lind, "How America's Rejection of Jews Fleeing Nazi Germany Haunts Our Refugee Policy Today," *Vox*, January 27, 2017, https://www.vox.com/policy-and-politics/2017/1/27/14412082/refugees-history-holocaust.

2. The "White Australia" Policy

Consider the history of Australia's former immigration law, known as the "white Australia" policy:

> In the last decades of the nineteenth century, concern was growing in the Australian colonies about the level of "coloured" immigration to Australia, particularly from China, and many colonies passed restrictive immigration legislation. Following Federation in 1901, one of the first pieces of Commonwealth legislation passed was the *Immigration Restriction Act 1901*, based on the earlier colonial legislation. The overall aim of this and other related legislation was to limit non-white immigration to Australia, particularly Asian immigration, and thereby preserve the predominance of the British within Australia.[†]

Is an immigration policy that accepts only white Europeans morally acceptable? Is *any* immigration policy that selects immigrants according to race, color, religion, or country of origin morally acceptable? Why or why not?

[†]National Archives of Australia, "Immigration Restriction Act 1901 (commonly known as the White Australia Policy)," 2017, http://www.naa.gov.au/collection/a-z/immigration-restriction-act.aspx. © Commonwealth of Australia (National Archives of Australia) 2018. CC by 3.0.

3. Ideological Tests

> **Washington Post**—Donald Trump called Monday for a Cold War-style mobilization against "radical Islamic terror," repeating and repackaging calls for strict immigration controls—including a new ideological litmus test for Muslim visitors and migrants—and blaming the current level of worldwide terrorist attacks on President Obama and Hillary Clinton. . . .
>
> The principal new initiative was what Trump called "extreme vetting" for "any hostile attitude towards our country or its principles, or who believed sharia law should supplant American law.[‡]

Trump's proposed ideological test for immigrants was short on specifics, although it seemed to entail more than the loyalty statement currently required under U.S. naturalization law, which asks for adherence to "the principles of the Constitution." Critics feared that Trump's test (ostensibly designed to identify terrorists) would be used to discriminate against Muslims. But what about a universal ideological test used to weed out dangerous extremists generally? Would you, for example, think it morally acceptable to use a test asking all applicants if they approved of (1) suicide bombings against people of other religions, (2) laws severely restricting the rights of women, or (3) making homosexuality a capital crime? Why or why not?

[‡]Karen DeYoung, "Trump Proposes Ideological Test for Muslim Immigrants and Visitors to the U.S." *Washington Post*, August 15, 2016, https://www.washingtonpost.com/world/national-security/trump-to-propose-ideological-testfor-muslim-immigrants-and-visitors-to-the-us/2016/08/15/3192fdba-62fc-11e6-be4e-23fc4d4d12b4_story.html?utm_term=.a3dd8fdc95be.

READINGS

The Morality of Migration

SEYLA BENHABIB

In announcing the Department of Homeland Security's policy directive on June 15 stating that undocumented migrant youths who meet certain conditions would no longer be deported, President Obama said that "It was the right thing to do." What he did not say was whether he meant "the right thing" legally or morally.

Obviously, he considered the action to be legal, even though this invocation of his administration's power drew strong criticism from many, including Supreme Court Justice Antonin Scalia. But the president's grounds for believing it moral were much less clear.

This should come as no surprise: the morality and politics of migration are among the most divisive issues in much of the world. In the United States, discussions of immigration flow seamlessly into matters of national security, employment levels, the health of the American economy, and threats to a presumptive American national identity and way of life. Much the same is true in Europe. Not a week goes by without a story of refugees from Africa or Asia perishing while trying to arrive at the shores of the European Union.

Nor are such developments restricted to the resource-rich countries of the Northern Hemisphere. The United Arab Emirates, Kuwait, Singapore, Israel and Jordan are countries with the *highest percentage share* of migrants among their total population, while the United States, the Russian Federation, Germany, Saudi Arabia, Canada and France lead in the *actual number* of international migrants. Migrations are now global, challenging many societies in many parts of the world.

Whereas from 1910 to 2012, the world's population increased slightly more than fourfold, from 1.6 billion to more than 7 billion, the number of people living in countries other than their own as migrants increased nearly sevenfold, from roughly 33 million to more than 200 million.

Migrations pit two moral and legal principles, foundational to the modern state system, against each other. On one hand, the human right of individuals to move across borders whether for economic, personal or professional reasons or to seek asylum and refuge is guaranteed by Articles 13 and 14 of the 1948 Universal Declaration of Human Rights. On the other hand, Article 21 of the declaration recognizes a basic right to self-government, stipulating that "the will of the people shall be the basis of the authority of government." Under the current regime of states, that fundamental right includes control over borders as well as determining *who* is to be a citizen as distinguished from a resident or an alien.

The international system straddles these dual principles but it has not been able to reconcile them. The irony of global developments is that while state sovereignty in economic, military, and technological domains is eroded and national borders have become more porous, they are still policed to keep out aliens and intruders. The migrant's body has become the symbolic site upon which such contradictions are enacted.

Why not advocate a "world without borders" then? From a moral point of view, no child *deserves* to be born on one side of the border rather than another, and it is deeply antithetical to our moral principles to punish individuals for what they cannot help being or doing. Punishment implies responsibility and accountability for one's actions and choices; clearly, children who through their parents' choices end up on one side of the border rather than another cannot be penalized for these choices.

A strong advocate of the right to self-government might retort that rewarding certain children for the wrongs committed by their parents, in this case illegal immigration, by legalizing undocumented youths is illogical as well as immoral and that "the right thing to do" would be to deport *all* undocumented migrants—parents and children alike. Apart from the sheer impracticality of this solution, its advocates seem to consider undocumented "original entry" into a country as the analog of "original sin" that no amount of subsequent behavior and atonement can alter.

But such punitive rigor unfairly conflates the messy and often inadvertent reasons that lead one to become an undocumented migrant with no criminal intent to break the law.

If conditions in a person's native country so endanger his life and well-being [that] he becomes willing to risk illegality in order to survive, his right to survival, from a moral point of view, carries as much weight as does the new country's claim to control borders against migrants. Immanuel Kant, therefore, called the moral claim to seek refuge or respite in the lands of another, a "universal right of hospitality," provided that the intentions of the foreigner upon arriving on foreign lands were peaceful. Such a right, he argued, belonged to each human being placed on this planet who had to share the earth with others.

Even though morally the right to hospitality is an individual right, the socioeconomic and cultural causes of migrations are for the most part collective. Migrations occur because of economic, environmental, cultural and historical "push" and "pull" factors. "We are here," say migrants, "because in effect you were there." "We did not cross the border; the border crossed us."

We do have special obligations to our neighbors, as opposed to moral obligations to humanity at large, if, for example, our economy has devastated theirs; if our industrial output has led to environmental harm or if our drug dependency has encouraged the formation of transnational drug cartels.

These claims of interdependence require a third moral principle—in addition to the right of universal hospitality and the right to self-government—to be brought into consideration: *associative obligations* among peoples arising through historical factors.

States cannot ignore such associative obligations. Migration policies, though they are often couched in nation-centric terms, always have transnational causes and consequences. It is impossible to address Mexican migration into the United States, for example, without considering the decades-long dependency of the rich California agricultural fields upon the often undocumented and unorganized labor of Mexican workers, some of whose children have now grown up to become "Dreamers" (so named after the Development, Relief, and Education for Alien Minors Act introduced to Congress in 2001). Among the three million students who graduate from United States high schools, 65,000 are undocumented.

The United States owes these young people a special duty of hospitality, not only because we, as a society, have benefited from the circumstances under which their parents entered this country, but also because they have formed strong affiliations with this society through being our friends, students, neighbors and coworkers. In a liberal-democratic society the path to citizenship must follow along these associative ties through which an individual shows him or herself to be capable and worthy of citizenship.

Migratory movements are sites of imperfect justice in that they bring into play the individual right to freedom of movement, the universal right to hospitality and the right of collectives to self-government as well as specific associative moral obligations. These rights cannot always be easily reconciled. Furthermore, international law does not as yet recognize a "human right to citizenship" for migrants, and considers this a sovereign prerogative of individual states. Nonetheless, the responsible politician is the one who acts with a lucid understanding of the necessity to balance these principles rather than giving in to a punitive rigorism that would deny, in Thomas Jefferson's words, "the right which nature has given to all men of departing from [and I would add, from joining with] the country in which chance, not choice has placed them" (1774).

Whether or not President Obama considered all these moral aspects of the matter, his handling of this issue shows that he acted as a "responsible politician," and not opportunistically as some of his critics charged. It was "the right thing to do."

The Moral Dilemma of U.S. Immigration Policy Revisited: Open Borders vs. Social Justice?

Stephen Macedo

IMMIGRATION POLICY AS A MORAL DILEMMA

How should we think about U.S. immigration policy from the standpoint of basic justice, especially distributive justice which encompasses our obligations to the less well-off? Does a justifiable immigration policy take its bearings from the acknowledgment that we have special obligations to "our own" poor, that is, our least well-off fellow citizens? Or, on the other hand, do our moral duties simply argue for attending to the interests of the least well-off persons in the world, giving no special weight to the interests of the least well-off Americans?

There are reasons to believe that recent American immigration policy has had a deleterious impact on the distribution of income among American citizens. According to influential arguments—associated with George Borjas and others—by admitting large numbers of relatively poorly educated and low-skilled workers we have increased competition for low-skilled jobs, lowering the wages of the poor and increasing the gap between rich and poor Americans. In addition to the effects on labor markets, there are other ways in which high levels of immigration may have lessened support for social welfare policies.

How should we think about the apparent ethical conflict between, on the one hand, the cosmopolitan humanitarian impulse to admit less well-off persons from abroad who wish to immigrate to the U.S. and, on the other hand, the special obligations we have to less well-off Americans, including or especially African Americans? Those with liberal sensibilities need to consider whether everything that they might favor—humanitarian concern for the world's poor, an openness to an ever-widening social diversity, and

support for distributive justice within our political community—necessarily go together.

These are vexing questions in politics as much as in political theory and moral philosophy. Recent events have made them even more central. President Donald Trump has revived the isolationist slogan "America first," and linked immigration to the loss of well-paying American jobs. His anti-immigration message is crude and cruel but he also speaks to real grievances. His message has resonated with millions of working-class Americans—especially white working-class men without a college degree—who have in many ways borne the brunt of globalization.

We have not paid sufficient attention to the domestic distributive impact of immigration (as well as globalized trade). High levels of immigration by low-skilled workers make fulfilling our moral obligations to the poorest Americans more costly and less likely. If that is true, does it mean that the borders should be closed and immigration by the poor restricted? That conclusion would be hasty: the moral terrain and the policy options are complex.

If high levels of immigration have a detrimental impact on our least well-off fellow citizens that is a reason to limit immigration, even if those who seek admission are poorer than our own poor whose condition is worsened. Citizens have special obligations to one another: we have special reasons to be concerned with the distribution of wealth and opportunities among citizens. The relative standing of citizens matters in ways that the relative standing of citizens and non-citizens does not. In this respect, I argue against "cosmopolitanism" with respect to the principles of social justice, and join Michael Walzer, John Rawls, David Miller, and Michael I. Blake, among others, in defending the idea that distributive justice holds among citizens.

What is the basis of these special obligations among citizens? I argue that it is as members and co-participants in self-governing political communities that we have special obligations to our fellow members.

Distributive justice is a weighty moral consideration that bears on immigration policy, but it is not the only one. We also have significant moral duties and obligations to poor people (and others) abroad; these are different in content from what we owe to fellow citizens and they may take priority. The large external effects of our policies may dominate smaller negative effects on distributive justice.

This chapter proceeds as follows. The first part describes the reasonable grounds for thinking that we face a dilemma in shaping U.S. immigration policy. I feature claims advanced by George Borjas and others in order to raise important moral questions while allowing that there is serious disagreement about the effects of immigration. In section two I consider the debate between "cosmopolitans"—who argue against the moral significance of shared citizenship and in favor of universal obligations of distributive justice—and those who argue for the existence of special obligations of justice among citizens. I seek to clarify the moral grounds for regarding shared membership in a political community as morally significant, but also emphasize that we have significant cosmopolitan duties. In the final section I return to the moral dilemma of U.S. immigration policy and offer some reflections on policy choices. It may be that on balance we should accept and manage ongoing high levels of movement back and forth across the U.S.–Mexico border.

One point is worth making before moving on. The perspective adopted and defended here is politically liberal. John Rawls and Michael Walzer (whose ideas I treat in some detail) are philosophers of the left in American politics. It might be thought that this limits the relevance of my argument, but this is not so. For one thing, the vast majority of Americans profess a belief in some liberal principles, such as equality of opportunity. While Americans are less supportive than Europeans of measures designed directly to reduce income disparities between the wealthy and poor, they overwhelmingly affirm that institutions such as public education should insure that every child has a good start in life, irrespective of accidents of birth. The question of whether we have special obligations to our fellow citizens is important independently of the details of one's convictions about what justice requires

among citizens. Even those who believe that "equality of opportunity" mandates only a modest level of educational and other social services may still think that the mandate holds among fellow citizens and not all of humanity. The general thrust of my argument should, therefore, be of relevance to those who do not accept the specific prescriptions of Rawls and Walzer.

THE CONTOURS OF THE IMMIGRATION DILEMMA

Over the past half-century, American immigration policies and practices became, in some important respects, more accommodating to the less well-off abroad. Some argue that this "generosity" has exacted a significant cost in terms of social justice at home.

The basic facts are striking. Immigration to the U.S. has trended upward since the end of World War II. Between 2001 and 2016, about one million foreign nationals per year became long-term permanent residents in the U.S. (including both new arrivals and adjustments to visa status). Whereas in 1970, less than 5 percent of the general population was foreign born, that percentage rose to 14 percent—or 45 million people—in 2015 (just under the historic record of 15 percent around the beginning of the twentieth century). Twenty-six percent of the current U.S. population—or 85 million people—are either immigrants or the children of immigrants. Over half the U.S. population growth since 1965 is due to immigration and were it not for immigration, it is estimated that the current population of the U.S. would be 252 rather than 324 million.

Patterns of immigration to the U.S. were shaped deeply by amendments to the Immigration and Nationality Act passed in 1965, emphasizing the principle of family reunification. The exact formulas are complicated, but "immediate relatives" of U.S. citizens (spouses, parents, and unmarried children under 21 years of age) can enter without numerical limit (and often number nearly half a million per year). An additional 226,000 annual admission priorities are extended to adult children and adult siblings of U.S. citizens, and spouses and children of legal permanent residents ("green card" holders). In 2010, family-based preferences accounted for 66 percent of annual immigration to the U.S.

U.S. policy also favors some migrants based on employment qualifications and skills (14 percent of the total in 2010) and others based on humanitarian grounds, as refugees and asylum seekers (13 percent of the total in 2010). There are also shorter-term skills-based green card programs, including the H-IB visa program.

The composition of the growing immigrant pool changed markedly after 1965, with the skills level and earnings of immigrants declining relative to the native U.S. population. Whereas in 1960, the average immigrant man living in the U.S. earned 4 percent more than the average native-born American, by 1998 the average immigrant earned 23 percent less. Most of the growth in immigration since 1960 has been among people entering at the bottom 20 percent of the income scale. This is partly because, as George Borjas observes, "Since the immigration reforms of 1965, U.S. immigration law has encouraged family reunification and discouraged the arrival of skilled immigrants."

The ethnic and racial makeup of immigration has also changed with the percentage arriving from Europe and Canada falling sharply and the percentage from Latin America and Asia rising.

On Borjas's influential if controversial analysis, recent decades of high immigration have tended to lower wages overall by increasing the labor supply, with the biggest negative impact being felt by the least well-off. Immigration from 1980 to 1995 increased the pool of high school dropouts in the U.S. by 21 percent, while increasing the pool of college graduates by only 4 percent. By 2013, half of U.S. workers with less than a high school degree were foreign born. This, argues Borjas, contributed to a substantial decline in the wages of high school dropouts and to a widening of the wage gap based on education. He argues that immigration between 1980 and 2000 had the effect of lowering the wages of the average native worker by 3.2 percent, while lowering wages among those without a high school diploma (roughly the bottom 10 percent of wage earners) by 9 percent. To put it another way, it is widely agreed that in the U.S. in the 1980s and 1990s there was a substantial widening of the wage gap between more and less educated workers. Borjas

has argued that nearly half of this widening wage gap between high school dropouts and others may be due to the increase in the low-skilled labor pool caused by immigration.

Of course, all Americans have benefited from cheaper fruits, vegetables, and the many other products and services that immigrants (including undocumented workers) help produce. Firms have also benefited from cheap labor. Wealthier Americans have also benefited from increased access to cheap labor to perform service work—as nannies, gardeners, etc. By decreasing the cost of childcare and housekeeping, immigration has helped highly educated women participate in the labor force. However, Borjas argues that native-born African American and Hispanic workers have suffered disproportionately because they are disproportionately low-skilled and own few firms, and often compete directly with low-skilled immigrants.

Borjas also observes that nations with notably more progressive domestic policies often have immigration policies that are quite different from the U.S. While U.S. immigration policy since 1965 has emphasized family ties rather than desirable skills, Canada pioneered a system in the late 1960s that gives greater weight to educational background, occupation, and language proficiency. Canada's policy favors better-educated and high-skilled workers and this seems likely to have distributive effects that are the opposite of U.S. policy. By increasing the pool of skilled workers relative to the unskilled, Canadian policy tends to lower the wages of the better off and to raise the relative level of the worse off. Australia, New Zealand, and other countries have followed Canada's lead and President Trump has argued that the U.S. should also move in that direction.

It seems quite possible that Canada's policy of favoring more educated immigrants helps lessen domestic income disparities, while seeming less generous from the position of poor people abroad. U.S. policy, by admitting predominantly low-skilled and low education immigrants looks generous to poor persons abroad but may worsen the relative standing of the American poor. As is now obvious, were the U.S. to follow Canada and impose an education test on immigration this would have a substantial impact on the ethnic and racial composition and national origins of immigrants to the U.S. It would, in short, substantially and disproportionately reduce immigration from Mexico and the rest of Latin America.

We should emphasize that Borjas's arguments are controversial, and many economists argue that he exaggerates the negative effects of immigration while downplaying the positive side. Economist David Card argues that "immigration exerts a modestly positive effect on the labor market outcomes of most natives," but not all, and not the least well-educated.

The *labor market argument* advanced by Borjas (and others including Steven A. Camarota and Karen Zeigler in this volume) describes one possible way in which recent decades of immigration to the U.S. may worsen distributive justice in the United States. There are several other pathways—political, cultural, and economic—by which recent high rates of immigration may harm the relative standing of poorer Americans. I will mention these briefly.

One response to the forgoing argument is that if immigration increases our collective wealth while worsening income disparities across rich and poor, why not welcome immigration and redistribute the surplus via tax and spending policies? Redistributive policies could compensate for the malign distributive effects of immigration, but immigration may undermine political support for social welfare and redistributive programs.

Nolan McCarty, Keith T. Poole, and Howard Rosenthal argue that recent patterns of immigration help explain why increasing inequality since the 1980s has come about in the U.S. without an increase in political pressure for redistribution. Since 1972, the percentage of non-citizens has risen and their income relative to other Americans has fallen. "From 1972 to 2000, the median family income of non-citizens fell from 82% of the median income of voters to 65% while the fraction of the population that is non-citizen rose from 2.6% to 7.7%." Meanwhile, a "large segment of the truly poor does not have the right to vote. Whereas in 2010, noncitizens were 9.2 percent of the general population," they were 13 percent of families with incomes below $7,500 per year. McCarty, Poole, and Rosenthal argue that the increasing proportion of non-citizens among the poor has shifted the position of the median voter—the voters likely to be the "swing voters" who decide close elections. Immigration to the U.S. has made the median *voter* better off relative to the median *resident*, and this as decreased median voters' likelihood of supporting redistribution.

Immigration may have, thus, both worsened the relative standing of the least-well-off Americans and also made it less likely that crucial "swing voters" would support redistributive programs. McCarty, Poole and Rosenthal point out that countries with smaller portions of non-citizens among the poorest—such as France, Japan, and Sweden—have not seen the sort of sharp increases in the proportion of national wealth going to people in the top 1 percent as in the United States.

This *median voter argument* suggests that recent patterns of immigration to the U.S. may not only worsen the relative lot of the least well-off Americans but also make it harder to enact redistributive policies. Excluding immigrants from social welfare services is one way to counteract these effects, but immigrants—including illegal immigrants in many places—will still be provided with a variety of social services, including education.

Consider next an additional possible impact of immigration on social justice. Feelings of solidarity and mutual identification that help support social justice may be undermined, at least in the short to medium term, by the increased racial and ethnic heterogeneity associated with immigration. Robert Putnam surveys a range of different forms of evidence suggesting that, "in ethnically diverse neighborhoods residents of all races tend to 'hunker down.' Trust (even of one's own race) is lower, altruism and community cooperation rarer, friends fewer." The fact that immigrant groups typically have higher fertility rates than natives amplifies the effect. Putnam and others thus argue that immigration-induced increases in ethnic and racial diversity can reduce social solidarity and undermine support for the provision of public goods, including programs aimed at helping the poor.

On the basis of their survey of the evidence, Stuart Soroka, Keith Banting, and Richard Johnston argue, "International migration does seem to matter for the size of the welfare state. Although no welfare state has actually shrunk in the face of accelerating international movement of people, its rate of growth is smaller the more open a society is to immigration." They further argue that, "The typical industrial society might spend 16 or 17 percent more than it does now on social services if it kept its foreign-born percentage where it was in 1970.

All of these empirical claims are controversial and the impact of immigration on a society's capacity to sustain redistributive programs is bound to be complex. Just how immigration and increased ethnic and racial diversity inhibit social spending is unclear: the rise of New Right political parties in Europe is associated with controversies over immigration, and mainstream parties may need to shift to the right in response.

Consider, finally, the argument advanced by John Skrentny in his contribution to this volume. He joins those who think that the direct economic impact of immigration on wages is likely small. Yet he argues that native white and black workers, in particular, may be disadvantaged in local labor markets by popular stereotypes that associate Latino and Asian workers—especially immigrants—with hard work and greater reliability. The availability of Latino and Asian immigrants in a labor pool may, therefore, put white and especially African American workers at a disadvantage.

To sum up. There are reasons to believe that the specific contours of American immigration policy over the last 40 years may have lowered wages at the bottom, by increasing competition for low-wage jobs, while also reducing political support for more generous social provision targeted at low-wage workers and the poor generally. The greater ethnic and racial diversity associated with immigration may also have lowered trust among groups and support for public goods provision. And, finally, pro-immigrant workplace stereotypes may disadvantage native workers, especially whites and African Americans. Vexed empirical issues surround all of these claims.

The questions before us include the following: if U.S. immigration policies appear to be liberal and generous to the less well-off abroad (or at least some of them), does this generosity involve injustice toward poorer Native Americans, including—or perhaps, especially—African Americans? If we have special obligations to our poorer fellow citizens—obligations that are sufficiently urgent and weighty—then U.S.

immigration policy may be hard or impossible to defend from the standpoint of domestic distributive justice.

Of course, the question of how we should respond to this—if it is true—is not straightforward. It does not follow that the most morally defensible policy—all things considered—is to enact more restrictive immigration policies. It might well be morally preferable to change the other laws and policies that allow the immigration of low-skilled workers to generate adverse effects on native-born poor. The inegalitarian distributive effects of immigration could be offset via publicly funded income support for low-wage workers, improved education and training for the unemployed, and other social welfare benefits for the less well-off. And yet, high levels of low-skilled immigration may also tend to lower public support for social welfare provision. This sharpens the dilemma.

We should not underestimate the complexity of the questions that surround policy choice in this area. Distributive justice is important, but other moral values are also in play, including humanitarian concern for all humans who are very badly off. Aside from the moral considerations that might help us rank various options, there is also the question of what package of policies might be politically saleable. This chapter can only scratch the surface of these issues.

COSMOPOLITAN VS. CIVIC OBLIGATIONS?

Let us step back and consider some framing moral issues. If the better-off have moral obligations to help the least well-off, why shouldn't those obligations focus on the least well-off of the world? Can we justify special obligations to our own poor, even if they are less poor than many others in the world?

Consider two ways in which we might care about the condition of the poor and seek to do something about it. We might care only about their absolute level of poverty or deprivation, or we might care about relative deprivation: the gap between the lives of the poorest and those of the richest. In response to the first concern we would engage in *humanitarian assistance* and seek to establish a floor of material well-being: a standard of decency below which no one should fall.

In response to the latter concern we would articulate and enforce principles of social or *distributive justice*: standards to regulate the major institutions of taxation, inheritance, social provision, wage policies, education, etc., which help determine over time the relative levels of income, wealth, and opportunity available to different groups.

Most people seem to accept that wealthy societies owe the first sort of concern to human beings generally. Via humanitarian assistance, wealthier societies should pool their efforts and seek to lift poorer countries up at least to a level of basic decency; exactly what level is adequate or morally required is an important question. This sort of cosmopolitan moral concern has been likened to the duty we all have to be "Good Samaritans" when we can save people in distress without undue cost to ourselves.

The latter species of concern—social or distributive justice—requires the establishment of institutions to regulate market inequalities: systems of progressive taxation, inheritance taxes, and the provision of social services. As noted, most Americans profess a belief that every child born in America should have a fair chance to attain good jobs—to compete based on his or her talents and effort—and this requires that governments raise taxes in order to provide good schools for all. Virtually everyone accepts some degree of progressivity in the tax structure so efforts to promote fair equality of opportunity are typically redistributive and constitute part of a system of distributive justice. Opportunity is one of the things we distribute by building public institutions—including tax-supported schools—alongside market institutions. As we have seen, immigration policies may also have an impact on the distribution of opportunities and rewards in society.

Do we have special moral obligations to our fellow citizens, especially obligations falling under the rubric of distributive justice? Do national borders matter with respect to our fundamental moral obligations to one another?

There are, roughly speaking, two opposed lines of thought. One emphasizes the moral arbitrariness of borders and the universality of our obligations to the less well-off. The other position holds that borders are morally significant, that we have special obligations to poorer fellow citizens, and that obligations of distributive justice in particular apply only among citizens. The first position is often referred to as a form of "cosmopolitanism": the idea that we are, in effect, citizens of the world. The latter position—which I argue for—goes under various names and I'll refer to it as the *civic view*.

The civic view holds that we have special obligations of mutual justification to our fellow citizens, and that the fullest obligations of distributive justice have special force among fellow citizens. With respect to people in the rest of world, our duties and obligations are different, though still quite important: fair dealing—including curbs on the exploitive potential of our corporations, and doing our fair share to address common problems (such as environmental dangers like global warming); more specific projects of historical rectification and redress in response to particular past acts of injustice; and humanitarian assistance to help lift other societies (insofar as we can) out of poverty.

Michael Walzer strikingly asserts that: "Distributive justice begins with membership; it must vindicate at one and the same time the limited right of closure, without which there could be no communities at all, and the political inclusiveness of existing communities." It seems to me that Walzer is on the right track here, though he is unclear about the moral grounds. He famously argues that moral arguments in politics should take the form of interpreting "shared social meanings." Principles of justice are justified in light of "the particularism of history, culture, and membership." Social goods should be distributed according to criteria internal to their social meanings, and these shared social meanings are located within particular political communities.

Given this account of the nature of moral argument and distributive justice, it is not surprising that Walzer would argue that distributive justice applies within ongoing political communities which are the natural homes of shared meanings. "[T]he political community is probably the closest we can come to a world of common meanings. Language, history, and culture come together (come more closely together here than anywhere else) to produce a collective consciousness . . . . the sharing of sensibilities and intuitions among the members of a historical community is a fact of life." For Walzer, the rejection of cosmopolitan obligations of distributive justice goes hand in hand with the claim that common understandings of values are shared within particular political communities but not across them.

Walzer's argument contains part of the truth, but it is also puzzling. Achieving shared and well-justified principles of justice is surely a worthy aspiration within political communities. But while shared meanings are an important goal of public argument, an achievement to be worked toward, the extent of shared meanings is not the proper ground for circumscribing claims of social justice.

Shared social meanings—common understandings, shared assumptions of various sorts—are important for sustaining a political system based on discussion and mutual justification, but they are not the basic thing when it comes to demarcating the range of those to whom we owe justice. The range of those with whom we should seek to establish common and publicly justified principles of justice are those with whom we share a comprehensive system of binding laws. Publicly justified "common meanings" are not the basis of political obligations but rather the goal of public argument and deliberation within our political community.

Walzer lays too much emphasis on consensus and shared meanings in another way as well: what we should want is a *justified* consensus that is the result of criticism and testing. Critical argumentation is essential to public justification because what we should work toward are common understandings that are sound, and their soundness is essential to their authoritativeness. The mere fact of agreement, the mere existence of shared conventions, is not enough.

David Miller has argued eloquently for the advantages to political communities of a shared national culture and a common language, for these can help support a collective identity and bonds of mutual sympathy and understanding, "Social justice will always be easier to achieve in states with strong national identities and without internal communal divisions." That again seems right, as far as it goes: social justice may be harder to achieve in very diverse societies. But

justice remains an important goal in divided societies. Some societies, such as Canada, seem able to generate impressive levels of support for social justice even amidst great diversity, partly by adopting effective multicultural policies. Social scientists have more work to do to understand the relationships among heterogeneity, social capital, and social justice.

Particular political societies—at least when they are well-ordered rather than tyrannical, oppressive, very deeply divided, or desperately poor—will tend to generate roughly common understandings among members including standards for how disputes and disagreements should be resolved. They may generate disagreements and conflicts galore, but these will be manageable if the society has working standards and practices for how disagreements should be dealt with and a reserve of rough agreement on the most important matters sufficient to sustain a common willingness to share a political order.

In his *The Law of Peoples,* John Rawls argues that the political community—or "people"—is the appropriate site of distributive justice: there are no obligations of distributive justice among human beings simply. We have humanitarian duties to relieve those in distress—as mentioned above—but we have no obligations across borders to regulate the relative well-being of better and worse off people (or to create institutions capable of doing so).

Many have found this puzzling. Rawls does not as a general matter share Walzer's emphasis on the authority of shared social meanings. Moreover, Rawls's general approach to justice encourages us to transcend morally arbitrary accidents of birth. There is a puzzle here.

When formulating principles of justice, Rawls's guiding thought is that we should put aside claims based on morally arbitrary differences and accidents of fate. We put aside claims to unequal rewards based on advantages flowing from accidents of birth: including the good fortune of being born into a well-off family, or with a superior genetic endowment. We regard these advantages as arbitrary when justifying to one another principles of justice to regulate the basic structure of society, which includes the system of property and market exchanges, incomes and inheritance taxation, and public institutions and policies of all kinds. We instead regard one another as free and equal persons, and imagine ourselves in an "original position" behind a "veil of ignorance": we ask which principles of social justice we would choose if we did not know the social position we would occupy. This helps us consider which principles of justice for regulating the design of the basic structure are fair to all, and so capable of being freely accepted by reasonable people whichever position they occupy in society. To affirm mutually justified principles to regulate basic social institutions is to affirm that we regard one another as moral equals.

The upshot of Rawls's thought experiment is his argument that two basic principles of justice would be chosen by citizens of modern pluralistic democracies:

1. Each person has an equal claim to a fully adequate scheme of equal basic rights and liberties, which scheme is compatible with the same scheme for all; and in this scheme the equal political liberties, and only those liberties, are to be guaranteed their fair value.
2. Social and economic inequalities are to satisfy two conditions: (a) They are to be attached to positions and offices open to all under conditions of fair equality of opportunity; and (b), they are to be to the greatest benefit of the least advantaged members of society.

Principle 2 (b) is also known as the "difference principle."

What is the relevance of all this to obligations across borders? If being born into a well-off family or with especially advantageous genes are to be regarded as morally arbitrary when thinking about justice, surely it seems equally arbitrary whether one is born in New Mexico or Mexico. One's place of birth with respect to nationality or political community seems quintessentially arbitrary. And yet, Rawls follows Walzer in arguing that obligations of distributive justice (such as the difference principle and the principle of fair equality of opportunity) apply only within the borders of political community, and only among co-participants in a shared political order. What can justify this?

Like Walzer, Rawls mentions the fact of greater diversity on the international scale: the fact of reasonable pluralism "is more evident within a society

of well-ordered peoples than it is within one society alone." Some have supposed that this invocation of diversity signals a retreat in Rawls's later writings with respect to his ambitions regarding justice. I think this interpretation is wrong, and, in any event, we should seek a better one if we can find it.

The diversity-based argument for limiting obligations of distributive justice to particular political communities is a non-moral account of why justice's sails need trimming: a matter of bowing before unfortunate necessities, a pragmatic or prudential concession rather than a full moral justification. I believe there is a moral justification for confining obligations of distributive justice to co-participants in particular political communities. But what is it?

THE MORAL SIGNIFICANCE OF COLLECTIVE SELF-GOVERNANCE

Borders are morally significant because they bound systems of collective self-governance. The arbitrariness of the location of borders does not stop them from being of great moral significance once a collectively self-governing people creates a common life within them, as Michael I. Blake, Anna Stilz, and others have emphasized. Citizens of self-governing political communities—together making and being subject to the law—share a morally significant special relationship. As members of a political community we are joined in a collective enterprise across generations through which we construct and sustain a comprehensive system of laws and institutions that regulate and shape all other associations, including religious communities and families. We are born into political communities and are formed by them. From cradle to grave (and beyond) our interests, identities, relationships, and opportunities are pervasively shaped by the political system and the laws that we collectively create, coercively impose, and live within. The basic values and choices of our political order pervasively shape the lives of those who reside within it.

The governments of self-governing political communities—at least so long as they are legitimate—are recognized by members to be capable of authoritatively resolving conflicts, and of taking decisions that bind us as members of the political community: our government as our agent enters into treaties, makes alliances, declares war, and conducts various undertakings in our name. Legitimate governments are capable of putting citizens under new duties, and this is an awesome moral power. We can be held collectively liable as citizens for the actions of our government, recognized by us and others to be our collective agent.

Americans take responsibility—and *should* take responsibility—for what happens in North Dakota and Mississippi in a way they do not for what happens in Chihuahua and Ontario. Citizens look to one another to jointly establish collective programs concerning health and welfare: they view themselves as jointly responsible in perpetuity for their health and welfare, culture, and territory.

Citizens have powerful obligations of mutual concern and respect, and mutual justification, to one another because they are joined together—as constituent members of a sovereign people—in creating binding political institutions which determine patterns of opportunities and rewards for all. A self-governing political society is a hugely significant joint venture, and we understand it as such. We have strong common obligations as fellow citizens because we collectively govern one another: we collectively make hugely consequential decisions. This could not simultaneously be true of the international society, and it is not. Membership in international bodies does not have the same significance because that membership is mediated by membership in primary political units, namely the "Member States" of the UN or its peoples: individuals are not governed directly by multilateral institutions. International institutions deal with a limited range of subjects.

Cosmopolitan distributive justice (as opposed to a duty to assist other peoples to become self-governing and well-ordered) makes no sense absent a cosmopolitan state and a cosmopolitan political community, which hardly anyone seriously argues for, and which we are not obliged to bring into being; though there are good reasons for strengthening international institutions. It is, moreover, hard to understand the reasonableness of making people responsible for the welfare of others without also making them responsible for their governance. It would be strange and unreasonable to sever ongoing responsibilities for the provision of health, welfare, and education from responsibilities for governance with respect to these matters.

Federations or unions of states such as Europe may voluntarily enter into increasing cooperative relations, but we understand European peoples to be doing this as a matter of mutual advantage and choice, not as an obligation of fundamental justice. It may be good for them but it is also up to them, as the people of the United Kingdom have recently affirmed.

To argue that membership in a political collectivity is morally significant in the ways I have begun to describe raises the further question: which political collectivities qualify? Does every political community have equal moral standing, or if not, which ones? Respect for basic human rights is one crucial threshold condition of legitimacy and international respectability. Liberal democracies qualify for full respect, but so do certain not-fully liberal and democratic regimes, which Rawls calls "decent" peoples. We need not go into the details here, but suffice it to say that the theory of legitimacy at work here is the following: *we ought to fully respect states that effectively protect citizens basic interests and provide working legal and political arrangements and within which (a) basic human rights are respected and (b) there are effective processes for giving everyone a say, for insuring that all groups within society are listened to, responded to, and effectively included in collective self-rule.* To respect such political societies is to respect distinctive forms of collective self-rule, forms of collective self-rule that may deviate from some of the features that we understand to be aspects of liberal democracy, but which nevertheless observe basic rights and take all members interests seriously into account, and thereby make legitimate law. If by our lights such communities go wrong in some respects we can nevertheless say that the mistake is theirs to make. Such political communities can be regarded as the fit custodians of the interests of their own citizens.

WHAT DO WE OWE TO NON-MEMBERS?

Space does not permit an extensive discussion of what the civic view might say about obligations to non-members, but it may be helpful to round out the account before returning to the problem of immigration.

First, societies have general duties of (a) *fair dealing* with one another, and this would include non-exploitation, the avoidance of force and fraud, and the duty to curb the capacity of one's citizens or corporations to harm or exploit others. This general duty of fair dealing includes doing our share to address common problems (avoidance of free-riding), including environmental problems such as global warming, disaster relief, and humanitarian assistance.

Second, they have specific obligations to other countries or groups growing out of particular relations of exploitation, oppression, or domination, which give rise to specific obligations of *rectification and redress*. (b) If we have exploited or oppressed poorer and weaker societies, or if we have allowed our corporations to do so, then we have debts to these other societies which require some sort of recompense.

I should emphasize that these first two categories almost certainly generate strong demands to strengthen international institutions and for reform in the way that countries like the U.S. conduct themselves in the world.

Finally, it seems right to say that well-off societies have (c) general *humanitarian duties* to relieve those in destitution or distress and to respond to gross and systematic violations of human rights. Our duty is to do what we can to relieve distress, to end suffering, to stop gross violations of human rights, and to get a society on its feet so that it can look after its own affairs. These duties may involve substantial resource commitments, and they would require rich countries like the U.S. to spend more than they currently do on assistance, if it could be shown that such assistance is effective (which it very often is not). The proper target of aid is helping societies to develop their own effective and legitimate political institutions which can secure the basic interests of all citizens.

Our general humanitarian duties include doing our fair share to provide safe harbor for refugees, whose basic needs are not being met in their home countries and who have no prospect for having them met as a consequence of well-founded fears of persecution. If we have contributed to the creation of the conditions that generate refugees then we have special obligations to address their plight. In the absence of specific connections and special responsibilities, we still have general duties to do our part along with others: to bear some significant cost to relieve suffering abroad.

Crucially, however, members of wealthier societies do not owe to all the people of the world precisely the same consideration that they owe to fellow citizens. Full justice holds within political communities because of the special moral relation that citizens share: as the ultimate controllers and subjects of extensive institutions of shared governance.

U.S. IMMIGRATION POLICY AND DISTRIBUTIVE JUSTICE

As we have seen, it is not implausible to think that America's immigration policy has contributed to rising inequality and distributive injustice in the U.S. over the last half century. Poor immigrants are better off for having been allowed to immigrate, but many have competed for jobs with less-well-off Americans, and social programs to address inequality may have been made less politically popular. What, from an egalitarian perspective at least, could possibly be wrong in the U.S. being more like Canada, by reducing overall levels of immigration and giving greater priority to immigration by the better educated and higher skilled?

Howard Chang rightly observes that the civic, or "liberal nationalist," policy on immigration seems anomalous,

> If the welfare of all incumbent residents determines admissions policies, however, and we anticipate the fiscal burden that the immigration of the poor would impose, then our welfare criterion would preclude the admission of unskilled workers in the first place. Thus, our commitment to treat these workers as equals once admitted would cut against their admission and make them worse off than they would be if we agreed never to treat them as equals. A liberal can avoid this anomaly by adopting a cosmopolitan perspective that extends equal concern to all individuals, including aliens, which suggests liberal immigration policies for unskilled workers.

Chang allows, of course, that the morally justified cosmopolitan immigration policy may be politically infeasible because Americans seem unwilling to embrace the right sort of cosmopolitan moral attitude.

I have argued, however, that there are good reasons for believing that we have special responsibilities for our fellow citizens, obligations arising from membership in a self-governing community. In shaping immigration policies, concerns about distributive justice are relevant and urgent, and these concerns are inward-looking rather than cosmopolitan, emphasizing the special obligations we have to our poorer fellow citizens. If the U.S. were to move toward a more Canadian-style immigration policy this could improve the lot of less-well-off American workers. Considerations of distributive justice—taken in the abstract—argue for the superiority of the Canadian system: this would mean limiting immigration based on family re-unification (perhaps limiting that preference to spouses and minor children), placing greater weight on priorities for education and other skills, and curbing undocumented or illegal immigration.

However, sound policy recommendations in this vexed area of policy need to take into account a wider set of moral considerations and a great deal more of the relevant context, including geography and the heavy residue of historical patterns and practice. So far as the context is concerned, the United States is not Canada, and the costs of pursuing a Canadian-style immigration policy in the U.S. could be prohibitive. Empirical description, and careful analysis and prediction, must be combined with moral judgment. I can only sketch a few of the relevant considerations in concluding, and it should also be noted that patterns of migration to the U.S. are shifting rapidly.

The U.S. shares a 2,000-mile long border with Mexico, and that border has marked large differences in development, income, and wealth. For decades, there have been high levels of migration from Mexico to the U.S., and the U.S. has frequently welcomed massive influxes of migrant workers. In the period from 1965 to 1986, 1.3 million Mexicans entered the U.S. legally along with 46,000 contract workers, but 28 million entered as undocumented migrants. The vast majority subsequently returned to Mexico, yielding a net migration to the U.S. of around five million

during that time. Patterns of migration and return are self-reinforcing: migration prepares the way for more migration as language, labor market skills, and personal contacts are acquired. Heightened border security in the late 1980s and 1990s had the perverse consequence that illegal migrants chose to remain in the U.S. far longer than they did when it was easier to leave and re-enter.

Over three million Mexicans enter the U.S. yearly on non-immigrant visas and there are well over 200 million short-term border crossings. The U.S. and Mexico (along with other Western Hemisphere nations) are committed to policies of open markets and free trade. Economic growth in Mexico has narrowed the wage gap between the U.S. and Mexico: GDP in Mexico is now over $17,500 per capita, making it a middle-income country. The birth rate in Mexico has also declined.

Remittances from the U.S. undoubtedly contributed considerably to economic growth in Mexico, and Mexican migration to the U.S. has been falling since the early 2000s. In 2013, China and India surpassed Mexico as the largest senders of migrants to the U.S., though other Caribbean and Central American countries—including Cuba, the Dominican Republic, El Salvador, and Guatemala—continue to send large numbers of migrants.

What is the most ethically defensible way of responding to concerns about immigration, including concerns stemming from social justice within the U.S.? We must consider the humanitarian costs of attempts to massively alter longstanding patterns of movement across our long and long-porous borders with Mexico and other Central American countries.

The approach long favored by some on the right, and now being implemented at least in part, is to try to limit legal migration and stop illegal immigration by more vigorously controlling the southern border, by constructing a security fence, and by other means, including increased arrests and deportations of undocumented persons.

Will this be effective? Policy changes in the U.S. seem to be having some effect. As this book goes to press, it appears that migration to the U.S. from Central American countries in general is down significantly: U.S. Customs and Border Protection reports that apprehensions of undocumented persons along the Southwest Border are down 64 percent from May 2016 to May 2017.

But this has been partly at the cost of imposing tremendous burdens on the 11 million undocumented persons living and working in the U.S. It is estimated that 60 percent of these people have been living in the U.S. for over a decade, and a third of those have American-born children who are therefore citizens. It may be that many or most of these people had no right to come here in the first place, but they came mainly for honorable and decent reasons: to help their families cope with often desperate poverty. The costs of disruption for those who have been here for any considerable amount of time, as law-abiding citizens, makes it immoral to not provide a path to regularized status.

Another way of curtailing illegal migration by poor workers would focus on stemming the demand for migrant workers in the U.S. We might institute a national identification card, increase penalties for forging identification papers, and vigorously punish employers who hire undocumented people. Obviously, if such policies were implemented effectively, the cost of low-skilled labor would increase considerably in many areas, especially in agriculture, but that would appear to be good insofar as wages rise at the bottom of the income scale. It is often said that illegal migrants do work that Americans are unwilling to do, but of course they are unwilling at the prevailing low wage, and that is just the problem from the standpoint of distributive justice. Suppose the wages were doubled and the work conditions improved significantly?

An alternative approach would be to accept and regularize the flow of migrant labor, as Massey, Durand, and Malone recommend. Such proposals include increasing the annual quota of legal entry visas from Mexico, and perhaps other Central American countries. In addition, instituting a temporary two-year work visa, which would be renewable once. Massey, Durand, and Malone have proposed making available 300,000 such visas per year. This would regularize and re-channel the flow of illegal migrants into a legal flow. The work visas would be awarded to workers not employers, so that workers would be free to quit. Fees for these visas plus savings in the Immigration and Naturalization Services budget could generate

hundreds of millions of dollars a year that could be passed along to states and localities with high concentrations of migrants, to offset the costs of some local services. Finally, Massey and his colleagues would curtail the priorities that are now provided to family members of those who become naturalized Americans: they would eliminate the priority given to adult siblings of naturalized citizens and legal permanent residents, and they recommend making it easier for relatives of U.S. citizens to get tourist visas, so they can visit and return home more easily.

It may be that the guest worker program component is most controversial. It has the advantage of directly addressing some of the underlying forces generating migration to the U.S. from Central America and elsewhere: poverty and the need for economic and social development. Massey and his colleagues emphasize that immigration is part of the development process and it is temporary. The poorest nations do not send out migrants. Developing countries typically send out immigrants for eight or nine decades, until growth at home relieves the pressures to leave. As we have seen, migration from Mexico has indeed been falling as predicted. Facilitating short-term migration and return would help promote growth elsewhere. While government-to-government foreign aid has a very poor track record, remittances sent home by migrant workers contribute considerably to economic development.

One moral problem with this approach is that it regularizes a system that would seem to impose some downward pressure on low-wage jobs in the U.S. It takes seriously the interests of poor people abroad and it benefits American employers, American consumers, and better-off Americans, but it does not fully address the special obligations we have to our poorest fellow citizens. The distributive justice problem could be dealt with by explicitly coupling these reforms with measures designed to improve the conditions of poorer and less well-educated Americans, whose economic prospects have deteriorated considerably in recent decades of globalized trade while elites have prospered. This would be appropriate and overdue in any case. While high levels of immigration by low-income people may make transfer payments less politically popular, a guest worker program, by excluding guest workers from many public benefits, could help address this problem.

A problem with this policy is the intrinsic status of guest workers. Adequate protections must be built into any guest worker program so that workers are not exploited and oppressed. A regulated guest worker program ought to be coupled with measures to require decent wages and work conditions, basic healthcare, protection from poisoning by pesticides, etc. However, if a guest worker in the U.S. becomes seriously ill the program might be designed so that he or she is entitled to a trip to the emergency room and then a one-way ticket home. Such provisions seem likely to be part of the price of getting Americans to accept a guest worker program, and they seem legitimate so long as work conditions, wages, and protections are such that we can regard the conditions of work as humane and reasonable. (If such provisions led to workers concealing and postponing treatment serious illnesses then we would need to re-think the acceptability of the provision.)

An additional track of immigration reform can only be mentioned here: greater emphasis on skills-based migration. Such policies have spread from Canada to many countries around the world. They may be advantageous for developed countries and have some specific advantages from the standpoint of domestic distributive justice, as discussed above. But there are serious questions concerning whether skills-based migration policies are causing a "brain drain" for sending countries. The benefits of remittances, and the likelihood that many migrants will return home, may outweigh the costs, but these issues deserve more attention than I can give them here.

CONCLUSION

There is reason to believe that current patterns of immigration do raise serious issues from the standpoint of social justice: high levels of immigration by poor and low-skilled workers from Mexico and elsewhere in Central America may worsen the relative and absolute positions of poorer American citizens. Furthermore, such immigration may lessen political support for redistributive programs. Nevertheless, as

we have also seen, the costs of "tightening-up" the border have been high: border security efforts have imposed great hardships and expense on migrant workers. Employer sanctions could be a more humane enforcement mechanism, but Americans have not had the political will to impose such measures.

I have argued that U.S. immigration policy presents us with the necessity of grappling with the tension between two important moral demands: justice to our fellow citizens vs. humanitarian concern with the plight of poor persons abroad. We have urgent reasons to shape major public policies and institutions with an eye to the distributive impact. Justice demands that we craft policies that are justifiable not simply from the standpoint of aggregate welfare—or the greatest good of the greatest number. We must consider the justifiability of policies from the standpoint of the least well-off among our fellow citizens. Immigration policy—as part of the basic structure of social institutions—ought to be answerable to the interests of the poorest Americans. An immigration policy cannot be considered morally acceptable in justice unless its distributive impact is defensible from the standpoint of disadvantaged Americans.

And yet, we must also consider the collateral costs of tight curbs on immigration. While domestic distributive justice is an urgent moral concern it does not, I would argue, take absolute or lexical priority over broader humanitarian concerns. Fostering development in very poor countries is a humanitarian imperative. If we can make significant contributions to this while bearing only small and uncertain costs in terms of domestic distributive justice, it seems likely that we should do so.

The proposals by Massey and his colleagues hold out the prospect of doing some real good for hundreds of thousands of migrant workers, their families, and countries of origin. It is possible that the best combination of policies would be something like the Massey proposals involving guest workers, coupled with more generous aid to poorer Americans.

This discussion has only meant to suggest the shape of certain moral considerations relevant to any defensible immigration policy.

Selecting Immigrants

David Miller

In the developed liberal democracies today, the immigration issue has become intractable as a result of three conflicting pressures. The first is the increasing number of people from developing countries who wish to enter, whether to escape poverty or civil war or simply to improve their material prospects. Polling by Gallup, for example, suggests that 38% of those living in Sub-Saharan Africa and 21% of those living in the Middle East and North Africa would prefer to migrate permanently.[1] The second is the increasing reluctance of citizens within those societies to accept large numbers of incoming migrants. In the UK, for example, an opinion poll in late 2013 found that 80% of those who were asked thought that current levels of net inward migration were too high, 85% thought that immigration was putting too much pressure on public services such as schools, hospitals and housing, and 64% thought that over the last decade immigration had not been good for British society as a whole.[2] Broadly the same picture holds across Europe.[3] The third is the diminished capacity of governments to control immigration flows by means that are judged acceptable by international law and opinion. Even setting aside the special case of the EU with its principle of internal free movement, the prevailing human rights culture stays the hand of governments who seek peremptorily either to prevent unwanted immigrants from entering or to deport them once they have gained a foothold inside.

Under these circumstances, developing a defensible policy for selecting which immigrants to admit, and on what terms, becomes a priority. In sketching the outlines of such a policy, I make three assumptions, which I shall not defend here (though I have done so elsewhere[4]). The first is that there is no human right to

David Miller, "Selecting Immigrants," CSSJ Working Paper Series, SJ034, April 2015. Reprinted by permission of the author.

immigrate: the simple fact of being refused entry by a state does not, in itself, violate anyone's human rights.[5] The second is that democratic states can legitimately shape their immigration policies in the light of their overall national goals and priorities, whether these are economic, cultural, environmental, humanitarian etc. An important aspect of national self-determination is deciding who is going to form part of the 'self' in future. The third is that this right of self-determination is nevertheless limited by what I call 'the weak cosmopolitan premise', according to which all human beings are equally entitled to moral consideration when agents (whether states or individual people) decide how to act towards them. This means in particular that a prospective migrant seeking to enter must have her claim considered, and if it is denied she must be presented with reasonable grounds for refusal.[6]

Selecting between potential immigrants is justifiable, therefore, but how should it be done? There are two dimensions that we need to consider: the first is the inherent nature of the claim to enter that the immigrant is making; the second is the nature of the connection (if any) that already exists between the immigrant and the receiving state. On one dimension, we have the familiar distinction between refugees and economic migrants, where refugees are those whose claim is based on the threat to their human rights created by remaining in their current state of residence, and economic migrants are all those who have an interest in moving to a new society, whether to study, to find work, or to pursue some personal project, but who cannot cite a threat to their human rights as grounds for admission. On the second dimension, there are those who qualify as what I call 'particularity claimants' and those who do not. Particularity claimants are people who assert that one particular state owes them admission by virtue of what has happened in the past. A clear case would be one in which a group of people have been led to believe that they had a right to immigrate should their circumstances require it.[7] Another example would be people who have performed some service for the state, and claim now that being allowed to immigrate is the appropriate form of recompense.[8] Particularity claimants might also be refugees or economic migrants, but what distinguishes them (and justifies the rather awkward label I am applying to them) is that their claim is held against *one particular state*, whereas refugees and economic migrants, although they have chosen to apply in one place, might in many cases find that their rights or interests were equally well served by being admitted elsewhere.

The distinctions I have drawn suggest two priority rules that states should follow in selecting immigrants: 1. *Refugees as a category should have priority over economic migrants*; 2. *Within each category, particularity claimants should have priority over others*. The rationale for the first rule is that states have an obligation to admit refugees (the nature and extent of which will be explored shortly) whereas they have no such obligation to admit economic migrants. The rationale for the second rule is that a state has more reason to acknowledge a claim that stems from an existing relationship with the immigrant than one that is general in nature. This, however, does not yet settle whether a refugee without a particularity claim should always get precedence over an economic migrant who has one. Consider the following case: suppose the UK Border Agency has (for some reason) to make a choice between two applicants for admission: a refugee from South Sudan, who can credibly show that her life is in danger because she has been an outspoken critic of the regime, but who has no previous connection to the UK, and a young man from Iraq who worked as a translator for the British Army during the Gulf War, but who can no longer find work (so he is poor but not yet in desperate straits). Who should be taken first? Well, perhaps the Sudanese, since time is of the essence and she needs immediate help. But maybe she can claim less than the Iraqi eventually: if the Agency has made an arrangement for refugees from Sudan to be accommodated in neighbouring Kenya, that may offer sufficient protection for her human rights. The Iraqi man, on the other hand, may have a desert claim that can

only be redeemed if he is provided with the opportunities that come with being allowed into Britain.

In presenting this case as a test of our moral intuitions, I have already assumed that the obligation to accept refugees is not unlimited, and therefore that there may justifiably be selection among those who are claiming refugee status. First, it is a responsibility that falls upon all states able to provide the necessary refuge, and each state, therefore, is only required to discharge its fair share of that responsibility. Ideally this would be done by entering into an international scheme for placing refugees according to each state's capacity to absorb them.[9] In the absence of such a scheme, it is permissible for states to enter into bilateral or multilateral agreements whereby states who receive more asylum applications that they are obliged to accept can pass asylum-seekers on to other places willing to take them in, provided always that their human rights will be adequately safeguarded in those places. Second, the obligation is an obligation to provide temporary sanctuary, and it only becomes an obligation to grant permanent residence in cases where it becomes clear that the refugee has no realistic prospect of returning safely to her own society within a reasonable space of time.

On these assumptions, receiving states may have to select, among those who can prove their claim to refugee status, people they will take in themselves and others who they will pass on under one of the arrangements outlined above. So what grounds for selection are permissible? Consider four possibilities: 1) The refugee's need for permanent settlement; 2) The causal role played by the receiving state in creating the situation from which the refugee is escaping; 3) The likely economic contribution of the refugee to the receiving society; 4) The degree of cultural affinity between refugee and host political community.

1) This seems a relevant consideration. Although the places to which refugees are transferred must be human rights compliant, and this means that they provide all the opportunities that are needed to live a decent human life and not just food, shelter and the other immediate necessities, under the kind of arrangement envisaged (realistically one in which rich developed states pass on a proportion of those

who apply for asylum to less developed countries) there will inevitably be less assurance that the same opportunities will continue to be available far into the future. This matters less if the stay is only going to be temporary.

2) Consider next situations in which the state to which the asylum-seeker applies is at least in part responsible for making her into a refugee. These will typically be cases in which it has intervened in her country of origin, creating conflicts between national or ethnic groups that expose her to threats of persecution—for example the position of some Iraqi Kurds after the Iraq war. The granting of asylum may then be viewed as a form of reparation.[10] This makes the refugee into a particularity claimant, and provides grounds why she should be admitted to the state in question rather than to some other place—her reparative claim is a claim against that state in particular, and may not be satisfied by a promise of refuge somewhere else (this will depend on the extent of her loss). As Souter argues, refugees' choices about where to claim asylum gain additional significance in these circumstances: 'after causing or contributing to their displacement, heeding refugees' wishes is the least that responsible states can do'.[11] Indeed they may be able to claim not just temporary asylum but permanent residence on reparative grounds.

3) Many states choose which immigrants to accept by examining whether they bring special skills that will contribute to the economy. But can this criterion also be used, legitimately, when deciding which asylum-seekers to admit? Keeping in mind that the refugee's claim is based on the threat to his human rights, not on his potential contribution, it might seem arbitrary to give him any kind of priority on this basis. Certainly it would be unacceptable if the asylum claim itself were to be assessed more generously in the case of those who were seen as having valuable skills. But assume that the latter claim is assessed strictly on the grounds of the seriousness of the threat to the asylum-seeker's human rights, could productive skill nevertheless count at the second stage, when deciding whether asylum is offered in the state of first entry or somewhere else? I believe this would be legitimate only in cases where the state is offering something more than asylum to the refugee—when it is offering permanent resettlement to someone who does not automatically qualify for it. States are surely permitted to do this, in the same way that they can offer resettlement to refugees who have been granted asylum elsewhere, and when they do so it is reasonable to take account of the refugee's prospective contribution.[12]

4) Can states select in favour of their cultural kin when deciding who to admit as refugees? The rationale for this is set out clearly by Carens, though it is not so clear whether he accepts it himself:

> As an empirical matter, it is almost certainly the case that a state's willingness to take in refugees will depend in part on the extent to which the current population identifies with the refugees and their plight. Moreover, other things being equal, it will be easier for the refugees themselves to adapt to the new society and for the receiving society to include them, the more the refugees resemble the existing population with respect to language, culture, religion, history, and so on.[13]

To take a concrete example, the wars in Syria and Iraq in 2014 led to calls in some quarters for traditionally Christian countries such as the UK to give priority to Christian refugees escaping from these countries. This was in justified in part on the grounds that Christian families were undergoing particularly severe persecution, but also on the grounds that Christian states had special obligations to people who shared their national religion. The first part of this claim is clearly relevant, but what about the second?

Such an argument from common culture seems hard to defend, unless it can be presented as a way of dividing responsibilities between states. In the Iraq/Syria case it was claimed that Muslim refugees would be more likely to be offered sanctuary by neighbouring Islamic states such as Jordan. Assuming this is true, and that states more generally are inclined to give precedence to those who share their citizens' cultural or religious values, then it would be justifiable for each state to take this into account. But without such a background, and considering the nature of the obligation towards refugees, cultural selection does not seem defensible.

I turn now to selection criteria for immigrants who make no claim to refugee status—'economic migrants' in the broad sense. Since states have discretion over whether to admit such immigrants in the first place, it might seem that they have *carte blanche* as to whom they select, even if this means choosing on grounds of race or national origin (such as occurred with the notorious 'White Australia' policy of the 1920s and 1930s). How can we show that this does not follow? It might appear to be ruled out by the human right against discrimination. But on closer inspection this turns out to be too weak an instrument, since there are contexts in which it seems perfectly permissible to discriminate on grounds, for example, of gender, language, or religion. It isn't a breach of human rights if a political party decides to draw up an all-women short list to select its candidate in a particular constituency, if a public broadcaster chooses only among those able to read the news in Welsh, or a church confines membership to those who belong to its own faith. So the human right against discrimination must be interpreted as prohibiting discrimination on grounds *that are irrelevant to the right or benefit being allocated.* Those who in the past defended selecting immigrants by race or national origin thought that they could justify using these criteria by appeal to the need to preserve the 'character' or 'moral health' of their societies. To defeat these arguments requires showing that such claims are either false, or irrelevant, for substantive reasons.

An initially more promising avenue is to argue that selecting immigrants on grounds such as race or religion is an injustice to some existing citizens, namely those who belong to the group or groups that the immigration policy disfavours.[14] By discriminating in this way, the state appears to be labelling these people as second-class citizens. As Michael Blake has put the point, 'the state making a statement of racial preference in immigration necessarily makes a statement of racial preference domestically as well'.[15] This will often provide states with strong reasons not to pursue discriminatory admissions policies, but a limitation of this approach is that it would not apply to a state that was already religiously or ethnically

homogeneous and whose members wished it to remain so.[16] Notice also that the argument hinges upon the injustice that is done to existing citizens whose status is lowered by the discriminatory policy, not on any wrong that is done specifically to the excluded candidates for admission, and this seems to put the emphasis in the wrong place.

Although an economic migrant cannot assert a right to be admitted, she does typically have a strong *claim*, based on how her interests will be advanced by moving—for example through working in a different kind of job, or for a much higher wage, than she could hope to obtain at home. According to the weak cosmopolitan premise stipulated above, to turn down such a claim without giving relevant reasons for the refusal is to show disrespect for the person making it. It is to treat her as though she were of no moral significance. This extends also to the selection of immigrants from the pool of applicants. It is not sufficient merely to put forward the general reasons in favour of immigration controls. If John is going to be granted entry while Jaime is turned away, the latter must be offered relevant reasons for his unequal treatment.

This appeal to weak cosmopolitanism explains why the state is not entitled to use merely arbitrary methods in choosing which immigrants to admit, but it does not yet settle which reasons should count in making the selection, and so far, therefore, does not explain what is wrong about using race, ethnicity, and other such criteria. One way to narrow down the list is to say that the reasons must be ones that the immigrants themselves can accept. It is obvious enough that no immigrant will regard her own skin colour as legitimate grounds for exclusion. But a problem then arises in cases where the receiving state and the prospective immigrant hold different views about what should count as relevant. Suppose, for example, that a state decides to admit only high-skilled immigrants on the grounds that it has a greater economic need for these than for low-skilled workers. An immigrant without the relevant skills might reject this on the grounds that he (and others like him) deserves a chance to improve his condition. So it is asking too much to say that the reasons the state gives must also be ones that the immigrants can accept (if 'can accept' means 'will in fact accept once these reasons are explained'). Instead the relevant condition is that the reasons the state gives for its selective admissions policy must be good reasons, reasons that the immigrants *ought* to accept given the general aims of the policy.[17]

A more difficult question is whether it can be justifiable to select in favour of those who already have the political or cultural attributes that will enable them to fit more easily into the society they are joining. Consider political attributes first: can liberal democracies choose immigrants who have already demonstrated their democratic credentials as opposed to those who espouse other political values, assuming that this can be reliably established? Most commentators, including strong liberals such as Carens, agree that states may exclude people who pose a threat to national security by virtue of the beliefs that they hold, such as those liable to engage in terrorist acts.[18] But in such cases it is the disposition to act, rather than the beliefs themselves, that forms the reason for exclusion. What about those whose political beliefs are such that they do not acknowledge the authority of the state they wish to join, even though they have no intention of sabotaging it by violent or other means? All states, not least liberal states, depend on their members complying voluntarily with their laws most of the time, and presumably a belief in the state's legitimacy is one of the main sources of compliance. Someone who lacks that belief may keep the law for other reasons (prudence, respect for the rights of others) but is likely to be less reliable in carrying out her duties as a citizen. So there is some reason for favouring already committed democrats when choosing immigrants. On the other hand, liberal democracies do not require all of their existing citizens to sign up personally to their founding principles: they are prepared to tolerate anarchists, fascists and others, leaving them free to express their beliefs and to attempt to persuade others of their correctness within the limits of the law. On balance, then, selection on political grounds would be justifiable only in cases where illiberal or anti-democratic immigrants were applying in sufficient numbers that their presence would create social conflicts or disrupt the working of democratic institutions.[19]

The argument that can be made for cultural selection raises different questions. We are contemplating here immigrant groups whose cultural affiliations are different from those of the majority of existing citizens—though we should also distinguish between cases where the existing state is already multicultural and has enacted multicultural policies (e.g. Canada), and cases in which it is more culturally homogeneous (e.g. Japan): the issue becomes more pressing in the latter circumstances. Immigrants who speak a different language, practise a different religion, or have a different lifestyle from the majority may pose two kinds of problem. The first is simply the cost of incorporating them into the host society on terms of equality. There will, for example, be the cost of translating public documents into a new language or of providing translators in courts and social service agencies; or if religion is the source of the division, the cost of accommodating religious practices where these impose different requirements on believers outside of the mainstream. Some of these costs can be passed to the immigrants themselves, but others will be borne by the state, and indirectly, therefore, by citizens at large.

There are of course likely to be compensating benefits that come with increasing cultural diversity. The point is simply that if we look at (economic) immigration as a practice that is governed by the logic of mutual advantage, both costs and benefits need to be factored in when considering selection policy. Some of the costs may only be apparent with hindsight, as it becomes clear what the equal treatment of minority cultures actually requires. This also applies to the second potential problem. Culture is not only a matter of belief or of practice, but also of personal identity. This raises a concern about the way in which culture can come to constitute a line of fracture within a political community, possibly leading to the formation of 'parallel societies', whose members have very little contact with those beyond their own community; and also a concern about the effects of cultural diversity on social trust, and through that on people's willingness to support welfare states and other instruments of social justice. These are by no means inevitable consequences of admitting immigrants with cultural backgrounds different from those of the majority, but they are *possible* consequences, and avoiding them may again prove to be somewhat costly, this time in the form of support for active integration programmes. This is the point at which the state's existing cultural character becomes important: a state that is already well-equipped with multicultural policies can more easily tackle these problems than one that is not. There is, however, no independent requirement that a state should embrace multiculturalism prior to deciding upon its admission policy. Democracies are entitled to decide how far they wish to protect their inherited national cultures, and how far to encourage cultural diversity within their borders.

To sum up, selective immigration requires that states give reasons for the policies they apply, and these reasons must relate to the legitimate purposes of the state itself, as manifested in its other policy decisions. Selection on economic grounds is the least controversial example, but other forms of positive discrimination cannot be ruled out: if a society wants to enhance its sporting reputation, for example, I cannot see why it should not seek to attract immigrants who will later qualify for the national teams. Giving reasons of this kind shows sufficient respect for those who are refused entry, disappointed though they may be. Recall that the later part of the discussion relates only to *economic migrants*. Where refugees are concerned, there is much less scope for selecting on grounds other than the refugee's own need for sanctuary and the opportunity for a decent life.

NOTES

1. N. Esipova, J. Ray, and R. Srinivasan, *The World's Potential Migrants: Who They Are, Where They Want to Go, and Why It Matters* (Gallup Inc., 2010–2011). Overall, 40% of those living in the poorest quartile of countries have expressed a wish to migrate—see P. Collier, *Exodus: Immigration and Multiculturalism in the 21st Century* (London: Allen Lane, 2013) p. 167.

2. See http://www.harrisinteractive.com/vault/HI_UK_News_Daily_Mail_Poll-Nov13.pdf.

3. See E. Iversflaten, 'Threatened by diversity: Why restrictive asylum and immigration policies appeal to western Europeans', *Journal of Elections, Public Opinion and Parties*, 15 (2005), 21–45.

4. For shorter defences, see D. Miller, 'Immigration: the case for limits' in A. Cohen and C. Wellman (eds.), *Contemporary*

Debates in Applied Ethics (Oxford: Blackwell, 2005); D. Miller, 'Is there a Human Right to Immigrate?' in S. Fine and L. Ypi (eds.), *Migration in Political Theory: The Ethics of Movement and Membership* (Oxford: Oxford University Press, 2016). My most complete treatment is D. Miller, *Strangers in Our Midst: The Political Philosophy of Immigration* (Cambridge, MA: Harvard University Press, 2016).

5. In some cases, however, it might *lead to* a violation of that person's human rights: the distinction is important.

6. Someone might ask why, if there is no human right to immigrate, states have to justify their refusal to those they exclude. But compare applicants for a job: no-one has a right to that job, but they are nonetheless entitled to be selected by a fair procedure, and to be given reasons for why they were not chosen.

7. For example the Ugandan Asians who held British passports but whose right to immigrate was abruptly removed by the Immigration Act of 1971. When Idi Amin came to power and threatened to expel them at short notice, the British Government recognized its obligation and allowed them to enter. The episode is described in R. Winder, *Bloody Foreigners: The Story of Immigration to Britain* (London: Little Brown, 2004), ch. 22.

8. Consider the case of the Nepalese Ghurkhas who, after serving in the British Army, have sought the right to reside in Britain after retiring. This right was granted to them by a High Court decision in 2008. According to the actress Joanna Lumley who spearheaded their campaign, 'The whole campaign has been based on the belief that those who have fought and been prepared to die for our country should have the right to live in our country' (http://www.gurkhajustice.org.uk/).

9. There is a substantial literature on refugee burden-sharing schemes, and the criteria that might be used to judge each state's quota. For a helpful review, see T. Kritzman-Amir, 'Not in My Backyard: On the Morality of Responsibility Sharing in Refugee Law', *Brooklyn Journal of International Law*, 34 (2009), Part III.

10. See J. Souter, 'Towards a Theory of Asylum as Reparation for Past Injustice', *Political Studies*, 62 (2014), 326–42 who provides a detailed analysis of the conditions under which asylum claims of this kind are valid.

11. Souter, 'Asylum as Reparation for Past Injustice', pp. 335–36.

12. Could those who are moved elsewhere under a burden-sharing arrangement complain about the unequal treatment they are receiving? I do not think so. The important point is that they are treated equally at the point at which their claim to asylum is assessed, and thereafter in ways that respect their

human rights. That the state does more for some refugees than it is obliged to do is not an injustice to the others.

13. J. Carens, *The Ethics of Immigration* (New York: Oxford University Press, 2013), p. 214.

14. It is followed in J. Carens, 'Who Should Get In? The Ethics of Immigration Admissions', *Ethics and International Affairs*, 17 (2003), 95–110, and at greater length in M. Blake, 'Discretionary Immigration', *Philosophical Topics* 30 (2002), 273–89, and M. Blake, 'Immigration', in R. Frey and C. Wellman (eds.), *A Companion to Applied Ethics* (Oxford: Blackwell, 2003). I also used the argument in an earlier discussion: D. Miller, *National Responsibility and Global Justice* (Oxford: Oxford University Press, 2007), ch. 8.

15. M. Blake, 'Discretionary Immigration', p. 284.

16. This is conceded by Blake in Blake, 'Discretionary Immigration', p. 285. See also M. Walzer, *Spheres of Justice* (Oxford: Martin Robertson, 1983, pp. 35–51) and the discussion in Blake, 'Immigration'.

17. A rather similar position is taken in Blake, 'Immigration and Political Equality', where it is formulated in the language of 'reasons that immigrants could not reasonably reject' (p. 971).

18. Carens, *The Ethics of Immigration*, ch. 9.

19. As Carens puts it 'the problem is not with any single immigrant's views, but with the collective effect of ideas hostile to democracy' (Carens, *The Ethics of Immigration*, p. 176).

Immigration and Freedom of Association

Christopher Heath Wellman

In this article I appeal to freedom of association to defend a state's right to control immigration over its territorial borders. Without denying that those of us in wealthy societies may have extremely demanding duties of global distributive justice, I ultimately reach the stark conclusion that every legitimate state has the right to close its doors to all potential immigrants, even refugees desperately seeking asylum from incompetent or corrupt political regimes that are either unable or unwilling to protect their citizens' basic moral rights.

This article is divided into four sections. First, I argue for a presumptive case in favor of a state's right to limit immigration as an instance of its more general right to freedom of association. In the second and third sections, I respond to egalitarian and libertarian cases for open borders. Finally, in the fourth section, I consider the permissibility of screening immigrants based upon their race, ethnicity or religion.

Christopher Heath Wellman, "Immigration and Freedom of Association," *Ethics* 119 (October 2008), 109–41. © 2008 by The University of Chicago. Reprinted by permission of The University of Chicago Press.

I. THE CASE FOR THE RIGHT TO CLOSED BORDERS

To appreciate the presumptive case in favor of a state's right to control its borders that can be built upon the right to freedom of association, notice both that (1) freedom of association is widely thought to be important and that (2) it includes the right not to associate and even, in many cases, the right to disassociate.

That freedom of association is highly valued is evident from our views on marriage and religion. In the past, it was thought appropriate for one's father to select one's marital partner or for one's state to determine the religion one practiced, but, thankfully, those times have (largely) passed. Today, virtually everyone agrees that we are entitled to marital and religious freedom of association; we take it for granted that each individual has a right to choose his or her marital partner and the associates with whom he or she practices his or her religion. Put plainly, among our most firmly settled convictions is the belief that each of us enjoys a morally privileged position of dominion over our self-regarding affairs, a position which entitles us to freedom of association in the marital and religious realms.

Second, notice that freedom of association includes a right to reject a potential association and (often) a right to disassociate. As Stuart White explains: "Freedom of association is widely seen as one of those basic freedoms which is fundamental to a genuinely free society. With the freedom to associate, however, there comes the freedom to refuse association. When a group of people get together to form an association of some kind (e.g., a religious association, a trade union, a sports club), they will frequently wish to exclude some people from joining their association. What makes it *their* association, serving their purposes, is that they can exercise this 'right to exclude.' "[1]

In the case of matrimony, for instance, this freedom involves more than merely having the right to get married. One fully enjoys freedom of association only if one may choose whether or not to marry a second party who would have one as a partner. Thus, one must not only be permitted to marry a willing partner whom one accepts; one must also have the discretion to reject the proposal of any given suitor and even to remain single indefinitely if one so chooses. As David Gauthier puts it, "I may have the right to choose the woman of my choice who also chooses me, but not the woman of my choice who rejects me."[2] We understand religious self-determination similarly: whether, how, and with whom I attend to my humanity is up to me as an individual. If I elect to explore my religious nature in community with others, I have no duty to do so with anyone in particular, and I have no right to force others to allow me to join them in worship.

In light of our views on marriage and religious self-determination, the case for a state's right to control immigration might seem straight-forward: just as an individual has a right to determine whom (if anyone) he or she would like to marry, a group of fellow-citizens has a right to determine whom (if anyone) it would like to invite into its political community. And just as an individual's freedom of association entitles one to remain single, a state's freedom of association entitles it to exclude all foreigners from its political community. There are at least two reasons that this inference from an individual's to a state's right to freedom of association might strike some as problematic,

however. First, presumably there are morally relevant differences between individuals and groups, and these differences might explain why only individuals can have a right to self-determination. Second, even if it is possible for groups to have rights, presumably the interests a group of citizens might have in controlling immigration are nowhere near as important as an individual's interest in having a decisive say regarding who he or she marries. Let us consider these two issues in turn.

In response to concerns about the differences between individuals and groups, let me begin by highlighting some commonly held convictions which illustrate that we typically posit at least a presumptive group right to freedom of association. Think, for instance, of the controversy that has surrounded groups like the Boy Scouts of America or the Augusta National Golf Club, both of which have faced considerable public pressure and even legal challenges regarding their rights to freedom of association. In particular, some have contested the Boy Scouts' right to exclude homosexuals and atheists, while others have criticized Augusta National's exclusion of women.[3] These cases raise a number of thorny issues. We need not adjudicate either of these conflicts here, however, because the requisite point for our purposes is a minimal one. Specifically, notice that even those who insist that the Boy Scouts should be legally forced to include gays and atheists or that Augusta National cannot justify their continued exclusion of women typically concede that there are weighty reasons in favor of allowing these groups to determine their own membership. That is, even activists lobbying for intervention usually acknowledge that there are reasons to respect these groups' rights to autonomy; the activists claim only that the prima facie case in favor of group self-determination is liable to be outweighed in sufficiently compelling instances (e.g., when society as a whole discriminates against women or privileges theism and heterosexuality over atheism and homosexuality). The key point, of course, is that questioning Augusta National's group right to determine its own membership does not require one to deny that groups have a presumptive right to freedom of association because one could simply assert that this presumptive right is vulnerable to being overridden. And because I seek at this stage to defend only a presumptive case in favor of a state's right to control its own borders, it is enough to note how uncontroversial it is to posit a group's right to freedom of association.

There is still room to question my slide from an individual's to a state's right to freedom of association, however, because, unlike the Boy Scouts and the Augusta National Golf Club, political states do not owe their membership to the autonomous choices of their constituents. The nonvoluntary nature of political states can raise complex problems for those who would defend a state's right to political self-determination (problems I address at length elsewhere), but here I would like merely to highlight some of the unpalatable implications that follow from denying a country's right to freedom of association.[4] In particular, consider the moral dynamics of regional associations like the North American Free Trade Agreement (NAFTA) or the European Union (EU). If legitimate states did not enjoy a right to freedom of association—a right which entitles them to decline invitations to associate with others—then they would not be in a position to either accept or reject the terms of these regional associations. Think of Canada's choice to join NAFTA, or Slovenia's decision to enter the EU, for instance. No one believes that it would be permissible to force Canada into NAFTA or to coerce Slovenia to join the EU. (Of course, nor may Canada or Slovenia unilaterally insert themselves into these associations!) And the reason it is wrong to forcibly include these countries is because Canada's and Slovenia's rights to self-determination entitle them to associate (or not) with other countries as they see fit. Put plainly, if one denies that legitimate states like Canada and Slovenia have a right to freedom of association, one could not explain why they would be righteously aggrieved at being forced into these mergers.

Indeed, there would be even more awkward implications because, without positing a right to freedom of association, we could not satisfactorily explain what is wrong with one country forcibly annexing another. Imagine, for instance, that a series of plebiscites revealed both that an overwhelming majority of Americans wanted to merge with Canada and that

an equally high proportion of Canadians preferred to maintain their independence. Would it be permissible for the United States to forcibly annex Canada? I assume without argument that, even if the United States could execute this unilateral merger without disrupting the peace or violating the individual rights of any Canadians, this hostile takeover would be impermissible. The crucial point for our purposes is that one cannot explain the wrongness of unilateral annexations like this unless one supposes that countries like Canada enjoy a right to autonomy, a right which accords Canadians the freedom to associate with others as they see fit.[5]

If the analysis to this point has been sound, then there is no reason to doubt that groups, even political states, can have rights to autonomy analogous to those enjoyed by individuals. Even if one agrees that legitimate states can have rights to self-determination, though, one might still question the argument sketched above on the grounds that the intimacy of marriage makes freedom of association immeasurably more important in the marital context than in the political realm. After all, in the vast majority of cases, fellow citizens will never even meet one another. On this point, consider Stuart White's contention that "if the formation of a specific association is essential to the individual's ability to exercise properly his/her liberties of conscience and expression, *or to his/her ability to form and enjoy intimate attachments*, then exclusion rules which are genuinely necessary to protect the association's primary purposes have an especially strong presumption of legitimacy."[6] Transposing White's reasoning, one might insist that, since there is no intimacy among compatriots, it is not at all clear why we need to respect freedom of association for groups of citizens.[7]

I concede that freedom of association is much more important for individuals in the marital context than for groups of citizens in the political realm, but my argument does not rely upon these two types of freedom of association being equally important. Notice, for instance, that being able to choose the associates with whom one worships is also less important than having discretion over one's marital partner, but no one concludes from this that we need not respect freedom of association in the religious realm. It is important to recognize that I seek at this stage to establish only that there is a prima facie case in favor of each legitimate state's right to control immigration (it will be the burden of the remainder of this article to show that competing considerations are not as weighty as one might think). Nonetheless, let me say a bit more about this presumptive case.

In my view, autonomous individuals and legitimate states both have rights to autonomy. This means that they occupy morally privileged positions of dominion over their self-regarding affairs. Such a position can be outweighed by sufficiently compelling considerations, of course, but in general people and states have a right to order their own affairs as they please. Freedom of association is not something that requires an elaborate justification, then, since it is simply one component of the self-determination which is owed to all autonomous individuals and legitimate states. As a consequence, I think that there is a very natural and straightforward case to be made in favor of freedom of association in all realms. Just as one need not explain how playing golf is inextricably related to the development of one's moral personality, say, in order to justify one's right to play golf, neither must one show that one's membership in a golf club is crucial to one's basic interests to establish the club members' right to freedom of association. And if no one doubts that golf clubs have a presumptive right to exclude others, then there seems no reason to suspect that a group of citizens cannot also have the right to freedom of association, even if control over membership in a country is not nearly as significant as control regarding one's potential spouse.

What is more, for several reasons it seems clear that control over membership in one's state is extremely important. To see this, think about why people might care about the membership rules for their golf club. It is tempting to think that club members would be irrational to care about who else are (or could become) members; after all, they are not forced to actually play golf with those members they dislike. But this perspective misses something important. Members of golf clubs typically care about the membership rules because they care about how the club

is organized and the new members have a say in how the club is organized. Some members might want to dramatically increase the number of members, for instance, because the increased numbers will mean that each individual is required to pay less. Other members might oppose expanding the membership because of concerns about the difficulty of securing desirable tee times, the wear and tear on the course, and the increased time it takes to play a round if there are more people on the course at any given time.

And if there is nothing mysterious about people caring about who are (or could become) members of their golf clubs, there is certainly nothing irrational about people being heavily invested in their country's immigration policy. Again, to note the lack of intimacy among compatriots is to miss an important part of the story. It is no good to tell citizens that they need not personally (let alone intimately) associate with any fellow citizens they happen to dislike because fellow citizens nonetheless remain political associates; the country's course will be charted by the members of this civic association. The point is that people rightly care very deeply about their countries, and, as a consequence, they rightly care about those policies which will effect how these political communities evolve. And since a country's immigration policy affects who will share in controlling the country's future, it is a matter of considerable importance.

These examples of the golf club and the political state point toward a more general lesson that is worth emphasizing: because the members of a group can change, an important part of group self-determination is having control over what the "self" is. In other words, unlike individual self-determination, a significant component of group self-determination is having control over the group which in turn gets to be self-determining. It stands to reason, then, that if there is any group whose self-determination we care about, we should be concerned about its rules for membership. This explains why freedom of association is such an integral part of the self-determination to which some groups (including legitimate states) are entitled. If so, then anyone who denies that we should care about the freedom of association of nonintimate groups would seem to be committed to the more sweeping claim that we should not care about the self-determination of any nonintimate groups. But, unless one implausibly believes that we should care only about intimate groups, then why should we suppose that only the self-determination of intimate groups matters? Thus, people rightly care deeply about their political states, despite these states being large, anonymous, and multicultural, and, as a consequence, people rightly care about the rules for gaining membership in these states. Or, put another way, the very same reasoning which understandably leads people to jealously guard their state's sovereignty also motivates them to keep an eye on who can gain membership in this sovereign state.

A second, less obvious, reason to care about immigration policy has to do with one's duties of distributive justice. As I will argue in the next section, it seems reasonable to think that we have special distributive responsibilities to our fellow citizens. If this is right, then in the same way that one might be reluctant to form intimate relationships because of the moral freight attached, one might want to limit the number of people with whom one shares a morally significant political relationship. Thus, just as golf club members can disagree about the costs and benefits of adding new members, some citizens might want to open the doors to new immigrants (e.g., in order to expand the labor force), while others would much rather forgo these advantages than incur special obligations to a greater number of people.

Finally, rather than continue to list reasons why citizens ought to care about issues of political membership, let me merely point out that citizens today obviously do care passionately about immigration. I do not insist that the current fervor over political membership is entirely rational, but it is worth nothing that anyone who submits that freedom of association in this context is of no real importance is committed to labeling all those who care about this issue as patently irrational. Thus, even though the relationship among citizens does not involve the morally relevant intimacy of that between marital partners, the considerations quickly canvassed above, as well as the behavior of actual citizens, indicate that we need not conclude that control over immigration is therefore of negligible

significance. If so, then neither the observation that (1) individual persons are importantly disanalogous to political states nor the fact that (2) freedom of association is much more important for individuals in the marital context than for groups of citizens in the political realm should lead us to abandon our initial comparison between marriage and immigration. As a consequence, we have no reason to abandon the claim that, like autonomous individuals, legitimate political regimes are entitled to a degree of self-determination, one important component of which is freedom of association. In sum, the conclusion initially offered only tentatively can now be endorsed with greater conviction: just as an individual has a right to determine whom (if anyone) he or she would like to marry, a group of fellow-citizens has a right to determine whom (if anyone) it would like to invite into its political community. And just as an individual's freedom of association entitles him or her to remain single, a state's freedom of association entitles it to exclude all foreigners from its political community.

Before turning to the case against political freedom of association, I would like to highlight two features of the view I am advancing here: (1) I defend a deontological right to limit immigration rather than a consequential account of what would be best, and (2) my view might be dubbed "universalist" rather than "particularist" insofar as it neither suggests nor implies that only distinct nations, cultures, or other "communities of character" are entitled to limit immigration. Consider each of these points in turn.

First, let me stress that I seek to defend a deontological conclusion about how legitimate states are entitled to act, not a consequential prescription for how to maximize happiness or a practical recipe for how states might best promote their own interests. I understand that groups can have weighty reasons to limit immigration in certain circumstances, but what the best policy would be for any given state's constituents (and/or for those foreigners affected) will presumably depend upon a variety of empirical matters, matters about which others are more knowledgeable. Thus, I doubt that any one-size-fits-all immigration policy exists, and I, qua philosopher, have no special qualification to comment on the empirical information that would be relevant to fashioning the best policy for any given state. However, if anything, I am personally inclined toward more open borders. My parents were born and raised in different countries, so I would not even be here to write this article if people were not free to cross political borders. What is more, my family and I have profited enormously from having lived and worked in several different countries, so it should come as no surprise that I believe that, just as few individuals flourish in personal isolation, open borders are typically (and within limits) best for political communities and their constituents. Still, just as one might defend the right to divorce without believing that many couples should in fact separate, I defend a legitimate state's right to control its borders without suggesting that strict limits on immigration would necessarily maximize the interests of either the state's constituents or humanity as a whole. My aim is merely to show that whatever deontological reasons there are to respect freedom of association count in favor of allowing political communities to set their own immigration policy.

I hasten to emphasize, however, that, while I conceive of freedom of association in deontological terms, I do not thereby suppose that it is necessarily absolute. I consider freedom of association a deontological matter because it is something to which a party can be entitled (it is something to which people can have a moral right), and I do not believe that matters of entitlement can be adequately cashed out in exclusively consequential terms. In saying this, however, I do not thereby commit myself to the view that such a right must be perfectly general and absolute. A right can be independent of, and largely immune from, consequential calculus without being entirely invulnerable to being out-weighed by all competing considerations. (Prince William has a right to marry anyone who will have him, for instance. And while this right gives him the discretion to marry any number of people, presumably it would be defeated if his marrying a particular person would set off a chain of events leading to World War III.) In this regard, my views tend to resemble those of W.D. Ross more than those of Immanuel Kant. Moreover, like Ross, I know of no algorithm for determining in advance when

and under what circumstances a party's right to freedom of association would be defeated. In the end, then, I see nothing contradictory about conceiving of freedom of association as a deontological consideration (and thus of speaking of a right to choose one's associates) and simultaneously conceding that the case in favor of freedom of association is merely presumptive.

The second aspect of my account worth highlighting is that my defense of freedom of association makes no mention of a political community's distinctive character or culture. I emphasize this to distinguish myself from those who argue that ethnic, cultural, or national groups have a right to limit immigration in order to preserve their distinctive characters. In particular, the most compelling treatments of the morality of immigration with which I am familiar are Michael Walzer's seminal discussion of membership in *Spheres of Justice* and David Miller's recent article, "Immigration: The Case for Limits."[8] Other ways in which my account diverges from theirs will become apparent in due course; for now, notice that Walzer and Miller both emphasize the importance of preserving culture. As Walzer puts it: "Admission and exclusion are at the core of communal independence. They suggest the deepest meaning of self-determination. Without them, there could not be *communities of character*, historically stable, ongoing associations of men and women with some special commitment to one another and some special sense of their common life."[9]

In a similar vein, Miller suggests that "the public culture of their country is something that people have an interest in controlling: they want to be able to shape the way that their nation develops, including the values that are contained in the public culture."[10] He is especially interested in political groups being able to preserve their distinctive identities because he believes that states must maintain a decent level of social solidarity in order to secure social justice. Unless compatriots sufficiently identify with one another, Miller argues, it is unlikely that the political climate will engender mutual trust or fellow feeling, elements liberal democratic states need if they are to inspire their constituents to make the sacrifices necessary to sustain a healthy democracy and an equitable welfare state.

In contrast to authors like Walzer and Miller, my account emphasizes that anyone is entitled to freedom of association. Thus, just as few would suggest that individuals have a right to marry only people of their own ethnicity, culture, nationality, or character, I do not believe that a group's right to limit immigration depends upon its members sharing any distinctive ethnic/cultural/national characteristics.

Now, I could certainly see why distinct cultural groups might in certain circumstances be more interested in or more inclined to exclude others, but I deny that they alone have the right to do so, since I believe that everyone—not just members of distinct nations—is entitled to freedom of association. To see why, think again of groups like the Boy Scouts or the Augusta National Golf Club. I presume that no one would suggest that the Boy Scouts are entitled to freedom of association only because they are all heterosexual theists or that Augusta National's claim to group autonomy depends upon their membership being all male. Indeed, if anything, it is just the opposite: the group autonomy of the Boy Scouts and Augusta National is challenged precisely because the former explicitly exclude gays and atheists and the latter has no female members. And since more diverse groups of scouts or golf club members would be at least equally entitled to freedom of association, there seems no reason to believe that only groups whose members share a distinctive characteristic are entitled to freedom of association. If so, then we need not suppose that only populations with distinct characters are entitled to limit immigration into their territories. To reiterate: even if it is true that countries whose populations understand themselves to be importantly distinct from (most) foreigners exhibit the greatest interest in excluding nonnatives, we should not infer from this that only these groups are entitled to control their territorial borders.

In sum, the commonly prized value of freedom of association provides the basic normative building blocks for a presumptive case in favor of each legitimate state's right to exclude others from its territory. But, while freedom of association provides a weighty consideration in favor of a state's right to limit immigration, it is obviously not the only value of importance. Thus, even if my reasoning to this point has been sound, the case in favor of a state's dominion is only presumptive and may be outweighed by competing considerations. With this in mind, let us now review the arguments in favor of open borders to see if they defeat a state's right to limit immigration.

II. THE EGALITARIAN CASE FOR OPEN BORDERS

Egalitarians survey the vast inequalities among states and then allege that it is horribly unjust that people should have such dramatically different life prospects simply because they are born in different countries. The force of this view is not difficult to appreciate. Given that one's country of birth is a function of brute luck, it seems grossly unfair that one's place of birth would so profoundly affect one's life prospects. Some believe that the solution is clear: political borders must be opened, so that no one is denied access to the benefits of wealthy societies. Although he couches his argument in terms of a principle of humanity rather than equality, Chandran Kukathas makes this point particularly forcefully: "A principle of humanity suggests that very good reasons must be offered to justify turning the disadvantaged away. It would be bad enough to meet such people with indifference and to deny them positive assistance. It would be even worse to deny them the opportunity to help themselves. To go to the length of denying one's fellow citizens the right to help those who are badly off, whether by employing them or by simply taking them in, seems even more difficult to justify—if, indeed, it is not entirely perverse."[11]

For several reasons, this case for open borders presents an especially imposing obstacle to the prima facie case for the right to restrict immigration outlined above. For starters, both its moral and empirical premises appear unexceptionable. How could one plausibly deny either that all humans are in some fundamental sense equally deserving of moral consideration or that the staggering inequalities across the globe dramatically affect people's prospects for living a decent life? Indeed, looked at from this perspective, sorting humans according to the countries in which they were born appears tantamount to a geographical caste system. As Joseph Carens famously argues: "Citizenship in Western liberal democracies is the modern equivalent to feudal privilege—an inherited status that greatly enhances one's life chances. Like feudal birthright privileges, restrictive citizenship is hard to justify when one thinks about it closely."[12] What is more, notice that advocating this position does not require one to deny the importance of freedom of association: an egalitarian who presses this objection can agree that we should generally be free to choose our associates, as long as the resulting associations do not lead to unjust arrangements. Thus, allowing states to limit immigration is regarded as problematic on this view only because countries cannot enjoy this form of freedom of association without people's life prospects being seriously affected by morally irrelevant matters, that is, factors entirely beyond their control.

Despite the intuitive appeal of this line of reasoning, I will counter this objection with two arguments. First, I suggest that the most compelling understanding of equality does not require us to guarantee that no one's life prospects are affected by matters of luck; more minimally, equality demands that we address those inequalities that render people vulnerable to oppressive relationships. If this is correct, then the particular theory of equality required to motivate the egalitarian case for open borders is suspect and should be rejected in favor of a theory of relational equality. Second, even if luck egalitarianism is the best theory of equality, it would not generate a duty to leave borders open, because a wealthy state's redistributive responsibilities can be discharged without including the recipients in the union. Consider each of these responses in turn.

I should begin by acknowledging the obvious appeal of luck egalitarianism. After all, it does seem unfair that some people's life prospects are dramatically worse than others when neither the poorly off nor the well off did anything to deserve their initial starting points. And it is hard to deny that the world would be better if everyone enjoyed roughly equal prospects for a rewarding life. It is important to

recognize, though, that luck egalitarianism is not the only game in town. In *Political Philosophy*, for instance, Jean Hampton recommends an approach she ascribes to Aristotle: "We want, he says, a society in which people treat each other as equals (no one should be allowed to be the master of another or the slave of another) and in which these equals treat each other as partners—or 'civic friends.' The way to get that is to pursue not exact equality of resources but sufficient equality to ensure that no one is able to use his greater wealth to gain political advantage over others in a way that damages their partnership."[13]

Now, one might be struck by Hampton's suggestion that we need not pursue "exact" equality, but I want to call attention to another, related feature of her view: its relational nature. As Hampton emphasizes, Aristotle is concerned with equality because he sees it as necessary to sustain the desired relationships among fellow citizens. We need not concern ourselves with securing exact equality, then, because (political) relationships are not undermined by slight disparities in wealth; clearly, compatriots can interact as political equals even if some have more than others, regardless of whether or not their unequal resources are deserved.

Others share Hampton's preference for relational theories of equality, but no one, to my knowledge, has better motivated this approach than Elizabeth Anderson.[14] Key to Anderson's defense of relational equality is the question: "What is the point of equality?" In her view, answering this question reveals most clearly why relational theories are preferable to those which fixate on luck. The crucial point is that we should care about inequality principally to the extent that subordinates are dominated in oppressive relationships. For this reason, Anderson insists that we should be "fundamentally concerned with the relationships within which the goods are distributed, not only the distribution of goods themselves."[15]

To appreciate the force of this point, compare two possible inequalities. The first exists between two societies, A and B. Assume that everyone in A is equally well off; everyone in B is doing equally poorly; and no one in either A or B knows anything of the other society's existence, since they are on opposite sides of the earth and have never had any contact. The second inequality mirrors the disparity between the As and Bs, except that it exists within a single society C. And because the Cs share a single political community, not only are they aware that others are faring considerably better/worse but also their relationships are affected by these inequalities. I take it as uncontroversial that the inequality among the Cs is much more worrisome than the same inequality between the As and Bs. In other words, whether or not we should care about the inequality between the As and Bs, clearly we should be much more concerned to eliminate the inequality among the Cs. Based in part upon reasoning like this, Anderson concludes: "Negatively, people are entitled to whatever capabilities are necessary to enable them to avoid or escape entanglement in oppressive relationships. Positively, they are entitled to the capabilities necessary for functioning as an equal citizen in a democratic state."[16]

Arguments like Anderson's convince me that we should be keenly aware of the relationships within which the goods are distributed, but I stop short of concluding that relational equality is the one correct theory of equality. In my view, luck equality matters, but it matters considerably less than relational equality. In other words, although I would not hesitate to eliminate the inequality between the As and Bs if I could do so by waving a magic wand, this inequality is not sufficiently worrisome that I would necessarily interfere in the internal affairs of the As in order to eliminate the inequality between them and the Bs. However, because I am much more concerned about the inequality among the Cs, I would be correspondingly less reluctant to demand that the wealthy Cs take measures to ensure that the less well off Cs are not entangled in oppressive relationships.

As a consequence, while I do not think that there is nothing of moral consequence to be gained from realizing luck equality, I do accept a more modest claim: even if achieving relational equality is important enough to trump other values like freedom of association, realizing luck equality is not important enough to deny people their rights to self-determination. And this more modest conclusion has important implications for the morality of immigration. Most obviously, even if we would prefer a world

with no inequality between the As and the Bs, eliminating this inequality is not important enough to justify limiting the As' right to freedom of association. In short, given that the moral importance of any particular inequality is a function of the relationship in which the goods are distributed, the lack of a robust relationship between the constituents of a wealthy state and the citizens of a poorer country implies that this admittedly lamentable inequality does not generate sufficient moral reasons to obligate the wealthy state to open its borders, even if nothing but luck explains why those living outside of the territorial borders have dramatically worse prospects of living a rewarding life.

Here two potential objections present themselves. First, although it is not false to say that the citizens of some countries are relatively well off while the constituents of others are relatively poorly off (as I do in my example of the As and Bs), this cryptic description is nonetheless misleading insofar as it fails to capture that, in the real world, those in the developed countries are staggeringly wealthy in comparison to the masses who are imperiled (when not outright killed) by eviscerating poverty. In short, given the radical inequality and objective plight that make Carens's reference to "feudal privilege" apt, it is not so easy to dismiss global inequality merely because it does not exist between compatriots. Second, because of the history of colonization, as well as the current levels of international trade (among other things), it is simply not the case that the world's wealthy and poor are unconnected and unaware of each other (as I stipulate in my example of the As and Bs). On the contrary, one consequence of the emerging global basic structure is that virtually all of the world's people now share some type of relationship, so presumably even relational egalitarians cannot dismiss the moral significance of global inequality. I think there are important truths in both of these objections, so I will consider each in turn.

To begin, the twin facts that the world's poor are so desperately needy and the world's wealthy are so spectacularly well off that they could effectively help the impoverished without sacrificing anything of real consequence is unquestionably morally significant, but in my mind these facts indicate that the real issue is not about equality. Rather than being exercised merely because some are relatively worse off through no fault of their own, we are (or at least should be) concerned simply because others are suffering in objectively horrible circumstances.[17] What is more, the reason that we may have a duty to help is not because mere luck explains why we are doing better than they (presumably we would be obligated to relieve their suffering even if our relative standing was fully attributable to morally relevant factors like our hard work). Instead, our duty to help stems most straightforwardly from samaritanism: one has a natural duty to assist others when they are sufficiently imperiled and one can help them at no unreasonable cost to oneself.[18] As a result, I am inclined to respond to the first objection in disjunctive fashion: if the less well off Bs are not doing terribly badly in objective terms, then the inequality between the As and Bs does not generate a duty on the part of the As to help the Bs. If the Bs are clearly suffering in absolute poverty, on the other hand, then the As may indeed have stringent duties to help, but these duties spring from a samaritan source rather than from the mere fact that the As are (for morally arbitrary reasons) doing better than the Bs.[19] If this is right, then even the previously unfathomable inequalities we now see in the real world do not sufficiently buttress the luck egalitarian's case for open borders.

Regarding the second objection, I am inclined to agree that the emerging global infrastructure entails that virtually all of us have increasingly substantial relationships with people all over the world. And as a relational egalitarian, it seems to follow that the more robust these relationships become, the more concerned we should be about the inequalities within them. But I can concede all of this without jettisoning my response to the egalitarian case for open borders because my account has never relied upon the claim that being fellow citizens of a country is the only morally relevant relationship.[20] On the contrary, my account requires only that the less ambitious (and more plausible) claim that the relationship among compatriots is one relationship with morally relevant implications for inequality. To see the significance of this point, notice what I would say about inequalities within a particular state. Even though I think that the

relationship shared among compatriots is relevant when assessing the inequalities among two people, I would never allege that no relationships within a state are morally relevant. Because familial relations are particularly liable to oppression, for instance, we might worry about the inequalities between wife and husband, between the parents and children, or among the children in a way that we would not among compatriots who are not members of the same family. For example, we would likely be less comfortable with a scenario in which a family paid for the sons but not the daughters to go to college than one in which one set of parents paid for the children's college expenses and another set of parents did not. Thus, there is nothing about my insistence on the moral relevance of the relationship among compatriots that forces me to deny the possibility of other relationships within the states which are significant for the purposes of inequality. And if I can acknowledge important relationships within a state, there seems no reason why I cannot accept that citizens of separate states can stand in relationships which matter from the point of equality. Most important, notice that conceding this last point does not undermine my response to the egalitarian case for open borders, because I can still insist that (whatever other relationships there are which matter from the standpoint of equality) the relationship between fellow citizens is one particularly important relationship which explains why we need not necessarily restrict the liberty of the better-off citizens in one country merely because nothing but luck explains why they are faring so much better than the citizens of a foreign state.

Finally, a persistent critic might counter that, even if the case based on luck egalitarianism fails, both samaritanism and the morally relevant relationships among foreigners explain why we have duties to those outside of our borders. In response, I suggest that these duties, even if stringent, can be fully satisfied without necessarily allowing those to whom we are duty bound entry to our country. That this is so will become apparent shortly when I explain why, even if luck egalitarianism is correct, it cannot shoulder the argumentative burden required of it by the case for open borders.

Before turning to this argument, though, it is worth nothing that, while he does not use the luck/relational equality terminology, Walzer implicitly endorses the position on equality for which I am lobbying here. This occurs most clearly in his important discussion of Germany's bringing in "guest workers" from countries like Turkey. Here Walzer argues that, while Germans are not morally obligated to admit these workers, they nonetheless may not bring the workers in as political subordinates. He writes: "Democratic citizens, then, have a choice: if they want to bring in new workers, they must be prepared to enlarge their own membership; if they are unwilling to accept new members, they must find ways within the limits of the domestic labor market to get socially necessary work done. And those are their only choices."[21]

Now at first glance Walzer's position seems curious. After all, if prospective immigrants have no right to entry, how can they have a conditional right to equality if admitted? (By comparison, if Miriam has no right that Patrick sell her his gently used copy of *Spheres of Justice*, presumably Miriam would thereby also lack the conditional right to a cheap price if Patrick chose to sell it to her.) One would think that the right to equal treatment either gives the prospective workers a right to equal treatment either gives the prospective workers a right to equal citizenship within Germany or it does not, but it could not generate a conditional right which depends upon the choice of the Germans. Reflecting upon the distinction between luck and relational theories of equality shows why this is not so, however. Walzer's positing a conditional right to equality-if-admitted makes perfect sense if he is implicitly presuming a relational theory of equality (as I believe he is), because such a theory implies that the same inequalities which would clearly be pernicious among compatriots might well be benign when present between foreigners. Thus, there is nothing inconsistent about Walzer's voicing no objection to an inequality between Germans and Turks, on the one hand, and objecting to this same inequality when it exists between two people (whatever their nationality) subject to the same political community within Germany, on the other hand.

In light of Walzer's analysis, we are now in a position to conclude the first prong of our critique of the egalitarian case for open borders with two points. First, this case depends upon a particular theory of equality, luck egalitarianism, which leading theorists have rejected on grounds that have nothing to do with immigration. Second, without explicitly weighing in on this topic, one of the most prominent and sophisticated discussions of immigration implicitly endorses relational equality by staking out positions which presuppose that the moral importance of any inequality is a function not only of its magnitude but also of the relationship in which the goods are distributed. For the sake of argument, however, let us assume that I am wrong to criticize luck egalitarianism. Suppose that luck egalitarianism is the best theory of equality, or that securing luck equality is as least as important as securing relational equality, or at the very least that realizing luck equality is sufficiently important to justify restricting people's rights to freedom of association. Even if we grant one of these assumptions, it would still not follow that legitimate states are therefore not entitled to freedom of association. To see why, consider how marital freedom of association is typically combined with the demands of domestic distributive justice.

Even the most zealous critics of inequality typically recommend neither that we must abolish marriage nor that wealthy couples must literally open up their marriages to the less well off. Instead, it is standard to keep separate our rights to freedom of association and our duties of distributive justice, so that wealthy people are able to marry whomever they choose and then are required to transfer a portion of their wealth to others no matter whom (or even whether) they marry. Admittedly, history includes radical movements like the Khmer Rouge, who abolished marriage because it was thought to be inconsistent with their quest for complete equality, but most egalitarians rightly shy away from this degree of fanaticism.[22] Indeed, consider this: despite the enormous disagreement about what type of responsibilities the likes of Bill Gates and Warren Buffet have in virtue of their staggering wealth, no one alleges that, unlike the rest of us, these billionaires are required to marry poor spouses. And just as our domestic redistribution of wealth among individuals has not led us to prohibit marriage, global redistribution does not require us to open all political borders. Instead, even if we presume that wealthy societies have extensive distributive duties, these duties are distinct and can be kept separate from the societies' rights to freedom of association. To reiterate: if wealthy couples need not open up their marriages to those less well off, why think that wealthy countries must open their borders to less fortunate immigrants? Just as relatively wealthy families are required merely to transfer some of their wealth to others, why cannot wealthy countries fully discharge their global distributive duties without including the recipients in their political union, simply by transferring the required level of funds abroad?[23]

Thus, no matter how substantial their duties of distributive justice, wealthier countries need not open their borders. At most, affluent societies are duty bound to choose between allowing needy foreigners to enter their society or sending some of their wealth to those less fortunate. In fact, David Miller has pressed this point even further, suggesting that it would be better if wealthier countries sent resources abroad. He puts it as follows:

> People everywhere have a right to a decent life. But before jumping to the conclusion that the way to respond to global injustice is to encourage people whose lives are less than decent to migrate elsewhere, we should consider the fact that this policy will do little to help the very poor, who are unlikely to have the resources to move to a richer country. Indeed, a policy of open migration may make such people worse off still, if it allows doctors, engineers, and other professionals to move from economically undeveloped to economically developed societies in search of higher incomes, thereby depriving their countries of origin of vital skills. Equalizing opportunity for the few may diminish opportunities for the many.[24]

If Miller is right about this, then the ardent egalitarian not only may be in no position to demand that affluent societies open their borders but she also may be forced to insist that states not do so, since sending aid abroad is a better way to rescue those most imperiled by poverty.

Even if legitimate states have no duty to open their borders to the world's poor, however, surely it would be unconscionable for a state to slam its doors on people desperately fleeing unjust regimes. After all, even authors like Walzer, who are in general prepared to defend a state's right to control its membership, make an exception for refugees.[25] The core idea behind this exception is that, unlike those who merely lack exportable resources, some asylum seekers are actively threatened by their states, and thus they cannot be helped by an international transfer of goods; their only escape from peril is to be granted asylum.

As implausible as it might initially seem, I suggest that, even in cases of asylum seekers desperately in need of a political safe haven, a state is not required to take them in. I adopt this stance not because I am unmoved by the plight of asylum seekers but because I am not convinced that the only way to help victims of political injustice is by sheltering them in one's political territory. In my view, these people might also be helped in something like the fashion in which wealthy societies could choose to assist impoverished foreigners: by, as it were, exporting justice. Admittedly, one cannot ship justice in a box, but one can intervene, militarily if necessary, in an unjust political environment to ensure that those currently vulnerable to the state are made safe in their homelands.[26] Let me be clear: I am not suggesting that this is always easy or even advisable, nor do I assert that states are necessarily obligated to take this course of action. I claim instead that where asylum seekers are genuinely left vulnerable because their government is either unable or unwilling to protect their basic rights, then their government is illegitimate, it has no claim to political self-determination, and thus it stands in no position to protest if a third party were to intervene on behalf of (some of) its constituents. Think, for instance, of the Kurds in Iraq. One way to help them is to allow them to emigrate en masse. Another option, though, is to use military force to create a safe haven and no-fly zone in Northern Iraq. And since the Iraqi government was the party threatening the Kurds, it had no right to object to this interference with its sovereignty. I suspect that Walzer stops short of this conclusion only because he wrongly, I think, respects the political self-determination of virtually all states, even those persecuting asylum seekers.[27]

Walzer and I diverge on this point, then, not because I am less impressed than he by the plight of asylum seekers but because he is more impressed than I by the claims to political self-determination of failed and rogue states, those regimes either unable or unwilling to secure their citizens' basic moral rights. Thus, I once again conclude that affluent societies have a duty to help but that it is a disjunctive duty: just as global poverty requires wealthy states to either export aid or import unfortunate people, the presence of those desperately seeking political asylum renders those of us in just political communities duty bound either to grant asylum or to ensure that these refugees no longer need fear their domestic regimes. Miller seems to me to get it just right when he suggests: "The lesson for other states, confronted with people whose lives are less than decent, is that they have a choice: they must either ensure that the basic rights of such people are protected in the places where they live—by aid, by intervention, or by some other means—or they must help them to move to other communities where their lives will go better. Simply shutting one's borders and doing nothing else is not a morally defensible option here."[28]

Before turning to what might be called the "libertarian" case for open borders, I would like to emphasize that nothing in the preceding critique of the egalitarian case for open borders is intended as a rejection of egalitarianism or as a defense of the status quo. On the contrary, I believe that most of us in affluent societies have pressing restitutive, samaritan, and egalitarian duties to do considerably more to help the masses of people in the world tragically imperiled by poverty, and I even think that one good way to provide this assistance is to allow more immigrants from poorer countries. If sound, the arguments of this section establish merely that egalitarian considerations do not by themselves generate a moral duty which requires wealthy countries to open their borders, in part because the egalitarian case for open borders depends upon a suspect theory of equality, but also because wealthy countries have the discretion to

discharge their distributive responsibilities in other manners.

III. THE LIBERTARIAN CASE FOR OPEN BORDERS

To motivate the libertarian case for open borders, Carens imagines the following scenario. "Suppose a farmer from the United States wanted to hire workers from Mexico. The government would have no right to prohibit him from doing this. To prevent the Mexicans from coming would violate the rights of both the American farmer and the Mexican workers to engage in voluntary transactions."[29] As this example illustrates, libertarian arguments against restricting immigration can take either of two forms, depending upon whether they focus on property rights or rights to free movement. The former emphasizes the rights of those within the state and contends that limiting immigration violates individual property owners' right to invite foreigners to visit their private property. The latter stresses the rights of foreigners, claiming that closing territorial borders wrongly restricts an individual's right to freedom of movement.

According to the first type of argument, states may not limit immigration because doing so wrongly restricts their constituents' rights to private property. The appeal of this idea is apparent: if a farmer owns a piece of property, then she occupies a position of moral dominion over that land which gives her the discretion to determine who may and who may not enter that land. If the farmer's government denies foreigners access to its political territory, however, then it thereby effectively denies the farmer the right to invite foreigners onto her land. Thus, since a state cannot limit immigration to its territory without also limiting its constituents' property rights, political communities clearly are not morally entitled to control who crosses their borders.

It is worth nothing that this argument is not skeptical of the moral importance of freedom of association; it merely questions why the state should get to enjoy this right when its doing so necessarily limits the ability of its individual constituents to do so. In a conflict between an individual's right versus a state's right, a libertarian will typically argue that the individual's right should take precedence. When the state as a whole gets to limit immigration, however, its doing so effectively curtails the rights of its citizens to unilaterally invite foreigners onto their land. And because inviting others to join one on one's privately owned land is one type of freedom of association, it is impossible to grant a state the right to control its borders without stripping property owners of their rights to freedom of association. So if either party should have priority in claiming the right to freedom of association, it is the individual, not the state.

In response, I concede that there is a conflict between a state's sovereignty over its territory and an individual property owner's dominion over her land, but in this case I am inclined to favor the claims of a (duly limited) state. I am a staunch defender of individual self-determination, but the crucial point here is that one cannot consistently insist that property rights are totally unlimited without committing oneself to anarchism. This is because political states are functionally incompatible with extending unlimited dominion to their constituents. States must be sufficiently territorially contiguous in order to perform their requisite functions, and achieving contiguity requires them to nonconsensually coerce all those within their territorial borders.[30] Thus, while it is perfectly intelligible to claim that individual dominion should always take precedence over state sovereignty, one cannot maintain this position without implicitly endorsing anarchism. To reiterate, effective political society would not be possible unless some crucial decisions were made by the group as a whole, and (as this example of the conflict between a state's controlling its territory and an individual controlling her land indicates) all areas of group sovereignty imply a corresponding lack of individual dominion. In light of this, I suggest that, in the choice between unlimited property rights and the anarchy it entails versus limited property rights and the statism it allows, one should favor the latter.

Of course, one might eschew anarchism and still suggest that individual property rights take precedence over a state's right to control its borders, but this position would require an additional argument designed specifically to show why the individual should take precedence over the group in matters of freedom of association. We should not presume in advance that such an argument could not be furnished, but there are several reasons to be skeptical of this approach.

To begin, notice that, in matters unrelated to immigration, we take it for granted that the group as a whole has a right to freedom of association. Consider again, for instance, Canada's participation in NAFTA or Slovenia's membership in the European Union. In these cases, everyone acknowledges that Canadians as a whole must determine whether they would like to join NAFTA and that Slovenians as a group should decide whether or not Slovenia will enter the EU. If each individual's right to freedom of association must always take precedence over the group's, on the other hand, then it follows that every single Canadian had the right to veto Canada's involvement in NAFTA or a single Slovenian citizen would be entitled unilaterally to block Slovenia's membership in the EU. I presume without argument that this position is untenable. And if no one thinks that individuals have the right to veto their county's entrance into associations like NAFTA or the EU, then we seem similarly committed to denying that individuals have a right to veto their country's immigration policy.[31]

At this point one might answer that a country's limiting immigration is in principle distinct from joining NAFTA, the EU, or even the merger between East and West Germany because the latter three are all acts of association, whereas restricting immigration is a refusal to associate. The idea is that, of course an individual may not appeal to the value of freedom of association to criticize any of these mergers because each expands her possibilities for association. But this carries no implications for whether an individual might rightfully object to her state's restricting immigration, which limits the people with whom one may associate.

The distinction between expanding and limiting association is a real one, but I nonetheless doubt that it will do the necessary work. To see why, consider an uncontested secession like Norway's break from Sweden in 1905. In this case, more than 99 percent of the Norwegians voted in favor of political divorce and Sweden as a country did not resist the separation.[32] Whatever one thinks about the justifiability of state-breaking, this seems like a paradigmatic case of permissible secession. If each individual's right to freedom of association trumps the state's right to self-determination in those cases in which the group as a whole seeks to disassociate from others, however, then Norway's secession was unjustified; it was impermissible because every last Norwegian (if not also each Swede) had the right unilaterally to veto the political divorce and the plebiscite in favor of separation did not garner unanimous consent. Again, I presume without argument that this position is implausible. And if an individual's claim to freedom of association does not trump her state's right in the case of secession, there seems good reason to believe that an individual's right would be equally impotent in the realm of immigration.

A second reason to doubt that an individual's dominion over her private property takes precedence over the state's control of its territorial borders stems from the twin facts that (1) an inability to invite foreigners onto one's land is typically not an onerous imposition and (2) bringing outsiders into the political community has real consequences for one's compatriots. I will explain below why being unable to invite foreigners onto one's land is in most cases not a huge limitation of one's dominion over one's property. To appreciate why inviting foreigners to live permanently on one's property has consequences for others, one need only reflect upon the implications of the relational theory of equality outlined above. In particular, recall Walzer's conclusion that affluent societies have no obligation to invite guest workers into their territory but that they are obligated to treat as political equals all those they do admit. The idea here is that once an individual enters the territory and becomes subject to the dictates of the state, she becomes more vulnerable than outsiders to political oppression.[33] Thus, Walzer rightly concludes that all those who enter the territory for an indefinite period must be welcomed as equal members of the political community. If so, however, this explains why a person's inviting foreigners onto her land has important moral implications for all of the state's citizens. This invitation does not merely entitle the invitee to stay on one's land; it morally requires all

of one's fellow citizens to share the benefits of equal political standing with this new member of the political community. And because the costs of extending the benefits of political membership can be substantial, it makes sense that each individual should not have the right unilaterally to invite in as many foreigners as she would like. It is only appropriate that the group as a whole should decide with whom the benefits of membership should be shared.[34]

Although I think the preceding considerations show why the libertarian is wrong to assume that the state's right to freedom of association must give way to individual property rights, I do think there is room for an intermediate position that accommodates in a principled way both associational and property rights, giving each right its due. And this is important because a state should not restrict individual dominion any more than is necessary. In particular, while I am skeptical that an individual has the right to invite foreigners to live on her land indefinitely, I do not see why property owners may not invite outsiders to visit for limited periods. In fact, one need not even object to a guest worker arrangement, as long as the worker does not stay too long.[35] Indeed, this strikes me as an appealing compromise, because allowing for these sponsored visits gives property owners greater dominion over their land than the status quo without creating any additional imposition upon their compatriots (since citizens are not obligated to extend the benefits of political membership to those foreigners visiting for a limited amount of time). What is more, this solution enables us to avoid the standard practical problem of foreigners entering the country on a limited visa and then staying indefinitely, because the state could require the property owner to be responsible (putting up collateral, perhaps) for all those she invites to visit. In the end, then, I am inclined to conclude that a property owner's dominion over her land might well entitle her to invite foreigners to visit her land but that it would not justify a more sweeping curtailment of a state's right to control immigration into its territory. And once we make room for this additional right for property owners, one gets a better sense of why the remaining restrictions upon their dominion over their property is rarely terribly onerous.

At this stage a libertarian might concede all that I have argued so far and still insist that states may not restrict immigration, not because doing so unjustifiably limits the property rights of its citizens but because it violates foreigners' rights to freedom of movement. Surely each of us has a right to migrate as we please; if not, then states would be justified prohibiting emigration or even free migration within the country. And just as our rights to freedom of movement allow us to leave or travel within our country, they entitle us to enter other countries as well. As Carens emphasizes: "No liberal state restricts internal mobility. Those states that do restrict internal mobility are criticized for denying basic human freedoms. If freedom of movement within the state is so basic that it overrides the claims of local political communities, on what grounds can we restrict freedom of movement across states?"[36] Thus, unless one is prepared to accept a state's right to deny either emigration or internal migration, consistency appears to demand that states not limit immigration either.[37]

My response to this second prong of the libertarian case for open borders is analogous to my arguments above: I concede that there is a right to freedom of movement, and I certainly believe that states must take great care not to violate the individual rights of either constituents or foreigners, but I do not think that the right to free movement is perfectly general and absolute. My right to freedom of movement does not entitle me to enter your house without your permission, for instance, so why think that this right gives me a valid claim to enter a foreign country without that country's permission? Some might counter that this response essentially denies the right in question, but this is not so. No one says that I am denied my right to marriage merely because I cannot unilaterally choose to marry you against your will. So, just as my freedom of association in the marital realm remains intact despite your right to not associate with me, there seems no reason why my right to freedom of movement does not similarly remain intact despite foreign states' retaining the right to exclude me. David Miller captures this point nicely:

The right of exit is a right held against a person's current state of residence not to prevent her from leaving the state (and perhaps aiding her in that endeavor by, say, providing a passport). But it does not entail an obligation on any other state to let that person in. Obviously if no state were ever to grant entry rights to people who were not already its citizens, the right of exit would have no value. But suppose that states are generally willing to consider entry applications from people who might want to migrate, and that most people would get offers from at least one such state: then the position as far as the right of exit goes is pretty much the same as with the right to marry, where by no means everyone is able to wed the partner they would ideally like to have, but most have the opportunity to marry *someone*.[38]

What is more, there is no inconsistency in insisting upon freedom of emigration and internal migration, on the one hand, and allowing states to restrict immigration, on the other hand. First and most important, distinguishing between immigration and emigration makes perfect sense given that freedom of association includes the option not to associate; one may unilaterally emigrate because one is never forced to associate with others, but one may not unilaterally immigrate because neither are others required to associate with you. Second, as we have seen above, immigration is importantly different because, unlike either emigration or internal migration, it can involve costs to those who must include you as an equal in their political community.[39] Third, a state that denies emigration (or perhaps even one that denies internal migration, for that matter) treats its citizens as tantamount to political property insofar as it forces them to remain in the union, regardless of their preferences. As unpleasant as it might be to be denied the right to enter a country, on the other hand, this rejection no more treats one like property than does a romantic partner who declines one's marriage proposal. Thus, there appears to be nothing inconsistent about requiring states to permit open emigration while simultaneously allowing them to limit immigration.

Notice, though, the following: just as I earlier suggested amending the status quo to give greater dominion to property owners, here we might explore ways to create more room for those interested in entering foreign countries. In particular, given that the pivotal issue involves the twin facts that (1) countries may not dmit people for indefinite periods without extending them equal membership rights and (2) groups of citizens have the right to control membership in their political communities, this suggests that even legitimate states do not necessarily have the right to bar foreigners from visiting for a duly limited period. The host countries might have a valid concern about huge numbers of visitors illegally staying beyond the terms of their visa, but, again, it is not clear that this worry could not be satisfactorily addressed by some mechanism such as the visitor putting up sufficient collateral. If so, then the arguments for limiting immigration offered in this article would leave much more room for freedom of movement than the status quo, since it would allow most people to travel freely around the world (as tourists, to family or doctors, or even to study or work) as long as they did not stay indefinitely in some place without the permission of the host political community.

Despite this important qualification, I am no more impressed by the second prong of the libertarian case for open borders than by the first. In both instances, the libertarian gestures toward an important right, but the existence of this right could defeat the presumptive case for a state's claim to control its borders only if the right is wrongly presumed to be perfectly general and absolute. In the end, then, neither the egalitarian nor the libertarian case for open borders undermines the case that can be made on behalf of a legitimate state's right to restrict immigration.

IV. A QUESTION OF CRITERIA

In *Who Are We?* Samuel Huntington worries not only about the raw number of immigrants entering the United States but is especially concerned that so many are from Mexico.[40] He views the United States as defined not just in terms of its distinctive American creed but also by its Anglo-Protestant culture. Thus, unless it more stringently limits the flow of Mexican immigrants, America will forever lose its distinctive—and distinctly valuable—character. This provocative

proposal raises a difficult and important question, a question to which Walzer and Miller give two distinct answers, neither of which I find fully satisfying. Assuming that states have the right to control who, if anyone, may enter their territories, does it follow that a country may adopt a policy that explicitly excludes people based upon their race, religion or ethnicity? What if a country wanted to admit only whites, for instance?[41] This question is especially difficult, I think, because, if the state is genuinely at liberty to exclude everyone, how could an applicant righteously complain about not being admitted? On the other hand, most take it for granted that, even if a business is not required to hire anyone, it may not adopt a policy to hire only whites. And if a company cannot select employees in this way, presumably a state may not screen potential immigrants according to this type of criterion.

Walzer explores this question in terms of "White Australia," Australia's erstwhile policy to admit only whites. Walzer concludes that Australians would in fact be permitted to admit only whites, but only if they ceded a portion of their territory to those who needed it to survive. He writes: "Assuming, then, that there actually is superfluous land, the claim of necessity would force a political community like that of White Australia to confront a radical choice. Its members could yield land for the sake of homogeneity, or they could give up homogeneity (agree to the creation of a multiracial society) for the sake of the land. And those would be their only choices. White Australia could survive only as Little Australia."[42] Thus, Walzer appears to believe that, while Australia was not at liberty to simply turn its back upon needy nonwhites, there is nothing inherently unjust about an immigration policy that discriminates based upon race.

Miller diverges from Walzer on this question, arguing that, even if the state is at liberty to exclude everyone, it wrongs potential applicants for admission by excluding them based on a category like race. As he puts it:

I have tried to hold a balance between the interest that migrants have in entering the country they want to live in, and the interest that political communities having (sic) in determining their own character. Although the first of these interests is not strong enough to justify a right of migration, it is still substantial, and so the immigrants who are refused entry are owed an explanation. To be told that they belong to the wrong race or sex (or have the wrong color) is insulting, given that these features do not connect to anything of real significance to the society they want to join. Even tennis clubs are not entitled to discriminate among applicants on grounds such as these.[43]

I must admit to being torn between these two views. I am tempted by Walzer's position because, as much as I abhor racism, I believe that racist individuals cannot permissibly be forced to marry someone (or adopt a child) outside of their race. And if the importance of freedom of association entitles racist individuals to marry exclusively within their race, why does it not similarly entitle racist citizens to exclude immigrants based upon race? At the very least, one must explain why the immigration case is dissimilar to the marital one. In the end, though, I reject Walzer's position because I think that such an explanation can be furnished. Yet I am also not entirely persuaded by Miller's explanation.

As noted above, Miller suggests that a state may not exclude immigrants based upon a category like race because doing so wrongly insults applicants of the rejected race. I am not sure that this account suffices, though. I do not doubt that the rejected applicants might feel horribly insulted, but I am not convinced that they have a right not to be insulted in this way. By analogy, I would expect a black person to be insulted by a racist white who would never consider marrying someone who is black, but I would not say that this black person has a right not to be insulted in this way. Because of these concerns, I would like to suggest an alternative explanation as to why states may not limit immigration according to racist criteria.[44] In doing so, I will focus upon the rights of those already within the political community rather than the rights of those who might want to enter. I shift the emphasis from foreign immigrants to citizens of the state whose policy is in question because, given the relational theory of equality detailed above,

it makes sense to presume that we may have responsibilities to our compatriots that we do not equally owe to foreigners.[45] In particular, we have a special duty to respect our fellow citizens as equal partners in the political cooperative. With this in mind, I suggest that a country may not institute an immigration policy which excludes entry to members of a given race because such a policy would wrongly disrespect those citizens in the dispreferred category.

Even if we assume that there is a special responsibility not to treat one's compatriots as less than equal partners, someone might still question how an immigration policy (which cannot evict any current citizens) could possibly affect any of a state's constituents. To see how such a policy might disrespect existing citizens, consider the analogous situation from the familial context. Rather than focusing upon racists who are unwilling to marry outside of their race, imagine a family of two white parents with two children, one white and another black. (For the purposes of this thought-experiment, imagine that white parents sometimes gave birth to black children, and vice versa.) Now, imagine the parents announcing that, as much as they would love to have a third child, they have decided against it for fear that she might be black. I take it as obvious how hurtful this announcement could be to the existing black child, even though the decision not to have any additional children obviously does not threaten his or her chances of coming into existence. In light of this analogy, it is not difficult to see how black Australians, for instance, might feel disrespected by an immigration policy banning entry to nonwhites. Even though this policy in and of itself in no way threatens blacks with expulsion, it sends a clear message that, qua blacks, they are not equally valued as partners in the political union. As Blake comments: "Even if a hypothetical pure society could close the borders to preserve itself, a modern multi-ethnic democracy could not do so without implicitly treating some individuals already present within the society as second class citizens. Seeking to eliminate the presence of a given group from your society by selective immigration is insulting to the members of that group already present."[46] Thus, unless Australia were already composed exclusively of white constituents (and no state is completely homogenous), it would be impermissible to institute immigration policies designed to approximate a "White Australia," not because such policies might insult potential black immigrants (though no doubt it would) but because they would fail to treat nonwhite Australians as equals. And because no state is completely without minorities who would be disrespected by an immigration policy which invoked racial/ethnic/religious categories, no state may exclude potential immigrants on these types of criteria.

A possible exception to this rule might be a religious state like Israel. When a country is designed as a state for Jews, it might be thought entirely appropriate to deny non-Jews entry. I am not so sure about this conclusion, however, because I do not see why a state's being designed to cater especially to a specific group should license it to disrespect those subjects not in the favored group. Thus, assuming that I am right that barring all but Jewish immigrants would treat the current non-Jewish citizens as less than equal members of the political community, only a state that was completely Jewish could permissibly adopt such an anti-non-Semitic immigration policy.

Of course, in the case of Israel, the moral horror of the holocaust makes it tempting to accept an immigration policy that excludes non-Semites. After all, as Hannah Arendt famously emphasized, an early but crucial step toward rendering the Jews vulnerable to inhumane treatment was stripping them of their citizenship. Against the backdrop of this tragic history, the idea of a state prepared to act as a safe haven for all and only Jews might seem unobjectionable. In my view, however, while this type of consideration could well justify Israel's controversial Law of Return (which automatically grants admission to all Jews), it would not justify Israel's admitting all and only Jews.[47] An immigration policy that summarily rejected all non-Jews might be acceptable for a state which included no non-Jewish subjects, but because roughly 20 percent of Israel's population is not Jewish, it may not adopt such an immigration policy. Even a wrong that follows on the heels of the utterly horrific wrong of the holocaust (like all second wrongs) does not make a right. To emphasize: whether or not we are sympathetic to the idea of a state designed especially to serve a specific racial, ethnic, or religious constituency, such a state is not exempt from the requirement to treat all of its subjects as equal citizens. So if I am right that restricting immigration according to racial, ethnic, or religious criteria wrongs the current subjects in the banned groups, then only a state completely devoid of people in the banned category could permissibly institute this type of immigration policy. As a result, Australia is not free to reject potential immigrants based upon their race, and even Israel is not free to exclude non-Jews simply because they are not Jewish.

CONCLUSION

In this article I have tried first to construct a presumptive case in favor of a state's right to set its own immigration policy and then to defend this prima facie case against the formidable arguments that have been made on behalf of open borders. If my arguments are sound, then we should conclude that, even if egalitarians are right that those of us in wealthy societies have demanding duties of global distributive justice and even if libertarians are correct that individuals have rights both to freedom of movement and to control their private property, legitimate states are entitled to reject all potential immigrants, even those desperately seeking asylum from corrupt governments.

NOTES

1. Stuart White, "Freedom of Association and the Right to Exclude," *Journal of Political Philosophy* 5 (1997): 373–91, 373.

2. David Gauthier, "Breaking Up: An Essay on Secession," *Canadian Journal of Philosophy* 24 (1994): 357–92, 360–61.

3. Some also object to the Boy Scouts' refusal to admit girls.

4. For an extended discussion of some of the issues associated with group autonomy, see chap. 3 of my book *A Theory of Secession* (New York: Cambridge University Press, 2005).

5. Here one might be tempted to object that Canada's right to independence is more straightforwardly accounted for in terms of its right to self-determination. But, as I shall argue below, it is misleading to contrast freedom of association with self-determination because freedom of association is actually a central component of the more general right to self-determination. In the case of political states, for instance, a state cannot fully

enjoy the right to political self-determination unless its rights to freedom of association are respected.

6. White, "Freedom of Association and the Right to Exclude," 381 (emphasis added).

7. It should be noted White is not necessarily committed to this line of argument because his analysis is explicitly restricted to "secondary" groups (which I take to be groups within states) which adopt "categorical" exclusion (i.e., exclusion based upon an individual's race, gender, sexuality, or religion).

8. See Michael Walzer, *Spheres of Justice* (New York: Basic Books, 1983), 31–63; and David Miller, "Immigration: The Case for Limits," in *Contemporary Debates in Applied Ethics*, ed. Andrew I. Cohen and Christopher Heath Wellman (Malden, MA: Blackwell, 2005), 193–206. In *Toward a Theory of Immigration* (New York: Palgrave, 2001), the only monograph I know of which defends a state's right to craft its own immigration policy, Peter Meilander takes a similar tack, arguing that legitimate national identities have a right to defend themselves against the threat posed by immigration.

9. Walzer, *Spheres of Justice*, 62.

10. Miller, "Immigration: The Case for Limits," 200. Miller also stresses the role that limiting immigration can play in curbing population growth, but his flagship argument features the importance of preserving culture.

11. Chandran Kukathas, "The Case for Open Immigration," in Cohen and Wellman, *Contemporary Debates in Applied Ethics*, 207–20, 211.

12. Joseph H. Carens, "Aliens and Citizens: The Case for Open Borders," *Review of Politics* 49 (1987): 251–73, 252.

13. Jean Hampton, *Political Philosophy* (Boulder, CO: Westview, 1996), 158.

14. Other prominent defenses include David Miller, "What Kind of Equality Should the Left Pursue?" in *Equality*, ed. Jane Franklin (London: Institute for Public Policy Research, 1997), 83–99; Jonathan Wolff, "Fairness, Respect, and the Egalitarian Ethos," *Philosophy & Public Affairs* 27 (1998): 97–122; Andrew Mason, "Equality, Personal Responsibility, and Gender Socialisation," *Proceedings of Aristotelian Society* 100 (1999–2000): 227–46; and Samuel Scheffler, "What Is Egalitarianism?" *Philosophy & Public Affairs* 31 (2003): 5–39.

15. Elizabeth S. Anderson, "What Is the Point of Equality?" *Ethics* 109 (1999), 287–337, 314.

16. Anderson, "What Is the Point of Equality?" 316.

17. Harry Frankfurt makes a similar point in "Equality as a Moral Ideal," *Ethics* 98 (1987): 21–43.

18. Incidentally, this point both explains, and is confirmed by, the fact that Chandran Kukathas's quote listed earlier is offered under the banner of a principle of "humanity" rather than one of equality.

19. I do not claim that Michael Blake would follow me in putting this point in terms of samaritanism, but in some important respects the position I outline here squares well with what he says about international distributive justice in his excellent article "Distributive Justice, State Coercion, and Autonomy," *Philosophy & Public Affairs* 30 (2001): 257–96.

20. This appears to be another respect in which my views diverge from those which Blake develops in "Distributive Justice, State Coercion, and Autonomy." According to Blake, the relationship among compatriots is singled out because the state's coercion is key to determining when relative equality is important.

21. Walzer, *Spheres of Justice*, 61.

22. As Jonathan Glover explains in his book *Humanity* (New Haven, CT: Yale University Press, 2001): "The idea of the family was attacked. People who were allowed to stay in their villages had to share everything, down to pots and pans. Communal meals for hundreds of families together were compulsory. Many families were split up, with men and women being forced to sleep in segregated communal dormitories" (303).

23. Here one might reassert the objection to my analogy between immigration and marriage. In particular, because political unions are not nearly as intimate as marriages, an egalitarian might consistently protect freedom of association in the marital realm without being similarly impressed with a state's right to craft its own immigration policy. I agree that it would be more of an imposition to restrict one's discretion to select one's spouse, but this concession does not trouble me because I need not press the marriage analogy as far as this objection presumes. My limited hope is that our family held and familiar views on marriage will confirm my contention about a state's right to control its territorial borders need not conflict with its duties of distributive justice, even when the latter are cashed out in starkly luck egalitarian terms. If this is right, then arguments like Peter Singer's (which compares refugees to people desperately clamoring for shelter from the fallout of a nuclear bomb) are fallacious because, unlike those exposed to the fallout (whose only hope is to be admitted to the shelter), potential immigrants can be effectively helped without being admitted into one's country. See Peter Singer, "Insiders and Outsiders," *Practical Ethics* (Cambridge: Cambridge University Press, 1993), 247–63.

24. Miller, "Immigration: The Case for Limits," 198–99. Thomas Pogge and Eric Cavallero have offered similar

arguments. See Pogge's "Migration and Poverty," in *Citizenship and Exclusion*, ed. Veit M. Bader (Houndmills: Macmillan, 1997), 12–27; and Cavallero's "An Immigration-Pressure Model of Global Distributive Justice," *Politics, Philosophy and Economics* 5 (2006): 97–127.

25. It is important to note, though, that those who make an exception for refugees (as defined by international law) apparently cannot do so on principled grounds. As theorists like Andrew Shacknove and Michael Dummett have pointed out, restricting the status of refugees to those who have crossed an international border because of a well-founded fear of persecution is morally arbitrary. See Andrew Shacknove, "Who Is a Refugee?" *Ethics* 95 (1985): 274–84; and Michael Dummett, *On Immigration and Refugees* (New York: Routledge, 2001).

26. Of course, interventions will typically take time, and in these cases the intervening state should not return the refugees to their home state (at least without protecting them) until the intervention is successfully completed.

27. For more on the permissibility of armed humanitarian intervention (as well as a more expanded critique of Walzer's position), see Andrew Altman and Christopher Heath Wellman, "From Humanitarian Intervention to Assassination," *Ethics* 118 (2008): 228–57.

28. Miller, "Immigration: The Case for Limits," 198.

29. Carens, "Aliens and Citizens: The Case for Open Borders," 253.

30. This inference from libertarianism to anarchism is admittedly very quick. I defend this claim at greater length in my essay "Liberalism, Samaritanism and Political Legitimacy," *Philosophy & Public Affairs* 25 (1996): 211–37. Very briefly, though, notice that even the most minimal state must nonconsensually force all constituents within the territory to do at least two things: (1) defer to the state's judgments regarding criminal punishments (e.g., individuals must refrain from vigilante justice) and (2) pay taxes so that the state has enough money to maintain its monopolistic coercive power over the criminal law.

31. A thorough-going libertarian might well deny that states are entitled to determine the terms of international trade, but of course this is not because there is anything distinctive about international trade. Such a libertarian will deny that a state has any moral dominion which each individual has not voluntarily surrendered. And since no state has garnered the morally valid consent of all of its constituents, staunch (and consistent) libertarians must reject all forms of statism.

32. In a referendum in August of 1905, 368,392 Norwegians voted in favor of political divorce and only 184 voted against.

33. Walzer (*Spheres of Justice*, 59) characterizes the situation of guest workers as follows: "These guests experience the state as a pervasive and frightening power that shapes their lives and regulates their every move—and never asks for their opinion. Departure is only a formal option; deportation, a continuous practical threat. As a group, they constitute a disenfranchised class. They are typically an exploited or oppressed class as well, and they are exploited or oppressed at least in part because they are disenfranchised, incapable of organizing effectively for self-defense."

34. One might object that this argument presumes a relational theory of equality, which a libertarian might reject. I do not worry about this argument's reliance upon the relational theory of equality, however, both because those drawn to libertarianism are likely to be much less uncomfortable with relational egalitarianism than with luck egalitarianism and because one cannot summarily dismiss all concerns regarding inequality on the grounds that they require some type of positive rights unless one is willing to embrace anarchism (since statism also requires the existence of positive rights).

35. I suspect that Walzer himself would not even object to this, since presumably a key factor triggering his concern about the Turkish guest workers in Germany was the extended duration of their stays.

36. Carens, "Aliens and Citizens: The Case for Open Borders," 267.

37. As Phillip Cole puts it, "one cannot consistently assert that there is a fundamental human right to emigration but no such right to immigration; the liberal asymmetry position is not merely ethically, but also conceptually, incoherent" (*Philosophies of Exclusion: Liberal Political Theory and Immigration* [Edinburgh, Edinburgh University Press, 2000], 46).

38. Miller, "Immigration: The Case for Limits," 197.

39. I should acknowledge that, when the level of welfare benefits varies considerably from province to province, the stakes of internal migration can also be much higher.

40. Samuel Huntington, *Who Are We?* (New York: Simon & Schuster, 2004).

41. Although this is less clear, it may be that a country which de facto discriminates according to these types of criteria may be just as blameworthy as one which has a de jure policy to do so. See, e.g., Dummett's discussion of British immigration practices in *On Immigration and Refugees*.

42. Walzer, *Spheres of Justice*, 47.

43. Miller, "Immigration: The Case for Limits," 204.

44. The view I advance here is similar to that which Michael Blake develops in "Immigration," in *A Companion to Applied Ethics*, ed. R.G. Frey and Christopher Heath Wellman (Malden, MA: Blackwell, 2003), 224–37.

45. My favoring the relational theory of equality also explains why I do not accept Carens's rejection of Walzer's view. Carens invokes the distinction between the private and public spheres to explain why, while you "can pick your friends on the basis of whatever criteria you want," you may not invoke categories like race to discriminate among applicants for immigration ("Aliens and Citizens: The Case for Open Borders," 267). For reasons that the relational theory of equality helps illuminate, though, even if one should not use racial categories to discriminate among applicants (for positions within the public sphere) within a given commu-nity, it does not follow that these categories may not be used when deciding who should get in to this community.

46. Blake, "Immigration," 233.

47. Defenders of Israel's Law of Return often cite the Convention on the Elimination of All Forms of Racial Discrimination Article I (3), which allows states to give a group preferential treatment in immigration (as long as no group is discriminated against). More important, in my view, is the historical context in which the Law of Return was enacted. Given how many Jews were massacred for lack of a political safe haven, it is altogether understandable that Israel would decide, with the Knesset's first law, to open its doors to Jewish people everywhere. (Here we might invoke the Convention on the Elimination of All Forms of Racial Discrimination Article I (4), which permits preferential treatment as a remedy for past discrimination.)

Freedom of Association Is Not the Answer

Sarah Fine

Cosmopolitan liberals have long argued that, contrary to prevailing practices and assumptions, there is a tension between liberal principles, on the one hand, and the coercively enforced borders and exclusive membership practices that are familiar features of nation states, on the other hand.[1] In that vein, it has become common to emphasize the liberal commitments to universalism and moral equality and to highlight the moral arbitrariness of birth place in order to question the relevance of borders in relation to a person's rights and opportunities. It is notable, too, that liberal principles are often regarded as the universalist antidote to the more particularist or exclusionary tendencies of the other features (sovereignty, nationality, democracy) that make up the modern state.

This is one of the reasons why Christopher Heath Wellman's article "Immigration and Freedom of Association" is so novel and interesting: Wellman puts forward what appears to be a distinctly liberal case for the state's right to exclude would-be immigrants.[2] As Wellman points out, we must not overlook the potentially exclusionary implications of the liberal commitment to freedom of association. There is a widespread and apparently uncontroversial view of the relationship between freedom of association and exclusion: few would argue with Amy Gutmann's statement that "the freedom to associate . . . entails the freedom to exclude."[3] Thus, if Wellman can establish that states—like individuals—should enjoy the freedom to associate and that this includes a right to exclude prospective members, then we would have clear foundations at least for the state's prima facie right to exclude.

In fact, Wellman's position appears to be doubly contentious; not only does he make a liberal case for a right to exclude voluntary immigrants, but he also maintains that states actually have the right to "close [their] doors to all potential immigrants, even refugees desperately seeking asylum from incompetent or corrupt political regimes that are either unable or unwilling to protect their citizens' basic moral rights" (109). In this respect he seems to go further than other

Sarah Fine, "Freedom of Association Is Not the Answer," *Ethics* 120, January 2010, 338–56. © 2010 by The University of Chicago. Reprinted by permission of The University of Chicago Press.

progressive political philosophers who have offered more qualified defenses of immigration restrictions.[4] In short, this is a bold argument, which makes a significant contribution to a most topical debate.

I outline the key points of Wellman's two-stage argument in Section I. In Sections II and III, I develop an internal critique of Wellman's position. The main target of my response is his central claim that "the commonly prized value of freedom of association provides the basic normative building blocks for a presumptive case in favor of each legitimate state's right to exclude others from its territory" (119). I highlight the way in which exclusion has the potential to harm the interests of would-be immigrants, and I point out some crucial distinctions between the state and associations in civil society.[5] In Section IV, I contend that, beyond the issues of external harm and the distinctiveness of the state, a successful defense of the state's right to exclude others from its territory could not rest on the appeal to freedom of association alone: it also would require a justification of the state's territorial rights, something that is conspicuous by its absence from Wellman's argument. The search for the normative foundations of the state's purported right to exclude would-be immigrants continues: freedom of association is not the answer.

I

There are two main steps on Wellman's path to the conclusion that states have the right to exclude all prospective immigrants. First, he seeks to establish that there is a prima facie case for the state's right to exclude; second, he aims to illustrate that the presumption in favor of a right to exclude is not outweighed by potentially competing "egalitarian" and "libertarian" considerations.[6]

Wellman's case for a presumptive right to exclude is quite straightforward. He begins with the claim that everybody seems to think freedom of association is important. Taking marriage and religion as his central examples, Wellman draws attention to the widespread agreement that people should be free to choose their own (willing) marital partners and their own (willing) religious associates. This, he suggests,

is indicative of a common conviction "that each of us enjoys a morally privileged position of dominion over our self-regarding affairs," or, in short, a commitment to individual self-determination (110). The freedom to associate is part of what it means to be self-determining.

And what does a commitment to freedom of association imply? Wellman contends that it includes "the right not to associate and even, in many cases, the right to associate and even, in many cases, the right to disassociate" (109). Freedom of marital association, for example, comprises a right to marry a willing partner but also the right not to marry a given suitor and even not to marry anyone. Freedom of religious association similarly means a right to associate with consenting others for religious purposes, as well as the right not to associate with anyone in particular or indeed anyone at all. Neither marital nor religious associational freedom includes a right to associate with nonconsenting others (110).

From these apparently uncontroversial liberal premises, Wellman reaches the following somewhat more controversial conclusion: "Just as an individual has a right to determine whom (if anyone) he or she would like to marry, a group of fellow-citizens has a right to determine whom (if anyone) it would like to invite into its political community. And just as an individual's freedom of association entitles one to remain single, a state's freedom of association entitles it to exclude all foreigners from its political community" (110–11).

Wellman then responds to a number of potential objections to his move from premises to conclusion. None of these objections deters him from confidently contending that he has established at least a prima facie case for a state's right to exclude all would-be immigrants (119). If the first part of Wellman's argument is correct, then, all other things being equal, we should favor states' rights to exclude over would-be immigrants' claims to be admitted.

The prima facie case, he acknowledges, could be outweighed by competing claims. First, the presumption in favor of a state's right to restrict immigration might be trumped by what Wellman calls "the egalitarian case for open borders." Wellman accepts that individuals and states have significant duties to outsiders living in abject poverty, and, in line with his relational view of equality, he maintains that, as relationships between insiders and outsiders become more "robust," the inequalities between them are a greater cause for concern (120–30). He argues, however, that states may choose to "export justice" rather than open their borders to immigrants.[7] Export options include, in Wellman's view, the transfer of aid to poor countries in place of admitting immigrants who are fleeing poverty, and, rather more contentiously, military intervention to protect those whose governments are "unable or unwilling to secure their . . . basic moral rights" instead of admitting refugees of corrupt or inept regimes (129).

Next, Wellman critically appraises "the libertarian case for open borders." Opponents might contend that the state's right to exclude illegitimately restricts the citizens' freedom to invite outsiders onto their property and/or the would-be immigrants' freedom of movement. Wellman argues that the state's "sovereignty over its territory" must take precedence over the individual citizen's right to invite others onto her property and, anyway, inviting people into the state for indefinite periods of time actually has far-reaching, costly consequences for one's fellow citizens, which means that this sort of decision should not be made unilaterally. Furthermore, the right to freedom of movement is not absolute: I have no right to enter your house without permission, so why should I have a right to enter another country without its consent (130–36)? Yet he claims that states should not interfere with self-determining individuals "any more than is necessary" (134). Hence, states can have no reasonable objection to individuals inviting outsiders onto their property or to foreigners entering the territory provided that these visits are for "duly limited" periods (136–37).

Despite these apparent concessions, Wellman does not shy away from his stark conclusion that "even if egalitarians are right that those of us in wealthy societies have stringent duties of global distributive justice, and even if libertarians are correct that individuals have rights both to freedom of movement and to control their private property, legitimate states are entitled to reject all potential immigrants,

even those desperately seeking asylum from corrupt governments" (141).

Wellman's defense of the state's right to exclude rests on two debatable claims. The first is that the state has a right to freedom of association, which is a component of its right to self-determination. All liberals are familiar with the claim that individuals have associational rights, and many would accept that groups formed by consenting individuals also can have associational rights. However, Wellman does not elaborate on the precise sense in which the state has a right to freedom of association. He does not explain whether we should understand the state as the right-holder or whether the state exercises the right on behalf of its citizens. At times he refers to "the citizens' right," at others he refers to the "state's right." If the state acts on behalf of its citizens as a collective body, then presumably the state has no right to exclude those with whom the citizens collectively choose to associate. He also does not reveal exactly how this purported collective right relates to the individual right to freedom of association. The citizens' (or the state's) right to freedom of association does not emerge from the citizens exercising their individual rights and choosing to associate together as a group in the first place; as Wellman acknowledges, ordinarily membership of the political community is nonvoluntary (112). Moreover, as he points out, the citizens' collective right to refuse to associate with outsiders may conflict with the associative rights of those individual citizens who wish to associate with the excluded outsiders (131). In lieu of a response to these questions about the nature of the state's right to freedom of association, Wellman simply suggests that there are some unpalatable consequences of denying that states have such a right. For example, without positing that right, he argues, we would be unable to identify the wrong that occurs when one state forcibly annexes another state (112–13). Despite the lack of clarification, let us accept for the sake of argument that the state may have a right to freedom of association.

The second controversial claim is that the state's freedom to associate includes a right to exclude would-be immigrants. In order to understand the basis of that claim, it is useful to distinguish between a state's right to exclude outsiders from its territory (from simply crossing its borders), its right to exclude them from settling within that territory, and its right to exclude them from membership of the political community (from acquiring citizenship status). Although Wellman obscures these distinctions by writing, interchangeably, of a state's right to "control immigration over its territorial borders," "close its doors," and "set its own immigration policy," it transpires that the central focus of his freedom of association position is actually the state's right to exclude would-be immigrants from obtaining citizenship status. Wellman's argument is that the citizens together ought to enjoy a collective right to determine the membership rules for their political community, and so it is the freedom of the citizens, as a group, to choose their fellow political associates that is at stake. Access to citizenship matters because "the country's course will be charted by the members of this civic association"— that is how Wellman connects the citizens' collective right to self-determination and their right to freedom of association (114–15). In short, Wellman is primarily concerned with the state's control of its "civic" boundaries, "which regulate membership."[8]

How does Wellman move from the contention that the state should have control of its civic boundaries to the argument that the state should have control of its "territorial" boundaries, "which regulate movement?"[9] At first it might appear as though the attempt to defend the state's right to exclude would-be immigrants from its territory by appeal to freedom of association is something of a nonstarter. David Miller, for example, swiftly dismisses this line of argument. According to him, it depends on the notion that "we have a deep interest in not being forced into association with others against our wishes," a notion that has little force in the context of the modern liberal state since it is implausible to claim that the "mere presence" of immigrants within the state's territory harms the (associational) interests of the citizens.[10] In that respect, Miller must be correct. The mere presence of immigrants within the state's borders cannot be a serious problem with regard to the associational rights of individual citizens—it is certainly compatible with their individual rights to associate freely within civil society, where they remain free to choose to associate, or not to associate, with newcomers and with other citizens in their private lives. In addition, it seems to be compatible with the collective right of citizens, as a group, to associate or not to associate with others in their political community.

The issue of movement across territorial borders and subsequent settlement (as opposed to full membership) only enters Wellman's argument insofar as he agrees with Michael Walzer that all long-term residents of a state should have the option of acquiring equal rights of membership to protect them against political oppression. For states to function effectively, Wellman contends, they must "nonconsensually coerce all those within their territorial borders" (131). The state, then, is both a nonvoluntary, coercive, territorial institution and the site (and representative?) of a self-determining political community. The requirement to offer citizenship status to long-term residents is a democratic one; in the absence of that guarantee, resident noncitizens are subject to the state's coercive authority without any say over the state's actions and they are comparable to "live-in servants," governed by a "band of citizen tyrants."[11] In other words, a democratic state is not entitled permanently to withhold citizenship status from those residing (for indefinite periods) within its territory. The citizens' collective freedom to associate (and to refuse association) does not extend to excluding long-term residents of the state from the political community.

Thus, while Wellman cannot defend the right to exclude outsiders from the state's territory by direct appeal to the citizens' individual or collective rights to freedom of association, because their mere presence within the state's territorial boundaries is not a problem from that perspective, the democratic state's right to exclude would-be immigrants from settling indefinitely in the territory indirectly becomes a necessary extension of the right to exclude them from full membership of the political community. The citizens' collective freedom to choose their political associates (their fellow citizens) relies on their freedom to exclude would-be long-term residents at the territorial borders. Wellman's defense of a right to exclude would-be immigrants by appeal to freedom of association therefore depends both on the assumption that states have a right to freedom of association and on the validity of the claim that all long-term residents must be offered the option of acquiring the complete rights of full membership; if the latter claim is without substance, then Wellman's argument would fail because the citizens could control access to membership of the political community and enjoy the collective right to freedom of association without controlling access to the state's territory.[12] Furthermore, the citizens' collective claim to freedom of association must be weighty enough to override not only the would-be immigrants' claims to become members of the political community but also their claims to settle in the state's territory.

Even if we do not challenge these two foundations of Wellman's position, the argument that the state has a right to exclude would-be immigrants by virtue of its right to freedom of association still fails on its own terms. In what follows, I raise three objections, focusing on harm to others, the distinctiveness of the state, and the absence of a justification for the state's territorial rights.

II

The first central problem emerges on closer inspection of Wellman's conception of self-determination. As indicated in Section I, Wellman describes the individual right to self-determination in the following terms: "Each of us enjoys a morally privileged position of dominion over our self-regarding affairs," and this is a position "which entitles us to freedom of association" (110). Although he does not elaborate on the idea of self-determination in the immigration discussion, in a previous article he notes that "it is not always clear when any given action is purely self-regarding," but "many people believe that we should be allowed to choose freely when our behavior is not harmful to others."[13] Behavior that is harmful to others wrongly causes them to be worse off than they would be otherwise (where "worse off" means that their interests are set back or thwarted).[14] Wellman's omission of the harm clause in the immigration piece is significant because, as I will show, the potential to cause harm to

others obstructs his path to the conclusion that the state enjoys a right to exclude.

To explain, there is no denying that Wellman's claim about the importance of individual self-determination has a good liberal pedigree. We are familiar with this as an argument in favor of allowing people the freedom "to be the authors of their own lives."[15] It is a "let them be" position and one that makes perfect sense with reference to the beliefs or actions of an individual. "You do not like the way that Ali chooses to live her life? If she is not harming anyone then you have no say in the matter. Let her be!" In Wellman's words, "it is *her* life."[16] The presumptive case lies with Ali.

From Wellman's conception of individual self-determination, we might extrapolate a comparable notion of group self-determination: groups enjoy a morally privileged position of dominion over their self-regarding affairs and should be allowed to choose freely when their behavior is not harmful to others. Matters become more complicated here because of the clear potential for groups illegitimately to restrict the autonomy of their own members. One common liberal response is to "let groups be" on the condition that the members of the group enjoy a right of exit.[17] The individual right of exit represents a form of safeguard against the group's potential to abuse its power.[18]

Yet the actions of groups affect not only the autonomy of their members; just like the actions of individuals, they may (directly or indirectly) affect third parties as well. When a private club in a residential area regularly arranges noisy late-night gatherings, the group's actions have spill-over effects for the local residents. In that way, while seemingly going about its own business, the private club has the potential to harm the interests of nonmembers. And, whereas a right of exit might go some way toward protecting the individual autonomy of the members, outsiders often are unwillingly exposed to the effects of a group's decisions. In such instances, where the nonmembers do not seek to interfere in the affairs of others for paternalist reasons, "let them be" is not an appropriate response to their appeals. Clearly, it is not the case that every action with potentially harmful effects ought to be prohibited, but, once the potential for harm to others enters the picture, the presumption in favor of the group members' freedom to do as they please is called into question, as is implied by Wellman's claim that "we should be allowed to choose freely *when our behavior is not harmful to others.*"[19] In fact, the potential for harm represents a good, if not a conclusive, reason for intervening in the group's affairs in order to prevent the harm.

There is also another way in which the actions of groups, unlike those of individuals, necessarily affect and even potentially harm third parties. As Wellman explains, "an important part of group self-determination is having control of what the 'self' is," and this is why he is so concerned with the citizens' freedom to select their political associates (115). Having control of that "self" means choosing "who is in and who is out," which, in turn, means including some people and excluding others.[20] The very act of excluding people may thwart their interests, either making them worse off than they are at present, or making them worse off than they would be otherwise, if they were left to act on their own plans and the group did not act to exclude them. For example, when a patch of green land, open to the general public, is purchased by a private group which plans to reserve the land for the use of members only, then current users of the land who are excluded from the group are made worse off. In another case, if a necessary condition of securing work in the teaching profession is membership of a national teachers' trade union, then qualified teachers excluded from the union are made worse off than they would be otherwise—exclusion bars them from pursuing their chosen career. Again, though not every action with potentially harmful effects can or should be prohibited, sometimes the interests in question are so substantial, and thwarting them is so detrimental to the well-being of the excluded, that exclusion itself becomes a cause for concern.

The potential to cause harm to others has important implications for Wellman's argument regarding the state's right to exclude. Would-be immigrants seek to leave one state and to enter another for a variety of reasons. Some effectively have no choice but to leave their state of origin, while others elect to move. Here

we might distinguish between those who are unable to live a minimally decent life in their present country and those whose basic needs are currently met but who wish to settle elsewhere in order to further their (various) interests. We know that emigration is generally accompanied by significant costs, including separation from family and friends, from a wider community, and from familiar surroundings, and often involves moving to somewhere unfamiliar, somewhere in which one is a stranger. It seems reasonable to assume, therefore, that those who are willing (or are forced) to incur such costs have substantial interests in living in another state and that thwarting their pursuit of those interests may be detrimental to the well-being of the excluded. This is particularly true if, as Wellman contends, in order to control access to membership of the political community, states must also enjoy a right to exclude outsiders from settling indefinitely within their territorial borders, because it means that those who are excluded from membership of the political community are unable to further any of their interests in long-term residence within the state (just as teachers who are excluded from the teaching union are unable to further their career interests).

Those who cannot live a minimally decent life in their country have an interest in meeting their basic needs. Wellman maintains that states must not ignore that interest but are free to "export justice" to them instead of granting them access to the state's territory and political community. Even if this were a plausible and legitimate option, it could not fully resolve the question of harm to would-be immigrants.[21] In a world where all the adverse political and economic (and, we might add, ecological and social) causes of forced migration had been eliminated, as Joseph Carens has emphasized, "people might have powerful reasons to want to migrate from one state to another."[22] Most importantly for our purposes, the interests in living in state *A* are not always interchangeable with the interests in living in state *B* or state *C*. Prohibiting outsiders from settling in and becoming members of a particular state hinders or prevents their pursuit of all the many familial, social, religious, cultural, political, or economic interests tied to residence and citizenship in that state, despite the fact that some, if not all, of their basic needs could be met elsewhere. Once more, this potential for harm to others represents a good, though not conclusive, reason against permitting the group to exclude some or all would-be members.

Therefore, while we may grant that there is a strong presumption in favor of individuals enjoying "dominion over their self-regarding affairs," group rights to self-determination are, by definition, always more troublesome, because groups consist of individuals who may be harmed by their group's actions and because the very act determining the group "self" is necessarily exclusionary, possibly at significant cost, even harm, to the excluded would-be members. Wellman thinks he establishes that there is a presumption in favor of the state's right to exclude prospective immigrants because he does not pause to consider the possibility that the act of exclusion is potentially harmful to them insofar as it thwarts the interests that they have in long-term settlement or in acquiring membership. And, as I have sought to illustrate, when the acts of a self-determining group are accompanied by potential harm to others, there does not appear to be a clear presumption on the group's side—the potential for harm represents a parallel reason to interfere with the group's actions.

III

In response, Wellman might wish to invoke the examples of marriage and religion again to illustrate that the refusal of a marriage proposal or exclusion from a religious group both may "damage the interests of others" and cause "pain or loss" in some sense, and yet everyone appears to assume that there is a clear presumption in favor of the refuser and the excluder in those cases.[23] However, this only serves to highlight why Wellman's inference from the examples of marriage and religion to the example of a state is problematic in the first place. While liberals are likely to accept that the presumption lies with the excluder in the marriage and religion cases despite the potential for causing "pain or loss" to the excluded, for many of them this is because there is something special about certain forms of association, which gives them a privileged status. They might argue, in line with

Amy Gutmann and Stuart White, for example, that there is a particularly compelling case for freedom of association, and by extension exclusion, in intimate or expressive contexts.[24] According to White's view, as quoted by Wellman himself, "if the formation of a specific association is essential to the individual's ability to exercise properly his/her liberties of conscience and expression, or to his/her ability to form and enjoy intimate attachments, then exclusion rules which are genuinely necessary to protect the association's primary purposes have an especially strong presumption of legitimacy."[25] The idea is that it would be objectionable to compel individuals to form or maintain intimate attachments against their will or to betray their own consciences. Does the modern liberal state enjoy a privileged status on a similar basis?

Although the liberal state obviously cannot be viewed as an intimate association, perhaps it has more of a claim to be viewed primarily as an expressive association, certainly not in the sense that it subscribes to a particular religious doctrine but at least insofar as it is (supposedly) committed to a set of principles that represent its liberal character. While there is a great deal of debate between liberals about how comprehensive or perfectionist those principles may be, and liberals of various stripes will disagree about the basic list and ranking, it is uncontroversial to claim that a liberal state is committed, in some way, to toleration, equality before the law, and individual liberty, for example. However, the liberal state's adherence to a basic set of common principles is not sufficient to suggest that it constitutes an expressive association. The label 'expressive association' implies, as Gutmann notes, "that the primary purpose of an association is expression of a point of view."[26] The members of liberal states are a diverse bunch, many of whom do not see themselves as making any sort of principled statement by remaining resident within the borders of a particular state. Citizens in a liberal state may endorse a variety of liberal principles, or may be indifferent to them, or may reject them altogether. Freedom of association within a liberal state is supposed to facilitate the citizens' freedom to express various points of view, including views antithetical to liberalism. When governments mistake the state itself for something akin to an expressive association with a single, comprehensive point of view, the result is often distinctly and disturbingly illiberal, as in the case of the American government's clampdown on communist views in the McCarthy era or the suppression of political opposition in the former Soviet Union. Hence, since the liberal state cannot claim to be primarily an intimate or expressive association, the initial case for exclusion then must be weaker than in the examples of marriage and religion.

Wellman acknowledges that freedom of association is "much more important for individuals" in the examples of marriage and religion, but he denies that this imperils his position regarding a presumptive right to exclude because he believes that "there is a very natural and straightforward case to be made in favor of freedom of association in all realms" (114). He points out that freedom of association for members of a golf club is obviously not as important as marital and religious freedom of association, and yet, "if no one doubts that golf clubs have a presumptive right to exclude others, then there seems no reason to suspect that a group of citizens cannot also have the right to freedom of association, even if control over membership in a country is not nearly as significant as control regarding one's potential spouse" (114).

The freedom of association principle, Wellman maintains, applies collectively to citizens of a state, just as it applies to members of a golf club. This argument by analogy is awkward again, though, because one might be reluctant to accept that a state has a presumptive right to exclude precisely because of the ways in which a state differs dramatically from a golf club. As a number of theorists have emphasized over the years, states are not like clubs.[27] For one thing, it is not possible today for would-be immigrants to get together and set up a state of their own. Moreover, it is generally fair to assume that exclusion from a golf club is unlikely to have a devastating impact on the life of the would-be member, whereas exclusion from a particular state—as the bearer of an enormous range of resources and options, many of which are not interchangeable with those on offer in other states and are not accessible to nonresidents and noncitizens—may have exactly that effect.

This suggests that there might well be a presumption in favor of a group's right to exclude would-be members in two quite different cases. The first case, as in the examples of marital and religious freedom of association, is when the associational freedom and accompanying exclusion are intricately connected to intimate attachments or expressive purposes. The second case, as in the golf club example, is when associations are not intimate or expressive but exclusion is generally fairly innocuous. Although Wellman invokes both sorts of case in his attempt to support the state's presumptive right to exclude, neither is relevantly comparable to that of the state, and so the examples do very little to help his cause. Interestingly enough, however, when particular clubs or associations start to look a bit more like states in the sense that outsiders have significant interests in becoming members and exclusion brings with it high costs to the nonmembers without serving clear expressive or intimate purposes, the argument in favor of exclusion seems weaker. That certainly appears to have been the view of the U.S. Supreme Court in the case of *Roberts v. United States*, 1984. The Court ruled that it was not unconstitutional to deny the U.S. Junior Chamber (Jaycees)—a nonintimate, nonexpressive, and formerly all-male association, which was understood to have clear career-enhancing advantages for its members—a right to exclude its regional chapters that chose to admit women as full members.[28] As Gutmann puts it, with reference to nonintimate, nonexpressive associations within civil society, there is no obvious presumption in favor of the excluders: "We cannot claim a presumption in favor of a right to exclude or a presumption in favor of a right not to be discriminated against without begging the question: which side carries the weight of argument in cases of conflict between the values of free association and those of nondiscrimination?"[29] With reference to the state and prospective members, we might rephrase Gutmann's statement and argue that we cannot claim a presumption in favor of the state's right to exclude or a presumption in favor of the would-be immigrant's interests in cases of conflict between the importance of free association and not harming others.

In summary, then, without denying that citizens have an interest in setting the rules of membership for their political community in order to maintain some control over the policy direction of their state, I have illustrated that, contra Wellman, the appeal to self-determination and freedom of association does not deliver a presumptive case in favor of a state's right to exclude would-be immigrants from settling within its borders and obtaining citizenship status. Excluding would-be immigrants from a state clearly has the potential to harm their interests to a significant degree, and this potential for harm also represents a good reason for challenging the citizens' right to exclude them. Groups may enjoy a presumptive right to exclude outsiders when the associations in question are intimate or primarily expressive or when exclusion is ordinarily reasonably "harmless," but the state does not meet the criteria necessary to qualify for that presumption.

Furthermore, once it becomes clear that the potential for harming the would-be immigrants' interests negates the case for the state's presumptive right to exclude based on the citizens' collective right to freedom of association, it is also apparent that Wellman's response to the "egalitarian" objection to the state's right to exclude is insufficient. Even if the state is able and willing to fulfill its duties to outsiders living in poverty or the victims of incompetent or brutal regimes by "exporting justice" abroad, excluding people who wish to pursue interests specific to that particular state is still potentially harmful, and that potential for harm remains an important challenge to Wellman's position.

Wellman might argue that he does directly confront that potential for harm to outsiders since he considers whether the citizens' right to exclude, grounded in their collective right to freedom of association, conflicts with the would-be immigrants' right to freedom of movement. In a sense, this is something of a red herring; as I emphasized at the outset, the citizens' collective right to freedom of association could not support a right to prevent outsiders crossing the state's borders anyway because their mere presence has no bearing on the citizens' individual or collective associational freedoms. Thus, it is not a surprise when Wellman concludes that the right to exclude is compatible with the rights of outsiders to enter the state's territory, provided that their visits are temporary. As the state is under no

obligation to extend the full rights of membership to temporary visitors, their presence within the state does not pose a problem for the citizens' collective right to self-determination and freedom of association. Hence, he stresses that his argument "would leave much more room for freedom of movement than the status quo, since it would allow most people to travel freely around the world (as tourists, to family or doctors, or even to study or work) as long as they did not stay indefinitely in some place without the permission of the host political community" (137). Nevertheless, again, this response does not serve to mitigate the harms that may accompany exclusion from permanent residence and citizenship. People who are not free to settle within a state are not at liberty to form or maintain long-term intimate relationships with citizens; to take advantage of the political, religious, and social options in that state; or, generally, to make a stable life for themselves there. The opportunity to travel "freely around the world" surely is of little comfort to those whose interests in settlement and membership are thwarted.

IV

Wellman does not deliver a conclusive case in favor of the citizens' position—that would require him to explain why the citizens' claim to self-determination is sufficiently strong to outweigh the harm to would-be immigrants. I will add that the argument in favor of preventing harm to the would-be immigrants seems more appealing once we recognize that we are not being asked to make a stark choice between self-determination and the interests of outsiders: while "having control of what the 'self' is" may be one element of group self-determination, it is not the only, or even a necessary, component. In the absence of full control over access to membership, a group still can be self-determining to the extent that it is free to set its own internal policy agenda without external interference. That freedom might be limited by the lack of control over membership rules, but liberal and democratic principles already constrain the extent of the citizens' discretion to control the membership of their political community. Wellman accepts the democratic requirement that long-term residents are offered citizenship rights, and presumably that same requirement extends to prohibiting the arbitrary expulsion of existing members. Moreover, as Walzer argues, in theory, states also could control membership by regulating birth rates and selectively awarding the right to give birth, choosing between different ethnic groups, or setting "class or intelligence quotas." This, he contends, "would require very high, and surely unacceptable, levels of coercion: the dominance of political power over kinship and love."[30] Therefore, since denying a group full control over membership rules is not an automatic denial of its right to self-determination, the citizens are not forced to sacrifice all control over their common life in order to prevent significant harm to others.

Nonetheless, aside from the issue that Wellman's argument about controlling the rules of membership is inconclusive, there is an additional difficulty for Wellman's defense of the right to exclude based on a commitment to freedom of association. As Wellman contends that citizens must enjoy not only a right to exclude would-be members from the political community but also would-be residents from the state's territory, his position calls for a further justification of the state's purported rights over that particular territory. To see why the freedom of association argument is insufficient here, consider the example of a private club. The club members might enjoy the right to exclude outsiders from membership and from using the club's property and resources, provided that they have rights of ownership over the premises. However, while a yoga group that meets in Central Park might be free to reject prospective members, it is not entitled to bar them from making use of Central Park itself because the park is not the members' property. In other words, Wellman's position begs the question whether citizens and/or their states have the relevant rights over the territory from which they wish to exclude others and thus whether they are within their rights not just to control the rules of membership but also to control settlement within that territory.

Perhaps a territorial argument is to be found lurking behind Wellman's claim that freedom of movement is not absolute: "My right to freedom of movement does not entitle me to enter your house without your permission . . . , so why think this right gives me a valid claim to enter a foreign country without that country's permission?" (135). The reason why one might agree that

Ali's right to freedom of movement does not entitle her to enter Ben's house without Ben's permission is that one assumes Ben is the legitimate owner of the house and that this grants him a set of rights over that property, including a right to exclude unwanted visitors. If states are the legitimate owners of their territory, then we would have good additional grounds for concluding that they enjoy a right to exclude outsiders from that territory. Yet, ultimately, Wellman does not appear to conceive of the state's relationship to its territory as one of ownership since, as we have seen, he contends that "even legitimate states," presumably unlike the owners of private property, "do not necessarily have the right to bar foreigners from visiting for a duly limited period" (136). And if, as is implied by Wellman's claims about visitors, the state's relationship to its territory is not one of ownership, in what sense does the state enjoy territorial rights?[31]

Wellman does refer to the specifically territorial requirements of states when he claims that, in order for states to fulfill their functional imperatives, they must be "sufficiently territorially contiguous" and this, in turn, means that states must (nonconsensually) coerce those within their borders (131). Elsewhere Wellman explains why he considers that it is legitimate for states to coerce their citizens in this way despite the value that he attaches to individual self-determination: "The reason that *I* have no moral right to be free from political coercion . . . is that, even if *I* would rather forego the benefits of political society, my state may permissibly coerce me in order to secure political stability for *my fellow citizens*."[32] States, he asserts, are necessary for people to enjoy the benefits of political stability and states must be territorial in order to fulfill those functions. Wellman employs the territorial contiguity point against Hillel Steiner's argument that individual citizens of a state should enjoy the freedom to associate with those not resident within that state and that the state's right to exclude illegitimately restricts that freedom.[33] However, although the purported territorial requirement might support the state's claim to coerce those within its borders, and thus may offer something of a general, consequentialist justification for a state's authority over territory (though not for any particular state's claims to its particular territory), it does not bear on the state's right to exclude would-be immigrants from settling in a territory. Once individuals are within the state's borders, they become subject to the state's authority. It will coerce them, as it coerces all other residents—excluding them is not a necessary condition for maintaining the state's territorial contiguity. Offering all long-term residents the option of becoming full members of the state may be "costly" for the existing citizens, as Wellman proposes, but that argument is not enough to support the state's right to exclude outsiders from settling in its territory either: just as the yoga group in Central Park is not entitled to prohibit nonmembers from making use of the park despite its control over its own membership rules, so the citizens of a state are not entitled to stop noncitizens from settling there, despite their claim to control access to membership, without a further entitlement to control access to the territory in the first place. Wellman must engage with this question if he is to establish that states have a right to exclude outsiders from settling within their territorial borders.

V

Wellman maintains that it is possible to defend a state's presumptive right to exclude would-be immigrants by appeal to the liberal commitment to freedom of association. He draws attention to the widespread conviction that individuals "should be allowed to choose freely when [their] behavior is not harmful to others," but I have argued that there is no clear presumption in favor of the state's position based upon the freedom to associate since exclusion from the state obviously has the potential to harm the interests of others—interests that would not disappear even if wealthy liberal states did, to use Wellman's words, "export justice" and thereby fulfill some of their duties to outsiders (128–29). The potential for exclusion to result in harm must be taken seriously, in line with Wellman's own argument, and more must be said about why the freedom of citizens takes precedence over the interests of the would-be immigrants, especially since states are neither intimate nor expressive associations. Moreover, freedom of association alone cannot deliver a right

to exclude would-be immigrants from entering and settling within a state: absent a further argument in support of states' rights over the territory they claim for themselves, we are left wondering whether states are entitled to control access to their territory at all.

NOTES

1. See, e.g., Joseph H. Carens, "Aliens and Citizens: The Case for Open Borders," *Review of Politics* 49 (1987): 251–73; and Phillip Cole, *Philosophies of Exclusion: Liberal Political Theory and Immigration* (Edinburgh: Edinburgh University Press, 2000).

2. Christopher Heath Wellman, "Immigration and Freedom of Association," *Ethics* 119 (2008): 109–41. Page numbers in the main text refer to this article.

3. Amy Gutmann, "Freedom of Association: An Introductory Essay," in *Freedom of Association*, ed. Amy Gutmann (Princeton, NJ: Princeton University Press, 1998), 3–32, 11.

4. See, e.g., Michael Walzer, *Spheres of Justice: A Defense of Pluralism and Equality* (New York: Basic Books, 1983), chap. 2; and David Miller, "Immigration: The Case for Limits," in *Contemporary Debates in Applied Ethics*, ed. Andrew I. Cohen and Christopher Heath Wellman (Oxford: Blackwell, 2004), 193–206.

5. This is an internal critique insofar as it seeks to illustrate that Wellman's freedom of association argument in defense of a right to exclude does not succeed on its own terms. Given the purposes of this article and the limits of space here, I do not develop an important external line of criticism recently advanced by Arash Abizadeh. To summarize very briefly, Abizadeh argues that state border control regimes subject would-be immigrants to coercion and democratic theory demands that coercion is justified to all those subject to it, where justification means rights of democratic participation. This simultaneously challenges any appeal to collective self-determination as the normative core of the state's right to exclude would-be immigrants: if those subject to coercion are entitled to participate in the relevant decision-making process, and coercion extends beyond the boundaries of the state, then the "self" is not simply equivalent to "all residents of the state" or "all members of the political community." For the full argument, see Arash Abizadeh, "Democratic Theory and Border Coercion: No Right to Unilaterally Control Your Own Borders," *Political Theory* 36 (2008): 37–65. I also make the case that democratic principles do not support a unilateral right to exclude in Sarah Fine, "Immigration and the Right to Exclude" (DPhil diss., University of Oxford, 2009).

6. In the final part of his article, Wellman explores the question of whether it is permissible for states to exclude would-be

immigrants primarily on the basis of their race, ethnicity, or religion, but I do not assess that aspect of his argument here.

7. Indeed, egalitarians may be committed to the conclusion that states have a duty to export justice rather than open their borders to "unfortunate people" if it is true that aid is a more effective response to poverty. See Wellman, "Immigration and Freedom of Association," 127–28.

8. Abizadeh, "Democratic Theory and Border Coercion," 38.

9. Ibid.

10. David Miller, *National Responsibility and Global Justice* (Oxford: Oxford University Press, 2008), 210–11.

11. See Walzer, *Spheres of Justice*, chap. 2.

12. For a challenge to Walzer's (and thus also to Wellman's) "bundling" of membership and residence claims, see Ryan Pevnick, "Social Trust and the Ethics of Immigration Policy," *Journal of Political Philosophy* 17 (2009): 146–67.

13. Christopher Heath Wellman, "The Paradox of Group Autonomy," *Social Policy and Philosophy* 20 (2003): 265–85, 265.

14. Christopher Heath Wellman, *A Theory of Secession: The Case for Political Self-Determination* (New York: Cambridge University Press, 2005), 11 n. 7, 12 n. 9. Wellman is following Joel Feinberg's analysis of the harm principle. For a full discussion, see Joel Feinberg, *The Moral Limits of Criminal Law*, vol. 1, *Harm to Others* (New York: Oxford University Press, 1987).

15. Wellman, *A Theory of Secession*, 2.

16. Wellman, "The Paradox of Group Autonomy," 266, author's emphasis.

17. See, e.g., John Stuart Mill, "On Liberty," in *On Liberty and Other Writings*, ed. Stefan Collini (Cambridge: Cambridge University Press, 1989), 91–92, where Mill considers the example of Mormons; and Chandran Kukathas, *Liberal Archipelago: A Theory of Diversity and Freedom* (Oxford: Oxford University Press, 2003), 95–96. It worth noting that this response is not considered sufficient by many (liberals and nonliberals alike), owing, e.g., to the possibility of crippling costs imposed on leavers—as in the case of "shunning."

18. Wellman is alert to the possibility that groups might illegitimately restrict the autonomy of their members; on that basis, he has argued that liberal principles point to a presumption (though not a conclusive case) against the sort of group rights that grant groups control over their own members. See Christopher Heath Wellman, "Liberalism, Communitarianism and Group Rights," *Law and Philosophy* 18 (1999): 13–40, esp. 33. Will Kymlicka refers to these as "internal restrictions," in contrast to "external protections" that defend the group

against the "larger society." See Will Kymlicka, *Multicultural Citizenship: A Liberal Theory of Minority Rights* (Oxford: Oxford University Press, 1995), 35, cited in Wellman, "Liberalism, Communitarianism and Group Rights," 14 n. 4.

19. Wellman, "The Paradox of Group Autonomy," 265, emphasis added.

20. Michael Walzer, "Exclusion, Injustice, and the Democratic State," *Dissent* 40 (1993): 55–64, 55.

21. Not to mention the various cases in which there is no apparent "export" alternative, as in the example of people who wish to emigrate to escape specific violent individuals.

22. Carens, "Aliens and Citizens," 258.

23. Mill, "On Liberty," 94–95.

24. See Gutmann, "Freedom of Association," 7–13; Stuart White, "Freedom of Association and the Right to Exclude," *Journal of Political Philosophy* 5 (1997): 373–91.

25. White, "Freedom of Association and the Right to Exclude," 381, cited in Wellman, "Immigration and Freedom of Association," 113.

26. Gutmann, "Freedom of Association," 11.

27. See, e.g., Cole, *Philosophies of Exclusion*, esp. 70–73; Carens, "Aliens and Citizens," 267–68; Melissa Lane, "A Philosophical View on States and Immigration," in *Globalizing Migration Regimes: New Challenges to Transnational Cooperation*, ed. Kristof Tamas and Joakim Palme (Aldershot: Ashgate, 2006), 131–43; and Jonathan Seglow, "The Ethics of Immigration," *Political Studies Review* 3 (2005): 317–34, 322.

28. For further discussion, see Gutmann, "Freedom of Association," esp. 8–9.

29. Ibid., 11.

30. Walzer, *Spheres of Justice*, 34–35.

31. For a selection of different arguments concerning the normative grounds for territorial rights, see Tamar Meisels, *Territorial Rights* (Dordrecht: Springer, 2005); Cara Nine, "A Lockean Theory of Territory," *Political Studies* 56 (2008): 148–65; Avery Kolers, *Land, Conflict, and Justice: A Political Theory of Territory* (Cambridge: Cambridge University Press, 2009); and Anna Stilz, "Why Do States Have Territorial Rights?" *International Theory* 1 (2009): 185–213.

32. Wellman, *A Theory of Secession*, 16–17, author's emphasis.

33. Hillel Steiner, "Hard Borders, Compensation, and Classical Liberalism," in *Boundaries and Justice: Diverse Ethical Perspectives*, ed. David Miller and Sohail H. Hashmi (Princeton, NJ: Princeton University Press, 2001), 79–88.

CHAPTER 21

Global Economic Justice

A plain fact of the moral life is that in ethical matters small and large, personal and abstract, we wrestle with issues of justice. Whatever our moral outlook, we must sometimes ask, What is just? **Justice** is about persons getting what is fair or what is their due. In the name of justice, we condemn racial discrimination, unequal pay for equal work, and judicial punishment based on a judge's prejudice. For justice's sake, we strive to treat people the same unless there is a morally relevant reason for treating them differently—that is, we try to treat equals equally. For reasons of justice, we act—or feel obliged to act—to change the way things are, to try to make the world or ourselves more just.

Among the more vexing questions of justice are those that emerge when we become aware of people in dire need of something we have, something we could easily supply. Then the questions are, Do we have a duty to give to the needy in order to somehow ease their misery? Do they have a right to some of what we have? If so, how much should we relinquish to them? Would we be justified in refusing to give? Such queries trouble us on two levels—*locally* (pertaining to needy people nearby: in our neighborhood, community, or country) and *globally* (regarding the poor and hungry in other countries). The former has always been a concern. The latter presses us harder than ever because, thanks to our technology and wealth, we now know a great deal about the suffering of people in distant lands and we have the wherewithal to do something about it. In this chapter, we explore the global question, What are our obligations to the impoverished, hungry, dying strangers who are half a world away and whom we will never meet?

ISSUE FILE: BACKGROUND

For many people, this moral issue is compelling because the wretchedness of the world's poor is profound and the economic gap between rich and poor is wide. According to the latest estimates, 1.2 billion people are living in extreme poverty, and about one in five persons in the developing world lives on less than $1.25 a day. About 99 million children under the age of five are underweight for their age—a sign of severe malnutrition. In developing countries, the mortality rate for children under five is forty-eight deaths per thousand live births, mostly from preventable causes.[1]

Economic inequality across the globe has always been with us, but now its scale is larger than most people realize. The eighty-five richest people on the planet now own as much as the entire poorest half of the world's population. People in the poorest half of the world's population possess only about 0.7 percent of the world's wealth. The richest 1 percent of people own almost half of all wealth—which amounts to $110 trillion. Perhaps it is not surprising that in 2005 the wealthiest 20 percent of the world's people consumed over 75 percent of its goods, whereas the poorest consumed only 1.5 percent.[2]

Most careful thinkers agree on such facts and react with dismay and sympathy, but they disagree on the proper moral response to the massive suffering. The disagreements hinge on which moral theory is accepted and on how certain elements of morality are interpreted.

One factor is our distance from those who need help. Suppose you come upon a child drowning in a stream. With very little inconvenience to yourself you could easily save her, and you are the only person in a position to do so. If you walk away, no one will be the wiser. Would you save her? Most people probably would, and many would think they had a *duty* to save her. That is, not to save her would be wrong.

But imagine that the child is not 20 feet away from you but 1 mile or 100 miles or 5,000 miles away. If you somehow had the power to rescue her despite the distance involved, would you be obligated to do so? Most of us assume that we have duties to help those close to us—our family, friends, neighbors, or fellow citizens. After all, we have relationships with these people, and we are often in a good position to aid them. But many believe we have no duty at all to help distant peoples, strangers with whom we have no social or emotional connection. Distance changes our moral obligations; charity begins at home. Others argue that distance is irrelevant. As one philosopher says, "It makes no moral difference whether the person I can help is a neighbor's child ten yards from me or a Bengali whose name I shall never know, ten thousand miles away."[3]

Another important element in debates over aid to the needy is the notion of rights. A **right** is a person's claim or entitlement to something, a moral demand that obligates others to act accordingly. Someone's **negative right** obligates others *not to interfere* with that person's obtaining something. Someone's **positive right** obligates others *to help that person* obtain something.

Many insist that people possess only negative rights—that is, persons are entitled to be free of coercion or harm or improper restraint. Those who take this line maintain that they have no duty to help the needy, whether near or far. Their obligation is to refrain from interfering in others'

lives. They may, out of a sense of charity, give to the destitute, but they are not *morally required* to give anything. Others argue that people have both negative and positive rights and that we are therefore obligated to aid the less fortunate, including the poor and hungry of the world. They may contend that everyone has a right to the necessities of life and that the affluent are, therefore, duty bound to provide them. The have-nots possess a right to the resources of the haves. Exactly how much the have-nots are entitled to, however, is a matter of debate.

Some argue that we must aid the needy of other lands because we have a **duty of beneficence**, a moral obligation to benefit others. The impoverished may not have a right to our resources, but we nevertheless should give what we can to them. If we can help the poor without sacrificing too much of what we have, the argument goes, we should do so.

For a few conscientious people, beneficence seems to require extraordinary sacrifice—they feel obliged to give until their own standard of living is jeopardized. Others accept a duty of beneficence toward the distant needy but try to balance it against other duties, including those to their families and to themselves.

People in this latter group often appeal to a common distinction in morality—that between obligatory and supererogatory actions. Obligatory actions are what duty requires; **supererogatory actions** are above and beyond the demands of duty. Supererogatory conduct is not required, but it is praiseworthy. Some think their duty of beneficence is limited and that giving more than required is supererogatory—commendable but optional. Others (many utilitarians, for example) do not recognize supererogatory actions. To them, duty demands that we benefit others as much as possible all the time. If maximum moral effort is required of all our actions, then no actions are supererogatory. On this view, we should give until it hurts, perhaps to the point of greatly reducing our own wealth.

MORAL THEORIES

Concerns about justice emerge in different regions of the moral life. As we saw in earlier chapters, they appear in deliberations about fair punishment for wrongdoing, an issue known as **retributive justice**. Questions regarding the fair distribution of society's goods (income, rights, welfare aid, etc.) are topics of **distributive justice**. The latter applies not only to justice within a society but also to justice among societies—for example, to the global distribution of wealth and resources among rich and poor countries and among rich and poor individuals.

Theories of distributive justice try to explain what makes a particular allocation of economic goods fair or just. They may be part of a broader moral theory such as Kantian ethics or utilitarianism, or they may stand alone as distinct conceptions of justice. Either way, they often have something interesting to say about the morality of helping or not helping impoverished people of distant lands.

Libertarian theories of justice emphasize individual liberties and negative rights. Exemplified in the writings of Robert Nozick, John Hospers, and others, these perspectives reject positive rights as a violation of personal freedom, because such rights force people to contribute to the welfare of others. The central point is that people have a right not to be interfered with and to do whatever they want with their own property as long as they do not violate the liberty rights of others. John Hospers expresses the view like this:

> The political philosophy that is called libertarianism . . . is the doctrine that every person is the owner of his own life, and that no one is the owner of anyone else's life; and that consequently every human being has the right to act in accordance with his own choices, unless those actions infringe on the equal liberty of other human beings to act in accordance with *their* choices.[4]

The libertarian asserts that we have no duty to help the poor and hungry of the world; we are

---

VITAL STATS:
The Planet's Poor and Hungry

- In 2010, 1.2 billion people lived in extreme poverty.
- Every day, 18,000 children under age five die from preventable causes.
- From 2011 to 2013, 842 million people suffered from chronic hunger.
- About 805 million people continue to go hungry.
- In 2012, 748 million people relied on unsafe drinking water.
- An estimated 801,000 children under five years of age die each year from diarrhea, mostly from unsafe drinking water and unsanitary conditions.

Data from United Nations, "Millennium Development Report 2014," http://www.un.org/millenniumgoals /reports.shtml (March 1, 2015); International Food Policy Research Institute, *2014 Global Hunger Index*, http:// www.ifpri.org/publication/2014-global-hunger-index (March 1, 2015); Oxfam International, "Working for the Few," 2014, http://www.oxfam.org/en/research/working-few (March 1, 2015); Centers for Disease Control and Prevention, "Global Water, Sanitation, and Hygiene," 2012, http://www.cdc.gov/healthywater/global/assessing.html (March 1, 2015).

---

not obligated to share our resources with those less fortunate. If we aid the needy, we do so as an act of charity, not because duty commands.

Critics of the libertarian doctrine say that it conflicts with commonsense morality. In strictly libertarian terms, we have no duty to save a drowning child even though we could do so with minimal trouble. But surely when saving her life costs us so little, the critics say, we have a strong duty of beneficence to pull her from the water. The notion that saving her is not morally obligatory but merely optional seems implausible.

Consequentialist or utilitarian theories have been marshaled both to commend the aiding of distant peoples and to deplore it. Taking a utilitarian tack, Peter Singer argues that we can increase the overall good, or utility, in the world if the affluent give large portions of their wealth to the needy in other countries. He thinks his approach would dramatically lower the standard of living for the rich and drastically reduce the suffering of the poor, resulting in a general decrease in misery, starvation, and death. He tries to show that transferring our surplus of goods to those who have little or nothing is not a supererogatory gesture but an inescapable moral obligation.

Others who argue in a consequentialist vein have ended up opposing aid to the world's starving millions. In their view, uncontrolled population growth is the cause of global poverty and starvation. They contend that in developing countries, population growth is usually unrestrained, so population increases over time, inevitably outstripping available food supplies. Famine soon follows, and many die; but then the balance between population and available food is restored. Giving the starving people food to avert famine would temporarily prevent mass starvation and allow the population to increase again—but that would only postpone the inevitable famine. When this catastrophe does come, many more people will suffer and die than if food were never donated. Thus, on consequentialist grounds, these critics of food aid argue that feeding the hungry in countries where population is unchecked will just lead to greater tragedy. Our moral duty, they say, is not to feed the hungry.

Critics question nearly every assumption behind this argument. They dispute the notions that population growth is the primary cause of famine, that giving food aid is the only option for preventing starvation, and that rich nations bear no responsibility for the plight of the poor in developing countries.

Egalitarian theories of justice hold that justice requires equal distribution of goods among all persons. Some egalitarians insist that everyone be allotted a certain minimum amount of vital goods such as food and medical care. Others claim that only a truly equal share of everything is just. Since all persons have equal value and deserve equal respect, they have equal rights to the world's resources. The world's food, for example, should be shared equally by everyone on the planet. This global equality is the supreme value, even though it requires taking goods from the better-off to give to the needy, thus curtailing the personal liberties of some for the betterment of others.

This latter point provokes considerable criticism from those who believe that individual liberties should take precedence over economic equality—libertarians, for example. They think ensuring that people can use their own legitimately acquired resources as they see fit is more important than guaranteeing that everyone's needs are met.

MORAL ARGUMENTS

Among the more influential arguments on obligations to the world's needy is Peter Singer's utilitarian case for making major personal sacrifices to aid impoverished, starving people. His argument is straightforward:

1. "[S]uffering and death from lack of food, shelter, and medical care are bad."[5]

2. "[I]f it is in our power to prevent something bad from happening, without thereby sacrificing anything of comparable moral importance, we ought, morally, to do it."[6]

3. Therefore, we are morally obligated to prevent suffering caused by the lack of these necessities.

Singer asserts that our moral duty applies to needy people regardless of their distance from us. "If we accept any principle of impartiality, universalizability, equality, or whatever," he says, "we cannot discriminate against someone merely because he is far away from us (or we are far away from him)."[7]

The argument shows, Singer says, that giving money to famine relief is not an act of charity—a supererogatory gesture—but a moral duty:

> Because giving money is regarded as an act of charity, it is not thought that there is anything wrong with not giving. . . . On the contrary, we ought to give the money away, and it is wrong not to do so.[8]

But how much should we give? The second premise requires a drastic change in conventional moral attitudes toward the extent of our obligations:

> [W]e ought to give until we reach the level of marginal utility—that is, the level at which, by giving more, I would cause as much suffering to myself or my dependents as I would relieve by my gift. This would mean, of course, that one would reduce oneself to very near the material circumstances of a Bengali refugee.[9]

Singer offers a weaker version of the second premise, even though he thinks the stronger one is closer to the truth: we are duty bound to prevent something bad from happening as long as we can prevent it without "sacrificing anything morally significant."[10] This principle would require us to contribute to famine relief when doing so would not cost us anything of real importance. If by aiding the poor we would have to forgo buying new clothes or a fancier car, so be it.

Even if we all adopted only the weaker principle, Singer says, society would likely be transformed:

> Even if we accepted the principle only in its moderate form, however, it should be clear that we would have to give away enough to ensure that the consumer society, dependent as it is on people spending on trivia rather than giving to famine relief, would slow down and perhaps disappear entirely.[11]

Critics of Singer's strong premise charge that it disregards essential features of the moral life. We may have a duty to help those in need, but we also have obligations involving rights. John Arthur contends, for example, that each person has rights that should not be relinquished even to help others in dire need. Each of us could help others by giving away a kidney or an eye—we could save a life or restore sight to a blind person, and our loss would not be comparable to the terrible loss experienced by someone who will die or be blind for lack of our help. But this much sacrifice is not obligatory:

> If anything is clear, however, it is that our [moral] code does not *require* such heroism; you are entitled to keep your second eye and kidney. . . . The reason for this is often expressed in terms of rights; it's your body, you have a right to it, and that weighs against whatever duty you have to help. To sacrifice a kidney to a stranger is to do more than is required, it's heroic.[12]

Singer's critics hold that desert is another factor we must weigh when deciding whether to give food to the hungry. As Arthur says,

> Suppose, for example, an industrious farmer manages through hard work to produce a surplus of food for the winter while a lazy neighbor spends his summer fishing. Must our industrious farmer ignore his hard work and give the surplus away because his neighbor or his family will suffer? What again seems clear is that we have more than one factor to weigh. Not only should we compare the consequences of his keeping it with his giving it away; we also should weigh the fact that one farmer deserves the food, he earned it through his hard work.[13]

Others who question Singer's view concede that we have an obligation to aid distant people but maintain that we also have a duty to help those with whom we have a special relationship. As one philosopher explains,

> I may have a duty to give of my surplus to help save drowning children in a distant land, but I have a stronger duty to help those with whom I have intimate or contractual ties.[14]

Like Singer, Garrett Hardin takes a consequentialist approach to the morality of aiding the needy, but he arrives at a very different conclusion. He argues that the rich should *not* aid the poor and hungry because doing so will only invite catastrophe for rich and poor alike.

His argument proceeds by way of metaphors, the best known being the lifeboat. Rich countries are lifeboats carrying the affluent people of the world in an ocean swarming with the drowning poor, who are desperately trying to scramble into the boats or grasp some of the food on board. Like a country, each lifeboat is limited in the number of people it can sustain, and to maintain a margin of safety it should carry fewer passengers than its maximum capacity. If a boat takes on any more passengers or throws vital supplies to the unfortunates swimming nearby, everyone—rich and poor—will perish. Either the boat will capsize, or those on board will slowly starve. Thus, the only reasonable option is to refuse to help the drowning people. Sadly, millions will be lost, but those already on board will be saved. The conclusion to be drawn, Hardin says, is that the moral duty of affluent countries is not to give aid to the starving, overpopulated ones.

Many take issue with Hardin's argument (and metaphors). A chief complaint is that the lifeboat argument is simplistic, that it ignores some hard facts about rich and poor nations. For instance, Hardin implies that the lifeboats of the rich have no interaction with the poor. But many deny this, asserting that for years rich countries have been taking advantage of poor ones and, therefore, bear some responsibility for the wretched plight of the impoverished:

> Haven't colonization and commercial arrangements worked to increase the disparity between the rich and the poor nations of the earth? We extract cheap raw materials from poor nations and sell those nations expensive manufactured goods (for example, radios, cars, computers, and weapons) instead of appropriate agricultural goods and training. The structure of tariffs and internal subsidies discriminates selectively against underdeveloped nations. Multinational corporations place strong inducements on poor countries to produce cash crops such as coffee and cocoa instead of food crops needed to feed their own people. . . . Hardin's lifeboat metaphor grimly obscures the fact that we have profited and are profiting from the economic conditions in the third world.[15]

QUICK REVIEW

justice—The morality of persons getting what is fair or what is their due.

right—A claim or entitlement to something; a moral demand that obligates others to honor it.

negative right—A person's right that obligates others not to interfere with that person's obtaining something.

positive right—A person's right that obligates others to help that person obtain something.

duty of beneficence—A moral obligation to benefit others.

supererogatory actions—Conduct that is above and beyond duty; not required, but praiseworthy.

retributive justice—Justice concerning the fair use of punishment for wrongdoing.

distributive justice—Justice concerning the fair distribution of society's goods.

libertarian theory of justice—A doctrine emphasizing individual liberties and negative rights, and rejecting positive rights as a violation of personal freedom.

egalitarian theory of justice—A doctrine holding that justice requires equal distribution of goods and social benefits among all persons.

The lifeboat metaphor suggests that supplies are fixed, but critics protest that the reality is far different:

> In the real world, the quantity has strict limits, but these are far from having been reached. . . . Nor are we forced to devote fixed proportions of our efforts and energy to automobile travel, pet food, packaging, advertising, corn-fed beef, "defense," and other diversions, many of which cost far more than foreign aid does. The fact is that enough food is now produced to feed the world's population adequately. That people are malnourished is due to distribution and to economics, not to agricultural limits.[16]

The gist of these counterarguments is that the survival of rich countries is not really at stake and that feeding the hungry will not necessarily capsize any boats. The critics conclude that Hardin offers no good reason for our not aiding the needy.

CHAPTER REVIEW

SUMMARY

Justice is about persons getting what is fair or what is their due. Distributive justice pertains to the fair distribution of society's goods and applies to both national and international issues. A central justice issue in global economics is, What is the moral duty of the affluent to the needy of the world?

In answering this question, libertarian theories—which emphasize negative rights—say that we have no duties to the poor. The poor have only negative rights of noninterference; they have no positive rights to be aided by others. Consequentialist theories have been used both to advocate helping the poor and to refrain from helping them, their proponents arguing that the overall benefits and harms of aid are the deciding factor. Egalitarian theories maintain that justice requires equal distributions of goods among all persons.

Peter Singer argues that we should make huge sacrifices to aid the impoverished of the world: if it is in our power to prevent something bad from happening without sacrificing anything of comparable moral importance, we should do it. Garrett Hardin contends that we have an opposite duty—not to help the needy. Both Singer and Hardin argue that their preferred course of action results in the overall best consequences.

KEY TERMS

justice (p. 820)
right (p. 821)
negative right (p. 821)
positive right (p. 821)

duty of beneficence (p. 821)
supererogatory actions (p. 821)
retributive justice (p. 822)
distributive justice (p. 822)
libertarian theory of justice (p. 822)
egalitarian theory of justice (p. 823)

EXERCISES

Review Questions

1. What is justice? How is the concept of justice related to issues such as racial discrimination and unequal pay for equal work? (p. 820)
2. To what does the phrase "economic gap between the world's rich and poor" refer? (p. 820)
3. What is a right? What is the difference between a negative and a positive right? (p. 821)
4. What is the duty of beneficence? (p. 821)
5. Give two examples of positive rights and two examples of negative rights. (p. 821)
6. What are supererogatory actions? (p. 821)
7. What is distributive justice? What is retributive justice? (p. 822)
8. What characterizes libertarian theories of distributive justice? (p. 822)
9. What characterizes egalitarian theories of distributive justice? (p. 823)
10. On what grounds do libertarians reject positive rights? (p. 822)

Discussion Questions

1. Do we have a duty to give to the needy to help ease their suffering? If so, under what circumstances do we have such a duty?
2. Would you have a moral duty to save a drowning child if you could easily do so with very little inconvenience to yourself? Why or why not?
3. Do you believe in positive rights—that is, rights that obligate others to help someone obtain something?
4. Are you a (distributive justice) libertarian? Why or why not?

5. What aspects of libertarian theories do you find most appealing? What aspects do you find most unattractive? What do you think is most plausible and implausible about egalitarian theories?

6. How do libertarians and egalitarians differ in their views about personal liberty?

7. Suppose you could transform society into a system of distributive justice based strictly on libertarian principles. What would be the real-world implications of such a change? What changes would we see in welfare, health care, poverty relief, and other programs based on positive rights? Who would be helped or hurt in this libertarian world?

8. How might the strict application of an egalitarian theory of justice change society? Who would likely be helped or hurt in such a system?

9. How strong is your duty of beneficence? Should you give to the needy only if you have resources to spare? Should you give until your own standard of living is reduced? Explain.

10. You may have a duty of beneficence to your immediate family, but do you have a similar duty to needy people in your neighborhood? To starving people in a faraway land? If you help your family live comfortably but refuse to aid anyone else, are you morally blameworthy? Explain.

FURTHER READING

William Aiken and Hugh LaFollette, eds. *World Hunger and Morality,* 2nd ed. (Englewood Cliffs, NJ: Prentice-Hall, 1996).

Lester R. Brown, *Tough Choices: Facing the Challenge of Food Scarcity* (New York: Norton, 1996).

Joel E. Cohen, *How Many People Can the Earth Support?* (New York: Norton, 1995).

Nigel Dower, "World Poverty," in *A Companion to Ethics,* ed. Peter Singer (Cambridge, MA: Blackwell, 1993).

Steven Luper-Foy, ed., *Problems of International Justice* (Boulder, CO: Westview Press, 1988).

William W. Murdoch and Allan Oaten, "Population and Food: Metaphors and the Reality," *BioScience* 25 (1975): 561–67.

Onora O'Neill, *Faces of Hunger: An Essay on Poverty, Justice, and Development* (London: Allen & Unwin, 1986).

Thomas Pogge, *World Poverty and Human Rights: Cosmopolitan Responsibilities and Reforms,* 2nd ed. (Cambridge: Polity Press, 2008).

Louis P. Pojman, "World Hunger and Population," in *Life and Death: Grappling with the Moral Dilemmas of Our Time,* rev. 2nd ed. (Belmont, CA: Wadsworth, 2000).

Michael J. Sandel, ed., *Justice: A Reader* (New York: Oxford University Press, 2007).

Robert N. Van Wyk, "Perspectives on World Hunger and the Extent of Our Positive Duties," *Public Affairs Quarterly* 2, no. 2 (April 1988): 75–90.

ETHICAL DILEMMAS

1. Averting Famine

For years the small nation of Malawi in southern Africa remained on the verge of famine, with high rates of acute child hunger, begging for emergency food aid from richer countries. But now the tables have turned, and Malawi is growing enough food to feed its people *and* sell much of the surplus to other nations. Rates of child hunger have dropped dramatically.

Why the change? With the soil in Malawi overfarmed and depleted, it was impossible for the country to feed itself. The situation improved only when Malawi began to ignore the advice of the World Bank and rich countries, which advised Malawi to get rid of fertilizer subsidies and to rely on the workings of free markets. After the disastrous harvest of 2005, Malawi reversed the trend and subsidized farmers' use of fertilizer—just as many Western countries do for their own farmers.

Malawi's success has prompted reappraisals of the capacity of agriculture to eliminate poverty and of a government's ability to spur self-sufficiency and growth through investments in agricultural production and know-how.*

If, as this story suggests, the World Bank and rich nations offered bad advice to Malawi, do they bear some responsibility for the subsequent food shortages? Does this story seem to support or undermine Garrett Hardin's views on helping the needy?

*Based on Celia W. Dugger, "Ending Famine, Simply by Ignoring the Experts," *New York Times*, December 2, 2007, http://www.nytimes.com/2007/12/02/world/africa/02malawi.html?scp=1&sq=ending+famine+simply +by+igno ring+the+experts&st=nyt&_r=0 (March 1, 2015).

---

2. Developed Countries Failing the Poor

UNITED NATIONS—In criticism aimed primarily at the United States, Japan and the European Union, a U.N. report said rich donor nations have failed to deliver on promises to help the world's poorest countries and must increase aid by $18 billion a year.

The report released Thursday also criticized the failure of rich and poor nations to reach a trade pact in seven years of negotiations that would expand global trade opportunities for developing countries to reduce poverty. It called for redoubled efforts to conclude negotiations.

The report was issued ahead of a Sept. 25 meeting of world leaders at U.N. headquarters to step up efforts to achieve the Millennium Development Goals, adopted by world leaders at a summit in 2000. The goals include cutting extreme poverty by half, ensuring universal primary school education and starting to reverse the HIV/AIDS pandemic, all by 2015. . . .

U.N. Secretary-General Ban Ki-moon told a press conference that the report "sounds a strong alarm."

> "The main message is that while there has been progress on several counts, delivery on commitments made by member states has been deficient, and has fallen behind schedule," he said. "We are already in the second half of our contest against poverty. We are running out of time.". . .
>
> Ban noted that total aid from the world's major donor nations amounts to only 0.25% of their combined national income, far below the U.N. target of 0.7%. The only countries to reach or exceed that target were Denmark, Luxembourg, the Netherlands, Norway and Sweden.[†]

Is the failure of rich nations to aid the world's poorest countries morally wrong? Is the giving of aid a moral obligation for rich nations—or a supererogatory act? What conclusion do you draw from the United States' failure to contribute its promised share of aid?

[†]Associated Press, "U.N. Report: Developed Countries Failing Poor," published on USAToday.com, September 4, 2008. © The Associated Press. Reprinted by permission.

3. Singer or Hardin?

CBC News—The Church World Service aid agency is warning that "immediate, massive intervention and assistance" are needed to prevent mass starvation in Kenya.

A team from the humanitarian agency reported recently that many fields are barren and cracked, dried out by the drought that is threatening a third of the east African country's population, or about 10 million people.

What was once among the most fertile land in Africa can now only support a few struggling plants suitable only for grazing cattle.

"We don't have any food," farmer Lizy Bimba, a Kwale resident, said in Swahili.

In one area, a local official reported that 85 per cent of 5,600 people are facing starvation, the Church World Service team said.

Other farmers have left the land to find what work they can.

"We have been forced to do this so that we get money to buy food," Musa Charo said in Swahili as he broke rocks to earn money to feed his 10 children.

The government declared the food shortage a national disaster on Jan. 16, the UN is appealing for international help and aid agencies warn that the problem will only get worse.[‡]

What would be the proper moral response of rich nations to this impending tragedy? Do you favor Garrett Hardin's approach in which rich countries would not send food aid? Or Peter Singer's path in which affluent individuals would be obligated to give much of their wealth to feed the hungry? Or a middle way in which the rich would have a duty to give some aid but would also have obligations to themselves and to their family and friends? Explain.

[‡]CBC News Staff, "Kenya Facing Mass Starvation: Aid Group." *CBC News*, January 31, 2009. Reprinted by permission of Canadian Broadcasting Corporation.

READINGS

From *Famine, Affluence, and Morality*

PETER SINGER

As I write this, in November 1971, people are dying in East Bengal from lack of food, shelter, and medical care. The suffering and death that are occurring there now are not inevitable, not unavoidable in

Peter Singer, excerpts from "Famine, Affluence, and Morality." *Philosophy and Public Affairs* 1(3): 229–36, 238, and 240–43. Copyright © 1972 Blackwell Publishing Ltd. Reproduced with permission of Blackwell Publishing Ltd.

any fatalistic sense of the term. Constant poverty, a cyclone, and a civil war have turned at least nine million people into destitute refugees; nevertheless, it is not beyond the capacity of the richer nations to give enough assistance to reduce any further suffering to very small proportions. The decisions and actions of human beings can prevent this kind of suffering. Unfortunately, human beings have not made the necessary decisions. At the individual level, people have, with very few exceptions, not responded to the situation in any significant way. Generally speaking, people have not given large sums to relief funds; they have not written to their parliamentary representatives demanding increased government assistance; they have not demonstrated in the streets, held symbolic fasts, or done anything else directed toward providing the refugees with the means to satisfy their essential needs. At the government level, no government has given the sort of massive aid that would enable the refugees to survive for more than a few days. Britain, for instance, has given rather more than most countries. It has, to date, given £14,750,000. For comparative purposes, Britain's share of the nonrecoverable development costs of the Anglo-French Concorde project is already in excess of £275,000,000, and on present estimates will reach £440,000,000. The implication is that the British government values a supersonic transport more than thirty times as highly as it values the lives of the nine million refugees. Australia is another country which, on a per capita basis, is well up in the "aid to Bengal" table. Australia's aid, however, amounts to less than one-twelfth of the cost of Sydney's new opera house. The total amount given, from all sources, now stands at about £65,000,000. The estimated cost of keeping the refugees alive for one year is £464,000,000. Most of the refugees have now been in the camps for more than six months. The World Bank has said that India needs a minimum of £300,000,000 in assistance from other countries before the end of the year. It seems obvious that assistance on this scale will not be forthcoming. India will be forced to choose between letting the refugees starve or diverting funds from her own development program, which will mean that more of her own people will starve in the future.[1]

These are the essential facts about the present situation in Bengal. So far as it concerns us here, there is nothing unique about this situation except its magnitude. The Bengal emergency is just the latest and most acute of a series of major emergencies in various parts of the world, arising both from natural and from man-made causes. There are also many parts of the world in which people die from malnutrition and lack of food independent of any special emergency.

I take Bengal as my example only because it is the present concern, and because the size of the problem has ensured that it has been given adequate publicity. Neither individuals nor governments can claim to be unaware of what is happening there.

What are the moral implications of a situation like this? In what follows, I shall argue that the way people in relatively affluent countries react to a situation like that in Bengal cannot be justified; indeed, the whole way we look at moral issues—our moral conceptual scheme—needs to be altered, and with it, the way of life that has come to be taken for granted in our society.

In arguing for this conclusion I will not, of course, claim to be morally neutral. I shall, however, try to argue for the moral position that I take, so that anyone who accepts certain assumptions, to be made explicit, will, I hope, accept my conclusion.

I begin with the assumption that suffering and death from lack of food, shelter, and medical care are bad. I think most people will agree about this, although one may reach the same view by different routes. I shall not argue for this view. People can hold all sorts of eccentric positions, and perhaps from some of them it would not follow that death by starvation is in itself bad. It is difficult, perhaps impossible, to refute such positions, and so for brevity I will henceforth take this assumption as accepted. Those who disagree need read no further.

My next point is this: if it is in our power to prevent something bad from happening, without thereby sacrificing anything of comparable moral importance, we ought, morally, to do it. By "without sacrificing anything of comparable moral importance" I mean without causing anything else comparably bad to happen, or doing something that is wrong in itself, or failing to promote some moral good, comparable in significance to the bad thing that we can prevent. This principle seems almost as uncontroversial as the last one. It requires us only to prevent what is bad, and not to promote what is good, and it requires this of us only when we can do it without sacrificing anything that is, from the moral point of view, comparably important. I could even, as far as the application of my argument to the Bengal emergency is concerned, qualify the point so as to make it: if it is in our power to prevent something very bad from happening, without thereby sacrificing anything morally significant, we ought, morally, to do it. An application of this principle would be as follows: if I am walking past a shallow pond and see a child drowning in it, I ought to wade in and pull the child out. This will mean getting my clothes muddy, but this is insignificant, while the death of the child would presumably be a very bad thing.

The uncontroversial appearance of the principle just stated is deceptive. If it were acted upon, even in its qualified form, our lives, our society, and our world would be fundamentally changed. For the principle takes, firstly, no account of proximity or distance. It makes no moral difference whether the person I can help is a neighbor's child ten yards from me or a Bengali whose name I shall never know, ten thousand miles away. Secondly, the principle makes no distinction between cases in which I am the only person who could possibly do anything and cases in which I am just one among millions in the same position.

I do not think I need to say much in defense of the refusal to take proximity and distance into account. The fact that a person is physically near to us, so that we have personal contact with him, may make it more likely that we *shall* assist him, but this does not show that we *ought* to help him rather than another who happens to be further away. If we accept any principle of impartiality, universalizability, equality, or whatever, we cannot discriminate against someone merely because he is far away from us (or we are far away from him). Admittedly, it is possible that we are in a better position to judge what needs to be done to help a person near to us than one far away, and perhaps also to provide the assistance we judge to be necessary. If this were the case, it would be a reason for helping those near to us first. This may once have been a justification for being more concerned with the poor in one's own town than with famine victims in India. Unfortunately for those who like to keep their moral responsibilities limited, instant communication and swift transportation have changed the situation. From the moral point of view, the development of the world into a "global village" has made an important, though still unrecognized, difference to our moral situation. Expert observers and supervisors, sent out by famine relief organizations or permanently stationed in famine-prone areas, can direct our aid to a refugee in Bengal almost as effectively as we could get it to someone in our own block. There would seem, therefore, to be no possible justification for discriminating on geographical grounds.

There may be a greater need to defend the second implication of my principle—that the fact that there are millions of other people in the same position, in respect to the Bengali refugees, as I am, does not make the situation significantly different from a situation in which I am the only person who can prevent something very bad from occurring. Again, of course, I admit that there is a psychological difference between the cases; one feels less guilty about doing nothing if one can point to others, similarly placed, who have also done nothing. Yet this can make no real difference to our moral obligations.[2] Should I consider that I am less obliged to pull the drowning child out of the pond if on looking around I see other people, no further away than I am, who have also noticed the child but are doing nothing? One has only to ask this question to see the absurdity of the view that numbers lessen obligation. It is a view that is an ideal excuse for inactivity; unfortunately most of the major evils—poverty, overpopulation, pollution—are problems in which everyone is almost equally involved.

The view that numbers do make a difference can be made plausible if stated in this way: if everyone in circumstances like mine gave £5 to the Bengal Relief Fund, there would be enough to provide food, shelter, and medical care for the refugees; there is no reason why I should give more than anyone else in the same circumstances as I am; therefore I have no obligation to give more than £5. Each premise in this argument is true, and the argument looks sound. It may convince us, unless we notice that it is based on a hypothetical premise, although the conclusion is not stated hypothetically. The argument would be sound if the conclusion were: if everyone in circumstances like mine were to give £5, I would have no obligation to give more than £5. If the conclusion were so stated, however, it would be obvious that the argument has no bearing on a situation in which it is not the case that everyone else gives £5. This, of course, is the actual situation. It is more or less certain that not everyone in circumstances like mine will give £5. So there will not be enough to provide the needed food, shelter, and medical care. Therefore by giving more than £5 I will prevent more suffering than I would if I gave just £5.

It might be thought that this argument has an absurd consequence. Since the situation appears to be that very few people are likely to give substantial amounts, it follows that I and everyone else in similar circumstances ought to give as much as possible, that is, at least up to the point at which by giving more one would begin to cause serious suffering for oneself and one's dependents—perhaps even beyond this point to the point of marginal utility, at which by giving more one would cause oneself and one's dependents as much suffering as one would prevent in Bengal. If everyone does this, however, there will be more than can be used for the benefit of the refugees, and some of the sacrifice will have been unnecessary. Thus, if everyone does what he ought to do, the result will not be as good as it would be if everyone did a little less than he ought to do, or if only some do all that they ought to do.

The paradox here arises only if we assume that the actions in question—sending money to the relief funds—are performed more or less simultaneously, and are also unexpected. For if it is to be expected that everyone is going to contribute something, then clearly each is not obliged to give as much as he would have been obliged to had others not been giving too. And if everyone is not acting more or less simultaneously, then those giving later will know how much more is needed, and will have no obligation to give more than is necessary to reach this amount. To say this is not to deny the principle that people in the same circumstances have the same obligations, but to point out that the fact that others have given, or may be expected to give, is a relevant circumstance: those giving after it has become known that many others are giving and those giving before are not in the same circumstances. So the seemingly absurd consequence of the principle I have put forward can occur only if people are in error about the actual circumstances—that is, if they think they are giving when others are not, but in fact they are giving

when others are. The result of everyone doing what he really ought to do cannot be worse than the result of everyone doing less than he ought to do, although the result of everyone doing what he reasonably believes he ought to do could be.

If my argument so far has been sound, neither our distance from a preventable evil nor the number of other people who, in respect to that evil, are in the same situation as we are, lessens our obligation to mitigate or prevent that evil. I shall therefore take as established the principle I asserted earlier. As I have already said, I need to assert it only in its qualified form: if it is in our power to prevent something very bad from happening, without thereby sacrificing anything else morally significant, we ought, morally, to do it.

The outcome of this argument is that our traditional moral categories are upset. The traditional distinction between duty and charity cannot be drawn, or at least, not in the place we normally draw it. Giving money to the Bengal Relief Fund is regarded as an act of charity in our society. The bodies which collect money are known as "charities." These organizations see themselves in this way—if you send them a check, you will be thanked for your "generosity." Because giving money is regarded as an act of charity, it is not thought that there is anything wrong with not giving. The charitable man may be praised, but the man who is not charitable is not condemned. People do not feel in any way ashamed or guilty about spending money on new clothes or a new car instead of giving it to famine relief. (Indeed, the alternative does not occur to them.) This way of looking at the matter cannot be justified. When we buy new clothes not to keep ourselves warm but to look "well-dressed" we are not providing for any important need. We would not be sacrificing anything significant if we were to continue to wear our old clothes, and give the money to famine relief. By doing so, we would be preventing another person from starving. It follows from what I have said earlier that we ought to give money away, rather than spend it on clothes which we do not need to keep us warm. To do so is not charitable, or generous. Nor is it the kind of act which philosophers and theologians have called "supererogatory"—an act which it would be good to do, but not wrong not to do. On the contrary, we ought to give the money away, and it is wrong not to do so.

I am not maintaining that there are no acts which are charitable, or that there are no acts which it would be good to do but not wrong not to do. It may be possible to redraw the distinction between duty and charity in some other place. All I am arguing here is that the present way of drawing the distinction, which makes it an act of charity for a man living at the level of affluence which most people in the "developed nations" enjoy to give money to save someone else from starvation, cannot be supported. It is beyond the scope of my argument to consider whether the distinction should be redrawn or abolished altogether. There would be many other possible ways of drawing the distinction—for instance, one might decide that it is good to make other people as happy as possible, but not wrong not to do so.

Despite the limited nature of the revision in our moral conceptual scheme which I am proposing, the revision would, given the extent of both affluence and famine in the world today, have radical implications. These implications may lead to further objections, distinct from those I have already considered. I shall discuss two of these.

One objection to the position I have taken might be simply that it is too drastic a revision of our moral scheme. People do not ordinarily judge in the way I have suggested they should. Most people reserve their moral condemnation for those who violate some moral norm, such as the norm against taking another person's property. They do not condemn those who indulge in luxury instead of giving to famine relief. But given that I did not set out to present a morally neutral description of the way people make moral judgments, the way people do in fact judge has nothing to do with the validity of my conclusion. My conclusion follows from the principle which I advanced earlier, and unless that principle is rejected, or the arguments shown to be unsound, I think the conclusion must stand, however strange it appears.

* * *

The second objection to my attack on the present distinction between duty and charity is one which has from time to time been made against utilitarianism. It follows from some forms of utilitarian theory that we all ought, morally, to be working full time to increase the balance of happiness over misery. The position I have taken here would not lead to this conclusion in all circumstances, for if there were no bad occurrences that we could prevent without sacrificing something of comparable moral importance, my argument would have no application. Given the present conditions in many parts of the world, however, it does follow from my argument that we ought, morally, to be working full time to relieve great suffering of the sort that occurs as a result of famine or other disasters. Of course, mitigating circumstances can be adduced—for instance, that if we wear ourselves out through overwork, we shall be less effective than we would otherwise have been. Nevertheless, when all considerations of this sort have been taken into account, the conclusion remains: we ought to be preventing as much suffering as we can without sacrificing something else of comparable moral importance. This conclusion is one which we may be reluctant to face. I cannot see, though, why it should be regarded as a criticism of the position for which I have argued, rather than a criticism of our ordinary standards of behavior. Since most people are self-interested to some degree, very few of us are likely to do everything that we ought to do. It would, however, hardly be honest to take this as evidence that it is not the case that we ought to do it.

* * *

[Another] point raised by the conclusion reached earlier relates to the question of just how much we all ought to be giving away. One possibility, which has already been mentioned, is that we ought to give until we reach the level of marginal utility—that is, the level at which, by giving more, I would cause as much suffering to myself or my dependents as I would relieve by my gift. This would mean, of course, that one would reduce oneself to very near the material circumstances of a Bengali refugee. It will be recalled that earlier I put forward both a strong and a moderate version of the principle of preventing bad occurrences. The strong version, which required us to prevent bad things from happening unless in doing so we would be sacrificing something of comparable moral significance, does seem to require reducing ourselves to the level of marginal utility. I should also say that the strong version seems to me to be the correct one. I proposed the more moderate version—that we should prevent bad occurrences unless, to do so, we had to sacrifice something morally significant—only in order to show that even on this surely undeniable principle a great change in our way of life is required. On the more moderate principle, it may not follow that we ought to reduce ourselves to the level of marginal utility, for one might hold that to reduce oneself and one's family to this level is to cause something significantly bad to happen. Whether this is so I shall not discuss, since, as I have said, I can see no good reason for holding the moderate version of the principle rather than the strong version. Even if we accepted the principle only in its moderate form, however, it should be clear that we would have to give away enough to ensure that the consumer society, dependent as it is on people spending on trivia rather than giving to famine relief, would slow down and perhaps disappear entirely. There are several reasons why this would be desirable in itself. The value and necessity of economic growth are now being questioned not only by conservationists, but by economists as well. There is no doubt, too, that the consumer society has had a distorting effect on the goals and purposes of its members. Yet looking at the matter purely from the point of view of overseas aid, there must be a limit to the extent to which we should deliberately slow down our economy; for it might be the case that if we gave away, say, forty percent of our Gross National Product, we would slow down the economy so much that in absolute terms we would be giving less than if we gave twenty-five percent of the much larger GNP that we would have if we limited our contribution to this smaller percentage.

I mention this only as an indication of the sort of factor that one would have to take into account in working out an ideal. Since Western societies generally consider one percent of the GNP an acceptable level for overseas aid, the matter is entirely academic. Nor does it affect the question of how much an individual should give in a society in which very few are giving substantial amounts.

It is sometimes said, though less often now than it used to be, that philosophers have no special role to play in public affairs, since most public issues depend primarily on an assessment of facts. On questions of fact, it is said, philosophers as such have no special expertise, and so it has been possible to engage in philosophy without committing oneself to any position on major public issues. No doubt there are some issues of social policy and foreign policy about which it can truly be said that a really expert assessment of the facts is required before taking sides or acting, but the issue of famine is surely not one of these. The facts about the existence of suffering are beyond dispute. Nor, I think, is it disputed that we can do something about it, either through orthodox methods of famine relief or through population control or both. This is therefore an issue on which philosophers are competent to take a position. The issue is one which faces everyone who has more money than he needs to support himself and his dependents, or who is in a position to take some sort of political action. These categories must include practically every teacher and student of philosophy in the universities of the Western world. If philosophy is to deal with matters that are relevant to both teachers and students, this is an issue that philosophers should discuss.

Discussion, though, is not enough. What is the point of relating philosophy to public (and personal) affairs if we do not take our conclusions seriously? In this instance, taking our conclusion seriously means acting upon it. The philosopher will not find it any easier than anyone else to alter his attitudes and way of life to the extent that, if I am right, is involved in doing everything that we ought to be doing. At the very least, though, one can make a start. The philosopher who does so will have to sacrifice some of the benefits of the consumer society, but he can find compensation in the satisfaction of a way of life in which theory and practice, if not yet in harmony, are at least coming together.

NOTES

1. There was also a third possibility: that India would go to war to enable the refugees to return to their lands. Since I wrote this paper, India has taken this way out. The situation

is no longer that described above, but this does not affect my argument, as the next paragraph indicates.

2. In view of the special sense philosophers often give to the term, I should say that I use "obligation" simply as the abstract noun derived from "ought," so that "I have an obligation to" means no more, and no less, than "I ought to." This usage is in accordance with the definition of "ought" given up by the *Shorter Oxford English Dictionary*: "the general verb to express duty or obligation." I do not think any issue of substance hangs on the way the term is used; sentences in which I use "obligation" could all be rewritten, although somewhat clumsily, as sentences in which a clause containing "ought" replaces the term "obligation."

From *Lifeboat Ethics*

GARRETT HARDIN

* * *

Before taking up certain substantive issues let us look at an alternative metaphor, that of a lifeboat. In developing some relevant examples the following numerical values are assumed. Approximately two-thirds of the world is desperately poor, and only one-third is comparatively rich. The people in poor countries have an average per capita GNP (Gross National Product) of about $200 per year; the rich, of about $3,000. (For the United States it is nearly $5,000 per year.) Metaphorically, each rich nation amounts to a lifeboat full of comparatively rich people. The poor of the world are in other, much more crowded lifeboats. Continuously, so to speak, the poor fall out of their lifeboats and swim for a while in the water outside, hoping to be admitted to a rich lifeboat, or in some other way to benefit from the "goodies" on board. What should the passengers on a rich lifeboat do? This is the central problem of "the ethics of a lifeboat."

First we must acknowledge that each lifeboat is effectively limited in capacity. The land of every nation has a limited carrying capacity. The exact limit is a matter for argument, but the energy crunch is convincing more people every day that we have already exceeded the carrying capacity of the land. We have

been living on "capital"—stored petroleum and coal—and soon we must live on income alone.

Let us look at only one lifeboat—ours. The ethical problem is the same for all, and is as follows. Here we sit, say 50 people in a lifeboat. To be generous, let us assume our boat has a capacity of 10 more, making 60. (This, however, is to violate the engineering principle of the "safety factor." A new plant disease or a bad change in the weather may decimate our population if we don't preserve some excess capacity as a safety factor.)

The 50 of us in the lifeboat see 100 others swimming in the water outside, asking for admission to the boat, or for handouts. How shall we respond to their calls? There are several possibilities.

One. We may be tempted to try to live by the Christian ideal of being "our brother's keeper," or by the Marxian ideal (Marx 1875) of "from each according to his abilities, to each according to his needs." Since the needs of all are the same, we take all the needy into our boat, making a total of 150 in a boat with a capacity of 60. The boat is swamped, and everyone drowns. Complete justice, complete catastrophe.

Two. Since the boat has an unused excess capacity of 10, we admit just 10 more to it. This has the disadvantage of getting rid of the safety factor, for which action we will sooner or later pay dearly. Moreover, *which* 10 do we let in? "First come, first served?" The best 10? The neediest 10? How do we *discriminate*? And what do we say to the 90 who are excluded?

Three. Admit no more to the boat and preserve the small safety factor. Survival of the people in the lifeboat is then possible (though we shall have to be on our guard against boarding parties).

The last solution is abhorrent to many people. It is unjust, they say. Let us grant that it is.

"I feel guilty about my good luck," say some. The reply to this is simple: *Get out and yield your place to others.* Such a selfless action might satisfy the conscience of those who are addicted to guilt but it would not change the ethics of the lifeboat. The needy person to whom a guilt-addict yields his place will not himself feel guilty about his sudden good luck. (If he did he would not climb aboard.) The net result of conscience-stricken people relinquishing their unjustly held positions is the elimination of their kind of conscience from the lifeboat. The lifeboat, as it were, purifies itself of guilt. The ethics of the lifeboat persist, unchanged by such momentary aberrations.

This then is the basic metaphor within which we must work out our solutions. Let us enrich the image step by step with substantive additions from the real world.

REPRODUCTION

The harsh characteristics of lifeboat ethics are heightened by reproduction, particularly by reproductive differences. The people inside the lifeboats of the wealthy nations are doubling in numbers every 87 years; those outside are doubling every 35 years, on the average. And the relative difference in prosperity is becoming greater.

Let us, for a while, think primarily of the U.S. lifeboat. As of 1973 the United States had a population of 210 million people, who were increasing by 0.8% per year, that is, doubling in number every 87 years.

Although the citizens of rich nations are outnumbered two to one by the poor, let us imagine an equal number of poor people outside our lifeboat—a mere 210 million poor people reproducing at a quite different rate. If we imagine these to be the combined populations of Colombia, Venezuela, Ecuador, Morocco, Thailand, Pakistan, and the Philippines, the average rate of increase of the people "outside" is 3.3% per year. The doubling time of this population is 21 years.

Suppose that all these countries, and the United States, agreed to live by the Marxian ideal, "to each according to his needs," the ideal of most Christians as well. Needs, of course, are determined by population size, which is affected by reproduction. Every nation regards its rate of reproduction as a sovereign right. If our lifeboat were big enough in the beginning it might be possible to live *for a while* by Christian-Marxian ideals. *Might.*

Initially, in the model given, the ratio of non-Americans to Americans would be one to one. But consider what the ratio would be 87 years later. By this time Americans would have doubled to a population of 420 million. The other group (doubling every 21 years) would now have swollen to 3,540 million. Each American would have more than eight people to share with. How could the lifeboat possibly keep afloat?

All this involves extrapolation of current trends into the future, and is consequently suspect. Trends may change. Granted: but the change will not necessarily be favorable. If—as seems likely—the rate of population increase falls faster in the ethnic group presently inside the lifeboat than it does among those now outside, the future will turn out to be even worse than mathematics predicts, and sharing will be even more suicidal.

RUIN IN THE COMMONS

The fundamental error of the sharing ethics is that it leads to the tragedy of the commons. Under a system of private property the men who own property recognize their responsibility to care for it, for if they don't they will eventually suffer. A farmer, for instance, if he is intelligent, will allow no more cattle in a pasture than its carrying capacity justifies. If he overloads the pasture, weeds take over, erosion sets in, and the owner loses in the long run.

But if a pasture is run as a commons open to all, the right of each to use it is not matched by an operational responsibility to take care of it. It is no use asking independent herdsmen in a commons to act responsibly, for they dare not. The considerate herdsman who refrains from overloading the commons suffers more than a selfish one who says his needs are greater. (As Leo Durocher says, "Nice guys finish last.") Christian-Marxian idealism is counterproductive. That it *sounds* nice is no excuse. With distribution systems, as with individual morality, good intentions are no substitute for good performance.

A social system is stable only if it is insensitive to errors. To the Christian-Marxian idealist a selfish person is a sort of "error." Prosperity in the system of the commons cannot survive errors. If *everyone* would only restrain himself, all would be well; but it takes *only one less than everyone* to ruin a system of voluntary restraint. In a crowded world of less than perfect human beings—and we will never know any other—mutual ruin is inevitable in the commons. This is the core of the tragedy of the commons.

One of the major tasks of education today is to create such an awareness of the dangers of the commons that people will be able to recognize its many varieties, however disguised. There is pollution of the air and water because these media are treated as commons. Further growth of population and growth in the per capita conversion of natural resources into pollutants require that the system of the commons be modified or abandoned in the disposal of "externalities."

The fish populations of the oceans are exploited as commons, and ruin lies ahead. No technological invention can prevent this fate: in fact, all improvements in the art of fishing merely hasten the day of complete ruin. Only the replacement of the system of the commons with a responsible system can save oceanic fisheries.

The management of western range lands, though nominally rational, is in fact (under the steady pressure of cattle ranchers) often merely a government-sanctioned system of the commons, drifting toward ultimate ruin for both the rangelands and the residual enterprisers.

WORLD FOOD BANKS

In the international arena we have recently heard a proposal to create a new commons, namely an international depository of food reserves to which nations will contribute according to their abilities, and from which nations may draw according to their needs.

Nobel laureate Norman Borlaug has lent the prestige of his name to this proposal.

A world food bank appeals powerfully to our humanitarian impulses. We remember John Donne's celebrated line, "Any man's death diminishes me." But before we rush out to see for whom the bell tolls let us recognize where the greatest political push for international granaries comes from, lest we be disillusioned later. Our experience with Public Law 480 clearly reveals the answer. This was the law that moved billions of dollars worth of U.S. grain to food-short, population-long countries during the past two decades. When P.L. 480 first came into being, a headline in the business magazine *Forbes* (Paddock and Paddock 1970) revealed the power behind it: "Feeding the World's Hungry Millions: How it will mean billions for U.S. business."

And indeed it did. In the years 1960 to 1970 a total of $7.9 billion was spent on the "Food for Peace" program, as P.L. 480 was called. During the years 1948 to 1970 an additional $49.9 billion were extracted from American taxpayers to pay for other economic aid programs, some of which went for food and food-producing machinery. (This figure does *not* include military aid.) That P.L. 480 was a give-away program was concealed. Recipient countries went through the motions of paying for P.L. 480 foods—with IOU's. In December 1973 the charade was brought to an end as far as India was concerned when the United States "forgave" India's $3.2 billion debt (Anonymous 1974). Public announcement of the cancellation of the debt was delayed for two months: one wonders why.

"Famine—[1975]!" (Paddock and Paddock 1970) is one of the few publications that points out the commercial roots of this humanitarian attempt. Though all U.S. taxpayers lost by P.L. 480, special interest groups gained handsomely. Farmers benefited because they were not asked to contribute the grain—it was bought from them by the taxpayers. Besides the direct benefit there was the indirect effect of increasing demand and thus raising prices of farm products generally. The manufacturers of farm machinery, fertilizers, and pesticides benefited by the farmers' extra efforts to grow more food. Grain elevators profited from storing the grain for varying lengths of time. Railroads made money hauling it to port, and shipping lines by carrying it overseas.

Moreover, once the machinery for P.L. 480 was established an immense bureaucracy had a vested interest in its continuance regardless of its merits.

Very little was ever heard of these selfish interests when P.L. 480 was defended in public. The emphasis was always on its humanitarian effects. The combination of multiple and relatively silent selfish interests with highly vocal humanitarian apologists constitutes a powerful lobby for extracting money from taxpayers. Foreign aid has become a habit that can apparently survive in the absence of any known justification. A news commentator in a weekly magazine (Lansner 1974), after exhaustively going over all the conventional arguments for foreign aid—self-interest, social justice, political advantage, and charity—and concluding that none of the known arguments really held water, concluded: "So the search continues for some logically compelling reasons for giving aid. . ." In other words, *Act now, Justify later*—if ever. (Apparently a quarter of a century is too short a time to find the justification for expending several billion dollars yearly.)

The search for a rational justification can be short-circuited by interjecting the word "emergency." Borlaug uses this word. We need to look sharply at it. What is an "emergency"? It is surely something like an accident, which is correctly defined as *an event that is certain to happen, though with a low frequency* (Hardin 1972a). A well-run organization prepares for everything that is certain, including accidents and emergencies. It budgets for them. It saves for them. It expects them—and mature decision-makers do not waste time complaining about accidents when they occur.

What happens if some organizations budget for emergencies and others do not? If each organization is solely responsible for its own well-being, poorly managed ones will suffer. But they should be able to learn from experience. They have a chance to mend their ways and learn to budget for infrequent but certain emergencies. The weather, for instance, always varies and periodic crop failures are certain. A wise and competent government saves out of the production of the good years in anticipation of bad years that are sure to come. This is not a new idea. The Bible tells us that Joseph taught this policy to Pharaoh in Egypt more than 2,000 years ago. Yet it is literally true that the vast majority of the governments of the world today have no such policy. They lack either the wisdom or the competence, or both. Far more difficult than the transfer of wealth from one country to another is the transfer of wisdom between sovereign powers or between generations.

"But it isn't their fault! How can we blame the poor people who are caught in an emergency? Why must we punish them?" The concepts of blame and punishment are irrelevant. The question is, what are the operational consequences of establishing a world food bank? If it is open to every country every time a need develops, slovenly rulers will not be motivated to take Joseph's advice. Why should they? Others will bail them out whenever they are in trouble.

Some countries will make deposits in the world food bank and others will withdraw from it: there will be almost no overlap. Calling such a depository-transfer unit a "bank" is stretching the metaphor of *bank* beyond its elastic limits. The proposers, of course, never call attention to the metaphorical nature of the word they use.

THE RATCHET EFFECT

An "international food bank" is really, then, not a true bank but a disguised one-way transfer device for moving wealth from rich countries to poor. In the absence of such a bank, in a world inhabited by individually responsible sovereign nations, the population of each nation would repeatedly go through a cycle of the sort shown in Figure 1. P_2 is greater than P_1, either in absolute numbers or because a deterioration of the food supply has removed the safety factor and produced a dangerously low ratio of resources to population. P_2 may be said to represent a state of overpopulation, which becomes obvious upon the appearance of an "accident," e.g., a crop failure. If the "emergency" is not met by outside help, the population drops back to the "normal" level—the "carrying capacity" of the environment—or even below. In the absence of population control by a sovereign, sooner or later the population grows to P_2 again and the cycle repeats. The long-term population curve (Hardin 1966) is an irregularly fluctuating one, equilibrating more or less about the carrying capacity.

A demographic cycle of this sort obviously involves great suffering in the restrictive phase, but such a cycle is normal to any independent country with inadequate population control. The third-century theologian Tertullian (Hardin 1969a) expressed what must have been the recognition of many wise men when he wrote: "The scourges of pestilence, famine, wars, and earthquakes have come to be regarded as a blessing to overcrowded nations, since they serve to prune away the luxuriant growth of the human race."

Only under a strong and farsighted sovereign—which theoretically could be the people themselves, democratically organized—can a population equilibrate at some set point below the carrying capacity, thus avoiding the pains normally caused by periodic and unavoidable disasters. For this happy state to be achieved it is necessary that those in power be able to contemplate with equanimity the "waste" of surplus food in times of bountiful harvests. It is essential that those in power resist the temptation to convert extra food into extra babies. On the public relations level it is necessary that the phrase "surplus food" be replaced by "safety factor."

But wise sovereigns seem not to exist in the poor world today. The most anguishing problems are created by poor countries that are governed by rulers insufficiently wise and powerful. If such countries can draw on a world food bank in times of "emergency," the population *cycle* of Figure 1 will be replaced by the population *escalator* of Figure 2. The input of food from a food bank acts as the pawl of a ratchet, preventing the population from retracing its steps to a lower level. Reproduction pushes the population upward, inputs from the world bank prevent its moving downward. Population size escalates, as does the absolute magnitude of "accidents" and "emergencies." The process is brought to an end only by the total collapse of the whole system, producing a catastrophe of scarcely imaginable proportions.

Such are the implications of the well-meant sharing of food in a world of irresponsible reproduction.

I think we need a new word for systems like this. The adjective "melioristic" is applied to systems that produce continual improvement; the English word is derived from the Latin *meliorare*, to become or make better. Parallel with this it would be useful to bring in the word *pejoristic* (from the Latin *pejorare*, to become or make worse). This word can be applied to those systems which, by their very nature, can be relied upon to make matters worse. A world food bank coupled with sovereign state irresponsibility in reproduction is an example of a pejoristic system.

This pejoristic system creates an unacknowledged commons. People have more motivation to draw from than to add to the common store. The license to make such withdrawals diminishes whatever motivation poor countries might otherwise have to control their populations. Under the guidance of this ratchet, wealth can be steadily moved in one direction only, from the slowly-breeding rich to the rapidly-breeding poor, the process finally coming to a halt only when all countries are equally and miserably poor.

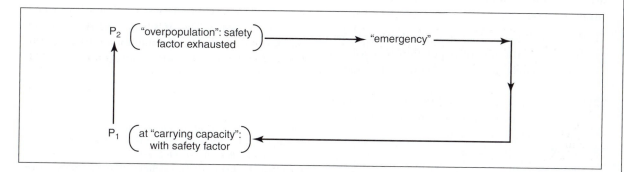

Fig. 1. The population cycle of a nation that has no effective, conscious population control, and which receives no aid from the outside. P_2 is greater than P_1.

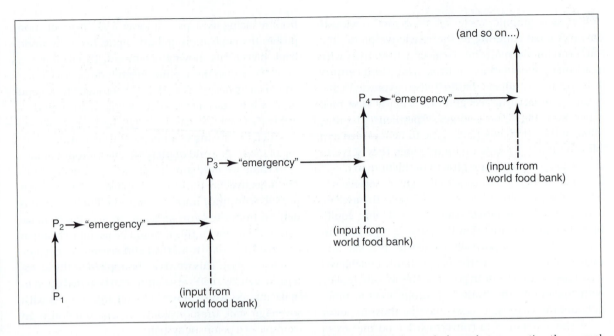

Fig. 2. The population escalator. Note that input from a world food bank acts like the pawl of a ratchet, preventing the normal population cycle shown in Figure 1 from being completed. $P_n + 1$ is greater than P_n, and the absolute magnitude of the "emergencies" escalates. Ultimately the entire system crashes. The crash is not shown, and few can imagine it.

All this is terribly obvious once we are acutely aware of the pervasiveness and danger of the commons. But many people still lack this awareness, and the euphoria of the "benign demographic transition" (Hardin 1973) interferes with the realistic appraisal of pejoristic mechanisms. As concerns public policy, the deductions drawn from the benign demographic transition are these:

1) If the per capita GNP rises the birth rate will fall; hence, the rate of population increase will fall, ultimately producing ZPG (Zero Population Growth).

2) The long-term trend all over the world (including the poor countries) is of a rising per capita GNP (for which no limit is seen).

3) Therefore, all political interference in population matters is unnecessary; all we need to do is foster economic "development"—*note the metaphor*—and population problems will solve themselves.

Those who believe in the benign demographic transition dismiss the pejoristic mechanism of Figure 2 in the belief that each input of food from the world outside fosters development within a poor country thus resulting in a drop in the rate of population increase. Foreign aid has proceeded on this assumption for more than two decades. Unfortunately it has produced no indubitable instance of the asserted effect. It has, however, produced a library of excuses. The air is filled with plaintive calls for more massive foreign aid appropriations so that the hypothetical melioristic process can get started.

* * *

REFERENCES

Anonymous. 1974. *Wall Street Journal* 19 Feb.

Borlaug, N. 1973. Civilization's future: a call for international granaries. *Bull. At. Sci.* 29: 7–15.

Boulding, K. 1966. The economics of the coming Spaceship earth. *In* H. Jarrett, ed. Environmental Quality in a Growing Economy. Johns Hopkins Press, Baltimore.

Buchanan, W. 1973. Immigration statistics. *Equilibrium* 1(3): 16–19.

Davis, K. 1963. Population. *Sci. Amer.* 209(3): 62–71.

Farvar, M. T., and J. P. Milton. 1972. The Careless Technology. Natural History Press, Garden City, N.Y.

Gregg, A. 1955. A medical aspect of the population problem. *Science* 121: 681–682.

Hardin, G. 1966. Chap. 9 *in* Biology: Its Principles and Implications, 2nd ed. Freeman, San Francisco.

———. 1968. The tragedy of the commons. *Science* 162: 1243–1248.

———. 1969a. Page 18 *in* Population, Evolution, and Birth Control, 2nd ed. Freeman, San Francisco.

———. 1969b. The economics of wilderness. *Nat. Hist.* 78(6): 20–27.

———. 1972a. Pages 81–82 *in* Exploring New Ethics for Survival: The Voyage of the Spaceship *Beagle*. Viking, N.Y.

———. 1972b. Preserving quality on Spaceship Earth. *In* J. B. Trefethen, ed. Transactions of the Thirty-Seventh North American Wildlife and Natural Resources Conference. Wildlife Management Institute, Washington, D.C.

———. 1973. Chap. 23 *in* Stalking the Wild Taboo. Kaufmann, Los Altos, Cal.

Harris, M. 1972. How green the revolution. *Nat. Hist.* 81(3): 28–30.

Langer, S. K. 1942. Philosophy in a New Key. Harvard University Press, Cambridge.

Lansner, K. 1974. Should foreign aid begin at home? *Newsweek*, 11 Feb. p. 32.

Marx, K. 1875. Critique of the Gotha program. Page 388 *in* R. C. Tucker, ed. The Marx-Engels Reader. Norton, N.Y., 1972.

Ophuls, W. 1974. The scarcity society. *Harpers* 248(1487): 47–52.

Paddock, W. C. 1970. How green is the green revolution? *BioScience* 20: 897–902.

Paddock, W., and E. Paddock. 1973. We Don't Know How. Iowa State University Press, Ames, Iowa.

Paddock, W., and P. Paddock. 1967. Famine—1975! Little, Brown, Boston.

Wilkes, H. G. 1972. The green revolution. *Environment* 14(8): 32–39.

A Critique of Lifeboat Ethics

William W. Murdoch and Allan Oaten

Should rich countries provide food, fertilizers, technical assistance, and other aid to poor countries? The obvious answer is "yes." It is natural to want to fight poverty, starvation, and disease, to help raise living standards and eliminate suffering.

Yet, after 25 years of aid, diets and living standards in many poor countries have improved little, owing partly to the population explosion that occurred during these same years. Death rates in poor countries dropped sharply in the 1940's and 1950's, to around 14/1,000 at present, while their birth rates declined very little, remaining near 40/1,000. Some populations are now growing faster than their food supply.

From William W. Murdoch and Allan Oaten, "Population and Food: Metaphors and the Reality" *BioScience*, vol. 25, no. 9 (1975), 561–67. © 1975 American Institute of Biological Science. Reprinted by permission of Oxford University Press.

As a result an apparently powerful argument against aid is increasingly heard. Its premise is simply stated. "More food means more babies" (Hardin 1969). Our benevolence leads to a spiral that can result only in disaster: aid leads to increased populations, which require more aid, which leads. . . . This premise mandates a radically new policy: rich countries can perhaps provide contraceptives to poor countries, but they should not provide food, help increase food production, or help combat poverty or disease.

This policy would result in the agonizing deaths, by starvation and disease, of millions of people. Consequently, one expects its advocates to have arrived at it reluctantly, forced to suppress their humanitarian feelings by inexorable logic and the sheer weight of evidence. Its apparent brutality seems a sure guarantee of its realism and rationality.

We believe that this allegedly realistic "nonhelp" policy is in fact mistaken as well as callous; that the premise on which it is based is at best a half-truth; and that the arguments adduced in its support are not only erroneous, but often exhibit indifference to both the complexities of the problem and much of the available data. We also believe that the evidence shows better living standards and lower population growth rates to be complementary, not contradictory; that aid programs carefully designed to benefit the poorest people can help to achieve both of these ends; and that such programs, though difficult to devise and carry out, are not beyond either the resources or the ingenuity of the rich countries.

In the next two sections, we analyze some of the standard arguments in support of nonhelp policies, by focusing first on the article "Living on a Lifeboat" (Hardin 1974) and then on "The Tragedy of the Commons" (Hardin 1968). We will consider the long-term effects of nonhelp policies and some possible reasons for their widespread appeal. Then we will summarize some of the evidence about birth rates that is available and seems relevant. This evidence suggests that if we are serious about halting the food-population spiral and minimizing deaths from starvation and disease (in the long-term as well as the short), then it may be more rational to help than to stand back and watch. Finally, we will estimate the costs of some aid and discuss some difficulties in achieving reduced birth rates.

MISLEADING METAPHORS

The "lifeboat" article actually has two messages. The first is that our immigration policy is too generous. This will not concern us here. The second, and more important, is that by helping poor nations we will bring disaster to rich and poor alike:

> Metaphorically, each rich nation amounts to a lifeboat full of comparatively rich people. The poor of the world are in other, much more crowded lifeboats. Continuously, so to speak, the poor fall out of their lifeboats and swim for a while in the water outside, hoping to be admitted to a rich lifeboat, or in some other way to benefit from the "goodies" on board. What should the passengers on a rich lifeboat do? This is the central problem of "the ethics of a lifeboat." (Hardin 1974, p. 561)

Among these so-called "goodies" are food supplies and technical aid such as that which led to the Green Revolution. Hardin argues that we should withhold such resources from poor nations on the grounds that they help to maintain high rates of population increase, thereby making the problem worse. He foresees the continued supplying and increasing production of food as a process that will be "brought to an end only by the total collapse of the whole system, producing a catastrophe of scarcely imaginable proportions" (p. 564).

Turning to one particular mechanism for distributing these resources, Hardin claims that a world food bank is a commons—people have more motivation to draw from it than to add to it; it will have a ratchet or escalator effect on population because inputs from it will prevent population declines in overpopulated countries. Thus "wealth can be steadily moved in one direction only, from the slowly-breeding rich to the rapidly-breeding poor, the process finally coming to a halt only when all countries are equally and miserably poor" (p. 565). Thus our help will not only bring ultimate disaster to poor countries, but it will also be suicidal for us.

As for the "benign demographic transition" to low birth rates, which some aid supporters have predicted, Hardin states flatly that the weight of evidence is against this possibility.

Finally, Hardin claims that the plight of poor nations is partly their own fault: "wise sovereigns seem not to exist in the poor world today. The most anguishing problems are created by poor countries that are governed by rulers insufficiently wise and powerful." Establishing a world food bank will exacerbate this problem: "slovenly rulers" will escape the consequences of their incompetence—"Others will bail them out whenever they are in trouble"; "Far more difficult than the transfer of wealth from one country to another is the transfer of wisdom between sovereign powers or between generations" (p. 563).

What arguments does Hardin present in support of these opinions? Many involve metaphors: lifeboat, commons, and ratchet or escalator. These metaphors are crucial to his thesis, and it is, therefore, important for us to examine them critically.

The lifeboat is the major metaphor. It seems attractively simple, but it is in fact simplistic and obscures important issues. As soon as we try to use it to compare various policies, we find that most relevant details of the actual situation are either missing or distorted in the lifeboat metaphor. Let us list some of these details.

- Most important, perhaps, Hardin's lifeboats barely interact. The rich lifeboats may drop some handouts over the side and perhaps repel a boarding party now and then, but generally they live their own lives. In the real world, nations interact a great deal, in ways that affect food supply and population size and growth, and the effect of rich nations on poor nations has been strong and not always benevolent.

First, by colonization and actual wars of commerce, and through the international marketplace, rich nations have arranged an exchange of goods that has maintained and even increased the economic imbalance between rich and poor nations. Until recently we have taken or otherwise obtained cheap raw material from poor nations and sold them expensive manufactured goods that they cannot make themselves. In the United States, the structure of tariffs and internal subsidies discriminates selectively against poor nations. In poor countries, the concentration on cash crops rather than on food crops, a legacy of colonial times, is now actively encouraged by western multinational corporations (Barraclough 1975). Indeed, it is claimed that in famine-stricken Sahelian Africa, multinational agribusiness has recently taken land out of food production for cash crops (Transnational Institute 1974). Although we often self-righteously take the "blame" for lowering the death rates of poor nations during the 1940's and 1950's, we are less inclined to accept responsibility for the effects of actions that help maintain poverty and hunger. Yet poverty directly contributes to the high birth rates that Hardin views with such alarm.

Second, U.S. foreign policy, including foreign aid programs, has favored "pro-Western" regimes, many of which govern in the interests of a wealthy elite and some of which are savagely repressive. Thus, it has often subsidized a gross maldistribution of income and has supported political leaders who have opposed most of the social changes that can lead to reduced birth rates. In this light, Hardin's pronouncements on the alleged wisdom gap between poor leaders and our own, and the difficulty of filling it, appear as a grim joke: our response to leaders with the power and wisdom Hardin yearns for has often been to try to replace them or their policies as soon as possible. Selective giving and withholding of both military and nonmilitary aid has been an important ingredient of our efforts to maintain political leaders we like and to remove those we do not. Brown (1974b), after nothing that the withholding of U.S. food aid in 1973 contributed to the downfall of the Allende government in Chile, comments that "although Americans decry the use of petroleum as a political weapon, calling it 'political blackmail,' the United States has been using food aid for political purposes for twenty years—and describing this as 'enlightened diplomacy.' "

- Both the quantity and the nature of the supplies on a lifeboat are fixed. In the real world, the quantity has strict limits, but these are far from having been reached (University of California Food Task Force 1974). Nor are we forced to devote fixed proportions of our efforts and energy to automobile travel, pet food, packaging, advertising, corn-fed beef, "defense," and other diversions, many of which cost far more than foreign aid does. The fact is that enough food is now produced to feed the world's population adequately. That people are malnourished is due to distribution and to economics, not to agricultural limits (United Nations Economic and Social Council 1974).
- Hardin's lifeboats are divided merely into rich and poor, and it is difficult to talk about birth rates on either. In the real world, however, there are striking differences among the birth rates of the poor countries and even among the birth rates of different parts of single countries. These differences appear to be related to social conditions (also absent from lifeboats) and may guide us to effective aid policies.
- Hardin's lifeboat metaphor not only conceals facts, but misleads about the effects of his proposals. The rich lifeboat can raise the ladder and sail away. But in real life, the problem will not necessarily go away just because it is ignored. In the real world, there are armies, raw materials in poor nations, and even outraged domestic dissidents

prepared to sacrifice their own and others' lives to oppose policies they regard as immoral.

No doubt there are other objections. But even this list shows the lifeboat metaphor to be dangerously inappropriate for serious policy making because it obscures far more than it reveals. Lifeboats and "lifeboat ethics" may be useful topics for those who are shipwrecked; we believe they are worthless—indeed detrimental—in discussions of food-population questions.

The ratchet metaphor is equally flawed. It, too, ignores complex interactions between birth rates and social conditions (including diets), implying as it does that more food will simply mean more babies. Also, it obscures the fact that the decrease in death rates has been caused at least as much by developments such as DDT, improved sanitation, and medical advances, as by increased food supplies, so that cutting out food aid will not necessarily lead to population declines.

The lifeboat article is strangely inadequate in other ways. For example, it shows an astonishing disregard for recent literature. The claim that we can expect no "benign demographic transition" is based on a review written more than a decade ago (Davis 1963). Yet, events and attitudes are changing rapidly in poor countries: for the first time in history, most poor people live in countries with birth control programs; with few exceptions, poor nations are somewhere on the demographic transition to lower birth rates (Demeny 1974); the population-food squeeze is now widely recognized, and governments of poor nations are aware of the relationship. Again, there is a considerable amount of evidence that birth rates can fall rapidly in poor countries given the proper social conditions (as we will discuss later); consequently, crude projections of current population growth rates are quite inadequate for policy making.

THE TRAGEDY OF THE COMMONS

Throughout the lifeboat article, Hardin bolsters his assertions by reference to the "commons" (Hardin 1968). The thesis of the commons, therefore, needs critical evaluation.

Suppose several privately owned flocks, comprising 100 sheep altogether, are grazing on a public commons.

They bring in an annual income of $1.00 per sheep. Fred, a herdsman, owns only one sheep. He decides to add another. But 101 is too many: the commons is overgrazed and produces less food. The sheep lose quality and income drops to 90¢ per sheep. Total income is now $90.90 instead of $100.00. Adding the sheep has brought an overall loss. But Fred has gained: *his* income is $1.80 instead of $1.00. The gain from the additional sheep, which is his alone, outweighs the loss from overgrazing, which he shares. Thus he promotes his interest at the expense of the community.

This is the problem of the commons, which seems on the way to becoming an archetype. Hardin, in particular, is not inclined to underrate its importance: "One of the major tasks of education today is to create such an awareness of the dangers of the commons that people will be able to recognize its many varieties, however disguised" (Hardin 1974, p. 562) and "All this is terribly obvious once we are acutely aware of the pervasiveness and danger of the commons. But many people still lack this awareness. . . " (p. 565).

The "commons" affords a handy way of classifying problems: the lifeboat article reveals that sharing, a generous immigration policy, world food banks, air, water, the fish populations of the ocean, and the western range lands are, or produce, a commons. It is also handy to be able to dispose of policies one does not like as "only a particular instance of a class of policies that are in error because they lead to the tragedy of the commons" (p. 561).

But no metaphor, even one as useful as this, should be treated with such awe. Such shorthand can be useful, but it can also mislead by discouraging thought and obscuring important detail. To dismiss a proposal by suggesting that "all you need to know about this proposal is that it institutes a commons and is, therefore, bad" is to assert that the proposed commons is worse than the original problem. This might be so if the problem of the commons were, indeed, a tragedy—that is, if it were insoluble. But it is not.

Hardin favors private ownership as the solution (either through private property or the selling of pollution rights). But, of course, there are solutions other than private ownership; and private ownership itself is no guarantee of carefully husbanded resources.

One alternative to private ownership of the commons is communal ownership of the sheep—or, in general, of the mechanisms and industries that exploit the resource—combined with communal planning for management. (Note, again, how the metaphor favors one solution: perhaps the "tragedy" lay not in the commons but in the sheep. "The Tragedy of the Privately Owned Sheep" lacks zing, unfortunately.) Public ownership of a commons has been tried in Peru to the benefit of the previously privately owned anchoveta fishery (Gulland 1975). The communally owned agriculture of China does not seem to have suffered any greater over-exploitation than that of other Asian nations.

Another alternative is cooperation combined with regulation. For example, Gulland (1975) has shown that Antarctic whale stocks (perhaps the epitome of a commons since they are internationally exploited and no one owns them) are now being properly managed, and stocks are increasing. This has been achieved through cooperation in the International Whaling Commission, which has by agreement set limits to the catch of each nation.

In passing, Hardin's private ownership argument is not generally applicable to nonrenewable resources. Given discount rates, technology substitutes, and no more than an average regard for posterity, privately owned nonrenewable resources, like oil, coal and minerals, are mined at rates that produce maximum profits, rather than at those rates that preserve them for future generations.

Thus, we must reject the temptation to use the commons metaphor as a substitute for analysis. Not all commons are the same: they differ in their origin, their nature, the type and seriousness of the problems they cause, the solutions that are appropriate for them, and the difficulty of implementing those solutions. In particular, we cannot rule out a proposal just because someone calls it a commons; a "solved" or benign commons may be the correct approach to some problems.

ON MALIGN NEGLECT

Hardin implies that nonhelp policies offer a solution to the world population-food problem. But what sort of solution would in fact occur?

Nonhelp policies would have several effects not clearly described in "Lifeboat" (Hardin 1974). First, it is not true that people in poor countries "convert extra food into extra babies" (p. 564). They convert it into longer lives. Denying them food will not lower birth rates; it will increase death rates.

These increases might not take effect immediately after the withdrawal of aid. Increases in local food production and improvements in sanitation and medicine would probably allow populations to continue growing for some time. (Death rates would need to increase almost three-fold to stabilize them.) Thus, in the future we could expect much larger populations in poor countries, living in greater misery than today. The negative relation between well-being and family size could easily lead to even higher birth rates. A "solution" that puts us back to prewar birth and death rates, at even higher population levels, is certainly not a satisfactory permanent solution.

Second, the rich countries cannot remain indifferent to events in poor countries. A poor country or a group of poor countries that controls supplies of a vital raw material, for example, may well want to use this leverage to its advantage; it may be very uncompromising about it, especially if its need is desperate and its attitude resentful, as would be likely. Just how intolerable this situation would be to the rich countries can be guessed at by recent hints of war being an acceptable means for the United States to ensure itself adequate supplies of oil at a "reasonable" price.

War is an option open to poor countries, too. China and India have nuclear weapons; others can be expected to follow. With Hardin's policies, they may feel they have little to lose, and the rich countries have a great deal to lose.

Thus we could look forward to continuing, and probably increasing, interference in and manipulation of the increasingly miserable poor countries by the rich countries. We do not believe this is a stable situation. One or more poor countries will surely want to disrupt it; recent events show that our ability to prevent this is limited. Alternatively, in the future, one or more of the rich countries may decide to help poor countries reduce their birth rates, but will then be faced with an even greater problem than we face today. In sum, malign neglect of poor nations is not likely to cause the problem to go away.

If Hardin's proposals are so defective, why are they attractive to so many people? We have already discussed Hardin's use of oversimplified metaphors, but there are other temptations.

An obvious one is the presentation of false choices: either we continue what we are doing, or we do nothing. Aid is either effective or ineffective; much of our aid has been ineffective, so all aid is, and it always will be. Such absolute positions are tempting because they save thought, justify inaction, never need reconsideration, and convey an impression of sophisticated cynicism. But they do not conform to the facts. Intelligent and effective aid, though difficult, is possible.

The apparent callousness of Hardin's proposals is itself a temptation. There is an implication that these policies are so brutal that they would not be proposed without good reasons. Conversely, those who argue for increased aid can be dismissed as "highly vocal humanitarian apologists" or "guilt addicts" (Hardin 1974, pp. 563 and 562). The implication is that these views *could* arise from unreasoning emotion, so therefore they *must* arise this way. Proposals for increased aid are then "plaintive cries" produced by guilt, bad conscience, anxiety, and misplaced Christian or Marxist idealism. But such argument by association is plainly misleading. Benign policies can also be the most rational; callous policies can be foolish.

BIRTH RATES: AN ALTERNATIVE VIEW

Is the food-population spiral inevitable? A more optimistic, if less comfortable, hypothesis, presented by Rich (1973) and Brown (1974a), is increasingly tenable: contrary to the "ratchet" projection, population growth rates are affected by many complex conditions beside food supply. In particular, a set of socioeconomic conditions can be identified that motivate parents to have fewer children; under these conditions, birth rates can fall quite rapidly, sometimes even before birth control technology is available. Thus, population growth can be controlled more effectively by intelligent human intervention that sets up the

appropriate conditions than by doing nothing and trusting to "natural population cycles."

These conditions are: parental confidence about the future, an improved status of women, and literacy. They require low infant mortality rates, widely available rudimentary health care, increased income and employment, and an adequate diet above subsistence levels. Expenditure on schools (especially elementary schools), appropriate health services (especially rural paramedical services), and agricultural reform (especially aid to small farmers) will be needed, and foreign aid can help here. It is essential that these improvements be spread across the population; aid can help here, too, by concentrating on the poor nations' poorest people, encouraging necessary institutional and social reforms, and making it easier for poor nations to use their own resources and initiative to help themselves. It is *not* necessary that per capita GNP be very high, certainly not as high as that of the rich countries during their gradual demographic transition. In other words, low birth rates in poor countries are achievable long before the conditions exist that were present in the rich countries in the late 19th and early 20th centuries.

Twenty or thirty years is not long to discover and assess the factors affecting birth rates, but a body of evidence is now accumulating in favor of this hypothesis. Rich (1973) and Brown (1974a) show that at least 10 developing countries have managed to reduce their birth rates by an average of more than one birth per 1,000 population per year for periods of 5 to 16 years. A reduction of one birth per 1,000 per year would bring birth rates in poor countries to a rough replacement level of about 16/1,000 by the turn of the century, though age distribution effects would prevent a smooth population decline. . . . [T]hese countries, . . . together with three other nations, including China, are poor and yet have brought their birth rates down to 30 or less, presumably from rates of over 40 a decade or so ago.

These data show that rapid reduction in birth rates is possible in the developing world. No doubt it can be argued that each of these cases is in some way special. Hong Kong and Singapore are relatively rich; they, Barbados, and Mauritius are also tiny. China is able to exert great social pressure on its citizens; but China is particularly significant. It is enormous; its per capita GNP is almost as low as India's; and it started out in 1949 with a terrible health system. Also, Egypt, Chile, Taiwan, Cuba, South Korea, and Sri Lanka are quite large, and they are poor or very poor. In fact, these examples represent an enormous range of religion, political systems, and geography and suggest that such rates of decline in the birth rate can be achieved whenever the appropriate conditions are met. "The common factor in these countries is that the *majority* of the population has shared in the economic and social benefits of significant national progress. . . . [M]aking health, education and jobs more broadly available to lower income groups in poor countries contribute[s] significantly toward the motivation for smaller families that is the prerequisite of a major reduction in birth rates" (Rich 1973).

The converse is also true. In Latin America, Cuba (annual per capita income $530), Chile ($720), Uruguay ($820), and Argentina ($1,160) have moderate to truly equitable distribution of goods and services and relatively low birth rates (27, 26, 23 and 22, respectively). In contrast, Brazil ($420), Mexico ($670), and Venezuela ($980) have very unequal distribution of goods and services and high birth rates (38, 42, and 41, respectively). Fertility rates in poor and relatively poor nations seem unlikely to fall as long as the bulk of the population does not share in increased benefits.

We have tried briefly to bring the major evidence before the reader. However, there is a large literature, well summarized by Rich, and the details of the evidence are well worth reading in their entirety.

This evidence is certainly not overwhelming. Its accuracy varies. There are many unmeasured variables. Some measured variables, like income and literacy, are highly interrelated. We have no evidence that we can extrapolate to other countries or to still lower birth rates. By the standards of scientific experiment, these data are not conclusive. But policy decisions such as those discussed here are always based on uncertainty, and this evidence is at least as convincing as simple projections of average birth and death rates now prevailing in poor nations. Certainly the evidence is good enough that we need to treat

the reduction of birth rates as a viable alternative to nonhelp.

A useful evaluation of the demographic transition hypothesis is provided by Beaver (1975), whose book became available only after we had completed the final revision of this article. Beaver restates the hypothesis as a set of assumptions, yielding specific predictions that can be tested against recent population data. These assumptions are similar to those given here, with some additional details and emphases. In particular, Beaver stresses the importance of a time lag of about 10 to 15 years before factors which tend to reduce birth rates can take effect. For example, both mortality decline and economic development reduce birth rates in the long run by raising expectations and confidence in the future, but both can increase birth rates in the short run by simply making it possible, physically and economically, for parents to have more children. The demographic transition hypothesis receives "strong empirical support" from a variety of statistical tests using recent Latin American data. Furthermore, the recent declines in natality in Latin America have been much more rapid than the declines in Europe during its demographic transition (see also Teitelbaum 1975).

COSTS, GAINS, AND DIFFICULTIES

We have neither the space nor the expertise to propose detailed food-population policies. Our main concern has been to help set the stage for serious discussion by disposing of simplistic proposals and irrelevant arguments, outlining some of the complexities of the problem, and indicating the existence of a large quantity of available data.

However, some kind of positive statement seems called for, if only to provide a target for others. We approach this task with trepidation. A full discussion of aid possibilities would require detailed consideration of political, social, and cultural complexities in a wide variety of recipient and donor countries. A thorough cost accounting would require detailed, quantitative knowledge about the relation between social conditions and the motivation for smaller families. Here we merely list some forms of aid, crudely estimate their costs, indicate some of their benefits and briefly discuss their feasibility.

Brown (1974a) estimates that $5 billion per year could provide:

- family planning services to the poor nations (excluding China, which already provides them); the cost includes training personnel and providing transportation facilities and contraceptives;
- literacy for all adults and children (a five-year program); and
- a health care program for mothers and infants (again excluding China).

To this we could add the following:

- 10 million metric tons of grain at an annual cost of $2 billion;
- 1.5 million metric tons of fertilizer, which is the estimated amount of the "shortfall" last year in the poor countries (U.N. 1974); the cost, including transportation, is roughly $1 billion; and
- half of the estimated annual cost of providing "adequate" increases in the area of irrigated and cultivated land in the poor countries (U.N. 1974), about $2 billion.

These costs may well be too low, although, according to Abelson (1975), the annual cost of an "effective" global food reserve is only $550 million to $800 million, compared with the $2 billion cited above. The estimates do suggest that aid on this scale, *properly designed and properly used in the recipient nations,* could make a sizeable improvement in social well-being.

The total cost is $10 billion. Still, these estimates are very crude. Let us suppose the real cost is $20 billion. Other wealthy countries could (and should) provide at least half of this. This leaves about $10 billion to be provided by the United States. Can the United States afford it?

In the past, U.S. aid has not normally been free. Indeed, India is now a net exporter of capital to the United States because it pays back more interest and principal on previous aid loans than it receives in aid. However, even giving away $10 billion is likely to have only minor effects on the U.S. economy and standard of living. It is about 1% of the GNP, about 10% of current military expenditure. It would decrease present and future consumption of goods and services in the United States by slightly more than 1% (because the cost of government accounts for about 25% of the GNP). It could result in a slight lowering of the value of the dollar abroad, unless other rich nations were also contributing proportionately. The most noticeable effects within the United States would be on the relative prices of goods and services and, as a consequence, on the poor in this country. Those items most in demand by poor countries would increase in price relative to "luxury" goods, so that the poor in the United States would be hurt more than the rich unless countermeasures were taken.

In short, although we must take care that the burden is equitably borne, the additional aid could be provided with only minor effects on the well-being of the U.S. population. Such a reduction in living standard is hardly "suicidal" or a matter of "human survival" in the United States, to use Hardin's terms. It is not a question of "them or us," as the lifeboat metaphor implies. This simpleminded dichotomy may account for the appeal of Hardin's views, but it bears no relation to reality.

The six measures suggested above should encourage economic growth as well as lower birth rates in poor countries. Adequate diet and health care improve work performance and reduce medical costs and lost work days. There is evidence (Owens and Shaw 1972) that agricultural improvements made available to small farmers can lead not only to improved diets and increased employment but also to greater productivity per hectare than occurs on large, capital intensive farms, and that the poor can save at very high rates provided they own or rent their economic facilities (e.g., farms) and are integrated into the national economy through a network of financial institutions. Since small farms are labor-intensive, agricultural improvements that concentrate on them are not only well suited to poor countries but make them less vulnerable to fluctuations in energy supplies and costs.

Improved living conditions probably would first decrease the death rate. Does this mean that the decrease in the birth rate must be very great just to compensate? Infant mortality is the major part of the death rate that can still be decreased easily in poor countries. Suppose a poor country has a birth rate of 40/1,000 per population and an infant mortality rate of 150/1,000 live births; India is close to this. These six dead infants (15% of 40) help motivate parents to have many babies. Suppose, in the next decade, conditions improve so much that infant mortality drops to zero— a ludicrous hope. This decrease would be exactly balanced if the birth rate dropped from 40/1,000 to 34/1,000. All 10 of the countries [mentioned above] dropped this many points (and greater percentages) in five years or less. Further, once mortality rates are very low, every reduction in the birth rate reduces population growth. These calculations are oversimplified, but they illustrate that even a great decrease in poverty-related deaths can be balanced by a modest decrease in births.

We can gauge the effect of lowered birth rates upon the food-population ratio. [Consider] currently projected rates of population growth and food production for the major areas of the world (U.N. 1974). These projections assume continued improvement in food production at previous rates; they do not assume increased success in programs against high birth rates. For the next decade, the annual percentage increase of population would be 0.2 to 0.4 greater than that of food supply in Africa, noncommunist Asia, and Latin America (although for the world in general food grows faster than population). A successful program that reduced births by 0.5/1,000 or more per year would quickly remove the projected imbalance between food and population, even allowing for increased survival. This effect would accelerate as gains in survival gradually declined, thus vastly reducing the amount of aid that would be needed.

Will the aid in fact be used in ways that help reduce birth rates? As a disillusioning quarter-century of aid giving has shown, the obstacles to getting aid to those segments of the population most in need of it are enormous. Aid has typically benefitted a small rich segment of society, partly because of the way aid programs have been designed but also because of human and institutional factors in the poor nations themselves (Owens and Shaw 1972). With some notable exceptions, the distribution of income and services in poor nations is extremely skewed—much more uneven than in rich countries. Indeed, much of the population is essentially outside the economic system. Breaking this pattern will be extremely difficult. It will require not only aid that is designed specifically to benefit the rural poor, but also important institutional changes such as decentralization of decision making and the development of greater autonomy and stronger links to regional and national markets for local groups and industries, such as cooperative farms.

Thus, two things are being asked of rich nations and of the United States in particular: to increase nonmilitary foreign aid, including food aid, and to give it in ways, and to governments, that will deliver it to the poorest people and will improve their access to national economic institutions. These are not easy tasks, particularly the second, and there is no guarantee that birth rates will come down quickly in all countries. Still, many poor countries have, in varying degrees, begun the process of reform, and recent evidence suggests that aid and reform together can do much to solve the twin problems of high birth rates and economic underdevelopment. The tasks are far from impossible. Based on the evidence, the policies dictated by a sense of decency are also the most realistic and rational.

REFERENCES

Abelson, P. H. 1975. The world's disparate food supplies. *Science* 187:218.

Barraclough, G. 1975. The great world crisis I. *The N. Y. Rev. Books* 21: 20–29.

Beaver, S. E. 1975. Demographic Transition Theory Reinterpreted. Lexington Books, Lexington, Mass. 177 pp.

Brown, L. R. 1974a. In the Human Interest. W. W. Norton & Co., Inc., New York. 190 pp.

——1974b. By Bread Alone. Praeger, New York. 272 pp.

Davis, K. 1963. Population. *Sci. Amer.* 209(3): 62–71.

Demeny, P. 1974. The populations of the underdeveloped countries. *Sci. Amer.* 231(3): 149–159.

Gulland, J. 1975. The harvest of the sea. Pages 167–189 *in* W. W. Murdoch, ed. Environment: Resources, Pollution and Society, 2nd ed. Sinauer Assoc., Sunderland, Mass.

Hardin, G. 1968. The tragedy of the commons. *Science* 162: 1243–1248.

——1969. Not peace, but ecology. *In* Diversity and Stability in Ecological Systems. *Brookhaven Symp. Biol.* 22: 151–161.

——1974. Living on a lifeboat. *BioScience* 24(10): 561–568.

Owens, E., and R. Shaw. 1972. Development Reconsidered. D. C. Heath & Co., Lexington, Mass. 190 pp.

Rich, W. 1973. Smaller families through social and economic progress. Overseas Development Council, Monograph #7, Washington, D.C. 73 pp.

Teitelbaum, M. S. 1975. Relevance of demographic transition theory for developing countries. *Science* 188: 420–425.

Transnational Institute. 1974. World Hunger: Causes and Remedies. Institute for Policy Studies, 1520 New Hampshire Ave., NW, Washington, D.C.

United Nations Economic and Social Council. 1974. Assessment present food situation and dimensions and causes of hunger and malnutrition in the world. E/Conf. 65/Prep/6, 8 May 1974.

University of California Food Task Force. 1974. A hungry world: the challenge to agriculture. University of California, Division of Agricultural Sciences. 303 pp.

The Case for Aid

Jeffrey Sachs

I have long believed in foreign aid as one tool of economic development. This is not an easy position to maintain, especially in the United States, where public misunderstanding, politics, and ideology all tend to keep aid an object of contempt for many people. Yet the recent evidence shows that development aid, when properly designed and delivered, works, saving the lives of the poor and helping to promote economic growth. Indeed, based on this evidence, Bill and Melinda Gates released a powerful letter to the public today also underscoring the importance and efficacy of foreign aid.

As experience demonstrates, it is possible to use our reason, management know-how, technology, and learning by doing to design highly effective aid programs that save lives and promote development. This should be done in global collaboration with national and local communities, taking local circumstances into account. The evidence bears out this approach.

Of course, I do not believe that aid is the sole or main driver of economic development. I do not believe that aid is automatically effective. Nor should we condone bad governance in Africa—or in Washington, for that matter. Aid is one development tool among several; it works best in conjunction with sound economic policies, transparency, good governance, and the effective deployment of new technologies.

Professor William Easterly of New York University has long been a vocal opponent of aid, and recently declared that the aid debate was "over," claiming victory for his theory that large-scale aid projects are doomed to fail. This blanket claim flies in the face of recent experience. Prof. Easterly has been proven wrong in both diagnosis and prescription.

During the past 13 years, the greatest breakthroughs in aid quantity and quality came from the field of public health (unlike other social sectors, such as education and sanitation, where aid increases were far less notable). As a result, the outcomes in public health in poor countries have also advanced markedly. Not only did aid quantities for public health improve; new public health institutions, such as the Global Fund to Fight AIDS, Tuberculosis, and Malaria and the Global Alliance for Vaccines and Immunization, were created to promote the effective delivery of the increased aid.

The approach of increased aid that is well targeted through innovative institutions has been enormously successful in improving public health in low-income countries. One could cite many examples ranging from the scale-up of vaccine coverage (largely through GAVI and UNICEF) to increased treatment coverage for HIV/AIDS and expanded tuberculosis control (through the Global Fund and the U.S. PEPFAR program), but I will focus specifically on malaria control, since Prof. Easterly was particularly pointed in his opposition to the mass scale-up of malaria control that has proved to be so successful. Fortunately, the global community did not heed Easterly's erroneous advice, and followed a path that the public health community strongly advocated.

At the turn of the new century, malaria was front and center of the global aid debate. Research by myself and others, and evidence garnered in the report of the World Health Organization (WHO) Commission on Macroeconomics and Health that I had the honor to chair, showed that in addition to being a health catastrophe, malaria imposes a significant economic burden, particularly in sub-Saharan Africa. Luckily, though, the world was starting to take notice. In 2000, the U.N. Millennium Declaration, The African Summit on Malaria, and the G8 Declaration all addressed the burden of malaria and committed the world to action. The debate soon turned to the issue of policy: how could the malaria burden be reduced?

Here we must look at some key details in order to keep aid in careful perspective. Starting in the late 1990s, malariologists at WHO, in academia, and in various government agencies around the world, described how malaria control could be made highly effective. The malariologists emphasized the ability of insecticide-treated bed nets to reduce the transmission of the disease. They also emphasized the urgency of shifting to a new generation of first-line medicines, notably those using artemisinin (a powerful anti-malaria drug developed by Chinese scientists) in combination with other medicines, because the old-line medicines (mainly chloroquine) were losing efficacy to growing drug resistance. The combination of bed nets and effective medicines (known in the jargon as "vector control" and "case management" respectively), supported by rapid diagnosis of infections, makes for a powerful one-two punch in saving lives and reducing malaria transmission.

Indeed, epidemiological theory and practical experience strongly suggested that if bed net coverage could be raised to a sufficiently high rate (typically around three-quarters, depending on local conditions), the transmission of malaria would be sharply reduced even for those not directly protected by their own bed nets. The "spillover" of protection to the non-users is called a mass-action effect, similar to the

way that high vaccine coverage protects even unvaccinated people because the disease stops spreading when fewer people are susceptible to infection. This mass-action phenomenon of course strongly argued for a malaria control strategy that would lead to a high level of bed net coverage.

There was one more detail of great policy significance: Not all bed nets are equal. The high-quality bed nets work not only mechanically (by covering the body) but also chemically, by a treatment with insecticide that repels or kills mosquitoes that land on the bed net. A bed net without insecticide treatment is far less effective than a treated net. Until the early 2000s, bed nets required frequent retreatment with insecticide (e.g. by bathing the nets in tubs filled with insecticide) in order to remain effective. Then, Sumitomo Chemical developed long-lasting insecticide-treated nets (LLINs) that were specially engineered to keep the insecticide intact even when the nets were repeatedly washed. The new nets could therefore remain effective for around five years or even more. Other companies, such as Vestergaard and BASF, also developed their own varieties of LLINs. This was a great breakthrough, but the new nets were more expensive to manufacture than the preceding generation of simpler nets.

All of these developments—new nets, new medicines, improved diagnostics, and a surging epidemic—were crucial to developing a successful malaria control policy after the year 2000. Taken together, they motivated the case for increased donor aid to support the mass free-distribution of LLINs and free access to the new generation of artemisinin-based medicines and rapid diagnostic tools. Without financial support, poor people could not afford either the LLINs or the new medicines. Attempts to sell the nets at a discount, known as social marketing, had very little take up, since many poor families simply lacked any cash income at all. The prospect of achieving "mass action" protection through social marketing was very small. Moreover, impoverished households would often scrape together the needed money only to buy the cheaper but ineffective nets, rather than the more expensive but more effective LLINs.

Governments of low-income African countries needed donor support for the scale-up effort since their own domestic tax revenues, even when amply allocated to public health, could not cover the costs of a basic primary health system including scaled-up malaria control. The financial calculations, laid out by the Commission on Macroeconomics and Health, showed that an impoverished country with a GDP of around $500 per capita, typical for a poor country in Africa, may be able to muster around $15 per person per year out of domestic revenues for primary health (directing 15 percent of domestic revenues to health, as the Abuja target for health spending recommends), while the costs of a basic public health system (measured in 2014 dollars) would be around $50–$60 per person per year.

Prof. Easterly would have none of it. He took special and early aim at these recommendations in his 2006 book *The White Man's Burden*, claiming that free nets "are often diverted to the black market, become out of stock in health clinics, or wind up being used as fishing nets or wedding veils." After this specious claim, he then went on to write that "a study of a program to hand out free [malaria bed] nets in Zambia to people . . . found that 70 percent of the recipients didn't use the nets." Yet this particular study, which was conducted by the American Red Cross and CORE, actually showed the program was a success, with high rates of net adoption. Prof. Easterly's claim misconstrued this and other evidence being developed by the ARC and others about the mass distribution of nets, which had found that the free distribution of malaria bed nets was achieving high coverage and adoption rates.

Prof. Easterly's arguments added to a highly visible narrative against the needed global action on malaria control. Yet despite this anti-aid narrative, a global turning point finally came in 2007–08. This turning point was helped by the early success of Kenya. Kenya's Minister of Health at the time, Charity Ngilu, led a government effort during 2006–7 to scale up mass bed net distribution based, in part, on the example of free LLIN distribution in the Sauri Millennium Village. Kenya's policies led to a sharp drop of malaria nationwide.

Next, WHO swung its powerful weight behind the mass free distributions of bed nets throughout sub-Saharan Africa. Soon after, U.N. Secretary-General Ban Ki-moon established the mass free distribution of bed nets as policy for all U.N. agencies, and called on the world's governments and NGOs to support the scale-up effort. Ban's leadership tipped the global scales decisively. Close to 300 million bed nets were freely distributed from 2008–2010, with the Global Fund to Fight AIDS, Tuberculosis and Malaria and the U.S. President's Malaria Initiative program paying for a substantial share of the scale-up.

The evidence is overwhelming that malaria declined precipitously as a result of these bold measures. WHO's latest report finds a stunning 51 percent drop in malaria deaths of African children under the age of five between the years 2000 and 2012. These results are historic. Roughly a half-million children, if not more, are being saved each year that otherwise would have succumbed to malaria. Even more success is possible, but only if development aid continues to back the effective control of malaria. The Global Fund is struggling to fill its request for $5 billion per year of funding, essential to supplement the health budgets of poor countries. Prof. Easterly's continued denunciations of aid, and his declarations that large-scale aid has failed, are injurious to the public support needed for the replenishment.

Across the board, the post-2000 improvements in public health in sub-Saharan Africa have been dramatic, strongly supported by scaled-up aid. Up to 10 million HIV-infected individuals are now receiving life-saving, anti-retroviral medicines thanks at least in part to aid programs. Tuberculosis (TB) patients are being treated and cured, with a global TB mortality rate drop of 45 percent since 1990, and an estimated 22 million people alive due to TB care and control from 1995–2012, thanks to Global Fund support, which provides the lion's share of donor financing to fight TB. With increased donor support, antenatal health visits, institutional deliveries, and access to emergency obstetrical care are all on the increase, contributing to a decline in sub-Saharan Africa's maternal mortality rate (the annual number of female deaths per 100,000 live births) from 850 in 1990 to 740 in 2000 to 500 in 2010. Deaths of children under five worldwide have declined from 12.6 million a year in 1990 and 10.8 million in 2000 to 6.5 million in 2012.

These successes demonstrate a key lesson: that well-designed aid programs with sound operating principles, including clear goals, metrics, milestones, deliverables, and financing streams, can make an enormous difference, and that such programs should be devised and applied on a large scale in order to benefit as many people as possible. Such quality design needs to be based on the details of best practices, such as the combination of medicines, bed nets, and diagnostics used in cutting-edge, community-based malaria control. The economics profession needs to do a much better job working with experts in other fields, such as public health, in order to design effective aid interventions that reflect the nitty-gritty of high-quality systems delivery. While Prof. Easterly begrudgingly admits that some health aid programs have worked, for him this contradiction seems to make no difference to his overarching claim that aid is doomed to fail, for reasons that are hard to explain. All the evidence and all the exceptions have not mattered to his rhetoric, or for that matter, to his harsh attacks on me personally.

The aid successes of the past decade have saved millions of lives, a worthy use of money (which has totaled just a tiny fraction of rich world income) on its own. Yet aid has delivered more than lives saved and improved. Various kinds of aid, including public health outlays, debt cancellation under the IMF and World Bank's Heavily Indebted Poor Countries initiative (providing debt relief and cancellation for the poorest countries), and other programmatic and budget support, have helped to put sub-Saharan Africa on a path of much higher economic growth and development. For the first time in decades, Africa's poverty rate has come down notably (from 58 percent in 1999 to 48.4 percent in 2010) and the region's economic growth is now around 5 percent per year, making it the region with the second fastest growth (following Asia).

Of course, aid didn't cause this success by itself, as there are many factors in play. But aid has helped. Research distinguishing the types and timing of aid has shown that development aid raises economic growth, though the effects will differ across countries and depend on the quality of aid. The malaria example is one of the clearest and most dramatic examples, but across the continent, aid has helped with improvements in education, agriculture, sanitation, infrastructure, and more.

In *The White Man's Burden,* Prof. Easterly declared, "You just have to do whatever you discover works with your modest resources to make a difference in the lives of poor people." Prof. Easterly's emphasis on "modest resources" mischaracterizes our real global situation. We are living in a world of great wealth. We need not accept the fallacy perpetuated by the rich that global resources available are quite so "modest," when total aid to sub-Saharan Africa in 2012 amounted to roughly 0.1 percent of the GDP of the donor countries (around $45 billion per year). We can and should mobilize more support. Just fractions of 1 percent of GDP of the rich countries can make a profound difference to ending extreme poverty throughout the world. Of course, we should also certainly agree to focus on what works, and take effective programs to large scale. The positive evidence since 2000 shows that well-designed aid has made a tremendous impact.

The issue is not "yes" or "no" to aid. Aid is needed, and can be highly successful. The issue is how to deliver high-quality aid to the world's poorest and most vulnerable people.

GLOSSARY

abolitionist—One who wishes to abolish capital punishment. (Ch. 18)

abortion—The deliberate termination of a pregnancy by surgical or medical means. (Ch. 9)

act-egoism—The theory that to determine right action, you must apply the egoistic principle to individual acts. (Ch. 5)

active euthanasia—Euthanasia performed by taking a direct action to cause someone's death; "mercy killing." (Ch. 10)

act-utilitarianism—A utilitarian theory asserting that the morally right action is the one that directly produces the most favorable balance of good over evil, everyone considered. (Ch. 4)

advance directive—A legal document allowing physicians to withhold or withdraw treatments if a patient becomes terminally ill and unable to express his or her wishes. (Ch. 10)

affirmative action—A way of making amends for, or eradicating, discrimination based on race, ethnicity, and gender. (Ch. 14)

animal rights—Possession by animals of (1) moral status; (2) strong moral considerability that cannot be easily overridden. (Ch. 12)

anthropocentrism—The notion that only humans have moral status. (Ch. 13)

anticosmopolitanism—The view that wealthy nations able to ease the suffering of the world's poor and oppressed have a moral obligation to do so, but they also have moral obligations to their own citizens that may be weightier than those concerning foreigners. (Ch. 20)

appeal to authority—The fallacy of relying on the opinion of someone thought to be an expert who is not. (Ch. 3)

appeal to ignorance—The fallacy of arguing that the absence of evidence entitles us to believe a claim. (Ch. 3)

appeal to the person—The fallacy (also known as *ad hominem*) of arguing that a claim should be rejected solely because of the characteristics of the person who makes it. (Ch. 3)

applied ethics—The application of moral norms to specific moral issues or cases, particularly those in a profession such as medicine or law. (Ch. 1)

argument—A group of statements, one of which is supposed to be supported by the rest. (Ch. 3)

begging the question—The fallacy of arguing in a circle—that is, trying to use a statement as both a premise in an argument and the conclusion of that argument. Such an argument says, in effect, *p* is true because *p* is true. (Ch. 3)

biocentrism—The view that all living entities have moral status, whether sentient or not. (Ch. 13)

capital punishment—Punishment by execution of someone officially judged to have committed a serious, or capital, crime. (Ch. 18)

categorical imperative—An imperative that we should follow regardless of our particular wants and needs; also, the principle that defines Kant's theory. (Ch. 4, 6)

cogent argument—A strong argument with true premises. (Ch. 3)

conception—The merging of a sperm cell and an ovum into a single cell; also called *fertilization*. (Ch. 9)

conclusion—The statement supported in an argument. (Ch. 3)

consequentialist theory—A theory asserting that what makes an action right is its consequences. (Ch. 4)

considered moral judgment—A moral assessment that is as free from bias and distorting passions as possible. We generally trust such a judgment unless there is a reason to doubt it. (Ch. 4)

conventional view (of sexuality)—The idea that sex is morally acceptable only between a man and a woman who are legally married to each other. (Ch. 15)

cosmopolitanism—The view that wealthy nations able to ease the suffering of the world's poor and oppressed have a moral obligation to do so and that this obligation is as strong concerning foreigners as it is concerning a nation's own citizens. (Ch. 20)

criminalization—Making the use (and possession) of drugs a criminal of defense. (Ch. 17)

cultural relativism—The view that an action is morally right if one's culture approves of it. (Ch. 2)

decriminalization—Allowing people to use drugs without being liable to criminal prosecution and punishment. (Ch. 17)

deductive argument—An argument that is supposed to give logically conclusive support to its conclusion. (Ch. 3)

deportation—The formal removal of a foreign national from a country for violating an immigration law. (Ch. 20)

descriptive ethics—The scientific study of moral beliefs and practices. (Ch. 1)

direct moral consideration—Moral consideration for a being's own sake, rather than because of its relationship to others. (Ch. 12)

distributive justice—Justice concerning the fair distribution of society's benefits and costs (such as income, taxes, jobs, and public service). (Ch. 4, 21)

divine command theory—A theory asserting that the morally right action is the one that God commands. (Ch. 4)

doctrine of double effect—The principle that performing a good action may be permissible even if it has bad effects, but performing a bad action for the purpose of achieving good effects is never permissible; any bad effects must be unintended. (Ch. 6)

drug—A nonfood chemical substance that can affect the functions or makeup of the body. (Ch. 17)

drug addiction—An intense craving for a drug and compulsive, uncontrolled use of the drug despite harm done to the user or other people. (Ch. 17)

drug dependence—A condition in which discontinuing the use of a drug is extremely difficult, involving psychological or physical symptoms. (Ch. 17)

duty of beneficence—A moral obligation to benefit others. (Ch. 21)

ecological holist—One who believes that the fundamental unit of moral consideration in environmental ethics is the biosphere and its ecosystems. (Ch. 13)

ecological individualist—One who believes that the fundamental unit of moral consideration in environmental ethics is the individual. (Ch. 13)

egalitarian theory of justice—A theory of justice holding that justice requires equal distribution of goods and social benefits among all persons. (Ch. 21)

emotivism—The view that moral utterances are neither true nor false but are expressions of emotions or attitudes. (Ch. 2)

equivocation—The fallacy of assigning two different meanings to the same term in an argument. (Ch. 3)

ethical egoism—A theory asserting that the morally right action is the one that produces the most favorable balance of good over evil for oneself. (Ch. 4)

ethics (or **moral philosophy**)—The philosophical study of morality. (Ch. 1)

ethics of care—A perspective on moral issues that emphasizes close personal relationships and moral virtues such as compassion, faithfulness, kindness, love, and sympathy. (Ch. 8)

eudaimonia—Happiness, or flourishing. (Ch. 7)

euthanasia—Directly or indirectly bringing about the death of another person for that person's sake. (Ch. 10)

extrinsically valuable—See *instrumentally valuable*. (Ch. 1)

faulty analogy—The use of a flawed analogy to argue for a conclusion. (Ch. 3)

feminist ethics—An alternative way of looking at the concepts and concerns of the moral life; an approach focused on women's interests and experiences and devoted to supporting the moral equality of women and men. (Ch. 8)

fertilization—See *conception*. (Ch. 9)

Golden Mean—Aristotle's notion of a virtue as a balance between two behavioral extremes. (Ch. 7)

greatest happiness principle—Mill's principle that "holds that actions are right in proportion as they tend to promote happiness, wrong as they tend to produce the reverse of happiness." (Ch. 5)

gun control—Laws and policies designed to restrict the possession, use, and availability of firearms. (Ch. 17)

harm principle—The view that authorities are justified in restricting some people's freedom to prevent harm to others. (Ch. 17)

harm reduction—A drug policy aimed at reducing the harm that arises from drugs and drug laws. (Ch. 17)

hasty generalization—The fallacy of drawing a conclusion about an entire group of people or things based on an undersized sample of the group. (Ch. 3)

hate speech—Spoken or written words used to insult, disparage, or attack people based on their social or ethnic group. (Ch. 16)

homosexuality—Sexual relations between people of the same sex. (Ch. 15)

humanitarian intervention—The act of a state (or states) going to war to defend people of another state against the murderous aggression of their own regime. (Ch. 19)

hypothetical imperative—An imperative that tells us what we should do if we have certain desires. (Ch. 6)

imperfect duty—A duty that has exceptions. (Ch. 6)

indicator words—Terms that often appear in arguments to signal the presence of a premise or conclusion, or to indicate that an argument is deductive or inductive. (Ch. 3)

indirect moral consideration—Moral consideration on account of a being's relationship to others. (Ch. 12)

individual racism—Person-to-person acts of intolerance or discrimination. (Ch. 14)

inductive argument—An argument that is supposed to offer probable support to its conclusion. (Ch. 3)

institutional or **structural racism**—Unequal treatment that arises from the way organizations, institutions, and social systems operate. (Ch. 14)

instrumentally (or **extrinsically**) **valuable**—Valuable as a means to something else. (Ch. 1)

intrinsically valuable—Valuable in itself, for its own sake. (Ch. 1)

invalid argument—A deductive argument that does not offer logically conclusive support for the conclusion. (Ch. 3)

involuntary euthanasia—Euthanasia performed on a person against his or her wishes. (Ch. 10)

jus ad bellum—The justification for resorting to war; the justice of war. (Ch. 19)

jus in bello—The moral permissibility of acts in war; justice in war. (Ch. 19)

justice—The morality of persons getting what is fair or what is their due. (Ch. 21)

just war theory—The doctrine that war may be morally permissible under stipulated conditions. (Ch. 19)

Kant's theory—A theory asserting that the morally right action is the one done in accordance with the categorical imperative. (Ch. 4)

legalization—Making the production and sale of drugs legal—that is, making their sale and production no longer a punishable crime. (Ch. 17)

legal moralism—The doctrine that the government is justified in curbing people's freedom to force them to obey moral rules. (Ch. 17)

liberal view (of sexuality)—The idea that as long as basic moral standards are respected, any sexual activity engaged in by informed, consenting adults is permissible. (Ch. 15)

libertarian theory of justice—A theory of justice that emphasizes individual liberties and negative rights and rejects positive rights as a violation of personal freedom. (Ch. 21)

managed care—A type of health insurance in which providers contract with a managed care plan to offer health care to a particular group of patients (members of the plan) at discounted costs. (Ch. 11)

means-ends principle—The rule that we must always treat people (including ourselves) as ends in themselves, never merely as a means. (Ch. 6)

Medicaid—A health insurance program supported jointly by the U.S. federal government and the states, with the former providing matching funds to the latter. It covers some low-income families, pregnant women, and people with disabilities. (Ch. 11)

Medicare—A federally funded U.S. health insurance program that covers people 65 and older, some adults under 65 with disabilities, and people with end-stage kidney disease. (Ch. 11)

metaethics—The study of the meaning and logical structure of moral beliefs. (Ch. 1)

moderate view (of sexuality)—The idea that sex is permissible, whether in marriage or not, if the consenting partners have a serious emotional connection. (Ch. 15)

morality—Beliefs concerning right and wrong, good and bad; they can include judgments, rules, values, principles, and theories. (Ch. 1)

moral philosophy—See *ethics*. (Ch. 1)

moral statement—A statement affirming that an action is right or wrong or that a person (or one's motive or character) is good or bad. (Ch. 3)

moral status (or **moral considerability**)—The property of being a suitable candidate for direct moral concern or respect. (Ch. 12)

moral theory—An explanation of what makes an action right or what makes a person or thing good. (Ch. 4)

natural law theory—A theory asserting that the morally right action is the one that follows the dictates of nature. (Ch. 4)

negative right—A person's right that obligates others not to interfere with that person's obtaining something. (Ch. 4, 21)

noncombatant immunity—The status of a person who should not be intentionally attacked in war. (Ch. 19)

nonconsequentialist theory—A theory asserting that the rightness of an action does not depend on its consequences. (Ch. 4)

nonmoral statement—A statement that does not affirm that an action is right or wrong or that a person (or one's motive or character) is good or bad. (Ch. 3)

nonstate actors—Individuals or groups that are not sovereign states. (Ch. 19)

nonvoluntary euthanasia—Euthanasia performed on a person who is not competent to decide the issue and has left no instructions regarding end-of-life preferences. In such cases, family or physicians usually make the decision. (Ch. 10)

normative ethics—The study of the principles, rules, or theories that guide our actions and judgments. (Ch. 1)

objectivism—The theory that moral truths exist and that they do so independently of what individuals or societies think of them . (Ch. 2)

pacifism—The view that war is never morally permissible. (Ch. 19)

passive euthanasia—Euthanasia performed by withholding or withdrawing measures necessary for sustaining life. (Ch. 10)

paternalism principle—The view that authorities are sometimes justified in limiting people's freedom to prevent them from harming themselves. (Ch. 17)

perfect duty—A duty that has no exceptions. (Ch. 6)

person—An entity with full moral rights. (Ch. 9)

physician-assisted suicide—The killing of a person by the person's own hand with the help of a physician. (Ch. 10)

pornography—Sexually explicit images or text meant to cause sexual excitement or arousal. (Ch. 15)

positive right—A person's right that obligates others to help that person obtain something. (Ch. 4, 21)

premise—A supporting statement in an argument. (Ch. 3)

prima facie principle—A principle that applies in a situation unless exceptions are justified. (Ch. 4)

principle of utility—Bentham's "principle which approves or disapproves of every action whatsoever, according to the tendency which it appears to have to augment or diminish the happiness of the party whose interest is in question." (Ch. 5)

psychological egoism—The view that the motive for all our actions is self-interest. (Ch. 5)

punishment—The deliberate and authorized causing of pain or harm to someone thought to have broken a law. (Ch. 18)

quickening—The point in fetal development when the mother can feel the fetus moving (at about sixteen to twenty weeks). (Ch. 9)

racial discrimination—Unfavorable treatment of people because of their race. Discrimination and preju-dice can be directed at traits other than race, including sexual traits. (Ch. 14)

racial prejudice—Racially biased opinions based on incomplete or erroneous information. (Ch. 14)

racism—The belief that distinct races exist, that significant differences (such as moral, intellectual, or cultural differences) among races can be distinguished, and that some races are inferior in these significant respects or otherwise deserving of dislike or hostility. (Ch. 14)

realism (as applied to warfare)—The view that moral standards are not applicable to war, which must be judged instead on how well it serves state interests. (Ch. 19)

refugee—Someone who has fled from his or her home country and cannot return because he or she has a well-founded fear of persecution based on religion, race, nationality, political opinion or membership in a particular social group. (Ch. 20)

retentionist—One who wishes to retain the death penalty. (Ch. 18)

retributive justice—Justice concerning the fair use of punishment for wrongdoing. (Ch. 4, 21)

retributivism—The view that offenders deserve to be punished, or "paid back," for their crimes and to be punished in proportion to the severity of their offenses. (Ch. 18)

right—A claim or entitlement to something; a moral demand that obligates others to honor it. (Ch. 21)

rule-egoism—The theory that to determine right action, you must see if an act falls under a rule that if consistently followed would maximize your self-interest. (Ch. 5)

rule-utilitarianism—A utilitarian theory asserting that the morally right action is the one covered by a rule that if generally followed would produce the most favorable balance of good over evil, everyone considered. (Ch. 4)

self-evident statement—An assertion that a person is justified in believing merely by understanding it, such as "No bachelors are married." (Ch. 4)

slippery slope—The fallacy of using dubious premises to argue that doing a particular action will inevitably lead to other actions that will result in disaster, so that first action should not be done. (Ch. 3)

social contract theory—The theory that morality arises from a social contract that self-interested and rational people abide by in order to secure a degree of peace, prosperity, and safety. (Ch. 5)

sound argument—A valid argument with true premises. (Ch. 3)

species egalitarian—One who believes that all living things have equal moral status. (Ch. 13)

speciesism—Discrimination against nonhuman animals just because of their species. (Ch. 12)

species nonegalitarian—One who believes that some living things have greater moral status than others. (Ch. 13)

speech codes—Campus regulations that ban the use of language or symbols thought to embody hate speech. (Ch. 16)

statement—An assertion that something is or is not the case. (Ch. 3)

straw man—The fallacy of misrepresenting someone's claim or argument so it can be more easily refuted. (Ch. 3)

strong affirmative action—The use of policies and procedures to favor particular individuals because of their race, gender, or ethnic background. (Ch. 14)

strong argument—An inductive argument that does in fact provide probable support for its conclusion. (Ch. 3)

structural racism—See *institutional racism.* (Ch. 14)

subjective relativism—The view that an action is morally right if one approves of it. (Ch. 2)

supererogatory actions—Conduct that is "above and beyond" duty; not required, but praiseworthy. (Ch. 21)

terrorism (as defined in Chapter 19)—Violence against noncombatants for political, religious, or ideological ends. (Ch. 19)

terrorism (the definition preferred by the U.S. Department of State)—Premeditated, politically motivated violence perpetrated against noncombatant targets by subnational groups or clandestine agents, usually intended to influence an audience. (Ch. 19)

therapeutic abortion—An abortion performed to protect the life or health of the mother. (Ch. 9)

torture—The intentional inflicting of severe pain or suffering on people to punish or intimidate them or extract information from them. (Ch. 19)

utilitarianism—A theory asserting that the morally right action is the one that produces the most favorable balance of good over evil, everyone considered. (Ch. 4)

valid argument—A deductive argument that does in fact provide logically conclusive support for its conclusion. (Ch. 3)

viability—The stage of fetal development at which the fetus is able to survive outside the uterus. (Ch. 9)

virtue—A stable disposition to act and feel according to some ideal or model of excellence. (Ch. 7)

virtue ethics—A theory of morality that makes virtue the central concern. (Ch. 7)

voluntary euthanasia—Euthanasia performed on a person with his or her permission. (Ch. 10)

weak affirmative action—The use of policies and procedures to end discriminatory practices and ensure equal opportunity. (Ch. 14)

weak argument—An inductive argument that does not give probable support to the conclusion. (Ch. 3)

zoocentrism—The notion that both human and nonhuman animals have moral status. (Ch. 13)

1. If John works out at the gym daily, he will be healthier. He is working out at the gym daily. So he will be healthier.

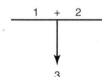

3. Ghosts do not exist. There is no reliable evidence showing that any disembodied persons exist anywhere.

5. The mayor is soft on crime. He cut back on misdemeanor enforcement and told the police department to be more lenient on traffic violators.

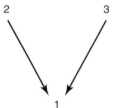

7. The president is either dishonest or incompetent. He's not incompetent, though, because he's an expert at getting self-serving legislation through Congress. I guess he's just dishonest.

9. Can people without strong religious beliefs be moral? Countless people have been nonbelievers or nontheists and still behaved according to lofty moral principles. For example: the Buddhists of Asia and the Confucianists of China. Consider also the great secular philosophers from the ancient Greeks to the likes of David Hume and Bertrand Russell. So it's not true that those without strong religious beliefs cannot be moral.

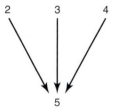

11. We shouldn't pay the lawnmower guy so much money because he never completes the work, and he will probably just gamble the money away because he has no self-control.

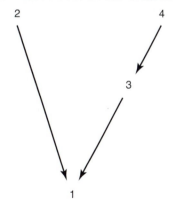

NOTES AND REFERENCES

CHAPTER 1: Ethics and the Examined Life

1. Paul W. Taylor, *Principles of Ethics: An Introduction* (Encino, CA: Dickenson, 1975), 9–10.
2. G. W. von Leibniz, "Discourse on Metaphysics," in *Selections*, ed. Philip P. Wiener (New York: Scribner, 1951), 292.
3. James Rachels, *The Elements of Moral Philosophy*, 4th ed. (Boston: McGraw-Hill, 2003), 51.
4. Jonathan Berg, "How Could Ethics Depend on Religion?" in *A Companion to Ethics*, ed. Peter Singer, corr. ed. (Oxford: Blackwell, 1993), 525–33.

CHAPTER 2: Subjectivism, Relativism, and Emotivism

1. Walter T. Stace, *The Concept of Morals* (1937; reprint, New York: Macmillan, 1965), 8–58.
2. Phillip Montague, "Are There Objective and Absolute Moral Standards?" in *Reason and Responsibility: Readings in Some Basic Problems in Philosophy*, ed. Joel Feinberg, 5th ed. (Belmont, CA: Wadsworth, 1978), 490–91.
3. Solomon Asch, *Social Psychology* (Englewood Cliffs, NJ: Prentice Hall, 1952), 378–79.
4. See, for example, Clyde Kluckhohn, "Ethical Relativity: Sic et Non," *Journal of Philosophy* 52 (1955): 663–77, and E. O. Wilson, *On Human Nature* (1978; reprint, New York: Bantam, 1979).
5. A. J. Ayer, "Critique of Ethics and Theology," in *Language, Truth and Logic* (1936; reprint, New York: Dover, 1952), 107.
6. Ayer, 112.
7. This scenario is inspired by some of Brand Blanshard's examples from "Emotivism," in *Reason and Goodness* (1961; reprint, New York: G. Allen and Unwin, 1978).
8. Blanshard, 204–5.

CHAPTER 4: The Power of Moral Theories

1. John Rawls, *A Theory of Justice*, rev. ed. (Cambridge, MA: Harvard University Press, Belknap Press, 1999).
2. Immanuel Kant, *Groundwork of the Metaphysic of Morals*, trans. H. J. Paton (1948; reprint, New York: Harper & Row, 1964), 88.
3. W. D. Ross, *The Right and the Good* (Oxford: Oxford University Press, 1930).
4. See, for example, Robert Audi, *Moral Knowledge and Ethical Character* (Oxford: Oxford University Press, 1997); and Russ Shafer-Landau, *Moral Realism: A Defence* (Oxford: Oxford University Press, 2003).

CHAPTER 5: Consequentialist Theories: Maximize the Good

1. Joel Feinberg, "Psychological Egoism," in *Moral Philosophy: Selected Readings*, ed. George Sher (San Diego: Harcourt Brace Jovanovich, 1987), 11–12.
2. Jeremy Bentham, "Of the Principle of Utility," in *An Introduction to the Principles of Morals and Legislation* (1789; reprint, Oxford: Clarendon Press, 1879), 1–7.
3. John Stuart Mill, "What Utilitarianism Is," Chapter 2 in *Utilitarianism*, 7th ed. (London: Longmans, Green, 1879).
4. Mill, Chapter 2 .
5. Mill, Chapter 2.
6. Judith Jarvis Thomson, "The Trolley Problem," in *Rights, Restitution, and Risk: Essays in Moral Theory*, ed. William Parent (Cambridge, MA: Harvard University Press, 1986), 95.
7. This case is based on one devised by W. D. Ross in *The Right and the Good* (Oxford: Clarendon Press, 1930), 34–35.
8. Paul W. Taylor, *Principles of Ethics: An Introduction* (Encino, CA: Dickenson, 1975), 77–78.
9. The points in this and the preceding paragraph were inspired by James Rachels, *The Elements of Moral Philosophy*, 4th ed. (Boston: McGraw-Hill, 2003), 111–12.
10. J. C. Smart, *Utilitarianism: For and Against* (Cambridge: Cambridge University Press, 1973), 68.
11. Fred Feldman, *Introductory Ethics* (Englewood Cliffs, NJ: Prentice Hall, 1978), 77–78.

12. Thomas Hobbes, *Leviathan*, 1651.

13. Hobbes, *Leviathan*.

14. John Rawls, *A Theory of Justice*, rev. ed. (Cambridge, MA: Harvard University Press, 1999), 10.

CHAPTER 6: Nonconsequentialist Theories: Do Your Duty

1. Immanuel Kant, *Fundamental Principles of the Metaphysic of Morals*, trans. Thomas K. Abbott, 2nd ed. (London: Longmans, Green, 1879), 1–2.

2. Kant, *Fundamental Principles of the Metaphysic of Morals*, 52.

3. Kant, *Fundamental Principles of the Metaphysic of Morals*, 55.

4. Kant, *Fundamental Principles of the Metaphysic of Morals*, 66–67.

5. I owe this point to James Rachels, *The Elements of Moral Philosophy*, 4th ed. (Boston: McGraw-Hill, 2003), 126.

6. C. D. Broad, *Five Types of Ethical Theory* (1930; reprint, London: Routledge & Kegan Paul, 1956), 132.

7. Thomas Aquinas, *Summa Theologica*, in *Basic Writings of Saint Thomas Aquinas*, ed. and annotated by Anton C. Pegis (New York: Random House, 1945), First Part of the Second Part, Question 94, Article 2.

CHAPTER 7: Virtue Ethics: Be a Good Person

1. Aristotle, *Nicomachean Ethics*, trans. W. D. Ross, book II, chapter 1 (eBooks@Adelaide, 2004).

2. Louis P. Pojman, *Ethics: Discovering Right and Wrong*, 4th ed. (Belmont, CA: Wadsworth, 2002), 165.

3. Rosalind Hursthouse, "Virtue Ethics," in *Stanford Encyclopedia of Philosophy*, Fall 2003 ed., ed. Edward N. Zalta, http://plato.stanford.edu/archives/fall2003/entries/ethics-virtue/ (January 9, 2015).

4. William K. Frankena, *Ethics*, 2nd ed. (Englewood Cliffs, NJ: Prentice Hall, 1973), 65.

CHAPTER 8: Feminist Ethics and the Ethics of Care

1. Alison M. Jaggar, "Feminist Ethics," in *Encyclopedia of Ethics,* ed. Lawrence C. Becker and Charlotte B. Becker (New York: Garland, 1992), 364.

2. Alison M. Jaggar, "Feminist Ethics," 363–64.

3. Sarah Clark Miller, "Feminist Ethics," in *Kantianism, Liberalism, and Feminism: Resisting Oppression*, ed. Carol Hay (New York: Palgrave Macmillan, 2013), 204–205.

4. Carol Gilligan, *In a Different Voice: Psychological Theory and Women's Development* (Cambridge, MA: Harvard University Press, 1982).

5. Annette C. Baier, "The Need for More Than Justice," *Canadian Journal of Philosophy,* supplementary vol. 13 (1988): 41–56.

6. Virginia Held, "The Ethics of Care as Moral Theory," in *The Ethics of Care* (Oxford: Oxford University Press, 2006), 10.

CHAPTER 9: Abortion

1. *Roe v. Wade*, 410 U.S. 113, 164–65 (1973).

2. *Roe*, 158, 162.

3. Mary Anne Warren, "Abortion," in *A Companion to Ethics*, ed. Peter Singer, corr. ed. (Cambridge, MA: Blackwell, 1993), 304.

4. John T. Noonan Jr., "An Almost Absolute Value in History," in *The Morality of Abortion: Legal and Historical Perspectives*, ed. John T. Noonan Jr. (Cambridge, MA: Harvard University Press, 1970), 56–57.

5. Warren, 312.

6. Mary Anne Warren, "On the Moral and Legal Status of Abortion," *The Monist* 57, no. 4 (1973): 56.

7. Judith Jarvis Thomson, "A Defense of Abortion," *Philosophy & Public Affairs* 1, no. 1 (1971): 48–49.

8. Thomson, 66.

CHAPTER 10: Euthanasia and Physician-Assisted Suicide

1. Larry Copeland and Laura Parker, "Terri Schiavo's Case Doesn't End with Her Passing," *USAToday*, March 31, 2005, www.usatoday.com/news/nation/2005-03-31-schiavo_x.htm (January 13, 2012).

2. I owe the notion of a good death "for the sake" of the person dying to Philippa Foot (in "Euthanasia," *Philosophy & Public Affairs* 6, no. 2 [1977]: 85–112); and to Helga Kuhse (in "Euthanasia," in *Companion to Ethics*, ed. Peter Singer, corr. ed. [Oxford: Blackwell, 1993], 294–302).

3. Issued June 1994 based on the reports *"Decisions Near the End of Life,"* adopted June 1991, and *"Physician-Assisted Suicide,"* adopted December 1993 (*JAMA*); updated June 1996.

4. Immanuel Kant, "Suicide," in *Lectures on Ethics*, trans. Louis Infield (New York: Harper & Row, 1963), 147–54.

5. Ronald Munson, *Intervention and Reflection: Basic Issues in Medical Ethics,* ed. Ronald Munson, 7th ed. (Belmont, CA: Wadsworth, 2004), 696–97.

6. Dan W. Brock, "Voluntary Active Euthanasia," *Hastings Center Report* 22, no. 2 (March/April 1992): 11.

7. I owe this point to Thomas F. Wall, *Thinking Critically about Moral Problems* (Belmont, CA: Wadsworth, 2003), 176.

8. James Rachels, "Active and Passive Euthanasia," *New England Journal of Medicine* 292, no. 2 (January 9, 1975): 79.

9. Winston Nesbitt, "Is Killing No Worse Than Letting Die?" *Journal of Applied Philosophy* 12, no. 1 (1995): 101–5.

10. J. Gay-Williams, "The Wrongfulness of Euthanasia," in *Intervention and Reflection: Basic Issues in Medical Ethics*, [selected by] Ronald Munson, 7th ed. (Belmont, CA: Wadsworth, 2004), 710–11.

11. Brock, 20.

CHAPTER 11: Delivering Health Care

1. Kaiser Family Foundation analysis of the 2013 and 2016 National Health Interview Survey, https://www.kff.org/uninsured/report/the-uninsured-a-primer-key-facts-about-health-insurance-and-the-uninsured-under-the-affordable-care-act/(December 17, 2017).

2. A. P. Wilper et al., "Health Insurance and Mortality in U.S. Adults," *American Journal of Public Health* 99:2289–95.

3. Michelle Long et al., "Trends in Employer-Sponsored Insurance Offer and Coverage Rates," Kaiser Family Foundation, March 21, 2016, https://www.kff.org/private-insurance/issue-brief/trends-in-employer-sponsored-insurance-offer-and-coverage-rates-1999-2014/.

4. OECD.org, OECD Data, "Health Spending," 2016, https://data.oecd.org/healthres/health-spending.htm;

Melissa Etehad and Kyle Kim, "The U.S. Spends More on Healthcare Than Any Other Country—but Not with Better Health Outcomes," *Los Angeles Times*, July 18, 2017.

5. OECD, "Health at a Glance 2017: OECD Indicators" November 10, 2017).

6. Kaiser Family Foundation, "US Improving in Health Care Quality, But Still Lagging Behind Other Countries, New Analysis Finds," September 10, 2016, https://www.kff.org/health-costs/press-release/us-improving-in-health-care-quality-but-still-lagging-behind-other-countries-new-analysis-finds/.

7. Commonwealth Fund, "US Health System Ranks Last Among Eleven Countries on Measures of Access Equity, Quality, Efficiency, and Healthy Lives," June 16, 2014, http://www.commonwealthfund.org/publications/pressreleases/ 2014/jun/us-health-system-ranks-last.

8. National Conference of State Legislatures, "Affordable Care Act: A Brief Summary," March 2011, http://www.ncsl.org/portals/1/documents/health/hraca.pdf. Reprinted by permission.

9. Tami Luhby, "Will Obamacare Survive the Tax Bill?" CNNMoney, December 15, 2017, http://money.cnn.com/2017/12/15/news/economy/obamacare-individual-mandate-tax/index.html.

10. *The Economist* (editorial), "Libertarians, Health Insurance, and Rights," September 2, 2009.

11. Norman Daniels, "Is There a Right to Health Care and, If So, What Does It Encompass?" in *A Companion to Bioethics*, ed. Helga Kuhse and Peter Singer (Oxford: Blackwell, 1998, 2001), 317.

12. John Rawls, *A Theory of Justice*, rev. ed. (Cambridge, MA: Harvard University Press, 1999).

13. Norman Daniels, 319.

14. Norman Daniels, 323.

CHAPTER 12: Animal Welfare

1. Peter Singer, *Animal Liberation*, 2nd ed. (New York: New York Review of Books, 1990), i.

2. Thomas Aquinas, *Summa Theologica*, from *Basic Writings of Saint Thomas Aquinas*, ed. and annotated by Anton C. Pegis (New York: Random House, 1945), Second Part of the Second Part, Question 64, Article 1.

3. U.S. Department of Agriculture, National Agricultural Statistical Services, *Livestock Slaughter: 2016 Summary*; USDA, NASS, *Poultry Slaughter: 2016 Summary.*

4. Tadlock Cowan, "Humane Treatment of Farm Animals: Overview and Issues," Congressional Research Service Report RS21978, May 9, 2011, www.nationalaglawcenter.org/assets/crs/RS21978.pdf (August 20, 2017); People for the Ethical Treatment of Animals, "Petition for Agency Action to Fully Comply with the Mandates of Humane Methods of Livestock Slaughter Act," December 11, 2001, www.peta.org/feat/usda/petition.html (December 3, 2006).

5. Lori Gruen, "The Moral Status of Animals," in *Stanford Encyclopedia of Philosophy*, Fall 2003 ed., ed. Edward N. Zalta, http://plato.stanford.edu/entries/moral-animal/ (February 23, 2015).

6. Jeremy Bentham, *An Introduction to Principles of Morals and Legislation* (1789; reprint, New York: Hafner, 1948), 311.

7. Peter Singer, "All Animals Are Equal," *Philosophic Exchange* 1 (1974): 106, 107–8.

8. Singer, "All Animals Are Equal," 109.

9. Singer, *Animal Liberation*, 77–78.

10. Tom Regan, "The Case for Animal Rights," in *In Defense of Animals*, ed. Peter Singer (Oxford: Blackwell, 1985), 21.

11. Regan, "The Case for Animal Rights," 22.

12. Regan, "The Case for Animal Rights," 24.

13. Mary Anne Warren, "The Rights of the Nonhuman World," in *Environmental Philosophy: A Collection of Readings*, ed. Robert Elliot and Arran Gare (University Park: Pennsylvania State University Press, 1983), 116.

14. Regan, "The Case for Animal Rights," 23.

CHAPTER 13: Environmental Ethics

1. National Academy of Sciences and the Royal Society, *Climate Change: Evidence and Causes*, "Summary," February 26, 2014, http://dels.nas.edu/resources/static-assets/exec-office-other/climate-change-full.pdf.

2. David Schmidtz and Elizabeth Willott, "Introduction," in *Environmental Ethics: What Really Matters, What Really Works* (New York: Oxford University Press, 2002), xvii.

3. Aldo Leopold, "The Land Ethic," in *A Sand Country Almanac* (Oxford: Oxford University Press, 1981), 237–65.

4. Immanuel Kant, *Lectures on Ethics*, trans. Louis Infield (New York: Harper and Row, 1963), 239–40.

5. Paul W. Taylor, "The Ethics of Respect for Nature," *Environmental Ethics* 3, no. 3 (1981): 198.

6. Tom Regan, "Animal Rights, Human Wrongs," *Environmental Ethics* 2, no. 2 (Summer 1980): 99–120.

7. Robert Elliot, "Environmental Ethics," in *A Companion to Ethics,* ed. Peter Singer, corr. ed. (Oxford: Blackwell, 1993), 291.

8. Elliot, 292.

9. This argument is a vastly oversimplified rendering of Robert Elliot's argument in "Faking Nature," *Inquiry* 25, no. 1 (1982): 81–93.

10. This example is adapted from Martin H. Krieger, "What's Wrong with Plastic Trees?" *Science* 179 (1973): 446–55.

11. Taylor, 207.

12. David Schmidtz, "Are All Species Equal?" *Journal of Applied Philosophy* 15, no. 1 (1998): 59.

CHAPTER 14: Racism, Equality, and Discrimination

1. Lawrence Blum, *"I'm Not a Racist But ...": The Moral Quandary of Race* (Ithaca, NY: Cornell University Press, 2002), 110. Copyright © 2002 by Cornell University. Used by permission of the publisher, Cornell University Press.

2. Tanya Maria Golash-Boza, *Race and Racisms: A Critical Approach* (New York: Oxford University Press, 2016), 3.

3. Blum, 133.

4. Blum, 131.

5. Michael James, "Race," in *Stanford Encyclopedia of Philosophy,* Spring 2017 ed., ed. Edward N. Zalta, https://plato.stanford.edu/archives/spr2017/entries/race/.

6. Blum, 147–64.

7. Blum, 8–9.

8. Blum, 1–2.

9. Eduardo Bonilla-Silva, *Racism without Racists* (Lanham, MD: Rowman and Littlefield, 2018), 2. Copyright © 2014. Used by permission of Rowan & Littlefield Publishing Group. All rights reserved.

10. Blum, 23–24.

11. Bonilla-Silva, 1.

12. Bonilla-Silva, 2.

13. Bonilla-Silva, 3.

14. Civil Rights Act of 1964, Section 601 of Title VI.

15. Terms used by Louis P. Pojman in "The Case against Affirmative Action," *International Journal of Applied Philosophy* 12 (1998): 97–115 (reprinted in *Philosophy: The Quest for Truth,* ed. Louis P. Pojman and Lewis Vaughn. 6th ed. [New York: Oxford University Press, 2006], 632–45). I attach very roughly the same meanings to them that Pojman does.

16. Pojman, "The Case against Affirmative Action," 98.

17. Albert Mosley, "The Case for Affirmative Action," in *Philosophy: The Quest for Truth,* ed. Louis P. Pojman and Lewis Vaughn, 6th ed. (New York: Oxford University Press, 2006), 630.

18. *Regents of the University of California v. Bakke,* 438 U.S. 265, 312 (1978).

19. Carl Cohen, in *Affirmative Action and Racial Preference: A Debate,* by Carl Cohen and James P. Sterba (Oxford: Oxford University Press, 2003), 25.

20. Ronald Dworkin, "Bakke's Case: Are Quotas Unfair?" in *A Matter of Principle* (Cambridge, MA: Harvard University Press, 1985), 294.

21. Cohen, *Affirmative Action,* 110.

22. Cohen, *Affirmative Action,* 27–28.

23. Judith Jarvis Thomson, "Preferential Hiring," *Philosophy & Public Affairs* 2, no. 4 (Summer 1973): 383–84.

24. Robert Simon, "Preferential Hiring: A Reply to Judith Jarvis Thomson," *Philosophy & Public Affairs* 3, no. 3 (Spring 1974): 318.

25. Thomson, "Preferential Hiring," 382–83.

26. Pojman, "The Case against Affirmative Action," 101.

CHAPTER 15: Sexual Morality

1. Gallup Poll, "Marriage," May 8–11, 2014, gallup.com/poll/117328/marriage.aspx (February 16, 2015).

2. Lawrence B. Finer, "Trends in Premarital Sex in the United States, 1954–2003," *Public Health Reports* 122 (January–February 2007), www.publichealthreports.org/issueopen.cfm?articleID=1784 (February 16, 2015).

3. Catherine Kaukinen, et al, ed., *Addressing Violence against Women on College Campuses* (Philadelphia: Temple University Press, 2017), 18–30.

4. Alison E. Hatch, *Campus Sexual Assault* (Santa Barbara, CA: ABC-CLIO, 2017), 3–4.

5. Vanessa Grigoriadis, *Blurred Lines: Rethinking Sex, Power, and Consent on Campus* (Boston: Houghton Mifflin Harcourt, 2017), xix.

6. Grigoriadis, xx.

7. Hatch, 16.

8. Hatch, 51.

9. Sacred Congregation for the Doctrine of the Faith, "*Persona Humana*: Declaration on Certain Questions Concerning Sexual Ethics" (December 29, 1975).

10. Thomas A. Mappes, "Sexual Morality and the Concept of Using Another Person," in *Social Ethics: Morality and Social Policy*, ed. Thomas A. Mappes and Jane S. Zembaty, 7th ed. (New York: McGraw-Hill, 2007), 171.

11. Alan H. Goldman, "Plain Sex," *Philosophy and Public Affairs* 6, no. 3 (Spring 1977): 267–87.

12. Goldman, 269.

13. Igor Primoratz, *Ethics and Sex* (London: Routledge, 1999), 173.

14. Goldman, 280.

15. Michael Ruse, "Is Homosexuality Bad Sexuality?" in *Homosexuality: A Philosophical Inquiry* (Oxford: Blackwell, 1988), 179–192.

16. Michael Levin, "Why Homosexuality Is Abnormal," *The Monist* (April 1984).

17. Timothy F. Murphy, "Homosexuality and Nature: Happiness and the Law at Stake," *Journal of Applied Philosophy* 4, no. 2 (1987).

CHAPTER 16: Free Speech on Campus

1. Erwin Chemerinsky and Howard Gillman, *Free Speech on Campus* (New Haven, CT: Yale University Press, 2017), 73. Copyright © 2017 by Erwin Chemerinsky and Howard Gillman. Reprinted by permission of Yale University Press.

2. Chemerinsky and Gillman, 98.

3. Sigal R. Ben-Porath, *Free Speech on Campus* (Philadelphia: University of Pennsylvania Press, 2017), 12.

4. John Arthur, "Sticks and Stones," in *Ethics in Practice: An Anthology*, ed. Hugh LaFollette (Oxford: Blackwell, 2007), 399.

5. *Survey: Half of U.S. College Students "Intimidated" When Sharing Views,* William F. Buckley, Jr. Program

at Yale (October 26, 2015), http://mclaughlinonline
.com/2015/10/26/the-william-f-buckley-jr-program
-at-yale-almost-half-49-of-u-s-college-students-
intimidated-by-professors-when-sharing-differing-
beliefs-survey/ (September 24, 2017).

6. Chemerinsky and Gillman, 10–11.

7. Richard Delgado and Jean Stefancic, *Understanding Words that Wound* (New York: Westview Press, 2004).

8. Chemerinsky and Gillman, 103–110.

9. Ben-Porath, 27-28.

10. Chemerinsky and Gillman, 20.

11. Delgado and Stefancic.

12. Chemerinsky and Gillman, 108.

CHAPTER 17: Drugs, Guns, and Personal Liberty

1. National Institute on Drug Abuse, "Overdose Death Rates," September 2017, https://www.drugabuse.gov /related-topics/trends-statistics/overdose-death-rates (December 29, 2017); Centers for Disease Control and Prevention (CDC). *Alcohol-Related Disease Impact (ARDI)*, Atlanta, GA: CDC (December 29, 2017); M. Stahre, J. Roeber, D. Kanny, R. D. Brewer, and X. Zhang, "Contribution of Excessive Alcohol Consumption to Deaths and Years of Potential Life Lost in the United States, *Prev. Chronic Dis.* 2014;11:130293 (December 29, 2017); Substance Abuse and Mental Health Services Administration (SAMHSA), "Tobacco" (December 29, 2017); SAMHSA, Center for Behavioral Health Statistics and Quality, "National Survey on Drug Use and Health," 2014 and 2015 (December 29, 2017).

2. Substance Abuse and Mental Health Services Administration, Center for Behavioral Health Statistics and Quality, September 4, 2014, "The NSDUH Report: Substance Use and Mental Health Estimates from the 2013 National Survey on Drug Use and Health: Overview of Findings," available at http://jpo.wrlc.org /bitstream/handle/11204/3782/2013%20 Subst%20Use%20and%20Ment%20Hlth%20 Ests.SAMHSA.pdf?sequence=1 (February 15, 2015).

3. National Institutes of Health, National Institute of Drug Abuse, "Medical Consequences of Drug Abuse," December 2012, http://www.drugabuse.gov/related -topics/medical-consequences-drug-abuse/mortality (February 15, 2015).

4. "Crime in the United States 2016—Arrests," FBI Uniform Crime Report (Washington, DC: US Dept. of Justice, September 2017), p. 2; Table 18, Estimated Number of Arrests, United States 2016; Table 21A, Arrests by Race and Ethnicity 2016; and email correspondence between the editor and Stephen G. Fischer Jr., Chief—Multimedia Productions, FBI— CJIS Division.

5. Pew Research Center, "America's New Drug Policy Landscape," April 2, 2014, http://www.people-press .org/2014/04/02/americas-new-drug-policy-land- scape/(February 15, 2015).

6. Pew Research Center, "America's New Drug Policy Landscape"; Abigail Geiger, Pew Research Center, "Support for Marijuana Legalization Continues to Rise," October 12, 2016, http://www.pewresearch .org/fact-tank/2016/10/12/support-for-marijuana -legalization-continues-to-rise/.

7. *The Merck Manual (Home Edition)*, "Overview of Drug Abuse," January 2009, http://merckmanuals .com/home/special_subjects/drug_use_and_abuse /overview_of_drug_abuse.html?qt=%22Overview %20of%20Drug%20Abuse%22&alt=sh (Feburary 15, 2015).

8. *The Merck Manual (Home Edition)*, "Overview of Drug Abuse."

9. Douglas Husak and Peter de Marneffe, *The Legalization of Drugs: For and Against* (Cambridge: Cambridge University Press, 2005), 34–35.

10. National Center for Health Statistics, "Suicide and Self-Inflicted Injury," "Assault or Homicide," 2013, https://www.cdc.gov/nchs/fastats/suicide .htm (December 31, 2017); National Center for Health Statistics, "All Injuries," 2014, https://www .cdc.gov/nchs/fastats/injury.htm (December 31, 2017); *American Journal of Medicine*, March 2016, vol. 129, iss. 3, 266–73.

11. David Degrazia and Lester H. Hunt, *Debating Gun Control: How Much Regulation Do We Need?* (New York: Oxford University Press, 2016), 121.

12. Philip J. Cook and Kristina A. Goss, *The Gun Debate: What Everyone Needs to Know* (New York: Oxford University Press, 2014), 22.

13. Degrazia and Hunt, 121–22.

14. Degrazia and Hunt, 12.

15. This definition is based on one given by Degrazia.

16. Degrazia and Hunt, 247–48.

17. Glen H. Utter and Robert J. Spitzer, *The Gun Debate: An Encyclopedia of Gun Rights & Gun Control in the United States* (Amenia, NY: Grey House, 2016), 274.

18. Hugh LaFollette, "Gun Control," *Ethics* 110 (2000).

19. ProCon.org, "Should More Gun Control Laws Be Enacted?" https://gun-control.procon.org/.

20. Jon Stuart Mill, *On Liberty* (1859).

21. James Q. Wilson, "Against the Legalization of Drugs," *Commentary*, February 1990, https://www.commentarymagazine.com/article/against-the-legalization-of-drugs/ (Feburary 15, 2015).

22. Husak, *The Legalization of Drugs: For and Against*, 92–95.

23. De Marneffe, *The Legalization of Drugs: For and Against*, 110.

24. John Q. Wilson, quoted in *Body Count: Moral Poverty . . . and How to Win America's War on Drugs*, by William J. Bennett, John DiIulio, Jr., and John Walters (New York: Simon & Schuster, 1996), 140–41.

25. Nelson Lund, "The Second Amendment and the Inalienable Right to Self-Defense," www.heritage.org, April 17, 2014.

26. Degrazia and Hunt, 149–50.

27. Degrazia and Hunt, 157–58.

CHAPTER 18: Capital Punishment

1. Death Penalty Information Center, "States With and Without the Death Penalty," 2016, https://deathpenaltyinfo.org/states-and-without-death-penalty; "Methods of Execution," 2016, https://deathpenaltyinfo.org/methods-execution (August 21, 2017); Death Penalty Information Center, "Facts about the Death Penalty," https://deathpenaltyinfo.org/documents/FactSheet.pdf; Death Row Population Figures from NAACP-LDF "Death Row USA (July 1, 2014)," http://www.deathpenaltyinfo.org/death-row-usa/DRUSAFall2014.pdf; Bureau of Justice Statistics: "Capital Punishment, 2013—Statistical Tables," http://www.bjs.gov/cp13st.pdf.

2. Facts about the Death Penalty," Death Penalty Information Center, www.deathpenaltyinfo.org (August 21, 2017); Bureau of Justice Statistics: "Capital Punishment, 2013," 2014–2016 figure from DPIC research; NAACP Legal Defense Fund, "Death Row USA."

3. "Facts about the Death Penalty," Death Penalty Information Center, www.deathpenaltyinfo.org (August 21, 2017); *Bureau of Justice Statistics Bulletin*, Capital Punishment, 2003 (November 2004), 10; Bureau of Justice Statistics: "Capital Punishment, 2013—Statistical Tables," http://www.bjs.gov/cp13st.pdf.

4. Gallup, "Death Penalty," http://www.gallup.com/poll/1606/death-penalty.aspx; "Facts about the Death Penalty," Death Penalty Information Center, www.deathpenaltyinfo.org (August 21, 2017).

5. Amnesty International, "The Death Penalty in 2016," April 11, 2017, https://www.amnesty.org/en/latest/news/2017/04/death-penalty-2016-facts-and-figures/ (August 21, 2017).

6. John Stuart Mill, "Speech in Favor of Capital Punishment," to the English Parliament, 1868, http://ethics.sandiego.edu/books/Mill/Punishment/ (January 26, 2015).

7. Louis P. Pojman, "Why the Death Penalty Is Morally Permissible," in *Debating the Death Penalty: Should American Have Capital Punishment? The Experts on Both Sides Make Their Best Case*, eds. Hugo Adam Bedau and Paul G. Cassell (Oxford: Oxford University Press, 2004), 60–61.

8. Ernest van den Haag, "On Deterrence and the Death Penalty," *Journal of Criminal Law, Criminology, and Police Science* 60, no. 2. (1969).

9. Richard C. Dieter, "Millions Misspent: What Politicians Don't Say about the High Cost of the Death Penalty," Fall 1994, www.deathpenaltyinfo.org/node/599 (January 26, 2015).

10. Igor Primoratz, *Justifying Legal Punishment* (Atlantic Highlands, NJ: Humanities Press International, 1989), 165.

11. Immaneul Kant, *The Philosophy of Law*, trans. W. Hastie (Edinburgh: Clark, 1887), 195.

12. Kant, 198.

13. Paul G. Cassell, "In Defense of the Death Penalty," in Bedau and Cassell, eds., *Debating the Death Penalty*, 201.

14. Cassell, 201.

15. B. M. Leiser, *Liberty, Justice and Morals: Contemporary Value Conflicts* (New York: Macmillan, 1973), 225.

CHAPTER 19: Political Violence: War, Terrorism, and Torture

1. James Turner Johnson, "Threats, Values, and Defense: Does the Defense of Values by Force Remain a Moral Possibility?" *Parameters* 15, no. 1 (Spring 1985).

2. James P. Sterba, "Reconciling Pacifists and Just War Theorists," *Social Theory and Practice* 18, no. 1 (Spring 1992): 21.

3. Thomas Aquinas, *Summa Theologica*, in *Basic Writings of Saint Thomas Aquinas*, ed. and annotated Anton C. Pegis (New York: Random House, 1945), Second Part of the Second Part, Question 40, Article 1.

4. Michael Walzer, "Moral Judgment in Time of War," *Dissent* 14, no. 3 (May–June 1967): 284.

5. U.S. Department of State, *Patterns of Global Terrorism 2003* (Washington, DC: U.S. Department of State 2004), xii.

6. *International Encyclopedia of Terrorism*, 1997 ed., s.v. "The Official View"; quoted in *A Military Guide to Terrorism in the Twenty-first Century*, U.S. Army Training and Doctrine Command, August 15, 2005, version 3.0, available at www.fas.org/irp/threat/terrorism/index (December 4, 2006), 1–3.

7. Mark Burgess, "A Brief History of Terrorism," Center for Defense Information, July 2, 2003, http://www.pogo.org/our-work/straus-military-reform-project/cdi-archive/a-brief-history-of-terrorism.html (February 24, 2015).

8. National Memorial Institute for the Prevention of Terrorism (MIPT), *Terrorism Knowledge Base*, www.tkb.org/Home.jsp (January 27, 2006).

9. National Counterterrorism Center, *2009 Report on Terrorism*, April 30, 2010, http://www.riskintel.com/wp-content/uploads/downloads/2011/10/2009_report_on_terrorism.pdf (February 24, 2015).

10. Council on Foreign Relations, "Types of Terrorism," *Council on Foreign Affairs*, http://cfrterrorism.org/terrorism/types.html (January 27, 2006).

11. U.S. Department of State, Office of the Historian, Bureau of Public Affairs, "Significant Terrorist Incidents, 1961–2003: A Brief Chronology," March 2004, http://fas.org/irp/threat/terror_chron.html (Feburary 24, 2015).

12. Terrence McCoy, "ISIS, Beheadings and the Success of Horrifying Violence," *Washington Post*, June 13, 2014, http://www.washingtonpost.com/news/morning-mix/wp/2014/06/13/isis-beheading-and-the-success-of-horrifying-violence/ (October 31, 2014).

13. Richard Falk, "Thinking about Terrorism," *The Nation*, June 28, 1986; note that this view was expressed long before the events of September 11, 2001.

14. Joseph M. Boyle Jr., "Just War Doctrine and the Military Response to Terrorism," *Journal of Political Philosophy* 11, no. 22 (2003): 157–70.

15. Haig Khatchadourian, *The Morality of Terrorism* (New York: Peter Lang, 1998), 31–32.

16. Michael Walzer, "Terrorism: A Critique of Excuses," in *Problems of International Justice*, ed. Steve Luper-Foy (Boulder, CO: Westview Press, 1988), 238.

17. Andrew Valls, "Can Terrorism Be Justified?" in *Ethics in International Affairs: Theories and Cases*, ed. Valls (Lanham, MD: Rowman and Littlefield, 2000), 65–79.

18. Thomas Nagel, "War and Massacre," *Philosophy & Public Affairs* 1, no. 2 (Winter 1972): 123–43.

19. Jan Narveson, "Pacifism: A Philosophical Analysis," *Ethics* 75, no. 4 (1965): 623–24.

20. Larry May, Eric Rovie, and Steve Viner, in *The Morality of War: Classical and Contemporary Readings*, eds. May, Rovie, and Viner (Upper Saddle River, NJ: Pearson/Prentice Hall, 2006), 200.

21. R. G. Frey and Christopher W. Morris, "Terrorism," in *Violence, Terrorism, and Justice*, eds. Frey and Morris (Cambridge: Cambridge University Press, 1991), 1–11.

22. Walzer, "Terrorism," 240.

23. Michael Walzer, "The Argument about Humanitarian Intervention," *Dissent* 49, no. 1 (Winter 2002), http://www.dissentmagazine.org/article/the-argument-about-humanitarian-intervention (February 26, 2015).

24. Stephen Nathanson, "Can Terrorism Be Morally Justified?" in *Morality in Practice*, ed. James P. Sterba, 7th ed. (Belmont, CA: Wadsworth/Thomson, 2004), 607.

25. From Jeffrey Goldberg, "Inside Jihad U.: The Education of a Holy Warrior," *New York Times Magazine*, June 2000; quoted in Louis P. Pojman, "The Moral Response to Terrorism and the Cosmopolitan Imperative," in *Terrorism and International Justice*, ed. James P. Sterba (New York: Oxford University Press, 2003).

26. Seumas Miller, "Torture," in *Stanford Encyclopedia of Philosophy*, Summer 2017 ed., ed. Edward N. Zalta, http://plato.stanford.edu/entries/torture/ (February 26, 2015).

CHAPTER 20: The Ethics of Immigration

1. Cari Lee Skogberg Eastman, *Immigration: Examining the Facts* (Santa Barbara: ABC-CLIO, 2017), 16.
2. Pew Research Center, "Key Findings about U.S. Immigrants," May 3, 2017, http://www.pewresearch.org/topics/search/?query=key findings immigration.
3. Pew Research Center, "Key Findings."
4. Ipsos Survey, "The Perils of Perception: Americans' Estimates of Number of Immigrants, Atheists, and Those Living Rurally Radically Out of Step with Reality," December 1, 2015, https://www.ipsos.com/en-us/perilsperceptions-americans-estimates-number-immigrants-atheists-and-those-living-rurally.
5. Pew Research Center, "Key Findings."; "5 Key Facts about U.S. Lawful Immigrants," August 3, 2017, http://www.pewresearch.org/fact-tank/2017/08/03/5-key-facts-about-u-s-lawful-immigrants/.
6. Pew Research Center, "Key Findings."
7. USA.gov, "Deportation," https://www.usa.gov/deportation; Pew Research Center, "Key Findings."
8. U.S. Department of State, "Refugee Admissions," https://www.state.gov/j/prm/ra/, (December 4, 2017); https://www.state.gov/j/prm/ra/; Pew Research Center, "Key Findings."
9. U.S. Census Bureau, "New Census Bureau Report Analyzes U.S. Population Projections," March 3, 2015, https://www.census.gov/newsroom/press-releases/2015/cb15-tps16.html.
10. Cari Lee Skogberg Eastman, *Immigration*, 121.
11. Cari Lee Skogberg Eastman, *Immigration*, 38.
12. Eduardo Porter, "Can Immigration Hurt the Economy? An Old Prejudice Returns," *New York Times*, February 14, 2017, https://www.nytimes.com/2017/02/14/business/economy/immigration-productivity-economists.html.
13. Jens Manuel Krogstad, Jeffrey S. Passel, and D'Vera Cohn, "5 Facts about Illegal Immigration in the U.S.," Pew Research Center, April 27, 2017, http://www.pewresearch.org/fact-tank/2017/04/27/5-facts-about-illegalimmigration-in-the-u-s/; Cari Lee Skogberg Eastman, *Immigration*, 79–85.
14. American Immigration Council, "Fact Sheet: Why Don't They Just Get in Line?" August 12, 2016, https://www.americanimmigrationcouncil.org/research/why-don't-they-just-get-line.
15. Cari Lee Skogberg Eastman, *Immigration*, 22–24.
16. Stephen Macedo, "The Moral Dilemma of U.S. Immigration Policy: Open Borders versus Social Justice?" in *Debating Immigration*, ed. Carol M. Swain (Cambridge: Cambridge University Press, 2007), 64.
17. Christopher Heath Wellman, "Immigration and Freedom of Association," *Ethics* 119 (2008): 109–41.
18. Stephen Macedo, "The Moral Dilemma," 64.
19. Stephen Macedo, "The Moral Dilemma," 64

CHAPTER 21: Global Economic Justice

1. World Bank, "Poverty Overview," October 8, 2014, http://www.worldbank.org/en/topic/poverty/overview (February 28, 2015); United Nations, Department of Economic and Social Affairs, "The Millennium Development Goals Report, 2014," July 30, 2014, http://www.un.org/millenniumgoals/2014%20MDG%20report/MDG%202014%20English%20web.pdf (February 28, 2015); UNICEF, "The State of the World's Children 2014 in Numbers," January 2014, http://www.unicef.org/sowc2014/numbers/ (February 28, 2015).
2. Oxfam International, "Working for the Few," 2014, http://www.oxfam.org/en/research/working-few (February 28, 2015); United Nations Development Programme (UNDP), "Human Development Report 1998: Consumption for Human Development" (New York, 1998), http://hdr.undp.org/sites/default/files/reports/259/hdr_1998_en_complete_nostats.pdf (February 28, 2015).
3. Peter Singer, "Famine, Affluence, and Morality," *Philosophy and Public Affairs* 1, no. 1 (Spring 1972), 23–32.
4. John Hospers, "What Libertarianism Is," in *The Libertarian Alternative*, ed. Tibor R. Machan (Chicago: Nelson-Hall, 1974), 3.
5. Singer, "Famine, Affluence, and Morality," 231.
6. Singer, 231.

7. Singer 232.

8. Singer, 235.

9. Singer, 241.

10. Singer, 231.

11. Singer, 241.

12. John Arthur, "Equality, Entitlements, and the Distribution of Income," *Philosophy for the 21st Century*, ed. Steven M. Cohn (New York: Oxford University Press, 2003), 677.

13. Arthur, 677.

14. Louis P. Pojman, ed., *Life and Death: A Reader in Moral Problems*, 2nd ed. (Belmont, CA: Wadsworth, 2000), 180.

15. Pojman, 175.

16. William W. Murdoch and Allan Oaten, "Population and Food: Metaphors and the Reality," *BioScience* 25, no. 9 (September 1975): 561.

INDEX